Triad and Tabut

A Survey of the Origin and Diffusion of
Chinese and Mohamedan Secret Societies in
the Malay Peninsula, AD 1800–1935

Mervyn Llewelyn Wynne

PART 1

First published in 1941

This edition published in 2024 by AMP Book House

Publisher's note
The publisher has gone to great lengths to ensure the quality of these reprints. but wishes to point out that certain characteristics of the original copies will, of necessity, be apparent in reprints thereof.

TRIAD AND TABUT

A survey of the origin and diffusion of
Chinese and Mohamedan

SECRET SOCIETIES

in

The Malay Peninsula
A. D. 1800 — 1935

by

Mervyn Llewelyn Wynne
Malayan Police

SINGAPORE :
PRINTED AT THE GOVERNMENT PRINTING OFFICE, SINGAPORE,
BY W. T. CHERRY, GOVERNMENT PRINTER.

Up from Earth's Centre through
    the Seventh Gate
I rose and on the Throne
    of Saturn sate,
And many Knots unravel'd
    by the Road;
But not the Knot of Human
    Death and Fate.

❀   ❀   ❀

Di-pusat alam beta menjalu,
Tujoh petala bumi di-lalu;
Dudok semayam di-atas bintang,
Lehat ka-bawah alam terbentang.
Sedang berjalan, berlengkar-lengkar,
Simpulan banyak dapat di-bongkar,
Choma satu ta'dapat di-puleh,
Nasib ma'ut yang kita peruleh.

(Rubaiyat of Omar Khayyam
Stanza 31
Transl. A. W. Hamilton)

FOREWORD

By W. L. BLYTHE, C.M.G.

Former Colonial Secretary, Singapore

Sometime Secretary for Chinese Affairs, Federation of Malaya

No-one can turn over the pages of the late Mervyn Wynne's *Triad and Tabut* without being impressed with the industry and erudition which have gone to its compilation. And this is the more surprising when one knows that this massive work was accomplished during such spare time as was available to a very busy Police Officer during a period when he was holding senior and responsible appointments. That he should have brought together so much material on the subject of secret societies is symptomatic of his energetic, restless temperament which was forever seeking perfection.

The author had hoped to continue his work by a more detailed analysis of the activities of particular societies in Malaya, but owing to the Japanese occupation of Malaya during which he died, this was never completed.

Wynne wrote at a time when Chinese Secret Society activity was just about at its lowest ebb in Malaya. For years there had been few prosecutions of persons for membership of such societies, and very little documentary evidence had been preserved. He was, therefore, handicapped by a lack of up-to-date material for comparative study and of members and officials of such societies who could be interrogated.

The main theme of his study is that there were two opposed roots from which the Chinese Secret Societies in Malaya stemmed. He frankly admits that he puts this forward as a theory, and the bases for this theory are repeatedly conjectural. From evidence now available it becomes clear that some of his conjectures were erroneous.

Immediately after World War II the operation of the law relating to the registration of Societies was suspended in the Malayan Union (now the Federation of Malaya) with the immediate result that Triad societies sprang up throughout the country, particularly in Penang and Perak with such rapidity that their membership soon reached scores of thousands, and as many as 1,000 persons were present at a single initiation ceremony. The result was that in certain areas, the Triads were in control, leaving the Civil Government almost powerless to check the spate of murder and extortion, robbery and piracy which ensued.

But one result of this was that when the time came to take strong action against society organisers, a mass of evidence was forthcoming both documentary and personal as to the organisation, ritual, history and operations of the Societies. And an examination of this evidence at the time and since makes it appear reasonably certain that there is not, and never was, a dual origin of the Chinese Secret Societies in Malaya from two roots—Han and Hung—as Wynne suggests.

A few specific examples of discrepancies in the development of the theory which are now discernible may here be given:—

    I. The suggestion that the Ghi Hok Society was of different origin from the Ghi Hin (p. 80) and not a part of it is completely disproved by the two "chops" shown in Volume I of Ward & Stirling's book *The Hung Society* (London 1925) on pages 29 and 76. The first of these has, horizontally "Ghi Hin Kongsi" and vertically "Ghi Hok Kwan"; the second:, horizontally, Ghi Hin Kongsi, and vertically "Ghi Hok Hoey Kwan". Both of these seals (which are also to be found in another document) show clearly that the Ghi Hok was a "Hall" of the Ghi Hin.

   II. The suggestion that the Three Dots Society (pp. 80, 128–151) is different in origin from the Triad Societies is not borne out by the evidence of old Secret Society members or by documents now available. The term "San Teën-hwuey" (Three Dots Society) was used in Canton as early as 1831 and in Penang as early as 1843, as an alternative to "Tien-ti hoey" or "Sam Hop Wui" to denote a Triad Society and it is still commonly used in Malaya to-day in this sense.

III.   The ritual of the Three Dots Society (p. 128-151).

There are many variations of the ritual of initiation used by Triad Societies, and they appear to increase with the passage of time. It can confidently be asserted that there is nothing in the Three Dots ritual as given by Wynne which would be out of place in the initiation ceremony of a Triad Society. Indeed a Triad "priest", (sinseh) who was asked about the "five portals" referred to by Wynne and regarded by him as being evidence of a difference from the normal "three gates" of Triad, at once replied: "Many people say that there are five gates but actually there are only three. The fact that they first of all pass under an 'arch' representing the East Gate of the City, and, after passing through the three gates pass through the "Heaven and Earth Hoop under the altar makes them think there are five gates. There are five 'arches' but only three of them are 'gates' ". Similarly there is ample evidence that some Triad societies have pricked the middle finger of the right hand, and some the middle finger of the left hand. And at one initiation ceremony the police found that left and right fingers were pricked indiscriminately.

IV.   The other document referred to under I above is a large wall-sheet signed by Wm. Cowan, Protector of Chinese, Perak, and dated 1897. It is referred to by Wynne at the top of p. 102, though it is incorrectly given the date 1890. It contains replicas of the membership diplomas and seals of the various societies. Of these, the diplomas of the Hai San, Ghee Hok, Hok Hin and Siong Peh Koan societies, all of which are listed by Wynne (p. 112) as 'Han' or 'Tokong' societies, bear the character "Hung" which indicates that they are branches of the Hung Brotherhood. The name Wah Sang shown in the list under "Tokong" and the name "Ho Seng" shown under "Triad" are, in fact, variants of the romanisation of the name of one society—the Ho Seng, whose diploma bears the "Hung" character. The diploma of the Kien Tek (Toh Peh Kong) does not bear the character "Hung" but there is other evidence that it was an offshoot of the Ghi Hin Triad Society.

In addition to the Malayan material, there is another field of research which has yielded useful information. During the last twenty-five years or so, a number of Chinese printed books on the subject of Secret Societies have been published in Shanghai and Hong Kong. Examination of these sources shows without doubt that the Ko Lao Hui or Elder Brother's Society in China is part of the Hung Brotherhood. It has the same traditional history, the same Ancestors and other traditional founders, and though its organisation and ritual differ from those of the Triad societies, its ritual verses repeatedly refer to membership of the Hung Family. Chinese sources invariably affirm that the Ko Lao Hui and the Triad Society are both members of the Hung Brotherhood, the former covering north and central China down to and including the Yangtze Valley, while the latter under various names: Heaven and Earth Society, Three in Harmony Society or Three Dots Society operates in the southern provinces, particularly Fukien, Kwangtung and Kwangsi, from which three provinces all the Chinese immigrants to Malaya came.

From all the evidence available, there would appear to be no reason to doubt the correctness of this contention, and if this is accepted, then the theory that these two societies were of different ideologies falls to the ground. It is true that there still remains the possibility of quarrels between societies which are members of the same Brotherhood, and this is what happened in Malaya, but a careful review of all the evidence available fai's to disclose that any society descended from the Ko Lao Hui ever existed in Malaya; the quarrels have been between societies which were within the Triad division of the Hung Brotherhood.

This is not the place to set out in detail all the arguments in support of this conclusion, but the summary given above may suffice to make it clear that the basic presumption: that there were two ideologically antagonistic origins of the societies in Malaya cannot be substantiated. It is quite true that in the secret society world in Malaya there have invariably been two camps bitterly opposed to each other, but there now exist any number of examples of Triad societies being rent asunder by internal quarrels, dividing into two societies, and thereafter becoming bitter enemies despite their common origin and their common use of the Triad ritual. The reason for the enmity in such cases is to be sought not in any ideological difference or separate source but in rivalry for power. Both are after the same thing—the demonstration of their own supremacy, and the benefits of prestige, influence and wealth which inevitably fall to the winner. Often the basis for the split is found to be the difference between language-groups, Hokkien versus Tiechiu, Cantonese versus Hakka, Cantonese versus Hokkien, and so on; sometimes it arises from a struggle for power between two "clan" groups, the Lims versus the Tans, the Lees versus the Chuas, and at other times antagonism between two groups tendering for a revenue "farm" or some other form of contract is the cause of dispute. Investigation along these lines is a surer guide through the maze of Chinese intrigue than is the invention of a mythical "Tokong" to explain the differences.

But the fact that the passage of time and research in a wider field have led to a re-appraisement of Wynne's theory does not detract from the value of the painstaking compilation of the material in this work. *Triad and Tabut* was never intended by the author to be published as it stands. His purpose in preparing it was two-fold : to bring together all the knowledge available on the subject so that a sound appreciation could be made therefrom, and to emphasize in the official circles to which the circulation of the work was to be restricted, the complexity and the danger of the problem of secret societies. It is not too much to say that these aims have been achieved. Not only have the Malayan Governments found this book of considerable practical use in the investigation of post-war secret societies, but the presentation of the theory enunciated therein, even though it has now to be abandoned, has kindled the enthusiasm of other searchers in the same field.

As the material contained in this book may be of interest and use to a wider group of research workers, permission has been given by the Governments of the Federation of Malaya and the Colony of Singapore for the issue of such copies as still remain, to libraries and centres of learning.

SINGAPORE, *4th July*, 1957.

Throughout this work, references will be found to various Appendices, but these did not survive the Japanese occupation of Malaya. There are also references to "Part II" and to chapters numbered from XXII onwards. These concern the projected second part of this work which was planned and partly written but was unfinished at the time of the Japanese occupation.

PREFACE

This work is an attempt to present from both the Chinese and the Malay standpoint, an aspect of Malayan history of importance to British officials who have contact with the people of the country.

The story of secret societies in their local environment has never been fully told and the present work is a contribution towards that end. It attempts to trace the activities of Chinese and Malay secret societies, working in concert in Malaya during the period of the British connection, and in so doing it becomes a history of the political and criminal under-currents which have flowed hither and thither in different parts of Malaya during the past hundred and thirty-five years.

The subject is a very wide one and any comprehensive attempt to depict its many-sidedness must take into account all the ingredients, racial, historical, religious, economic, political and criminal which go to its composition.

In presenting these factors we have tried to preserve a balance between them, while deliberately emphasising a few salient features not previously brought to notice—such for example as the presence not of one, as generally accepted, but of *two* secret Chinese confederations in Malaya—in order to adjust to the main theme the relative importance of each and to give shape to their variant manifestations arising in the text.

In the treatment of a subject so obscure, wherein there is so much room for individual opinion to differ, we have thought it best to offer some of the evidence in its original form by extracts *in extenso* from the published authorities, so that readers as they proceed, may form their own judgment upon the presentation of the facts.

For the most part the story unfolds itself chronologically by means of these extracts, set out in what we believe to be their proper sequence. We have sought not to burden the reader with new theories on old themes, except where generally accepted views are at variance with fact.

Nor do we desire to pose as an authority upon a subject so difficult and contentious.

We seek only to help to remove some of those perplexities which in the past have baffled our administration and to place in a clearer light some of the questions which present themselves for future solution, by fitting a true interpretation to them and by drawing them into a correct historical perspective.

By bringing together into one place, all relevant evidence known to us, we hope to enable those best qualified to judge, to provide final answers and to draw final conclusions.

It is inevitable that in the treatment of our subject, facts hitherto generally accepted again come under review and as a result, a revision of some historical values and a re-adjustment of certain aspects of local history become necessary.

In this regard we are only concerned to trace and attempt to evaluate the importance of the different threads which, woven together during the last century, have combined to form the present-day undersurface fabric of secret societies in Malaya.

The work is therefore, a compendium of information and reference not hitherto readily available, correlated as far as may be, to the main argument and blended to form an historical background to the modern problem.

This method has necessarily meant a compilation of considerable bulk which some readers will condemn, objecting that long extracts are tedious and unnecessary and should be abridged or condensed or replaced by references to published works. These volumes are not, however, intended for the general reader, but will serve, we hope, as a work of fully documented historical interest as well as of present-day practical value to Government officials in a field of research always remote from the official eye throughout the whole period of the British connection.

It would have been easy to write a comparatively succinct history of the subject, giving references instead of extracts, opinions instead of the foundations upon which they rest, and conclusions instead of the road leading to them; but the ground-work is so wide and obscure, many of the references so inaccessible and diverse, and the sources of information so meagre, that any such attempt at abridgement would fail to be of practical use: nor would it carry conviction in the absence of some half-way house, wherein the historical sources may be deposited, consulted and weighed, independent criticism be exercised and judicial conclusions be arrived at, based upon the application of individual experience to recorded history and ascertained fact.

The present work attempts to supply this need. It seems the lesser of two evils that the work should be comprehensive and comparatively convincing, rather than brief and inconclusive.

References to authority will be found freely interspersed in the text, a method which, although a little awkward, is less tedious than a slavish use of footnotes, and is unavoidable in some form or other in these days when the cry of justification for every statement or opinion is so insistent.

An old saying runs :—

> "What is hits is history.
> "What is missed is mystery".

This work attempts to clear away some of the "mystery" attaching to the things present, but not seen in the background of Malayan life.

If and when some measure of acceptance has been accorded to the main contentions raised herein, then only will it be profitable to write a concise history of the subject, suitable for the general reader, unburdened by lengthy extracts, and using perhaps, the present work as a general reference.

Portions of the earlier chapters are printed in heavy type for emphasis. These passages are the "bridges" that link the main argument together and help to adjust the reader's perspective.

We are aware that the work is doubtless bestrewn with mistakes of fact and that there is perhaps much available material which has not been examined. We feel, however, that the main lines of its arguments are fairly clear cut and hope that their study may stimulate the interest of others who have personal knowledge of this fascinating subject.

Since the work was completed in December, 1936, we have added an introduction in the belief that a general survey of the sources from which all secret societies appear to spring, would be of at least speculative interest, while helping to focus attention upon the relation of the subject to some of the modern problems of Colonial administration.

The introduction is not an integral part of the main work and may be conveniently omitted by those readers who are interested only in the factual presentation of the subject.

As regards orthography and the romanisation of foreign language words, we have adopted no system. In extracts we have followed the spelling in the original. For the rest, we have been more concerned with the pursuit of facts and their correct interpretation, than with the niceties of spelling.

For the many imperfections in our work, we ask our readers' indulgence.

IPOH,
PERAK, F.M.S.
1st December, 1939.

ACKNOWLEDGMENT

We beg to acknowledge our indebtedness to the following ladies and gentlemen who have given us assistance and facilities for research :—

Professor RANDLE, Librarian, India Office, Whitehall;
Mrs. F. CARDEW, Assistant Librarian, Royal Asiatic Society, London;
Miss I. EDWARDS, Assistant in the Library of the Royal Asiatic Society;
Mrs. M. DAVIS, Assistant Secretary, Royal Asiatic Society;
Mr. J. F. COWGILL, O.B.E., Assistant Superintendent, Indian Police, Delhi.

Our best thanks are due to Sir RICHARD WINSTEDT, K.B.E., C.M.G., D.LITT., late of the Malayan Civil Service and presently Director of the Malay section of the School of Oriental Studies, London, and to Dr. V. W. W. S. PURCELL, D.LITT., of the Malayan Civil Service, for having read most of the work in typescript, and for valuable criticisms upon it, the one from the Malay, the other from the Chinese standpoint.

Our special thanks are offered to Sir HERBERT DOWBIGGIN, late Inspector-General of Police, Ceylon, for having read the complete typescript with the professional interest of a Police Officer of long experience, some of whose interesting notes on different points arising in the text appear in their appropriate context.

To Sir CECIL CLEMENTI, G.C.M.G., late Governor of the Straits Settlements and High Commissioner for the Malay States we tender our warmest thanks, not only for having read the work in typescript but for having brought to official notice whatever merit it may possess; and without whose kindly interest and encouragement the work could never have been published.

To the Governments of the Straits Settlements and the Federated Malay States are due our thanks for acceptance of the work for printing at the public expense. The Malayan Governments are in no way responsible for the form of the work or for opinions expressed in it, which are entirely our own.

We are much indebted to Mr. K. J. N. DUTHIE and Mr. G. E. DEVONSHIRE, both Assistant Superintendents of the Federated Malay States Police, for their help and advice in the proof-reading and in particular to Mr. DEVONSHIRE for having undertaken unaided the onerous task of compiling the index.

CHE MOHAMED SHERIFF BIN IBRAMSHA, typist in the Police Headquarters Office, Ipoh, has been most helpful in typing revisions for the press: while Mr. CHING YIT CHEW of the same office has re-drawn the maps and illustrations for publication.

We have to thank Mr. W. T. CHERRY, Government Printer, Singapore and his assistants Mr. F. R. VINE, Mr. W. D. S. JENNINGS and Mr. V. B. K. NAIR for their unfailing help and courtesy in printing.

Lastly, we gratefully acknowledge the help and guidance in our labours of those from whose works we have so freely quoted and to whom individual acknowledgment is made in the text.

CONTENTS

INTRODUCTION

THE NATURE OF SECRET SOCIETIES

This introduction is a speculative essay for the consideration of readers interested in first causes. It is divided into the following sub-heads:—

1. THE HUMAN FACTOR IN COLONIAL ADMINISTRATION

In his inaugural address to the Oxford Summer School on Colonial Administration in June, 1938, the Secretary of State for the Colonies, the Rt. Hon'ble Malcolm MacDonald, restated that the purpose of the British Empire was the gradual spread of freedom among all His Majesty's subjects in whatever part of the earth they live, and went on to say:—

> "The spread of freedom in British countries overseas is a slow, sometimes a painful evolutionary process. The pace varies from place to place, according to local conditions. There may even sometimes be inevitable set backs. But over the generations the evolutionary process goes on...... Our main effort is to teach those peoples to stand always a little more securely on their own feet...... The objective will be reached in different places at different times and by many different paths. Before it is reached, there may be re-arrangements of political divisions: units at present separate, may be combined, others may be split up into component parts. The important thing is to ensure so far as is possible that whatever changes are necessary should be so effected as to be in harmony with the general aim".

This statement emphasises two points, the evolutionary process in British imperial policy and the ultimate objective of a harmonious whole.

In the same series of lectures Professor R. Coupland referred to another principle of imperial policy now well established namely, that the units of the Empire are not property but peoples, who are an end in themselves and whose active co-operation towards the attainment of that end is an essential factor in Colonial administration.

In the pursuance of this general aim, one of the most important pre-requisites in the equipment of the administrator is a knowledge of the peoples with whom he is called upon to deal. Knowledge of man is, therefore, of primary importance if the goal of imperial endeavour is to be attained.

But the scientific study of man only began in the last century and is still in its infancy. Casson in *The Discovery of Man* (1939) says page 328:—

> "The story of man that began with the tentative inquiries of the curious into evidence which they could not understand has ended in a fully organised research which summons to its aid every conceivable assistance from any competent quarter. The activities of man are various and manifold. To unravel them you need every device which man has himself invented. In the unravelling, the discerning will recognise the various qualities of the human soul, which are revealed by the uncovering of human history and pre-history. To watch man growing in complexity is to watch the greatest and only certifiable miracle in history. To observe civilisation taking shape is to see one of the real marvels of the earth".

In his recently awakened interest in himself scientific man has employed as his chief instruments of investigation archaeology and anthropology, both sciences of late development in the history of human research.

The former is costly and has languished not only on that account, but because of man's innate dislike of examining himself objectively, lest scientific discovery in this field should upset established dogma.

The importance of anthropology on the other hand, has been admitted, not only as a theoretical science, but also in the practical sphere of British Colonial administration.

In his interesting lecture to the Oxford Summer School in June, 1938, upon the subject of applied anthropology, Professor Radcliffe-Brown said:—

> "Social anthropology......aims at investigating, from a theoretical point of view, the nature of human society and of such social phenomena as systems of morality, law, religion, etc. It does this by systematic comparison of societies of diverse types, and, while it does not and cannot neglect the complex societies of civilised peoples, it devotes its attention chiefly to the simpler societies of non-European peoples...... The colonial administrative officer is a practitioner...... The question we have to consider is, to what extent and in what way the social anthropologist can supply the Colonial administrator with knowledge that can be of use to him in his practical task".

It becomes evident from the foregoing that if freedom be the purpose of Empire, one branch of social anthropology both theoretical and practical, which is of value to the Colonial administrator, is a comparative study of those secret societies among both civilised and uncivilised peoples, which tend to restrict that freedom, by the establishment, unseen by the administration, of *imperia in imperio*. Secret societies are, generally, of two kinds, beneficent and maleficent but always restrictive, and exercise a powerful influence upon the behaviour of the individual, both within and without the British Empire.

By its very nature the subject is obscure and presents almost insuperable difficulties to objective study. Its importance, however, particularly in Malaya, where "secret societies" have been a bugbear of the administration throughout the whole period of the British connection,—cannot be gainsaid. That the subject is worthy of study in the interests of good government will not be denied, and that it has an application far beyond the local Malayan scene, with roots reaching down to the fundamental beliefs of man, will become evident from what follows.

The subject, upon closer acquaintance becomes so vast that the term "secret society", the only presently accepted term for the phenomenon, becomes an inadequate vehicle to describe its ramifications. In the absence of any other accepted term, repetition of this expression in this work, will, we fear, become wearisome to the reader.

It seems almost as if a separate branch of social anthropology might be opened for a more comprehensive study of the subject and some new name be coined for the science of the secret societies of man. Such terms as "esoteric, or cabbalistic anthropology" or "crypto-symbolism" suggest themselves for the branch itself, but a name to describe all the aspects and paraphernalia of the subject is more difficult to find. If not too fanciful, we suggest "ethno-arcana" a kind of arcanan "Golden Bough", to embrace all its attendant and correlated manifestations and phenomena.

These phenomena affect man's belief, man's history and man's political development and cannot be dissociated. The work that follows is confined to an examination of these phenomena in the miniature setting of Malaya, where the recent admixture of races has enabled their several roots to be separately identified, before the passage of time has obliterated them.

Enough will appear to show that the subject is worthy of much wider attention. Some of its manifestations in other parts of the world have been indicated in their appropriate context, but the present work is generally confined to an investigation of the subject among the Chinese and Mohamedans in the Malay peninsula.

Casson *op. cit.* page 322 has said:—

> "Without the continuous refreshment provided by new outlooks and men of vision, anthropology might have remained always as a simple collection of unrelated ethnological *data*, and all anthropological work might have consisted of treatises on strange tribes and unknown people. Without the stimulus of excavation, archaeology might have remained the mere collecting of unusual objects and their classification without any realisation of their cultural value or their chronological relationships. Anthropological studies did in fact remain for long ages in this state and were only removed to a higher plane by the realisation of the deeper implications behind the *data* and of the important conclusions to be derived from them. Slowly, the *data* from different regions were correlated and the conclusions drawn. Archaeology only became a comparative study when excavation had revealed the relationships between apparently isolated cultures".

The branch of anthropology of which this work treats is one which has suffered, not so much from a lack of *data*, as from an absence of—"the realisation of the deeper implications that lie behind them and the important conclusions to be drawn from them".

The field of investigation presented, is none other than the study of the arcana of the human mind among the thousands of races and tribes that compose the citizenship of the Empire. This leads us into untrodden paths of anthropogeny and psychogenesis and the aspects of those subjects which affect the fundamental beliefs of Man and their manifestations in his religion, his behaviour and his attitude to life at the present-day. Professor Radcliffe-Brown said in his lecture in the summer of 1938:—

> "The fullest utilization of anthropological knowledge, theoretical and factual, can only be brought about by the creation of a science of applied anthropology. I believe that it would be to the great advantage of every Colony to place on the staff at least one person competent in applied anthropology to act as adviser on native affairs........
>
> I have to admit that the applied anthropology of which I have been speaking, does not exist—except for isolated attempts to interpret native institutions in the light of anthropology. The Royal Anthropological Institute has recently set up a committee on applied anthropology, an indication of rapidly increasing interest in the subject. There is, therefore, some hope that at some time in the future such an applied science may exist and fulfil its function of connecting the theoretical investigations of the social anthropologist with the practical activities of the Colonial officer".

Finally he said:—

> "Regretfully I have to admit that the theoretical science of human society is as yet in a very undeveloped state. The establishment of an effective applied anthropology must depend on the progress of the pure theoretical sciences and it is therefore this, that we have to make our principal aim".

The foregoing statement of the present position shows that the authorities are alive to a deficiency in our present Colonial administrative equipment and are prepared to "remove to a higher plane" the science of human society and thereby place it on a comparable basis with the other handmaidens of the Colonial administrator, archaeology and anthropology. Proof of this intention has been given by the Secretary of State in his *Review of the Colonial Empire, April 1938 to March 1939* in which he has emphasised the importance of Colonial research in a special chapter on the subject in which he says:—

> "Research is not just a test-tube matter: it must concern itself with human happiness...... Among other developments during the year......arrangements have been made for my Department to be represented on the Committee of applied anthropology of the Royal Anthropological Institute".

And a separate section of the report has been devoted to the year's results in archaeological research within the Empire.

Professor Radcliffe-Brown's view that the theoretical sciences must be the vanguard of progress in the sphere of applied anthropology meets with the initial difficulty that science is itself divided upon the method of that advance.

Hocart in his prologue to *Kingship* (1927) says:—

> "A fierce battle is now raging between the historians of two parties......
> those who deny that the same thing is ever invented twice and who, therefore,
> assert that if two customs in parts of the world ever so remote......show some
> resemblance, they must come from the same source: on the other hand......
> the die-hards......who automatically turn down every attempt at tracing common
> origins, with the equally confident assertion that similar ideas occur to men inde-
> pendently in different parts of the world...... Such contradictory views would
> be impossible if we had first determined the origin and growth, say, of our own
> religion and its collaterals, and then ascertained the processes by which they have
> evolved and diverged...... Our first duty then is to trace the actual course of
> events, thence to deduce our laws of development".

Until science shall have decided upon the method of investigation, between these two opposing schools,—known as the Evolutionist[1] and the Diffusionist—we are unlikely to register much progress in applied anthropology.[2]

Hocart says *op. cit.* page 2:—

> "This investigation can have little use unless sooner or later we make up our
> minds whether all the forms that will come under review have a common origin
> or not: ultimately we shall, I think, be driven to the conclusion that they have:
> but that cannot be until a large array of the facts has been collected which bears
> no other interpretation; for we can never actually see these common origins,
> we can only infer them: and in the end it is a question whether or not we are
> forced to do so, by the accumulation of evidence".

We have noted above that definite official steps have recently been taken towards the accumulation of this evidence and towards the general development of applied anthropology within the Empire, but until a final decision has been reached upon the direction whence man has come, the direction in which he should go must remain in doubt.

One branch of this new science may perhaps be devoted to esoteric anthropology, or the study of the secret societies of the human race, which on closer acquaintance will be found to possess a remarkable similarity throughout the world, and therefore, *prima facie* present a wide and promising field for fruitful research. For example, the Triad society of China, with which this work begins, bears a close resemblance to some aspects of Freemasonry. Indeed, masonic signs are found the world over in both ancient and modern cultures and among civilised and savage peoples and for this reason independent workers in this field have themselves felt the need for some central depository, wherein the known *data* on this subject could be correlated and evaluated and whence authoritative conclusions could be drawn.

The eminent Freemason, J. S. M. Ward in his work *Freemasonry and the Ancient Gods* (1921) has recorded this need in the following passage page 123:—

> "I advocate the formation (within the Masonic body) of a lodge of anthropological
> research...... My contention is that Freemasonry derives originally from those
> primitive rites which first taught a boy whence he came, then prepared him to be
> a useful member of society, and finally taught him how to die and that death
> did not end all".

And again page 340:—

> "It will be essentially a lodge of research...... It will adopt the anthropo-
> logical attitude...... The lodge will co-ordinate facts collected from every source.
> It will place them on permanent record in its library and make that library one
> dealing with Man, not with the dead bones of history...... We particularly want
> to attract travellers and students of anthropology, who can speak from personal
> experience. Such men would be invaluable".

In this passage we see that the idea of a school of applied anthropology, albeit solely in the interests of masonic research, was being advocated several years before the semi-official proposal of 1938.

As we ourselves have no connection with Freemasonry, we are unable to say whether there exists or not, a masonic lodge of anthropological research. We can however say that the records of such a lodge would be of pre-eminent practical value to students of applied anthropology in the Colonial Empire.

We make this assertion with confidence, because of the existence of that strange link of resemblance with what passes for Freemasonry, that appears to bind together the arcana of most if not all civilisations and races of mankind.

These arcana in turn provide the basis for the beliefs, customs and laws of races, which in sum, form that human society, which it is the purpose of applied anthropology to investigate, and of Colonial administration to preserve in happiness.

Seeing that these arcana or esoteric beliefs are a common factor throughout the whole of human society, no more promising starting-point for social anthropological research, would seem to offer.

Ward *op. cit.* pages 119, 124 and elsewhere propounds the theory that:—

"Freemasonry originated from the primitive initiatory rites of pre-historic man".

Without venturing an opinion upon this contention, we may say that a system of secret society initiation similar to that of Freemasonry and applied to many various

Footnote.—(1) This is also known as the "Comparative", or the "Independent Origins", school.
Footnote.—(2) A concise survey of the present position of science in this field, written by Professor Malinowski of the University of London and supported by a full bibliography, will be found in the *Encyclopaedia Britannica*, under "Social Anthropology".

purposes, is to be found in almost every country in the world at the present-day and that certain masonic signs, may be traced back to greatest antiquity in almost all ancient civilisations.

Ward *op. cit.* page 329 ff. quotes the following periods and countries, races and religions among which this common factor is to be found to-day, if not among living peoples, then among drawings and statuary left behind by them. Thus:—

"In Asia.—China, Malaya, India (both among Mohamedans and Hindus including caste-marks of the latter) Ceylon.

In the Near East.—Turkey, Arabia. The Dervishes, the Druses (who claim to be the descendants of the actual builders of Solomon's temple): the Crusaders: Knights Templar: etc., ancient Assyrians and all Mohamedans in the Near East.

In Africa.—Ancient Egypt, Modern savage Africa including British and Portugese East Africa: The Hausas of West Africa. The Senussi of North Africa. The Negroes of the Nile basin and the modern Egyptians.

In Europe.—Ancient Greece and Rome: Mithra-ism: Mediaeval Italy and England, and all countries of modern Europe.

In America.—Ancient central America. Ancient and modern Mexico: and the American Indians.

Other countries.—Ancient West Indies, Ancient Peru, Australia, Easter Island and New Guinea".

So much for Ward's list. Many other examples might be given.

At this reference Ward *op. cit.* page 327 has, among others, the following special references to China and Malaya:—

"Abundant evidence has been given throughout this book that certain signs, grips and symbols are known and used with the same essential meaning, all over the world and at all periods of the history of man on earth. For example: In China there is:—

    (1) Use of masonic phrases in the ancient Chinese classics.

    (2) An ancient religious system, now apparently extinct, which taught its doctrines by the use of masonic symbols, the allegory of a temple built in a desert, and had an organisation similar in almost every way to a masonic lodge.

    (3) The existence of a perfect network of secret societies with pass-words, grips, and rituals, of which, however, little is known and further investigation is urgently required.

In Malaya:—

    (1) Secret societies and strange initiatory rites are known to exist.

    (2) The presence of Mohammedanism almost certainly means that similar signs to those in use in Turkey among the dervishes would be found by a careful investigator; but more information is required".

In seeking for an explanation of this very remarkable phenomenon, we must bear in mind what Ward says *op. cit.* Preface page vi:—

"Freemasonry is still and always has been, a secret society. In its very essence, written documents are anathema. To this day our oath proves this and it is only during the last two hundred years that any deviation from this rule has been winked at".

From this we realise two facts; First, that in theory Freemasonry and its proto-types the world over, are all secret societies with an *oral* tradition and ritual and without documentary proof of any corporate existence whatever. Recognition is by sign or hand-grip, many of which are common to the whole human race. Second, that the precise origin of Freemasonry, the best known and wealthiest of all secret societies with limitless resources for research, is itself in dispute. Indeed, a vast library exists upon the subject without finality of origin having been reached.

These two facts alone give some indication of the difficulty which faces the student in the objective study of this important matter. Of course in practice, documents do exist, which have reached the profane and from which independent researchists and interested observers have made records for comparative study.

Few of these documents can be vouched for, because all secret tradition is oral and only the initiated can certify them, and they mindful of their oaths, will rarely disclose their clandestine formulæ. This obvious and initial difficulty tends to enshroud the subject of secret societies in pseudo-mystery, which encourages the layman to pooh-pooh their existence altogether, or else to explain them away as something which they are not. This attitude raises a further practical difficulty by creating an atmosphere of reserve almost of tabu, regarding secret societies among the general population, the vulgar, who are encouraged, or encourage themselves to ignore them, in apprehension of the powerful and unseen forces which these societies are popularly believed to possess and which may exact vengeance upon the too inquisitive. They are neglected too by the historians, with one or two brilliant exceptions.

Arnold Lunn *Revolutionary Socialism* (1939) says on page 44:—

"The influence of secret societies is a subject of controversy......
An historian who concerns himself with secret societies, risks a certain loss of professional prestige, for he risks being regarded as a sufferer from a conspiracy complex; but the question as to whether a particular conspiracy exists cannot be disposed of by proving that cranks have believed in non-existent conspiracies".

The result produced may be psychological, but it is none the less effective, and while leaving beneficent secret societies unaffected, it encourages the organisers of maleficent secret societies to trade upon this disinclination of the uninitiated to probe too deeply into their activities.

xviii

Professor Max Muller, says:—

"We must guard against rejecting as absurd what we cannot understand at once or what seems to us fanciful or irrational. I know from my own experience how, what seemed to me for a long time unmeaning, nay absurd, disclosed after a time a far deeper meaning than I should ever have expected".

As the writers of the *Palestine Commission Report* 1937 pertinently remark, page 8:—

"Popular instinct draws away from what is strange".

Because of the natural gregariousness of Man, he prefers to believe only what he can see, and hates and fears, or ignores what he does not understand. For this reason the barrier of mystery which is made to surround the subject as part of its protective armament, increases his instinct to draw away from a too close investigation of the phenomena of secret societies. In the case of beneficent societies no harm ensues from their exclusiveness.

But against maleficent secret societies whose power is known, whose vengeance is feared, and whose genius for concealment opposes an almost impenetrable wall to objective study, there can be no excuse for disinclination or apathy in investigation.

A recent manifestation of esoteric anthropology in Colonial administration is afforded by the Aba riots which occurred in the south-east of Nigeria in 1929, in which some 10,000 women took part and much damage was done.

Miss Perham *Native Administration in Nigeria* (1937) page 206 ff. gives an interesting account of these riots in which the women of the Ibo tribe combined to resist what they believed to be a move to impose a government tax upon them. They called themselves the "messengers of god" or the "spirit of womanhood" and believed themselves irresistible and immune from death. They bound their heads with ferns and carried palm leaves in their hands. Miss Perham *op. cit.* page 209 says:—

"It is interesting to note that no Europeans understood the exact significance of these last symbols, though nearly all the native witnesses assumed that they meant war".

We learn, however, from Frazer *The Golden Bough* (abridged ed. page 705) that in the realm of esoteric anthropology, the fern is believed to be an emanation of the sun's fire and is supposed to possess the power of revealing hidden gold and the treasures of the earth and, in addition on homeopathic principles, the fern is regarded as the best possible cure or preventive of injury by fire.

The palm is, of course, an universal emblem of fertility and thence of womanhood. Miss Perham *op. cit.* page 214 says:—

"There is no evidence that the Nigerian women had protected themselves with any special magic, but they had certainly armed themselves psychologically with a sense of security".

A possible explanation of the symbols they bore might be, that the fern represented their worldly goods, protected by its nature-magic properties: and the palm represented their inviolable womanhood.[1]

There is really nothing peculiar or inexplicable in the action of the Ibo women in 1929. Before going to war they assumed what they believed to be the armour of invulnerability, like the Taoist his talisman, the knight his coat of mail or the modern soldier his testament.

The same faith or superstition is common to the world and is to be found in the background of almost any rebellion anywhere. In the case of the Ibo, it happened to be in the foreground, and, therefore, drew undue attention to what is, after all, common to the human race. Another recent example was the Burma rebellion 1932–34.

Miss Perham does not ascribe the Ibo riots to any secret society organisation, with which, of course, African tribes are honey-combed, but suggests that secret society influence may have lain behind the outbreak. On page 218, she says:—

"Beneath the peculiar local symptoms lies a pathological condition, common to the whole of negro Africa. It is produced by the sudden strain, thrown upon primitive communities by the strong, all-embracing pressure of European influence. There are examples in various parts of the world of primitive peoples unexpectedly rebelling, after years of apparent acquiescence in European rule......

One relief for the desire for re-assertion is found in the formation of secret societies, or of quasi-Christian bodies, independant of white control, whose proceedings express at once European influence and an anti-European attitude. The "Watch-Tower" movement in southern Africa, with its apocalyptic hopes of the fall of Christendom, "Satan's organisation", clearly belongs to this category".

Miss Perham need not have restricted her view to Africa or to primitive peoples. The danger of this latent pathological condition has given many manifestations of its presence among diverse races within the Empire in recent years, and is widespread in the depths and shadows of the human mind throughout the world. Miss Perham concludes on page 220:—

"The gap that lies at present between Africans and the ever-shifting administrative officers, who represent to them the British Government, can only be bridged by *knowledge* and over that bridge it is we, who have to go three-quarters or more of the way, to meet them......

Yet such research is still regarded as a luxury which can be indulged in only when there is time and money to be spared from other enterprises, none of which can succeed apart from the human factor".

Here Miss Perham's insight touches upon a vital question, namely, Is our Imperial mission to be discharged as an objective or a subjective responsibility?

Footnote.—(1) P. Amaury Talbot *In the Shadow of the Bush* (1912) gives further information on this subject among the Ibo.

Lionel Curtis *The Commonwealth of God* page 608 has noted the same dilemma of the British administrator in India in the following pregnant passage:—

"The impact of British ideas on Indian society was thus complicated by the opposite and no less powerful influence to which the English were subject in India. They tended to acquire a certain distrust of the principles underlying the society by which they themselves were produced. The policies which appealed to them were such as England could not follow to the end without renouncing the law of her being.

The West in adjusting its relations to the East was hampered by the tendency of its representatives to lose their grasp of its own essential ideas".

Apart from the maintenance of order and security, (even without the intervention of law) no amount of "government" can make any real appeal to the illiterate and inarticulate "governed", unless its principles follow the law of their being, its tendencies inspire their confidence and its purposes are represented to them subjectively, with simplicity and clarity in their own language, and with a full explanation of its purpose from their point of view and with sympathetic understanding of what their reactions will be. This is the subjective approach which meets with an instant response and controls thereby the human factor.

The other, the cold objective approach is an artificial thing without appeal and, therefore, without command over the human factor, except what may be extracted by the threat of pains and penalties.

Generally speaking British Colonial administration is objective and to make it otherwise, we are met with an immediate difficulty well expressed by Casson in his Introduction to *The Discovery of Man* (1939) in his opening passage on page 13:—

"It will remain always one of the strangest of all enigmas of human history that however proper may be the study of Mankind by Man, yet it is invariably the ultimate study in which he indulges. For millennia man has in fact taken peculiar pains to study almost anything but himself. He has avoided self-analysis and the study of human origins and developments as if they were the plague. In this he was moved, I think, by that curious but fundamental motive which is inherent in human nature, which inhibits a human being from self-examination lest he be charged by his fellows with a kind of morbid indecency. Man to live and survive, must in the earliest stages of his existence, be completely objective.

* * *

Curiosity into human matters *per se* belongs to a stage when society is more secure, more confident and more capable of recognising self-consciousness as a virtue rather than as a dangerous luxury".

Casson here touches the important point revealed by Miss Perham above. He continues:—

"All inquiry into human relations and origins is a form of self-consciousness. We still use the term self-conscious as a term of reproach, "self-analysis" as an occupation for the unstable and the unworthy and in all our curricula of education the hardest objectivity is encouraged in the young, and considered an essential ingredient of the mature. "Subjective" as a term, has none of the merits accorded to its opposite "objective": "impersonal" has some quality superior to "personal". Here, indeed, is a long-standing prejudice in the human race, born of the need for survival, bred in the hard school of selection. It accounts for a hundred strange abberations of the mob, for a thousand minor aspects of persecution and repression.

In the early stages of human history, when the need for such self-consciousness, or analysis became so evident that not all the reactions of established authority can subdue it, such activities are relegated to a particular place and sphere in social organisation. They are dealt with by medicine-men, by an organised priest-craft and by publicly appointed experts. Only so can they be canalised into safety and the explosive material that they represent be insulated and isolated".

It is here, canalised into secret societies, that the social anthropologist will find that explosive material to-day, as in the Aba riots of 1929, insulated and isolated in the arcana of human belief. It is only by a subjective approach, that these arcana may be broached.

Mr. Bernard Shaw in his *Adventures of a Black girl in her search for God* wittily refers to the difficulty of overcoming these fundamental, almost sub-conscious, taboos which impede research, where he says, page 38:—

"When it comes to getting a move on, you (scientists) are all of the same opinion: stop it, flog it, hang it, dynamite it, stamp it out".

With such obstacles to progress has research to compete!

It would seem that belief in Special Creation which connotes belief in a more favourable status for those who accept it and a correspondingly less favourable status for those who do not, raises an unconscious but almost insuperable barrier to successful subjective approach, free from the taint of patronage or condescension.

But it is not only upon interesting speculations as to the origin of man, that the subject of esoteric anthropology touches. It concerns three vitally important practical matters:—

(1) The happiness of the human race and more particularly that part of it for which British administration is responsible.

(2) The control of violence, that "explosive material" referred to above and hence the control of the causes of war and rebellion.

(3) The control of crime.

These may be large claims, but they seem nonetheless capable of proof. We hope the following pages will prove them.

We can no longer afford to pooh-pooh the power of secret societies in the political sphere, with the story of Europe since the Great War before us. In the past twenty years we have seen movements which began as underground secret societies, bearing all the stigmata of such organisations, break surface and assume political power in one country after another. In Russia in 1917: in Italy in 1922: in Egypt, Turkey, Germany, Spain and elsewhere, there have sprung up powerful forces from secret society beginnings, some of which even now menace the peace of the world.

D. W. Pike *Secret Societies* (Oxford University Press, 1939) in his Introduction page 4 has:—

> "To-day, the secret society has become the weapon of diplomacy, a very important factor in the affairs of nations...... Events move so quickly that the assassin of to-day may be the national hero of tomorrow. A secret society may become the official Government of a country before its very existence is suspected abroad".

An investigation of these forces must, therefore, be worthwhile at this perilous juncture in our history and may perhaps be undertaken by the applied anthropologists and other scientists, lest they take root unrecognised within the Empire itself and undermine its foundations.

It is at this point that we approach the subject of this essay—the nature of secret societies and although it may seem perhaps presumptuous to attempt to undertake an exploration of such an abstruse subject, its importance is sufficient justification for the attempt, as it touches the problem of Colonial administration at so many vital points.

In this regard, the Secretary of State in his address to the Summer School in June, 1938, said:—

> "Colonial policy must not be a hotchpotch business, concocted at random each day according to the exigencies and seeming requirements of that particular moment, and perhaps undone the next day, when what is expedient seems to have changed. It must have thought, plan and design: it must be constantly inspired by some great main purposes. Nor must these purposes have application only here and there, in this Colony or that. If they are right, they should be the consistent motive force behind policy throughout the whole Colonial Empire".

The present work finds encouragement in these words, because it attempts to demarcate and identify in the infant sphere of applied anthropology, some of the motive forces, powerful but covert, at work among the people in one corner of the Empire.

Colonial policy cannot in our view have thought, plan and design and must inevitably meet with set-backs and reverses, unless these covert forces are rendered recognizable and are thoroughly understood, so that they may be readily canalised if the need should arise, into paths of safety.

To illustrate this point, we may quote three widely separated examples of "explosive material" (to which detailed reference is made in the text) wherein the generative force lay in the arcana of the human mind and the organisation and precipitating cause in a secret society, and all leading to war, namely:—

> In China.—The Taiping rebellion (1850) and the Boxer rebellion (1900).
> In Malaya.—The Perak war 1874–75.
> In Egypt.—The Sudan campaign 1882–1885.

It may sound fantastic, but is nevertheless true that the same signs and formulæ, most of them common to Freemasonry, are to be found at work as a hidden agency in the complex organisation of these otherwise vastly different antagonisms.

The same agency that General Gordon overcame in China in 1864, destroyed him at Khartoum in 1885.

We will now set ourselves to our task, but the authorities to guide us in an investigation of the phenomenon of secret societies are exceedingly meagre, as a reference to the *Encyclopaedia Britannica* under this heading will show. The general tabu which lies upon the subject and which has been explained above, no doubt accounts for this meagreness.

The subject of secret societies occupies but two and a half columns of the *E.B.* and the contributors are J. H. Driberg for the general and African section; and J. S. M. Ward (whose work has already been referred to) for the Chinese section.

The general section is confined almost exclusively to a discussion of the age-grades, fertility cults and magico-religious rites and governmental systems of present-day African tribes[1] and includes no survey of the secret societies of Europe or Asia, apart from Ward's article on China.

Chamber's Encyclopaedia offers a little more help. An article therein by Northcot W. Thomas gives information condensed from Hasting's monumental *Encyclopaedia of Religion and Ethics* and contains the following:—

> "Among civilised peoples the secret society is often political in its objects......
> On the other hand societies which originally had ulterior objects such as the Freemasons, may become purely social in their functions.
> Among non-civilised peoples secret societies often take a more prominent place than among ourselves, partly because they may fulfil judicial and other functions ......partly because, in the absence of any competing organisation, any body of men is able to impose its will on the unorganised mass.
> * * *
> Generally speaking the rites of secret societies and of initiation generally are to be explained as *firstly*, the removal of the candidate from the profane world for, *secondly*, a period of instruction prior to admission to the ranks of the adults or initiates, and *thirdly* a ceremony or series of ceremonies to remove him from the world in which he has lived as a candidate and to readmit him to the profane world".

Footnote.—(1) For West Africa, Butt-Thompson's *West African Secret Societies* (1929) seems a safer guide.

This definition though true of some types of secret societies is too circumscribed for general application and takes no account of the fundamental difference between those ranges of secret societies which are essentially religious, mystical and beneficent, and those which are essentially irreligious, magical and maleficent.

The truth seems to be that in the study of secret societies all of which are based in varying degree upon the arcana of the human mind, we must carefully follow the logic thread of cause and effect if we wish to arrive at satisfactory conclusions upon the whole abstruse subject.

This brings us to the fountain-head of first causes.

In his delightful book *The Story of Mankind* (1922) Van Loon begins:—

"We live under the shadow of a gigantic question-mark.

Who are we? Where do we come from? Whither are we bound?

Slowly but with persistent courage, we have been pushing this question-mark further and further towards that distant line beyond the horizon, where we hope to find our answer. We have not gone very far.

We still know very little but we have reached the point where with a fair degree of accuracy, we can guess at many things".

Unfortunately the first cause of man is still in dispute, which adds its own particular difficulty to the study of this subject and in some measure accounts for the absence of authoritative *dicta* to guide the student. Mr. H. G. Wells in *The Fate of Homo Sapiens* (1939) has recently drawn a rather gloomy picture of what may become of us if we do not make a serious attempt to decide whence we have come and whither we are bound and act in concert upon that decision for the welfare and harmony of us all.

2. THE EMERGENCE OF MAN

As the subject begins and ends with man and his beliefs, we must start with a glance at Man's own beginnings.

We are here met with the initial difficulty that science and religion are divided upon the question.[1] Religion teaches man's special creation, science his evolution. The opposing beliefs may be roughly shown thus:—

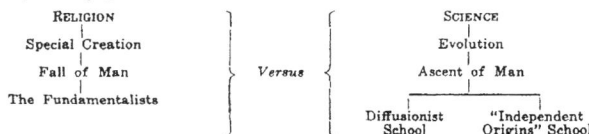

RELIGION
|
Special Creation
|
Fall of Man
|
The Fundamentalists

Versus

SCIENCE
|
Evolution
|
Ascent of Man
|

Diffusionist School   "Independent Origins" School

In this essay we will be guided by the views of the most eminent members of the Royal Anthropological Institute. Professor Elliot Smith *Early Man* (1931) says on page 13:—

"The true history of the creation of Man, which we now call evolution is not to be confused with the ancient traditions. It is a new field of inquiry which after more than a century of passionate controversy is now for the first time being cultivated calmly and seriously.

* * *

Each new discovery......gives renewed confidence in our attempts to reconstruct our pedigree and probe into the sources of our being...... It is generally admitted that all living members of the human family belong to the same species *homo sapiens*.

* * *

Whatever criterion may be adopted as racial distinctions......there are certain outstanding features, which the man in the street is competent to recognise without any special training for differentiating six well defined types of mankind: the aboriginal Australian: the Negro: the Mongol: the Mediterranean: the Alpine and the Nordic races. However much these various racial strains have become intermingled during the last fifty centuries, most educated people are familiar with their distinctive features.

* * *

The divergent streams that set out from the original home of the common ancestors of these sharply contrasted peoples cannot be brought together east of Mesopotamia.

* * *

The hypothetical centre of the species *sapiens*......the spot from which all these distribution areas seem to radiate was somewhere in the neighbourhood of Western Asia...... If the implication of these distributions is accepted, we may tentatively assume that the species *sapiens* probably lived somewhere in the region between India and North Africa and from this centre they radiated out in different directions in groups which became segregated respectively in six different areas and assumed the distinctive characters of the fundamental races of the species".

Sir Arthur Keith in the same series of published lectures (*Early Man*) says on page 49:—

"This widespread organisation of mankind into many and diverse types was and is, Nature's way of evolving higher types. I use the word "higher" merely

---

Footnote.—(1) For a reconciliation of the standpoints of religion and science, *see* Herbert Spencer *First Principles* (ed. 1900) Chapters I and V.

to indicate that the races which replaced others whether by evolution or substitution, were the better adapted for the needs of the time and the locality and in this sense only were they higher; they need not have been larger brained. The general trend of evolution had been to give man better knowledge of his surroundings and from being their slave, to make him their master to a greater or lesser degree......
It was under such conditions of unconscious competition that there were produced the races which we find in possession of the world at the dawn of the historical period".

The necessity to include a glance at the genesis of man himself in any survey of the development of secret associations or beliefs among the Human family, is thus revealed.

In all investigation we must proceed from the known or at least from a working hypothesis, if we wish to advance towards the unravelling of the unknown.

In the sphere of Colonial administration where we have commitments and imperial responsibilities among all six of the fundamental races of the Human family, to attempt to understand the problems involved by any other less fundamental method of approach, is bound to meet with confusion and ultimate failure.

In beginning at this point we incidentally greatly simplify our particular subject, as will shortly appear.

Recent archaeological research by Sir Leonard Woolley[1] has brought Old Testament history vividly to life. So far from refuting the Bible story, excavation has, with the adjustment of a few dates or periods, largely confirmed it.

Abraham was the first historical modern man.[2] He was born in the year B.C. 2000 at Ur in southern Mesopotamia on the Euphrates river, and Sir Leonard Woolley could probably point out the house he lived in. The city of Ur was at the time of Abraham's birth, the capital city of the Sumerian Kings.

To our minds this date may appear remote—pre-historical—but in fact it is but yesterday in the time-register of the world. Archaeology has also shown that Abraham and his generation were men much like ourselves, leading city or country lives just as we do, and probably complaining about the weather.

Abraham was not the first man, but he was the first historical figure, whose full story has come down to us.

His importance lies not only in this fact, but in the still more important fact that when grown up and living the pagan existence of his fellow citizens, he received a *revelation and a promise* from a divine being, who later declared himself to be Yahweh or Jehovah, the revealed God of the Jews, the Christians and the Mohamedans and whose first prophet was Abraham. This is one of the earliest and certainly one of the greatest recorded events in human history.

But we must remember that the revelation of God to Abraham was not the first, it was the *second* traditional revelation of God to Man, and it is of comparatively recent date.

Before considering the first revelation and the traditions surrounding it, we should adjust our perspective to the age of the world and the place of modern man in it. Woolley helps us to do so in the following passage from *Digging up the Past* page 12:—

"In these days, natural science is unfolding before us a panorama, which, to our great-grandfathers seemed in its beginnings, blasphemous. To them it undermined the foundations of belief, to us it establishes it, though upon a base broader and more rational. Science reckons time in millions of years and stretches space to infinity: the wider outlook does not make us one bit less interested in the things of to-day and tomorrow and may seem scarcely to affect our practice, but it is there, part of our consciousness and the more it is explored the better we can understand ourselves. Archaeology is doing the same thing in a smaller field. It deals with a period limited to a few thousand years and its subject is not the universe not even the human race, *but modern man.* We dig, and say of these pots and pans, these beads and weapons, that they date back to 3000 or 4000 B.C. and the onlooker is tempted to exclaim at their age and to admire them simply because they are old.

Their real interest lies in the fact that they are new.

If mere age were the standard, all that we unearth is insignificant, compared to the dinosaur's fossil egg and, for that matter: what is six thousand years in the life of the human race, when we have to calculate that in terms of geological periods?

The importance of our archaeological material is that it throws light on the history of men very like ourselves and *on a civilisation which is bound up with that of to-day".*[3]

This passage supplies the setting for the present work, which deals with an aspect of the life of modern historical man, and we take as our starting point the modern year B.C. 2000.

It will also help us to keep our proper perspective, particularly in Malaya where so many ancient races intermix, to realise that in our current year 1937 the day that dawns tomorrow will be for the Chinese a day in the 13th year of the 77th sixty-year-cycle (*i.e.* the year 4,634): for the Hindu a day in the 5,037th year of the *Kali Yuga* era: for the Siamese a day in the 2479th year of the Buddhist era: for the Jews a day in the 5698th (or *Annus Mundi*) year, reckoned from the Jewish date of the creation B.C. 3761: for the Malays and other Mohamedans a day in the 1355th year since the flight of Mohamed from Mecca to Medina: and so forth. This pageant of years illustrates the diversity of human belief around us in the simple sphere of time alone and may help us to realise the vastly greater diversities in other spheres of human society.

Footnote.—(1) *See his works:—Ur of the Chaldees* (1929). *Digging up the past* (1930) *Abraham* (1935).
Footnote.—(2) This distinction is sometimes claimed for Akhenaten of the 18th dynasty of Egypt (c. 1388 B.C.).
Footnote.—(3) The italics are ours.

But in all this complex of origins and beliefs, there remains *one common factor among the peoples of the earth* and that is the similarity, we may say the identity, of their arcanan formulæ,—the signs and symbols of their secret societies.

Surely, if the purpose of the British Empire is to ensure that the evolutionary process shall go on and lead at different times and by different paths to the final objective, an investigation into something tangible, a veritable common factor, albeit seemingly unimportant, which binds all those races together, must be worthwhile?

Another investigator has drawn attention to another common factor, that of language, which awaits investigation upon similar lines. Hocart *Kingship* (1927) page 15 has:—

> "We all know that a single family of languages has long extended from Iceland to the Bramaputra: but we are in continual danger of forgetting that another family, even more homogeneous, stretches from Madagascar through Indonesia as far as Hawaii and Easter Island. Now, if two languages could between them in less than four thousand years cover two hundred and fifty degrees out of three hundred and sixty that go round the globe, how much easier for a single religion, which has had at least six thousand years in which to do so"?

The same writer records the disinclination of scientists noted by Casson above, to investigate along these lines and for the same reason. Hocart *op. cit.* page 14 has:—

> "The essence of science is to guess and then set about to accumulate facts bearing on this guess, to prove it or disprove it, or, in more learned language, science advances by means of working hypotheses. If we are not allowed to use these, we might as well pack up our learning, for we shall never achieve more than collections of facts.
>
> There is no harm in trying the hypothesis of common origin but numerous scholars and historians of high repute refuse even to go so far. This is partly due to a fear of losing caste by being confounded with those wild men who seized upon the most superficial resemblances in every part of the world to prove that the Ten Lost Tribes of Israel had been there. Partly this reluctance springs from very vague or erroneous notions about the races of the world east of India".

It is perhaps due to these sub-conscious inhibitions that even in Malaya, were the maleficent power of secret societies is well-known and constantly in public evidence, there has been no deep-level excavation, aimed at unearthing and identifying the roots of those pernicious secret fraternities which have kept the community in fear; the underworld in thrall and the Government on tenterhooks, during the past hundred years.

In his *Outline of History* (1920) Mr. H. G. Wells gives us in condensed form in Chapters VIII to XIV the currently accepted views of science, based on modern researches in geology, anthropology and archaeology, upon the ancestry of man. This ancestry began about 50,000 years ago with early palaeolithic (early Stone Age) man, known to science as Neanderthal man, during the Fourth Ice Age in Europe and Western Asia. This race of men died out and were replaced in the post-glacial period, by men of the later palaeolithic period (about B.C. 35000 to 15000) known as reindeer man, who in turn gave way to neolithic (or new stone age) man, who appeared in Europe some 12,000 years ago and probably earlier in Asia and North Africa, and who is still with us.

Neolithic man arrived at the stage of *homo sapiens* and is the true ancestor of the modern human race. With him agriculture and civilisation began and is still going on.

For those who find the contemplation of man's evolution through geological periods unreal, Van Loon *The Story of Mankind*, has provided a chart (*op. cit.* page 11) which vividly contrasts the pre-history of man with his brief historical period of the last 6,000 years.

It was, perhaps, during the early part of the neolithic period, between B.C. 12000 and B.C. 2000, that the first revelation of God to man was made, which is enshrined in the biblical tradition of the Creation. Science has already furnished much historical material, gathered for the most part in Egypt and Mesopotamia, covering the period B.C. 5000 to B.C. 2000 but the date of the "creation" or first revelation of God to man, has not yet been fixed.

Archbishop Ussher's *Notation* (A.D. 1650) placed the date of the Creation as B.C. 4004, but this date is no longer tenable.

We know of two traditional events which took place during the early neolithic period subsequent to the first revelation. These were:—

(1) The fall of man after the first revelation (or "creation").

(2) The flood, which, according to tradition was the punishment of man for that fall.

The "neolithic" date of the "creation" is unknown, but may be placed at the beginning of the neolithic period, about B.C. 12000. The approximate date of the flood in the Euphrates valley has been fixed by science at about B.C. 4200. Knowledge of these events comes to us from Mesopotamian sources and we do not yet know whether evidence exists of their having affected other than the Mesopotamian peoples, but we do know that there exists among the Chinese the tradition of a flood in the Yellow River basin of China at about that epoch.[1]

We know that the city of Ur was the capital of the powerful Empire of the Sumerians at the time of the birth of Abraham, an empire which had flourished in that region since about B.C. 5000 or earlier of which King Sargon of Akkad, a semite (B.C. 2528) was one of the later and greatest rulers, and which collapsed about B.C. 2170.

We do not know whence the Sumerians came, but by tradition they came from the East. They gave their cuneiform (wedge-shaped) script to the Mesopotamian or Babylonian region and some scholars have detected a similarity between Sumerian and Chinese script.

A common human origin in the Central Asian Plateau

We must here make a brief examination of the evidence in support of the theory of a common human origin in the Central Asian Highlands.

Footnote.—(1) *See* below under, "The Flood".

Couling *Encyclopaedia Sinica* (1917) page 531 has:—

"Sumerian is the primitive script of Babylonia from which in course of time were developed all the varieties of Cuneiform. It was originally pictorial, but had already taken on conventional forms in the time of the earliest extant specimens of the language that is, between 3000 and 4000 B.C. Some scholars have found so much similarity between Sumerian and Chinese writing that they have conjectured the two races to be kindred tribes who once lived together in the highlands of Central Asia. The latest exponent of this theory is Dr. Ball, lecturer in Assyriology at Oxford, who has published an essay[1] towards a comparative lexicon of the two languages".

The theory of a Central Asian highland origin of the Sumerians is of the utmost importance to our subject. Since Dr. Ball's thesis appeared, there have been three major discoveries in archaeology which have a bearing on it. These are:—

(1) In 1906–8, German and Turkish excavators at the site of a Turkish village Boghaz Keui near Angora, first investigated by Perrot in 1861, discovered several thousand tablets in cuneiform belonging to a Hittite culture of about B.C. 2000 of which some three thousand have not yet been deciphered. Among those already transcribed are actual dictionaries with words in parallel columns in Hittite, Sumerian and Assyrio-Babylonian, belonging to the period B.C. 1350–1300.

(2) From 1922 onwards Sir Leonard Woolley has carried on at Ur the vastly important researches already referred to, which threw much more light on the Sumerians, but have as yet failed to fix their origin. In *Ur of the Chaldees* (1929) Woolley says, page 16:—

"At a date we cannot fix people of a new race made their way into the Euphrates valley, coming whence we do not know and settled down side by side with the old inhabitants.[2] These were the Sumerians. Quoting probably some legend of the Sumerians themselves, the Old Testament says that "the people journeyed from the East and came into the plain of Shinar (which is Babylon) and dwelt there", and of recent years excavations so far away to the east as the valley of the Indus river, have produced remains of an early civilisation which has certain elements in common with what we find in Mesopotamia. The Sumerians believed that they came into the country with their civilisation already formed, bringing with them the knowledge of agriculture, of workmanship in metal, of the art of writing—"since then", said they, "no new inventions have been made". And if, as our excavations seem to show, there is a good deal of truth in that tradition, then it was not in the Euphrates valley that the arts were born, and though it is not likely to have been in the Indus valley either, later research may well discover some site between these two extremes where the ancestors of our Sumerians developed the first real civilisation of which we have any knowledge".

(3) The third discovery was that made in the Indus valley alluded to by Woolley. In 1924, Mr. R. D. Banerji excavating at Mohendjodaro near Harappa discovered a whole city of the dead which bears some likeness to the Sumerian cities of Mesopotamia.

The position up-to-the minute has been summarised by Casson in *The Discovery of Man* (1939) page 304 ff. thus:—

"The Sumer was a fully-developed civilisation which must have come from an earlier period—yet the latest date assignable to it is about 3000 B.C.

The origins of civilisation are thus seen to recede into a remoter past. The Sumerians were themselves immigrant into Mesopotamia and the aboriginal people whom they replaced or absorbed lived at an even earlier date. But it was the Sumerians who established the outlines of civilisation in Mesopotamia. Whence they came and what was their own earlier history is among the many problems which still await solution.

                        *   *   *

During the course of the Mesopotamian excavations on Sumerian sites a small number of unusual seal stones had been identified which appeared to be importations from elsewhere. Their origin was unknown...... The excavations in the Indus valley showed where they came from, for the sites of Harappa and Mohendjodaro produced large numbers of them. Clearly India was their place of manufacture. The contact was established.

                        *   *   *

The fact that the inhabitants of the Indian sites were in touch with Mesopotamia in B.C. 3000 was of vital importance. *Perhaps both cultures originate in a common source.*

                        *   *   *

If the Indian is derivative together with Sumerian culture from a common source, then both must have separated off from the parent stock at a very early date, certainly before either invented the art of writing.

Until the wastes of Western Turkestan and the plateaux of Baluchistan and Iran have been more fully explored we must suspend judgment.

                        *   *   *

In China archaeology is a very recent growth, barely a few years old......
Excavations by Chinese archaeologists cannot be said to have reached a stage when it is possible for the outlines of Chinese history and pre-history to be written with clarity.

                        *   *   *

Footnote.—(1) *The New Accadian* (Proc. Soc. Bibl. Archaeology) 1889–90: and *Sumerian and Chinese*, 1913. See also article by Rev. H. W. White entitled "Chinese and Sumerian" *The New China Review* Vol. II (1920) page 37.
Footnote.—(2) River and marsh folk of a primitive type.

One notable discovery deserves mention, namely the fixing of a neo-lithic age for Chinese pre-history and *the realisation that that age is dependent upon a similar culture that stretches right across Asia to eastern Europe.*
The uniformity of early Asiatic culture is indeed remarkable. The same history is touched on again by recent excavations in the highlands of Persia where a primitive culture, using highly skilled painted pottery, shows a community with both East and West".

Looked at dispassionately, we must admit that the excavated researches of archaeology, as compared with the area of the earth's surface are infinitesimal. In China, with a living uninterrupted civilisation of some 4,000 years, the surface has hardly been scratched. And yet wherever the work has been undertaken it shows the same finger pointing backwards to a single remote ancestry of Man. The sign-posts of esoteric anthropology point a still more vivid finger towards the same conclusion. And not only east and west, but north and south, in both hemispheres and in all continents and islands the same signs and symbols of what may be referred to under the generic name of freemasonry are to be found to-day, preserved in the arcana of all or most tribes and races and suggesting insistently a common origin.

Sir Percy Sykes *The Quest for Cathay* (1936) supports the view that the pre-historic source of the Aryan race may be found in the buried cities beneath the Gobi desert of to-day, where some 10,000 years ago the sand encroaching upon their grazing lands, precipitated an eruption towards the west of those nomad Aryan tribes inhabiting this once most fertile tract. Le Fevre *An Eastern Odyssey* (1935) Appendix II, surveying the results of archaeology in the Gobi to date, shows that too little is as yet known of the area to enable an opinion to be formed.

It may yet be proved that the Sumerians moved from the Gobi westward of the Pamirs prior to B.C. 10000 and thence to the Euphrates valley in B.C. 6000.

Casson says above, that if the Indian and Mesopotamian cultures of B.C. 3000 split from a common parent stem, they must have split before the invention of writing. If this be so, does not the universal use of common and well-understood signs and symbols all relating to man's beliefs among the nations of the earth to-day, in all states of culture, suggest that that split may have occurred before even the dawn of human speech?

Or, may it not have been, that the fear and tabu that surrounded man's first religious promptings or revelation caused him to use his new-found speech for his physical needs alone and to preserve his pre-speech sign-language for the things of the soul: and even after the invention of writing, to prefer to transmit *orally* his ancient sacred tradition?

The Sumers and Mount Meru

To return to the origin of the Sumerians, we may perhaps on the strength of the foregoing summing up of present knowledge, offer a suggestion for what it may be worth. The "eastern tradition" of the Sumerians has led to confirmation in the Indus valley. There is no reason why it should stop there. Unfortunately we do not know, as between Sumerian culture in the Euphrates and the Indus valley, which was the chicken and which the egg.

We do know that Sumerian tradition in Mesopotamia taught two things:—

(1) That the Sumers came from the east.

(2) That they arrived with a fully developed culture.

And from other sources we know that their arrival must have been about 6000 B.C. With these facts and the sign-post of the Indus valley before us to point the way, we may be permitted to seek a clue to their original common parentage in "the highlands of central Asia" which tower between India and China. This Indo-Aryan *nidus* has been suggested as the source of the original common stem by many scholars and is the subject of the thesis of Dr. Ball in 1913 referred to above.

In the Central Asian mountain mass, which radiates from Tibet and which includes the highest mountains in the world, there is a range known to the Chinese and to geography as the Kw'en Lun 崑崙 mountains.

Couling *Encyclopaedia Sinica* has the following about this mountain range:—

"A name both geographical and mythical. In geography it means the great range of mountains which beginning in the Pamirs in the west, divides Tibet from Chinese Turkestan and dwindles away eastward in the hills which divide the Yangtze and Yellow river basins. The range is regarded by geologists as the true backbone of Asia, being an earlier elevation than the Himalayan chain, south of Tibet".

Upon this testimony borne out by many authorities, the Kw'en Lun mountains are the true and original physical link between east and west Asia across the Pamirs—"the roof of the world".[1]

Couling continues:—

"In legend, Kw'en Lun is a mountain of Central Asia, perhaps to be identified with Hindu Khush: but Taoist and other fables make it the central mountain of the world. The Sai Wang Mo (西王母) Queen mother of the west, lives there with her fairy legions: There is the fountain of immortality and thence flow the four great rivers of the world.[2]

Many of the legends are evidently Hindu in origin and Kw'en Lun is the same as Sumeru".

In Hindu mythology, Mount Meru is the central mountain of the universe, round which all heavenly bodies revolve.

We have been unable to trace the origin of the name Sumeru, as given by Couling, for the mountain known in Asiatic mythology as Meru. There can be no doubt however that Couling's reference is to Mount Meru. It has been suggested to us that the prefix is analogous to the Sanscrit adjectival prefix Su—meaning "auspicious" or "golden", but the

---

Footnote.—(1) *See* map page xlviii *infra*.
Footnote.—(2) Actually the following four great rivers rise in the area—Yellow, Yangtze, Mekong and Salween.

authority for this and for its use by Couling is absent. We suggest another explanation below.

Chambers *Encyclopaedia* gives:—

"Meru. In Hindu mythology a fabulous mountain in the centre of the world, 80,000 leagues high. It is the most sacred of all mythical mountains and the abode of Vishnu".

We here reach an interesting point in that the *Encyclopaedia Britannica*, identifies Mount Meru, with the existing town of Merv, or Maur in modern Russian Turkestan, which occupies the same site as the ancient oasis and town of the same name, situated in the depression of the Hindu Kush range which stretches from the Caspian to the Pamirs. This site is in the "wastes of western Turkestan", referred to by Casson above. *The Encyclopaedia Britannica* says:—

"In the Hindu (the Puranas), Parsi, Arab tradition, Merv is looked upon as the ancient Paradise, the cradle of the Aryan families of mankind, and so of the human race. Under the name of Mouru the place is mentioned with Balkh in the geography of the Zend-Avesta, which dates probably from at least 1200 B.C.".

As the origin of the Aryan race has not yet been determined might not the tradition which identifies it with the oasis of Merv and thence with Mount Meru and thence with the origin of the human race be true?

Archaeology alone can supply the answer perhaps by excavation of the oasis of Merv.[1]

We have seen that the Taoist tradition has the same association, for it was there that Si Wang Mo lived with her immortals. Without suggesting an identity between the Hindu name of the mountain and the Sumers, we are entitled to enquire further into the identity of Si Wang Mo and here we are in good company.

Couling *op. cit.* page 518 says:—

"Si Wang Mo (西 王 母) is a name which occurs in ancient Chinese works and has given rise to a remarkable variety of opinions among sinologues. The characters simply translated mean West-King-Mother, meaning Queen Mother of the West: but the puzzle is to know to whom or to what the term applied. The following solutions have been suggested:—

Mayers, says it was a fabulous being of the female sex and adds that modern writers take it as the name of a region or of a sovereign.

Legge, in his translation of the *Bamboo Books* renders it "Western Wang Moo" and "the chief of Wang Moo".

Faber, translating Lei Tz (列 子) (Laotius) gives *die mutter des West-Koniges*.

Hirth, translates it as "Mother of the Western King", but again speaks of it as "a place, an imaginary abode of a fairy queen".

Eitel, regards it as probably a mere transliteration of some non-Chinese name. In translation he gives both "The people Si-wang-mu and the chief of Si-wang-mu".

La Couperie, thought it was the title of a line of sovereigns of the Wa-sun nations.

The early Jesuit missionaries, thought it meant the Queen of Sheba and *Forke* has elaborated this theory.

Chavannes takes it as the name of a barbarous tribe.

De Groot, speaks of Si Wang Mu as "a mystic queen" of the Sien (仙) or immortals.

The latest theory advanced by a foreign scholar is that of *Giles*, who identifies Si Wang Mu with Hera (Juno).

All references required for the above, with a study of the Chinese allusions and the exposition of Giles' theory will be found in Giles' *Who was Si Wang Mu?* in *Adversaria Sinica* page 1".

With such a wealth of supposition before us, there is perhaps room for the theory that the name may refer to the goddess of that region whence the Sumerians came? If we take the suggestions of Eitel and de Groot (above) and place them side by side, we may be as near the truth as not. The "Si" of the name, if a transliteration, may not stand for west (西) sai but for immortal (仙) sien and placing "Si" and "Mu" together we would then get "Immortal mother". "Wang" may mean in Chinese either: King, prince, ruler, royal or to govern. (The term for a queen is more properly 皇后 Wang Hau). This transposition would give Si Mu Wang meaning Queen Si-Mo "Immortal mother-ruler", or "Royal and immortal mother".

Here we approach the conception that Si Wang Mu of the Kw'en Lun mountains may be the Great Goddess of Nature. The west, where these mountains lie from China, is associated by the Chinese with the Moon and the female principle in Nature, hence Si Wang Mu may even stand for the Moon Goddess. (See Chapter III *infra*).

Disregarding as dangerous the similarity between the name Sumerian and the Hindu name of Mount Meru and the Chinese name for the goddess Si-Mu, we have nevertheless the two remaining Mesopotamian Sumerian traditions to support the general inference, namely, that they came from the east and that they arrived with a ready-made culture.

The Soma and Mount Meru

This leads us to a final hypothesis based upon Vedic mythology.

In the Avesta the plant known by the Sanskrit name of *Soma* grew on the slopes of Mount Meru and when pressed, gave forth a sacred intoxicating juice, which was *mixed*

Footnote.—(1) Oudendyke *Ways and Byways in Diplomacy* (1939) page 182 says:—
"The ruins of Old Merv date only from the thirteenth and fifteenth centuries, but the place is one of the oldest known in history. It is mentioned in Zoroaster's writings and the local legends maintain that our common ancestor Adam learnt the art of agriculture there. The various ruins cover tens of square miles, an impressive graveyard of an ancient civilisation."
Meakin *In Russian Turkestan* (1903) page 296 says of Merv:
"To-day there are still forty miles of ruins that have never been properly explored by archaeologists".

with milk to form the nectar of the gods, the wine of immortality. Thus, in Book IX of the *Rigveda* which is devoted to the Soma ritual we read:—

> "We have drunk the Soma;
> We have become immortal;
> We have won the light;
> We have won the gods".

As Chambers' *Encyclopaedia* (1930) says:—

> "Soma in Indian literature, Haoma in the *Avesta*, is the name of a drink pressed (*Su* = press out) from a plant and mixed with milk. The intoxicating qualities of the drink won it great popularity in Indo-Iranian times.
>
> Naturally the exhilaration caused by the drink led to its being treated as divine and the god Soma appears already in the *Rigveda* as a most potent power...... He is a guardian of natural order, supporter, or creator of heaven and earth...... As Indra drinks deep draughts of Soma to strengthen him to win the rains from the demons who hold them back, so Soma as a god is present and identified with the drink or the plant: he grows on the mountains, but also he is brought down to earth by an eagle, perhaps the lightning.
>
> In the later Vedic period he is constantly identified with the moon, which is conceived as the heavenly receptacle of the Soma which the gods drink...... As practised in later Vedic times the Soma sacrifice is accompanied by an elaborate ceremonial, and an animal sacrifice forms an essential preliminary.
>
> The use of substitutes for the real Soma is in this period frequently mentioned, whence it is probable that the true soma grew only in the mountainous regions once inhabited by the Indo-Iranians. This may help to explain the fact that the cult. evidently extremely popular in Vedic times, plays no serious part in mediaeval or modern Hinduism, though even now it is not entirely extinct".

The *Encyclopaedia Britannica* says, page 965:—

> "Soma, in Vedic India personified the plant *asclepias acida*[1] whose sap, fermented, is an intoxicant. As a Bacchus-like god, Soma is lauded in 114 hymns of the *Rig-veda* and as a co-equal of Indra, Agni and Rudra in other Books. Its uses, like its name (*haoma* in the Avesta), go back to Iranian times, and it was prized both in India and Iran as a medicine conducing to longevity. The celestial variety, distinct from that of earth, was drunk by the gods, and incited Indra to establish the universe. In the post-Vedic epics, Soma is the Moon who wanes when drunk by gods but is replenished by the Sun.[2] For the theft of the first soma by Indra's eagle, *see* Zeus, Odin, etc.".

Rev. S. Beale *Buddhism in China* suggests that Mount Sumeru the abode of the gods, may derive its name from the root Suma meaning "heavenly water". This must refer to the intoxicating soma juice. The Buddhist Mount Sumeru became divided into 13 concentric circles or stages, representing separate heavens. Beyond the summit of Sumeru lay Nirvana the highest spiritual heaven of Buddhism.[3]

If we now return to Woolley and the Sumerians and read again in Chapter I of *Ur of the Chaldees* that:—

> "The Sumerians believed that they came into the country with their civilisation already formed...... If, as our excavations seem to show, there is a good deal of truth in that tradition, then it was not in the Euphrates valley that the arts were born, and though it is not likely to have been the Indus valley either, later research may well discover some site between these two extremes where the ancestors of our Sumerians developed the first real civilisation of which we have any knowledge".

Could that other site be the Vedic mountain of Meru where the moon was worshipped and the Soma milk drunk on a site near perhaps to modern Merv?

The Moon Goddess of Egypt

Opposed to the Central Asian plateau theory, is the school of Professor Elliot Smith, which designates Egypt as the home of modern Man. It was there, this school maintains, where barley was indigenous, that irrigation and agriculture began and prepared the way for a settled form of human life. The storage of barley led to the discovery of beer-making. Professor Elliot Smith *In the Beginning* (1928) page 36 has:—

> "The beer was regarded as the divine (*i.e.* life-prolonging) essence of the sacred barley, which, again, was identified with the body of the god Osiris. In every part of the world each civilisation imitated its Egyptian prototype and had its sacred drink,—wine, ambrosia, amrita, soma, kava, manguey, mead, etc., to confer immortal life upon its gods. The settled mode of life......was already...... creating the conditions that led to the domestication of cattle and, probably for the first time in the history of mankind, the use of cow's milk as food for human beings. The realisation of the fact that the milk of the cows they had domesticated could be used for feeding human children seems to have made so profound an impression on the earliest Egyptians that they regarded the cow as a divine being, a foster-mother of mankind, whom they identified with the Great Mother who was the source of all human life. They already regarded the moon as the controller of woman's life-giving functions, and so they added to the symbols of the divine milk-giver the moon's disc as one of her insignia: and in course of time identified the sacred cow with the sky in which the moon moved".

Footnote.—(1) Akin to the common milkweed and also known as the moon-plant. Both names are significant. For Soma rites in particular relation to religious beliefs, *see* Hocart *Kingship* page 10: Chapter VI (Ambrosia) : page 142: pages 210-13 and 219.
Footnote.—(2) *See* Macdonell *Vedic Mythology*, and Keith *Religion and Philosophy of the Veda.*
Footnote.—(3) *See* also Ward and Stirling *op. cit.* Vol. II pages 19-22 and page 24.

And *op. cit.* page 85:—

"The Celestial Cow, Hathor, not only conferred life upon mortals by giving them birth; she also sustained them throughout life by giving them the divine milk, and at death she conveyed them to the sky".

The Moon Goddess of Ur

Woolley in *Abraham*, page 79 ff. says:—

"Ur was the city of Nannar, the Moon God...... Nannar was not only the god of Ur, but its King, so that it was but fitting that his house should be the city's ultimate stronghold.

* * *

This walled platform was the Moon-god's terrace and on the terrace stood the Ziggurat, which was the chief glory of the city and the core of its worship......

* * *

The shrine of Nannar......was the most sacred thing in Ur. A mountain of brickwork, one might say, and rightly, for the ziggurat was a "High Place" an artificial hill made by men who had once worshipped their gods on mountain tops and, finding nothing of the sort in this flat delta-land, had set to work to build one. They called it the "Hill of Heaven" or "the Mountain of God" and they planted trees on its stages as if in imitation of the real hills of their ancient home, so that its terraces were hanging gardens and the shrine was ringed about with green. In that shrine which men call heaven, was the statue of Nannar and there was his bed-chamber, to which the priestess went by night to become the bride of the god: and once a year the priests in procession brought the image down the long flights of stairs to carry it outside the city to its summer temple, where was celebrated the mystic marriage, on which depended the fertility of the soil and the renewal of Nature".

May not the Ziggurat of the Sumerians at Ur, which was staged and terraced, have been an artificial representation of the mount of Meru?[1]

Woolley again has in Chapter III of *Ur of the Chaldees* a description page 70, of a frieze found at Al Ubaid just outside Ur (illustrated at Plate VIII (a) in his work) showing:—

"Men seated on stools milking cattle. On the other side of the byre two men, shaven and wearing the fleece petticoat which in later times seems to survive as the official dress of priests and priest-Kings, are putting milk through a strainer into a vessel set on the ground, while two others are collecting the strained liquid in great store jars.

It is a typical scene of pastoral life, but the costume of the actors makes it likely that it is something more than this. There were in later days at least, sacred farms attached to the temples and here we may have priests preparing the milk of the Mother-goddess Nin-Kharsag which was the nourishment of Kings".

Is it too much to hazard the suggestion that the frieze may represent the preparation of Soma? And again at the same reference Woolley has:—

"That the very domestic looking picture of milking has a religious bearing is made more likely by the fact that in the same frieze there was introduced between the figures of walking cattle, a small panel of a curiously incongruous character: it shows a bearded bull rampant in hilly country on whose back is perched a lion-headed eagle apparently attacking him and tearing at his rump: this certainly is an illustration of some mythological legend and its presence here cannot but affect our view of the frieze as a whole".

May not the lion-headed eagle be Indra's eagle mentioned in the *Rig-veda* which brought down the soma-plant to earth and thus brought immortality to man? The legend is, of course, common to many beliefs.

Mediaeval Christian belief also provides examples, as the following references show. Jehan de Mandeville *Early Travels in Palestine* (*circa* A.D. 1350) page 276 quoted by W. Edwards in *A Mediaeval Scrap-heap* (1930) page 88 says:—

"Of Paradise.......wise men told me that the Earthly Paradise is the highest place in the earth: it nearly touches the circle of the moon. From a well in the highest part spring four rivers, *viz*:—
Pison or Ganges of India
Gyson or Nile of Egypt
Tigris of Assyria and Armenia
Euphrates of Media and Persia"

and again, Ranulf Higden a benedictine monk of Chester author of the English mediaeval chronicle *Polychronicon* (c. 1150) R.S. 1. 73 quoted by W. Edwards *op. cit.* page 88 says:—

"The fame of Paradise has remained unquestioned for six thousand years, but its exact site could never be determined".

Higden *op. cit.* R.S. 1. 321 decides that Paradise is not situated in the Fortunate Isles in the Western Sea but that it is in the extreme parts of the East. Its situation is high because Noah's flood did not reach it. It is of vast extent because, of its four great rivers, the Nile is said to rise near the Atlas Mountains of Ethiopia: the Tigris and Euphrates from the mountains of Armenia at the foot of the Caucasus (*ibidem* 66–78).

The Meaux Chronicle (*circa* A.D. 1460) R.S. 1. 146 says that the good in the Earthly Paradise were fed with celestial food which came down from Heaven once a day in a fiery flame (? lightning).

Dr. Coulton in *A Mediaeval Garner* page 464 quotes a fourteenth century Italian legend, according to which three monks entered the Earthly Paradise where they saw a tree of

---

Footnote.—(1) For comparative purposes, a restoration of the Ziggurat at Ur will be found at Plate IX (b) in *Ur of the Chaldees* and a recent illustration of Mount Meru will be found in Hocart's *Kingship* to face page 179. In both illustrations the plintha, stages or terraces of each are shown.

glory whose leaves were of gold and a spring which gave eternal life to those who drank of it. Here we have in mediaeval Europe legends pointing an analogy between the Christian idea of Paradise and the story of Mount Meru.

Putting aside the sound similarity of the names Sumeru, Sumer and Si Mu, the foregoing hypothesis would link Si Wang Mu of the Chinese with the Vedic Mount Meru and the sacred cow of Egypt and India and the latter with the moon goddess of the Sumerians of Mesopotamia in B.C. 4000, and would fit the traditions of the Sumerians themselves. The only recommendation for any theory is that it should fit all the known facts.

There is thus presented the possibility that the origin of the Sumerians may be found in the oasis of Merv.

The Ararat Area and the Tibetan Area of secret society diffusion

What is important to our subject in the theory of a common human origin in the Central Asian plateau is the fact that since the beginning of the Christian era up to the present time, there appear to be in the world two chief centres of distribution of esoteric or secret society knowledge and praxis, both situated in Asia, and both closely associated with man's survival after the flood and subsequent early religious diffusion. For purposes of this work we name these two areas:—

      (1) The Ararat Area.
      (2) The Tibetan Area.

The dominant fact in this context is, that the signs and esoteric formulae of secret societies the world over, practically all of which may be traced back to one or other of these two sources, are largely *identical*. This fact provides the strongest possible argument for thinking that at some period in the history of neo-lithic man, the first revelation of the Supreme Being came to him at one single place, whence it has been diffused to the ends of the earth.

That *single* place may perhaps have been the mountain of Meru, or the oasis of Merv.

3. THE GENESIS OF HUMAN BELIEF

Just as it has been necessary to a general comprehension of our subject to glance at what is known of man's common ancestry, so we must survey in brief what science has to show of the origin of his "religion", which has a still closer bearing upon the particular subject of the nature of those arcana of the human mind which form the hard core of all belief.

We may introduce this vast subject with the words of Potter *The Story of Religion* (1930) page 13:—

"Once religion and life were one. It is a very significant fact that the word "religion" does not once occur in the old Testament. There was no need of the word, for everything was religious. In all primitive societies it was so. Law was simply the will of the gods. Morals were determined by religious taboos".

Without being dogmatic we may say that the history of religion is the history of man and until we know more of the one we cannot properly understand the other.

Man began as a pagan.

The *British Encyclopaedia* says of Paganism:—

"All Paganism is at heart a worship of Nature in some form or other and in all pagan religions the deepest and most awe-inspiring attribute of Nature was the power of reproduction...... To ancient pagan thinkers as well as to modern men of science, the key to the hidden secret of the origin and preservation of the universe lay in the mystery of sex.

Two energies or agents, one an active generative (male) and the other a feminine passive or susceptible one, were everywhere thought to combine for creative purposes and heaven and earth, sun and moon, day and night were believed to co-operate to the production of being. Upon some such basis as this rested almost all the polytheistic worship of the old civilisation and to it may be traced back, stage by stage, the separation of the divinity into male and female gods, the deification of distinct powers of nature and the idealisation of man's own faculties, where every power of his understanding was embodied as an object of adoration and every impulse of his will became an incarnation of deity. But in each and every form of polytheism we find the slime track of the deification of sex".

The theme of man's first belief has a vast library of its own. A few authorities only have been consulted by us.[1]

The consensus of opinion is that primitive belief began with fear and centring round the mystery of reproduction and fertility had developed at the dawn of history into belief in the divinity of Kings, where we find it established in the Nile Valley and at Ur of the Chaldees about B.C. 6000.

Professor Elliot Smith leader of the Diffusionist school has presented the case for the Nile Valley as the source of Man's belief.[2] It must be left to the future to decide between the Diffusionist and the Evolutionist schools, and if the decision finally goes to the Diffusionists, the claims of Egypt against those of the Central Asian Plateau as the birthplace of neo-lithic culture, still remain to be assessed.

Of the beginnings of awareness in primitive man for the need of combination if he was to survive at all H. G. Wells *Outline of History* page 66 has:—

"Confused under the stimulus of the need and possibility of co-operation and a combined life, neolithic mankind was feeling out for guidance and knowledge. Men were becoming aware that personally they needed protection and direction, cleansing from impurity, power beyond their own strength. Confusedly in response to that

---

Footnote.—(1) Haeckel *The Riddle of the Universe* (1899) : Herbert Spencer *First Principles* (1900) : Fraser *The Golden Bough* (1900) : Crawley *The Mystic Rose* (1902) : Winwood Reade *The Martyrdom of Man* (1872) : H. G. Wells *The Outline of History* (1920) : Curtis *The Commonwealth of God* (1938) and Gerald Heard *The Source of Civilisation* (1935).

Footnote.—(2) *See* his *The Ancient Egyptians* (1923) : *Human History* (1930) *In the Beginning* (1928) ; and *The Diffusion of Culture* (1933).

demand, bold men, wise men, shrewd and cunning men were arising to become magicians, priests, chiefs and kings. They are not to be thought of as cheats or usurpers of power, nor the rest of mankind as their dupes. All men are mixed in their motives: a hundred things move men to seek ascendancy over other men, but not all such motives are base or bad. The magicians usually believed more or less in their own magic, the priests in their own ceremonies, the chiefs in their right. The history of mankind henceforth is a history of more or less blind endeavours to conceive a common purpose in relation to which all men may live happily, and to create and develop a common consciousness and a common stock of knowledge which may serve and illuminate that purpose. In a vast variety of forms this appearance of Kings and priests and magic men was happening all over the world under neolithic conditions. Everywhere mankind was seeking where knowledge and mastery and magic power might reside: everywhere individual men were willing, honestly or dishonestly to rule, to direct, or to be the magic beings who would reconcile the confusions of the community...... These neolithic men were full of the fear of some ancient old man who had developed into a tribal god, obsessed by ideas of sacrificial propitiation and magic murder...... Neolithic man under the sway of talk and a confused thought process, killed on theory; he killed for monstrous and now incredible ideas, he killed those he loved through fear and under direction. Those neolithic men not only made human sacrifices at seed time: there is every reason to suppose·they sacrificed wives and slaves at the burial of their chieftains; they killed men women and children whenever they were in adversity, and thought the gods were athirst. They practised infanticide. All those things passed on into the Bronze age".

It is here that we find Abraham in Ur in B.C. 2000 when he reached the parting of the ways and took the decisive step which changed the history of the world as described by Woolley below.

Hocart *Kingship* page 7 says:—

"The earliest known religion is a belief in the divinity of Kings...... When history begins there are kings, the representatives of gods".

Hocart *op. cit.* propounds the theory that there is an analogy between natural and human history and that what has descended to us as man's mythological belief and oral tradition, can be penetrated by comparative study in all the fields of science and can be ultimately established as sober history (page 207). In the sphere of religion he sees the phenomena of nature and the abstract entities such as mind, speech, justice, etc., personified in primitive belief.

Thus, the sun was personified as man, the moon as woman, and the union of heaven and earth takes place by proxy. The proxies are the king and the queen, and thence any bride or bridegroom.[1]

The development and ramifications of this system of ideas which seems to fit so much of the common belief of man, he expresses by the term "divine kingship", and poses the question (page 209): may we not have here the solution of the whole problem of the common origin of human belief?

In support of this view Hocart presents the student with the results of his observations in two further spheres of comparative anthropological research among various races and religions, namely:—

(a) Coronation or installation ceremonial.

(b) Initiation rites into age-grades, religious castes, religious societies and religious arcana.

Briefly summarised the results are as follows:—

UNDER (a) CORONATION CEREMONIAL

In Chapter VII *op. cit.* he sets out twenty-seven constant features of coronation ceremonial found throughout the world, and discusses those points common to these twenty-seven, which are present, so far as present knowledge goes, among various races and religions taken at random.[2]

UNDER (b) INITIATION RITES

In Chapter XII *op. cit.* Hocart discusses those points gathered from our present deficient knowledge, which are common both to the twenty-seven features of the coronation ceremonial and to the religious initiation rites of various races and religions taken at random.[3]

Footnote.—(1) Cf. the custom among the Malays of regarding the bride and groom as royalty on their wedding day (*raja sa'hari*), a custom common all over the world.

Footnote.—(2) Tabulated, these Coronation rites are:—

Race or religion			Reference			No. of points in common
Brahman (Hindu) ...	...	...	Satapatha Brahmana	...	...	18
Fijian (Pagan) ...	...	...	Present-day practice	...	...	17
Cambodian (Buddhist)	...	...	A. Leclere Cambodge	...	...	13
Egypt ...	...	...	Hocart Kingship page 83 footnote ...	...	...	13
Hebrew ...	...	...	Hocart page 86 ...	...	...	6
Roman	...	...	Hocart page 87 ...	...	...	15
Byzantine	...	...	Hocart page 89 ...	...	...	11
Abyssinian	...	...	Hocart page 89 (footnote) ...	...	...	5
Christian	...	...	Woolley Coronation rites ...	...	...	15

Footnote.—(3) Tabulated, these Initiation rites are:—

Race or religion			Reference			No. of points in common
Brahman	...	...	Hocart op. cit. page 135			12
Fijian ...	...	...	do. 136	...	...	8
Melanesian	...	...	do. 137	...	...	6
Eleusinian	...	...	do. 139	...	...	13
Mithraic	...	...	do. 141	...	...	12
Australian aborigines	...	...	do. 147	...	...	14
African tribes:						
(i) Kipsiki (Kenya)	...	...	do. 149-150	...	...	11
(ii) Ruanda ...	...	...	do. 151	...	...	16
Christian	...	...	do. 150	...	...	11

Hocart's results are examined further in section 6 below.

The theory that the origin of historical man's belief is to be found in the doctrine of the Divinity of Kings is a vast separate study[1] in the sphere of comparative esoteric anthropology. Enough has been indicated to show its scope and the direction whither it may be expected to lead.

In *Ur of the Chaldees* page 48 Woolley writes:—

> "Sumerian Kings were deified in their life-time and honoured as gods after their death......and when the chroniclers wrote in the annals of Sumer that "after the Flood, Kingship again descended from the Gods" they meant no less than this".

Again in *Abraham* (1936) Woolley discussing the function of the temple among the Sumerians, says page 88:—

> "The Sumerian temple was much more than a place of worship...... The priests were judges and the temple was a court of law, but much besides legal business was transacted in its precincts. Ranged round the courtyard......forming part of the temple were factories and workshops, offices and the house of the Moon-god's business manager, buildings not religious in themselves but bearing witness to the fact that in a theocratic state Nannar was King as well as god and needed his civil service as much as his priesthood. Indeed, the whole organisation of worship was on the lines of a royal Court. The God had his Minister of Finance and Ministers of War and of Agriculture, his Master of the Harem, his transport officers, his archive keepers and his Treasury staff......
>
> But all these various activities were in theory and largely in fact, subordinate to that ritual of worship, on whose strict observance depended the welfare of the State".

The First Revelation or "Creation" and the Fall of Man

At a date vastly antecedent to the Sumerian epoch, there had occurred in Christian tradition the first revelation of God to man. No date can be ascribed to this event, but it was followed in Bible tradition by man's disobedience and his fall, the site of which is given as the Euphrates valley.

But as the tradition of the fall of man, or something like it, is commonly met with in most religions, the site as given in the Bible may only refer to the locality covered by the Bible tradition.

The Flood

The date of this event in the Euphrates valley has been fixed by science at about B.C. 4200. The flood is recorded in the Bible tradition as the punishment of man for his fall after the first revelation. As the tradition of the great flood is also met with in most ancient religions, it follows that men other than those in the Euphrates valley, were affected by it. There is historical evidence that the Sumerians of the Euphrates valley suffered a flood and carried on after it.

In Gen: X—32 we read that after the flood, the families of the sons of Noah were re-distributed over the earth and the first two verses of Chapter XI read:—

> "And the whole earth was of one language and of one speech. And it came to pass as they (Noah's descendants) journeyed from the east, that they found a plain in the land of Shinar and they dwelt there".

The "land of Shinar" is generally believed by the authorities to refer to the Sumer. Woolley's excavations prove that the Sumers were established in the Euphrates valley for at least 1,000 years before the flood of B.C. 4200 and that their culture survived and continued after it.

The re-distribution of man after the flood, as recorded in the biblical tradition, was not confined to that part of the earth's surface covered by that tradition. What differentiated pre-deluge men from post-deluge men was the *confusion of tongues*, by whatever means it arose.[2]

May we not suppose that, although men's language differed after the flood, their pre-deluge or perhaps even their pre-speech sign-language remained as a means of communicating with one another upon the arcana revealed to or developed by their common ancestors?

The Tibetan Area and the Ararat area of religious diffusion

Be that as it may, we have suggested that if the first revelation was confined to a single people at a single place, that place may have been in the central Asian plateau rather than in the Euphrates valley. On the subject of religious origins Max Muller *Last Essays* (written in 1893) page 118 has:—

> "There has never been in the whole history of the world what could be called an entirely new religion. Every religion we know presupposes another religion, as every language presupposes an antecedent language. Nay, it seems almost impossible to conceive the possibility of an entirley new religion quite as much as of an entirely new language. Mohamedanism presupposes Christianity, Judaism and a popular faith prevailing among the Arab tribes. Christianity presupposes Judaism and Greek philosophy. Judaism presupposes an earlier and more widely spread semitic faith, traces of which appear in the inscriptions of Babylon and Nineveh. Beyond the religion of the Mesopotamian Kingdoms, there seems to have been an Accadian religion and beyond that our knowledge comes to an end. The ancient religion of Zoroaster again presupposes the Vedic religion, while the Vedic religion points to a more ancient Aryan background. What lies beyond that common Aryan religion is again beyond the reach of history, more, even of conjecture. But

---

Footnote.—(1) This thesis has been expounded by Fraser *The Golden Bough* Part 1: Elliot Smith *Human History* (1930) and *The Diffusion of Culture* (1933) Perry *Gods and Men* (1927) and by Wells *The Outline of History* Chapters XII, XVI and XIX, and receives fresh support from Woolley's recent excavations at Ur.
Footnote.—(2) For a survey of flood traditions see Yearsley *The Story of the Bible* (1933) page 61: also Fraser *Folk-lore in the Old Testament*, and Peake *The Flood*.

it may certainly be stated that as no human race has ever been discovered without any language at all, neither do we know of any human tribe without something like a religion, some manifestation of a perception of a Beyond, or that sense of the Infinite beneath the Finite, which is the true fountain head of all religions".

This passage suggests the same division for ancient religious sources of diffusion, as we have just noted for secret society origins. In each case the line of pursuit into antiquity loses itself in prehistory after the Accadian (Sumer) and Vedic points are passed.

The following plan suggests the possible evolution of these two fixed centres of diffusion of both the esoteric and exoteric doctrines of the earth:—

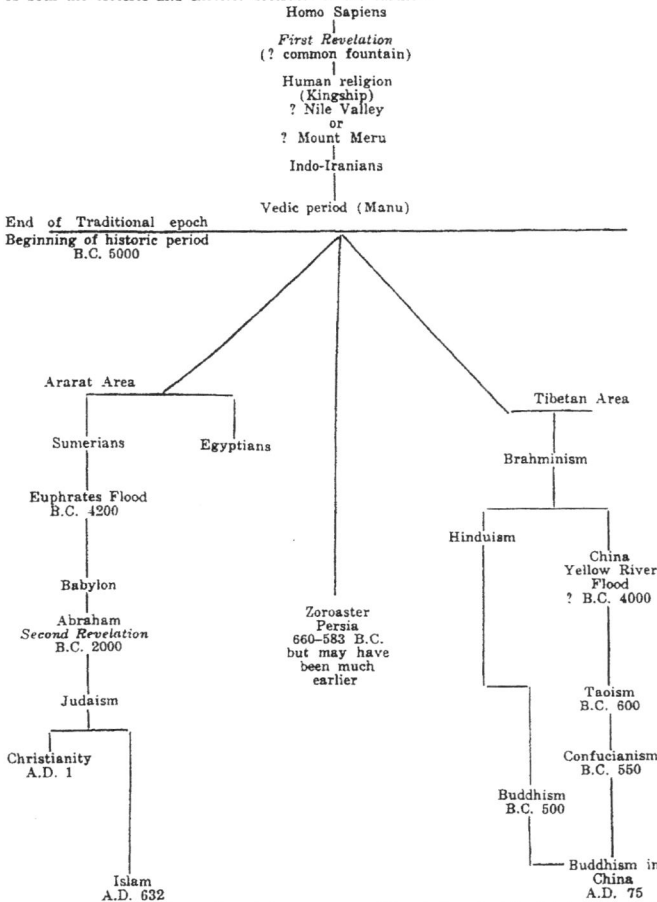

Homo Sapiens

First Revelation
(? common fountain)

Human religion
(Kingship)
? Nile Valley
or
? Mount Meru

Indo-Iranians

Vedic period (Manu)

End of Traditional epoch
Beginning of historic period
B.C. 5000

Ararat Area

Tibetan Area

Sumerians   Egyptians

Brahminism

Euphrates Flood
B.C. 4200

Hinduism

China
Yellow River
Flood
? B.C. 4000

Babylon

Abraham
Second Revelation
B.C. 2000

Zoroaster
Persia
660–583 B.C.
but may have
been much
earlier

Taoism
B.C. 600

Judaism

Confucianism
B.C. 550

Christianity
A.D. 1

Buddhism
B.C. 500

Buddhism in
China
A.D. 75

Islam
A.D. 632

This rough plan is not intended to prove anything, it is only intended to suggest the possible point of bifurcation of the two foci of secret society lore which dominate the study of the subject in its modern setting.

Thus, to the Ararat area may be traced, for example, the sources of secret society praxis in Judaism, Christianity and Islam; and to the Tibetan area those of Hinduism, Buddhism, Taoism and Shintoism; while pagan rites in the modern world have features common to both sources, a fact which seems to suggest for them an affinity with the prehistory belief of man in the divinity of kings.

The relationship between Judaism, Christianity and Islam

We should perhaps here notice the common religious sources inherited by Judaism, Christianity and Islam in the Ararat area.

Dr. Maude Royden *The Problem of Palestine* (1939) page 29–30 has:—

"Those who like very ancient stories indeed can believe, if they wish, that the Arabs are descended from Shem, one of the three sons of Noah. They are Semites, as the Jews are, but perhaps we had better accept the suggestion of an able historian Bertram Thomas in *The Arabs* (page 357) who says that "Shem was an environment rather than a grandfather". We are not, however, compelled to jettison the ancient tradition that the Arabs are descended from Abraham through Ishmael. In any case, anthropologists and historians alike agree that Arabs, Jews, Assyrians, Phoenicians, Ethiopians and Armenians all belong to the Semitic family.

* * *

Mahomet, greatest of Arabs and one of the greatest of men, was born in Mecca in Arabia about the year A.D. 570. He came with a message from God, the character of this message has been greatly misunderstood outside the Moslem world and still is so. Modern western men think of Mohamedanism or "Islam" as a new religion founded by a prophet called Mahomet somewhere in the seventh century A.D. Mahomet never thought of it so, neither do the Arabs to this day. To them Mahomet was a man sent by God to recall his erring children to the true faith proclaimed by Abraham, Isaac and Moses. As Richard Coke says in *The Arabs' Place in the sun* page 36:—

"He saw himself as the latest prophet of the historic Semitic line, come as a "plain warner" to his people, a legitimate successor to Moses, Jesus and all the ancient teachers, who had come to preach the same lesson, but in vain".

To the Moslem, Jews and Christians alike are heretics. They have wandered from the purity of the faith, though they are still more to be respected than absolute heathen. Their prophets are the prophets of Islam also, and moreover they are held to be *more* the prophets of Islam than of Judaism or Christianity, because Islam has kept the tradition where we, Jews and Christians, have fallen away. Abraham, Isaac and Moses, therefore, belong to the Moslem rather than to the Jew. Jesus Christ was a great prophet also, but he failed to recall men to the pure faith, while Mahomet seven hundred years later succeeded".

* * *

And on page 36:—

"One who is neither a Moslem nor a Jew may be allowed to reflect upon the extraordinary fitness of the religion to the hour. Here was a Prophet who proclaimed a God of righteousness, unity and law, whose claim to the worship of men was universal, not narrowed to a chosen people, nor beyond the reach of the ordinary man.

* * *

Islam has made the Arab the conqueror of his conquerors. From its very nature it is a missionary religion, and it was not by any fault or mis-teaching of Mahomet that its spread was to be connected with the sword, any more than it was the fault of Moses that Jehovah became the god of one nation only, nor of Christ that heretics and unbelievers were made by Christians to expiate their heresy in blood and torment".

It is necessary that the true position of Islam *vis-à-vis* Christianity, thus lucidly described by a modern Churchwoman, should be presented to the reader, not only because of the dominant place of Islam in the Empire, but also because of the contribution of Islam to secret societies in the modern world, as outlined in Chapter X below.

4. DUALISM, OR THE TWO ROADS TO FULFILMENT

Throughout all religions whether they belong to the stem of "revealed" monotheism or to the polytheism of nature worship, or to ethical codes such as Buddhism and Confucianism, there runs a common feature of mysticism, from which derives a dualism in their praxis; the one path the ascendant, leading through pure mysticism to the higher levels of esoteric knowledge, the other, the descendant, leading through magic to the lower and debased cults. A further reference to dualism, therefore, becomes necessary at this point, because some acquaintance with what is understood by the term, is essential for a study of the nature of secret societies.

Haeckel *The Riddle of the Universe* (1899), defines dualism as the system which admits two ultimate realities, in contrast to monism which holds that the ultimate reality is one.

We are not here concerned with metaphysics, but with the practical effect on human affairs of the existence of the dualist principle.

This ancient underlying concept appears to develop from the fact of the two principles in nature, male and female, light and darkness, etc. The conception is usually ascribed to the teaching of Zoroaster, a Persian, believed to have lived 600 B.C. but to whom some scholars ascribed a very much earlier date. In monotheism dualism is represented by the struggle between Good and Evil or God and Devil, the Ormudz and Ahriman of Zoroaster. In its historical application to monotheism, men seem to have been obliged to learn to hate the devil before they could learn to love God. The danger in this is that men may fear the devil so much that they worship him in fear and propitiation as much as they worship God in love and reverence.

The *Encyclopaedia Britannica* (ed. 1925) has the following in respect of dualism in ethics and theology:—

"In the domain of morals, dualism postulates the separate existence of Good and Evil, as principles of existence. In theology the appearance of dualism is sporadic and has not the fundamental, determining importance which it has in metaphysics. It is a result rather than a starting-point. The old Zoroastrianism, and those Christian sects (*e.g.* Manichaeism) which were influenced by it, postulates two contending deities Ormuzd and Ahriman (Good and Evil) which war against one another in influencing the conduct of men. So, in Christianity, the existence of Satan as an evil influence, antagonistic to God, involves a kind of dualism. But generally speaking this dualism is permissive, inasmuch as it is always held that God will triumph over Satan in His own time. So, in Zoroastrianism, the dualism is not ultimate, for Ahriman and Ormuzd are represented as the twin sons of Zervana Akarana, *i.e.* limitless time, wherein both will be finally absorbed. The postulate of an Evil Being arises from the difficulty, at all times acutely felt by a certain type of mind, of reconciling the existence of evil with the divine attributes of perfect goodness, full knowledge and infinite power. John Stuart Mill (Essay on Religion) preferred to disbelieve in the omnipotence of God rather than forgo the belief in His goodness. It follows from such a view that Satan is not the creation of God, but rather a power coeval in origin, over whose activity God has no absolute control".

In the Christian religion the difficulty is explained by the Omnipotence of God on the one hand and the exercise of free-will by man on the other, who is free to choose his own course of life.

This concept is of first importance to our subject as it supplies the key to that debased esoterism which is generally employed to cloak a maleficent secret society.

Dualism divides a religion into two halves or sides, the exoteric and the esoteric.

Hocart *Kingship* (1927) discussing an aspect of this subject says page 106:—

"The idea became a favourite theme of Tibetan art. The following equivalences are the result:—

King = God = sky = æther = spirit = soul.
Queen = goddess = earth = matter = body".

The theme constantly recurs throughout the rituals of the secret society world in the East. (*See* Chapter III below).

The former is the open aspect corresponding with the Sun, male, light; the latter the hidden aspect, corresponding with Moon, female, darkness. Each of these aspects has in turn its two sides, the right and the left. The right is the simple doctrine in each case which is usually unexceptionable if sometimes bigoted and fanatical: the left has again two sides, the pure and mystic and the debased. The latter or left-esoteric is a degraded form of the true doctrine, perverted with magic for ends other than those of religion, usually politics or crime, but still retaining the cloak of religion and the essential privacy for plotting, that such a cloak provides.

To keep the real character of the debased side secret, its followers find it necessary to protect their identity and their real designs from all but the initiated, by the use of pseudo-religious secret formulæ.

The relationship of the upright to the debased is something as follows:—

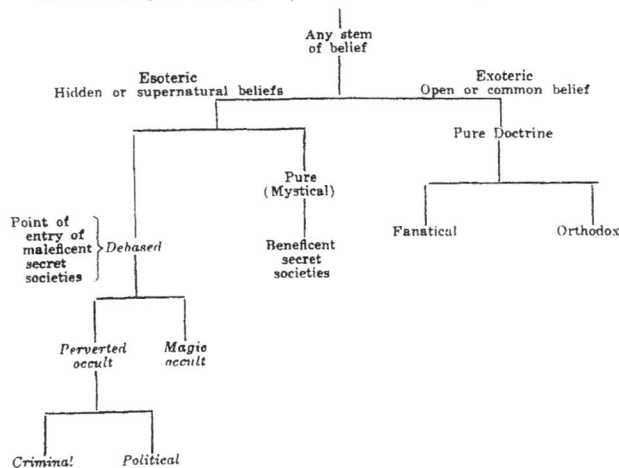

Any stem
of belief

Esoteric
Hidden or supernatural beliefs

Exoteric
Open or common belief

Pure Doctrine

Pure
(Mystical)

Point of
entry of
maleficent } *Debased*
secret
societies

Beneficent
secret
societies

Fanatical

Orthodox

*Perverted
occult*

*Magic
occult*

Criminal

Political

The point where esoterism becomes "debased" in the above chart, is usually the point of entry and organisation of the maleficent secret society, which from that point on, can pursue an underground course in comparative safety in any one of three directions:—

(1) The simple and less harmful occult (black magic).
(2) The perverted occult used for political purposes, including political assassination.
(3) The perverted occult used for frankly criminal purposes, including robbery and murder for personal gain.

We have now arrived at what seems to us the essence of the nature of secret societies, and it is, therefore, necessary to correct any misconception on this point.

Not all secret societies, but only those springing from the debased side of esoterism as shown in the above chart, are evil.

Secret societies have been shown to be bound up with what for a better name we must call the *primitive mysteries* with which man has, since the dawn of the human race, persistently concerned himself. These are:—

The nature of the creator of the Universe.
The origin and end of man.
The life of the soul after death.

In the pursuit of this hidden knowledge, two paths have been trodden by man:—

The one—beneficent, of high aspiration, in pursuit of divine truth for its own sake.
The other—maleficent—of low intrigue for selfish human ends.

Both have used the methods of secret initiation, oaths, signs and ritual, the one for a good, the other for an evil purpose.

In general, these secret paraphernalia bear a close resemblance sometimes an identity, and are found among all peoples and all cultures throughout the world. A close inspection of such detail of this paraphernalia as is available to the outside often shows, however, that what appears at first to be identical is in fact the same thing *reversed*, thus emphasising the ancient dualism that runs throughout the subject.

The position is well expressed by Mrs. Webster *Secret societies and subversive movements* (1928) page 3:—

"In the study of secret societies, we have a double line to follow—the course of associations enveloping themselves in secrecy for the pursuit of esoteric knowledge and those using mystery and secrecy for an ulterior and usually a political purpose".

In the present work, we are only concerned with the latter, which embraces not only political but frankly criminal purposes. It is this fact that makes their study an essential part of every Police Officer's equipment in the fight against crime and in the preservation of internal security in any country.

For reasons explained above, the study of maleficent secret societies is intertwined with two subjects, which have only a countervailing relevancy namely, religion and freemasonry.

We would have preferred to omit all reference to these two subjects in a work of this kind, but to have done so would have left the subject incomplete. Their inclusion, therefore, is unavoidable.

No disrespect is intended to any religion and no reflection is cast upon the purity of British freemasonry. We trust that no cause of offence will be found in either regard.

Le Plongeon in *Sacred mysteries among the Mayas* (1903) page 53 ff. has:—

"The idea of a sole and omnipotent Deity, who created all things, seems to have been the universal belief in early ages amongst all the nations that had reached a high degree of civilisation. This was the doctrine of the Egyptian priests.

The Doctrine of a Supreme Deity composed of three parts distinct from each other, yet forming one, was universally prevalent among the civilised nations of America, Asia and the Egyptians. The priests of Egypt, Chaldea, India and China ......kept it a profound secret and imparted it only to a few select, among those initiated into the sacred mysteries".

This assertion has been made by many writers, yet lacks historical proof. All we can say with certainty is that the same signs and formulæ are to be found throughout the world conveying the same meaning anent those sacred mysteries.

We have been at some pains to show whence these signs and formulæ may have arisen from a single source, and how that source may have bifurcated into the two historical foci of diffusion, the Ararat area and the Tibetan area as they exist to-day. We must now return to the history of Abraham, who it must be remembered is a prophet of Islam as well as of Jewry.

The Second Revelation and Promise

Woolley in *Abraham* (1936) Chapter VI, gives a vivid picture of the religion of Ur— a polytheism of the grossest type at the time of Abraham. Some five thousand names of gods of this period have been unearthed. The patron god of Ur was the Moon-God Nannar who was worshipped as King of Ur and Lord of Heaven. His consort was Nin-Gal. Woolley op. cit. says page 195:—

"It would have been strange indeed, if the household of Terah, living at Ur in the days when "Your fathers served other gods". (Josh. XXIV 2) had been other than followers of the Moon-God......and if the father of Abraham was called Terah Nannar it can only be because he was under the special protection of that deity. We can take it as certain that the worship of the Moon-God was the faith in which Abraham was brought up".

And page 198:—

"Abraham from the moment he appears as an independent person, the head of his house, cannot be suspected of Moon-worship: since, therefore, that had been the worship of his father and of himself in his youth the "conversion" of Abraham becomes a tangible fact".

For convenience in survey we may divide the epochs of human belief in the Ararat area into the following periods:—

(1) The Pagan period pre-Abraham.
(2) The old Testament Biblical period from Abraham onwards.
(3) The "Seven Centuries" (B.C. 50—A.D. 650) which span the period between the advent of Christ and the advent of Mohamed.

We must now glance briefly at these periods, for which purpose we include in the "Ararat area" the following territories:—

Asia Minor, Persia, Mesopotamia, Arabia, Syria, Egypt and the Eastern Mediterranean.

The Pagan Period.—The recent work of archaeologists has vastly extended the vista of this period backwards and brought within the realm of established historical fact, what has hitherto been a legendary vision.

"Religion" in the pre-deluge (c. B.C. 4200) epoch in the Ararat area seems to have centred around the worship of Baal (abomination), as the source of life and around the adoration of the organs of procreation as the emblems of the highest mystery—the mystery of Life itself.

For purposes of reference we may call this pagan period the period of the primitive mysteries. The measure of this period we do not know. It might extend to 10000 or 50000 or 100000 B.C. The quality of paganism is referred to on page xxx above. (Genesis of Man's Belief).

The Old Testament Biblical Period.—The punishment of man inhabiting the Ararat area for his adherence to this primitive belief, and the "abominations" committed therewith, was, in bible history, the deluge of the Noachian epoch (B.C. 4200).

The second revelation of the supreme Godhead came to the people of this area after the flood, through Abraham, as narrated in Chapter XII of the Book of Genesis.

We know that about B.C. 2000 Abraham and his family who were not Sumerians but belonged to the Aramaean nomad tribe of the Habiru (Hebrews) left Ur and migrated northwards to Haran.

It was at Haran, after the death of his father Terah that Abraham received his revelation and promise and it was from Haran, another city of the Moon God, that he led his tribe into Palestine—the Promised land where the history of the tribe begins the history of the western world.

Woolley *Abraham* page 187 says:—

"Abraham did not come away from Ur empty handed...... He brought with him those stories of the creation and of the Flood which, moralised by his descendants, have been as history or as parable treasured by half the world for four thousand years. He brought with him the laws of Ur and handing them down through the generations of his house, laid the foundations of that Mosaic code which is still the Law of the Jews and has been professedly adopted by most Christian nations as the basis of their own systems.

But it is as the founder of a new religion that Abraham interests us most...... The modern world is permeated with religious ideas either taken directly from the Jewish scriptures or inculcated by the Christian and Mohamedan faiths which were in large measure founded on them.

*   *   *

There is no evidence whatsoever to show that any esoteric knowledge was treasured by the ancestors of Abraham, concerning whom we know nothing at all. On the other hand it is expressly stated by early Hebrew tradition that in Mesopotamia, the patriarchal family shared in the common paganism of the time and place......

The old Testament explicitly attests something in the nature of a revelation granted to Abraham, and it would certainly seem to imply something in the nature of a conversion of the man, such as later tradition has attributed to him".

This passage does not mean that Abraham himself may not have possessed esoteric knowledge. He no doubt possessed in full the esoteric knowledge connected with the worship of the Moon Goddess and the other gods of the Sumerians among which he was born and from which he turned away.

His conversion may perhaps represent the point of bifurcation in belief, at which the mind of western man first rejected polytheism and the worship of man, the lower road, and grasping the ideal of the worship of one god, followed the higher.

Woolley *Abraham* page 190 has:—

"Somehow or other Abraham freed himself not merely from the accidentals of paganism but from an element essential to it, so that his personal freedom was a turning point in the religious advancement of the world".

Finally, Woolley *op. cit.* sums up as follows page 290:—

"In the history of Abraham and in that of the Hebrew people as recounted in the Old Testament, we can watch the gradual evolution of a conception of God to which Christian and Moslem are alike in debt. Abraham did not create that conception out of nothing nor receive it ready made from others, nor indeed, did he himself attain to it. He was bred in the crude paganism of the time. When circumstances made that untenable as a whole he was able to discard its grosser elements and to hold fast to the little in it which was, potentially at least, true and eternal. Here was the parting of the ways and Abraham took the decisive step. It was for future generations to explore the road from this".

This is, perhaps, the bifurcation from the lower to the higher road, the point of emergence of dualism in religion, the struggle between the worship of God and the worship of Man, a comprehension of which is so essential to an understanding of the subject of esoteric anthropology.

This parting of the ways in the World's religious history might perhaps be illustrated thus:—

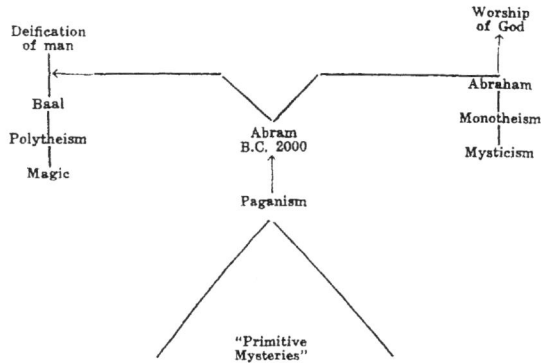

```
                                                              Worship
                                                              of God
                                                                ↑
        Deification                                              |
        of man                                                 Abraham
          ↑                                                      |
          |←──────────────         ──────────────→            Monotheism
        Baal                                                     |
          |                         Abram                      Mysticism
        Polytheism                  B.C. 2000
          |                                                    
        Magic                                                  
                                       ↑
                                       |
                                    Paganism

                        \                            /
                         \                          /
                          \                        /
                           \                      /
                            \    "Primitive      /
                             \   Mysteries"     /
                              \               /
```

Woolley concludes:—

> "In the history of his descendants there were many backslidings into idol-worship, which endangered alike the racial identity of the Hebrew people, and the conservation of the faith entrusted to them, yet there was always a remnant that kept to the straight path".

Throughout the whole of the old Testament, there runs the story of the conflict[1] between belief in the "Primitive mysteries" (Baal) of the pagan epoch and belief in the Divine revelation (Yah weh) or between the "abominations" of man, and the law of God.

The struggle has run true to form in the world right up to the present-day.

If we substitute for Baal, the concept of the *deification of Man* represented by the worship of sex and the belief that Man is his own creator and the arbiter of his own destiny, and contrast it with belief in the Divine omnipotence of God, we arrive at a tenable explanation of the two rival forces, the believers in the worship of God, as opposed to the believers in the deification of man, constantly at war in the world of men. Belief in the Divine Revelation is still paramount in the world to-day.

The former faith comprises among others the adherents of Judaism, Christianity and Islam, but there are many backsliders in each faith. There are they who pursue world domination, first through the power-house of secret societies, then through political revolution and conquest, instead of the evolution of human happiness through the benign influence of revealed religion. The one seeks through force the control of man's destiny and the domination of the world, the other seeks through law the development of the fellowship of Man.

And the Promise

The promise that Abraham brought with him from Ur, was fulfilled in the history of the Israelites in Palestine, until their last dispersal by Hadrian in A.D. 135.

Since then, belief in the validity of the ancient promise has been kept alive by a section of what is now known as Jewry. This section, known to the modern world as Zionists, regards final possession of Palestine by Abraham's descendants as inalienable and awaits a lasting fulfilment which shall re-unite them as a nation with Jerusalem as their capital city.

This unshaken belief received a recent impetus from the "Balfour Declaration" of 1917, which took world Jewry by storm and forms the sombre background of the present political situation in Palestine,[2] in which we see religious belief and political aspiration presented in vivid colours among the modern problems of British Colonial administration. The place of secret societies in the political arena of modern Palestine, receives notice in its appropriate context in the body of this work.

The Period of the Seven Centuries (B.C. 50—A.D. 650)

After the fulfilment of the biblical prophecy by the coming of Christ, there intervened in the Ararat area a period of some seven centuries before the rise of Mohamed.

This period was filled with the conflict between the Christian tradition and the Primitive mysteries, each striving for supremacy, the one cult of evil the other of good, or satanism

---

Footnote.—(1) Examples of this conflict may be seen in the story of the Golden Calf of Aaron (Exodus 32) : the "curses" (Deuteronomy 27) : the struggle between Reho-boam and Jero-boam (1st Kings Chapters 12 and 13) etc., etc.
Footnote.—(2) For a concise and unbiassed statement of the present position, *see* Dr. Maude Royden *The Problem of Palestine* (1939) ; and *The Palestine Royal Commission Report* (1937).

versus godhead, or the struggle between the two opposing principles which we call dualism and which we have seen emerge as "religion" from primitive man's examination of his own conscience and the revelation and promise vouchsafed to Abraham.

This struggle became epitomised for Englishmen during this period or later, by the story of St. George and the Dragon which is a symbol of the triumph of good over evil.

5. THE DISSEMINATION OF NEOLITHIC CULTURE

At some period of human history subsequent to the appearance of neolithic man and prior to the Second revelation to Abraham in B.C. 2000, a culture with clearly marked features seems to have been slowly disseminated throughout Asia and across the Pacific to America.

This culture was the first vehicle of diffusion of esoteric knowledge throughout the world and seems to have sprung from a single source.

Professor Elliot Smith is the leading authority on this subject.[1] He gives the birth-place of this sunstone culture as the valley of the Nile.

Wells *Outline of History* has the following interesting notice of this movement, backed by the authority of Professor Elliot Smith.

Wells *op. cit.* page 72 says:—

"At some period in human history there seems to have been a special type of neolithic culture widely distributed in the world, which had a group of features so curious and *so unlikely to have been independently developed in different regions of the earth,* as to compel us to believe that it was in effect *one culture.* It reached through all the regions inhabited by the brunet Mediterranean race and beyond through India, further India, up the Pacific Coast of China, and it spread at last across the Pacific and to Mexico and Peru.[2]

It was a coastal culture, not reaching deeply inland...... This peculiar development of the neolithic culture which Elliot Smith called heliolithic or "Sunstone culture" included many or all of the following odd practices:—

(1) Circumcision.
(2) The *couvade, i.e.,* the practice requiring the *father* on the birth of a child to perform certain acts and abstain from certain foods.
(3) The practice of massage.
(4) The making of mummies.
(5) The raising of megalithic monuments (*e.g.* Stonehenge).
(6) Artificial deformation of the heads of the young by bandages.
(7) Tattooing.
(8) Religious association of the Sun and the serpent (in China, the dragon).
(9) The use of the symbol known as the "Swastika" for good luck.

This odd little symbol spins gaily round the world: it seems incredible that men would have invented and made a pet of it twice over.

Elliot Smith traces these practices in a sort of Constellation all over this great Mediterranean—Indian Ocean—Pacific area. Where one occurs, most of the others occur. They link Brittany with Borneo and Peru.

* * *

For thousands of years from 15000 to 1000 B.C. such a Sunstone neolithic culture and its brownish possessors, may have been oozing round the world, through the warmer regions, drifting by canoes often across wide stretches of sea.

And its place of origin may have been as Elliot Smith suggests the Mediterranean and North African region. It must have been spreading up the Pacific coast and across the island stepping stones to America, long after it had passed on into other developments in the areas of origin. Many of the peoples of the East Indies, Melanesia and Polynesia were still in this heliolithic stage of development when they were discovered by European navigators in the seventeenth century. The first civilisation in Egypt and the Euphrates-Tigris valley probably developed directly out of this widespread culture".

Here then we get a picture of the dispersion of man eastwards from the Tibetan area and indeed during many milleniums prior to the fixation of the Tibetan area as a centre of religious diffusion.

It suggests in a rational way how early Man with his sign language and primitive mysteries came to be dispersed over the face of the earth taking with him certain peculiarities such as sun and serpent worship, mummification and the use of the swastika symbol which are, among many other practices, closely associated with the rituals of secret societies in the modern world.

For example: Both in China and Japan the ruling house claims descent from Heaven, while in China up to A.D. 1912 the Dragon (Serpent) was the emblem of Imperial authority and the Emperor sat upon the Dragon Throne.[3]

Again, in regard to the making of mummies, Elliot Smith *In the Beginning* page 64 has:—

"There is now a vast collection of evidence to show that all initiation ceremonies, not only those of medicine-men in Australia and North America, but also those of members of secret societies in every continent, are modelled essentially on the ritual of mummification".

Footnote.—(1) *See* Elliot Smith *The Diffusion of Culture.*
Footnote.—(2) The temple of Kukul Can in Mexico excavated by Dr. S. G. Morley of the Carnegie Institute of Washington since 1923 bears a resemblance to the Ziggurat of Ur restored by Woolley.
Footnote.—(3) *See* Johnston *Lion and Dragon in North China* (1910) pages 385-390 also Perry *The Children of the Sun* (1923).

Again the swastika, (*Sanscrit* = well-being) the most ancient of symbols is of two kinds depending apparently upon the relevance of the earth's motion to the Sun *viz:*—

With points going left,
away from the Sun.
Female, Earth, Moon, Death.

With points going right,
towards the Sun.
Male, God, Sun, Life.

Its origin and association with secret societies are referred to by Ward in *Freemasonry and the Ancient Gods* (Chapters VI and VII).

In both of its symbolic aspects, it appears to belong to the left stem of secret societies or the deification of man. With points to the left, it represents the female principle, or saktism and is the sign of Kali (Ward *op. cit.* page 11). With points to the right it is the male or true Swastika, representing life and the axe, or hammer of Thor (*ibidem* pages 74 and 237).[1]

Chamber's *Encyclopaedia* has the following:—

"A widespread religious symbol......which according to some, was intended to represent the Sun, being found associated with the worship of Aryan sun-gods (Apollo, Odin).

Similar devices occur on the monumental remains of the ancient Mexicans and Peruvians; on an object from the burial mounds of the United States; and in Tibet. ......In Germany the swastika or hakenkreuz has been taken as a badge by the anti-semites".

The most recent examination of the emblem published in English[2] suggests that it is a Sumerian sign for "god of the mountains". This conclusion from an independent quarter, supports, perhaps, the suggestion made above of an association between the Sumerians and Mount Meru.

So much for the diffusion of the arcana of secret societies eastwards from the Tibetan area. This diffusion may have been unconscious through the spread of the helio-lithic culture, many milleniums before the dawn of history in B.C. 5000. There was, no doubt, a secondary and perhaps conscious diffusion eastwards during the historical period, which may have corresponded roughly with the conscious diffusion westwards and southwards from about 2000 B.C. onwards, after the second revelation which we have roughly traced above.

To the list of customs of the sunstone culture given by Wells, there might be added another common practice, which may have been diffused both East and West from the common fountain of Mount Meru. That practice is the worship of a sacred mountain, natural or artificial, traces of which, some living and some dead, but all associated with Kingship, are found almost universally among the human family. As examples we have the Ziggurat of Ur: The pyramids of Egypt: The pagodas of Burma, Siam and China: The altar of Heaven at Pekin: The *stupa*, tope, or barrow of India and the Pacific islands: The castillo of Mexico, (exemplified in the temple of Kukal Can excavated by the Carnegie Institute 1923–1930): the "sacred mountain" in African tribal rites and, to give a local example, the *panchapersada* of the Malay coronation ceremony and the "Meru" shrines of the Balinese who, alone among the Indo-Polynesian peoples of the Malayan Archipelago, have retained their pre-Islamic Hinduism, and with it the name as well as the conformation of the sacred mountain itself.[3]

Mount Meru in Malaya and Indonesia

Hindu ascendancy in what is modern Malaya and the Netherlands Indies, covered a period of a thousand years (c. A.D. 450–1450) during which the Empire of Sri Vijaya was paramount for some seven hundred years (A.D. 670–1377) in Malaya, Sumatra and Java. According to Malay tradition, it was ruled over by the dynasty of Sailendra, or "Kings of the Mountain".[4]

In Malay history, the coming of their first kings is connected with the sacred mountain of Mahameru (*see Malay Annals* 18, 20 and 29) Wilkinson, *Dictionary* 1932 ed. has:—

"Mahameru (Sanscrit) The "Great Meru" or Indian Olympus: more specifically the mountain mass of Kailas at the source of the Indus and Brahmaputra and near the source of the Ganges. Mahameru is regarded as the home of the gods and is identified in Indonesia with some of the loftier peaks such as Merapi and Dempo in Sumatra; and Sumeru in Java, of which a summit still bears the name Mahameru".[5]

This association, no doubt, accounts for the *pancha persada* in the Malay coronation ceremony. But it is among the Balinese, where Hindu ascendancy has remained an isolated outpost to the present-day, that the tradition of Mount Meru is strongest. A description and illustration of a typical Balinese temple or *puru* is given by Miguel Covarrubias *Island of Bali* (1937), pages 264–269; and a comparison with Woolley's description of the Temenos of Ur in B.C. 2000 emphasises the striking likeness between them, and again suggests a common origin in Mount Meru.

Footnote.—(1) It is from the latter that it has been adopted as the symbol of hitlerism, which we must remember, was a secret society before it became from 1933 onwards a world power.
Footnote.—(2) *Real History of the Swastika* by Rev. N. Walker. (Lutterworth Press 1939).
Footnote.—(3) Nor does there appear any reason to exclude the tumulus of Greece, the spire of Christianity or the dome of Islam.
Footnote.—(4) *See* Winstedt *History of Malaya* (1935) page 24.
Footnote.—(5) For further light upon the historical connection between the Hindu Mount Meru and modern Malaya, see:—
　(i) T. Braddell. *Sagantang Maha Miru J.I.A.* Vol. V (1851) pages 176–177.
　(ii) R. Braddell. *Study of Ancient Times in the Malay Peninsula J.R.A.S.M.B.* Vol. XIV. Part III (Dec. 1936) pages 55–56.

A detailed comparison would be out of place here, but we may point out that whereas in the Temenos, the Ziggurat or "stepped-pyramid" upon the uppermost stage of which stood the shrine of Nannar, was the "holy of holies (Heaven) the most sacred thing in Ur, the chief glory of the city and the core of its worship", so the third and innermost shrine of a Balinese *Pura* is the *Meru*, or representation of the sacred mountain of Hinduism, the ancient name of which has been preserved and which is constructed of wood and thatch in varying sizes of three, five, seven, nine or eleven tiered roofs, or steps.[1]

6. THE ARCANA OF HUMAN BELIEF

We may be permitted to assume that the dissemination of the sunstone culture of Professor Elliot Smith, was accompanied by a diffusion of man's earliest esoteric knowledge derived perhaps from the first (traditional) revelation of God to man.

All of this knowledge would have been oral and much of it conveyed, no doubt, by sign language at an epoch when the process of speech may not yet have been fully developed. We may also suggest that the "single source" attributed to this culture by some scholars may have been the Mount Meru of Hindu and Chinese mythology, or the oasis of Merv at the foot of the Hindu Kush of history, whence we have further suggested the Sumerians may have come.

Of the sunstone diffusion, Wells says (above) :—

"The first civilisation in Egypt and the Euphrates valley probably developed directly out of this widespread culture".

This last hypothesis would be met by the foregoing assumption.

We may further assume that from the second (historical) revelation of B.C. 2000, there followed a second propagation of esoteric knowledge emanating from it and mingling, no doubt, with the earlier "mysteries", and extending perhaps the system of sign language and fixed formulæ to convey their meaning.

This secret knowledge deriving in part from the "abominations", and in part from the "revelations", became crystallised into the arcana of human belief.

We may briefly survey at this point some of these actual *cabala*, without investigating further their origin or significance. For convenience these may be summarised under three heads, *viz*:—

(A) Symbols.

(B) Ceremonies.

(C) Signs and grips.

    (A) *Symbols.*—Some of the commoner and universal ones are:—
        (1) The tau cross.
        (2) The rose or *vesica piscis* (see Chapter III page 45 *infra*).
        (3) The ankh.
        (4) The equilateral triangle.
        (5) The serpent.
        (6) The swastika.

These symbols generally speaking, are associated with the reproductive principle and with solar or stellar cults, and astrological lore, and appear to represent:—
        (a) The nature of god and the origin of man and the earthly duties incumbent upon man ("the lesser mysteries").
        (b) The fate of man after death and the mystery of the cross ("the greater mysteries").[2]

    (B) *Ceremonies and their emblems.*—Three ceremonies are *common to the whole human family viz*:—
        (1) The coronation or installation of a king, sultan or chief.
        (2) The celebration of marriage.
        (3) The ritual of initiation, whether into manhood, priesthood, or membership of any religious, or secret secular fraternity.

Each of these ceremonies employs certain objects, acts and procedure which, in turn:—
        (a) Are common to that ceremony to-day throughout the whole human family.
        (b) Are imbued to a greater or lesser degree with a common esoterism.
        (c) Are reproduced to a greater or lesser extent, *in all three ceremonies*.

This means that there is a double interpenetration, or link of association between the three ceremonies, firstly, through observances common to any one ceremony throughout the world: and secondly, through features common throughout the world to all three ceremonies.

Some of these interdependent and analogous features have been tabulated for us by Hocart in *Kingship* (1927) Chapters VII, VIII, X, and XII, and may be conveniently reproduced here in still more concise form.

Some of them will come to our notice later in Chinese and Mohammedan secret society initiation ceremonies in Malaya.

Hocart has labelled these features each with a serial index letter, which he retains constant for the three ceremonies among the different races quoted by him. (*See* page xxxi footnotes 2 and 3 above).

Footnote.—(1) Readers interested will find material for comparison in Woolley *Abraham* page 79 ff. and *Ur of the Chaldees* Chapter IV Covarrubias *Island of Bali* (1937) page 264 ff.; and in Foran *Malayan Symphony* pages 287 and 253 and Hocart *Kingship* Chapters XIV and XV.
    Footnote.—(2) *See* Ward *Freemasonry and the Ancient Gods* pages 231-240: Churchward *Signs and Symbols of primordial man.*

(B) Ceremonies and their emblems.

For convenience, we will retain Hocart's index letters, which are based upon his interpretation of the theory of divine Kingship. Consequently, the coronation ceremony takes pride of place in Hocart's work and the three ceremonies present the following standard features to our notice, thus:—

Serial number	Hocart's Index Letter	Coronation (Standard features)	Marriage	Initiation	Notes
1	A	The theory that the King:—(a) dies (b) is reborn (c) as a god ..	The bride-groom represents the Sky¹ the bride the Earth² the setting and rising sun gods³ ..	The theory that the initiate (a) dies (b) is reborn³ ..	A.—(1) Cf. the Malay wedding ceremony in which the bride and bridegroom are regarded as royal persons on their wedding day (raja sahari). Skeat Malay Magic page 387. (2) Cf. the Brahman observance of the bridegroom and bride as Siva and Parvati. (3) Cf. the three "twice born" castes of India.
2	B	Preparation by fasting with or without other austerities ..	Preparation by abstinence	Preparation by austerities	—
3	C	Exclusion of women and strangers and provision of an armed guard ..	—	The proceedings are strictly secret	—
4	D	A silence is observed, as in the presence of death ..	—	The symbolic death of the initiate —	—
5	E	A ritual combat in which the King is victorious ..	Conflict and victory⁵ ..	—	E.—(4) Cf. the Malay custom of a mimic battle for the person of the bride upon the arrival of the bridegroom at the bride's house. (Skeat op. cit.). (5) Cf. the more primitive custom of marriage by capture.
6	F	Admonition to adhere to certain rules	Marriage vows	Two primary oaths:— (1) To reveal none of the mysteries to the profane .. (2) To observe the code of rules and obligations, subject to death or excommunication ..	—
7	G	Drinking of ambrosia and distribution of food ..	Husband and wife eat out of the same vessel ..	Libations of wine, often mixed with other ingredients, are made⁶ ..	G.—(6) Cf. the blood-brotherhood of the Chinese, drunk in blood and wine; of Malays in blood and milk.
8	H	The people indulge in antics or buffoonery ..	Pranks played on the newly married pair ..	—	—

xlii

(B) Ceremonies and their emblems—continued.

Serial number	Hocart's Index Letter	Coronation. (Standard features)	Marriage	Initiation	Notes
9	I	Assumption of robes, three in number[1]	Wedding garments	Initiation robes[2]	I.—(1) Symbolising the three cauls of the womb, or re-birth. (2) Frequently white as in Freemasonry and in the Triad of China, symbolising re-birth.
10	J	Ceremonial bathing (lustration)	Sprinkling with holy water[3]	Ceremonial purification	J.—(3) Cf. the Malay custom at royal weddings of the bride and bridegroom bathing together and also the ritual bathing of the raja and his consort at Malay coronations. Skeat *Malay Magic* page 387.
11	K	Inunction	In India, clarified butter is poured in the bride's hand and later the pair are annointed with scented oil	—	
12 13 14	L M N	Ritual sacrifice .. / Acclamation and rejoicing / A feast is held	Wedding feast	A feast is frequently held[4]	N.—(4) Cf. the symbolic slaying of the white horse (the sky) and the black ox (the earth) and the feast provided at the conclusion of the Chinese Triad ceremony.
15	O	The King is crowned (the head)	The crown has disappeared in the West except in Russia, where the whole marriage ceremony is called the "matrimonial coronation"	The bishop's mitre corresponds to the crown	O.—(i) Cf. the red fillet or turban worn by the initiate in the Chinese Triad ceremony. (ii) Cf. A similar observance in the Chinese Three Dot Brotherhood. (iii) Cf. A similar but white headdress used in the Malay White Flag ceremony.
16	P	He puts on shoes (the feet)	Like the King who becomes a god in coronation and whose feet cannot thereafter touch the ground, the bridegroom in many places is made to stand upon skins, etc.	The Hindu "twice-born" boy receives a pair of shoes	P.—(i) The coronation shoes have been discontinued in the English ceremony since George II. (ii) Cf. the "grass sandals" worn by the priest and the initiate in the Chinese Triad ceremony. (iii) Cf. the "left shoe" given to the initiate in the Chinese Three Dot Brotherhood. (iv) Cf. the grade known as *kasut* (shoe) in both the White and Red Flag societies of the Malays.

(B) Ceremonies and their emblems—continued.

Serial number	Hocart's Index Letter	Coronation (Standard features)	Marriage	Initiation	Notes
17	Q	He receives other regalia conferring sovereignty such as: a sword, a sceptre, staff or baton, sometimes tipped with an eagle: a seal: a ring: a shepherd's crook: a seven fold parasol, etc.	The Wedding ring ..	The Hindu "twice-born" boy receives a staff and an umbrella. The Buddhist monk retains a fan and parasol. The bishop his crozier ..	Q.—(i) Cf. the sacred emblems in the Triad ceremony among which are the banner of the *victorious* brotherhood. The magic sword; also the red staff. (ii) Cf. the umbrella carried by the initiator at the Three Dot ceremony (page 188). (iii) Cf. also the official known as the *Pojong* (umbrella) in the Red Flag society of the Malays.
18	R	He ascends a throne ..		The Bishop has a throne	S.—(i) For the origin of the three steps of Vishnu as recorded in the *Ramayana* and the *Satapatha Brahmana* etc. of Vedic mythology *see* Hocart *Kingship* pages 214-221. (ii) Cf. the three steps in the ritual of both the Triad and the Three Dot societies of China.
19	S	He takes three ceremonial steps or paces ..	In India, the bride and bridegroom take seven steps to the North-East, corresponding to the three steps of Vishnu in the Indian coronation rite	The three paces constantly recur in the ritual of secret society initiations	
20	T	Perambulation or symbolic procession around his dominions	In the Russian rite the pair with crown held over their heads, circumambulate the assembly	The perambulation of the initiates constantly recurs	
21	U	He receives a new name	The wife takes the husband's name (in the west)	In many secret societies the novice receives a new name!	U.—(1) Cf. the Triad ceremony of China in which they all take the surname Hung = inundation.
22	V	Installation of the Queen	The consummation of marriage	Puberty rites	
23	W	Installation of the vassals or officials as minor gods		The appointment of lodge officials of a secret society	
24	X	The priests conducting the ceremony are dressed as gods, sometimes with masks		This feature constantly recurs among more primitive rituals ..	
25	Y	These masks are sometimes those of animals, thus identifying the priest with a beast ..		This feature constantly recurs among more primitive rituals ..	
26	Z	A King may be consecrated more than once, going up one step each time in the hierarchy of Kingship ..		There are many advancing degrees of initiation and re-consecration in almost all rituals	

Despite the difficulties of investigation in a sphere so abstruse over so wide a field, and despite the obstacles raised by displacement, divergence and religious prejudice, the foregoing analogies are not arrived at by guess work, as the following two facts help to show:—

(1) In the *Satapatha Brahmana* Book V pages 3, 5, 20 ff. it is stated in explicit terms, that at his coronation the King is reborn from the womb of sovereignty.[1]

This ancient concept portrays the *fact* of natural birth,—the result of human marriage and *belief* in the supernatural rebirth of Kings at the coronation ceremony, as of common origin.

(2) Similarly, strange as it may seem, the salient features of coronation as given above, re-appear in a corresponding form to-day in the ceremony of initiation to manhood (secret rites of puberty) among the Australian aboriginal tribe of the Kurnai in South-East Australia.[2]

These two facts seem vividly to draw together from the ends of the earth, the common threads of the three great universal ceremonies of coronation, marriage and initiation among the human family.

(C) *Signs and grips.*—This section of the arcana although widespread, indeed universal, is, like the oral ritual of every secret society, jealously guarded from the profane.

We are, therefore, forced back upon surmise. The common praxis appears to be that each society uses in public:—

(a) A general or pass sign to enable a member to make himself known to any brethren present.

(b) A particular sign to convey special information, such as warning, distress, etc.

Having thus made contact with a brother, each grade or degree has its own individual sign of recognition by hand-grip, pass-word, or positioning of common articles, (of attire etc.).

Some of such used in the West are given in Morgan *Freemasonry* (1826) and others are indicated by Ward *Freemasonry and the Ancient Gods*, pages 93–118 under "Masonic signs and grips the world over", etc. Many others in use among Chinese and Malays will come to notice in the chapters that follow.

We have omitted from the above citation of cabala any mention of *customs* as these are a dangerous guide and do not necessarily connote any esoteric quality.

Nevertheless, the features of the Sun-stone culture referred to in the preceding section were, no doubt, absorbed into the arcana of belief, if they did not derive in the first place from them, and some re-appear among the above cabala; others, like circumcision and human sacrifice, are unmentioned therein; others again have lost their arcanan quality and become nothing more than empty survivals.

Among the fundamental esoteric features of belief, some have doubtless been refined and sublimated and absorbed into the great established religions of the world and others, rejected by them, have doubtless been adopted into the rites and rituals of secret societies both beneficent, and maleficent, to supply that quality of "mystery" without which they would lack appeal.

This process, we suggest, supplies the explanation of the presence throughout the world of to-day and yesterday of those forms of "Freemasonry" common to the whole human family and referred to at the beginning of this Introduction, where their rough distribution is recorded.

For the method of their diffusion in the pre-Abrahamic period, we must be guided by the opinion of Professor Elliot Smith upon the spread of the Sun-stone culture. For the method of their diffusion from Abraham's day, we have an historical line to follow.

7. THE TRANSFUSION OF SECRET BELIEF BETWEEN ASIA AND EUROPE

(A) Diffusion from the Ararat area South and West

We have suggested above how the secret formulæ and sign-language of the "primitive mysteries" may have been carried by the Sumerians from the Tibetan area of Mount Meru to the Euphrates basin. May we be permitted to suggest that in the diffusion of these formulæ westward and southward from the Ararat area which may have accompanied the redistribution of man after the flood, the sign-language was found to be all the more necessary after the confusion of tongues had made the communication of the verbal tradition difficult? Acceptance or rejection of this theory must depend upon acceptance or rejection of the Bible tradition.

We may assert with more confidence that the religious arcana of the Euphrates valley were carried westward with that migration towards the Mediterranean coast which began with Abraham's family.

The Phœnicians

This brings the trail of esoteric knowledge to the Mediterranean basin, the home of the Phœnicians. Wells *Outline of History* page 150 has:—

"Along the eastern end of the Mediterranean the Phœnicians, a Semitic people, set up a string of independent harbour towns of which Acre, Tyre and Sidon were the chief and later they pushed their voyages westward and founded Carthage and Utica in North Africa. Possibly Phœnician keels were already in the Mediterranean by 2000 B.C.".

And on page 108:—

"They were great seamen because they were great traders. Their Colony of Carthage, founded before 800 B.C. by Tyre, became at last greater than any of the older Phœnician cities, but already before 1500 B.C. both Sidon and Tyre had settlements upon the African Coast.

* * *

Footnote.—(1) *See* Hocart *op. cit.* page 77.
Footnote.—(2) *See* Howitt *Native Tribes of South-East Australia* page 526; also Hocart *op. cit.* page 147.

At her zenith Carthage probably had the hitherto unheard of population of a million...... As well as a coasting trade she has a considerable land trade with Central Africa. She sold negro slaves, ivory, etc., to all the Mediterranean people and her ships went out into the Atlantic and coasted along Portugal and France northward as far as the Cassiterides (the Scilly Isles, or Cornwall) in England to get tin".

We may assume that to the Phœnicians was due in some measure the spread from the Ararat area to Central Africa and to Europe of those religious arcana which are to-day common to the world, in the formulæ of secret societies.

This view finds support from Ward *Freemasonry and the ancient Gods* who in discussing the vexed question of the origin of Freemasonry says on pages 154–155:—

"Perhaps the truest answer as to whence Masonry comes......is that given in the *Layland-Lacke MSS* (c. 1436 A.D.) in the Bodleian Library which says:—
Q. Where did it (freemasonry) begin?
A. It began with the first men of the East, who were before the first men of the West.
Q. Who brought it to the West?
A. The Phœnicians.
Q. How came it into England?
A. Pythagoras, a Grecian,[1] travelled to acquire knowledge in Egypt and Syria and in every other land where the Phœnicians had planted Freemasonry, and, gaining admission into all lodges of masons, he learned much and returned and dwelt in Magna Graecia. Here he formed the great lodge at Crotona and made many masons some of whom travelled to France and there made many more, from whence in due time the art passed into England".

In further support of the view that the arcana of freemasonry were transmitted from Ur of the Chaldees to the Phœnicians, in the epoch following the migration of Abraham along the same route, we may quote an article entitled *Whence come you?* by H. C. Faxon a past master mason in Vol. XXIX (1939) of *The Pentagram*, a Masonic periodical published in Singapore by the District Grand Lodge of the Eastern Archipelago.

He poses the question page 220:—

"Can any evidence be adduced as to a possible medium of the transmission of the (masonic) rituals from Chaldea to Jerusalem"?

To which he replies *inter alia* as follows page 221:—

"From time immemorial the secrets of the mysteries have been most zealously guarded and have been transmitted from generation to generation, from teacher to disciple by word of mouth. The solution of the problem must, therefore, lie in the discovery of some existing race, nation, or community of individuals whose traditional history, legends or customs directly connect the present with the far distant past. It is suggested that such a community does exist at the present-day in the Druses of Lebanon—the direct descendents of those ancient Phœnicians, whose ruler was Hiram, King of Tyre".

The importance of the Druses of Lebanon to the general subject of the diffusion of religious arcana from the "Ararat area" southward and westward and the further strange link which their belief furnishes with the "Tibetan area" of diffusion in addition, is referred to in Chapters X and XXXIII of this work.

(B) RE-DIFFUSION OF WESTERN THOUGHT EASTWARDS

After the penetration of the Phœnicians westward, European thought was re-diffused eastwards during the Empire of Darius I, (B.C. 520) whose tributaries came from the Oxus and the middle east; and again under Alexander the Great (B.C. 330), the seeds of whose conquests bore a fruitful harvest in the fertile lands of Ferghana, Sogdiana and the Oasis of Merv for near a thousand years.

What re-diffusion of western arcana of belief in Central Asia accompanied these political eruptions we can only speculate upon, but it is a fairly safe assumption that they all belonged ultimately to the Ararat tradition and had not yet co-mingled to any great extent with those of the Tibetan area.

(C) DIFFUSION OF "RELIGIOUS" ARCANA FROM THE TIBETAN AREA SOUTH AND EAST

We have noted above, under "The Sumers and Mount Meru" section, the Taoist legend of Si Wong Mo and her association with Mount Meru where is:—

"The fountain of immortality and whence flow the four great rivers of the world".[2]

Whether the diffusion followed the rivers we cannot say, but we can state positively that the territories through which these rivers flow are permeated with an identical esoterism traceable to a common depository in the Lamaism of Tibet.[3]

Whether these arcana which bear a close resemblance, are in turn traceable back from Tibet to a common ancestry in the central Asian plateau only archaeology can say.

It would seem probable that it was from the Tibetan area of diffusion that these arcana found their way to America. We may trace them roughly *via* the Yellow River basin to Japan.

(D) THE PERIOD OF THE GREAT EXTRAVASATION OF ARCANA FROM THE TIBETAN AREA TO THE WEST

Whatever the manner of diffusion of religious arcana throughout the world in the pre-history and pre-Christian eras, there intervened a period in recent world history in which successive irruptions of eastern thought flowed into the western world.

Footnote.—(1) Pythagoras of Samos, who lived in the sixth century B.C., a philosopher and mathematician and the founder of a secret society system with initiation by blood-brotherhood.

Footnote.—(2) The Yellow River and the Yangtze of China: the Mekong of French Indo-China and the Salween of Burma. (*See* page xxvi, footnote 2 *supra*). *See* also page xxix *supra*, where the rivers are given as the Ganges, Nile, Tigris and Euphrates. It seems probable that the rivers really meant were: Euphrates, Indus (Sutlej), Ganges and Brahmaputra.

Footnote.—(3) For a modern authoritative description of which, *see* the writings of Alexandra David-Neel.

The slow change of climate that had replaced the swamps of central Asia by "steppes" or wide grazing lands, favoured the rise of a virile race hardened by a nomadic life necessitated by an annual movement between summer and winter pastures.

This steppe-belt swept across the heart of Asia from the Volga to Lake Baikal and cradled a multitude of hardy nomadic tribes whom we know as the Mongolian races and who are popularly referred to in their rôle of early invaders of the west as "Huns", a derivation from the name of one of the tribes known to history as the Hiung Nu.

Wells *Outline of History* Chapter XXIX Section 4, says of these people:—

> "There can be little doubt that the Hiung Nu, the Huns, and the later people called the Mongols, were all very much the same people and that the Turks and Tartars presently branched off from this same drifting Mongolian population. Kalmuks and Buriats are later developments of the same strain. We shall favour the use of the word "Hun" as a sort of general term for these tribes".

With the expansion westward of the Chinese Empire under the Western Han dynasty (B.C. 200—A.D. 25), the southern Huns were partly civilised and assimilated by the Chinese, the northern Huns were turned still further westward to the borders of Europe. Wells *loc. cit.* continues:—

> "In the opening century of the Christian era, the Chinese Empire was strong enough to expel and push off from itself the surplus of this Mongolian nomadism, which presently conquered North India and gathered force and mingled with Aryan nomadism, and fell at last like an avalanche upon the weak-backed Roman Empire".

About A.D. 450 there arose the Hun leader Attila whose legions attacked the Roman Empire and gave their name but little of their blood to modern Hungary. The Huns thereafter withdrew to the Oxus or dissolved into the surrounding populations and disappear as "Huns" from history.

What degree of Tibetan arcana, if any, "the Huns" may have imported to the west, during the first 500 years of the Christian era, we do not know. We mention them only as the fore-runners of a mighty and sustained irruption from the far East, which descended upon Europe by the land route 800 years later.

Meanwhile Islam arose and among its vast conquests A.D. 630–750 had converted to that faith the Hun tribes that had settled near the Oxus. Among these was the Seljuk clan of Turks, one of the Mongol tribes who gave their name to Turkestan.

When the Moslem Empire began to weaken under the Sunni-Shiah schism, which split it up into separate kingdoms, a revival took place under the Seljuk Turks who were Sunnis. They conquered the decaying Abbasid (Sunni) Khalifate of Baghdad and over-ran the Shiah kingdoms in Asia Minor, Palestine and Egypt and swept on to the walls of Constantinople. The capture of Jerusalem by the Seljuk Turks in A.D. 1073 provoked the struggle between Islam and Christendom for possession of the Holy City, which we know as the Crusades, and which lasted from A.D. 1097 to 1244, when Jerusalem was finally recaptured by Islam and remained in Moslem possession until A.D. 1918.

There is proof that the period of the Crusades saw much assimilation of both the Tibetan and Ararat arcana of belief among those men from the east and men from the west engaged in it, who for long periods dwelt in Palestine together on terms of close association with, among others, the Assassins of Alamut, who were also represented among the Turkish forces (*see* Chapter X).

But the last and greatest influx of eastern thought and influence by the land route to the west, was that of the Mongol conquest under the dynasty of Genghis Khan.

The same fertile region about Lake Baikal whence began the Hun migrations westward in the fourth century, and whence sprang the powerful Turkish Kingdoms in the sixth, saw also the rise in the twelfth of that great Mongol dynasty of the Khans—Genghis, Mangu and Kublai are the best known to history—which was destined to build an Empire from the China Sea to the Baltic in the thirteenth.

The founder of this dynasty[1] was a mythical nomad Mongol named Budanstar whose eighth descendant was Yesukai, the ruler of a tent-city of 40,000 tents at Karakoram, on the River Orkhon, which flows into Lake Baikal.

Footnote.—(1) The dynasty was roughly as follows:—

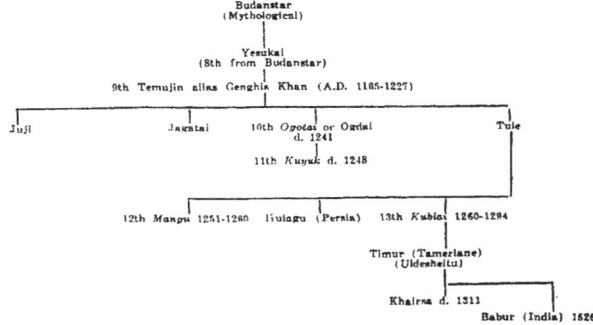

The history of the rise of this dynasty and its European conquests is given in condensed form in the *Encyclopaedia Britannica* under *Mongols*: by Wells *Outline of History* Chapter XXXIV, and in the *Travels of Marco Polo*.

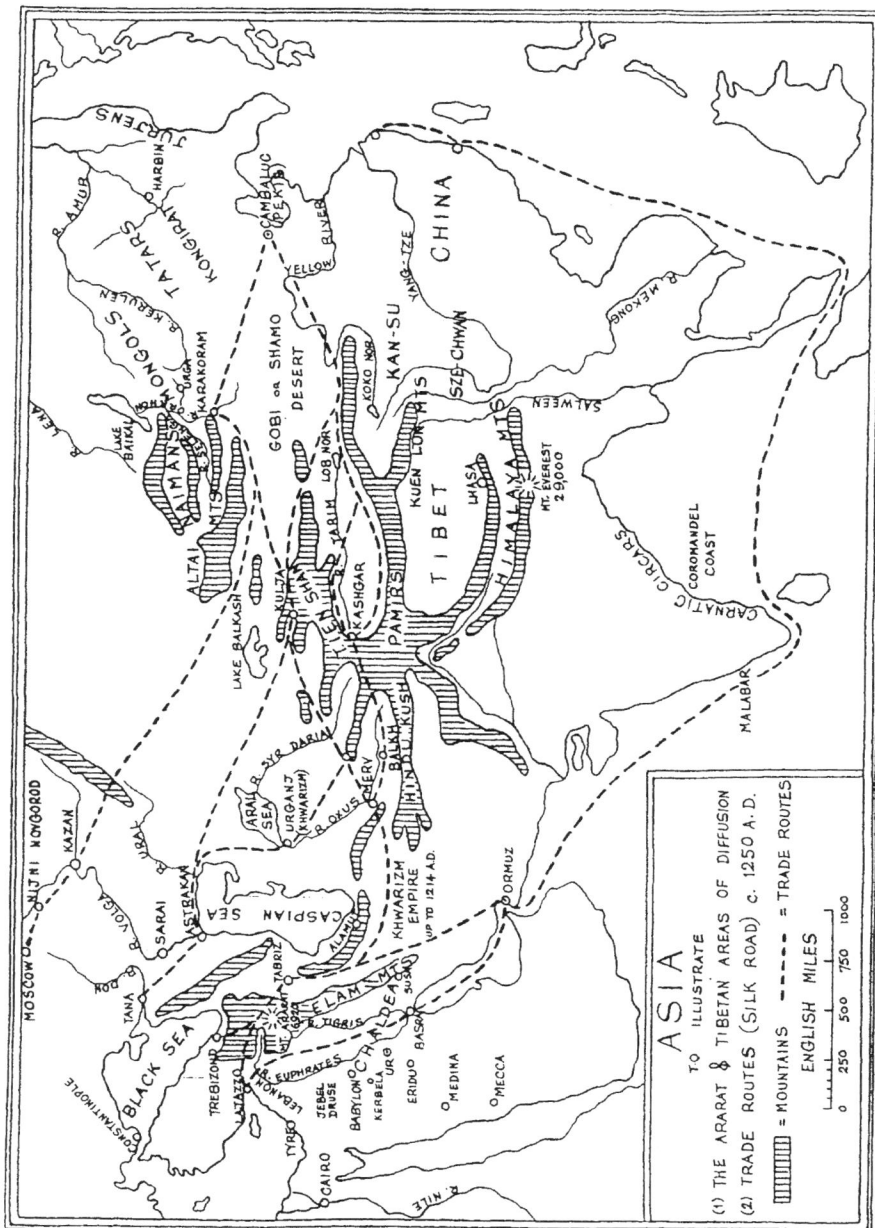

ASIA
TO ILLUSTRATE
(1) THE ARARAT & TIBETAN AREAS OF DIFFUSION
(2) TRADE ROUTES (SILK ROAD) c. 1250 A.D.

⊞⊞⊞ = MOUNTAINS   - - - - = TRADE ROUTES

ENGLISH MILES

0   250   500   750   1000

The blood-brotherhood of the Mongols

One final feature of Mongol religious or social structure merits our attention. This was the custom of *anda* or blood-brotherhood to which Fox *op. cit.* has the following reference on page 71:—

> "The old men say that when two make themselves *anda*, then they both have one life. "One does not leave the other and they guard each other's life"......
> They then exchanged gifts and made a feast by a cliff......and at night they slept under one blanket".

Blood-brotherhood[1] is a basic feature of secret society organisation the world over and the *anda* custom of the Mongols, while presenting nothing new, would furnish a predisposition among them to combination by secret *formulæ*.

The "religious" composition of the Mongol hordes

This then suggests the arcanan composition of that conquering avalanche that swept into the "Dark Age" of Europe in the thirteenth century, carrying with it, no doubt, elements of the Yin Yang of China, the native shamanism of the Mongols, the blood-brotherhood peculiar to themselves and the *débris* of Buddhist, Nestorian and Islamic beliefs.

By their coming, the mechanical process of diffusion of the arcana of the Tibetan and Ararat areas from the China seas to the Baltic, was complete. The great rushing together of the peoples of Asia and Europe, the final cross-over co-mingling and inter-penetration of human beliefs in modern times had taken place, and from this dark vortex there arose again those *foci* of esoteric knowledge, which have become the rallying points of modern secret societies.

8. THE DEVELOPMENT AND CHARACTER OF MODERN SECRET SOCIETIES

It remains to suggest the process whereby some of the arcana of primitive belief after their diffusion and rediffusion throughout the human family, and after refinement by the doctrines of the great religions of the world, which rejected their grosser aspects, broke off and became in turn the core of secret organisations, whether for beneficent or maleficent purposes, according as they followed the higher road in search of atonement for their higher selves through mysticism, or the lower road in search of gratification of their worldly ambitions through deception and magic.

We are not concerned here with those secret associations which formed themselves along the higher road and for beneficent purposes. They are religious in the modern sense and are pure and holy and outside the scope of this work, except in so far as they share what are, or what appear to be, the same arcana as the maleficent societies and are, therefore, sometimes used by similar but debased secret associations belonging to the lower road, as a convenient and unsuspecting "host" or camouflage, to cover worldy designs.

But it is in the struggle that has continued since Abraham's day between the polytheism of the deification of man and the monotheism of the worship of God, that the breeding-ground of maleficent secret societies is to be found.

"Bold men, wise men, shrewd men and cunning men" have continued to arise and become "magicians, priests, chiefs and kings", and they are so continuing to arise in the world of to-day.

At the root of almost every one of these successive bids to rule the world there has lain a core of secret intrigue which has supplied the recruiting machinery and the directive brain for the final attempt. These secret associations have usually been at first wreathed in the arcana of "religion" to make them more attractive to unsuspecting recruits. Their political complexion has only revealed itself when the time was ripe. Their organisation as maleficent secret societies all seem to bear a common stamp of deception and treachery, which in the course of the past thousand years in the western world may be traced to the system of one single man.

The secret society system of Abdullah bin Maimun

Among the succession of bold and cunning men who sought by deception and magic to enthral his fellows, there arose about A.D. 870 in the Ararat area, a Persian of wide learning and purely materialist outlook who had been brought up in the doctrine of gnostic dualism then prevailing in Persia and Irak.

His name was Abdullah bin Maimun and he devised a system of secret society organisation among the Shiah Mohamedans of his day, of which the object is given by Reinhart Dozy in *Spanish Islam* (page 403) as follows:—

> "To unite in the form of a vast secret society with many degrees of initiation, free-thinkers who regarded religion only as a curb for the people, and bigots of all sects: to make tools of believers in order to give power to sceptics: to induce conquerers to overturn the Empire they had founded: to link together into one body the vanquished and the conquerors: to build up a party numerous, compact and disciplined which in due time would give the throne if not to himself at least to his descendants......an extraordinary conception which he worked out with marvellous tact, incomparable skill and profound knowledge of the human heart. The means he adopted were devised with diabolical cunning".

To each degree of initiation he admitted only those whom he could rely upon to accept the revelation of that degree until he gradually reached the final "mystery" to which only his immediate followers were admitted and revealed therein that religion and morality were nothing but an imposture and an absurdity.

Footnote.—(1) *See* Chapter II page 18-19 *infra:* also Fraser *Golden Bough* Abridged. ed. pages 113 and 202 and Tylor *Anthropology* Vol. II page 148.

1

The aftermath of this vast Mongol or "Mogol" conquest was the rise of the "Mogol"[1] Empires *viz*:—

    The Manchu in China
    The "Mogol" in India
    The Khajiar in Persia
    The Ottoman in Turkey

all of which only disappeared from history in the nineteenth and twentieth centuries (*see* Chapter III).

Another result was the permanent opening of the land routes between Asia and Europe, which the accompanying map helps to fix in the mind.[2]

The questions which rise to the mind at this point are these:—

What quality of esoteric knowledge, if any, did these advancing hordes which had already over-run China, bring with them to Europe from the shores of Lake Baikal? and what degree of diffusion of these arcana in the west followed upon this eastern avalanche, which struck Europe just when the struggle between Cross and Crescent for possession of Jerusalem was coming to a close?

To attempt an answer to such abstruse questions touching a period the factual history of which is still largely in obscurity, may seem presumptuous, but a recent able work by Ralph Fox *Genghis Khan* (1936) offers us considerable help.

First, we should remember that Christianity had been percolating eastward for many centuries through Nestorian missionaries and had flourished in China between A.D. 600 to 850 (*see* page 53 Chapter IV *infra*) secondly, that the effects of the rise and conquests of Islam A.D. 630–750 were felt far beyond the confines of the first Moslem Empire and Mohamedan missionaries who arrived both by sea and by the caravan routes across central Asia were already at work in South China (Canton) and in the western provinces of Kansu, Shensi, Szechuan and Yunnan, by the middle of seventh century. Fox *op. cit.* page 20, gives us the following picture of central Asia east of the Moslem Khwarizmian Empire (modern Russian Turkestan): and of the Pamirs: Chinese Turkestan (or Sin-Kiang): and in the Chinese province of Kansu at the beginning of the twelfth century:—

> "The trade routes from China to the west were no less disturbed throughout the twelfth century. The Khitans driven out of Northern China by the Manchurian Kin or Jurgens, built a new Empire for themselves in central Asia. Their centre was in the lands of the Uighur and in Eastern Turkestan, but their conquests spread at one time as far west as Bokhara and Samarkand, the two great homes of central Asian trade and Islamic culture.
>
> Their Empire was known as the *Kara-Khitai*, the Empire of Black Cathay.
>
> Another Kingdom, that of the *Hsi-Hsia*, inhabited by the Tibetan Tangut or Hsia, held the debouches into China proper, the ancient caravan road through the Lop Nor region...... Both these states......were centres of ancient culture. Their walled cities contained Buddhist temples and libraries, Nestorian churches and Mohamedan mosques (in which)......the heritage of Alexander's great campaign was mingled with the purely Chinese...... To their Moslem subjects, these Kara-Khitan conquerors, with their train of Tangut and Uighur followers were merely ignorant idol-worshippers".

This description provides us with a picture of the confluence of religious arcana in central Asia east of the Pamirs at the beginning of the twelfth century, before the coming of the nomad Mongol conquest.

Fox *op. cit.* page 53, thus divides for us the nomad mongol races whose home lay between the shores of Lake Baikal and the sources of the Amur:—

> "Tribes of two races lived on the lands these rivers watered—the Tatars, whom men later called Mongols, and the Turks".[3]

> "Since A.D. 1009 the Kerait were Christians, converted by the Nestorian bishop of Merv in central Asia, while among the Naiman, pagan shamanists and Christian priests alike were to be found. The Kerait were much mixed with the Mongols and spoke the Mongol tongue".

Despite the admixtures of Buddhism, Christianity and Islam, the prevailing religion of the Mongols was shamanism. Thus Fox *op. cit.* page 45 has:—

> "The Mongols did not believe in any god, but in the spirits of nature and the mighty power of the blue sky".

And again on page 27:—

> "The sky is his (the Mongol's) supreme spirit, his god. But the winds, the stones, the rivers, the forests, all have their spirits, mostly evil. The shaman, the medicine-man, can commune with them and is, if not the master of nature, at least its confidant".

And lastly on page 98:—

> "Buddhism and Christianity were widespread among them, though the old shamanist sorcerers still kept their influence".

Footnote.—(1) The word "mogol" is a faulty romanisation of the Arabic mughal, which was itself a corruption of the name "mongol".
Footnote.—(2) The position of Samarkand is shown on this map, east of Merv, but the name has been omitted by mistake (*See* also page 153 *infra*).
Footnote.—(3) The divisions of these races given by Fox can best be shown by a table.

	Tatars (Mongols)				Turks	
Merkits	Kongirat	Taijint		Kerait		Naiman

Dozy continues:—

"The rest of mankind—the "asses" as Abdullah called them—were incapable of understanding such doctrines. But to gain his end, he by no means disdained their aid. On the contrary he solicited it, but he took care to initiate devout and lowly souls only into the first grades of the sect.

His missionaries were inculcated with the idea that their first duty was to conceal their true sentiments and adapt themselves to the views of their auditors ...... They won over the ignorant and vulgar by feats of legendemain which passed for miracles...... In the presence of the devout they assumed the mask of virtue and piety...... By means such as these, the extraordinary result was brought about that a multitude of men of diverse beliefs were all working together for an object known only to a few of them".

This system is of the highest importance to a comprehension of the nature and true aims of maleficent secret societies in the western world. Abdullah was its first practitioner in the Ararat area whence it spread throughout the West. Whether Abdullah invented it or adopted it from further East we do not know.

We can only say that the system in its subsequent elaborations in the West provided the pattern and method of organisation of subversive secret societies in the world to-day.

The system was elaborated in nine degrees and taught in the Dar-ul-Hikmat (House of knowledge) lodge in Cairo in A.D. 1000 and from its teaching there sprang the sect of the Assassins of Alamut, a teaching which found its way to Malaya at the beginning of the nineteenth century through the Thuggist deportees from India as described in Chapter X of this work.

In its elaborated form the teaching of the last five degrees reversed the teaching of the first four and so perpetrated a gradual and calculated fraud upon the proselyte from which he was unable to withdraw because of the penalty of death which his oaths, already taken, would exact.

This teaching has been summarised by Von Hammer *History of the Assassins* (1818) page 36 ff. as follows:—

"To believe nothing and to dare all was the sum of this system, which annihilated every principal of religion and morality and had no other object than to execute ambitious designs with suitable ministers, who daring all and knowing nothing are the best tools of an infernal policy: a system with no other aim than the gratification of an insatiable lust for domination".[1]

This is the pattern of every subversive secret society that has arisen in the West since the foundation of the Dar-ul-Hikmat lodge in Cairo in A.D. 1000 and is clearly based upon the principle of the deification of man as opposed to the worship of God.

The common identifiable features are, a cloak of false religion and a core of political revolution. In the world of men to-day religion and politics cannot be dissociated, any more than in the days of Abraham at Ur.

First human thought gave birth to human belief, belief to law and law to the state, whether that "state" be an African tribe or a world-wide Empire.

To return for a moment to the anthropologists.

Before a political *modus vivendi* can be found in the world between those who wish to maintain the present order, based on the worship of God and those who would replace it with other systems based on the deification of man, a final decision must be made upon the nature and origin of man himself and the genesis of his beliefs.

A decision as between Evolution and Special creation must be made, for if the source and method of man's appearance on the earth be left in doubt, whither shall governments attempt to direct the course of his development? There seems no obstacle to the acceptance of evolution and the concurrent acceptance of Divine revelation to man at one or more periods of his evolutionary history, when he had reached a stage at which he could understand the message. There seems to be no grounds except those of sentiment, for rejection of this view.

The Royal Anthropological Institute cultivates the science of man, upon the accepted basis of his evolution.

The steps now being taken by the Colonial office in conjunction with the Royal Anthropological Institute referred to at the beginning of this essay, may result in Colonial administration being based upon the same principle.

A further step might then follow by which human relations in the sphere of international law might be similarly adjusted and some of the causes of friction among the human family be thereby eliminated.

To-day colonial law and administration remain based upon belief in special creation, as Sir Arthur Keith *Darwinism and its critics* (1935) pages 27-28 has noted:—

"Strangely enough, two great departments of human endeavour were left untouched by the publication in 1859 of Darwin's *The Origin of Species*—namely, politics and business. Even to-day seventy-five years after its publication, British politicians think and legislate as if neither Charles Darwin nor Herbert Spencer had ever existed".

Belief in the theory of Evolution is a religion which rejects the theory of a more favourable status for any one section of humanity and sets all men upon a common basis of ascent towards their ultimate evolutionary destiny.

If human science should ultimately prove that all human society has a single origin, all human belief a single source and that all members of the human family do but stand upon different rungs of the same evolutionary ladder, which all are ascending; and if human society itself should, in turn, accept that proof and adjust its inter-relationships and

---

Footnote.—(1) This and the two preceding extracts are in part repeated at pages 158 and 161 of the main work where attention is again directed to the importance of the systems of Abdullah bin Maimun and Hasan bin Saba as the prototype of the modern subversive secret society. No apology is needed for thus underlining what we believe to be a point of great importance.

governments accordingly, the science of applied anthropology and the study of the secret societies of man, which forms part of it, may claim to have helped clear the path towards a wider human understanding.

The nature of secret societies in the modern world

This brings us to a consideration of the practical place of secret societies in the modern world.

The position may be summarised as follows. There are, in most countries, three categories of maleficent secret society constantly active viz:—

(1) The political revolutionary.
(2) The pseudo-"religious".
(3) The frankly criminal.

In western countries they usually remain under cover until their activities break surface in political upheavals, or out-breaks of crime.

In the east and particularly in those countries under western rule (the so-called "Colonial countries") they are usually all proscribed by law. Nevertheless the structure of society in "Colonial" countries is such that the western governments depend upon eastern sources for their information. This enables the illegal to co-exist with the legal, and sometimes almost to supersede it, and *imperia in imperio* to flourish.

Thus, Coulet *Les sociétés secrètes en terre d'Annam* (1926) goes further and maintains that in the secret society world in "colonial" countries, the illegal can become the whole basis of organised civil society. On page 286 *op. cit.* Coulet says:—

"En effet, la société secrète ne se cache pas sous les formes d'une société civile quelconque. Bien au contraire, elle est et veut être exactement cette société civile".

For this reason the problem of control of secret societies is more formidable in "Colonial countries" than in the West, where the ties of loyalty and the restraints of public opinion are stronger, the sources of information more tappable and the danger signals more easily discerned.

The tendency of governments whether in the East or West is, therefore, generally to ignore or discount what is carefully concealed from its view. No one who is not a member ever sees these societies at work and only a few hear vaguely of their supposed existence. But what harm do they do or can they do? and why make a fuss about them?

The same might be said of disease. Until it strikes us, we are hardly conscious of its existence and yet it would overwhelm us, were it not for the constant battle waged against it, by the unseen armies of medicine, hygiene and research.

If the foregoing diagnosis of the nature of secret societies is acceptable, it follows that on the maleficent side, those societies which attain to political eminence in any country are of great importance because of the power for evil they wield over their supporters who are made helpless victims of an unseen force they are unable to oppose—the State. The world has many such examples to offer at the present epoch. States built upon the principles of revolutionary secret societies such as Russia and Germany represent now, just as in Abraham's day, the triumph of the deification of man over the worship of God.

The most thoughtful book recently written on this aspect of the subject is Coudenhove-Kalergi's *The Totalitarian State against Man* published in 1938 with an Introduction by Mr. Wickham Steed.

Wickham Steed welcomes this book[1]:—

"As a contribution of outstanding value to the clarification of thought at a moment of supreme crisis in the political history of the world...... Meantime the fight against the totalitarian state, with its ideal of enforced "like-mindedness" among the sons of men, is a holy war for the freedom of the human soul".

Coudenhove-Kalergi himself *op. cit.* page 20 says:—

"We are living through the most dangerous revolution in the history of the world—the revolution of the State against mankind. We are living through the most dangerous idolatry of all ages—the deification of the state".

This is the language of political philosophy; but, in its essentials, the struggle is the same as that between Baal and Yahweh in Abraham's day, the struggle between the deification of man and the worship of God, which under a myriad secret, "religious" and political disguises has kept the world in turmoil throughout recorded history.

The two camps may, for purposes of contrast and identity with the two schools of man's arcanan belief, be set out once again hereunder using the words of Coudenhove-Kalergi *op. cit.* Chapter I, as quoted by Wickham Steed "Introduction" pages 8–9:—

DEIFICATION OF MAN (The Might State)	WORSHIP OF GOD (The Right State)
1. Man is the crown of creation.	1. Man is a creature of God.
2. The State is many men and, therefore, more than any man. The State is, therefore, a demi-god or god and the master of mankind.	2. The State is a creature of Man and the servant of mankind.
3. Man is a means.	3. Man is an end and not a means.
4. The State alone is an end in itself.	4. The State is a means and not an end.
5. The State is a building, man the building material.	5. The State is a machine, built for the service of man in the struggle against chaos and anarchy.

Footnote.—(1) In the Introduction thereto, pages 10—11.

DEIFICATION OF MAN (The Might State)	WORSHIP OF GOD (The Right State)
6. The value of man is exactly as great as his service to the State.	6. The value of the State is exactly the value of its services to human beings.
7. The State is everything.	7. The Man is a being and the State is his tool for good or for evil.

The modern political setting of the above[1] does not alter the age-old antagonism in the formulæ, it rather emphasises it by heightening the contrast.

Herbert Spencer *First Principles* (ed. 1900) pages 4–7 in discussing this subject, points out that the Might State is based upon primitive belief in the divinity of Kings; while the Right State is founded upon the modern belief in the sacredness of the individual.

Among the sharpest weapons with which the struggle between the right and the left has been maintained down through the ages since Abraham, have been the teeth and claws of maleficent political secret associations usually camouflaged under a pseudo-religious cloak.

To satisfy ourselves that we have emerged from our investigation into the nature of secret societies, with the thread of cause and effect intact, we may quote the following passage from Coudenhove-Kalergi *op. cit.* page 32 :—

"Those who think of politics in terms of power, picture the world as biological and dynamic, as a ceaselessly moving struggle between forces. In their eyes, States, peoples, classes and parties are living beings which grow, blossom and fade, which wage a fight for power and existence, the issue of which depends on their strength, their ruthlessness and their adroitness......in accordance with the law that nature allows of no armistice, but only of growth or decay, development or degeneration—the same law of nature that imposes a struggle for existence on beasts and plants.[2]

Those who think of politics in terms of law, picture the world as architectural and static. They see states, peoples, classes, professions and parties as given quantities, as material for building a political and social construction in accordance with the eternal laws of stability and harmony...... Thus, the politics of power are rooted in earthly laws, the politics of law in heavenly laws".

The struggle between the forces of world revolution and world evolution born at Abraham's parting of the ways in B.C. 2000 and sustained through the centuries, underground by secret societies, above ground by war, has run true to type in all parts of the world down to the present-day.

Subjective description of the aims of modern secret societies

Now let us examine briefly a subjective description of modern secret societies taken from the writings of acknowledged European members and leaders of some of them.

Dr. Gerard Encausse ("Papus") in his *Traité méthodique de magie pratique* (1927) refers to a book by Hoëné Wronski *L'Apodictique Messianique* (published in 1825 and no longer procurable), in which the latter has given an analysis of mysticism in its relation to secret societies. In this work[3] Wronski, endorsed by Papus in his own book, gives the aim of mystic associations to be: *participation in creation*, and their practical purpose to be: *direction of the destinies of the earth*. In further explanation, Papus *loc. cit.* quotes Wronski as saying :—

"Because man has been as yet unable to discover scientifically his destiny upon this earth, he has formed himself into societies for the cultivation of supernatural arts and sentiments, through whose aid he professes to forsee that destiny "by a cabalistic interpretation of the traditions of Holy Scripture", and by means of which he seeks to direct that destiny through the agency of special missions given to chosen men in all ranks of society".

Of the aims of modern secret societies Wronski says :—

"As the supernatural efforts made by this association of chosen mystics to take part in creation, can neither be practised nor discussed in public, and as this association is equally debarred from attempting openly to direct the destinies of the world, because Governments would promptly step in to oppose it, therefore, this association of mystics can of necessity only act *through secret societies*.

Thus, actually, it is in the heart of mysticism that all secret societies which have existed and still exist upon our globe, are born. Secret societies controlled by this association of mystics have dominated and, governments notwithstanding, continue to dominate the world. These secret societies are formed when needed and are detached into groups distinct and apparently opposed, professing respectively and in turn the most contrary opinions of the day, so as to be able to direct apart and with confidence, all parties—political, religious, economic and literary.

In order to receive common direction, they are again united to an unknown centre, where is hidden this powerful source—the association of mystics, which seeks invisibly to control all earthly sceptres".

Here, for what it may be worth, and from within the circle of secret society organisation itself, we are presented with a subjective description of the chief aim of modern maleficent secret societies.

The parallel between this description and the system of Abdullah bin Maimun is immediately apparent.

This aspect of our subject is referred to in more detail in Chapter XXXIII of the main work. It covers the sphere of what is often referred to as the power of the "hidden hand".

Footnote.—(1) This has recently been ably reviewed in *Conservatism the only way* by Reginald Northam (1930).

Footnote.—(2) *i.e.*, Nature-worship.

Footnote.—(3) The extracts from it that follow are available in fuller detail in *Light-bearers of Darkness*. Anon (1930).

The Hidden Hand

No attempt to explain the nature of secret societies can afford to ignore altogether what the popular mind calls the "Hidden Hand". This term is used to connote some active sinister agency which delights in bringing to nought, through the influence of indeterminate secret means, the best intentions of civilised man.

Gentle fun has been poked at this popular conception in a recent book[1] which the author has respectfully dedicated to all believers in the Hidden Hand.

We take no sides in this matter, but relying upon the discoveries of science in the sphere of archaeology, anthropology, ethnology and psychology, we may say that there exists in the human mind both savage and civilised, certain ingrained prejudices and inhibitions.

These are ultimately based upon religion—human belief, and we know them as "tabus".

Much study has been given to the tabus of the savage, much less to those of civilised man, of which we may here quote two:—

(1) The study of the origin of man himself.

(2) The application of preventive medicine to venereal disease.

Like all tabus, both are based on fear. In the first case the fear that investigation might upset established dogma. In the second the fear that knowledge of prophylaxis might lead to licence.

So far as science has been allowed to progress in the breaking down of both these prejudices, it has proved the fear to be unfounded. The work now in hand in Britain by the Committee of Applied Anthropology on the one hand, and the society for the Prevention of Venereal Disease on the other, may perhaps succeed in removing these civilised tabus altogether.

The association of both these tabus with ultimate religious sanction is obvious and needs no elaboration. The one rests upon acceptance of the theory of the evolution of man, as opposed to his special creation as a finished product: the other upon the relations of the sexes and the mystery of life itself, with which all religions are ultimately bound up.

At this point we reach again the subject of that ancient dualism which obtrudes itself in all religions and has been explained above as the source of all secret societies good and bad, both in the ancient and the modern world and among both savage and civilised man.

So long as such tabus remain as obstacles past which enquiry may not proceed, so long will they, in their dualist aspect, provide the opportunity and the excuse for maleficent secret societies to pander to their fears, with all the deception, crime and misery that ensues. For example: the origin and destiny of man is the essence of mysticism: and a perverted mysticism is the stock-in-trade of maleficent secret societies. Secondly: the sex tabu is intimately connected with both religious and secular prostitution and the latter in the modern world has become a traffic controlled by fear and operated largely by members of maleficent secret societies.

So long as tabus remain unexplained, so long do they invite any agency, good or bad, to use the fear they engender to its own ends.

This power may be consciously exercised upon humanity by some agencies to a good end, by others it may be cunningly applied in any desired direction.

The technique of the evil application of this power through pseudo-religion embodied in a secret society, was provided by Abdullah bin Maimun in A.D. 870, since when it has not altered, and is still active.

To this extent only it seems to us, can it be said that there exists an agency in the world consciously exercising a will to deceive and mislead the unaware. This to the external observer may look like the working of a "hidden hand".

The Black Hand

This name also has an association with secret societies. The term is commonly used as a euphemism for political assassination, the outcome of political secret society intrigue.

Many ephemeral political secret societies in the west have from time to time adopted the name for their own transient organisations. The association of the colour black with night and the Yin principle of the Chinese: the left side in dualism, the principle of darkness, evil and death is constant. Cf. black magic: necromancy (fr. G. nekros and L. niger): blackmail and the judge's black cap. The very word "sinister" conveys the same idea.

The modern profession of political assassinator began (see Chapter X) with Hasan Saba and the Assassins of Alamut in A.D. 1090 and had, therefore, an origin in a genuine secret society of the left.

That the profession still flourishes in the modern world is proved by a glance at any encyclopaedia under "Assassination", where a list will be found of some score of heads of States assassinated during the present century alone.

Several recent political murders in Europe have been the work of a Pan-slav organisation known in the present century as *The Black Hand*[2] with headquarters in Belgrade. This society was responsible for the murder of King Alexander and Queen Draga of Serbia in 1903, and for that of the Archduke Francis Ferdinand of Austria and his wife at Sarajevo, capital of Bosnia, on 28th June, 1914. This latter act, while giving terrorist expression to Yugo-slav discontent at Austro-Hungarian repression, precipitated the World War 1914–1918.

Again, members of the Black Hand murdered King Alexander I of Yugo-Slavia and M. Barthou, French Foreign Minister in Marseilles in October, 1934, which shocked the conscience of the World.

Truly, the baneful influence of secret societies in the politics of to-day, renders their study a matter of importance to our rulers, lest by another stroke they should plunge the world yet again into a devastating war.

Footnote.—(1) *Portraits of Mean Men* by John Gwyer (1938).
Footnote.—(2) A concise and up-to-date account of the Serbian Black Hand society is given by Pike *Secret Societies* 1939 page 134 *et seq.* For an historical survey of the Black Hand, *see* Professor R. W. Seton-Watson *Sarajevo* (1926).

The exercise of supernatural powers

Finally, although the existence and exercise of supernatural powers may be a fairy-story to the average matter-of-fact Englishman, it is not necessarily so to the observant or enquiring administrator. Here is a modern subjective description of how one aspect of oriental magic "works", taken from Maurice Collis' *Trials in Burma* (1938, Chapter I "The Astrologer").[1] For the truth and accuracy of the predictions made by this method, covering a period of some ten years (1921–1931) Mr. Collis as District Magistrate, Rangoon, and an officer of the Indian Civil Service himself vouches. He says:—

> "A *zada* is a private astrological chart, with commentary and supporting calculations and it so happened that I had a *zada*; for only the year before in Mandalay, I had met the senior member of the corps of astrologers which, in King Thibaw's time, had advised the Government, and he had drawn me a *zada*. It was beautifully done on palm leaf, a little work of art. This I sent to the Abbot of the Taung-Yin monastery, who was a mystic and practised meditation as a way of entry into truth and had made a study of astrology".

Collis had his "fortune told" by this man which proved amazingly accurate and continues:—

> "At the time I did not attach more importance to the monk's statements than one can attach to matters outside one's comprehension, but prompted by a desire for knowledge, I asked him how he knew these things. He replied:—
>
> > "In astrology there are the empiric rules of the ancients upon which an intuitive faculty is brought to bear. My method is this—I get up at dawn and taking a chart (*zada*) work out the positions and their meanings according to the old rules. A number of possibilities emerge, which have to be balanced and interpreted before a definite finding on the particular case can be given. I concentrate *my* mind, as in the manner before entering meditation and cause it to dwell on the possibilities. At that juncture a shape or representation (*na-meik*) takes form for me as before some inner eye. The shape is the shape of things to come and I can translate it into words, which I thereupon write down" ".

Collis did not find this description easy to follow, nor will the reader, but it is, at all events, an attempt to describe to the uninitiated something outside their comprehension. Much of the work that follows will attempt a similar exercise.[2]

9. THE PLACE OF SECRET SOCIETIES IN THE PROBLEM OF COLONIAL ADMINISTRATION

Examples are given in the body of this work showing unmistakably the important relationship between secret societies and British administration in both the political and criminal sphere.

This is sufficient justification for attempting to analyse and identify the multitudinous cross-currents in the underworld of secret societies in Malaya, which also has a bearing upon similar Colonial problems in other parts of the Empire.

It is not so much what is happening to-day in this sphere that matters, as what has already happened in the past and what will happen tomorrow, next year and in ten years time.

It is not the conditions of to-day that so much concern the thinking administrator— if he does not know them at first hand, almost any informed person can tell him what they are, and anyway they are past the point where they can be cured and must be endured. But it is the conditions to which to-day will lead that matter most and to know this, he must know the road whence that long succession of nights and days we call history has come, and what has happened on the way.

As Bacon says "He who is without a knowledge of history cannot rule". He becomes just the shuttlecock of contending forces: he feels but cannot identify and, therefore, cannot control.

In this search of the past the better to read the future, the wise administrator familiarises himself as best he may with those great modern currents, movements, influences and discoveries, racial, historical, religious, social and anthropological that lie within his ambit and rigorously rejects the comfortable voice that whispers "Nothing ever happens". The truth is that something is happening all of the time every day, from day to day. With almost imperceptible gradualness, the new wine of the West is bulging in the old bottles of the East and the stresses and strains of a constantly changing mental and material environment are being taken up by a rigid administrative machine too often out of date, or maladjusted to its task.

The wise administrator knows how to choose his instruments, how to keep them in tune and how to use them to ease the tension at the danger points and to adjust the machine to the changing load, the fresh demands, and the increasing strain, so as to keep the bottles from bursting.

In this task there can be nothing of greater value than knowledge of the underlying and invisible causes which give rise to fermentation—that "dangerous explosive material", in the popular mind. Among these causes in Malaya must be reckoned those secret societies, whose invisible web touches Asiatic life at all points and a knowledge of which must command a foremost place in the armament of Colonial administration.

Acceptance of the principle that the component units of our Empire are not "property" but "peoples" has placed in the foreground of Imperial policy to-day, the political necessity to understand the cultures of the indigenous races which compose our Colonial Empire. The need for this change of emphasis arises from the spread of knowledge from the west;

Footnote.—(1) Other remarkable first-hand subjective experiences of the supernatural, by a Colonial administrator in the sphere of African witchcraft, will be found in Hives and Lumley *Ju-Ju and Justice in Nigeria* (The Bodley Head 1930).

Footnote.—(2) For other first-hand descriptions see Alexandra David-Neel, *With Mystics and Magicians in Tibet* (1931), particularly Chapter VIII "Psychic phenomena".

the development therefrom of a critical faculty among subject races: and the rise of an intense national sentiment throughout the world, since the war of 1914–1918, which has ruffled the placid waters.

The nineteenth century belief that East is East and West is West has been exploded by the facts of the twentieth. The shrinkage of the world by the development of swift communications and the power and persuasiveness of hostile propaganda have, like a plague-laden wind, brought in their train serious danger to the solidarity of our Empire.

The conditions of to-day demand those re-adjustments in Colonial policy pronounced at the Oxford Summer School, if disaster to our Empire is to be averted.

In the forefront of this policy is a realisation of the vitality and efficacy of indigenous institutions, a growing appreciation of their value for purposes of Government and a set purpose to employ for the future indirect methods of Colonial administration based upon them. Herein lies a danger. If this development is to prove successful, a prerequisite is an understanding by administrative officers not only of native institutions themselves, as they are presented to the European gaze, but a comprehension of those vital hidden springs and sources whence these institutions in turn derive—the underside of native culture and organisation and the powers and influences that govern them. These elements form the basic fundamentals of the human factor in Colonial administration. They are foreign to the British administrator and require to be carefully disentangled and studied before they can be understood and success in their direction and control be assured. We hope the chapters that follow will help towards this end.

Conclusion

Since the foregoing was written the calamity of another great war has come upon the British Empire. Within a generation, a breath in the life of man, the rule of Force has twice challenged the rule of Law and the challenge has again been accepted, with all the tragedy and destruction that acceptance involves. Already the minds of thinking men are at work to devise a means whereby the recurrent pestilence of war may be permanently banished from the world.

Before the solution can be found, more knowledge of man himself may be required; and a foundation be laid only after an answer has first been given to the simple question: whence has he come and whither is he bound?

On 16th December, 1918, General Smuts said:—

"There is no doubt that Mankind is once more on the move. The very foundations have been shaken and loosened and things are again fluid. The tents have been struck and the great Caravan of Humanity is once more on the march".

Among the leaders of the Caravan are those who, through self-seeking, vanity and the subversive power of maleficent secret societies, would lead it to destruction.

Unless a decision is first made upon the doctrine of man's evolution, as opposed to his special creation, any effort to adjust the present conditions of his existence to his future development, so as to eliminate the cause of war, is almost foredoomed to failure, because it may be founded in opposition to truth.

The question is: has the human family or part of it, fallen; or is the human family the whole of it, still climbing upward? When this question was put to a great Prime Minister of England in the middle of the last century he replied, "I am on the side of the angels". That remains the position of England to-day.

We must first decide whether it is true that certain chosen sections of the human family are fallen angels, seeking to regain a lost paradise, which other less fortunate sections have never yet known; or whether the whole human family is slowly and painfully advancing together according to the will of the Divine architect along parallel roads of evolution from a lower to a higher form. Upon this decision, which must be made for us by science, the Church and Parliament, would seem inevitably to rest the success or failure of man's future endeavours to find himself and in so doing to avoid war and his own destruction. In arriving at the answer to this simple yet fundamental question, a greater knowledge of man himself, than we now possess or at least admit, would seem to be necessary so that the hatreds, prejudices, vested interests and taboos, which to-day divide, may be resolved into their component parts and be reforged in the furnace of human trial into links to bind the whole human family into one vast army of co-operation in its great adventure upon the road upward to its destiny.

So long as doubt remains on this fundamental question, so long will individual men and nations, from motives of greed, selfishness and ambition, make that doubt their excuse to attempt the hegemony of mankind. Until we are able to decide which way we are facing and base our policy on that decision, so long will the human family remain under the pall of fear, the threat of Force and at the brink of the abyss of war, where ascent is impossible and descent imminent, instead of moving together along the path of human progress, co-operation and enlightenment.

Professor Elliot Smith *In the Beginning* (1932) says on page 5:—

"We are apt to forget the extent of our debt to the antiquity and the all-pervading influence of our great heritage. At every moment of our lives events that happened centuries, and in many cases thousands of years, ago in distant parts of the world are shaping our behaviour and intimately affecting our innermost thoughts, in particular our attitude to the modern events around us. We *are part of* the great social current formed of a multitude of intermingling streams that have come down from remote ages and distant lands to carry us along with it".

In the deeper and wider investigation of the origin and destiny of man, which must precede his efforts to find a *modus vivendi* for the whole human race, some help may be obtained from a closer examination of those latent disruptive forces of which this work treats, which throughout human history have periodically come to the surface of human affairs and attempted to overthrow the accepted order of society, by revolution instead of evolution and by the imposition of the rule of Force in place of the rule of Law.

At the moment of writing, the world is asking England to state her "war aims" in the new conflict: to this question the Foreign Secretary has replied in general terms—"the rehabilitation of the rule of law". This reply is an admission that forces have gained an ascendancy in the world over which the leaders of our civilisation have lost control.

May not some of these forces have their roots and mainspring in the secret maleficent conclaves widespread throughout the world, a corner of whose cloak this work attempts to lift?

As the *Palestine Commission Report* of 1937 says: "Popular instinct draws away from what is strange". It is easier and more comforting to dismiss the very thought of what is unknown with the mental decision "I don't believe it", rather than to accept its existence as a working hypothesis and investigate it searchingly. In very many modern books on political and sociological subjects we find a mention of undefined "underlying causes" and frequently the tacit admission that these were in turn believed to be due to secret societies also undefined and unidentified. As a great Imperial race with a trusteeship for millions of our fellow men upon the proper discharge of which our leaders have recently publicly expressed doubts, we owe it to ourselves and to them in a darkened world to investigate thoroughly every hypothesis which may lead to a better understanding of the problems of our imperial mandate.

The chapters that follow may shed some light upon these dangerous and uncharted waters.

PART I

CHAPTER I

THE HUNG LEAGUE OR TRIAD SOCIETY IN CHINA FROM THE EARLIEST TIMES UP TO A.D. 1900

Although the Triad Society in China is of great antiquity, colonial governments in eastern Asia knew practically nothing of its history, ritual and secret governance until A. D. 1866, in which year there was published in Batavia, in English, the first authentic history of the society under the title 天地會 *Thian Ti Hwi, The Hung League, or Heaven and Earth League* being "a secret society with the Chinese in China and India". To the author, Gustave Schlegel, at that time interpreter in Chinese to the Government of the Netherlands Indies, are due the grateful thanks of those who, coming after him, have found his work their standard guide to the study of this difficult subject. Schlegel's material was largely obtained from a bundle of books seized by accident in the house of a Chinese suspected of theft at Padang, Sumatra, in 1863. These books were at first unintelligible to him, whose pioneer labours still stand as a monument to his industry and scholarship. The earliest available notice of the Triad Society is a paper written by Dr. Milne, a Protestant missionary in Kwangtung, in July, 1821, and published in 1826 in *Transactions of the Royal Asiatic Society, Volume I, Part II*. This paper was used by Schlegel in the preparation of his classic study and will be referred to later. Other papers used by him, some of which have been re-examined for purposes of this compilation, are given on page vi of Schlegel's preface.

The next available reference is a paper by Lieut. Newbold published in 1841, in the *Journal of the Royal Asiatic Society, Volume VI, page 120*. The author was then serving in the garrison of the Straits Settlements.

The opening paragraph of Newbold's paper is:—

"Various associations have long existed in China of which secrecy was at an early period the prominent feature, since the jealousy of the imperial government declares the association of even five persons to be illegal, and punishes the crime of belonging to these associations with death. Among these fraternities may be enumerated:—

1. The Great Ascending Society.
2. The Society of Glory and Splendour.
3. The Union of the Three Great Powers—Heaven, Earth and Man. (*i.e.* The Triad Society).
4. The White Jackets.
5. The Red Beards.
6. The Short Swords.
7. The White Water Lily. (*i.e.* White Lotus).
8. The Sea and Land Society.
9. The Righteous Rising Society, etc.

The third of these associations (No. 3 above), which, from all that can be gathered, assimilate in their origin, is the one that prevails in Canton and obtains almost exclusively in the Straits of Malacca and the vast islands of the Indian archipelago, and which will principally form the subject of this notice. It is commonly known under the terms of: Tien-Ti-Hui (天地會) or San-ho-hui (三合會) and is sometimes divided into two branches, the Canton and the Fukien, to which provinces most of the Chinese emigrants belong....

The secret nature of the Tien-Ti-Hui or Triad Association of Heaven, Earth and Man, and the natural dread of its members to violate their solemn oath of secrecy, render it a matter of great difficulty to arrive at the truth and to penetrate into its early history and origin".

Newbold omits to give the source of his information for the nine names quoted by him, and the characters in Chinese are not given. The list, however, is interesting, proving that such names were already known to English students in Malaya in 1841. Newbold claims for all these "various associations" an affinity even an identity with the Hung League. It will be part of the purpose of this work to attempt to identify some of them with the parent stem to which they properly belong. According to Schlegel, *op. cit.* page 4, the following names are the only ones which may properly be applied to the Hung League because they are the only names by which it refers to itself:—

(1) The Hung League or Flood Family.　洪家
(2) The Heaven and Earth League.　天地會
(3) The Three United League.　三合會

The Triad Society takes this, its popular name, from the last of these, namely the 三合會 (Sam Hop Wui) or "Three-United-League" so called because the League is based upon the bonds existing between Heaven, Earth and Man. The more general Chinese term and the one whereby the Society at large will be referred to hereafter in this compilation is the Hung Ka 洪家. Hung means "flood" or "deluge" or "inundation" and Ka means "family", hence Hung or "Inundation League", a name which

c

Schlegel suggests (*op. cit.* p. xii) denotes the universality and brotherhood of the League) On the other hand, the history of China recorded in the *Shu King* (書 經) or Book of History, which dates from about the 24th century B.C., begins with an account of an inundation of the Yellow River, described in terms which have suggested to some students an identity with the biblical deluge and in which the labours of the Great Emperor Yu (禹), compare with those of Noah. If this view should come to be accepted, a more literal explanation of the name Hung Ka would present itself, namely "The survivors of the flood", and a link with biblical history be thereby established)

Of the two other names:—

(4) The Incense Burners. 聞 香

(5) The White Lotus or White Lily Sect. 白 蓮 教

by which it has been referred to in China, Schlegel at the same reference, is careful to say that they are names "which the people probably gave to this League". Reasons will be given later for a revision of this view. The third source of original research upon the nomenclature of the Hung League used in the present work, is *The Triad Society or Heaven and Earth Association,* by William Stanton of Hongkong, first published in the *Chinese Review Volumes XXI and XXII, 1899* and reprinted in book form by Kelly & Walsh in 1900.

The following extract from Couling's *Encyclopaedia Sinica* published in 1917 provides to some extent a condensed introduction to the history of our subject.

Under "The Triad Society" Couling has:—

> This society, also known as the Heaven and Earth Society and the Hung League, is the most famous of all the secret sects of China. Its own records do not agree as to the date of its inception, one set giving A.D. 1674, the twelfth year of K'ang Hsi, while another gives sixty years later under Yung Cheng.
>
> *   *   *
>
> Rebellions followed: one in Formosa in 1787, as the result of oppression of the Society by military officials; one in 1814 in Kiangsi, one in Canton 1817, where there were numerous executions. In 1832, the Triad members were again in trouble for assisting the Yao tribes against the Peking Government. By this time, they had also established themselves in Siam, in the Dutch East Indies and in India.
>
> In 1850 they were again in rebellion in Kwangtung and Kiangsi and hence were supposed to be in league with the T'ai P'ing rebels, but this is incorrect)
>
> *   *   *
>
> (The Triad members were certainly encouraged by the T'ai P'ing movement, and fought from 1850–1856 in Kiangsi and Fukien. Sometimes parties cut off from one would join the other, *e.g.* the Triad Society held Shanghai city in 1853–1854 for fifteen months, and when compelled to evacuate it joined the T'ai P'ing forces. They were never anti-foreign.)
>
> The organisation when carried beyond China lost a good deal of its political meaning and became more of a friendly society. Nevertheless the British and Dutch authorities disapproved of it, as it screened its members from the law, and sometimes levied blackmail. At first, registration only was insisted on, but later suppression was found necessary even in California, Siam and Australia. In 1845 membership was made a penal offence in Hongkong, with a punishment of branding on the cheek and three years' imprisonment, but this soon became a dead letter, and in 1857 a band of 800 coolies, probably all Triad members, worked loyally for the English against the Manchus.
>
> In 1887 all Chinese secret societies were prohibited by the British, as the result of their incessant quarrels amongst themselves. At this time there were 156,440 Triad members in the Straits Settlements alone. The pioneer missionaries, *Milne* and *Morrison,* with others, had begun to write about them as early as 1825, but the accidental finding by the police in 1863 at Padang (Sumatra) of a number of their books and paraphernalia led to much more information being searched out than had been obtained before. *Schlegel,* at that time the official in charge of the matter, wrote a book embodying his discoveries.
>
> *   *   *
>
> Portuguese and Malays are sometimes admitted to the brotherhood, and certain modifications of the signs have been introduced for their benefit.

Under "Secret Societies" Couling *op. cit.* has:—

> In the proceedings of the Missionary Conference of 1890 a valuable paper by *Rev. F. H. James* was given dealing with the secret sects of Shantung, of which fifty-two had been studied, with a list of some of their literature. Information concerning such was obtained with great difficulty, those who had left the societies, *e.g.* on becoming Christians, being afraid to give much. The establishment of a Republic (A.D. 1912) and the Declaration of Religious Liberty has rendered the previously existing societies out-of-date, but no study of fresh material on the subject has been reported, and it is probable that as far as the history of the secret sects is concerned, the confusion is too great even for the Chinese themselves to unravel. Societies originally political became also religious with the addition of fresh blood or in new conditions, and *vice versa;* some died out or were persecuted into silence, to be revived perhaps under a new name and in another place, with or without modifications in doctrine and organisation; large societies divided and the parts developed differently; while the literature was mostly in manuscript, and often had to be hurriedly destroyed. On the other hand, a study of the present-day beliefs of members of such societies ought to be valuable, as it is well known that many of the most spiritually-minded of the Chinese belong or did belong to them. It is impossible to say how many of the sects still exist, but in 1896 they were said to average anything from 20,000 to 200,000 members per province.

We have not been able to consult the Rev. James's paper for the purposes of this work, but his observations concerned the province of Shantung and we will later present grounds for thinking that at least one of the secret organisations to be found in that province is also to be found in Malaya, distinct from the Hung League.

In the kaleidoscope which Couling's description of the secret society world in China presents to the mind and in spite of his discouraging view that the confusion is too great even for the Chinese themselves to unravel, we will attempt in the following chapters to identify the two main stems into which we believe that world in China to be divided.

For this purpose we must glance at Chinese history.

THE DYNASTIES OF CHINA

The rise and fall of China's dynasties has a direct bearing upon the history of her secret societies. These dynasties are given as a note at the end of this chapter and are taken from Werner's *Dictionary of Chinese Mythology (1932) page 623.* Werner's list is not necessarily acceptable to all sinologists.

The sequence of these dynasties covers a period of some 4,000 years, and for purposes of sketching the outline and influence of the Hung League upon such an enormous historical canvas, we may roughly divide it into three main epochs and one transitional period, namely :—

1.	The Traditional or religious age	From greatest antiquity down to the end of the Ming dynasty (A.D. 1644).
2.	The Transitional period ..	A.D. 1644—A.D. 1700.
3.	The Political or revolutionary age (150 years)	From about fifty years after the beginning of the Ts'ing dynasty (say A.D. 1700) to the end of the Taiping Rebellion, A.D. 1864.
4.	The Degenerate age ..	(a) In China, A.D. 1865 to the present time.
		(b) Overseas, A.D. 1800 to the present time.

THE INVASIONS OF CHINA

We should here note the following historical facts relating to invasions of China during the past 800 years.

The Tartars obtained their first permanent footing in China proper early in the twelfth century A.D. In A.D. 1127 the Manchus or Eastern Tartars invaded the country and captured all the provinces north of the Yellow River. They continued their progress slowly southwards during succeeding years but were unable to possess a foot of ground south of the Yang-tze river. During this time South China remained steadfast to the rule of the Chinese Emperors of the Sung dynasty.

Meanwhile the Western Tartar (Mongolian) Emperor Genghis Khan[1] about A.D. 1207 had consolidated his empire which then included a great part of Central Asia and bordered of the western frontier of China.

The 14th Emperor of the Chinese Sung dynasty sought the aid of Genghis Khan to drive out the Manchus from the north of China. A long war ensued ending in the destruction of the Manchus who were driven beyond the Great Wall. The Mongols occupied the Chinese provinces won from the Manchus and finally in A.D. 1280 took possession of the whole of China with Kublai Khan son of Genghis Khan as first emperor of the Yuan 元 (Mongol) dynasty. In 1368 the leader of a local Chinese insurrection set up his own standard and marched against Peking, defeating the imperial army north of the Yellow river. The Emperor fled beyond the frontier and the Tartar (Mongol) rule came to an end. The leader of the successful rebellion became the first emperor of the Ming (Chinese) dynasty, with his capital at Nanking.

The third Ming Emperor moved the capital to the old Tartar capital at Peking.

In the sixteenth century incursions by the Tartars began again on the north and north-west frontiers and during the reign of the seventeenth and last Ming emperor, China became the prey of rebel armies. The leader of one of these opened the gates of Peking to the Eastern Tartars (Manchurians) and in 1644 the son of the Chief of these Tartars was declared first emperor of the Ts'ing dynasty. Thus after 400 years the Manchus reimposed their rule upon the Chinese.

The south maintained its independence for many years and it was not until the accession of Kang-hi, second Ts'ing Emperor in 1662 that all China became re-united in subjection to the Manchus.

The Manchus were again driven out by the Chinese in 1912 and an uneasy republic followed.

In 1937, China was again invaded, this time by the Japanese employing western methods of warfare and on a scale much greater than any previous invasion in her history. The outcome of this latest invasion has yet to be seen.

From 1674 onwards there were constant insurrections particularly in the south against the power of the Manchus. In these rebellions political secret societies took

---

Footnote.—(1) For the historical detail of his campaigns, *see* Ralph Fox *Genghis Khan* (1936).

a leading part, particularly the Triad Society, whose history we must now examine in closer detail under the rough divisions given above.

(1) THE TRADITIONAL OR RELIGIOUS AGE
(condensed from Schlegel)

The beginnings of the Hung League are lost in antiquity, but commentators agree that the League in origin was a religious society of lofty aims, whose motto was 順天行道 sun t'in hang to—"Obey heaven and act righteously", and whose ritual was connected with the ancient mysteries and with the journey of the human soul from Heaven to Earth and back through the underworld, to Heaven ;)a theme common to most ancient religions, and presented to the Christian mind in Bunyan's *Pilgrim's Progress*. The date of the Hung League's origin in its traditional or religious form must be placed about B.C. 3,000, but it also contains much evidence of the later influence of Buddhism.

The ritual of the League today bears testimony to its ancient origin and has a close resemblance to that of western Freemasonry, a subject fully treated in Ward and Stirling's work, *The Hung Society (3 volumes)* published in 1925, a book commended to those interested in that aspect of this subject.

Schlegel also discusses this question in his Introduction page xxix ff.

Another reference-book for comparative study from the view-point of freemasonry is *Secret societies of all ages (2 volumes)* by G. W. Heckethorn—London, 1897. This work does not appear in the bibliography of Ward and Stirling and was apparently not consulted by them.

Both Ward and Stirling are practising freemasons, while Heckethorn who appears to have been an apostate, gives in *Volume I* of his work a fairly full description of the ritual of freemasonry, thereby offering a comparison with that of the Hung League.

Heckethorn also gives examples of how freemasonry has from time to time lapsed into unworthy channels in various western countries, which offers a further comparison with the degeneration of the Hung League, a subject further discussed in Chapter XXXIII *infra*.

ROOTS IN THE TRADITIONAL PERIOD

The Hung League claims for itself a high antiquity. Schlegel illustrates this from the 32nd answer in his edition of the ritual:—

"Since the time that the foundation of the world was laid, we bear the name of Hung."

and the 220th answer:—

"Yin (陰) and Yang (陽) united
Heaven and Earth joined
First produced the sons of Hung
In myriads combined."

The second outstanding characteristic of the Hung league is the high level of its moral principles. This is implicit in its rituals and is stressed by all commentators.

Thus Schlegel in his Introduction page xii:—

"So we find in the formulary of oath and in the statutes and laws of this League, a spirit of fraternity, devotion, filiality and piousness, which offers not the least idea of rebellion or murder; and on every page the member of the Hung League is reminded of the object "Obey Heaven and act righteously."

Stanton *op. cit.* page 14 has:—

"Triadism is nothing without Buddhism. Nearly all the religion there is about it, and there is a great deal in the ritual, is Buddhist".

Ward, an eminent freemason, in his preface to *The Hung Society Volume I, page iii* has:—

"I have no hesitation in saying that the original object of the ritual had nothing to do with politics.) The ceremonies like masonry, had a threefold purpose: first to teach sound morality and more especially brotherly love: secondly by a dramatic allegory to indicate what *its* initiates thought befell a man after death: thirdly to give instruction regarding the mystical journey, whose end is atonement with the Supreme Being, by whatsoever name we may call Him".

We need not multiply examples of what is freely acknowledged by observers, but we must here lay emphasis upon the three characteristics of the Hung League, that it teaches morality, acknowledges a Supreme Being and avers the existence of an after-life.

These points are of great importance for subsequent comparative study with another Chinese secret association, discussed in the next chapter, which acknowledges none of these things.

With regard to the moral principles taught by the Hung League and their similarity to those of freemasonry, Schlegel in his Introduction page x has:—

"It will probably be objected that the workings of the Hung League and of the Society of Freemasons are quite different: that the object of the latter is thoroughly peaceful, whilst the Hung League has carried civil war and murder wherever it went. We do not deny these facts, but we must bear in mind that circumstances have forced the brotherhood to become a political body and that it is impossible for any Society to be held responsible for the acts of all its members ....Freemasonry has likewise.......been used as a cover for political conjurations.......".

Again Schlegel at the same reference quoting "Excellent words of exhortation of the Hung league" gives:—

"Converse with virtuous friends and renounce heartless companions. If people insult you, injure you, revile you, abuse you—how ought you to take it? You ought to bear it, suffer it, endure it and forgive it. Don't ask immoral people to drink wine with you. Don't believe those who are righteous with their mouths and unrighteous in their hearts. Do not frequent people who turn you a cold shoulder and are without heart or faith. Do not despise people whose fortune has turned, for you will only be for a few years a lamb and an inferior. Always, remember in your actions the fundamental principles of Heaven 天本, of Earth 地本 and of yourself 自本."

Despite the fact that during the past 100 years, when for the first time a study of the subject has become general among Europeans, we find the story of the League punctuated with rebellion, robbery, and murder, we must remember that these incidents were not necessarily the sole contribution of the Hung league to the history of the time. As Schlegel *op. cit.* page 6 says:—

"Not all the horrors committed in the name of the Heaven and Earth League ought to be considered as its acts."

The acts of rebellion and outrage attributed to the league naturally attracted more attention from Europeans during the nineteenth century, but this should not blind our judgment of the character of the association as a whole. During this disordered period of Chinese history and particularly among Chinese overseas, the tail may have wagged the dog and the efforts of European colonial governments were concentrated therefore upon the suppression of the League as being all bad, whereas the dangerous and criminal elements so conspicuous during this period, may have been representative of only a part and that a comparatively minor part of the League's activities and true character.

Upon this aspect of our subject Schlegel in his Introduction page xxxix writing in 1865 has:—

"In the eyes of the present members of the Hung League the Tartars have forfeited their claims and must therefore be exterminated. Theirs is a sacred war of righteousness against tyranny—of humanity against oppression and vice. If our supposition that the Hung League has existed since antiquity is correct, they must have waged continually a war for the defense of righteous principles—for the same reason they will consider such a war righteous against everyone who oppresses them or whose government they think hurtful to the people) be they Tartars, Mongols, Chinese or Europeans. They mean to represent in the world the combat of light against darkness........and the means they use thereto are not considered unlawful by them........The Chinese are not a savage or unruly people: they are fully alive to the horrors of anarchy and to the benefits of order. They will suffer hardships and misfortunes, if these are in the natural order of things, but they will submit less to tyranny than any other Eastern nation."

Finally Schlegel Introduction page xxxvii has:—

"In conclusion we do not think it improbable that the Hung league, is the depository of the old religion of the Chinese consisting in the belief in a single and undivided God, worshipped symbolically by the adoration of light, which in all religions has been considered as His essence."

With such precepts, it is impossible to regard the Hung league in its original or traditional form as anything but a virtuous or religious association, impregnated later with the teachings of Buddhism, which has since become debased to secular uses as a result of external or other circumstances. A thorough comprehension of this fact is necessary to a proper understanding of the place of the Hung league in the secret society world of China.

Schlegel concludes his survey of this aspect of the subject *op. cit.* page 6 with the words:—

"Whatever may be now (A.D. 1865) the condition of the Hung league, it had once and has still two sure and trusty bases, fraternity and morality. We do not doubt that when peace will be restored to China, either by the overthrow of the Manchu dynasty, or by the people gradually submitting peaceably to its rule, the Hung League will be able to purify itself from all political and criminal elements and become again what it most surely was formerly, a band of brethren following the great precepts taught by Christ and Confucius "As ye would that men should do unto you, do ye also unto them likewise"."

In the chapters that follow, there will be unfolded a story of the struggle of the Hung league during the eighty years that have elapsed since these words were written, which will, we believe, support the view that the League is probably still the backbone of that "sacred war of righteousness against tyranny, of humanity against oppression" which is being waged afresh in China to-day.

THE SACRED NUMBERS

Some reference to this subject is necessary to a comprehension of the numbers now used by Chinese secret societies, all of which have their roots in the traditional period. We learn the following about Chinese numerology from *Mémoires concernant les Chinois* (*Volume VI*) by the Jesuit Father Amiot extensively quoted by Schlegel. In Chinese belief, discussed more fully in Chapter III *infra*, there are two principles of nature from which everything is derived. These are known as the Yin (陰) or female and the Yang (陽) or male: and in combination these two principles are represented by the symbol ☯ the "Yin Yang" or "Grand primordial". This symbol represents "unity" or the number 1. Yin and Yang united form "harmony" (和) out of which were produced the three powers (三才) Heaven, Earth and Man. One being alone, cannot beget anything, but it can produce everything, because it contains in itself the two principles whose harmony and union produce everything. In this sense, one produces two, two produces three and by three all things are produced. Heaven and Earth form what we call Time. Heaven is male (Yang) and Earth is female (Yin).

The numbers 1 to 10 combine these two elements of Yang and Yin, the odd being the 'perfect' or male or heavenly numbers, the even being the 'imperfect' or female or earthly numbers. The odd numbers added together make 25, and the number of Heaven is 25. The even numbers added together make 30 and the number of Earth is 30. The number of man·perfected is 15.

The intimate union of Heaven, Earth and Man is expressed by the symbol △ which is composed of the characters " 入 " "to enter" or "penetrate" and " 一 " "one", so the symbol signifies three united, penetrated or blended into one. It is the union of the three powers (三才) Heaven, Earth and Man which together rule, create and nourish all things.

The similarity between this and the teaching of Pythagoras will be seen. The third of the "perfect" numbers is 5 the number of God or the Supreme ruler, Shang Ti (上帝) and has a particular association with the Hung League, whose founders were five: with five lodges and five banners. (*see* Schlegel Introduction pages XIII and XX).

The fourth is 7 the number of the world and of death. The fifth is 9 the number of perfection or of the celestial beginning.

Two other numerical combinations common among the Chinese must be noted.

THE PAT KWA (八卦) OR "EIGHT SUSPENDED"

To the Emperor Fuh Hi (B.C. 2953) is ascribed the invention of lines to express thoughts. These combinations of lines numbering 64 are represented symbolically by the figure of the "Pat Kwa" or eight diagrams or "eight suspended", so called because they were the original eight diagrams devised by Fuh Hi from which the others were composed and they were hung up everywhere for the instruction of the people.

The "Pat Kwa" is commonly found in combination with the symbol of the Yin Yang mentioned above. This combined symbol, reproduced below, although commonly met with in the secret society world of China, is not particularly associated with the Hung League.

THE MAGIC SQUARE

Tradition records that the Chinese Emperor Yu (禹) who lived B.C. 2205 was walking one day by a tributary of the Yellow River, after the Great Flood of that period and saw a tortoise rise out of the water with a peculiar dotted pattern on its back which the Emperor resolved into the following arithmetical form which contains the Yin Yang numbers, 1 to 9 referred to above—

4	9	2
3	5	7
8	1	6

This figure is familiar in all countries today as the numbering upon the modern "shuffle-board". The numbers added together in whichever way, always total 15 which is

Footnote.—(1) For further explanation of the significance of the sacred numbers, *see*—
    Schlegel Introduction page xix.
    Ward and Stirling Volume III page 75 ff.
    The Sacred 5 of China (Geil) 1926, page 170.
    Les Sociétés Secrètes en Chine (Lt.-Col. Favre 1933) page 205. Note 39.

Footnote.—(2) For the mathematical rules for making magic squares *see Encyclopaedia Britannica* xvii 310 ff.; and for examples of their use in religions *see Encyclopaedia of Religion and Ethics* (ed. Hastings) III pages 445, 457 and 449, also—
    Magic White and Black, Hartman, page 86.
    Islam in India, Herklots (ed. W. Crooke 1921) Chapters XXVII and XXVIII.
    The Kingdom and People of Siam, Bowring, Vol. I pages 152-153.
    Malay Magic, Skeat, page 555 ff.

the number of 'Man' perfected. The sum of the nine figures is 45, which is the number of dots seen by the Emperor Yu on the back of the tortoise. (*see* Schlegel Introduction page XIX ff.).

In Chinese secret society ritual the magic square is not a mere mathematical curiosity, but contains a definite esoteric meaning and permeates Chinese religious cults as well as secret society rituals and is also used, as will be mentioned later, in an initiation ceremony amongst Malays. (*see* Chapter XXIX *infra*).

(From the foregoing traditional sources, a group of sacred numbers possessing a mystical significance has been absorbed into the ritual and statutes of the Hung league.)

These sacred numbers are:—

2	×	9	=	*18.*	2 × 36	=	*72.*
3	×	7	=	*21.*	36 + 72	=	*108.*
3	×	12	=	*36.*	30 × 12	=	*360.*

These numbers will repeatedly recur when we come to discuss the present day organisation of the Hung league in Malaya and its Mohamedan prototypes.

THE ORIGIN OF THE NAME 義興 GHEE HIN

(The Hung league has been subjected to repression and persecution from time to time in China and almost continuously in its political or reconstituted form under successive Manchu emperors) since the *"Sacred edict"* of the second Manchu emperor Kang Hsi A.D. 1670, repeated by his successor Yung Ching and directed equally against Buddhism, Christianity and secret societies. (This led to the adoption by the secret society world in China of innocent sounding names or "watchwords", camouflage titles by which they might be known without attracting the attention of their Manchu rulers.)

(The names thus assumed were indistinguishable from the names of numerous harmless "friendly societies" which were then, as now, very common, and were formed for purposes of mutual help and which have always been a feature of Chinese communal life.)

Some of these names are relevant to our subject, and we will here refer particularly to the origin of the name 義興 Yi Heng or Ghee Hin or "Patriotic Rise Society", by which the Hung league is known today in Malaya. The age-old practice of secret societies of adopting innocent-sounding or *camouflage titles* for their branches, should here be clearly noted, as it will re-appear again and again as a commonplace in Malaya today, not only of Chinese, but also of Mohamedan secret societies.

Schlegel tells us (*op. cit.* page 17) that the watchword of the Hung league is the word 義 "Yi" in Cantonese: "Ghee" in Hokkien meaning, variously "virtuous", "patriotic", "righteous". This is recorded in the Traditional history of the league.

The name by which the Hung league is universally known in Malaya and the Dutch East Indies and probably elsewhere overseas, is the 義興公司 Ghee Hin Kung Sz or "Patriotic rise society". We would naturally expect to find the source of any name for the league buried in the traditional age. But this name appears to be peculiar to the league overseas and there is no recorded use of it as applied to the league in China proper.

The Hung documents published in the works of Schlegel, Stanton and Ward and Stirling, wherein this name appears are exclusively "overseas" documents and do not refer to documents of the league in China proper. In the documents published by Dr. Milne which refer exclusively to China proper, the name does not appear.

The question then presents itself: whence is this name derived? and in seeking for the answer, we must record our only divergence from the conclusions of Schlegel.

We will show in the next chapter that the same character 義 is also the designation of a lodge of a secret society in China which differs from the Hung league. The only authority who has attempted to explain the origin of the name "Ghee Hin Kung Sz" is Schlegel and his reference (*op. cit.* page 4) is as follows:—

"These three names (*i.e.* Hung League: Heaven and Earth League and Three United League) are the only ones that may properly be applied to the league: all the other names are only "watchwords".

The statutes of Shantung, found in Japara, Java, in 1851, have given us the clue to these watchword names. The first chiefs of the lodge there (*i.e.* in Shantung province) were six men living in the district of Lung Chau (龍州縣) on the ridges of the Hau Hui mountains.

The first of these headmen was named 洪其海 Hung K'ei Hoi, who took the watchword 義興 pronounced Yi Heng in Cantonese, and Ghee Hin in the Hokkien speech, and which means "Patriotic Rise" or "Rise of Justice".

The second headman was named 黃其青 Wong Kei Ts'ing, who took the watchword 海山 Hai San, meaning "Sea and Land".

The third headman was 周 元 斉 Chau Yun Ts'ing who took the watchword 大 刀 Tai Tao, which means "Large Knife or Sword".

The fourth was 沈 利 章 Chin Lei Chang, who took the watchword 小 刀 Siu Tao, which means "Small Knife" or "Dagger".

The fifth was 蘇 元 勳 So Yuen Hiun, who took the watchword 柄 擔 Peng Yen, which means "Handle and Eaves".

The sixth was 鄭 枝 龍 Ching Chi Lung, who took the watchword 菫 子 T'ung Tsz which means "The Boy".

These watchwords were probably adopted because the three abovementioned genuine names were too well known by the Tartar government to be openly adopted. Concealed under these watchwords they might be confounded with the numerous "friendly societies" for mutual help existing in all parts of China and the islands of the Indian Archipelago."

Schlegel does not say at this point that from the "watchword" of the first headman above is derived the name "Ghee Hin Kung Sz" but we are left to infer this. He only offers the reference as a "clue" to the name and suggests that this watchword among others was "probably used for purposes of concealment".

Later, on page 31 of his work, still relying upon the fidelity of this clue, he alters his inference from theory to fact by the following:—

"In the province of Shantung the brotherhood (meaning the Hung League) has the following diploma.

It is a square of white linen....containing in the centre the celebrated diagrams of the Emperor Fuh Hi (*i.e.* the Pat Kwa). Within this figure is the symbol called the Yin and Yang. The characters on the upper margin of the diploma are 義 興 公 司 the watchword of the Ghee Hin Kung Sz "The Patriotic Rise Society". To the right is written the name of the member to whom the diploma is given and to the left are the characters 記 號 Ki Ho "mark". Circulars, diplomas, receipts, etc., are stamped with the common seal of the society. On the greater one which is *square*.......are the characters 義 興 館 Ghee Hin Kwan "Hall of Ghee Hin". On the smaller one, a square inch in size, are engraved the characters:— 義 興 公 司 Ghee Hin Kung Sz or "Society of the Ghee Hin."

An illustration of this diploma is given at the end of Chapter V. It is upon this evidence, all of which comes exclusively from the bundle of documents found in Japara, Java, in 1851 and not from those found at Padang Sumatra in 1863 that the belief rests which has been generally accepted, that the name "Ghee Hin" is in origin a "watchword" or "cover label" for the Hung league overseas.

Prima facie there are no grounds disclosed in the documents found at Japara including the "watchwords" given above and the diploma of the Shantung lodge just described, to identify them either superficially or definitely with the Hung league in China, or even to connect them with the documents found at Padang, Sumatra, and used by Schlegel for his work, which latter unquestionably belonged to the Hung league. Furthermore on page 26 *op. cit.* Schlegel gives a description of the drawings in the book found at Japara in 1851 together with the statutes of the Shantung Lodge and the diploma described above. These drawings illustrate a difficult journey which in Schlegel's interpretation, described the physical approach to the Shantung lodge of the Hung league in China, and assumed that a similar explanation would fit conditions in Malaya or the Dutch East Indies. Thus he has page 26:—

"In the Indian Archipelago the Chinese build their lodges in deep forests, in places only known to the brotherhood. There the feared Hung family holds its re-unions, whilst guards perched on their lofty seats, keep a sharp look-out for strangers or policemen who might approach and detect their secret meeting place."

Whatever conditions of secrecy the persecution of the Hung league in China after the Sacred Edict may have imposed, no similar precautions were required in colonial countries overseas in 1850, where the existence of the league was hardly suspected by local governments and no repressive measures had yet been taken against it except in Hong Kong (1845). This discrepancy has been noted by Ward and Stirling *op. cit.* Volume I page 24 where the view is expressed with which we agree, that the description of the journey in the book found at Japara is an allegory and refers to something different from and *antecedent* to the ritual of the Hung league. Ward and Stirling Volume I, page 25 have:—

"We thus see that this description of the journey, which Schlegel thought described the actual path to a real lodge, is the description of the road which the initiate is supposed to have followed, previous to his arrival at the Hung Lodge."

From these considerations we are forced into a slight divergence on this single point from the conclusions of Schlegel regarding the source from which the name "Ghee Hin Kung Sz", has been derived. We believe that the documents found at Japara in 1851 belonged to something different from and antecedent to the Hung league ritual; but before presenting the evidence upon which this view rests, it is necessary to introduce the reader to the existence of another and separate secret brotherhood among the Chinese which appears to have hitherto been largely confused with the Hung league, or at least to have failed to find its proper place in the commentaries of European observers upon the secret society world of China. This second secret brotherhood we present in the three following chapters and return to offer a final opinion upon the source of the name "Ghee Hin" at the end of Chapter V.

(2) THE TRANSITIONAL PERIOD A.D. 1644–1700

After the overthrow of the Ming (Chinese) dynasty by the victorious Manchus (Tartars) in the middle of the seventeenth century the Hung league changed its purely religious complexion and became primarily a band of political and revolutionary crusaders and took up the cause of the overthrown 明 Ming (Chinese) dynasty against the alien 清 Ts'ing (Manchu) conquerors.

"Drive out the Ts'ing and restore the Ming", became the chief slogan of the reconstituted League during this period. Although possibly embracing all China during the Traditional epoch, the cradle of the Hung league from the time of its re-constitution into a revolutionary society, was the two provinces of Canton and Fukien. The new revolutionary slogans, which became common at this time were incorporated into the ancient ritual and became guiding principles, passwords and tokens of the league.

The Manchu rulers of the Ts'ing dynasty (A.D. 1644) were soon alive to the danger of the secret confederation against them and persecuted the league with great severity, thus increasing the need for secrecy among the members. The Sacred Edict issued in A.D. 1662 during the reign of the second Manchu Emperor (Kang Hsi) inaugurated the drastic Manchu persecution of the Buddhists and Taoists which included persecution of the Hung league. The Manchus confused membership of the league with membership of the Christian Church which was then (1650) obtaining a foothold in China through the missionaries of Loyola. Persecution of both Christians and of the "brothers" of the Hung league continued unabated, but was unsuccessful in either crushing Christianity or in stamping out the secret Hung league, which to disguise itself adopted at this time many "aliases".

Although all attempts of the Manchu Government at suppression failed, the resistance of the league was sharpened by persecution. The league degenerated into a band of rebels and robbers sworn to drive out of China the hated Manchu usurpers. The league's numerical strength increased enormously, particularly in the provinces of Canton and Fukien, which were the spear-head of resistance to the Manchus, and with which two provinces, Malaya is peculiarly linked.

(3) THE POLITICAL OR REVOLUTIONARY AGE A.D. 1700–1865

In order that the reader may form a connected picture of the series of events which caused the transformation or re-constitution of the ancient Hung league into a secret political revolutionary party, using the ancient world-old ritual, still found today in some form among all nations, co-mingled with the slogans of a patriot crusade, which are still in use in the branches of the league in Malaya today, we must examine in greater detail the "Traditional History" upon which the present-day ritual of the Hung league is largely based. The following account is condensed from Schlegel *op. cit.* pages 7 to 19.

According to the most common records of the league it was in A.D. 1674 that a band of militant monks, belonging to the Shaolin (少林) monastery in Fukien province,[1] rendered good service to the second Manchu Emperor Kang Hsi in defeating an invading army of the Selu State (modern Inner Mongolia), against whom his regular soldiers had been unsuccessful. He rewarded them at first, but afterwards, at the instigation of two ministers, had the monastery surrounded by troops and set on fire at night, when the monks were asleep. Only five monks (now styled the five Patriarchs of the league) escaped; the others, numbering one hundred and twenty-eight, were killed or burnt to death.

At one point in the story the five refugees seeking water to quench their thirst found a stream in which was floating a white porcelain bowl, with the characters on it 反清復明 fan ts'ing fu meng "Overturn the Ts'ing and restore the Ming dynasty". On seeing it the five monks exclaimed "This is the will of God".

Being pursued by a troop of horse they fled to a hill and there saw a peachwood sword shoot out of the ground on which was carved the characters 二龍爭珠 yi lung chang chu "Two dragons contending for a pearl" and near the point of the sword were the same characters as those found on the porcelain bowl "Overturn Ts'ing restore Ming".

Two women onlookers took up this miraculous sword and routed the pursuing soldiers with it.

After many hardships the five that escaped met Ch'en Chen-nan 陳近南 a discarded minister of state, and then a student of Taoism. He received them kindly, inflamed their desire for revenge and as a means of obtaining their object, proposed the establishment of the T'in-tei-wui (天地會) or Heaven and Earth Association or "Hung (Deluge) Family" (洪家): for the reconstituted Triad Society was started under both designations.

There are several variations of this story, which admits of a mystical interpretation, but all accounts agree that the latter-day Hung league owes its origin to an infamous act of treachery, in the burning of the Shaolin monastery and the massacre of most of its inmates, after they had done good service to the Manchu cause.

Footnote.—(1) For notice of another Shaolin monastery in Honan province, *see* Chapter VII *infra.*

The following is a brief record of the salient historical events in the story, insofar as they affect the present-day ritual in Malaya.

THE TRADITIONAL HISTORY OF THE HUNG LEAGUE

The foundation of the Hung league as it is known today, dates unquestionably from the destruction of the Shao Lin monastery. The year of this event is uncertain, but may with safety be placed later than either the date in the ritual (A.D. 1662) or the popular story date, A.D. 1674. Probably A.D. 1700 would be a safe approximation. Another version attributes the destruction of the monastery to an order of the provincial Manchu judge of Foochow, during the reign of the third Manchu emperor Yung Ching (A.D. 1723–1736). Be that as it may, the five monks journeyed from Foochow to the town of Shek Seng (石城) in the province of Kwangtung where they met the abbot of a monastery there named 萬雲龍 Wan Yun Lung, who became the first president and national grand-master of the now reconstituted Hung league. The abbot and the five monks mixed their blood with wine and swore to "drive out the Ts'ings and restore the Mings". They all adopted the name 洪 Hung and took as their watchword the word 義 Yi (Cantonese) : Ghee (Hokkien) meaning "Patriotism" "Righteousness" or "Rectitude".

A month later the abbot at the head of an army of monks gave battle to a Manchu army and was himself killed, although the monks ultimately defeated the Manchu troops in a battle lasting three weeks. After this victory the five monks dispersed themselves over five provinces of China in order to raise troops and money for their crusade against the Manchus. A Taoist priest named 陳近南 Ch'an Chen Nam, mentioned in the "popular" version of the history, who had thrown in his lot with the monks, succeeded the abbot as national grand-master.

The five monks[1] had been helped and befriended during their escape from the Shao Lin monastery by five horse-dealers,[2] who also decided to throw in their lot with the monk-crusaders.

The five monks each founded a principal lodge of the reconstituted (political) league in the five provinces of Fukien, Kwangtung, Yunnan, Hunan and Chekiang. The five horse-dealers each founded a minor lodge in the five provinces of Kansu, Kwangsi, Szechuan, Hupeh and Kiangsi.

Each lodge was given a name[3] by its founder, (*vide* Schlegel *op. cit.* page 18).

Stanton *op. cit.* page 38 gives a rather different English rendering of the Chinese names of the lodges, but it should be noticed that none of the names is associated with the watchword 義 興 or "Patriotic Rise" by which name the Hung league is known in Malaya.

The foundation names of the lodges and their watchwords are not referred to by any other original researchists.

The five monks thereafter became the heads of the five principal lodges, or the "Five Patriarchs or ancestors" of the ritual: and the five horse-dealers of the five minor lodges, or the "Five Tiger-Generals".

Footnote.—(1) The names of the five monks were :—

Footnote.—(2) The names of the horse-dealers were :—

蔡囿忠	Tsai Tak Chung		吳天成	Wu T'in Cheng
方大洪	Fung Tai Hung		李色智	Lei Shih Chi
馬超興	Ma Chui Hing		洪大歲	Hung Tai Sui
胡囿帝	Wu Tak Tai		姚必達	Yau Pei Tat
李色開	Lei Shih Kai		林永超	Lam Yeong Chau

Footnote.—(3) The names of the lodges were :—

Principal lodges

	Province			Name of lodge founded by the monks		
1.	Fukien	..	..	Green Lotus Hall	..	..青蓮堂
2.	Kwangtung	..	..	Hall of obedience to Hung	..	..洪順堂
3.	Yunan	..	..	Hall of our Queen	..	..家后堂
4.	Hunan	..	..	Blended-with-Heaven Hall	..	..參天堂
5.	Chekiang	..	..	Extensive-conversion Hall	..	..宏化堂

Minor lodges

	Province			Name of lodge founded by the horse-dealers		
6.	Kansu	..	..	Phoenix District	..	..鳳凰郡
7.	Kwangsi	..	..	Golden orchid District	..	..金蘭郡
8.	Szechuan	..	..	Established-Law-District	..	..建章郡
9.	Hupeh	..	..	Happy-Border District	..	..麻浦郡
10.	Kiangsi	..	..	Dyke-West District	..	..隴西郡

The following extract from an article entitled "Chinese Secret Societies" by Frederick Boyle, which appeared in *Harper's Magazine,* issue of September, 1891 gives a variant rendering of the "traditional history" of the political Hung league in brief.

The T'ien-Ti, or Hung League, claims an immemorial antiquity. "Since the foundations of the Earth were laid", says its catechism, 'we bear the name of Hung', again, 'Yin and Yang, Heaven and Earth, accoupled, produced the sons of Hung in myriads leagued'. But(the only distinct evidence of great antiquity with which I am acquainted, lies in the honour paid to Liu pi, Chang-fi, and Kwan-yu,)heroes who flourished, as they say about 184 A.D. The fact is that we should not expect to hear of the T'ien-Ti before the Manchu conquest. In those early days its motto was, 'Obey Heaven and do Righteousness'. That motto still heads every page of its hand-books, but in practice it is over-ruled by the eternal 'Hoan Cheng, Hok Beng' Drive out the Tartar, restore the native line. The league in its present form dates from 1664 A.D., twenty years after the Manchu conquest. At that time the Eleuth or Olot Tartars revolted against their Manchu suzerain, and reduced him to the greatest straits. This is history. By the tradition of the T'ien-Ti, a certain Buddhist abbot saved the empire, taking the field with his monks. The grateful monarch made them such presents that Tang-Sing, his favourite, determined to ruin them. By false reports he obtained an edict commanding him to destroy those traitors, and he fired the monastery. Five inmates alone escaped, by a series of miracles; they are now reverenced as the 'five ancestors'. For years they were hunted over the province of Hok-kien. At length, walking on the banks of the Sam-ho (lit. Three Rivers) River, they beheld a censer floating, on the bottom of which was inscribed the new motto, 'Overthrow the Ching' (the Manchu), 'restore the Ming' (native dynasty). With this watchword they took up arms. Many thousands joined them, and they routed the imperial army. But their hero Bang-lung fell. Thereupon the second-in-command dismissed every man to his home, there to enlist recruits and to preach eternal hatred to the Tartar. Thus the Hung League was formed.

We may venture to believe this story in the main. Putting romance and marvels aside, it tells how /a benevolent association was transformed into a ruthless conspiracy by persecution. Thus one of the vanguard general's replies in the book of ritual may be understood. The master asks him, 'Do you know that there is a Greater and a Less T'ien-Ti?' He answers 'Yes. The Greater was founded in Heaven; the Less at the waters of the Three Rivers', that is, on the banks of the Sam-ho."

GEOGRAPHICAL DISTRIBUTION OF THE HUNG LEAGUE

Geographically the five principal lodges comprise the three southermost maritime provinces of China, namely Chekiang, Fukien and Kwangtung, with Hunan lying inland to the north and contiguous with Kwangtung: and Yunnan due west of Kwangtung, with one province, Kwangsi, lying between them. The five minor lodges are again contiguous with the five principal lodges namely Kwangsi, between Kwangtung and Yunnan; Kiangsi immediately inland of Fukien and between it and Hunan: Hupeh to the immediate north of Hunan and Kiangsi, with Szechuan immediately west of Hupeh; and Kansu immediately north of Szechuan, the whole forming a contiguous block of territory of which the five main provinces and two of the minor provinces (Kiangsi and Kwangsi) lie all together and *south of the river Yangtze.* Of the three remaining minor Hung provinces lying to the north of the Yangtze (Hupeh, Szechuan and Kansu), two lie in the Yangtze valley itself (Hupeh and Szechuan) and one, Kansu, between the Yangtze and the Yellow river.

Evidence will be offered in the next chapter to show that in the Yangtze valley and the area north of it, the re-constituted Hung league had a powerful rival association, which was also both secret and anti-dynastic. It is probable that on account of this fact the re-constituted(Hung league never made much headway north of the Yangtze.)

Evidence, to be offered in subsequent chapters, will support the belief that historically as well as geographically, the Hung league during its re-constituted or political era has remained generally entrenched *south of the line of the Yangtze.*)

The province of Shantung lies north of the Yangtze in the valley of the Yellow river and is not included among the list of principal or minor provinces of the re-constituted Hung league. This point is of importance for the following reasons: firstly because geographically, historically and ritualistically there is nothing to connect the Hung league with the province of Shantung, whereas there are historical grounds given in the next chapter for associating that province closely with a rival secret fraternity to the Hung league: secondly because Schlegel's work on the Hung league is based to some slight extent upon "a Chinese book full of drawings found in 1851 at Japara (Java) with the statutes of the Shantung branch" and upon these documents rests the claim put forward by Schlegel (*op. cit.* Preface Page 4) that "the statutes of Shantung found in Japara have given us the clue" to those names (other than the three standard names which the Hung league applies to itself) by which the Hung league has been referred to in countries outside China: thirdly because among these other names or "watchwords" is that of the 義 興 Ghee Hin or "Patriotic rise" society, by which the Hung league is universally known today in Malaya and the Dutch East Indies, and the clue to which Schlegel suggests (*see* page 7 *supra*) is to be found in the documents found in Japara (Java) in 1851.

We find this view open to some question and a summary of our own conclusions on the point is given at the end of Chapter V.

FLAGS OF THE HUNG LODGES

The five principal lodges, and the associated subsidiary lodges of each, have a triangular flag of the following colours. (*see* Ward and Stirling, Volume I, page 156, and Schlegel, page 36) :

Ward mentions that the five colours are those of the five elements and discusses the allegorical meaning of their use and the parallel in this connection between the Hung observance and a certain degree in Freemasonry.

The flags are :—

		Colour
1.	Fukien and Kansu	.. Black with a border of green.
2.	Kwangtung and Kwangsi	.. Red with a border of white.
3.	Yunnan and Szechuan	.. Yellow or Carnation pink with a border of red.
4.	Hunan and Hupeh	.. White with a border of green.
5.	Chekiang and Kiangsi	.. Green with a border of black.

We are not here concerned with any further description of these flags, beyond noting the fact that "overseas" Hung lodges, wherever found, all have their own identification flags of the above colours according to their origin, and that all these are *triangular* in shape.

THE TAIPING REBELLION A.D. 1850–1864

The league's ramifications grew apace and its new revolutionary character soon showed itself in a series of open rebellions against the Manchus during the first half of the nineteenth century, which culminated in the T'ai peng (太 平 or "Universal Peace") Rebellion of A.D. 1850–1864.

Although this revolutionary movement covering a period of 15 years, is often referred to by Europeans as the "Triad war", its origin was complex and its beginning was unconnected with the Hung league.

(It is only after the rebellion was well established that evidence becomes available to show that the Hung league was giving it support.) The degree and duration of that support is still in some doubt. The rebellion began among the Hakka (Kheh) Chinese in the province of Kwangtung, whose leader 洪 秀 全 Hung Sio Chun was a visionary who taught a pseudo-Christianity of his own invention, although he was not himself a baptised Christian. (The insurrection was anti-dynastic and aimed at throwing off the yoke of the Manchu oppressors.) Its support by Christian converts among the Chinese, as well as by large numbers of the Triad society, seems to have been an important incident in the main movement rather than merely accidental, as some writers maintain. What is important to note here is that (the rebellion was anti-Manchu and was supported by Christian Chinese converts and the pseudo-Christians or "Society of God-worshippers" (上 帝 曾) of its founder: and, largely in consequence of this, by foreign sentiment: thirdly it was supported at different times by large numbers of the Hung league) to such an extent that the rebellion has been referred to by many writers as a purely Triad movement.

Technically this may be incorrect, but actually, the "Taipings" and the "Triads" became for sometime indistinguishable in the public mind, both Chinese and foreign. What is also important to note is that the rebellion enormously affected the Hung league and unquestionably if not perhaps deservedly, blazoned it forth as an instrument of rebellion and thereby increased the Manchu fear of the league and their persecution of it.

A fuller account of the Taiping rebellion and its influence upon the Hung league in Malaya is given in Chapter IV.

THE HUNG LEAGUE AND THE REVOLUTION IN CHINA A.D. 1911

There is reason to suppose that the Hung league inspired the revolution in China of 1911, and so achieved its purpose of driving out the Ts'ing (Manchu) dynasty. In this connection the following extract from Heckethorn *op. cit.* Volume II, page 133, is relevant:

"Towards the end of the year 1895, a number of Mohammedans rose against the Chinese Government and captured the capital of the province of Kansu; the secret societies in Central

China joined the Mohammedan insurgents. Their success, however, was of short duration; in the month of December of the same year the insurrection was crushed, and some fifteen of the leaders were captured and beheaded. Others made their escape. Among these was Sun Yat Sen, or, as he is also called, Sun Wen, a medical man, well known in Hong Kong.

We further discuss Sun Yat Sen's connection with the Hung league in Chapters XXVII and XXXII *infra*.

On this subject Ward and Stirling, Volume I, page 8, have:—

"Since the T'ai P'ing rebellion the society appears to have kept somewhat in the background, but there are reasons for thinking that they (The Triads) secretly inspired the successful revolution which finally overthrew the Manchu Dynasty, and established the Republic.

There are certain facts which strongly support this view, for example we know that Dr. Sun Yat Sen was a member of the Hung Society, hence the significance of the first official action of that Chinese leader who was the first President of the Republic and entered into office on 1st January, 1912. Soon after assuming office, as reported in 'The Eastern Review' for March, 1925, page 101, he resigned in order to facilitate a general settlement by enabling Yuan Shi Kai to unite all parties under his Presidency, and, in place of his former office, was appointed Provisional President in Nanking. He announced these changes to the whole populace in front of the famous Ming tombs, and then solemnly informed the Spirits of the Mings that the Manchus and their despotism had been driven out and that China was once more under Chinese rule, although this time as a Republic. As there is independent evidence that Sun Yat Sen was a member of the Triad Society, it is certainly significant that although he was a Christian, he thus paid reverence to the ancient traditions of the Hung Society."

It would not seem unreasonable to suppose that this ceremony marked the fulfilment of the task of the latter-day Hung League (1662–1912).

It does not follow that the "Political Age" of the Hung League ended in 1912. It may well be that Chiang Kai Shek is at the present time employing "Hung braves" for special services in support of the Nanking regime inaugurated by Dr. Sun Yat Sen. Again, the loss of Manchuria and the invasion of China by Japan in 1937 might well invite today a resurgence of the Hung league in its political form.

(4) THE DEGENERATE AGE A.D. 1865 ONWARDS

Whatever the true reading of the signs may be, it is certain that the character of a large section of the league utterly degenerated both in China and overseas during the nineteenth century and became an instrument of terror and oppression to their countrymen and a source of anxiety and embarrassment to constituted authority. This leads us to an examination of the "Degenerate period" of the league's activities with which in Malaya this compilation is chiefly concerned, but without the foregoing historical sketch it would be largely incomprehensible.

(a) In China Proper including Hong Kong—

If we care to accept the theory that the Revolution of 1912 was the crowning achievement in China of the Hung league, then we may post-date the beginning of the degenerate period of the league *in China itself* as from 1912, otherwise the period should date from the end of the Taiping Rebellion in the middle of the last century (A.D. 1864).

Stanton, *op. cit.* pages 26, 27 and 28, gives some details of the league's criminal activities in Hong Kong from 1845 onwards.

Referring to the "lodges of the Triad Society" found in Hong Kong, Stanton mentions four by name on page 27 but without Chinese characters, which we have interpolated, *viz.*:—

Man On   安萬

Fuk I Hing   福義興

Hoi Luk   海陸

and on page 91 :—

Fuk On She   福安社

On page 27 he mentions that these were the chief lodges that caused disturbances in Hong Kong in 1886 and that the Man On was hostile to the Fuk I Hing (Hok Ghee Hin). On page 28 he mentions that the members of the Man On and Hok Ghee Hin were Hok-los (*i.e.* Teo Chews) and states that at the time of writing (1900).

"It is estimated that about a third of the male population of the Colony and many females are more or less active members."

Devonshire, in an article on "Chinese Secret Societies" in the *Malayan Police Magazine* (issue of July, 1931), refers to the society's recent excesses in China Proper. But here again we must remember in the words of Schlegel quoted above "Not all the horrors committed in the name of the Heaven and Earth league, ought to be considered as its acts". The next Chapter introduces to the reader a secret association whose responsibility for outrage is probably much greater and whose existence has been largely ignored by writers in the past.

(b) Overseas—

But the ramifications of the league had never been confined to China. Wherever the Chinese went overseas during the eighteenth and nineteenth century, a period when the political activity of the league in China was at its height, they took the ritual and secrets of the league with them and established lodges all over the world which remain to the present day in those countries where the Chinese have permanently established themselves. These include French Indo-China (aboriginal), Siam, Malaya, the Dutch East Indies, Burma, India, and parts of Australia, America and England.

Whatever justification and political objective the league might have had in China proper during the last two centuries, there was no good reason or excuse why its revolutionary aims and secret ritual should have been fostered in overseas lodges under a stable non-Chinese Government, except on the grounds of the natural exclusiveness of the Chinese and the fact that the secret and self-contained organisation of the league provided a ready-made instrument whereby Chinese settlers in foreign countries, speaking a language not then generally understood, could govern themselves and their community as an *imperium in imperio*, thus avoiding interference by or friction with the local authorities, who welcomed these industrious settlers and were glad to appoint their leader, usually the headman of the local Hung lodge, to be "Kapitan China", to rule his own community "according to Chinese laws and customs" (usually those of the league) and to be answerable always to the local authorities for crimes committed by, or questions affecting, members of the local Chinese community.

As was only to be expected, the league thus transplanted overseas, lost most of its political significance and quickly degenerated among its lowest *strata* into an organised machine of oppression and extortion, encased in the powerful armature of secrecy and backed by the death penalty for "traitors", and proof, therefore, against treachery from within and interference from without. The aphorism "Dog does not eat dog" is unknown among the Chinese, whose whole social edifice is largely built upon a system of battening upon one another.

So long as overseas lodges were content to feed upon their own fat and confine their extortions to the non-members of the league in their own communities and so long as no rival lodges were founded which demanded a share of the profits, the system of government of Chinese overseas through a "Kapitan China" worked fairly well. But the demoralising misuse of the ancient ritual and secret organisation of the league for solely selfish and criminal purposes soon broke down the unity of the earlier overseas lodges. To this was added the influx of other Chinese settlers from different provinces of China speaking again in different dialects, who brought their own secret lodges and their own headmen with them. These were not necessarily lodges of the Hung league and they soon found themselves at loggerheads with the older established lodges. This led to riots, with the result that the local authority was at length forced to intervene for its own protection against gang rule. This process has repeated itself in most countries overseas with a settled Chinese population.

(c) In Malaya—

In Chapter V we attempt to trace briefly how this process had developed in Malaya up to about the year 1850 and to sketch the establishment and development of the different secret lodges in the Straits Settlements down to the point in fairly recent history (A.D. 1867), when these secret Chinese gangs had allied themselves for their own purposes with similar secret criminal gangs amongst the indigenous Mohammedan population, a confederacy which is still at work underground in Malaya today.

But these modern developments have not had a single isolated root in the Hung league. Their origins are more complex and spring partly from other causes, underlying the history of Malaya during the nineteenth century and which must next command our attention.

Some of these other causes may be summarised as follows:—

(1) The existence of another secret Chinese organisation known as the Han League or the Ko Lao Hui (哥老會) or "Society of the Elder Brethren", active in China during the nineteenth century, which seems to share a common origin with the Hung League and whose members seem to have come to Malaya about the same time or shortly after the Hung. This circumstance may have given rise to that rivalry and hostility to the Triad Society which has been such a prominent feature in the secret society history of Malaya. This subject is dealt with in Chapter II.

(2) The state of civil war which existed in South China during the second half of the nineteenth century, particularly that between the Cantonese and Hakkas (Khehs) and the echoes and repercussions of this hatred between immigrants to Malaya from among these tribes during that period. This subject is dealt with in Chapter IV.

(3) The state of war which existed between Kedah and Siam, between 1821 and 1850, during which several rebellions by exiled Malays living in Penang and Province Wellesley, were secretly hatched in Penang with Chinese aid. This subject is dealt with in Chapters V and XIII.

(4) The effect upon the Malayan criminal field of the transportation from India to Malaya of over 1,500 convicted Indian Mohamedan and Hindu "Thugs" during the years 1830–1850. This subject is dealt with in Chapter X.

In Chapter V we resume again the study of the "Degenerate Age" of the Hung league in Malaya.

We must now consider the Han league or Ko Lao Hui or society of the Elder Brethren and the features which it shares with, as well as the points in which it differs from, the Hung league.

NOTE
THE DYNASTIES OF CHINA

Name of Dynasty		Duration
Mythical Rulers (Seven)		2953–2357 B.C.
Patriarchs (Two)		2357–2205
Hsia 夏		2205–1766
Emperor Yu 禹	2205–2197	
Shang 商		1766–1121
Yin 殷 Dynasty (Change of name)	1401–1121	
Chou 周		1121– 255
Kingdom of Chou	1121– 770	
Ch'un Ch'iu 春秋 (Period of the Annals)	770– 464	
Chan Kuo 戰國 (Warring States)	464– 221	
Ch'in 秦		255– 206
Han 漢 "Former" (Ch'ien 前) or "Western" (Hsi 西)	B.C. 206– 25 A.D.	
Han 漢 "Later" (Hou 後) or "Eastern" (Tung 東)	25– 221 A.D.	
The Three Kingdoms (San Kuo 三國)		221– 265
Wei 魏 (in North)	220– 265	
Minor Han 漢 or Shu 蜀 (in West)	221– 265	
Wu 吳 (in South)	222– 280	
Western Chin (Hsi Chin 西晉)		265– 317
Eastern Chin (Tung Chin 東晉)		317– 420
Period of Division between North and South (Nan Pei Ch'ao 南北朝)		420– 589
Sung 宋 (Liu Sung 劉宋)	420– 479	
Ch'i 齊	479– 502	
Liang 梁	502– 557	
Ch'en 陳	557– 589	
N. Wei (Pei Wei 北魏)	386– 535	
W. Wei (Hsi Wei 西魏)	535– 557	
E. Wei (Tung Wei 東魏)	534– 550	
N. Ch'i (Pei Ch'i 北齊)	550– 589	
N. Chou (Pei Chou 北周)	557– 589	
Sui 隋		589– 618
T'ang 唐		618– 907
The Five Dynasties (Wu Tai 五代)		907– 960
Posterior Liang (Hou Liang 後梁)	907– 923	
„ T'ang (Hou T'ang 後唐)	923– 936	
„ Chin (Hou Chin 後晉)	936– 947	
„ Han (Hou Han 後漢)	947– 951	
„ Chou (Hou Chou 後周)	951– 960	
Tartar Dynasties		907–1234
Liao 遼 (K'i Tan 契丹 or Iron Tunguses)	907–1125	
W. Liao 西遼 (Hsi Liao 西遼)	1125–1168	
Kin or Chin 金 (Nu Chen 女真 or Golden Tunguses)	1115–1234	
Sung 宋 (Northern Sung, Pei Sung 北宋)		960–1127 A.D.
Sung 宋 (Southern Sung, Nan Sung 南宋)		1127–1280
Yuan 元 (Mongol)		1280–1368
Ming 明		1368–1644
Ts'ing 清 (Manchu)		1644–1912
Republic or (Min Kuo 民國)		1912

CHAPTER II

THE HAN LEAGUE (SOCIETY OF THE ELDER BRETHREN) IN CHINA FROM EARLIEST TIMES UP TO A.D. 1900

THE PEACH GARDEN TRIO

(Throughout the ritual of the Triad society there is frequent reference to three persons "who took an oath in a Peach Garden") and whose names are

Liu Pei 劉備) or Liu Yuan-te (劉玄德)

Kwan Yu (關羽)

Chang Fei (張飛)

These three are referred to as "The Peach Garden trio" and the Triad ritual records that it was in imitation of this trio that the Five Ancestors of the Triad took their oath in the Red Flower Pavilion after the burning of the Shao Lin Monastery. The story of this Peach Garden trio, which antedates the story of the reconstituted Hung League (A.D. 1700) by many centuries, must next command our attention, for the reason that (it is not only woven into the fabric of Hung League ritual, but the Peach Garden trio are also claimed as the "ancestors") of another secret Chinese association known as the Han Liu (漢流) the "Sons of Han", or Han League, or Ko Lao Hui (哥老會) the "Society of the elder brethren", a study of which forms the main subject of this chapter. The *Peach Garden trio* therefore provide one of the links between the Hung League and the Han League. The ritual of the latter may well be found by those best qualified to judge, to contain "that missing degree or degrees", which (according to Ward and Stirling *op. cit.* Vol. III. page 117) the nature of the Hung ceremony postulates".

We will return later to this aspect of our subject.

The story of the Peach Garden trio is contained in the Chinese annals known as the *Sam Kwok Chi Yin Yi* (三國志演義) or *Romance of the Three Kingdoms or States* (A.D. 221–265), a modern translation of which by C. H. Brewitt-Taylor in 2 Volumes was published in 1925.

The following are extracts from Chapter I of this work and give the origin of the Peach Garden trio:—

"The rise of the fortunes of Han began with the slaughter of the white serpent. In a short time the whole Empire was theirs and their magnificent heritage was handed down in successive generations till the days of Kuang-Wu, whose name stands in the middle of the long line of Han. This was in the first century of the western era and the dynasty had then already passed its zenith. A century later came to the throne the Emperor Hsien, doomed to see the beginning of the division into three parts, known to history as "The Three Kingdoms".

The descent into misrule hastened in the reigns of the two Emperors Huan and Ling, who sat in the dragon seat about the middle of the second century. The former of these two paid no heed to the good men of his court, but gave his confidence to the palace eunuchs. He lived and died, leaving the sceptre to Ling, whose trusted advisers were the General Tou Wu and the Grand Tutor Ch'ên Fan.

These two, disgusted with the abuses resulting from the meddling of the eunuchs in affairs of State, plotted their destruction. But the chief eunuch Ts'ao Chieh was not to be disposed of easily. The plot leaked out and the two honest men fell, leaving the eunuchs stronger than before.

The government went quickly from bad to worse, till the country was ripe for rebellion and buzzed with brigandage.

At this time in Chulu was a certain Chang family, of whom three brothers bore the name of Chio, Pao and Liang respectively. The eldest Chang Chio was an unclassed graduate who devoted himself to medicine. One day while cutting simples in the woods, he met a venerable old gentleman with very bright eyes and fresh complexion, who walked leaning on a staff. The old man beckoned Chio into a cave and there gave him three volumes of the "Book of Heaven." "This book" said he "is the Way of Peace. With the aid of these volumes you can convert the world and rescue mankind. But you must be single-minded, or, rest assured, you will greatly suffer".

With a humble obeisance Chang Chio took the book and asked the name of his benefactor. "I am Hsein of the Southern Land of Glory," was the reply, as the old man disappeared in thin air. The new possessor of the wonderful book studied it eagerly day and night and strove to reduce its precepts to practice.

Chang Chio began to have a following of disciples whom he initiated into the mysteries and sent abroad throughout the land. They, like their master, could write charms and recite formulæ and their fame increased his following. He began to organise his disciples. He established thirty-six circuits, the larger with a myriad or more members, the smaller with about half that number. Each circuit had its chief who took the military title of General.

With the growth of the number of his supporters grew also the ambition of Chang the "Wise and Good". He dreamed of Empire.....

To his brothers, Chang Chio said, "For schemes like ours always the most difficult part is to gain the popular favour. But this is already ours. Such an opportunity must not pass". And they began to prepare. Many yellow flags were made and a day chosen to strike the blow.

Then they wrote letters to the chief eunuch, Fêng Hsü, and sent them by a follower, who alas betrayed their trust and discovered the plot.....

The plot having thus become known the Changs were forced at once to take the field. They assumed grandiose titles, T'ien Kung, (天 公) or Celestial Duke; Ti Kung, (地 公) or Terrestial Duke; Jên Kung, (人 公) or Duke of Humanity, and in these names[1] they put forth this manifesto:—

"The good fortune of the Hans is exhausted and the Wise Man has appeared. Discern the will of Heaven, O ye people, and walk in the way of righteousness, whereby alone ye may attain to peace".

Support was not lacking. On every side people bound their heads with a yellow turban[2] and joined the army of the rebel Chang Chio, so that soon his strength was exceeding great, and the official troops melted away at a whisper of his coming.

*　　　　*　　　　*

Chang Chio led his army into Yuchow, the northern of the eight divisions of the country. The Prefect was one Liu Yen, a scion of the Imperial House. Learning of the approach of the rebels, the Prefect put out notices calling for volunteers to serve against the rebels. One of these notices was posted up in Cho district, where lived one of whom much will be heard later. This man was no bookish scholar only, nor found he any pleasure in study. But he was liberal and amiable, albeit a man of few words.

He was a descendant of a Prince whose father was the Emperor Ching, (the occupant of the dragon throne a century and a half B.C.) His name was Liu Pei, or more commonly Liu Yüan-tê.

Yüan-tê was twenty-eight when the outbreak of the rebellion[2] called for soldiers. The sight of the notice saddened him and he sighed as he read it. Suddenly a rasping voice behind him cried, "Noble Sir, why sigh if you do nothing to help your country?" Turning quickly he saw standing there a man about his own height, with a bullet head like a leopard's, large eyes, a pointed chin, and a bristling moustache. He spoke in a loud bass voice and looked as irresistable as a runaway horse. At once Yüan-tê saw he was no ordinary man, and asked who he was.

*　　　　*　　　　*

"Chang Fei is my name; and I am usually called I-tê" replied the stranger. "I live near here where I have a farm; and I am a wine-seller and a butcher as well. And I like to become acquainted with worthy men. Your sighs as you read the notice drew me toward you".

Yüan-tê replied, "I am of the Imperial Family, Liu by name, and my distinguishing name is Pei. An I could I would destroy these rebels and restore peace to the land, but alas I am helpless".

"I am not without means", said Fei "Suppose you and I raised some men and tried what we could do".

This was happy news for Yüan-tê and the two betook themselves to the village inn to talk over the project. As they were drinking, a huge, tall fellow appeared pushing a hand-cart along the road. At the threshold he halted and entered the inn to rest awhile and he called for wine. "And be quick" added he "for I am in haste to get into the town and offer myself for the army."

Yüan-tê looked over the new-comer item by item and noted his huge frame, his long beard, his dark brown face and deep red lips. He had eyes like a phœnix and fine bushy eyebrows like silkworms. His whole appearance was dignified and awe-inspiring. Presently Yüan-tê crossed over, sat down beside him and asked his name.

"I am Kuan Yü," said he: "I used to be known as Shou-ch'ang (Long as Eternity), but now am usually call Yun-ch'ang (Long as a Cloud)." I am a native of the east side of the river, but I have been a fugitive on the waters for some five years because I slew a ruffian who, since he was powerful, was a bully. I have come to join the army here".

Then Yüan-tê told him his own intentions and all three went away to Chang Fei's farm where they could talk over the grand project. Said Fei, "The Peach trees in the orchard behind the house are just in full flower. To-morrow we will institute a sacrifice there and solemnly declare our intention before Heaven and Earth, and we three will swear brotherhood and unity of aims and sentiments; thus will we enter upon our great task".

All three being of one mind, next day they prepared the sacrifices, a black ox, a white horse and wine for libation. Beneath the smoke of the incense burning on the altar they bowed their heads and recited this oath:—

"We three, Liu Pei, Kuan Yü and Chang Fei, though of different families, swear brotherhood and promise mutual help to one end. We will rescue each other in difficulty, we will aid each other in danger. We swear to serve the state and save the people. We ask not the same day of birth but seek to die together. May Heaven, the all-ruling, and Earth, the all-producing, read our hearts and if we turn aside from righteousness or forget kindliness, may Heaven and man smite us".

They rose from their knees. The two others bowed before Liu Pei or Yüan-tê as their elder brother, and Chang Fei was to be the youngest of the trio. This solemn ceremony performed, they slew other oxen and made a feast to which they invited the villagers. Three hundred joined them, and all feasted and drank deep in the Peach Garden.

The next day weapons were mustered. But there were no horses to ride. This was a real grief, but soon they were cheered by the arrival of two horse dealers with a drove of horses. "Thus does Heaven help us," said Yüan-tê and the three sworn brothers went forth to welcome the merchants. They were from Changshan and went northwards every year to buy horses. They were now on their way home because of the rising. They also came to the farm, where wine was set before them, and presently Yüan-tê told them of the plan to strive for tranquility. The two dealers were glad, and at once gave them fifty steeds, and beside, gold and silver and a thousand catties of steel fit for the forging of weapons. After the merchants had taken their leave, armourers were summoned to forge weapons.....

*　　　　*　　　　*

Before many days it was announced that the rebellion had actually broken out and the leader, Chêng Yüan-chih, had invaded the district with a huge army. The three heroes went out to oppose them with five hundred men.

*　　　　*　　　　*

....The drums rolled for the advance. The rebels also came forward. Then Yüan-tê suddenly retired. Thinking this was their chance, the rebels pressed forward and were led over the hills. Then suddenly the gongs sounded for the ambush to discover itself and the rebels were attacked on three sides. They lost heavily and fled to the provincial city. But the Prefect led out the men he had to assist in the battle and the rebels were entirely defeated and many slain".

Footnote.—(1) The association of these titles with the Heaven, Earth and Man of the Triad Society will be noted.

Footnote.—(2) The rebels are known to history as the Yellow Cap or turban rebels— 黃 巾 賊 A.D. 184.

This story contains many features of interest the significance of which will become more apparent in later chapters. Attention may usefully be drawn here to the following. The fortunes of the Han dynasty are described as beginning after the death of the serpent, the symbol of wisdom in most ancient religions. After a period of magnificence the Han dynasty decayed and its misrule was challenged by the three born brothers Chang Chio (張 角), Chang Pao (張 寶) and Chang Liang (張 樑) whose crusade was based on the "Book of Heaven", which was "the way of peace", leading to the rescue of mankind and who were enjoined to remain single-minded in this crusade, or great suffering would ensue. Instead they "dreamed of Empire" and power and organised their followers in *thirty-six* circuits. They raised the standard of the "Yellow Cap" rebellion, while claiming at the same time to be guided in their attempt forcibly to overthrow the Han dynasty, by the teaching of the Book of Heaven and the Way of Peace. In assuming command of the rebellion they adopted the titles of the trinity now appropriated to the Hung League. They were in turn challenged by three sworn brothers, described respectively the first as "liberal and amiable but no scholar" the second as "a wine-seller and butcher", the third as "a fugitive on the waters from justice" who to confirm their oath of brotherhood sacrificed a black ox to the Earth goddess and a white horse to the sun, symbols common to the rites of many ancient beliefs. The three sworn brothers were aided in their enterprise by two horsedealers reminiscent of those already met with in the Triad society tradition and who also appear as apostles in the tradition of the spread of Buddhism. The story ends with the victory of the three sworn brothers, the champions of the Han, over the three born brothers who claimed to be rescuers of mankind and the champions of the "book of heaven" and the "way of peace".

The whole story suggests an allegory in which the three born brothers and their disciples, the Yellow Cap rebels, represent the return of wisdom to the earth under the banner of Buddhism, following the earlier death of the serpent: and the three sworn brothers and their Han army represent the prevailing state of ignorance which the new wisdom failed to conquer because its apostles were unworthy of the task they had been set and did not remain single-minded but "dreamed of empire" and were themselves vanquished.

If this interpretation should be correct, the application of the story to the Chinese secret society world would, in turn, logically show the three *born* brothers to represent the Hung league identifying at the same time the Yellow cap rebels with Buddhism and the Hung league: and would show the three *sworn* brothers to represent another league, hostile to the Hung and supporting the Han dynasty, and the material magnificence for which it stood.)

It is the purpose of this chapter to introduce the reader to this second league, the Han league, which we believe to be an even more potent force than the Hung league in the secret society life of China.

After his death the second of the Peach Garden trio, Kwan Yu (關 羽) received posthumous honour and is recorded as having been *deified under the name of Kwan Ti* (關 帝) *and worshipped as the God of War.*)

Ward and Stirling have the following note on this circumstance (*op. cit.* Vol. I page 2 Note 2).

This is usually regarded as historical but it bears a striking similarity to mythological legends dealing with the Divine Triad and the slain god.

Whether it be myth or history the picture of Kwan Ti is or was up to the Revolution of 1911 universally popular and could be found in almost any home in China. The fact of his deification as the god of war by the Ming emperor Wan Li) (A.D. 1573–1620) probably explains this popularity and has not necessarily any connection with his partnership in the Peach Garden oath.[1]

It may be objected that the constant references to the "oath of the Peach Garden" in the Hung ritual rules out the assumption that the three sworn brothers could have any but a beneficial association with the Hung league, but it is noteworthy that they are not claimed as "ancestors" of the Hung, nor have they any place in the Hung hierarchy. Only the example of their oathtaking is referred to in the Triad ritual as symbolic of the power of sworn brotherhood and worthy of imitation.

We refer again to the allegorical aspect of the Peach Garden story in Chapter III below.

Every Chinese from Pekin to Hainan and from Shanghai to Tibet knows this story which has become an integral part of Chinese life. It is the basis of that "sworn brotherhood"(結拜 or 結盟) so beloved of the Chinese mind, so universal in Chinese social relations, covering every shade of purpose from a guarantee of commercial integrity. such as the Co-Hong (結 行) monopoly, to murder or rebellion, and so baffling to the uninitiated.

Footnote.—(1) For the association of Kwan Ti with the Ko Lao Hui *see* page 26; and with the Triad society and the Three Dot Brotherhood, *see* Chapter IX *infra.*

The oath of blood brotherhood is of course very widespread, being found among races in all parts of the world (*see* Ward and Stirling Volume III, Chapter IX).

Sworn brotherhood is one of the foundations of the Chinese genius for organisation and one of their principal engines of oppression and exploitation of their own kind. Its practice is by no means confined to the criminal classes.

Its prevalence in all walks of Chinese life, among the *literati*, officials, merchants, artisans, peasants and bandits, combines the purposes of an insurance policy and a trades union, and explains much of that Chinese exclusiveness, self-reliance, and inscrutability which is at once the wonderment and the despair of the European official.

Some writers on the Triad society see the possible origin of the Hung League itself in the Peach Garden story, but this view is not sustained by other authorities. Furthermore, the names of the Peach Garden trio, although appearing frequently in the Hung ritual, do not appear in the genealogical table of the founders of the Hung league (Schlegel page 23). A new interpretation of the story which seems to fit the facts, has been offered above.

None of the authorities consulted on the Triad society (neither Milne, Newbold, Tomlin, Hoffman, Schlegel, Stanton nor Ward and Stirling) makes any reference to the Han Liu or Ko Lao Hui, although Newbold, Schlegel and Ward and Stirling refer to the "Peach Garden trio" in the following terms:—

Newbold, in his paper *JRAS*. Vol. VI (1840) page 120 gives a translation of Chapter I of the SAN KWOH (History of the three Kingdoms) made for him by Rev. Tomlin of Malacca in 1838, and suggests therein the origin of the Hung League itself. The suggestive passages quoted by him are those given above from Brewitt-Taylor's translation.

Schlegel, who used Newbold's paper, but who also does not mention the Ko Lao Hui, of the existence of which he was probably also unaware, contents himself with the following general reference to the story of the Peach Garden trio as contained in the history of the three Kingdoms. Schlegel page 2:—

"The Chinese annals afford many illustrations of such fraternal bonds (*i.e.* as the Hung League). One of the most renowned to which the Hung League alludes at every moment, is that sworn between Liu Pei (劉 備) Chang Fei (張 飛) and Kuan Yü (關 羽). This alliance was sworn during the civil wars, that desolated the Chinese empire, between the overthrow of the Han dynasty and the establishment of the Eastern Chin. These wars lasted 168 to 265 of our era. It was in the year A.D. 184 that the Western Chinese revolted against the Emperor. They wore yellow turbans around their heads and were called therefrom, the yellow-cap-rebels (黃 巾 賊). As is generally the case in China, the Emperor was too weak to subdue these rebels. He issued a proclamation, calling upon all the valiant of the empire to enlist and fight against the insurgents. Two men Liu Pei and Chang Fei, having read this proclamation, went to a tavern to speak about it. Liu Pei himself was an offspring of the reigning dynasty of Han. Whilst sitting there, a certain Kuan Yü joined them. Animated by a common spirit, these three men sought to devise the means of restoring peace in the land. At the proposal of Chang Fei, they came together the next day in the Peach Garden behind his house, and being assembled under the peach-trees, they sacrificed a black ox and a white horse and having offered incense, they knelt down and swore the oath of fraternity. Liu Pei was named "first brother" of the League. Having enlisted volunteers they succeeded after a long war in subduing the "yellow caps" and in restoring peace to their country".

In "the Traditional History" of the Hung League (Schlegel page 15) the Peach garden trio are mentioned in the following terms (describing the oath taken by the *Five* ancestors of the *Hung* in the *Red Flower Pavilion*.):—

"They (the Five Ancestors) then agreed to unite themselves at this place before Heaven and Earth, just like Liu Pei, Kuan Yü and Chang Fei who had sworn together an oath in the Peach Garden, to remain friends for life and death".

See also the corresponding passage in Ward and Stirling Vol. I page 41.

Ward and Stirling Vol. I page 1 and 2 give the following interesting historical sketch:—

"At the time of the downfall of the Han Dynasty, about A.D. 221 the Western Provinces of China broke into revolt and the Emperor found it impossible to subdue them. In this emergency he issued a general call for volunteers, which was responded to by three men: Liu Pei, himself a cadet of the Han Dynasty, and his two friends, Kuan Yü and Chang Fei. These three men met on a certain day in a peach garden and having burnt magic incense sacrificed a black ox and a white horse, offered up prayers, and bound themselves by a special oath of fidelity.

'It is from this incident, in all probability, that the Triad Society derives its custom of sacrificing a black ox and a white horse at an initiation.' This ceremony is of vast antiquity, and is found in many parts of the world. The sacrifice of black cattle, symbolising the Earth Goddess of the underworld, usually preceded any attempt to visit that place. The Horse is the emblem of the Sun, and the whole ceremonial is discussed in Vol. III. The significance of the colours is fairly obvious. They represent the contending forces in Nature;—day and night; good and evil; male and female;—and are represented in the West by the black and white pillars of the Rosicrucians, and by the black and white banner of the Knights Templar. In Chinese symbolism we get the Yin and the Yang which are respectively black and white[1].

Liu Pei was named "First Brother" or Leader, and, loyally supported by the other two, he organised an army which after many struggles conquered the rebels. The Han Dynasty was, however, on the verge of collapse, and when this event happened China became split up into three kingdoms.

The story of the Three Kingdoms is one of the most romantic and famous in Chinese history, and even to-day incidents connected with this epoch are frequently enacted on the Chinese stage. The Three Kingdoms became known as Wai, composed of the central and northern provinces,

_____

Footnote.—(1) The Yin and Yang symbol is described in Chapter I *supra* and referred to again in Chapter III *infra*.

having its capital at Lo Yang; Wu, consisting of the provinces south of the Yang Tze river, now known as Hunan, Hupei, Kiangsu and Chekiang, with the capital at Nankin;—and Shu, which covered the western province, with Chengtu as its capital.

At the collapse of the central government Liu Pei, who was a Chihli man of royal descent, assumed the title of Emperor of Shu. In this he was loyally supported by his two sworn brethren, but Kwan Yi was captured during the fighting and put to death by Liu Pei's enemies. (Posthumous honours were conferred upon him in memory of his unswerving loyalty to his friend, and he was deified under the name of Kwan Ti and worshipped as the God of War. This honour was conferred on him by the Ming Emperor, Wan Li, and he became to the military what Confucius is to the literary.

After its formation, the Hung Society adopted him as its tutelary deity, and his picture is always found in the shrine in the Hall of Loyalty and Patriotism. In adopting him they were no doubt influenced partly by the fact that he was essentially the soldiers' god, but their main reason was that in China he has always stood for the embodiment of loyalty to a sworn brother. At the same time it must be remembered that he was equally popular among the uninitiated, and at any rate up to the time of the establishment of the Republic his picture could be found in almost any Chinese merchants' shops".

THE HISTORY OF THE HAN LIU (漢 流) OR KO LAO HUI (哥老會) IN CHINA UP TO 1900.

It is necessary to the building up of our background to tax the reader's patience further with an introduction to the Han Liu or Ko Lao Hui, another secret organisation in China, which seems to have found its way to Malaya—doubtless in truncated and degenerate form, a circumstance which provides an explanation of that enmity and hostility which has been such a prominent feature of the history in Malaya of those Chinese secret organisations which have hitherto been lumped together as "branches of the Triad Society".

The independent authorities on this subject appear to be few. The following have been consulted:—

Playfair	..	..	.. Article in *The China Review* 1886—87, Vol. 15.
Boyle	..	..	.. Article in *Harper's Magazine* September 1891.
Heckethorn	..	..	*Secret Societies*, 1896 Vol. II page 136.
Couling	..	..	*Encyclopaedia Sinica*, 1917.
Rev. J. Hutson	..	..	Article in *The New China Review* Vol. II No. 1 of February, 1920.

The last named is by far the fullest account and provides the chief material for this chapter.

The authorities quoted who, it must be remembered, do not appear to have consulted one another, claim three different periods of origin for the Ko Lao Hui, namely:—

(1) A modern military conspiracy dating only from the T'ai P'ing rebellion A.D. 1848 (Boyle and Heckethorn).

(2) A military crusade, set on foot by the "three ancestors" or "trio of the Peach Garden" and dating from the end of the Han dynasty, say A.D. 184. (Hutson). Schlegel's comments upon the Peach Garden Trio given above also support this view.

(3) A religious fraternity originating in the Totemistic age (age of magic), with roots in hoary antiquity, probably representing the most ancient demon worship. (Hutson and to some extent Couling).

Hutson agrees that the Han League assumed the complexion of a military crusade towards the end of the Eastern Han dynasty (A.D. 184) from which epoch dates the "trio of the Peach Garden" and in this respect it provides a parallel—although of an older vintage—to the "political age" of the Hung League.

Boyle's account, while denying its ancient lineage, agrees with the view of Hutson that the Ko Lao Hui in its militant form looks further back than the Hung League beyond the Ming dynasty (A.D. 1368—1644) to the Han (B.C. 260—A.D. 25) for the restoration of the pure Chinese stock.

According to Hutson the Han Liu or "Descendants of the Han dynasty", and the Ko Lao Hui or "Society of the Elder Brethren", may be regarded as indistinguishable.

Before proceeding to the history of the Han League in China and to the evidence of its presence in Malaya, it may help to sustain the reader's attention to give at this point a summary of the chief points of interest which will appear from a study of that evidence.

(1) There is a common link between the Hung league and the Han league in the "Peach Garden trio", discussed above. References to the Peach Garden trio in the Hung ritual will be found in Schlegel on the following pages 2, 15, 74, 87, 97, 99, 131, 175, 188, 189 and 217.

(2) The origin of the Han league may ante-date that of the Hung league and the ritual of the Han league may provide that "missing degree" which Ward and Stirling have noted as being absent from the Hung ritual (*see* Chapters VII and VIII *infra*).

(3) In their respective allegorical interpretations discussed in Chapter III the Han may be found to represent the rule of darkness or Earth or "Nature" or Ts'ing (青) while the Hung represents the rule of light or Heaven or Meng (明).

(4) In the allegorical sense the struggle and rivalry between the Han and the Hung in China and overseas, may be interpreted as the struggle between the Yin (陰) and the Yang (陽) principles in Chinese cosmogony or between Evil and Good in the physical world. (*see* Chapter III).

(5) The documents of the Han league as furnished by Playfair refer particularly to the cypress, ts'ung, (松) and fir-tree, pak (柏) which as we shall see in Chapter VI below, were special emblems in the ritual of the Toh-peh-kong society of Penang, which was hostile to the Ghee Hin (Hung) society of Penang and between whom both the Penang war of 1867 and the Larut Wars of 1862–1873 in Perak were fought. References to the cypress and fir-tree occur also in the Hung ritual, but only as emblems of life on this earth, of which they are universal symbols in most religions.

(6) The documents of the Han league suggest that other more modern names for secret societies in use in Malaya, such as the Ts'ung Shun (松 信) and Ts'ung Pak (松 柏) usually found as rivals to the Hung, may also be identified with the Han league.

(7) The ritual of the Han league according to Hutson refers at every turn to the dragon, Lung, (龍), the emblem of imperial authority and power, which also finds a place in the document furnished by Playfair and is constantly found in secret society documents in Malaya, but is not commonly associated with those of the Hung league.

(8) The ritual of the Han league provides for the inclusion of women on a large scale, thus emphasising the Yin (陰) or female principle in its origin. This feature is absent from the Hung ritual which is associated with the Yang (陽) or male principle.

(9) The Han league is identified below with the Ghee Hoa Khun (義 和 拳) or "Boxer" rebellion of 1900 and with the Ghee Hoa Tong (義 和 堂) in French Indo-China of the present day, both of which appear in modern times to be purely political and criminal gang associations, which the Hung league has never professed to be.

(10) Of the Han league's eight lodges given by Hutson, three are named respectively Ghee (義) "rectitude", Shun (信) "sincerity" and Wu Hok (五 福) "Five Happinesses". These may provide among them the origin of the name of the Ghee Hok (義 福) Society of Singapore which has always been hostile to the Ghee Hin lodge of the Hung league.

(11) The suggestion will be made and supported by other evidence in subsequent chapters that the origin of the Ghee Hok Society of Singapore, the Toh Peh Kong Society of Penang, the Hai San society which fought the Ghee Hin in Perak during the Larut Wars, and ultimately the Sa Tiam Hui or Three Dot Brotherhood which is today found throughout the whole of Malaya and neighbouring countries, may all be found in the Han league.

It should be recorded here that the series of papers by Hutson in the *New China Review* which were republished in book form in 1921 under the title *"Chinese life on the Tibetan foothills"*, are the work of an accurate and independent observer to whom the student of these matters owes almost as much as he does to Schlegel. Hutson's papers contain a mine of precise information upon the underside of Chinese life unobtainable elsewhere.

In his Preface to the 1921 edition of his work, this modest scholar says:—
"These studies were never intended for public consumption, but for personal benefit and enlightenment: and it was only at the request of several friends, coupled with the fear of permanent loss owing to the disturbed state of the country, that I was induced to submit them for publication.
The object of the studies was to obtain the Chinese view point concerning the many mysterious customs and practices which perplexed me in daily intercourse with this people.
It should be stated that no foreign text books have been consulted: questions of a scientific, ethnological and comparative nature have been set aside in order to present the local view of the subject in hand. The writer does not claim to have fully attained his end or to have exhausted the information obtainable on any given subject, while variations may be found in almost every county in the province, to say nothing of the whole of China.
The little city of Kwan Hsien, which lies 40 miles to the northwest of Chengtu in the province of Szechuan is the hub of the "Tibetan Foothills". It was from this centre, so richly endowed with natural beauty, so famous for its ancient yet efficient irrigation system, so crowded with a teeming cosmopolitan population, that these pages were gradually compiled.

We now proceed to the evidence.

Hutson's paper[1] on secret societies *New China Review* Vol. II No. 1 of February, 1920 begins :—

"During the past twenty years the writer's calling has often brought him into close contact with and even into sharp opposition to secret society organizations in Szechuan. The chief difficulty in studying such societies is, of course, that they are secret, and the divulging of details is likely to be severely punished.

The difficulty all missionary societies have had in getting a foothold in Szechuan is due to the Tang Tzu Hang (黨子行), or Confucian Society.

The plots of the literati culminated in the riots of 1895. From that year till about 1902 new influences were brought into play by bringing the more lawless elements of society into action. This period might be called the Hypnotic Period; it includes the Yu Man-tzu rebellion of 1898, the Boxer upheaval of 1900, and the local Boxer trouble of 1902, when the Boxer bands even entered the provincial capital.

From 1902 a new phase begins, when the Chien Tzu Hang (韱子行), or Tally Society, made a movement toward the Church to capture it for political purposes, both protective and aggressive. The period ended in the Revolution of 1911.

To be clear, it may be stated here that the Tally Society is the same as the Han Liu (漢流), or Ko Lao Hui (哥老會), and the period may be named the Han Liu period.

After 1911 those who had entered the Church for political reasons tried to get possession of Church property or to start self-governing causes of their own; but always for political or personal advantage. This might be called the Self-government Period.

The first three of the above periods exhibit phenomena important not only now, but acting even in remote antiquity.

The writer believes that this ancient West China fraternity originated in the Totemistic age. That age, which was one of magic, has left many traces, especially in these societies. The frequent mention of the dragon in the organization of the brotherhood abundantly proves its Totemistic origin. The leading Elder Brother is spoken of as the "Dragon's Head." The baser sort, who make a living by roving, are called "Rolling Dragons." And a score of similar instances might be given.

Not to go further back than the end of the Chou (周) dynasty, B.C. 1122-225 we may divide the society of the time into three classes:—

    (1) followers of Confucius—the reform party;

    (2) followers of Lao-Tzu—a mystical party;

    (3) followers of Nature—a reactionary party that developed into the Han Liu fraternity. These three schools of thought can be distinctly seen in the secret society organizations of West China to-day.

The Confucian Society, Tang Tzu Hang (黨子行)

The School, or Society, is very ancient and has always borne an agnostic stamp, both in literature and religion.

The worship of Confucius is a very real thing in China, and the substitution of a tablet for an image, a change made by the Republic, is very superficial. But few, if any, of the Confucian schools have ever been satisfied with the worship of Confucius alone, but freely indulged in the worship of ancestors, and have invited the aid of the Shaman brethren when expedient or when sickness or death in the family made it necessary. Thus, the Confucian scholar may also be a follower of both the mystical and naturalistic schools.

It is readily understood that the class of persons who enter the Confucian Society is different in caste and calibre from those of other societies; but it must be remembered that the agreement is equally binding and the political consequences even more serious than in the case of other societies, and it has been the source of revolutionary activities of great importance.

The Tang Tzu Hang, or Confucian Society is *par excellence* the society of the official, scholar, and student. In its present form it dates at least from the Tang dynasty, when the followers of the "Peach Orchard" trio refused to recognise the Tang and clave to the Han (漢) and Liu (劉) and are called Han Liu. Though the characters are different, some Chinese give this explanation of the Han Liu (漢流).

The Mystical or Hypnotic Sect, Chiao-fei (教匪)

The Hypnotic School (No. 2 above) has always been closely connected with the Taoist sect, with charms, trances, and spells of various kinds; and it may be that some of the exploits attributed to ancient heroes were done under hypnotic influence. The trances, etc., are brought about by regular training of mind and body, a rigid concentration of spirit, and complete submission of the being to the domination of some particular demon: when the training is complete the whole person is under the mesmeric control of the demon.

The rallying centre of these hypnotic sects is generally a living goddess of mercy, usually a girl of sixteen or eighteen or even younger; doubtless the remnant of a cruder, naturalistic system of great antiquity.

Footnote.—(1) The importance of this paper and the frequent references to it in subsequent chapters, has suggested its reproduction here in bold type, for the convenience of the reader.

There is quite a long list of these sects which have caused insurrection and bloodshed in different parts of the country. These religious fanatics, *chiao fei*, have caused much more difficulty to the government than the ordinary *ku-fei* (喝匪) (*v. inf.*). The latter rob for their sustenance, and having stolen enough they live luxuriously till there is need for another raid to get more funds. But the religious fanatics are of a very different character.

Such societies seek first by charms and vegetarian vows to win the rich and landed classes. They promise immortality as the reward of large liberality and abstinence from fornication, wine, and pork. The entrance fee is generally small, but members have only the common purse; even rice and clothing are held for the common use.

Having gained a footing among the rich, they next win over the village headmen, and finally the retainers of the district magistrate. When trouble arises, the magistrate may send to suppress it and may even raid the Society's headquarters; but care is taken that the propagandists are protected and escorted to their resorts in the southern mountains.

Such societies may differ in the charms they use and the idols they worship; but they have mesmeric hypnotism and fanatical trances as their common feature.

In this category are included the—

> White Lotus Society (白蓮敎),
> The Arabic or Square Heavens Society (天方),
> The Eight-Diagram Society (八卦),
> The Red Lantern Society (紅燈敎),[1]
> The United Fists Society (義和拳),[1]
> The Big Sword Society (大刀會),
> The Lamp-wick Society (燈花敎), and others.

The many rebellious movements and rebel leaders with which and with whom these Societies are connected will be found in history.

In Szechuan many people knew the boxer arts before 1900, especially round such centres as Paoning (保寧), Mienchou (綿州), and Chin Tang hsien (金堂); but there was not enough strength or organization for a rising.

The hypnotic arts are still practised in secret in different part of the province, but more especially in the North, their original home. The vows used are many and various, but the chief are for the purification of the body and of the mouth. Their charms also are very abundant, the chief ones being the Kao Wang (高王符) charm and the Goddess of Mercy (觀音) charm.

In 1905 a hypnotic sect entered Szechuan from Shensi and disturbed the eastern and southern parts of the province. It was known as the Ching Cha Chiao (清察敎), or Clear Tea Society. Its charms were similar to those of the Red Lantern Society; but the vows were different and seem to have originated in the Yangtze provinces, for the "tea-planter's ballad" was used in the religious observances.

During the short reign of Hsuan Tung a religious sect drilled and caused trouble in eastern Szechuan; but they never got out of control owing to the severe measures taken against them by the authorities.

The Reactionary School, or Han Liu (漢流)

This is our third great class of secret societies (No. 3 above). It must be borne in mind that our division is by no means arbitrary. It is quite possible for a person to belong to all three classes; on the other hand there has sometimes been strife, especially between the Hypnotic and the Reactionary Schools.

Investigating the origin of this School we find it begins in hoary antiquity, and probably represents the most ancient demon worship. The class tenaciously holds to natural depravity, resists external reforms, and through the ages has made licentious liberty the chief ideal of life.

The heroes worshipped are the "Peach Orchard" trio of the Han dynasty; but they have also a system of Shamanism probably of much earlier date, and including all manner of sorcerers' and wizards' art.

Among other terms the brethren call themselves *tsa-men ti-hsiung* (咱們弟兄), "We brethren." *Tsa-men* is of northern origin and Shamanism had its capital in Northern Asia; hence I believe this brotherhood to be Asiatic Shamanism. This system of Shamanism has very wide ramifications in Central Asia, where neither race nor religion seems to debar any one from joining the secret conclaves. On the Tibetan border Chinese and aboriginals make sworn covenants for mutual protection and assistance in business matters. No Chinese could prosper in barter trade with Tibetans unless he was a member of this Society; he would most likely be robbed and killed on his first journey.

The sorcery practices which are such a feature in this brotherhood are presided over by a system of lay Taoist priests called *ho-chu-tao* (夥居道). These men, though knowing all the arts of the exorcist and much of the doctrine of Tao, are not celibates or hermits, as in the regular priesthood, but have their homes among men and around their ancestral tablets.

Footnote.—(1) Particular note must be made of the Chinese names for the Red Lantern Society and United Fists Society given in this list, because these are the names by which the "Boxers" were commonly known during their rebellion in 1900. (*see infra*).

The Society delights in sorcery and wizardry, and on the slightest pretext members present one another with a "pacification concert." Such occasions as a sickness in the family, a slight bodily injury, an unlucky omen, etc., are seized on as excuses for a midnight orgy to expel some troublesome demon. At the close of such uproarious nocturnal performances the baser sort amuse themselves by committing robberies on their way home in the small hours.

The weird music connected with Shaman worship needs to be heard, for no pen can describe the uncanny effects; the drum of the temple, the blast of the trumpet, the conch horn of the wizard, the hooting cow's horns of the priests, the clash of cymbals, the crash of gongs, the howling of demon-oppressed people, the cry to departing spirits, are all directly or indirectly related to this brotherhood.

Many primitive and objectionable customs are still practised in the sect. Marriage by capture is by no means unknown, and to many it is the ideal method. Eating the liver and the heart of an enemy, or distributing parts of his body to distant places for others to eat; the sacrifice of human victims to the flags or to the spirit of a fallen comrade, are customs still practised.

The Society has thus earned the name ho-êrh-liu (和 而 流), or loose profligates.

The Szechuan Ku-lu-tzu (喎 嚕 子)

The province was practically depopulated by the robber bands of Li Tzu-cheng (李 自 成) Chang Hsien-chung (張 獻 忠), Wang San-huai (王 三 槐), and others. Many were slaughtered, many fled. Afterwards immigrants from Hupei, Hunan, and other provinces occupied the deserted soil and bound themselves by oaths for mutual protection against remnants of robber bands or returning émigrés.

Many old inhabitants returned, to find their lands in possession of strangers. Such people, the weak taking to beggary, the strong to robbery, together with the scattered remnants of the earlier robber bands, all together received the name of ku-lu-tzu.[1]

This term is peculiar to Szechuan and it was contracted into ku-fei (喎 匪). The explanation of this is not satisfactory. The Kuang Yun (廣 韻)[2] says that ku resembles the sound of quacking and gabbling, while lu means flattering words such as beggars use. The Cheng Tzu Tung (正 字 通)[3] speaks of tu-lu (吐 嚕) as meaning ko-hsi (可 惜), a term of pity. In some parts evilly disposed beggars are still called tu-lu-tzu, so it is possible that it is a term of pity, and meant, pity the poor aborigine. Some explain by saying the ku-fei were to be feared because of their number and character while the lu-fei were to be pitied because of their extreme poverty. This explanation, which seems reasonable, makes the term ku-lu-tzu mean robbers and beggars; and it may have been applied by the Mongol and Manchu troops who came to the province to restore order.

As the Ts'ing dynasty gradually got control of the country the ku-lu-tzu were dispersed, and began to be spoken of as pi-fei (痞 匪), which means obstructionists. They were also jokingly called hsien-ta-lang (閑 打 浪), or idle wavebeaters; this is now contracted to ta-lang-êrh, and seems to mean one who lives by his wits or his luck.

These obstructionists lived in blue tents, and were used as entertainers at funerals or festivities. On such occasions they pitched their tents at the door of the dwelling house where they were invited and opened a gambling booth for the entertainment of the visitors.

Such entertainers were divided into two distinct classes, the red cash and the black cash fraternity. The latter made secret vows amid the sacrificial burnings of the incense hall, carried arms, and lived by burglaries. The red cash fraternity occupied themselves with slitting open cash bags or cutting off the last 200 cash on a string of cash. If any red cash brother got caught and was branded on the face he was at once degraded into the black cash brotherhood. These two classes exist to-day, the red cash people being gamblers and pickpockets by daylight while the black cash brethren live by burglary in the dark.[4]

The settlers from other provinces naturally hated all ku-lu-tzu, and called them "rats" because of their nocturnal habits and because they so readily disappeared on the approach of the enemy. In the south of the province any one with the look of an aborigine is still called a rat. But the curse has come home to roost, for in Hupei and Hunan all Szechuanese are now called by this term, whatever their extraction. In retaliation the Hupei people in Szechuan are contemptuously termed "Hupei bean-curd."

In spite of Government and settlers (in the Szechuan Province) the ku-lu-tzu have never been exterminated, and they continue to style themselves the Han Liu.

The terms "Han Liu" and ku-lu-tzu or, ku-fei (喎 匪), seem synonymous, the former being used by the brethren, the latter being applied to them by the officials. The former term implies their wish to preserve the ancient Han ideals and aspirations as against Mongol and Manchu influences. The other term, ku-fei indicates that the officials regard them as malcontents and opponents of law and order.

Footnote.—(1) This term should be particularly noted as it was one applied to the "Boxers" in 1900.

Footnote.—(2) The name of a Chinese rhyming dictionary.

Footnote.—(3) The name of a cyclopaedia.

Footnote.—(4) The red and the black cash must not be confused with the red and the black flags, to be mentioned later.

For many years before the Hsien Fêng reign (A.D. 1851-62) the "Yellow River was at peace," that is, was free from rebellion. Then the *ku-fei*, rose[1] in revolt under the leadership of Lan Ta-shun (藍 大 順) and Li Tuan-ta (李 短 韃). The different characters of these two are shown by their nicknames, "Lan hurry up," and "Li go slowly." Though not natives of Szechuan Province they easily persuaded the *ku-fei* to join them against the Manchus. The revolt was quelled by Hunan troops under Viceroy Lo Wen-chung. The remnants of Lan's marauders were scattered in Tsung Ching-chou, Kuan-hsien, and Tai-I hsien. These districts west of the Min River seem to have been also the chief refuge of Chang Hsien-chung's bands, which no doubt accounts for the lawless, ungovernable character of the population there.

After Lo Wen-chung's coming the *ku-fei* began to be called *tu-fei*, but the former term is still known and is sometimes applied to them by officials. The term *tu* was used of the aboriginal tribes, and *fei* probably meant they were not fit to be classed as men, *fei-jen* (非 人). This term, *fei-jen* (匪 人), has been systematically applied to all aborigines all over China.

The meaning of Han Liu is also variously given; some regard it as meaning simply brigands; others say the name means the descendants of Liu Pei (劉 備) of the Han dynasty; but it most likely means the descendants of the obstructives and outcasts of the Han period.

It may safely be said that there is now little or no difference between Han Liu, *ku-fei*, *tu-fei*, *pao-ko* (胞 哥), *ko-lao* (哥 老), and *chiang-hu* (江 湖); all are somehow linked up in one great fraternity. The prestige of some brethren extends over several provinces and it would be highly interesting to trace the connection between the Dragon throne and the rolling dragons of the provinces.

The Ko-lao-hui and the Han Liu

With the advent of Lo-Wen-chung and the suppression of Lan Ta-shun's revolt about 1855, a new secret society organization seems to have been introduced into the province of Szechuan in the shape of the Ko-lao-hui. Some Chinese state that it was introduced by the government as a check to the Han Liu. It is more generally held, however, that Lo's Hunan braves brought it with them. Many of these soldiers settled in Szechuan and their brotherhood gradually amalgamated with that of the Han Liu. It would seem as if there was also a union with some piratical elements. The term *chiang-hu* (江 湖), so often used, means "rivers and lakes" and is supposed to mean "rovers of the waters." The terms *to-pa-tzu* (抢 把 子), "helmsman"; *ma-tou* (碼 頭), "anchorage"; *hai* (海), "sea"; *shui* (水), "water"; all seem to point to a piratical origin, but are in constant use in the fraternity.

Lodges of the Ko Lao Hui

The Ko-lao-hui was originally divided into eight lodges, each known by a distinctive character[2], as follows: (1) *jen* (仁), "benevolence"; (2) *i* (義), "rectitude"; (3) *li* (禮), "propriety"; (4) *chih* (智), "wisdom"; (5) *hsin* (信), "sincerity"; (6) *san-yuan* (三 元), "the Taoist trinity"; (7) *ssu-hsi* (四 喜), "four joys"; (8) *wu-fu* (五 福), "five happinesses."

All recognize the Benevolent Lodge as being not only the senior, but also the aristocratic part of the brotherhood. Its members are called (清 水 胞 哥) "clear-water womb-brothers"; their conduct is more enlightened and their customs more rigid than in the other lodges. This Benevolent Lodge is now amalgamated with the Western Lodge of ancient Han Liu, and I believe their character-marks are interchangeable.

In the second, or Rectitude Lodge, are massed the turbid-water (渾 水) womb-brothers, probably the real Han Liu members; all the lawless elements in the district adjoining Chengtu are mustered under this Rectitude mark.

In these districts, strange to say, a few belong to the Benevolent Lodge, the majority to the Rectitude Lodge, and the other lodges are mere empty names. In districts on the Yangtze, however, it is not so; there, some of the other lodges are fully occupied and organized; the Ko-lao-hui element seems the stronger there, while in the Chengtu districts the Han Liu element predominates.

Those in the Rectitude Lodge call the brethren of the Benevolent Lodge by the term "uncle." It is sometimes easy to mistake the sworn adoptive relationships for those of blood.

Each lodge has twelve grades of membership, *pai* (排) or *tai* (代).

The first consists of the presiding elder (坐 堂 大 爺), *tso tang ta yeh*, and the vice president, *ti tiao* (提 調) *ta yeh*. The former position is a very important one, since all believe that the success of their meetings rests on the virtues of their president.

The second grade is called *Wu sheng* (武 聖). Few dare assume the responsibilities of this grade, for their lot in life will then be poor and mouldy and their luck mean and miserable. Some Buddhist or Taoist priests are generally found to shoulder the responsibilities.

The third grade is known as *Hsuan Hou* (桓 侯) *san yeh*, Hsuan Hou being Chang Fei (張 飛), of the "Peach Orchard" trio.

Footnote.—(1) This rising was contemporaneous with the Dagger Society rebellion in Amoy of 1853. The Dagger rebels many of whom came from Szechuan were probably members of the Ko Lao Hui. (*see* Chapter IV).

Footnote.—(2) Particular note should be made of these names for purposes of later comparison with names found in Malaya.

The fourth grade stands with no representative, in fact no one would be allowed to take a position under the grade even if willing. The cause is superstition; *ssu* (四), "four," is akin in sound to *shih* (事), "trouble," and is the same except in tone as *ssu* (死), "death."

The fifth grade is called *Kuan shih* (管 事) *wu yeh*. This is a very important position, occupied by two men at each "anchorage," known as the red flag and the black flag managers (紅 旗), and (黑 旗), *Hung chi* and *hei chi Kuan shih*. Most power is in the hands of the former, while most of the drudgery falls to the latter, who is generally a man of inferior ability or one who has been degraded to that position for some misdemeanour. Sometimes, however, a rich man with plenty of money to lose and no brains for managing business may be made black flag leader. From the sixth grade downwards the grades are simply known by numbers. But number seven is another grade without a representative, its positions being mere empty names. This is owing to the character for "seven" being akin in sound to the character "to slice."

The eighth grade is called *lao pa* (老 八), or *jao pa* (么 八), and the last grade is called *lao jao* or *hsiao lao jao* (小 老 么)[1].

Any one may buy his way to the top of the Society, *i pu teng tien* (一 步 登 天), "rising to heaven at one step." Such a one enters the Benevolent Lodge as a senior brother, and is called *hsien pai* (閒 排) *ta yeh* or leisure-grade brother." Another term for such is *mao ting* (帽 頂), or "cap top."

The entrance fee for one and all is 1,280 cash. A candidate, *hsin fu* (新 福), must find some one to introduce him and also a guarantor for his good faith. All recruits first enter the grade *lao jao*, but those with ability soon get promoted. On entrance the introducer and guarantor must have presents and all along the line superiors must be honoured and humoured with gifts. The rank and file of the Rectitude Lodge on meeting the elders of the Benevolent Lodge have to show respect by a three-fold kotow. This is called "one shot with three reports" (一 砲 三 響), *i pao san hsiang*. If the knocks of the head on the ground are not distinctly heard it is considered a lack of reverence.

Meetings are generally held in out-of-the-way villages or in some large secluded temple. They are called *kai tang* (開 堂), "to open the hall"; *shao hui* (燒 會), "meeting to burn (incense?)"; *tso fang shou* (做 方 手), which probably means the "crossing of the hands to the four points of the compass"; *tso hsien shih* (做 賢 事), "practising the acts of the worthies."

These gatherings are generally held at the time of some festival such as the Single Sword Festival (單 刀 會), the 13th of the 5th moon; the Ching Ming (清 明) Festival, about April 5; the Yu Lan (孟 蘭), Festival in the 7th moon; and at the New Year. (In this way Society business may be done in better security and the officials are deceived) Expenses are met by contributions and entrance fees from novices, by fines for misdemeanours, etc. An elder brother of the Benevolent Lodge is generally invited to preside or "sit on the dragon's head" (坐 龍 頭), *tso lung tou*. He is treated with great respect and formality.

On a dais in the centre of the meeting place is a tablet to Kuan Yu, which is worshipped by all. Before the tablet swords are hung from the roof, and it is supposed that the fear of a sword falling on them will prevent people from worshipping with wrong motives.

Younger members are detached to guard the entrances; they scrutinize every comer so as to guard against attack or surprise by the officials.

The red and the black flag leaders make orations, which are mere gibberish to the uninitiated; the list of members' names is presented on the dais and worshipped; the president reads aloud the rules of the Society; the novices are introduced by their guarantors to the *Kuan shih* of the 5th grade and he announces their nomination and reception into the lodge.

The following oath is then read: 我們今夜晚結拜一不當卯子二不當眼睛如有當眼子常眼睛照香而死照鷄而亡. The meaning is roughly this: "We are met here in conclave to-night; if there should be any false ones come to spy they may die as this incense and perish as this fowl." The incense is then ignited and chopped in two; the chicken's head is chopped off, the blood drained into a bowl of wine, and all the company drink it.

The new members must then worship the tablet beneath the suspended blades, repeat the above oath and drink of the wine. Matters of discipline are attended to; some members are degraded and some expelled. Where time for repentance is allowed, the offender has to kneel before the tablet and apply a dagger to his thigh till the blood flows freely. This is called *pu chiao-tao* (撲 尖 刀), "falling on the knife." The culprit may choose another way of showing penitence—by putting nails on the ground, points upward, and rolling on them naked till his body is bloody. This is called *Kun ting pan*, (滾 釘 板), "rolling on the nailed board."

The wretch to whom the tribune refuses space for repentance is at once led out to some grove or other secluded spot and despatched with the sword; the body is thrown into the river or left to be devoured by dogs.

Those who have done meritorious service to the whole Society or for the senior brethren are raised in rank and honoured by the assembly.

The president then announces that the particular meeting will be known as such and such a hill or water or hall; this enables new members to refer to their initiation without divulging the place of meeting. The novices who first enter the Society and have their positions defined later

---

Footnote.—(1) These terms evidently mean "Eighth grade brother": "Little eight" and "Little tenderfoot", respectively.

are said "to first ascend the hill and then plant the willow." The reverse is said of those who before entering state what position they will hold; and it is these who provide the midnight feast for the assembly.

A member absenting himself from the meetings is punished by being reduced in rank for the second offence, and excluded from the Society for the third. This means he will no longer have the Society's protection; and though while law and order are maintained he may be safe, when there are disturbances he will most likely pay for broken vows with his life.

Each district has an "anchorage" (碼頭), ma tou, also knowns as kung-kou or tang-kou since the use of kung-tang (公堂) has been forbidden by law. Each anchorage has a resident elder living in the hall. These halls are often in the houses of the elder brother himself. He keeps a register of affiliated halls and of his own sworn brethren; he entertains guests from a distance and advises or helps brethren who appeal to him for protection or money. Members from other districts should notify their arrival; otherwise if they get into any trouble they will get no help till they have owned their fault. The elder brother of a hall has tremendous power; his orders (上覆), shang-fu, ought to be obeyed without questioning by every loyal Han Liu.

Certain classes, such as barbers, chairbearers, etc., are not allowed to enter the Society. Persons who try to pass themselves off as chiang-hu "rivers and lakes", a degree of the brotherhood (see above) or pretend to higher rank than they really hold are punished by a special tribunal.

The book of rules of the Society is called hai-ti-shu, "book of the sea-bottom"; its chief tenets are filial piety, rectitude, benevolence and reverence.

The use of passwords is common. Without knowing the password an entrance might possibly be got into a secret meeting; but I am told it would be practically impossible for the offender to get out alive.

Within the Rectitude Lodge there are cliques whose influence is wholly evil; these are called hui-fei, "Society rascals."

Women play a large part in the Society; leading women being called nu-kuang-kun (女光棍) or "female polished sticks." Youths have a juvenile society organized on the model of the adult Society and known as the pang (棒) pang hui or Cudgel Society. They exchange cards, make vows, conduct fights and organize petty persecutions of those whom they dislike.

Each anchorage has a ying-pin-hui (迎賓) with a fund for the entertainment of visitors.

The salutations of the Society are very complex. The general term for them is tiu-chien-tzu (丟筮子), or "casting the tally." Salutations to the chief, second, third, and fifth grades are by placing the hand on the shoulder, elbow, forearm or wrist. Between equals the salutation called "right and left twist (左右歪子), tso-yu-wai-tzu, is used. Thus the status of members can be recognized at once without enquiry.

A country robber is known as pang-ke, "cudgel guest," and the keeper of a robber's den is called (窩戶) wo-hu. Such a keeper has great influence, and may be the helmsman of an anchorage. He receives a large share of the booty. Stolen goods are hidden for a time, then taken into the capital and pawned for a term of years. Later they are dyed and altered and sold to second-hand dealers. The helmsman is nearly always acquainted with the reasons for murders, arsons and robberies in his locality and with the means used.

I have learned on good authority that many people go from home ostensibly on business, but really for dishonourable purposes, for work they can do at a distance with a good conscience, though they would not degrade themselves by doing it near home. If they should happen to relieve of his goods some notable in the Society, the property will soon be restored if he applies in the proper quarter at once, before it is sold or pawned.

It must not be supposed that only the poor and illiterate compose the Han Liu Sodality: many sons of the country gentry join through love of money and adventure. Thus robberies are not made by the poor and half starved so much as by the strong and able-bodied who are in comfortable circumstances. In fact, but for the connivance and help of the rich it would be impossible for the rogues to carry on their depredations. People say that when a robber gang is equipped for action and makes its appearance at dead of night it is a terrifying sight. Torches are fixed in their caps or hats, their faces are painted with hideous colours, they are armed with battering rams, swords, clubs, crowbars, and latterly with rifles and Mauser pistols. Their attack is sudden and determined, but at the slightest alarm they retire, carrying with them what silver and valuables they have been able to secure. Prior to the raid some servant has been bribed to reveal where the silver is kept.

If any of the gang should be caught, there is danger that secrets may be let out; but some of the descendants of Lan Ta-shun's bands will defy torture and scorn death. No officials can get their secrets either by torture or cajolery; and no severities used on them seem to have any moral effect on the rest of the gang; indeed it sometimes seems as though the more are killed the more the membership grows.

The chief Han Liu ideal is liberty, which means to them anarchy, selfishness and depravity, and it may be said that the Society is always "agin the government." They are under a kind of military rule, make their own laws and reserve all rights of interpreting and administering them.

There is, however, a growing tendency to social equality and the senior brother does not enjoy the same blind obedience as formerly. Among certain classes his word is no longer law. The tendency is to follow a popular man apart from his social standing; but such a man soon finds himself in a difficult and dangerous position.

In such an organization there must be jealousy and strife. Even in peaceful times deep enmity may exist on personal grounds, between two anchorages in the same street. These factions have been compared to two tigers in the same forest,—fighting must ensue. Suspicion and envy develop into hatred and murder. Officials take advantage and use one faction against another; then secrets are divulged, mutual recriminations follow, and hatred is engendered which may last for generations, one victim after another on both sides being murdered in revenge. A son's duty to avenge a parent's wrong cannot be shirked.

Such conditions produce in members a cruel and relentless disposition, and foster a suspicious and revengeful nature.

As already mentioned, the place held by women in this secret society is not a small one. Many are sworn members, and the mothers and wives are often able assistants of male members. They spy out the land, hide the booty and screen the guilty. It is a rare thing for a woman to be put to death for implication in robbery and it must be remembered that the mother of adventurous sons will also rear daughters of a similar character, who in turn become the mothers of a new generation of desperate adventurers; and thus a constant succession is assured in spite of official reprisals on the males. Here lies a social problem of immense importance, which might well tax the heart and brain of some great statesman. If brute force could cure the moral and social ills of this people it would by this time have had some effect; but torture and capital punishment have proved futile, and nothing short of a moral and spiritual regeneration will change the Han Liu adventurer into a law-abiding citizen.

This regeneration seems especially necessary for the female population, for the saying, "She who rocks the cradle rules the world" is true in Western China—she who carries the baby rules the land. So long as we have a race of women vicious enough to murder their own offspring in large numbers, to bind their daughters' feet, to abet the men in every crime, so long we shall have a race of brigands and buccaneers to terrify the country at every opportunity.

The hypnotic sects work secretly with the wiliness of serpents till they gain a secure hold; the naturalistic sects are full of bluster and pantomime, yet their propaganda is secret and swift. When either of these elements gains the upper hand the whole district is made to quake. Their methods of blackmail are inimitably ingenious; their revenge on traitors, swift and unswerving. Their cruelties to enemies are indescribable. When their passions are roused their victim will be hacked to pieces, each person cutting off just as much as he desires of the common enemy's flesh. The more daring and cunning he has been the more is his liver and gall wished for, since it is believed that by eating these one's own valour and cunning will be increased.

Before the Revolution of 1911 and the organization of the Railway League, the Society men always had to be reckoned with; but since that date their influence has been supreme, and no one dare give offence to them, however much grieved or injured. If a society rascal is arrested neighbours dare not refuse to bail him out, and whole families may be ruined for the divulging of a secret. The best policy for all is to humour the members and avoid any action that would rouse their wrath.

The Railway League (同志會), tung chih hui

The Han Liu, true to its ancient traditions, is still the enemy of all reform, and is ever ready for any pretext of making trouble. The proposal to introduce railways into the province (of Szechuan) caused the formation of the so-called Railway League, in Chinese, "The Society of united purpose for protection of the way". It was really an amalgamation of the Confucian Society with the Han Liu for the purpose of opposing a railway system financed by foreign capital. The new name should not mislead the student; it was simply a revival of the revolutionary brotherhood reinforced by the addition of the weaker Confucian Society. The League leaders were the Han Liu leading elder brothers, and the organization was the anchorage system of the Han Liu.

A rebellion broke out first in Kwan hsien and the other districts already specified as full of brigand stock. The lawless wretches carried devastation and anarchy wherever they marched. They got more than they expected or wanted, but at the downfall of the Manchus they immediately set up the Han Republic (大漢), Ta Han. With the new government many of these outlaws got wealth and were decorated with medals for services rendered to the country, were much honoured by the Republican party, and became honoured officials of the new government. At that period the people had no one to appeal to for redress, since a magistrate was less powerful than a robber; as the Chinese said, "Robbery was done according to law." The poor fled their homes and suffered terribly, and the rich were blackmailed and bullied without mercy. Only those who passed through that crisis know how paralyzing was the grip of the Han Liu octopus.

Later on such taunts were thrown at the Szechuan Republican party that they determined to reform and started a new Society called the Hsi hua Kung hui (西華公會)[1]. The purpose was to dissolve the Railway League and then to eradicate the lawless elements of the She hui (社會) or Republican party, raising the rest to a higher standard of citizenship. A system of badges was instituted by which the senior brethren in each country might be recognized, and each clan head was made responsible for all of his name in his district.

Once more the Han Liu Society was faithful to itself, refused to acknowledge the new Society and declined to be reformed. The difficulty thus created was only relieved by an official order

Footnote.—(1) "The West China Association".

to dissolve all Secret Societies, making all alike illegal.   The new Society melted its silver badges, but it seems impossible to hope for the extermination of the Han Liu, which, in spite of all adversity, has thriven for so many centuries.   There have been later attempts at reform but they seem futile.   The society has entered into ninety per cent. of the homes, permeated all society, controlled well-nigh every institution in Western Shu and probably in a much wider area''.

Several interesting points of comparison present themselves between the above description and the initiation ritual of the Sa Tiam Hui or Three Dot Brotherhood as practised in Malaya to-day and discussed in Chapters VIII and IX *infra*.

At no point do these comparisons coincide with the ritual of the Triad Society and the belief that the Han Liu formulary is of separate and distinct origin and not a truncated version of the Triad ritual, is thereby strengthened.

The following is Playfair's article (from *The China Review*, 1886–1887, Vol. 15.) which introduces us to the only known extant document of the Ko Lao Hui and provides several further interesting points of comparison.

The article is given in full:—

THE KOLAO 哥 老 SECRET SOCIETY.

At the end of August 1886 two men were arrested by the Shanghai Police and brought before the Mixed Court charged with attempting to extract money from shopkeepers.   So far the case was in no way unusual.   The extraordinary feature of it was that, when arrested, one of the prisoners attempted to swallow some documents he had concealed on his person, and these turned out to be three tickets of membership in the well-known Kolao 哥老 Secret Society.   I availed myself of my position as assessor to secure one of the tickets and the following is a description of it—

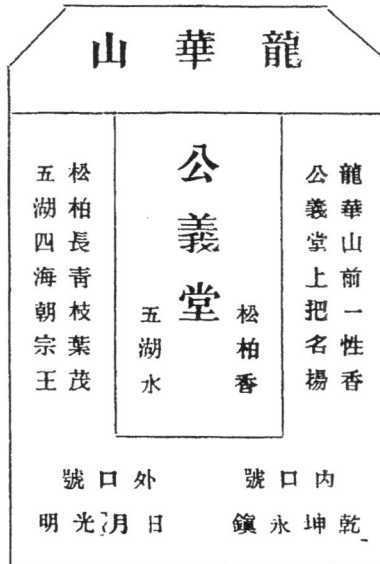

```
                山   華   龍

   五 松                        龍 公
   湖 柏          公              華 義
   四 長                        山 堂
   海 青          義       松     前 上
   朝 枝                   柏     一 把
   宗 葉          堂   五   香     性 名
   王 茂              湖         香 揚
                      水

        號 口 外              號 口 內

        明 光 月 日          鎮 永 坤 乾
```

The material is linen and the stamp is a parallelogram measuring about $3'' \times 6''$, the top corners truncated.   The upper segment, about ¾ inch deep, bears an inscription, black on a white ground, which I will designate 'A'.   There is a central parallelogram measuring $1½'' \times 4''$, also containing an inscription in black on a white ground (B).   The remainder of the ticket consists of a strip an inch wide running round three sides of the central parallelogram; the right side I shall refer to as 'C', the left side as 'D' and the portion at foot 'E'.

'A'.   Horizontally in large characters 龍 華 山 Lung-hua Shan.   I have not been able to localise this hill, but it is probably in the Hukuang provinces.

'B'.   In the centre of the upper portion written vertically in large characters 公 義 堂, which might be translated "Hall of Patriotism".

To the right of the upper portion in smaller characters, written vertically, 督辦國字號羅 "Lo, controller of the section distinguished by the character Kuo".   This does not form part of the original ticket, but is affixed from a separate stamp.   (Not shown in specimen reproduced).

To the right of the lower portion, in medium sized vertical characters, 松 栢 香 Perfume of fir and cypress.

To the left, similarly, 五 湖 水 Water of the Five Lakes.

On the upper portion of 'B' is impressed obliquely a red seal bearing in seal character the inscription 都 統 龍 莽 "The Superintendent of Lung Hua". (Not shown in the reproduction).

'C' and 'D' contain each two lines of a rhyming quatrain, written vertically in small characters.

'C'. 龍 華 山 前 一 性 香
     公 義 堂 上 把 名 揚

'D'. 松 栢 長 青 枝 葉 茂
     五 湖 四 海 朝 宗 王

(The sixth character in the first line 性 is a misprint for 炷). The translation is as follows:—

"Before the Lung-hua mountain set a stick of incense flame; within the Kung-yi Hall "go win yourself an honoured name; the cypress and the fir o'erhead their leaves in green "luxuriance spread; the five lakes and four seas one universal lord proclaim".

'E'. Contains two lines written horizontally and may be divided into two sections, right and left.

Right 內 口 號 Inner password;
乾 坤 永 鎮 Heaven and Earth keep watch continually.

Left 外 口 號 Outer password;
日 月 光 明 The Sun and Moon shine clear.

It may be added that the Kolao Society resembles Freemasonry and it is not essentially seditious. Its members have, however, so often used the organization for evil purposes, that membership is forbidden by Government under severe penalties.

In this important article by Playfair special note should be made of the references to the Lung-hua Mountain: the cypress and fir tree: water and lakes, which will recur.

The following extract is from the article by Frederick Boyle, published in *Harper's Magazine*, September, 1891 pages 601–602:—

"The Ko-Lao Hwey, or League of the Elder Brother dates only from the time of the Taiping rebellion, when, as report goes, General Tseng-Kuo-fan himself established it during the siege of Nanking. This is a very dangerous association, said to be growing in strength continually. As the T'ien-Ti has its home in Hok-Kien and as the Wu-Wei Keaou in Nanking, so the Ko-Lao makes its headquarters in Hunan and Honan, the central provinces. It claims to represent the pure Chinese race, the sons of Han, to whom the inhabitants of the South and West are almost as foreign as are the Tartars. These malcontents look behind the Ming dynasty, as the name "Elder Brother" implies, to the imperial line of Tang, which is supposed to be extinct long ago, but doubtless a scion will be forthcoming when the throne is vacant. The society consists of soldiers mostly, but it is understood that some affiliates occupy very high positions indeed, as we should expect when they advocate such a policy. A very desperate and disreputable band they are by all accounts, numbering a large proportion of the bad characters in those districts where they have influence. Mr. Balfour says, however, "There is not the slightest doubt that if one of their old generals were to raise the standard of rebellion, he might have a hundred thousand men about him in the time it takes to spread the news from Nanking to Hankow".

The Ko-Lao is, in fact, a military conspiracy. Its agents commonly travel as doctors, carrying news from one centre to another, and making proselytes as they go. The ceremonial of initiation is said to be elaborate, but I have heard no details. An association of old soldiers designed to overthrow the civil power is naturally turbulent. The Ko-Lao has broken out several times during its brief existence. In 1870 and 1871 it raised serious disturbances in Hunan, but the grand movement was disconcerted by a lucky chance. A secret letter containing the plan for blowing up the powder-magazine at Hukow was delivered to the wrong person. It named several of the chief conspirators, who were seized and promptly executed. In that neighbourhood the society was suppressed for a while. But its attraction for the men of the central provinces, who hate their kinsfolk all round, must be very strong".

Although very superficial, the foregoing shows that the Society was active at the time of the T'ai P'ing rebellion, which event in China (1849–64) and its connection with the Hakka (Kheh) tribes and thence its influence upon the immigrant stream into Malaya in the second half of the nineteenth century, is discussed in Chapter IV *infra*.

There is also the probable association of the Dagger Society of Amoy with the Ko Lao Hui.

The Dagger Society Rebellion in Amoy of 1853, which had close connection with Singapore is also referred to in Chapter IV.

Although the Headquarters of the Ko Lao Hui are given by Hutson as Szechuan, and by Boyle as Honan, the Society appears from Playfair's notice, to have been widely dispersed, and there seems to have been no historical obstacle to its members reaching Malaya during the nineteenth century, most likely perhaps, amongst Hokkien, Teochew, and Hakka immigrants.

Dyer Ball *Things Chinese* (1903) page 656 has:—

"An association which has attracted some attention lately is the Ko Lao Wui which has its Headquarters in the province of Hunan, the army being honeycombed by this political associations which, like the Triad, has for its object the overthrow of the present dynasty.....It was believed by some to be answerable for the riots a few years ago directed against foreigners in Central China".

Some of these riots taken from Dyer Ball's list *op. cit.* page 611–612 were:—

July 1st 1886.	Serious riot at Chung King (Szechuan).
May–Sept. 1891.	Wide-spread anti-foreign and anti-missionary riots throughout Central China.
May 29th 1895.	Anti-foreign riots in Szechuan Province.

March 16th 1898.	American Mission in suburbs of Chung King (Szechuan) sacked by mob, one Chinese medical assistant murdered.
July 8th 1898.	Protestant and Catholic missions attacked by rioters at Shum-ching-fu in Szechuan.
Oct. 15th 1898.	Rioting at Ho Chou 50 miles from Chung King (Szechuan) American and French mission places attacked and burnt.
1899–1900.	*The Boxer Rebellion. Widespread massacre of foreign missionaries.*
August 15th 1902.	Murder of two missionaries at Chengchou Hunan.

It will be noticed that (these anti-foreign mission riots largely centre round the provinces of Szechuan and Hunan, the home of the Ko Lao Hui.) Hutson *op. cit.* states that (the Boxer rebellion was in fact, a rising of the Ko Lao Hui against foreigners.) (*see* note below on the *Boxers*).

Dyer Ball *op. cit.* page 656 writing in 1903 continues:—

"Its (Ko Lao Hui) organisation is in all probability on somewhat similar lines to that of the Triad Society....... It is described as resembling freemasonry and not essentially seditious, *but opportunities for a thorough study of it have not yet been afforded to those interested in such subjects*....... Instead of seeking to re-establish the Ming Dynasty, it would appear to look further back, even as far as to the T'ang Dynasty....... The Ko Lao Hui Society is known to have been in existence for the past twenty years, and there are great numbers of men connected with it distributed over the provinces of Kiangsu, Anhui, Hunan, Hupeh, Kiangsi and *Kwangtung*".

As the Cantonese themselves were mostly wedded to the Triad the above-mentioned "men from Kwangtung" would most likely be Hakkas, a sketch of whose history is given in Chapter IV.

The following is an extract from Heckethorn's *Secret Societies* Vol. II page 136:—

The Ko Lao Hui.—The secret society which at the present day (1896) seems most powerful in China, is that known by the above name. (It was at first a purely military association, whose object was mutual protection against the plunder and extortion practised by the civil officials in dealing with the pay and maintenance of the troops.) It is believed that the initiation consists in killing a cock and drinking the blood, either by itself, or mixed with wine. It is also believed to use a planchette whose movements are attributed to occult influence; gradually persons not connected with the army were admitted; the ticket of membership is a small oblong piece of linen or calico, stamped with a few Chinese characters. The possession of one of these, if discovered, entails immediate execution by the authorities.

The Society is anti-foreign and anti-missionary, and is believed to be at the bottom of all the riots against foreigners, and especially against foreign missionaries, which have lately occurred in China. In 1891 the Ko Lao Hui, which is also anti-dynastic, caused inflammatory placards to be posted up in various parts of the Empire, which the authorities immediately tore down, only to be posted up afresh; the Society also distributed anti-missionary pamphlets, with titles such as this: "The Devil Doctriners ought to be killed," wherein the missionaries are charged with every kind of crime against morals and life; The Roman Catholics are more severely handled than the Protestants.

In September, 1891 it would appear that the society was organising a rising against the Government, and a Mr. C. W. Mason a British subject, and a fourth-class assistant in the British Customs at Shanghai, was implicated in the project, he having been instrumental in introducing arms and dynamite into the country for the use of the conspirators. He was sentenced to nine months' imprisonment, with hard labour, and he was sent out of the country in September, 1892. In November, 1891 a famous Ko Lao Hui leader named Chen-kin-Lung fell into the hands of the Chinese Government. He had been staying at an inn with about thirty of his followers. Gagged and bound, he was taken on board a steam-launch kept ready to start and carried to Shanghai. His examination was conducted with the greatest secrecy by the magistrate and deputies of the Viceroy and the Governor. On his person were found several official documents issued by the Ko Lao Hui, and a *short dagger* with a poisoned blade. He was addressed in the despatches as the "Eighth Great Prince", and was evidently the commander of a strong force. Three examinations were held, but Chen preserved the strictest silence. Torture was employed but in vain; the only words that could be extracted from him were "Spare yourselves the trouble and me the pain; be convinced that there are men ready to sacrifice their lives for the good of a cause which will bring happiness to this country for thousands of generations to come". Then more gentle means were employed, but with what result is not known. The Ko Lao League has various offshoots, which being known to be in reality mutual aid societies, are secret societies in name only, and therefore attract but little attention from the Government. One of the largest of these offshoots is the "Golden Lily Hui", which flourishes in the western provinces of China. Its members are divided into four sections, respectively marshalled under the white, the black, the red, and the yellow flag.

The foregoing is interesting as showing that the Chinese authorities were drastic in their suppression of the Ko Lao Society and that the society was anti-dynastic and anti-Roman Catholic.) The latter fact suggests a reason for the secret society attack on Roman Catholics in Singapore in 1851. (*see* Chapter VI). A further point of interest is the mention of the ceremony of initiation also referred to by Hutson which although *similar* to the Triad, belongs to a different organisation and corresponds more with that of the Three Dot Brotherhood of to-day (*see* Chapter VIII). Again there is reference to "Offshoots of the Ko Lao Hui", of which the Three Dot Brotherhood and its affinities might well be one, particularly as they are referred to as being "mutual aid societies", and are secret societies in name only and therefore attract but little attention from the government. The insistence upon the "mutual aid" was a cardinal point in the Toh-Pe-Kong society of Penang (referred to in Chapter V) and also in the Three Dot Society and its Malay affinities today, whereas in the latter-day Triad Society the cardinal point has always been the overthrow of the Manchu dynasty—"mutual aid" being an incidental.

Finally there is an interesting reference to the flags of the society as being white, black, red and yellow. Of these Hutson also makes reference to the red and black flags of the Ko Lao Hui.

Our two last references are of more recent date. Couling *Encyclopaedia Sinica* (1917) has:—

ELDER BROTHER SOCIETY, KO LAO HUI 哥老會

A secret brotherhood which had been known for some time to exist, when three membership tickets were found in 1886 on a man arrested in Shanghai. (The Yangtze valley riots in 1891 were believed to have been caused by Elder Brothers, the object being to embroil the Manchus with the foreign powers.) An early origin is claimed for the cult in Szechuan; in its present form it dates from the beginning of the Manchu rule, but while anti-dynastic it was pro-T'ang and not pro-Ming.

The Society builds itself on three famous friendships recorded in Chinese annals, and each member calls the others "Brother". There is an elaborate ritual, a system of secret signs with many grades of membership, and there is said to be a considerable resemblance to Freemasonry. The Society, which consists of eight guilds, early divided into East and West, the latter being the stronger, especially in Szechuan, Kansu and Shensi. In 1900 they became mere bandits, and in 1911, getting the upper hand of the Revolutionaries, with whom they had allied themselves, they were responsible for the massacre of at least 10,000 Manchus in Hsi-an fu, as well as of some of the missionaries.

The three membership tickets found in 1886 are those referred to in Playfair's article given above.

Couling writing in 1916 had not Hutson's observations on the Ko Lao Hui to help him.

Finally the most recent reference is taken from Sir Eric Teichman's *Affairs of China* published in 1938.

On page 296 Sir Eric Teichman has:—

The secret societies are seldom heard of in the treaty ports. But the foreigner who lives or travels in the more remote interior, if he delves at all below the surface in the northern provinces, will soon be brought in contact with the *Ko Lao Hui*, the all-pervading, subterranean Brotherhood, which rules in secret the lives of millions of the Chinese peasantry. If trouble or disturbances are brewing in the neighbourhood, the *Ko Lao Hui* are pretty sure to have a finger in the pie. In the early 'nineties their activities in central China came to the attention of the foreign public through the antics of a Mr. Mason, a young man in the Chinese Customs Service, stationed at the treaty port of Chinkiang, who became associated with a projected rising of the *Ko Lao Hui* against the Dynasty. Mr. Mason, who was arrested by the British consular authorities, and whose adventure ended with a sentence of deportation and imprisonment, wrote many years later an entertaining book about his strange experiences. The present writer came into contact with the Brotherhood in Szechuan nearly thirty years ago, when the storm of impending revolution was rumbling through the land and burst for the first time in western China in August of 1911. He recalls the armed bands of peasants roaming through the countryside, equipped with antiquated weapons and bearing red standards and mysterious devices. When the members of the Brotherhood are on the warpath they are best avoided by the foreigner. The magic rites and incantations, groping back into the mysticism of a long-gone past, rouse the peaceful peasantry of China into a kind of ecstasy, when they behave in ways that are strange and unaccountable. This is the explanation of what happened in the rising of the Boxers and similar rebellions in the past.

The book by Mason referred to by Teichman deserves our further attention. It is called *The Chinese Confessions of C. W. Mason* published in 1924 by Grant Richards It was written when Mason was nearing sixty years of age and is a personal account of his connection with the Ko Lao rebellion of 1891, and the circumstances which led him to engage in this enterprise.

Granted that Mason was morbid and mentally "different" from other young men of his day, he was nevertheless an educated Englishman with three or four years service in the Chinese Maritime Customs, when he became involved in this wild adventure which brought his career in the Customs to an end.

The first point of interest in his story is that he was (and if he is alive still is) a member of the Ko Lao Hui: no doubt the only Englishman ever to have been admitted a member: secondly that his book is more an explanation of the causes and mental processes which led him to his adventure than a description of the adventure itself: thirdly that it is in no way an *exposé* of the Ko Lao Hui and we look in vain in his work for any description of initiation, ritual or rules of the society. Needless to say it would be of intense interest to the student of these matters to obtain such, even if only in rudimentary form, from the only Englishman, probably, who knows them, indeed from the only single known source whence they may be obtained at first hand.

It should here be remembered that there exists no authoritative account or disclosure of the rules and ritual of the Ko Lao Hui, such as we have of the Hung league in the work of Schlegel. Apart from Hutson's observations, we give in succeeding chapters some fragmentary and truncated references to what the Han league ritual probably contains, but the power and vengeance of the league is such that its secrets appear to have been preserved inviolate up to the present day.

Mason's book is chiefly interesting because it gives us an insight into the "philosophy" of the Ko Lao Hui, if we may identify the ethic expressed by him, with that of the Ko Lao Hui of which he was a member, and in view of the absence of any other references to the subject except those of Hutson, it may be as well to devote a paragraph to an examination of this philosophy, for purposes of comparison with that of the Hung league.

THE ETHIC OF THE KO LAO HUI OR HAN LEAGUE

Hutson on this subject says above:—

(The Han Liu or Ko Lao Hui tenaciously holds to natural depravity, resists external reforms, and through the ages has made licentious liberty the chief ideal of life")

And again:—

"The chief Han Liu ideal is liberty, which means to them anarchy, selfishness and depravity and it may be said that the society is always "agin the government". They are under a kind of military rule, make their own laws and reserve all rights of interpreting and administering them".

And again:—

"Their methods of blackmail are inimitably ingenious: their revenge on traitors swift and unswerving. Their cruelties to enemies are indescribable".

Mason *op. cit.* page 39 bases his adhesion to the Ko Lao Hui upon "the inevitable consummation of innate character and years of cogitation" The results of this cogitation he discloses in a remarkable and introspective document written by him in 1891 which he gives in his book (page 40) and entitled "D.P." which he explains variously as Decision and Purpose or the struggle in his mind between following the dictates of Duty or Pleasure in the circumstances in which he found himself as a member of the Ko Lao Hui into which he had been led by one of his Chinese servants.   In this document he defined "Pleasure" as follows:—

(a) The object of life is ambition or the acquisition of Power.

(b) Power means being able to punish your enemies and guard oneself against punishment by them. To be immune from all law except one's own conscience. To be able to seize and enjoy with impunity whatever gratifies the appetite, such as countries, estates, buildings, works of art and ornament, wine and women.

(c) Since such Power is nullified if an enemy can conquer you, or seize or damage your person, the essential of Power is physical force sufficient to overcome other physical force. One must have an army superior to other armies with the necessary strongholds and supplies.

(d) An army consists of a multitude of strong men and in order to be able to control and order them, one must feed and clothe and pay them well and (win their devotion by some sort of fanaticism,) such as persuading them that you are the vice-regent of God and able to bestow precious honours in the form of tinsel decorations and tin-pot titles.)

(e) One can obtain the money and influence necessary for these things only by becoming the King of a country and robbing ten million families of part of their earnings in the form of taxation in order to equip one million ablebodied soldiers.

(f) I therefore decided that the immediate object of "P" is to become a King.

One must assume that Mason became imbued with this philosophy at least partly from his membership of the Ko Lao Hui as it exhibits a remarkable likeness to the ideals of the society as recorded by Hutson.

It would also seem as if some of the leaders of present-day Europe have become followers of the same creed. (This creed is the "worship of man" or of purely material ends) a subject to which we shall refer more fully later in relation to (the worship of God) which latter (seems to have been the pristine ideal of the Hung League) as discussed in Chapter I.

Mason's document proceeds to discuss the means of attaining his object and develops into a disquisition upon the right use of physical force, ruthlessness, charlatanry and unscrupulousness in the pursuit of personal ambition. He finally reached a state of mind in which the positions of Duty and Pleasure were reversed and he conceived "Pleasure" to represent "a tame acquiescence in accepted ethics" and "Duty" to demand that he should "pin his faith to an overt act" and follow his fortune by throwing in his lot with the Ko Lao Hin rebellion, then (1891) being hatched.

He says on page 47:—

If I chose the philosophy of Pleasure by which I meant virtue and propriety, culture and law, I must refuse to have anything more to do with Chinese conspiracies. If on the other hand I chose the philosophy of Duty, by which I meant sacrificing my ease and reputation to the stern demands of ambition, I must cast in my lot with the Ko Laos and become a rebel to the Chinese government and a renegade in the eyes of my compatriots. I chose the latter.

A further example of how the Ko Lao philosophy had worked upon Mason's mind is given by him on page 46:—

"The religion of which I was being made the unconscious martyr was what we should call the religion or schism of Antichrist. The Devil, as we call one half of god, had hold of me and was determined to make me the champion of crime: and as my entire education and early environment had chained me to the religion of virtue, I was subjected to a cruel internal struggle........ Nevertheless it was I whom the Devil chose to fasten on for the painful gospel of persuading the world that *virtue and not vice was a crime*".

In a study, however superficial of the criminal under-world in its modern international aspect and of the secret associations which bind it together, this reversal of the accepted ethic is constantly met with and the proposition continually presented to the mind that Good is Evil and Evil is Good. This proposition seems in its Chinese setting to be the obtrusion of the Yin over the Yang principle and is the common creed of anarchism and nihilism and to its inspiration is due a definite proportion of that revolutionary violence, which from time to time has shocked the conscience of the world throughout recorded history.

D

THE WHITE LOTUS OR WHITE LILY SOCIETY (白 蓮 教)

Scattered references to this society occur in the writings of observers already quoted and the concensus of opinion has hitherto apparently been that the White Lotus is an earlier name for the Hung league.

This view appears to rest firstly on the mention by name of the White Lotus in the "Sacred Edict" (A.D. 1662) and again in the edict of the Emperor Kien Lung in 1761, before the names by which the Hung league is now known came into general use: secondly upon the association of the White Lotus with Buddhism with which the Hung League is impregnated and thirdly because the insurrections of the White Lotus in comparatively recent history (*see* Stanton page 2–6) have arisen in the south and west of China where geographically the Hung league of today is paramount.

In the absence of any material for comparative study such as the ritual or statutes or oaths of the White Lotus society, it is not possible to arrive at a conclusive view as to its original identity with the Hung league in the latter's Traditional Age, but there are reasons for thinking that in its revolutionary period the White Lotus belonged to the Han stem rather than the Hung stem in the secret society world of China. The original confusion of the White Lotus with Buddhism in the official mind of China may have arisen from a confusion between the name of the society and the early "Lotus School" of Buddhism founded by Hui Yuan (慧 遠) in A.D. 416: while the geographical diffusion of the society may from causes mentioned in Chapter IV have been entirely fortuitous.

Hutson definitely places the White Lotus in the category of the mystical or hypnotic sect of the Han league and further evidence will be offered to support this view.

Couling *op. cit.* 1917, says of this historical association:—

WHITE LOTUS (OR LILY) SOCIETY, Pai lien chiao 白 蓮 教 must not be confounded with the Lotus School of Buddhism founded by Hui Yuan, and arose in the reign of the Mongol Emperor Wu Tsung (A.D. 1308–1312), owing to persistent misrule.

It was given a religious turn by Han Shan-T'ung 韓 山 童, (the grandson of the founder) declaring the advent of Maitreya to be near. He himself was palmed off as a descendent of the Sung dynastic family, and rose in rebellion. Red turbans were the distinguishing mark of his followers. He was captured early and executed, and his son 韓 林 兒 carried on the revolt, and was actually proclaimed Emperor; but he died in 1367 at Nanking and the prize of the Empire fell to his friend Chu Yuan-chang, the first of the Ming rulers.

Towards the close of the Ming Dynasty, when misrule and disorder again prevailed, the White Lotus Society, reappeared. In the reign of T'ien Chu'i (1621–1628) they joined forces with a rebel leader who had actually been proclaimed Emperor, but was defeated and slain in battle.

In 1761 Ch'ien Lung issued edicts against this and other sects, but in 1794 the White Lotus Society broke out in rebellion again, in Hupei and West China, around the person of a youth represented as a descendant of one of the Ming Emperors. This rebellion took ten years to repress. In the first four months 20,000 members of the sect were beheaded, but nevertheless the movement spread over six provinces and cost untold money and lives.

In 1814, in Chia Ch'ing's reign, a daring insurrection broke out in the palace itself, which was ascribed to the White Lotus Society, though the White Feather and other organisations were also accused. In 1815, a White Lotus army suffered defeat in Shensi and this was their last open revolt, though the Nien fei[1] who worked such havoc in the north at the time of the T'ai P'ing rebellion were probably largely recruited from the other Society.

It is said to survive under the name of the Tsai Li 在 理 sect, whose members abstain from wine, opium and tobacco, but were strongly disliked by the Manchu authorities to the end.

Edkins also stated in 1886 that the White Lotus still existed as a small purely religious sect in the neighbourhood of Te chou in Shantung.

Quite apart from its universal observance by Buddhism, the adoption of vegetarianism by the Han league at certain times of the year is noted by Hutson in another of his papers, quoted in Chapter XXXII below, in connection with the observance of the Ninth Moon festival by a sect of the Han league in Malaya. This observance which is apparently shared by the White Lotus, appears to have been another cause of confusion in the Chinese official mind up to a quite recent date, between the White Lotus and Buddhist vegetarianism.

Thus we learn from Couling *op. cit.* that the fifteenth patriarch of the Jasper Pool Society (瑤 池) one of the most important Buddhist vegetarian sects in China to-day, had already been twenty years in prison at Hanyang in the year 1902, on a false charge of being the leader of a contingent of White Lotus insurrectionists in 1881. A full account of the Jasper Pool society is given in the *Chinese Recorder* Volume XXXIII.

THE BOXERS 義 和 團 Ghee Hoa Tu'an

Couling *Encyclopaedia Sinica* page 59 has:—

This is the name given to the anti-foreign disorders of 1900. The organisers called themselves 義和團 "The public-spirited harmonious band" By others the band was called 土 匪 T'o Fei "Bandits", or 義 和 拳 Ghee Hoa Kh'un "The public-spirited harmonious boxers", so termed from the boxing antics that distinguished it.

Footnote.—(1) Nien fei probably refers to the soldiers of the Manchu General Nien Kang Yiu (年 庚 堯) who opposed the Taiping rebels (1860) and whose soldiers were known to the long-suffering populace as "Nien's brigands" Nien fei (年 匪).

Couling's English rendering of the Chinese does not follow the "Schlegel school" and perhaps "The Righteous and United Band" would be a more orthodox translation of the name.

These Chinese names take us directly to the names applied to the "mystical or hypnotic sect" of the Han Liu or Ko Lao Hui given by Hutson above c.f. The United Fists Society (義 和 拳) Ghee Hoa Tu'an and the nickname 楬 匪 Ku Fei or "brigands" mentioned by him. (pp. 23–24 above).

Couling continues:—

> The fraternity was a revival of an association long existing and never wholly extinct in Shantung, which had its rise in political unrest. What had been under a ban for long was officially recognised and welcomed in 1900 under the title of "Volunteers". They received help from Government funds. Once started and officially encouraged, the Boxer movement spread with great rapidity. As it developed it gathered strength from certain magical ideas that possessed the members. Some youths were found to be susceptible to charms and were sedulously trained. These were taught certain gibberish and by continuous mutterings of these incantations they became initiated until finally they were under the spell 上 法 . These magic arts stirred the popular fervour......especially did the mysterious and miraculous working of the Red Lamp Society (紅 燈 照) (cf Hutson above) confirm the magic powers of the initiated and increase the wave of terror and inspiration that passed over the people. The Red Lamp Society was started by a woman and young girls wearing red trousers and girdles joined it in great numbers.
>
> *   *
>
> Whether the movement was instigated by the Government or arose independently of it is not quite clear: but this much is plain that the movement was led to rely on Imperial favour and protection and a Prince became its President. The Government in turn was emboldened by the rise of such a powerful instrument to try conclusions with the foreigners and drive them out of the country.

The identity of the "Boxers" with the "Hypnotic Sect" of the Han Liu and thence with the Ko Lao Hui rests upon the following further considerations.

Hutson op. cit. says:—

> "The difficulty all missionary societies have had in getting a foothold in Szchuan is due to the TANG TZU HANG (黨 子 行) or Confucian Society. The plots of the literati culminated in the riots of 1895 in Szechuan. From that year till about 1902 new influences were brought into play by bringing the more lawless elements into action. The period might be called the Hypnotic period; it includes the YU MAN TZU rebellion of 1898, the Boxer upheaval of 1900 and the local (Szchuan) Boxer trouble of 1902, when the Boxer bands even entered the provincial capital (of Szchuan i.e. Cheng Tu). From 1902 a new phase begins when the CH'IEN TZU HANG (欛 子 行) or TALLY SOCIETY made a movement towards the Church to capture it for political purposes, both protection and aggression. The period ended in the Revolution of 1911.
>
> To be clear it may be stated here that the TALLY SOCIETY is the same as the HAN LIU or KO LAO HUI, and this period may be name the Han Liu period".

In this passage, Hutson identifies the *Boxers* with the KO LAO HUI. According to him therefore the Boxer Rebellion of 1899–1900 was an outbreak of the KO LAO HUI in China against foreign missions.

This at first sight seems contradictory, because we know the Ko Lao Hui was anti-dynastic as well as anti-foreigner, and we know from Playfair and elsewhere that the Manchu Government rigorously suppressed the Ko Lao Hui, whereas we know from history that the Boxer "rebels" in 1900 were fostered and encouraged by the officials of the Manchu Government. The explanation may be that the *literati* or confucian element amongst the Chinese, joining forces with Manchu officialdom, took advantage of the widespread anti-foreign riots throughout China during the decade 1886 to 1896 which were organised by the Ko Lao Hui and decided to guide this anti-foreign feeling into a profitable channel instead of trying to suppress it, and so fostered and directed it against the general encroachment of Western nations upon China (as evidenced by the trade expansion and the opening up of fresh Treaty Ports,) in the hope of driving Europeans entirely out of China. If this be the explanation, the result was just the opposite to that desired.

Dyer Ball *Things Chinese* page 657 has:—

> "The dreadful Boxers which created such disturbances in the North, and were encouraged by the Chinese officials *were also a Secret Society, based to some extent on the same principals and ceremonials as the Triads.* They believed largely in hypnotism and one of their tenets was that they could render themselves invulnerable in fight. They imposed on numbers of people, who joined them in crowds".

Dyer Ball does not anywhere suggest that the Boxers were identical with the Ko Lao Hui, but he was writing in 1903 and Hutson's researches were not published till 1919–1920. With regard to Dyer Ball's reference to the well known "hypnotic arts" of the Boxer rebels, compare the following passage in Hutson op. cit.

> "In Szechuan many people knew the Boxer arts before 1900, especially round such centres as Pao Ning, Mien Chou and Chin T'ang hsien, but there was not enough strength or organisation for a rising. The hypnotic arts are still practised in secret in different parts of the province, but more especially in the north, their original home".

The following further description of the Boxers by Dyer Ball at the same reference discloses other points of similarity with Hutson's description of the KO LAO HUI. Dyer Ball goes on to quote:—

> "The Boxers include not only boys of from 12 to 16 but girls of the same age, and they form separate branches. The branch in which the girls belong is known as the HUNG TANG CHIU (紅 燈 照) or *Red Lantern* Shrines; They carry about with them red lanterns...... The boys branch is called the I WO TUN (義 和 團) (There follows a description of the method of self-hypnotism). When anyone joins the Boxers he puts *pieces of red cloth round his head,* stomach and legs, and dons two shoulder straps on which are characters which mean "Protect China and kill the foreigners".

In Chapter XXVII *infra* we identify the 義和拳 Ghee Hoa Kh'un or "Boxers" or Ko Lao Hui, or Han Liu of Pekin in 1900 with the 義和堂 Ghee Hoa Tong in Annam at the present-day, which has been the mainspring of anti-catholicism and insurrection throughout the period of French ascendancy in Indo-China.

Some evidence will, at the same time be offered to suggest that similar arts from a common source, may lie behind the peasant unrest in Burma, which broke out in 1930 and still continues.

THE GORMOGONS

The origin of this Society which appeared in England as a rival to Freemasonry in 1724, has interested the following writers: Heckethorn: Thomas Frost and Ward and Stirling and has not yet been satisfactorily explained. Ward and Stirling *op. cit.* Vol. III, page 125 say:—

> "The Hung Society has numerous points of similarity with Freemasonry, and the question therefore arises whether a mysterious and supposedly Chinese Society called the Gormogons, which appeared in England in 1724, and possibly earlier, and set itself up as a rival to Freemasonry, was indeed derived from the contemporary Hung Society or from some other Chinese Society at that time active in the Far East".

Thomas Frost in *The Secret Societies of the European Revolution 1776–1876,* Vol. I, page 26 has:—

> "An attempt was made during the second quarter of the eighteenth century to graft upon the Masonic Order the rites and mysteries of the GORMOGONES, said to have been brought from China and to have been practised in that country for centuries. Very little information concerning this Society is accessible. It is said to have been introduced into England by a Chinese Mandarin who was suspected of being a Jesuit Missionary: but it is not known whether the supreme chapter of the order had its seat in Paris or in Rome. Masonic authors, though they have very little to tell us concerning the Gormogons, agree in regarding it as a Jesuit enterprise. Kloss conjectures that it was an attempt of the disciple of Loyola to promote Romanism and regain their influence in England: and Findel surmises that Ramsay, who was an adherent of the Jacobite faction, had something to do with the experiment, which was however a failure. The order was dissolved in 1738 having been in existence 13 years: and it is a curious co-incidence if nothing more, that the first Papal Bull against the Freemasons was fulminated in the same year".

Heckethorn *op. cit.* Vol. II, page 93 says:—

> "The order of the Gormogons founded in England in 1724, was said to have been brought by a Chinese Mandarin or Jesuit Missionary from China and to possess extraordinary secrets. It is supposed to have been an attempt of the Jesuit, by the help of Masonic Ceremonies to gain converts to Catholicism....... I have vainly endeavoured to trace the origin and meaning of the term Gormogon—according to one account I have seen, it was also called the Order of the Gormons......".

We offer the suggestion for what it may be worth, that the name Go-mo-gon may be a romanisation of the Chinese 哥老館 KO LAO KWUN which—pronounced phonetically might be GO-MO-GON, the letter 'L' of the original having possibly become 'M' for euphony. Besides similarity in the name, there are one or two other points which suggest identity with the Ko Lao Kwun. Ward and Stirling give the first official notification published by the Gormogon Society on 3rd April, 1724, which opens with this passage:—

> "Whereas the truly Antient Noble Order of the Gormogons instituted by......the first Emperor of China......and of which the Great Philosopher Confucius was Oecumenical Volgee, has lately been brought into England by a Mandarin......".

This suggests a connection with the Tang Tzu Hang or Confucian Society (黨子行) mentioned by Hutson, and thence with the Han Liu and Ko Lao Kwun.

The Pope issued a Papal Bull against Freemasonry in 1738, after which date the Gormogons lost ground in England and seem to have entirely disappeared after the Act suppressing secret societies was passed in England on 12th July, 1799. In *The History of Freemasonry* (Gould) Vol. IV, page 379, there is an illustration of a jewel of the Gormogon Society on which there is a sun inside an inscription which is *surmounted by a dragon.* The presence of the dragon suggests a connection with the "dragon throne" and "rolling dragons" mentioned by Hutson above.

A date in this jewel claims the foundation of the Gormogons (? KO LAO KWUN) to have been 6,000 years before the Christian era.

This again suggests that the antiquity of the KO LAO HUI or Han Liu may be as great or even greater than that of the Hung League (Traditional Period).

If, as we suggest in a later chapter, a whole range of secret societies in Malaya is based on the *Han* or *Ko Lao* foundation, as opposed to the *Hung* or *Triad* family, we have here perhaps an explanation of the source of that incessant strife between "rival" Chinese secret societies in Malaya, the rivalry being that of entirely different foundations and not merely that between different branches of the same great brotherhood.

CHAPTER III

THE RELIGIOUS BACKGROUND OF CHINESE SECRET SOCIETIES

We have now made the acquaintance of the two main stems from which the great body of secret societies in China appear to spring, and it would be well at this point to sketch in the religious background from which these two stems in turn derive, and to suggest the manner and the degree in which the secret society world of China influences the daily lives of the Chinese people in their social intercourse.

In Chapter I reference has been made to the Yin (陰) and the Yang (陽) or the "order of the universe" as understood by Chinese minds. We must now take a wider glance at the religions of China.

de Groot *Religion in China* (1912) page 1 says:—

> It is a matter of common knowledge that there are three religions in China *viz.*, Taoism, Confucianism and Buddhism. There is however a saying in that country, "It contains three religions and yet it is only one religion."

Rev. W. E. Soothill in his *Three Religions of China* page 5 has:—

> Let us now turn to a consideration of the terms used by the Chinese for their "religions". I have told you that there are three recognised religions or "isms". These are known in their own language as the San Chiao (三 教) and are commonly spoken of as the Ju (儒) Shih (釋) Tao, (道) San Chiao. I give them in their usual Chinese order. The first of these is the Ju Chiao, usually styled by Europeans Confucianism, so called after its founder K'ung Fu-tze, latinised by the early Roman missionaries as Confucius. The word Ju means cultured or learned. Hence, Ju Chiao means the cult of the learned. The second is the Shih Chiao. The word Shih is an abbreviation for Shih-chia-mu-ni (釋 迦 牟 尼), the Chinese form of Sakyamuni, one of the names of the Buddha, Shih Chiao, therefore, stands for Buddhism. The third term is Tao Chiao. The word Tao means "The Way". The foundation of the Tao Chiao, that is to say, Taoism, is attributed to Lao Tsu, or Laocius, about whom more will be said later.

de Groot *op. cit.* page 2 continues:—

> The fact is that the three religions are three branches growing from a common stem, which has existed from prehistoric times: this stem is the religion of the Universe, its parts and phenomena. This *Universism* as I will henceforth call it, is the one religion of China. As these three religions are its three integrant parts, every Chinese can feel himself equally at home in each, without being offended or shocked by conflicting and mutually exclusive dogmatic principles.
>
> In the age of Han, two centuries before and two after the birth of Christ, the ancient stem divided itself into two branches, Taoism and Confucianism, while, simultaneously Buddhism was grafted upon it.
>
> Indeed Buddhism at that time found its way into China in an universistic form called Maha-yana, and could therefore live and thrive upon the ancient stem. It is a remarkable co-incidence that this greatest moment in the development of religion in China was synchronous with the birth of Christ and Christianity.
>
> Buddhism being merely the engrafted branch may be left aside for the present, in order that our attention may be confined in the first place to Taoism and Confucianism the bifurcation of ancient Universism. This universism was Taoism: the two terms are synonymous.
>
> In the Han period it produced a branch which however did not give birth to any new religious elements or doctrines. This was Confucianism, the State religion, destined to become the pre-eminent branch, sapping and destroying under the control of the principle of intolerance, the vitality of the Buddhist branches, and preventing Taoism from growing into a religion of paramount importance. The Chinese Empire one and undivided was created in the third century before our era............
>
> In organising the young Empire its statesmen built up a political constitution taking naturally and systematically for their guides the principles, rules and precedents of the old time, embodied in the ancient literature............
>
> Thus there arose a classical, ultra-conservative State constitution, which, handed down as an heirloom to all succeeding dynasties, exists to this day. The religious elements contained in the classics were necessarily incorporated with that constitution, together with the political, since everything mentioned in the classics was to be presumed and developed as a holy institution of the ancients: in other words those religious elements became the *state religion*. This religion, therefore, is now fully two thousand years old. The basic principle, Universism, is of course older, much older than the classical writings (*i.e.* of Lao Tze, Confucius and Mencius) by means of which it has been preserved. As is the case with many origins, that of China's Universism is lost in the darkness of antiquity............
>
> We have now to see what these (religious) principles are and what, accordingly is the character and core of the ancient and present religion of East Asia.
>
> Universism is Taoism. Indeed its starting point is the Tao (道) which means the Road or Way, that is to say, the road or way in which the Universe moves, its methods and its processes, its conduct and operation, the complex of phenomena regularly recurring in it, in short, the order of the world, nature, or natural order. It actually is in the main the annual notation of the seasons producing the process of growth, or renovation and decay: it may accordingly be called "Time the creator and destroyer."

de Groot on page 8 has:—

> "There is indeed in the Chinese system no God beyond the cosmos, no maker of it, no Yahweh, no Allah. Creation is simply the yearly renovation of nature, the spontaneous work of Heaven and Earth repeating itself in every revolution of the Tao......Its pristine principles are contained in the classics, which are the holy bibles of Confucianism and Taoism.

And on page 11:—

> Ancient and modern authors are wont to define the Tao of the Universe as "the way of the road (道) of Yin (陰) and Yang (陽)". The Yin is assimilated with the Earth, which is cold and dark, and the Yang with Heaven, which is warm and luminous: they are respectively the female and the male of cosmos, its *anima* and its *animus*,

In the Li Ki the most voluminous collection of classical books we read "Man is a product of the beneficial operation of Heaven and Earth, or of the copulation of the Yin and the Yang and the union of a Kwei (鬼) with a Shen (神). Thus ancient philosophy described Man as a compound of a Kwei and a Shen, two souls respectively related, as the context of this passage suggests, with the Yin or terrestial matter and with the Yang or immaterial celestial substance.

In the same great classic we read:—"Tsai Ngo said"— "I have heard the words Kwei and Shen, but I do not know their meaning" and Confucius replied "The khi (氣) or breath (i.e. Yang soul) is the full manifestation of the Shen; and the p'oh (魄) (i.e. Yin soul) is the full manifestation of the Kwei: the union of the Kwei with the Shen is the highest of all doctrines. Living beings must all die and the soul which must then return to earth is that which is called Kwei. But while the bones and the flesh moulder in the ground and imperceptably become the earth of the fields, the Khi or breath departs to move on high as a shining light".

This instructive paragraph is the fundamental dogma of Taoist and Confucianist psychology. It teaches that the universal Yang and Yin are divided into an indefinite number of souls or spirits, respectively called Shen and Kwei: the Shen represents light, warmth, productivity, life, which are the special qualities of the Yang, and the Kwei darkness, cold, sterility, death, which are the attributes of the Yin. The soul of man like that of any living being, consists of a Shen and a Kwei or p'oh: his birth is an infusion of these souls, his death is their departure, the Shen returning to the Yang or Heaven, the Kwei to the Yin or Earth. His body is, like Heaven and Earth, composed of the five elements. Accordingly, man is a part of the Universe, a microcosm, born spontaneously from and in the macrocosm. His Shen is of course his principal soul, contributing his intelligence and life: his Kwei represents his qualities of the opposite kind".

Again on page 16:— "With these dogmas before us, we may now say that the old groundwork of the Chinese system of religion is an Universistic Animism. The Universe being in all its parts crowded with Shen and Kwei: the system is moreover, polytheistic and poly-demonistic.

Again on page 45:— "The man who has gained the Tao (道) is the perfect man. We know that the operations of the Tao of the Universe are those of the Shen (神) or gods, which are the parts of the Yang or celestial half of the universe: it is then a logical conclusion that the man who has the Tao actually is such a god, and that the Tao is called Shen Tao (神道). "The Tao of Divinity" or "The way of the gods". We all know this word in its Japanese form Shinto: indeed Taoism has existed from an early date in the Land of the Rising Sun.

Again on page 89:— "To the students of the history of ancient and modern religions, it is of some value to know that Man in Asia, in times much older than the Christian era, possessed positive ideas about holiness and divinity and about magical wisdom and art which such divinity conferred: and that it is possible by the help of Chinese books to define these ideas satisfactorily as products of an all-dominating Universism, rooted in a remote antiquity.

Lastly on page 177 de Groot has this significant passage:— "Deification of man (anthropo-theism) and worship of man (anthropo-latry) are main features of the Universistic religion, but doubtless antedate it.

Worship of man after his death may have been the oldest religion of the human race. It certainly prevailed in Eastern Asia before the rise of other gods. It is mentioned in the classical and other writings of Chinese so often and in such detail, that it must have been the core of the ancient faith. It was a natural and logical continuation of the worship of the living— in the first place of fathers and mothers, the highest authorities in family life according to the Order of the World itself".

And on page 181:— "Highest among the Taoist gods are the parts and forces of the Universe. Chaos, before it divided itself into the Yang and the Yin, occupies the principal place in the pantheon and under the name of Pwan Ku (盤古) the deified Yang, the universal warmth and light is named Tung Wang Kung (東王公) or Royal Father of the East, and as such he holds sway in a kind of paradise in the Pacific Ocean. The deified Yin, the universal cold and darkness, is his consort, Si Wang Mo (西王母) or "Royal Mother of the West,"[1] who wields the sceptre in the Kwun Lun (崑崙) paradise, over myriads of Sien (仙) "fairies", "immortals".

We have referred in the introduction to the connection between religion and secret societies and we must here briefly indicate the association of the foregoing outline of religion in China with the development of secret societies in that country.

The Rev. W. E. Soothill in his Three religions of China page 4 has:— It is impossible to divide the Chinese into three separate mutually exclusive churches or religious communities, as is the case, say, with Roman Catholics, Greek Catholics, and the Reformed branch of the Christian Church. Those writers, therefore, who speak of so many hundred millions of Chinese Buddhists have as much right to these as others would have who claimed the same hundreds of millions for Confucianism or Taoism. There are, it is true, a certain number of the educated who are strictly Confucianist, and who heartily despise both Buddhism and Taoism. Their number, however, is quite limited, for there are few among them who do not summon Buddhist or Taoist monks, or indeed both, to perform the rites for the dead, or consult their divinities in case of sickness or distress. The Buddhist and Taoist clergy, an unlettered class, for the most part confine themselves to their respective cults, and while a few of the laity devote themselves, some solely to Buddhism, some solely to Taoism, the great mass of the people have no prejudices and make no embarrassing distinctions; they belong to none of the three religions, or, more correctly, they belong to all three. In other words, they are eclectic, and use whichever form best responds to the requirement of the moment, or for which on any occasion they use religion.

Again on page 84 Soothill has:— The numerous secret societies which have honeycombed the nation for the most part have been associated with Taoism. The Boxer madness was the latest instance of this. Thousands and hundreds of thousands believed that, possessed of Taoist charms, weapons could not harm

Footnote.—(1) Further reference to Si Wang Mo is made in the introduction to this work.

them, and that the horsehair whip blessed by the priest could turn back upon the marksman the bullet he fired.

The history of Taoist influence on Chinese history has yet to be written. It has been greater than is generally realised. Emperors have been its devotees. It may have been the cause of the burning of the ancient books by China's Napoleon, Ch'in Shih Huang. For hundreds of years it influenced the Court of China, and affected both politics and the national religion. It has adopted all that it possibly could from Buddhism, except the higher elements, established its heaven, modelled in clay its lurid hell, filled it with all the horrid torments which the barbarous mind can invent, and deified Laocius and a multitude of others, as well as the various forces of Nature.

Finally on page 310 Soothill has:—

Many secret societies have existed and still do exist. Some of them have been formed purely and simply for political purposes often anti-dynastic, though generally they have been politico-religious. Others have been formed for religious purposes only, the members pledging themselves to abstain from flesh, from intoxicants, and from tobacco. Nor has abstinence been the only rule of such a society, for the patron saint, or divinity of the society, has become also the patron saint of each member, and been especially worshipped by him. Some of these societies have undoubtedly assisted in the development of a kind of personal religion, independent of domestic religion. As a rule they are associated with the Taoist religion, and though proscribed by law, perhaps *propter hoc*, they have flourished from time to time over a wide area. Their tendency, in the long run, has been to degenerate into political organisations, which indeed is the real cause of proscription. At times they have caused rebellions, and fostered a fanaticism, such as made itself so terribly felt during the Boxer outbreak of 1900.

We have seen in Chapter I the close association between the Hung league and Buddhism and the foregoing sketch of Taoism will help to show the existence of what appears to be a similar close association between the Han league and Taoism.

The third or State religion of China, Confucianism, to which belong the *literati* and the official class under the old *régime*, seems to have occupied a central position from which it persecuted with impartiality "heresy" of all descriptions. Thus de Groot *op. cit.* page 43 has:—

We find the school of Confucius in close alliance with the State, which has entirely assimilated itself with it imbued with a fanatical animosity against everything religious and ethical which cannot be covered by the idea of "classicism" and against all teachings not built upon the foundations of these holy writings. Crusades against false doctrines are preached by the Shu King (經 書) one of the holiest among the classics, in a chapter assumed to have been written in the 23rd century before our era. Confucius himself declared cultivation of heresy to be injurious. And Mencius whose writings too are classical, laid upon the shoulders of all future ages the duty of persecuting heresy. He categorically defines heresy as everything which departs from the teachings of Confucius and the sages of a still greater antiquity. The *literati,* including the Mandarins, who are recruited from their midst by means of the State examinations, have always been persecutors of false doctrine: indeed it is they who uphold the government that is based upon the only true Confucian doctrine. The common people, deprived of schooling, are free from fanatical Confucianism. They have the privilege of supplying the victims and martyrs for the blood-drenched altar of intolerant officialism. Such are the reasons why the Chinese State would naturally persecute Christianity and Islam and also Buddhism and other numerous religious communities or sects which this religion has called into existence among the people.... Under the recently deposed dynasty (de Groot was writing in 1912) persecution was very severe. Imperial resolutions and decrees relating to persecution of sects may be counted by hundreds. Many uprisings of sects, smothered in streams of blood are declared by imperial decrees and resolutions to have been preceded by bloody persecutions under full imperial approval.

But the State religion, or Confucianism, was itself not free from secret society influence, as we learn from the observations of Hutson given in Chapter II.

We read in his independant testimony:—

The difficulty all missionary societies have had in getting a foothold on Szechuan is due to the Tang Tsu Hang (黨 子 行) or Confucian society. The plots of the *literati* culminated in the riots of 1895, etc.

And again:—

The Tang Tsu Hang or Confucian society is *par excellence* the society of the official, scholar and student. In its present form it dates from at least the Tang dynasty (A.D. 600–900), when the followers of the "Peach orchard trio" refused to recognise the Tang and clave to the Han.

We here get a glimpse into the religious background of the secret society world of China which confirms the view that the Han league in its esoteric aspect is derived from or based upon the classical, or conservative, or reactionary elements in the religion of China namely, Taoism and Confucianism; while the Hung league appears to derive in its esoteric or allegorical sense from the teachings of Buddhism.

COMPARISON OF THE TWO MAIN STEMS IN THE CHINESE SECRET SOCIETY WORLD

Granted a common origin in remote antiquity for both the Hung and the Han league, it may be helpful to give at this point a rough comparative analysis of the differences in their developed characteristics, as suggested in the two preceding chapters and in the writings of the authorities quoted therein.

In attempting this analysis we offer the following main conceptions for the reader's acceptance:—

    (1) The Han is antecedent to the Hung.
    (2) Both are susceptible of a threefold parallel interpretation, *viz.:*—
        (a) Allegorical, or ritualistic, or "religious".
        (b) Historical.
        (c) Political.

(3) The allegorical interpretation represents the Han as the Yin (陰) element and the Hung as the Yang (陽) element in human relationships.

(4) Just as the Han precedes the Hung, thus supplying the "missing degree" in the Hung ritual commented on by observers, so we submit does admission to the Han represent man's physical birth, and his journey through this world, while admission to the Hung as noted by all observers, represents man's physical death and his journey through the under-world back to heaven.

(5) The allegorical concept further presents the Yin or Han as worshipping the physical senses, or material interests or, as we say, the worship of this world or the worship of man, while the Yang or Hung represents the struggle of individual man towards the light of a world-to-come, and the worship of an unseen supreme being or God.

(6) The historical interpretation presents the Yin or Han as developing through the Taoist doctrine of Lao Tze, perverted to the "worship of man"; and the Yang or Hung as developing through the Buddhist religion of self-perfection towards the worship of God, but debased to serve political ends.

(7) The political interpretation presents the characteristics of the two leagues as we have seen them develop from their pristine traditional age, through the rebellious anti-dynastic era, down to the present degenerate period and suggests that the two leagues may at the present day have already entered upon a further period of political resurgence and rivalry, each in support of one of the two *régimes* which are struggling for supremacy in China to-day.   We return to this subject in a later chapter.

(8) One point remains.   *Is the story of the Peach Garden trio allegorical?*

The story of the Peach Garden trio (Chapter II above) is generally accepted as historical, but from a comparison of the two main stems of Chinese secret society development as now presented, it would seem that the story may also be an allegory, representing again the struggle between the Yin and the Yang.

A logical interpretation of the allegory would seem to be that the three *born* brothers Chang Chio, Chang Pao and Chang Liang, who for purposes of their crusade took the names Lord of Heaven, Lord of Earth and Lord of Man respectively, represented the trinity of the Hung League with which these names are so closely bound up and were the torch-bearers of Light in a darkened world: while the three *sworn* brothers whose individual characters as given in the story suggest affinity to that "licentious liberty" which is the ideal of the Han league, represented the powers of Darkness; and the victory of the latter over the Yellow cap rebels, the triumph of Darkness over Light.

This view is not necessarily refuted by the facts as far as they are at present known and other observers are silent on the point.[1]

It remains to note that the three *sworn* brothers of the Peach Garden story have no honoured place in the Hung league tradition.   It is only the fact of their oath taking and the power and unity which it gave them, that is held up for emulation in the Triad ritual.   The fact may be that the oath of the Peach Garden was merely adopted into the Hung tradition as a convenient symbol, associated with an historical incident and dating from an epoch in which the Hung and the Han ethic or the Yang and the Yin principle were in active conflict.[2]

The authorities are silent upon the origin of the colour yellow adopted by the "Yellow Cap" rebels, but the suggestion is here made that the rebellion may have been a Hung League or "Yang" challenge to the "Yin" or decadent materialism of the magnificent Han epoch.   Some support is found for this view which would also explain the origin of the colour yellow in a work *Tibet's Great Yogi Milarepa*[3] edited with an introduction by Dr. W. Y. Evans-Wentz in which we are told:—

Throughout Tibet and extending into......parts of Mongolia there are three chief schools of Buddhist philosophy.   In Tibet these schools are—
(1) "The Yellow Caps" or Gelug Pa, the established church of northern Buddhism, wielding through its spiritual head, the Dalai Lama, both spiritual and temporal power.
(2) "The Followers of the Apostolic Succession" or Kargyut Pa.
(3) "The Red Caps" or Adi Yoga School, the unreformed church.
The Yellow Caps acknowledge the superiority of the Red Caps in all questions connected with magic and the occult sciences.

The "Yellow Cap" rebellion (A.D. 184) took place historically about a hundred years after the advent of Buddhism to China (A.D. 75), and its leaders, who in the peach garden story received their inspiration from the miraculous acquisition of the "book of Heaven" which was the "Way of Peace" and who "initiated their disciples into its mysteries" may perhaps have been converts to the new religion of Buddhism, as well as champions of the

Footnote.—(1) But *see* Pearl Buck, *The Chinese Novel* (1939) pages 33–34 and 43–44 where she comments upon the allegorical interpretation placed upon this story by the Chinese *literati* of the past.

Footnote.—(2) For a description of the ancient annual Yin Yang fertility rites in China, *see La Civilisation Chinoise*—Marcel Granet Paris 1929—especially Chapter IV "Rivalités de Confréries" page 229 ff.

Footnote.—(3) Also spelled Milarespa.   The name of that most popular Tibetan poet and ascetic, who lived in the eleventh century A.D.

Comparative analysis of the opposing characteristics of the Han and the Hung League, deriving from a common origin in the ancient Chinese belief in the "Yin Yang" or Dual element in nature.

陰 YIN — 和 — 陽 YANG

	YIN		Harmony 和 三才	YANG		
Allegorical	Historical	Political		Political	Historical	Allegorical
1. Left hand side						1. Right hand side
2. Female						2. Male
3. Black						3. White
4. Numbers 2, 4, 6, 8, 10			The three Powers "Universism" (de Groot)			4. Numbers 1, 3, 5, 7, 9
5. Incomplete			Taoism Confucian-Buddhism			5. Complete
6. Symbol:—						6. Symbol:—
7. Earth			The Yellow Cap Rebels 黃巾 賊 A.D. 184			7. Heaven
8. Darkness			The Peach Garden Trio			8. Light
9. The West						9. The East
10. Night						10. Day
11. Rest (passive)						11. Motion (active)
12. Cold						12. Heat
13. Moon						13. Sun
14. Immutability						14. Mutability
15. Negative (cf. Boaz)						15. Positive (cf Jakin)
16. Physical Birth						16. Physical Death
17. Man's journey on Earth						17. The Journey of the Soul after death
18. Imperfection						18. Perfection
19. Mammon						19. God
20. "Evil" (鬼)						20. "Good" (伸)
21. The Worship of Darkness (荫) or Nature						21. The Worship of Light (明) or of a Supreme Being
22. The Worship of Man hence, ancestor worship						22. The Worship of God (Shang Ti 上帝)
	23. The Worship of Man		The Worship of Confucius. B.C. 500 (Tang Tzu Hang 养子行) (Hutson) B.C. 255		23. The Worship of God	
	24. Magic, Shamanism Demonology				24.	
	25. Lao Tze (老子) B.C. 600				25.	
	26. Taoism (道)				26. Buddhism in China circa A.D. 75	
	27. The Worship of Lao Tze. (Chiao Fei 教匪) (Hutson)				27.	
	28. The Nature School of Taoism. ("Tsa Men Ti Hiung 咱門兄弟" "We Brothers") (Hutson)				28.	
	29. The Han Liu 漢流 circa A.D. 1000				29. The Hung league Political period A.D. 1700	
		30. The Han League	30. The Hung League		
		31. Reactionary Anti-Manchu Pro-Han	31. Ethological		
		32.	32. Anti-Manchu		
		33.	33. Pro-Ming		
		34. The Ko Lao Hui circa A.D. 1750	The Doctrine of the Mean	34. The Society of God-worshippers 上帝會 A.D. 1845		
		35. Hostile to Christianity		35. The Tai Ping Rebellion (A.D. 1850-1864)		
		36. Hostile to Foreigners		36. Tolerant of Christianity		
		37. Stronghold north of the Yangtze		37. Tolerant of Foreigners		
		38.		38. Stronghold south of Yangtze		
		39. The Tally Society 鐏子行 Chien Tzu Hang (circa A.D. 1800) (Hutson)		39.		
		40. The Boxer Rebellion A.D. 1900		40.		
		41. The "puppet" regime in North China to-day	The Revolution in China 1911	41. The K.M.T. in China to-day		
		42. Materialist		42. Regenerate		
		43. Collectivist		43. Individualist		
		44. Rule of Force		44. Rule of Law		
		45. The "Might" State		45. The "Right" State		

Hung tradition; and it may well have been from this point that the Hung tradition became impregnated with Buddhism. The fact that the Yellow Caps acknowledged the Red Caps as their superiors in magic and occultism is not without its significance in the same context.

In the absence of any authoritative views on this point, we prefer in the analysis which follows, to show the story of the Peach Garden Trio as the point of bifurcation of the Hung and the Han secret society stems in historical times, albeit the real point of cleavage may have been many centuries earlier.

We will now attempt to present a tabulated comparative analysis of the chief characteristics of these two main stems with their respective religious, historical and political background.

ESOTERISM IN CHINESE SECRET SOCIETY RITUAL

This rough analysis shows the historical ties that have bound up Chinese beliefs with Chinese politics, and with the secret associations which, we suggest, lie behind both.

There is depicted too the dualism of man's origin, as understood by the Chinese, and how this dualism seems to reflect itself in the two main branches of China's secret society world.

This dualism, the left and right of man's nature, is the basis of ancestor and fertility worship and bears a close analogy to similar beliefs in other world religions, and indeed, to the "left" and "right" in human affairs in the world to-day.

These analogies have been widely discussed by many observers and we need only note here a few points of special interest to our subject, which may have escaped the observation of others.

The "lingam-yoni" emblem of Hinduism and more particularly the sacred cowrie shell of the Hindus, which has the same significance, bears a close resemblance in form to the Yin Yang symbol of China.

The conventional or non-realistic form of the "lingam-yoni" is the two intertwined equilateral triangles known in the west as the "Shield of David" or the square and compass of freemasonry.[1] The triangle on its base, the active agent, the compass, is the male principle; and that on its apex, the passive agent, the set square, the female.

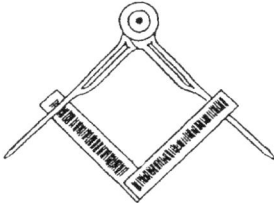

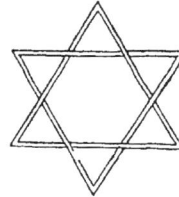

The equilateral triangle comes to us from the first proposition of Euclid, (B.C. 300) in which by the intersection of two equal circles which, we may suggest correspond to the Yin and Yang, and the juncture of their centres with their point of intersection, the triangle is evolved.

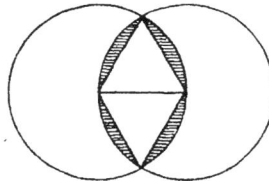

Not only does the triangle thus appear, but the intersecting segments of the Yin and Yang circles present the form of the *Vesica Piscis* or "fish-bladder" or womb, the universal religious emblem of female guardianship or preservation, containing within it the triangle, or emblem of all things created; in fact, the two triangles of the "Shield of David", the one on its apex, the female, the other on its base, the male.

Applied to Chinese belief, (*vide* p. 6 *supra*) we suggest that the two circles represent the circle of darkness, the moon (月) and the circle of light, the sun (日), or the Yin and the Yang of the Taoist cosmos and of the Han league, intersecting instead of coinciding; the one thus producing within itself two and the two producing all things, or the

Footnote.—(1) Known in masonry as the "Seal of Solomon".

Heaven, Earth and Man of the Hung league, of which the equilateral triangle is the symbol, and the character (明) meng "light", the sign.

It is not our intention to plunge into a discussion of the esoterism which lies behind and beyond the tenets and ritual of the Han and the Hung league, but as this esoterism pervades our subject at every turn, it cannot be totally ignored. We will content ourselves with one example suggesting the significance of the Hung slogan 反清復明 Fan Ts'ing fu Meng "Overturn Ts'ing restore Meng" and taken from Ward and Stirling *op. cit.* Volume I page 6:—

> The Ming (明) dynasty meant originally the Dynasty of "Light", while there are two characters in Chinese pronounced "Ts'ing", one indicating the dynasty of the Manchus *viz.*: (清), and the other meaning "dark" or "darkness" (青) Although the English word "Darkness" best conveys the general idea to Western minds, in reality the meaning is much more subtle. Ts'ing (青) in Chinese means "clear" and the radical really denotes "colour in nature", whether it be black, blue or green. The antithesis is between *Light* 明 representing *Spirit*, and *Darkness* 青 representing, the *material Universe*.
> Hence I have used the word "Dark" so as to convey the opposition to the Divine light. The mystical meaning is "the light of the spirit engulfed in the material envelope". Ts'ing 青 also means the vital force in man and also the passions with the character for 'heart' added 情 (*see* de Groot *The Religious system of China* Volume IV pp. 10 and 17 sq.). When written, the dynasty 清 is distinguished from darkness (青) by the addition of the character for "Water". Therefore, all that is required to alter an allegory of the fight between Darkness and Light into a political one, teaching that its followers should overthrow the Manchu, is to insert these three drops of water in front of the character of Darkness. Thus it is only necessary to read for the dynasty Ts'ing 清 the word ts'ing 青 darkness and for the dynasty Ming 明 the word meng 明 light, to recover what was probably the original meaning of the Hung ceremony throughout.

Stanton, *op. cit.* page 33 in his account of the traditional history gives the Chinese characters for the slogan "Overturn Ts'ing restore Ming" found by the Hung patriarchs on the blade of the miraculous sword (*see* page 9 *supra*) as 反泪復泪 which present an even more vivid contrast between 'darkness' and 'light' and intensify the esoteric significance of the slogan and its association with the Yin and Yang principle.

He says:—

> Carved on the hilt of this miraculous sword were two dragons struggling for a pearl, typical of two emperors contending for empire and, near the point, the characters 反泪復泪 fan ts'ing fu meng "subvert Ts'ing restore Meng".

Stanton does not give the source or authority for the use of the characters 泪 and 泪 to represent the dynasties of Ts'ing and Meng, nor are those characters recognised by Chinese lexicographers.

The character 反 fan means according to Giles, "to turn back, to turn over, to turn wrong-side-up: contrary, opposite, to rebel", so that, esoterically, their use by Stanton is exactly appropriate to convey the idea of the "fall of man", and the Emperor of Light (Yang) contending with the Emperor of Darkness (Yin) to re-establish the rule of light in the physical world.

Some readers may see in all this an explanation of the perplexing world conditions of to-day. Beginning with the Russian revolution of 1917, the *Zeitgeist* of what was formerly Christendom seems to have swung further and further to the left (Yin) until the religious principles of the preceding (Yang) period have been almost eclipsed: established standards of political morality forsaken, leading to the overthrow of the former values and principles of civilised intercourse: civilisation itself brought to the verge of destruction by the challenge of Force against Law; and man himself threatened with a return to the jungle.

These conditions have called forth from the leaders of the western world to-day a cry for "moral rearmament", a swing away from the Yin and a return to the Yang for the preservation of that civilisation so painfully built up in Europe during the past five hundred years.

A similar phenomenon is observable in China under the nationalist (K.M.T.) government which launched a "New Life" movement in 1934 aimed at that moral re-armament which has now been taken up in the west.

Another concurrent movement has still more recently (1938) appeared in China, sponsored again by the K.M.T. government and called "The Spiritual Mobilisation Movement" which has declared self-sacrifice and patriotism to be its keynotes and the spiritual unity of the people: national resistance to invasion and the national salvation of China to be its objects. This movement has spread to Malaya where in April, 1939, oaths in support of it, similar to those taken in China, were taken by the leaders of the Chinese community.

These movements towards moral re-armament seem unconsciously to have a common source in what may perhaps be the rising desire among thinking men and women both in the East and West to overthrow the domination and false values of the perverted Yin and to re-establish in the world of to-day the standards and principles of the Yang.

DIFFUSION OF COMMON ESOTERIC FEATURES

In contemplating the esoteric similarities that seemingly lie behind secret society forms throughout the world, we are reminded of two facts; firstly, as mentioned in the introduction to this work, in the remote past all secret societies seem to have taken their beginning from the religious forms which arose in one or other of the two areas dominated by the highlands of Tibet in the East and Mount Ararat in the West of Asia, both of which areas have an historical association with the survival of man after a great deluge: secondly, in the comparatively recent past, that is to say since A.D. 1250 up to about the period of the Great War of 1914–1918 as pointed out by Sir George MacMunn in the *The Romance of the Indian frontiers* (1931) page 53, there have been four great Tartar dynasties ruling the whole of Asia from the Pacific to the Bosphorus; the Manchu in China: the Mogul in India: the Khajiar in Persia and the Ottoman in Turkey.

The Mogul was the first to go in A.D. 1857, the Manchu the next in A.D. 1912 and the other two disappeared just after the Great War (*see* Parker *A thousand years of the Tartars* (1925).

To the common origin of these great Tartar dynasties deriving from the eastern or "Tibetan area" and to the fact that they conquered and over-ran the western or "Ararat area" after the twelfth century A.D., may perhaps be ascribed in some measure the preservation of those esoteric features common to most secret societies down to the present-day. Two examples will suffice.

THE MICROCOSM IN THE MACROCOSM

The Chinese concept, quoted by de Groot above, that man is part of the Universe "a microcosm born spontaneously from and in the macrocosm" was known to the Greeks four centuries before the Christian era.

Dr. Charles Singer in one of his works *From Magic to Science* (1928) page 67 has:—

> The *Timaeus* of Plato became one of the most influential of all the works of antiquity and especially it carried the central dogma of mediaeval science, the doctrine of the macrocosm and microcosm.

It is not an unreasonable conjecture that if this belief had its true origin in the Yin Yang of the "Tibetan area" it may have penetrated to Europe "across the roof of the world" by means of those contacts in the pre-Christendom period, referred to in the Introduction to this work.

Dr. Singer *op. cit.* introduces us to the work of the eleventh century English writer Byrhtferth of Ramsey (circa A.D. 970–1020) whom he refers to as follows on page 141:—

> In the belief of the men of the Dark Ages, there was a close relationship between the external and the internal world, the macrocosm and the microcosm. Thus they discerned a parallel between the four ages of man and the four seasons, between the humours of the body and the solstices and equinoxes, between the four elements and the four cardinal points, and so on.
> Such a scheme is elaborated in the following diagram[1] drawn up by Byrhtferth of Ramsey (circa A.D. 1000) . . . . . whose copious commentary on Bede may be regarded as the final product of the nature-knowledge of the Dark Age.

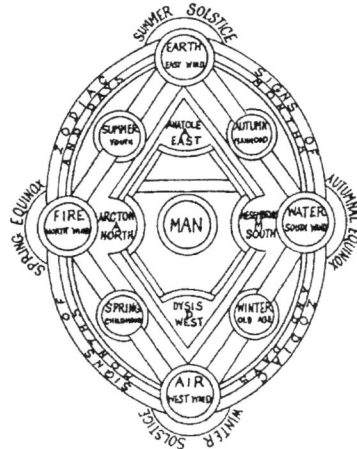

Footnote.—(1) The diagram is Fig. 52 on page 143 in Dr. Singer's work and is a modified version in English of the original as re-drawn from a Greek and Latin MSS. copy, dated A.D. 1110 in St. John's College, Oxford.

For purposes of reproduction herein the diagram has been further simplified, the main features only being shown.

The diagram is of particular interest as illustrating the diffusion of those esoteric features latent in the Yin Yang principle.

Thus for example we see again in it the ellipse formed by the two intersecting circles and enclosing the two equilateral triangles: and in addition we see the idea of "Time" and the elements of nature embraced within its perimeter, the whole enfolding at its centre "the spirit of Man in its material envelope".

Dr. Singer continues on page 143:—

> This diagram is remarkable for associating the initials of the four cardinal points (Arcton, Dysis, Anatole, Mesembrios) with the letters of the name ADAM, to whom in the text the name protoplast is attached..... It is therefore probable that the scheme which Byrhtferth introduces had arrived in England before the eighth century.

Lastly in Chapter VI of the same work, Dr. Singer introduces us to the writings of the abbess Hildegard of Bingen (A.D. 1098–1179) who elaborated a complete science of the universe illuminated with drawings based upon her visions, and having as its main structure her conception of the relation of the macrocosm and microcosm. Several of these illustrations are reproduced in Dr. Singer's work and vividly suggest an inspiration drawn from the Chinese principle of the Yin Yang. In discussing the sources of Hildegard's scientific knowledge (op. cit. pp. 234–239) Dr. Singer comes to the conclusion that although she repeatedly claims that her knowledge was revealed to her in waking visions, it nevertheless reflected the earlier Greek philosophies of Aristotle and Plato which were then beginning to be re-diffused in the West, after the "Dark Ages", through the Arabic translations of those works.

This view would still permit acceptance of the conjecture that their true origin may be found in the Yin Yang principle of China.

THE VESICA PISCIS

Our second example of the diffusion of esoteric features is that of the *vesica piscis* or "fish bladder" mentioned on page 42 above.

This symbol permeates heraldry and freemasonry and is found in some form in all religions and in the signs of the Hung league.[1] It is discussed by Ward in *Freemasonry and the Ancient Gods* page 247 ff., but its association with the fish is nowhere made plain, unless we are to trace it to the first manifestation of Vishnu, "the Preserver", who according to Brahmanism first appeared in the shape of a fish, the form of life from which the higher animals derive. The similarity in shape between the ellipse of Euclid's first proposition and the body of a fish will be noted. The *vesica piscis* is the universal emblem of the female principle in Hinduism, "the circlet of bones" the female pelvis, the "doorway of life" in that religion. It is too, the halo, or nimbus, or *aureole*, the protective ellipse appearing in Christian symbolism, statuary and painting and is always depicted therein as encircling the body or head and as being of *gold*.

Thus, in the description of one of the visions of Hildegard of Bingen, given by Dr. Singer op. cit. page 216 we read:—

> I saw a fair human form and the countenance thereof was of such beauty and brightness that it had been easier to gaze upon the Sun. The head thereof was girt with a golden circlet through which appeared another face as of an aged man.

The numerous coloured illustrations of these visions reproduced in Chapter VI of Dr. Singer's work, present a recurrent picture of the two concentric circles of the macrocosm (which we liken to those of the Yin Yang) and depict man, the microcosm, within the orbit of the inner human figure, which forms the circle of darkness and upon whose head rests the golden circlet.

This symbol is identical with the sacred "ichthys" of Christianity, defined in the dictionary as: "A symbol in the form of a fish connected with Christ because the Greek letters gave the initials of the Greek words "Jesus Christ, Son of God, Saviour". The two constant features of the emblem are its association with the fish and its workmanship of gold.

There is a Malay folk-tale dating from the Hindu period and given by Fraser in *The Golden Bough* (abridged edition) page 676 ff., which is seemingly connected with the *vesica piscis* or "fish bladder". In this story the King of Indrapura fell in love with the adopted daughter of a rich merchant, who to protect her, caused a golden fish to be made, and into it put the soul of his adopted daughter and hid the fish in water. The jealous queen tortured the girl whose name was Bidadari, but could not kill her because her soul was in the golden fish. To save herself from further torture she told the queen of the fish. The queen then procured the fish and fastened it round her own neck and so had Bidadari in her power. By day the queen wore the fish and Bidadari lay in a swoon and at night she put the fish in water and Bidadari revived. The King learned the secret and took the fish from the queen and released it in water and Bidadari recovered and married the King of Indrapura.

We have in this story what seems to be an allegory of the external soul's troublous journey through this world under the protection of the *vesica piscis*. In Malay lore Bidadari became a nymph of Indra's paradise and is a kindly fairy who presides at the union of lovers.

Interest in the *vesica piscis* as the sign of the Yin or female, or "left" principle in human affairs, is not merely academic, but appears to have a direct connection with the

Footnote.—(1) *See* Ward and Stirling *op. cit.* Vol. I pages 110, 114 and 117.

practice of "black magic", voodoo and sex rites throughout the world[1] and with much of the sedition, terrorism and political unrest which has swept the British Empire since the rise of Communism twenty years ago. Its effects in India in blood and bomb worship to appease the hungry goddess Kali, the female attribute of Siva, may be read in popular form in Sir George MacMunn's books: *The Underworld of India* and *The religions and hidden cults of India*. Its effects in Malaya through the advent of Thuggism from India and the later alliance of that cult with the Han league in Malaya, will be noted in subsequent chapters. Thus MacMunn in the former work has:—

> The modern Bengal secret murder cult and the Babbar Akali movement are tinged with the same fervour that animated the darkest side of Thuggism. And it is just this presence of some ancient horror existing beneath the outer surface of perfectly reasonable political aspirations, which has been a source of trouble to many a kind viceroy desiring only India's good.

As shown in Chapter II, knowledge of the Han league ritual is still meagre and fragmentary as compared with the full exposition of the Hung league ceremony provided us by Schlegel in 1866. Some further fragments of what is probably a truncated form of the Han league ceremony appear later in this work, particularly in Chapters IX and XXXI, but until a full and reliable text of the whole ceremony of initiation is obtained, no very successful attempt can be made to interpret its esoteric meaning.

The nature which seems to be ascribed by the Chinese to the Yin principle with which the Han ceremony is allied, provides, nevertheless, a general guide to the probable esoteric interpretation of the Han and we shall have occasion to draw attention in subsequent chapters to what seems to be a fundamental association between the "Han ethic" and present political unrest in Burma, French Indo-China, Palestine and the West Indies, where the presence of "some ancient horror," unsuspected by those on the spot, often outruns the "reasonable political aspirations" of the people and leads to the acute embarrassment of the local government.

Those readers who may be further interested in the esoteric significance of the Hung ritual on the other hand, as exemplifying the Yang principle and in its similarity with rituals found in the religions of the world, will find a full discussion of the subject in Ward and Stirling *The Hung Society* Vols. II and III and in *Freemasonry and the Ancient Gods*, another work by Ward published in 1921[2].

SECRET SOCIETY INFLUENCE UPON CHINESE EVERYDAY LIFE

It remains only to make some reference to the practical influence exercised by the two main secret society currents upon the everyday life and social and economic relationships of the masses of China.

Of the political and criminal influences exercised by them, the subsequent chapters of this work largely treat.

An opinion upon this aspect of our subject has recently been expressed by an American writer K.S. Latourette in his work *The Chinese, their history and culture* 2 Volumes, published in 1934 from which the following extracts are taken:—

Latourette Volume II page 98–99 has:—

> Commerce, like industry has been by small units organized in guilds. Firms are family or partnership affairs, and the need of organization for protection against each other and outsiders has forced those of the same trade together into guilds which in their essential features resemble those formed by craftsmen. They have their officers, their membership, their regular meetings, and their rules. Through them are negotiated many of the transactions with merchants of other cities. They fix the minimum prices which their members can charge and exact penalties for infringement of these or of other regulations. They serve as benevolent societies to assist impecunious members. They tend to be wealthier than the craft guilds and many of them own sumptuous halls which are not only places of business but centres of social life. Merchant guilds have often been very powerful and have even coerced officials or the general community.
> In addition to the guilds organized by particular crafts, professions, or types of business there have been, what are usually called in English, 'provincial guilds'. Uniting the natives of a province or city who reside in another city, they are evidence of the strong local loyalties found in China, as elsewhere, and of community discrimination in favour of natives and against outsiders. The provincial guilds provide social and business rendezvous, give aid to indigent fellow-provincials, and at times assist in promoting the business interests of their members.
> So strong has been the habit of working through guilds that in some cities an organization like a guild and including most of the merchants of the locality has become the governing body of the entire community. Notable instances have been seen in Swatow and Newchwang.
> Moreover, secret societies, so prominent a factor in Chinese life, have entered into commerce. Organizations of that character of more than local extent sometimes bring together members of related businesses and occupations in an entire region—boatmen on the Yangtze, for example, and some of the shippers.
> These societies and the guilds have often been a force in politics and even in international affairs. For instance, the guilds were largely responsible for the boycott of American trade in 1907 which was induced by the ill-treatment of Chinese immigrants to the United States by American officials.

Again Volume II page 199–201 Latourette has:—

> The family has been the strongest universal social unit in China. However, as we have seen, it has been and is but one of several types of unit. Another has been the secret societies. These have played and continue to play a very important part in the life of China, probably much

---

Footnote.—(1) *See The History of witchcraft and demonology*, by Montague Summers (1926) in the *History of Civilisation* series.

Footnote.—(2) Other interesting works on this subject are: *Freemasonry in China* Giles: *Symbolism East and West* Murray-Aynsley: and *Signs and Symbols of Primordial Man* Churchward.

more so than do the numerous fraternal organizations in the United States. Often they have had an active and influential part in politics. It is estimated that to-day about half the adult males who can lay claim to any influence are members. Almost everywhere they must be reckoned with by those who would understand the life of a community. Just how ancient are those now in existence is a matter of doubt, although some of them claim to have begun hundreds of years ago. Certainly organizations of this general type have long had a share in Chinese life. The Red Eyebrows and Yellow Turbans, prominent in civil wars in Han times, appear to have been fraternal bodies. Repeatedly in seasons of disorder others have come to the fore. Since the societies are secret, it is impossible to give a full and satisfactory account of them. Sometimes, as we have seen, they have religious features. Often they have solemn and binding vows of brotherhood, and they may have secret codes. Frequently, too, their discipline is very severe, exacting of members strict obedience to the commands of their officers. Some are to be found among the Chinese abroad and fill a prominent role in the lives of the emigrants. Such, for example are the tongs among the Chinese in the United States. These tongs, it may be added, seem to be peculiar to Chinese colonies in America and were, perhaps, originally organizations for legal and benevolent services to their members.

One of the most famous and powerful of the secret societies has been the Ko Lao Hui, or Association of Elder Brothers. It is said to have an elaborate ritual and its members are reported to take an oath of brotherhood.

It is believed to have been responsible for numerous outbreaks and riots from time to time and of late years sometimes to have taken to banditry. It has been much feared and revenge visited for any violence to its members has added to the dread felt for it.

Sir Eric Teichman in *Affairs of China* (1938) page 296 refers to the Ko Lao Hui as "the all-pervading subterranean brotherhood" which rules in secret the lives of millions of the Chinese peasantry.

Latourette continues at the same reference:—

Chapters of another, the Red Spears, are often started as a farmer's protective society. Then ruffians frequently obtain the weapons and the power, compel all residents to join and pay fees or submit to their demands, struggles ensue with adjacent groups or with the authorities, and disorder is accentuated. Still another has been the Triad Society (San Ho Hui), also known as the Hung Society and the Society of Heaven and Earth. Just how far back it goes is uncertain, but it has been implicated in more than one rebellion and has probably appeared under various guises and aliases. It is organized by individual chapters as well as by a general brotherhood. Opposed to the Manchus, it was associated with the beginnings of the T'ai P'ing rebellion. The White Lily and the White Cloud Societies are also famous. Both probably originated near the beginning of the twelfth century. Both appear to have been founded by Buddhist monks and were originally religious and Buddhist in character. Both repeatedly fell foul of the state and were responsible for outbreaks, some of them serious.

Secret societies have played an important part in recent politics. A large proportion of the leaders of the country belong to them. Indeed, it is said to be impossible for an aspirant for power in the state long to be successful without membership in one of them. As a rule a man joins only one and not many contrary to the practice in the United States. A connection with more than one is said to work disadvantageously for him.

Again Volume II page 202–203:—

Chinese society has been and is an interplay of groups, some of them united by blood, some by economic ties, and some by political, professional, or religious interest. By the custom of "sworn brotherhood" men not otherwise bound to each other pledge reciprocal fidelity, perhaps professing to hark back for a precedent to the famous "Peach Garden Oath" taken during the Three Kingdoms by Lui Pei, Chang Fei, and Kuan Yu. It is believed that it was such a relationship which in 1898 led Yuan Shih-k'ai to reveal to Jung Lu, Kuang Hsu's plan of action and so precipitated the fateful *coup d'état* of September of that year.

All these many kinds of associations make Chinese society extraordinarily complex. They are one reason why the uninitiated foreigner finds particular problems and situations in politics and business so difficult to understand. Even an intelligent Chinese frequently fails to know all the elements involved.

This American observer writing as recently as 1934 claims that the secret associations of China occupy as powerful a place to-day in the politics, commerce and daily intercourse of the people as they have ever done in the past.

This view, if true, gives the present-day European official an inkling of what may lie behind the Chinese mind when as so often happens, the leaders of the Chinese community approached upon an apparently simple subject, present what seems to be an illogical point of view, resort to equivocation, or, retiring within themselves, assume an attitude of baffling obscurantism.

A more pronounced view is stated by Coulet in his *"Les sociétés secrètes en Terre d'Annam"* (1926) in which page 23, he poses the question:—"Without attempting to investigate their remote and still obscure origin, what is the nature of these societies? What is their organisation and what the ideal that activates them?

To which he replies that his book, based on official records, will attempt to show:—

Par l'analyse des éléments magique, religieux et profanes, qui se trouvent dans toutes les sociétés secrètes d'Annam, que la société secrète chez les Annamites est une phénomene social, précis dans son essence et défini dans ses manifestations. Toute société secrète en terre d'Annam est: (a) magique par ses symboles: (b) religieuse par ses rites et ses statuts: (c) profane par son organisation materielle, la réunion intime de ces trois éléments formant un tout harmonieux et un "être social" puissant de vie.

The chapters that follow will show that secret societies in Malaya to-day present a somewhat similar if less aggressive parallel to that *imperium in imperio* attributed to them in French Indo-China by Coulet in the passage above.

The existence of secret society influence in business relationships among the Chinese in Malaya to-day is shown by the following extract from the *Review of Chinese Affairs,* issued for official use by the Chinese Secretariat, Singapore. The issue of June, 1939, page 27 has:—

> Among the Chinese in Malaya there have existed from the earliest times associations of persons engaged in the same trade or business for the purposes of mutual assistance and protection, and for the settlement of disputes. In the early days, the various lodges of the Triad Society which until 1890 were not illegal, fulfilled some of the functions normally covered by trade associations. They were large mutual benefit and protection societies covering between them practically the whole of the Chinese population. The spheres of influence of the various lodges were mainly territorial, but, in so far as it is customary for Chinese establishments carrying on a particular trade to group themselves together in one area, the tendency was for those engaged in particular trades to join particular lodges, though a particular lodge might embrace several trades in its own territorial sphere. Examples of this tendency still persist in Singapore among the unlawful hooligan "societies" which are the descendants of the Triad lodges. For example, the Cantonese sawmills at Kallang are under the control of the Lo Kwan gang of the Khwan Yi Society, the Cantonese and Hakka Quarry Workers of Pulau Ubin are all members of the Tai Hok Society, the Cantonese wharf coolies are all members of the Hung Yi Khwan Society. And it is true to say that where this tendency persists no one can engage in the particular trade in the particular area without acknowledging the claims of the controlling society.
>
> A more particularised form of trade association is the Guild. From the earliest times until recent years the Trade Guilds were the only organisations catering exclusively for the interests of persons engaged in particular trades. They have existed in China from very ancient times and included mastercraftsmen, journeymen, and apprentices. They were particularly common in Malaya among the old-established trades such as tailors, shoemakers, goldsmiths and carpenters. The usual type is governed by a committee composed of employers and employees. Rates of wages, hours of work, holidays and terms of apprenticeship were decided by the guilds. In addition they frequently fulfilled the role of Friendly Societies, providing funeral benefits for the members, and accommodation for unemployed.

Latourette refers to banditry, a common plague of the peasantry in China, as having a close association with the secret society world. Upon this subject, Sir Eric Teichman *op. cit.* page 295 has:—

> Closely associated with Chinese brigandage are the secret societies with which China is and always has been honeycombed: the Triads and White Lotus in the south and the Ko Lao Hui ("The Brotherhood of Elders") the Big Knives, Red Spears, Boxers and others in the northern provinces.

The geographical distribution of Triad in the south and Ko Lao Hui in the north given in this passage should be noted.

Sir Eric Teichman continues:—

> The secret societies are mysterious and nefarious, a strange mixture of freemasonry and magic rites, co-operation, terrorism and sedition.
>
> For three hundred years their main impulse was that of secret revolutionary agitation against the Manchu dynasty. Rebellions, revolutions and disturbances invariably brought their activities to light. They were associated with the T'ai P'ing rebellion in the nineteenth century, with the Boxer rising and the revolution which resulted in the abdication of the dynasty in 1912. And during the troubled years of the Republic their activities were manifested in the recurrent waves of brigandage and civil war. No doubt they played their part in the rebellions of the Communists against the Nanking government: and they are probably to-day proving a thorn in the side of the Japanese.

It is safe to say that the Japanese invasion of China has given an enormous impetus to the political and criminal activities of the secret society under-world in China proper, a circumstance which cannot fail to have its effect, in turn, among the Chinese overseas.

Not all of this activity is necessarily patriotic, nor even in support of the Chinese cause: much of it, may well be exercised selfishly and traitorously on behalf of the invaders.

Some of it may spring from fresh causes and new alignments and loyalties, but most of it will be based upon the age-old systems and rivalries of the past.

Chinese history shows that the north has always been ready to make terms with the invader, while the south, largely due to the influence of the Hung league, has remained for three hundred years implacably hostile to him.

For this reason alone, an attempt to analyse the history of these powerful underground combinations and unravel their mutual relationships in the recent past, should be helpful in estimating the direction of their present-day political and other developments under the stress of actual invasion and may, perhaps, offer a pointer to the navigator in the turgid and uncharted waters of modern Chinese political intrigue.

We would only add to the comment of Sir Eric Teichman above, that if the southern half of the secret society world of China (the Hung) is proving a thorn in the side of the Japanese, some elements of the northern half, the Han, may well be found in support of the Japanese puppet *régime*. Grounds for this view are offered in Chapters XXVII, XXXI, XXXII and XXXIV *infra*.

CHAPTER IV

THE HISTORICAL BACKGROUND OF THE HAN AND THE
HUNG LEAGUES OVERSEAS

We must now briefly refer to the historical contacts between the Chinese and those peoples bordering on Malaya and to European relations with those peoples during the nineteenth century.

These early contacts would seem to have left behind them the taint of Chinese secret society influence which is still alive to-day in the countries affected, as a source of political embarrassment to the western powers.

EARLY RELATIONS BETWEEN BURMA, CHINA AND SIAM

The progenitors of the present Burmese race are believed to have come from the central Asian highlands. Their language belongs to the Tibeto-Burman branch of the Tibeto-Chinese language and their written language derives from the ancient square Pali. Their religion is the purest form of Buddhism extant, and their system of *pon-gyi* or monks, vowed to poverty and celibacy and the religious education of the people, presents the highest form of religious discipline and community-service to be found in the East.

The first great historical epoch of the Burmese as a race begins about A.D. 1000 when they set up their capital at Pagan in central Burma. About A.D. 1272 the Burmese invaded China and were defeated and in turn were invaded by the Tartars (Southern Sung dynasty) who took and sacked Pagan which has remained a ruin.[1]

For several centuries thereafter Burma was divided into separate states, the two chief being Ava in the north (Upper Burma) and Pegu in the south (Lower Burma).

During the sixteenth, seventeenth and eighteenth centuries the Kingdom of Siam stretched down as it does to-day through the neck of the Malay Peninsula to the Bay of Bengal and held a thriving trading port south of Pegu at Mergen (modern Mergui) in the province of Tenasserim. In the middle of the eighteenth century the Lower Burmans of Pegu successfully invaded Upper Burma and sacked the northern capital Ava.

The Upper Burmans retaliated and re-conquered Upper Burma, captured Pegu from the Lower Burmans and Tenasserim from the Siamese and invaded Siam proper, finally in A.D.1766 capturing and burning Ayuthia, the then capital of Siam, just north of modern Bangkok. Various Chinese invasions of Burma through the Shan States during the same period were repulsed by the Burmese. The Burmese were finally driven out of Siam by the Sino-Siamese General Phya Tak (1767–1782) whose career is referred to in Chapter XIII *infra*, but the war did not end till 1793.

This series of wars established the unification of Burma including the Shan States under a single dynasty, which remained in power until the coming of the British in the nineteenth century.

RELATIONS BETWEEN BRITISH INDIA AND BURMA 1824–1900

In 1824 the Burmese invaded British India and the first Burma war followed. The Burmese made peace in 1826 and the provinces of Arakan and Tenasserim were ceded to Britain. In 1852 the second Burma war with British India broke out and the whole of Lower Burma was annexed to the Indian Empire. In 1879 the then King of Burma, King Mindon, died and was succeeded by his son Thibaw (1853–1916) who practised barbarities upon his people and showed hostility to Britain, finally issuing in October 1885 a proclamation calling upon all Burmans to drive the British into the sea. The third Burma war ensued. Upper Burma was occupied and annexed to British India in 1886 and King Thibaw was deported to India. Guerilla warfare followed, but the country was finally pacified by 1890.

This brief sketch shows the early Chinese Tartar contacts with Burma across the Burma-China border and the later stormy period when Burma and Siam were at each others throats *via* the southern route. The significance of these contacts in the spread of secret society influences from China among the peoples affected, will appear in later chapters. The seeds of these contacts may perhaps remain in the heart of the Burmese people to-day, as they do among the people of Annam, and may in some measure provide a focus for, if not an actual cause of present-day political unrest in Burma.

RELATIONS BETWEEN FRANCE, CHINA, INDO-CHINA AND SIAM 1800–1907

In the painful process of opening up China to western trade in the nineteenth century, France as well as Britain took a foremost part, not only in China proper but upon China's southern borders.

Before the rise of western power in Asia, China had for centuries claimed suzerainty, albeit largely of a shadowy kind, over the whole of that vast land tract stretching from

---

Footnote.—(1) For an account of this period *see* Maurice Collis, *She was a Queen* (1937).

Tibet and the valley of the Irrawaddy to Manchuria. In the last reign of the Manchu dynasty 1875–1908, China lost Upper Burma to Britain; Annam and Tongking to France; part of Manchuria to Russia; besides Korea and Formosa to Japan.

The influence of France in what is now French Indo-China began in 1789 when Pigneau de Behaine, a French missionary, aided Gia-Long (1802–1820) to seize the throne of Annam which had been rendered vacant by a rebellion. French activity waned during the period of the French Revolution, but in 1862 the French established a colony in Cochin with Saigon as capital and in 1863 made the Kingdom of Cambodia adjoining it, a French protectorate. In 1867 they added three provinces of southern Annam to their colony of Cochin-China. In 1873 they captured Hanoi, capital of Tongking province, against the opposition of bands of Chinese pirates. A commercial treaty with Annam followed, but in 1882 renewed fighting broke out in the delta of the Song Koi and regular Chinese troops were employed to assist Annam against the French. The Chinese were finally defeated by the French at Foochow in 1883. By a treaty of 1884, Annam and Tongking, despite the protests of China, acknowledged the suzerainty of France.

Adjustments of territory between France and Siam followed during 1893–1907. In 1897 French power in what is now French Indo-China was finally established and a French Governor with residence at Hanoi took the place of the viceroy of the King of Annam in Tongking. In 1900 the small territory of Kwangchow in south China opposite the island of Hainan, was added to French Indo-China.

The cause of active French intervention in Annam in 1862 was the continued hostility of the Annamites to French missionary effort. Some fifty Roman Catholic priests had been murdered within a few years, besides many thousands of the people who had embraced the Christian religion.

The French campaigns of the later nineteenth century increased the hostility of China to the foreigner and his religion, an hostility which led ultimately to the "Boxer" outbreak of 1900.

Since the establishment of French power in Indo-China in 1884 there has been a history of continual revolt against the French, having for its object the restoration of the independence of Annam.

This revolutionary movement has been almost entirely fostered by what we identify in Chapter XXVII *infra* as the Han league which, true to its origin and character, has increasingly employed in its furtherance of this object "magic in its symbols, religion in its rites and a gross materialism in its organisation", together with an implacable hatred of Christian proselytism.

A succinct and detailed account of these rebellions covering the period 1886–1916 and based upon official records is given in a work already referred to, *Les sociétés secrètes en Terre d'Annam* by G. Coulet published in Saigon (Librarie C. Ardin) in 1926.

RELATIONS BETWEEN BRITAIN AND CHINA 1800–1860

The East India Company established itself in south China in 1635 and there grew up a trade in opium between India and China which before 1767 rarely exceeded 200 chests. In that year it amounted to 1000 chests and in 1792 the British Government sent an embassy under Lord Macartney to Pekin in order to place the relations of Britain and China on a proper footing. The mission was not successful. In 1800 an imperial edict was issued from Pekin forbidding the import of opium and threatening Chinese who smoked it with heavy punishment. A trade in smuggled opium then began. In 1816 a second British mission to Pekin also failed. In 1834 the charter of the East India Company expired after two hundred years trading with south China. The head of the East India Company at Canton was in that year replaced by a representative of the British government, who was unable to carry on trade with the Hong merchants as his predecessors had done, but nevertheless determined to expand trade on a basis of equality. On the other hand the Chinese government was equally determined not to acknowledge the claim to equality and to suppress the import of opium.

In 1839—just a hundred years ago,—Lin Tseh Su was appointed Governor-General of Canton with orders to bring the "barbarians" (the British) to reason. As a result of his measures, Great Britain declared war for the first time upon China in 1840.

In such an unequal struggle there could be but one outcome and peace was signed at Nanking on board H.M.S. "Cornwallis" in August, 1842, by which the island of Hong Kong was ceded to Great Britain: the ports of Canton, Amoy, Foochow, Ningpo and Shanghai were opened to British trade and residence: agreement was reached to recognise the Christian religion and to conduct official correspondence on terms of equality.

Nothing was said in the Treaty about the trade in opium, and the smuggling traffic continued as before. During the post-treaty period, troubles between Great Britain and China continued owing to this traffic, particularly at Canton where in 1856 the Governor-General Yeh Ming Chin refused to meet the British envoy Sir John Bowring. This refusal led to war being declared a second time upon China by Great Britain with whom France joined as an ally. This is known as the "Arrow" war, from the name of an opium ship concerned in its cause.

Canton was captured in December, 1857, and Governor-General Yeh sent a prisoner to Calcutta. A joint commission of the allies Britain and France, took over the temporary government of Canton and the powers laid their demands before the emperor. A draft treaty was concluded at Tientsin in 1858 between the powers and China which was to be ratified within a year, by which the former treaty of Nanking (1842) was confirmed and in addition China undertook to exchange diplomatic agents on equal terms with Britain: to protect Christian missionaries and their converts: to permit British subjects to travel in the interior of China for trade or pleasure: to open five additional "Treaty ports" to foreign trade (Newchwang, Cheefoo, Swatow and the islands of Formosa and Hainan) and to open the Yangtze river to the trade of foreign vessels.

Treaties on the same lines were made with France, Russia and the United States. In the revision of the tariff regulations which followed this treaty, opium was included among the legitimate articles of import and an arrangement made whereby a foreign official was accepted by China for the collection of all maritime duties:

Upon the return of the representatives of the Powers in 1859 for ratification at Pekin within the year, they found that the Chinese had meanwhile changed their minds, re-fortified the approaches to Tientsin and were prepared to oppose by force ratification of the Treaty.

The powers were unable to capture the defences at Taku and after a severe engagement had to withdraw.

A third expedition was immediately prepared by the Powers under the same plenipotentiaries and with a force of 20,000 men, the Taku forts were taken in August, 1860, and a combined march made upon Pekin. The Emperor (Hsien Fung) fled and his brother Prince Kung undertook to negotiate with the Powers. In October 1860 the Treaty of Tientsin (1858) was ratified at Pekin and opportunity was at the same time taken to obtain an additional indemnity from China, together with the cession to Britain of the Kowloon peninsula (2 square miles) on the mainland opposite Hong Kong.

Thus ended the attempt of China to keep herself aloof from the rest of the world: and with the year 1860 there opened a new era in Chinese relations with foreign powers.

In the years that followed many additional "Treaty Ports" were added by negotiation. The "New Territory" on the mainland, adjoining Kowloon (376 square miles) was leased by Britain in 1899 and added to Hong Kong.

The anti-foreign feeling engendered in the Chinese mind by these treaties imposed by a *force majeure* and which are nowadays referred to as the "unequal treaties", was to find its first coherent expression in the "Boxer" rebellion of 1898–1900 referred to below.

THE EAST INDIA COMPANY'S TRADING STATIONS IN THE STRAITS OF MALACCA

1. **Malacca.**—Malacca is the oldest European settlement in Malaya, having been in the hands of the Portugese, the Dutch and the British at different times since A.D. 1511. It did not cease to be Dutch until 1824 (*see* Winstedt *History of Malaya* 1934, page 204 ff.).

2. **Ujong Salang.**—About 1760 the directors of the East India Company became anxious to establish a naval base and trading centre near the Straits of Malacca to counteract the paramount Dutch trading influence in Malaya with headquarters at Malacca and in the archipelago generally.

In 1771 Francis Light the employee of a Madras firm and the Captain of a "country" trading vessel, endeavoured to find a suitable site and during the years 1771 to 1786 he used the harbour of Ujong Salang or "Junk Ceylon" as it was called (the place now known as Tongkah or Puket on the West Coast of Siam) as a trading base for his Madras firm.

"Junk Ceylon" was known at that time to be rich in tin, and Light's activities there attracted thither increasing numbers of immigrant Chinese tin-miners from China.

3. **Penang.**—In 1786, the directors of the East India Company under pressure from Warren Hastings, made their decision upon a trading base and Light bought the island of Penang from Kedah on the Company's behalf.

If we exclude the transient seventeenth century claim of Patani, Penang is, therefore, the oldest original British settlement in Malaya.

Its settlement by Light attracted Indian traders from Madras and Chinese immigrants from China.

From 1786 to 1805 Penang was a dependency of Bengal and was under trial by the East India Company as a trading station.

In 1800 the territory of Province Wellesley was purchased from the Sultan of Kedah and added to Penang.

In 1805 Penang was promoted to be "the fourth Indian presidency" with a large staff of officials from India. (Bombay, Madras and Bengal, being the other three Presidencies).

4. **Singapore.**—In 1819 the Settlement of Singapore was founded by the genius of Sir Stamford Raffles. This new trading centre immediately attracted large numbers of Chinese and Indian immigrant settlers.

So much for the dates in Malay history which have a bearing on our subject. The full story of the East India Company's Trading Stations in the Malay Archipelago is given in Chapter I of L. A. Mills *British Malaya 1824–1867*, published in 1925. The story of the English pioneer traders in Malaya is given in Winstedt's *History of Malaya* (1934) page 97 ff.

The following facts should also be noted—

In 1824 final agreement was reached between England and Holland and the British returned to occupy Malacca.

In 1826 the settlements of Malacca and Singapore were transferred from the supervision of Bengal to the control of the Penang or Eastern Presidency, still under the East India Company.

In 1830 owing to heavy and unremunerative expenditure, the Penang Presidency was abolished, the staff of officials was greatly cut down and the three "Straits Settlements" were reduced to the status of an East India Company "Residency", with the centre of administration still in Penang.

The rapid growth of the trade of Singapore soon made it the most important of the three settlements and in 1832 the capital of the administration was transferred to Singapore.

Between 1830 and 1867 Penang and Malacca gradually sank to a condition of less and less trading importance in comparison with Singapore.

In 1867 the control of the Straits Settlements was transferred from the Government of India to that of the Colonial Office in London.

It will be seen from the foregoing that up to the date of the "transfer" in 1867 there was much more and longer-established Indian influence both official and racial in Penang than in either Malacca or Singapore.

In 1870 the first Chinese-speaking government official in the Straits Settlements, Mr. W. A. Pickering, was appointed from the Chinese Maritime Customs Service[1] to be "Protector of Chinese", Singapore. This marked the first step towards the building up within the Straits Settlements' Civil Service, of a corps of European officers, qualified to handle Chinese affairs at first hand.

It also marked the first departure from that method of indirect rule or rule by proxy which had been the sole means of government under the East India Company namely, through the Headmen or "Kapitans" of each community, whether Malay, Arab, Indian or Chinese, under which, as Emerson says in *Malaysia—A study in direct and indirect rule (1937)* page 26 :—

> "Operating through close-knit secret societies......the Chinese established governments for themselves......and lived their own lives subject to a minimum of interference from above".

For the "Kapitan" system there was substituted "an affirmative governmental control" or attempted direct rule of the Chinese, in place of the *imperium in imperio* of the East India Company's *régime*, and thus began that struggle between government and Chinese secret societies in Malaya, the story of which is traced in the following chapters.

The publication of Schlegel's book (Chapter I *supra*) in 1866 and the appointment of Pickering in 1870 combined to give the various governments in Malaya then taking shape under British control, their first introduction to the realities and perplexities of that struggle.

THE IMPORTANCE TO THE SECRET SOCIETY HISTORY OF MALAYA OF EVENTS IN CHINA BETWEEN 1842–1868

It must be remembered that during the first half of the nineteenth century large numbers of immigrant Chinese from the two southernmost maritime provinces of China, Fukien and Kwangtung, and from the southern inland province of Kwangsi and from the island of Hainan, were streaming to the "South seas" encouraged by the increase in trade of the Western powers and by the economic growth of the Straits Settlements and the Netherlands Indies after the Napoleonic wars.

To these incentives were added the disturbed internal condition of south China itself, which began with the Taiping rebellion in 1849 and the opportunities for profit which the nascent tin mining industry in Malaya and the Netherlands Indies offered to the business instincts of the southern Chinese.

This powerful immigrant stream altered the course of history. It changed the direction of Malaya's economic orientation from India to China: made Chinese cities of Penang and Singapore and led directly to British intervention in Perak in 1874.

The extent to which this statement is true may be judged from the following figures. In Penang in 1820 there were 7,800 Chinese in a total population of 35,000: in 1860 there were 20,000 in a total population of 60,000: in 1930 there were 176,000 in a total population of 359,000. In Singapore in 1820 there were 3,000 Chinese in a total population of 5,000: in 1860 there were 50,000 in a total population of 80,000: in 1930 there were

---

Footnote.—(1) Established under the Treaty of Tientsin in 1860.

421,000 in a total population of 567,000[1]. The preponderance of alien communities in the Federated Malay States (exclusive of the Colony and the Unfederated States) at the present-day, is illustrated by the official estimate of population in 1935 viz., Malays 643,000: Chinese 717,000: Indians 387,000: Others 30,000, in a total population of 1,777,000.

We must therefore examine more closely the circumstances that gave rise to this influx in order to gain a clear estimate of the quality and antecedents of those Chinese immigrants who were destined to affect so greatly the subsequent history of their adoptive country.

Emphasis must here be placed upon the importance of historical events in influencing the direction of Chinese secret society cross-currents in Malaya. These cross-currents are identified more closely in the two following Chapters, but their sources in Malaya are to be found in historical events in China during the same period, outstanding among which were :—

(1) The Treaty of Nanking, 1842, which granted toleration to Christian missionaries and their converts. In the Treaty of Tientsin 1860, this was extended to protection.

(2) The Taiping rebellion (1850–1864) which in a sense gained its momentum from this protection.

(3) The migration to the south of China of the Hakkas who were the backbone of that rebellion.

(4) The struggle for "living-room" in the Canton province between the native Cantonese (Puntei) and the Hakka immigrants 1850–1868.

(5) The Small Knife rebellion of Amoy of 1853.

(6) The growing hostility of the Chinese to the infiltration of the foreigner 1860–1900, which led to frequent anti-foreign riots, anti-missionary massacres and finally to the "Boxer" outbreak of 1900.

Some of these events are briefly noted below.

THE ADVENT OF CHRISTIANITY TO CHINA

The Christian religion like other religions has not escaped association with secret societies in China and so we must give a brief outline of its advent to that country.

Christianity was first brought to China by Nestorian missionaries about A.D. 625 and flourished for 200 years but shared the persecution of Buddhism in about A.D. 840 and did not survive. It was re-introduced by the order of St. Francis, and in A.D. 1307 Corvino, a Franciscan, was appointed bishop of Pekin, then known as Cambalu, or Cambulac, by Pope Clement the Fifth.

Roman Catholicism flourished under the Mongol dynasty (1280–1368) particularly under Kublai Khan, but was persecuted out of existence under the early Ming Emperors, until it was again re-introduced by Jesuits of the order of Loyola in A.D. 1580.

By the beginning of the eighteenth century the hostility of the Tartar Government was aroused against Christians (Jesuit converts) because of the suspicious similarity between their rituals and activities and those of the Triad society, then at the beginning of its "political period" and pledged to drive out the Tartar rulers. For a description of Jesuit initiation rites and a comparison between them and Freemasonry and Triad rites, see Heckethorn op. cit. Volume I page 285.[2]

Official persecution of Christians and members of the Hung league continued unabated until Christianity became again tolerated in 1842. Membership of the Triad Society remained outlawed and the period from 1800 to 1850 in south China is one of frequent Triad risings.

By the Treaty of Nanking (1842) a measure of toleration for the Christian religion was granted, which was strengthened into protection for Christian missionaries and their Chinese converts by the Treaty of Tientsin (A.D. 1860).

THE GENESIS OF THE TAIPING REBELLION 1830–1850

There are many published accounts of this strange episode in the internal history of China, none of which satisfactorily explains the nature and degree of secret society influence which all observers admit to have been present in this struggle. In an attempt to present this aspect of the revolt, and to canalise its less familiar under-currents, we prefer to be guided by such native Chinese sources as exist; and by the original investigations of the Rev. E. J. Eitel and Commander Brine, R.N. extracts from whose work on the subject are given below; and to draw inferences from some of the views already expressed in the preceding chapters.

First, we must anticipate the extract from Rev. Eitel by borrowing at this point two statements from it.

Footnote.—(1) Official census Report 1931.
Footnote.—(2) There is a full bibliography in a recent work The Power and secret of the Jesuits, Fülöp-Miller, 1930.

Eitel says :—

(1) The whole Taiping rebellion from its first faint beginning in Kwangsi to its suppression through the fall of Nanking was started, sustained and controlled to the end, by Hakkas from the Canton province.

(2) Both oral tradition and their own geneological records agree in pointing to the north of China as the original home of the Hakkas where it is said they were located at the end of the Chow dynasty (B.C. 255). Most family chronicles which I have examined mention the province of Shantung as the original dwelling place of their forefathers.

It is a matter of history that owing to successive persecutions, the Hakkas migrated southwards after the fall of the Chin dynasty (A.D. 419) and ultimately established themselves in the province of Kwangtung from the beginning of the Ming dynasty (A.D. 1368).

A second influx of Hakkas into the southern districts of Kwangtung province began in A.D. 1730, and from being men of the north they became men of the south, sojourners in a province not their own and conserving their own language and customs and refusing assimilation with the native Cantonese, with whom they lived on terms of open hostility, a position they have maintained to the present-day.

We may reasonably assume that they have also adhered in the main to whatever secret society allegiance their forefathers bore in the province of Shantung, and this, from the preceding chapters we know could only have been to the Han league. This view is strengthened by the historical fact that under the Han dynasty before their geographical transplantation, the Hakkas enjoyed a position of imperial favour and preferment (*see* Eitel below). We have referred in Chapter II to the White Lotus sect whose rebellions in the south have been commonly identified with those of the Hung League and to the fact that Hutson alone among observers, has identified the White Lotus with the Han League which, in turn, would identify the White Lotus with the vanquishers of the "Yellow Cap" rebels of A.D. 184. From this it seems possible that the rebellions of the White Lotus, although occurring in the territorial sphere of the Hung League were in fact inspired by the Han League. Without more precise knowledge of the tribal identity of the leaders of the various White Lotus rebellions, we can do no more than suggest their probable origin among the Hakka immigrants south of the Yangtze river.

The Taiping rebellion sprang from a pseudo-Christian cult known to history as the Shang Ti Kau (上 帝 教) lit. the Doctrine of God or, as it is commonly, though less correctly, called "The Society of God-worshippers" as explained in full below.

The view that this cult owed its true derivation, paradoxically enough, to the Han league rather than the Hung, is sustained by the following translated extract from the well-known Chinese encyclopaedia *Chi Yuen* (辭 源) which gives :—

Shang Ti Kau (上 帝 教), the doctrine of God. This is the name of a secret society formed by a Cantonese named Chu Kau Tho 朱 九 濤 during the reign of Toh Kwong 道 光 (1821–1850). Its leader, Hung Siu Ch'un (洪 秀 全) made use of Christian missionary work for revolutionary purposes. The society copied the Christian religion and called God, Tin Fu 天 父 (Father of heaven) Jesus Christ, Tin Heng 天 兄 (Elder brother of heaven) and looked upon Jesus Christ as the elder son of God and Hung Siu Ch'un as the second son of God. The object of this revolutionary movement, unlike that of the 三 合 會 Sam Hup Wui (Hung League) was not that of restoring the Ming dynasty. During the years of the Taiping rebellion the 上 帝 教 or Society of the Doctrine of God was sometimes confused with the Sam Hup Wui, but this is an error.

Later evidence will tend to show that the purpose of the Taiping rebels was the restoration of the Han. The same Chinese encyclopædia *Chi Yuen* gives the following interesting link between the Society of God-worshippers and another secret society, the Three Dot Brotherhood, which is of great importance in Malaya. We give an account of this Brotherhood in Chapters VIII and IX *infra*, wherein we suggest its identity with the Han League :—

Sa Tiam Hui 三 點 會 the Three Dot Society, a secret society in the reign of Toh Kwong 道 光 of the Tsing dynasty (1821–1850). It professed the Doctrine of God (上 帝 教), with Hung Siu Ch'un (洪 秀 全) as its chief.

In this single reference from a purely Chinese source, there is support for the view expressed above that the Taiping rebellion although launched perhaps by accident, perhaps by design, under the banner of a pseudo-Christianity, belonged essentially to the Han camp.

This view receives further support from the following considerations:—

The *Chi Yuen* reference above mentions a certain Cantonese named Chu Kau Tho (朱 九 濤) as being the real founder of the Society of God-worshippers. A reference to this man occurs in a Chinese work called *History of the T'ai P'ing Rebellion*, 'Tai P'ing Tin Kwok Kak Men Sz' (太 平 天 國 革 命 史) written by Wong Chung K'ei (王 鍾 麒) in the modern Chinese encyclopædia called *Maan Yau Ch'un Shu* (萬 有 全 書) and published in 1929 by the Commercial Press, Shanghai. On page 3 of this work we read in translation—

About the middle of the reign of T'o Kwong (1821–1850) a Cantonese named Chu Kau Tho started a secret society in Kwangtung Province on the lines of the former White Lotus Society (白 運 教).

His purpose was to make money for himself by deceiving the credulous and to this end he spread the rumour that he possessed magical powers. He claimed, among other things to have made a bronze incense bowl in which he could sail the seas. He gained a large following, amongst whom were two men named Hung Siu Ch'un (洪 秀 全) and Fung Wan San (馮 雲 山). After joining the society of Chu Kau Tho, Hung Siu Ch'un went to Canton to undergo the Provincial Examination; and while in the city he met a foreign missionary preaching in the market place and became interested in this missionary's words. Later he obtained a copy of a book called *Keng Sai Leung Yin* (緊 世 良 言) "Good words for exhorting the age", which contained translations from the Old and New Testament of the Christian Bible.

After the death of Chu Kau Tho, Hung Siu Ch'un began to feel that the doctrine of his late teacher lacked popular appeal and so with the aid of Fung Wan San he began to preach a new doctrine based upon what he had learned of Christianity. This he called Shang Ti Kau (上 帝 敎) or the Doctrine of God and named his newly formed society the "Three Dot Brotherhood" or Sa Tiam Hui (三 點 會). In 1836 Hung Siu Ch'un and Fung Wan San went to Kwangsi to preach his doctrine.

No hint is given at this reference of the origin of the name "Three Dot" nor, in the literature of the rebellion which we have seen, does the name anywhere appear, nor does it seem to have been a "popular" name for the "society of God-worshippers" among the profane during the years of the rebellion.

It has been suggested to us that the term expressed the "Trinity" or three essences, or three leaders of the religious movement which later became the Taiping rebellion, but we do not know the origin of this view nor have we seen any evidence to support it and we offer what seems to be a better explanation of the name in Chapter VIII *infra*.

The *Maan Yau Ch'un Shu* reference is interesting in other respects. It mentions Chu Kau Tho as being the real "founder" whose name is also given in the *Chi Yuen* extract above, and whose claim to magical powers fits the mystical sect of the Han league. The mention of the White Lotus suggests that Chu Kau Tho was a member or renegade member of the White Lotus which, it will be remembered Hutson (Chapter II *supra*) definitely assigns to the Han League.

If we accept the *Maan Yau Ch'un Shu* evidence, we would have to admit that the real genesis of the movement which became the Taiping rebellion is to be found in the Han League and that those "Christian" and Triad attributes assumed by the Taiping rebels were merely accidental accretions.

This view is sustainable even after a closer examination of the facts surrounding the genesis of the rebellion which is made below. We must remember that after the ban on Christianity was raised in 1842, Christian converts in south China greatly increased, especially amongst the Hakkas (Khehs).

Whether due to this circumstance, or to mere coincidence, the seeds of the Taiping rebellion were fostered in an atmosphere of pseudo-Christian teaching and among a people, the Hakkas, alien to the soil of the rebellion and whose revolutionary sympathies belonged, if the foregoing supposition is accepted, not to the native Hung League of the south, but to the northern Han League, which paradoxically was essentially hostile to Christian proselytism. In the complexity of the revolutionary movement known to foreigners as the Taiping rebellion, in which both "Taipings" and "Triads" took part against the dynasty, the true distinction between the two components of the rebellion may be found in the immemorial hostility between the Han and the Hung league, whose only common factor was anti-dynasticism.

This view, if acceptable, would explain much that has hitherto been obscure in the movement and would render intelligible the historical demand made by the leaders of the "Taipings" at the outbreak of the revolt, that before they would recognise assistance from the "Triads" they required the latter's renunciation of membership of the Hung league, which we may assume meant "a change of flags" and adherence to the Han.

It would also explain the absence of anti-foreign sentiment in the Taiping rebellion itself, which would have been a leading feature in a purely Han league rebellion. This may have been due to the fact that the "Taipings" launched their rebellion against the Manchus under the false colours of a "Christian" crusade and under the protection granted to Christian converts by the Nanking Treaty. The "Taipings" could not, therefore, afford to quarrel with the foreign element under whose religious banner they were enabled to organise and, with typical Chinese adjustment to circumstance they accepted the paradox as a concession to their disguise.

This would be but another example of that opportunism or perhaps deliberate pretence, or colour-protection which is second nature to all subversive secret society intrigue, and which in the case of the Taiping rebellion, successfully hoodwinked the natural enthusiasm of foreign Christian missionaries into support for its cause, and would explain the ultimate paradox that when its camouflage had worn threadbare after fifteen years of struggle, the rebellion itself was finally suppressed by foreign Christian forces commanded by General Gordon, the most Christian of them all.

It would also help to explain how several decades later, Sun Yat Sen was able to combine the revolutionary forces of both the Han and Hung leagues for the final assault upon the Manchu power.

THE STORY OF THE TAIPING REBELLION 1850–1864

We must now give a brief account of the Taiping rebellion itself, already referred to in Chapter I, whose special importance to Malaya is to be found in the fact that its ranks were largely composed of those very southern Chinese who, during the period of the rebellion, were supplying the immigrant stream to the south seas; and in the fact that the spirit of lawlessness engendered by the rebellion was twice prominently reflected in Malaya during those years: first in the Singapore riots of 1854 and secondly in the Penang riots of 1863 and 1867, which are discussed fully in a later chapter.

In 1813 there was born to a small Hakka farmer about thirty miles from Canton a son named Hung Siu Ch'un (洪秀全) who for reasons connected with his earlier history became a half crazy religious visionary. If we accept the *Maan Yau Ch'un Shu* evidence above, he had probably earlier become a member of the White Lotus Society.

In 1844 according to the presently accepted historical version, one of Hung Siu Ch'un's Hakka followers founded a religion on a Christian model, although himself not a baptised Christian, and called it Shang Ti Kau (上帝教) or the "Doctrine of God".

Again, if we accept the *Maan Yau Ch'un Shu* evidence, the basic organisation upon which the Shang Ti Kau rested was the White Lotus revival of Chu Kau Tho, with the Doctrine of God superimposed thereon by Hung Siu Ch'un and his associates. Everything that follows supports this view.

All authorities maintain that the "Society of God-worshippers" or "Taiping rebels" were not members of the Triad society and it is upon historical record that Hung Siu Ch'un refused the aid of Triad recruits unless they foreswore membership of the Hung league. The popular view nevertheless seems to have identified the "Taipings" with the Triad Society.

The fact that Hung Siu Ch'un's own surname was Hung (洪) "Inundation" the same as that of the Hung league, and that many of his followers on joining him changed their surnames to his, seems to be without significance as a reason for identifying the "Taipings" with the Triads.

Although it does not cover the whole period, the most faithful account we have seen of the Taiping rebellion is that by Commander Brine, R.N. *The Taeping Rebellion in China* published in 1862. This work is based upon original documents and information obtained in China by the author, who took part in many of its episodes.

The following facts are condensed from Brine's work :—

The leader of the movement Hung Siu Ch'un was not himself a revolutionary, but a disappointed candidate for literary honours under the Chinese imperial system of competitive examination. On one of his visits to Canton in 1833 for examination purposes, he was given a parcel of nine protestant tracts in Chinese called Keng Sai Leong Yin (劝世良言) "Good words exhorting the age", by a Cantonese named Leong Ah Fah who came to China from Malacca, where he had become a convert to Protestantism under the missionary Dr. Milne. In China the missionary Dr. Morrison ordained Leong Ah Fah as a native preacher of the gospel. The nine books contained whole chapters from the New Testament according to the first Chinese translation of Dr. Morrison, which was a very imperfect and misleading translation[1] as well as sermons, texts and other miscellaneous religious exhortations composed by their author Leong Ah Fah, who had had them printed in China about the year 1832. Hung Siu Ch'un accepted the gift of the books but did not at that time read them[2].

After further failure to pass the first examination in 1837 Hung Siu Ch'un's health broke down and he became subject to trances and visions, in which he saw a venerable man from Heaven who commanded him that all men should turn to him and all treasures flow to him for the salvation of the world from its perverseness.

In 1843 after he had regained his health and was employed as a teacher in a village near his home, a relative named Li (李)[3] happened to look through the books "Good words exhorting the age" and told Hung Siu Ch'un something of what they contained[4]. Hung Siu Ch'un then took up their study for the first time and professed to find in them the explanation of his earlier visions.

Brine has :—

"He then understood the venerable old man who sat upon the highest place and whom all men ought to worship to be God, the Heavenly Father: and the man of middle age, who had instructed him, to be Jesus the Saviour of the world".

Learning from the books the necessity of baptism, Hung Siu Ch'un and his friend Li administered baptism to one another and began to teach the new religion or Doctrine of God in which Hung Siu Ch'un assumed the roll of the younger brother of Jesus.

Footnote.—(1) Brine *op. cit.* page 93.

Footnote.—(2) According to the *Maan Yau Ch'un Shu* evidence Hung Siu Ch'un would at this time have been himself a disciple of the White Lotus revival of Chu Kau Tho.

Footnote.—(3) Probably 李秀成 who later became "Chung Wong" 忠王 or "Faithful King" of the Taipings.

Footnote.—(4) The exact titles are given in Brine *op. cit.* page 95.

His first two converts were Fung Wan San (馮雲山) and Hung Tai Jin (洪大全) both Hakkas of his own village.   Fung Wan San is referred to in the European literature of the Taiping rebellion as the real founder of the "Society of God-worshippers".   We may accept this view with reserve, because, from the evidence of the Chinese sources above,[1] the true fact may have been that Fung Wan San merely gave a pseudo-Christian twist to the White Lotus revival of Chu Kau Tho.   What is certain is that Fung Wan San was of great importance in the early days of the movement and one of the chief organisers of the subsequent rebellion.

The second convert Hung Tai Jin was a man of different stamp.   For various reasons he did not join the rebellion at its outset and was actually employed by the London Missionary Society as a Christian catechist in Hongkong between 1855–1858.   When he ultimately joined the rebellion in 1859, he was appointed the "Shield King" in the same year, after most of the original leaders were dead.

In 1844, Fung Wan San went into the country of the Miau-tsze (苗子) tribe in Kwangsi, and made many converts there.

In 1846 Hung Siu Ch'un and Hung Tai Jin visited Canton for the purpose of being baptised by the American missionary I. J. Roberts then working there, but they were unsuccessful.

In 1847 Hung Siu Ch'un joined Fung Wan San in Kwangsi where there were already some 2,000 converts, and from this time onwards the movement adopted the name "Society of God-worshippers" (Shang Ti Hui) or, if we accept the evidence of the *Maan Yau Ch'un Shu*, it was also known from now on as the Sa Tiam Hui or Three Dot society. Admission was by a form of baptism a description of which is given by Brine *op. cit.* page 81 (footnote) which bears a resemblance to the form of initiation to the "Three Dot Brotherhood" which in turn we identify with the Han League[2].

The movement attracted the attention of the authorities and Fung Wan San was arrested and put in gaol, but was subsequently removed from Kwangsi to his native province of Kwangtung and there set at liberty.   Some of the converts in Kwangsi now began to experience ecstatic fits and trances, among whom was Yang Siu Tsing (楊秀清) whose utterances gave him a commanding position in the movement.

These utterances and their association with a spurious version of Christian teaching were condemned at the time by foreign sentiment as being blasphemous, but in reality no claim was made that they were the sayings of God Almighty in our sense, but merely that they were, in the ordinary shamanist manner, met with everywhere among the adherents of the Han Liu school, the messages of the "god" pronounced through the mouth of the medium[3].   The pseudo-Christian atmosphere given to these pronouncements by the two mediums Hung Siu Ch'un and Yang Siu Tsing was mere embellishment obtained from the nine books "Good words exhorting the age".

As the movement progressed Yang Siu Tsing became the recognised medium of the "Heavenly Father" and another member of the society named Siau Chiu Kwai (蕭朝貴) was the recognised medium of the Elder Brother, or "Jesus", in the belief of the converts, while Hung Siu Ch'un was the recognised representative on Earth of the two Heavenly persons, and was known as the Second or Younger Brother, thus completing the "Trinity".

There was in all this no hint of politics or rebellion.   Thus Brine *op. cit.* page 95 has :—

Up to the year 1850 with the exception of a few expressions of hatred to the ruling power, it does not appear that Hung Siu Ch'un was anything more than a religious enthusiast whose mind had soured by want of success in his literary career.

From the year 1848 onwards the provinces of Kwangtung and Kwangsi were in a state of unrest due to "risings of local banditti" unconnected with the Society of God-worshippers.   The local Manchu forces were unable to control the local bandits who were Cantonese natives of the province (pun-tei) and not Hakkas, and furthermore appear to have been largely composed of members of the Triad Society.   In 1850 a dispute arose in the Kwei district of the province of Kwangsi between the Punteis and the Hakkas over a girl who was taken as a concubine by a rich Hakka after she had been allegedly promised in marriage to a Puntei.   The local officials were unable or unwilling to control the situation and in September, 1850, fighting began between the Punteis and the Hakkas, large numbers of the latter seeking refuge and protection in membership of the Society of God-worshippers, which was very numerous in that district.   From then onwards the character of the followers of Hung Siu Ch'un changed and he espoused the cause of the Hakkas in the dispute and became violently anti-dynastic and from that moment, the Taiping rebellion may be said to have begun.

Hung Siu Ch'un made a large number of converts, chiefly from among his own people the Hakkas.

Footnote.—(1) *i.e.* the *Chi Yuen* and the *Maan Yau Ch'un Shu.*
Footnote.—(2) *See* Chapters VIII and IX *infra.* This bears out the view of Hung Siu Ch'un's earlier association with the White Lotus.
Footnote.—(3) This again supports the origin of the Taipings in the mystical sect of the Han League (*see* Hutson Chapter II *supra*).

As the movement progressed Hung Siu Ch'un took command of it under the name T'ai P'ing T'in Kwok Wong (太 平 天 國 王) or "Emperor of the Heavenly Kingdom of Universal Peace", from which title the movement which soon assumed the form of a rebellion against the Manchus, took its rather inappropriate name of T'ai P'ing (太 平) "Universal Peace" Rebellion.

Hung Siu Ch'un saw a parallel between himself and the rebel leader Chu Yuan Chang a Buddhist priest who led the White Lotus rebellion of A.D. 1367 against the Tartar government of his day and became the founder of the glorious Ming dynasty. From this time onward Hung Siu Ch'un appears to have regarded himself as the founder of a new dynasty which he called the Tin Teh (天 德) Heavenly Virtue Dynasty and himself assumed the title of Tin Teh T'ai P'ing Wang (天 德 太 平 王) or first Emperor of the Heavenly Virtue and Universal Peace dynasty and from now on was known as Tin Wang (天 王) or Heavenly Prince or King. From this moment the original quarrel was forgotten and instead, a common anti-dynastic front was formed and Hung Siu Ch'un appears to have been joined by large numbers of "Punteis" including graduates and men of influence. Among the latter were several leaders of the Hung League who had been engaged in recent rebellions of their own, but Hung Siu Ch'un seems at this early period to have refused their services until they foreswore membership of the Triad and became members of his own society.

Be that as it may, from this point (March 1851) onwards the issue became one between "the rebels" meaning the Taipings and the Government forces.

A flood of proclamations, praiseworthy rules, and organisational decrees mixed up with his doctrinal exhortations[1] were issued by Hung Siu Ch'un, who appointed at this time his lieutenants with grandiose titles, as follows:—

Fung Wan San to be Southern King
Yang Siu Tsing to be Eastern King
Siau Chau Kwui to be Western King
Wei Cheong Fye to be Northern King
Shek Tat Hoi to be Assistant King.

He placed Yang Siu Tsing the Eastern King and the 'familiar' of the 'Heavenly Father' in the place of authority next to himself, and the rebellion was on.

We need not follow the fortunes of the rebellion in further detail, except to say that it achieved an astonishing success during the next twelve years and was actively supported in its later stages by the Hung League, either as opportunists upon the common anti-Manchu front, or as acknowledged allies of the Taipings.

In 1852 the rebels about 10,000 strong moved north from Kwangsi through Hunan, and captured Chungsha and reached the Yangtze river in December. They captured Wuchang and Hankow early in 1853 and descended the Yangtze, capturing Nanking in March 1853. Their forces then numbered about 100,000. In April Sir George Bonham, British Ambassador to China visited the Taipings at Nanking, where ten years earlier the first treaty between England and China had been signed.

At this time Chinkiang 50 miles down stream from Nanking was held for the Taipings by Loh Tai Kong (羅 大 綱) a Triad society chief, who had joined the God-worshippers.

In 1853 the Chinese part of Shanghai City was occupied by bands of the Triad Society and was held for the Taipings until 1855. The "Small Knife" rebellion mentioned below, was taking place at the same time at Amoy.

In May 1853 part of the Taiping army went north to Tientsin which it failed to capture and returned in 1855. In 1857 the Triad Society was in rebellion in Fukien province and the Mohamadan Chinese in Yunnan were also in revolt.

In 1856 the second war with Britain, (the "Arrow" war) had broken out at Canton.

In 1858 Lord Elgin's expedition sailed up the Yangtze to Hankow, but finding it all in the hands of the Taiping rebels, the treaty which ended the second war was signed at Tientsin.

In 1860 the Imperial troops attacked the Taipings in Nanking but were signally defeated. After the ratification of the treaty of Tientsin in 1860 the Manchu Government sought the aid of the foreigners to suppress the Taipings and General Gordon in command of a mixed force captured Nanking from the Taipings in 1864 and the rebellion was at an end.

It is not really surprising that the whole rebellion should have assumed in both the popular and the official mind, an identity with the Triad Society which was either part of it, or in active, if separate, support of it, and whose declared object for 150 years had been the overthrow of the Ming dynasty and which was so much better known than the obscure "Society of God-worshippers," which had only come into existence from the combination of curious circumstances described above.

Footnote.—(1) *See* Brine *op. cit.* page 125.

The true explanation may be that, taking advantage in the time honoured manner of the cover afforded by the pseudo-Christian doctrine of the half mad but harmless Hakka visionary Hung Siu Ch'un and the protection to Christianity granted by the treaty of Nanking (1842), the ever watchful Han league represented by the Hakkas Fung Wan San, Yang Siu Tsin and others who may well have been members of the White Lotus Society under the earlier leadership of Chu Kau Tho, seized upon this opportunity for a fresh revolt and appropriated the "Society of God-worshippers" to their own political purposes : and while using the visionary Hung Siu Ch'un and his religious mysticism as a convenient tool, really directed the movement by methods of shamanism towards the well worn political objective of overthrowing the Manchu and restoring the Han Dynasty.

This explanation would remove many of the perplexities and contradictions in the recorded story of the rebellion, and help to clarify opinion upon the share taken in it by the Han and the Hung leagues respectively.

This view is further strengthened by the fact that the rebels wore red turbans, the immemorial identity colour of Han league rebellions, and by the further statement in a document[1] issued by the rebels to a deputation of foreign consuls in 1861. This document is couched in the usual pseudo-Christian jargon of the rebels and contains the following :—

*   *   *

"But in the time of the Ming dynasty, the Tartar devils, originally serfs from beyond the Northern frontier, stole into China and usurped the emblems of Royalty, making unclean and polluting the land to a degree that no tongue can tell of.

*   *   *

At these their sins, the Heavenly Father being exceeding wroth would have destroyed the world. Then Jesus, the Heavenly Elder Brother, out of his mercy and loving kindness towards mankind, sent down the true and holy Lord, the Heavenly King, to wash out the stains of the Northern serf, and to set up anew the house of Han. (i.e. to re-establish a purely native dynasty)".

It seems from this extract highly improbable that the authors of this document could be anything but members of the Han League masquerading under the camouflage of the Society of God-worshippers.

Despite the conclusion that in the application of what we may call the Yin Yang or Han-Hung theory to the Taiping rebellion, the fact appears to emerge that the rebellion belonged essentially to the Han camp, the circumstances surrounding it and the fact that coming from the south it was identified in the popular and official mind with the Hung league, undoubtedly gave an enormous impetus to the revolutionary objectives of the Hung League, more perhaps than the Han, and for this reason we have shown the Taiping rebellion as belonging to the Hung camp in the analysis given on page 41 *supra*, although it may more probably belong to the other.

The story seems to reveal in fact an anti-dynastic alliance between the Han and the Hung, and later chapters will show that this alliance was probably revived by Dr. Sun Yat Sen in his final assault upon the Manchu power.

One circumstance more should be remembered, namely, that it was between the dates of the treaties of Nanking 1842, and Tientsin 1860 whereby protection for Christian proselytising in China was secured, that this devastating upheaval took place, for which in the eyes of Chinese officialdom, the foreigners and the protestant religion were mostly to blame.

After the suppression of the rebellion with foreign aid in 1864, the sequel was to be seen in the intensification of anti-foreign and anti-mission feeling between 1865 and 1900 during which period a succession of massacres and riots already referred to took place, culminating in the Boxer rebellion, a purely Han League outbreak in 1900.

THE HISTORY OF THE HAKKAS

We must now glance at some of the other disintegrating movements going on contemporaneously in south China during the years of the Taiping rebellion, and to understand these we must include an extract from Rev. E. J. Eitel's history of the Hakka people, published in the *China Review* Vol. 11 1873–74, which is as follows :—

"It is but quite lately through the famous Taiping rebellion that the Hakkas have obtained a place in the annals of the Middle Kingdom. Before that time no historian ever mentioned them so far as I am aware..... Both oral tradition and their own geneological records agree in pointing to the north of China as the original home of the Hakkas, where it is said they were located at the close of the Chow dynasty (B.C. 255). Most family chronicles which I have examined mention the province of Shantung as the original dwelling place of their forefathers— a few refer to the borders of Shansi and very few also to the borders of Anhui..... Again tradition as well as their own family records mention the period during which the Ts'in dynasty (B.C. 249–209) reigned, as a time when all the different clans of Hakkas were subject to a general bloody persecution. This seems to have been the first cause that cut the ancestors of the Hakkas adrift from their ancient quarters in the north of China and started them in that long continued course of erratic wanderings which carried them after the lapse of a thousand years to the extreme south, and imbued their descendants of the present-day with the restless spirit of vagabonds and rovers..... With the fall of the Ts'in dynasty however, their fortunes mended and in the course of the succeeding dynasties they enjoyed not only peace but Imperial protection, individuals of their number being even raised to high official appointments, especially

Footnote.—(1) Brine *op. cit.* page 323 and published in Parliamentary Papers on the Rebellion 1862.

under the Han dynasties (B.C. 202—A.D. 203) and during the reign of the Ch'in dynasty (A.D. 265–419). But this very preferment probably brought on the Hakkas the wrath of the dynasty immediately succeeding, for most of their family records mention further shifting of quarters and renewed immigration at the time of the downfall of the Ch'in dynasty (A.D. 419). Even the few tribes of Hakkas that had in spite of persecution, faithfully clung to their native mountains in Shantung had to flee now to the south of Honam and to the mountainous regions in the south-east of Kiangsi and to the very borders of the Fokien province.

The rise of the T'ang dynasty (A.D. 628) compelled the Hakkas again to strike their tents. This time it would seem, a separation took place; the majority of their clans taking refuge in the mountains of Fokien whilst a few hovered on the high mountain chains which separate the Kiangsi and Kwangtung provinces.

*　　*　　*

Since the rise of the Mongol dynasty (A.D. 1280–1333) the Hakkas seem to have made their first appearance within the borders of the Canton province. But they do not appear to have settled down there permanently or in large numbers till the beginning of the Ming dynasty (A.D. 1368) when disturbances in the Fokien province compelled those Hakkas, whose ancestors had been peaceably settled there for centuries, to take refuge in the Canton province. So over-whelming were the numbers of Hakkas issuing from Fokien into the Kia-ying-chow prefecture, that they drove everything before them and took exclusive possession of the whole of Kia-ying-chow, which to the present-day forms the head-quarters of the Hakka people. About the same time when the Hakkas entered the Canton province from Fokien, an influx of Hakka clans from Kiangsi took place into the districts north-west of Kia-ying-chow.

The Hakkas found pleasant quarters in the Canton province. But the roving spirit that possessed their ancestors would not let them rest. Besides, the Hakkas, being not only an industrious but also an exceedingly prolific race, soon found their quarters in Kia-ying-chow and in the neighbouring districts of the Hwuy-chow and Chau-chow prefectures too narrow. Numbers of them pushed farther into the heart of the Canton province, either wandering about on the tramp as stone-cutters, barbers or blacksmiths, or settling down here and there, first on uncultivated land and tilling that, then recruited by fresh contingents from Kia-ying-chow encroaching upon the fields of the Puntis, and gradually gaining ground by continual feuds with them. The outbreak of political disturbances at the beginning of the seventeenth century gave a new impetus to this movement, and about the year 1730 A.D. hordes of Hakkas poured into districts even to the west and south-west of Canton, settling down especially in the Fa-yuen, Hoh-shan and Sin-ning districts.

*　　*　　*

But the most important epoch in the history of the Hakkas opened with the rise of the Taiping rebellion. I do not propose here to follow the fortunes and misfortunes of these rebels, whose exploits have become a matter of history. Suffice it here to state that the whole Taiping rebellion, from its first faint beginning in Kwangsi to its suppression through the fall of Nanking, was started, sustained and controlled to the end, by Hakkas from the Canton province. The rebel Emperor, his ministers or kings, as they were styled, his generals and administrators, were all Hakkas, though thousands of Chinese of other than Hakka extraction swelled the ranks of the Taiping rebels. The fact that a handful of Hakkas contrived to raise such a powerful rebellion which but for the ill-advised and thankless interference of the foreign powers would most certainly have resulted in the downfall of the Manchu dynasty, and the equally astonishing fact that, through all the vicissitudes of their march from Kwangsi to Nanking, they succeeded in retaining the supremacy among the ill-assorted cohorts of rebels from all the eighteen provinces,—these facts, I say, speak volumes for the power there is in those rough sons of the soil. It is well known that both the English and French commanders, during the last war with China[1], came to the conclusion that there is better material for good soldiers in these simple-minded but stalwart Hakkas than in any other tribe of Chinese who contributed contingents to the so-called "Bamboo Rifle Corps".

THE HAKKA-PUNTEI WAR 1855–1868

During the middle years of the nineteenth century the struggle in the province of Canton between the Hakkas (Khehs) and the native Cantonese (Puntei) for land and the right to live broke into open conflict.

This civil war in Kwangtung doubtless owed its inception to the quarrel in Kwangsi in September 1850, referred to above, which became the Taiping rebellion and was carried on contemporaneously with it as the latter moved further north. This bitter struggle helps to explain the secret society hostility between the Cantonese and Hakka immigrants to the Straits Settlements during those years.

As will be shown in a later chapter the Hakkas in Penang and afterwards in Perak formed the bulk of the Hai San (海 山) secret society, whose struggle with the Ghee Hins (Cantonese) for the possession of the Larut tin-fields gave rise to the Larut wars of 1862–73.

The Rev. Eitel's article quoted above contains the following account of the Hakka struggle for existence in the Canton province:—

A sad episode in the latest history of the Hakka race is the internecine war carried on more recently (1855 to 1868) in the south-western districts of the Canton province between Puntis and Hakkas. The following notes have been placed at my disposal by Mr. W. F. Mayers who through his position in the Consular Service and his intimate acquaintance with some of the highest native officials was enabled to collect trustworthy information, and are a valuable contribution to the history of the Hakkas. I subjoin these notes literally as they were written down in November 1868:—

"The original influx of Hakka immigrants into the districts west of the Canton River and south of the West River is said to have taken place during the reign of the Emperor Yung-cheng (A.D. 1723–1735) since which period, by their industry and thrift, they have become possessed of much of the land formerly owned by the Punti clans, to whom the original immigrants became hired labourers.

Footnote.—(1) The capture of the Taku forts 1860, *vide* page 51 *supra*.

For very many years clan fights have been common between the two races, but the mutual antipathy grew to a climax after 1854, in which year the Hakka clans located there remained for the most part faithful to the Government, during the Hung-t'ow rebellion which was largely joined by the Puntis until suppressed by the Viceroy Yeh. At this time Hakka and Punti clans dwelt interspersed over all the south-west districts, notably Sun-hing, Sun-wui, Yan-p'ing, Hoi-p'ing, Hoi-ming, and Hok-shan. After the suppression of the Hung-t'ow rebellion, the ill-feeling between the two races took the shape of an internecine warfare, in which the authorities were powerless to interfere.

Up to the year 1860 little was heard by Europeans of this obscure contest, although attention was drawn from time to time to its existence through the discovery of shipments of arms and even the despatch of armed steamers from Hongkong to assist one or other of the belligerent parties. The Hakkas greatly outnumbered by their foes, were gradually driven from their homes and villages, and formed wandering bands of from a few hundred to many thousands in number.

During 1862 the contest in the western districts was at its height, and Imperial authority was entirely suspended in several districts.

Towards the end of that year large bodies of the Hakkas were driven towards the coast, and fell upon the fortified town of Kwang-hai, westward from Macao, which they stormed and occupied for a considerable length of time, until driven out by an Imperial force co-operating with the Punti clans.

This was the first overt act of official interference in the contest.

The number of wandering Hakkas was at this time estimated at fully 200,000, but famine and pestilence rapidly thinned their numbers, whilst thousands were carried off by Punti incursions and sold to the crimps for "exportation".[1]

During 1864 the remnants of these wandering outcasts, who had become half banditti, half-refugees, were collected at various points in the mountains of the western districts, such as No Fu, Kum Kai, Ng Hang and Chek Shui.

Here, amid the security of mountain fastnesses, they established little republics, in which they tilled the ground, built habitations and defended themselves as best they could against the incursions of their Punti enemies who beleaguered every pass.

Numberless officials of high and low degree, were sent to seek a means for reconciling the conflicting parties; but whereas the Hakkas demanded only liberty to live, whilst the Puntis steadfastly refused to be sheltered by the same heaven with them, no result could be achieved.

Up to the summer of 1866 matters stood in this posture, the principal points of assembly being Ng Hang, in the Sun Hing district No Ki in the Yan P'ing district, and Tsao Chung on the sea coast beyond Kwanghai, where the more lawless bands had established themselves and maintained relations with the coast pirates.

On the arrival of the new Governor of Kwangtung, measures were resolved upon for bringing this difficult question to a settlement either by force or by persuasion, and in September 1866 a body of 8,000 troops was despatched to the western districts under the superintendence of the Grain Intendant of Canton, for the purpose of compelling the Hakkas to give up their arms and to disperse, with which end in view a sum of 200,000 Taels was set aside to be distributed in the proportion of Taels 8 to each adult and 4 to children and youths, with passes and protection to enable them to reach Kwangsi, Hainan and other parts of the country where waste lands exist on which it is hoped they will settle.

In October 1868, the Hakkas at No Ki, to the number of some 7,000 accepted these conditions, and dispersed. The band at Ng Hang, which is very much more numerous, than that at Ts'ao Chung will be taken in turn.

The Punti clans will then remain in complete possession of the country; whilst, if the intentions of the Chinese authorities are carried out, Hakka colonies will be formed in remote districts.

It is estimated that at least 150,000 have perished within the last four or five years (1864–1868).

A very large number of Hakkas will undoubtedly still remain throughout the western districts, but wherever their clans have been intermingled with a Puntei population they have been ousted and overwhelmed".

Referring to the Hakka-Puntei War, 1864–1866, Dyer Ball in his *Things Chinese* page 326 says:—

"A dreadful internecine strife in which 150,000 at least perished, took place between the Hakka and the Punteis in the south-western districts of the Canton province from A.D. 1864–1866, and arms, and even armed steamers were procured from Hongkong by both parties."

These same years 1864–1868 form the background of the iniquitous coolie traffic between south China and the Straits Settlements, and of another "dreadful internecine strife" which was taking place between Hakkas of the Hai San society and Punteis of the Ghee Hin society in the Larut district of Perak in which "arms and even armed steamers" were being procured from Penang by both parties.

THE DAGGER SOCIETY OF AMOY (小 刀 會)

There was a third cause of unrest in south China in the middle of the nineteenth century, apparently unconnected with either the Taiping rebellion or the Hakka-Puntei war, which had an important influence upon the secret society history of Singapore. This was the Dagger Society of Amoy, of which the following information is on record:—

Stanton in *The Triad Society* page 15 has:—

"While the T'aip'ings were fighting the Manchu power from Kwangsi to Nanking, the Triads rose in other parts of the Empire. About 1849 Ch'en Ch'ing Cheu (陳 慶 眞) a Singapore Chinaman employed in a foreign firm in Amoy established in that city a branch of the Triad Society to which he gave the name of *The Dagger Society*. Before long, several thousands joined it.

In 1851 information of this reached the Provincial Government and a Tao-Tai was sent to Amoy to investigate into the character of the society and to suppress it. Ch'en Ch'ing Cheu was arrested and subjected to horrible torture to induce him to confess.

In consequence of his being British born the English Consul interposed and demanded his rendition. The Chinese authorities lied as to where Ch'en Ch'ing Cheu was detained and before

Footnote.—(1) This was the origin of much of the notorious "coolie traffic" to the South Seas.

the Consul discovered his whereabouts, he was tortured to death and placed dressed in his usual manner in a sedan chair and left at his master's door.

The leadership of the society was then taken up by an energetic character named Huang Wei 黃 潤 . This man used his power as the leader of the society to screen from the Chinese authorities a wealthy man Huang Te Mei (黃 德 美) from whom the authorities had already squeezed an immense sum of money.

Huang Te Mei then joined the Dagger Society.

In 1853 a further attempt was made by the Chinese authorities to extort money from him, in consequence of which Huang Wei 黃 潤 with two thousand followers rose in arms to see his friend righted. MANY OF THE LEADERS IN THIS INSURRECTION WERE SINGAPORE CHINAMEN.

Having captured two small towns and augmented their forces to 8,000, they marched on Amoy and captured it."

In this passage Stanton identifies the Dagger Society with the Triad Society and in doing so he appears to copy an error made by George Hughes, evidently an officer of the Chinese Consular service who in 1872 published an interesting article entitled *The Small Knife rebels. An unpublished chapter of Amoy History* in *the China Review* Vol. I 1872-73 from which the following extract is taken. It was evidently from this article by Hughes that Stanton took his facts. Hughes says :—

There had existed for many years amongst the Chinese of Java, Singapore, Malacca and Penang, a secret society, the Siao t'ou hui, (小 刀 會) or Dagger society, the ostensible object of which, was mutual assistance and protection. It contained men of all classes and its rules were so strictly observed that, it is said, piratical members meeting on the high seas the vessels of other leading brothers, were content to accept the sign of the society, and to allow the vessels to pass on unmolested. This society was originally called (三 合 會) San ho hui, *i.e.* the society of the three (powers) united, or, as it has been aptly translated, the Triad Society......
It became the 天 地 會 or the Society of Heaven and Earth, during the reign of Chien-lung (about 1795) when its object was distinctly political, and it had attained such magnitude and power as to seriously endanger that Monarch's government[1].

This society or an offshoot of it, was introduced into Amoy, about the year 1848-9, by a Singapore Chinaman named Tan-keng-chin 陳 慶 真 , a compradore in the employ of Messrs. Jardine Matheson & Co. The society rapidly took root, and in 1851, numbered some thousands of members, when, the suspicions of the provincial Government at Foochow being excited, the Viceroy despatched to Amoy, to investigate its character, and to suppress it, a resolute old anti-foreign Taot'ai, named Chang 張 , the same who served as Wei yuan to the Governor-General Lin, when 20,291 chests of opium, were surrendered by the British, and burnt at Canton, in 1839. Chang's first act was to arrest Tan Keng Chin, on a charge of conspiring against the Government; the only evidence against him was a book, found in his house, containing the names and residences of the members of the society; but this was deemed sufficient, and Tan was subjected to horrible torture to make him confess further particulars. Meanwhile Tan Keng Chin, being a British-born subject, the English Consul on hearing of his arrest, went, accompanied by three other gentlemen, to the Taot'ai's Yamên, to demand his rendition.

* * *

The Consul was not successful in obtaining possession of Tan, who was tortured to death. His body was found on the following morning, on opening Jardine Matheson's Hong, dressed as usual, and seated in a sedan chair, opposite to his master's door.

Hutson (Chapter II *supra*) places the Big Knife (大 刀) Society in the Han League camp, where we believe the Dagger (小 刀) Society also properly belongs. The only other reference to the society we have seen is by Pickering who in *JSBRAS* Vol. I (1878) page 65; writing in 1878 has :—

"Some years ago the leader of the 'Sio To' or Small Knife rebellion at Amoy was a Straits-born Chinese and there are doubtless now in the Straits several old T'aip'ing rebels."

THE DAGGER (SMALL KNIFE) REBELLION IN AMOY 1853

The only first hand description of this rebellion we have seen is that of Hughes in the *China Review* Vol. I 1872-73 whose account is as follows :—

After giving a description of the Society itself quoted in the preceding section, ending with the death of Tan Keng Chin, Hughes continues :—

The leadership of the society now appears to have fallen on a man of low extraction, but of great energy and force of character, named Hwang wei, or in the local dialect, Un wee 黃 潤 . At this time there lived at Amoy one Hwang tê mei, or, locally, Un teck bé 黃 壋 美 a merchant once possessed of great wealth. This man bore a high character, for honesty and benevolence, and was exceedingly popular amongst the poor classes. He had been compelled to accept the post of salt monopolist, of the prefectures of Chang Chow Foo, and Chin Chew Foo, an office greatly dreaded on account of its holder having to return to the salt Commissioner a certain fixed sum, far above what he could collect. The salt Commissioner himself, being precisely in the same position *vis-à-vis* the Board of Revenue, had usually compelled one of the richest merchants to accept the post. This office resulted, it is said, in losses to the amount of $800,000.

Smarting under this, (duress) and at a second attempt to force the post of monopolist upon him. he probably (although this is not admitted by my informants) joined the society. At all events, it is certain that he advanced money to it, and was on terms of intimacy with Hwang, otherwise Un-wee. This second attempt to impose the detested office upon Un-teck-bé was seized upon by Un-wee as a means of securely enmeshing this wealthy and influential man in the society. Some 2,000 members of it, now styled the Siau-tou-hui, 小 刀 會 or Dagger Society, rose under Un-wee, at his native village Sim Thay 審 宅 on 14th May 1853, and proclaiming that they sought to right Un-teck-bé (without his authority, and against his wishes, he always declared)

Footnote.—(1) This is doubtless an error. It seems more likely that this piratical society was a branch of the Ko Lao Hui rather than of the Triad Society.

marched on and captured Hai-têng-hsien, 海澄縣 , Cheo-bay, 石碼 , Chau-chow-foo (which they only held for three days) and finally Amoy where, on arrival, the society was found to consist of about 8,000 men, controlled by a Council of six persons, three of whom were Singapore Chinamen, and at whose head was Un-wee. Many of the subordinate positions, such as centurions and leaders of ten,[1] were also held by Singapore Chinese.

This was the force that captured Amoy (on 16th May 1853), and retained possession of it until the 11th November following. On the 27th May a fleet of Imperial Junks entered the port and landed 500, or 600, soldiers who marched on the city. They were met by the rebels, and, after a brief skirmish, driven back to their junks, which immediately left. This defeat, considered by the rebels as an auspicious omen, greatly elated them, and strengthened their numbers. Preparations for extending the war were made, and requisitions issued for the stores, ammunition, etc., stolen from the arsenals, on the capture of the city, for which compensation was promised to the holders. Proclamations for the repression of disorder, and the administration of justice, in which nearly all breaches of regulations were punishable by death, were put forth by the rebel leader Hwang-wei, or Un-wee, who now styled himself "Appointed by Imperial Decree of the Emperor of the Han (Chinese) Ta Ming dynasty,[2] Commander-in-Chief of the forces for the conquest of the Fukien Province".

*   *   *

On the 4th July, the Imperialists landed between 4,000, and 5,000 men, some ten miles to the N.E. of Amoy. The rebels responded by erecting a barricade at their advanced station six miles from them, and on the 7th, the Imperialists having approached, a melée took place, when the Imperialists were driven back with a loss of 18 heads. On the same day about 42 Imperial Junks appeared off the harbour, and attacked some 25 rebel junks. After two hours' fighting, in which it has been computed by witnesses, that about one shot in a thousand took effect, the fleets parted, the Mandarins standing out to the six Islands, and the rebels returning into harbour. On the following morning the rebel junks went out to the six Islands, and engaged the Imperialists. The action was fought at a sufficient distance to avoid injury to each other, and the Imperialists left next day 9th July 1853. About this period the contributions to the rebel coffers falling short of anticipation, an attempt was made to raise funds by the levy of Port charges. As the Proclamation is a curiosity in its way, I copy it hereunder:—

"By Hwang. Appointed by Imperial decree of the Emperor of the Han[2] (Chinese) Ta-ming dynasty. Commander-in-Chief of the forces for the conquest of the Fukien Province. An order for the guidance of the merchant shipping.

"I, as Commander-in-Chief, received an Imperial order to come to Amoy, to relieve the people, not to harm them, to put down oppression, not to commit oppression, for by means of their strength, and by a display of power, those Tartar miscreants had embittered the whole living population. People of all classes asserted their innocence to the Gods, both above and below; and merchants, too, had long been suffering their cruel injuries.

"Accordingly I beg hereby to notify to the merchant shipping of Amoy, that all such ships as are engaged in import or export trade are to be duly provided with passes or papers, which will enable them to leave, or enter, the port, on their voyages to and fro, without danger of obstruction."

[Annexed was a scale of charges temporarily fixed upon which everyone was called upon to obey.]

*   *   *

A desultory campaign of several months duration followed at Amoy between Huang Wei and the Provincial Manchu troops.

Finally an arrangement was made whereby the rebels were allowed to evacuate the city on 11th November 1853 and they sailed away in junks, mostly to Singapore and elsewhere in the South Seas. One report stated that Huang Wei was delivered over to the Mandarins by his own relatives for torture and execution. Another, that he escaped to Saigon.

After the evacuation, the Imperial troops entered Amoy and carried out a wholesale slaughter of the innocent inhabitants graphically described by Hughes.

There is no historical reason to suppose as suggested by Pickering above, that the Small Knife rebellion was allied with the larger Taiping rebellion which was going on at the same time.

In this connection Brine op. cit. page 260 has a footnote:—

"The city of Amoy was captured and held about the same period (1853) by a large force of local rebels, who, for a time, raised the Taiping Standard, although totally unconnected with the Taipings."

The Dagger rebels are referred to by Schlegel op. cit. page 6 in the following terms:—

"Not all the horrors committed in the name of the Heaven and Earth League ought to be considered as its acts. There are lots of pirates who assume the name because it is feared, but who do not in fact belong to the Hung League at all. So the robbers who desolated Amoy in 1853 took the name of "Small Knife".

Schlegel omits at this point to say that "Small Knife" is one of the watchwords appearing in the Statutes of the Shantung Lodge found at Japara, Java in 1851 discussed under "Origin of the name Ghee Hin" page 7 supra.

Although Hughes and Stanton assume that the Small Knife rebels were members of the Hung League the evidence supports the view that they were members of the Han. Seven facts seem fairly clear, namely:—

1. Chinese from Singapore were interested from the outset in the Small Knife rebellion in Amoy in 1853.

Footnote.—(1) Fore-runners of the "Ten-men Corps" of the Communist movement in Malaya at a later date.

Footnote.—(2) Note again this acknowledgment of the Han mission of the Dagger rebels, as opposed to the Ming mission of the Triads.

2. The rebels claimed to have a mission to re-establish the Han dynasty under the title of the Tai Meng (大 明).

3. The rebels called themselves the Small Knives which is one of the "watchwords" of the Shantung Lodge as given by Schlegel (page 7 *supra*), who at the same reference gives another of the same family of watchwords as the "Big Knives".

4. Hutson (Chapter II *supra*) identifies the "Big Knives" with the Ko Lao Hui or Han League.

5. The Small Knife rebellion was unconnected with the Taiping rebellion then in progress, which sought to re-establish the Han under the title of the Tai Peng (太 平) or Universal Peace Dynasty.

6. We may fairly safely assume that the Small Knife rebels were members or allies of the Han League and hostile to the Hung or Triad Society.

7. After their failure the Small Knife rebels set sail for Singapore where they arrived in large numbers at the end of 1853 and within six months the Han and the Hung were in open conflict in Singapore. (see Chapter VI *infra*).

THE GROWTH OF ANTI-FOREIGN AND ANTI-DYNASTIC SENTIMENT IN CHINA 1870–1900

We have noted above the importance of certain events in China between 1842 and 1868 to the political and economic conditions developing in the Straits Settlements during the same period. Their effect upon anti-foreign sentiment among the Chinese generally and upon the Chinese secret society under-world in Malaya was no less important. For example, whatever its exact genesis in China, the Dagger rebellion in Amoy had a direct connection with the Chinese disturbances in Singapore in May 1854 which are loosely and inaccurately recorded by the Malayan authorities as having been due:—

> "To a refusal of the Ghee Hok (Hokkiens) to join with the Ghee Hin (Cantonese) in a subscription to help the T'ai p'ing rebels in China who had been driven out of Amoy by the Manchu (Imperialist) troops."

It seems on the evidence more probable that the "Ten days riot" as it was called, in May 1854, in Singapore of which a full account is given in Chapter VI *infra* was occasioned by the traditional hostility of the Ghee Hins (Hung League) to the defeated Dagger society elements (Han League) from Amoy, whose irruption into Singapore in large numbers may well have been resented by the vested interests of the Hung. The circumstances indeed suggest a close connection between, if not identity with, the Dagger Society rebels in Amoy in November, 1853 and the Ghee Hok rioters in Singapore in May 1854.

The following extract from *Play and Politics* by W. H. Read shows this. On page 82 Read has:—

> "Matters remained much in the same state till May, 1854. When in the autumn of 1853, the Chinese rebels at Amoy in China were driven away by the Imperial troops, numbers of them seized junks, and made the best of their way to Singapore, and in such crowds, that the number of immigrants that season instead of amounting to about eight or ten thousand as usual, aggregated upwards of twenty thousand. Most of them belonged to the secret societies and nearly all were of the three tribes Macao, Taichoo, and Amoy. They joined in Singapore the two great Hoeys, Toantay and Ghehok. A quarrel soon arose between these two, which after smouldering for some time, burst into a riot, the ostensible cause of which was a quarrel about a trifle of five catties (7 lbs.) of rice".

Similarly the "Arrow War" in China 1856–58 and the events leading up to the Treaty of Tientsin (1860) were reflected in anti-British sentiment among the Chinese in Singapore, recorded as follows by Song Ong Siang in *One hundred years of the Chinese of Singapore* (1923) page 105 ff.:—

> "On the 2nd of January, 1857 all the shops in Singapore were closed, the markets were deserted, and the boatmen and hack-gharry syces refused to work. The grievance alleged was that the new Municipal and Police Acts, which had come into force, had not been explained, and their objects were not understood by the natives. The strained state of affairs in China over the "Arrow" incident, which shortly after culminated in the second China War, had given rise to some feelings of ill-will on the part of some of the lowest classes of the Chinese towards the European community in Singapore, and an attempt to induce a shop-keeper to open his shop resulted in a riot in which the Police were roughly handled.
>
> The merchants lost no time in nipping the trouble in the bud. The Sheriff, who was an officer annually elected among the European merchants, convened a meeting on the same day, and a deputation of nine Europeans with Messrs. Whampoa (Hoo Ah Kay) and Tan Kim Cheng, called on the Governor and asked him to issue a proclamation in Chinese promising explanation of the unpopular acts which was done that very day.
>
> "To this there was a counter proclamation which was posted over the Government circular, to the effect that no faith was to be put in the Governor's promise to have the law explained, that he only wished to gain time, and secure provisions; while the Chinese were quite ready to sweep away every "barbarian" from the island. The shops were however, opened shortly afterwards, and general business was resumed."

As we shall see in later chapters "Messrs. Whampoa and Tan Kim Cheng" were probably the heads of the Han and the Hung League respectively, in the Singapore of that day.

The great disintegrating movements in China described above coincided with the growth of foreign influence and the acquisition of trade and territorial interests by western powers in both north and south China.

This helped to undermine the waning Manchu power. South China adapted itself more quickly to the changed conditions, but the north remained implacably hostile to the influence and religious encroachments of the foreigner. The history of the years 1870 to 1900 are eloquent testimony to this.

Dyer Ball *Things Chinese* page 611 ff., gives a list of some thirty major outbreaks against foreigners and foreign missions in China during these thirty years.

A similar campaign of murder of foreign missionaries at the same epoch in Annam led to the drastic intervention of the French in that country in 1868.

During the last thirty years of the nineteenth century this latent revolutionary urge in China developed a twofold character. The political slogan of the Hung League in the south "Drive out the Ts'ing and restore the Ming" was taken up in the north during these years by the cry of the Han League "Drive out the foreign barbarians".

European writers explain the political slogan of the south as an expression of the hatred of the Chinese for their Manchu rulers. However true that may have been in the seventeenth century, it underwent a change in the eighteenth due to the exactions and the maladministration of the native Chinese officials, appointed under the Manchus by the system of open competitive examination. The Chinese officials doubtless blamed their own misdeeds upon the rapacity of their Manchu masters, which was cold comfort to the suffering Chinese multitudes.

The nineteenth century saw the advent of numbers of European merchants and foreign ambassadors who broke down by force the traditional exclusiveness of the Chinese and imposed upon the already weakened Tartar rule the hated "unequal treaties".

These developments fundamentally changed the character of the revolutionary urge in China and directed it firstly against the native Chinese administration and the *literati* class, which held the people in the grip of official extortion behind a facade of orderly Government and secondly against the foreigner whose demands for rights in China and for compensation for wars he had himself imposed upon her, drove the people to recognise as the two chief instruments of their misery, their own Chinese officials and the foreigner and all his works.

This view appeared to be falsified by the circumstances of the Taiping rebellion, whose precipitating cause and chance of success, seemed by an accident to be bound up with the fortunes of Christianity, the religion of the foreigner. Hostile relations with the French however, soon followed the Taiping rebellion in 1882–1886 and China was brought to her knees by Japan in the Sino–Japanese War of 1894–95. By the end of the nineteenth century the Chinese had made up their minds upon the value of the foreigner to them.

We get a clear view of this development from Mason's curious book *Chinese Confessions* (referred to in Chapter II) where, in a document written by him in 1890 he has, on page 42:—

> "In all recent rebellions the popular cry has been "Down with the usurping Tartars, restore the native Chinese dynasty of the Mings". Does this amount to anything in reality? I think not. The Manchus have ruled China for two hundred and fifty years and there are no Ming pretenders left. The people are not fools. They know that it is not the poor little Tartar clans in Peking who oppress them, but the Chinese bureaucracy of the provinces and counties who enrich themselves by "squeeze" in lieu of salaries. Therefore a really popular war-cry must suggest something in the form of democracy or republic as it was in Puritan England and Revolutionary France".

And again on page 81:—

> "It was the young Mandarins of my own age who treated me as one of themselves and inducted me into plots..... These young Mandarins were rather State conspirators aiming at a large revolution, but the rank and file of the Ko Laos to tell the truth, were little better than brigands".

This revealing passage discloses one of the ingredients of that revolutionary explosion which was soon to convulse the whole of China, the Revolution of 1912.

Another ingredient was hatred of the foreigner. This hatred showed its first sharp intensity in the anti-foreign "Boxer Rebellion" at the turn of the century.

The swiftness and rigour of the retribution exacted by the powers from China for that outbreak, stemmed for a time the rising tide of revolution which was then being slowly harnessed by Sun Yat Sen.

It will be seen in a later chapter that this astute revolutionary did not depend upon the Hung League alone for the success of his plans, but seems to have organised the underground forces of both the Han and the Hung league for his final assault upon the decrepit Manchu *régime* and the encroachment of foreign powers.

In attempting to evaluate these political cross-currents and adjust them to the situation in China to-day, it must be remembered that they were the first-fruits of China's awakening from a slumber never before disturbed by the west, since the beginning of the world's history.

Secondly they all occurred in the short space of the last century which is but China's yesterday.

E

Lastly, in the words of Rabindranath Tagore, the most important single fact of the nineteenth century is that, in spite of Rudyard Kipling's couplet, the East met the West in China.

The nature of that impact has been sketched in this Chapter: its reverberations are still to-day sounding about our ears.

THE BOXER REBELLION 1899–1900

The study of this episode is outside the scope of this work. In Chapter II *supra* we have identified the "Boxers" with the Ko Lao Hui and thence with the Han League.[1]

It is from their self-hypnotism for the purpose of making themselves invulnerable in battle and their consequent posturing that the "Boxer" rebels received the name by which they are known to foreigners.

It is probable that in origin, the movement was but one of many rebellions of the hypnotic sect of the Han league against the Manchu power. It may, indeed, have been the flowering of that Ko Lao Hui plot, in which Mason was involved in 1891 (Chapter II).

But it seems equally probable that just as the Taiping rebellion was switched from an innocent religious revivalist beginning, to a Han political purpose in a Hung historical setting, so the Manchu rulers and Chinese officials took advantage of the powerful anti-foreign sentiment among the Han League to divert the Boxer movement from themselves and direct it against the second objective of the league, the extermination of the foreigner. As a result of their partial success the rebellion is recorded in history as a purely anti-foreign and particularly anti-Christian-missionary movement. Thus Dyer Ball *Things Chinese* page 612 says of it:—

"The terrible Boxer rising was fostered by the Chinese Government, Chinese officials aiding and abetting them, and Chinese soldiers fighting with them in a war of extermination against all Westerners, and resulted in the dreadful seige of the Legations in Peking, the fighting in Tientsin and operations in North China and the taking of the Taku forts etc. It may not be amiss to call attention to the number of murdered missionaries, many of them slaughtered in cold blood, some by order of officials with a slight semblance of legal procedure. These massacres took place in 1899 and 1900. One mission alone, the China Inland, lost 48 members and 12 children. The total Protestant loss was 135 adults and 53 children. If the Roman Catholic losses are added and the martyred native Christians, it will be one of the greatest persecutions in history".

History seems to be repeating itself to-day in north China, where the Han league may once again be compelled by political jugglery to fight the battles of its own enemies against the Western powers. The so-called "puppet" *régime* set up by Japan in 1937 with Chinese co-operation, has a strong anti-foreign bias. This co-operation may perhaps come from a section of the Han league. (*see* Chapters XXI and XXXIV *infra*).

We may conclude by noting the different characteristics of the Taiping rebellion with which the Triad Society was associated, and the Boxer rebellion fifty years later which we identify with the Ko Lao Hui.

TAI PING[2] (Hung League in appearance)

1. Date A.D. 1850.
2. Origin. Kwangtung.
3. Anti-dynastic.
4. Supported by Chinese Christians and foreign missionaries.
5. European adventurers mixed freely with the Taipings.
6. Opposed by the Chinese Government (Manchu).
7. Suppressed by General Gordon in command of Chinese Imperial troops on behalf of Chinese Government 1864.
8. White was the colour of initiation to the Triad Society.

BOXER (Han League)

1. Date A.D. 1900.
2. Szechuan.
3. Anti-foreigner and anti-missionary.
4. Chinese Christians and foreign missionaries were massacred.
5. No foreigner's life was safe with the Boxers.
6. Supported by Chinese Government officials (Manchus).
7. Suppressed by foreign international intervention, with foreign troops (1900).
8. Red was the distinguishing colour of the Boxer braves.

As we progress with our subject, these features, or a local modification of them, will continually re-appear and roughly represent the line of cleavage in the Chinese secret society world of Malaya, during the nineteenth century.

Footnote.—(1) The practice of the "boxer" arts is connected with the Shaolin monastery of Honan. *See* Chapter VII *infra.*

Footnote.—(2) The rebellion was of complex origin, more Hung than Han in outward appearance, but probably basically a revival of the White Lotus and belonging essentially to the Han League.

CHAPTER V

THE HUNG LEAGUE AND THE HAN LEAGUE IN
MALAYA 1800–1850

There is no more fitting opening to a survey of the history of the Hung league in Malaya than the summary given in Professor Mills' *History of British Malaya 1824–1827* pages 203–210, which represents the presently accepted view of Chinese secret society activity in the Straits Settlements during the last century. A condensed extract is as follows, with the documentation which is very full, omitted:—

During the first forty years or so of the existence of Singapore, it was afflicted by a constant series of Chinese gang-robberies. Bands of from twenty to one hundred made frequent attacks at night on native and sometimes isolated European houses. The thieves were not very brave, and a determined resistance often frightened them away; but on many occasions they were successful, and for years the police were unable to prevent these attacks.

Gambling and robbery however faded into insignificance when compared with the activities of the secret societies. Although as a rule the respectable Chinese were not members, the whole of Chinese society in the Straits was permeated by these covert and often dangerous organisations. This state of affairs was not confined to British Malaya: in Sarawak, the Dutch East Indies, and in China itself the same conditions existed. A genius for combination is a predominant characteristic of the Chinese: from one point of view China itself might almost be regarded as a congeries of associations for agriculture or commerce. The villages form agricultural societies in which each man has his part, so that farming may be more efficiently carried on; and merchants unite in associations for trade. Benevolent societies to provide for needy members and ensure their decent burial are also very numerous. It need therefore cause no surprise that societies were formed which, despite their ostensibly benevolent purposes, might be described with fair accuracy as the *Pirates and Robbers Co-operative Association.* Many of them tried to be an *imperium in imperio*, to enjoy the benefits of British rule and at the same time ignore any laws which did not suit their convenience. Moreover the societies were often bitterly hostile to one another, and their rivalries periodically culminated in bloody street-fights in which dozens of Chinese sometimes were killed. It is noteworthy however that on these occasions no attempt was made to attack Europeans unless they interfered to stop the fighting. The rival mobs would suspend operations and allow them to pass through their midst unscathed.

* * *

The genuine Hué riots in Singapore were of two kinds, those between the rival branches of the Thian Tai Hué and the quarrels of the Kongsis. Most of the Chinese in the Straits came from the maritime provinces of China where the inhabitants were notorious for their turbulence. A large number of the immigrants were criminals, the lowest and worst class of Canton and other cities. Furthermore the people of the different provinces, and sometimes of the districts of the same province, hated one another bitterly, and for generations had carried on bloody feuds. The inhabitants of each province moreover were united in Kongsis, or associations. These were mutual benefit societies intended to assist needy members, carry out various religious rites, give aid in all disputes, etc.

* * *

Unfortunately the Chinese who migrated to the Straits carried their ancestral feuds with them as well as their Kongsis. Turbulent, often criminal, and well-organised, every condition was favourable for carrying on in Penang or Singapore the quarrels in which they had engaged at home. Many of the riots in the Straits and notably the ten days' riot of 1854 the most bloody of all, in which 400 Chinese were killed, were really provincial faction fights. The Kongsis cut across the lines of the other secret societies, the branches of the Thian Tai Hué, which accepted members from every part of China. Many Chinese belonged to both organisations, so that those who were brothers in the Thian Tai Society cut one another's throats with great zest as members of rival provincial Kongsis.

* * *

The Triad Society in the Straits Settlements retained the worst, and but few of the better features of the degenerate parent organisation. It was divided into local lodges each under its Master and Generals, while all were affiliated with the headquarters in China. Where possible the lodge, with its elaborate buildings and defences, was erected in some inaccessible tract of jungle, and guards were stationed to keep off intruders. When this could not be done the meetings were held in the homes of the Lodge Masters.

In the Straits Settlements the patriotic motive of the League, the overthrow of the Manchus could find no expression, and the Hué therefore became a mutual benefit society of a peculiar kind. The age-old ritual with its exhortations to brotherly love and works of righteousness was retained, and the Thian Tai Hué did much good work in settling disputes between members and giving them assistance when necessary. A large number of the members however were Chinese criminals of the lowest class, and the headmen were often unscrupulous. Many of the Chinese pirates and robbers who infested Singapore belonged to the League. The ritual contained an elaborate code of passwords whereby the other members could avoid molestations if they chanced upon their lodge-brethren in the discharge of their professional duties.

The greatest emphasis was laid upon the solidarity of the order. Members were forbidden under severe penalties to submit their disputes to a court of justice: all quarrels were to be decided by the headmen of the lodge. Chinese who were not members but who had a dispute with a "brother" were also compelled to resort to the same tribunal. The statutes of the lodges contained elaborate provisions designed to defeat the ends of justice. When a member had committed a crime all other members were required to co-operate in his defence. Witnesses against him were bribed not to appear, and if necessary murdered; if the criminal had to fly the country his escape was provided for, while if he were fined, the amount was paid by the Society. Members were also forbidden to give any assistance whatever to the police, and were required to take part whenever a riot was determined on. The penalties for breaking these and the other laws were merciless floggings, mutilation and death.

The method by which new members were enrolled was equally criminal. The Triad Society was regarded with terror by the Chinese, for example, blackmail collected from the brothels and small shop-keepers was a regular part of its income in the Straits and there were very few who dared to disobey its orders. When a Sinkheh, or newly arrived coolie came to British Malaya, and the local headmen wished him to become a member, he was ordered to join the Society on pain of death. If he refused, he was executed. Abdullah Munshi, the protégé of Raffles, who in disguise attended a meeting of the Hué about 1825 saw one man who remained obdurate beheaded.

* * *

The secrecy of the society was no mere fiction: up to about 1860 very little was known of its procedure, and still less of its actual members. One principal reason for this was that before 1867 very few officials in the Straits Settlements could speak Chinese, or were intimately acquainted with their customs. Abdullah gleaned some information at the risk of his life, and the police from time to time secured a little more; but it was not until Schlegel's book, based on documents seized by the Dutch police, was published in 1866 that the governments obtained much authoritative knowledge of it. No assistance could be obtained from Chinese who were not members, for to them it was an impalpable, ever-present menace. A man's own brother might be a member and he would never know it. The laws of the Society were no idle enactments: how many times their penalties were inflicted will never be known. It is certain however that for many years after 1819 the bodies of Chinese were found in Singapore and Penang with the mark of the Triad Society neatly carved upon them. The murderers were very rarely caught. Chinese who had suffered from the League dared not give evidence against it, or even, complain of wrongs inflicted upon them. There are cases noted in the Straits Records where Chinese who had been robbed and nearly killed by members of the Society refused to prosecute so that the culprits escaped scot free. English law, Pickering declared, proved to be ill-adapted for such a situation; and the Indian Government refused to follow the example of the Dutch and Spaniards by giving the police and the courts extraordinary powers to deal with the Hués.

As the century advanced the original Triad Society in the Straits became divided into about a dozen different Hués, all offshoots of the parent organisation, but bitterly hostile to one another. Their strength was unknown: in some cases it was a few hundreds, in others it extended into the thousands. Periodically the feuds between the rival Hués found vent in faction fights; and for a few hours or days the streets of British cities were filled with howling mobs of armed men. Eventually the police would subdue the rioters, bury the corses, and all would be quiet till the next time.

The aim of the headmen of the societies was to create an *imperium in imperio*, to enjoy all the benefits of life in a British settlement, and at the same time be free to do as they chose, and govern the Chinese as they pleased, without any interference. In fact, they wished to ignore the constituted government altogether. As a rule they were prosperous and eminently respectable individuals who took no overt part in proceedings, but gave their orders and left it to their gangs of ruffians to carry them out. Whatever happened, they had an unimpeachable alibi. It was an intolerable situation, yet one which it was extraordinarily difficult to alter.

The problem of the Chinese secret societies arose only a few years after the foundation of Penang. In 1799 several of them were already established there, and giving trouble to the Resident; while as time advanced, the question became more serious. Daring robberies, frequent murders, constant interference with the course of justice, all were traced to the Hués. And there the matter ended: it was known that powerful and criminal associations were at work; but to convict the members or seriously to hamper their activities was usually found impossible. Then, from about 1846 to 1885, came a series of riots in Penang, Malacca, and Singapore. In all there were about twelve serious outbreaks. Some of them assumed very large proportions, as for example the Kongsi riots at Singapore in 1854, when 400 Chinese were killed, and for ten days the whole island was the scene of pitched battles between the rival factions. The police finally subdued the rioters and no attack was made upon the European quarter of the city. How serious the situation might have become was shown in Sarawak in 1857. In that year the local branch of the Triad Society terrorised the whole Chinese population of 4,000 into revolting, sacked the capital, and nearly murdered Raja Brooke and his staff. The Hué had been encouraged to rise by the belief that the Raja was in disgrace with the British Government, and that no retribution would follow his murder. In their mad venture however the Chinese had quite failed to take into account the Orang Laut, the Sea-Dayaks who had now become the faithful allies of the Raja. In a few days they were assailed by 10,000 of the dreaded ex-pirates, and a mere handful of the rebels escaped into Dutch territory. As the number of Chinese in the Straits increased the riots became bloodier and more frequent.

Colonel Cavenagh, the Governor of the Straits from 1859 to 1867, managed to abate the Singapore riots by a very ingenious device. It was known though it could not be proved that these fights were always engineered by the Lodge-Masters of the Societies, and therefore, whenever one broke out, these headmen were sworn in as special constables. They were sent out to patrol the streets, with a guard of police to see that they did not weary in well-doing. Most of these gentlemen were portly and well-nourished, accustomed to an easy life, and by no means in training to enjoy hours of walking in hot streets under a blazing sun. So after a brief taste of this unwonted exercise the riot would suddenly come to an end.

The problem of dealing with the Societies was not finally solved until their suppression in 1889, during the governorship of Sir Cecil Smith. Fourteen years before that time it had been deemed impossible to destroy the Hués, and it was therefore decided to bring them under the control of the Government. In 1877 a new branch of the administration, the Chinese Protectorate, was formed, with officials well acquainted with the Chinese language and customs. The Government was very fortunate in securing as the first head of the department W. A. Pickering who not only knew the Chinese well, but also had their confidence to a remarkable degree. The duties of the department were to protect the Chinese from any injustice, and by explaining to them the meaning of new laws by which they felt themselves aggrieved, to prevent the former riots of protest. The Secret Societies were compelled to give a list of their members, and afford information as to their actions. Strict surveillance was kept over their proceedings: Pickering himself for example sometimes attended lodge meetings. The Hués were no longer protected by the abysmal ignorance of the administration and its inability to secure information. In a few years their power for ill had greatly diminished, and the evil practices which had formerly characterised them were largely abandoned. By 1878 members of the same Hué dared to appear as witnesses in the law-courts against one another, and offenders were handed over to the police by their Lodge-Masters. The Hués and Kongsis were of real assistance to the authorities in keeping the Chinese under control. Pickering considered that by 1878 the headmen honestly tried to prevent their men from breaking the laws and thus involving them in trouble with the Government. The presidents of the rival lodges also co-operated with one another, and settled thousands of petty disputes which would otherwise have encumbered the work of the law-courts. They also prevented many riots from becoming serious.

Apart from the Hués and from gambling however the Chinese were a remarkably law-abiding and peaceful race, easy to control. They did not run amok or make treacherous attacks like the Malays, or assault Europeans and indulge in religious riots like the Hindus and Mohammedans in India. They paid their taxes, and attended to their own affairs. Schlegel put the whole case in a nutshell when he wrote: "Whenever due regard is paid to the prejudices of the nation, and when care is taken to explain to them the necessity or expediency of a new law or regulation, the Chinese, the most reasonable and cool of all Eastern races, will remain at ease, and the existence of their secret society will not endanger in the least their quietness." So far as gambling and their Hués were concerned the Chinese did indeed offend grievously against the law; but they regarded these matters as their own private concerns, and looked upon the interference of Government as merely another inexplicable trait of the Western barbarians among whom their lot was cast. The Chinese formed two-thirds of the population of the Straits Settlements; but they were never a menace to their security. It is a fact of the utmost significance that during the worst riots the bulk of the garrison at Singapore was usually left in barracks: the Governors realised that the danger to Europeans was slight, and that only the police were required to restore order. It is true that if the reins of authority were relaxed the Chinese were apt to get out of hand, but even then they confined themselves to fighting amongst themselves. A comment passed by the Governor-General of India on the riots 1854 aptly described the whole attitude of the Chinese towards the British Government: "There was in this peculiar case an outrageous violation of all laws, with little if any resistance to constituted authority".

This summary admirably presents in miniature the surface picture of secret society intrigue in the Straits Settlements during the nineteenth century, up to the time of the official suppression in 1890, and restates the official view that all these troubles began and ended with the Triad Society. This view however offers no explanation of the fact that the intrigues and riots continually recurred between supposedly friendly branches of one great fraternity.

A fresh view is now offered in explanation of this peculiarity by suggesting, and we hope by proving in the Chapters that follow, that not one but two great rival and hostile fraternities have all along been represented unobserved in the under-ground world of Malaya, the one the Hung league introduced to the reader in Chapter I, the other the Han league introduced in Chapter II.

THE COMING OF THE HUNG LEAGUE TO MALAYA

As we have seen in Chapter IV, the majority of Chinese in the Malay Peninsula are immigrants from, or the local-born descendants of immigrants from the southern maritime provinces of China, chiefly:—

PROVINCE			TRIBES
Fukien	..	..	Hokkiens, Hokchews and Hakkas.
Kwangtung	..	..	Cantonese, Hakkas, Teochews (or Hoklos).
Kwangsi ..	..	..	Kwongsais and Hakkas.
The Island of Hainan		..	Hylams (or Hainanese).

The Hakkas, as we have seen, have no province of their own and those in Malaya who are locally known as Khehs, come chiefly from the large Hakka colonies in the provinces named above. Hakka colonies are also to be found in China in the provinces of Kiangsi and Chekiang.

Cantonese and Kwongsai immigrants are often spoken of together in Malaya as "men from the two Kwangs", for the reason that the Canton or West River (西江) Si Kiang is the water-way of both the Kwangsi and Kwangtung provinces, and Canton city is the "home port" of settlers from both provinces.

With the majority of Chinese settlers in Malaya coming from the three "Hung league" provinces of Fukien, Kwangtung and Kwangsai, the Malayan lodge of the Triad society became a transplantation of the provincial lodge of Canton, whose settlers and adventurers appear to have preceded to the South Seas those of Fukien province. Mills op. cit. page 205 has:—

How early it (the Triad Society) appeared in the East Indies is unknown, but in the nineteenth century it was spread broadcast over British Malaya, Sarawak and the Dutch possessions". Wherever the coolie came, the Hung league followed".

We propose to show that not only did the Hung league follow, but also the Han league or Ko Lao Hui, that distinct and rival confraternity which seems to be represented in modern times by the Three Dot Brotherhood or Sa Tiam Hui. Of the two, the latter with its adjuncts and variant appellations appears to be the more active, the more dangerous, and the more widespread not only in China, but also in Malaya and neighbouring countries to-day. Ward and Stirling op. cit. Vol. I page 156 discussing the subject of Triad lodge flags and in reference to the lodge of the province of Kwangtung have:—

The flag is red with a white margin, the characters being written on the red part of the flag itself and denominating the Kwangtung and the Kwangsi provinces. The first lodge in these provinces was founded at Canton and was called "The Hall of Obedience to Hung" (洪順堂). A subsidiary lodge was founded in the province of Kwangsi and was called the "Golden Orchid" (金蘭郡). It is apparently from this lodge that the Ghee Hin Society of Singapore is derived.

The reasons for this deduction are not given, but the history of the Triad Society in Malaya seems to support it,

It is however highly improbable that the Triad "Mother Lodge of Malaya" if we can speak of such a thing, was founded in Singapore, a comparatively new city. It is much more likely that the earliest foundation was in Siam and later in Malacca or Penang, and that the Malayan Headquarters of the Triad has only since the middle of the nineteenth century been established in Singapore, probably about 1850.

There is little or no evidence to guide us in a search for the origins of the Triad in Malaya. This is due to four causes:—

(1) The Chinese community governed itself largely through the league up to 1870.

(2) The secrecy of the league prevented members on pain of death, which was then a common penalty for "traitors", from disclosing information, and those Chinese who were not members could offer no assistance to the authorities and lived in constant fear of the league.

(3) Until the appointment of Pickering in 1870 there was no European official in Malaya who understood the Chinese or their language and none whose duty it was to study the Chinese and their customs. Furthermore, no colonial government knew anything about the Triad society until the publication of Schlegel's work in 1866.

(4) Upon the suppression of the Triad society in 1890, which had then been officially registered in Malaya since 1870, all the records were destroyed.

Ward and Stirling *op. cit.* Vol. I page 17 and footnote 2, comment as follows upon this circumstance:—

When the Triad society was formally suppressed (1890) everything from the Mother Lodge was burnt......including all documents and the Charter.

It seems a great pity that such interesting historical documents should have been destroyed, as they formed part of the history of the Straits Settlements..... A better procedure...... would have been to send them to the British Museum in London, where they would have been in safe keeping, and could always have been referred to by students.

We know that the Triad society in Malaya and elsewhere in the South Seas assumed or received the name Ghee Hin Kung Sz (義興公司) which can be translated "Justice and prosperity society" (Stirling) if an innocent benefit-society-like title is required, or, as "Society of the rise of the Patriots" (Schlegel) if a more formidable or revolutionary title is wanted.

Conclusions upon the origin of this name are given at the end of this Chapter.

We also know that at some period the Malayan foundation of the Hung league took as its motto 結萬爲記 Kit Maan Wai Kei "Combine myriads for a clue (or record)" a slogan which constantly recurs in its documents. Apart from this, we are singularly without information upon the advent of the Triad society to Malaya.

In respect of records of the activity of the Triad society in Malaya during the early nineteenth century we are in slightly better case and these records form the subject matter of this and the following Chapter.

THE COMING OF THE HAN LEAGUE TO MALAYA

Owing to what we hold to be the confusion from the outset, between the Hung league and the Han league, there is still less to guide us in our search for the coming of the Han league or Ko Lao Hui to the Malay Peninsula.

Newbold *op. cit.* refers in 1840 (in an extract given in full below) to "The Fokien society recently established in the town of Singapore" which bore enmity to the Cantonese Ghee Hins.

Then there is a reference by Abdullah Munshi (given below) to the Keng Tek Kung Sz founded in Singapore in 1835 which may well have been "the Fokien Society" referred to by Newbold five years later.

Again there is the Kheng Tek Hui (慶德會) founded in Singapore in 1831 and fully discussed in Chapter XXVII *infra,* which is probably the same foundation as that referred to by Abdullah Munshi.

Whether these early foundations in Singapore represented the advent of the Han league to Malaya under the name of the Ghee Hok society (義福公司) which may be translated the "Justice and Happiness Society" or the "Happy Patriots Society", we are unable to say.

We do know that about 1840 the Ghee Hok society made its presence felt in Singapore as a rival confederacy to the Ghee Hin, but both were believed to be branches of the Triad society.

Ample evidence will, we believe, be offered to show that the Ghee Hok Society was in fact a foundation of the Han Liu in Singapore and evinced nothing but hostility to the Triad society.

Similarly in Penang about the same time (1844) there arose a society known as the Toh Peh Kong, which from the time of its appearance was implacably hostile to the

Ghee Hin (Triad) of Penang. The Toh Peh Kong, we also propose to prove, was in fact a foundation of the Han Liu and the representative in Penang of the Ghee Hok society of Singapore.

Not to lay ourselves open to a charge of forcing facts to fit a theory, we propose to designate that series of Chinese secret societies in Malaya which have consistently shown themselves hostile to the Triad, by the name of "Tokong" a term the meaning of which will be explained later on. The names of the two rival camps in Malaya will henceforth be referred to accordingly, *viz.*:—

> Triad (The Hung league)—The Ghee Hin Kongsi and its affiliations.
> Tokong (The Han league)—The Ghee Hok Kongsi and its affiliations.

The origin of the name Ghee Hok is probably to be found in the Ghee (義) or "rectitude" lodge of the Han Liu, mentioned by Hutson in Chapter II.

EARLY ACTIVITIES OF THE HUNG LEAGUE IN THE COLONY AND ADJACENT TERRITORIES

Having thus obtained a general view of the subject matter of this and the following Chapter, it is necessary to trace as far as possible from the time of its foundation in each Settlement in the Straits, up to the year 1867, the history and fortunes of each one of the local Chinese secret societies which collectively are known as the Triad society, and upon that evidence to attempt to separate the several societies into the two rival camps of Triad (Hung) and "Tokong" (Han) to which we believe them properly to belong.

We will take the Settlements in the following order:—
>   (1) Junk Ceylon or Ujong Salang
>   (2) Penang
>   (3) Malacca
>   (4) Singapore

and as far as possible trace in each the beginnings and early history of the following associations active during the first half of the nineteenth century:—
>   The Ghee Hin Kongsi
>   The Hai San
>   The Ho Seng
>   The Wah Sang
>   The Ghee Hok
>   The Toh Peh Kong.

Junk Ceylon or Ujong Salang (NOW KNOWN AS PUKET OR TONGKA)

In the days of Francis Light, (1772–1786) Chinese, particularly Cantonese and Hokkiens, were already engaged in tin-mining in the island of Junk Ceylon, referred to in Chapter IV *supra*.

The territory was then nominally Siamese, but was evidently claimed by Kedah.

Anderson in his *Considerations relative to the Malay Peninsula J.I.A.* Vol. VIII pages 283–284 has:—

> In Captain Light's account of Junk Ceylon, he says:—
>   The King of Quedah claims the dominions of these seas that is between Salang and Mergui..... After the loss of Siam (alluding to the conquest of that country by the Burmese) the Malays got possession of the Island (Junk Ceylon) and the Laksamana of Quedah maintained an absolute authority, treating the Siamese as slaves, until an accident inspired the islanders with the idea of liberating themselves, which they performed in one night. The Laksamana constantly regretted the loss of this island and offered me (Light) 8,000 men when it was proposed by Mr. Hastings (Warren Hastings) to establish a settlement there.

We are not informed whether the Chinese settlers assisted the Siamese islanders to liberate themselves, but it is possible that they did so, in view of subsequent intrigues in Penang.

It will be seen from what follows that about the year 1825, a plot was suspected between the Ghee Hins of Penang and their compatriots in Junk Ceylon, arising out of a political intrigue, details of which are given below, between Low Ah Chong, the then leader of the Hai San society in Penang and the Raja of Ligor (himself said to be half Chinese). This plot had as its object the seizure of Penang by the Siamese, then at war with Kedah and was to be aided by a simultaneous rising of the Ghee Hins resident in Penang.

The Chief Minister of the Raja of Ligor at this time (1825) was in touch with Low Ah Chong and is stated to have been a Chinese named Choo Lee, who may himself have been a member of the Junk Ceylon Ghee Hins.

The Siamese expedition was duly fitted out in 1825 and was declared to be for the purpose of subjugating Selangor in alliance with the Penang Ghee Hins, so as to put the British authorities in Penang off their guard. The Governor of Penang (Fullerton) believed however that the expedition was in fact intended for an attack on Penang and that it may have been inspired by the "liberation" of the island of Junk Ceylon from Malay rule in the preceding century, referred to by Light in the extract from Anderson given above.

The Siamese town and Province of Ligor or Lakon, was situated on the East Coast of the peninsula almost opposite Junk Ceylon on the West Coast. The Province of Ligor at the time of the Kedah-Siam war 1821–1848, evidently comprised the whole of Siamese territory south of the Isthmus of Kra, and may have included Junk Ceylon itself, although in the *Straits Settlements Factory Records* Vol. 132 (1830), there is frequent reference to correspondence between the Governor of Penang and the Raja of Salang, which makes it look as if the Province of Salang (including Junk Ceylon) on the West Coast, was distinct from the Province of Ligor on the East Coast.

Be that as it may, the liaison between the Ghee Hins of Penang and Junk Ceylon persisted right up to the year 1867, as will be shown in Chapter XVI *infra*.

Traces of this liaison are also to be found in the early history of the Singapore Triad foundation. Indeed as late as October 1874, we find references in official records to a suspected liaison, for political purposes, between the then ex-Sultan Ismail of Perak and the "Raja of Tongka", the latter evidently the counterpart of the former Raja of Salang. The references are these:—

In the *Precis of evidence taken at the enquiry as to the complicity of Chiefs in the Perak outrages* published in 1876, page 33 (Summary) Item 38 reads:—

"That about this time (Oct. 1874), ex-Sultan Ismail summoned a meeting of all the chiefs of the Ulu and Ilir to consider whether they would submit to the British authority in Perak, or whether they would combine and attack Bandar Bahru and drive the British out of Perak".

On page 9 of the Appendix to this publication, an extract from Appendix IX, letter from ex-Sultan Ismail to the Governor dated 8/9/1874 reads:—

"It is mentioned in one of our friend's letters that we have asked assistance of the Raja of Tongka. As to that, we have never in any way done so, to go against our friend's wishes".

And on the same page Appendix X. Letter from the Governor to Ex-Sultan Ismail dated 12/10/1874:—

"We are glad to learn......that our friend was not concerned in the intrigues said to be going on between people in Perak and the Raja of Tongka".

As will appear later in Chapter XVI there were probably good grounds for these suspicions of the Governor (Clarke) and the part probably played by the Chinese secret society under-world in these intrigues is therein recorded. It suffices for the moment to point out here a probable secret society connection between the intrigues of Perak and Tongka in 1874 and those of Penang and Junk Ceylon at an earlier epoch. It is probable, therefore, that it is to Junk Ceylon and to the territory of the Raja of Ligor that we should look for the origin of the Mother Lodge of the Triad society in Malaya. We shall have more to say of the influence of Sino-Siamese intrigue in Malayan affairs when we discuss in a later Chapter the activities of Tan Kim Ching of Singapore (*aet.* 1829–1892).

Penang.—After the foundation of Penang in 1776, Chinese in large numbers came thither from Junk Ceylon and Sarawak, as well as from China, who seem at first to have been, for the most part, Cantonese and Hakkas of the pirate type. These settlers doubtless brought the Hung and the Han leagues with them. The earliest available Penang records (1825) show that in that year, the Ghee Hin and the Hai San, two separate and distinct secret societies, both composed of Cantonese, and both with ties in Junk Ceylon, had then amongst others been firmly established in Penang, the Ghee Hin for 24 years, the Hai San for about three years. This evidence given below, would fix the dates of the foundation of these two societies in Penang approximately as: Ghee Hin in 1800, the Hai San in 1820.

Even before 1800, Chinese secret societies had made their presence felt in Penang, as the following references show:—

Newbold in his *Account of the British Settlements in the Straits of Malacca* 2 Vols. London 1839 has in Vol. I page 13 the following:—

The secret fraternities in which they (the Chinese settlers) enrol themselves for mutual protection and support, prove powerful engines for political combinations, as the Dutch have repeatedly experienced during their long administration in Java and in the Malay States. In China itself, these societies are deemed so dangerous to the Government as to be interdicted under penalty of death.

At Penang in 1799, they set the administration in defiance and strong measures were necessary to reduce them to obedience. Even in the present-day, the ends of justice are frequently defeated both at Penang, Malacca, and Singapore: by bribery, false swearing, and sometimes by open violence owing to combinations of these fraternities, formed for the purpose of screening guilty members from detection and punishment.

In European Settlements, they are under the general control of an officer, or headman, styled "Capitan", who receives a salary from Government, and is responsible in some measure, for the orderly conduct of his countrymen, whose representative and official organ he is. Their interior affairs, disputes, and private interests are arranged by the heads of their respective "Kongsis" or fraternities.

Mills, *op. cit.* page 208 refers to the same incident:—

"The problem of the Chinese secret societies arose only a few years after the foundation of Penang. In 1799 several of them were already established there, and giving trouble to the Resident, while as time advanced, the question became more serious".

The official records of this early period have not become available to us, and have therefore not been consulted for purposes of this work.

In 1825, Kedah and Siam were at war, and Governor Fullerton became aware in that year of the existence of an intrigue between the Chinese secret societies in Penang and the Siamese invaders of Kedah, having as its object a possible attack upon Penang.

The following Minute of Governor Fullerton, extracted from *The Burney Papers* Vol. II Part I January–June 1825 pages 211–213 and dated 10/6/1825, illuminates the position at that date:—

I now lay before the Board a paper of information received from Mr. Maingy. I beg leave at the same time to submit copies of letters received from the Rajah of Ligore, with draft of my reply thereto. These letters were delivered by four envoys, with whom I have had a conversation, the substance of which corresponded entirely with the letters and reply.

The Board will perceive a striking coincidence between the information of Mr. Maingy, and the subject of the letters. The information states it to be the intention to send troops on pretence of going to Perak, to halt on Kreean River, and wait a favourable opportunity for attacking the Island. The main drift of these letters goes to shew the necessity of sending troops to Perak, a fabricated letter said to be from Perak, requiring assistance is produced, the object is evidently to blind us as to the true object of sending troops to the Kreean. I trust that the Board will be satisfied that the hostile intention of the Rajah towards this Island is now sufficiently manifest to authorize our acting against him, should a favourable occasion present itself for the destruction of his means of aggression.

The Board will perceive the employment of persons to set fire to the town, again alluded to; on this point I confess I am not so well informed as on external proceedings, having relied principally on the Police for discovery of internal enemies. From a conversation held by me with the principal Chinese inhabitants, substance of which I annex hereto,[1] there seems not a vestige of doubt, notwithstanding the depositions of the asserted heads of the Kongsee, or Clubs, that Low Achong is at the head of one of them, the "Hysan Kongsee"; the information may, if necessary, be supported on oath. This being so is indeed as notorious as the sun at noonday, and I have obtained the same information from a variety of channels. If any persons are engaged to aid the views of the Rajah on the Island, we may be assured the members of these Kongsees are they, and it would be most desirable to obtain, if possible, by a seizure of papers, or otherwise, the names of those belonging to it. I must at the same time confess my firm belief that had an immediate search taken place at the house where they are known to assemble, instead of trusting to the asseveration of the reported heads, we should have got at the names, as well as the object of these meetings. Having furnished the Superintendent of Police with the late information from Mr. Maingy, I still hope he will succeed in obtaining a clue to the discovery of those employed on account of the Rajah. In the meantime, a due regard to the preservation of order requires that Achong should be kept for the present in close custody, and not allowed to hold communication with any person whatever.

The great object and purpose of Police is to watch and discover such machinations of the evilly disposed, and it is impossible for me to conceal my regret that on the present occasion the Police has shown itself to be so deficient. As to those clubs, I can only express my surprise that they have ever been allowed to exist, composed of the very lowest and most worthless of our population, a class of people without tie or connexion on the Island, ready for any mischief, holding such meetings with closed doors, administering oaths of secrecy. I can hardly conceive an Instrument better fitted for the subversion of any regular Government; and I am only withheld from submitting a Proclamation for their immediate suppression, in the hopes that the important object of the discovery of persons, may still be attainable.

Connected with this, there is another subject on which it seems desirable that information should be obtained and recorded. I allude to the manner in which the Macao Chinese obtain footing on the Island. I have been informed, by respectable authority, that they are brought here from China on speculation by Captains of ships, and sold as slave debtors to the highest bidders, the purchase money being repayable to the purchasers by a given portion of their labour. This practice seems to me to have rather close affinity to actual slave trade, and I propose that a full and complete statement of the mode and manner of carrying on the transaction be obtained from the best authority, in order that we may judge of the expediency of allowing or preventing the continuance of the practice.

Annexed to the above Minute is the following statement, undated, of Choa Shim Yip a Hokkien goldsmith of Penang, taken by R. Caunter, Assistant Superintendent of Police, Penang, about 1st June 1825, and bearing the endorsement *Bengal Secret and Political Consultations* Vol. 331. Dated Fort William, Calcutta 17/6/1825. Extracted from *The Burney Papers*, Vol. II Part I pages 237–239:—

Information of Shimyep or Sihimyen, a Chinese man of the tribe Choah,[1] prisoner in the House of correction—

Informant is by trade a goldsmith, and has been for some time employed of a master goldsmith, a Macao Chinese named Hinneoo of the tribe Cheong,[2] who lives near the market place in George Town. Whilst in this man's employ about eight months ago, informant was invited to join a Kungsee or Club, to which his master belonged, the head man or manager of which is the Chinese watchmaker Appoo. All persons joining the club were obliged to do so under an oath that they would, when required, or in any public commotion, join the members thereof. This club is termed the Ghe Chin, and is very numerous. Informant understood that they had stores of spears and other weapons which were deposited in different places some he heard were kept in the house or premises of the arrack Farmer. On joining, each member pays five dollars entrance money, and takes the aforesaid oath.

Not having the means of paying the entrance money, and not wishing to take the oath prescribed, informant never joined the club.

The Macao Chinese have two other clubs of this kind in George Town, one of which is called the Hoo Sing, and the other the Hy San and held one near Ujong Passir, and the other in the Prangin Road. Following is a list of the Head men, or managers of these clubs and places they are held in:—

	PLACES	MANAGERS	OCCUPATION
Ghe Chin	Church Street	Boon Appoo	Watchmaker
Hoo Sing	Ujong Passir	Hoh Hew	Shopkeeper
Hy San	Prangin Road	Loh Allak	Shopkeeper

Footnote.—(1) *See* below. Statement of Chua Shim Yip taken by R. Caunter about 1st June, 1825.
Footnote.—(2) *i.e.* Cheong Hin Yew.

Informant has heard that Achong, Lowe Ammee's son is a member of both the Ho Sing and Hy San clubs, and that when he lately went from here to Ligore, he was desired to communicate to the Siamese that there were but few people now at Penang, and that it was a good opportunity for attacking it if the Siamese were inclined to do so. Upon being asked who informed this, he gives no direct answer and only says he heard so.

Caunter added the following note to the above statement from his personal knowledge:—

There are seven or eight Chinese clubs (or Hooeys) in this island, some of which have been established several years. The avowed object of these institutions is the relief of indigent brethren and particularly to defray in a decent manner the funeral expenses of members dying without that means. Owing to the propensity of the Chinese to conspiracies, these Hooeys are, I understand, strictly forbidden in China. Here they are formed chiefly, if not solely, among what are termed the Canton or Macao Chinese of whom there may be about three thousands (3,000) in this Island. The Chinchoo Chinese may, if they please, become members of these associations, and some of the Chinchoos are said to belong to them but they are chiefly composed of the Canton Chinese, between whom and the Chinchoos great jealousy and often hostility prevails.

When the Rajah of Ligore was at Kedah about two and a half or three years ago, he carried on a good deal of secret correspondence with the Canton or Macao Chinese of this place, got numbers of them to go in some junks he equipped, and sent them to cruise to the northward of and about Junk Ceylon, where they were reported, and I believe with some truth, to have committed atrocious acts of piracy.

The informant Choah Shimyep is a Chinchoo (i.e. Hokkien) Chinese.

Other evidence to the same effect is contained in the same Volume of *The Burney Papers* at the following references. Page 106:—

"Statement dated 5/5/1825 of Che Toah Hokkien the principal Chinese merchant in Penang, given to H.E. The Governor (Fullerton) in person, in which he says that he thinks the Siamese (in the person of the Raja of Ligor) have designs on Penang and have "an arrangement with Low Ah Chong, head of the Macao Chinese in Penang, numbering up to 1000, to help them".

On page 107:—

"The above is corroborated by a letter from the ex-Sultan of Kedah to H.E. the Governor, in which he says that Low Ah Chong is treated with the greatest respect by the Raja of Ligor".

Again in *Straits Settlements Factory Records* Vol. 101 (1825) pages 1346-7, there is a record of an examination of Low Ah Chong, head of the Hai Sans in Penang (mentioned above) by the Governor in Council on 4/5/1825, relative to the suspected plot of that year against Penang. The following is an extract from this examination:—

EXTRACT OF CONSULTATION HELD AT FORT CORNWALLIS (PENANG) ON 12TH MAY, 1825

Examination of Achong, son of Lowe Ammee before Council on Wednesday, 4th May, 1825

Q. How many boats did you understand were prepared at the northward ports of Quedah?	A. About 300, all new, viz. at Purlis 120, at Traang a little more than 100, at Quedah, 80.
Q. What did you understand to be the object of their equipment?	A. To go to Salengore.
Q. Who gave you this information?	A. The King of Ligore's Minister, Choo Lee, a Chinaman.
Q. Did you enquire of the Rajah of Ligore himself?	A. Yes, at first he said no, then he acknowledged he did intend doing so.
Q. How many men fit to bear arms did you see at Ligore?	A. About 15,000 Siamese besides about 1,000 Chinese and 8,000 Malays.
Q. How are they generally armed?	A. With musquets without bayonets.

The following extracts are taken from the same source,[1] being an examination of the titular Heads of the Ghee Hin and Hai San in Penang 1825 viz:—

(1) Ghee Hin	..	..⎰ Mun Ah Fu *or*
		⎱ Boon Ah Poo
(2) Hai San	..	.. Ho Ah Kow

Although the information given to the Governor by these two head-men is scanty and probably largely untrue, the record is nevertheless interesting:—

EXTRACT OF CONSULTATION HELD AT FORT CORNWALLIS ON 19TH MAY, 1825

"The President lays before the Board the following examination of the chiefs of three Chinese clubs in George Town, delivered to him by the Sitting Magistrate.

EXAMINATION OF THE CHIEFS OF CHINESE CLUBS

(1) Examination of Mun Affoh.—Commonly called Appoo, Chinese watchmaker of George Town, President of the Hooey or club designated Nghee Hung Khoon (i.e. Ghee Hin).

This club has been established about 24 years, the objects of it "relief of sick and distressed members". On joining, 1½ dollar entrance money is paid by each member. This club is a general one, and composed of Canton Chinese of different classes. Tradesmen, mechanics, planters, seamen, &c., only 4 or 5 Chinchoo Chinese belong to it, who are Nakodahs, and seafaring men. Meetings held twice a year,—viz., on the 13th of the 1st, and 13th of the 5th Chinese month the latter is the anniversary of the institution. Members enter this club under an oath to assist their poor brethren and further the benevolent objects of the society, and not to be concerned in any bad or improper acts. The present property of the society is about 70 dollars in money and a house in Church Street for holding their meetings in. The books of this club have been examined in which there appear—

Entered	..	..	..	..	..	720 Members
Dead	..	..	..	..	..	43 „
Left	..	..	..	..	..	209 „
Remaining	..	..	..	..	..	468 „

In former years this club is said to have been much larger than it is at present. Mun Affoh has been elected President during life; the former President died about 18 months ago. Lowe Achong, Ammee's son is declared not to be a member of this club".

Footnote.—(1) *Straits Settlements Factory Records* Vol. 101 1825 pages 1476-1480.

DESIGNATIONS OF CHINESE CLUBS IN PRINCE OF WALES ISLAND MAY, 1825.

The following is a "return" of Chinese clubs (secret societies and district associations mixed) in Penang in May, 1825, compiled by R. Caunter, Superintendent of Police, extracted from *Straits Settlements Factory Records* Vol. 101 (1825) page 1604:—

Where Situate	Designation of the clubs	Present No. of members	How long established	No. of meetings held annually	Name of President		Remarks
GEORGE TOWN							P. signifies Permanent or for Life. A. Annual these letters are intended to shew how the heads of the clubs to which they are placed have been chosen. Khoon, in Chinese, I am informed, signifies an almshouse or place of refuge for poor and distressed. Clubs or societies called Hoey Khoon exist and are allowed in China being benevolent societies, but they are not permitted to engage their members under an Oath, the doing which in that country would be treasonable. All secret associations or meetings are most strictly prohibited there and are considered and treated as seditious assemblies. Such in Chiuu are denominated Tin-Tee-Huey.
Church Street	Nghee Hung-Khoon	468	about 24 years	2	Mun Affoh *alias* Appoh	P.	
Prangin Road	Woh Sung-Khoon	147	" 15 "	4	Loh Aloke	P.	
Ujong Passir	Hoy San-Khoon	393	" 2 "	2	Hoh Akow	P.	
Prangin Road	Choong Chang-Khoon	175	" 4 "	3	Ow Yong Sow	A.	
Prangin Road	Wye Chow-Khoon	160	" 1 year	3	Lee Ahang	A.	
King Street	Yan Woh-Khoon	17	" 20 years	3	Chan Achoon	A.	
King Street	Yeng San-Khoon	16	" 30 "	3	Chung Ayyat	A.	
		1,376					

(*Signed*) R. CAUNTER.
S.P.

(2) Examination of Hoh Akow.—Chinese shopkeeper of George Town, President of the Hooey or club designated "Hoysan Khoon" (*i.e.* Hai San).

This club has been established about three years and is a general one for all Canton Province Chinese; these belong to it: tradesmen, shopkeepers, mechanics, planters, and others. No oath is administered or required from persons joining this club, but a certain sum as entrance money is paid which varies from 1 to 5 dollars, according to the circumstances of the members. This institution possesses no funds in money but has a house in Beach Street Ujong Passir which cost 400 dollars. Two meetings a year are held by this club, *viz.*, in the 3rd and 7th months. The objects of this Institution are aid and relief to sick and distressed members, and the granting of decent burials to such of their brethren as die indigent, and cannot defray that expense. When sums are required for charitable purposes they are raised by collections from among the members of the society the expenses of their club dinners at the annual meetings are defrayed in the same manner. The books of this club show—

Entered	..	..	..	..	568	Members
Dead	..	..	..	..	11	„
Left	..	..	..	..	164	„
Remaining	..	..	..	..	394	„

Lowe Achong is declared not to belong to this club 10th May, 1825.

(Signed) R. FULLERTON.

Ordered that Achong son of Low Ammee, now in custody of the Police be retained for further examination and until further orders.

The following extract is from the same source, being an examination by the Governor of Penang of four leading Chinese merchants on the subject of the Ghee Hin and Hai San societies. It is interesting as tending to confirm the suspicions of political intrigue at that time between the Siamese and the Chinese secret societies, against the Malays and against British interests. *Straits Settlements Factory Records* Vol. 101 (1825) :—

EXTRACT OF A CONSULTATION HELD AT FORT CORNWALLIS ON 10TH JUNE, 1825

(Enclosure 6 in the President's Minute)

"Examination.—Of Che Seong, Che Toah, Beng, and Kiat, the head Chinese merchants of George Town, by the Honourable the Governor and Chief Judge, at the Recorder's Chambers, on Thursday the 9th June, 1825.

The four Chinese merchants were informed that it was probable they might be called upon to repeat on oath any declaration which they might make, and were therefore cautioned to consider well the replies they made to any questions put to them.

They unanimously declared it was notorious amongst the Chinese that Achong, son of Lowe Ammee is the head of the Hysan Congsee or club. They were ready to swear to it. This club has been established about 2 years. It consists of about 1,000 members of the lowest class of Macao Chinese, day labourers, carpenters, gardeners, &c. they are all poor, not a merchant or respectable trader amongst them. They are all looked upon as bad characters; good people do not join such clubs. All the proceedings are secret. They have two large meetings in the country in the year.

"The house at Ujong Passir, where the meetings are chiefly held is not a large house. Such clubs are strictly prohibited in China, and they ought not to be allowed here. It would, in the opinion of informants, be very desirable to put a stop to them. They are of opinion that since the seizure of Achong, the head of the Hysan club, the meetings have been suspended. The Macao Chinese, who were employed in the Rajah of Ligore's service a few years ago, belong to the Hysan and Gehin clubs. They do not think it would be easy to discover the names of all the people belonging to the clubs. It is a well understood fact that Achong went to Ligore and endeavoured to get appointed "Captain" at Perak. He was concerting to convey 200 or 300 Chinese from this island to join the Chinese at Perak, and to carry his views into effect.

"Appoo is the head of the Gehin club; Hochong is the next in rank. This club is equally numerous and the persons composing it equally bad as the Hysan club. Many of the members are sea-faring people; they are connected with the Chinese residing in Pegu, Siam and the adjoining countries".

Again in the *Straits Settlements Factory Records* Vol. 129 (1829) there is an account of "Chinese Hoey Khoons or clubs, as existing in Prince of Wales Island (Penang) in June, 1829" by I. Pattullo, then Superintendent of Police, and afterwards Government Secretary.

A *précis* of this report is given below in confirmation of the Caunter report above.

Like all accounts of the period, it is without Chinese characters to help us and confuses what came to be known as the "dangerous" or secret societies, with the harmless Hoay Kwans or genuine district or tribal "mutual benefit" associations. The Pattullo account mentions the following associations. We have suggested the probable Chinese characters for some of them :—

    (1) Nghee Hunge (Ghee Hin) (義兄 or 義興)

    (2) Choon Sin   (   )

    (3) Wah Sang   (華生)

    (4) Yeng San   (   )

    (5) Hoy San   (海山)

    (6) Yan Woh   (人和)

    (7) Wye Chow   (惠州)

    (8) Ho Seng   (和勝)

    (9) Chong Chang (   )

Information extracted from the Pattullo account (1829) is as follows:—

(1) Nghee Hung (Ghee Hin)—Cantonese: long established: formerly very numerous but latterly decreasing, many members having gone to Junk Ceylon.[1]
Kongsi house in King Street: present membership 150: Retiring President Ah Poo, Watchmaker: New President to be Hoo Chong.

(2) Choon Sin—A harmless Hokkien Hoay Kwan.

(3) Wah Sang[2]—Established 20 years by "a class of Chinese who come from the mountain tracts near Canton". Club house in Prangin Road: present membership 175.

(4) Yeng San[3]—A Cantonese association, "long established by traders from Sambas in the island of Borneo" (i.e. Sarawak).

(5) Hoy San[4] (Hai San)—Established 8 or 10 years ago: composed of Cantonese and a few Chin Chews (Hokkien). Present membership 200, formerly 400. Has a club house in Ujong Passir. President Hok Ah Keow (absent): acting President Hong See Hoey.

(6) Yan Woh[5]—Established upwards of 30 years, composed of "a certain class of Chinese coming from Kahang Chow, a hilly part of Canton province". It was originally established (like number (4) above Yeng San), by traders from Sambas. No oath is taken by members.

(7) Wye Chow—The district association of the Cantonese from the Wai Chow prefecture of Canton. The Wai Chow Cantonese also compose the membership of the Ho Seng, which is a secret society.

(8) Ho Seng—The secret society of the Wai Chow Cantonese allied at this time to the Ghee Hin: no particulars given.

(9) Chong Chang—The district association of the Cantonese from the Chung Fa district of Canton, harmless.

Of the above, No. (1) Ghee Hin, No. (3) Wah Sang, No. (5) Hai San, No. (8) Ho Seng belong to the category of secret societies and these only need concern us, the Ghee Hin and Ho Seng were Cantonese and later allied themselves with the White Flag society of the Malays and the Wah Sang and Hai San, being or becoming predominantly Hakka, later allied themselves with the Red Flag Malays. (See Chapter XIV and XVI infra).

From the above extracts we gather the following information, viz.:—

(1) In 1825 in Penang the four following secret societies—

Ghee Hin (羨典) or Nghee Hung (? 義兄)

Ho Seng (和成)

Hai San (海山)

Wah Sang (華生)

were already firmly established there. The first three were mainly composed of Cantonese membership. The fourth was composed of Hakkas.

(2) One of the leaders of the Hai San was a Cantonese named Low Ah Chong and the association, as its name implies was a piratical one, distinct from the Ghee Hin, but acting in concert with it and both were in support of the Siamese invaders of Kedah.

(3) The headmen in Penang at this time were:—

Ghee Hin	{ Boon Ah Poo, watchmaker, Church Street. / Hoo Chong
Ho Seng	Ho Hiu, shopkeeper, Ujong Passir.
Hai San	{ Ho Ah Kow, Ujong Passir. / Low Ah Chong / Hong See Hoey
Wah Sang	Low Ah Luk, shopkeeper, Prangin Road.

From evidence which will appear later, it is certain that although Cantonese members seem to have predominated in the earlier Hai San and consequently they did not quarrel at that time with their fellow Cantonese in the Ghee Hin, the character of the Hai San in Penang changed between the years 1845–1860, and owing perhaps to the influx of Hakkas due to the wars in south China (see page 60 supra) it became increasingly Hakka in membership, and consequently increasingly hostile to the Cantonese.

During the same period the former Hakka society in Penang, the Wah Sang, seems to disappear from the records and may have been absorbed into the Hai San as the latter became purely Hakka.

We learn from Vaughan Notes on the Chinese in Penang J.I.A. VIII that in 1854, "the Hye San is composed of Keh Langs" (i.e. Khehs or Hakkas) and by 1860, the transfer of the Hai San to the opposite camp, hostile to the Ghee Hins, was complete.

Footnote.—(1) The Membership given is as shown by the "books" and probably only includes the headmen. The reference to Junk Ceylon is interesting in view of the Sino-Siamese political intrigues of the period, against Kedah mentioned above.

Footnote.—(2) This is evidently the earliest purely Hakka secret society in Penang. Its name later disappears from recorded history and it evidently became merged in the Hai San, which from about 1850, and onwards was purely Hakka. It probably was or became an "anchorage" of the Han league and belonged to the "Tokong" camp.

Footnote.—(3) Evidently a harmless tribal association, but may have had a piratical origin.

Footnote.—(4) This is the Hai San, which like the Ghee Hin may have had an original foundation in Junk Ceylon in the eighteenth century. It was probably chiefly Cantonese until about 1850, when it became almost exclusively Hakka, and thence forward showed its hostility to the Cantonese of the Ghee Hin. It was probably of piratical origin.

Footnote.—(5) Evidently the harmless tribal association of the Ka-Yin-Chiu Hakkas.

In the Rules of the Kian Tek (Toh Peh Kong) society dated 30/12/1844, the Hai San society is mentioned in Rule 11 (*see* Appendix II) which reads:—

"If those who have joined our society on this day or on another day, and join any of the following three Congsees *i.e.* Ghee Hins, Ho Seng, or Hy San and the fact be proved against those persons, they will be immediately expelled the society and their children and grand children will not be permitted to succeed them".

This shows that in 1844, the Hai Sans were still considered to belong to the camp of the Ghee Hins.

The *Penang Riot Commission Report 1868*, nowhere makes special mention of the Hai San Kongsi, other than the above, and it is clear from subsequent events that at some time between 1845 and 1867, the Hai San (Hakkas) joined forces with the Toh Peh Kongs (Hokkiens), and in the *Riot Report of 1868*, the name "Toh Peh Kong" seems to have included the Hai Sans, although the latter are unmentioned.

The year of alliance may well have been about 1860, just before the outbreak of the Larut wars (1862–1873) in which the name of the Toh Peh Kong, seems in turn to give place to that of the Hai Sans as the rivals of the Ghee Hins in Larut, whereas in Penang, the name Toh Peh Kong remained as that of the antagonists of the Triad.

It seems clear that both the Toh Peh Kong Kongsi, and the Hai San Kongsi, were foundations of a similar kind, the one of Hokkiens, the other originally of Cantonese, which became later absorbed by Hakkas, and both were hostile to the Triads.   This strengthens the earlier submission that they both were or became "anchorages" or lodges of the Ko Lao Hui.

For purposes of this work we prefer to label them as both belonging to the "Tokong" camp, whose common factor was hostility to Triad.

The next notice of the Triad society in Penang in point of time, seems to be the paper by Lt. Newbold *Chinese Secret Triad Society J.R.A.S.* VI 1840 quoted in Chapters I and II.

On page 133 Newbold has:—

"In Java, Rhio, and many other Dutch Settlements they (the Triads) have from time to time concocted dangerous conspiracies against Government and risen into open rebellion.

At our own Settlement of Penang in 1799, the Kongsis uniting, set Government at defiance, and were only reduced to subjection by the most vigorous measures.......

According to Major Low, Superintendent of Province Wellesley, the Chinese at Batu Kawan sugar plantations, nearly all belong to one Kongsi and were very turbulent before 1829, having turned out on several occasions to the sound of a buffalo horn, against the civil power.......

The same intelligent observer, whose functions as a magistrate gave him many opportunities of observing the practical effects of these organisations at Penang, remarks that when a Chinese is apprehended for, or accused of, a crime, however atrocious it may be, his whole Kongsi are unanimous in their endeavour to get him off.   Subscriptions for counsel, high bribes to adverse witnesses to keep them away, and to forthcoming ones to perjure themselves; dreadful threats to conscientious witnesses and connivance at the escape or secreting of the accused, are the means resorted to as matters of course.   When one Kongsi is opposed to another by the criminal accusation of an individual of one of them, no bounds can be assigned to the use which is made of these illegal means.

The foregoing passage, although written in 1840 is almost equally applicable to secret society conditions in Malaya to-day.

A final extract from Newbold's paper *op. cit.* is of great interest.

After reference to the Hung league's activities at that time (1840) and earlier, in Siam, he quotes (page 135) a statement of a Chinese of long residence in the Straits Settlements, which appeared in the *Chinese Repository* (reference not given) in which the deponent bewails the power of the Hung league in the settlements in the South Seas. The statement contains the following:—

Secret societies have arisen up in all the settlements, but they are all emanations of the Triad society......   They have assumed the names of the Hae-Shan-Hwuy "the Sea and Land society" (海 山 會) and the E-Hin-Hwuy (義 興 會) "the Righteous rising society".

These two associations are scattered over all the settlements and they all obey the orders and restrictions of the heads of their respective societies, whom they call 'the Great Brother'. This stock is divided into four, eight, or twelve great stems as the case may be, and from these stems there issue scores of branches.   Every stem and every branch has its Headman who is designated "senior brother".   Emigrants from China are called sinkehs.   As soon as they arrive at any settlement, the brotherhood send persons to invite them to join the confederacy if they decline they are forthwith persecuted.   However the two above-named societies often wrangle, and if you belong to the one and not to the other, you are equally persecuted".

With reference to the plunder obtained by members of these societies by criminal means, the statement says:—

"One half goes to the society and one half to the member who captured the plunder".

As we shall see later on, the two secret societies in Penang which were to cause most trouble and lead to British intervention in Perak were the Ghee Hin (Triad) and the Hai San ("Tokong") mentioned above.

Malacca.—Newbold on page 130 *op. cit. J.R.A.S.* VI 1840 records that the *Peking Gazette* of 7th October, 1817, stated that the Triad society was then powerful in Canton. He continues:—

"It is not unreasonable to infer that the Chinese colonists at Malacca, in Java, Borneo, and other parts of the Indian archipelago at an early period after emigration would find the advantages of binding themselves together as a means of defence and self protection in a foreign land: Many of them had probably been members of associations already alluded to (The Hung league) in their native land. Hence the numerous "Kongsis" or public clubs with which we find them invariably linked, particularly at the mines and plantations in the interior. Be that as it may, the particular tenets of the secret society of Tien-ti Wui have of late years gained ground. According to the calculation of a Chinese, himself one of the fraternity, the number of sworn brethren in our settlements in the Straits cannot be less than 7,000. During the Dutch administration it was nearly broken up, but has, however, again reared its head under the more lenient and perhaps too liberal policy of the English. Shortly after taking possession of Malacca in 1825 (i.e. after the English re-took possession from the Dutch) they became so numerous and riotous as to excite the attention of the Government".

Newbold gives an extract from the *Malacca Observer* of 1826 which says:—

"It is reputed that the brotherhood (i.e. the Triad society in Malacca) are able to muster four thousand strong from the different plantations and tin mines in the interior, added to those at Malacca itself. They are all either Canton or Macao men, no Fokien man being allowed to enter their body, as the natives of that province speak another dialect".

Then follows a recital of murders and outrages committed by the society (doubtless the Ghee Hin) in Malacca in 1826, whose headquarters appear to have been at the tin mines at Lukut, outside Malacca territory.

Newbold goes on to record that in 1828, the Malays of Sungei Ujong raided the treasure chest of the Ghee Hins at the tin-mines at Sungei Ujong and stole the treasure after great slaughter. A reprisal was made one night in September 1834 when the Ghee Hins rose and plundered and murdered every man, woman and child in Lukut upon whom they could lay hands, including Tengku Busu, the owner of the mines, who was their employer and a relation of the Sultan of Selangor.

Newbold in his *Account of the British Settlements of the Straits of Malacca* 1839, 2 Vols. has in Vol. II page 33 the following account of this incident in his Chapter on the history of Selangor:—

"The Lukut mines are situated several miles inland, near the banks of a river of the same name...... The Chinese who formerly worked these mines on their own account, paid a tenth of the produce to Selangore. Latterly I believe, Tuanku Boosu took upon himself the entire direction. In September, 1834, the Chinese miners from 300 to 400, in number, rose one dark rainy night upon their Malay employers, fired their houses and massacred them indiscriminately. Tuanku Boosu was slain and many of his followers...... The Chinese who were mostly of the Triad Society were hotly pursued by the Malays...... The plunder obtained by the Chinese is said to have amounted to 18,000 Spanish dollars.......
This murderous business it is strongly suspected was aided and abetted, if not concocted by certain Chinese merchants living under the protection of the British flag at Malacca".

Newbold in his paper *J.R.A.S. VI (1840)* gives a description, (page 144) of the Ghee Hin headquarters in Malacca in 1835, to which he gained admittance and which had branches at Lukut and Sungei Ujong.

His article includes a reproduction of the following original Triad documents which he states were obtained from members in Penang and Malacca:—

(a) A Certificate of Membership, similar to Illustration No. 8 in Stanton *The Triad Society* page 85. Name, number, place and date of holder are not shown (they were probably on the back).

(b) A Circular document containing the names of the eight genii and the legend "Overthrow Ts'ing and restore Ming".

(c) A Circular document containing ten exhortations to good conduct—Nothing to identify it with Triad.

Newbold's interesting article concludes with a translation of the Thirty-six oaths: the Thirty-six rules: and some of the ritual and Triad constitution, with a note upon the points of likeness between Freemasonry and the Triad society.

His translations from the Chinese were done for him by the Rev. Tomlin of Malacca.

Singapore.—Singapore was founded in 1819, thirty-three years later than Penang. On the subject of its population at the time of its foundation McNair in *Prisoners their own Warders* pages 34 and 38 has:—

Our new possession (Singapore in 1819) then contained in round numbers about

120	Malays
30	Chinese.

In the course of a year the population had risen to 5,000.

In January 1824, the first regular census was taken—the population then consisted of:—

74	Europeans
4,580	Malays
3,317	Chinese
756	Indians
1,925	Bugis
16	Armenians
15	Arabs

Total .. 10,683.

Chinese secret society activity began, therefore, very much later in Singapore than in Penang, Malacca, or even Sungei Ujong (Lukut). But we may assume that the Triad lodge from Penang had established itself in Singapore by the year 1825. Newbold in his paper *Chinese Secret Triad Society J.R.A.S.* Vol. VI 1840, on page 134 has:—

"They, (the Ghee Hins) are even strongly suspected of concerting and executing most daring robberies and murders, particularly at Singapore, where a large body resides among the jungles and fastnesses in the interior of the island. This body consists chiefly of the emigrants from Canton and there does not exist much goodwill between it and the Fokien Society lately established in the town of Singapore".

This reference to the Fokien society lately established in Singapore is of particular interest as it is almost certainly the earliest published reference to the Ghee Hok 義福 society, whose acquaintance we have made on page 70 *supra*.

The passage also helps to fix the date of the foundation of the Ghee Hok society as between 1830 and 1840, a point upon which the authorities are silent.

This date would suit the assumption made elsewhere, that the Ghee Hok foundation in Singapore was the parent of the Toh Peh Kong foundation in Penang of 1844, the latter becoming identified with the Hai San and the Red Flag of the Malays and finally with the present-day Three Dot Brotherhood. Furthermore it seems to clinch the fact that the "Fokien society" mentioned, was in fact the Ghee Hok, because the passage specially mentions that there was little love lost between it and the Ghee Hin in Singapore.

All the subsequent history of the Hung league in Singapore is a history of the incessant warfare between the Ghee Hin and the Ghee Hok.

Even granting that both societies had degenerated into purely criminal associations, the bitter internecine strife which even now still persists between them in Singapore, does not suggest that they were ever fellow-branches of the same parent stem.

As regards nomenclature, the Ghee Hin as representing the Malayan foundation of the Triad society of China, has remained fairly constant as the Ghee Hin, wherever met with throughout the history of the Peninsula, whereas its enemy and rival "Tokong" has been disguised under a variety of names in the different localities, and at the various epochs, chief of which are:—

PLACE				PERIOD	NAME
Singapore	..	..	..	1830–1890.	Ghee Hok
Penang	,.	..	..	1844–1867.	Toh Peh Kong
Larut	..	..	..	1862–1874.	Hai San
Throughout Malaya	..		..	1890–Present day.	Sa Tiam Hui (Three Dot)

It is at least a reasonable explanation to suggest that the variations in name of the opponent of the Ghee Hin were due to the desire of "Tokong" to disguise itself within the folds of Triad and to adopt "watchwords" indistinguishable from those attributed to the different branches of Triad, but in reality probably representing the different "anchorages" in Malaya of the Ko Lao Hui.

In order not to appear to insist too strongly upon the theory that the Hai San and Toh Peh Kong societies of Penang, and the Ghee Hok society of Singapore, were in fact lodges or 'anchorages' of the Ko Lao Hui, we prefer, as explained at the beginning of this Chapter, to coin the name "Tokong" to represent that range of societies which have all along shown themselves to be separate from and hostile to the Triad (Ghee Hin) Mother Lodge in Malaya, and will hereafter in this compilation use the word "Tokong" in this sense, except when from the context it bears another meaning. Similarly the Sa Tiam Hui or Three Dot Brotherhood and its later ally the Red Flag society of the Malays, will be included under the generic term "Tokong", in contradistinction to the name "Triad" and its later ally, the White Flag society.

The earliest first hand record of Triad activity in Singapore, is an account published by Munshi Abdullah in his *Hikayat* of a visit paid by him to a Triad initiation ceremony at 'Tanglin Besar' about 1824.

This account has been translated by Braddell and published in *Journal of the Indian Archipelago* Vol. VI page 550 entitled *Concerning the Tan Tae Hoey of Singapore* and is included in this compilation as Appendix I.

Apart from the vivid picture it presents of the *imperium in imperio* already established in Singapore by Chinese secret societies within five years of its foundation, Abdullah's account is historically interesting for the following facts disclosed therein:—

(a) Abdullah's guide was "the son of a Malacca Chinaman, a member of the society" and from internal evidence was an important officer-bearer of the Singapore lodge, suggesting that the Singapore Triad lodge was founded from Penang or Malacca and not direct from China.

(b) Abdullah's reason for risking a visit to the lodge was a rumour that the Triads were preparing in their jungle fastness in the interior of the island, to attack Singapore, with reference to which his guide says:—

"Yes, it is true, they intend to attack the town......they have sent letters to their friends at Malacca and Pinang to ask for their consent and co-operation".

This suggests that the Singapore lodge was at that time under the control of Malacca and Penang; and provides a parallel to the plots for the seizure of Penang, which we have seen above, were afoot about this year 1824–1825.

(c) Abdullah enquired of his guide the extent of the organisation, who replied:—

"In Singapore in town and country, there are about 8,000 members: there are others at Malacca, Sungei Ujong, Lokat, (Lukut) Lingga and Pulau Pinang, all belonging to the same Society".

Although the number of members given for Singapore is probably exaggerated, being more than the total Chinese population of Singapore in 1825, as given elsewhere, the passage helps to confirm what we already know of the organisation about this time.

(d) Abdullah asked his guide whether any other races besides Chinese were admitted as members, to which he replied:—

> "How could they? as they would certainly divulge. Moreover if Malays or other Mussulmen were admitted, they could not believe in our God (Dato) neither could they drink spirits nor yet blood".

It was probably not until criminal Mohamedan elements from India were let loose amongst the population of Singapore and Penang some years later (Chapter X) that the process of inoculation of the Mohamedan communities of those towns with the secret society virus first began, an inoculation which led through the mixed blood of the descendants of these Indian criminals, to the establishment of the White and Red Flag societies in Penang. (Chapters XII and XIV).

The Triad outrages in Singapore in 1824, referred to by Abdullah at the end of his article, are probably the same "riots" as are mentioned by Song Ong Siang in *One hundred years of the Chinese of Singapore* (1923) page 25:—

> "Towards the close of the year 1824, for the first time, some riots occurred among the Chinese in which several persons were killed and wounded".

Buckley in his *Anecdotal History* speaks of Singapore as being in a lawless state in 1831.

The Singapore Police then numbered some 20 Constables and the town boundaries were from Kallang River to the present Yacht Club and from the sea-front to about Tank Road. (Song Ong Siang *op. cit.* page 29).

The following extracts from Buckley *op. cit.* page 213 refer to the years 1831 and 1841 in Singapore:—

> "The place was in a very lawless state at this time, several murders being reported in one week, and no proper measures being available to trace the criminals or to secure life and property in the out-lying parts of the town. Very little was known of Singapore beyond the hills behind the town; the rest of the island was covered with jungle with a few isolated reclaimed spots. While a gang of Chinese convicts were working on a road, a number of Chinese ran out of the jungle and rescued ten of the convicts by carrying them off and knocking off their irons. The whole police force, eighteen strong, was mustered and recovered five of the convicts. It was said at the time that a Secret Society exceeding one thousand men, was established in the jungle, and that they had actually an armed fort there".[1]
>
> There is a note of Mr. Braddell's that in July, 1830, there was activity in the Resident Councillor's office on the subject of Chinese Hoeys, or secret societies, and that a letter was written with a list of questions to the Superintendent of Police. This seems to have been the first mention of the secret societies in Singapore.

On pages 365 and 366 (1841).

> The following is from a Journal kept by Major Low giving a description of Singapore 1840 and 1841:—
>
> "The Chinese uphold here as they do in other places where they have settled out of China, the Kongsis or secret societies of which the Emperor of China is so much afraid. The chief one here is the Tean Tay Hueh, which boasts it is believed, about from five to six thousand members, who are bound by oath to support each other on all occasions, and to screen their brethren from public justice: but reserving to their secret tribunal the power to punish offences committed within the society, by its own members, but not by others against it—all such being given up to English law. I have not learnt what the badge of this lodge is, for everything regarding it is about as mysterious as Freemasonry, of which it is a perverted type. The meetings of the society are held at a temple in the outskirts of the suburbs at Kampong Glam. The Society is governed by a Council of four officers, each of whom represents a tribe. The tribes are the Amoy, the Kheh, the Teouchoo, and the Macao. Some of these societies are avowedly for good purposes, such as relieving distress within the limits of the Chinese population.

If this account of Major Low may be accepted, it makes it quite clear that in 1840 in Singapore the Triad society was established as a single unit with four sub-divisions or branches one for each dialect Hokkien, Hakka, Teochew and Cantonese all using the same lodge, presumably (as mentioned elsewhere) on different nights.

This fact seems to corroborate the view that "The Fokien society recently established in Singapore" mentioned by Newbold in 1840 in his paper *J.R.A.S.* VI, which was hostile to the Triad in Singapore, must be something quite distinct from the Hokkien branch of the Triad society, mentioned above by Major Low.

The two rival camps into which Singapore secret societies were divided as early as 1841, is further illustrated by the following extract from *Play and Politics* by W. H. Read page 91:—

> The chief Hoeys in Singapore were the Teantay and the Ghehok, which as early as 1841, numbered some ten thousand members. These, on initiation, were separately sworn to observe certain rules and regulations, of which some were:—
>
> You shall not reveal the proceedings of the society to any but a brother.
>
> You shall not cheat or steal from a brother, or seduce his wife, his daughter, or his sister.
>
> If you do wrong or break these laws, you shall come to the society to be punished, and shall not go to the authorities of the country.
>
> If you commit murder or robbery against a member, you shall be dismissed for ever from the society, and no brother will receive you.

Footnote.—(1) This may have been the one visited by Munshi Abdullah *see* Appendix I.

> If a brother commits murder or robbery, you shall not inform against him, but you shall assist him to escape, and prevent the officers of justice from arresting him.
> If a brother is arrested and condemned, you shall do all you can to assist his escape.
> A number of signs by which members might recognise one another, were also communicated.
> Some of these eighteen[1] secret societies were undoubtedly harmless, mere charitable associations but these were few and unimportant. The others formed an *imperium in imperio*, and were consequently, fraught with danger to the general peace.
> The riots in 1854, which will be hereafter alluded to, were, undoubtedly, originated and maintained by these societies; and almost all the fights which subsequently took place, in the streets of Singapore were due to the turbulent spirit which they fostered.

Song Ong Siang in *One Hundred Years of the Chinese in Singapore* (1923) page 57 has:—

> In 1842 and 1843 owing to an inadequate and inefficient Police Force, there was a long series of armed gang-robberies in Singapore by Chinese which led to a Public Meeting on 10th February, 1843, at which the following resolution was passed:—
> "That it is an understood fact that many Chinese shopkeepers and traders in the town, particularly the native-born subjects of China, pay regular sums to the "Hueys" or Brotherhoods (organised associations of Chinese for unlawful purposes) as protection money for their own property or as a contribution in the nature of blackmail, and that such payments should be made a penal offence".

This appears to be the first recorded reference to the payment of protection money, which is the ordinary revenue of a secret society, being the blackmail levied by its bullies, upon the meek and helpless of their own kind, usually petty traders, hawkers, prostitutes and sly gambling and opium dens, and paid by such as a form of insurance against molestation. Protection money is the curse of Malaya. Its levy is a challenge to authority; its payment an accusation.

In 1846, a riot occurred in Singapore on the occasion of the funeral of the headman of the secret society whose temple was in Rochore.[2] The incident is mentioned by Song Ong Siang pages 70–72, and by Read page 91, but details are lacking. The riot was evidently the result of a trial of strength between the Ghee Hin and the Ghee Hok.

The following extract from Buckley referring to an incident which occurred in 1850, illustrates again the two camps into which the secret societies were divided.

Buckley, page 537 has:—

> "The following shows how the secret societies carried on their proceedings in those days:—
> A case which exposes to view the criminal and pernicious tendency of the system of the Hoes was brought before the Criminal Session last Saturday, and Tan Ah Tow, one of the headmen and judges at the Kongsi house at Rochore, was put on his trial charged with misprison of felony and an aggravated assault. It was fully proved by the evidence produced, that five Chinamen, the owners of a boat which had been stolen, had succeeded after a search of fourteen days in finding it in the Serangoon river with a number of weapons in it, commonly used by our petty pirates, securing three of the thieves at the same time, whom they were conducting to the Police Office, when they met the prisoner at Gaylang who ordered them to let go the thieves, who were his men, and directed them to appear at the Kongsi house on the 9th, of June, when he would decide upon the merits of the case. Fear compelled them to act as they were directed. On the appointed day they went all five to the Kongsi house, found there only one of the thieves, about thirty other Chinese, and the prisoner in the chair, who directed them to return all the articles found in the boat to the thieves, and to keep the boat, while they were told they would be punished. Not submitting to that decision, the prisoner directed them to be beaten, which was done with fists, stones, and the handles of umbrellas. Found guilty, the Hon'ble The Recorder sentenced him to imprisonment for six months, and to a fine of 200 dollars.
> The Court house during that trial was crowded by a number of the leading men of the society, who, at the close of it, manifested great satisfaction at the penalty; some even were heard to say that the penalty being levied by a collection, the same would come to one cent a head, there being 20,000 members of the society in the Island. It ought to be noticed that each person on entering the Society, pays two dollars entrance fee, has not to pay any monthly contribution, but is bound to pay any sum when called upon by the Kongsi. It is of common occurrence to see the 'hoe' raising sums of 500, 1,000 and 2,000 dollars in a few days, and it can easily be ascertained, the Police Authorities being acquainted with the fact that 20,000 dollars were raised in 8 days on account of the disturbances at the burial of the late chief of the society, (the 1846 riot mentioned above) besides the burial expenses, which amounted to nearly 5,000 dollars".

This concludes the record of the Han and Hung leagues in Malaya down to the year 1850. In a brief survey of this early period we will bring this chapter to a close. It is first necessary, however, to make an interpellation at this point, in order finally to dispose of the evidence surrounding the origin of the name Ghee Hin as applied to the Hung league overseas and to record our conclusions thereupon, before our survey of this period may be complete.

CONCLUSIONS UPON THE ORIGIN OF THE NAME GHEE HIN (義興) AS DENOTING THE HUNG LEAGUE OVERSEAS

The presently accepted view

In Chapter I (pages 7-8 *supra*) we have stated the presently accepted view of Schlegel that the name Ghee Hin by which the Hung league is universally known in

---

Footnote.—(1) He included secret societies and district or clan associations in this total.
Footnote.—(2) This was probably the Ghee Hok ("Tokong") headquarters at this time.

Malaya and the Netherlands Indies, derives from one of the "watchwords" of the "Shantung lodge". This view is based upon certain documents found in Japara, Java in 1851, which have hitherto been accepted as belonging to the Hung league.

Reasons for rejecting the accepted view

We offer the following reasons for rejecting the presently accepted view. Much of the evidence in support of its rejection is contained in the foregoing chapters :—

(1) There is no evidence anywhere of the existence at any time of a lodge of the Triad society in the Shantung province of China.

(2) Schlegel appears to have been unaware of the existence of the Han league or of the society of the Elder Brethren.

(3) The home of the Han league was in north China and the "Shantung lodge" referred to by Schlegel as belonging to the Hung league, was more probably the lodge of the Han league in the province of Shantung.

These three reasons are supported by the following further considerations.

(4) The original home of the Hakka people was in north China in the province of Shantung. The Hakkas were favourites under the Han dynasty and might therefore be naturally expected to belong at a later epoch to the Han league whose purpose was the restoration of their benefactors.

(5) After the series of persecutions of the Hakkas (B.C. 250–209: A.D. 420: A.D. 618 and A.D. 1206–1368) and their consequent dispersal to south China, particularly to the provinces of Fukien and Kwantung, we may assume that they brought with them the Han league from their "home" province, Shantung.

(6) When emigration to the South Seas from the province of Kwangtung and Fukien began after the Napoleonic wars, the Hakkas whose distressful condition in those provinces has been noted, were among the first emigrants to seek "living-room" overseas. We may assume that the Hakkas took the Han league, the secret organisation of their "home" province Shantung, with them overseas, as much for their own protection and tribal cohesion as for any other purpose. By this process it would not be surprising to find documents of the Han league originating from the province of Shantung, at Japara in Java in 1851.

(7) If the true origin of the name Ghee Hin as applied to the Hung league overseas is nowhere traceable in the records of the Hung league, it should, we submit, be sought in those of the Han, among which, we suggest, were the documents found at Japara in 1851.

Arguments in support of the rejection of the accepted view

We offer the following reasoned arguments in support of our rejection of the accepted view :—

(1) Nothing was clearly known to Europeans about the Hung league in China proper or among the Chinese overseas until Schlegel published his work in 1866.

(2) Schlegel's work is primarily based upon documents in use among the Chinese overseas and obtained from three entirely different sources in the Netherlands Indies, as recorded on page 1 of the preface to his work, namely :—

(a) A bundle of documents found at Padang, Sumatra, in 1863.

(b) A bundle of documents found at Japara, Java, in 1851.

(c) Two Chinese manuscripts lent to him by the Batavian society of Arts and Sciences for the purposes of his studies in 1864.

(3) Schlegel records that—

(a) the first of these bundles contained "the laws, statutes, oaths, mysteries of initiation, catechism, description of flags, symbols and secret signs, etc., of a secret society at Padang, numbering about 200 members".

(b) the second bundle contained "a Chinese book of drawings, with the statutes of the Shantung branch".

(c) the third source "contained the whole of the catechism, history, description of the rites, lodges, flags, secret signs and implements, enriched with a series of drawings".

(4) We may assume two things from the above namely, that sources (a) and (c) contained similar material and doubtless provided Schlegel with the main basis for his work: that the second bundle source (b), contained material different from the other two bundles and provided Schlegel with much food for thought.

(5) The second bundle contained—

(i) The statutes of the Shantung branch.

(ii) A diploma of the Shantung lodge.

(iii) A book of drawings believed by Schlegel op. cit. page 26 to describe the physical approach to the Shantung lodge.

It does not appear as if Schlegel used this bundle to any great extent in his work, because he only makes a few casual reference to the "statutes" and does not give a full description or translation of them: he refers (*op. cit.* page 1) to the two other bundles, particularly the third, as having provided "the most valuable contributions" to his work. He suggests (page 4) that the "statutes" of Shantung have given the clue to the name Ghee Hin, while on page 31 he states this, as a fact, without however the production of any definite evidence to support his asseveration. He gives a description of the book of drawings on page 26, but does not attempt to include these drawings or an explanation of them in the pattern of his work and dismisses them as being the physical description of the approach to the Shantung lodge and without significance either allegorically or in respect of the actual Hung ritual, in which they are not mentioned. In effect, he dismisses the second bundle in the following terms:—

    (*a*) that the statutes give us six watchwords which "were probably adopted" by the Hung league for purposes of concealment. These six watchwords are:—

        義興 Ghee Hin "Patriotic Rise"

        海山 Hai San "Sea and Land"

        大刀 Tai Tao "Big Knife"

        小刀 Siu Tao "Dagger"

        柄檐 Peng Yen "Handle and Eaves"

        童子 Tung Tze "The Boy"

from which we are left to infer that No. 1 watchword above, is the origin of the "overseas" name of the Hung league.

    (*b*) that the diploma confirms the above inference.

    (*c*) that the book of drawings has no allegorical or ritualistic significance and may be ignored.

(6) Ward and Stirling *op. cit.* Vol. I page 25 have rejected the view in (*c*) above, in terms quoted on p. 8 *supra*, and we must therefore examine Schlegel's description of this book of drawings more closely. On page 26 *op. cit.* he has:—

    In the book found at Japara is a description with drawings of the approaches to the Shantung lodge. A stone road leads to the first pass called the "Heaven Screen Pass" 天防關. Past this is the "Earth net pass" 地羅關. Next come the "Sun Moon pass" 日月關 at which each brother is obliged to pay one mace and two candareen (about a shilling). After this comes a stone bridge over a river which leads to the Hall of Fidelity and Loyalty 忠義堂 where are the shrines of the five ancestors flanked to the right by the Council room 羅事堂 and to the left by the Court 理事堂. Here the brother must produce his capital (three cash) and his diploma. From this there is a long road along the mountains of Hwui ling 惠嶺 girded on one side by this mountain and on the other side by the sea. At the end of this road is the "Outside moss pass" 出苔關 called also the Pavilion of the Black river 黑河亭. Thirteen Chinese miles further on is the Golden sparrow frontier 金雀界, so called from the name of the mountain at whose foot it lies. Past this frontier are four buildings. Over the front of one are the words "Patriotic rise which enlarges the Empire 開國義興 Hoi Kwok Ghee Hin". The second is called the Palace of Justice 義殿, with the civil entrance 入相 to the left and the military entrance (? exit) 出將 to the right. The lodge follows immediately and twenty-four miles farther is the "Look up and fathom pavilion" 仰沁亭 which is at the foot of the Yin-Yang mountain 陰陽山 near the sea. From here if the brother wants to see the Goat-head island 羊頭嶼 he must go in a boat and sail one day. On this island is the Rock-grotto-cavern 石洞門 where ammunition is stored.

No one reading this description even without a knowledge of the esoteric character of Chinese secret society rituals, could fail to become aware that it must be an allegory, and not a physical description of the approach to a particular lodge. Schlegel interprets the reference to Goats-head island as a reference to the island of Formosa. Ward and Stirling *op. cit.* Vol. I page 25, probably more correctly, interpret it as a synonym for the Isles of the Blest.

It will be noticed that the inscription or slogan Hoi Kwo Ghee Hin 開國義興 "Patriotic Rise which enlarges the empire" appears in the above description. We agree with Ward and Stirling Vol. I page 24 that the whole description is an allegory and refers to a journey that the candidate is supposed to have taken before he reaches the point of initiation at the door of the Hung lodge, where he begins his second and mystical journey through the underworld.

We suggest further that the first journey is that of man through the physical world from birth to death and that it is represented in the secret society world of China by the Han league ritual; just as the second journey is that taken after death and is represented exclusively by the Hung ritual.

This view seems to be strengthened by the following further considerations:—

(7) The *Traditional History* of the Hung league as given by Schlegel and others makes no mention of any Shantung lodge. The five principal and five subsidiary lodges of the Hung league are clearly given in the history (*see* footnote p. 10 *supra*) and the Shantung lodge is not among them. Further, as far as the records show, the Hung league has at no time been known in China or in Hongkong by the name of the Ghee Hin society, nor by any other of the "Watchwords of the Shangtung lodge". Further, whatever the conditions in China, there was no need for the overseas Chinese of those days to seek to disguise the Hung or any other league in the Netherlands Indies or elsewhere under any "watchword" as the league was not illegal, in fact, it was the governing organ of the Chinese overseas.

(8) Further, Schlegel evidently was unaware of the existence of the Han league or Ko Lao Hui at the time (1866) he wrote, because neither name appears anywhere in his work, albeit there is much to contrast between the Han and the Hung leagues and they may have a common origin in dim antiquity. This is probably the cause of the confusion between them existing in European minds, a confusion which the Chinese themselves in their exclusiveness have done nothing to dispel.

(9) But the question which above all others rises to the mind in this connection is; why the Shantung lodge?

We do not know how Schlegel satisfied himself on this point, but *prima facie* it seems in the highest degree unlikely that there was a lodge of the Hung league in the province of Shantung (山東省) at all. If there ever was one, that an identifiable copy of its "statutes" should have found its way to mid-Java in 1851, seems equally unlikely, because it is only of very recent years that northern Chinese in any number have emigrated to the South Seas.

(10) In the absence of any other explanation, Schlegel's careful and guarded interpretation has been accepted because, without it we have hitherto had no introduction to the universal use in the South Seas of the name "Ghee Hin" to signify the Hung league.

But if we accept the watchword 義興 Ghee Hin "Patriotic Rise" on the Japara diploma as a watchword of the Hung league, we must also accept the other watchwords given by Schlegel *op. cit.* page 4 from the *statutes of the Shantung Lodge* as belonging to the Hung league. Among these are:—

海山 Hai San "Sea and Land"

大刀 Tai Tao "Large Knife or sword"

小刀 Siu Tao "Small Knife or poignard"

and these three watchwords have been identified in Chapters II and IV above, as belonging to the Han league. Schlegel had not the observations of Hutson to guide him and the possibility of there being a second secret league other than the Hung present in the South Seas probably never occurred to him and he therefore felt quite justified in identifying the Japara documents with the Hung.

(11) With Hutson's researches to guide us, it seems more probable that the Japara documents belonged to the Han league, a lodge of which might reasonably be expected to exist at that time in the province of Shantung which lies away to the north in the valley of the Yellow River, divided by some two or three provinces and by the Yangtze basin from those southern provinces in which the true lodges of the Hung league were founded. Further, as shown in Chapter III, just as the south and south-west of China has always been predominantly influenced by the Hung league, so the north and north-west has all along been under the influence of that different and apparently hostile secret brotherhood known variously as the Ko Lao Hui or society of the Elder Brethren or the Han league.

(12) At the same time we know that southern Chinese chiefly Hakkas in large numbers belonged at that time (1866) to the Han league (*see* Chapter IV) and the parent lodge of the Han league in the South Seas may well have been situated in Shantung with a branch established by immigrant Hakkas in Java, just as the parent lodge of the Hung league we know to have been in Canton, with branches in Sumatra and elsewhere in the South Seas.

(13) We should here notice that the Han league was in active revolt against the Manchus in the valley of the Yellow River and throughout the Shantung province in 1851-1855 (Hutson *op. cit. China Review* Vol. II 1920, pages 77–78) and that one of the names by which the Han league or a section of it, is known is the 大刀會 Tai T'o Hui "Big Sword Society" and that there are eight known lodges of the Han Liu each known by a distinctive character of which the No. 2 lodge is known as the Rectitude

(義) lodge "under which are mustered all the turbulent elements of the Han Liu". The Japara documents were found in Java in 1851 (Schlegel *op. cit.* Preface page 1) and there was a disturbance among the Chinese in Japara (in the province of Samarang, Java) in 1852 due to secret society causes which, we suggest, were connected with the Yellow River rising in China. This disturbance was put down by the Dutch Government with the aid of troops. The incident is referred to by Schlegel *op. cit.* Introduction page xl.

(14) Another possible explanation which could only be checked by a re-examination of the Japara documents if they still exist, is, that the Shan tung or "Eastern Hills" therein mentioned did not refer to the province of Shantung in China but to some locality in mid-Java known to the immigrant Chinese as "Eastern Hills".

(15) Lastly we submit that, granted the existence in 1850 of the two rival associations in the Netherlands Indies, there is no clear ground for maintaining that secret documents of one association found in Java in 1851 should have any necessary connection with secret documents of the other association found twelve hundred miles away in Padang Sumatra, twelve years later in 1863.

The foregoing seems to suggest that the "watchword of the Shantung lodge" given by Schlegel may have referred exclusively to the Han Liu established in Java by immigrant Hakkas, and have had nothing to do with the Hung league.

We feel that Schlegel would be the first to admit this hypothesis. He did not claim infallability for himself and says in his Preface:—

> Much remains still to be studied and we do not presume that the present work contains all possible information.

Reasons for accepting an alternative view

So much for our divergence from Schlegel on the point of the *Statutes of the Shantung Lodge*, but our excursion has not yet brought us any nearer to an explanation of the origin of the use of the name Ghee Hin 義興 in the Netherlands Indies and Malaya to signify the Hung league, to which end we submit these further considerations:—

(1) Schlegel introduces us to the name for the first time on page 31 of his work in the following terms:—

> In the province of Shantung the brotherhood has the following diploma, which is called the red bill 紅罩 Hung Tan.

ORIGINAL   TRANSLATION

It is a square piece of white linen, the middle of which is occupied by an octagonal figure in which is drawn the celebrated diagram of the Emperor Fuh-hi (B.C. 2953)[1]. Within this figure is the symbol of eternal change, of the struggle between light and darkness, rest and motion called Yin (陰) and Yang (陽). The characters on the upper margin of the diploma are the watchword of the I Hing Kung Sze 義興公司 "The Patriotic rise Society". To the right is written the name of the member to whom the diploma is given and to the left are the characters 記號 Kei Ho or "Mark". Circulars, diplomas, receipts, etc., are stamped in vermilion with the common seal of the society. On the greater seal which is square......are the characters 義興館 I Hing Kwan "Hall of I Hing". On the smaller one ......are engraved the characters 義興公司 I Hing Kung Sze "Society of I Hing" (*i.e.* Ghee Hin).

This is the only introduction Schlegel gives us to the name which is universal for the Hung league in the Netherlands Indies and Malaya and his only explanation of its use is that it is taken from a "diploma of the Shantung lodge" found in Japara Java in 1851. The fact that this document is

Footnote.—(1) *See page 6 supra.*

called a 紅 単 Hung Tan or "red sheet of paper" does not identify it with the Hung 洪 ("inundation") league. On the other hand the colour red is closely associated with the Han league. The fact that the diagram on the document contains the "Yin Yang" or "Grand primordial" sign and the "Pat Kwa" or eight diagrams would seem to identify it more with Taoism and the Han league (*see* Chapter III above) than with the Buddhist tradition of the Hung league. The Yin Yang sign is as noticeably absent from the documents of the Hung league we have seen, as the equilateral triangle of the Hung league is present therein.

(2) The fact that a very similar type of Malay membership card (*see* Appendix X) written in Arabic character and containing the, eight diagrams, has been found in Penang relating to the Mohamedan "Red Flag Society" with which we identify the Han league, suggests that Schlegel's diploma belongs to the latter fraternity. We offer for acceptance the view that Schlegel's Ghee Hin (義興) diploma was in origin a document of the 義 or Rectitude lodge of the Han Liu (discussed in Chapter II) as there is little or nothing to connect it *prima facie* with the Hung league, by which it seems to have been "borrowed" as a camouflage label overseas.

This view would help to explain other similar "watchwords" such as the Ghee Wo 義和 of the "Boxers" at Pekin: the Ghee Hok 義福 in Singapore: the Siu Tao 小刀 in Amoy: the Hai San 海山 of Penang and later of Perak and others which have been throughout, the historical rivals to the Ghee Hin in Malaya and the Netherlands Indies, and which we know to belong to the Han league.

The only other commentators on the name "Ghee Hin" which we have found are Ward and Stirling who have no explanation to offer.

In Vol. I page 6 *op. cit.* they have:—
"Later we find the Triad calling itself the Ghee Hin society which means the "Justice and Prosperity Society". No doubt the object of this change was to lead Government officials to think that it was merely one of the numerous "Friendly Societies" which existed then as now, all over China".

Again Vol. I page 13 *op. cit.* we find:—
"In the days when the Triad society was an authorised and recognised body, it was known as the Ghee Hin Society and had its own Temple in Singapore".

Again Vol. I page 132 *op. cit.* we see:—
"The certificates issued by the Hung society vary somewhat in the different lodges....... The most important is the Grand Diploma of the Ghee Hin Society, the mother lodge of the Triad society, and the society of which most of the other lodges (in Malaya) are offshoots or branches".

Lastly Vol. I page 156 *op. cit.* they say:—
"The first lodge in the province of Kwangtung and Kwangsi was founded at Canton and was called "The Hall of Obedience to Hung". A subsidiary lodge was founded in the province of Kwangsi and was called "The golden orchid". It is apparently from this lodge that the Ghee Hin society of Singapore derived".

These references all have the same vagueness about them and in the main but echoes of the views of Schlegel, and do not help towards discovering the real origin of the name Ghee Hin.

(3) We know from the extracts from the *Straits Settlements Factory Records* and from other sources given in this Chapter, that the name Ghee Hin,—therein called the "Nghee Hung", as applied to the Triad society in the British and Dutch possessions in the East, was well known to the authorities even before A.D. 1800, so that the date of the adoption of the name must be very much further back than the discovery of the *statutes of the Shantung Lodge* at Japara in 1851.

In a wider search for the origin of the name we have no dependable Chinese characters to guide us earlier than Schlegel's researches (A.D. 1850). We nevertheless offer for consideration the following possible explanation:—

Schlegel *op. cit.* Introduction page xxxvii has:—
"We might also compare the three degrees in Masonry of Apprentice, Fellowcraft and Master to the terms of the Hung League *viz.*:—

結 弟 Kit Tai "Sworn Brother"
義 兄 Ghee Hiung "Adopted Brother"
義 伯 Ghee Pak "Righteous Uncle"

which mean, the younger brethren; those of the same degree: and the elder brethren.

We offer as a conceivable alternative explanation, that the name given to the second grade 義兄 may have provided the original watchword or designation of the overseas Hung league namely 義兄公司 Ghee Hin Kung Sz, meaning "Society of Adopted Brothers", and may be the origin of the variant romanisation "Nghee Hung" of the *Straits Settlements Factory Records*.

(4) Schlegel page 233 mentions that in the Triad slang, the term for the second grade 義兄 is also used to express 同等者 or "those of the same degree" which would give the meaning "Society of those of the same degree", which would be both rational and in consonance with Chinese practice.

(5) In this connection attention may be drawn to the names of two monks mentioned in the *Traditional History* (Schlegel *op. cit.* page 15) with whom the five founders stayed in the ancestral temple of Kao Khi: their names were 萬兄 Wan Hiung (Maan Hing) and 義兄 I Hiung (Nghee Hung). With these names may conceivably be associated the name of the Hongkong lodge 萬安 and the original "overseas" name might thus have been 義兄.

(6) Again in Stanton *op. cit.* page 72 we have an illustration of a Triad document which incontestably belongs to the Hung league and which contains in disguise some of the better known couplets from the Hung ritual and begins with the well-known:—

初進洪門結義兄 Ch'u chin hung mun kit yi hiung "Enter Hung doors, with patriots combine".

These references provide some grounds for thinking that the original watchword for the Hung may have been 義兄 Ghee Hiung, adopted brothers, as being definitely identifiable with the Hung tradition, rather than 義興公司 Rising patriots, which seems more properly to belong to the Han.

(7) There is also the fact that the characters 義兄 Ghee Hin meaning "fellowcraft" and 義興 Ghee Hin meaning "patriotic rise" have a similar sound and tone in Chinese, and it would be in conformity with the well known Chinese habit of playing on words and with the Triad practice of disguising itself in something other than itself, if the overseas Hung league were found to have "adopted" the watchword of a Han league lodge namely 義興 Ghee Hin or "Patriotic Rise" in place of 義兄 Ghee Hin or "Righteous or Adopted Brother" thus to avoid drawing undesirable attention to itself, especially after the unwelcome discovery by Europeans about 1825 of the other names by which it openly acknowledges itself, *viz.*, The Hung league, the Heaven and Earth league, and the Three United league. This explanation would also preserve to the Hung League its watchword of 義 which Schlegel translated as "patriotism" while preserving at the same time to the Han league its second lodge name of 義 which Hutson translates as "rectitude".

This explanation would also support the belief in a deliberate conspiracy to silence between the Hung and the Han and in pursuance of a deliberate policy of confusing the one with the other among Chinese overseas, so as to keep the European authorities in the dark as to their separate identities and so help to preserve their individual independence.

This is only a guess and perhaps a bad guess, but it does suggest a rational explanation of something which remains unexplained, as well as retaining the real identity of the term 義興 in the 義 or "Rectitude", or No. 2 lodge of the Han league, where we believe it properly to belong.

Survey of the Han and the Hung Leagues in Malaya up to 1850

Having expressed our conclusions upon the matter of the name Ghee Hin, we will now briefly review the admittedly fragmentary references quoted in this Chapter to the coming of the Han and the Hung leagues to Malaya and their activities during the first half of the nineteenth century.

Piecing the earlier fragments together we get a picture something as follows:—

During the eighteenth century two main stems of the Hung league, or what passed for the Hung league, were already widely diffused throughout the South Seas, including Borneo, Java and Siam.

These were known by the names of the Ghee Hin (義興) (Triad) and the Hai San (海山) ("Tokong") societies. The former was unquestionably the South Seas branch of the Triad society of China, while the precise character of the latter remains in some doubt. Both seem to have been at that time chiefly composed of "Macao" Chinese a fairly elastic term, which probably included Chinese from both Canton and Kwangsai provinces, and probably owing to this fact the two societies do not appear at that time to have been hostile to one another, although remaining separate and distinct.

It can hardly be correct to suppose that they were both branches of the same society, seeing that they were both evidently composed originally of similar components. There is some evidence to show that the Hai San members were sea-going pirates, as opposed perhaps, to the landsman members of the Ghee Hin, which suggests, from what we have seen in Chapter II, and the association of the Han league with "waters and lakes", that the Hai Sans were not a branch of the Hung league, but were an 'anchorage' of the Han Liu. To avoid insistence upon what may after all be rejected as untenable, we prefer to designate what the Hai San and their affinities later became, by the name of "Tokong", in contradistinction to the Triad of the Ghee Hins which has remained constant in name and character throughout.

The Ghee Hin and probably the Hai San were established at Junk Ceylon in the eighteenth century and it seems fairly certain from the records that it was from Junk Ceylon that they found their way to Penang.

At the beginning of the nineteenth century and more particularly after the political adjustments in Malaya and the Netherlands Indies following the Napoleonic wars, when modern economic development began in those countries, the stream of migration from south China to the South Seas began in earnest. The first comers were Cantonese, followers of the earlier eighteenth century Cantonese migration to the south, and they were quickly followed by the Hakkas, the "Jews" of China, that distressful tribe whose very name 客家 Hakka or Kheh in the northern Pekin dialect means "strangers" and who had been driven from their northern home in Shantung by the persecutions and dispersals of an early epoch. In south China they were a wandering and landless people whose struggle with the native Cantonese (Punteis) for existence gave an impulse to their search for new homes in the colonial countries of the south.

The Hakka emigrants no doubt took their ancestral Han league organisation with them overseas, but wherever they went in the South Seas they found their arch-enemies the Cantonese and the Hung league already entrenched against them. In the early days of their colonial settlement the two tribes seem to have arranged a *modus vivendi* until, with the growth of vested interests in the Chinese underworld, the old bitterness broke out afresh in the new countries and finally ranged the tribes and their rival leagues against one another in two implacably hostile camps.

The Hokkiens from the Hung league province of Fukien followed the Cantonese in point of time as emigrants to the south, and no doubt those among them who were already members of the Hung league in China naturally joined that camp overseas. Those Hokkien emigrants who were unattached to the Hung league in China, doubtless shrewdly saw the advantages of ranging themselves against the entrenched power of the Cantonese and therefore on arrival joined the Han league.

We suggest that from this process there arose the fact, puzzling to earlier observers, that ever since the secret society problem in Malaya first came to notice, Hokkiens in large numbers have been found in both camps.

Be that as it may, we know from the records quoted that the Ghee Hin was founded in Penang about 1790 and the Hai San about 1820.

During the period of the Siam-Kedah War 1821–1848, and particularly about 1825, the Ghee Hins and Hai Sans in Penang were intriguing with their compatriots in Junk Ceylon and with the Siamese, for the seizure of the island of Penang.

By 1825, the Ghee Hin had become firmly established also in Singapore, where similar intrigue to seize the island of Singapore seems to have been afoot. As fresh immigrants from China, who were not Cantonese arrived in Penang and Singapore they established their own secret societies, notably:—

The Wah Sang, in Penang by Hakkas about 1810.

The Ghee Hok in Singapore by Hokkiens, about 1835.

The Toh Peh Kong in Penang by Hokkiens, in 1844.

There is little evidence before 1850, to help us to decide the origin of these three associations, but from Vaughan in 1854, quoted in full in the next Chapter, and from other sources given therein, we can reasonably assume that the Ghee Hok in Singapore was the parent of the Toh Peh Kong in Penang.

The Toh Peh Kong in Penang which was absorbed by the Hai San of Penang, during the period that the Hai San changed into hostility to the Ghee Hin, bears strong points of resemblance to what we know of the Han league or Ko Lao Hui. As a result, it would perhaps not be unreasonable to assume that the Ghee Hok of Singapore and the Toh Peh Kong of Penang were both 'anchorages' of the Ko Lao Hui.

The period of change of the Hai San into hostility to the Ghee Hin (1845–1860) was the period in which the Hai San lost its Cantonese complexion, and became almost exclusively Hakka, thus reproducing in Malaya the conditions then obtaining in South China during the Hakka-Puntei War, referred to in Chapter IV.

There remains only the question of the relationship between the Ghee Hok society of Singapore, and the Dagger society of Amoy.

Here there is little to guide us, but it does seem fairly certain that the Dagger society was a branch of the Ko Lao Hui, and unconnected with the Triad. The piratical character of the former is remarked on by Hutson (Chapter II).—Furthermore, at the time of the Small Knife (Dagger society), rebellion in Amoy in 1853, the Taiping rebellion, partly identified with the Triads, was in full swing near by, in which the Dagger supporters might have joined, had they not belonged to a different camp.

Lastly, Hughes' article on the Small Knife rebellion given in Chapter IV, need not be taken too literally where he says that the Triad society of China, in the shape of the Small Knife society, was introduced into Amoy, for the first time in 1848, by a Chinese from Singapore. Chapter I above, shows how the Triad society developed in the Fukien province. The Triad was certainly not introduced into the Fukien province from Singapore! The "Chinese from Singapore", mentioned by Hughes, is doubtless genuine, but he was probably a headman of the Ghee Hok society of Singapore, founded about 1835, who provided the funds from Hokkien residents in Singapore, to stage the Dagger society rebellion in Amoy of 1853.

There is no evidence other than Hughes to suggest that the Small Knife rebellion was a Triad society outbreak, the indications are all the other way, and we must remember that according to Hutson, the Ko Lao Hui was just as anti-dynastic as the Triad.

We prefer to think that the Dagger rebellion of Amoy was an incident independent of the Triad society, probably financed largely by the Hokkien Ghee Hok society of Singapore, the parent of the Toh Peh Kong society of Penang, both of which were from their foundation, the rivals of Triad in Malaya, and both of which, with their affinities we designate henceforth as "Tokong" in this work.

We conclude this *précis* with a picture of the two rival camps already established in Singapore and Penang in 1850, *viz:*—

In Singapore.—The Ghee Hin (Triad) *versus* the Ghee Hok ("Tokong").

In Penang.—The Ghee Hin (Triad) *versus* The Toh Peh Kong ("Tokong").

This picture is not one of a territorial or tribal division of Cantonese against Hokkiens. It is one of two hostile underground armies arrayed against each other, whose soldiers were bound to one another by the most stringent and secret oaths, whose breach meant death. There is ample evidence to show that in Singapore in 1850, the Ghee Hins included at least four tribes, namely "the Amoy (Hokkiens) the Kheh, (Hakka), the Teouchoo (Teochews or Hok-los) and the Macao (Cantonese), *vide* Major Low's account quoted by Buckley *supra*.

The Ghee Hoks seem to have been chiefly Hokkiens throughout.

Again in Penang in 1850, the Ghee Hins, according to Vaughan, included chiefly Cantonese, but professed universality, while the Toh Peh Kong, originally Hokkien, was in 1854 still faithful to itself, and its membership remained according to Vaughan "nearly all Babas and Chinchews".

We must now resume the historical narrative, including a closer examination of the Toh Peh Kong society of Penang.

CHAPTER VI

THE HAN AND THE HUNG LEAGUES IN THE COLONY, 1851–1867

Having drawn together the earlier threads of Triad and "Tokong" in Malaya, we will confine ourselves in this Chapter to recording the activities, in Singapore and Penang only, of these two organisations during the period 1851–1867.

Singapore.—The year 1851 saw an organised campaign of outrage against the Chinese Roman Catholics in the country districts of Singapore Island.

It seems probable from such evidence as presents itself in a study of this campaign, that the Ghee Hin (Triad) headquarters in Singapore were at this time in Kampong Glam and the Ghee Hok ("Tokong") headquarters were in Rochore. This point is of some importance in helping to explain some later references.

THE ANTI-ROMAN CATHOLIC RIOTS OF 1851

Authorities are silent upon the reason of this campaign and attribute it generally to the "Chinese secret societies". If we accept the submission that the Ghee Hok society ("Tokong") was a branch of the Ko Lao Hui, we find from Chapter II that the Ko Lao Hui was anti-missionary as well as anti-dynastic. This fact would supply an explanation of the Singapore campaign, if we allow that the campaign was probably the work of the Ghee Hok society exclusively, upon which point the authorities are again silent.

It is more reasonable to suppose that it was attributable entirely to the Ghee Hok ("Tokong") rather than the Ghee Hin (Triad) seeing that the Taiping rebellion was at that time in full swing in China, under the banner of a pseudo-Christianity and that it was largely supported by the Triad society in China and by those Christian sympathies which were being attacked in Singapore. (see Chapter IV).

Another point to bear in mind is that, at the same epoch, the Roman Catholic converts in Annam were being subjected to a similar but more prolonged and more savage campaign of persecution by the secret organisation which we later identify as belonging to the same "Tokong" camp as the Ghee Hok of Singapore, the Boxers of Peking and other affinities of the Han league.

Another reason for the campaign was doubtless jealousy at the refusal of Christian converts in Singapore, backed by their Roman Catholic priests, to join the Ghee Hok society, thus depriving the society of influence over them, and giving rise to this attempt at coercion.

Song Ong Siang in *One Hundred Years of the Chinese of Singapore* (1923) page 82 has:—

> (1850) "The interior of the Settlement had been for some time in a disturbed state, owing to the steady persecution of the Chinese converts to the Roman Catholic faith by the "Hoeys", whose headmen found that the conversion of the Chinese in the interior had the effect of placing everywhere throughout the land, men who did not require the protection and assistance of the Hoeys, while as it were, acting as a check upon their activities. The result was a general attack in 1851 upon the Christian Chinese in the country districts. The disturbances lasted for over a week, and Indian convicts were sent out in gangs to follow the rioters into the jungles and disperse them; finally it required the presence of the military to quell them".

Major McNair in *Prisoners Their Own Warders* has:—

> "Over 500 Chinese were killed, and among them many of the well-to-do Christian converts who had become planters".

Buckley in his *Anecdotal History* page 542 has:—

> (1851) "The interior of the island had been in a most disturbed state, owing to an active persecution having broken out against the Chinese converts to the Roman Catholic Church, who were scattered over the island as planters, and whose numbers were steadily increasing. A very slight pretence was laid hold of for putting in practice a general sacking and pillaging of the plantations belonging to the Christian Chinese, and for carrying off individuals and holding them to ransom in large sums. These proceedings were generally ascribed to the influence, more or less openly exerted, of the Tan Tae Hoe, and probably of the other secret societies, from whose ranks the Christian converts were withdrawn, and whose power and influence were of course diminished in proportion to the success of the Roman Catholic missionaries. Besides withdrawing members from these secret societies, the conversion of the Chinese in the interior had the effect of placing everywhere throughout the island, men who were subject to influences adverse to the interests of the societies, who were thus deprived of that complete immunity from surveillance which constituted one of the sources of their power. With these Chinese converts disseminated throughout the island, the Hoes could no longer hold their meetings, or execute sentence on refractory or defaulting members, with the same security which they had enjoyed when there was no check upon their proceedings. This led to a general attack upon the Christian Chinese throughout the island".

The first demand for registration

The following are extracts from a leading article in the *Penang Gazette* of the 23rd October, 1852, advocating the registration of Chinese secret societies. The demand no doubt arose from the attention directed to the subject by the anti-Roman Catholic campaign of the previous year.

The Gee Hin society held a meeting in Singapore on the Tanah Merah road on the last Sunday in September, (1852) for the purpose of admitting a number of new members, chiefly persons in the employment of European merchants. Constable Berthier proceeded to the place with a Jemedar and two peons, where he found about 250 persons assembled. He seized a number of books and papers, flags with inscriptions, diplomas printed on cloth, "a red execution truncheon," stamps, and pins to draw blood. We hope Mr. Dunman[1] will seize an opportunity so favourable for ascertaining whether the English Acts against secret confederations are to be considered as in force here, that is if the Constable has not merely made one of those blind rushes, devoid of any well considered aim, and leading to no tangible legal evidence, by which the Police occasionally illustrate their zeal at the expense of their character for discretion. In that case we shall probably have actions for trespass, damages against the Constable and peons, and a great triumph to the Gee Hin. It is not a little strange that after all the trouble the Chinese secret societies have given to the executive, the resolutions of public meetings, presentments of Grand Juries[2] and memorials to the Legislature that have been directed against them, these Acts have never been practically made a part of the law of this Settlement. If they in fact are not, it is quite impossible for the police to deal with these societies. As for suppressing Chinese hoes, it is as hopeless as the suppression of gambling, even if it were as desirable, which it certainly is not. The greater number of the Chinese societies are for commendable objects, and even those that are most dangerous or doubtful in their operation, have, to a certain extent, similar objects with the most unexceptionable. To us it has always appeared that the first step in dealing with these societies, is to put an end to the singular system of coquetting with them, in which both the executive and the police have so much indulged, and into which they have no doubt felt themselves driven by their uncertainty as to the state of the law. The government should either openly recognize their existence, as fully as it does that of the Chambers of Commerce or any other unchartered association, or it should have no dealings with them whatever. The Chinese are a shrewd people well able to draw the right conclusion from the inconsistent and humiliating policy of the ruling power, now denouncing the hoes through its Judges on the bench now leaguing with their leaders through its Superintendents of Police, and now recognizing them through its Governors and Resident Councillors as more powerful in the Settlement than itself, and virtually confessing its inability to protect life and property without their aid. The difficulty of dealing with the hoes has been exaggerated. At one time we almost allow ourselves to forget their existence, for in the East there is a strong tendency to postpone the trouble of thinking and acting as long as possible. Then comes some event that roughly startles us into a sense of the unremitting operation and the dangerous power of the hoes, and we call out for severe and impracticable remedies. We can no more suppress dangerous hoes than we can suppress gambling and gang robbery. But we can, to a large extent, check them by a sensible and consistent policy, just as we can encourage them by a foolish and vacillating one. We cannot prevent men from associating, but we can heap difficulties in the way of their turning their associations to bad purposes. We hear a great deal about the imperfections and absurdities of the English law. But it strikes us that the law shews a good deal of common sense, and of that wisdom which comes from experience, with reference to this very subject. It provides the means of dispersing assemblies for unlawful purposes. It makes it felonious to administer or take unlawful oaths of the very kind that are taken by every member of a Chinese secret society on admission, and which form the very foundation of the society. Amongst the oaths expresaly prohibited by law are an oath to obey the orders or commands of a committee or body of men not lawfully constituted, or of a leader or commander or other person not having authority by law for that purpose; an oath not to inform or give evidence against any associate, confederate or other person; an oath not to reveal or discover any illegal act done or to be done, and an oath not to reveal or discover any illegal oath or engagement. The law goes on so far as to declare such oaths felonious, for whatever object the association may be formed. On the other hand it protects friendly societies, and prevents their being converted to evil purposes, by providing for the registry of their office-bearers, rules, members &c. and thus striking at the root of that mystery which is the natural hotbed of mischief. All this seems to us a business-like system, very credible to John Bull's practical sense, and just as well adapted for plotting Chinese as for plotting Englishmen. In fact it may be doubted whether legislation can do much more. An act of Parliament cannot make energetic and intelligent magistrates, or acute and honest policemen, nor can it inspire the lower orders of Chinese and other natives with independence and moral courage. What is the use of legislating further for a community that has not energy enough to work the laws it has already got? Compel all the Chinese societies to declare their objects and register their office-bearers and members, and you at once break up their secrecy and see with whom you are dealing. You learn the power and the ramifications of each and the very clan names will disclose much of its peculiar strength and weakness, and of the jealousies and hostilities that prevail between it and others. This kind of information the Police are in fact continually groping for, and possess to a partial extent. Why not procure it in a complete and accurate manner, and as a matter of right, by forcing the law? The mere registering of the societies would go far to check an abuse of their powers, because the office-bearers and influential members would feel they were in the hands of the Government, and liable to suffer in their own persons, if any unlawful oath or object which they had concealed, ever came to light. Besides, it is always best to proceed by gradual steps in effecting a fundamental change in a policy bearing on the habits and feelings of a people. Begin by registering in a manner least likely to give annoyance, and the more respectable Chinese will second government in reconciling their countrymen to the movement.

*   *   *

When this system had been in operation for some time, the Police authorities would be in a position to judge whether any future means of surveillance were necessary. There is a feeling that the Continental system of police is better adapted for an Asiatic community than ours. Granting this, consistency demands that whatever power of surveillance our laws accord should be fully availed of by the executive. But whatever may be at least done should be done cautiously. The Gee Hin is believed to have about thirteen thousand members at Singapore. They have been allowed to develop their society unchecked, to build halls, to acquire property, and to follow the coffins of their chiefs to the grave in crowds to which the burial of an African king affords the only parallel. It would be equally unjust and foolish to attempt suddenly to enforce the law against 13,000 men, even if we had ample proof of their having taken unlawful oaths.

Footnote.—(1) The Magistrate, afterwards Inspector-General of Police, Straits Settlements.
Footnote.—(2) English law was in force at this time in the Straits Settlements. The Indian Penal Code was not introduced until 1871.

The registration of secret societies advocated in this article did not become law in the Straits Settlements until twenty years later (1870). The disturbed state of public opinion about this time is again illustrated by the following:—

Song Ong Siang *op. cit.* page 83 has:—

> "Again in their presentment of August, 1853, the Grand Jury drew attention to the necessity of adopting stringent measures to detain witnesses in very grave cases until the trial of prisoners, particularly where the "Hoeys" were concerned, as it was believed that witnesses were frequently tampered with, and disposed of by the secret societies, consequently defeating the ends of justice and encouraging crime. Notwithstanding these repeated warnings of the Grand Jury and the strong comments of the local papers, the Government did not appear to realise fully the seriousness of the danger to the population, due to the growing activities of the various secret societies and the great accession to their strength by the arrival of rebels from China, who had been routed by the Imperial troops.[1]
>
> Then like a bolt from the blue occurred in May, 1854, the biggest Chinese riots that have ever been known in Singapore".

Before proceeding to a description of the 1854 riots, a note is necessary on the Teochews, who now, for the first time occupied a foremost position in secret society affairs in Malaya, which they have never relinquished.

Dyer Ball in *Things Chinese* page 346 has:—

> "Hok-Lo (Teochew) this name is applied to the inhabitants of certain parts of the North-eastern portion of the Canton province, who differ in speech, manners, and customs from the rest of the population. Their language is near akin to the Fukkienese, but has several dialects. The Swatow dialect is spoken at that port, and the Hoi-fung and the Luk-fung in the districts so named.
>
> The Hok-lo occupy the whole of some districts and are scattered through other parts, having migrated from the Fukkien province a few centuries since. It is estimated that within the Canton province there are about three million Hok-lo speakers.
>
> In dress they differ slightly from the Cantonese, and they, often in common with the Fukkienese, wear turbans. They are a rougher, wilder set of men than the Cantonese...... Many Hok-lo have gone abroad...... by the census of 1891 there were 43,791 Teochews in the Straits Settlements. "Teochew" is the term applied generally to them in Singapore, Penang, and the Malay States, while "Hok-lo" is the name by which they are generally known by the Cantonese speakers in China. The former name being derived from the departmental city of Ch'ao Chao Fu (in local dialect—Tiu Chiu Fu or Teo Chew Fu) to which the different districts from which many of the Hok-los came, belong; while Hok-lo means " men from the Hok province, *i.e.* Fukien province".

The Teochews, formerly known in Malaya as Ahyas, have a turbulent history in Malaya and although they are of Hokkien origin their domicile is now the province of Canton (Swatow) and there is no love lost between them and the Hokkiens. In extensive tribal squabbles they usually range themselves on the side of the Cantonese, but are constantly engaged in squabbles of their own.

THE GREAT HOKKIEN-TEOCHEW RIOTS OF 1854

Song Ong Siang *op. cit.* page 87 has:—

> The outstanding event of the year 1854 was the *émeute* between natives of Fukien and Kwangtung. The ostensible cause was a quarrel on the 5th of May between a Hokkien and a Cantonese about a trifle of five catties of rice. Mr. Vaughan cites this riot as an illustration in support of his contention that most of the riots that occurred in Singapore did not originate with the secret societies, and says that on this occasion the solemn obligations of the secret societies were thrown to the winds, and members of the same Hoey fought to the death against their own brethren.

Buckley gives the following origin of the riot:—

> It arose between the Hokkiens and the Teochews from the province of Quantung because the Hokkiens refused to join in a subscription to assist the rebels who had been driven from Amoy by the Imperial Chinese troops.

We have not been able to consult the official report on these riots, but the origin is probably no more clearly stated therein than in the above extracts.

What seems quite clear, is that the riots were between the Ghee Hok society (Hokkien) and the Ghee Hin society, which latter included at that time four branches namely, Hokkien, Hakka, Teochew and Cantonese. (*vide* Major Low's account quoted in Chapter V (1841)).

We can nowhere find an authoritative statement upon the exact difference between the Ghee Hin and the Ghee Hok in Singapore, or what it was that caused all the hostility and bloodshed, which has marked the rivalry of these two societies in Malaya, nor any satisfactory explanation why all this rivalry should exist if, as the accepted view seems to suggest, the Ghee Hin and the Ghee Hok were merely the Cantonese and Hokkien branches of the Triad society in Malaya. Nor does such a view explain the existence of the "Hokkien Ghee Hin" which we know to have been the recognised Hokkien lodge of the Ghee Hin (Triad) foundation in Malaya.

We must, therefore, look elsewhere for an explanation and we find it, we submit, in the reasonable supposition that the basic cause has all along been the *historic hostility between two essentially different secret Chinese organisations,* namely, the Hung league or Triad society (Ghee Hin) and the Han league, or "Tokong" family of secret societies, amongst which the Ghee Hok is to be found.

Footnote.—(1) This refers to the Dagger rebellion in Amoy 1853. *See* Chapter IV.

The Singapore Ghee Hok society ("Tokong") was, as we have suggested in Chapter V, the local representative of the Han league of China, while the Singapore Ghee Hin (Triad) was the local representative of the Hung league.

The Ghee Hok (Han) had recently (1853) received a large accession of strength from the arrival in Singapore of the defeated "Small Knife" rebels from Amoy.

The Ghee Hin (Hung) had hitherto been numerically superior in Singapore and would naturally resent this threat to their vested interests.

This picture of the two rival camps would dispose of Vaughan's contention quoted by Song Ong Siang above, because members of the same tribe would legitimately be found on both sides, depending upon whether their ultimate allegiance lay with the Han or the Hung league.

The real *casus belli* was doubtless to be found in the events which had just then occurred in Amoy (the Dagger rebellion) but whether the immediate cause was the refusal of the Singapore Ghee Hins to subscribe funds to assist the defeated Dagger rebels then returning in large numbers to their friends, the Singapore Ghee Hoks, or whether it was the refusal of the Ghee Hoks to support the Ghee Hin's Triad rebellion, then also in progress in China, it is impossible without further evidence to say.

It is clearly stated by Buckley that the quarrel originated between the Hokkiens (*i.e.* the Ghee Hoks) and the Teochews (*i.e.* members of the Teochew branch of the Ghee Hins in Singapore) thereby of course involving all members and all branches of the Ghee Hins against the Ghee Hoks. A trivial incident between a Hokkien (Ghee Hok) and a Cantonese (Ghee Hin) precipitated the conflict, much in the same way as a similar trivial incident precipitated the Penang riots of 1867 (*see* Chapter XVI).

To return to the riots of 1854, Read, in his *Play and Politics* refers to the Ghee Hins and Ghee Hoks on page 93 :—

> "The meetings of these societies were held in temples on the outskirts of the town, or in the jungle surrounding it. These societies were governed by a council of officers selected from the various Chinese tribes, of which the principal were the Amoy, the Keh, the Taichoo (*i.e.*, Teo Chew) and the Macao. Europeans, on their early morning rides in the forties, frequently met members of these societies returning from their meetings held in the jungle, and numbering many hundreds, if not thousands.
>
> Matters remained much in the same state till May, 1854. When in the autumn of 1853, the Chinese rebels at Amoy in China, were driven away by the Imperial troops, numbers of them seized junks, and made the best of their way to Singapore, and in such crowds, that the number of immigrants that season, instead of amounting to about eight to ten thousand as usual, aggregated upwards of twenty thousand.
>
> Most of them belonged to the secret societies, and nearly all were of the three tribes, Macao, Taichoo, and Amoy. They joined in Singapore the two great Hoeys, Teantay and Ghee Hok. A quarrel soon arose between these two, which, after smouldering for some time, burst into a riot, the ostensible cause of which was a quarrel about a trifle of five catties (7 lbs.) of rice".

Buckley in his *Anecdotal History* gives the following account of the 1854 riots page 585 :—

(1854) :—

> This was the year of the biggest Chinese riots that have been known in Singapore, which upset the whole island for ten or twelve days. It arose between the Hokiens, from the province of Hokien in China, and the Teo Chews from the province of Quantung, because the Hokiens refused to join in a subscription to assist the rebels who had been driven from Amoy by the Imperial China Troops. We proceed to give an account of them at some length, with the proceedings that subsequently took place in connection with them. The riots arose, as they have done since, without any apparent cause, as the small dispute which commenced them was not, of course the real *casus belli*, which originated in the proceedings of the secret societies, with a predetermination to fight out their quarrels in spite of the authorities. There were 400 or more persons killed, a great number wounded, and about 300 houses burned. The police force proved to be in good order and quite equal to what could be expected from their small number as compared with the thousands of Chinese. The military in the Settlement only numbered about 300 in all, and after providing for the necessary guards there were only 150 to 180 men available. The whole community turned out as special constables, and to them, as in after times, the return to law and order was principally due.

Friday, 5th May, 1854 :—

> On Friday, the 5th May, about mid-day, a dispute arose between two Chinese, the one a Hokien man and the other a Macao man, about the weight of a catty of rice which the one was selling to the other. High words ensued, and the quarrel of each was quickly adopted by his countrymen among the bystanders. Blows followed, and the report being rapidly circulated through the neighbouring streets, the adherents of each faction came pouring in by hundreds to take part in the broil, which then assumed a very alarming character. The fighting spread into the adjoining streets, in all of which the shops were at once closed, and sticks, stones and knives were used freely on the streets, and bricks thrown from the upper windows whenever an opportunity offered of assailing their enemies on the street. Several shops and houses were broken into, rifled of their contents and the inmates maltreated, and the work of plunder once commenced would soon have become general throughout the town, had not the military made their appearance, after Mr. Dunman, the Superintendent of Police, had stated his inability to suppress the riot.

*   *   *

> The Governor then listened to Mr. Dunman's opinion, and the troops were sent for; when they came, quietness generally ensued...... The troops were dismissed to their barracks, and the evening passed over without any signs of a serious intention to renew the riot. Many flattered themselves that the affair was at an end, and that nothing more would be heard of it.

Saturday, 6th May, 1854:—

The following morning, however, was calculated to undeceive all those who thought that the Chinese had had enough of it the day before. They must have been busy organising themselves during the night, for in the morning with day-break the fighting and plundering began in different parts of the town, and, in spite of the Police, the shops and houses of many of the Chinese inhabitants were broken and pillaged. Wherever, in fact, a few of the one faction happened to have their houses or shops in a locality inhabited chiefly by the other, they were set upon at once, their goods either stolen or destroyed, and themselves severely bruised or wounded and in some instances murdered.

* * *

At noon the Europeans met and determined to offer their services as special constables. They proceeded in a body to the Police Office, where they were met by the Governor and Resident Councillor. About seventy gentlemen, comprising the greater part of the European residents and a few of the commanders of merchant vessels lying in the harbour, were sworn in, Mr. W. H. Read being the first to be sworn; he has written an account of the matter in his book at page 95, in the chapter called *The Chinese Secret Societies.*

* * *

Sunday, 7th May, 1854:—

On Sunday, a strong body of the special constables was ordered to be on duty by 4 o'clock in the morning; and it was fortunate that this was done, as there were evident symptoms that an extensive system of depredation had been determined on for that day...... The regular police were wholly knocked up with the work of the two previous nights and days, and the body of special constables on duty had almost the entire charge of the town. They were divided into parties, each numbering eighteen or twenty men, and headed by two Magistrates.

* * *

A little before six o'clock, an attempt was made to commence operations by plundering a house at the corner of Circular Road and South Bridge Road, but luckily one of the patrolling parties happened to be near, and were in time to prevent it, and to disperse the mob. Considerable rioting took place in Philip Street (where the rioters were armed with knives and swords), Market Street, and Amoy Street, where a party of seven special constables and four police peons took upwards of fifty of the rioters into custody.

Colonel Butterworth and the authorities now became thoroughly awake to the extent of the danger which threatened. All the *pukats* and other Chinese boats, which were swarming with men and afforded the most convenient receptacles for plunder, were ordered into the middle of the river to prevent communication with the shore, and seven boats belonging to the men-of-war were kept rowing about to prevent any attempt at landing, and other signs of more prompt action became apparent, should any further attempts at plunder be made. These measures and the attitude assumed by the authorities and European community appeared to frighten the rioters from any further serious attempt in town, and they then betook themselves to the suburbs and country in the vicinity.

* * *

About eight in the evening an armed party of Chinese with banners and gongs made their appearance at Rochore, defied the police to fight, and proceeded to break open and pillage the houses and shops of some of the inhabitants. The constables fired over their heads at first, but that having no effect the officer ordered his men to fire upon them before they would disperse. Two men were shot dead, and several were wounded. In the town all remained comparatively quiet during the night, both the Marines and Sepoys being posted in the town for fear of any outbreak.

Monday, 8th May, 1854:—

The scene of operations appeared on Monday to have been fairly transferred to the country districts, and murder, burning and pillage prevailed in all directions. In the Tanglin districts, a number of houses and *bangsals* were attacked and burnt, several persons were killed, and numbers wounded. In the Bukit Timah district the Police stationed at the village of Bukit Timah were threatened with an attack by a large body of men, and were at last so closely pressed that they were obliged, in self-defence, to fire upon the Chinese, several of whom were wounded.

* * *

In the Payah Lebar district, the persons belonging to the two tribes which chiefly inhabit that locality had entered into a compact that they would not molest each other, but the Teochew people violated the agreement by turning out considerable bodies and attacking the Hokien Chinese who were taken quite unprepared as they relied on the engagement which had been made. A number of houses were plundered, several burnt to the ground, and the inmates killed and wounded. A large body went to the Station which had been recently established at the village of Gaylang, and told the Jemadar that they intended to burn the village, that if he did not interfere they would not harm him, but if the contrary, he and his party would all be put to death. The Jemadar refused to parley with them and on their attempting to attack the village, fired several times, after which the Chinese retreated. One man was killed and several wounded. All the Chinese *pukats* were that evening turned out of the river by a party of special constables.

Tuesday, 9th May, 1854:—

On Tuesday, a number of houses were burnt in Tanglin, and persons killed or wounded. One of the magistrates on his way to town having learned that a party of some hundreds were advancing from Bukit Timah, immediately turned back, and assisted by four special constables and a few peons, Boyans, and Chinese, formed a barricade at the first Station on the Bukit Timah Road. They then advanced along the road towards Bukit Timah, and near Cluny encountered a large body of Chinese, armed, and having gongs and banners. This party was driven back for some distance, shots being exchanged with them. They, however, so greatly outnumbered the magistrate's force that the latter was obliged to give way for about one hundred yards, then Constable Berthier with a party of peons at this time came up, and thus reinforced they returned to the attack and succeeded in driving back the Chinese, who at last took shelter in a *bangsal* and some negotiations ensued. In the meantime, another party, consisting of a Magistrate, a number of special constables, and police peons, &c., went round by the hills and through the jungle. They met a very large body of Chinese, whom they repeatedly fired upon and at last forced to give way, some taking to the jungle, but the greater part retiring upon the other body of their countrymen, whom they joined in the *bangsal*. Fifteen Chinese were killed in this affray, and many more must have been wounded.

A detachment of troops was sent out to help them, but being without a guide, missed its way and did not join the specials until the evening. In the Payah Lebar and Siglap districts, the unfortunate Hokien people continued to suffer severely, the huts being everywhere burnt by their enemies, who murdered men, women and children. The corpses in this and other localities were found in many instances frightfully mutilated. A Magistrate with a party of fifty Malays, &c., went out to Thomson Road, from whence they followed a number of armed Chinese to near Serangoon, but owing to the obstruction offered by the jungle they did not succeed in bringing them to a stand. Several prisoners were taken. In the evening a party of forty Malays were sent to Siglap to reinforce the police. A party of some hundreds of Chinese, armed, and having flags, gongs and horns, attempted to pass the Police Station at the fifth mile-stone in Thomson Road, in the direction of town, but the Jemadar and police peons stationed there opposed their progress, and on their still persisting, fired several rounds upon them, when they retired. They afterwards returned to within half a mile of the Station, but finding that the police were on the alert they did not attempt to advance.

In the evening, at about seven o'clock, the Police were fired upon from a house in Church Street at a short distance from the Police Office, on which Mr. Dunman, Sitting Magistrate, proceeded to the spot with a party of Sepoys and having read the Riot Act, the house was fired into and then entered, a quantity of arms being found in it, and several prisoners taken.

* * *

Wednesday, 10th May, 1854:—

On Wednesday, the 10th, the disorder in the country districts still prevailed. It was resolved to despatch the steamer *Hooghly* with Sepoys and Malays to be landed at different points round the island so as to co-operate with the parties which had been sent out, and especially with a detachment of Sepoys under Colonel Cameron, which proceeded towards Buddoh, information having been brought in that the Chinese had collected in force near that place.

The road about two miles beyond Buddoh was over a hill, and on the crown of this a barricade was found, placed across the public road so as to effectually stop all passage. It was not quite finished, but it was apparently intended to be made of considerable strength and was protected by an attap roof. No one was on the watch, or considerable resistance might have been offered. Colonel Cameron, who was on horseback on the right flank of the detachment, caught sight of about one hundred and thirty Chinese apparently waiting for dinner. For a minute they appeared stupified at the appearance of the military, and then bolted into the jungle in all directions. The soldiers came up at a run and immediately opened fire, but the jungle came so close up to the spot where the Chinese were found, that they were out of sight in a moment. Only four men were made prisoners.

* * *

A little further on, on the opposite side of the road, a new house was met with, surrounded by a strong stockade about twelve feet high, and from this and another hut near it, a number of Chinese were observed to flee into the jungle. The whole of these buildings were burnt down, and the stockade across the road having been destroyed, the party returned towards Singapore.

* * *

Thursday, 11th May, 1854:—

On Thursday quiet prevailed in town. From the country, the different parties landed from the *Hooghly* at Changi, Serangoon, Thomson Road, and Kranji, returned to Singapore. The Changi division came upon the remains of the stockade destroyed on the previous day by Colonel Cameron, which was still burning. The party which landed at Kranji found the Chinese gathered in force with arms, and about twenty armed Chinese having fired at them, they were obliged to return the fire. Two men were seen to drop down dead and one man was wounded in the arm. The headman of the village and some others were captured and brought to town. The people at the village said they had armed themselves, as they were afraid, having heard that the Hokien men were going to attack them that evening. This statement was so far corroborated by the fact that letters had been received in town from parties in the village in which the anticipated attack had been mentioned.

The other divisions did not meet any opposition. The whole of the roads radiating from Singapore to different parts of the island were thus traversed from one end to the other, and with good effect, as the Chinese are described to have been quite surprised at seeing these large parties of armed men approaching them from the back of the island. The Malays are said to have behaved very well under the European gentlemen by whom they were accompanied.

* * *

Friday, 12th May, 1854:—

On Friday, a Chinese was found murdered near the foot of Government Hill. Two Malays were also murdered by Chinese in the Payah Lebar district. Several parties of armed Chinese were seen in this district and chased, but took refuge in the jungle, where, for want of guides, it was found impossible to follow them. A large force was reported to have assembled in the jungle, between the Serangoon and Gaylang Roads. Four detachments of Sepoys, each of twenty men, were stationed on Thomson Road near the fifth mile stone, in the Tanglin District, in Gaylang at Dr. Little's bungalow, and on the Bukit Timah Road at the house of Mr. M. F. Davidson, still called Dalvey.

Saturday, 13th May, 1854:—

On Saturday morning a Chinese was murdered in the Tanglin district. The police tried to beat the jungle between the Gaylang and Serangoon Roads, but all the paths were found to be obstructed by trees being felled across them, the logs, by which the swamps are crossed, removed, &c. In various districts, besides burning down the houses, the nutmeg, cocoa-nut, and other fruit trees were cut down by the rioters.

The riots subsided, after having lasted for ten or twelve days, and murder, fire-raising, robbery, and wanton destruction of houses, plantations, gardens, and fruit trees, having happened daily during that time.

There was great uneasiness at Malacca, all kinds of rumours being propagated there about what was occurring in Singapore. The secret societies in Singapore wrote to Malacca inviting their friends there to commence a riot, but without effect. A public meeting was held at the Residency, Mr. J. H. Velge in the Chair, and resolutions adopted calling on the Government to take immediate steps to prevent similar disturbances there.

In Johore, there was some trouble, as the coolies were short of rice, the supplies from Singapore being temporarily stopped, as all trade was suspended.

The lock-ups and gaol were crowded with prisoners, about five hundred men having been arrested, and a special sessions was held on Tuesday, the 6th June, before Colonel Butterworth Sir Wm. Jeffcott, the Recorder, and Mr. Church.

* * *

The Sessions lasted seventeen days. Six men were sentenced to death, but only two were executed; sixty-four were sentenced to various terms of hard labour, and eight were transported for fourteen years. There were about two hundred and fifty prisoners tried.

These extensive extracts are given so as to convey an authentic atmosphere to this description of a Chinese secret society outbreak in Singapore eighty years ago. The most recent comparable outbreak was in 1928 (*see* Chapter XXVII *infra*).

In 1863 there occurred another week's rioting in Singapore, the cause of which is not clearly stated in the published authorities, some of whom refer to it as faction fights, some as clan fights, and some as a secret society war. It was probably due to a dispute over the disposal of a consignment of prostitutes from China, and followed the main line of cleavage between Ghee Hin and Ghee Hok and their affinities, which by this time were becoming numerous.

These riots are referred to by Buckley, Read and Song Ong Siang (page 124), but their story does not add to our knowledge.

It was during these riots, which occurred during Sir Orfeur Cavenagh's Governorship (1858–1868), that the plan was adopted, which Read claims as his own, of swearing in the headmen as special constables, and keeping them on duty in the streets until the riots ceased. Cavenagh in his book *Reminiscences of an Indian Official* has the following references to the disturbances of his day on page 256:—

The two great difficulties to contend with in ruling over Chinese are the influence of these secret societies, and their own gambling propensities. Although the Hooeys offer no open opposition to the Government they are ever striving, with the view of increasing their own powers, to compel their members to submit to their decision disputes of every description, whether of a civil or a criminal nature, and thus to frustrate the action of the legal tribunals and diminish their authority. As regards gambling, although it might be practicable to bring it under some control, it is impossible to prevent it. Large bribes were paid to the subordinate officers in the police by the keepers of private gaming houses to connive at their breaches of the law, and the force was thus demoralized.

On page 255–6:—

Owing to disputes between the different secret societies the island of Singapore had been on various occasions the scene of serious disturbances, resulting in loss of life; as these disturbances frequently arose from collisions occurring between rival parties accompanying processions in their passage through the town, with the view of preventing future breaches of the peace, I prohibited all processions; and, upon the recommendation of the commissioner of police, to whom the heads of the societies, apparently respectable citizens, were well known, I directed that, in the event of any riot taking place, these gentlemen should be at once summoned and sworn in as special constables, and compelled to take an active part in quelling the disturbance. This arrangement did not at all suit their views, as, although willing to urge others to fight, they did not care about having their own heads broken; hence quarrels between the members of the several secret societies became comparatively rare, and no riot of sufficient importance to necessitate the employment of troops to quell it occurred at Singapore during my term of office.

Schlegel *op. cit.* on page xi of his Introduction says of this period in Singapore:—

"Wherever a just mode of governing them has been adopted, the Chinese have never been troublesome. Singapore, always cited as a refutation of this fact, owes the unruliness of her Chinese population to the defects of her own government. We fully acquiesce with Mr. Oliphant's judgement in his *Narrative of the Earl of Elgin's Mission to China and Japan* 1857 Vol. 1 page 20 where he says:—

At present there is a population of 70,000 Chinamen in Singapore, and not a single European who understands their language. The consequence is that, in the absence of any competent interpreter, they are generally ignorant of the designs of Government, and, regarding themselves still as Chinese subjects, are apt to place themselves in an antagonistic attitude, whenever laws are passed affecting their peculiar customs. No effort is made to overcome a certain exclusiveness arising hence; and this is fostered by the secret societies, which exercise an important moral influence upon the minds of all, but more particularly the ignorant portion of the population.

* * *

It is a sheer impossibility to try and eradicate the Hung league where it exists. Notwithstanding the military expeditions of the Netherlands Indies Government to Borneo, the league still (1866) flourishes there. It exists at Sumatra; and even Java, always thought to be free of this Brotherhood, is not without its members.

In 1867, in July and September, there were again riots between the Ghee Hin and Hok Hin (福 興) which latter society here comes to notice for the first time. Little appears to be on record about the Hok Hin and we can only suppose that it was an off-shoot of the Ghee Hok. It is mentioned separately in the list of societies suppressed in 1890. We should place the Hok Hin therefore in the category of "Tokong" societies.

In connection with these 1867 riots in Singapore referred to by Song Ong Siang *op. cit.* page 145, it must be remembered that July and August, 1867 saw severe riots in Penang between the two camps of Triad and "Tokong" dealt with in Chapter XVI below, of which the Singapore riots of the same year were no doubt an echo.

It would probably be true to say that the sixties of the last century marked the beginning of the real prosperity of the Chinese in Malaya: and the arrival of great numbers of ignorant immigrants in search of the new El Dorado provided the secret societies with a constant supply of just that raw material upon which to thrive and to practise their blackmail and with a ready means of making easy money by supplying this immigrant army with the relaxations they most wanted, namely, opium, gambling and women.

A comparable process was taking place in America about the same time when the army of Irish immigrants was received into the welcoming and supporting arms of the Tammany octopus, in return for their vote and the political power that went with it.[1]

The process of conversion of a section of the Ghee Hin and Ghee Hok from being the two governing bodies of the Chinese community into two rival camps of bullies as we know them to-day in Singapore, was probably hastened by these circumstances, and the sources of revenue of these gangs to-day remain pretty much as they began, namely, in squeezing the innocent newcomer and fleecing him in gambling and in the supply of illicit chandu, and in levying "protection" money on prostitutes and other defenceless members of society.

In August, 1867 a bill had been introduced into the Legislative Council with the following "objects and reasons":—

> It has long been felt that some legislative enactment was required to deal with the secret societies so common in the Colony, but great difficulties have existed as to the manner in which the subject might be treated, owing to the element of secrecy in a country where the officers of Police have no knowledge of the language of the greater number of persons forming such combinations..............
>
> The societies are believed to have their origin in praiseworthy and benevolent motives, but, after a little time, are apt to degenerate into unlawful combinations. It is proposed by the present bill to require all societies to be registered under certain rules......., and to give notice of their meetings.

The bill was ultimately shelved. (see Song Ong Siang page 146). Events were, however, occurring in Penang at this time, to which we must now turn our attention.

Penang.—By 1867 in Singapore the cleavage between the Ghee Hin (Triad) and Ghee Hok ("Tokong") was complete and, although misunderstood by the authorities, this cleavage was discernable by them in the constant succession of disturbances due to the rivalry between the two camps and the scramble for money and power in the underworld of a "new" country. But it was only in that year that an outbreak occurred in Penang which was to furnish evidence of a similar cleavage there, which was destined to lead to British intervention in Perak and to the formation of secret political alliances between the Chinese and Malays, which exercised a paramount influence on events at the time, and which have continued in existence to the present-day. But we anticipate.

SECRET SOCIETY SYSTEM AT WORK IN PENANG 1851–1854

The following extracts from Vaughan's valuable paper *Notes on the Chinese of Penang J.I.A.* Vol. VIII 1854 give a picture of the coolie traffic in Penang at that date and the working of the secret society system, with which that traffic was bound up. Vaughan says:—

*   *   *

> The Chinaman on landing in the Straits is called a "Singke" or new man or new friend, by the Chinchew, and "Sin Hak" by Macao men. Those immigrants are thus obtained. One or more of the Chinese merchants charter a vessel and leave Pinang in April or May for Macao or Amoy. On arriving at the destined port, the charterer, who usually proceeds in the vessel as super-cargo, sets a number of agents to work. These men go about the country and cajole the unsuspecting people, by promises of a speedy fortune and return to their native land, to accept the bounty money, which varies according to the respectability of the victims. They are then huddled on board. The agents receive a dollar a head. The immigrants are usually overcrowded on shipboard but treated well on the whole. They arrive in the months of January, February and March. The anchor is scarcely cast when the resident Chinese flock on board to buy Singkes as they term it. The charterer gets for a master workman, either tailor, goldsmith or carpenter, 10 to 15 dollars, for a cooly 6 to 10, for a sickly man 3 to 4 or less. The Singke then agrees to serve for 12 months, receiving food, clothes and a few dollars for his services. Should he be an expert workman and fall in with a generous master, he may receive more than the sum agreed on. The Singke costs 2 to 4 dollars per mensem for food and clothing. If not paid for, they are detained on board ship (if convenient) or in a godown, until a purchaser turns up. Should the charterers be forced to the latter alternative the Singkes are not well treated. Complaints have been lodged before the Sitting Magistrate at different times on this ground and the Singkes were set at large after signing a bond promising to pay the passage money.
>
> Their agreements are generally faithfully fulfilled; at the end of the 12 months the Singke is at liberty to enter his master's service on a monthly stipend or to seek his livelihood elsewhere. He is also then admitted into one of the Hoes, and into the Kongsee of his tribe. Very few Chinese remain clear of the Hoes, but as few will acknowledge themselves members it is difficult to arrive at the truth. From 2 to 3,000 Chinese land annually at Pinang and spread from thence to Province Wellesley and the Siamese and Malay territories.
>
> The natives of Quang-tung are more robust and hard working than the Fuh-kien or Chin-chew and other tribes. All the carpenters, blacksmiths, shoemakers, and other laborious tradesmen are of the first; a few are goldsmiths, tailors and shopkeepers; they are excellent

---

Footnote.—(1) Chinese immigrants were also crowding to America at this epoch, taking with them their secret societies which came to be known there as Tongs (堂). The "Tong wars" of American city life, no doubt, derive from the same two stems of Han and Hung described in these chapters, whose traditional hostility is probably the ultimate cause of Chinese internecine strife the world over

squatters and may be called pioneers to the Chin-chews. After completing their 12 months servitude as Singkes, many get an advance of money from their friends, soon clear a piece of forest land, plant vegetables, plantains and indigo at first, and eventually spice trees. After felling the jungle the ground is measured, boundaries fixed, and a grant obtained from the Government Land Office. The returns are so slow, that in a few years they are forced to sell their grants to satisfy creditors. Chin-chew men are the usual purchasers. The plantations which are at present in the hands of Chin-chew shopkeepers were made by Quantung men. These last indulge in arrack and opium and gamble a little.

Fuh-kien or Chin-chew men are tailors, goldsmiths, shopkeepers, merchants and owners of spice plantations and constitute the most wealthy portion of the native inhabitants. They are much addicted to gaming and opium.

The chiefs of all the Hoeys are well known by reputation. For the last three or four years they have been on very amicable terms, but before that several desperate street rows took place and some lives were lost.

* * *

On the third moon of this year (1853 or 54) the Sin Neng Kongsee and Hye San Hoe quarrelled at "poh", several men were dangerously wounded, much property destroyed, and the two clubs involved themselves in a law suit which has not yet concluded, six months after the fight. A great deal of ill-nature has been displayed on both sides, a Hye San man was plundered of a large sum of money, and several grown trees of a Sin Neng man were destroyed.

This shows the Hai San to have been still active at this date, but as we shall see from later extracts, it had now become entirely a Hakka society. The "Sin Neng Kongsee" referred to was a Cantonese district association, (Hoay Kwan) and not a secret society, but would nevertheless be identified with the Ghee Hins in a riot. Vaughan continues:—

"The Hoes have two great days in the year, viz:—in the third moon, when they worship the dead, and in the seventh moon, when they worship the evil spirits. In the latter they assemble in town and have a great feast. I have visited these assemblies and there were at least 3,000 members of the Ghee Hin in the Kongsee house and the adjacent street on one occasion. There are no stated meetings, but whenever an offender is to be tried, notice is sent round, and the members of the Hoe assemble. If the culprit is pronounced guilty, he is flogged, fined, expelled, or punished in any way the elders judge fit.

On one occasion while a constable was on his rounds, he was alarmed on passing the Ghee Hin Kongsee house, by cries issuing from the building, at the same time a man rushed out followed by others.

The police finding the door open went in and seized the elders, as they sat in solemn conclave and took them to the police office, the pursued and pursuers being also taken up; the former had his hand cut open and severe bruises appeared about his person. He declared that the elders had nothing to do with the assault, but that the pursuers were bad men and against the order of the head man had assaulted him; he also admitted having been before the Hoe for some misdemeanour. There was no doubt the Hoe had ordered him to be flogged and that he managed to force his way past the door-keeper. Evidence could not be procured and the chief and officers were released.

The most influential man in the Gee Hin, who was arrested on the above occasion, is a Chinese, born in Bengal, and a watchmaker by trade. He had been on the island for 50 or 60 years and is remarkable for his benevolence. He has a small hospital for lepers and poor creatures afflicted with any other diseases, in which there are generally 15 or 20 patients at a time. He gives a great deal of money away in charity and buries all paupers who have not belonged to any Hoe or Kongsee, or have not paid up their subscriptions to these institutions, for which purpose he keeps a number of rough coffins ready at hand. He has a wonderful influence over his people. At one of their feasts, I walked to the Hoe at about 10 p.m. and found the street in front of the house crowded with initiated Chinese. Fearing a disturbance, I sent for this man, who is named Appoo, and told him it would be better to send the men in doors and keep them quiet. He immediately gave an order for them to retire and shut the gates and in 5 minutes the street was deserted, and where a minute or two before all was noise and confusion the greatest silence prevailed. He is much respected by all classes. He may be recognized any day by his black beaver hat, being the only Chinaman that wears one.

This passage refers to Man Ah Fu *alias* Boon Ah Poo, whom we have met in Chapter V as President of the Penang Ghee Hin in 1825.

This man's Indian origin as given by Vaughan, invites an interesting speculation as to how far his influence may have been responsible for the formation of those Indian and Malay alliances with Chinese secret societies, which came into existence in Penang between 1830 and 1867, and whose development is discussed in Chapters XIV and XV *infra.*

Vaughan concludes:—

"It is believed in Penang that the rebels in China[1] are members of the Hoe."

THE KONGSEES, (DISTRICT OR CLAN ASSOCIATIONS) AND HOES (SECRET SOCIETIES) IN PENANG 1854

The following extracts from Vaughan *op. cit.* clarify the position regarding clan associations and secret societies in Penang at that date:—

A. Kongsees (district or clan associations)—
(1) Cantonese (Macaos)—"The Chinese of Penang may be divided into two classes, the Macao and Chinchew. The former includes Khehs and Ahyas (*i.e.* Hakkas and Teo Chews). The latter are natives of Fukkien and the north western provinces. Keh-langs and Ahyas come from the province of Quangtung on the borders of Fukkien. Nearly all the former belong to the city of Kiaying and its environs. The latter are from Chao-chau-fu and the neighbouring towns.

Footnote.—(1) This refers to the Taiping rebellion then in progress in China, and probably also to the Dagger rebellion in Amoy.

Macao men are divided into six great Kongsees or Friendly societies, or clubs, *viz*:—Sin Neng, Hiong Shan, Chen Sang, Yu Kin Chew, Chong Far, Win Tai Kwan. And seven lesser Kongsees:—Nam Hoi, Sen Tak, Poon Ngwi, San Wi, San Oon, Hok San, Howi Peng.[1]

These clubs must be distinguished from the Hoes or Triad societies, from which they materially differ; they are however confounded by Europeans. Kongsees are formed by men of the same town, village or district, and no other natives are admitted.

The above titles are the names of certain localities in the province of Quangtung. ·The six first clubs have houses with rooms for their sick and indigent, where they are lodged and fed, and on dying are buried at the expense of the Kongsee. They have no oath of secrecy or signs to distinguish each other. Each member subscribes according to his means".

(2) Hokkiens (Chinchews)—"The Chinchew men do not divide themselves thus, but each "Seh" or tribe has a club of its own, conducted exactly as the Macao clubs. The only difference is that Chinchew will admit Macao men of the same tribe; while the latter are more exclusive and will not admit a stranger. There are a great many Chinchew Kongsees; the principal are:—Long Say Tong, established by the "Seh" Lee; Leong Sang Tong, by the "Seh" Khoo;[2] Kew Leong Tong by the "Seh" Tan; Poo Soo Tong by the "Seh" Cheah.

Country born (*i.e.* Straits born) Chinese have a club called Sip Gee Seeah (*i.e.* "The Twelve Surnames Club"). They elect twelve Towkays or trustees".

B. Hoes (or secret societies)—

"In addition to these Kongsees there are five Hoes or Triad societies, *viz*:—The Gee Hin, Ho Seng, Hye San, Chinchin (or ring), Toh Peh Kong. The two first approach nearer to the famous Triad society of China than the last three. The Gee Hin corresponds with the Tien Teh Hoe, or "heaven and earth", fraternity. The term Tien Teh is also used as a name for the deity.

The three last have been formed in Penang, and differ but slightly from the others. The whole five may be considered one, having different names and separate rules for internal management and although some of the signs differ they are known to all the Hoes. The separation was evidently caused for convenience sake, by each tribe, if we may judge from the apparent exclusiveness of each.

The Gee Hin is principally composed of Macao men, though professing universality.

Ho Seng admits all classes and even Malays, Portugese, Klings, and Jawi Pukans[3] belong to it.

Hye San is composed of Keh Langs (*i.e.* Hakkas).

Toh Peh Kong is nearly all Babas and Chinchews.

Chinchin is composed of Chinchews and all classes.

The Gee Hin is said to number about 15,000 members in Penang and Province Wellesley; but this amount is not to be depended on, as the number given by several members of the Hoe varies from one to twenty thousand:—

Ho Seng from three to five thousand.
Chinchin from two to three thousand.
Toh-Peh-Kong three to four thousand.
Hye San one to two thousand.

Females are not admitted.

*　　　*　　　*

Although these Hoes profess not to assist a guilty man, yet it is a well known fact that they do so. When a brother commits a crime he has nothing to do but exonerate himself before the Hoe, and it is an easy matter for the members to believe him innocent. Both Hoes and Kongsees do some good in adjusting petty quarrels and punishing slight offences, but in more serious crimes they carry out the same principle, and force men to compromise them. A most flagrant case occurred at the Criminal Sessions in the month of June last, which will serve to exemplify the manner in which the ends of justice are defeated.

In the third moon the members of a Kongsee were worshipping the dead at the Macao burial ground. A mendicant having displeased them, was beaten, and died from the effects of the blows. Some fellow beggars of the deceased complained to the Police, the perpetrators of the deed were arrested, and a Coroner's Jury returned a verdict of wilful murder against them. On the opening of the Sessions not a witness was to be found. These men had lived for years at the burial ground and subsisted on the generosity of the frequenters, they were too poor to have left the island without assistance, it therefore may be inferred that the Kongsee bought them off and paid their passage to China. Such cases are not uncommon, for at every Sessions cases are thrown out for want of evidence. It is quite apparent that the Fraternity is the root of all evil here. Were they suppressed, the Chinese would be brought under the influence of our laws and made to respect them, but at present the Hoe is looked up to as the only legitimate Court of Justice, and Magistrates, Judges, Courts of Judicature etc. are viewed as merely engines of tyranny".

From the above it seems clear that in 1854 there were in Penang two distinct sets of Chinese secret societies *viz*:—

(*a*) The Ghee Hin and the Ho Seng "corresponding with the Triad society of China".

(*b*) The Hye San, Chinchin, and Toh Peh Kong "formed in Penang and differing but slightly from the others".

The above was written by Vaughan some ten years before the first recorded trial of strength in Penang (1863) between the Ghee Hin and Ho Seng on the one side, and the Hye San, Chinchin, and Toh Peh Kong on the other. It was written, too, some twelve years before the publication of Schlegel's work.

Footnote.—(1) These are names of districts in the Kwang Chow and Wai Chow prefectures of the Canton province, the accepted modern romanised spelling of which is:—

　　i. San Ning; ii. Heong Shan; iii. Chen Shang (Hakka); iv. ? Kia Ying Chew; v. Chung Fah; vi. ? Tung Kwan; vii. Nam Hoi; viii. Shun Tak; ix. Phun Yu; x. San Wui; xi. Sin On (Hakka); xii. Hok San (Hakka); xiii. Hoi P'eng (a sub-district of San Ning).

These districts have an important bearing on Perak history and are further discussed in Chapter XVII *infra*.

Footnote.—(2) For a note on the "Leong San Tong" of the Seh "Khoo", *see* Chapter XXVII.

Footnote.—(3) This word and its variations is explained in Chapter XII *infra*.

Vaughan's writing throughout gives evidence of his careful and accurate observation.

Allowance can therefore be made for Vaughan's observation above that:—

> The whole five may be considered one, having different names and separate rules for internal management, and although some of the signs differ, they are known to all the Hoes.

Although it is usual down to the present-day in Malaya, to find all Chinese secret societies "considered one, although some of the signs differ"; we may perhaps take it as proved that there are in fact as we have tried to demonstrate in the foregoing chapters, two opposing camps in the Malayan secret society world to-day, each having different signs, a different ritual, and a different origin.

In any community, it is of course greatly to the advantage of the underworld therein that it should be "considered as one" by the authorities, because it is thereby enabled to preserve its appearance of an united front and, when the occasion arises, to offer combined resistance to official interference. Furthermore, by concealing from the authorities its own divisions and therewith its own weaknesses, it reduces the danger of successful official attack upon the sanctuary of its *imperium in imperio*.

It is a reasonable assumption that the Toh Peh Kong society of Penang was a counterpart at this time (1854) of the Ghee Hok in Singapore.

Both Ghee Hok (Singapore) and Toh Peh Kong (Penang) were largely composed of Hokkiens (or Chinchews as they were then called).

The Ghee Hoks of Singapore already had at this time a history of thirty years war against the Ghee Hins of Singapore.

The hostility of the Toh Peh Kongs of Penang against the Ghee Hins of Penang had not yet at this time (1854) openly shown itself. A submission is put forward in Chapter VIII that the Ghee Hok of Singapore and the Toh Peh Kong of Penang were both "anchorages" of the Han league and identical with the Three Dot Brotherhood ("Tokong"). This would explain the reason for their common hostility to the Ghee Hin (Triad).

IDENTIFICATION OF THE NAME TOH PEH KONG, AND OF THE NAMES OF OTHER SECRET SOCIETIES IN PENANG, 1854.

To assist in subsequent identification, it will be well to give here the probable Chinese characters for the Toh Peh Kong and other secret societies in Penang referred to by Vaughan. The absence of Chinese characters from the records of that day render this desirable. The name Toh Peh Kong represents the characters 大伯公 pronounced in Hokkien Toa Peh Kwun. This is the Hokkien name for the "'God of Earth" or the "God of Money" known in Cantonese as 土地公 T'o Tei Kung (*see* Giles dictionary).

Temples of the god Toa Peh Kwun are to be found everywhere in Malaya to-day.

Vaughan in *Manners and Customs of the Chinese* p. 35 writing in 1854 says:—

> The household gods of the Chinese are represented by idols, or "Tokongs" or "Topehkongs" as they are called by the Malays; or by pictures of deified personages.

The name of Toa Peh Kwun has found its way into the Malay language, and represents to-day the "localese" for a Chinese temple. *Vide* Wilkinson's dictionary:—

Tokong (Chinese)	=	A Chinese temple, a "Joss" house.
cf. To-pe-kong	=	The "Joss" or god itself.

and in the 1932 edition:—

To-pe-kong (Chinese)	=	"Joss", image, or picture over a Chinese shrine.

Also *To-pekong, Tapekong,* and *Dato Pekong;* also used loosely of a Tamil temple.

Another variant met with among Malays is that of Dato Peking or Dato Pekin, *i.e.* "The god of the capital city of China".

We know from its Rules (*see* Appendix II) that the Toh Peh Kong society was also known by the alternative name of Kien Tek 建德 "Established Virtue Society". This alternative name is also met with in the variant form Kien Hok 建福 "Established Happiness". We also know from its Rules that this society was founded in Penang in 1844 and Vaughan above tells us that in 1854 it was chiefly composed of Hokkiens and Straits-born Chinese "Babas".

It is probable that the name of the universal Hokkien household god Toh Peh Kwun was chosen so as to provide the society with an innocent-sounding title, a Taoist religious background, and a tacit acknowledgement of its Han league allegiance all in one. The more precise and "business" name was Kien Tek. The latter appears on two documents of the society, reproductions of which are contained in a Chinese manuscript book made by the then Governor of the Straits Settlements, Sir Cecil Clementi Smith in 1890, and very kindly lent in 1938 for purposes of this work by Sir Cecil Clementi, former Governor of the Colony. This book is entitled—*Impressions* (prints from wood-blocks) *of the Seals and Tickets of Membership of those Chinese secret societies in the Straits Settlements suppressed 1889–1892.*

The following is a reproduction of the seal of the Kian Tek T'ong (建德堂) taken from this book.

Another reproduction of the same seal is to be found in a framed record of similar seals, made by Cowan when Protector of Chinese, Perak, in 1890, and now hanging in the office of the Protector of Chinese in Ipoh.

SEAL OF THE KIAN TEK T'ONG

Examining this octagonal seal which by its shape suggests the "Pat-kwa" of the Han league, we get the following lay-out:—

and the following translation:—

SEAL OF THE KIAN TEK T'ONG

ASSOCIATION BRINGS ENLIGHTENMENT, CO-OPERATION DISPELS MISUNDERSTANDING

Our brethren since of old have inhabited the beautiful deep lakes
And to-day our only wish is to remain united in heart
We vow to rejoice together in peace and to render mutual help in times of danger
Rectitude knows no oppression nor cruelty, nor does it infringe our rights
We rely upon Heaven for the disposal of all our affairs
At all times we show respect to virtue and morality
Upon taking the oath of alliance we refrain from offering opposition
For the setting of this seal increases the law's severity.

There is nothing in these antithetical verses corresponding with, or even reminiscent of Triad ritual, whereas the first line of the opening stanza suggests the "rivers and lakes" of the "Tokong" camp.

The mention of "rectitude", suggests the Rectitude lodge of the Han league mentioned by Hutson in Chapter II *supra*.

The Ipoh specimen of this document bears at the foot, outside the octagon, the additional characters:—

地　　　　出
頭　　　　水

in juxtaposition, meaning perhaps:—

"The source of the waters", with the character 忠 chung, meaning "loyalty" set between the two couplets. This again suggests the "water-motif" of the Han league (*see* Chapter VIII *infra*).

The second document is a Summons to a meeting of the Kian Tek Thong.

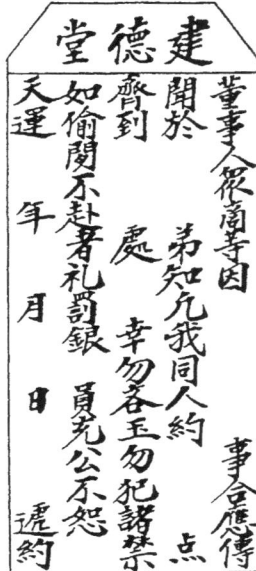

Rough translation:—

In the matter of .... the Committee of the Kian Tek Thong hereby notify brother .... that he and all comrades are required to go to .... (place) at .... o'clock.

Do not fail nor offend against the rules.

Absentees will be fined $........ without excuse.

Sent on .... day .... month .... year of Thin Wan.

There is nothing remarkable in this document other than its identification with the Kian Tek society and thence with the Han league. Another similar summons which we have also identified (pages 104 and 149) with the Han league is given by Stanton *op. cit.* page 91 fig. 12.

IDENTITY OF THE NAMES OF OTHER SOCIETIES MENTIONED BY VAUGHAN

Other societies in Penang in 1854 mentioned by Vaughan above are:—

(1) Ho Seng. The characters for this society (和 勝) "Peaceful Victory" appear among the Clementi-Smith wood-prints of 1890. This society was a Ghee Hin (Triad) foundation in Penang up to the end of the 1860's but seems as will be shown later, to have joined the Toh Peh Kong ("Tokong") camp in Perak in the 1870's.

(2) Hai San (海山) "Sea and Land" we have already met in Chapter V. From an indeterminate foundation in Penang at the beginning of the nineteenth century, during which early epoch it appears to have lived on terms of

non-aggression with the Ghee Hin (Triad) camp, it absorbed Hakkas into its ranks and according to Vaughan above it was entirely Hakka by 1854. From then on it belonged to the Toh Peh Kong ("Tokong") camp and was implacably hostile to the Triad.

(3) Chinchin. This society does not appear among the Clementi-Smith woodprints. Vaughan gives it the alternative name of the "Ring" and says it was composed of Hokkiens and "'all classes" (which probably included Malays). As the word "Chinchin" is the Malay for "ring" the name may not be Chinese at all, but a purely Malay name.

We think, however, that it may be a corruption of the characters 見 簽 Chien Ch'ien meaning "On seeing this tally" used by the Fuk On She (福安社) society of Hongkong (pages 13, 112 and 149) on their form of summons by "tally" or bamboo splint (*vide* Stanton *op. cit.* page 91 fig. 12). This would associate the "Chinchin" society with the Tally society of Hutson and thence with the Han league. Another alternative might be an identity with the modern society in Penang, the Ch'im Ch'ian (潛戰) or "Hidden Fight" society (*see* under "Penang" in Chapter XXVII *infra*).

CHINESE TERMS FOR CLAN AND DISTRICT ASSOCIATIONS AND FOR SECRET SOCIETIES

As will be seen from the *Straits Settlements Factory Records* (1825–1830) Chapter V *supra* and from the extracts from Vaughan under "Kongsees and Hoes" quoted above, considerable confusion existed at that time in the official mind between the genuine and harmless clan or district associations, and the secret societies whose members were bound by an oath of secrecy.

This confusion was also commented on in the *Penang Riot Commission Report*, 1868, and has continued to some extent down to the present-day. Vaughan has sought to differentiate between the two, by labelling the former, *i.e.* clan associations "Kongsees", and the latter *i.e.* secret societies "Hoes".

These terms will, however hardly suffice, for the reason that "Kongsee" or Kung Sz (公司) is commonly used to denote a secret society, *e.g.* Ghee Hin Kung Sz, while "Hoe" or "Hoay", or Hui or Wui (會) is commonly used in the expression "Hoay Kwan" (會館) to denote a harmless clan or district association.

For this reason we cannot follow Vaughan, and must use terms more closely allied to Chinese usage, and more in harmony with modern practice in Malaya.

Dyer Ball in *Things Chinese* p. 172 says:—

> "The division of the people of China into clans is analogous to that of the Scottish clan in many respects and is provocative of feud and disaster to themselves and others sometimes, as well as of protection at other times to those belonging to the same clan, as was the case a few generations ago amongst the Highland clans of Scotland...... These petty wars are waged so fiercely that in some instances they approach the vindictiveness displayed in the Italian vendetta.
>
> It should however, be observed that the system of clans is more marked in the south of China and most especially so in the Kwangtung and Kwongsai provinces.
>
> The secret societies especially in the Straits Settlements take their rise in the clan system to a great extent".

Vaughan quoted above, referring to the Cantonese and Hokkiens in Penang in 1854 says:—

> "Macao men are divided into six great "Kongsees" or Friendly societies or clubs"[1] and seven lesser "Kongsees".[2]
> "These clubs must be distinguished from the Hoes or Triad societies, from which they materially differ; they are however confounded by Europeans".

This confusion has continued throughout Malayan history in greater or less degree to the present-day.

Vaughan continues:—

> "Kongsees (amongst the Macaos) are formed by men of the same town, village, or district (in China) and no others are admitted. The first six clubs (Prefectural associations, referred to above) have houses with rooms for their sick and indigent, where they are lodged and fed, and on dying are buried at the expense of their "Kongsee".
> They have no oath of secrecy, or signs to distinguish each other. The Chinchew men (Hokkiens) do not divide themselves thus, but each Seh (姓) or tribe has a club of its own, conducted exactly as the Macao Clubs".

The above description fits very well what is known to-day in Malaya as a 會館 Hoay Kwan or Wui Kwun, meaning a guildhall, club-house, friendly or mutual benefit society.; or district or clan association premises.

The modern designation for a secret society, or underground (illegal) association of any kind remains 會 (Hoay or Wui) or less usually 公 司 (Kung Sz).

Footnote.—(1) He then names six prefectures (府 fu) of the Canton Province.
Footnote.—(2) He then names seven districts (州 chau) within the above prefectures.

The word "Kongsee" or "Kongsi" is the form in the Malay language of the Chinese characters 公司 Kung Sz, which term is used both in Chinese and Malay primarily to mean a "trading company" or legitimate business of any kind.

In Chinese the term Kung Sz conveys the meaning of secret and illegal society, only when used after the name of such illegal society e.g. Ghee Hin Kung Sz.

In Malay the word "Kongsi" means a partnership or association of any sort, or a barracks or house occupied by Chinese labourers. Used in conjunction with the Malay word "gelap" = "concealed", "dark", "covert" (whether expressed or implied by the context) it has no other meaning than that of secret society ("Kongsi gelap") whether of Chinese, Malay, Indian or any other kind.

When referring to a Chinese Friendly society, or district or clan association premises, Malays who understand this difference, often use the Chinese word "Hoay Kwan" given above, which is never used nowadays of a secret (dangerous) society.

The necessity for some classification of terms was also noted in 1867 by the Commissioners in their Report on the Penang Riots. *Vide* paras. 30, 31 and 32 of the Report[1] *viz:*—

* * *

Erroneous opinion regarding Hoeys

30. "There is an opinion generally entertained that the Chinese Hoeys are necessary and beneficial to the Chinese community as Benefit societies. The Commissioners are therefore anxious before leaving the subject of the societies, to record that this opinion is erroneous".

31. Every Chinese tribe has its own Benefit society, which is entirely free and independent of any Hoey. It is only a member of a tribe, who can be head of it, and he is appointed the head in virtue of his social position in the tribe. The head of a Hoey, on the contrary, may be a member of any tribe, and members of the same tribe are frequently to be found in different Hoeys.

Explanation of terms

32. "The word Hoey means brotherhood, society of association, and the word Congsee or Kongsee, so frequently used in this evidence means company. A Hoey is a secret society, a Kongsee is any company, but the word is frequently made use of to denote a Hoey. The Kongsee house is the meeting house or club of the Hoey".

* * *

The Commissioners themselves appear to have become confused between a "Hoey Kwan" and a "Hoey", in the absence of the Chinese characters to guide them.

For the sake of clarity in this work, the following terms only will be used to signify the meanings as given:—

Hoay Kwan (會 館)	=	Chinese Friendly society, or clan or district association, or club. (This is also sometimes spelt Whay Kwan).
Hoay (會)	=	Chinese secret society. (This sound is spelled variously by the authorities "Hwui", "Hui", "Hue", "Hoe", "Hoey", "Whay", "Wui", etc.
Kongsi Gelap	=	A secret society (of nationality as may be specified), *i.e.* Malay kongsi gelap, Tamil kongsi gelap, etc.

THE PERIOD 1855-1866 IN PENANG

The records of secret society history in Penang between 1855 and 1865 are meagre. There is mention in the *Penang Riot Commission Report*, 1868 and elsewhere, of a disturbance which took place in Penang in 1863 between the Red Flag and the Toh Peh Kong society. Para. 28 of the Report reads:—

In the year 1863 a fight took place between Che Long's society, (the Red Flag) and the Toh Peh Kong society, after which the two societies became friendly, and entered into an alliance for offensive and defensive purposes.

The official record of this (1863) disturbance has not been traced by us. If it were available, it might shed important light upon our subject.

This passage is the first, and 1863 the first year in which there occurs an official reference to the existence of the Flag societies among the Malays of Penang, whose origin is discussed in Chapters XIII and XIV below.

The following extracts from the *Official Report of the Administration of the Straits Settlements* for the years 1865 and 1866, provide the only other material we have been able to find covering this period of Penang history.

Penang Administration Report 1865 under "Burglary"

There were ten serious cases, of which four originated in quarrels between Chinese secret societies. The first case was one in which several members of one society attacked the houses

---

Footnote.—(1) *See* Chapter XVI *infra.*

of three Chinese of a rival Hoey, and plundered or destroyed the whole of their property, eleven men were charged with the offence, four were acquitted, and the remaining seven sentenced to imprisonment with hard labour for eighteen months.

*   *   *

The third arose from a Hoey disturbance, six men entered and plundered the house of a Chinaman, and wantonly killed three pigs, they were seized, tried and sentenced to eighteen months' incarceration in the House of Correction.

*   *   *

The seventh was a Hoey case, the house of a Chinese blacksmith having been attacked by an armed gang, there was only one man inside who effected his escape, but the body of one of the burglars was found outside the next morning, it is supposed that he had been shot by some Malays employed by the owner, to watch the premises.

The eighth was another Hoey case, the cooley lines and mill house of a wealthy Chinese sugar planter, were attacked by about three hundred men, armed with muskets and spears, and a large quantity of property, including live stock, carried off, a Police punghuloo and four peons proceeded to the estate as soon as the notice of the outrage reached his station, the main body of the rioters had retired, but the Police came into collision with a party of about thirty, who, upon being challenged, opened fire upon the peons, the fire was returned, and one of the Chinese shot dead upon the spot, the others took to flight, followed by the Police, but owing to the darkness of the night, they succeeded in effecting their escape.

Penang Administration Report 1866 under "Assault"

There was only one assault which calls for remark. A body of Malays had collected, with a view of attacking a rival society, and the leaders of the party assaulted the punghooloo of the district on his attempting to disperse the crowd, one was arrested and bound over to keep the peace in two sureties of five hundred dollars each, the other who was a resident of Quedah, made his escape, but was subsequently punished by the Siamese authorities for having organised a body of armed men for the purpose of making an incursion into British territory.

These incidents which were evidently typical of conditions during the years between 1855 and 1866, provide evidence of rival societies both among Chinese and Malays and were the flutter of the storm that was to break over Penang and Province Wellesley in 1867 in the first open struggle in that settlement between Triad and "Tokong". The story of this struggle forms the subject of Chapter XVI below, wherein we resume the study of this aspect of our subject. It should be remembered that the law at this time was the Law of England. The Indian Penal Code (Macaulay 1860) was not introduced into the Straits Settlements until later. Hence the use of the terms "Burglary" and "Assault" above.

AN INVESTIGATION INTO THE CHARACTER OF THE TOH PEH KONG SOCIETY, PENANG IN 1867

It is necessary here to undertake an investigation into the name, character and rules of the Toh Peh Kong society of Penang in 1867, in order to demonstrate its differentiation from the Ghee Hin or Triad camp and its identity with the Han league or "Tokong".

In this task we are fortunate in having a copy of the Rules of the Toh Peh Kong society published in 1868 (*see* Appendix II) to guide us.[1]

The Name

From these rules and from the *Penang Riot Commission Report* of which they form part (*see* Chapter XVI *infra*), we know that the Toh Peh Kong society (大伯公) of Penang in 1867 was also known as the Kien Tek (建德): the Kin Hok (建福) and the Hok Keen (福建).

The following evidence proves that this society was something different from the Triad foundation.

(1) Vaughan, in his *Notes on the Chinese of Penang* (*JIA* 8) quoted above, writing in 1854 says:—

There are five Hoeys or Triad societies in Penang, *viz:*—

The Ghee Hin,
The Ho Seng,
The Hye San,
The Chinchin (or ring),
The To-pe-kong.

The first two approach nearer to the famous Triad society of China than the last three.

The last three have been formed in Penang, and differ but slightly from the others.

(2) The *Penang Riot Commission Report* 1867 (para. 14) states as one of its findings that:—

The Toh-pe-kong society or Hoey was instituted in Penang about twenty-four years ago (*i.e.* 1844) under one Khoo Ten Pang.

(3) In the preamble to the Rules (Appendix II) the following occurs:—

The Kian Tek society hereby begin and publish their rules as follows . . . .

On the twenty-first day of the fifteenth moon of the year Kah Sin being the thirty-fourth year of To Kong (30th Dec. 1844) this combination was begun at Jelutong in the coconut plantation of Yew Hua, in the interior of it, and there it was that the society was established.

Footnote.—(1) Three copies of the rules were obtained during the Penang enquiry and are fully authenticated. *See* page 47 of the "Evidence" section of the *Penang Riot Commission Report* 1867.

There is ample evidence in the *Penang Riot Commission Report* 1867 to show that the Toh Peh Kong society was identical with the Kian Tek society founded in Jelutong in 1844. It is true that variant spellings of Kian Tek appear in the evidence without prejudice, all referring to the Toh Peh Kong society, *viz*:—Hok Kian, Kian Hok, etc. The *Penang Riot Commission Report* makes this clear in para. 4 of the Report, *viz*:—

> The names of these ...... societies are the Ghee Hin and the Toh-pe-kong, otherwise called Kian Tek ....

(4) The origin of the name "Kian Tek" is suggested in the translated rules of the society (Appendix II), where, under "Secret signs of the Kian Tek society" the following appears:—

> Kian made property in Penang, Tek bound himself on oath in a flower garden.

to which a note is added by the Commissioners in reference to the "flower garden" as follows:—

> Flower in Chinese is Hua, the name of the man Yew Hua (*see* above) in whose plantation at Jelutong the society was formed.

This explanation of the name would only be for colour-protection and would not necessarily convey the real significance of the foundation to unearth which, we shall have to dig deeper.

(5) Before leaving the superficial or "business" name, Kian Tek, we may refer to a similar name (Chapter V above) applied, about the same epoch, to the Han league foundation in Singapore namely Keng Tek. Whether there is identity between the Keng Tek Kung Sz founded in Singapore in 1835 and the Kian Tek founded in Penang in 1844 we are at present unable to say. The present-day Kheng Tak society of Singapore is fully discussed in Chapter XXVII *infra*.

The Precise Origin of the Name Kian Tek

The following considerations may lead to a fuller understanding of the name and nature of the Toh Peh Kong foundation in Penang:—

(1) In the Kian Tek rules (Appendix II) there appears the following interesting clue:—

> The Seong and the Pek trees, which even in the summertime are green, are our people. The grass and the dried trees are not our brethren.

These names refer to the (松) ts'ung (Hokkien, Siong) a fir tree, and (柏) pak (Hokkien, Peh) a cypress tree, which in fact occur in Hung ritual (Schlegel p. 68, Ward and Stirling, Vol. I p. 81 (2), and elsewhere).

The verse in the Hung ritual runs:—

> When a withered tree meets Spring it sprouts again.
> When the eight sages crossed the sea, they put golden flowers in their hair.
> The Princess rides on horseback along the road.
> The fir (松) and cypress (柏) groves are our home.

This verse is reminiscent of the world-old fertility cult and tree-worship, (*see* Ward and Stirling, Vol. III p. 29 and Frazer *The Golden Bough*, abridged edition (1935), p. 109 ff.).

(2) Although references to these two trees occur in the Hung ritual, just as do frequent references to the "Peach Garden Trio" (*see* Chapter II), it is to the Han league and its nature-worship more than to the Hung league, that both the worship of the "Peach Garden Trio" and the worship of the "Fir tree and Cypress" seem properly to belong. The references to both in the Hung ritual are only incidental, whereas they constantly recur, even in such meagre documents as we have believedly belonging to the Han league, with which is wrapped up the Ko Lao Hui and other adjuncts of "Tokong" in Malaya.

(3) The names of the Cypress and Fir trees are also given as "pass words" in the rules and secret signs of the Kian Tek (Toh Peh Kong society).

The *Penang Riot Commission Report* 1867 page 81 has:—

> How to call out a reinforcement in time of great need.
> When you meet a member raise both your hands above your head and clap both palms together in order to produce a sound. If the reason of your coming be asked, you shall say thus:—
> Seong (Casuarina) and Pek (Ara tree) send us to procure a reinforcement.

Again, page 82:—

> How to recognise one by the features
> Pass the fingers of your right hand over your eyebrows, as if you are wiping them, such recognition will cause merriment. Tong (Summer), Cheong (green), Seong (Casuarina), and Pek (Ara tree) are our people. Pass your fore-finger between your lips, touching them at the same time.[1]

Footnote.—(1) The translation is not very good, but in the absence of the original, it must stand.

(4) If we now refer to Playfair's article on the Ko Lao society of China (page 29 *supra*), it will be seen that the "cypress and fir tree" motif is strongly represented therein, appearing twice in the document supplied by him.

This seems to provide further ground for believing that the Toh Peh Kong society of Penang had its origin in the Ko Lao Hui.

(5) Be that as it may, the clue of the cypress and fir-tree, translated as the local Malayan "ara (fig) tree" and "casuarina (fir) tree" in the *Penang Riot Commission Report* 1867, takes us to a list of the "nine branches of the Triad society in Singapore in 1879" given by Pickering in *J.S.B.R.A.S.* Vol. III (July 1879) in which is mentioned: "No. 5, The Siong-Peh-Koan", the Chinese characters of which are given in a footnote there as 松柏館. This seems to connect the Toh Peh Kong society of Penang in 1867, with the Siong Peh Koan of Singapore in 1879. In considering this point, we must bear in mind that Pickering in common with Schlegel had probably never made the acquaintance of the Han league or the Ko Lao Hui and that he assumed, as has been assumed ever since, that what properly belonged to the Han league, was merely "one of the local branches of the Triad society", the Hung.

(6) It is also worth noting that with the character for wood (木) removed from the two characters given by Pickering above (柏) and (松), there remain the two characters 白 Peh and 公 Kung, which may perhaps conceal, in their form and sound, but not in their meaning, the true origin and reason for adopting the common and harmless name Toh-peh-kong (大伯公) as the style which the Han league assumed in Penang from 1844 to 1868. This would only be in keeping with the common Chinese practice of playing on words.

(7) Or, again as suggested above, the name Toh-peh-kong may more correctly conceal the Malay word *To* (=*Dato*, a god or shrine), followed by the Chinese words 柏松, meaning the "Shrine of the Cypress and Fir tree".

(8) The Malay equivalent of the "cypress and fir tree" given in the *Rules of the Kian Tek society* 1867 (Appendix II) is of itself interesting. The translator, uncertain perhaps what rendering to give, or perhaps for some other reason, selected the names of two local trees to represent 松 Seong, fir tree, and 柏 Pek or Peh, cypress, namely "casuarina" for fir tree, and "ara" for cypress; and to make the meaning clear has added the romanised sound of the Chinese name which each is intended to represent, thus:—

> "Casuarina (Seong) and ara (Pek)", which sounds obviously stand for Pickering's:—

> 松 Siong (or Ts'ung), and

> 柏 Peh (or Pek).

The Malay synonyms chosen are very apt. Both the casuarina and the ara tree are evergreens and are thus appropriate to represent the tree worship or fertility cult, which we believe to lie behind the Toh Peh Kong observances.

(9) Furthermore, the Malay name for the casuarina tree is *Ru*, the etymology of which is not given by Wilkinson in his dictionary, ed. 1932, but the name suggests the Arabic word *Ruh* (روح), pronounced in Malay *Roh*, of which Wilkinson *op. cit.* gives the following meaning:—

> "The life-spirit: the quickening spirit of life":

Etymology apart, it may not have been a coincidence that the translator chose the *pokok Ru* (casuarina), to represent the esoteric qualities of the fir tree. Grant Allen *The Evolution of the idea of God*, p. 96 says that the Tahitians put young casuarina trees on graves. This no doubt is symbolic of the continuity of the life-spirit after physical death.

(10) Schlegel *op. cit.* Introduction p. xxxiv has:—

> The pine and cypress are, since the remotest antiquity the symbols of eternal life.

Their use by the Han league for a similar purpose would therefore be appropriate.

(11) Again, something more than accident is seen in the translator's selection of the ara tree to represent the cypress. The Malay name *ara* means a fig tree, and the fig tree is a universally sacred tree and a universal emblem of fertility.[1]

Grant Allen *op. cit.* Chapter VII (Sacred Trees) emphasises the place of evergreens in general and of the cypress-tree in particular, in the worship of the Greeks, Etruscans, Romans, Phœnicians, Arabs, Persians, Hindus, Chinese and American nations.

The Rules

The rules of the Kian Tek (Toh Peh Kong) society of Penang contain further material offering an explanation of the origin of the hitherto unexplained rivalry and hostility between Triad and "Tokong" in Malaya:—

(1) The Kian Tek rules and secret signs in general refer to little else than battle, murder and sudden death, *e.g.*

The secret signs include:—

Signs used in time of fighting and disputing.

How to rally or renew hostilities.

How to obtain aid when insulted.

How to call for reinforcements when hard pressed.

How to enter and withdraw from a fight.

How to escape after committing murder, etc.

(2) The rules include:—

Rule 8.—If outsiders commit any wrong to the members of our society, the society will enquire into it, and if the facts be proved then we will go forward and fight them with all our might, so that others will not laugh us to scorn.

These provisions emphasise that spirit of lawlessness and "natural depravity" recorded by Hutson (p. 33 *supra*) as typical of the Han league and are totally alien to the spirit of the Hung.

(3) Lastly we find in the Kian Tek rules, provision for *the hereditary principle* in the admission to membership. Thus:—

Rule 11.—If those who have joined our society on this day, go on another day and join any of the following three societies, *i.e.* The Ghee Hins, Ho Seng, or Hai San[2] and the fact be proved against those persons they will be immediately expelled from the society, and their children and grand-chidren will not be permitted to succeed them.

Rule 12.—The members of our society are to understand that their children will succeed them in their respective places. In the case of those having no issue, their brothers or the issue of their brothers will take their respective places. (Also Rule 20.)

These provisions besides being specifically directed against the rival Triad camp are in opposition to the purely elective principle in the membership of the Hung constitution.

(4) In the hereditary principle of the Toh Peh Kong membership, we see the idea of continuity and ancestor-worship,—the worship of man which permeates the Han ethic, in contradistinction to the freedom and individualism in the elective principle of the Hung league. (*See* page 41 *supra*).

(5) The three rules quoted point to three important principles in the character of the Toh Peh Kong society which differentiate it from the Hung league, and, we submit, definitely identify it with the Han, *viz:*—

    (*a*) It was a fighting society of unprincipled bullies who made "licentious liberty" in the words of Hutson "its chief ideal of life".

    (*b*) It was, by its constitution, the sworn enemy of the Triad foundation.

    (*c*) It observed the hereditary principle in its membership and administration, thus preserving that continuity implicit in ancestor-worship, and in the nature-school of the Han league.

These three features alone demarcate clearly the line of cleavage between the Han (Yin) and the Hung (Yang) foundations.

Footnote.—(1) *See* Frazer *Golden Bough* abridged ed. pages 136 and 580–81: Ward and Stirling *op. cit.* Vol. III page 29 ff. and 34 (Sacred Bo (*i.e.* Fig) Tree): also Skeat (*Malay Magic* page 68) and Schlegel *op. cit.* Introduction pages xxxiv–xxxv.

Footnote.—(2) *See* Note on the allegiance of the Hai San society page 113 below,

(6) The three following "findings" of the *Penang Riot Commission Report* 1867, help to confirm this view:—

> (a) Para. 12.—The Ghee Hins of Penang consist chiefly of the labouring and artisan class, and are principally men from Canton.
>
> (b) Para. 15.—The Toh-Peh-Kong society was founded by men from the Ho-kien province of China who have always been antagonistic to the Cantonese.
>
> (c) Para. 33.—The Toh-Peh-Kong was, from the day of its foundation, antagonistic to the Ghee Hin society.

In the face of this evidence we are forced to discard as a heresy the view that all Chinese secret societies in Malaya may be considered as one, and that all are branches of the Triad society.

THE SIGNIFICANCE OF THE SPLIT BETWEEN TRIAD AND "TOKONG" IN MALAYA 1867

From the foregoing considerations and from the researches of Hutson (Chapter II *supra*) it may be propounded that the Han league and its affiliations, represent in China to-day the age-old fertility worship, or deification of humanity, so fully treated of in its religious aspect in Frazer's *Golden Bough;* while on the other hand the Triad society or Hung league represents in its religious aspect, the belief in the principle of an omnipotent God-head and a revealed religion. The main framework of this proposition has already been set up in Chapter III *supra*. We return in Chapters XXXII and XXXIII to a consideration of the political aspects of these two schools of belief, and their manifestations in the secret society world of to-day.

In the Malayan sphere the anti-Roman Catholic riots of 1851 in Singapore are an indication of the hostility of "Tokong" to "revealed" religion; in French Indo-China the history of the same struggle between 1868 and 1926 has been recorded by Coulet *op. cit.*, while in China the long series given in Chapter II, of anti-missionary riots and rebellions during the second half of the last century, culminating in the Boxer outbreak of 1900, is evidence of the same spirit. The main conclusion we arrive at along this line of reasoning is, once again, that the Toh Peh Kong society of Penang, and therefore the whole range of "Tokong" societies in Malaya, had their origin in the Han league of China: as distinct from the Ghee Hin society and its affinities, which was and has remained the true representative in Malaya of the Triad society of China.

This conclusion provides an explanation for what must otherwise remain unexplained, namely the open rivalry and hostility which has characterised the history of the Ghee Hin (Triad) and Ghee Hok "Tokong" in Singapore, and the Ghee Hin (Triad) and Toh Peh Kong "Tokong" in Penang, during the nineteenth century.

The same conclusion applied to the conditions of the present-day, supplies in part an explanation of the rivalries of the modern Chinese secret societies, including the Sa Tiam Hui or Three Dot Brotherhood, and the White and Red Flag societies of the Malays. These aspects of our subject are treated of in Chapters VIII, IX, XIV, and XXIV, below.

Turning to the political (anti-dynastic) aspirations of the Han league (Ko Lao Hui) in China during the nineteenth century, we find it associated with the Dagger society rebellion in Amoy (1853), and with the Boxer rebellion (1900).

As regards the Dagger (Small Knife) society, there are no documents belonging to it available for examination, but the account of Hughes given in Chapter IV makes it plain that the "Small Knife" rebels of Amoy in 1853 claimed a *fiat* to restore the Han dynasty, as distinct from the claim of the Triad to restore the Ming. This tends to show that the Dagger society of Amoy was an offshoot of the Ko Lao Hui and not of the Triad society.

Similarly, the Boxer rebellion of 1900 was in origin as much an anti-Manchu movement at it was anti-foreigner and anti-foreign-mission. But throughout its struggle, it preserved its distinctive characteristics, which clearly differentiate it in its "religious" and political aims from the Triad, and identify it with "Tokong" and the Ko Lao Hui.

In Chapters XXVII and XXXIV *infra* we show the connection between the Han league and Japanese secret societies, which presents an explanation for the basis of the present-day Chinese "puppet" *régime* in north China and for the powerful anti-foreign sentiment among the Chinese which proceeds from it.

We suggest therein that the same agencies which split the Chinese in Malaya into two hostile camps in 1867, may be in operation to effect the same result in China proper to-day.

NAMES APPLIED TO THE HAN AND HUNG LEAGUES IN CHINA AND OVERSEAS UP TO 1867

We will conclude this chapter with a statement of the various names by which the Han and the Hung leagues appear to have been known from the earliest recorded times in China and overseas up to A.D. 1867.

· In Chapter II pages 16 and 17 we have given the story of the Yellow cap rebels (A.D. 184) and on page 18 have suggested that the Yellow caps represented the first insurrection of the Hung league and Buddhism against the decadence of the Han dynasty, whose protagonists "the Peach Garden trio" defeated the Yellow caps and themselves became the founders of the Han league, or Han restorationists, as recorded by Hutson page 22 *supra*.

In Chapter III pages 40–41 we have suggested that the story may be an allegory, but whether history or allegory it is from this epoch that the two stems of the Chinese secret society underworld become, for the first time, clearly distinguishable. From this epoch onwards historical records help to preserve the distinction. Thus Stanton *op. cit.* page 1 refers to the activities of the Yellow turban and Red eyebrow secret societies at the beginning of the Christian era, which staged rebellions in the north-eastern provinces of Hupeh, Honan and Shantung. We have noted how yellow or white have been the distinguishing colour of the Hung league and red that of the Han, the one the colour of "light", the other that of earth, no doubt the symbolic colours of the two segments of the Yin Yang. This would suggest that the "Yellow turbans" belonged to the Hung and the "Red eyebrows" to the Han league.

Next, Stanton at the same reference quotes the first mention of the White Lotus or White Lily society which rose in rebellion about A.D. 1300 and which he identifies with the Red turban rebels of A.D. 1350. The White Lotus is identified by Hutson (page 23 *supra*) as belonging to the Han league and other indications seem to confirm this view. This would tend to corroborate the identification by Stanton of the White Lotus with the Red turbans who doubtless also belonged to the Han league. By identifying the White Lotus with the Han league we might seem to contradict the colour theory of white for Hung and red for Han, but the White Lotus and the White Feather (below) are the only instances in which the theory does not apply and there may be another explanation for this divergence. The White Lotus was again in rebellion in A.D. 1621–1628 and 1761–1794.

Next, Stanton mentions the "Three Incense Sticks": the "White Feathers" and the "Eight Diagrams" (Pat Kwa), which rose in the year 1814 in the provinces of Honan, Shantung, Chihli (modern Hopei), Shensi and Kansu provinces and which he again identifies with the White Lotus.

Hutson (p. 23 *supra*) identifies the Eight diagrams with the Han league and territorially this rebellion belonged to the area of the Han league. .Otherwise there is little to help us to confirm Stanton's identification.

After the 1814 rebellion the White Lotus seems to disappear from history except as noted on page 34 *supra*, and its place seems to have been taken by the Ko Lao Hui in north China where the latter was responsible for the rebellions and anti-foreign outbreaks north of the Yangtze subsequent to the Treaty of Tientsin (1860).

Stanton *op. cit.* p. 8, writing in 1900 and referring to the Ko Lao Hui says :—

At the present time the provinces of Hunan, Hupeh, and Szechuan are reported to be the hot-bed of the society.

This view is supported by the subsequent researches of Hutson.

On p. 13 *supra* we give the names by which the "branches of the Triad society" were known in Hong Kong in 1900 as recorded by Stanton: and, from internal evidence, we hazard·the guess that both the Han and the Hung leagues were represented among these societies in Hong Kong and that probably of those mentioned, the Hok Ghee Hin, the Fuk On She and the Hoi Luk belonged to the Han and the Maan On belonged to the Hung league.

As regards Malaya, numerous names, most confusing to the reader, are scattered throughout the foregoing pages. These we have gathered together and attempted to place in their respective camps of Han and Hung, or Triad and "Tokong", in the schedule that follows.

NAMES APPLIED TO THE HAN LEAGUE AND HUNG LEAGUE IN CHINA AND TO THEIR PROTO-TYPES IN MALAYA FROM EARLIEST TIMES UP TO 1867

THE HAN LEAGUE (YIN 陰)

Serial number	Common Name	Characters	Period in use and place	Authority
	IN CHINA			
1.	The Red Turbans (Eyebrows, or Spears)	紅巾 or 眉 or 矛	Earliest times.	Doubtful.
2.	White Lotus Society	白蓮教	Earliest times to present-day in North China.	
3.	Han Liu	漢流		
4.	Ko Lao Hui or Society of the Elder Brethren	哥老會	A.D. 1000 to A.D. 1860.	Hutson and Stanton.
5.	The Arabic or Square Heavens	天方會		
6.	The Eight Diagrams	八卦		
7.	Big Sword Society	大刀會	A.D. 1860–1902.	
8.	Dagger Society	小刀會		
9.	Chien Tzu Hang or Tally Society	帳子行		
10.	Red Lantern Society	紅燈經		
11.	"Boxers" or United Fists	義和拳		
12.	Lamp Wick Society	燈花教		
13.	Pure Tea Society	清茶教		
14.	Loose profligates or mystical or Hypnotic Sect.	和尚流 or 教子	Present-day.	
15.	Robbers & Beggars	履嘮子		
16.	Robbers (Ku Fei)	膃匪		
	IN HONG KONG			
17.	Hok Ghee Hin (Hokkien Patriotic Rise Society)	福義興	Hong Kong 1845–1900.	Stanton.
18.	Fuk On She "Happiness & Peace"	福安社		
19.	Sea & Land Society (Hoi Luk)	海陸		
	IN MALAYA ("Tokong")			
20.	Hai San (Sea & Land)	海山	Penang & Larut. 1825–1875.	Newbold, Fullerton, Caunter, Pattullo, Vaughan.
21.	Wah Sang	華生	Penang 1825–1850. Singapore 1830–1890	Do.
22.	Ghee Hok	義福	Penang 1844–1867	All commentators. Vaughan 1868 Penang Riot Commission Report.
23.	Toh Peh Kong	大伯公 or 土地公	Penang 1844–1867	Do.
24.	Kien Tek or Kian Hok	建德 or 建福	Penang 1844–1867 Singapore 1867–1890	Song Ong Siang Vaughan.
25.	Hok Hin	福興	Penang 1844–1890	Vaughan.
26.	Chin Chin or Chin Chian	見貞 or 存貞 戰	Singapore 1850–1890	Pickering.
27.	Siong Peh Kong	松柏公所	Penang 1850 to present	Vaughan.
28.	Leong Sang Tong (Seh "Khoo" Kongsi)	誠山堂		

THE HUNG LEAGUE (YANG 陽)

Serial number	Common Name	Characters	Period in use and place	Authority
	IN CHINA			
1.	The Yellow caps (or turbans)	黃巾	A.D. 184.	Doubtful.
2.	Hung Ka	洪家	Earliest times to present-day.	Schlegel.
3.	Heaven and Earth League (Tin Tei Hui)	天地會		
4.	Three United League (Sam Hop Hui)	三合會		
	IN HONG KONG			
5.	Maan On (Myriad Peace)	萬安	Hong Kong 1845–1900	Stanton.
	IN MALAYA (Triad)			
6.	Ghee Hin or Nghee Hung	義興 or 義兄	Universally in Malaya and the South Seas 1800 to present-day.	All commentators.
7.	Ho Seng	和勝	Penang 1825 to 1865.	Fullerton, Caunter, Pattullo, Vaughan.
8.	Teantay (sic) (i.e. Tin Tei Hui)	天地	Singapore 1825 to 1850.	Read.

NOTE ON THE ALLEGIANCE OF THE HAI SAN SOCIETY.

One name in the foregoing list (No. 20) the Hai San society calls for some comment. It was distinct from, but seemingly not actively hostile to, the Ghee Hin from the time of the earliest overseas records. In Malaya it became hostile thereto between the years 1845–1860. If, as we suppose, the Hai San was in origin a foundation of the Han league, this change was inevitable so soon as a sufficient divergence of interest between the Punteis and the Hakkas in the fast growing economy of Malaya made itself felt. So long as the Chinese as a whole were concerned to preserve their identity and to prevent themselves from being swamped by the Indian immigrants, this common interest would override faction. As soon as the Chinese were established at the head of Malayan commerce, the factional and secret society cleavage made itself apparent in the scramble for underground power. The change in the composition of the Hai San from "Puntei" to Hakka membership, sharpened this antagonism for reasons given in Chapter IV.

The foregoing schedule covers roughly those names to which the reader has been introduced up to this point. A large number of other names will come to notice in subsequent chapters and these will be scheduled at intervals in the same way, so as to reduce confusion in the readers' mind.

Most of these new names will be placed without difficulty in one camp or the other.

From about this epoch 1870, the Han league in Malaya (or "Tokong") seems to have adopted for itself the generic name of Sa Tiam Hui or Three Dot Brotherhood which we have already met in Chapter IV p. 54–55, wherein it has been suggested by a Chinese source to be identical with the "Doctrine of God" of the Taiping rebellion, which in turn we have suggested was identical with the White Lotus and thence with the Han league. Some authorities including those in Malaya, have confused the Sa Tiam or Three Dot with the Hung league and regard the name Sa Tiam as a generic name for the Triad society in Malaya in the same manner as the name Ghee Hin is so used. To emphasise the error of this view and to throw into sharp contrast the wide difference between the ritual of Triad and that of the Sa Tiam or "Tokong", we proceed to give in the following chapters a sketch of the Triad ritual, followed in Chapters VIII and IX with an examination of the Sa Tiam Hui and a sketch of its ritual.

In Chapter XXIX we present a comparative table of these analogies and differences in combination with similar rituals among Malays.

This ends our survey of the actual history of Chinese secret societies in Malaya up to 1867. We resume the historical narrative in Chapter XVI below.

CHAPTER VII

SKETCH OF THE RITUAL OF THE TRIAD SOCIETY

TEXT OF THE TRIAD RITUAL IN ENGLISH

Like all secret and persecuted sects the tradition and ritual of the Hung league is oral.

There is extant no authoritative and comprehensive printed Chinese work on the society and its ritual. Such Triad rituals as exist are in manuscript, copied or written down from memory by lodge officials for their own convenience and contain therefore, an infinite variety of alternative readings.

It is a tribute to the vitality of the Hung league that such Chinese manuscript texts as have been found by Colonial authorities, bear in the main a close resemblance to each other and preserve the purity and meaning of the ritual in a remarkably full degree.

The various texts of the Triad ritual, or parts thereof, printed with English translation and consulted for purposes of this work are as follows:—

1. Milne Text (1821) in *Transactions of the Royal Asiatic Society.* Vol. I Part II page 240 (1825).
2. Tomlin Text (1840) in Newbold's article, *J.R.A.S.* 1840, pages 121–129; 137–142; 146–150.
3. Hoffmann Text (1849) in *The Chinese Repository* Vol. XVIII June 1849, pages 281–295.
4. Schlegel Text (1866) *The Hung League* (Batavia 1866).
5. Penang Riot Commission Report Text (1868) *Proceedings of the Legislative Council of the Straits Settlements.* Vol. 1867–1869.
6. Pickering Text (1878) incomplete. *J.S.B.R.A.S.* No. 1 (1878) and No. 3 (1879)
7. Stanton Text (1900) *The Triad Society,* (Hong Kong 1900).
8. Ward and Stirling Text (1925) *The Hung Society* (London 1925).

With the exception of Nos. 1, 3, and 7, these texts are translations from copies of the ritual obtained overseas, *i.e.* in either Java, Sumatra or Malaya.

Nos. 1 and 3 are from original sources in China but are incomplete and were made before the publication of Schlegel (No. 4).

As regards the character and quality of the above texts:—

No. 1 is the pioneer translation of parts of the ritual and was used by Schlegel.

No. 2 is a straight translation by the Rev. J. Tomlin of Malacca from a single Chinese original. It is incomplete but interesting and contains a long translation from the *History of the Three Kingdoms* (A.D. 220–277) which Tomlin suggests refers to the origin of the Triad society, a point dealt with on page 19 *supra.*

No. 3 authorship is not given but it is recorded by other authorities as being by Dr. Hoffman. It contains a translation of the *Thirty-six Oaths.*

No. 4 this is the earliest classic translation giving both English and Chinese, and was laboriously built up by Schlegel by comparison with a large number of Chinese originals.

No. 5 is a straightforward translation, evidently by a Chinese clerk, of a single copy of the ritual found in Penang during the war of 1867. From internal evidence this copy appears to have belonged to the Hok Chew section of the Penang Hokkien branch of the Ghee Hin (Triad) society. The translator had a copy of Schlegel to help him.

No. 6 is built up from a number of originals found in Singapore and elsewhere in Malaya and borrowed from the lodges themselves, which were then recognised by Government. It gives the ritual of the Singapore Hokkien branch of the Ghee Hin (Triad) society. It is unfortunate that it is incomplete.

No. 7 (Stanton) is built up from a number of rituals obtained in Hong Kong, many of which show a connection with Malaya.

No. 8 (Ward and Stirling) is the most recent, and the most polished version so far published, built up from a number of original rituals and from the foregoing texts which served as a guide.

ESTIMATE OF OUR PRESENT KNOWLEDGE BY MONSIEUR PAUL PELLIOT

One of the world's leading authorities on this subject M. Paul Pelliot, editor of *T'oung Pao* (通報), the most important European journal dealing with Chinese subjects, published the following *resumé* of our present knowledge on this subject, when reviewing Ward and Stirling's work *The Hung Society* (3 Vols. pub. 1925). This important article appeared in *T'oung Pao* Vol. XXV in 1928 pages 444–448 :—

Il y a déjà toute une littérature sur la Triade (三 合 會) ou "Hung League" (洪 會) ou "Société du Ciel et de la Terre" (天 地 會) et sur les autres organisations secrètes chinoises; on en trouvera l'enumération dans la *Bibliotheca Sinica*, 1894–1900 et 3989; les principaux travaux sont ceux de Schlegel, de Giles et de Stanton. Comme de juste, c'est dans les régions où des Chinois vivent sous le contrôle d'Européens, en particulier aux Indes néerlandaises et dans les Etats malais, qu'il a été possible d'obtenir les renseignements les plus précis. Un Européen réussit même à se faire admettre comme membre de la Hung league avant que cette association eût été déclarée illégale à Singapour en 1890; c'était W. A. Pickering, "protecteur" des Chinois à Singapour, et qui a donné quelques informations sur les sociétés secrètes chinoises dans le *Journ. of the Straits Br. of the R.A.S.* de 1878 et 1879. Il a laissé en outre des notes abondantes que conserve le Protectorat des Chinois. M. Stirling, qui fait partie du Protectorat des Chinois depuis 1909, a connu ces notes[1] et a en outre eu l'occasion d'intervenir assez souvent contre les réunions, aujourd'hui prohibées, de la Hung league. Dans son livre *Freemasonry and the Ancient Gods*, M. Ward demandait, des informations supplémentaires sur les sociétés secrètes chinoises. M. Stirling, maçon lui-même, s'offrit à les lui fournir. Le present ouvrage est né de cette collaboration.

Le premier volume est particulièrement intéressant; les traductions de documents fournies par M. Stirling l'occupent en majeure partie, et elles sont accompagnées de planches qui reproduisent beaucoup de pièces et d'insignes authentiques de la Hung league. Les vol. II et III, dus à M. Ward, sont des plus discursifs, aussi bien comme texte que comme illustration; ce qui s'y rapporte directement à la Chine—histoire du bouddhisme, du taoïsme, renseignements sur la Secte du Lotus blanc, etc.—est entaché des erreurs traditionnelles, plus quelques autres.

Même après cette grosse publication, magnifiquement éditée, nous devons bien constater que nous ignorons à peu près tout de l'histoire de la Triade. M. Stirling reproche à l'ouvrage de Schlegel, paru en 1866, d'être souvent inexact parce que Schlegel ne connaissait pas le jargon spécial de l'association; il n'a pas tort, mais on aimerait à être sûr que ses propres versions sont fidèles. En tout cas, au t. I, 64–70, M. Stirling donne la traduction des *36 serments*; une planche insérée après la page 66 reproduit ce qui devrait être le texte des *serments 24–29*; il n'y a aucun rapport entre ce texte chinois et la traduction.

A côté du rituel, l'histoire même de la Triade pique notre curiosité. Non pas qu'à la suite de Schlegel on doive admettre un lien direct entre la Triade chinoise et la franc-maçonnerie occidentale. Mais, quand une société secrète a couvert de ses loges toute la Chine du Sud, l'Indochine, l'Insulinde, et a essaimé jusque'en Inde, en Australie et en Californie, on aimerait à savoir où et comment elle est née et quelles ont été les étapes de son progrès. Mais comme sources historiques extérieures à la secte, nous en sommes toujours réduits à l'insurrection de Lin Chouang-wen (林 爽 文) à Formose en 1786–1788. Lin Chouang-wen était un des chefs de la Société du Ciel et de la Terre (cf. aussi De Groot, *Sectarianism*, 340–347; Haenisch, dans *Ostasiat. Zeitschr.*, IX, 182) Tout le reste, nous le devons aux récits que la Société elle-même transmet à ses nouveaux membres, et ici nous entrons de plain-pied dans la légende. Les textes traduits par M. Stirling, tout comme ceux résumés par Stanton, mettent à l'origine de la Triade l'intervention de moines guerriers du (少 林 寺) Chao-lin-sseu sous K'ang-hi, en 1674 selon certains récits; et on nous dit que le Chao-lin-sseu était dans la préfecture de Fou-tcheou au Foukien (I, 80). Mais si les moines guerriers du Chao-lin-sseu sont célèbres dans la tradition chinoise, leur monastère était au Ho-nan, et il est évident que le récit de leur intervention sous K'ang-hi est imité de la légende plus ancienne des 13 moines guerriers du Chao-lin-sseu du Ho-nan qui auraient assisté l'empereur T'ai-tsong des T'ang dans sa lutte contre (王 世 充) Wang Che-tch'ong en 621. D'autres éléments du récit sont empruntés au roman légendaire brodé sur les voyages de Hiuan-tsang, le (西 游 記) *Si yeou ki*.[2] Mais sans caractères chinois, il est impossible de poursuivre dans le détail l'étude des éléments très variés qui se sont amalgamés dans ce récit traditionnel, et où l'étude de la mythologie populaire chinoise trouverait beaucoup à glaner.

L'ouvrage de MM. Ward et Stirling est à peu près muet sur les rapports mutuels des diverses sociétés secrètes. Un texte de 1813 (De Groot *Sectarianism*, 470) mentionne au Kiang-si le (添 弟 會) T'ien-ti-houei qui n'est probablement qu'une autre orthographe de (天 地 會) T'ien-ti-houei, "Société du Ciel et de la Terre"; un autre texte de 1814, mentionne le même (添 弟 會) T'ien-ti-houei au Kouang-si, et signale au Kouang-tong l'activité du (三 合 會) San-ho-houei (*ibid.*, mais avec une fausse lecture "San hoh-hwui"); le San-ho-houei est la "Triade"; aucun des textes historiques de De Groot ne nomme la (洪) Hung league. Il n'y a pas de doute de l'identité actuelle du T'ien-ti-houei et de la Hung league; et il est très probable qu'on a raison de les identifier encore le San-ho-houei, encore que ces divers noms aient pu couvrir à l'origine des groupements analogues, mais autonomes, et qui existaient dans des régions différentes. Il semblerait que le centre ancien du T'ien-ti-houei eût été le Foukien et celui du San-ho-houei le Kouang-tong. D'après Dyer Ball *Things Chinese*, 549 la Triade ou San-ho-houei, créée au Foukien et au Kouang-tong pour résister à la conquête mandchoue, était en pleine dégénérescence au milieu du XIXᵉ siècle quand l'un de ses membres, (洪 秀 全) Hong Sieou-ts'iuan, la transforma et la galvanisa en greffant sur elle un pseudo-christianisme, qui fut la doctrine de la grande insurrection des T'aip'ing; l'*Encyclopaedia Sinica*, s.v. Triad society, nie au contraire que Hong Sieou-ts'iuan ait rien eu à voir avec la

Footnote.—(1) On est un peu étonné que la bibliographie à la fin du Vol. III passe entièrement sous silence les articles publiés par Pickering. Il n'est pas non plus fait mention de la traduction française de l'ouvrage de Schlegel, parue autographiée à Saigon (la *Bibl. Sinica* l'ignore également).

Footnote.—(2) Cf. Vol. I page 100, ou la note ne distingue pas entre les véritables *Mémoires de Hiuan tsang* ou (西 域 記) si yu ki, et le roman beaucoup plus tardif auquel ses voyages ont servi de cadre et qui est intitulé (西 遊 記) Si yeow ki. Dans le texte. "a priest of T'ang" est naturellement le (唐 僧) T'ang-seng du roman, c'est-à-dire Hiuan-tsang.

Triade: Si nous consultons les maigres informations que le "Ts'eu yuan"[1] (辭 源) fournit sur les sociétés secrètes, nous voyons qu'il ignore le nom de la Hung league et du T'ien-ti-houei (sous ses deux orthographes) ; sous San-ho-houei, il rappelle la fondation traditionnelle de la secte en 1674 par des moines du Chao-lin-sseu (mais sans faire mention du Fou-kien) et l'insurrection de Lin Chouang-wen à Formose; sous (上 帝 敎) Chang-ti-kiao, "Religion du Seigneur d'en haut" (terme d'inspiration protestante ici), il est dit que cette doctrine fut fondée au Kouang-tong par (朱 九 濤) Tchou Kieou-t'ao puis développée pour des fins politiques par Hong Sieou-ts'iuan, le "frère cadet de Jésus", et que, contrairement à ce que certains contemporains ont pensé, elle n'a rien de commun avec le San-ho-houei; mais sous (三 點 會) San-tien-houei, ou Société des Trois points, il est spécifié que c'est là une branche du Chang-ti-kiao et que Hong Sieou-ts'iuan en fut l'un des chefs; ces diverses données ne sont conciliables qu'en admettant que le San-tien-houei est à séparer absolument du San-ho-houei. Tout cela demeure très obscur. Pour qu'on pût s'orienter un peu, il faudrait reprendre l'ensemble des textes, tâcher de voir à quel moment et en quel lieu les diverses dénominations se rencontrent et en particulier à quelle date le nom de la Hung league apparait pour la première fois. Le livre de MM. Ward et Stirling, qui n'est pas sans importance par ce qu'il contient, vaut peut-etre surtout en nous faisant mieux sentir que, sur le sujet qu'il traite, nous ne savons encore à peu près rien.

In this article M. Pelliot records the following important opinions :—

    (1) Even after the publication of Ward and Stirling we must admit that we are still almost entirely ignorant of the history of the Triad society...... The chief value of Ward and Stirling's work is to make us feel more clearly than before, that we still know almost nothing of the subject of which it treats.

    (2) Apart from the insurrection of the Triad society in Formosa A.D. 1786–1788, which is history, all the rest of the Triad traditional story rests upon the legends of the society itself and is without historical or other confirmation.

    (3) The traditional foundation of the society (Political period) in A.D. 1674 was laid by the militant monks of the Shaolin Monastery (see page 9 supra) which is placed in the Foochow prefecture of the Fukien province. But if these monks of Shaolin are the same as those who are renowned in Chinese tradition, then their monastery was in the province of Honan and not in Fukien. If this assumption is correct, the story of their adventure in A.D. 1674 would be a borrowed imitation of the much older legend of the thirteen militant monks of the Shaolin monastery in Honan who assisted the emperor T'ai Tsung (太 宗) of the T'ang dynasty in A.D. 621.

    (4) The Shaolin monastery of Honan in A.D. 621 was associated with the "boxer" arts.[2]

    (5) The Three Dot society was associated with the Taiping rebellion A.D. 1850, and is absolutely distinct from the Triad society.

The above are important conclusions and have been already discussed in this work with the exception of (3) and (4) which refer to a connection between the "Boxer" arts and the monks of a Shaolin monastery in Honan in A.D. 621, upon which subject we here insert a note.

THE SHAOLIN (少林) MONASTERY IN HONAN PROVINCE

    M. Pelliot in a footnote to his article above has the following :—

        For further information about the Shaolin monastery of Honan, see T'oung Pao year 1923 pp. 245–264, particularly p. 253: also year 1927 p. 179. For a description of the boxer arts of Shaolin see the texts collected in the Yat Chi Lau (日 知 錄) of Kou Yen Wou and which are completed in the Kai Yu Ts'ong K'ao (陔 餘 叢 考) of Chao Yi (趙 翼) 41, pp. 14–15.

        Plate No. 433 in Chavannes' Mission Archeologique reproduces some mural paintings illustrating the warlike exercises of the monks of the Shaolin monastery of Honan.

We have not investigated these references because they have not become available to us, but we can testify to the "earlier tradition" of the Shaolin monastery being alive among the Chinese of the Malay Peninsula to-day.

Between thirty and forty years ago there died in Singapore a well-known Chinese named Leng Tsai Yuk (靚 仔 玉) or "Handsome Jade" who was reputed to possess supernatural powers, which he was popularly believed to have learnt "from the monks of the Shaolin monastery". This no doubt meant no more than that he was practised in the "boxer" arts", of which Hutson in Chapter II supra has given us an account.

The fact that there is in Honan province to this day a Shaolin monastery with an authentic history going back a thousand years earlier than the date of the Triad traditional story and associated with the magic and mysticism of the Han league, suggests once again that the Han is anterior to the Hung and that the ritual of the re-constituted

---

Footnote.—(1) We have given the extracts from the Chinese encyclopædia called Chi Yuen 辭 源 or "The sources of speech" here referred to, in Chapter IV supra under "Genesis of the Taiping rebellion".

Footnote.—(2) The references to this subject are given by M. Pelliot (see below) but the material has not been available to us for purposes of the present work.

Hung league A.D. 1674 may have borrowed the story of the genuine monastery in order to add political point to its new anti-dynastic crusade. Without investigating the subject further, we may even suggest that the boxer arts of the Han league may have descended from a Han Liu school of magic founded in a monastery in Honan by the followers of the "Peach Garden trio", who defeated the Yellow Cap rebels in that part of China in A.D. 184 and who belonged by inference to what became the Han league. Honan is not a traditional Triad province, but lies within the territory of the Han league. There is no reason why the original Shaolin monastery might not be that situated in the Honan province and have been dedicated to the practice of mysticism, nor why its name and the exploits of its monks in A.D. 621 should not have been borrowed for the purpose of reconstituting the Hung league in its political mission in A.D. 1674.

This would provide but a second common link (the first being the Peach Garden Trio) between the origin of the Han and the Hung leagues in the Yellow cap rebellion of A.D. 184.

M. Pelliot suggests that, in order to get the hang of this obscure subject, it would be necessary to collect and study together all the available texts and to attempt to see at what moment and where the various societies met and particularly the date on which the name "Hung league" first appears as applied to the Triad.

We have not the facilities for undertaking such a task, which would have to include a study of Han league as well as Hung league texts, the former at present non-existent.

There is still a deal of matter in the Triad ritual which remains obscure and defective and awaits the publication of a new and authoritative text complete with the Chinese character and commentary, and embodying the labours of the earlier workers in this field with the results of later researches.

It is not to be supposed that the last few decades have seen the last of the Han and the Hung organisations, whose vitality has carried them through eighteen hundred years.

SKETCH OF THE TRIAD RITUAL

We must now give a brief account of the salient features of the Triad ritual.

The Hung league is governed in theory by the Grand Masters of the five Principal lodges in China as given in Chapter I.

The officials of each lodge whether in China Proper, or abroad are:—

1. The President 大哥 (Tai Ko) Elder Brother.
2. Two Vice-Presidents 二哥 (Yi Ko) Second and 三哥 (Sam Ko) Third Brother.

   The Vice-President is also known as the "Incense Master" 香主 (Heung Chu).

   These are the Grand lodge officials, in addition to whom every branch lodge has the following:—

3. One Master 先生 (Sin Shang) Teacher.
4. One Instructor 白扇 (Pak Shin) White Fan.
5. Two Introducers 先鋒 (Sin Fung) Vanguard.
6. One Executioner 紅棍 (Hung Kwan) Red Staff.
7. Ten Councillors 議事 (Yi Sz) Councillor.
8. One Treasurer 櫃匙 (Kwai Shi) Key of the Safe.
9. One Receiver 收櫃 (Sau Kwai) Receiver of the Safe.
10. One Assistant Receiver 代收櫃 (Toi Sau Kwai) Assistant Receiver.
11. Agents, detectives 草鞋 (T'so Hai) Grass Shoes.
12. Messengers 鐵板 (T'it Pan) Iron Planks.
13. Recruiters 帶馬 (Tai Ma) Horse Leaders.

Frederick Boyle in his article in *Harper's Magazine* of September 1891 says:—

> It appears to be certain that there is no supreme Grand Master of the T'ien-Ti, but it has a central government.
>
> There are five Grand lodges in Fuk-kien, Kwang-tung, Yun-nan, Hunan, and Che-Kiang to one of which all branches are subordinate. The Masters of these, in some sort of council, direct the society in all parts of the world such is the theory, at least. Every local lodge has its President, two Vice Presidents, a Master, two Introducers, a Cashier, and thirteen Councillors, of whom eight form a "quorum".

Stanton *op. cit.* page 40 has:—

> The nearest approach to a Grand lodge in modern times was probably that of the Kwang, Huei, Shao, Ghee Hin, Tai Kung Sz (廣惠肇義興大公司) in Singapore before the split that occurred in it shortly after the death of the Great Brother or Grandmaster Ho Yim[1] about 1870.

Footnote.—(1) Not identified.

Before his death Cantonese Hokkiens and Teochews held meetings in the same lodge-room on different nights and all looked to him as their chief. After his death discord broke out amongst the members and splits occurred. This led to great bitterness of feeling and fights between the various sections of the society.

At the present time (1900) it appears by the Certificates of Membership and Seals, that the Kwangtung-Kwangsi is the principal division, but in their lodges they use the flags and devices of the other Sections and burn incense to their respective Patriarchs; as well as to their own.

Ward and Stirling Vol. I page 13 mentions that the Ghee Hin society in Singapore, purchased in 1872 house No. 4 China Street, to be the Mother Temple of the Hung league in Malaya. This temple or lodge room ceased to exist in 1890 upon the suppression by Government of the Triad society in Malaya.

There is a considerable difference of opinion amongst the published authorities about the titles and functions of lodge officials in Malaya.

For instance, neither Schlegel nor Pickering make any mention whatsoever, of the "White Fan" or, Instructor (白扇) and make the Master (先生) perform the functions of the White Fan.

Stanton says that "White Fan" is given in some texts as another name for the Master who is also called the Instructor (先生).

Ward and Stirling give the ritual verbatim for two separate officials viz:—

    (1) Master (先生).

    (2) Instructor or White Fan (白扇).[1]

The titles, functions and relevent importance of the Triad lodge officials, are closely connected with the subject of our enquiry, as will be seen when we come to discuss the officials of Malay secret societies (Chapter XXIX).

It is probable that the variations in the titles of lodge officials and in the ritual, are due to an unconscious confusion in the minds of some, between a Hung, or Triad lodge and a Han, or Three Dot Brotherhood lodge.

The following, for purposes of later comparison, are the main features of the ritual of initiation into the Triad (Ghee Hin) society, and follow the sequence of Ward and Stirling Vol. I page 23, et seq., except where otherwise noted.

(A) PREPARATION OF THE CANDIDATE FOR INITIATION

    1. He must put on new or at least freshly washed white cotton coat and trousers.

    2. His right arm, shoulder and breast are made bare.

    3. The left leg of the trousers are rolled up above the knee.

    4. His shoes are replaced by a pair of grass sandals.

    5. A strip of red cloth is tied around his head.

(B) PREPARATION OF THE OFFICIALS FOR THE CEREMONY

    1. The Master (先生) is dressed in white.

    2. The Vanguard (先鋒) and other principal officials are also in white the Vanguard in addition has a strip of red cloth round his head.

(C) OPENING THE LODGE

The Master then recites the "Traditional History" (see Chapter I) outside the entrance to the Temple proper, and concludes by giving the candidates the first initial signs and passwords.

The Master then enters the Temple or Lodge proper and consecrates it and each of the sacred articles used in the ceremony viz:—Flags of the five ancestors, banner of the lodge: seven starred banner (of the constellation of the Great Bear) : the banner of the victorious brotherhood: the magic sword: the sacred writing materials: the magic mirror: the Hung lamp: the foot-rule, etc., each with the appropriate verse.

He then lights the various lamps on the altar: pours out tea and wine in libation: distributes the various flags to the different office-bearers of the lodge who take up their stations.

The Red Staff and the Vanguard are posted outside the East gate.

The lodge is then opened with the symbolic slaughtering of the "white horse and the black ox".

These preliminary proceedings occupy about one hour.

(D) DESCRIPTION OF THE TEMPLE

The Temple is an imaginary walled city through which a symbolic journey is taken during the process of initiation.

Certain ceremonies take place outside the city walls (noted later) and the candidates are then admitted by the East gate and journey towards the West.

Footnote.—(1) See Pickering J.S.B.R.A.S. No. 3 July, 1879, page 2. Schlegel op. cit. page 47. Stanton op. cit. page 42, and Ward and Stirling op. cit. Vol. I page 15.

Inside the "city walls" *i.e.*, within the cleared space prepared for the initiation, there are three doorways through which the candidate must pass, each usually represented by wooden uprights with a piece of red paper stretched across.

The first doorway is the Hung door, Hung mun (洪門) at which certain ceremonies take place.

The second doorway leads to the "Hall of Loyalty and Justice".

The third doorway leads to the "City of Willows", within which is the "Red Flower Pavilion", within which **again** is the altar with sacred emblems, where the Oath of the Brotherhood is taken.

The following rough plan showing the main features will assist the reader to follow the description of the ceremony given below:—

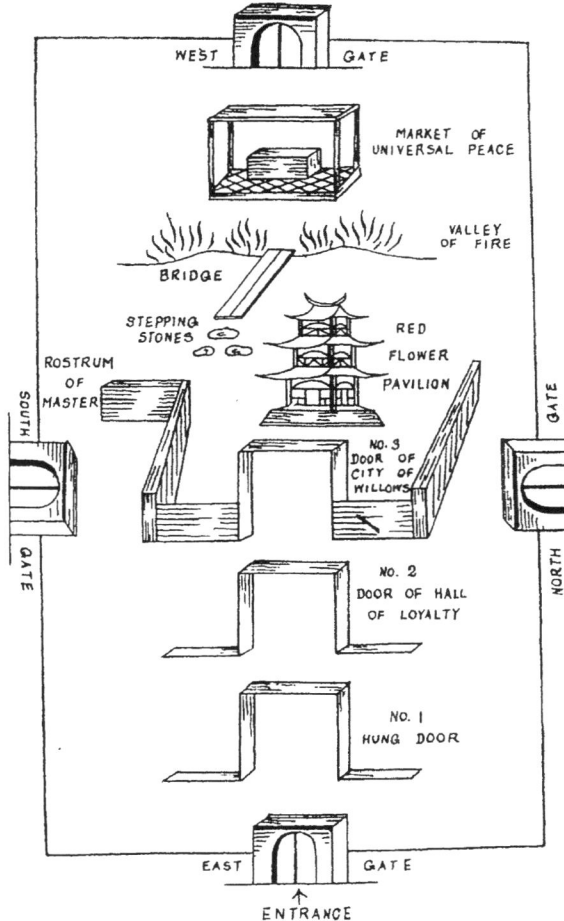

This plan of a Hung lodge may be compared with that of a Han (Three Dot Brotherhood) lodge given in Chapter IX *infra*.

We have now to examine the sequence of the Triad ritual of initiation more closely.

THE CEREMONY OF INITIATION—FIRST PART

The initiation ceremony proper begins by the candidates being formed up in pairs in charge of the Vanguard, outside the East gate of the imaginary city. The other officers of the lodge being in their places as above (C), the following theatricals take place:—

An Alarum is sounded, which the Red Staff (Executioner) reports to the Master, who orders one of the Generals to go out and see what it is. The General returns with the Vanguard who prostrates himself before the Master and reports his arrival with new recruits for the Hung league.

After catechising the Vanguard, during which he says "Whence come you" and the Vanguard replies on behalf of the candidates "From the East", the Master gives the Vanguard the magic sword from the altar and a Warrant Flag. The Vanguard returns with these to the waiting candidates and bids them prepare to enter the East gateway of the "city".

Meanwhile the brethren immediately within the gateway form an "Arch of Swords", those on one side swords of steel, those on the other side swords of brass. The candidates are then bidden to enter with the left foot first and immediately pass under the arch of swords and are led towards the first of the three doors or Hung Mun (洪門).

Here the Vanguard places the magic sword on the ground between the pillars of the Hung door and bids each candidate to kneel upon it, while the two "Generals" guarding the door cross their swords above his head, thus forming the "Triangle of Steel", framing the candidate.

This triangle represents Heaven, Earth and Man and is one of the most solemn emblems of the Hung league, whence the league derives its alternative name of Triad society and also its familiar seal[1] viz:—

While kneeling, each candidate is given three lighted incense sticks ("joss sticks") and is ordered to hold them with the lighted ends pointing downwards to Mother Earth.

The candidates then give their names and particulars to the Master and repeat after him a solemn affirmation, which includes a promise to obey the Thirty-six Oaths, etc., failing which "may my life be extinguished even as I now extinguish this incense stick".

Each candidate then plunges his lighted "joss" sticks into a bowl of earth so that they are extinguished.

The master then asks:—

"What are these swords (held by the Generals guarding the doors) that are held over you used for"?

And the Vanguard replies for the candidates:—

"To behead traitors".

Master—"Which are the harder, these swords or your necks"?

Vanguard—(for candidates) "As our hearts are truly loyal and sincere, our necks are harder than your swords".

The General of the main body then cries in a loud voice "Pass On".

This ceremony is repeated at the next two doors and in some rituals 12 of the 36 laws are sworn at each door.

After passing the third door, the City of Willows is reached, wherein stands "The Red Flower Pavilion" in which is the Altar upon which stands the precious white censer.

After symbolic washing of the face in a bowl with water taken from the "Three Rivers", the candidates are led before the altar in the Red Flower Pavilion where the Thirty-six Oaths are administered in the following way[2]:—

CEREMONY OF INITIATION—SECOND PART

The administration of the Thirty-six Oaths:—

(1) The Master pointing to the censer on the altar says:—

"What is the weight of the censer"?
The Vanguard (for the candidates) replies
"Five Katties thirteen Tahils".

Footnote.—(1) See Ward and Stirling Vol. I page 56 Note 4.

Footnote.—(2) The detail of this ceremony is important for comparative purposes later with that of:—(i) The Toh Peh Kong (Chapter V). (ii) The Sa Tiam Hui ritual (Chapter IX). (iii) The White and Red Flag societies ritual (Chapter XXIX).

Signifying (Ward and Stirling Vol. I page 58, Note 5) :—

(a) The five original lodges and the thirteen provinces of China proper (excluding Manchuria).

(b) (Mystically) the five senses of man or his sub-divisions and the twelve signs of the Zodiac with the sun which passes through them and the effect of these on man.

Master, "What characters are on the bottom of the Censer"?

Vanguard, "Four—Overthrow Ts'ing and restore Ming".

(2) Each candidate is now given nine blades of grass and three sticks of incense ("joss sticks") which, with ritual, are placed in the censer. At the same time the Master places a sheet of yellow paper, with the thirty-six oaths written thereon, on the altar near the censer. (This paper is known as the "Yellow Quilt").

Two pieces of dry wood are lighted.

A pair of red candles are lighted.

Three cups of wine are filled from a jug.

(3) The Assembly now kneels down and the Vanguard addresses a long prayer to "Pwan Ku" who according to the Taoists first separated Heaven and Earth out of Chaos.

(4) After the prayer the assembly rises and makes the eight salutations, viz:—

To Heaven as our father;
To Earth as our mother;
To the Sun as our brother;
To the Moon as our sister-in-law;
To the five Founders;
To Wan Yun Lung;
To all the brethren;
To the ancient Glory of the Order.

THE TRIAD DISCIPLINARY CODE

The scroll containing the thirty-six oaths is unrolled and all kneeling, the master reads them out.

A few, condensed from the version of Ward and Stirling Vol. I page 64 ff. are given below for comparative purposes, viz:—

Having entered the Hung gate:—

(1) The first duty of a brother is to honour his parents.

(2) A member must not gamble with a brother separately but only in a gambling house or in company.

(3) A member must not because he is strong, impose on the weak or despise the small, nor must he quarrel with a brother on account of his wife.

(4) A member must not break the laws of the country. If he does so and is arrested he must sustain his cause alone. The society will in no way be responsible for his actions and he must avoid bringing disrepute upon the brotherhood.

(5) A member must not thoughtlessly break a law, nor may he do harm to a brother, nor be covetous nor a receiver of bribes.

(6) A member must not seduce the wife of a brother.

* * *

(12) When the members of the Great Family are at variance with a member's own brother, he shall not help his own brother to defeat the members of the Hung family.

* * *

(14) A brother must not secretly steal another brother's property.

(15) If on the occasion of a birthday or funeral, a brother's parents are in need of money for the celebrations, a brother must inform the society and ask all the brethren to assist him.

* * *

(17) If a brother die and leave behind him a widow who desires to marry again, a brother may not take her as his wife. Thus the brethren must be very careful in making enquiries before they marry.

* * *

(24) A brother must not misuse his power as a member of the Hung family, or with four or five others start a street fight, cause a riot or impose on the weak.

(25) If a brother cheats another brother the matter must be reported to the society and left for it to judge.

* * *

(28) A brother must not join with three or four others and go here and there making mischief. From the beginning of his career, a man should have a definite occupation, which will enable him to provide for himself and he should take particular care not to cause disturbance or harm to others.

*   *   *

(30) If a brother leaves home and cannot supervise his wife's conduct at home, and if a brother see her in adultery, he must let it be known to the brethren, catch the adulterer and revenge his brother.

(31) If a member recognises in a candidate a man of bad character he must not permit him to become a brother. Should, however, a brother commit a crime and be obliged to run away, the brethren must assist him to escape and must not betray their brother in distress for the sake of any reward. Should a brother be summoned before the officers of the government (*i.e.* the Manchu Government) and be made to confess, he must carefully avoid implicating the other brethren. Whosoever dareth to disobey, may his eyes be torn out, may he die in the Great Ocean, may his descendants for a hundred generations live in misery and may the spirits of his ancestors find no rest and be damned.

Ward and Stirling, Vol. I page 69, have the following note on the above:—

> "This oath (No. 31) is evidently from the terrible severity of the penalty, considered the most important clause of the Thirty-six. On the one hand candidates of notorious character must not be proposed, but on the other hand, once a brother, always a brother, and even a crime does not dissolve the member's right to protection and assistance. Such a clause renders it very difficult for any civilised Government to recognise this society. No brother dare break this obligation, because he has involved not only his own fate and that of his descendants, but by breaking this obligation calls down a curse on his ancestors, the most terrible crime the Chinese can imagine".

*   *   *

(34) It is not permitted for any brother to propose for election any person known to be employed by the Government (*i.e.* the Manchu Government), or anyone who, for the sake of reward desires to learn the secrets of the society.

*   *   *

Ward and Stirling, Vol. I page 65 Note 1, have the following general note on the Thirty-six Oaths:—

> "These oaths really inculcate the moral teachings of the Triad society and for the most part are unexceptionable. It should be noted that they are really a cursing formula, similar to the ceremony in the Western Church, known as the Commination Service, held on Ash Wednesday".

So "unexceptionable" is the wording of this version of the 36 Oaths that we suspect in not to be genuine, but to be a translation of one of the "watered-down" editions commonly available during the period of registration in Malaya, 1870–1890, as a concession to the feelings of Government.

The complete Triad disciplinary code is composed of:—

The thirty-six oaths,
The ten rules,
The seventy-two articles of law,
The twenty-one regulations.

The provisions of these tend to become very much mixed up in the various published texts, but contain in some versions much stronger wording than anything given by Ward and Stirling.

We will, therefore, interpolate here some of the variant readings found in Schlegel and in the *Penang Riot Commission Report*, 1868, which convey what is probably much nearer the real message of the Triad disciplinary code.

The keynotes of this code are three, namely:—

(1) Secrecy,
(2) Mutual help in trouble,
(3) Respect for the women-folk of fellow-members.

These keynotes re-appear in the Code of the Malay White Flag society. *See* Chapter XXIX *infra.*

(1) SECRECY

Schlegel, 36 oaths No. 2 (page 135) has:—

"To keep secret everything from your wife and family, for fear that something might leak out before strangers: even so that as a father you do not tell it to your son, and as an elder brother you do not tell it to your younger brother".[1]

Schlegel, 36 oaths No. 10 (page 137) :—

"You must live and die together and be attached to each other as if you were born from one womb. Do not give out untruth for truth, and deceive the brethren, neither shall you conceal the Police and betray the trust of the brethren".[2]

Schlegel, 36 oaths No. 27 (page 141) :—

"If the master has appointed a meeting you shall most surely not conceal policemen within the precincts, in order to show them secretly the secrets. To conceal them is to mix serpents among dragons".[3]

Schlegel, 72 laws No. 18 (page 154) :—

"If a brother of the Hung league lends clandestinely his diploma and proof of membership to other people in order to curry favour with them, or if he sells them for money and betrays the secrets, he shall be put to death".[4]

Schlegel, 10 rules No. 5 (page 166) :—

"The brethren shall not bring policemen clandestinely within the Council, in order to show them formalities and objects......and falsely let him pass for a brother. Punishment: Death.

(2) MUTUAL HELP

Schlegel, 36 oaths No. 7 (page 137) :—

"You ought to consider the affairs of the brethren as your affairs. If one of them has smuggled or escaped the duties or has some secret affairs, or trades in smuggled goods, or cheats strangers, or the Police, you must keep it secret and not let it leak out".[5]

Schlegel, 36 oaths No. 16 (page 139) :—

"If you know that a heavy price is set upon a brother, and you do not think about saving him......but betray him to the Government, or if you give yourself the thread in hands or lead the way to make him prisoner and injure in this way a brother may you be struck by thunderbolts".

Schlegel, 72 laws No. 10 (page 153) :—

"If a brother, having committed a crime, enters the house of a brother and beseeches him to help him to escape over the frontiers, and if this brother does not help him to escape or prevents him from escaping, he will be punished......".[6]

Schlegel, 72 laws No. 26 (page 155) :—

"If a brother is seized for a crime by Government soldiers and is transported, and if the brethren do not advance and free him forcibly and prevent the soldiers, they shall be punished......".

Schlegel, 72 laws No. 58 (page 159) :—

"If a brother has committed a crime and is seized by the authorities and suffers imprisonment and all the brethren have contributed money and entrusted this money to one brother, that it may be used in mitigation of the punishment of the arrested brother and if this brother pockets the money himself he shall be put to death".

Schlegel, 72 laws No. 59 (page 159) :—

"If a brother has killed someone in the public interest and wishes to escape to another district or country, if then a traitor informs against him so that he is caught, the traitor will be put to death".[7]

Schlegel, 21 regulations, No. 5 (page 162) :—

"If a brother commits robbery afloat or ashore he shall observe well the signs of recognition before he acts...... He who knew certainly that it was a brother but pretended not to have recognised him......shall be punished......".[8]

Schlegel, 21 regulations No 8 (page 162) :—

"If a brother has become implicated with the authorities, or if a price is set upon his person, it shall not be allowed to betray him to the authorities and be the leading thread by which a brother is caught".[9]

(3) RESPECT FOR FELLOW MEMBERS' WOMEN-FOLK

Schlegel, 36 oaths No. 5 (page 136) :—

(Part)...... "Neither shall you seduce the wife or concubine of a brother".

Schlegel, 36 oaths No. 30 (page 142) :—

"You must observe the etiquette of this society and keep its regulations. When the wife or concubine of a brother passes you on the road, you shall not address her rudely or dally with her, for this is a heavy offence against propriety".[10]

Footnote.—(1) This is the same in the *Penang Riot Commission Report (P.C.R.)* version of the 36 oaths No. 4 (page 130).

Footnote.—(2) This is the same as *P.C.R.* 36 oaths No. 16 (page 131).

Footnote.—(3) This is the same as *P.C.R.* 36 oaths No. 30 (page 132).

Footnote.—(4) This is the same as *P.C.R.* 21 regulations No. 8 (page 128).

Footnote.—(5) This is the same as *P.C.R.* 21 regulations No. 9 (page 129).

Footnote.—(6) This is the same as *P.C.R.* 36 oaths No. 6 (page 130).

Footnote.—(7) This is much the same as *P.C.R.* 36 oaths No. 8 (page 130).

Footnote.—(8) This is much the same as *P.C.R.* 36 oaths No. 24 (page 132).

Footnote.—(9) This is the same as *P.C.R.* 36 oaths No. 8 (page 130).

Footnote.—(10) This is the same as *P.C.R.* 21 regulations No. 16 (page 129). It is also repeated in Schlegel, 21 regulations No. 17.

Schlegel, 72 laws No. 53 (page 158) :—

"If a brother, seeing the wife or concubine of another brother, is young and good-looking and relying upon his power (so that the other brother dares not to withstand him) appropriates her to himself and takes her as his wife, he shall be put to death".[1]

The punishment allotted for breach of most of the foregoing rules is death, and the punishment is usually exacted.

This helps the reader to realise the enormous power which lies behind the disciplinary code of the Triad society.

We shall have occasion later on in Chapter XXIX to compare this code with that of the Three Dot society.

We must now resume our summary of the Triad ritual.

THE TAKING OF THE OATH

After the conclusion of the reading of the Thirty-six Oaths by the Master, he breaks a bowl, saying:—

"As the pieces of this bowl can never be re-united, so no brother can escape the responsibilities he has incurred in taking the 36 oaths, transmitted to us by our five ancestors".

The candidates are then taken through the West gate where the paper on which the oaths were written is burnt so that they may ascend to the gods who will henceforth watch over their enforcement.

The ashes are taken back to the Red Flower Pavilion where the oath is ratified by the decapitation of a live white cock.

As he strikes off the cock's head the candidate says:—

"As I thus strike off the head of this white cock, Ah Ts'at (i.e. Mr. "Seven") so may my head be struck off if I, like Ah Ts'at prove a Traitor".

Ah Ts'at is the traitor monk Ma Ghee Hok (馬儀褔) the seventh in prowess in the monastery.[2] Seven, it should be noted, is the number of death.

The Master holds a bowl in which are the ashes of the Thirty-six Oaths and a few drops of the cock's blood are allowed to fall into the bowl and are mixed by the master with the ashes. Into this mixture red rice-wine is poured.

The candidate then drinks a cup of tea, after which the White Fan (Instructor) steps forward and says:—

"Stretch forth the middle finger of your left hand, which I shall prick, so that a few drops of blood may fall into the bowl held by the master".

Which being done, the Instructor continues:—

"In this manner, our ancient founders, the five monks of the Shaolin monastery, pledged themselves by an oath of eternal brotherhood.

You, my brothers, as a sign of your obedience and sincerity, will now in turn drink of the liquid contained in this vessel and thereby become blood brothers of all the members of our order. As you drink, bear in mind the solemn oaths you are thereby ratifying.

Henceforth the Hung society is to you as Father and Mother, its friends are your friends, its foes, your foes, where the brotherhood leads you must follow and from you absolute obedience to the orders of its duly appointed officers is demanded".

Each candidate then in turn takes a sip from the vessel while repeating a verse and then every other brother assembled also drinks from the bowl.

Thus the Triad oath is ratified.

Ward and Stirling Vol. I page 72 Note 3 have the following:—

"......Modern Chinese do not usually drink red wine and its retention in this ceremony indicates great antiquity.

Frazer in Taboo page 249 says:—

"The juice of the grape is naturally conceived as the blood of the vine[3] the fact that three kinds of blood or life namely that of the vine, of the cock, and of the candidate are mingled, is significant, as calling to witness the vegetable, the animal of the human kingdom, to the sanctity of the oath, represented by the ashes".

EXPLANATION OF THE SACRED SYMBOLS, PASSWORD AND UNIVERSAL SIGN

There follows an explanation by the White Fan (Instructor) to the candidates, of the sacred symbols lying on the altar.

After which the Instructor gives each candidate the Password "Pun" (本) = Self or Personal: and the Pass sign, spreading out the five fingers of the Right hand at full stretch.

PAYMENT OF THE ENTRANCE FEE

Each candidate then pays over his entrance fee.

This fee according to Schlegel (page 148) is a sum of 600 "cash"—the universal brass coin of China, in use for over a thousand years, about the size of a halfpenny with

Footnote.—(1) This is the same as P.C.R. 36 oaths No. 11 (page 131).
Footnote.—(2) See version of Traditional History in Ward and Stirling Vol. I pages 36–37.
Footnote.—(3) See under soma and batu kawi in Chapter XI.

a square hole in the middle, of value about 100 to the Chinese dollar. Schlegel gives the then (1866) value of this payment in "local currency" as "nearly two rupees" and gives the detail of this payment as follows:—

360 cash for "making clothes" (*i.e.* the book of the ritual);
108 cash for the "purse" (Certificate of Membership);
72 cash for "instruction" (the 36 oaths);
36 cash for the "traitorous subject" (the white cock);
21 cash for buying fruit (paid during the ritual);
3 cash to be kept by the candidate.

Total   600.[1]

The Penang Riot Commission Report Text page 126 has the following verse:—

"I entered the City saw the temple and paid 4 by 9.
The Blue Lotus in the mountain are 72.
108 were paid in the Hall of Fidelity and Loyalty.
In the joss house (at the altar) I paid 36.
I paid at the end of the bridge 21 for fruits.
After deducting these there remains a balance of three.
My Mother told me at the Flower Pavilion not to give away these three to anyone".

Owing to the vagaries of "local currency" in overseas countries, the amount of the candidate's entrance fee has varied in different lodges (between a dollar and a third and five Straits dollars *see* Ward and Stirling Vol. I pages 23 and 174) but it seems to be based nevertheless on the original 600 cash. This point will be found to be of some importance in connection with the entrance fees in present-day Mohamedan secret societies in Malaya discussed later on.

ISSUE OF CERTIFICATE OF MEMBERSHIP

Following payment of the entrance fee, the Master gives the candidate his certificate or diploma of membership, known variously[2] as the—

Hung Piu (洪票) Hung Diploma.

Yiu P'ing (腰屏)—The Purse or Waist-belt.

Hung Tan (紅單 or 洪單)—The Hung Bill.

THE MYSTICAL JOURNEY

The Master then addresses the candidates as follows:—

"I must explain that you should now take a long symbolical journey—owing, however to our limited space you must content yourself with supposing that you have taken this long, dangerous and arduous journey and listen attentively to the incidents connected therewith, which will be revealed to you in the course of the questions which I shall address to you and which will be answered by the Vanguard on your behalf".

Master (to Vanguard)—Whence come you?
Vanguard—From the East.[3]
Master—At what time?
Vanguard—At sunrise.

*   *   *

Master—How many came with you?
Vanguard—Two others, making three.
Master—How is it that you now come alone?
Vanguard—The sworn brother went before me, the adopted brother followed after me.

This refers to the three souls which according to the Chinese, dwell within a man: the ritual refers only to that soul which "descends into Hell"—*cf.* the Western "Body, Soul and Spirit" (Ward and Stirling Vol. I page 79 Note 1).

The ritual of the mystic journey is long and is given in Ward and Stirling Vol. I pages 77–101, and Schlegel pages 61–112. Schlegel includes it in the *Catechism (see* para. A above) but it more naturally comes after the initiation ceremony proper, as placed by Ward and Stirling.

The two extracts from it given above are included for purposes of later comparison with Malay initiation ceremonies.

The mystical journey is supposed to be taken in the Hung boat, and for a full explanation of its esoteric meaning, *see* Ward and Stirling Vol. III page 101.

Footnote.—(1) *See* also Ward and Stirling Vol. I page 75 Note 3.
Footnote.—(2) *See* Schlegel page 28; Ward and Stirling Vol. I page 132, and Stanton page 71.
Footnote.—(3) The soul is supposed to enter matter in the East, (Ward and Stirling, Vol. I page 77 Note 1). *See* also Introduction and Chapter IX).

The striking similarity between the adventures of the Hung hero during the Mystic Journey, and the legends belonging to other countries, of Knights who have similarly travelled in a world which is not this world, provides material for speculation and suggests that these legends either enshrine genuine knowledge of what befalls a man after death, or else are all descended from a common primitive ancestor and have been merely superficially influenced by the different races, whence they are drawn.[1]

THE TEN RULES

The Mystical Journey ends with an "obligation" pronounced by the Vanguard on behalf of the newly admitted candidates which reads thus:—

"A Censer with incense stands in the Red Flower Pavilion.
"Before which the Five Ancestors swore the oath of blood brotherhood.
"Perform your duties in the temple in ... (*name of place where lodge meets*).
"The gathering place of all Hung Heroes within the four seas.

Thereafter the candidates are ordered by the Master to be taken round the lodge to be tested by other members, the Vanguard still acting as sponsor.

Thereafter the ten rules of the Triad society are read out to the candidates.

The wording of these rules again varies very much in the different texts, but generally speaking, appears to be unexceptionable in the original version, but objectionable in some of the more modern variant versions.

These rules differ from the Thirty-six Oaths in that, in the main they indicate the practical advantages which membership bestows and the correct method of obtaining those advantages (Ward and Stirling Vol. I page 104 Note 7).

Schlegel pages 152–165 adds the—

Seventy-two Articles of Law of the Hung league;
and the
Twenty-one Articles of the Regulations.

But these seem mostly a repetition of the 36 Oaths and the 10 Rules. Other texts omit these.

The lodge official after reading the rules, demands a final proof of membership and the Vanguard replies for the candidates the well known verse:—

"At parting, the Five (Ancestors) a verse composed
Which Hung Braves carry undisclosed,
But if to a Brother this is shown
He'll know that he is not alone".

TERMINATION OF CEREMONY

This terminates the ceremony of initiation and afterwards the brethren sit down to a banquet for which the Black Ox and the White Horse were symbolically slaughtered earlier in the ceremony.

Before quitting the lodge, the brethren change from their Ming robes (white) to their ordinary clothes.

The ceremony as sketched falls into three divisions:—

(*a*) The Traditional History.
(*b*) The Initiation.
(*c*) The Mystical Journey.

The first has been strongly tinged with political matter, the second less so, while the third has been but little tampered with for political objects.

The whole represents a sacrament in which the initiate is baptised, confirmed, and makes his first communion during the process of the ceremony.

TRIAD SECRET SIGNS, PASSWORDS AND SLANG TERMS

By custom the Chinese as a race do not shake hands.

There are, therefore, no "grips" in use as secret signs amongst members of the Triad society proper. The methods of recognition used by Triad members may be sub-divided as follows:—

(1) Signs made by the hand or hands alone.
(2) Signs made by the body, or hands and body combined.
(3) Signs made by means of the clothing.
(4) Signs made by peculiar methods of movement or positioning or handling of common articles.
(5) Test phrases and slogans from the ritual.
(6) Triad slang terms.

Some of the hand signs are very ancient and common in secret rituals throughout the world. (*see* Ward and Stirling Vol. I pages 108–121).

Footnote.—(1) *See* Ward and Stirling Vol. I page 101 Footnote.

Some of these ancient hand signs and hand and body signs follow with remarkable fidelity the form of the Chinese character for the word they represent (*see* illustrations in Ward and Stirling Vol. I to face pages 96 and 120, also 72, 86, and 116). This fact provides matter for further speculation upon the origin of the earliest primitive mysteries. (Ward and Stirling Vol. I page 110).

The chief signs made by means of clothing are:—

(1) Right Lapel of coat collar turned in.

(2) Right Cuff of coat sleeve rolled up inwards.

(3) Left Trouser end rolled up inwards.

The chief signs made by peculiar movement are:—

(1) On entering a brother's house, enter Left foot first.

(2) If on a road, twigs are met with, placed carefully in a methodical way, signifying the presence of robbers in hiding near by, the twigs must be moved to one side with the Left foot, and must not be trodden on or stepped over.

The chief signs made by positioning common articles are:—

(1) If in need of money place hat under *left* arm, crown to the body, inside of crown facing outwards.

(2) If carrying a stick or umbrella between 1st to 20th of the Chinese month,. place one finger on the side of the handle to the front.
From 21st of the month, two fingers must be to the front.

(3) On meeting a stranger on the road believed to be a brother, take off hat and hold it with the *left* hand, crown outwards with three fingers of Right hand on crown.

(4) In times of disturbance or when going to sleep, place before doorway or on floor by sleeping-berth a bowl of water with parang laid across bowl and a small cup of water placed on blade of parang.

THE SIGNS MADE BY HANDLING COMMON ARTICLES

These signs are very numerous and chiefly concern the handling of tea-cups; match boxes: matches: chop-sticks: opium pipes: and materials for chewing betel-nut and are given in Ward and Stirling Vol. I pages 123–127, with illustrations and also in Schlegel pages 183–218 and Stanton pages 99–117.

The six commonest signs with tea-cup, match box and matches are illustrated in Ward and Stirling Vol. I to face page 126.

TEST PHRASES AND SLOGANS FROM THE RITUAL

These are given in Ward and Stirling Vol. I pages 127–128 and Stanton pages 97–98.

TRIAD SLANG TERMS

Like Freemasonry and many other ancient secret associations, the Triad society has its own secret language and special terms for common objects.

Some of these are given in Ward and Stirling Vol. I pages 129–131. Schlegel pages 230–234: Stanton pages 91–96: and the *Penang Riot Commission Report* page 124.

This completes a sketch of the main features of the Triad ritual and its accompaniments and is here inserted for convenience of easy reference and comparison with current local deviations from this ritual in Malaya, referred to in subsequent chapters.

CHAPTER VIII

THE THREE DOT BROTHERHOOD

The subject matter of this chapter is of peculiar complexity, but it is important that it should be discussed and as far as possible cleared up early in this work, if what follows in subsequent chapters is to bear the significance on the Chinese side, which we believe it to have.

In his article in *T'oung Pao* in 1928 quoted in full in the preceding chapter, M. Pelliot says:—

> These various data are irreconcilable unless we admit that the Three Dot Brotherhood is absolutely separate from the Triad society.

In an article entitled "Historical notes on Chinese political societies", in the *Review of Chinese Affairs* for May, 1934, an official document published monthly by the Chinese Secretariat, Singapore, there is the following:—

> The first political society of modern times to be noted is the Triad society, or Heaven and Earth association, or Hung league, colloquially referred to as the Sam Tim Wui.[1]

This statement represents the presently accepted official view.

We will attempt in this chapter to explain the divergence between the British official view and that of the French savant.

Although a generic name by which the Hung league is popularly, if vaguely, known in Malaya is that of the Sa Tiam Hui, the opinion, supported by that of M. Pelliot above and by such evidence as is available, will be submitted in this and following chapter, that the name is a misnomer when applied to the Hung league, from which it seems to be a separate and distinct organisation, having nothing in common with the Triad society, except perhaps a name borrowed from the Triad story, but even this seems doubtful, an initiation ceremony of which we know very little, some of which, but not all, is similar to the Triad ritual and with secret signs some of which, but not all, are similar to Triad signs.

Apart from a casual reference here and there among various writers to the name alone, and apart from notes on the ritual appearing in the *Malayan Police Magazine* given in Chapter IX *infra*, the only published notice of the Three Dot Brotherhood is in Ward and Stirling, who in *op. cit.* Vol. I page 176, have the following:—

> The Sa Tiam, or Three Dot Brotherhood. A Thieves' society.
>
> This society exists throughout the Malay Peninsula and its objects are to further crime. The members share the proceeds of robbery according to rank and the size of their subscription. They are composed of three grades, the first containing persons of intelligence and influence— these are the real heads of the Order and take the biggest share of the plunder: the second rank seem to constitute the executive officers, while the third are subject to the higher ranks and do not make much out of the nefarious activities of the society. Promotion, however, is quite possible. A member of the second rank may be promoted in 24 months if his conduct is quite satisfactory to the heads of the Order, and becomes one of them; while a member of the third rank must wait 36 months before he can achieve second rank. For specially meritorious conduct, however, more rapid promotion is granted.
>
> The ceremonial and ritual, signs and passwords are very similar to those in use in the Triad society and are clearly based on it: but it is dangerous to know one or two signs without knowing them all, and essential to be acquainted with the passwords, for the society has no hesitation in carrying out the death penalty on a traitor.

Prima facie this description bears a marked resemblance to the Ko Lao Hui of Hutson pages 25–28 *supra*.

Schlegel *op. cit.* who has made the most comprehensive study hitherto published of the origins of the Triad society and the names by which it has been known, does not mention the Three Dot Brotherhood as being one of them. This significant omission suggests *prima facie* that the Three Dot is something other than the Triad, a view held by those few writers who have mentioned the Three Dot, and supported by such additional evidence as we now propose to adduce.

It should be noted here that the name "Three Dot" as applied to a secret organisation in China is apparently quite modern, dating only in China proper from the period of the Taiping rebellion (1850) and in Malaya from about the time of the suppression of dangerous societies (1890). This may account for Schlegel's omission to mention it. But in order to identify the camp to which it belongs and its peculiar character, it has been thus early interpolated into this work so as to dispose of the subject of its origin and allegiance under the Yin Yang theory propounded in Chapter III *supra* and thus to simplify subsequent references.

Footnote.—(1) This is the Cantonese pronounciation of the Hokkien Sa Tiam Hui (三 點 會) or Three Dot Brotherhood.

Although frequent reference is made in Ward and Stirling *op. cit.* to the Three Dot Brotherhood as a secret organisation in Malaya separate and distinct from the Triad society, we have been unable to find any explanation of the origin of the association itself, nor of the origin of the name, nor the place where, the period of time when the name first came to notice and how and when it came to be applied colloquially, if erroneously to the Triad society (Ghee Hin) in Malaya.

ORIGIN OF THE THREE DOT BROTHERHOOD TO BE FOUND IN THE HAN LEAGUE

We propose to show in this chapter that the origin of the Three Dot Brotherhood is to be found in the Han league. Before presenting the evidence in support of this view it is necessary briefly to recapitulate the causes of the existing confusion, which has led to all secret societies in Malaya being regarded for official purposes as "different branches of the Triad society", and in doing so to attempt to clear away some of the *débris* of erroneous conclusions which have led to this confusion.

In Chapters V and VI we have referred to some of the causes of this obscurity and have emphasised that throughout the observations of all earlier commentators upon the secret society phenomenon in Malaya, there has run an awareness of a rivalry and hostility in the secret society underworld, which could not be properly explained, if in truth all societies belonged to a single brotherhood governed by the most stringent code of conduct with death as the penalty for breach of it.

This inconsistency led the Penang riot Commissioners in 1868 to include in their report a sub-section dealing with the "Erroneous opinion regarding Hoeys", but they were themselves without sufficient *data* to establish the causes of this "erroneous opinion" which has persisted to the present-day.

We have presented in the preceding chapters what we believe to be the two main stems of the secret society underworld of China, the Han (or "Tokong",) and the Hung (or Triad) emanating respectively from the Yin and the Yang principle in Chinese cosmogony, and have shown how these two stems have been transplanted to Malaya.

It remains for us to identify the Three Dot Brotherhood with one or the other.

We believe the Three Dot Brotherhood to belong to the Han league or "Tokong" camp of the two great rival organisations.

It is not enough to say that the history of Chinese riots and bloodshed in Malaya during the past 150 years is the history of the rivalry between different local branches of the same thing "the Triad society, known locally as the Sa Tiam Hui".

It is nearer the truth to say that it has been the story of an undersurface war, waged unceasingly between two distinct and hostile organisations and these we suggest are and have always been the Triad society and all its branches—Cantonese, Hokkien, Teochew, against the "Tokong" camp or Three Dot Brotherhood and all its affinities (mainly Hakkas and Hokkiens).

Without some such explanation as this for the bitter rivalry of the two opposing Chinese "factions" which to-day seem to be known generically as the Ghee Hin (Triad) and the Three Dot ("Tokong") the undersurface history of Malaya during the period of the British connection is incomprehensible.

Furthermore, this warfare was not confined throughout to a struggle for a free market in local extortion, blackmail and traffic in women, but was carried to its bitterest extent in the Larut wars, where the land hunger of the rival Punteis and Hakkas in their native country, which we have mentioned in Chapter IV, was transferred to the local scene.

Moreover, the same rivalry and hostility has no doubt coloured all the social and commercial relations of the Chinese in Malaya down to the present time and is probably an important factor in deciding political loyalties in the Sino-Japanese war to-day.

INITIAL DIFFICULTIES IN THE CLARIFICATION OF EXISTING CONFUSION

In attempting to clear away the *débris* of confusion, we are met with the following initial difficulties :—

    (1) Foreign authorities nowhere give a clue to the possible origin of the Three Dot Brotherhood.

    (2) The published authorities either do not mention the existence of the Toh Peh Kong or Kien Tek society of Penang (1867) or do not attempt to suggest the relationship between it and the Triad society in Malaya, other than that they were mutually hostile.

    (3) The published authorities admit that in Singapore in the middle of the last century, the Ghee Hin society (Triad) had a serious rival in another society loosely referred to as the Ghee Hok society.

    (4) The authorities refer to the existence in Malaya of a Hokkien branch of the Ghee Hin (Triad) society commonly known as the Ghee Hok lodge, but there does not appear to be anywhere any explanation offered of

the relationship between this Ghee Hok (Triad) lodge or "Hokkien Ghee Hin" and the Ghee Hok society proper, which latter, all agree, has been throughout the past century in Malaya and up to the present date, the enemy and rival of the Ghee Hin (Triad) and its various branches including the Hokkien Ghee Hin or Ghee Hok lodge of the Triad society.

(5) Confusion has consequently resulted in the published records between :—

    (a) the Hokkien Ghee Hin (Triad) lodge or Ghee Hok lodge of the Triad society; and

    (b) the rival society to the Triad in Malaya usually referred to as the "Ghee Hok" society.

(6) In the official list of "Dangerous Societies" suppressed by law in Singapore in 1890 some of which are given in Ward and Stirling Chapter I page 180, there is separate mention of :—

    (a) the Hokkien Ghee Hin society or Ghee Hok lodge of the Triad; and

    (b) the Ghee Hok society,

suggesting that they were then (1890) regarded as two separate societies. This same differentiation is also evident in the *Government Gazette* notifications of the suppression period 1890–1893 (*see* Chapter XXI *infra*).

(7) In Chapter V we have suggested the origin of the name of the Ghee Hok society in Singapore and have identified it with the Han league of Hutson.

In Chapter VI we have identified the Toh Peh Kong society of Penang (1867) with the Ghee Hok society of Singapore and therefore with the Han league.

The Penang Riot Commissioners of 1868 have identified the Toh Peh Kong society and the Kian Tek or Kien Hok society of Penang of 1867 as being one and the same, and as being the aggressors throughout against the Triad in the "Penang War" of that year.

We are here met with the difficulty that after having added such a bloody page to the history of Malayan secret societies as recently as 1867, the names Toh Peh Kong and Kian Tek seem to have almost entirely disappeared from subsequent Penang records, although both names are mentioned subsequently in *Government Gazettes*, the Toh Peh Kong in 1885 and the Kian Tek in 1890 (*see* Chapter XXI below).

(8) Ward and Stirling *op. cit.* make no reference to either the Toh Peh Kong or the Kian Tek societies of Penang, although they are the only extensive commentators upon the Sa Tiam Hui.

(9) The first and only published reference to the Sa Tiam Hui by an European observer which we can find prior to the publication of Ward and Stirling's work is that by Heckethorn *op. cit.* Vol. II page 133, where he refers to the Three Dot Brotherhood's activities in Sarawak in 1889. The full reference is given in Chapter XXI below. Even in this reference the Sa Tiam Hui is identified in accordance with the presently accepted view, with the Ghee Hin (Triad) society in Sarawak.

GENERAL ACCEPTANCE OF THE OBSCURITY

Resignation to this condition of confusion both in the popular and in the informed mind is illustrated by the following extracts :—

The popular view.—

(1) W. H. Read's *Play and Politics* page 91 has :—

    The Chief Hoeys in Singapore (since A.D. 1850) were the Teantay (*sic*) and the Ghehok (*sic*) which as early as 1841 numbered some ten thousand members.

By the Teantay the writer means the Ghee Hin (Triad) society, and by the Ghehok he means the rival society to the Triad, and therefore obviously not the Ghee Hok lodge of the Triad, otherwise known as the Hokkien Ghee Hin.

(2) C. B. Buckley *Anecdotal History* Vol. II page 723 (writing under date 1865) has :—

    "For some years there had been trouble at times arising from secret societies among Klings, both Hindu and Mahammedan, called the Red and White Flag societies........ In 1864 serious disturbances had taken place (in Singapore) during the Moharram Festival, and in May this year (1865) Governor Cavanagh and Mr. Dunman forbade the procession. In October (1865) what was called the "Great Conspiracy Case" against six of the head members was heard, two of whom were men of standing, Mr. Dunman and Mr. Weir giving them remarkably good characters in matters of business. They were all convicted and sentenced to two years' imprisonment. This broke up the societies practically, which had been established after (the manner of) the Chinese Ghi Hin and Ghi Hok societies, with which it was supposed they were connected".

The informed view.—

(3) J. D. Vaughan *Notes on the Chinese of Penang, J.I.A.* VIII· (1854) :—

There are five Hoes or Triad societies, *viz:*—

The. Ghee Hin,
Ho Seng,
Hye San,
Chinchin (or ring),
To-pe-kong.

The first two approach nearer to the famous Triad society of China than the last three. The Ghee Hin corresponds with the Tien Teh Hoe...... The last three have been formed in Penang and differ but slightly from the others.

(4) Ward and Stirling, Vol. I page 180 :—

The Ghee Hok became a very powerful lodge and was inclined to be hostile to the Mother Temple of the Ghee Hin.

(5) Ward and Stirling, Vol. I page 139 :—

It seems probable that the White Flag society was founded by members of the Ghee Hin society in order to obtain control of members of the Malay Police and that the Red Flag society was founded by the Ghee Hok, a somewhat similar society to the Ghee Hin and a rival to it.

From the above and from further extracts from the same source, given elsewhere, it will be seen that as early as 1854 there was already felt to be some intangible difference between those who belonged to the Ghee Hin (Triad) society and its adjuncts and those who belonged to its rival society referred to as Ghee Hok in Singapore, and by Vaughan more exactly as the Hye San, Chinchin, and To-pe-kong in Penang.

These latter we have already labelled with the omnibus term of "Tokong" and in this chapter we also place the Three Dot Brotherhood within the "Tokong" camp.

Henceforth in recording the rivalries between Triad and "Tokong" the Three Dot Brotherhood must be understood to be included in the latter. The evidence which justifies this inclusion is given below.

THE WATER-MOTIF IN THE HAN LEAGUE

We have drawn attention in the preceding chapters to the references as they arose, to *water* in connection with the Han league. Thus, Hutson Chapter II in his description (page 25) of the *Elder Brethren society* has :—

It would seem as if there was a union with some piratical elements. The terms so often used "rivers and lakes" is supposed to mean "rovers of the waters". The terms helmsman, anchorage, sea and water, are in constant use in the fraternity and seem to point to a piratical origin.

The White Lotus or Water Lily society which Hutson has identified with the Han league also carries the same suggestion in its name. The catchwords of the Toh Peh Kong society of Penang (Appendix II) and which we have identified with the Han league (Chapter V) and the association of the Toh Peh Kong generally with the green of nature, conveys the same idea.

The seal of the Kian Tek society of Penang (Chapter VI) which is identified with the Toh Peh Kong presents the same characteristic (*see* page 102 *supra*).

Many other similar allusions to water in association with "Tokong" and the Han league will occur in subsequent chapters.

It is therefore perhaps safe to say that there runs throughout the Han league and its affinities a latent *water-motif* which helps to identify it with nature and the Yin principle in the Chinese cosmos, (Chapter III) and with the "Tokong" camp in Malaya.

In this connection it is relevant to note that in the teaching of Lao Tze, water is a pattern of humility and a symbol of the Yin.

Thus, in the *Tao Teh King*   (道 德 經) Book of Reason and Virtue (Legge's translation page 52) we read :—

The highest excellence is that of water. That excellence appears in its benefitting all things and in its occupying without striving to the contrary, the low place which all men dislike.

And again page 104 :—

What makes a great State? Its being like a low-lying, down flowing stream. It so becomes the centre to which tend all the small states under Heaven. To illustrate from the case of all females: the female always overcomes the male by her stillness and the process may be considered a sort of abasement.

We have here the *water motif* of the Ko Lao Hui and the Han league directly associated with the Yin or female principle.

ORIGIN OF THE NAME THREE DOT BROTHERHOOD

With these difficulties and obscurities before us, we will present the various conjectures as to the origin of the name "Three Dot", with the grounds in support of each. These are:—

(1) An origin in the short form of the Chinese character for water, (氵) known as the "three drops of water" form.

(2) An origin in the "Doctrine of God" of the Taiping rebels.

(3) An origin in the San Ch'ing (三 清) or Three Pure Ones, the members of the Taoist trinity.

(4) An origin in the Tally society of the Han league.

(1) Origin in the short form (氵) of the characters shui (水) "water".— Dr. Milne in his paper on the Triad society published in 1825 in *Transactions of the R.A.S.* Vol. I Part II page 240, refers to the composition of the character 洪 Hung, which contains the hidden number 321, thus:—

> 氵   for 三 three;
>
> 八   pah (eight) for 百 pah (one hundred);
>
> 廿   yah, the short form for twenty;
>
> 一   one.

Schlegel refers to the same thing on page xxxviii of his "Introduction" and again on page 86 where it occurs in the text (Note 1).

Dr. Milne remarks further that the character 氵 , the short form of the character 水 shui, "water", is ordinarily referred to by Chinese as the 三 點 水 sa tiam shui or the "three dots form of the character for water", or more simply, "the three dots water".

As a whole character in which it is used *viz:*— 洪 Hung, stands for the Hung league, it is commonly held that the three dots at the side of that character supply the origin of the popular name for the Hung league in Malaya, the Sa Tiam Hui, or Three Dot society. This view does not seem to us to be very convincing, particularly as it is held in ignorance or disregard of the water-motif in the Han league.

The assumption that the name "Three Dot Society" has its origin in the three dot form of the character for water, is held by the same school of thought to be strengthened by the fact that the traditional gravestone of Wan Yun Lung[1] (the abbot mentioned in the *Traditional History* page 10 *supra*) bears an inscription in sixteen characters, to each of which "three drops of water" have been added, making 48 drops of water in all.

This simply means that the short form or "three dot" form of the character for water, namely 氵 has been engraved beside each character of the inscription on the tombstone. (*see* Schlegel, page 18 and Plate No. 1).

Pickering *op. cit.* in his account of the same incident in the *Traditional History* (translated from a different source from that of Schlegel) has a somewhat similar reference:—

> The Sien-Seng, Kin Lam, erected a tombstone (to Wan Yun Lung) and on this tablet were engraved six characters; to each character was added the character 氵 sui—"water".

Ward and Stirling Vol. III page 40 have this:—

> Before leaving the subject (of the significance of the white cock in Triad ritual) it is well to bring to mind the title of the Thieves' society. The society is called the Three Dot Brotherhood, which probably refers to the three dots, representing three drops of water, which were depicted on each side of the grave of Wan Yun Lung.
>
> In view, however, of the importance of dotting the tablet at a funeral with cock's blood[2] it seems probable that there is a reference to this custom in the name of the Brotherhood, for we see by the Three Dot ritual that towards the end of the ceremony, the initiates are supposed to be ghosts, since they go round the lodge the reverse way of the Sun.
>
> As the corpse of a cock plays an even more prominent part in the rites of the (Three Dot) society than it does in the original Hung ceremony, there seems good reason to think that the title of the Brotherhood is indeed connected with this funeral custom, though in what precise way we cannot as yet decide.

The foregoing represents the presently accepted, if shadowy basis for the origin of the name "Three Dot", as applied to the Triad society in Malaya. It all rests on the assumption that the Three Dot is identical with the Triad and that therefore the name must be borrowed from the Triad ritual, or at least its origin repose within the Triad story. Although perhaps plausible from this aspect, we are unable to accept the view, because we believe it to be based on a false premise and we hold with M. Pelliot above, that the Three Dot is entirely separate and distinct from the Triad society.

Having regard to the connection between the Ko Lao Hui and its parent the Han Liu (漢 流), we must note the fact that the characters for Han Liu also bear three drops of water at the side of each. It is therefore just as reasonable, if not a great deal more so, to suppose, in view of the latent water-motif in the Han league, that the particular three drops of water from which the Three Dot society takes its name,

---

Footnote.—(1) Wan Yun Lung (萬 雲 龍) was First President and National Grand Master of the reconstituted Hung league circa A.D. 1735.

Footnote.—(2) Vermilion ink is sometimes used for this purpose as a substitute for cock's blood. *See* Ward and Stirling Vol. III page 39 Note 1.

derive from the characters of the Han Liu, a "Tokong" and Red Flag foundation, rather than from the inscription on Wan Yun Lung's tomb, which belongs to the Triad and White Flag foundation, hostile to the Three Dot society.

This surmise offers an explanation of what has never otherwise been explained, namely, the persistent rivalry between Triad and Three Dot and its affiliations and the essentially religious origin of the former (though now degenerate) and the essentially criminal character of the Three Dot.

(2) Origin in the "Doctrine of God" of the Taiping rebels.—In Chapter IV (pages 54–55 *supra*) under "Genesis of the Taiping rebellion" we have quoted the reference in the Chinese encyclopædia *Chi Yuen* which states that the Three Dot Brotherhood was a secret society founded in the reign of the Emperor Toh Kwang (1821–1850) and that it professed the Doctrine of God, with Hung Siu Ch'un, the Taiping rebel leader, as its chief.

At the same reference we have quoted another Chinese source the *Maan Yau Ch'un Shu* published in 1929 which repeats the statement in the *Chi Yuen* above.

These statements offer no explanation of the name, but it has been suggested that the name might derive from the "essences" of the three leaders of the movement—the Taiping trinity.

Following upon this, we have been at some pains in Chapter IV to suggest that the whole of the Taiping rebellion may have been an insurrection of the White Lotus society, which has been identified by Hutson as belonging to the Han league.

The process by which the Han league may have come to adopt such a protective colouring in the Taiping rebellion, has been already explained in Chapter IV.

In this regard M. Pelliot in his article in *T'oung Pao* (1928) quoted in Chapter VII has :—

> The meagre information in the *Chi Yuen* states specifically that the Sa Tiam Hui or Three Dot is a branch of the Doctrine of God society and that Hung Siu Ch'un was one of its chiefs. These various data are irreconcilable unless we admit that the Three Dot is absolutely separate from the Triad. All this remains very obscure.

If the Three Dot was in fact founded as a new society in the reign of Toh K'wong it would agree with the finding of the *Penang Riot Commission Report* para. 14, in respect of the Toh Peh Kong society *viz:—*

> The Toh Peh Kong society was instituted in Penang about twenty-four years ago (*i.e.* 1844).

It would also agree with the statement in the actual rules of the society (Appendix II) :—

> The Kian Tek society hereby begin and publish their rules as follows...... On the twenty-first day of the fifteenth moon of the year Kah Sin, being the thirty-fourth year of Toh Kwong (30th December, 1844) this combination was begun at Jelutong.

We can hardly accept these bald statements as being conclusive evidence that the Three Dot Brotherhood dates only from the period of the Taiping rebellion and is identifiable only with that tatterdemalion rabble, which has long since disappeared as an isolated phenomenon from the political arena in China, while the Three Dot Brotherhood remains one of the most powerful criminal organisations among the Chinese in Malaya.

We may perhaps more safely accept the statement of the *Maan Yau Ch'un Shu*, (pages 54–55 *supra*) that the germinal element in the Taiping rebellion was the "secret society started by Chu Kau Tho about the middle of the reign of Toh K'wong (circa 1835) on the lines of the White Lotus society", around which nucleus the Taiping rebellion and with it the Three Dot Brotherhood with its pseudo-Christian accretions, subsequently matured.

If we accept for the Three Dot an origin in the White Lotus revival of Chu Kau Tho, we must allow that the Three Dot was essentially of mystical Han league origin and may proceed to investigate with the aid of Hutson whence its name may have been derived in the background of Taoism. We must bear in mind that the name Three Dot is nowhere mentioned by Hutson and may therefore be a name confined to south east China and the South Seas, although from other evidence and from the declared character of the association itself, it may be clearly identifiable with the criminal elements in the Han league or Ko Lao Hui of China proper, of which Hutson gives such a vivid account.

(3) An origin in the San Ch'ing (三 清) or Three Pure ones of the Taoist Trinity.—There is a conceivable derivation of the "Three Dots" from the San Ch'ing or the "Three Pure Ones", who form the Triad of T'aoist gods namely:—

Yuk Ch'ing (玉 清)—Pearly Azure.

Shang Ch'ing (上 清)—Upper Azure.

T'ai Ch'ing (太 清)—Supreme Azure.

Of these three, Werner, in *A Dictionary of Chinese Mythology* (1932) page 400 says:—

> The San Ch'ing or Three Pure Ones, are the manifestation of Lao Tzu, who was deified for his intellectual and moral qualities. The Triad is a modern imitation of that of the Buddhists. The function of this Triad is also similar, namely, instruction and benevolent interference for the good of humanity.

Again Hutson *op. cit.* Book IV Chapter I on the subject of the supernatural, page 377 has:—

> Setting up the altar for the purpose of divination is an elaborate affair. A chart belonging to the sorcerer is hung up over the family gods: in this chart the San Ch'ng have a prominent place.......
>
> The three pure ones are believed to be peculiarly fitted for the work of frightening away demons.

This reference identifies the functions of the "Three Pure Ones" with shamanism and the "Tokong" cult.

The close association of the Hung league (Triad) with Buddhism and of the Han league ("Tokong") with Taoism, suggests that these "three drops of water", from which the authorities suggest the Three Dot gets its name, may quite conceivably be, not the three drops of water associated with the inscription on Wan Yan Lung's tomb, but the "three dots" in the character 清 used for the 三 清 or Three Pure Ones of the Taoist trinity, or indeed the name Sa Tiam may possibly be an euphemistic term for the Taoist trinity itself. (*see* page 55 *supra*).

Again, it is but the "three drops of water" which differentiates the hated Ts'ing dynasty 清 from the rule of Nature, Ts'ing 青 *see* pages 42–43 *supra*.

Further, it may possibly be that having regard to the Chinese delight in playing on words, the 三 清 "Three Pure Ones" above, give their name to the 安清幫 An Ch'ing Pang ("Society for the Pacification of the Ts'ing Dynasty") otherwise known as the modern 青幫 Ch'ing Pang or "Green Association" which we discuss in full in Chapter XXXI and which we identify therein with "Tokong".

(4) Origin in the Tally society of the Han league.—Pursuing further the belief that the origin of the Three Dot is to be found in the Han league, we offer a final alternative derivation of the three drops of water in the description of the Elder Brethren or Ko Lao society, to which Hutson has introduced us. Such a derivation is at least as plausible as the foregoing, and better explains the origin of the three dots of water if we emphasis the "water-motif", with which the Han league is associated and the "piratical" elements in the Ko Lao which suit the known criminal character of the Three Dot society better than a Triad derivation of the name.

Hutson in his article given in Chapter II, after pointing out its great antiquity, says that the Ko Lao Hui is generally held to have been introduced into Szechuan (the province for which he speaks) by the braves of Viceroy Lo Wen Chung from Hunan Province in 1855, who quelled the Han Liu revolt of that year in Szechuan.

He goes on to say:—

> Many of these soldiers (Hunan troops of Lo Wen Chung) settled in Szechuan, and their brotherhood (Ko Lao Hui) gradually amalgamated with that of the Han Liu. It would seem as if there was also a union with some piratical elements. The term Chiang Hu (江 湖) so often used, means, "rivers and lakes", and is supposed to mean "rovers of the waters". The term To Pa Tsu (舵 把 子) "Helmsman"; Ma T'au (碼 頭) "anchorage"; Hai (海) "seas"; Shui (水) "water", all seem to point to a piratical origin, but are in constant use in the fraternity.

Again under "Lodges of the Ko Lao Hui", Hutson has:—

> 義 or "Rectitude" lodge.
>
> In the second or rectitude lodge are massed the turbid-water womb-brothers (潭 水 胞 哥) probably the real Han Lui members. All the lawless elements in the district of Chengtu (Szechuan) are mustered under this rectitude mark.

These two passages suggest that the piratical elements among the Chinese immigrants to Malaya, of whom there were large numbers amongst the Hakkas, Cantonese and Hokkiens of the earlier period, may well have formed a Ko Lao Hui lodge or lodges on arrival in opposition to the Triad in "Junk Ceylon" and Penang, there being no reason to suppose as stated in Chapter II that the Ko Lao Hui was confined to Hunan and Szechuan.

Indeed, the earlier history of the Hakkas as given in Chapter IV, suggests a direct channel for the flow of the Ko Lao Hui brotherhood into Malaya.

At the end of Chapter IX below we give a derivation of the catchword of the Three Dot Brotherhood ("Kiam Jee") from the Ch'ien Tzu Hang or Tally society of Hutson, within the Ko Lao Hui or Han league. The evidence on this point necessarily rests upon the ritual (Chapter IX) and cannot therefore be inserted here.

The trend of the evidence here given is nevertheless the same, namely to identify the Three Dot with the Han league.

Again the "Rectitude Lodge" of the Ko Lao Hui suggests an origin for the Ghee Hok (義 福) lodge in Singapore, (*i.e.* a Hokkien (福) branch of the Rectitude (義) lodge of the Ko Lao society of China, which throughout its Singapore history was at war with the Triad there.

Again, the Hai San (海 山) Kongsi which we have seen in Chapter V was established in Penang (about 1820) as distinct from the Ghee Hin (Triad) there, suggests again from its name, an association with those "piratical elements" referred to by Hutson.

The general association of water with the Ko Lao Hui, suggests that the origin of the Sa Tiam Hui, or Three Dots of Water society is more likely to be found in the Han league, in which according to Hutson the motifs of "crime" and "water" are implicit, rather than in the Triad, where the addition of "three drops of water" is only a minor incident of which we hear nothing further, and whose tenets are at variance with the Three Dot and whose origin is probably distinct.

We showed in Chapter VI that the Toh Peh Kong of Penang in 1867 was by its own rules, a fighting or criminal society and was impregnated with the "Han ethic" referred to in page 33 *supra*.

We present in the Chapter that follows, what little is known of the ritual of the Three Dot Brotherhood which will demonstrate to what a degree it differs from the Triad ritual outlined in Chapter VII above.

A comparison between the description of the Han league ritual given by Hutson in Chapter II and that of the Three Dot Brotherhood in Chapter IX below will present so many points of similarity that we invite acceptance of the view that they belong to the same stem. A comparison between the ritual of the Hung league as given in Chapter VII and of the Three Dot Brotherhood as given in Chapter IX below, will present so many points of difference that we invite acceptance of the view expressed by M. Pelliot and borne out by the evidence produced, that the Three Dot is something totally different from the Triad. We ask in addition for acceptance of the view that the Three Dot Brotherhood in Malaya is identical with the Han league or "Tokong" camp.

From the allegorical or esoteric standpoint we suggest that the ritual of the Three Dot society represents physical birth and man's journey through this world: while the Triad ritual represents his physical death and the journey of his soul to the next.

THE CRIMINAL CHARACTER OF THE THREE DOT BROTHERHOOD

The character of the Three Dot in Malaya is that of a thieves' society, which is in consonance with the Han ethic as described by Hutson but is totally alien to the spirit of the Triad.

Whether it bears a similar character in China we are unable to say, but anyone interested in the Thieves' society in China proper will find a recent and lively description of the practical working of what he calls therein the "Thieves Guild", in Digby's *Down Wind* (1939) page 110 ff.

In identifying the Three Dot in Malaya with the "Tokong" camp in Malaya, we necessarily bracket it with the Mohamedan Red Flag society in Malaya, to which we introduce our readers in Chapters XII, XIV and XVI below. The Red Flag will be found to bear a similar criminal character and to have allied itself with the Toh Peh Kong society of Penang in 1863. The latter we have already identified with the Three Dot. Thus the *Penang Riot Commission Report* 1868 para. 28 reads:—

> In the year 1863 a fight took place between Che Long's society, the Red Flag, and the Toh Peh Kong, after which the two societies became friendly and entered into an alliance for offensive and defensive purposes.

We show in Chapter X how the Indian criminal cult of Thuggism was carried to Penang between 1825–1860 and draw attention to some points of similarity between the rules and rituals of the Toh Peh Kong, the Three Dot Brotherhood and those of Thuggism. In Chapter XIV we show how Thuggist elements penetrated the Red Flag society, thus identifying for practical purposes the Three Dot and the Red Flag as belonging to the "Tokong" camp in Malaya.

Other evidence will be offered to show that the Chinese foundation of the Three Dot Brotherhood in Malaya received an access of strength from Indian criminality through the deportations of Thugs and other convicts from India to the Straits Settlements during the early part of the nineteenth century, and finally in later chapters evidence will be offered to show how the operation of Chinese and Indian organised criminality in Malaya, through Three Dot (Toh Peh Kong) and Thuggist influences at work in Penang, later infected the indigenous Malay population, leading to the development of the dangerous Red Flag society or Bendera Merah amongst the Malays of Penang.

A POSSIBLE DERIVATION OF THE TERM "SAMSENG"

A common term in Malaya for a hooligan is "samseng" for which word the dictionaries offer no etymology. The word is more "localese" than Chinese.

It is commonly used in reference to secret society bullies and gangsters, the more daring and lawless of whom belong to the "Tokong" camp.

We have suggested above under Origin No. (3), a derivation of the name "Three Dot" from the "Three Pure Ones" of the Taoist trinity. If this association is correct it may supply the etymology of the Malay word, derived from *Sam Ch'eng* (三 清) the three guardian devils of the Three Dot Brotherhood.

During the earlier stages of Chinese secret society development in Malaya, members of the Triad society were known among Malays as Sam Hop men from the name of the Hung league then commonly used (三 合 會), "Three United League".

By analogy, it is conceivable that a common earlier mode of reference among Malays and others to members of the Han league, and unrecorded by observers, was Sam Ching men, whence the Malay word "samseng" may have originated.

Another possibility is that the word samseng is adopted from the Chinese words 三 姓 *Sa seh* (lit. "Three Surnames"), pronounced in Hakka *Sum Siang,* and that the three surnames are those of the "Peach Garden Trio" of Chapter II, who were the patrons of the Han league and thence of the Three Dot Brotherhood. The expression sam seng (三 姓) to mean a hooligan is unknown in Chinese. The authorities are silent on the point. We shall refer to this term again in Chapter XXII *infra* when discussing the origin of the Sa Jee (三 字) or "Three Character" society in modern Singapore.

CHAPTER IX

SKETCH OF THE RITUAL OF THE THREE DOT BROTHERHOOD

There are only two published references to a Three Dot ritual, separate and distinct from that of the Triad. These are:—

    (1) Ward and Stirling *op. cit.* (1925) Vol. I pages 176–179, and Vol. III pages 117–120.

    (2) C. B. Cooper (1933). Article in the *Malayan Police Magazine* March, 1933.

No complete authoritative text of the Han league or Three Dot ritual, either in Chinese or in translation, has ever appeared in print, or indeed, so far as is known to us, even exists.

There are, however, certain other notices available to the student, of what we believe to be either the ritual of the Han league under one or other of its disguises, or, at all events the ritual of the "Tokong" camp in Malaya in one or other of its manifestations. These are:—

    (3) The observations of Rev. J. Hutson (1920) given in Chapter II of this work.

    (4) The confessions of C. W. Mason (1924) who was a member of the "Elder Brethren" in 1891. These can be read in his book referred to in Chapter II above.

    (5) The rules of the Toh Peh Kong society of Penang (1868) given in Appendix II to this work.

    (6) A fragment of the ritual of the Ch'ing Pang 青帮 or Green Association of modern China, published in the *China Review*, London, December, 1934, and given in Chapter XXXI below.

Although the publication of Ward and Stirling's work ante-dates the late Mr. Cooper's article by eight years, a comparison shows that the former account is taken direct from Cooper's description, which was in existence in 1924 and available to be seen by a privileged few, although not published until much later.

For this reason we give only Cooper's account in full below, because it was recorded by him at first hand.

Cooper's account is as follows:—

NOTES ON THE SA TIAM OR THREE DOT BROTHERHOOD

(Recorded in 1924—published in 1933.)

"The following facts have come to my knowledge in connection with a case concerning a branch of the brotherhood in North Johore. The society, I understand, extends throughout the Peninsula, and the same ritual applies, and the same signs, tokens and passwords are in use certainly in Negri Sembilan, Kuala Lumpur, Bentong and Pahang, and I believe among the robbers of Perak.

I used formerly to hold the opinion that every member of the brotherhood throughout the Peninsula participated in the proceeds of a robbery but I now think I am correct in saying that it is only the members of the particular branch committing the crime that do, and it is likely that even among these all do not benefit if the result be small.

Members are of three grades or ranks, and an initiate may enter at once into the first or highest rank; this depends on the candidate his intelligence or influence and the benefit and use he may be to the society. About this more will appear later.

There is a fixed contribution. A moderately well-to-do candidate may contribute as much as three hundred dollars, a poor one only seven; but thirty dollars seems to be a more usual figure. Shares in the proceeds of crime seem, however, to depend on the amount contributed and I have reason to believe that the contributor of seven dollars hardly ever receives a share, his contribution being more or less in the nature of an insurance against molestation. This applies to a member of the third or lowest class who is liable to be called on for his services without sharing in the proceeds. I take it that a member of a higher class is entitled to share irrespective of the amount of his contribution.

More will appear later as to the ceremonial attending the initiation of members of different ranks. Those of the first rank appear to possess considerable power, including power to inflict punishment and death on an offender or traitor. They hold enquiries and are in a similar position to magistrates as regards the affairs of the society. The second rank seem to be in the nature of executive officers and the third or lowest are subject to the orders of the higher. The signs will be dealt with later. A member of the second rank may in twenty-four months, provided his conduct is good, be on recommendation promoted to the first rank. In the case of a member of the third rank the period is thirty-six months. Either may, however, before the expiration of that period be promoted for specially meritorious service.

The ceremonials and ritual signs and passwords seem to be akin to the Triad, but my knowledge of Triad societies is not extensive enough to warrant any definite opinion.

I understand that it is dangerous to be acquainted with one or other of the signs without knowing them all and it seems to be particularly important to be acquainted with the passwords. I am assured that many people have met their deaths owing to inability to answer questions correctly even although they have handed out a sign.

I have reason to believe that the description given of the initiation ceremonial is correct and that no detail has been omitted. I also believe that the signs, tokens and words given later are complete or very nearly so. The ceremony of initiation is of the utmost importance. On it many of the passwords are based and the supreme test of a person's membership among strangers is the questioning to which he is submitted as to the points of his initiation. In bygone days in some districts as many as forty candidates would come forward for admission at one time and the occasion which I understand was held once a year often lasted from shortly after sunset to dawn.

Ceremony of Initiation

Description of the lodge.—The place where the initiatory ceremony takes place is carefully prepared as follows:—

Five uprights with connecting rods, similar to trestles, about three to four feet high are prepared. These are well made and portable and are kept for the purpose. They are stood upright one after the other so as to form five arches or portals.

At the far end facing the last trestle is an effigy (usually a picture) of the datoh[1] on a stand of sufficient height to enable a man on his knees to crawl under. Immediately in front of the datoh is a large bowl, a parang and a cup. On the further side of the datoh on the ground side by side are a lighted torch and a parang, the torch being on the left and the parang on the right; and immediately behind and between these, a dead fowl killed by having its neck wrung.

To the left a fire is lighted. Further down is a man selling fruit, cana or olives, and further again, placed zig-zag, three stones or pieces of paper representing stones. On the right of the trestles and about midway is a man selling water. Each trestle has a man to right and left of it armed with a parang and holding joss sticks; and either before the whole place or on the first trestle are the characters "Kiam Jee".[2]

The Five Portals

Candidates are admitted in pairs, this I take it being if they are many in number, but I am not clear on this point.

The candidate approaches the first portal on his knees where he is stopped by its guardians and asked what he wants; he replies "I seek my brethren". He is then questioned as to whether he will preserve inviolate the secrets of the brotherhood and on his replying in the affirmative he is given a lighted joss stick and an oath is administered. At the conclusion the candidate extinguishes the joss stick and I understand he declares that if he breaks his oath as the light of the joss stick is extinguished so may the light of his life be put out, but I am not quite clear on this point. The guards then pass him through the portal by tapping him on the back with their parangs, he passes on, on his knees, to the second portal where the same ceremony is observed, and so on until the fifth portal is passed and he halts opposite the large bowl before the datoh.

The candidate is accompanied by an official or master of ceremonies. This individual passes outside the portals while the candidate is passing through. He holds over his right shoulder an umbrella. If the date be from the first to the twentieth inclusive of the current month he rests his first finger on the shaft of the umbrella; if subsequent thereto the first and second fingers, the thumb and remaining fingers being below. This is important as one of the secret signs is based on this.[3]

In the large bowl before the datoh is a mixture of fowl's blood, arrack, sugar and other ingredients. To this will be added the blood of the candidates as mentioned below.

The taking of the Oath

The candidate, having passed the fifth portal, is in a kneeling posture before the bowl. Here the middle finger of his *right* hand is pricked and blood squeezed out. The candidate puts his finger to his tongue, dips it into the bowl, and again puts it to his tongue. The small cup is now dipped into the mixture in the bowl, a parang placed across the mouth of the bowl, and on the blade of the parang the filled cup is stood. The candidate with hands behind his back and kneeling leans forward and applying his lips to the cup drinks some of the contents.

The candidate now passes under the stand on which is the effigy of the datoh[4] and on the further side is confronted with the lighted torch stuck in the ground on the left and the parang on the right. Here kneeling he crosses his hands and seizes the torch in his right hand and the parang in his left, before him being the corpse of the strangled fowl. I understand, but on this point I am not quite certain that he then repeats an oath to the effect that as the torch

---

Footnote.—(1) Kuan Yu or, Kuan Ti, the God of War *see* page 18 *supra*. Cf. Hutson page 26 *supra* who has, "On a dais in the centre of the meeting place is a tablet to Kuan Yü, which is worshipped by all".

Footnote.—(2) *See* note on "Kiam Jee" at the end of this chapter. It is unfortunate that Cooper, like Stirling, does not give these characters, nor any clue to them.

Footnote.—(3) Cf. the similar but not identical Triad sign referred to on page 127 *supra*.

Footnote.—(4) *See* note below, "The portrait of Kwan Ti".

is extinguished so may his life be put out if he betrays the secrets of the brotherhood, and with hands still crossed puts out the torch by beating it against the ground. I gather, but here again I am not clear that he rests the parang on the corpse of the fowl and again repeats an oath that as the bird has been killed so may it befall him if he reveals the secrets of the brotherhood. With regard to this part of the ceremony I desire it to be clear that although this seems to be substantially what happens I cannot undertake to say that what I have described is the exact sequence and order of what takes place.

Lay-out of a lodge of The Three Dot Brotherhood

This diagram is inserted for the convenience of the reader and follows that of Stirling *op. cit.* Vol. I page 166, which in turn is based on the description of the ceremony by Cooper. The value of this diagram does not necessarily lie in its accuracy of detail, but in the help it gives to fix in the mind the essential difference between a Triad lodge (*see* page 119 above) and a Three Dot ("Tokong") lodge.

For the most part Three Dot initiations in Malaya are conducted with the greatest secrecy, in inaccessible jungle retreats and with make-shift paraphernalia. Nevertheless, the essential materials are always present which make it immediately distinguishable from the Triad ceremony.

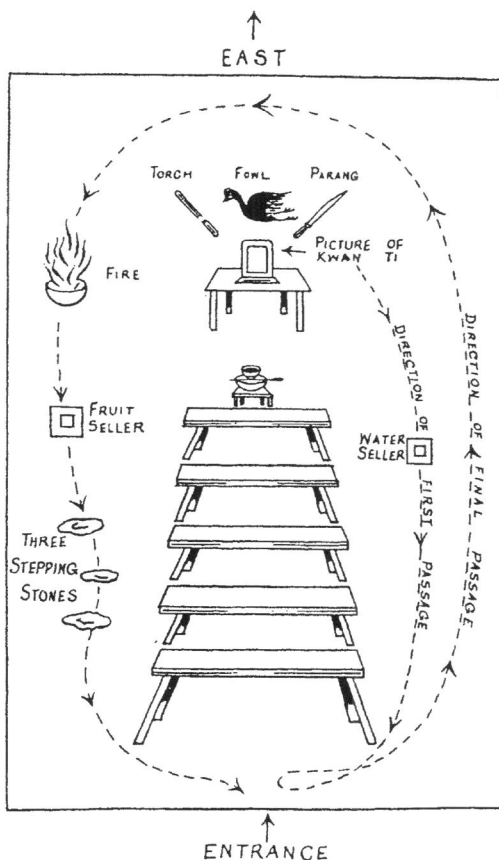

The oath being accomplished the candidate springs to his feet and it appears that his admission is accomplished; it still remains for him to pass in review before the assembled brethren and to be instructed in the signs, tokens and words.

I am not clear as to whether the candidate is instructed before he passes in review or whether he passes in review first. I am inclined, however, to believe that he is instructed on some points at least before the final passing in review as this concludes with an exit which would naturally take him out of the ceremony. This, however, is clear; that at some time subsequent to his final oath he is instructed, and that an official of the society is appointed to instruct him on any points on any subsequent occasion should him memory fail him in any particulars.

The Perambulations

The candidate now passes in review. His right arm and shoulder are bared by being taken out of the sleeve and should his coat have buttons it is fastened with two buttons. The end of his left trouser leg is rolled up and fastened in a knot by being twisted and turned inwards or towards the leg. The left lapel or left side of the coat or baju neck is rolled inwards. This is one of the signs.

The candidate in passing in review first turns to the right and perambulates the assembly three times clockwise, passing outside the portals. He is met on the right of the portals by an official who presents him with a cup of water. For this he pays a cent. This is a point of importance as subsequent tests by way of questions are directed to this. Having circled the assembly three times clockwise he turns and circles the assembly three times in the opposite direction. On his final round, and after passing the datoh, he approaches the fire; this he steps or leaps over. He then approaches the fruit seller and purchases a cana or olive for twenty-one cents. This again is of importance as it forms a test on subsequent occasions of the *bona fides* of a professed member. He finally approaches the stones or papers representing stones. On the first he places his right foot, this being the foot by which an exit is made, on the second his left foot and on the third his right foot zig-zag as the stones are placed. This is symbolically his exit as an initiate from the ceremony of initiation.

The Appointment to Grades

After all the candidates have been admitted they assemble at the entrance facing the first portal. Those who have been admitted directly into the first rank are then seated. The first man is given a fan; his forehead is bound with a red cloth and stuck in the band so as to come over the candidate's forehead is a small rod attached to which is a piece of paper on which is a drawing representing the datoh. The second man is similarly treated only in his case the rod is placed at the back of the head and he is not given a fan. The remaining members of the first class among the new initiates are given nothing. The other new members now make obeisance on their knees to their colleagues of the first rank.

They now make way for the new members of the second rank who seat themselves. To the first man is given a fan, to the second a left shoe. This appears to be a symbol that whereas the first is not required to bestir himself the other may be required to travel in the business of the society. It is apparently only symbolical as the second rank are subject to the orders of the first. The second rank have obeisance made to them by the new members of the third rank. These do not assume the seats occupied by the two higher ranks but are on the ground the whole time.

One final point remains to be touched on. It would appear that at the close of the ceremony the effigy of the datoh is moved and carried to the entrance of the assembly-place by members of a certain rank. I am inclined to this view rather than that the datoh is carried from the entrance to its position fronting the fifth portal at the commencement by the members mentioned. Whatever it be, it is only members of the first and second rank who are privileged to touch the datoh and assist in the carrying. Members of an inferior rank are not permitted to do so.

Secret Signs of the Three Dot Brotherhood

The signs of the Brotherhood are many in number, and I have endeavoured to classify them roughly. I emphasize that it is dangerous to know only one or two of the signs, as this may lead to questioning and so the imposture be revealed. I have referred to passwords. These are nearly all based on the ritual of the initiatory ceremony and it is important that their points be remembered as questions are directed to these features :—

I. The General or Universal sign.—Join the thumb and first finger of the right hand so as to form a loop or circle with the thumb, overlapping top joint of first finger. Extend the other three fingers.[1]

Footnote.—(1) This is the sign of Earth *see* illustration No. F.2 to face page 116 in Ward and Stirling *op. cit.* Vol. I. Its appropriateness as the universal sign of the Three Dot society which we identify with the Han league and with the Yin or female or earth principle has been explained in Chapter III. The sign itself is that of the *vesica piscis* (see page 45 *supra*) and is totally different from the universal sign of the Triad (*see* page 124 *supra*).

II. To demonstrate one's membership to the casual observer.—This of course can be done by any of the other signs but under this head I include the following :—

(a) Left side of collar rolled inwards.

(b) Right cuff or sleeve rolled and twisted inwards into a knot, the knot being next to the skin.

(c) End of left trouser leg twisted into a knot as in (a) supra.

(d) Alternatively to (b) the whole arm and shoulder may be bared by removing arm from the sleeve. If the coat has buttons it should be fastened with two buttons, the right side of the coat passing under the arm. (This is an important sign when passing through districts infested with robbers. I know of one contractor who habitually did this and although he frequently had as much as two thousand dollars on him he was never molested.)

(e) When carrying a stick or umbrella and if the date be from the 1st to the 20th of the current Chinese month the first finger should be on the side of the stick to the front or top and the thumb and other fingers on the other side; if the date be subsequent to the twentieth let the first and second fingers be on top or to the front.

III. On entering a room or house do so left foot first on leaving a room or house do so right foot first. (In this connection vide the initiatory ceremony when the candidate has passed in review).

IV. In the dark.—If in the dark and hearing a noise strike a match and throw it up, and repeat three times in all.

V. When Washing.—Dip face towel thrice in water. Then fold twice, a third at a time, from right to left so that it is threefold. Wring out thrice. Open out and hold between thumb and first finger of each hand, with the back of the hand out. Throw towel once round between the hand and then put right hand inside the towel, palm up, and pile towel on right palm with left hand. With towel on right hand start on right side of jaw and wipe up right side of face over forehead and down left side to chin.

VI. In everyday social intercourse :—

(a) When offering a cup either (1) hold cup by rim between thumb and first two fingers. The hand is then over the mouth of the cup, or (2) hold cup between thumb and second finger, touching rim with first finger, the hand being on the side of the cup, palm down, or (3) the cup may be held by the handle with first finger through, thumb above and second finger supporting it below. In every case a little of the contents should be spilt.

(b) When receiving a cup (as a counter-sign) take with same hand as the offerer holds it. If offered as in (1) receive cup by bottom in same manner, the back of hand being downwards. If offered as in (2) received in same manner as offered. If offered as in (3) form general sign with both hands, the tips of both thumbs and forefingers touching. Grip cup between both second fingers, one on each side.

(c) When offering a box of matches or similar object either (1) hold between thumb and second finger, these resting on either end the first finger rests on the striking part of the box, but does not overlap so as to come on top or (2) hold in palm of hand with ball of thumb on top of box and forefinger curled round one end. In this position the second and other fingers are curled below the box.

(d) When receiving a box (as a counter-sign) accept with the same hand as the offerer holds it. If offered as in (1) receive in a similar manner but rest first finger over the edge of the box so as to overlap the top. If offered as in (2) receive similarly and curl second finger so as to engage second finger of offerer below the box.

(e) When offering another a light strike match towards self holding lighted end towards self between the first two fingers of right hand, extending the hand towards the person to whom the match is offered. The person accepting takes the match between the first and second fingers, palm towards himself, and applies to it to his cigarette. I understand that if he desires to light a pipe he turns the lighted end inwards (presumably for convenience). In any case before throwing it away which he does to the right and backwards he first turns the burnt end of the match outwards, the match being between the first and second fingers.

(f) When offering a cigarette offer the tin or packet with two cigarettes projecting beyond the others. When accepting a cigarette offered as above, with the back of the first and second fingers held together press the two projecting cigarettes level with the others. Then pick out a cigarette.

(g) To light a cigarette hold cigarette between the first and second fingers of the left hand with end to be lighted towards self between first and second fingers and apply to end of cigarette towards self. When alight turn wrist and put cigarette to mouth, the palm being outwards. The match is turned round between fingers, burnt ends outwards, and thrown away backwards from between the first and second fingers.

(h) When drinking from a cup hold by handle as in VI (a) (3). When drinking from a glass hold between second finger and thumb, the first finger crooked over the rim. Spill a little before drinking.

(i) When eating, if taking anything with a spoon do not rub bottom of spoon on rim of vessel or plate. With chopsticks do not level them by pressing them on table but against the palm of the hand.

(j) When smoking chandu hold pipe, left hand near mouth, with finger or fingers on top as in holding a stick, vide II (e), the other hand between bowl and mouth with thumb and forefinger on top and other fingers below and bowl to the right. If offering mouthpiece turn pipe between hands, shifting finger or fingers as the case may be so as to be on top at the finish as before.

VII. When attacked on road; form general sign with both hands; extend right hand towards attacker, and bending elbow of left arm place the tip of thumb and forefinger joined to left shoulder. (Also see those paras. dealing with passwords at the end of this article.)

VIII. To ward off attack on a house; place before doorway a large bowl containing water. Across this lay a parang. On parang blade stand a small cup of water. (In this connection refer to the similar arrangement at the initiation ceremony). If attacked in house before the foregoing sign can be prepared take a cup in left hand, and holding it towards assailant, break by striking bottom with a parang, hammer or other implement.

IX. (a) If hungry and desiring a meal take a cap or other headgear and place top of crown on stomach so that the interior of hat faces outwards. (The converse denotes repletion).

(b) If, on entering a house, you desire to sleep the night, place hat with right hand on right shoulder, resting crown on shoulder, interior facing up. (Conversely with crown up denotes an intention to stay only a little while). To show membership place hat crown down on table or chair.

(c) If in need of pecuniary assistance, with right hand place hat under left arm, crown against left side of body and interior facing innerside of left arm.

X. If it happens that one meets twigs stretched across a path or an obstruction such as a stick placed across the way a little height above the ground or Chinese characters traced in the dust or sand it is probable that people are in hiding. It is necessary to demonstrate to them that one is a brother to avoid molestation :—

(a) If twigs or stones be across the path they must not be stepped over but carefully shifted on one side with the toe of the left foot.

(b) If there be writing the same applies. In passing obliterate with the tip of the left foot or shoe.

(c) If a stick be met placed at a height across the path place first and second fingers of left hand on stick, thumb and other fingers under. Turn left side to obstruction and step over it sideways, left leg first.

XI. In the house of a stranger if you desire to ascertain if you can stay with him place shoes, when taken off, so that one points towards the interior of the house and the other towards the door. If owner of house is able to put you up he will alter shoes so that both point towards the interior of the house. If he is unable to do so he will place shoes so that both point outwards to the doorway.

XII. The signs of the different ranks :—

(a) The First Rank.—Take a piece of paper and fold it down and across. Turn down the corner which when opened out is the centre of the sheet, in a fold. Then make a further fold outwards and a final and third fold inwards so that the corner of the paper is threefold. On opening it out a design of three diamonds, one within the other, will be disclosed in the centre of the paper.

(b) The Second Rank.—Fold paper once and make similar folds in one of the corners which, when the paper is unfolded, represents the middle of one side. When opened out a design of three triangles, one within the other, will be disclosed in the middle of one side.

(c) The Third Rank.—Fold paper down and across and then diagonally, and fold as before that point which will be the centre of the paper when unfolded. When opened three octagonal figures one within the other, will appear.[1]

Of passwords in the strict sense there appear to be none or very few and I use the word in its wide sense to include answers to questions. These appear to be often put, when a sign is offered, as a further test of a person's *bona fides* and the questions are usually on the points of the candidate's initiation. It is apparently essential that on being questioned he should be able to retail the main points as thus :—

I was present at a *wayang* = theatrical performance. (in Malaya, the initiation ceremony is referred to by this term).

I passed the five portals.

I took an oath.

Footnote.—(1) *Cf.* illustrations reproduced in Appendix X.

I drank blood.

I worshipped the datoh.

I saw a dead fowl and swore on it.

I drank water for which I paid one cent. (The price is important).

I ate a fruit for which I paid twenty-one cents. (The price is important).

I passed out over the stones right foot first.

The following are further questions :—

Q. "How many eyes have you?"

A. "Three." (Here the candidate usually puts his hand to his face, first finger on right eye, third on left eye and second between, but this is not essential).

Q. "How is it that you have three eyes when others have only two?"

A. "My first eye is to see the datoh, my second to see my brothers, and my third to regard myself".

Q. "How many times do you eat?"

A. "Three and half, namely—rice once; fruit once; water once; and a half thus." (Here apply the tip of the second finger of the right hand to the tongue.)[1]

The following questions and answers may be used if held up in the road :—

The person held up says :—

"This coat is mine and has a chop" (here he should touch the back behind the left shoulder blade with the right hand). "The chop is "Kiam Jee"."

Q. "What 'Seh'?" (Surname).

A. "Seh 'Ang' (Hokien sound for 'Hung') (or 'Ang Chew').[2] Do you now intend to rob me?"

The answer should be "No", we were only joking".

The foregoing is as complete an account and description of the signs, questions and answers as I have been able to obtain. I must again emphasize the danger of knowing only one or two signs as they will provoke questions and countersigns which unless answered will inevitably reveal the fraud with unpleasant results.

This concludes Cooper's very interesting notes. It will be observed that although he describes a different aspect of the subject, his account nevertheless bears a general family likeness to similar matters mentioned by Hutson (Chapter II) as belonging to the Ko Lao Hui or society of Elder Brethren.

This is the more remarkable when we remember that Cooper, an advocate and solicitor of Johore Bahru, was not a Chinese scholar, nor a special student of secret society matters, although extremely well-informed upon things Chinese in general, and that the medium of his information for the above notes was probably not Chinese as in the case of Hutson, but Malay. The resemblance becomes all the more remarkable when we consider the distance and circumstances dividing the observations of Hutson in a purely Chinese environment in Szechuan and the account of Cooper recorded in a purely Malay environment in Johore, in a secret society case in 1923, in which Malays and Chinese were jointly concerned.

INCIDENCE OF THE THREE DOT CATCH-WORD "KIAM JEE" IN THE MALAY RED FLAG CEREMONY.

In 1934; we obtained from an ex-penghulu of Johore a description of the initiation ceremony of the Malay Red Flag society. This description is given *in extenso* in the "Johore" section of Chapter XXVIII *infra*, and the catechism, which was supplied to us in both Malay and romanised Hakka, is given *verbatim* in Chapter XXIX, where it more conveniently belongs for comparative purposes, and where it is identified with that of the Three Dot Brotherhood.

To avoid repetition of the whole, the following questions and answers which have a bearing on the subject of this Chapter, have been extracted from that catechism.

Initiator   Q. Awak datang mana?

Catechist   A. Saya datang mata hari mati, mahu pergi mata hari hidop. (*i.e.* From West to East, the reverse of the Triad ritual).

Q. (Challenge by the initiator as he seizes the coat of the catechist). Ini baju saya punya?

A. Bukan. Saya punya. Ada surat.

Footnote.—(1) *Cf.* the Malay version in the Red Flag ceremony given in Chapter XXIX *infra*.

Footnote.—(2) This no doubt stands for the character 紅 ang or hung = red. Ang Chew may stand for 紅 旗 or the Hung Chi or Red Flag of Hutson (*see* page 26 *supra*) *cf.* also a similar question and answer in the Malay fragment given below in this chapter. There is no reason to assume that the surname referred to is 洪 hung = inundation, which is the surname adopted by all members of the Triad (*see* pages 1 and 10 *supra*); but it would be in keeping with the Chinese practice of playing on words that this reading should be accepted by the profane, which would help to maintain the confusion among the uninitiated between the Triad and the Tokong camps. The extract from the Malay version of the Red Flag ritual which follows, helps to clarify this point.

Q. Apa surat?
A. Ada chop belakang.
    (The Chinese version has, "Kiam Jee Ho", for "chop").
Q. Apa bangsa chop?
    (The Chinese version has "what colour" (色).
A. Bangsa bendera merah.
    (The Chinese version is "The colour is red").

We here find the "password" of the Three Dot society "Kiam Jee" meaning "chop" or "label", noted by Cooper above, appearing in the Malay ritual of the Red Flag society: and the colour red, which is consistently identified with the Han league, appearing in the same context.

We discuss below the probable derivation of this "password", identifying it through the Tally society of Hutson, with the society of the Elder Brethren and the Han league.

THE CEREMONY OF BAPTISM IN THE SOCIETY OF GOD WORSHIPPERS.

In Chapters IV and VIII *supra* we have referred to the stated origin of the Three Dot Brotherhood in the Society of God Worshippers, who became the Taiping rebels in 1850–1864.

Brine *op. cit.* page 81 gives a description of the "baptism" ceremony among the God-Worshippers, which is mildly reminiscent of the Three Dot initiation ceremony as given by Cooper.

THE PORTRAIT OF KWAN TI (關帝)

This item of the regalia is clearly the central though not the most important feature in the Three Dot lodge ceremony. It is variously referred to as an effigy (as by Cooper above) and as a portrait, a tablet, the Dato' and the Toh Peh Kong: but all accounts agree that whatever its form, it represents Kwan Yu, the second of the Peach Garden trio (Chapter II) in his deified form of Kwan Ti (*see* page 18 supra). One might almost expect to find the origin of the name "Three Dot", hidden in this representation of the God of War, the symbol of physical force in the world, as opposed to the spirituality which underlies the Triad ceremony and its watchword "Obey heaven and act righteously".

We are here met with a difficulty, namely, *Does the portrait of Kwan Ti occupy an official place in the Triad ceremony as well as in that of the Three Dot?*

If we take Schlegel as our guide, we will find no mention of the effigy of Kwan Ti either in the appurtenances of a Triad lodge nor in the Triad ceremony itself. The references to the "Peach Garden trio" in Schlegel's work, whether singly or collectively, are given at the foot of page 20 *supra*. The only other reference in Schlegel is *op. cit.* page 52 where "the birthday of the God Kwan" is mentioned among the festivals celebrated by the brethren of the Hung league, on which day each member contributes 72 cash to society funds.

This observance can be explained as being merely an incidental acknowledgment of the debt the Hung league admits it owes to the Peach garden trio as the originators of the symbolic oath of the Peach garden, which they use in their ritual—an incidental acknowledgment, but nothing more.

Similarly none of the other Triad texts (quoted in Chapter VII) assign any place of honour in the ritual to the Peach Garden trio in general, or to Kwan Ti in particular.

This omission notwithstanding, we are faced with the fact that both Stanton *op. cit.* page 41 and Ward and Stirling *op. cit.* Vol. I page 15, allege the common presence of the portrait of Kwan Ti in Triad lodges. In addition, Ward and Stirling in their illustrations (*op. cit.* Vol. I to face pages 24 and 40) show the portrait of Kwan Ti among the paraphernalia that purports to belong to a Triad lodge. But we must remember that these illustrations are *artificial*. They are photographs of a conglomeration of articles found in various lodges in Malaya, all of which were believed to be "branches of the Triad society", but some of which, no doubt, were "Tokong" lodges. These articles were found by officers unaware of the existence of the Han league side by side with the Hung. The portrait of Kwan Ti may, therefore, quite innocently, but erroneously have become included among the essentials of a Triad lodge, whereas it may properly belong exclusively to a Three Dot lodge.

Or again, the general popularity of the portrait of Kwan Ti among the Chinese community which has no connection with secret society matters, may have suggested to Triad lodge officials to include it in lodge appurtenances as a convenient camouflage or as a useful means of confusing the authorities, both in Hong Kong and Malaya, in regard to the separate nature of the two hostile secret society camps. This is only conjecture, but the point requires an explanation, which further research may provide.

Stanton's work in common with that of Ward and Stirling may unconsciously confuse and intermix what belongs exclusively to the Han league, with the detail of the Hung league praxis, with which alone they were familiar.

Thus, Stanton *op. cit.* page 42 has:—

> In some Cantonese lodges candidates during initiation have to crawl between the legs of this officer (the Second Brother or Incence Master) as a typical representation of being born into the Hung family: in such lodges the Second Brother is styled the Ah Ma = Mother.

As we believe the Han league ritual to symbolise physical birth and life in this world, it would seem probable that Stanton was here confusing Han league with Hung league ritual, since we know the latter to symbolise physical death and the soul's journey to the next.

The wording of the passage suggests that Stanton was himself aware of a considerable variation from the orthodox Hung practice "in some Cantonese lodges" in Hong Kong. These may have been Han or Three Dot lodges, the names of which in Hong Kong we have suggested on page 111 and 112 *supra*.

Again Stanton *op. cit.* page 42 has:—

> Many persons, especially women, are initiated without ever going to a lodge.

We know from Hutson that women are freely admitted to the Han league, while the consensus of authoritative opinion is that women are not admitted to the Hung. This fact again suggests that Stanton has confused Hung and Han praxis, which latter would include the presence of a portrait of Kwan Ti in what he took to be a Hung lodge.

Thus, on page 41 *op. cit.* Stanton has:—

> But on account of the (Triad) society being illegal in most places, and there being always a desire to keep the work secret, these shrines *except the one to Kwan Ti*, appear only at initiations, and then only on paper.

This passage suggests that the shrine or portrait of Kwan Ti is a permanent fixture in a Triad lodge. This we believe either to be an error of fact or else a camouflage introduced by Triad lodge officials as colour-protection. We know from Hutson that the portrait of Kwan Ti is the central object of worship in a Han league initiation. He says, page 26 *supra*:—

> On a dais in the centre of the meeting place is a tablet to Kuan Yu, which is worshipped by all.

Cooper's description above bears out this important feature in respect of the Three Dot ceremony.

Three final considerations provide almost conclusive reasons why the portrait of Kwan Ti may not be associated with the Hung at all, but must belong to the Han league. These are:—

(a) If Kwan Ti's portrait really occupied such a prominent position as Stanton and Stirling suggest, or even took any distinguishable part in the Triad ritual, we must expect to find the portrait or effigy the recipient of one of the *Eight Salutations* (*see* page 121 above), which conclude the Triad ceremony. But it is unmentioned therein.

(b) In the story of the Peach Garden Trio (Chapter II) the three sworn brothers of whom Kwan Ti was the second, were the supporters of the Han dynasty and the conquerors of the three born brothers (the Yellow Cap rebels), who, we have suggested (page 18 *supra*), were the protagonists of the Hung league. If such be the position, we would not expect to find Kwan Ti revered by the Hung league.

(c) In the story of the Peach Garden Trio and before he became the god of war, Kwan Ti had been "a fugitive on the waters", because he had committed a murder (*see* page 17). As war is consecrated to killing and killing is forbidden by Buddhism, we would be as unlikely to find honour done in a Buddhist temple to the god of war as in a Triad lodge, whose motto is "obey Heaven and act righteously".

The uncertainty surrounding the presence or absence of the portrait of Kwan Ti in the Triad ceremony, may thus be attributable to that same confusion between the two main stems of the secret society world, which has characterised past researches; and its inclusion by Stanton and Stirling in the Triad lodge appurtenances may be due to their natural anxiety to account for the portrait by including it in the one ceremony known to them (Triad), whereas it may properly belong exclusively to the other ("Tokong").

Other features of the Three Dot ceremony which we must now notice, lend colour to this belief.

SOME FURTHER OBSERVATIONS ON THE THREE DOT CEREMONY

First we should notice that the Three Dot ceremony is invariably held at night from sunset to dawn and that it is worked from the west to the east which suggests its identity with the left or Yin or female principle (Chapter III) and with the Han league, as opposed to the Hung ceremony which is worked from the east to the west and is frequently held in the daytime.

Further, there is reason to believe that a black fowl is used in the Three Dot ritual as opposed to the white cock of the Triad, but this point awaits confirmation.[1] It is also

Footnote.—(1) *See* note at end of this Chapter page 151.

not certain whether a female fowl is used in the Three Dot ritual, which might have its own special significance in the application of the Yin Yang principle to the ceremony.

It should be noted that the white cock of the Triad is alive until it is decapitated by the candidate as the final act of taking the thirty six oaths, whereas the (? black) fowl of the Three Dot is already dead by strangulation when the ceremony begins.

At an initiation meeting of the Three Dot society among Hakkas and Teochews held in the jungle near Bangi, Selangor, in 1922, upon which a successful Police raid was made at night, a young Hakka woman decorously attired was found to be taking part.

The darkness and the difficulty of approach unobserved by outlying scouts, prevented observation to determine the part assigned to the woman. From this, and other similar cases reported, it seems probable however that at some Three Dot initiations among Chinese, a woman takes the place of the effigy of Kwan Ti.

This does not necessarily apply to Red Flag initiations among Malays, but in this connection we have heard of a roast pig (unclean to Mohamedans) being used at a Red Flag ceremony in Perak in 1933, presumably in substitution of the Toh Peh Kong. This is without confirmation.

We have indeed heard of a secret society initiation which took place near Woodleigh, Singapore, some 20 years ago, in which the Police raiding party found an unclothed Chinese woman in a sitting posture, which suggests that the particular ceremony was a Three Dot one and that the woman was acting in substitution for the god. In the past there has been so little systematic investigation into the factual details of such cases that much more careful and comparative examination is necessary, before any final conclusion can be drawn upon their esoteric significance.

These incidents, however, suggest the occasional substitution of a living woman for the Toh Peh Kong or "Tokong" in the Three Dot ceremony.

As the candidate is required to pass crawling beneath the stand upon which the "Tokong" rests, the substitution would serve to emphasise the esoteric meaning of physical birth, which we believe to be implicit in the Three Dot ceremony.

INTERPRETATION OF THE THREE DOT CEREMONY

The foregoing points are of interest from the interpretative angle.

Ward and Stirling *op. cit.* Vol. III pages 117–120 furnish an interesting commentary on the symbolic meaning of the Three Dot ceremony, in which they arrive at the following two main conclusions:—

    (1) It would seem that the ceremony represents in some measure the missing degree or degrees, which the nature of the Hung ceremony postulates.

    (2) The ceremony denotes the descent of the soul into matter, or physical birth, and the journey of man through this world.

These conclusions exactly fit the Yin Yang theory as presented in Chapter III and identify the Three Dot with the Ko Lao Hui or Han league which is antecedent to the Hung, the ceremony of the former representing physical birth, the latter physical death and the journey of the soul through the under-world.

In this connection *see* also Ward and Stirling Vol. II pages 177–178, section entitled "Masonic parallels in the Triad and Three Dot ceremonies". What concerns us chiefly in the Three Dot ritual as given above are those features which will re-appear in the Malay ceremony of initiation into the Red Flag society, which we identify as the Mohamedan prototype of the Han league in Malaya, and which is fully discussed in Chapter XXIX and to which frequent reference is made in Chapters XXI and XXIII below.

PROMINENT THREE DOT FEATURES OF INITIATION

For convenient reference, the prominent Three Dot features are:—

    (1) The initiation takes place from sunset to dawn and is worked from West towards East.

    (2) There are five gates instead of three as in the Triad ritual.

    (3) The initiates stoop or crawl under the gates or trestles.

    (4) The initiates travel straight up the lodge.[1]

    (5) The initiate kneels before the god or Toh Peh Kong who is Kwan Ti second of the Peach Garden trio and the god of war with a bowl in front of him.

    (6) In the bowl there is a mixture of fowl's blood, Chinese wine (arak) and sugar.

    (7) The middle finger of the *right* hand of each initiate is pricked, and blood squeezed out into the bowl.

    (8) The candidate puts a finger on his tongue, dips it in the bowl, and again puts it on his tongue. (The sign of secrecy).

Footnote.—(1) These features according to Ward and Stirling Vol. III pages 117–118 symbolise the comparatively swift descent of the soul into matter or physical birth.

(9) A small cup is filled from the mixture in the bowl, the sword or parang is placed across the bowl and the cup is placed on the blade of the parang.

(10) The candidate still kneeling and with his hands behind his back, leans forward and sips the contents of the cup, thus causing his reflection to fall in the bowl.

(11) Thereafter he passes kneeling or crawling beneath the stand upon which rests the effigy of the Toh Peh Kong (variously referred to in Malaya as the "Dato" "The Dato Peking" "The Topekong" "The Tokong", etc.).

(12) He then finds himself kneeling between a lighted torch on his left and a parang on his right with the corpse of a strangled fowl in front of him.

(13) Crossing his hands he takes the torch in his right hand and the parang in his left, and takes the oath of the Brotherhood. "As this torch is extinguished so may my life be put out if I betray the secrets of the Brotherhood".

(14) With hands still crossed he beats out the torch on the ground.

(15) He then lays the parang on the corpse of the fowl and repeats the oath. "As this bird has been slain, so may it befall me if I reveal the secrets of the Brotherhood".

(16) The candidate then rises to his feet and circumambulates the lodge three times in a clockwise direction, i.e. following the course of the sun. (This is said by Ward and Stirling to typify life on this earth, viz., Youth, Manhood and Old Age). There is similar ambulation in the Triad ceremony.

(17) As he reaches a point at the beginning of the first circuit he purchases a cup of water for one cent, symbolising baptism, or the obliteration of the memory of former lives.

(18) On completion of the three circuits, he then travels three more times in the opposite direction, typifying physical death.

(19) He thereafter jumps over a fire, symbolising the crossing of the mouth of hell.

(20) He there meets a fruitseller, and purchases a fruit for twenty-one cents symbolising the purchase of the fruit of eternal life in Paradise.

(21) He then reaches three stepping stones (represented by pieces of paper) placed zig-zag. He steps on these with the right foot first, symbolising the crossing of the river separating Paradise from the City of the Gods.

This ends the ceremony of initiation proper, and it is possible that it is here at this point that we find the candidates at the beginning of the Triad ritual, awaiting admission to the next degree, the Hung door.

PROMINENT FEATURES OF INVESTITURE

After completion of the Three Dot initiation proper, the following are the prominent features of the investiture ceremony which succeeds it:—

(1) There are three grades of investiture (Hutson suggests twelve). Admission to these is governed by the intelligence, influence and social position of the candidate, and the amount of his subscription on admission.

　　(a) The heads of the order who take the largest share of the proceeds of robbery.

　　(b) The executive officers who hunt up recruits and carry out initiations.

　　(c) The rank and file, who have to prove themselves by carrying out the nefarious work of the society.

(2) Promotion from one grade to the other is possible either on a time scale or by accelerated promotion on merit. Normally grade (c) serve 36 months before promotion to grade (b) and grade (b) 24 months before promotion to grade (a).

(3) Throughout the initiation the candidates are accompanied by an official carrying an umbrella.

(4) After the initiation ceremony, the initiates assemble before the first portal in three groups according to the grade to which they are to be admitted.

(5) The initiates of grade (a) group being seated, the first of them receives a fan and his forehead is bound with a red cloth. Into this band is inserted, in front over his brow, a small rod to which is attached a piece of paper having on it a drawing of the god, or Toh Peh Kong. (Kwan Ti).

(6) The second initiate of grade (a) also has his head bound with a red cloth into which a similar rod and paper is stuck at the back of his head. He is not given a fan.

(7) The remaining members of the first rank are given nothing, but all new members make obeisance on their knees to their comrades of the first rank, and way is made for those of grade (b).

(8) The members of grade (b) being seated, the first man of them receives a fan.

(9) The second man of grade (b) receives a left shoe.

(10) The remaining members of the second rank receive nothing, but all members of the third rank make obeisance to those of the second rank.

(11) Members of grade (c) do not sit down and are not given any emblem.

(12) This completes the investiture, and at its close the effigy of the Toh Peh Kong is carried to the entrance by members of the first and second ranks.

There is nowhere any explanation offered as to why the fowl must be killed by strangulation. Nor is there any explanation given as to the reason for the presence of sugar in the bowl at the ceremony. These two features suggest a connection with Thuggist rites. (see Chapter X).

In the dedication of the members of the Three Dot to a life of criminality, there is also seen a parallel to the belief among Thugs that the cult of murder in the service of Kali has a divine origin. In Chapters XII, XIV and XV *infra* we show how Indian Thuggism has become blended with the Three Dot society in Malaya.

CONCLUSION ON THE ORIGIN OF THE THREE DOT SOCIETY CATCH-WORD "KIAM JEE"

Both Stirling and Cooper mention the use in the Three Dot society of the catch-word, or "chop", Kiam Jee, but in neither case is the meaning of the expression or the Chinese characters given. The catch-word appears to be peculiar to the "Three Dot" as distinct from the Triad ritual, and its further exploration provides a valuable clue to the origin and connections of the Three Dot Brotherhood.

Enquiry made from Mr. Stirling in 1935 failed to obtain the Chinese characters or meaning of the phrase.

The term is used apparently by members as a sort of pass-word, and its meaning must be known to thousands of Chinese in Malaya, but for some reason it does not appear to have been hitherto disclosed.

The following explanations of this term are now offered, which, if either of them finds acceptance, will tend to confirm the view that the Three Dot society has an origin in the Han league.

(1) The Malay source in Johore, previously mentioned, when asked to obtain the Chinese characters for the term Kiam Jee, later produced the following characters written in a Chinese hand:—

　　　謙 Kiam ＝ "modest, humble";

　　　字 Jee ＝ "word, letter or (Chinese) character".

pronounced as above in Hokkien, Teochew, and Hakka. No explanation of the term accompanied the two characters, and the Malay source could himself furnish none.

The characters as supplied by him, do not at first sight contain any meaning, nor offer any clue to help in their elucidation.

If we now refer to the beginning of Hutson's article given in Chapter II we find mention of the Ch'ien Tzu Hang (籤子行) or "Tally Society", which he there states is the same as the Han Liu, or Ko Lao Hui.

The Chinese name for the "Tally Society" is romanised above by Hutson in the Szechuan dialect. If we romanise the name in the Hokkien dialect we get:—

　　　　　Ch'ieng Jee Hang

　　and in Hakka—

　　　　　Tsiam Jee Hang.

The meaning of this character 籤 Ch'ien, Ch'ieng or Ts'iam, is given as follows by Giles (No. 1697) :—

"A label: To make a note of: To record".

　籤貼子 "To paste on a label".

From which we get 籤子 Ts'iam Jee ＝ A label.

Giles continues:—

"Same sound as:—

　　No. 1698 籤 "A slip of bamboo: A lot as used for divination: A warrant: a tally".

Which in turn is interchangeable with:—

　　No. 1714 籤 (Pronounced in Hokkien *Ch'ieng* and in Hakka *Ch'iam*) "A bamboo slip: A lot used for divination: To send (as constables) To sign: To endorse:" Hung Kiam Jee—A strip of red paper or label in a letter, or parcel on which the address is written.

籤字 Ch'iam Jee ⎫

籤名 Ch'iam Miang ⎬ To sign, to affix a signature.

籤押 Ch'iam Kap ⎭

From this we find a close affinity between the name of the Tally society (which is the same as the Ko Lao Hui) and the catch-word of the Three Dot society "Kiam Jee". The affinity becomes even closer when we realise the context in which the catch-word always appears, namely:—

"the chop is Kiam Jee" (see ritual above).

The word "chop" signifying "mark" "seal" "brand" or "trade mark", is closely akin to the meaning "label" or "signature" which we find in the name of the Tally society.

Again Hutson in Chapter II has:—

"The salutations of the society are very complex. The general term for them is 丟 筶 子 Tiu Kiam Jee, or "casting the tally".

As sound and meaning and context are all three thus demonstrably similar, it seems highly probable that the origin of the catch-word "Kiam Jee" is to be found in the Chinese name of the Tally society of Hutson. (*see* Chapter VIII page 134). It also seems probable that, as so often happens with Chinese characters, the two characters 謙 字 Kiam Jee, put forward by the Malay source, and which give the exact sound in Hakka, are a substitute for

either 幟 子 pronounced in colloquial Hokkien Ch'iam Tzu

or 籤 子   ,,   ,,   ,,   Ch'iam Tzu

or 筶 子   ,,   ,,   ,,   Ch'iam Tzu

or 筶 字   ,,   ,,   ,,   Ch'iam Jee.

all of which are possible combinations of characters to represent the name of the Tally society (Kiam Jee Hong) or "Society of the Elder Brethren" (Ko Lao Hui) which belongs to the Han league in China and to the "Tokong" camp in Malaya.

Although we believe the foregoing to represent the probable origin of the expression Kiam Jee, it would be unsafe to dismiss the possibility of other origins, until more is known.

In this connection Plate No. 12 in Stanton *op. cit.* page 91, which refers to the Fuk On She of Hong Kong in 1900 (*see* Chapter V), may be an actual specimen of such a "Tally", as is referred to by the term "Kiam Jee" and the first two characters in this Plate *viz:*— 見筶 Chien Ch'iam, "Upon seeing this tally", may provide the name for Vaughan's "Chin Chin" society which we have already identified with the Han league in Chapter V (*see* also Chapter XXVI below).

(2) A second explanation of the term is that the characters 謙 字 Kiam Jee or "Humble Word" of the Malay source mentioned above, stand for the characters 劍 仔 which can have the same sound "Kiam Jee", and anyway mean "Small Sword". This name suggests the Dagger society of Amoy mentioned in Chapter II, which also belonged to the "Tokong" camp.

The recorded name of the Dagger society is 小 刀 Siu To or "Small Knife" society, but the possibility of its being also known behind the scenes in Malaya as the 劍 仔 Kiam Jee or Small Sword society, cannot be altogether ruled out.

A main objection to this explanation is, however, that it takes no account of the recurrent association in the Three Dot ritual of the term "chop" (mark, label, tally) with the expression Kiam Jee, for example, Ward and Stirling, Vol. I page 119:—

A. "This coat is mine and has a "chop" on it.
Q. "What "chop" "?
A. The "chop" is Kiam Jee.

The last line could, of course, mean "The chop or mark of the Small Sword society" or "The sign of the Dagger society of Amoy".

Either of the two foregoing explanations is possible, and both point to a Han league origin. For the present we prefer the first which seems the more probable derivation.

This concludes our examination of such fragments of the actual Three Dot ritual in use in Malaya as have come to our notice. Comparison will show a close family likeness between the fragments given in this chapter, and the following general descriptions:—

    (*a*) the Han league of Hutson (Chapter II);

    (*b*) the Rules of the Toh Peh Kong of Penang (Chapter VI and Appendix II);

    (*c*) the fragment of Red Flag ritual given by the Johore source (Chapter XXIX);

    (*d*) the "Han ethic" of Mason (Chapter II);

    (*e*) the Green Association in China to-day (Chapter XXXI);

all of which we place under the banner of "Tokong" in Malaya.

DISSIMILARITY BETWEEN TRIAD AND THE THREE DOT BROTHERHOOD ESTABLISHED

If we briefly survey the material now before us in this and the two preceding chapters, we will find nothing to justify the presently accepted official view that in Malaya, "the Triad society is colloquially referred to as the Sa Tiam Hui". Granted the incompleteness of our present knowledge, we submit that at every comparable point the Sa Tiam Hui identifies itself with the Han league. There may be some superficial similarity in the jargon of the two rituals, but any positive point of comparison which presents itself, suggests that the Three Dot belongs to the Yin and the Triad belongs to the Yang stem of the secret society world as outlined in Chapter III. To mention a few points:—

    (*a*) The Three Dot ritual nowhere refers to the political campaign of the Triad to "drive out the Manchus", but "Tokong" as a whole seems to have accepted a political creed to "drive out the foreigners" from China.

(b) The Three Dot creed is frankly criminal and its similarity in this respect to the Italian Mafia has been noted by Ward and Stirling *op. cit.* Vol. I page 137 a point referred to again in Chapter XXXIII *infra.* The Triad although debased has never professed anything but the highest religious principles and political motives.

(c) The initiation ceremonies of the two are quite different. That of the Three Dot appears to represent physical birth and the things of this world: that of the Triad, physical death and those of the next.

(d) The criminal character of the Three Dot has attracted to itself in Malaya the criminal elements of the Thuggist cult imported from India, and represented to-day by the Red Flag society discussed fully in later chapters, which is in alliance with the Three Dot.

(e) The Triad creed no matter how debased it may have become, remains an exhortation to "obey Heaven and act righteously", whereas the only purpose of the Three Dot, like that of the "Elder Brethren", of the Han league and the devotees of Thuggism, both Mohamedan and Hindu, is robbery, murder and depravity.

We have here in juxta-position and clearly distinguishable, the two schools of secret association, referred to in the introduction to this work, namely the worship of man as opposed to the worship of God, symbolised by the ancient dualism in the Yin Yang of China (Chapter III).

Hitherto no such distinction has been drawn between the two secret confederations in Malaya, both of which have become tarred with the same official brush and have remained confused under the generic name of "Triad societies", while remaining under the surface essentially distinct and utterly hostile, as predicated by M. Pelliot and, we submit, now proved by the foregoing evidence.

To assist the reader, we offer the following table to show the probable line of this traditional cleavage with its local Malay accretions,[1] on the basis of the Yin Yang and Han Hung divisions of the secret society world in Malaya:—

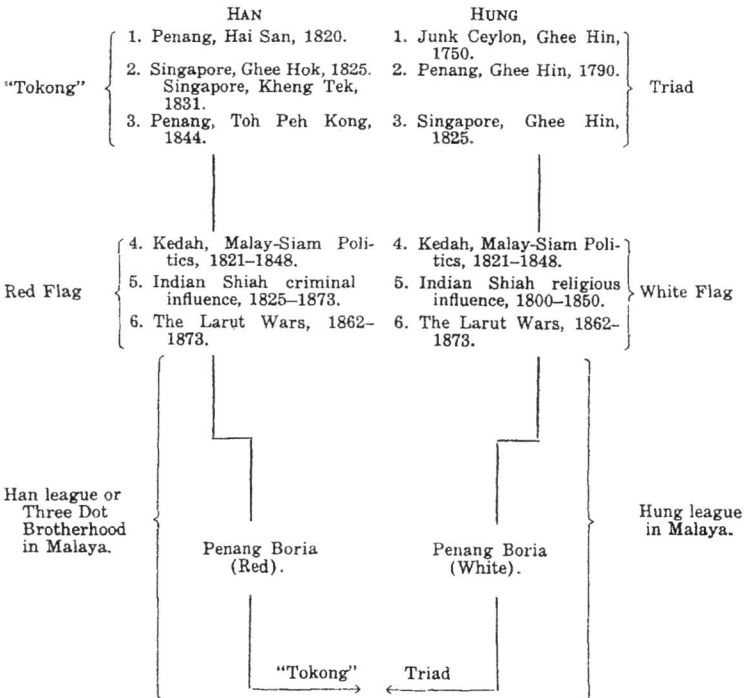

	HAN	HUNG	
"Tokong"	1. Penang, Hai San, 1820.	1. Junk Ceylon, Ghee Hin, 1750.	Triad
	2. Singapore, Ghee Hok, 1825. Singapore, Kheng Tek, 1831.	2. Penang, Ghee Hin, 1790.	
	3. Penang, Toh Peh Kong, 1844.	3. Singapore, Ghee Hin, 1825.	
Red Flag	4. Kedah, Malay-Siam Politics, 1821–1848.	4. Kedah, Malay-Siam Politics, 1821–1848.	White Flag
	5. Indian Shiah criminal influence, 1825–1873.	5. Indian Shiah religious influence, 1800–1850.	
	6. The Larut Wars, 1862–1873.	6. The Larut Wars, 1862–1873.	
Han league or Three Dot Brotherhood in Malaya.	Penang Boria (Red).	Penang Boria (White).	Hung league in Malaya.
	"Tokong" ⟶	⟵ Triad	

Footnote.—(1) These are explained in the chapters that follow.

In our submission the main line of cleavage between "Tokong" and Triad in Malaya has remained fairly constant up to the present-day, despite the multitudinous cross-currents and divergent interests of modern secret society intrigue, and notwithstanding the enormous increase in the Chinese immigrant population.

The same line of cleavage between the Mohamedan proto-types of Triad and "Tokong", namely the White Flag and the Red Flag, to which we must now turn our attention, will also be found to have remained fairly clearly defined up to the present-day.

TERMINOLOGY

When the time comes to refer in the same breath to the two Chinese camps of Han and Hung and the two Moslem camps of Red and White Flag, we shall call them respectively by the generic names of Triad (Chinese) and Tabut (Moslem)—terms which suggest the title of this work. The word Triad already connotes in the presently accepted Malayan view, its opposite number "Tokong". The meaning of the word Tabut is explained in its appropriate context in Chapters XI and XII *infra*. Succeeding chapters attempt to show how, by a long, circuitous and historical route, Triad and Tabut have come to be bound up in Malaya in two secret hostile confederations of the left and the right, thus:—

$$\left.\begin{array}{l}\text{``Tokong'' and}\\\text{Red Flag}\end{array}\right\} \longrightarrow \longleftarrow \left\{\begin{array}{l}\text{Triad and}\\\text{White Flag}\end{array}\right.$$

This concludes for the present our survey of the purely Chinese secret society field in Malaya. We must now introduce our readers to the genesis of those Mohamedan secret societies with which Triad and "Tokong" are in underground alliance.

NOTE

THE WHITE COCK AND BLACK FOWL AS SYMBOLS OF THE MYSTICAL MARRIAGE OF THE SUN GOD AND EARTH GODDESS

(1) Sir J. G. Fraser *Adonis* (1932 edition) pages 33–35 has:—

Among the Oraons, a primitive hill-tribe of Bengal, the marriage of the Sun and the Earth is annually celebrated by a priest and priestess who personate respectively the god of the Sun and the goddess of the Earth.

* * *

The rite is celebrated in the month of May, when the *sal* tree is in bloom, and the festival takes its native name (*khaddi*) from the flower of the tree. It is the greatest festival of the year. "The object of this feast is to celebrate the mystical marriage of the Sun-god (*Bhagawan*) with the goddess-earth (*Dharti-mai*), to induce them to be fruitful and give good crops".

* * *

In the afternoon the people all gather at the sacred grove, and the priest proceeds to consummate the sacrifice. The first victims to be immolated are a white cock for the Sun god and a black hen for the Earth goddess; and as the feast is the marriage of these great deities, the marriage service is performed over the two fowls before they are hurried into eternity. Amongst other things, both birds are marked with vermilion just as a bride and bridegroom are marked at a human marriage; and the earth is also smeared with vermilion, as if it were a real bride, on the spot where the sacrifice is offered.

* * *

Meantime the acolyte has collected flowers of the *sal* tree and set them round the place of sacrifice, and he has also fetched the holy water from the priest's house. A procession is now formed and the priest is carried in triumph to his own abode. There his wife has been watching for him, and on his arrival the two go through the marriage ceremony, applying vermilion to each other in the usual way "to symbolise the mystical marriage of the Sun god with the Earth goddess".

(2) Again, D. W. Pike *Secret Societies* (1939) page 56 mentions that the approach to Voodoo temples in the West Indies is sometimes "through an avenue of spears set in the ground and surmounted by the bodies of black and white hens".

CHAPTER X

THE SECRET SECTS OF ISLAM

INTRODUCTION

It is necessary at this point to turn from the East to the West and to direct the attention of the reader to those secret society influences which, in like manner to the Chinese, were carried during the early years of the nineteenth century by the immigrant stream from India to Malaya, where they have taken root.

For this purpose we must transfer our examination from the eastern or "Tibetan area" of secret societies to the "Ararat area" in western Asia, where we shall find to exist in the secret society under-world, that same dualism which we have discussed in the introduction and encountered in the Yin Yang of China.

Before leaving the east we should notice that a similar conception of dualism to that which we have seen in the cosmogony of China, permeates the Brahminical system of India and that the Indian system also has its origin in the Tibetan area, or more precisely in that Indo-Aryan mythological paradise of Mount Meru, the home of Indra, where we have suggested in the introduction the home of the Taoist "Mother of the West", the deified embodiment of the Yin of Chinese cosmogony, may also be found. A detailed reference to the secret sects of Hinduism is outside the scope of this work, as they do not greatly affect Malaya, with the single exception of Thuggism, referred to later in this chapter. The importance of Thuggism lies in the fact that it was imported into Malaya in the nineteenth century and that it embraces both Hindus and Mohamedans among its votaries.

The left and right of the Chinese system discussed in Chapter III *supra*, is in some degree paralleled in the Hindu system, of which the left, or mystical side is again subdivided into (a) the gross Nature or fertility worship of left-handed saktism which forms part of the secret society world of India and (b) the more restrained right-handed saktism, which worships the reproductive principle by the more decorous means of imagery.

In Malaya, we shall find the left-handed saktism of the Hindus in the form of Thuggism, join forces in the local under-world with the depravity of the left-hand Han league of the Chinese, to form the Red Flag society.

In forming this alliance Thuggism, true to its Indian character in which it embraces both Hindus and Mohamedans, induced a large section of Malayan Islam to follow it and to this extent only is the dualism of Hinduism of importance to our subject.

We must now briefly consider the dualism of the Ararat area, whence the secret sects of Islam directly derive.

The earliest "dualist" cult in the west of which there is historical record, appears to be Nature-Sabeism, a link between the "styes of paganism" or unadorned fertility worship of the pre-Abrahamic era,[1] and the "church" of the Essenes which followed, and which appears to have been based on the teaching of the Persian Zoroaster[2] (B.C. 660) and upon the Jewish mystics, the Kabbalists. The Essenes were followed in turn by the Gnostics of the first century A.D., who seem to have derived their dualist teaching also from the Kabbalists with an admixture of neo-platonism. There followed the Carpocratians of the second century A.D., with whom began the tendency towards a return to Nature-worship and to the *deification of humanity* in historical times in the western world.

From this point in the secret society under-world of the west, there began the war between the two contending principles, which we have already seen at work in China— the sensual conception of man as God (the Yin) and the spiritual conception of man reaching up to God and attempting to achieve atonement with Him (the Yang). The latter in a passive way is also the Buddhist concept of human destiny. In both cases self-annihilation in the source of Life is the aim; the one, the left, seeks it by the "lower road", the other, the right, by the higher. In the third century A.D. in the west, we have the teaching of the Persian Manes, which was pure dualism, known to history as Manichaeism or Mithraism.

It was founded, not on Christian teaching, but on the Zoroastrian conception of Ormuzd and Ahriman, the existence of two opposing principles in the world, light and darkness, good and evil, as in the Yin Yang of China.

Thus, according to Manes, all matter is absolute evil and humanity itself is of Satanic origin and the first human beings, Adam and Eve, are represented as the offspring of devils. A similar doctrine was taught by the Kabbalists among whom we find in de Pauly's translation of *Zohar* (Book of Light) Vol. I page 315, Eve is represented as cohabiting with the serpent. Manichaean demonology prepared the way for the

Footnote.—(1) *See* Introduction.
Footnote.—(2) Known as Mazdaism.

propitiation of the powers of darkness, which we find widespread in the 4th century A.D. as a secret religious rite. The "monstrous gnosis of Manes" was a desecration of the pre-Christian sacred traditions and the forerunner of that sacrilegious cult that was destined to invade and seduce some sections of Christianity during the period of the seven centuries (B.C. 50–A.D. 650) and to infect Islam later with the same heresy.

In the case of Christianity we may, for purposes of this work, call this poison Satanism and in the case of Islam we may call it left Sufism. In other words we may say that the Yin principle in the secret society under-world of China is represented in the same sphere of Christendom by Satanism and in the same sphere of Islam by left Sufism.

This view will correct any impression given that the cult of evil (or the Yin) as it appears to be enshrined in the Three Dot society is peculiar to China. It is as well to realise that the same phenomenon is to be found both in Christendom and in the Moslem world.

Before we can proceed to examine the elements composing the secret society world of Islam, we must examine these two "isms" more closely, remembering that both Christianity and Islam belong to the "Ararat area": that Christianity preceded Islam in that area by some six hundred years: that Islam accepts the prophets in the Christian bible as authentic, and that pure Islam makes no distinction between religion and politics.

SATANISM

We need only say here that the cult of the "left" principle, as defined by Chinese beliefs in Chapter III, is known in the west in its extreme debased form, by the generic name of satanism, associated generally with the worship of the serpent, the dragon of China: and with the emblems of generation (virility and fecundity), with the Devil or anti-Christ and with desecration of sacred Christian emblems.

In the Christian era the worship of the right principle and of a revealed God has driven satanism or the left principle underground.

And yet, the incidence of satanism is widespread in the civilised under-world to-day.

The only difference is, perhaps, that in the cult of evil in Christendom and Islam, as compared with China, many disguises are adopted, which render it less easy to identify.

If the suggestion put forward in Chapter III, of the "left" and "right" stems in the Chinese secret society under-world, each with its subdivisions into "religion", history and politics, is acceptable, the same explanation may with profit be applied to the secret society sphere of Christianity and Islam and of the world at large.

Satanism or the worship of the left, is to-day a secret cult among "civilised" peoples, associated with occultism, black magic, charlatanry and crime, whereas in the pagan or traditional epoch of the world's history, it was the open adoration of sex and the propitiation of the gods associated therewith, the gods of the mystery of life.

The worship of the left remains in Christianity the challenge of the warlock; and in Islam that of the shaman, to the divinity of God.

The common features which distinguish the left wherever met with are:—

    (a) In the religious sphere:—The worship of the reproductive principle, symbolising man himself as the source of life.

    (b) In the historical sphere:—The worship of man as god and as the source of all knowledge and wisdom.

    (c) In the political sphere:—The worship of force and materialism or the doctrine that "might is right", as opposed to the rule of law, which protects the sanctity of human life as belonging to God.

This is the ancient dualism discussed in the Introduction, the application of which to the secret society under-world in China has been given in the preceding chapters. Without some such general guide, the study of secret societies as a world-wide phenomenon, remains confused and unbalanced. With this guide, the subject becomes clarified and comparatively manageable and comprehensible.

SUFISM

Mohamed condemned the asceticism and monasticism of Christianity. Nevertheless by the second century of Islam (A.D. 800) Moslem practitioners in mysticism and asceticism were already numerous. They were known as "Sufis" from the garments of *suf*, "wool", which they wore as a mark of distinction and were at first devoted to the quietistic way of life, in imitation of the monasticism of Christianity. But by degrees the practice of Sufism bifurcated, the right remaining pietistic and aesthetic, while the left under some teachers deserted the way of theosophical speculation, adopted pantheism and became debased and perverted, practising black magic as opposed to mysticism: seeking to achieve annihilation of self and atonement with the Supreme being by "the lower road" and through excesses based not on spirituality, but on sensuality, catalepsy and charlatanry.

Thus, Nicholson in *The Mystics of Islam* (1914) has:—

    The Sufi theosophy tends to abolish the distinction between good and evil......and leads to the deification of the hierophant.

Encyclopaedia Britannica (1935) under Sufism has:—

Sufi fraternities......became widely spread before A.D. 1100 and gave rise to Dervish orders most of which indulge in the practice of exciting ecstasy by music, dancing, drugs, and various kinds of hypnotic suggestion.

Although it has never officially indulged in the sex extravagances of other religions or cults, this left-hand sufism of Islam is analagous to the left-hand saktism of the Hindus and by the same process of perversion and debasement of the mystical to the magical, approaches the satanism of debased Christianity, without the grosser desecrations of the latter.

The worship, in the sense of the propitiation, of Satan—*Shaitan* of the Malays (Ar. "the burnt one"), or *Iblis* (Gr. diabolos, "the prince of darkness) and his cohorts, or the left principle in nature, became common among certain Shiah sects of Islam and found its way to Malaya as shown in a later chapter.

This propitiation of the evil principle (the Yin) amounting in some cases to the worship of Evil in the guise of Good, is the basis of that "Satanism" which is active in most countries of the world to-day under secret society cover, providing at once the impulse and the excuse for much of the crime and rebellion that falls within the law of civilised countries. Some acquaintance with its existence and power is therefore essential to a comprehension of the secret society system and the problems of rule within the British Empire, with which it, as a very "human factor", is bound up.

The mischief that can be wrought by Sufi practitioners is vividly exemplified in the career of the Dervish, Mohamed Ahmad of Dongola, who in 1881, in the Sudan declared himself the Mahdi of the "Twelver" sect of Shiah Islam (*see* below) which led to the First Sudan war and the death of General Gordon.

Thus, Bermann in *The Mahdi of Allah* (1931) whose account is sponsored in an Introduction by Mr. Winston Churchill has, page 74:—

Among the Persians who carried their begging bowls through the Soudanese villages, the Sufi were numerous. Most of them would probably belong to the lower degrees of the great mystical community—to the common herd, that is shepherded with words. But was not some old Dervish, some opium-smoker and hashish-swallower in miserable rags—was he not perhaps, under his rags and under his dreamy lethargy a Sufi of high degree, a *urefa*, who believed he was justified in regarding himself as divine? a dreamer of those last magnificent dreams of participation in God? Did not, perhaps, the Dervish Mohamed Ahmad learn from some Sufi sage the innermost secret of this mystic doctrine that for one of the *Illuminati* it is even permissible to lie: that he is not obliged to practice what he teaches to the lowly ones: that there exist degrees of virtue that change according to the different grades by which knowledge and intellect are ascending to the Godhead: and that the uppermost grade may dispense with goodness—because the saint is soaring upwards into so much higher regions?

We cannot be certain of this because no record remains, but from a comparison with the teaching of Abdullah bin Maimun given below, it will be seen that the Sudan rebellion was Sufi-inspired. A Bedouin arab named Abdullahi bin Mohd. Adam after experiencing visions, signs and tokens, recovered from serious illness by drinking a draught given him by Mohamed Ahmad and thereupon declared Mohamed Ahmad to be the expected Mahdi (Messiah). The signs and omens were favourable. Mohamed Ahmad was accepted as the Mahdi.

What followed belongs to history.

Another and more prolonged challenge by sufism to the Empire arose in Somaliland in 1899 where a dervish leader Mohamed bin Abdullah, accredited by his followers with supernatural powers, declared himself to be the Mahdi and caused the Colonial Office much trouble for many years. He came to be known as the "Mad Mullah", and an almost incessant campaign was waged against him between 1900 and 1920. In the latter year the dervish force was destroyed, chiefly through the co-operation of the Royal Air Force and the Mad Mullah died an exile in 1921.

In the story of the Mahdi and of the Mad Mullah we see again one of the results of the deification of humanity—a result which we have already seen in the story of Hung Siu Ch'un in the Taiping rebellion and which is being re-enacted on a larger scale in the world to-day.

It is one manifestation of that "ancient horror" existing beneath the outer surface of "perfectly reasonable political aspirations" to which Sir George MacMunn refers. In this work we are chiefly concerned with its criminal and political manifestations among the Chinese and Mohamedan secret societies in Malaya.[1]

THE SUNNI AND SHIAH DIVISIONS OF ISLAM

Islam means "submission to the will of God" and as a religion is popularly supposed to be fanatically united and free from sectarianism, secret societies and other disintegrating influences, but this is very far from the truth.

To obtain a grasp of this aspect of our subject, it is necessary briefly to record some of the early history of Islam, to show how it came to be divided into its two main sects the Sunni and the Shiah.

Footnote.—(1) Those interested in its manifestations elsewhere will find further factual information in two recent anonymous books *Light Bearers of Darkness* (1930) and the *Trail of the Serpent* (1936). This aspect of our subject in its general application, is referred to again in Chapter XXXIII *infra.*

The following facts are condensed from the *Encyclopaedia of Islam* and other standard works:—

After the death of the Prophet Mohamed in A.D. 632, the next three Khalifs or leaders of Islam, were Abubakar, Omar and Osman.

The last named was murdered in A.D. 656. A struggle then took place for the leadership, or Khalifat, which caused a schism in the ranks of Islam, which has lasted to this day. That struggle was primarily between the elective and the hereditary principle in the succession.

On the death of Osman, the elders elected as the fourth Khalif, Ali bin Abu Talib, who had married the Prophet's daughter Fatima. Ali's father was the Prophet's uncle, so that Ali was both cousin and son-in-law of the Prophet.

Ali had by Fatima two sons, Hasan and Husein.

Ali's election was resisted by the Prophet's youngest widow and favourite wife, Ayesha, daughter of Abubakar, 1st Khalif, and her supporters, who thought that the Khalifat should pass to Ayesha's line.

Ali suppressed the rebellion against his authority, and took Ayesha prisoner.

The family dispute over the succession was embittered by the assassination of Ali in A.D. 661 at Kufa. The question of his successor to the Khalifat, permanently divided the Mohamedan world in the following manner.

The supporters of the elective principle to the Khalifat called themselves the Sunnis or the "orthodox" from *sunna* = a path, while they named the supporters of Ali and Fatima, the shiahs, *i.e.* the "sectarians" or partisans.

The Shiahs do not regard themselves as sectarians, and call themselves Al-adiliya, or the right people, but they are universally known as Shiahs.

Of some 235 millions of Moslems about 150 millions are Sunnis. The Shiahs are broken up into numerous sects. There are only some 12 millions adherents of the early Shiah tradition.

The Ali-Fatima line with their children Hasan and Husein are commonly referred to as the "Alids" or the "Fatimites". The two sons Hasan and Husein are commonly referred to as the "Saidani".

Upon the murder of Ali, the leadership was claimed by a cousin of Osman the third Khalif, named Mutawiya, who was then Governor in Syria, and who quickly gained control in Syria, Egypt, Yemen and Persia.

Mutawiya secured the abdication of Ali's elder son Hasan, although Shiah tradition holds that Hasan was poisoned.

Mutawiya became Khalif in "the year of union" (A.D. 661) and made the title hereditary.

Mutawiya was succeeded by his son Yezid I (679–683).

Ali's second son Husein had acknowledged Mutawiya, but did not acknowledge Yezid.

Husein left Medina to lead a rebellion against Yezid in Irak. The rebellion was crushed before Husein joined it and he and his followers were surrounded by Yezid on the plain of Kerbela where Husein was killed. His death or martyrdom, as the Shiahs call it, is known as the tragedy of the Kerbela and, coupled with the earlier death of his brother Hasan, is celebrated annually by the Shiahs in India and Persia at the Festival of Moharram—variously termed The Ashura (10th day of Moharram) Festival: The Taziah Festival: and, mistakenly, "The lamentation for Ali", etc.

Amongst Shiah Mohamedans this Festival is observed with the greatest reverence, since Ali and his two sons are venerated by them as martyrs, to whom are attributed semi-divine powers. A re-incarnation of Mohamed the twelfth Shiah Khalif is awaited by the Shiahs as the Mahdi or Messiah.

The orthodox Sunni Mohamedans reject this theology as heretical and perverted and, of course, totally ignore the observance of the Moharram Festival.

A description of the festival as observed in India is given in Chapter XI.

In India, owing to the Shiah tradition of the poisoning of Hasan and the martyrdom of Husein, the colours most in evidence during the festival are Green (representing poison) for Hasan and Red (representing the martyr's blood) for Husein.

The schism in Islam over the Khalifat which caused the two main historical divisions of the faith into Sunni and Shiah, gave rise at the same time to those secret sects among the Shiahs, to which we must now refer. Sectarianism in Islam is found almost exclusively among the Shiahs who adopted and developed the mysticism of the Sufi school and among whom a separate schism developed, upon the death of their 6th Khalif, Jaafar.

In this schism, there was again a "left" and a "right" school. The left school acknowledged Ismail the elder son of Jaafar as seventh Khalif and were known as the "Seveners" or Ismailis, because they recognised seven Khalifs only.

The right school acknowledged Abu Hassan Musa, the younger son of Jaafar, as seventh Khalif and supported the Alid succession thence to the twelfth Khalif, Mohamed Al Mahdi, whose return to earth as the Messiah they await. They were known as the "Twelvers" or Imamias and represent the "orthodox" Shiah doctrine. The left school or Seveners pursued a vagrant course which is best shown in the following table of the early Khalifat succession and the schisms which divided it:—

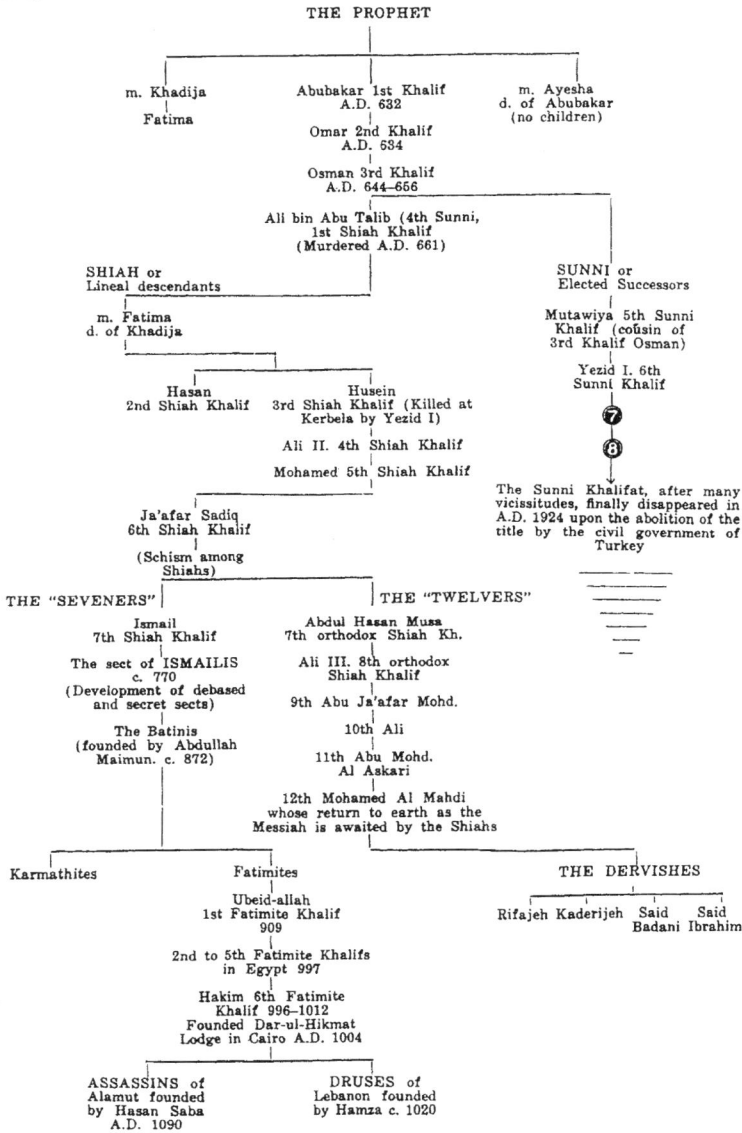

THE PROPHET

m. Khadija
Fatima

Abubakar 1st Khalif
A.D. 632

Omar 2nd Khalif
A.D. 634

Osman 3rd Khalif
A.D. 644–656

m. Ayesha
d. of Abubakar
(no children)

Ali bin Abu Talib (4th Sunni,
1st Shiah Khalif
(Murdered A.D. 661)

SHIAH or
Lineal descendants

m. Fatima
d. of Khadija

SUNNI or
Elected Successors

Mutawiya 5th Sunni
Khalif (cousin of
3rd Khalif Osman)

Yezid I. 6th
Sunni Khalif

7

8

Hasan
2nd Shiah Khalif

Husein
3rd Shiah Khalif (Killed at
Kerbela by Yezid I)

Ali II. 4th Shiah Khalif

Mohamed 5th Shiah Khalif

The Sunni Khalifat, after many
vicissitudes, finally disappeared in
A.D. 1924 upon the abolition of the
title by the civil government of
Turkey

Ja'afar Sadiq
6th Shiah Khalif

(Schism among
Shiahs)

THE "SEVENERS"

Ismail
7th Shiah Khalif

The sect of ISMAILIS
c. 770
(Development of debased
and secret sects)

The Batinis
(founded by Abdullah
Maimun. c. 872)

THE "TWELVERS"

Abdul Hasan Musa
7th orthodox Shiah Kh.

Ali III. 8th orthodox
Shiah Khalif

9th Abu Ja'afar Mohd.

10th Ali

11th Abu Mohd.
Al Askari

12th Mohamed Al Mahdi
whose return to earth as the
Messiah is awaited by the Shiahs

Karmathites

Fatimites

Ubeid-allah
1st Fatimite Khalif
909

2nd to 5th Fatimite Khalifs
in Egypt 997

Hakim 6th Fatimite
Khalif 996–1012
Founded Dar-ul-Hikmat
Lodge in Cairo A.D. 1004

THE DERVISHES

Rifajeh   Kaderijeh   Said   Said
Badani   Ibrahim

ASSASSINS of
Alamut founded
by Hasan Saba
A.D. 1090

DRUSES of
Lebanon founded
by Hamza c. 1020

Malays are Sunni Mohamedans and consequently, one would expect to find the Moharram festival totally ignored in Malaya, but the fact is that, besides some Shiah influence of long standing in Perak, referred to in Chapter XXII, there is also a good deal of recently imported Shiah influence at work in Penang, which has grown up during the nineteenth century from direct contact with Indians.

The nature of this Shiah influence in Penang, both religious and criminal, must next claim our attention.

THE SECRET SOCIETIES OF ISLAM

The origin of the Red and White flag societies long known to exist in Malaya first attracted the attention of observers at the beginning of the present century and the opinions upon their origin, expressed by various writers are given in Chapter XV below. Among the most influential of these opinions is that of the Rev. Dr. Luering an accomplished Malay and Arabic scholar of Ipoh, who discerned a connection between the local Red and White flag societies and the ancient secret sects of the Shiahs. For this reason it is necessary at this point to give a brief account of these secret sects. The whole subject in its general relevance is reviewed in Chapter XXXIII and XXXV *infra*.

The chief historical secret religious sects found among the Shiah Mohamedans are:—

    The Dervishes
    The Ismailis
    The Batinis
    The Karmathites
    The Druses of Lebanon
    The Yezidis
    The Fatimites
    The Assassins.

The Dervishes.—The Dervishes are sufis and are chiefly found in the near East[1] and Africa and therefore only affect our subject indirectly. Allusion has already been made to the sufi-inspired rising of the Dervishes in the Sudan in 1881, which led to Gordon's death.[2] The following notice taken from Heckethorn *op. cit.* Vol. I page 132 will serve as an introduction to the Dervishes:—

> The name is Persian and means mendicant. They are also called Fakirs and are a monastic order of Islam. Mohamed prohibited the introduction of monks into his religious system; but thirty years after his death, monks made their appearance, and it is supposed that there are now seventy-two orders of them. But twelve of these are, undoubtedly, older than Islam.
>
> The four chief orders of Dervishes are:—
>
> 1. The Rifajeh, who carry black flags, and wear black or dark brown turbans. They practise juggler's tricks such as swallowing daggers, eating fire, charming serpents, etc.
> 2. The Kaderijeh, with white flags and turbans; they are chiefly fishermen.
> 3. The Said Badani, whose founder Said Achmed el Bidani, is the greatest saint of the Egyptian Moslems. Their colours are red and white, and they are divided into several sects. They wear an absurd costume and act as buffoons.
> 4. The Said Ibrahim, with green flags and turbans. All that is known of them is that they have a monastery at Alexandria.

Beyond noting the fact of their existence, their Shiah origin as shown in the foregoing plan and some of their peculiarities, the sect of the Dervishes need not detain us. Ward in *Freemasonry and the Ancient God* alleges, page 1 ff. that freemasonry exists among the Mohamedans of India and the Ararat area, and on page 3 ff. he gives part of the ceremony of initiation into one of the orders of Dervishes (the Mevlevi). Superficially No. 3 above (Said Badani) might seem, as suggested by Dr. Luering, to have a connection with the White and Red Flag societies in Malaya, but in fact this does not appear to be so (*see* Chapter XII and XV below).

The Ismailis.—This sect arose from the schism among the Shiahs themselves after the death of the sixth Shiah Khalif Ja'afar as explained above. The Ismailis, supported Ja'afar's elder son Ismail. Abu Hassan Musa became the "orthodox" Shiah Khalif and the Ismailis formed their own sect. Ismail's son Mohamed disappeared about A.D. 770 and the succession lapsed for a time until about A. D. 872 when Abdullah bin Maimun[3] placed himself at the head of the Ismaili faction. Abdullah bin Maimun was a Persian of wide learning and a pure materialist brought up in the doctrine of gnostic dualism. He professed adherence to the orthodox Shiah creed while proclaiming a knowledge of the mystic doctrines which the Ismailis believed to have descended through Ismail to his son Mohamed, who had disappeared in A.D 770.

Footnote.—(1) An account of the Sufism of the De. s in India will be found in Herklots *Qanun-i-Islam* ("Islam in India") ed. W. Crooke 1921 pages 287–296.

Footnote.—(2) We may note in passing that General Gordon destroyed a secret society of the left in China in 1864 (*see* page 58 *supra*) and was himself the victim of one at Khartoum in 1885. The remarkable feature of those two wars is that they were inspired by a similar agency, a fact which this work hopes to demonstrate.

Footnote.—(3) For a fuller notice of this strange man, *see* Introduction.

By this means Abdullah bin Maimun became the accepted leader of the sect, which he proceeded to develop upon the lines of a gross materialism, under the form of a secret society.

Reinhart Dozy *Spanish Islam* English translation page 403 gives the following description of this project:—

> To link together into one body the vanquished and the conquerors: to unite in the form of a vast secret society with many degrees of initiation, free-thinkers, who regarded religion only as a curb for the people,[1] and bigots of all sects; to make tools of believers in order to give power to sceptics: to induce conquerors to overturn the Empire they had founded: to build up a party, numerous, compact and disciplined, which in due time would give the throne if not to himself, at least to his descendants, such was Abdullah bin Maimun's general aim—an extraordinary conception which he worked out with marvellous tact, incomparable skill and a profound knowledge of the human heart. The means which he adopted were devised with diabolical cunning.
>
>   *   *   *
>
> It was not among the Shiahs that he sought his true supporters but among the Ghebers, the Manicheans, the pagans of Haran and the students of Greek philosophy. On the last alone could he rely, to them alone could he gradually unfold the final mystery and reveal that Imams, religions and morality were nothing but an imposture and an absurdity. The rest of mankind, the "asses" as Abdullah called them, were incapable of understanding such doctrines. But to gain his end-he by no means disdained their aid. On the contrary, he solicited it, but he took care to initiate devout and lowly souls only in the first grades of the sect.
>
> His missionaries, who were inculcated with the idea that their first duty was to conceal their true sentiments and adapt themselves to the views of their auditors, appeared in many guises and spoke as it were, in a different language to each class.
>
> They won over the ignorant and vulgar by feats of *legerdemain* which passed for miracles, or excited their curiosity by enigmatical discourse. In the presence of the devout they assumed the mask of virtue and piety. With mystics they were mystical and unfolded the inner meaning of phenomena or explained allegories and the figurative sense of the allegories themselves.
>
>   *   *   *
>
> By means such as these the extraordinary result was brought about that a multitude of men of diverse beliefs were all working together for an object known only to a few of them.

This doctrine is important as it has consciously or unconsciously set the pattern and the method for subversive secret societies in the western world ever since it was launched by Abdullah bin Maimun in Persia and Irak,—the Ararat area of secret societies, in A.D. 870. Its close resemblance to the ethic of modern Leninism and Hitlerism will be noted. Did Abdullah bin Maimun invent this doctrine or evolve it or did he borrow it from elsewhere? We are unable to say; but among the inheritors of his system were the Karmathites, the Druses of Lebanon and the Assassins of Alamut, the second of whom have a religious tradition connecting them with China and the third of whom seem to have a latter-day connection with the Red Flag society in Malaya through the Thugs of India, as shown in subsequent chapters.

The system of Abdullah bin Maimun is clearly that of the worship of man as opposed to the worship of God and bears more than a superficial resemblance to the "Han ethic" and the Elder Brethren society (Chapter II).

The vast importance of the doctrine of Abdullah bin Maimun in shaping the future course of secret society history in the western world, cannot be exaggerated.

Every feature of disguise, treachery and deception to gain a political end, appears in his system which is *par excellence* the anarchic concept of governance for the benefit of the few "in the know"—the doctrine of gross materialism that sanctions any means for gaining an end, when that end is world domination,—the doctrine that might is right.

The Batinis and Karmathites.—Having assumed the leadership of the Ismaili faction about A.D. 850, Abdullah bin Maimun formed within it in A.D. 872, a secret sect which he called the Batinis (Ar. *batin* = secret, esoteric, magical) with seven degrees of initiation.

One of his initiates was Karmath who founded a separate faction of the Batinis, based on physical violence as a means of return to material chaos, as opposed to the more subtle method of Abdullah of instilling doubts in the minds of believers and developing a state of mental anarchy, aimed at the substitution of a natural for a revealed religion as a means of gaining the same end.

We see these two schools vividly portrayed in the modern world by the exponents of Leninism following the path of Abdullah and those of Hitlerism following that of Karmath, whose followers met destruction in Egypt about A.D. 1170 at the hands of Saladin. Of the Karmathites Von Hammer *History of the Assassins* (Engl. trans: 1835) says:—

> For a whole century the pernicious doctrines of Karmath raged with fire and sword in the very bosom of Islam, until the widespread conflagration from the Euphrates to Alex ndria was extinguished in blood.[2]

There is no historical barrier to the conjecture that the system of Abdu bin Maimun may have its origin in the Ko Lao Hui of China.

Footnote.—(1) Lenin, a modern practitioner of this creed, has called religion "the opium of the people".

Footnote.—(2) See also de Sacy in *Mémoires sur la dynastie des Assassins* in *Mémoires de l'Institut Royal de France* Vol. IV 1818, wherein he quotes the 14th century Arab historian Nowari.

The Druses of Lebanon.—Some colour is lent to this conjecture by the tradition that exists among the strange sect of the Druses that they had an origin in China.

Thus, Couling *Encyclopaedia Sinica* has:—

Druses or Druzes—A mysterious people who have been known in the Lebanon mountains since the twelfth century, but whose origin is unknown. They themselves state that they came from China; they expect at the end of all things to be re-established in their ancestral home, and meanwhile all good Druses, at their death, are supposed to go to China.

The *Encyclopaedia Britannica*, 14th ed. 1935, has:—

The Druses are the adherents of an esoteric religion founded in the 11th century A.D. by the Fatimite Khalif of Egypt Al-Hakim, the son of a Russian mother who proclaimed himself an incarnation of God, established a reign of terror at Cairo and finally disappeared mysteriously in A.D. 1021.

They take their name from his missionary Ismail-ad-Darazi[1] who preached the cult of Al-Hakim among the Syrians. Their origin is probably mixed: their traditions derive them from Arab colonists, but some of their chief families claim Turkoman or Kurdish descent.

* * *

The Druses believe that......when the tribulation of the faithful has reached its height, Hakim will re-appear to conquer the world and render his religion supreme. Then Druses, believed to be dispersed in China will return to Syria. The combined body of the Faithful will take Mecca and finally Jerusalem and all the world will accept the faith.

* * *

Not only is the charge of secrecy rigidly obeyed in regard to the alien world, but full initiation into the deeper mysteries of the creed is permitted only to a class designated "Aqils" (Ar. the intelligent) in contra-distinction from whom all other members of the Druse community, who whatever may be their positions or attainments, are called Jahil, the Ignorant. About 15 per cent. of the adult population belong to the order of Aqils.

* * *

Their meeting houses are plain unornamented edifices in which the women assemble at the same time as the men, a part of the space being fenced off for them by a semi transparent black veil. It has been frequently asserted that the image of a calf is kept in a niche and traces of phallic and gynæcocratic worship have been vaguely suspected, but there is no authentic information in support of either statement.

Silvestre de Sacy *Exposé de la religion des Druses* (1838) says that the Druses are divided into three degrees: profanes, aspirants and wise, to whom their doctrine is gradually unfolded under the seal of the strictest secrecy, to ensure which, signs and passwords are employed some of which are common to Freemasonry.[2] The catechism of the Druses which resembles that of the Freemasons can only be learnt from the "akals" a small group of higher initiates, who only reveal its mysteries to the aspirants after the application of severe tests and the taking of oaths of secrecy.

Of their secret doctrine de Sacy *op. cit.* says:—

It is a secret cult rendered to the head of a bull or a calf roughly made of gold, silver or bronze which they keep in a box hidden from all eyes and opened only for the veneration of the initiates.

The claims of the Druses to our attention are these:—

(1) They have preserved themselves intact, in the very centre of the "Ararat area" from the year of their foundation A.D. 1020 to the present-day, over 900 years of unbroken sectarianism maintained with fanatical determination.

(2) They have a tradition connecting them or their beliefs with China. This connection may conceivably be with the Si Wang Mu of the Taoists and Mount Meru of the Hindus and thence through the Sumerians to Lebanon (*vide* Introduction).

(3) They have a strong if debased religion founded on dualism.

(4) They possess a religious and social structure organised as a secret society and having many points of resemblance to the Hung league of China and the Freemasonry in the West.

(5) They are interested and skilled in political intrigue and mix in disguise with the outside world.

For these reasons their potential importance in the sphere of political secret society intrigue within the British Empire cannot be ignored.

But the same confusion between the Hung and the Han analysed in Chapter VIII may here be again in evidence and "the resemblance to the signs and password" Freemasonry" noted by observers in the Druse cult, may in fact be a resemblance not to Freemasonry and the signs and catechism of the Hung league, but to those of the Elder Brethren and the Han league—the Yin stem and not the Yang.

This view would accord with their origin in the left or Ismaili schism of the Shiahs, themselves the sufi-ridden branch of pure Islam, the worshippers of Hakim and adherents of the deification of man.

Footnote.—(1) "Ismail the Tailor" (Durzi).
Footnote.—(2) Further information upon this aspect is given under "Druses" in the Introduction to this work. *See* also *Freemasonry and the Ancient Gods* (Ward) page 8; and *Ars Quatuor Coronatorum* Vol. IV pages 7-19 (Rev. Hasketh Smith).

Some support is lent to this view by the vague references to the worship of the Golden Calf and to phallic and gynæcocratic practices among the Druses, which suggests the association of the *lingam-yoni* observances of the Yin and the worship of man in the person of Hakim, in place of the worship of Allah.

The story of the Golden Calf of Aaron is told in the Bible[1] wherein the worship of Baal is associated with burnt offerings, eating and drinking: nude dancing: "priests of the lowest of the people" and a feast on the 15th of the Eighth moon; which latter corresponds with the Mid-autumn festival of the Chinese when the moon is worshipped.

This again suggests association with the left or Yin stem and identity with "the abominations" and the worship of man—particularly as it was followed in the two bible instances, by two unmistakable manifestations of the wrath of God.[2]

The Yezidis.—Another secret sect still alive in the "Ararat area" which claims our passing attention is The Yezidis. This sect is frankly satanistic and of uncertain origin. The *Encyclopaedia Britannica* (1935) says of it:—

> A religious sect, numbering about 50,000 persons, dwelling chiefly in the neighbourhood of Mosul. Their own name for themselves is Dasni, but they are called by their neighbours Yezidi; the origin of both names is uncertain, but the latter is probably derived from the Persian Yazdan, God. Their religion was probably originally an offshoot of Mazdaism, but it has absorbed elements from Christianity and Islam, for they regard Christ as an angel in human form and recognise Muhammad as a prophet with Abraham and the other prophets, and practise circumcision and baptism. They regard the devil as the creative agent of the Supreme God, and seek to propitiate him as the author of evil; they avoid mentioning his name and represent him by the peacock. Their sacred books have been translated by F. Nau, *Recueil de textes et de documents sur les Yézidis* (1918).

They live mostly in the Caucasus where their chief town is Sheikh Adi, near Mosul, named after their traditional founder, a Persian mystic about A.D. 1150.

They are also found in Armenia and Kurdistan and are hated and persecuted by Christians and Moslems alike. Their doctrine shows traces of Iranian beliefs, with Zoroastrian, Manichaean and Nestorian admixtures.

They worship a black serpent, or Fallen Angel, in the form of Malik Taous, or Angel Peacock, whom they regard as the creative agent of the Supreme God, forgiven since his fall from grace and now restored to his heavenly rank.

Such accounts as have been recorded tend to identify Yezidi practices with the sex rites and orgies of black magic, voodoo and satanism.[3]

The Fatimites.—The immediate successors of Abdullah bin Maimun were the Fatimites.

The founder of this sect was Ubeid-allah (c. A.D. 900) whom the Abbasides declared to be a grandson of Abdullah bin Maimun. The sect took its name from its professed adherence to the left Shiah schism and the belief that the true doctrine of the Prophet had descended through Ali (4th Sunni and 1st Shiah Khalif) husband of Fatima the Prophet's daughter, to the 7th Shiah Khalif Ismail (*see* plan page 156) and thence through the Ismaili sect to Abdullah bin Maimun. Ubeid-allah laid claim to be the Mahdi and founded the Fatimite dynasty of which he was known as 1st Khalif (c. A.D. 909). Under the 4th Fatimite Khalif, Egypt fell into the power of the Fatimite dynasty and under the 6th Fatimite Khalif, Hakim, there was founded in Cairo the Dar-ul-Hikmat lodge or "House of Knowledge". This was the Grand Lodge of the secret society of Abdullah bin Maimun and added two more degrees to the system of the Batinis, making nine degrees in all.

THE DAR-UL-HIKMAT LODGE OF CAIRO A.D. 1004

We must examine this remarkable organisation at closer range as it supplies the key to the character of Mohamedan secret societies in general and bears resemblances to the internal organisation of the Elder Brethren of China. Dar-ul-Hikmat means literally in Arabic the "Abode of practical knowledge", but in Malay usage *Ilmu Hikmat* means magic and sorcery and nothing else. It is not difficult to realise from what we have seen of the doctrine of Abdullah bin Maimun, that the name was deceptive and meant in reality "Abode of magic and charlatanry". In this setting the "Elders of the Abode of Magic" under the mantle of Islam in Cairo in A.D. 1000, approach still nearer to the character of the Elder Brethren of the Ko Lao Hui of China at the same epoch.

Footnote.—(1) Exodus XXXII: Deuteronomy XXVII Verse 15: First Kings XII Verse 28 *et seq.*

Footnote.—(2) These are points for comparative study only. Those readers interested will find descriptions of two recent visits to the Djebel Druses by Englishmen, and actual contact—under very different circumstances in the two cases—with the subject of the Golden Calf in *Twixt Hell and Allah* by Waterhouse, an English soldier of the French Foreign Legion, published in 1930: and in *Adventures in Arabia* by Seabrook, published in 1928. Both accounts appear to be well authenticated. The latter has many interesting photographs.

Other references will be found in *Secret Sects of Syria*, Springett, *The Arabs and Druses at Home*, Ewing: *Journal of the Geographical Society* (1858) article by Graham, page 262.

Footnote.—(3) The following are references to this sect:—

Les Yezidis, L. Menant (1892) : *Scheich Adi, der grosse Heilige der Jezidis*, R. Frank (1911) : The cult of the Peacock Angel (1928) R. H. W. Empson: *Adventures in Arabia*, Seabrook. The last named gives a lively account of a visit he paid to the Yezidi "mysteries" at Sheikh Adi in 1928. Mrs. Stevens *By Tigris and Euphrates* (1923) has an interesting chapter on the Yezidis and an appendix upon the sacred books containing an illustration of their secret script.

The parallel remains constant as we shall see in the chapters that follow, until finally we find followers of both schools in an historical alliance in Malaya in A.D. 1850, an alliance to which they seem to have remained faithful down to the present-day.

The following account of the Dar-ul-Hikmat lodge derives from the account of the 14th century historian Nowari.[1]

The method of enlistment and initiation was as follows:—

Proselytes were divided into two main classes—the learned and the ignorant.

To these the "Dais" or fully initiated priors of the order used different methods of approach.

The learned, they flattered, agreed with and applauded for their wisdom. Towards the ignorant they assumed an air of superiority, impressed them with their own knowledge and confused them with perplexing questions on the Koran.

The First Degree.—Thus, in initiating the proselyte whether learned or ignorant into the first degree, the Dai assumed an air of profundity and explained that religious doctrines were too abstruse for the ordinary mind, but must be interpreted by men who, like the Dai, had a special knowledge of this science. The initiate was bound to absolute secrecy concerning the truths to be revealed to him and obliged to pay in advance for these revelations.

The Second Degree.—In the second degree, the initiate was persuaded that all his former teachers were wrong and that he must place his confidence solely in those Imams endowed with authority from God.

The Third Degree.—In the third, he learnt that these Imams were those of the Ismailis—seven in number ending with Mohamed son of Ismail who had disappeared in A.D. 770.

The Fourth Degree.—In the fourth, he was told that the prophets preceding the Imams descending from Ali, were also seven in number—namely, Adam, Noah, Abraham, Moses, Jesus and the first Mohamed and finally Mohamed son of Ismail. So far nothing was said to the initiate in contradiction to the broad tenets of the left schism in the Shiah sect of Islam.

The Fifth Degree.—With the fifth degree, the process of undermining his religion began. He was now told to reject tradition and to disregard the precepts of Mohamed.

The Sixth Degree.—In the sixth, he was taught that all religious observances—prayer, fasting, etc., were only emblematic, that in fact all these things were devices to keep the common herd of men in subordination.

The Seventh Degree.—In the seventh, the doctrine of Dualism and of a greater and a lesser deity were introduced and the unity of God, the fundamental doctrine of Islam, was destroyed.

The Eighth Degree.—In the eighth, a great vagueness was expressed upon the attributes of the first and greatest of these two deities and it was pointed out that real prophets were those who concerned themselves with practical matters, such as political institutions and good forms of Government.

The Ninth Degree.—Finally in the ninth degree, the adept was shown that all religious teaching was allegorical and that religious precept need only be observed in so far as it is necessary to maintain order, but the man who understands the truth may disregard all such doctrines. Abraham, Moses, Jesus and the other prophets were, therefore, only teachers who had profited by the lessons of philosophy. All belief in revealed religion was thus destroyed.

It will be noticed that in the last five degrees, the whole teaching of the first four is reversed and therefore shown to be a fraud. Fraud in fact constituted the system of the society. In the instructions to the Dai, every artifice is described for enlisting proselytes by misrepresentation. Above all, care was to be taken not to put before proselytes doctrines that might disgust them, but to make them advance step by step.

Von Hammer *op. cit.* (Engl. translation) pages 36, 38 sums up as follows against the Dar-ul-Hikmat secret society of Hakim:—

> To believe nothing and to dare all was the sum of this system, which annihil ᵈ every principle of religion and morality and had no other object than to execute ambiti :signs with suitable ministers, who daring all and knowing nothing—since they consider ʻhing a cheat and nothing forbidden—are the best tools of an infernal policy: a system with no other aim than the gratification of an insatiable lust for domination, and one which, instead of seeking the highest of human objects, precipitates itself into the abyss and mangling itself, is buried amidst the ruin of thrones and altars, the wreck of national happiness, and the universal execration of mankind.

This is the pattern of every secret revolutionary political society that has arisen in the west since the foundation of the Dar-ul-Hikmat in A.D. 1004.

Footnote.—(1) It is quoted by de Sacy *op. cit.* Vol. I page 74. It also appears in Dr. F. W. Bussell *Religious Thought and heresy in the Middle Ages* (1918) page 353 and in Von Hammer *op. cit.* and in Yarker *The Arcane Schools,* page 185.

H

The Assassins of Alamut.—The atheistical tradition of Abdullah bin Maimun did not descend to the Druses, who retained genuine if debased religious belief. The true line of descent of the Ismaili doctrine came through the "Assassins" of Alamut of whom we must now give a brief account taken from the authorities already quoted and from Heckethorn *op. cit.*

In the eleventh century, a Persian named Hasan bin Saba, a native of Khorasan and a professed Shiah of the left schism, was in training at the Dar-ul-Hikmat lodge in Cairo. He had partially qualified for the degree of Dai, or initiate, when he quarrelled with the heads of the Ismailis in Cairo and had to quit Egypt. Having absorbed some of the secret doctrines he returned to Persia where he began to teach and gradually gathered followers.

He devised a system which was to become infamous, by introducing the doctrine of physical violence among his adherents with the object of gaining world-domination, by means of the wholesale assassination of those who opposed them.

In A.D. 1090, he captured the rock-fortress of Alamut near the southern shore of the Caspian in Persia, and there he founded the secret society of the "Assassins" which preserved the speculative doctrines of the Ismailis, but added one peculiar feature, the employment of secret assassination against all enemies.

He reduced the nine degrees of the Dar-ul-Hikmat lodge to the original seven of Abdullah bin Maimun and gave each rank or degree the following names:—

1. Sheik ul Jebel. Sheik of the mountain fortress of Alamut. Supreme and absolute ruler of the order.
2. Dai-ul-Kerbal. Grand priors of the order, of which there were three.
3. Dai. Prior, or full initiate.
4. Refik. Associate, or those partially initiated.
5. Fedavi. Devotee. A band of resolute youths ready to carry out the blood-thirsty orders of the Sheik. They were not initiates.
6. Lasik. Novices or lay-brothers.
7. The Common people. Labourers and artisans who were simply blind instruments. Some authorities name the last degree Batini or affiliates.

Designs against religion were not of course openly admitted by the order. Strict conformity with the Shiah doctrine of Islam was demanded from all the lower ranks, but the "adept" was taught to see through the deception of faith and works. He believed in nothing and recognised that all acts and means were indifferent, and that only the secular end was to be considered.

Thus, the final object was domination by a few men consumed with the lust of power under the cloak of religion and piety, and the method by which this was to be established was the wholesale assassination of those who opposed them.[1]

THE VALLEY OF THE "ASSASSINS"

Marco Polo has given some account of the methods employed in training the instruments of this conspiracy. Near the fortress of Alamut there was the valley of the Mulebat, surrounded by mountains, which came to be known as the valley of the Assassins.[2]

In this valley, Hasan Saba is said to have constructed gardens cultivated and peopled to resemble a paradise. His method is said to have been to administer to the "fedavis" of his order and unsuspected by them hashish (Indian hemp).

While under the influence of hashish they were transported to the valley, where they were left for a fortnight to enjoy the delights of an earthly paradise. Hashish was then administered to them again and they were taken before the Sheik ul Jebel to whom they made vows to undertake any service he might command, in order to regain the bliss of the valley.

DERIVATION OF THE NAME "ASSASSIN"

This use of hashish is said to have given the name to the society, *viz. hashishiyin* = the hashishites, whose end was murder, hence the modern meaning of "assassin".

Another derivation given is from the Arabic word *hass* meaning "to destroy" or "to kill".

Another suggested derivation is from a word *asasa* meaning "to lay snares".

A common error is the belief that the assassins killed their victims by the use of hashish. This, the authorities agree, was not so. They killed their victims invariably with the dagger, they themselves being fortified thereto with hashish.

According to Heckethorn, the Assassins committed their murders dressed in white with a red sash round the waist, the emblems of innocence and blood.

The fortress of Alamut was captured in A.D. 1256 by the Tartar (Mongolian) leader Hulagu and the sect of the Assassins was broken up and dispersed but the survivors found refuge in Egypt and India and the sect has never been exterminated.

Footnote.—(1) Mrs. Webster *Secret societies and subversive movements* (1928) page 46.
Footnote.—(2) *See* book by Freya Stark of the same name, published in 1934.

THE MONGOL CONQUEST OF THE WEST (A.D. 1220)

We should here note that the Mongol conquest of the Mohamedan Seljuk Empire of the decaying Khwarizm-Shahs (modern Russian Turkestan) in the Ararat area mentioned in the Introduction, began in A.D. 1217. By 1220, the army of Genghis Khan (1165–1227) was at the gates of Samarkand which was captured in the same year. Genghis Khan died in 1227 on his way back to his tent-capital at Karakoram. His conquest of the West was completed by his dynasty,[1] which carried the western frontier of the Mongol Empire to the Adriatic and the Baltic seas.

It was to the Mongol General Hulagu, a younger brother of Mangu Khan, that the duty was assigned to exterminate the Assassins in 1256, after which Hulagu established his own dynasty in Persia.

It is a fair assumption that the blood brotherhood of the Mongols (*anda*) referred to by Ralph Fox in *Genghis Khan* (1936) which may have been the Ko Lao Hui of Hutson—accompanied the Mongols to the west and mixed with the secret sects of Christendom and Islam in the Ararat area.

Meanwhile Islam had been pressing south-eastward into India.

THE ISMAILI SECT IN INDIA

The Mohamedan conquest of India from A.D. 1191 onwards, is referred to below.

During the period of conquest the Shiah sect of the Ismailis became established throughout India.

The secret society of the Assassins derived from the Ismailis in the manner described above. After the Mohamedan conquest of India, there arose in that country a secret fraternity known as the Thugs, which included both Shiah Mohamedans and Hindus whose creed was murder, and whose origin is believed by many authorities to derive from those survivors of the society of the Assassins who found their way to India after the sack of Alamut, although this link has never been proved.

The origin of the Thuggist cult is thus described by MacMunn in *The Under-world of India* page 194:—

> The origin of the cult is lost in history and wrapped in mystery. Col. Sleeman thought it might owe its origin to the early wanderings of Tartar and Mogul tribes, then pagan, in the provinces of India.
> The Hindus claim for it a divine origin in the meddling of Bhowani with the affairs of men and certain it is that Thugs whether Moslem or Hindu, observed Hindu ceremonies which undoubtedly pointed to a Hindu origin.[2]
> It has been likened to the cult of murder and robbery known to exist in Persia in Sassanaian times and to that of......the Assassins—a cult of which in its harmless modern form the Aga Khan is head. In any case its origin is a mystery not likely now to be unravelled.

We must acquit the Aga Khan[3] at once of any association with the Thuggist cult. He is the head of the Ismaili sect, whose origin we have set out above, and which is represented among the Shiahs of India of to-day by the Khojas a trading sect of Islam, who have nothing to do with Thuggism. That fact does not exclude the view that the Thug may derive from an unreformed branch of the Assassins of Alamut, just as the desecrations of modern Satanism exist only by reason of the sacredness of Christian belief.

The secret society of the Assassins is still in existence in Persia, Syria and India.

THE NATURE OF THE THUGGIST CULT

Of Thuggism itself MacMunn *op. cit.* page 192 has:—

> It was a vast secret society which both Moslems and Hindus joined, based perhaps on some hatred of the wealthy and fortunate, as persons whose property should rightly be given to others: and immediately devoted to the conception of Kali another name for the female side of Siva, the Hindu God of life, death, birth and burial, whom men must fear and please......Under her form of Bhowani, the Thugs rendered her homage, swearing their allegiance to her both as directress and protectress. Their cult was in effect, the obtaining of wealth for their own personal use and in the heart of every initiate there soon arose a sacred joy in depriving people of their lives for the mere sensual gratification thereof—a form in fact of Sadism and of that unholy joy with which Soviet female executioners have put their prisoners to death.

We see in this description a likeness to the Han ethic and the depravity of the Ko Lao Hui and to the underlying principle of the deification of man who by the teaching of the cult constitutes himself the arbiter of the lives of his fellowmen, for the purpose of his own material gain. This is the creed of the Assassins of Alamut based on t' doctrine of Abdullah bin Maimun. The fact that Thuggism developed in India onl er the advent of Islam and after the dispersal of the Assassins in A.D. 1256, is the strongest argument in favour of giving it an Islamic rather than a Hindu origin. Because of the importation of Thuggism into Malaya from India in 1825 a more detailed examination of its secret formulæ and ritual becomes necessary, and is given later in this chapter.

Footnote.—(1) Ogotai 1227–1241: Mangu Khan 1251–1260: and Kublai Khan 1260–1294.
Footnote.—(2) It will later be shown that Thugs both Hindu and Moslem also observed Shiah Mohamedan feasts which gives Thuggism just as strong a claim to Shiah origin.
Footnote.—(3) The present Aga Khan is an influential representative of international Islam. For a sketch of his life *see The Controlling Minds of Asia* by Sir Ikbal Ali Shah (Herbert Jenkins 1937).

Because of the link between Thuggism and the Red Flag society in Malaya, recorded in Chapters XII and XIV *infra*, it is necessary at this point to refer briefly to the early association of the secret society of the Assassins—from which we believe Thuggism to derive—with the White Cross Knights Hospitaller and the Red Cross Knights Templar of the Crusade period in the Ararat area. This association draws together the ends of one important knot in the world-wide web of secret societies, as well between Freemasonry and the Knights Templar, as between east and west or the Ararat and Tibetan areas of secret society diffusion.

THE KNIGHTS HOSPITALLER AND THE KNIGHTS TEMPLAR

The eleventh and twelfth century in the "Ararat area" covered the period of the crusades and the foundation of the Knights Hospitaller and Knights Templar.

The following facts are taken from Tenison *Short history of the order of St. John of Jerusalem* (1922) and other sources.

A hospital in Jerusalem for Christian pilgrims to the Holy sepulchre was first founded and endowed by Neapolitan merchants in A.D. 1014, Jerusalem being then under Mohamedan (Saracen) rule.

In 1073, Jerusalem was captured from the Saracens by the Seljuk Turks.

In 1099, the first crusade captured Jerusalem from the Turkomans and in the same year Peter Gerard organised the Hospitallers into a regular constituted religious order clad in a black habit with a white cross of eight points. In 1113, the Pope formally recognised the order and in A.D. 1118, the order became a military one, and was reconstructed in three divisions, Knights, Chaplains and Serving Brothers. It also included Dames of the order. This was the order of the Knights Hospitaller.

It followed the rule of St. John the Baptist, and afterwards became the Order of the White Cross Knights of Malta.

In the same year (1118) a rival order was founded by a band of nine French gentlemen led by Hugo de Payens for the protection of pilgrims to the Holy Sepulchre,

The order was presented with a house as headquarters near the Temple of Solomon, from which fact it took its name, the Knights Templar.

In 1128, the order was recognised by the Council of Troyes and by the Pope and a rule drawn up under which the Knights Templar were bound by vows of poverty, chastity and obedience. They followed the rule of St. Benedict.

The second crusade promoted by Louis VII and the Greek and Germanic Kings was a failure and in 1152, the Knights Hospitaller and Knights Templar prevented Jerusalem from falling once again into the hands of the Egyptian Sultan, Saladin.

It was in this crusade that the Templars adopted the red cross and red cap to distinguish them from the white cross of the Hospitallers.[1]

In 1170, Saladin again marched from Egypt against the Christian Kingdom of Jerusalem and attacked Gaza, southern stronghold of the Christians. Gaza was saved but at a cost to the Templars of nearly a fifth of the brethren and some 2,000 of its citizens.

By 1172, the Kingdom of Jerusalem had shrunk to little more than a strip of the coast, forty miles broad at most from Ascalon to Tiberias; and Amalric (Amaury) then King of Jerusalem sought help in vain from Europe to stem the Moslem advance. It was in these circumstances that the Templars and the Assassins first appear to have come into close contact.

Campbell *The Knights Templars* pages 78–81 has:—

    In 1172, help was offered from an unexpected quarter, for the Assassins were ready to unite with the Christians. This sect, founded by the Persian, Hassan el Homeiri (Hasan Saba), late in the preceding century, was feared throughout the East. Its numerical strength was not large, but these fearless fanatics had been very successful in destroying everyone who opposed them and even the mighty Saladin had been forced to make peace with the chief of the organisation.

    The Assassins had established themselves in the castle of Alamut in 1090, and three-quarters of a century later were in possession of a number of fortresses in Lebanon. Sinan bin Suliman, who commanded the order in 1172, proposed that the Assassins should co-operate with the Latins against Islam, and that all his followers should adopt Christianity.

The proposal was not accepted for reasons given by Campbell at the same reference.

The fact that it had been entertained marked the beginning of a degeneration among the Christian population of Jerusalem which was destined to affect in time the order of the Knights Templar itself.

By the year 1187, the Christians in Jerusalem other than the members of the two orders of Knighthood, had degenerated to such an extent by contact with other races, that a contemporary chronicler quoted by Tenison page 12 says of them:—

    Corruption became so diffused throughout the land of Syria that other nations now draw an example of uncleanliness from the same source which formerly had supplied them with the elements of spiritual truth.

Footnote.—(1) *See* Campbell *The Knights Templars* (1937) page 45.

In the same year 1187, Jerusalem was captured by Saladin, who offered the Knights their freedom if they would renounce the Cross. This they refused. Thus, after 88 years Jerusalem again came under the domination of Islam. Saladin showed much magnanimity to the defeated Knights and Christians.

In 1191, King Richard Cœur de Lion led the third crusade, but was unable to recapture Jerusalem owing to dissension among his allies, the French and German armies. It was at this period that his life is said to have been spared by the Assassins. After Richard's return to England in 1192, the disunion spread among the two orders of Knighthood and friendly rivalry changed to animosity.

From this point the corruption already sown among the Christians in Syria seems to have spread to the Templars who appear to have begun to live on terms of close intimacy with the Assassins, despite the struggle which continued for another hundred years between the Cross and the Crescent for possession of Jerusalem.

Thus, referring to the first crusade of King Louis IX of France in A.D. 1244 (the seventh crusade of history) Campbell *op. cit.* page 188 has:—

> Louis was at length convinced that little help was to be expected from the efforts of his brothers to raise a force in Europe. The King, therefore, entered into negotiations to acquire assistance in the East so that Egypt would be forced to release the Christian prisoners. For a time there seemed to be hopes of an alliance with the Mongols,[1] whose messengers Louis had met in Cyprus and who again sought him at Acre, but the discussions came to nothing. Then there was the project of an alliance with the Assassins. Before giving their aid to Louis, they asked, as they had asked of Amalric, (in 1172) that he should relieve them of the tribute paid to the Temple. The emissaries explained frankly that while it was easy for the Assassins to remove an opponent, they would find no advantage in killing the Grand Master of the Temple. The only result would be the appointment of another Grand Master equally formidable. The negotiations with the Assassins likewise proved abortive.

And on page 189:—

> Louis was in Syria for nearly four years after his return from Egypt (A.D. 1248). Most of those who had survived the expedition had sailed back to Europe, and his following was at one time less than two thousand men. The long negotiations with different princes had tried the patience of his nobles and given rise to quarrels among the Franks. The Temple and the Hospital resented the suggestion of alliance with the Assassins; Damascus was supported by the Temple while the Hospital urged Louis to combine with Egypt against the Damascenes; and the King was constantly assailed by one faction or another.

This split between the White Knights of the Hospital and the Red Knights of the Temple came to a head about A.D. 1253 after the departure of King Louis to Europe at the close of the seventh crusade. Tenison *op. cit.* page 26 says:—

> The ever-smouldering animosity between the Templars and the Hospitallers flared up anew ......and to the scandal of Christendom they decided their quarrel in a pitched battle, in which the Hospitallers were victorious.

During the second half of the twelfth and the whole of the thirteenth century there was a growing suspicion in Christendom that the Templars had some underground understanding with the Assassins with whom they had previously been at war. There is a large body of evidence in support of this suspicion and the opinion upon it of Dr. F. W. Bussell, D.D. *Religious thought and heresy in the Middle Ages*, page 796–797 (note) is:—

> It cannot be disputed that the Templars had long and important dealings with the Assassins and were, therefore, suspected not unfairly of imbibing their precepts and following their principles.

Against this, there is the view of Campbell *op. cit.* page 347:—

> The orthodoxy of the Temple is claimed to have been undermined by the influx of heretics during the thirteenth century, especially the Albigensians, a number of whom found refuge in the Order after the crusade against them. The theory most frequently advanced, however, is that the Templars were infected with heresy through living in the East on terms of intimacy with the adherents of other religions. A number of the leaders are said to have turned to Islam and introduced Moslem practices throughout the Temple. It is undeniable that there was close friendship between the chiefs of the Temple and a number of Moslem sultans at various times and that the brethren showed less fervour for the holy war in later years. The tolerance which the Order exhibited towards the infidel was bound to be distasteful to the Church and the fanatical Christians, and it may be true that the Temple included in its ranks, brethren who had adopted the Moslem religion. That the Order as a whole was heretical, however, is not only incapable of proof, but is contrary to all presumption. Equally improbable is the theory that the Temple followed the secret doctrines of the Assassins.

The truth seems to be that some of the order adopted from the Assassins the double doctrine of Abdullah 'bin Maimun as taught by Hasan Saba.[2]

By the end of the thirteenth century the order of the Knights Templar w ʳ discredited. The order was impeached in 1307 before the Inquisitor of France upon following charges:—[3]

    (1) Denial of Christ and defiling of the Cross.

    (2) Adoration of an idol.[4]

    (3) A perverted sacrament performed.

    (4) Ritual murders.

    (5) The wearing of a cord of heretical significance.

Footnote.—(1) i.e. Hulagu.
Footnote.—(2) On this point *see* Ward *Freemasonry and the Ancient Gods* page 269 ff.
Footnote.—(3) As given by Ward *op. cit.* page 277.
Footnote.—(4) Known as Baphomet, believed to be a corruption of Mahomet.

(6) The ritual kiss (osculum in ano).[1]
(7) Alteration in the ceremony of the Mass and an unorthodox form of absolution.
(8) Authorisation of the practice of unnatural vice.
(9) Treachery to other sections of the Christian forces.

The order was abolished after prolonged enquiry by Pope Clement V at the Council of Vienna in A.D. 1312. In France, many of the Knights including the Grand Master Jacques de Molay, were burnt at the stake as heretics between 1310 and 1314.

Springett *Secret Sects of Syria* quotes King and Von Hammer to prove that:—

> The constitution of the Templar order is a servile copy of that of the Assassins. The statutes of the latter prove the fact beyond gainsaying. They were found upon their captives at the capture of Alamut by the Mogul Hulagu in the year 1335[2] when by a singular coincidence, Khalif and Pope were busy exterminating the model and the copy in the East and West at one and the same time.

The whole of the evidence for and against the Templar heresy is given with full documentation by Mrs. Webster *Secret Societies and Subversive Movements* (1928) pages 49–73.

The importance of the Templar heresy to our subject lies in the following facts:—

(1) The Templars became a debased secret society concealed in the cloak of a religious fraternity with a ceremony of initiation and secret oaths and a ritual, which at some points, appears to have resembled the left or Yin stem of the Yin Yang and to have been based on that depravity and licence or "Han ethic", which we have seen to be the doctrine of the Three Dot society of China.

(2) It appears to have derived from the teaching of Abdullah bin Maimun through the contact of the Crusaders with the Assassins.

(3) The Assassins sprang from the same root as the Druses. The Druses have retained a tradition of Chinese origin in their faith which also contains many elements common to Freemasonry.

(4) Freemasonry in the West has a traditional connection with the Templars, from which it seems possible that if the debased or heretical section of the Templars represented the Yin of China, Continental Freemasonry may derive from the Yin stem; and British Freemasonry which has remained pure and has a close resemblance to the Triad society of China, may spring from the Yang or non-heretical section of the Templars.

This conjecture, if sustained, would provide both the origin and the explanation of the likeness between Freemasonry and the Hung league.

We return to a general survey of this aspect of our subject in Chapter XXXIII *infra*.

THE ADVENT OF ISLAM TO INDIA

We must now turn eastward again and consider the connection between the Shiah sect of the Assassins in India and the Shiah society of the Thugs in India and their joint connection with events in Penang during the nineteenth century.

Before doing so, a note upon the advent of Mohamedanism to India is necessary. The following is taken from Herklots' *Qanun-i-Islam* (Islam in India) ed. Crooke 1921, pages 4, 9 and 15:—

> The first contact of militant Islam with India occurred in the Khilafat of Walid, when in A.D. 712, Muhammad, son of Qasim, son-in-law of Hajaj, governor of Persia, invaded Sind. But the force of this Arab movement on the western frontier was exhausted when it reached the Indus valley, and the first effective step towards the conquest of India for the new Faith was taken by a dynasty founded by a Turkish slave at Ghazni between Kabul and Kandahar. The greatest of these princes, Mahmud, between 999 and his death in 1050, made a series of raids with the object of plunder and the destruction of the temples and idols of the Hindus. It was not the intention of Mahmud to occupy the country, and the real task of conquest was undertaken by Muhammad Ghori, ruler of a petty kingdom between Ghazni and Herat, who, after some preliminary attempts, invaded India in 1191, and though he was at first checked by Prithiviraja, the Chauhan Rajput King of Ajmer, defeated and slew the Hindu leader in the following year. The conquests of Muhammad Ghori were extended by his lieutenant, Qutbu-d-din, and by 1206 the Muhammadans had mastered northern India from Peshawar to the Bay of Bengal. From that time until 1526, thirty-four Kings reigned at Delhi, Slave Kings, Khaljis, Tughlaqshahis, Sayyids, and Lodis. But their hold over northern India was precarious, and the country was repeatedly raided by bands of fierce Mongols from central Asia. The Tughlaqshahis fell before Taimur the Lame, who occupied and sacked Delhi in 1398. The Sayyids and Lodis succeeded to a kingdom ruined by the foreign invaders and convulsed by the struggles of rival claimants. The time was ripe for the coming of a stronger ruler, when in 1526, Babur, King of Kabul, defeated Ibrahim Lodi on the historical field of Panipat in the Karnal District of the eastern Panjab, and founded the Mughal Empire.

Footnote.—(1) What may be an echo of this rite appears in the initiation ceremony of the Red Flag society in Malaya. *See* Chapter XXIX *infra*.

Footnote.—(2) The accepted historical date of this incident is A.D. 1256.

In that year, Mangu Khan, reigning Mongol Emperor (A.D. 1251–1260) sent his younger brother Hulagu from Karakoram (near Urga) to Persia to punish the Assassins for creating trouble in the Western part of the Mongol Empire which at that time stretched from the Adriatic to the Yellow Sea.

After the sack of Alamut, Hulagu set up his own dynasty (1256–1353) as rulers of Persia under the name of the Il Khans of Persia. He himself died about A.D. 1275 and his dynasty began to disintegrate after the death of the Il Khan Abu Said in 1335.

This may have involved a further sacking of Alamut in that year, which may account for Springett's date.

His son, Humayun, a gallant soldier, but addicted to opium eating and possessed of less energy and enterprise than his father, was obliged to take refuge in Persia while his Indian dominions were occupied by Sher Shah, an Afghan officer in Bihar, who led the Hindostani Musalmans against the Mughals. After his death Humayun recovered his kingdom in 1556, and on his death, the result of an accident, his eldest son Akbar (1556–1605) succeeded to the throne.

It is unnecessary here to describe in any detail the foundation, extension, and ultimate decay of the Mughal Empire. Four Emperors, Akbar, Jahangir, Shahjahan, and Aurangzeb, reigned between 1556 and 1707. The policy of Akbar, known as the Great Mogul, was devoted to conquest, consolidation, fiscal and social reorganization. He practically discarded orthodox Islam, and aimed at establishing a new eclectic religion, known as the Divine Faith, while his sympathies led him to conciliate his Hindu subjects and to repress Musalman bigotry. During the rule of his successors, Jahangir and Shahjahan, the empire retained its magnificence, the Court ceremonies were conducted with splendour, splendid buildings were erected, but the administration was less efficient, and though persecution of the Hindus occurred, the rapprochement with the faith of the masses of the subject races were encouraged by royal marriages with Rajput princesses. Thus, the loss of constant streams of fresh recruits from Kabul and central Asia was compensated by the devotion to the Mughal throne of the Rajputs, the most virile of the Hindu tribes. Under Aurangzeb a fanatical Sunni Musalman, the policy of toleration was abandoned, and the destruction of Hindu temples and idols and the imposition of the Jisya or poll-tax on unbelievers alienated the Rajputs and led to the rise of the Maratha power in the Deccan. Between the death of Aurangzeb in 1707 and the establishment of British supremacy in Bengal after the battle of Plassey in 1757, the empire gradually fell into decay.......

Thus, in northern India, tribes like the Rajputs and Jats, or other castes which have accepted Islam, have both a Hindu and a Musalman branch, and members of the latter often supplement the orthodox ritual of Islam by Hindu marriage or death rites, follow Hindu rules of succession to real and personal property, and, particularly in time of trouble, reverence the local village deities. Even on the north-west frontier and in Baluchistan, where Hindu influence is practically absent, Islam has in a large measure failed to supersede the primitive animism.......

We should note this growth of Moslem and Hindu eclecticism. Its diffusion, as we shall see in the next chapter, spread to the observance of religious festivals both in India and Malaya. These festivals in turn played no small part in the background of the Thuggist cult in Malaya and in fostering the spread of the Red Flag society in Malaya down to the present-day.

SKETCH OF THE CHARACTERISTICS AND RITUAL OF THUGGISM[1]

The name "Thug" is believed to derive from the Hindi *thag* = a cheat, a swindler.[2]

The sect is a secret religious fraternity, who devote themselves to the commission of wholesale murder and live upon the plunder obtained from their victims.

Although in the main, composed of professing Moslems of the lower classes in India, the sect exhibits its eclecticism—deriving, perhaps, from the cynicism of Abdullah bin Maimun and Hasan Saba—by regarding murder as a religious rite, performed in honour of the Hindu goddess Kali, wife of Siva, the destroyer, and by taking part in the Hindu festival of the Durga puja appropriated to the same goddess. By this concession to the religion of the country of its adoption, the sect attracted Hindu devotees in large numbers, so that at the time of its exposure by British officials in the early nineteenth century, the sect presented the remarkable appearance of a secret murder society composed of both Moslems and Hindus, for, "in the shadow of Kali, Moslem and Hindu are brothers".

Similarly, Hindu members of the Thug cult, took part in the annual Shiah festival of the Moharram.

The origin of the sect of the Thugs in the Assassins of Alamut has not been proved. What seems probable is that the Assassin cult was grafted on to the technique of the much more ancient Hindu cult of Kali and strangulation took the place of the dagger as the method of obtaining victims to appease the goddess.

If we cannot say definitely that there is identity of origin, we can say that the ancient dualism that we have seen in the Yin Yang of China and in secret sects of the Ararat area, re-appears in the Thuggism of India. Thus, Ameer Ali, a Thug and the source of our present knowledge of the sect, quoted by Meadows Taylor *op. cit.* (*see* Appendix IV) gives the following explanation of the origin of the sect:—

In the beginning of the world according to the Hindus, there existed a creating and destroying power, both emanations from the Supreme Being. These were at constant enmity with each other, and still continue to be so. The creative power however, peopled the earth so fast that the destroyer (Siva) could not keep pace with him, nor was he allowed to do so, but was given

Footnote.—(1) This section is condensed from the following authorities:—
Asiatic Researches Vol. 13 (India Office Library) article by Dr. Sherwood entitled—
Of the murderers called phansigars Madras, 1816.
Ramaseena The language of the Thuggs W. H. Sleeman. Calcutta, 1836.
Rambles and Recollections W. H. Sleeman. Revised edition Smith, 1915.
Confessions of a Thug Meadows Taylor, 1839. Revised edition Stewart,
Thugs and Dacoits of India Hutton, 1857.
Thug, or a million Murders Col. J. L. Sleeman, 1933.
Prisoners their own Warders Maj. McNair, 1899.

Footnote.—(2) Two following definitions should also be noted:—

Dakaiti *or* Dacoity } = Systematic gang robbery with violence, committed by armed bands.

Thagi *or* Thugee } = The religion of a body of professional assassins, both Hindus and Mohamedans, devotees of Kali, the Hindu goddess of destruction.

permission to resort to every means he could to effect his object. Among others, his consort Devi, Bhowani or Kali......assembled a number of her votaries, whom she named Thugs......and endowed them with superior intelligence and cunning in order that they might decoy human beings to destruction.

The method employed by the Thugs in India was to band together in gangs and assume the appearance of ordinary traders, and after insinuating themselves into the confidence of unsuspecting fellow-travellers, to kill them by *strangulation.* Hence, they are also known as *phansigars* = stranglers, from *phansi,* a noose.

They were bound by secret oaths of brotherhood, taken at an initiation ceremony, and they carried on systematic assassination on a large scale. They considered murder a pious rite and their profession a lofty one.

The sect appears to have come into existence in India about the thirteenth century under the early Mohamedan rulers of India. This date would about coincide with the dispersion of the Assassins of Alamut (A.D. 1256). The British Government became aware of the existence of the sect at the beginning of the nineteenth century and carried on a campaign of extermination against the Thugs in 1820–1857. During this campaign, over 4,000 were arrested, of whom over five hundred were hanged, and of the remainder, over 1,700 were transported for life to the East India Company's penal settlements at *Penang* and Singapore.

This campaign, largely put a stop to Thug murder by strangulation, but thereafter the sect practised murder by datura (thorn-apple) poisoning instead.

The sect is still in existence in India and traces of its influence are still to be found in Malaya.

The two principal festivals of the Thugs, whose Mohamedan adherents are, of course, Shiahs, are:—

The Shiah Moharram festival, or lamentation for Husein (lunar calendar)[1] and the Hindu festival of the Dussera, or Durga-puja (solar calendar).

The following extracts from Heckethorn's *Secret societies of All Ages* gives in concise form the origin, ritual, and history of the Thugs. Fuller extracts on the subject from *Confessions of a Thug* are given in Appendix IV[2] to this work.

Heckethorn *op. cit.* Vol. I pages 245–250 has:—

Name and Origin:—

    Shortly after the conquest of Seringapatam in 1799, about a hundred robbers, called Phansigars, were apprehended in that province; but it was not known then that they belonged to a distinct class of hereditary murderers and plunderers, settled in various parts of India. In 1807, between Chittoor and Arcot, several Phansigars were apprehended, and information was then obtained which ultimately led to a full knowledge of the association infamous under the name of Thugs, though the name by which they were known to one another, and also to others, was *Phansigars,* that is, "men of the noose". The name Thug is said to be derived from *Thaga,* to deceive, because the Thugs get hold of their victims by luring them into false security. They were particularly numerous in Mysore, the Carnatic, in the Balaghat Districts, and in the Pollams of Chittoor. As to their origin, Sleeman considers them descended from remnants of the army of Xerxes, which invaded Greece; but more probably their origin is more recent. The date assigned by themselves to their first establishment in India coincides with the destruction of the Assassins of Alamut. It is not improbable, in fact, that some of the fugitives who fled from the swords of the Moguls made their way to India; and the existence of Ishmaelites in India, under the name of *Borahs,* was known before the existence of the Thugs as an organised sect had been detected. Now, the Thugs in the Ramasee, or cant of the Thugs, always call themselves *Borah,* which they do probably for the purpose of disguising their real pursuit; for there is a sect, numerous in Hindustan, known by the name of *Borahs,* and whose members are chiefly peaceful traders. Some sects of Thugs call themselves *auliya* = saints.

Practices and worship of Thugs:—

    One common mode of decoying young men having valuables upon them is to place a young and handsome woman by the wayside, and apparently in great grief, who by some pretended tale of misfortunte draws him into the jungle, where the gang are lying in ambush, and on his appearance, strangle him. The gang consists of from ten to fifty members; and they will follow or accompany the marked-out victim for days, nor attempt his murder until an opportunity offering every chance of success, presents itself. After every murder they perform a religious ceremony called *Tupounee;* and the division of the spoil is regulated by old established laws— the man that threw the handkerchief, or *Roomal,* gets the largest share; the man that held the hands, called the *Shumseea,* the next largest proportion, and so on. In some gangs their property is held in common. Their crimes are committed in honour of Kali, who hates our race, and to whom the death of man is a pleasing sacrifice.

    Kali (derived from *Kala*=time), or Bhowany, for she is equally well known by both names, was, according to the Indian legend, born of the burning eye, which Shiva, one of the persons of the Brahmin trinity, has on his forehead, whence she issued, like the Greek Minerva out of the skull of Jupiter, a perfect and full-grown being. She represents the evil spirit, delights in human blood, presides over plague and pestilence, and directs the storm and hurricane, and ever aims at destruction...... She has her temples, in which the people sacrifice cocks and bullocks to her; but her priests are the Thugs, the "sons of death", who quench the never-ending thirst of this divine vampire.

Traditions:—

    Like all similar societies, the Thugs have their traditions. According to them, Kali in the beginning determined to destroy the whole human race, with the exception, however, of her faithful adorers and followers. These taught by her, slew all men that fell into their power.

Footnote.—(1) *See* notes on these festivals in Chapter XI.
Footnote.—(2) *See* also a recent publication *Bombay in the Days of George IV* by F. D. Drewitt (1935) pages 318–325 and Sir George MacMunn's *The Under-world of India.*

The victims at first were killed by the sword, and so great was the destruction her worshippers wrought, that the whole human race would have been extinguished had not Vishnu, the Preserver, interfered, by causing the blood thus shed to bring forth new living beings, so that the destructive action of Kali was counteracted. It was then this goddess, to nullify the good intentions of Vishnu, forbade her followers to kill any more with the sword, but commanded them to resort to *strangulation*. With her own hands she made a human figure of clay, and animated it with her breath. She then taught her worshippers how to kill without shedding blood. She also promised them that she would always bury the bodies of their victims, and destroy all traces of them. She further endowed her chosen disciples with superior courage and cunning, so as always to ensure them the victory over those they should attack. And she kept her promise. But in the course of time corrupt manners crept in even among the Thugs, and one of them, being curious to see what Kali did with the dead bodies, watched her as she was about to remove the corpse of a traveller he had slain. Goddesses, however, cannot thus be watched on the sly. Bhowany saw the peeper, and stepping forth, thus addressed him: 'Thou hast now beheld the awful countenance of a goddess, which none can behold and live. But I shall spare thy days, though as a punishment for thy crime, I shall not protect thee as I have done hitherto, and the punishment will extend to all thy brethren. The corpses of those you kill will no longer be buried or concealed by me; you yourselves will be obliged to take the necessary measures for that purpose, nor will you always be successful, though I leave you the *Kussee*, or sacred pickaxe, to dig the graves; sometimes you will fall under the profane laws of the world, which will be your eternal punishment. Nothing will remain to you but the superior intelligence and skill I have given you and henceforth I shall direct you by auguries only, which you must diligently consult'. Hence their superstitious belief in omens. . . . .

Initiation :—

To be admitted into this horrible sect required a long and severe novitiate, during which the aspirant had to give the most convincing proofs of his fitness for admission. This having once been decided on, he was conducted by his sponsor to the mystical baptism, and clothed in *white garments*, and his *brow crowned with flowers*. The preparatory rite being performed the sponsor presented him to the *guru*, or spiritual head of the sect, who, in his turn, introduced him into a room set apart for such ceremonies, where the *Hyemader*, or chiefs of the various gangs, awaited him. Being asked whether they will receive the candidate into the Order, and having answered in the affirmative, he and the *guru* are led out into the open air, where the chiefs place themselves in a circle around the two, and kneel down to pray.

Then the *guru* rises, and lifting up his hands to heaven says: O Bhowany Mother of the World (this appellation seems very inappropriate, since she is a destroyer), whose worshippers we are, receive this thy new servant; grant him thy protection and to us an omen, which assures us of thy consent. They remain in this position until a passing bird, quadruped, or even mere cloud, has given them this assurance; whereupon they return to the chamber, where the neophyte is invited to partake of a banquet spread out for the occasion, after which the ceremony is over. . . . .

* * *

Certain persons, however, are excepted from the attacks of the Thugs. These belong to some particular tribes and castes, which the hierophant enumerates; persons who squint, are lame, or otherwise deformed, are also exempt; so are washerwomen, for some cause not clearly ascertained; and as Kali was supposed to co-operate with the murderers, women also were safe from them, but only when travelling alone, without male protector; and orthodox Thugs date the deterioration of Thuggism from the first murder of a woman by some members of the society, after which the practice became common.

* * *

Suppression :—

When the existence of the society was first discovered, many would not believe in it; yet in course of time the proofs became so convincing that it could no longer be ignored, and the British Government took decided measures to suppress the Thugs. A Thuggee school of industry in connection with the Lahore gaol was established, but closed again about 1882, the prisoners being allowed their freedom under ticket-of-leave. The crimes some of them had committed, indeed, almost exceed belief. One Thug who was hanged at Lucknow in 1825, was legally convicted of having strangled six hundred persons. Another, an octogenarian, confessed to nine hundred and ninety-nine murders, and declared that respect for the profession alone had prevented him from making it a full thousand, because a round number was considered among them rather vulgar. But in spite of various measures on the part of Great Britain, there is a regular government department in India for the suppression of Thuggism, the sect could not be entirely destroyed: it is a religious order, and as such has a vitality greater than that of political or merely criminal associations. It was still in existence but a few years ago, and no doubt has its adherents even now, though the modern Thugs resort to drugging and poisoning instead of strangling. It always had protectors in some of the native princes, who shared their booty, and such may now be the case. The society has a temple at Mirzapore, on the Ganges.

The reader will recognise points of similarity in the above description (as amplified in Appendix IV) between the secret society of the Thugs of India and the Three Dot society of China.

The importance of this similarity to British administration in Malaya lies in the fact that despite the suppression of Thuggism in India, both secret societies are to be found to-day in Malaya, where they are in underground alliance in the Red Flag society. The channel of importation of Thuggism to Malaya is given below.

The importance of Thuggism to British administration and political evolution in India lies in the fact that despite the suppression of its criminal activities in India, it has an undying religious basis which has found a political and revolutionary outlet in modern bomb worship. Thus, MacMunn *Religions and Hidden Cults of India* page 172 has :—

A bomb-parast (bomb worshipper) is one who has put a bomb in the shrine of Kali that he may worship it and gloat with hungry Kali on the blood that may flow when he shall throw it.

The fact emerges that Thuggism lives to-day in the political if not in the criminal sphere of Indian life, as the mainspring of Indian terrorism.

It is "the ancient horror existing beneath the outer surface of perfectly reasonable political aspirations".[1]

Sir Charles Spencer a retired officer of the Indian Civil Service, writing in the *Morning Post* of 11th September, 1933, said:—

> No sane Government can tolerate the presence of anarchical bodies in its midst. Therefore, the only sound policy is to treat the Bengal terrorists as Government once treated the Thugs. A special department should be formed for tracking and hunting down these pests of society and it should be made an offence, punishable with death, to belong to an organisation whose creed is the assassination of officials.

In this paragraph is exposed the doctrine of the perverted Yin, linking a thousand years in direct sequence from the Batinis of Abdullah bin Maimun to the Indian political terrorists of to-day.

THE ADVENT OF THUGGISM TO MALAYA

In 1844, an officer of the Madras army was made superintendent of convicts at Singapore and in 1848 a similar post was created in Penang.[2]

Major J. F. A. McNair afterwards Colonial Engineer held one of these appointments and in 1899 published a history of penal establishments in the Straits Settlements entitled *Prisoners their own warders* from which the following extracts are taken to show the coming of Thuggism to Malaya:—

> The first penal settlement was at Bencoolen, the Banka-Ulu of the Malays, to which convicts were transported from India about the year 1787, much about the same time that transportation to Australia for English convicts was sanctioned by our laws........

> *   *   *

> In the year 1823, there were between 800 and 900 of these Indian convicts at our settlement of Bencoolen, on the south west coast of Sumatra; and when this place was conceded to the Dutch by the London treaty of 1825, these convicts were removed to Penang and were subsequently distributed amongst the three settlements of Penang, Malacca and Singapore...... We think, the account which we are about to give of these Indian convicts at Singapore, will abundantly show how considerably this important settlement has benefited by their early introduction...... Moreover, when released from imprisonment upon a ticket-of-leave, they were absorbed innocuously into the native community, and again contributed to the advantage of the place in the various occupations they had recourse to, in order to obtain an honest livelihood........

We think, that the chapters that follow will show that the release of this criminal stream and its subsequent absorption into the native community, was not an unmixed blessing for Malaya. McNair continues:—

> We are not, of course, greatly concerned with the original crimes committed by those Indian convicts, and for which they had received a sentence of transportation. Suffice it to say that ......in the case of convicts for life, the crimes were for the most part those of murder, Thuggee, and dacoity: while those sentenced to a term of years had been tried and convicted of frauds and forgeries, robbery with violence and such like misdemeanours. "Thuggee" we all know, though it will bear repetition here, was in full operation all over India from very early times, but at the beginning of this century it engaged the serious attention of the Indian Government and it was found to be an hereditary pursuit of certain families who worked in gangs......and they committed countless numbers of murders all over the country. Thugs were a bold, resolute set of men, and as a rule divided themselves into groups, consisting of a leader, a persuader, a strangler, a scout and a gravedigger, but all the gangs, happily for India, were finally broken up under Colonel Sleeman about 1860. Some of the men were hanged, and many transported to our penal settlements in the Straits of Malacca. Dacoity was in some parts of India akin to Thuggee, for the leaders carried with them in the same way a sacred instrument, which was devoted to Bhowani. In the case of the Thugs, this was a pickaxe, but with the Dacoits, it was an axe with a highly-tempered edge..........

> *   *   *

> In the year 1826, there was a change of government in the Settlements,......and the seat of government was fixed at Penang, that being our oldest settlement in these seas. On this change taking place many more of the Indian convicts from Penang were sent down to Singapore....... From the accounts given in the newspapers of that day, the convicts were at this time treated with great indulgence if of proved good behaviour, being permitted after their work was over, to engage themselves as servants to the residents, who in the scarcity of labour at that time, and the fitness of the convicts for such service, were content to give them a very liberal wage. In the early days of penal colonies this had not infrequently occurred, and some of these old convicts have been known to amass considerable sums of money, and, indeed to become possessed of landed property in the town. Occasionally, even in those days convicts were employed as orderlies and servants to public officers..........

> *   *   *

> In 1832, the seat of government was transferred to Singapore which had by this time become the most important of the three settlements...........
> There were about 1,100 or 2,000 Indian convicts in Singapore, divided into six classes and employed in various ways as already narrated.

> *   *   *

> It was in the year 1841, that it was decided to erect a jail for the Indian convicts on a site near the Bras Basah Canal immediately below Government Hill, now known as Fort Canning. In this brick building the defaulters and those in irons were placed......and those employed in positions of trust were allowed to erect small huts for themselves in the style of a native village just outside the wall, in which they were allowed to have their wives and families........

> *   *   *

Footnote.—(1) MacMunn *The Under-world of India* page 197.
Footnote.—(2) Mills *British Malaya* page 89.

In the year 1857, there were 2,139 convicts from different parts of India, Burmah and Ceylon in this jail, but upon an average until the prison was broken up, there were 1,900 always under control. The men from India were...... Thugs and Dacoits from different parts of the Bengal presidency, and mostly from round about Delhi and Agra; felons from all parts of the Madras and Bombay presidencies, and a few from Assam and Burmah, chiefly Dacoits.

* * *

On the separation of the Straits Settlements from British India in 1867, it was arranged that the Indian life-convicts at Singapore should be transferred to Port Blair in the Andaman Islands. In the course of correspondence which took place on the subject, His Excellency the Governor of the Straits Settlements proposed, in respect of those convicted who were to continue in the Straits, that a liberal use of the power of pardon should be granted to those whose crimes and whose subsequent character warranted it. The Government of India agreed to this proposal, with the proviso that pardon should be conditional on convicts not returning to India, without the special sanction in each case of the Government of India; and that this sanction would not be given in any cases in which the crime was "Thuggee" or "Dacoity" or robbery by administering poisonous drugs, or other form of organised crime, or in the case of mutiny or rebellion accompanied with murder.

Accordingly, the Straits Government authorities submitted lists of convicts whom they recommended for pardon.

After consulting the local governments concerned, the Government of India issued orders, in each case, authorising the release and return to India of some of the convicts, granting conditional pardon to others, and refusing release on any account to the remainder.

This decision did not commend itself to the Straits Government, and His Excellency the Governor suggested the deputation of a special officer from India to enquire into the matter.

.... On the receipt of his report, the Government of India granted unconditional releases in certain cases, while in others the convicts were pardoned on condition that they did not leave the Straits.

* * *

Of those who were pardoned unconditionally, many returned to their own country; but when they arrived there they found things so uncongenial that they returned to the Straits and settled down as shopkeepers, cowkeepers, cartmen, etc., and most of them sought and obtained employment either with private individuals or in the Public Works Department.

* * *

When the old Singapore jail was put an end to in 1873, some six years after the transfer of the Straits Settlements to the Crown, the convicts then under confinement were removed to the Andaman Islands, at that time not long established as a penal settlement in India; while those on a ticket-of-leave were permitted to merge into the population, continuing to earn their livelihood as artisans, cowkeepers, cart drivers and the like.

The foregoing presents a clear picture of the channel whereby Thuggism became infused among the indigenous population of Malaya. The total number of Thug deportees to the Straits Settlements between 1830 and 1848 was 1,700, of whom we may assume the larger proportion ultimately gained their freedom and became assimilated. This figure is arrived at from the statistics given by W. H. Sleeman *op. cit.* (edition 1933) page 8, where he gives the total of transportees to Penang between 1831 and 1837 as 1,059.

Hutton, in *Thugs and Dacoits of India* (1857) gives transportees to the end of 1840 as 1,504, and the same authority gives 174 transportees for the period 1841 to 1847 and 24 transportees for the year 1848.

There were no doubt, further Thug deportees after 1848 of whom we have found no record. The authorities quoted give a total of 4,244 Thugs dealt with by the courts in India during the period 1830–1848 of whom 504 were hanged.

We have also to bear in mind that in addition to the purely Thug element, a large number of criminals including dacoits, professional poisoners and members of criminal gangs and tribes perhaps totalling in the aggregate more than the Thugs themselves, were liberated in the Straits Settlements between the years 1825 and 1873 on condition that they did not return to India.

These "bandi-wallah" as they were known locally, became by local inter-marriage the progenitors to a large extent of the Jawi-bukan ("not-Malay") or Jawi-pekan, or "Peranakan", community, whose stronghold is in Penang, and whose criminal proclivities and associations with the Red and White Flag societies in Malaya are discussed in subsequent chapters.

We submit that it may have been thus, through the Batini-Assassin-Thug link, that the perverted Shiah doctrine of the Dar-ul-Hikmat lodge of Cairo of A.D. 1004,—which in turn, may have had its origin in the Yin Yang of China,—reached Sunni Malaya eight hundred and thirty years later. Its criminal influence remains to the present-day.

TRACES OF THUG SLANG IN THE MALAY LANGUAGE

There remains only to note the presence in the Malay language of possible traces of "Ramaseena" or Thug slang.

W. H. Sleeman in his *Ramasee* or vocabulary of the peculiar language used by the Thugs (1836) says:—

Their peculiar dialect the Thugs called "Ramasee", and every word entered in this vocabulary is Ramasee in the sense assigned to it, while but few of them are to be found at all in any language with which I am acquainted.

The following "Ramasee" words are taken from Sleeman and the Malay words are taken from Wilkinson's dictionary ed. 1932.

Ramasee	Malay
1. Roomal=The handkerchief or noose of cloth, with which the Thugs were wont to strangle their victims.	1. Rumal ⎱ = A face towel: a handkerchief. Ramal ⎰
2. Bora=A Thug in contradistinction to Beetoo, any person not a Thug.	2. Bura=(Singapore slang). Chucked out, evicted, outcaste.
3. Nishan=Emblem, name for the Thug emblem, the sacred pickaxe.	3. Nesan=Grave stone, from the Persian nishan = emblem.
4. Pilao=Omen on the left hand.	4. Pelak ⎱ = Evil spirits, or influences Pilak ⎰ lurking about a locality.

Other traces of what may be Thug influence in the Boria performance of modern Penang are noted in Chapter XII.

We must now examine the connection between Thuggism and the observance of certain annual religious festivals in India and show how these festivals have developed in a distorted form among the Indian immigrant stream and the indigenous Malay population in Malaya during the nineteenth century.

CHAPTER XI

SOME RELIGIOUS FESTIVALS OF ISLAM AND HINDUISM

We have seen in the last chapter how the criminal cult of Indian Thuggism possessing the vitality of religious sanction, became diffused in Malaya.

We must now examine the character of some of the annual religious festivals of Shiah Islam and Hinduism as celebrated in India, which provided the religious background of the Thuggist cult in India up to about A.D. 1850. We may take that year for convenience as the year of the official suppression of Thuggism in India.

In this investigation it will be revealed that some of those Indian festivals most closely associated with the Thuggist cult are to be found in Malaya to-day, where they have been merged into the common "religious" background of the Mohamedan, Hindu and Chinese secret society under-world.

The festivals which it is necessary to bring to the reader's notice are:—The Moharram festival of Shiah Islam; the Durga-puja or Dasera festival of the Hindus: the Holi festival of Hinduism: the Akhiri Chahar festival of Sunni and Shiah Islam; and the Mandi Safar festival of the Malays.

It may seem that these descriptions are tedious and unnecessary—they certainly render this chapter somewhat disjointed,—but an understanding of the background and development of the secret society under-world in Malaya is impossible without them. The reader's indulgence is, therefore, sought in advance.

THE MOHARRAM, OR TEN-DAY SHIAH FESTIVAL

This festival is observed in present-day Malaya mainly in Penang in a distorted form and under a mutilated name and is known as the Boria. The explanation of this name is given in Chapter XII *infra*.

We will first give a general description of the festival as observed in India and then examine some of its component parts in closer detail. The following terms used in the description are also in use in Malaya and require explanation at this point *viz:*—

Ta'ziah, Tabut, Kudu, and *Panja.*

The following definitions are taken from Wilkinson's Malay dictionary editions 1903 and 1932:—

(1) **Ta'ziah** تعزية (Arab) lamentation (for Ali). *Memberi ta'ziyah*=to lament at a funeral. [This word does not appear in the 1932 edition].

(2) **Tabut** تابت (Arab تابوت). The Ark of the Covenant. A Kling idol. (Penang only) a Hindu image or processional emblem. (Singapore) = Kudu.

The 1932 edition has:—

Ark-emblem, box-like framework of lath with sides of coloured paper, carried in procession on the 10th Muharram to commemorate ...... the death of Husein.

Loosely, any processional emblem whether Moslem or not, and so applied to images carried in procession by Hindus (*cf.* Kudu (Penang) = Tabut Kling).

The emblem known as tabut in Malaya ...... is known also as Durga (Persian dargah=Kerbela shrine) and gives its name to the Muharram month=bulan Hasan Husein and (from the illuminations) bulan api. (Sumatra) bulan tabut.

(3) **Kudu** کودو (Singapore) a Kling idol.

The 1932 edition has:—

(Singapore from Tamil?) image of a Hindu God (as borne in procession round the streets.)

(4) **Panja** پنج The name given to a large image of the human hand, the hand of Hasan (grandson of Mohammed). This is carried about Penang at the Muharram to excite people.

The 1932 edition has:—

> "Hand with five outstretched fingers. *Cf.* Pancha. Used of the red hand-emblems carried in the Muharram processions, to represent the blood-stained hand of Husein".[1]

The following general description of the Muharram festival is taken from Sir Lewis Pelly's translation of the *Miracle Play* (of Hasan and Husein) published in 1879 Vol. I (Introduction) page xvii:—

> The Martyrdom of Hasan and Husain is celebrated by the Shiahs all over India during the first ten days of the month of Mohurrum, which begins when the new moon which ushers in the month is first seen. Attached to every great Shiah's house is an Imambarrah—a hall or enclosure—built expressly for the celebration of the anniversary of the death of Husain. The enclosure is generally arcaded along its sides, and in most instances it is covered in with a domed roof. Against the side of the Imambarrah directed towards Mecca is set the *tabut*—also called *tazia* or model of the tombs at Kerbela. In the houses of the wealthier Shiahs these *tabuts* are fixtures, and are beautifully fashioned of silver and gold, or of ivory and ebony, embellished all over with inlaid work, the poorer Shiahs provide themselves with a *tabut* made for the occasion, of lath and plaster, tricked out in mica and tinsel. A week before the new moon of the Mohurrum they enclose a space called the *tabut khana*, in which the *tabut* is prepared; and the very moment the new moon is seen a spade is stuck into the ground before "the enclosure of the Tombs", where a pit is afterwards dug, in which a bonfire is lighted and kept burning through all the ten days of the Mohurrum solemnities. Those who cannot afford to erect a *tabut khana*, or even to put up a little *tabut* or *tazia* in their dwelling house, always have a Mohurrum fire lighted, if it consist only of a nightlight floating at the bottom of an earthen pot or basin sunk in the ground. It is doubtful whether this custom refers to the trench of fire Husain set blazing behind his camp, or is a survival from the older *Ashura* ("ten days") festival which is said to have been instituted in commemoration of the deliverance of the Hebrew Arabs from Pharaoh and his host at the Red Sea; or from the yet more ancient Bael fire; but, in India these Mohurrum fires, especially among the more ignorant populace, Hindus as well as Mohammedans, are regarded with the most superstitious reverence, and have a greater hold on them even than the *tabuts*. . . . .
>
> The *tabut* is lighted up like an altar, with innumerable green wax candles, and nothing can be more brilliant than the appearance of an Imambarrah of white stone, or polished white stucco, picked out in green, lighted up with glass chandeliers, sconces, and oil lamps arranged along the leading architectural lines of the building, with its *tabut* on one side, dazzling to blindness. Before the *tabut* are placed the "properties" to be used by the celebrants in the "Passion Play", the bows and arrows, the swords and spear, and the banners of Husain, &c., and in front of it is set a moveable pulpit, also made of the richest materials, and covered with rich brocades in green and gold. Such is the theatre in which, twice daily during the first ten days of the month of Mohurrum, the deaths of the first martyrs of Islam are yearly commemorated in India. Each day has its special solemnity, corresponding with the succession of events during the ten days that Husain was encamped on the fatal plain of Kerbela, but the prescribed order of the services in the daily development of the great Shiah function of the Mohurrum would appear not to be always strictly observed in Bombay.
>
> During the four days after the *tabuts* have been carried to the houses of those who do not possess permanent representations of the tombs of Kerbela, there is little unusual excitement to be observed among the Shiahs in any Indian city, and the time is usually devoted to paying visits to the various *tabut khanas* and Imambarrahs. Women and children as well as men, are allowed to enter them, and Hindus and Christians, if they please, may join the company. Only the Sunni Mohammedans are denied and under the English rule prevented admission,. . . . . . but always on the fifth day the banners of Husain are taken in procession through the streets, and his horse is paraded, attended by men wearing *murchals* (peacock tails) and *chauries* (whips made of Yak tails, or shreds of ivory or sandalwood), and *aftabis* (banners embroidered in gold with the figure of the sun), which are recognised everywhere in the East as the most imposing insignia of royalty and empire; on the seventh day, the marriage of Cossim[2] with Fatimah is represented by a wedding procession through the streets by torchlight, a quire of young men chanting funeral dirges, in place of the usual troop of dancing girls, going before the bridegroom, who is distinguished by a gold or silver umbrella held over his head; and on the tenth, in commemoration of the death of Husain on that day of the month, the *tabuts* are carried to the Mohammedan cemetery, as representing "the plain of Kerbela", and at. . . . . . Bombay into the sea, which there does not simply stand mystically for the Euphrates, but is regarded as the River itself, seeing that in a sense it may be said to flow down the coast of Western India. When Husain's horse is brought into the arena of the Imambarrah, and his little sons and daughters and nephews appear on the scene, raised on thrones carried on men's shoulders, the rage and agony of the people become perfectly uncontrollable; for which reason no representations of the dead Husain, or of his children, or horse, are allowed to be taken through the streets of Bombay, for fear of exciting outrages against the Sunnis.
>
> On the 10th of Mohurrum every house in which a *tabut* is kept, or in which one has been put up for the occasion, sends forth its separate cavalcade or company to join the general funeral procession, which in the native Mohammedan States sometimes assumes the character of a solemn military pomp. First go the musicians, with pipes and cymbals, high horns, and deafening drums, followed by the arms and banners of Hasan and Husain, and the ensigns and crests, in gold and silver, or other metals of Ali and Fatima, and these by a chorus of men chanting a funeral dirge, followed in turn by Husain's horse. Next come men bearing censers of burning myrrh and frankincense, and aloes wood and gum benjamin, before the *tabut* or model of the tombs of Hasan and Husain, which is raised aloft on poles, or borne on an elephant.

Footnote.—(1) These definitions are a little confusing. Simplified they are:—

Taziah { i. The ceremony of mourning for the death of Husein and, or, the Alids (*see* Chapter X).
{ ii. Same as *tabut*.

Tabut { i. Model of the tomb of Husein at Kerbela in the Euphrates Valley (Chapter X).
{ ii. The Ark of the Covenant.

Kudu   A Hindu processional emblem or effigy.

Panja { i. A Mohamedan processional emblem.
{ ii. An emblem representing the hand of the murdered Husein.

Footnote.—(2) *i.e.* the marriage of Husein's son Kasim with Hasan's daughter Fatima.

Models of the sepulchre of Ali also and of Mohammed at Medina, and representations of the seraph-beast *Burak*, on which Mohammed is said to have performed his journey from Jerusalem to Heaven, are also carried along with the *tabut*. There may be one or two hundred of these separate funeral companies or cavalcades in the general procession, which is further swollen by crowds of faquirs and clowns or, "Mohurrum faquirs", got up for the occasion in marvellously fantastic masquerade, figuring, one, "Jack Priest", another, "King Tatterdemalion", and others, "King Clout", "King Raggamuffin", "King Double Dumb", and a hundred others of the following of the "Lord of Misrule", or "Abbot of Unreason", of our Catholic forefathers. An immense concourse of people, representatives of every country and costume of central and southern Asia, runs along with the procession. In Bombay, after gathering its contingent from every Shiah household as it winds its way through the tortuous streets of the native town, the living stream at length emerges on the Esplanade......"the plain of Kerbela"—for the day.

The confused uproar of its advance can be heard a mile away, and long before the procession takes definite shape through the clouds of dust and incense which move before it. It moves headlong onward in an endless line of flashing swords, blasoned suns (aftabis) and waving banners, State umbrellas, thrones, and canopies, and towering above all the *tabuts*, framed of the most elegant shapes of Saracenic architecture, glittering in silver and green and gold, and rocking backwards and forwards in high air, like great ships upon a rolling sea, with the rapid movement of the hurrying crowd, beating drums, chanting hymns, and shrieking, "Ya Ali", Ai Hasan, Ai Husain, Husain Shah "drowned, drowned, in blood in blood; all three, fallen prostrate, dead Ya Ali! Ai Hasan! Ai Husain, Husain Shah!" until the whole welkin seems to ring and pulsate with the terrific wail. Ever and anon, a band of naked men, drunk with opium or hemp, and painted like tigers or leopards, makes a rush through the ranks of the procession, leaping furiously, and brandishing their swords and spears and clubs in the air.

* * *

The temporary *tabuts* are taken out into the bay as far as they can be carried, and abandoned to the waves, into which all the temporary adornments of the permanent *tabuts* are also thrown. This operation has a wonderfully cooling effect on the mob. Their frantic clamours suddenly cease. In fact the mourners of Hasan and Husain having buried their *tabuts* in the sea, seize the opportunity to have a good bath; and a little after the sun has finally dropped below the western horizon, the whole of the vast multitude is seen in the vivid moonlight to be slowly and peacefully regathering itself across the wide Esplanade into its homes again, and the Saturnalia into which the last act of the Mystery of Hasan and Husain has degenerated in India is closed for another year.

Up country where the *tabuts* are carried to the Mohammedan cemeteries, and Sunnis and Shiahs meet face to face before the open graves of Hasan and Husain, the feuds between them, which have been pent up all the year, are often fought out to a bloody end. The custom of carrying the *tabuts* into the sea at Bombay no doubt contributes to the peace with which the Mohurrum is observed by the Mohammedans of that city.

The 11th and 12th of Mohurrum should be spent in meditation by the graves in which the *tabuts* have been laid, and in Bombay by the sea; but as a spectacle the Mohurrum celebration is over with the wild masquerade of the tenth day.

The following more formal description of the Ta'ziah is taken from the *Encyclopaedia of Islam:*—

Ta'ziya. (Arab). *The Passion Play of the Shi'is.*

Among the Shi'is the word means in the first place the lamentation for the martyred imams. In particular, however, it is *mourning for Husain*. The tabut, a copy of the tomb at Kerbela, in popular language is also called *ta'ziya*. It is a model kept in the house, often very richly executed. *Ta'ziya* however means particularly the mystery play itself. The time for its performance is the first third of the month of Muharram especially the 10th *Roz-i-Katl*, the day of the murder of Husain and of the Ashura festival. The local usages in Persia and in the Shi'i regions of Mesopotamia and India are very varied. In a wider sense the plays include the street processions such as the cavalcade with Husain's horse, the marriage procession of Husain's son al-Kasim with Hasan's daughter Fatima (*see* below) the procession to the cemetery with the *tabut*, all popular celebrations of a kind at which the deepest grief does not exclude a part being played by comic figures.

Lastly *ta'ziya* means the actual performance of the passion play itself. The stage is erected in public places, in caravanserais, even in mosques and in *imambara* (enclosures) specially erected for the festival. The chief properties required for the stage are a large *tabut*, receptacles in front to hold lights, also Husain's bow, lance spear and banner. The participators in addition to the players are the *rawza-khwan*, the poet, (*lit.* he who pronounces the eulogy for the dead). He speaks the introduction and with gestures indicative of lamentation chants a *khutba* with many hadiths in a voice of lamentation surrounded by a choir of boys called *pesh-khwan*, (*lit.* announcers) while the *nuwa-hannana*, dressed as mourning women, utter the lamentations of the women and mothers. The spectators are separated according to sexes. They are given *muhr*, cakes of earth from Kerbela steeped in musk, on which they press their foreheads in abject grief. While on the stage the hunger and particularly the thirst of the martyrs is most realistically expressed, water and other refreshments are provided for the spectators.

* * *

The motives and to a great extent the words are the same in the great number of such plays which are often touched up and expanded by the poets. The commonest are Persian but they also exist in Arabic and Turkish. The term drama can only be applied with reservation to the series of sometimes 40–50 independent tableaux which constitute the performance ......

More important, and also more serious, is the fact that these spectacles produce a completely biassed view of the figures of early Muslim history upon the Shi'is.

* * *

The fury against the Sunnis is so pronounced that non-Muslims are tolerated as spectators but certainly not non-Shi'a Muslims. National hatred of Arabs (and also Turks) is seen in such scenes as that in which Husain's widow Shahrabanu returns to her home in Persia or the young Fatima II is rescued by a Persian king.

The scenes......have grown out of various sources, but the material and the words are often old; verses of the Kur'an interpreted from the Shi'a point of view, and particularly old traditions with Shi'a bias, which are clothed in a form calculated greatly to impress the hearers ...... On the other hand songs of lamentation are still written in modern times.

In their elaborate form, the *ta'ziya* are recent and at one time could not be carried through without opposition from the mollas, on account of their crude dogma and irreligious accompaniment of dances and processions. It is probable that ancient rites of earlier mythological festivals like the Tammuz and Adonis cults have survived in the subsidiary plays which in India have been adapted by some Sunnis and even Hindus; the banners for the processions, a large staff, the hand which is carried round by those who summon to the festival and is now interpreted as the hand of Husain which was cut off, have thus their ancient prototypes. That the significance of the sacred properties has altered is shown by the fact that among the Shi'a Tatars the tabut is called the "marriage house of Kasim". In many places there are accompanying rites with water, which were originally indigenous; *the throwing of the tabut into water among the Indian Shi'is may be due to Hindu influence*. Even the style of the mourning garments is partly influenced by earlier forms. But the passion play itself is the popular expression of that religious feeling which has its roots in the historic fact of Kerbela.

The foregoing extracts provide respectively a general description and an authoritative explanation of the character of the festival and its Indian Shiah background, but do not help to identify the festival with any such observances in Sunni Malaya.

For this purpose we must examine the detail of the Indian ceremony much more closely and record in this chapter the clues which identify the Moharram festival of India with the annual Boria season in Malaya.

To these clues we shall refer back in the next chapter, in which the origin and development of the annual Boria in Penang is discussed and its significance explained.

The following extracts from Herklots are, therefore, of the greatest importance to our subject in drawing together the ends of another important knot in the secret society web which, in this case through the Batini—Assassin—Thug link, appears to bind the west with the east, and the Ararat area with the Tibetan area of secret society diffusion.

How these clues present themselves and are identified in the Malayan scene is worked out in the next chapter.

The following is taken from Herklots *Qanun-i-Islam* (ed. W. Crooke 1921) Chapter XIV pages 151–185, with the documentation omitted.

The Muharram Festival

The name Muharram means that which is "forbidden" or "taboo", and hence "saved", the first month of the Musalman year.

The Prophet is said to have fixed the 10th or Ashura of Muharram as a time of fast, which was subsequently transferred to Ramazan. The Muharram seems to have been originally a harvest feast.

The Muharram festival begins on the evening when the new moon becomes visible, but by the Musalman calculation from the morning following.

Special buildings are provided in which they set up the standards (*'alam*), the cenotaphs of the martyrs (*ta'ziya, tabut*), the royal seats (*shahnishin, dadmahall*), the representations of Buraq, the mule on which the Prophet made his journey (*mi'raj, isra*) to Jerusalem and to Heaven.

They are known as the "Ten Day houses" (*'ashurkhana*), "the house of the cenotaphs" (*ta'ziyakhana*), or "the Faqirs' lodging" (*astana*). Strangers are not allowed to approach these buildings as they must be kept pure for prayers.

*   *   *

The moment they see the new moon they do the "mattock-wielding" rite (*kudali marna*). They recite the Fatiha over sugar in the names of the martyrs, and go to the spot selected for the fire-pit (*alawa*). A sod of earth is turned and a day or two after the pit is dug. It is 1½ to 8 cubits in diameter, with a low wall built round it, and every year it is dug in the same place. After the pit is dug they light fires in it every evening during the festival, and ignorant people, young and old fence across it with sticks or swords.

In Surat, where the Muharram rites are more fully performed than in other parts of Gujarat, on the evening of the eighth day of the feast children are dressed in green, and clothes are sent to families connected by betrothal. Besides dressing as tigers, men and boys often join hands and go about singing the Muharram dirges, dressed like Hindu Gosain ascetics or half-Hindu, half-Musalman Husaini Brahman beggars.

The Ashurkhana of southern India is replaced in the north by the Imambara, "the place of the prayer-leader". . . . . .

Every night the funeral elegies are sung by boys trained for the duty, and Faqirs and friends keep vigil (*shab-bedari*). In south Gujarat after the fourth day the mourning changes to merriment and masquerade, and the only observance till the tenth day is the offering of sherbert at the side of the roads to children and travellers. This seems to be, in part, a reaction after the intensity of the mourning, partly, an imitation of the revelry at Hindu festivals like the Holi or fire feast. In Hyderabad, from the first to the seventh day, except the recital of the Fatiha and of the benediction (*durad*), reading of the Koran and the dirges with preparation of food and sherbert, nothing else is done. On the seventh day of the moon, by the ignorant on the seventh day of the month, the standard of the martyr Qasim, distinguished by a little silver or gold umbrella fixed on it, is paraded. He is one of the sacred bridegrooms, for at the age of ten he was betrothed to Fatima, daughter of Husain, and was slain in battle. . . . .

On the tenth day in Hyderabad all the standards and the cenotaphs, except those of Qasim, are carried on men's shoulders, attended by Faqirs, and they perform the night procession (*shabgasht*) with great pomp, the lower orders doing this in the evening, the higher at midnight. On that night the streets are illuminated and every kind of revelry goes on. One form of this is an exhibition of a kind of magic lantern, in which the shadows of the figures representing battle scenes are thrown on a white cloth and attract crowds. The whole town keeps awake that night and there is universal noise and confusion.

Many Hindus have so much faith in these cenotaphs, standards and the Buraq, that they erect them themselves and become faqirs during the Muharram. In Gujarat, as the cenotaphs pass in procession, poor Hindu and Musalman men and women, in fulfilment of vows, often throw themselves in the roadway and roll in front of the cenotaphs. Others hang red cotton threads round their necks, mark their brows with white powder and live for the time on alms given by friends.

Whenever the Muharram, according to the lunisolar calendar, chances to coincide with Hindu festivals, such as the Ramanavami, the birth of Rama, the Charakhpuja, or swing festival, or the Dasahra, serious riots have occurred as the processions meet in front of a mosque or Hindu temple, or when an attempt is made to cut the branches of some sacred fig-tree which impedes the passage of the cenotaphs. Such riots, for instance, occurred at Cuddapa in Madras in 1821, at Bhiwandi in the Thana District, Bombay, in 1837. In the latter case the riots were between the Sunni and Shi'a sects. In the case of some disturbances at Hyderabad it is said that Hindus who act as Muharram Faqirs sometimes take the part of the Musalmans against their co-religionists, and during this time do not eat any meat save that of animals which have been slaughtered by the Musalman ritual (*zabh*).

On this day at Hyderabad almost everybody, men, women, old and young, especially those who are unmarried, seldom the married, wear a Faqir's necklace (*seli*), made of cotton thread, silk, or hair, and bracelets (*Gajra*), made of coloured silk or flowers. Intelligent people think it unlawful to wear these ornaments as it is contrary to the Law. But in India, people obey more than the obligatory (*farz*) rites, the rubbing of perfumed powder (*abir*) on the faces of their children, dressing them in green clothes, and wearing such garments themselves. The higher and the more respectable of the middle classes content themselves with merely tying a necklace on their necks and a bracelet on their wrists.

During the festival many persons adopt the garb and mode of life of Faqirs, some wearing this dress on the fifth, a few on the second, and still fewer on the sixth or seventh.

The following are some of these classes in southern India:—

(1) The Seliwala vulgarly called Suheliwala (*suhela* "easy, feasible"), wear a Faqir's necklace (*seli*, *anti*), made of coloured thread. This is emblematical of the two classes of Faqirs, known as Azad, "free, unrestrained", and Benawa, "those who possess no worldly goods", who become Faqirs through grief for the fate of the martyrs. They usually wear a hair necklace, but during the Muharram it is made of green or red thread, the former colour being said to represent that to which the corpse of Hasan was reduced soon after his death from the effects of poison, the latter the blood which fell from the body of Husain on the battlefield. . . . . . After offering the Fatiha over these things they first put a small bracelet or necklace round one of the banners (*shadda*) and then on their own wrists or necks. If the bracelet is worn only on one arm it is always the right. They wear the usual costume of Faqirs.

(2) The Benawa or "indigent" are also called Azad, "unrestrained" or Alif shahi, because they make a black line like the Arabic letter Alif or A down the forehead and nose. They wear on the head a tall Persian woollen cap (*taj*, *topi*), a shawl or turban with a gold band round it (*Mandil*), and on the neck a piece of cloth with a slit in the centre of its breadth through which the head is passed, and to which a collar is sewn on. One-third of the cloth hangs behind as low as the calf, and two-thirds is tucked in front into the waistband (*kamarband*), so as to form a sort of bag to receive the contributions of the faithful. . . . . . .

Faqirs of this class form a band (*guroh*) with various ranks and titles, under a director (*murshid*) or a leader of the troop (*sarguroh*), whom all agree to obey. Under him there is, first, the Khalifa, who is second in command, like a Wazir to a King; secondly, the Bhandari Shah, house steward or chief of the commissariat; thirdly the Izni Shah, the "caller" or adjutant who assembles the troop and conveys orders; fourthly, the 'Adalat Shah, the "lawgiver", who is the director of movements or quarter-master; fifthly, the Kotwal, or chief police officer who maintains order and dicipline; sixthly the Dost or "friend" seventhly, the Al-hukm-i-lillah, or commander; eighthly, the Amr-i-lillah, or God's officer; ninthly, the Naqibu-l-fuqara, the Faqirs "leader", who marches in front of the troop and proclaims the praises and attributes of God, as an example to the other Faqirs. . . . . .

(3) The Majnun, the word Majnun means "possessed by the Jinn, demented". They dress with a kind of fool's cap or long sugar-loaf cap of paper with a queue of paper hanging behind and trailing on the ground ornamented with gold leaf. Sometimes this cap is made with panes of glass all round in the form of a lantern, with strips of tinfoil (*begar*) or tinsel, or white and red net-work paper hanging from the outside. Inside this they put a candle when they walk about at night. Instead of the cap they some-times wear a shawl, a red sheet or a piece of cloth, while others have a string of ripe lemons, dangling round their heads. Round the neck a red, yellow, or white scarf is twisted and worn in the shape of a necklace, (*baddhi*, *hamel*), or a shawl or handkerchief is passed through rings. . . . . . .

Thus equipped they go to the 'Ashurkhana and dance a circular whirling dance (ghumna) to the sound of the tambourine (daf). . . . . . .

(4) The Laila take their name from the famous Bedouin love story of Laila and Majnun, told by Persian poets, especially Nisami. The man who represents Laila has the whole of his body, from head to foot, glued over with cotton wool covering even his waistcloth, the only dress he wears. In his hands he holds a cup, sometimes full of pounded sandalwood or sherbert, or a human skull cap, a coco-nut shell, or the Calabash (chippi) of a turtle, and a fan or paper nosegay. On his head he wears a three-cornered paper cap.

(5) The Bahrang or Bharbhariya, "foolish chatterer", has his whole body covered with red ochre (lal geru) mixed with water. His head is covered with a shawl, hand-kerchief, or coloured cloth with a small flag fixed in the top of it, and like the Majnun he wears shoulder-bells (hamela) made of cloth. On his legs he carries tinkling bells (ghungru, ghanti, zang), and he wears breeches (gurji). His loins are tightly girt, and as he dances he kicks his posteriors with his heels, calling out, " 'Ali! 'Ali! 'Ali! Zang!". . . . . .

(6) The Bagla or Bagula represent paddy birds (ardea torra) ten or twelve men, all of the same height, smear their bodies all over with cowdung ashes, wear white paper caps on their heads, and loin-cloths. They go about holding each other by the waist and imitate the call of the paddy-bird. One of them calls himself Bhiri or Bahri Shah, "King hawk", and dashes at the paddy-birds, who escape and hide in the crowd, while some times they catch one and run round to prevent him from escaping.

(7) The Jalali or Khaki are one of the regular Musalman Orders, founded by Sayyid Jalalu-d-din, a disciple of Bahawal Haqq, the Suhrwardi Saint of Multan, whose shrine is at Uchh in the Bahawalpur State. Khaki means "dust-covered". They have no special dress, but wear fancy caps of various shapes and immense turbans made of straw, leather, or mat on their heads, rosaries and necklaces made of fruits. Some have their faces half blackened, their bodies covered with pipe-clay, garlands round their necks, and dried pumpkins hanging from their bodies. One of the band carries a hideous female doll which he says is the grandmother of one of the spectators, while others have a mock club made of leather with which they strike any poor man or woman who comes in their way. . . . .

(8) The Jogi is one of the Hindu Orders of ascetics. Men dressed like them come to the 'Ashurkhanas playing on the guitar (sitar), tambourine (daf), the small drum (dholki), and small tambourines (khanjari), sing songs and funeral dirges with much skill.

(9) The Sabetan and the Tan-be-sar, "the head without a body, the body without a head", is a trick played by a man concealing his head in a hole or under a bed and showing only his body while another buries himself, leaving only his head over-ground. A blood-stained sword is laid near them and the ground is stained to imitate blood.

(10) Khogir Shah, "King Saddle". A man dressed like a Jalali wears a Musalman saddle on his neck and red and white strings tied round his head.

(11) Sharabi, "The Drunkard", is dressed like a Jalali and has a mark like the Arabic letter A painted on his forehead, while he carries a bottle full of sherbert and water, repeating mock verses from the Koran in praise of wine and drinking freely. Much debate goes on between him and the other Muharram Faqirs about the use of wine or pork. Sometimes he wears a leather Brahmanical cord (janeo, zunar) round his neck.

(12) Qazi-i-la'in, Qazi-be-din, "The cursed and irreligious Law Officer". He wears a sleeveless shirt, his beard and moustaches are made of flax, and he counts a rosary while he preaches various absurdities contrary to the Law of Islam.

(13) Khodun-garun, "Digging and burying". He wears on his head a straw cap or turban encircled with ropes, his body is covered with a mat through a hole in which his head is thrust, his waist is encircled with ropes, on his shoulder he carries a spade and on his back is a screen. He goes about singing, "I throw down and bury whom I please; for a small grave I charge a hundred rupees, five for a big one". Then he seizes a rustic and pretends to bury him.

(14) The Nanakshahi or Nanakpanthi are followers of the Sikh Saint Nanak (A.D. 1469—1539). Four or five men assume this dress with coloured strings (seli) round their necks a spot of lampblack in the centre of their foreheads, their faces smeared with sandalwood paste, on their necks a handkerchief in which a small copy of the Koran (hamail) is fixed as an amulet a necklace of conch-shell such as that worn by Rajputs, and two coloured sheets round their waists. They carry a couple of clubs, visit 'Ashurkhanas, and, striking the clubs together, sing verses in honour of Husain.

(15) The Ghagriwala are so called because they wear on their thumbs brass rings (ghagri), inside which are little tinkling brass balls. Their dress is either white or red, their faces and bodies are rubbed over with cowdung ashes. They wear on their heads a sheet with coloured threads or fringes hanging to it, on their ears a feathered plume (turra), round each arm handkerchiefs tied like those of the Majnun, armlets (bazuband, bhujband), a waist cloth and a tinkling ornament (tora) on the right ankle. One of them, lamp in hand, goes in front, and two standard bearers carry white, green or red colours. All of them with the exception of the 'Adalat Shah wear rings on the right thumb, and these they rattle as they sing ballads of the Martyrdom, and the praises of Husain. In front of them a couple of Ramaniya, or dancing-boys, walk, each having a painted earthen pot with gravel inside or a yak-tail fly-flapper (Chamar), and so they dance and sway their legs, stopping or sitting down at the end of each verse. The leaders walk on each flank of the procession, and two men carry spears or long

bamboos covered with coloured paper in front. While the troop halts they tie the spears crossways and stand with them so as to keep off other troops while they recite verses in honour of their spears.

(16) The Garuri-Shah are snake charmers or buffoons. They dress like the Jalali, each wearing a feather ornament (*turra*) on his turban and carrying the pipe (*pungi*) played by jugglers, Jogis, and snake charmers. When they halt they do juggling tricks.

(17) Chindi Shah, "the Ragman" ties rags round his body from neck to feet and walks through the bazars without saying a word.

(18) Khandar Shah, "the Tatterdemalion", or "King Clout", wears rags, a tattered quilt (*khandari*) and short breeches (*cholna*) reaching to the knees. They beat each other with a ragged handkerchief and at the Ashurkhanas fall down and roll on the ground.[1]

* * *

Coolies carry jars full of sherbert in the procession which at night is accompanied by torches, and fireworks are discharged and as they walk they shout "Shah Husain! Ya Imam! Ya "Ali!" When they come to an Ashurkhana they walk thrice round the fire-pit and throw wood on it, the superintendent recites the Fatiha over food, some sherbert is poured into the pit and the attendants are fed. Other people, Hindus as well as Musalmans, vow to give flags, sherbert, food, money, to light lamps, perfumes and flowers if they are blessed with a child.

On the tenth day, known as Shahadat ka roz, "the Day of Martyrdom", between 9 a.m. and 3 p.m. all the standards are taken to an open place near the sea, a tank or river, known as Karbala ka Maidan, "the plain of Karbala".

When the standards and cenotaphs are brought to the water edge, the Fatiha is recited in the names of the martyrs over food and sweetmeats, some of them are distributed, and some regarded as sacred and brought home. The tinsel is removed from the cenotaphs, and the standards which they contain are removed. Then the structures are dipped in the water. Some are thrown away, others reserved for future use. Men and boys, Hindus as well as Musalmans, try to catch the drops of water which fall from them and rub it on their eyes to strengthen the sight. Then the standards are packed up and the food is distributed. . . . . .

Those who have acted as Faqirs during the festival now lay aside the garb of mendicants and wash themselves and their ornaments. The members of every band, before removing their Faqir dress, offer the Fatiha over sweetmeats, give some to their leaders, and eat the rest themselves. Some do not change their dress for three days. On this, the Day of Martyrdom, food is cooked in every house, the Fatiha is said over it in the name of Maula, "Lord". 'Ali, and the martyrs, and it is distributed to friends or given in charity.

* * *

On the tenth of the following month, Safar, dirges are sung and prayers offered for the souls of the martyrs, and on the fourteenth day, which corresponds to the twentieth of Safar, they observe the commemoration of the union of their heads and bodies (sar o tan) in the grave at Karbala.

The rites observed in southern India, of which the above is mainly an account, differ greatly from the distinctive mourning observances in the north where no buffoonery such as that of the Muharram Faqirs takes place. Mummery of this kind is also practised by the Sunni Musalmans in Bombay, while the Shi'as regard it as a real time of mourning. This is said to be largely based upon spirit beliefs and ghost-scaring borrowed from the Hindus. Such customs naturally are more prevalent in those parts of the country where the Musalmans are largely converts from Hinduism.

Much of the above description will be found to fit the present-day Boria as observed in Penang. (*See* Chapter XII *infra*).

THE HINDU FESTIVAL OF THE DUSSERA[2] OR DURGA-PUJA

The following description of this festival is taken from Buck's *Faith, Fairs and Festivals of India* (Calcutta 1917) pages 100–107:—

Durga Puja.

This festival is especially celebrated in Bengal and the *Puja* holidays are enjoyed by immense crowds. The goddess Durga, daughter of the Himalaya mountains and wife of Siva, goes for a ten days' visit to her father's home . . . . . .

Durga is the central figure of the *Markandeya Purana*. She is the personification of the creative energy and centre of the universe; she pursues the demons who wage war against the gods; ten-armed, she stands on a lion with swords in her hands, and subdues her foes, among whom is one with a buffalo-head, named Mahisasura. With her are Kartik, the god of war, Ganesha, the elephant-headed deity who rides on a rat, Sarasvati, the goddess of learning, and Lakshmi, the goddess of love and good fortune. These are the deities of the Durga Puja.

The ceremonies continue for ten days. Throughout the first three days images, sometimes gorgeously decorated, are set up by wealthy people in their houses, where costly entertainments are given. On the seventh day bathing commences and on the final day images are carried in procession with great pomp and immersed in the river. During the ceremonies, goats are

---

Footnote.—(1) Herklots goes on to enumerate some fifty-two different classes of such *faqirs* that commonly take part in the festival in India. The above eighteen classes are sufficient for purposes of identity with the Boria festival in Penang.
Footnote.—(2) Also spelt Dassora or Dasehra.

sacrificed—some substituting pumpkins for the animals—and everyone wears his best clothes. After the immersion, children reverence their elders and are blessed in return; friends embrace and the occasion is one for forgiveness and the settling of differences.

The Shastras prescribe a long series of offerings, fasts, recitations, and sacrifices for the ten days' festival known as *Durga-Ashtami* (tenth day of Durga), and the ceremonies in Northern India chiefly consist of dressing the hair and adorning Durga's image and offering food during the first five days; on the sixth day the goddess is awakened in the *bel* tree in the evening and on the following day she is brought forth and worshipped. Sacrifices commence on the evening of the eighth and continue on the ninth day. Finally, the goddess is dismissed or put to rest on the tenth day, dust and mud are thrown, and thereafter there is great rejoicing.

The form of the festival varies somewhat in different parts of the country.

Dussehra.

In the North and West of India, the last day (of the Durga Puja) is termed *Dussehra* (tenth day), and is especially observed, for it was then that Rama gained his great victory over Ravana. People polish the instruments of their profession at this time and also clean, plaster, and whitewash their houses and generally put things in order.

The *khaujan*, or wagtail (motacella alba), is looked for and omens taken from its situation, for it bears a holy *tilak* (caste mark): if near lotus flowers or among elephants, cows, horses, or snakes, it forebodes conquest and good luck; if, however, on ashes, bones, or refuse, evil may follow and the gods must be propitiated; Brahmans must be fed and a medicinal bath taken.

In the villages, little figures of Durga are made out of cowdung; these are highly decorated and placed on the walls of houses; offerings are made and barley is sown before them; on the eighth or ninth day these are thrown into a river or pond accompanied by shouts of *jae* (victory).

In the towns, the tenth day is generally celebrated by the *Ram Lila* a play performed in an open plain on which is set up a huge wicker-work image of the demon Ravana, filled with fireworks. An enclosure, at some little distance, represents *Lanka* (Ceylon) and the principal events of the rescue of Sita by Rama, as recorded in the Ramayana, are acted. Little boys are dressed up as the goddess and monkeys, while Hanuman, the monkey-general, is to be seen, with an enormous tail, acting as a bodyguard for the hero. The closing act consists in the advance of Rama in his chariot towards Ravana, against whom he shoots an arrow which causes a series of explosions the demon catches fire in mysterious fashion, catherine wheels revolve on his head, and he rapidly sinks in a heap of ashes amidst the shouts of the spectators. Sita is then rescued by Rama, and carried off in a chariot with further applause.

The *Dussehra* marks the close of the rains and the four months' absence of the gods: it is the signal, as it were, for the recommencement of joyful festivals of all kinds; further, it has always been specially observed by the military classes, who consider it auspicious to set out on an expedition just afterwards.

HINDU AND MOSLEM ECLECTICISM

Herklots *op. cit.* (ed. 1921) Chapter I, has the following upon the subject of Hindu and Moslem participation in the Durga Puja and Moharram festivals:—

In Bengal, before the recent crusade against idolatry, it was the practice of low-class Musalmans to join in the Durga Puja and other Hindu festivals. They are very careful about omens and auspicious days, and dates for weddings and other rites are fixed after consulting Hindu Pandits. Hindu deities, like Sital who control small-pox, and Rakshya Kali who protects her votaries from cholera, are worshipped during epidemics. In Bihar Musalmans join in the worship of the sun, and some of them visit Hindu temples. But the most important deviation from the standard rules of Islam is the widespread worship of Pirs and Saints. Facts of the same kind are reported from other parts of the country. In the Central Provinces Musalman Ahirs or cowherds perform their marriages Hindu fashion, and at the end call in a Qazi who repeats the Musalman prayers and records the amount of the dowry and settlement. Kurmis, Hindu peasants in Bihar, keep the Musalman feast of the Muharram and fast at Ramazan. The Lambadi carriers in Madras combine the Musalman rite of marriage with the original tribal ritual. The shrine of Qadirwali Sahib in the Tanjore District, Madras, is visited by crowds of Hindu women, and the Hindu princesses send large gifts to the Nagor mosque from the Palace. Particularly in the north, the saint Salar Mas'ud, otherwise known as Ghazi Miyan, is worshipped by crowds, the majority of whom are Hindus, and in many places Hindus share in the procession of the Ta'ziyas or Tabuts, the cenotaphs of the martyrs Hasan and Husain, at the Muharram festival. Much of this fusion of beliefs and rites is, of course, due to the eclectic character of Hinduism, which readily accepts the worship of any Saint or even of a martyr because he was slain in battle with the Hindus, whose advocacy with the Higher Powers is supposed to be effectual. But it also points to the close association of Hinduism and Islam among the lower-class votaries of both religions, a union based upon the ethnical identity of the two bodies.

In upper India, as a whole, the relations of Sunnis and Shi'as are marked, if not by friendliness, at least by mutual toleration. The Muharram processions of the Shi'as are generally conducted without opposition, and Sunnis sometimes take a part, even if it be subordinate, in these celebrations. But elsewhere instances of tension, and occasionally of active opposition, have occurred. In 1709, there were serious disturbances at Lahore in consequence of an order that in the Khutba or bidding prayer the Shi'a form "Ali is the Saint of God and heir (*wasi*) of the Prophet of God", should be added. In 1872, there were serious riots between the followers of the rival sects in the city of Bombay, and again during the Muharram of 1904 which culminated in a refusal to bring out and immerse the cenotaphs. The Ghair-i-Mandi sect and the Sunnis have come into conflict in southern India.

One French writer has noted the similarity between the Mohamedan Muharram and the Hindu Durga-puja festivals.

Garcin de Tassy, in *Particularités de la religion Musulmane dans l'Inde* Paris (1831) has:—

En lisant la description......de ces fêtes on croira souvent qu'il s'agit de fêtes hindous. Telle est par exemple la solemnité du *Ta'ria* ou deuil, établie en commemoration du martyre de Husein, laquelle est semblable en bien de points à celle du Durja-puja. Le dixième jour les Hindous précipitent dans la rivière la statue de la déesse au milieu d'une foule immense, avec un grand appareil et on sonne de mille instruments de musique: la même chose a lieu pour les réprésentations du tombeau de Husein.

The following extract further shows the same eclecticism and is taken from Yule's *Hobson-Jobson*[1] page 319:—

> It is to be remembered that these observances (*i.e.* the Muharram festival) are in India by no means confined to Shiahs. Except at Lucknow and Murshidabad, the great majority of Mohamedans in that country are Sunnis, yet here is a statement of the facts from an unexceptionable authority:—
>
> > Extract from the *Journal of the Royal Asiatic Society* Vol. XIII page 369. Article by Mir Shahamat Ali:—
> >
> > The commonality of the Mussalmans and especially the women have more regard for the memory of Hasan and Husein than for that of Mohamed and his Khalif. The heresy of making *ta'ziyas* on the anniversary of the two latter Imams, is most common throughout India: so much so that opposition to it is ascribed by the ignorant to blasphemy. This example is followed by many of the Hindus especially the Mahrattas. The Muharram is celebrated throughout the Dekhan and Malwa with greater enthusiasm than in other parts of India. Grand preparations are made in every town on the occasion as if for a festival of rejoicing, rather than of observing the rites of mourning as they ought.
> >
> > The observance of this custom has so strong a hold on the mind of the commonality of the Mussalmans, that they believe Mohamedanism to depend merely on keeping the memory of the Imams Hasan and Husein in the above manner.

Again in Smith's edition (1915) of W. H. Sleeman's *Rambles and Recollections* in the footnote on page 483 appears the following passage:—

> These events (the Hasan-Husein procession of the Muharram) are commemorated (in India) yearly by noisy funeral processions. Properly, the proceedings ought to be altogether mournful and confined to the Shiah sect, but in practice Sunni Mohamedans and even Hindus, take part in the ceremonies, which are regarded by many of the populace as no more solemn than a Lord Mayor's Show.

Whatever the conditions in India and elsewhere may be, it is true to say that Malay (Sunni) participation in the Moharram festival, along with Indian Shiahs and other nondescript Indian Mohamedans and Hindus, has always been confined in Malaya to Singapore and Penang, chiefly the latter place, and it is probably true to add that this participation owes its origin to purely Indian influence, partly Shiah, partly Thug and partly Hindu (Tamil). The share that each exercised in the evolution of the present-day festival in Penang is discussed in Chapter XII.

THE HOLI FESTIVAL OF HINDUISM

The Holi, or Ten-day vernal festival of the Hindus, is the saturnalia of India and terminates with feasting, drunkenness, obscenity and a bonfire on the last day of the Hindu month Phalgun, which corresponds to the 16th March.

For an account of the Festival see Buck, *Faiths, Fairs and Festivals of India.*

Its importance in our context is that it is observed in Malaya and although varying in different areas in India and among different castes, it contains certain common features, which re-appear to some extent in Malaya and which are:—

(1) The mixing of all classes and sexes in rough horseplay in honour of the God of Love (generally Krishna).

(2) The singing of coarse "love songs" and the temporary abjuration of certain restraints of everyday life.

(3) The throwing of red powder (*abir*[2]) and yellow water (*kunkuma*) from beakers (*gulabdan*) as an accompaniment to the two preceding features.

(4) The lighting of bonfires at night and the pretence of jumping through the fire.

(5) Dancing, clowning and buffoonery sometimes accompanied by a mock fight between the men of one village and the women of another. The women are armed with stout bamboos and the men defend themselves with leather shields and stag horns.

(6) Drinking and the ritual of the homa (soma) or nectar of the Gods, or of immortality (*see* Introduction).

The whole festival is one of sex and fertility worship and presents in India the picture of bands of noisy and excited revellers parading the streets, unrestrained in demeanour, gesture and speech: singing songs and shouting jests, their dress drip wet and bespattered with daubs of red powder and yellow water. They thus symb the spirit of the festival and the desires aroused by it.

In a minor way and usually without the accompaniment of women in public, this festival may be seen to be observed by Hindus in Malaya, but its importance lies in the fact that it has become confused with the celebration of the Moslem festival of the Moharram, a confusion which it is necessary to remove by thus separately identifying the Holi and its main features, to which we shall refer again in Chapter XII *infra.*

Footnote.—(1) The term "Hobson-Jobson" is curiously enough the Anglo-Indian "argot" or British Tommy's slang term for the Hasan Husein festival itself.

Footnote.—(2) This red powder is said to represent the lees of wine decocted from the juice of the *soma* plant and mixed with other ingredients, to make the sacred Haoma or Homa, the elixir of life of the Vedanta (*see* Introduction): Cf. below *A soma element in the Boria.*

CONFUSION OF THE MOSLEM FESTIVAL OF THE MOHARRAM WITH THE HINDU FESTIVALS OF HOLI AND DURGA-PUJA

Another fact of importance conducing to confusion is that because the Mohamedan is a *lunar* calendar and the Hindu a *solar* one, the lunar festival of the Moharram coincides in the date of its observance with both the solar Durga-puja (Dussehra) and the solar Holi once every thirty six years or so, the former in October the latter in March.

This fact is used in India as an opportunity and an excuse for communal hatred to be unleashed and for the paying off of old scores. These years of coincidence were in the past century;—1809–10: 1845–46: 1881–82: 1917–18 approximately, but whether the celebrations of these years were accompanied by any excessive rowdiness in Penang, or elsewhere in Malaya, we are unable from the records to say.

On this subject Sleeman, *Rambles and Recollections* (ed. Smith) has the following on page 482:—

> The Muhammadan festivals are regulated by the lunar,[1] and those of the Hindoos by the solar year, and they cross each other every thirty or forty years, and furnish fair occasions for the local authorities to interpose effectually. People who receive or imagine insults or injuries commonly postpone their revenge till these religious festivals come round, when they hope to be able to settle their accounts with impunity among the excited crowd. The mournful procession of the Muharrum when the Muhammedans are inflamed to madness by the recollection of the really affecting incidents of the massacre of the grandchildren of their Prophet, and by the images of their tombs, and their sombre music, crosses that of the Holi (in which the Hindoos are excited to tumultuous and licentious joy by their bacchanalian songs and dances) every thirty-six years; and they reign together for some four or five days, during which the scene in every large town is really terrific. The processions are liable to meet in the street, and the lees of the wine of the Hindoos, or the *red* powder which is substituted for them, is liable to fall upon the tombs of the others. Hindoos pass on forgetting in their saturnalian joy all distinctions of age, sex or religion, their clothes and persons besmeared with the red powder, which is moistened and thrown from all kinds of machines over friend and foe; while meeting these come the Muhammadans, clothed in their green mourning, with gloomy downcast looks, beating their breasts, ready to kill themselves, and too anxious for an excuse to kill anybody else. Let but one drop of the lees of joy fall upon the image of the tomb as it passes, and a hundred swords fly from their scabbards; many an innocent person falls; and woe be to the town in which the magistrate is not at hand with his police and military force........

THE MOHARRAM FESTIVAL IN THE WEST INDIES (TRINIDAD)

But it was not only into Malaya that the stream of Indian settlers imported these curiously eclectic festivals of Islam and Hinduism during the nineteenth century.

A somewhat similar process seems to have taken place in the West Indies where to-day in Trinidad, two festivals are observed and are known there as the Puja[2] and the Taja,[3] which represent respectively the Holi festival of the Hindus and the Moharram festival of Islam.

Thus, Yule *Hobson Jobson* page 688 has:—

> The word Ta'ziya has been carried to the West Indies by the coolies whose great festival, whether they be Mohammedans or Hindus, the Muharram has become. An attempt to carry "ta'ziyas" through the streets of one of the towns in Trinidad in spite of orders to the contrary, led in 1884 to a sad catastrophe (riots).

The serious riots which occurred in Trinidad in 1937 whose precipitating cause was no doubt economic, may well have had a much deeper pre-disposing cause in under-surface organisations of religious or even criminal origin, similar to those in Malaya described later in this work, and which may have a common origin in the Moharram festival.

For purposes of comparison with the Penang *Boria* we offer a brief description of the Puja and the Taja festivals in the following chapter, together with a brief analysis of the community scene in which they are set in the West Indies.

It may well be found that, as in Malaya, these festivals exert in the West Indies a powerful influence upon social disorder, with tap-roots in the religious and criminal under-world of both India and Africa.

THE DERA PANJA

Among the Mohammedans of southern India, the festivals of the Moharram and the Durga-puja appear to have undergone a further process of hybridisation.

In Madras, the Moharram is also known as the Dera Panja and both Mohammedans and Hindus take part and rowdyism without any specific criminal or religious cause is a usual annual feature, as the following extract from the Madras *Police Intelligence Journal* dated 27th April, 1935, shows:—

> Except for the dispersal of a crowd on the 12th April during the Dera Panja procession, Muharram passed off quietly in Madras city.

Footnote.—(1) The Muhammadan year consists of twelve lunar months of 30 and 29 days alternately. The common year, therefore, consists of only 354 days. But when intercalary days in certain years are allowed for, the mean year consists of only 354⅓ days. Inasmuch as a solar year consists of about 365¼ days, the difference amounts to nearly 11 days, and any given month in the Muhammadan year consequently goes the round of the seasons in course of time.

Footnote.—(2) The name Puja suggests the Durga-puja of India, but the observances appear to be those of the Holi. *See* Chapter XII.

Footnote.—(3) The name Taja is, no doubt, a corruption of *Ta'ziah*. It is also known there as the "Hassan-Hussein" and is confined in the West Indies to British Guiana and Trinidad, where the Indian population is most numerous.

An unusually large number of persons carrying *Aftabgiries* (long-handled fans) escorted the Dera Panja on the night of the 12th April, 1935. They became over-enthusiastic in their fanning, and in waving their fans knocked off the turbans of some constables. They then began to fan the Dera Panja still more vigorously making their religious fervour a cover for prodding the police with the fan handles, and ended by deliberately poking the constables in the back when they were looking the other way. As they were preventing the progress of the procession, the police proceeded to push them back, and to clear the space round the Panja, whereupon stone-throwing began.

The Dera Panja is the Procession of the Emblem of the Hand (of Husein) and although the name has a different derivation, the festival bears an affinity to that of the Durga Puja of the Hindus (the Dussera).[1]

The "hand-emblem" Pancha (sanscrit) = five; or Panja (Hind.) = a hand, with five fingers outstretched, is a sign used by Hindus, as distinct from the emblem of the hand of Husein used by the Shiah Mohamedans, and its use is of interest as showing the process of hybridization of the festivals of the Moharram and the Durga-puja.[2] The following extract is taken from *Faiths, Fairs and Festivals of India*, Buck, page 75 :—

> A common sign used by people of various denominations in India, is that of the out-stretched hand. It is called by Hindus the *abhaya hasta* (protecting hand) or *varada hasta* (beneficent hand) and may be seen stamped upon the walls of temples and houses to protect the inmates against ill-luck; on bullocks to preserve them from disease; on sacred trees worshipped by women; and on the wall of a room in which a maiden's maturity ceremony takes place. It is usual for a person to smear *kunkuma* on his hand and imprint the mark on the walls of a freshly constructed building, both inside and out, or on the walls of a temple when a new idol is installed, and on clothes at weddings. The colours used are usually red or yellow.

The reference to *Kunkuma* in this extract requires a further explanation. It is the *Kunguma* of the Penang Malays and is used both in the Holi festival of Hinduism in India: the Puja festival in Trinidad and the Boria festival in Malaya. It is allied to but not identical with the *ayer kunyit* = yellow (saffron) water, of the Malays which is used freely upon other Malay ceremonial occasions; whereas *Kunkuma* is exclusively connected in Malaya with the Boria, and elsewhere with the use of *Soma* (see Introduction) and the licence associated therewith. We must now examine more closely this Hindu importation into the religious observances and festivities of Sunni Malaya.

A SOMA ELEMENT IN THE PENANG BORIA?

The drunkenness which accompanies the observance of the Holi festival in India appears to provide the sanction for drinking which is a feature of the debased Mohamedan festival of the Moharram as seen both in the Boria of Penang and in the Taja of Trinidad described in the next chapter.

Other features of the Holi festival which re-appear in the debased Moharram are the use of the red powder *(abir)* and the yellow (saffron) water *(Kunkuma)* with which the Holi revellers bespatter one another and which appear to have their origin in Hinduism and the *soma* tradition of Mount Meru, and which have caused such a *furore* among orthodox Malays during recent years (see Chapter XXX *infra*).

Of the *soma* tradition (*Haoma* or *Homa* of the *Avesta*) explained in the Introduction, we need only say here that in Vedic mythology the intoxicating juice of the *soma* plant when mixed with milk represents the nectar of the gods (Indra): the wine of immortality among men; the elixir of life: the heavenly water, which enables men to achieve atonement with the gods.

In seeking for an explanation of the origin of the red powder and yellow water used in the Holi and in the Boria, we are reminded that the Vedic ritualists recognised *two elements*[3] in the immortal property of Soma, the one a food, the other a beverage.

In the absence of any other explanation it may possibly be that the red powder *(batu kawi)* and the yellow water *(ayer kunguma)* used in both in the Holi and the Boria may represent these two elements.

The Hindustani word for the red powder *abir* does not seem to have found its way into the Malay language, but the sanscrit word *kunkuma* for the yellow or saffron used in colouring the other element, appears to be well represented in Malay and to bear in itself an affinity to the root *soma*.

Thus, Wilkinson in his dictionary (edition 1932) gives the following spellings for the Malay word for saffron. Kumkuma, Kunkuma, Kuma-kuma, Kungkuma, Koma-koma.

Cf. also the following Malay words given by Wilkinson:—

Kesoma (from Sanscrit *Kawi Kusuma*) = a term used in Java as a poetical name for a flower: a plant: also handsome, noble, victorious in love, of noble or royal birth.

Footnote.—(1) Cf. Wilkinson's dictionary (1932 edition) :—
Durga
Durgah } (Persian) Muharram processional emblem (*see* Tabut).
Dargah
Footnote.—(2) It is also worth noting that the outstretched hand is the universal "Membership" sign of the Triad society of China (*see* Chapter VII).
Footnote.—(3) For the precise significance of these two elements *see* Hocart *Kingship* (1927) pages 59–60 quoting the *Satapatha Brahmana.*

This word may derive direct from the sanscrit *soma*.[1]

There is also the female name Kalsom which Wilkinson says is commonly given to "Jawi-pekan" women, which may derive from the Sanscrit, *Kali Soma*.

Among these affinities there may be found the explanation of the presence in the modern Malay Boria of the red powder and the yellow water, which are used freely but in a more restrained manner than in the Holi festival of India.

THE AKHIRI CHAHAR OR CHAR SHAMBA OBSERVANCE OF SUNNI AND SHIAH ISLAM IN INDIA

One further Indian feast-day demands our passing attention as it too, appears to have found its way to Malaya and to have become intertwined with the Boria observance.

This is the Akhiri Chahar holiday, observed on the last Wednesday of the Moslem month, Safar.

Herklots *op. cit.* page 189 has the following description of the ceremonies observed on this day:—

> This is the last Wednesday of the month Safar, the second month of the Mohamedan calendar...... On this day every Musulman early in the morning writes, or causes to be written, the seven *Salams* or greetings......on the leaf of a mango tree, or of a sacred fig-tree, or on that of a plantain......they then wash off the writing in water and drink it, in the hope that they may be preserved from affliction and enjoy peace and happiness. This is a Sunni observance but Shiahs consider the day unlucky and call it Charshumba-i-Suri "The Wednesday of the Trumpet", that is, of the Day of Judgment, an opinion now held in Hyderabad, and hence baths are usually taken the day before...... Some of the lower orders employ dancing girls to sing and dance in the garden or at home and regale themselves with "toddy" (sendhi) and other liquors.

Again on page 108 Herklots records that it is customary in India to grant sepoys a day and a half's leave for the observance of the festival of Akhiri Chahar, known to the Malays as *Mandi Safar*.

THE MANDI SAFAR FESTIVAL OF THE MALAYS

Finally, we must notice the Sunni Malay observance known as the Mandi Safar (or Bathing-Day of the month Safar) in which can be discerned features similar to some of those of the Moharram, the Durga-puja and the Akhiri Chahar of India.

The following references to this Malay observance day indicate in some degree the nature of these borrowed similarities.

Hamilton in *J.R.A.S.B.* No. 82 (1920) page 141 has:—

> In Singapore and Malacca (Muharram) performances in imitation of those in Penang are held during the month of Safar from the 20th of the month onwards, so as to terminate on *Mandi Safar* with the usual bathe and feast.

Wilkinson *Papers on Malay Subjects: Life and Customs* Part I (edition 1920) page 40 has:—

> ....Safar the second month, is regarded as unlucky...... The last Wednesday of the month is a religious event, a day of penitence and ceremonial purification from the sins of the world: but it has been turned by the light-hearted Malays into a sort of bathing-picnic known as the "Mandi Safar".

We must now examine in some detail the social and religious development of the domiciled Indian community in Penang during the second quarter of the nineteenth century. This development took place during the period of absorption of criminal elements in circumstances explained in Chapter X *supra*, and in conditions of inter-breeding and partial assimilation with the indigenous Malay population, under the communal name of "Jawi-pekan".

In this process, there were drawn together threads from all the Indian festivals mentioned in this Chapter. These threads some criminal, some religious, became knit together to form the warp and weft of that unique festival, the Penang Boria, described in the following chapter.

Footnote.—(1) Again Wilkinson has:—
Kawi (batu kawi) = cinnabar, vermillion.
Kusum = a shrub, a herb.
Kesom (daun kesom) and in Penang *daun chenohom*=a fragrant edible leaf.
Kesumba = yellow-red dye.

CHAPTER XII

THE ORIGIN AND CHARACTER OF THE MALAY BORIA

We have seen in the preceding chapter what the Moharram festival is, and we have now to show how a religious festival of Shiah India came to be transplanted to Sunni Malaya and to be there distorted into a criminal orgy known as the Boria.

SHIAH INFLUENCE IN PENANG, MALACCA AND SINGAPORE

Distinct from an earlier latent Shiah element in Perak, discussed in Chapter XXII, there was imported into Malaya during the first half of the nineteenth century direct Shiah influence from India, through two separate channels, viz:—

(a) Shiah *religious* influence through Indian traders and Indian native regiments; shortly referred to as the *garrison influence.*

(b) Shiah *criminal* influence through the transportation of Thugs and other criminals from India to the Penal establishments in Singapore and Penang between the years 1825 and 1860; shortly referred to as the *Thug influence,* particulars of which, as affecting the indigenous population, have been given at the end of Chapter X *supra.*

We must now examine more closely the share of the Indian garrison and resident Indian traders in moulding the early social habits of the three settlements. In doing so, we must bear in mind that the immigrant stream, particularly in Penang, remained predominantly Indian up to about 1830, as was only natural at an epoch when the Straits Settlements still formed a Presidency under the East India Company (Chapter IV). The ratio of Indian immigrants to the rest of the population during these early formative years and the race and caste of these Indians here becomes of some importance to our subject.

In this regard, Mills *British Malaya 1824–1867* page 42 has:—

Within two years of the occupation of Penang its population numbered about 1,000. During the following years it steadily increased until by 1804 it had grown to 12,000.[1]

From the very beginning the bulk of the population were Malays. *Next in point of numbers came Indians,* then Chinese and finally a varying number of half the races from Burma to Celebes.

A. DIRECT SHIAH RELIGIOUS INFLUENCES

Of the extent of Shiah influence brought in by Indian traders and other free Indian immigrants it is not easy to form an opinion. We learn however, from Buckley's *Anecdotal History of Singapore* page 375, that in May, 1842, in Singapore, the Government "refused to allow the Klings[2] to have a procession and to carry their Taboot about the town".... This must refer to the celebration of the Shiah Mohamedan Festival of the Moharram and there is nothing to show in the reference, that the celebration was anything but a religious one, unlike what it later became when criminal influences had bound it up with Chinese secret societies. The name "Kling"[2] was at that time universally applied in Malaya to Indian traders, both Hindu and Moslem.

Footnote.—(1) From the following population figures given by Mills *op. cit.* page 212, we note the Indians holding their predominance in Penang up to 1830, while the Chinese by that date had outstripped them in the other Settlements:—

SETTLEMENT			YEAR	INDIANS	CHINESE	TOTAL (with Malays and others)
Penang	..	..	1830	8,858	8,963	34,000
			1850	7,840	15,457	43,000
			1860	10,618	28,018	60,000
Province Wellesley		..	1830	1,087	2,259	46,000
			1850	1,913	8,731	65,000
			1860	3,514	8,204	65,000
Malacca	..	..	1830	2,830	4,797	30,000
			1850	3,258	6,882	46,000
			1860	1,026	10,039	62,000
Singapore	..	..	1830	1,913	6,555	17,000
			1850	6,261	27,988	60,000
			1860	12,971	50,000	81,000

It is not known whether the Indian regiments of the garrison and Indian convicts are included in the above figures for Indians, but presumably they are.

Footnote.—(2) *See* Yule *Hobson-Jobson* (1886) page 372 where the following definition is given:—

"*Kling,* is the name applied in the Malay countries including our Straits Settlements to the people of Continental India, who trade thither or are settled in those regions and to the descendants of such settlers".

And again Wallace *Malay Archipelago* (ed. 1880) page 20):—"The Klings of Western India are a numerous body of Mohamedans and ...... are petty merchants and shopkeepers".

Of probable Shiah influence imported by the Indian regiments of the East India Company, we can speak with more confidence. The view generally held is that Shiah influence from this source was first brought to Penang in A.D. 1845 by the men of the 21st Madras Native Infantry stationed there in that year.

The source of this opinion appears to be a statement in an article by Haughton published on page 312 of No. 30 of the *J.S.B.R.A.S.* in 1897 and quoted below. Further research on this point has disclosed that there were other regiments who may have introduced it at a much earlier date.

Haughton's informant was probably quite correct in stating that the Moharram festival in Penang was imported by the Indian troops of the early Penang garrison, but the festival was probably observed by the military in Penang and perhaps in Malacca, from the beginning of the nineteenth century.

INDIAN NATIVE MILITARY UNITS WITH EARLY SERVICE IN THE STRAITS SETTLEMENTS

The following are particulars of those Indian Regiments as far as we have been able to learn them, which had early contact with the Straits Settlements. They mostly came from Madras and Bengal.

(1) Penang.—The first regiment mentioned by name as having been stationed in Penang is the 25th Bengal Native Infantry.

Mills *op. cit.* page 140 has:—

> Captain Henry Burney was ...... appointed an ensign in 1809 in a regiment of Bengal Native Infantry and took part in the conquest of Java 1810–1811 and in 1811–1814 was stationed at Penang with his regiment the Twenty-fifth.

(2) Malacca.—In *Frontier and Overseas Expeditions from India*,[1] Vol. VI page 339 (Calcutta 1911) we read that Indian detachments sent to Malacca in 1831, being reinforcements for the Naning (Malacca) war[2] were:—

Four Coys. of 29th Madras Native Infantry.

Half Coy. of Madras Artillery.

One Coy. of Madras Engineers.

These units were followed in 1832 by the following further reinforcements direct from Madras to Malacca:—

Fifth Madras Native Infantry.

Four Coys. of 29th M.N.I.

At the same reference two Coys. of 46th M.N.I. were sent in 1832 from the garrison in Penang to Malacca.

These units all ante-dated the 21st M.N.I. of Haughton by fifteen years.

(3) Singapore.—The following information kindly supplied in 1935 by Dr. Randle, Librarian of the India Office, relates to the recorded movements of the 21st M.N.I.:—

> A detachment of the 21st Madras Infantry embarked from Madras to Penang on 4th April, 1846. Troops and followers of the 21st M.N.I. proceeded to Singapore on 11th April, 1846. They appear to have left Penang and Singapore between April 1849 and July 1849.

From this, it would appear that the 21st M.N.I. had as much contact with Singapore as with Penang, and that the originators of the Moharram festival in Penang would more likely be found in the 29th, 5th or 46th Regiments Madras Native Infantry, rather than in the 21st M.N.I.[3]

The identity of the individual Indian regiments which formed the early garrison in the Straits Settlements is not, however, of so much importance as the composition by race, caste, or religion of these regiments, most of which in the Madras and Bengal armies, prior to the Indian Mutiny, were composed of much the same material.

Footnote.—(1) War Office Library, Whitehall.

Footnote.—(2) *See* also Mills. *op. cit.* page 125.

Footnote.—(3) The following list of East India Company Regiments and other garrison troops stationed in Singapore between 1826 and 1851 appeared in the *Singapore Cathedral Courier* of February 1936:—

Year (approx.)		Year (approx.)	
1826	Bengal Artillery.	1836	26th Regt. British Infantry.
1827	{ 25th Regt. Native Infantry.	1837	Madras Horse Artillery.
	{ 58th Regt. Bengal Native Infantry.	1838	The Royal Irish.
1828	3rd Batt. Madras Artillery.	1839	Bombay Artillery.
1829	4th Regt. Madras Native Infantry.	1840	The 13th Regiment.
1830	13th Regt. Bombay Native Infantry.	1841	Bengal Volunteer Regiment.
	{ 47–49 Madras Engineers.	1842	27th Regt. Madras Native Infantry.
1831	{ 7th Regt. Bengal Native Infantry.	1843	2nd Madras European Light Infantry.
	{ 43–50 Madras Artillery.	1844	2nd Native Veteran Batt. Madras.
	{ 29th Regt. Madras Native Infantry.	1845	48th Regt. Madras Native Infantry.
1832	23rd Regt. Madras Native Infantry.	1846–49	21st Regt. Madras Native Infantry.
1833	49th Regt. British Infantry.	1850–51	{ 20th Regt. Madras Native Infantry.
1834	39th Regt. Madras Native Infantry.		{ Bengal Artillery.
1835	8th Regt. Madras Native Infantry.		

The only available reference to this subject appears to be the *Report of the Royal Commission appointed in 1859*[1] *to enquire into the organisation of the Indian army.*[2]

The following questions and answers in the printed evidence of this report, page 252, are relevant:—

THE RECRUITING AND COMPOSITION OF INFANTRY CORPS

Q. 1. What are the races, tribes, or castes of which the native infantry of the Madras army is composed?

A. 1. Mussulmans, chiefly from South Arcot and adjacent parts, Teloogoos from the northern division, Tamulians from the Malabar coast, Tranquebar Pariahs, a low and numerous class; also native Christians, many of whom are now sepoys in the native army.

Q. 2. What districts are the several races, tribes, and castes drawn from?

A. 2. From all the districts and divisions of the presidency of Madras, south of the river Kistnah.

Q. 3. Have any races, tribes, or castes been excluded from enlistment, either by the regulations or the practice of the Madras army?

A. 3. Many regiments in the infantry have for many years always recruited from certain districts, commanding officers have used their own discretion in obtaining drafts of men either from the northern or southern division of the army, but no particular races or castes have been excluded by order.

In Appendix 22 of the same Report, page 26, we find a:—

Return showing the number, caste and country of the Native Officers of each regiment regular and irregular of each Presidency, so far as can be stated from the records of this House.

The return is dated, September, 1858, and we learn as follows from it:—

Under Bengal.—The 25th Bengal Native Infantry is not mentioned but all the existing Bengal regiments, being 7 regular and 12 irregular, were composed of much the same material, and one may suppose that the 25th Regiment prior to its disappearance was similarly composed, namely: "Mohamedans, Brahmins, Rajpoots and Hindoos of inferior description, the latter predominating".

Under Madras.—The Madras Artillery was chiefly composed of "Mohamedans Brahmins, Telingas[3] (Gentoo) and Tamils". These men came mostly from "the Central Carnatic, Madras, Vellore, Southern Carnatic, Trichinopoly, Mysore and Hindustan".

The Madras Engineers were composed of "Christians 115, Tamils 177, Telingas 100, Mohamedans 51, other castes 350" and came chiefly from "Northern and Southern Carnatic, Mysore and the Madras Presidency".

The Madras Native Infantry was composed of 52 regiments, comprising in all:—

Mohamedans	15,000
Telingas	15,000
Tamils	4,000
Brahmins and Rajpoots	2,000
"Other castes"	2,000

[4]

The foregoing supplies us with a guide to the composition of those Indian Regiments probably responsible for introducing the Moharram festival to Malaya and we see that they contained the same mixed Mohamedan and Hindu elements from Central and South India described in Herklots (Chapter XI *supra*) as being the chief supporters of the Moharram festival in India.

LEAVE CUSTOMARILY GRANTED TO INDIAN TROOPS FOR THE MOHARRAM FESTIVAL

On this point Herklots *op. cit.* page 108 says that the time usually occupied for the performance of the Moharram for which leave is generally given to Musalman sepoys is thirteen days but if pressed for time, ten days.

Haughton in his article quoted below also mentions this customary leave granted to the Penang garrison.

We may presume, therefore, that the majority of sepoys of the early Penang garrison were if not Shiahs, at least supporters of the Moharram and that when the festival was first introduced into Penang it corresponded very closely to Herklots' description written in 1832, which, when applied to Penang, is a description of goodnatured horse-play among Indian Shiah Mohamedans, with doubtless a number of Hindu members of the regiment joining in the festivities, supported by such other Indian

---

Footnote.—(1) *i.e.* immediately after the suppression of the Indian Mutiny 1857-58.

Footnote.—(2) Parliamentary paper. India Office Library.

Footnote.—(3) Yule *Hobson-Jobson* page 694 gives:—

Telinga.—This term in the last century was frequently used in Bengal as synonymous with "sepoy".

Footnote.—(4) These men came from the following countries in the following numbers:—

Hindustan	2,000
Northern Circars	17,000
Central Carnatic	9,000
Southern Carnatic	5,000
Mysore	3,000

civilian settlers as happened to come from those parts of India where the festival was customarily observed.   It seems clear from Herklots' description that there were always elements of friendly disputation in the observance which may well have been importations from the Durga-puja or the Holi of the Hindus (*cf.* the passage where he describes the digging of the fire-pit on the first day "and ignorant people young and old fence across it with sticks and swords").   But the whole festival was homogenous and essentially one of mourning for the Alids particularly Husein, and there is nowhere any hint of an undercurrent of hostility or rivalry between those taking part, and no separate or "opposition parties" of the supporters of Hasan on the one side and the supporters of Husein on the other, such as were later to become such a prominent feature of the distorted Penang observance, which came to be known as the Boria.   For an explanation of this later local development, we must look elsewhere.

B. DIRECT SHIAH CRIMINAL INFLUENCE

(1) We should here note two features in the Moharram festival, as described by Herklots, which bear a resemblance to similar criminal features of Thuggism.   These are:—

> (a) The reference to *the mattock (pickaxe) wielding rite.* (*op. cit.* page 157 and page 176 *supra*).
>
> (b) The group of players referred to as the Khodun garun *The diggers and buriers* (*op. cit.* page 178 and page 178 *supra*) whose chant "I throw down and bury whom I please", suggests the Thuggist cult.

We shall have occasion to refer again to this group, who may be actually represented in the modern Boria.

(2) We have been unable to find the original records of the individual criminals transported to the Straits Settlements during the years 1825–1867, but the extracts from McNair, *Prisoners their own Warders*, given in Chapter X above, will give the reader some idea of the position.   McNair records the presence of over 2,000 transported felons from India in Singapore in 1857, of whom we know from other evidence given in Chapter X, some 1,500 were Thugs.   Most of these, who survived their sentences, were, according to McNair, "merged into the population" of the Straits Settlements, together with large numbers of other Indian convicts who, under the "ticket-of-leave" system, appear to have had sufficient liberty to enable them to set up in civil life and raise families of "Jawi-pekans".

THE RISE OF THE JAWI-PEKAN COMMUNITY

The Jawi-pekans or Peranakans as they are now more commonly known, were, as we shall see, a link in the transition of the Moharram festival from a religious celebration to a hooligan masquerade.

The process of liberating India's worst criminals to enable them to become merged in the growing population of the Colony, continued from 1825 to 1873 and doubtless a large part of the criminal history of Malaya among southern Indians and Malays can be traced to this cause.

The following extract from Vaughan's *Notes on the Chinese of Penang J.I.A.* VIII 1854, illustrates the rise of the Jawi-pekan community in Penang and their debasing effect upon the manners of the time:—

> The Chinese in Penang ...... are so attached to the habits of their forefathers, that notwithstanding an intercourse for the last 60 years with natives of all countries, they have jealously adhered to their ancient customs, and no doubt the European settler in China would recognise in the "Baba" of Penang and his peculiarities, a strong resemblance to his progenitors.
>
> It is not so with the Mohammedan and Hindoo settlers.   These have gradually intermixed their religious ceremonies.   To a Musjid in George Town, consecrated to the memory of a Mohammedan saint, both races subscribe indiscriminately and they imitate each other, as well as the Chinese, on their holidays by firing crackers and beating gongs.   On the continent of India, they utterly despise and hate each other, and could not under any circumstances suffer a junction, especially in religious affairs.   Caste is very much laid aside here.   I have seen Mussulmen seated in the houses of orthodox Hindoos eating off the same board.   The Hindoo also takes the Malay woman to wife.   Such a proceeding in Bengal would render him an outcast for ever, but here he does not lose his caste.   I have seen a Hindoo and Muslim bathe in the same tank, the water from the latter's body falling on the former, and *vice versa.*   Such a sight in India would be a novelty indeed.
>
> *   *   *
>
> On mentioning the Chinese game of Tigers, I am reminded of the manner in which the "Gamin" or Jawi-Pukan of Pinang, (a mixed breed between a Kling or Bengalee and the Malay) personates that animal.   In the Mohorum feast several of these men go about with their bodies painted like tigers, a tail stuck on behind, and a chain round the waist, which is held by others who are supposed to be their keepers.   They are generally muscular, clean made fellows and imitate the movements of a wild beast admirably.   They carry the resemblance so far and work themselves up to such a pitch of excitement, that if a live kid is thrown to them they will seize it, tear the poor creature to pieces and suck the blood.   There are families that bear the soubriquet of tigers.   The child is taught to personate the animal by the father as soon as the former is strong enough to bear the fatigue.   On going round the town and country they collect a great deal of money and are allowed to seize any articles of food that may be exposed for sale on the road side.

The blood-sucking custom mentioned, savours strongly of the cult of Kali.   MacMunn *The Under-world of India* page 188 describes a Kali-worshipper known to have destroyed thus a thousand kids in one day with his powerful jaws.

Again in Vaughan's *Notes on the Malays of Penang J.I.A.* Vol. II (New Series) 1858 he has the following:—

Allusion has been made to the offspring of Malay mothers and Kling or Bengali fathers; they are called Jawi bukans, Jawi pukans, and Jadi bukans indiscriminately, the last term is most commonly used in Pinang. The children of Chinese by Malays come under the same designation when they adopt the mother's nation, but those that follow their father's are termed Babas. It is difficult to ascertain which is the right epithet or the origin of the terms; the first means literally "not a Malay", the second, "the Malay of the village", and the last "not made" or "is not made".

Jawi bukan appears to be the right term and no doubt was originally used by the Malays to distinguish the half breeds from themselves; "Jawi pukan" might also have been early used to distinguish the inhabitants of the towns from those of the country; and the last term appears to be a corruption of either; it is however the usual name given to all half breeds except those that adopt the Chinese customs. The Jawi bukans possess all the courage of the mother combined with the activity, intelligence and cunning of the father; they easily acquire habits of business, prove smart traders, and a great number have amassed considerable fortunes; they compete successfully with European and Chinese merchants, and of course gain a great ascendency over their fellow countrymen. Those of the poorer classes possess the same good qualities, but chance affords the one an opportunity of rising to opulence while the other sinks into the drunkard or opium smoker; with few exceptions they are all addicted to the above vices as well as gaming; they prove the smartest seamen and policemen, but unfortunately their predilections render them untrustworthy.

For purposes of this chapter we do no more than point to this channel of Shiah influx, which we have noted more fully in Chapter X and which we will refer to as the "Thug Influence" in the Moharram.

We will now pass on to a description by Vaughan of the Moharram festival in which Thug influence is very marked in the behaviour of the "Jawi-pekans" of that epoch. This description provides an interesting cross-section of the transition period during which the Penang Moharram changed from a religious observance to a civil, and ultimately, criminal revel.

THE MOHARRAM FESTIVAL IN MALAYA 1858

The following extracts from Vaughan's *Notes on the Malays of Penang J.I.A.* Vol. II (New Series) 1858, contain the earliest published description of the Moharram while still a religious festival and before its complete transition into the performance known as the Boria, a name evidently unknown in Vaughan's day. (Sub-heads have been added for convenience).

Description of the Moharram as celebrated by Jawi-pekans in Penang, 1858:—

The Jawi bukans are addicted to making vows; as a return for any particular gratification, they promise to undergo certain penances, pilgrimages etc., which they scrupulously fulfill; this custom is derived from their fathers. They join heart and soul in all the amusements of the Mohorum and Dusserah festivals and will perform every species of buffoonery for the purpose of obtaining money.

They disguise themselves in a variety of ways to prove amusing, some dress as beggars of various nations, others as birds and beasts; some of them study the habits and movements of wild beasts so well, especially the tiger, that their imitations of the brute are splendid, some assume the attire of Europeans and dance various fashionable dances including the polka, their performances are rewarded by showers of cents principally subscribed by Europeans and Portuguese who are attracted out on such occasions; their love of fun and devilry leads them to imitate burlesquely all the ceremonies observed by the Mahomedans and Hindus of India, to the amusement of bystanders. They also form bands, led by some desperate fellows, and attack parties of Klings or Bengalies who may be devoutly parading with their images; the attack begins in fun but eventually ends in blows and even bloodshed; the principal work of the Police is to watch these bands of Jawi bukans who issue from their houses merely for the purpose of annoying the real devotees. Such scenes are despised by the Malays, they will not join in them nor will the most respectable portion of them visit the town during the celebration of heathen festivals,—no milder term can they apply to the orgies of the Mohorum, and they identify them with all other heretical rites.

No fusion of the Malays with the Moharram in 1858:—

At Pinang there are two mosques and, in order to insure a full house, the people assemble in each every alternate Friday.

The religion of the Malay is uncontaminated by Hindu example, so that he regards with disgust the orgies celebrated by the natives of India at the Mohorum and other seasons, and the pious will not leave their houses to show how they despise the folly of their corrupt brethren. The only holidays observed by the Malay are the Hari Rayah and Hari Suffur Mundi and Rayah Haji.[1]

The first is celebrated on the day after the New Moon is seen which follows the fast month, and the second on the last Wednesday of the month Suffer (Safar).

The Hari Rayah is simply a feast day; and on the second holiday (Mandi Safar) the Malays bathe in a stream which flows past the tomb of a local Saint; by doing so they believe in a sort of regeneration, and profess to believe that they are spiritually cleansed.

The third festival is held on the tenth day of the Mohorum month, but is unattended with processions or any outward demonstration; it is called Hari Rayah dul Hajira.[2]

Footnote.—(1) These are:—
   (i) *Hari Raya Puasa*. The first day of the tenth month (Shawal) marking the end of the fast of Ramathan.
   (ii) *Hari Raya Haji*. The tenth of the twelfth month (Dzu-l-Hijja) marking the hundredth day from the first of the ninth month (Ramathan). This period of 100 days is frequently observed as a fast by those who have made the pilgrimage (Haj).
   (iii) *Mandi Safar*. The last Wednesday of the second month (Safar) evidently identical in name and purpose with the Akhiri Charhar of India (*see* Chapter XI).
Footnote.—(2) This is an error. For "Mohoram" we should read "Zul Hajira" the 12th month of the Mohamedan calendar, better Dzu-l-Hijja. The feast referred to is Hari Raya Haji.

But influence of Indian religious customs was beginning to be felt among Malays :—

> The Malays do not naturally believe in the intercession of saints or holy men but from intercourse with natives of Hindustan they are gradually being corrupted on this head; there are several saints' tombs or cenotaphs in Pinang to which the Malays contribute their offerings with Bengalies and Klings to propitiate the shades of the worthies whose bones lie buried far away. One monument is erected over the grave of a holy man that died in Pinang, it is regarded with great respect by all classes and periodically vast multitudes visit the tomb and pray for the old man's intercession; the Malays do not join in considerable numbers, but all that know of the tomb believe in its virtues. The orthodox party under the guidance of the head Malay priest (Abdul Gunny), regard all such innovations with horror, nothing beyond the pages of the Koran is received by them.

The foregoing notes of Vaughan seem to establish clearly the following points :—

(1) That in the year 1858, in Penang (and probably in the other Settlements as well) and probably for the preceding twenty years or more, the Moharram festival in a rather orgiastic form was well established.

(2) It was celebrated by Shiah Indians, Hindu settlers and "Jawi-pekans", the descendants of Shiah Indians who had married Sunni Malay women.

(3) It was already regarded by some as an annual revel and included features of the purely Hindu festival of the Dussera or Durga-puja (see Chapter XI), the chief festival of the Thugs (see Chapter X).

(4) It was made the occasion for the formation by "Jawi-pekans" of "bands led by desperate fellows" which attacked, supposedly in fun, parties of devout Shiah worshippers carrying the Taziah or Tabut, and often led to bloodshed.

(5) "The principal work of the Police was to watch these bands of Jawi-pekans who issue from their houses merely for the purpose of annoying the real devotees".

(6) These "desperate" Jawi-pekans were probably drawn from that element of Indian criminality imported into Penang when it was a convict settlement.

(7) The pure-bred Malay of Penang of this period despised these revellers and remained entirely aloof from participation in their "heathen festivities".

(8) The influence of Indian religious customs was nevertheless, beginning to be felt at this time among the pure-bred Malays.

(9) The propitiation of holy places, or *keramat*, was becoming usual among the common people, in imitation of Indian sufism.

THE PERIOD OF DEGENERATION OF THE MOHARRAM FESTIVAL IN MALAYA 1860–1890

The foregoing description presents the character of the Moharram in Penang up to about 1870. The same description would probably hold good for the celebration of the festival in Malacca and Singapore up to the same date.

A process of degeneration set in as the Thug influence began to predominate, particularly after the religious influence of the Penang garrison consequent upon the Indian mutiny had been withdrawn; and a period ensued when the pure-bred Malay began to be more and more drawn into the celebration, for reasons unconnected with religious observance, to which we must now refer.

But another process had been taking place in Penang between the years 1830 and 1870 side by side with the debasement of the Moharram and due to the same cause, the Thug influence, then being merged into the population.

This process we can only guess at, but there is ample evidence to show its results in the formation among the "Jawi-pekan" community of two Mohamedan secret societies as counterparts to or in imitation of, the two long established Chinese secret society camps of Triad and "Tokong". These two Indo-Malay secret societies came to be known as the White and the Red Flag societies and their development as a separate phenomenon is discussed in Chapters XIV and XV *infra*.

The two flag societies were well established by 1860 and about that year or a little later, formed an unholy underground alliance with the two Chinese camps respectively, the White with Triad and the Red with "Tokong". This alliance projected the traditional hostility of Han and Hung among the Mohamedans of the Malay peninsula, dividing such of them as fell under its power, into two hostile underground camps similar to those of the Chinese under-world.

The benefits sought from membership of the flag associations were identical with those of the Chinese, namely secrecy, mutual help and protection of their women, which latter consideration, no doubt, appealed to Mohamedans living in a mixed community and also implied the exploitation by them of the women folk of non-members, or of those of the opposite camp. These secret sodalities had a particular attraction for the Indian criminal elements then merging into the population and once established, were not to be easily uprooted. In fact, they remain to the present-day.

During their formative years a means was found of making the position of the flag associations more secure by borrowing the religious cloak of the Moharram festival and using it as the explanation and excuse for their existence.

We find, therefore, that by degrees the celebration of the Moharram in Penang was appropriated almost entirely by the two flag associations, who felt safe from official interference on the plea of religious observance, and year by year the Moharram was used as a public trial of strength between them, until finally all pretence of religious observance faded from the festival. This process must have been completed by about the year 1865, when we begin to find references in the records to the "rival" parties of Hasan and Husein,—"each going on either side of the street and when they meet a fight ensues". We also find that those of the Hassan party carried white flags and those of the Husein party red flags.

Such a development had no sanction in the Moharram festival of the Alids, in which the colours used in India were green for Hasan to represent his traditional death by poison and red for Husein to represent his. traditional murder. (Chapter X). We suggest the origin of the white and red flag association colours in Chapter XV *infra*. Nor was there any religious sanction for the division of the celebration into two hostile parties "the Hasan" and "the Husein", when the whole purpose of the observance was one of mourning alike for Ali and his two sons.

We see in these developments the total distortion and debasement of the Moharram in Malaya, when once it had been appropriated by the two flag associations, until it became the annual battle-ground of the White and Red Flag societies and eventually changed its name from the Moharram to the Boria, and became linked underground with the two rival Chinese camps of Triad and "Tokong".

This was the position reached in about 1865, when official attention was first directed to the conditions which had by then developed, but the process by which they had arisen remained unknown. We discuss this aspect of the subject further in Chapter XIV *infra*.

THE EMERGENCE AND CHARACTER OF THE BORIA FROM 1870

The name by which the Moharram festival is known to-day in Malaya is "The Boria".

A description by Hamilton of the modern Boria performance is given in Appendix V.

It is not clear when this word first came to be applied to the festival. The name does not occur in the *Penang Riot Commission Report* of 1868, which uses only the phrase "Moharram Festival".

The word must have been in common use by 1890 to find its way into Clifford and Swettenham's dictionary (incomplete) of 1895. It does not occur in Marsden, or in earlier works, so we may assume that it came into general use between 1875 and 1890. This would be after the religious influence of the Penang garrison had been withdrawn and would cover a period when pure-bred Malays of Penang first began to take part in the festival, which up to then, had been chiefly supported by Indians and "Jawi-pekans".

There are four published references to the Boria,[1] but it is not clear from any of them whence the term is derived.

Wilkinson's dictionary (ed. 1932) has:—

Boria (Hind.) Muharram minstrels or singers of carols. At the Moharram, especially in Penang, it is (or was) the custom for bands of serenaders in fancy dress to visit houses of prominent citizens and sing topical songs. Such bands are known as "Boria".

Although Wilkinson claims a Hindi or Hindustani origin for it there is, in fact, no such word in Hindustani.

Haughton in his article (below) says it is a Persian word meaning a mat and quotes Forbes dictionary, but the word does not appear in Forbes (ed. 1866), nor in the other Hindustani lexicons of. the period.

The word *boriya* (بوریا) is, however, given in Ram Narain Lal's *Students' Practical Hindustani Dictionary* published in Allahabad in 1913, in which its origin is given as Persian and its meaning "a mat made of palm leaves or rushes".

It seems, however, unsafe to accept Ram Narain Lal's authority uncorroborated, for although his rendering exactly fits the meaning assigned to the word by Haughton's informant (below), the word had evidently been current in this meaning for some twenty-five years at least prior to the appearance of Narain Lal's dictionary (1913) and its inclusion therein may, therefore, be a case of intermutation, or displacement or assimilation of meaning. If the word is, in fact, Persian and was associated with the mats which Herklots describes as being used as coverings by some of the participants in the Moharram, one would reasonably expect to find the word among the great number of Persian and Hindustani renderings for the different paraphernalia of the Moharram procession included in Herklots' meticulous description, but it is not so included.

There is in Hindustani a word of Hebrew origin *Bora* meaning "a sack" or "canvas bag", which is the nearest we can get to a "mat" in that language.

It seems safer to seek the origin of the name within the nomenclature common to the Moharram festival itself as given by Herklots, and in doing so we shall not be disappointed.

Footnote.—(1) These are:—
    (i) Article by H. T. Haughton in *J.S.B.R.A.S.* No. 30 July, 1897 pages 312–313.
    (ii) Notice by R. J. Wilkinson in *Papers on Malay Subjects*. Life and Customs Part I page 40 (ed. 1920).
    (iii) Article by A. W. Hamilton in *J.S.B.R.A.S.* No. 82 1920 pages 139–144.
    (iv) A booklet in Malay entitled *Boria dan Benchana-nya* ("The evil influence of the Boria") by Mohamed Yusop bin Sultan Mydin Published in Penang in 1922.

THE ETYMOLOGY OF THE NAME "BORIA"

The clue to this search is to be found in Haughton's article (*J.S.B.R.A.S.* No. 30 July, 1897 page 312–13) which is as follows:—

"In Part II of Clifford and Swettenham's *Malay English dictionary*, under the head of Boriah, I find *Boriah*, بوريا A topical song. *Bacha boriah* باچ بوريا To sing a topical song.

No derivation of the word is given. The use of the word is chiefly confined to the pantomimes or mimic plays which are acted by Malays in Penang Town during the month of Muharam. It is of Persian origin according to Forbes, and means a "mat" in Hindustani. The following account of the word which I have received from an Indian in Penang will throw some light on the subject, as I believe, fanciful derivations of the word have been suggested.

"The plain meaning of the word Boriah in the Hindustani and Deccan language is a place of prayer (praying carpet), and in Malay they call it *tikar* (a mat). Formerly in the year 1845, the 21st Regiment was transferred from Madras to Penang. The Muhammedans of the Regiment used to be given ten days' leave in the month of Muharram for the purpose of mourning for the grandsons of the prophet. These Military men used to form parties and sing songs of mourning. For instance, representing four persons, Nanak Shah, Jogi Majnun, Balva Ghaghri, and Boria, they used to dress up in clothes made of mats and mourn for Husain, and used to recite the following piece of poetry:—

> Boria the best of its kind;
> Boria everywhere in the world;
> Boria the beautiful (was) seen;
> Sacred and pure Boria. .
> In the countries of Madras
> The Boria is made of grass;
> Fences are made with bamboo;
> Boria is green in colour, etc., etc.

"But in Penang the name of Boria is from the 21st Regiment, and has become celebrated. Now-a-days the Malays have given their own different names to it, but they call all of them Boria for the purpose of asking charity for them. In Madras wherever the Regiment is the Boria play is performed."

We should specially note the following points in the foregoing *viz:*—

(1) Clifford and Swettenham give the local meaning of the word to be: *A topical song.*

(2) The Boria is an adaptation from, or a local burlesque of, the Moharram.

(3) The importation of the festival is ascribed to the 21st Regiment of the Madras Native Infantry in 1845.

(4) Parties of "mourners" dress up in mats and represent four persons known as:—

> Nanak Shah
> Jogi Majnun
> Balva Ghaghri
> Boria

(5) The mourners recite poetry in praise of something called "Boria", which is sacred, green in colour and associated with the vegetable kingdom, or Nature.

(6) The name *boria*, by a process of prosopopœia, is applied both to a person and to a symbol of nature-worship.

We shall refer to the first point later. The second and third points have been discussed above. The fifth and sixth points are of interest as suggesting that the eclecticism remarked upon by Herklots in the Moharram of India (Chapter XI *supra*) had so far developed in its counterpart in Penang during the period 1870–1890, as to include in the debased Boria performance, elements of the nature worship and fertility cult of the Holi festival of the Hindus. What symbol of nature-worship the green and sacred boria is intended to represent in the verses quoted, we are unable to say, but we may be permitted to suggest that it may have been the soma-plant of Mount Meru referred to in the last chapter.[1]

But it is with the fourth point that we are here primarily concerned in our search for the etymology of the name, for which we now offer the three following alternative derivations:—

(1) If we refer back to the description of the Moharram in India as given by Herklots (pages 177–178 *supra*) we find among the names of those who

---

Footnote.—(1) Cf. the veneration of the green in nature of the "Tokong" foundation in Penang at the same period, page 107 *supra* and Appendix II, under "Passwords".

dress themselves up to represent different orders of sufi faqirs, the following:—

The Majnun Fakirs
The Laila Fakirs
The Bharang or Bhar-Bhariya.
The Jogi
The Khodun-garun
The Nanak Shahi
The Ghagriwala

We submit for acceptance that the "four persons" in the Boria mentioned by Haughton are identifiable in the Herklots' description of the Moharram as follows:—

Haughton	*Herklots*
1. Nanak Shah	1. The Nanak Shahi
2. Jogi Majnun	2. { The Jogi / The Majnun Faqirs
3. Balva Ghaghri	3. The Ghagriwala
4. Boria	4. The Bhar-bhariya or "Foolish Chatterers".

We suggest that the true origin of the name Boria is to be found in a corruption of the Hindustani term Bhar-bhariya,[1] or "Foolish Chatterers", the reduplicative prefix of which has been dropped.

The alternative name given by Herklots for the Bhar-bhariya is the *Bharang* the meaning of which Forbes gives as:—

Silly, artless, having the quality of telling secrets without reserve.

This is exactly the quality of the "topical songs" familiar in the modern Boria performance.

Although it seems probable that we have the true derivation of the Malay word *Boria* in the corrupt and shortened form of the Hindi word *Barbarya*, in one of its variant spellings, two alternative derivations suggest themselves.

(2) The Hindustani word *Barbarahut*=gibberish, chatter; is given in Platts' dictionary (ed. 1895) and suggests the Thug-slang or *Ramaseena* word *Boreeahut* or *Bore*, given at the end of Chapter X *supra*, which means: "loud talking, bellowing, uproar". We have seen in that chapter that some Thug slang words have found their way into Malay and this might be another example, conceivably shortened by Malays into "Boria", suggesting the uproar of the Moharram festival.

(3) Lastly, there is a Sanscrit word in use in Hindustani *Bharya* (بهاريا) meaning a wife or married woman. This word is given by Platts *op. cit.* (edition 1895) with a secondary meaning *viz:*—"A musical mode; or the wife of a deity presiding over a musical mode". This secondary meaning is absent from the earlier lexicons and it is tempting to connect it with the topical songs of the Penang Boria in preference to the Persian mat derivation of Haughton, but there seems no more substantial basis for the one than for the other.

OTHER SUGGESTED DERIVATIONS

It is true that in Herklots' description of the fancy dress worn by the groups of devotees in the Moharram there is frequent mention of the use of mats and matting. This may explain the acceptance by Haughton of his Indian informant's derivation, but the presence of mats is a minor incidental with no particular claim to furnish a new name to an ancient festival, thereby suggesting a change of title to "the Prayer-mat festival", which is without any particular point.

On this analogy many other more conspicuous impedimenta of the Moharram procession would have a prior claim. Furthermore, the use of mats and matting has been dropped from the Boria, but the "Foolish Chattering" has been retained.

Footnote.—(1) The Hindustani lexicographers have the following references to this word:—

Fallon (1879)   *Bharbharya* بهر بهزيا (Hindi). Adj.:—
   (i) Babbling, gossiping, unable to keep a secret.
   (ii) Open, candid, frank, without guile.
   Also spelled:—
   Barbarya بزبزيا n.m. A chatterer, murmurer, grumbler.

Forbes (1866)   As above and also has these additional words:—
   Bharang بهز نكّ Simple, undesigning, silly, artless, having the quality of telling secrets without reserve.
   Bariya بريّاي n.f. Boast, exultation.

Platts (ed. 1895)   As above and also has this additional word:—
   Barbarahut بزبزاهت Muttering, chatter, gibberish, light-headed talk.
   Barbarahut karna To mutter, to talk gibberish, to blabber, to rave.

Another more fanciful origin of the name might be found in the word:—

Bohora, a sect of Ismaili Shiahs of Guzerat and the Deccan, who might be expected to be represented in the Penang Moharram and from whose name Haughton's informant might have taken the name of the person he calls "Boria".

Another word, *Bora*, is the name by which Thugs of Behar and Bengal are known among themselves in the *Ramasee* slang; and as such devotees might also be expected to be present in the Penang Moharram, their name might have become corrupted to represent the debased Boria performance. None of these fanciful derivations have much to recommend them.

The importance of Haughton's contribution

Haughton's article provides the essential clue to the etymology of the name Boria by recording the four names which we can clearly identify with the Moharram of India, before these names became obliterated, and the fourth of which he records as that of a person represented in the performance.

As the name can hardly stand for a mat and a person at one and the same time, we think it a safe inference to conclude that it stands for the "Foolish Chatterers" of Herklots. In other respects Haughton's article is most valuable in linking the genuine Moharram festival of India with the burlesque performance of the modern Boria performance from which the clues provided by Haughton have long since disappeared.

The only names given by Haughton which have found a permanent place in the Malay language are Majnun and Jogi and in neither case was the channel of absorption that of the Moharram.

Wilkinson's dictionary (ed. 1932) has in this context:—

Majnun. Mad, Behaving as one possessed, Used specially of children who mimic frenzy in Minangkabau Hasan-Husein processions.

The name is, of course, that of the hero in the popular Persian romance of Laila and Majnun, who are known throughout the Moslem world and whose fame came to Malaya with the advent of Islam circa 1450. Wilkinson gives Jogi=Hindu ascetic: but does not connect the name with the Jogi of the Moharram festival of India, still less with the Boria of Penang. Had it not been for the timely article of Haughton these important links would have been lost.

Predominance of Penang in the development of the Boria

We have now traversed with the aid of Vaughan and Haughton the transition period of the Moharram festival in Malaya from 1860 to 1895, until it emerges as the modern Boria described by Hamilton in Appendix V.

Attention has throughout been focussed upon the process of its development in Penang. This is not only because the available records refer almost entirely to that settlement, but also because Indian influence has been both older and stronger in Penang than elsewhere in the peninsula, and also because Penang was the cradle of the Indo-Malay secret flag associations which formed themselves there during the first half of the nineteenth century, and appropriated the Boria performance as their own particular vehicle of public expression (under a religious cloak) during the second half. The last and most important reason for the predominance of Penang is the fact that it was there in the *Penang Riot Commission Report* of 1868, that official attention was first drawn to the alliance which had by then been established between the two Indo-Malay flag associations and the two Chinese secret societies of Triad and "Tokong".

It should not be inferred however that this process of Sino-Malay criminal alliance was peculiar to Penang. There can be little doubt but that it was taking place concurrently in all three settlements unobserved. Even on such occasions as it broke surface elsewhere and attracted attention to itself, little or no record seems to have been made, no doubt because its significance was not recognised or understood.

From Buckley *op. cit.* page 375 we learn that in May, 1842, the Government in Singapore "refused to allow the Klings to have a procession and to carry their Taboot about the town", lest riots should ensue.

From Buckley again page 723 we learn that:—

For some years there had been trouble at times arising from secret societies among Klings, both Hindu and Mohammedan called the Red and White Flag societies...... In 1863, serious disturbances had taken place in Singapore during the Moharram festival and in May, 1865, the Government forbade the procession...... The societies......had been established after the manner of the Chinese Ghi Hin (Triad) and Ghi Hock (Tokong) societies, with which it was supposed they were connected.

It was not until the publication of the *Penang Riot Commission Report* of 1868 that the Government received its first insight into the existence of this alliance. But even then its potentialities for evil were not recognised, though they were soon thereafter to spread from the criminal to the political sphere and to bring about British intervention in the Malay States. Meanwhile the Boria pursued its annual way as the outward and visible sign of that invisible alliance whose tentacles in the political sphere we examine in Chapters XIII and XVII *infra*.

THE MODERN BORIA

For over twenty years, from Haughton in 1897 to Hamilton in 1920, there was no published reference to the annual celebration of the Boria which during this period seems to have followed an undeviating course as the public expression of the Indo-Malay flag associations.

In 1920, there appeared a short notice by Wilkinson *Papers on Malay Subjects (Life and Customs)* Part I, page 40, which pictures the Boria's harmless aspect and shows that by that year the break with its religious origin was complete. He says:—

The Boria Performance.

"......... The Moslem year is a lunar year unconnected with seasonal events. It begins with the month of Muharram. The first day of the year is not marked by any festivities, nor does the month itself contain any special Sunnite holidays, but Indian Shiite influence shows itself in Penang in the Boria performances and in lamentations over the death of the Prophet's grandson Husein. A "Boria" is a troupe of strolling minstrels generally dressed and drilled as soldiers and headed by a Captain and an Army Chaplain. The troupe visits the houses of wealthy or popular Moslems and serenades them till paid to go away. The songs are sometimes eulogistic and sometimes comic: the tunes are admirably suited for their purpose—pleasing at first and monotonous after a time, so that the troupe is gladly welcomed and gladly dismissed. The religious element is absent from the boria performances and there is no apparent reason for their association with the month of Muharram".

In the same year there appeared the full notice by Hamilton *J.S.B.R.A.S.* No. 82 (1920) pages 139-144, which is given in Appendix V. A comparison between Hamilton's description and that of the conventional Indian festival (Chapter XI) demonstrates vividly the metamorphosis which the latter had undergone in Malaya before reaching its present form.

The causes of this distortion and their relation to the concurrent development of the flag associations of the Malays, are discussed in Chapters XIV and XV *infra*.

Meanwhile, the following two extracts from Hamilton's article call for passing notice. He says:—

In Singapore and Malacca, Boria performances in imitation of those in Penang are held during the month of Safar from the 20th onwards, so as to terminate on Mandi Safar, with the usual bathe and feast, but though popular at one time, only one Boria troupe exists now in Singapore against forty to fifty in Penang.

The explanation of this peculiarity which tends to confuse the Boria with the Mandi Safar festival, with which it properly has nothing to do, is probably to be found in remnants of the garrison influence dating from the celebration of the Akhiri Chahar festival at an earlier epoch in Malaya.   Another explanation may be found in the practice, common among Sunnis in respect of the celebration of the Moharram, which they do not normally observe, of transferring the observance from a sacred to a profane month to suit convenience. This practice is condemned by the Prophet.[1]

Again Hamilton says:—

"Once upon a time the advent of the Boria season was rather dreaded by the more peaceful Mohammedans in Penang on account of the frequent collisions which took place between the two factions of the red and the white flags, the followers of two noted Sayids of Acheen Street and Jelutong respectively, who had formed secret societies in imitation of and in conjunction with the Chinese. But of recent years this unruly element has died and only an echo remains in an occasional piece of red or white cloth tied to a stick or some challenging allusion in the chorus of one of the troupes concerned".

This reference to two Sayids of Penang and their connection with the white and red flag societies and with the Boria should be noted, as we shall have occasion to refer to them again in Chapters XXIV, XXV, XXVI, XXVIII and XXX.

THE EVILS OF THE MODERN BORIA

The fourth and last published notice of the Boria is a booklet entitled *Boria dan Benchana-nya* ("The evils of the Boria") by Mohamed Yusoff bin Sultan Maidin, chief clerk in the Education Office, Penang, and himself a member of the Jawi-pekan community, which was published in 1922. A few important extracts from this booklet are given below and fuller extracts with supplementary notes appear in Appendix VI. The author is a bitter opponent of the Boria and wrote his booklet partly in reply to Hamilton's article (Appendix V) and thereby involved himself in an unwelcome controversy in Penang (noticed under Chapter XXX *infra*) which ended in a suit at law.

Mohd. Yusoff bin Maidin's object in publishing his attack was to have a stop put to what he stigmatises as an ignorant and degrading performance, which brings public contempt upon Penang Malays and the Mohamedan religion.

He gives it as his opinion that the Boria originated with the Indian criminals deported thither when Penang was a Penal settlement, in the following words:—

"Maka daripada lapaz[2] yang tersebot itu nyata-lah yang permainan *boria* atau *borai*[2] itu bukan permainan Melayu dan bukan permainan yang dimulakan oleh orang[2] Melayu, kerana lapaz[2] itu semua-nya bahasa Hindustani belaka: jika demikian nyata-lah permainan itu dari

---

Footnote.—(1) *See* Sale's *Translation of the Koran: Preliminary Discourse* page 116 and page 139 note (1). Also Herklots *op. cit.* page 139.

Footnote.—(2) Standing for a Hindustani word *Burai*, = evil, wickedness, mischief; from which he suggests the name boria may derive.

India asal-nya, dibawa oleh orang² yang kena buang dari India yang datang ka Pulau Penang pada masa Pulau Penang ini mula² dibuka oleh keraja'an Inggris: kerana pada masa itu Pulau Penang telah dijadikan "Penal Station" oleh keraja'an India, dan banyak orang² Bengali yang bersalah besar dihantarkan kesini........

Both the Indian criminal origin suggested herein and the Indian garrison origin of Haughton have been discussed above. The truth seems to be that the Boria partakes of the nature of both sources, but because the religious inspiration has long since departed, it draws its present-day strength solely from its developed and widespread political ramifications through the flag associations; and from its criminal coherence throughout Malaya under the banner of Tabut.

Mohamed Yusop who is admittedly biassed, emphasises the criminal origin throughout his booklet and includes two other interesting references to what may be Thug or at least criminal Hindu features in the Boria. These are:—

> The Mandi Kerbala;
> The Koli Kallen.

THE MANDI KERBALA

In reference to the "Mandi Kerbala" or finale of the Boria, which is a grotesque distortion of the throwing of the Taz'iah into water at the close of the Indian celebration, Hamilton *op. cit.* has:—

> "These nightly revels continue until the evening of the 10th Moharram when they are continued all night until the following morning. Then the jaded troupe wends its way to some previously selected pleasure-ground near a stream, where after a short "mandi" or cleansing, they devote themselves to the enjoyment of a well-spread table..... until they disperse homewards soon after noon, tired but supremely happy".

Mohamed Yusop has:—

> *Mandi Kerbala.*—Maka pada hari yang ka-sepuloh daripada bulan Muharam itu beridarlah sakelian ahli Boria ka-padang Kerbala kerana mandi tolak bala. Ada pun yang di-katakan padang Kerbala itu ialah kebun² China atau tepi² sungai; di-situlah mereka itu pergi mandi dan ayer yang mengalir itu berkuasa, konon, menghilangkan bala daripada sa-saorang. Maka pada pemandanganku tempat itu bukan-nya tempat menolak bala; ialah tempat mengambil bala, kerana di-situlah terbuka beberapa botol arak dan jin yang memabokkan sakelian ahli² Boria itu, dan di-situlah juga mereka berjudi sahingga hilang wang di-dalam pinggang masing², dan terkadang berkelahi pula sama sendiri-nya, berpechah-pechah kepala dan kena tangkap. Ada pun mandi Kerbala itu suatu pekerjaan yang tiada boleh tidak bagi ahli² Boria itu; jika siapa² tiada pergi di-katakan Boria bangsat.
>
> Maka ada pula satengah daripada mereka itu memakai "nada"¹ di-tangan-nya ia-itu gelang yang di-perbuat daripada benang bulu kambing dan benang perak, dan memakai kain kuning dan baju kuning saperti orang² Berahman; dan di-sangka-nya ia-itu suatu pekerjaan yang wajib di-jalankan. Pada tiap² tahun maka pada hari Kerbala itu pergilah mereka itu ka-tepi sungai kerana mandi tolak bala, dan di-situlah di-buang nada dan kain baju kuning itu, dan mandi bersintok limau. Dan di-sangka-nya ayer sungai itulah, konon, yang menghilangkan bala-nya. Maka hal ini tiada dapat aku mengerti dari manakah datang bala itu dan darimanakah tumboh aturan yang karot ini, dan apakah sebab mereka itu menyangkakan ayer sungai itu berkuasa pada menerimakan bala mereka itu. Maka pada pikiranku aturan ini suatu tiruan daripada ugama Hindu dan pakaian kuning itu pun aturan Hindu jua, kerana orang² Hindu lah yang selalu pergi mandi menolak bala di-tepi² sungei yang terutama sekali di Kashi suatu tempat di-dalam India selatan. Maka di-situlah berhimpun sakelian Hindu² pada tiap² tahun kerana mandi tolak bala. Maka di-sabelah utara India sakelian bangsa Berahman itu mandi selalu pergi tolak bala di-Sungai Gangga (Ganges) kerana di-sangka-nya sungai itu sungai yang bertuah dan banyak Sami turon mandi di-situ, dan sungai itu, konon, berkuasa pada menghilangkan penyakit manusia, dan menyuchikan sa-saorang daripada sial dan malang-nya. Barangkali aturan inilah yang di-tiru oleh ahli² Boria yang di-kasehi itu, dan perbuatan pada tiap² tahun.

The foregoing description suggests that the modern Malay observance of mandi Kerbala or the tenth day of the Moharram (*i.e.* the Ashura festival of Indian Shiahs)² is a hybridization of the following features referred to in Chapter XI:—

(1) The casting of the Taziah or Tabut (Ark of the Covenant) into water on the tenth day of the orthodox Shiah festival of the Moharram.

(2) The "cleansing from sin", implicit in the Akhiri Charhar observance in India.

(3) The ceremonial bathing which concludes the Durga-puja festival of Hindu India.

(4) The soma-drinking rites of the Hindu festival of Holi.

(5) By a light-hearted substitution, or use of metonymy, the Shiah Mohamedan celebration of the "tragedy of the field of *Kerbala* "(*i.e.* the death of Husein which means nothing to Malays) is adopted as an occasion to indulge in the Malay animistic rite of *tolak bala* or aversion of evil by propitiatory offerings and the sprinkling of holy water.

The river Kashi mentioned by Mohamed Yusoff is probably that tributary of the Ganges which joins it at Patna. This river is mentioned by Sleeman *op. cit.* as a sacred river of the Thugs and the boundary of their operations in Bengal. The appearance of the river in the present context suggests the persistence of Thug influence in the *Mandi Kerbala.*

Footnote.—(1) A bracelet, *see* Herklots' description of the Moharram Chapter XI *supra.*
Footnote.—(2) Wilkinson's dictionary (ed. 1932) gives:—
Ashura.—The celebration of the 10th Muharram. Historically the Hebrew Day of Atonement now associated with the fate of Husain. A passage in the *Bustan Salatin* says:—"On the tenth day of Muharram, the day of atonement, the Ark came to rest on Mount Judi" (*i.e.* Ararat).

In regard to the liquor drinking bemoaned by Mohamed Yusoff for which we have suggested a religious sanction in the *soma* rites of the Hindus, it is worthwhile noting that the month of Moharram is known among Malays as the month of the Ashura or *bulan sura* and among the religious the 10th day is observed as a fast when a broth made of egg, onion, maize etc., known as *bubur sura*, is partaken by the devout. This observance is a purely religious one and quite distinct from the orgies of the mandi Kerbala, which, to a pious Malay is a profanity; but the two observances may, nevertheless, derive from a common source.

It is interesting, too, to note in passing, those light links in the background of the *Mandi Kerbala* observance, which seem in the arcana of the Malay mind, to join the flood of Ararat (B.C. 4,200) with his own secret flag associations of to-day.

We have noted in Chapter I, among the Chinese, what appears to be a similar connection between a flood of antiquity and their secret societies of the present-day.

This connection seems to derive among Mohamedans from the Ararat area of diffusion of esoteric knowledge and among the Chinese from the Tibetan area. A common link may lie behind each. (*See* Introduction and Chapter X).

We must now pass to the second important feature of the modern Boria mentioned by Mohamed Yusoff.

THE KOLI KALLEN OR "FOWL-THIEVES' PERFORMANCE"

This feature of the Boria, does not appear to have been mentioned by any other writer on the subject but is of considerable importance from the criminal standpoint.

Mohamed Yusoff has (in translation) :—

> During the season of the Boria, which is performed at night during the ten nights, another performance is given in Penang during the daytime which is still more contemptible from its very name than the Boria, and which is known as the "Koli Kallen" or "Fowl thieves Performance".

The description of this feature by Mohamed Yusop is as follows:—

> Ada pun permainan Koli Kallen itu di-jalankan pada siang hari, ia-itu dalam antara satu hari bulan hingga sapuloh hari bulan Muharram juga; dan permainan itu lebeh kurang sama juga saperti Boria itu, tetapi terlebeh hina lagi, kerana nama permainan itu sudah sedia hina. Ada pun ma'ana "Koli Kallen" itu di-dalam bahasa Keling "penchuri ayam"; dan pakaian dan kelakuan orang² yang bermain itu pun sangat munasabah dengan nama permainan itu. Maka di-pakai-nya pakaian yang chemar² saperti orang² gila, dan di-tudong-nya muka-nya dengan sapu tangan yang berlobang berbetulan dengan mata-nya dan mulot-nya; dan pergilah mereka itu dari satu pintu ka-satu pintu meminta sedekah. Ada yang memberi lima puloh sen, ada yang memberi saringgit.

> *   *   *

> Dan apakah nyanyi-nya? Ia-lah lafaz² yang hina di-atas diri-nya dan di-atas ibu bapa-nya, di-sebut-nya dengan tiada mengerti ma'ana-nya. "Siapa sakelian anak Koli Kallen?": ma'ana-nya siapa sakelian anak penchuri ayam; Maka apabila di-lihat oleh China, Hindu, Nasrani dan orang² Puteh. akan kelakuan orang² Melayu demikian, apakah ingatan-nya apabila tertawa ia gelak² melihat kumpolan orang² gila itu? Tiadakah kita mengerti lagi yang mereka itu menghinakan kita, dan tertawa mereka itu kerana kebodohan kita? Dengan sebab perbuatan satu pehak daripada kaum Melayu, sakelian orang² Islam nampak hina pada pemandangan dan timbangan bangsa² yang lain². Maka apabila di-sebut lafaz Melayu itu, terlintaslah segala sifat² kehinaan itu di-dalam pikiran bangsa² yang lain² itu. Ada pula satengah-nya memakai pakaian perempuan, dan menari saperti ronggeng, dan berjalan sapanjang jalan raya dengan berkelubong dan berkain batek dan kebaya renda dan bergelang berantai dan berkeronsang. Subahana-allah, hai Melayu! Adakah kamu pernah melihat bangsa² lain melakukan pekerja-an yang bodoh saperti ini? Sayugia-nya hendaklah kamu buangkan segala perangai dan kelakuan yang chemar² itu, dan- tirukan segala aturan dan jalanan bangsa² lain yang telah mendapat kemajuan, supaya kaum Melayu pun dapat melangkah kamedan tamaddun.[1]

The main features of "the koli kallen" as noted above are:—

(1) It is performed during the daytime of the ten days of the boria season, whereas the Boria troupes proper, perform only at night.

(2) The troupes wear dirty clothes and cover their faces with cloth masks, with holes cut for eyes and mouth.

(3) They chant nonsensical words, such as "who are the children of koli kallen?" meaning, according to Mohd. Yusoff:—

> "Who are the children of fowl thieves?"

(4) Some of those taking part dress as women, and wear anklets and other jewellery.

Examining these features more closely we find:—

(1) The first point suggests that the performance and therefore its origin is something distinct from the Boria, which we have seen derives from the Moharram—if it were not something different, there would be no occasion to make separate mention of it.

(2) The second point suggests at once the fancy dress of the *Khodun garun*, or "diggers and buriers", one of the groups of faqirs mentioned in the Herklots' description of the Moharram (Chapter XI.)

(3) The third feature is evidently intended to be in praise of crime and also suggests the "gibberish" or foolish chatter of the Bhar-bhariya.

Footnote.—(1) Transl: = "and so enter the realms of culture".

(4) The fourth feature introduces a sex factor absent from the Moharram festival, but present in the Durga-puja or Kali festival of Hinduism, which was also the chief festival of the Thugs.

Taken together, the four features suggest the survival from the nineteenth century of the Thug criminal tradition in the boria season, as a separate and distinct episode—and also a separate source of revenue—from the Boria performance itself.

EXAMINATION OF THE NAME KOLI KALLEN

But there is a further reason for thinking that the koli kallen may have a separate Thug derivation, allied with the Moharram festival, but distinct from the Boria. This is to be found in the derivation of the name itself.

Mohd. Yusoff in the passage above says the name comes from the two Tamil words *koli* a fowl, and *kallen* a thief.[1] We think that this derivation is probably an error. The influx of Tamils into Penang and Malaya generally, in sufficient numbers for their language to find its way into the Boria performance, dates only from the rise of the rubber industry in the present century.

It seems much more probable that in common with the Boria performance as a whole, the term "koli kallen" is of Hindustani origin and derives from the Moharram festival. We suggest that the name is a corruption of *"Khodun Garun"*—The diggers and buriers of the Herklots' description. The transition of the name may be not so much a corruption as a conscious or unconscious paronym.

This view is strengthened by the fact noted above, that the fancy dress of the Khodun Garun as described by Herklots, corresponds with that of the koli kallen as described by Mohd. Yusoff.

The suggestion of criminal origin in Mohd. Yusoff's term "The fowl thieves", is also sustained in the derivation from the Khodun Garun group of the Moharram, whose chant "I throw down and bury whom I please", has a distinctly Thuggist flavour. It is probable too, that we have in Mohd. Yusoff's derivation, the origin of that character hitherto so persistently applied by informed opinion, both to the Red and White Flag societies themselves, and to their "mutual benefit" branches among Kampong Malays—namely, that they are of no importance, being merely "kongsi churi ayam".

It is probably among the growing number of Jawi-pekans, that we should seek the cause of the slow seduction of the pure-bred Malays from their earlier attitude of contemptuous aloofness from the Moharram,—which was after all a religious festival of their own faith—to their ultimate support of and participation in the later Boria, the bastard offspring of an alliance between Indo-Malay and Chinese secret societies which had, not a religious but a criminal origin.

The form which the Boria took namely, of bands of strolling players singing topical songs during the first ten days of the new (lunar) year, for such profit as they could make, in substitution of the groups or troupes of mourners in the Moharram procession, was probably influenced to some extent by a similar existing practice among the Hokkiens prior to the Chinese Revolution of 1912 of which Doolittle in *Social life of the Chinese* (1866) Vol. II page 28, writing of Foochow at that time has:—

> Bands of musicians and play-actors are very busy during the first half of the first month. In mandarin establishments and in temples of the neighbourhood (Foochow), there is a vast amount of theatricals performed in this interval. Between the first and the fifteenth it is common for bands of music to call on respectable and wealthy families in the day time and if their services are not promptly declined, commence playing. After playing three times they stop and expect to receive a present of money. The amount given is voluntary and optional. These players come professedly to present their congratulations to the families they visit, on the arrival of another new year.

Evidence will be offered in a later chapter to show the extent of present-day Chinese interest in the organisation of Boria troupes in connection with secret society matters; and we may at least assume that the existence of a practice in Foochow similar to the Boria may have made the Hokkiens of Penang predisposed to look with favour upon a similar custom among the Indians and Malays of their adoptive country; and may have made easier those alliances for offensive, defensive and mutual benefit purposes, between secret societies of both races in Penang which we examine in greater detail in Chapters XIV and XV.

THE MOHARRAM FESTIVAL ELSEWHERE IN THE COLONIAL EMPIRE

Before leaving this aspect of our subject it is of interest to note that by a process not unlike that in Malaya, the Moharram festival is also found in a more or less distorted form elsewhere in the Colonial Empire. We will mention only Ceylon and the British West Indies.

Footnote.—(1) This is "dog-Tamil". *Koli* means a fowl, but *kallen* is the name of a criminal tribe of Tamils who are thieves by profession. The usual Tamil word for "thief" is *thiruden*: nevertheless among the mixed population of Penang the expression *koli kallen* can, no doubt, convey the meaning of "fowl thief".

"HOBSON-JOBSON" IN CEYLON

Sir Herbert Dowbiggin, former Inspector-General of Police Ceylon writes (1938) :—

In Ceylon Hobson-Jobson is celebrated as an annual festival. A fire-pit is always provided at the same place each year and the enthusiasts run over the hot embers with bare feet.[1]

In Ceylon Hobson-Jobson has no religious or political significance. It is just a happy occasion. Reference is made to young men dressing up and acting as tigers in the Moharram festival in Malaya. This is a notable feature of Hobson-Jobson in Ceylon.

The description of the transition stage of the Boria in Penang from a religious festival to a hooligan masquerade exactly describes Hobson-Jobson as carried out in Ceylon. It is interesting to note that the Malays in Ceylon are the descendants of those Malays who came to Ceylon to join the old Ceylon Rifle Regiment which was disbanded in 1865...... The Malays in the old Rifle Regiment joined the Police and it is the descendants of these men who have kept Hobson-Jobson alive in Ceylon. The Malays who came to Ceylon must have brought this custom with them.

This interesting note shows that the Moharram festival of Shiah India reached Buddhist Ceylon during the nineteenth century by way of Sunni Malaya.

The Moharram also travelled to the west direct from India during the same or an earlier epoch, as already noted in an extract from Yule (page 182 Chapter XI above).

TABUT IN THE BRITISH WEST INDIES AND BRITISH GUIANA

As a result of its westward passage we also find a distorted form of the Moharram of India mixed with other features firmly established in the West Indies of to-day.

In explanation of the form the celebration has taken there, it is desirable briefly to survey the racial elements of those dependencies, among whom it has taken root. The following facts are based on information taken from MacMillan *Warning from the West Indies* (1936) and refer to Jamaica and Trinidad only.

In Jamaica, which has a population of about one million, the preponderance of the African community (77 per cent.) eliminates from consideration the influence of its Indian[2] settlers who are but 3 per cent. Jamaican *mores* are therefore based upon the arcana of African voodooism, while the propinquity of Jamaica to the island of Haiti and San Domingo where voodooism flourishes, emphasises this characteristic and leaves no room for the development of purely Indian religious influences.

In Trinidad, with a population of some 380,000, the percentages of racial division are to-day roughly, African 40, Indian 36, Mixed (Creole) 20 and White 4, and in consequence the Shiah Mohamedan and Hindu influence imported by East Indian labourers, traders and settlers in the eighteenth century has not been swamped, but has developed side by side with the African which, by comparison with Jamaica, it has tended to absorb. Similar racial conditions to those of Trinidad appear to have developed in British Guiana, and to have resulted in the establishment in both territories of well-defined Hindu and Mohamedan annual festivals of a debased kind, but both clearly derived from the Durga-puja and Holi festivals of Hinduism, and the Shiah Mohammedan festival of the Moharram, respectively. In addition, the Christian festival of Shrove Tuesday has also become established in the two chief towns of Trinidad and has appropriated to itself features borrowed, no doubt, from the Moharram, which give it a character to-day oddly akin to that of the Boria of Penang. The following description of these three festivals as observed in the West Indies to-day, for which we are indebted to Mr. A. de K. Frampton of the Malayan Agricultural Department, apply, therefore, to Trinidad and British Guiana alone.

In the British West Indies particularly in Trinidad and British Guiana (Demerara) three annual festivals are observed by the native population. These are known locally as:—

    (1) The Puja.

    (2) The Taja or Hassan Hussein.

    (3) Carnival (observed only in Trinidad).

The chief features of each are as follows:—

    (1) The Puja is a solar festival observed only by the Hindu section of the community.[3]

    (2) The Taja or Hassan Hussein is a lunar festival of the Mohamedans observed during the first ten days of the Mohamedan New Year and is identical with the Moharram festival of India. But whereas in India the religious significance remains uppermost, in the West Indies the devout section of the orthodox Shiah Mohamedan community remains entirely aloof from the celebrations, which are regarded by them as a sacriligious orgy.

    In the West Indies, the festival is called a "rum-spree" and in addition to the dregs of the Mohamedan community, the chief body of those taking part are the Hindu and mixed African (Negro) population, together with the indigenous Christian labouring classes, who all make high holiday together, accompanied by much drinking and jollification. The celebration is chiefly confined to the agricultural labouring classes, the towns-people taking little part in it. It is usual in prosperous times for the employers of estate labour to make a grant from estate funds towards the cost of the estate "taja". The "taja" from which the festival takes its name is a large bamboo and paper pagoda and the name is doubtless a corruption of

Footnote.—(1) This suggests a hybridization of the festival in Ceylon with Hindu rites.

Footnote.—(2) In this section "Indian" means British Indian or East Indian from Continental India: and must not be confused with Red or other "Indian" influence from America.

Footnote.—(3) From its description it is identical with the Holi festival of India (*see* Chapter X).

the word "taziah". These "taja" sometimes reach a height of thirty feet and are constructed upon a rectangular earthen base in the rough shape of a recumbent human figure.[1]

Groups of "worshippers" from the various labour forces follow each estate "taja" which is carried in procession towards the villages. These groups "dress up" much as in the orthodox form of the procession in India as described by Herklots, and "mourn" the death of Hassan and Hussein with singing and chanting. Numbers of them carry short staves and engage in fencing across fire and in stick fighting with rival processionists in which old scores are paid off. There is drinking, mumming and quarelling among the various groups in the processions and on the last day of the festival the "taja" is carried to some nearby water's edge usually the sea shore and is then cast into the water.

Police permits are required for these processions and an authorised route prescribed. Permits are only issued against letters from responsible persons, such as estate managers, recommending the applicants.

The whole observance in the West Indies seems to present a fairly close reproduction of the festival as existing in India to-day.

(3) The Carnival is a solar festival of the Christian community and is held on the Monday and Tuesday preceding Ash Wednesday and its observance is almost exclusively confined to the townspeople of Port of Spain and San Fernando in Trinidad. Its origin is doubtless to be found in the Carnival of Southern Europe imported by the French in the eighteenth century and its observance in the West Indies resembles the "Mardi Gras" celebrations in the South of France at the present-day. Although a supposedly exclusive Christian vernal festival all communities including Europeans participate in it in Trinidad where it is enthusiastically observed as a free-for-all revel. Troupes of singers and musicians in fancy-dress, many of them European troupes, compete for prizes given for the most attractive turn-out and form processions of decorated lorries circumambulating the town and singing comic topical verses composed each year for the occasion. These verses are sung to well-known and long established tunes which have a peculiar African rythm and the verses themselves refer to topical subjects such as the merits of a departing Governor, the unpopularity of some recent restriction or the sins of the Inspector-General of Police. The troupes taking part in costume represent such groups as the "Dancing Dolls": "Chinese bandits": "the Foreign Legion" and such like, and as they pass by in lorries they throw confetti and coloured streamers at the crowd while singing to the strains of a four stringed guitar (quarto). They are known as the Calypso Singers, the origin of the name being perhaps a corruption of a Spanish name for the festival.

In the streets large crowds of all communities walk in procession singing, drinking and dancing. They all wear masks and many carry sticks which provide opportunity for working off old scores and large scale disturbances often result. The verses proposed to be sung at the festival are first subjected to a Police censorship to prevent obscenity and scurrility but even so the season is a heavy tax upon Police resources.

THE EUROPEAN CARNIVAL[2]

Fraser *Golden Bough* (abridged edition) pages 301–307, describes the meaning of the European observance and says on page 586:—

> The resemblance between the Saturnalia of ancient and the Carnival of modern Italy has often been remarked: but in the light of all the facts that have come before us, we may well ask whether the resemblance does not amount to identity...... If the view here suggested of the Carnival is correct, this grotesque personage is no other than a direct successor of the old King of the Saturnalia, the Master of the revels, the real man who personated Saturn (the God of the sown and sprouting seed) and, when the revels were over, suffered a real death in his assumed character. The King of the Bean in Twelfth Night, and the mediaeval Bishop of Fools, Abbott of Unreason, or Lord of Misrule, are figures of the same sort and may have had a similar origin.

Again, Grant Allen *The Evolution of the Idea of God* (1931 edition) page 294 has:—

> Nor can I resist a passing mention of the Moharram festival, which is said to be the commemoration of the death of Hosein, son of Ali...... This is a rude piece of acting...... and it ends with a sacred Adonis-like or Osiris-like procession, in which the body of the saint is carried and mourned over...... In Bombay after the dead body and shrine have been carried through the streets amid weeping and wailing they are finally thrown into the sea, like King Carnival. I think we need hardly doubt that here we have an evanescent relic of the rites of the corn-god, ending in a rain charm, and very closely resembling those of Adonis and Osiris.

We have seen (Chapter XI) a similar comparison drawn in Pelly's description of the Moharram festival in India. Having regard to the fact that Judaism, Christianity and Islam belong to the same stem of revealed religions and, therefore, possess identical arcana of belief, the similarities are not so far-fetched as might at first appear.

Footnote.—(1) This practice is not referred to by Herklots (Chapter XI) as belonging to the Moharram, and is doubtless an importation from elsewhere *cf.* the secret initiation ceremony of the Bora among Australian bushmen described by Ward *Freemasonry and the Ancient Gods*, page 354 and also Ward and Stirling *The Hung Society*, Vol. I page 56, footnote 2.

Footnote.—(2) *Chambers Encyclopaedia* gives the derivation of the name from the Italian *Carnevale* (or late Latin *Carne Levamen*) ="a solace of the flesh"; which it says has been incorrectly explained as meaning "farewell to flesh" and adds:—

> Without doubt the forms and customs still preserved in the celebration of the Carnival originated in the heathen festivals of spring-time and they still remind us of the Lupercalia and Bacchanalia of southern Europe.

The Encyclopaedia Britannica gives the derivation of the name from *Carnem levare*="to remove flesh", which it says is altered in Italian to *Carnem vale*="flesh farewell".

If the Carnival of Trinidad be of Spanish origin, rather than a French importation, the Mohamedan occupation of Spain in the eighth century, and the Spanish occupation of the West Indies in the sixteenth and seventeenth centuries may have left the imprint of the Moharram upon it.

Penang not necessarily the home of the Boria

Apart from speculation upon its origin, the following points of interest emerge from the above description of the West Indies carnival *viz:*—

(1) The musical troupes and topical songs of the Trinidad carnival bear a close resemblance to those of the Penang Boria as given by Hamilton (Appendix V), with this difference, that whereas the Boria parties perform as part of the Hasan-Husein festival, this feature is transferred in Trinidad to the Calypso singers of the Carnival.

(2) Just as we have seen features of the Hindu vernal festival of Holi appear in the Penang celebration of the Moharram in the nineteenth century, so resemblances to its successor the Penang Boria, and even perhaps to the Saturnalia of Rome, appear in the Trinidad carnival of to-day.

(3) It is also disclosed that Penang is not necessarily the "home of the Boria" as claimed by Hamilton, but that the Boria under a different name appears to flourish with even greater freedom in the West Indies, and possibly elsewhere.

(4) The Taja festival in Trinidad is celebrated by Mohamedans, Hindus, Negroes and others, but it is probable that the imported criminal element present in Penang, from the special causes explained above, is absent in the West Indies. Despite the catholicism of the celebration in Trinidad we learn that there the orthodox Shiah Mohamedans paradoxically remain aloof, and that it is the dregs of the population that take part, a term which, no doubt, includes a considerable criminal element.

(5) This circumstance may account for the incidence of riots which have occurred as noted by Yule, but there is nothing in the festival itself to provoke rioting in the absence of those underground forces which we have noted as being present in Penang. This raises the interesting speculation whether or not like conditions due to the same or variant causes, might not exist in the West Indies, unknown to the authorities, and even perhaps in other parts of the Empire, whereby local crime, riots and political differences might be found to be fostered under the same debased religious cloak. The severe labour riots in Trinidad in 1937 might perhaps have had a focal point of organisation in undersurface fraternities similar to those of Penang and feeding from a like source which MacMunn has described as "some ancient horror, existing beneath the outer surface of perfectly reasonable political aspirations".

If absent in Trinidad this "ancient horror" is certainly present in a social and religious if not in a political form in Jamaica as readers of Miss Z. Hurston's *Voodoo Gods* (1938) will understand. What influence, if any, upon the labour troubles in Jamaica of 1935–1937 this ancient horror may have had, we are unable to say.

We resume in Chapter XXX *infra* the investigation of the Penang Boria in its modern setting and disclose therein the link between its annual observance and the persistence of the flag associations under its colour protection.

We must now turn to an examination of the emergence and counter-play of the Penang fraternities upon the early nineteenth century political stage in Siam and Kedah.

For convenience in the following chapter we shall refer to the two Chinese fraternities of Han and Hung, by the single generic name Triad; and the two Indo-Malay Red and White Flag associations by the generic name of Tabut unless, by the context, a more restricted meaning is obviously intended.

CHAPTER XIII

POLITICAL INTRIGUES OF TRIAD AND TABUT IN SIAM,
KEDAH AND PENANG A.D. 1767–1850

The early history of Penang is bound up with that of Siam[1] and Kedah. Some of the undercurrents of this early period have already been touched upon in Chapters IV (historical) and V (political) and we have now to examine afresh the course of those undercurrents, with particular reference to Siamese and Kedah history, in order to expose to view as far as the available records allow, the share of Triad and Tabut in the political intrigues of the period. We must also examine the political development of what may have been the germinal rudiments of the White and Red Flag societies among the Malays of Penang, which have survived up to the present-day, camouflaged as social clubs, football associations and the like, and which furnish an annual proof of their survival under the colour-protection of the Penang Boria.

CHINESE INFLUENCE IN SIAM 1767–1850

A glance at Sino-Siamese relations north of Kedah at the beginning of the nineteenth century, is necessary if we are to understand the probable undercurrents in the Kedah-Siamese war, 1821–1848, in which Penang and British policy were particularly interested.

The eighteenth and the first half of the nineteenth centuries saw continual warfare between Siam and the Burmese Kings of Ava and Pegu. (*See* Chapter IV).

The following facts of Siamese history are condensed from Sir John Bowring's *Kingdom and People of Siam* 2 Vols., published in 1857.

In 1766, the Burmese after besieging Juthia (Ayuthia) the old capital of Siam just north of Bangkok, for a period of two years, captured it and drove out the King of Siam who died an exile. That dynasty thereupon came to an end and an interregnum ensued.

In 1767, there arose a Siam-born Chinese war-lord named Pin Tat or Tia (? Chia) Sin Tat who took the Siamese name Phya Tak, or Tarksing. The history of this remarkable man, as recorded by Bowring *op. cit.* pages 349–362, is as follows (condensed) :—

> The first king of Siam established at the new capital of Bangkok was an extraordinary man of Chinese origin, named Pin Tat. He was called by the Chinese Tia Sin Tat, or Tuat. He was born at a village called Bantak in northern Siam, in March 1734. At the capture of Ayuthia by the Burmese in 1766, he was thirty-three years old. Previous to that time he had obtained the office of governor of his own town of Tak under the title of Phya Tak. During the reign of the last King of Ayuthia, he was promoted to the office of governor of the city of Kam-Chengphilet, which was the capital of the western province of Northern Siam. He obtained this office by bribery and was called to Ayuthia on the arrival of the Burman troops as a member of the Council. But when sent to resist the enemy, he, with his followers, fled to Chantaburi (Chantabun), a town on the eastern shore of the Gulf of Siam. There he united with many robbers and pirates and subsisted by robbing the villages and merchant-vessels. In this way he became the great military leader and had a force of more than ten thousand men.
> At the end of the year 1767, General Phya Tak loaded all the war-boats he had completed with the provisions of war, and sent a number of his troops with the boats across the gulf to the mouth of the river of Paknam, while he himself with ten thousand men went overland to Bangkok and usurped the throne with Bangkok as his capital.
> At the end of the year 1768, he was King of all southern Siam, and of the eastern province bordering on the Gulf.
> In 1772, the fourth year of his reign, Phya Tak made an expedition into the Malay Peninsula, with the design of taking possession of Lagor. In this province, the Governor appointed by the King of Ayuthia, when the Burmans were victorious had assumed the supremacy and declared himself King of Lagor, and his children—three princes and princesses. Many noblemen with their families had fled from Ayuthia and taken up their residence at Lagor, and other towns in the Malay peninsula. Though he had not failed frequently to hear of the achievements of Phya Tak, the King of Lagor felt his power sufficient for defence against Phya Tak, besides he was sure the Burmans would ere long return with redoubled force, and revenge themselves upon the usurpations of Phya Tak.
> When Phya Tak arrived with his navy and armed forces by land, the King of Lagor prepared for defence, but some became alienated from their king, and some were the spies of Phya Tak. The King of Lagor lost confidence in his power to oppose the invading army, left the city privately at night, and fled in haste to Patani, a town in the Malay Peninsula, on the western coast of the Gulf of Siam, and placed himself under the protection of his former friend, the Raja of Patani. When King Phya Tak learned this, he wrote to the Raja that if he did not give him up he would come with an armed force and lay the country of Patani waste.
> The Raja of Patani, immediately gave up the King of Lagor to the Siamese messengers, who took him prisoner to King Phya Tak. In the meantime Phya Tak had taken Lagor, captured the royal family, and many noblemen of high rank, with their property and servants; and a few days after the capture of the King of Lagor, returned to Bangkok with all his booty. The King of Lagor had a daughter to whom Phya Tak gave a place in his harem, and on her account saved the lives of all her family, allowing her father his freedom in the capital.

Footnote.—(1) In June, 1939, the Government of Siam changed the name of their country to Maung Thai, or in English Thailand. This is a reversion to a former ethnological name for the people of Siam. For comment upon the possible political significance of the change, *see* Chapter XXXIII *infra*.

At the end of three or four years, the daughter of the King of Lagor presented King Phya Tak with a son. Phya Tak was delighted, declaring that an heir to the throne of Lagor was born. Fearing no longer that the King of Lagor would wish to avenge his former enemies, he allowed him to return to Lagor, restored to him his former office and gave up to him all the captives he had taken from the country. This was in the year 1776. From that time to the present, the government of Lagor has been administered by the descendants of the King of Lagor taken captive by Phya Tak; and through the power of this province, fifteen or sixteen townships of the Malay country have been made subject to the Siamese King, among which are Kedah, Patani, Kalantan and Tringano.

After reconquering Siam from the Burmese and making himself King of the whole of Siam, Phya Tak was attacked with insanity, became unpopular and was murdered in 1782. He was succeeded by one of his Siamese Generals who reigned from 1782 to 1811 and founded the present dynasty and whose son reigned from 1811–1825.

The following sketch taken from a map in Bowring Vol. II illustrates the territorial divisions of the northern section of the Malay Peninsula about 1850 and shows the communications towards Kedah and Junk Ceylon:—

LIGOR AND QUEDAH
1850

———————— HIGHWAYS

–·—·—·— STATE BOUNDARIES

Bowring *op. cit.* Vol. II page 49 has the following note upon *Ligor*,[1] as it was in the first half of the nineteenth century:—

> The true name of the district of Ligor (called by the Siamese, Muang Lakhon or the Lakhon Kingdom) is according to Pallegoix *Nakhon si Thamarat.* It was founded by the King of Ayuthia (ancient Siam) about four centuries and a half ago. It had two dependencies, Thalung and Songkhla, governed by relatives of the King of Ligor. There have been frequent but unsuccessful attempts to detach the kingdom from its dependence upon Siam, but at the present time (1855) intimate alliances between the King's family and that of the most influential nobles of Siam will serve to cement the friendly relations of the two countries.
>
> Ligor has 150,000 inhabitants of whom three fourths are Siamese: the rest consist of Chinese, Malays and some of the aboriginal races.........

And the following note on Patani (*op. cit.* Vol. II page 48):—

> *Patani* or Thani is another of the dependencies of Siam. It has a population of about 100,000 of whom more than half are of the Siamese race...... The province was formerly altogether in the hands of the Malays and revolted against the Siamese, who conquered the inhabitants and carried away the majority of them into slavery.

Writing of Siam's relations with China in 1850, Bowring has the following (*op. cit.* Vol. I page 4):—

> Siam itself pays tribute to China: the King of Siam seeks from the Emperor at Peking, a special recognition of his right to reign. He sends every three years his envoy to the Chinese capital. There is no doubt that the Siamese receive in remission of duties upon the cargoes of the tribute-bearing ships, more than an equivalent for the tribute they bear and the Government of China in no respect interferes with that of Siam, nor do the Chinese in Siam enjoy any other privileges and advantages than those which result from their superior industry, activity, aptitude for business, perseverance and capital. Yet the external forms of vassalage continue to be observed rather out of reverence for ancient traditions and usages, than from any power which China possesses to enforce the rights of sovereignty, or any disposition on the part of Siam practically to submit to them.

Bowring *op. cit.* Vol. I Chapter VIII gives an account of the junk trade between Siam and China, chiefly between Kwangtung and Fukkien ports, as in the case of the Straits Settlements. In Vol. II pages 140–200 he makes frequent reference to the presence of Malays (Moormen) at the Bangkok Court during the mission of Mr. Crawford (1822): and on page 249 ff., he refers to the prominence of Cantonese and Hokkiens in the life of Bangkok: again on page 394 he gives the following figures for estimated population of Bangkok (1855): Chinese 200,000, Siamese 120,000, Malays 15,000, others 70,000.

THE FLAG OF SIAM

Finally, in Vol. I page 478 Bowring has:—

> Each division of the army has its silk or cloth banner, generally decorated with lions, dragons or fabulous monsters. The royal flag has a white elephant on a scarlet ground, surrounded by a white edge.

ESTIMATE OF TRIAD INFLUENCE IN SIAM 1800–1850

At the time of the rise of the Chinese General Phya Tak 1767–1782, who was a freebooter before he was a king, the Triad society was very active in China (*see* Chapter I) and was already well established in the "south seas" and in Siam (*see* Chapter V). Bowring *op. cit.* Vol. I page 81, says that in 1850 the computed population of Siam was 6,000,000, of whom 2,000,000 were pure Siamese, 1,500,000 were Chinese, 1,000,000 Malays, etc. This provides a formidable body of material for the activities of the Triad society. In contemplating the opportunities for Triad expansion in Siam we have to remember that there was a Chinese King of Siam in the person of Phya Tak about the time of the foundation of Penang; that at that epoch Triad influence was strong at "Junk Ceylon"; that Siam was herself nominally a vassal state of China and sent triennial tribute to the Emperor; that Siam maintained close commercial and cultural ties with South China; and that there was in 1825 a half-Chinese "Raja" of Ligor with a Chinese Prime Minister (Chapter V). From these considerations we may reasonably assume that Siam was much more heavily infected with Triad influence at the beginning of the nineteenth century, than even Malaya had become by 1850, for the reason that the process had been going on longer, the numbers and opportunities were greater, the conditions more favourable and the opposition seemingly less.

We may, therefore, ask: how have the Siamese prevented the Chinese from assuming a dominant role in Siam and usurping political power through secret society influence? Bowring *op. cit.* Vol. I pages 86–87 answers this question thus:—

> The Siamese have managed to keep the Chinese in tolerable subjection though not without serious controversies and tumults. The insurrection which took place in the year 1847 had its origin in the imposition of a new tax...... (Two Siamese provincial Governors were beheaded by the Chinese insurgents and a fort seized, before they were subjugated). It was supposed that a general rising of the Chinese was intended and it is very doubtful whether the Siamese Government could have maintained itself against any extensive combination.

Footnote.—(1) The alternative spelling of Lagor.

One may be permitted to speculate how far Triad and "Tokong" intrigue had worked its way into the provincial governments of Siam by 1850. It is not too much to suppose that in outlying provinces with a large Chinese population there must have arisen something like an alliance between the local government and the Chinese secret societies, to enable the government to exist.

The view we have formed upon this subject is, that evidently from the first influx of Chinese to the south seas, Siam became and has remained a stronghold of Triad and is a country in which "Tokong" has never gained much foothold. The trend of the evidence already given in Chapter V (pages 71–74, 76 and 78 *supra*) supports this view and all the evidence which will appear at random upon the subject in this and subsequent chapters will, we think, also sustain it. We give here three specific examples:—

(a) Kok Chai, a prominent Chinese of Penang about 1840, (whom we identify in the Selangor section of Chapter XXI *infra* as a head of Triad), was employed by the Raja of Ligor in Penang during the period of the Kedah-Siam war 1821–1848.

Thomson *Glimpses into life in the Far East*, gives an account of this man in which he says:—

> His father had been a leading merchant in the early days of the settlement. This Kok Chai was then (1840) agent in Penang for the Siamese Government and a man of consequence among the Kedah Malays and Siamese, the latter treating him with the greatest respect.

(b) Tan Kim Ching a Singapore-born Hokkien of wealth and influence (*aet.* 1829–1892) whom we identify in a later chapter as the head for many years of Triad in Malaya, maintained throughout his career close official relations with Siam.

Song Ong Siang *One hundred years of the Chinese of Singapore*, (1923) says of him, page 92:—

> Mr. Tan Kim Ching was Consul-General and Special Commissioner for Siam in the Straits Settlements and had the title of Phya Anukul Siamkitch Upanick Sit Siam Rath conferred upon him by the King of Siam. He had great influence on the Chinese outside the Colony, especially in the northern States bordering on Siam, *viz.*, Kelantan, and Patani. In Sir Andrew Clarke's time he was instrumental in settling a difficulty which had arisen between the Siamese government and Perak, for which he received a special letter of thanks from the Governor.

We shall see in succeeding chapters the great political influence wielded by this man on behalf of Triad in Malayan affairs.

(c) Schlegel *op. cit.* page 51 gives a form of circular letter used in Siam for calling a meeting of the Triad society lodge in that country (暹 羅 國 開 香 帖 式).

From this we are entitled to infer that Triad must have held a recognised and predominant place among the Chinese of Siam in 1860.

SPECULATION UPON MODERN SECRET SOCIETY TRENDS IN NEIGHBOURING COUNTRIES

It is not out of place to mention here that if Siam appears to have always been a Triad enclave, perhaps because King Phya Tak was himself a Triad member, the trend of the evidence in subsequent chapters will suggest that both French Indo-China and Burma were and have remained strongholds of "Tokong". This point may be of some importance in explaining modern political trends in these countries.

For example, in Chapter XXXIV *infra*, we identify Japanese secret societies radically with the "Tokong" group, whose historical antagonism to foreigners and to western missions in China has been mentioned in Chapter II under "The Boxers" pages 34–36) and Chapter IV (pages 64–66). This characteristic has been mirrored in the history of French Indo-China during the same period, and is again showing its face under Japanese direction to-day. Again, evidence of the existence of the Malayan Red Flag society in Burma will come to notice later.

In referring to the hypnotic arts of "Tokong" as practised by the Boxers and their claim to render themselves invulnerable thereby,—also employed against the French in Indo-China—Sir H. L. Dowbiggin remarks "This is typical of the last Burma rebellion 1932–1934.

What connection, if any, there may be between the Burma rebellion and the Red Flag society of Malaya in Burma, we are, of course, unable to say, but the fact of the existence of "Tokong" and Red Flag influence in Burma, side by side with a highly organised rebellion against a foreign government, using "boxer arts" and lasting for a period of two years, suggests that there may have been one.

The only feature that conflicts with this view is that Burma is Buddhist which we associate throughout with Triad. The explanation may be found in the Red cap school of Buddhism referred to on page 40 *supra*.

As regards Malaya and the Netherlands Indies the balance of underground power as between Triad and "Tokong" seems to have been from the first fairly evenly maintained.

Evidence will be offered to show that in Malaya certain towns and areas have at one time or another been claimed as the exclusive sphere of influence of one or the other camp, but at no time does this influence appear to have extended to a whole state or settlement.

The following map illustrates what seems to us to be the distribution of preponderating Triad and "Tokong" influences in the South Seas, namely:—

1. *Triad dominant.*—(1) Kwangtung, (2) Siam.
2. *Tokong dominant.*—(1) Szechuan, (2) Yunnan, (3) Annam (French-Indo-China), (4) Burma.
3. *Triad and Tokong influence fairly evenly diffused.*—(1) Fokien, (2) Kwangsi, (3) Hongkong, (4) Junk Ceylon, (5) Malaya, (6) the Netherlands Indies.

THE "SOUTH SEAS"
to illustrate
the distribution of
TRIAD AND "TOKONG"
influence,
A.D. 1768–1850.

Lastly, we have the evidence of recent (1939) events in Siam whereby pressure has been put upon Chinese "secret societies" (unspecified) by the Siamese government, the nature of which is not known. Enough has appeared in the press, however, to suggest that the political stronghold of Triad (K.M.T.) in Siam is being attacked indirectly by the forces of "Tokong" or the "puppet" regime in north China, through pressure applied by the Japanese upon the Siamese, to break the Triad link.

This stratagem seems to involve application of the "Han ethic" discussed in Chapter II (page 33) to social and racial conditions in Siam, a policy better known to-day by its modern political label of "Pan-asianism".

This digression is of interest only to show the probable nature and degree of Chinese secret society influence in southern Siam in 1821, when the Raja of Ligor invaded Kedah, and to suggest that Triad has remained paramount in Siam since then, until attacked to-day by its age old rival "Tokong".

The evidence in subsequent chapters, fragmentary and inconclusive though it is, will we think, generally support this view.

THE EARLY POLITICAL HISTORY OF PENANG.

To keep in perspective the course of events which we have now to describe, it will be well to record the successive increases of population which took place at Penang down to 1867 and to note the composition by race and ratio of this population.

In 1788, the population of Penang Island was about 1,000 of whom almost all were Malay fishermen and pirates.

In 1804, the population had risen to 12,000 among whom Malays, chiefly from the mainland (Province Wellesley), predominated (6,000), then Indians, chiefly Mohammedan traders known as Chulias[1] (4,000), then Chinese about (2,000).

Footnote.—(1) On this word which is included in Wilkinson's dictionary (1932 ed.). Yule *Hobson-Jobson* page 159 has:—
  CHOOLIA. A name given in Ceylon and in Malabar to a particular class of Mahommedans and sometimes to Mahommedans generally. There is much obscurity about the origin and proper application of the term. According to Sonnerat, the Chulias are of Arab descent and of Shiah profession of faith.

By 1820, the population of Penang had increased to 35,000, consisting of 12,000 Malays, 9,000 Indians, 8,000 Chinese and 6,000 "others".

The increase in trade attracted the pirates who became a serious menace about this time in the Straits of Malacca. Mills *op. cit.* (page 222) states:—

> Penang received annual attention (from pirates) from the date of its foundation, and the pirates built villages on the neighbouring islands, and in Kedah and Perak. Penang's trade suffered severely and in 1826 raids were still frequently made into the harbour at night to capture prisoners (slaves) for sale at Galang. As late as 1830, the pirate squadrons on their return home from their annual cruise were accustomed to sail through the middle of the harbour between Penang Island and Province Wellesley as it saved them the trouble of rowing around the Island.

The population of Penang in 1830 still numbered about 35,000 of whom 10,000 were Chinese and the remainder being Malays 12,000; Indians 9,000; Europeans 1,800; "others" 2,200. In Province Wellesley, the population had increased from 6,000 in 1820 (of whom 5,500 were Malays and 250 each Indians and Chinese) to about 40,000 in 1830, of whom 35,000 were Malays, 2,000 Chinese, 1,000 Indians and 2,000 "others".[1]

THE "KAPITAN" SYSTEM

About this time (1804) Penang's population is described by the Penang Magistrate, Dickens, in *Notices of Penang J.I.A.* as composed of:—

> British subjects: Foreigners both European and American: People of colour descended from European fathers and Asiatic mothers (Eurasians): Armenians: Parsees: Arabs: Chulias (Mohammedan Indians from Madras): Malays from the Peninsula, Sumatra and the Eastern Islands (N.E.I.): Buggis from Borneo, Celebes and other Islands of the China Seas: Burmese from Pegu: Siamese: Javanese: Chinese: with Mussulmans and Hindoos from the Company's territories in India.

A serious problem soon arose owing to the absence in the Island of any legally established criminal code or courts of law.

Petty civil cases were tried by the "Kapitans" of the Chinese, Malays and Chulias. *These "Kapitans" were prominent natives of each community appointed by the Penang Government (then under the East India Company) to assist in maintaining law and order among their own countrymen.* The more serious cases, civil and criminal, were tried by the Superintendent or his Assistants. The office of Superintendent was shortly afterwards raised to the status of Lieutenant-Governor.

In 1807, for the first time a Recorder's Court was established by the Company for the disposal of both civil and criminal cases according to the law of England.

It should here be particularly noted that in the early days of Penang, government through the system of "Kapitans" was not confined to the Chinese, but there were also "Kapitans" appointed by the Government over the Malay and "Chulia" communities.

This system would naturally bring the leaders of each community into contact with one another, if only through similarity of appointment and, therefore, similarity of interest.

We may take it for granted that all or most of the Chinese "Kapitans" so appointed were the heads of Triad and "Tokong" of that day; they could not have held their positions if they were not, and, as will appear later, they have so continued to be, up to recent times.

It is easy to imagine that the Malay and Indian "Kapitans", who saw the numerically inferior Chinese so well organised under the temples of the Triad and "Tokong" lodges, much to the advantage of their Chinese "Kapitans", set about imitating them, a process which first centered round the mosques in different parts of the town, and later developed into secret societies using as we shall see a truncated Triad or "Tokong" initiation ceremony, with headquarters in separate premises camouflaged as "mutual benefit societies" and, since 1890, as football clubs and such-like.

It may well be, that in the old "Kapitan" system there is to be found a social nucleus and political pre-disposing cause for the formation of secret societies among the Malay and Indian communities, to enable them to keep abreast of the ready made Chinese secret fraternities of Triad and "Tokong".

Footnote.—(1) By 1860, the population position was roughly as follows:—

Settlement	Europeans	Malays	Indians	Chinese	Others	Total
Penang	2,000	19,000	10,000	28,000	1,000	60,000
Province Wellesley	100	52,000	3,500	8,500	900	65,000
Total ..	2,100	71,000	13,500	36,500	1,900	125,000

The religious and criminal pre-disposing causes we have discussed in Chapters X and XII.

THE KEDAH-SIAMESE WAR OF SUCCESSION 1821–1848

Apart from primary sources such as *The Straits Settlements Records*[1] and *The Burney Papers*, both of which have been examined for purposes of this work, the most modern published authorities for this period are, Professor Mills *British Malaya 1824–1867* Chapter VIII (published in 1925) and Sir R. Winstedt's *History of Malaya* Chapter VIII (*J.R.A.S.M.B.* March, 1935). Winstedt's recent survey is the more penetrating and should be read with this chapter.

This subject has already been touched on in Chapter V, but only to show the intrigues of Triad and "Tokong" in this struggle. We now have to sketch from the meagre evidence, the probable association existing between the two belligerents and the two rival Chinese secret society camps respectively; and to trace from this background of war, the emergence of the Mohamedan White and Red Flag societies, whose presence was first officially acknowledged in 1867, but which are known to have been in existence since 1830 and actively hostile to one another since about 1860.

Briefly, the Kedah Malays lost their country to the Siamese in 1821 and their Sultan was a fugitive from his own country and lived in Penang and Malacca from 1821 to 1848.

Mills *op. cit.* page 161 has:—

> After 1821, there was a constant series of attacks on the Siamese garrisons by bands of (Malay) exiles from Kedah ...... joined by many professional pirates, who combined a little fighting against the Siamese with a great deal of looting and piracy.

The British officials in Penang refused to assist the Sultan of Kedah to regain his throne, acting upon the unpopular Article 13 of the Burney Treaty of 1826 with Siam, which reads as follows:—

> The Siamese engage to the English that the Siamese shall remain in Quedah, and take proper care of that country and of its people; that the inhabitants of Prince of Wales Island[2] and of Quedah shall have trade and intercourse as heretofore; the Siamese shall levy no duty upon stock and provisions ...... which the inhabitants of Prince of Wales Island or ships there may have occasion to purchase in Quedah...... The English engage to the Siamese that the English do not desire to take possession of Quedah, that they will not attack or disturb it, nor permit the former Governor of Quedah (the ex-Sultan) or any of his followers to attack, disturb or injure in any manner the territory of Quedah, or any other territory subject to Siam.

Lastly, the East India Company pledged itself not to allow the ex-Sultan to live in Penang, Province Wellesley, Perak, Selangor or Burma.

During these years, three important rebellions were secretly hatched by the Malays of Penang and Province Wellesley with the object of driving the Siamese out of Kedah. These rebellions took place in 1831, 1836 and 1838–1839.

THE FIRST KEDAH REBELLION 1831

Of this rebellion, Mills records:—

> Three thousand Kedah Malay exiles living in Province Wellesley crossed the frontier and drove the Siamese out of Kedah. The rebels were joined by hundreds of Malays from Penang and most of their supplies were sent by *sympathisers in Penang*...... The attack came as a complete surprise to both the British and to the Siamese Governments, for although the plans for the rising were made at Penang and were known to hundreds of Malays, not one betrayed them.

It is inconceivable that this secrecy was maintained without an organisation among the Malays behind it.

We know that at this period Triad in Penang was coquetting with the Siamese (Chapter V) and, although there is nothing in the archives to show it, we suggest that the "sympathisers in Penang" who supported the Kedah Malay rebels against the Siamese were those Chinese of Penang who belonged to the opposite camp to Triad namely, "Tokong" or what later became "Tokong"; and that the secret organisation behind the Malays was the Red Flag society or the loose association between the Malays and their Chinese sympathisers, which later became the Red Flag.

There is independent evidence to show that the association between Triad, the Siamese and the Patani Malays which we submit, either then was, or later became, the White Flag, was already in existence in Penang about this time, 1831.

Thus, Saiboo, witness No. 68 of the *Penang Riot Commission Report* (1868) on page 73 of the printed evidence says:—

> I am 34 years of age. The White Flag society was established before I was born.

This would put the date of the foundation of the White Flag as prior to 1830. It is a fair inference that the Kedah rebels of this period obtained their arms and ammunition from Chinese on the lookout for concessions as well as from sympathetic European sources, just as we shall see both White and Red Flag Malays did in the Penang riots of 1867 (Chapter XVI) and in the Larut wars 1862–1873 (Chapter XVII).

Footnote.—(1) *i.e. Penang Factory records* of the East India Company.
Footnote.—(2) *i.e.* Penang.

And it is logical to suppose that from the underground association between "Tokong" Chinese in Penang and the Kedah rebels, secretly pursuing an unlawful purpose during the years of struggle 1821–1848, there arose that secret liaison which became the Red Flag society.

It is certainly remarkable that, *if* the political birth of the White and Red Flag societies took place during the struggle of the Kedah Malays, supported by "Tokong", against the Siamese allied with Triad, there should be no historical record of the fact in any of the published authorities. A search of the records in the India Office[1] covering this period, has failed to disclose any mention of it. The secrecy which guarded these associations is perhaps the explanation. We may assume that had any inkling of the kind been known to the East India Company's Officers in Penang prior to 1867, the Penang Riot Commissioners of that year would have mentioned it in their Report, wherein the first official reference to these societies occurs.

Notwithstanding the absence of any mention by name of these societies in the records of the period, the following extracts from those records provide evidence of the use of flags and their colour by the belligerents and make mention of the "intrigues" and "associations" formed among the Malays of Penang and Province Wellesley, having as their object the restoration of the Sultan of Kedah. One of the early leaders of this combination was Tengku Long Puteh.

Major James Low in his *Retrospect of British Policy in the Straits of Malacca, 1786–1839*, published in the *Burney Papers* Vol. V Part I page 139 has:—

> In 1828, Tuanku Long Puteh brother-in-law, and Tuanku Din (or Kudin) nephew, of the ex-raja (ex-Sultan of Kedah) settled themselves in Province Wellesley without permission and commenced intriguing with the inhabitants with the view of recovering Kedah.
> In 1829, Kudin (or Tuanku Din) attacked Kedah aided by certain other influential Malays[2] and by ryots of the Hon'ble Company, but he was driven back.

There is frequent mention at this reference, of Tengku Long Puteh as being a notorious rebel and pirate of that period. The British at that time (1830) were in support of the Siamese against the Malays.

Again at page 141, *op. cit.* Low has:—

> In October, 1830, Tuanku Soliman, a younger brother of the ex-raja of Kedah who was allowed by the Siamese to live at Kotah a place close to the eastern boundary of Province Wellesley and situated on the Pry (Prai) river, began to excite the ryots of the Prai district to disaffection.

Begbie in his *Malayan Peninsula* (Madras 1834) has the following on Tengku Din (or Kudin), and the rebellion of 1831, page 127:—

> The Siamese by their numberless atrocities rendered the oppressed Kedans (Kedah Malays) ripe for resistance, as soon as they could obtain a leader on whom they could depend. They naturally looked to the ex-royal family of Kedah for a chief at a time when their King himself was a prisoner, guarded by his allies (i.e. the British in Penang) and they found him in Tuanku Koodeen, the nephew of the deposed monarch or (as he was contemptuously referred to by the Siamese) "the former Governor" of Kedah. But the Siamese dreaded this warrior as much as his own party looked up to him, and endeavoured in the most dastardly manner to rid themselves of their opponent. The following statement of the transaction is founded upon a letter which appeared in the *Singapore Chronicle* of 5th January, 1832. I believe it to be substantially correct and therefore give it to the public. I have already stated that Tuankoo Koodeen was a nephew of the King of Kedah but I have not mentioned that his father was an Arab of Palembang, from whom it is probable that he derived that indomitable perseverance and fortitude which so eminently distinguished him in the struggle which he maintained for the liberties of Kedah.
> The Tuankoo was ...... compelled to submit to the trying vicissitudes of penury and obscurity and deemed himself happy in being permitted to reside in Province Wellesley and enjoy a fancied security under the British flag. The Siamese dreading his courage and talents hired some ruffians to assassinate him ...... by blowing up his house ...... at night. They so far failed in their object that the Tuankoo escaped, but his wife and three children were killed by the explosion.
> Exasperated by this ...... Tuankoo Koodeen stirred up the minds of his countrymen, and excited them to assert their independence by an appeal to arms. So successful was his summons, that from Province Wellesley alone it is stated that five thousand Malays flocked to his standard and as many hundred from Pulo Pinang. With this force he retook the fort of Kedah from the Siamese on 24th April, 1831, and would probably have maintained it to this day (1834), had it not been for Article 13 of the Siamese Treaty (Burney Treaty) in which the English engage that they will not:—
> "permit the former Governor of Queda, or any of his followers to attack, disturb or injure in any manner the territory of Queda, or any other territory subject to Siam".
> ...... Tuankoo Solyman, the King's brother, residing on the confines of Province Wellesley, made a demonstration of joining Tuankoo Koodeen with three thousand men, but his movements being closely watched by four Companies of the 46th Madras Native Infantry, he hesitated, and never declared himself.

On 4th October, 1831, Tengku Din was driven out of the Fort of Kedah by the Siamese and rather than submit, committed suicide.

From this passage we learn that Tengku Din was of Arab descent which may have had its own significance in respect to the cause which he espoused. Begbie mentions Tengku Din's standard but does not give its colour. This omission is made good by

---

Footnote.—(1) Given by Mills *op. cit.* in his *Bibliography* under *Primary sources*.
Footnote.—(2) The names of these are given in a footnote as follows:—
Tengku Jaffar and Tengku Dagang, sons of Tengku Long Puteh; Panglima Marwar; Che Man; Panglima Itam; Imam Isnein; Che Hajji; Panglima Husein; Panglima Mim; Che Bhio; Awang Lahal and Che Akil.

another writer (*see* below) from whom we learn that it was red.   Thence we know that from the first, the Kedah rebels supported by "Tokong", were fighting under a banner which may have given its political colour to the later Red Flag society of the Malays.

THE SECOND KEDAH REBELLION 1836

Mills *op. cit.* page ·162 has :—

In 1836, the Straits government was again compelled to assist the Siamese.   The ex-Sultan of Kedah had received permission to leave Malacca for a visit to Deli, Sumatra ...... Instead he went to Bruas in Perak and began to collect a fleet for the invasion of Kedah ...... The Siamese called upon the British to fulfil the terms of the Burney Treaty ...... Two warships were sent to Bruas to bring him back by force if necessary.   The Malays resisted ...... but their fleet was destroyed and the ex-Sultan captured and sent to Malacca and his pension reduced.

Although this attempted rebellion was frustrated, it is interesting to note that its focal point was Bruas, which as we shall see in subsequent chapters, was an active centre of Red Flag intrigue a hundred years later.

THE THIRD KEDAH REBELLION 1838–1839

Mills *op. cit.* page 162 has :—

In 1838, another rebellion broke out in Kedah.   A force of Malays entered the country from British territory (*i.e.* Province Wellesley) and for the second time expelled the Siamese ...... The Government of the Straits, holding itself bound by the Burney Treaty at once blockaded the Kedah coast.   The British warships did not attack the Malays, but by preventing the arrival of arms and reinforcements from Penang, they contributed largely to the failure of the rebellion ...... In 1839, the Siamese reconquered Kedah and drove out the rebels.

An intimate glimpse of the British rôle in this third rebellion is obtained from Captain Osborn, R.N., who took part in the blockade, in his book *Quedah, or Stray leaves from a Journal in Malayan waters* (London, 1857).

Writing of the blockade by the British of the Kedah coast in 1838, Osborn has, pages 22–26 :—

Returning ...... to Singapore about the end of July (1838) we were ...... to learn that Malay war-prahus to the number of forty had made their appearance at the opposite and western end of the Straits.

They had, we learnt, fitted out on the Sumatran coast at a place called Batu Puteh ...... and carrying 2,000 fighting men, the pirates (*i.e.* Kedah Malays) had taken advantage of our absence from the Penang Station to capture from the Siamese government the important province of Quedah.

This fleet of prahus, styled by us a piratical one, sailed under the colours of the ex-Rajah of Quedah ......

*   *   *

Money, arms and prahus had been secretly collected at Batu Puteh and there the chiefs raised the old red flag of Quedah and there was no lack of enterprising and disaffected spirits to join them.   A Prince Abdullah, a descendant of the ex-Rajah was the nominal head of the insurrection ......   Their plan of operation was ably laid down by a Tengku Mahomet Said.

*   *   *

Arms, powder and other stores were liberally but covertly supplied from European as well as native traders at Penang: the payment to be hereafter made in rice and other products of the rich land of Quedah.[1]

*   *   *

Leaving Penang in September (1838) we first proceeded to the town of Quedah, lying at the mouth of a river of the same name.   On an old Portuguese fort which commands the town ...... the Malayan colours were flying and Tengku Mohamed Said was found to be in command.

We here learn that the Malay rebel flag was red.   Whether, as Osborn suggests, this was the original flag of the Sultan of Kedah, we have been unable to confirm, but whether as a co-incidence or for some other reason, the fact remains that the Kedah rebels with "Tokong" aid fought under the Red Flag against the Triad-saturated Siamese. We also learn that "Tokong" concession-hunters were behind the aid granted to the rebels whose success would be their opportunity.   We shall see this process at work in its most cut-throat form, after British intervention in Perak (Chapters XVIII to XX *infra*).

Osborn *op. cit.* gives a few further glimpses of conditions during the third rebellion, and with them some references to flags.   He says on page 35 :—

The Fort of Quedah hoisted its (Malay) colours and ...... we placed ourselves in line across the entrance of the river out of gunshot, and anchored to commence the blockade.

Page 67 :—

The Malays in Quedah had to dispose of their produce in Penang and procure in return arms, powder and salt and our duty was to prevent them.

Page 74 :—

The vessel ...... (was) employed to keep up the communication between the Malay chieftains in Quedah province and their friends in Penang.

Page 199 :—

On 16th March, 1839, a Siamese flag was seen waving on a tree at the mouth of the Jurlong river north of the Quedah river.

If the colour of this flag had been given as white, we would have had direct evidence of the participation of the other Flag society.

Footnote.—(1) Here we note the arms dealers getting into position to claim payment later by concessions from the victors.

EVIDENCE OF A SECRET MALAY ASSOCIATION IN THE STRUGGLE

(1) We come now to an extract from the *India Political and Foreign Consultations:* being, a proclamation issued by the Governor of Singapore,[1] in 1839, warning British subjects in the Straits Settlements against aiding the Kedah "rebel" leaders, Tengku Mohamed Said and Tengku Mohamed Taib, "their followers and associations", which suggests the suspected existence of a secret organisation behind the rebels.

The proclamation[2] dated 6th February, 1839 is as follows:—

Whereas, with the view of upholding the faith of traders and of preserving our friendly relations with the Government of Siam it has become necessary to co-operate with that power in the recapture of Quedah conformably with the 13th Article in the Treaty of Bangkok dated the 20th June, 1826, and whereas many British subjects have joined the present piratical attack upon this capital by Tuanku Mahomed Saad and Tuanku Mahomed Taib and their followers and associations. This is to give public notice that such subjects above mentioned, as do not peaceably return to their homes within ten days after the promulgation of this Proclamation will subject themselves to all the penalties attached to British subjects found in open arms against their own Government and that of an ally........

And in order that no one may hereafter plead ignorance of the circumstances under which Quedah has recently been captured by Tuanku Mahomed Saad and others, it is hereby further notified that the former Rajah of Quedah has written to the Governor of Singapore, a letter dated 3rd October, 1838, disclaiming any participation in the capture of Quedah from the Siamese, by those now in possession of that country.

(2) The unofficial view of the Penang Europeans upon the struggle is given by Thomson *Glimpses of life in the Far East* pages 156–157 where he has:—

In 1831, Tuanku Kudin, a chief of Malay royal blood headed an insurrection against his Siamese conquerors. He was successful at first and regained temporary possession of his native country. But England's assistance was now given to Siam and he was reduced ...... and died a hero's death with a remnant of his adherents while defending Kedah Fort ...... Kedah was again devastated and Province Wellesley replenished with settlers; lands rose in value and rents ruled high ...... In 1838, a man called Tuanku Mahomed Saad, a prince of royal blood raised another insurrection against the Siamese and carried many people away with him from Penang and Province Wellesley. Rents fell and the value of land in the English Settlements again became normal. Tuanku Mahomed Saad drove the Siamese out of Kedah beyond Singora; but the English and Siamese were now allies. He was consequently beaten back, escaping only to be laid hold of by the East India Company's Government as a pirate, and to be dealt with as such. Kedah this time was utterly destroyed ......

Even in this reference we see an admission that organisation was carried out on a large scale in British territory against Britain's ally Siam, by Malays whose activities could only have been made possible by the use of secret methods.

THE RESTORATION OF THE KEDAH DYNASTY 1848

To get the full sweep of the circumstances surrounding the restoration of the Kedah dynasty we must retrace our steps a little in history. These circumstances are thus presented by Winstedt, *History of Malaya (J.R.A.S.M.B.* 1935) 194–196:—

In 1836, the ex-Sultan of Kedah, Ahmad Taju'd-din having got leave to reside at Deli in Sumatra quitted Malacca, but sailed instead to the Perak estuary and settled at Bruas, where the Raja Muda visited the prince who had conquered Perak at Siam's behest in 1818. Captain James Low was sent at once to point out to the Sultan of Perak that any co-operation with the ex-Sultan would give Siam an excuse for once more invading Perak. Ahmad Taju'd-din adopted his old tactics of passive resistance; he refused to leave Bruas and collected there several hundreds of his old adherents for another descent on the Siamese in Kedah. "Surely the English will not be displeased if I can retake Kedah" he wrote to Salmond the Resident Councillor of Pinang. The Company was not going to let this breach of the Burney Treaty bring Siam so far south: H.M.S. Zebra proceeded to Bruas, and after an affray in which one seaman was killed and four wounded secured the ex-Raja, who was then sent to Malacca. But the preparations for a second Kedah war went on and "the war-whoop at Penang was still heard urging two half-civilised races to deeds of carnage".

In March, 1838, the ex-Sultan discovered a paladin in his nephew, Tengku Muhammad Said, "at this time there is Tuanku Muhammad Said who has become enlightened by Allah's grace, and has been directed by Allah to return to Kedah. Let all my chiefs and relatives who wish to partake of the mercy of Allah assemble at Merbok river." A Kedah fleet drove back a Siamese fleet at Kuala Merbok. Kedah fort fell and the Siamese defenders were massacred. The Malays took Perlis and Trang. Their force was estimated at 10,000. They marched north, sacking villages and Buddist temples. One column reached the Patani river, another invested Singgora for three months but was driven back to Kedah by 500 Chinese[3] and 2,000 Siamese. Meanwhile the indomitable Chau Phya, Raja of Ligor, had crossed the Kedah frontier with 1,500 men. He came, he saw, he conquered. To Britain's shame, British gun-boats blockaded the Kedah coast.

The war of 1839 convinced Ahmad Taju'd-din Halimshah that he would never recover his throne by arms. Accordingly in 1841 he sent his eldest son, Tengku Daik, with a letter from Governor Bonham to declare that in the event of further Malay insurrection the Straits Government would not assist to quash it. The Chau Phya was dead, and Bangkok was tired after twenty years of guerilla warfare that had ruined Kedah and not benefitted her suzerain. In 1842, the Siamese officials were recalled and the Sultan allowed to leave Malacca and return, though parts of his former kingdom were placed under independent Rajas. The English Company still refused the Sultan's request for an alliance pledging it to maintain him on the throne.

Guerilla warfare had now become a Malay habit. In 1843, Ahmad Taju'd-din seized Krian, claiming it to be a province of his State. Perak invoked the British for the assistance Low's treaty had pledged in 1826, whereupon the Governor warned Sultan Shahabu'd-din not to use force against his aggressor, advised Ahmad Taju'd-din to relinquish an insupportable claim, and

Footnote.—(1) Bonham, 1837–1843.
Footnote.—(2) Extract from the *Burney Papers,* Vol. III Part II page 490, *India Political and Foreign Consultations,* Range 195 Vol. VIII.
Footnote.—(3) We suggest that these Chinese were probably Ghee Hins (Triad and White Flag), supporting Siam against the Red Flag.

asked the new Chau Phya of Ligor to remonstrate. Ahmad Taju'd-din was informed that his Pinang annuity of $10,000 would be withheld till he had kept the peace for a year. At last in 1848, he retired from Krian at the threat that the British would expel him by force. Soon afterwards he died; by July, 1850, Colonel Blundell was addressing his successor, Sultan Zain-al-Rashid Shah.[1]

There is a curious and unexplained feature in the story of this restoration namely, why did Ahmad Tajuddin the ex-Sultan of Kedah suddenly drop his paladin and nephew Tengku Mohd. Said in 1841 and send his son Tengku Daik to make terms with the infidel Siamese?

The circumstances of this ingratitude and desertion are made plainer in a letter[2] dated 11th December, 1846, from the Governor of Singapore (Butterworth 1843–1855) to the Government of India referring to the restoration of the Kedah dynasty.

Extracts from this letter are as follows:—

With reference to my letter under date the 26th August last (1846) I have now the honour to report that Tuanko Dye, *alias* Tuanko Zeinoon Rashid, Ebene, Murboom, Sultan Ahamad Tajudin Hallim Shah, Governor of Quedah, the eldest surviving son of the late Rajah of Quedah, has returned from Ligore, having been duly recognised by the King of Siam as successor to his father.

2. The return of Tuanko Zeinoon Rashid to Quedah was most opportune, for the country bordering our territory had been thrown into considerable excitement by the untoward proceedings of Tuanko Mahomed Saad, the chieftain who was sent by Mr. Bonham as a state prisoner to Calcutta in 1841, and remanded to Penang in September, 1843.

3. Tuanko Mahomed Saad, after the receipt of the letter to my address dated the 29th January 1844, having proceeded to Quedah, located himself at Kotah, and then and there commenced levying taxes on the inhabitants of the District of Prye, upon which he professes to have some claim in right of his wife. Not content with this, he undertook an expedition a few months since, with about 150 followers, ... to secure possession of the tin mines, at Pulie, under the charge of Hadjee Dultam, the revenue, dues and tolls on which, amounting to about 2,000 dollars annually, are collected by the Quedah Government at the mouth of the Muda river by a person named Tuanko Ibrahim.   *   *   *

6. At this period, Tuanko Zeinoon Rasheed, Ebene, Marhoom, Sultan Ahamad Tajudin Hallim Shah, reported his return to Quedah, and his determination to proceed against Tuanko Mahomed Saad ......   *   *   *

7. Tuanko Mahomed Saad was easily defeated and he is now a fugitive; it is generally believed, but nothing certain is known of his movements, that he has proceeded towards the southern end of the provinces, some say with a view of inducing the Rajah of Perak to espouse his cause but I think this improbable, for the old Rajah must have heard too much of the said Tuanko Mahomed Saad to trust him. Moreover his family have all come to Penang, where I have ordered that they shall be permitted to remain unrecognised and unmolested, so long as they keep quiet and in the event of the smallest hostile movement, that Act X of 1839 shall be enforced against them.

Mills *op. cit.* page 163, has the following, covering the reasons for the restoration:—

The failure of this insurrection (*i.e.* that of Tengku Mohamed Said in 1838) convinced the old Sultan (Ahmad Tajuddin) that he could never regain his kingdom by force. So in 1841, he sent Tengku Daik his eldest son to Bangkok to beg for pardon and reinstatement. Bonham, the Governor of the Straits Settlements was very sceptical of success, but with the approval of the Supreme Government he gave Tengku Daik a letter to the Prah-Klang.[3] In it he urged that the Sultan should be restored to his throne and warned the Siamese that the Company had grown weary of bolstering up their power in Kedah. Should another revolt occur, the Straits Government had been ordered not to assist in its suppression. The old Sultan's petition was made at a propitious moment. The Emperor of Siam had at last learned that there was no profit to be obtained from governing as a Siamese province a distant state whose inhabitants were resolved not to submit to alien rule. The experiment had been tried for twenty years and the only result had been a constant series of rebellions in which the prosperity of Kedah had been ruined. Had the Raja of Ligor been alive, the decision might have been different, but the Sultan of Kedah's implacable enemy was now dead.

In 1842, the Emperor of Siam accepted the Sultan's submission, removed the Siamese officials from Kedah and restored to him the greater part of his former kingdom ......

The East India Company hoped that it was at last freed from Siamese entanglements, but it was soon undeceived. In 1843, the Sultan of Kedah seized the Krian district of Perak claiming it as part of his kingdom ...... Finally in 1848, the Governor of the Straits Settlements compelled him to restore Krian to Perak by the threat of force ...... Until 1909, Kedah remained a Siamese dependency, ruled by the descendants of the restored Sultan. By the Treaty of Bangkok in 1909, Siam renounced its rights of suzerainty and the state became a British dependency.

The view that the restoration took place because "the King of Siam had at last learned that there was no profit to be obtained from governing a distant state whose inhabitants were resolved not to submit to alien rule" does not seem to be borne out by later history, since Siamese political intrigues continued in Kelantan and Trengganu until 1909.[4] Furthermore, the Malay state of Patani which is as far from Bangkok as Kedah, is to-day a part of Siam. It may have been the threat of losing British support which caused this remarkable change of heart at Bangkok just after the successful suppression of the third Malay rebellion. but it seems at least as likely that it was due to the death of the old Raja of Ligor in 1842, followed by the waning of Ghee Hin (Triad) support of the Siamese cause in Kedah, or perhaps to direct Triad representations *sub-rosa* in Bangkok.

Footnote.—(1) The former Tengku Daik.
Footnote.—(2) The *Burney Papers* Vol. IV Part II pages 200, 201, 202. *India Political and Foreign Consultations,* Range 197 Vol. LIV No. 36.
Footnote.—(3) *i.e.* Siamese Minister for Foreign Affairs in Bangkok.
Footnote.—(4) *See* Swettenham *British Malaya* pages 310–329.

It might even have been due to direct intervention by Triad and "Tokong" who had been supplying munitions to each side for ten years without a decision, on an extended credit basis. Their concession hunters, hopeful of large profits, may have cut off supplies so as to force the issue. We shall never know, because the intimate history of the relations between the heads of Chinese secret societies and the Siamese and Malays of the Peninsula in the nineteenth century will never be written.

It is nevertheless significant that such an abrupt change of heart overtook Bangkok during the visit of Tengku Daik.

Was a bargain struck in Bangkok with Triad wire-pullers in the background, whereby the Malay dynasty was to be restored only if the Kedah court undertook to accept Triad and White Flag influence in Kedah, instead of the "Tokong" and Red Flag support upon which they had hitherto relied, thus giving Triad the supporter of Siam in the struggle, first pick of the spoils in Kedah after the restoration, to the discomfiture of "Tokong"? There is no evidence to enable us to draw even an acceptable inference, but the bargain suggested if it was ever made, would help to explain several incidents in subsequent history, as well as the trend of later cross-currents in the secret society intrigue of Malaya.

We offer two examples only:—

(1) Within a year of his "restoration" (1842), the Sultan of Kedah had seized the Krian district of Perak, from which he was only expelled by the British by a threat of force in 1848, after a reduction of his pension had failed to dislodge him.

What could have impelled him to undertake a fresh war against his own people so soon after restoration by the infidel Siamese, except the promise of aid from Triad anxious to get a footing in the tin fields of Larut?

Winstedt, in the quotation given above, explains this act by the sentence "Guerilla warfare had now become a Malay habit". We suggest another and more concrete reason.

(2) From Governor Butterworth's letter to the Government of India of 11th December, 1846, quoted above, we see that in 1848, the Raja Muda of Kedah, Tengku Zain-al-Rashid, visited Ligor where he was recognised by Siam as the successor of Sultan Ahmad Tajuddin who died shortly afterwards (1849).

We also see in para. 6 of the letter that Tengku Mohamed Said, nephew of the Sultan, leader and hero of the rebellion of 1838, which so nearly gave Ahmad Tajuddin back his throne, was thereupon promptly disowned by the restored Kedah royal house, who so shortly before had acclaimed him as their "paladin". The letter reports Tengku Zain-al-Rashid's "determination to proceed against Tengku Mohamed Said, who with British aid, was subsequently easily defeated and is now a fugitive ...... towards the southern end of the provinces, some say with a view of inducing the Raja of Perak to espouse his cause". What is the explanation of this *volte face*, unless it be that Triad diplomacy had detached the Sultan of Kedah from his former Red Flag supporters and had attached him to the White Flag?

The fact mentioned in paragraph 7 of the letter, that Tengku Mohamed Said allowed his family to take refuge in Penang, suggests that he felt that they would be safe among his Red Flag friends there.

Although these extracts prove nothing, they help to direct attention to the period and the circumstances most likely perhaps to have fostered the political growth of the White and Red Flag societies among the indigenous Malays of Penang and Province Wellesley, and show a link of sympathy on the ground of self-interest between Triad and the Siamese or foreign faction among the Malays of Kedah on the one hand, and "Tokong" and the "nationalist" Kedah Malays on the other.

The story of the activities of Tan Kim Cheng of Singapore and of his "king-making" in Perak on behalf of Triad at a later date (Chapters XVII, XVIII and XIX) suggests that the power he later represented, may have been no less active in Kedah politics earlier in the century.

During the decade (1850–1860) that succeeded the Siam-Kedah struggle, it is easy to suppose that a cementing of friendship took place in the alliance of Triad with White Flag and "Tokong" with Red.

The secret ceremonies of initiation and criminal habits of Triad and "Tokong" were probably adopted during this period by the White and Red Flag and their political antagonism was sharpened, which was to break out anew in the Larut wars 1862–1873 and in the Penang Riots 1867.

CHAPTER XIV

THE EMERGENCE OF "TABUT" IN MALAYA 1830–1867

In preceding chapters, we have caught glimpses of the march of Islam eastwards from the Levant through Persia, down the frontier passes of Afghanistan into the plains of India, whence the Sunni doctrine came to Malaya about A.D. 1450 from the coasts of Coromandel and Malabar, reinforced by Arab missionaries direct from the Hadramaut.

We have seen the invasion of Malaya by the baser elements of Shiah Islam and Hinduism through the artificial influx of Indian criminality 350 years later, bringing with it the eclecticism of Hindu religious observance, the two epitomised in the degenerate Moharram festival, alien to the local scene.

We have seen something of the nature of Sufi mysticism, which in Malaya has remained almost exclusively within the domain of the Arab practitioner.

We have seen the advent to Malaya of the two great stems of Chinese esoteric belief, which we call secret societies, and we have seen the beginning of a movement among the other immigrant races in the early nineteenth century to organise themselves upon lines similar to the Chinese underground camps of Triad and "Tokong".

But the picture we have been building up has been only the background of a stage upon which we must now ring up the curtain.

True, the background as drawn has a world-wide sweep, whereas we are only concerned in this work with the detail of one tiny corner of the Imperial picture. But without this background whose subdued but all-pervading tone is the arcana of man's mind, anything we might record of secret societies in the Malayan corner would have no real meaning unattached to the main gigantic theme, the vast turmoil that is human life and relationship. Any purely local record would have but a transitory significance,— a seven-days' wonder, or perhaps just, "a matter for the Police".

But with the background thus roughly sketched in, we may, if we care to attempt it, trace the sources of those arcana which are the core of "religion". They are the mainsprings of human action, and so to the wise administrator, his touchstone.

In this chapter, we get closer to our subject and begin to paint in its more intimate Malayan features. The modern actors begin to appear before the backcloth we have been weaving, each to play his part in the story of the *dessous des cartes* in that secret society world of Malaya, which has now to be disentangled and presented to the reader.

We wish to make it clear that in handling the material of secret societies whether beneficent or maleficent, we are handling the material of religion.

We have already indicated the origin and character, judged by our standards, of the main stems in this secret society cosmos as it affects Malaya. In doing so we do not wish to sit in judgment upon what is after all largely relative, nor to appear to condemn nor yet to commend, what is essentially secret and sacred in the belief of others.

In some degree, the essence of every creed is secret, in that it is concealed from the profane. Secrecy in belief is a criterion of nothing except of the will to perpetuate and preserve. The purpose of that preservation may be good or bad. Generally speaking, when its objects are anti-social or chaotic, we say they are bad and when they are pure, idealistic and spiritual, we say they are good. But the presence or absence of secrecy depends in its degree upon the law, and the law in turn depends upon belief. What is condemned under one set of circumstances and under one law, is condoned or applauded under another; what is legal under one code is illegal under another; what must be destroyed in one country, must be preserved in another. These considerations determine the degree of secrecy which may enwrap any creed at any one time in any one place, with the proviso that at any moment, what is legal to-day, may become illegal tomorrow. For this reason all the arcana of human belief have a degree of secrecy or mysticism about them for their ultimate preservation, if not for their immediate protection against sudden attack or exposure.

This element of secrecy may constitute a breach of law, but is not necessarily evidence of evil intent.

Thus secrecy, whether inherent in the doctrine itself, or demanded by its illegality, is a leading feature of all associations, religious or political, formed round the arcana of human belief and which, for lack of a better name, we call secret societies. (*See* Introduction).

We will now introduce these phenomena as they appeared among the Mohamedan community of Singapore and Penang during the nineteenth century.

THE EMERGENCE OF THE WHITE AND RED FLAG SOCIETIES (TABUT) 1830–1867

Singapore.—The earliest recorded reference to the celebration of the Moharram occurs in Buckley's *Anecdotal History* page 375 where he says that in May, 1842 :—

> The Government in Singapore refused to allow the "Klings"[1] to have a procession and carry their Taboot about the town.

Again Buckley refers to a riot which took place in Singapore in February, 1857, occasioned by Police intervention to prevent obstruction during the celebration of what, from the following description, must have been the Moharram festival of that year.

Buckley *op. cit.* page 645 has :—

> The enforcement of the Police and Conservancy Acts[2] by the Police gave rise to another disturbance in February (1857) confined however to one section of the native population, the Klings, and was unfortunately attended with considerable bloodshed and loss of life. The Imam of the Mohamedan mosque in Telok Ayer Street had obtained a license to celebrate a festival extending over several days, on the condition that the proceedings should terminate each evening at ten o'clock. On the evening of the 5th February, Arthur Pennefather, one of the Police Inspectors going his rounds between ten and eleven, accompanied by a Police Sergeant and several peons, found a large assemblage of Klings at the mosque, completely blocking up the road in Telok Ayer and Japan Street, there being also obstructions in the shape of stakes and plantain trees stuck in the ground.[3] The Inspector ordered the obstructions to be removed by the peons, but this was resisted by the Klings. The Inspector then sent to the Police station for a reinforcement, he himself remaining on the spot with the Sergeant. Seven or eight policemen presently arrived, some of them armed with loaded muskets. The Inspector then again ordered the Imam to remove the obstructions, and on his declining to do so, the police peons were ordered to take up the stakes. On their attempting this, the mob assailed them with sticks and stones, and the sergeant and one of the peons were knocked down, the latter being rendered senseless. He was taken up by some of his comrades, and the party retired towards the Police Station in Telok Ayer Street, followed by the mob, who continued to throw missiles. When near the Station the Police fired over the mob, who retreated, and the party then gained the Station. The mob then assailed the Station with brickbats, stones, etc. and the Police replied by firing from both the ground and upper floors. One person was shot dead, one died next day from his wounds, and eleven others were so severely wounded that they were sent to Hospital. Inquests were held on the bodies of the persons killed, and in both, verdicts were returned of justifiable homicide. The Commissioner of Police (Mr. Mackenzie, the Resident Councillor) after the first inquest, with the consent of the Governor, dismissed the Inspector, Sergeant, and one of the peons, and reduced some of the native police, who had been concerned in the affair, in rank. This decision was come to because the Commissioner was of opinion that the conduct of the Inspector was most rash and precipitate, that fire arms had been used without sufficient cause and that this had provoked the riotous and illegal attack of the mob. Considerable excitement was induced amongst the European residents by this decision of the Commissioner; they thought it was not justified in face of the verdict of the coroner's jury, who had completely exculpated the police from blame, and they also conceived it was calculated to prejudice the interests of Inspector Pennefather, against whom proceedings had been taken before the Police Magistrate, which resulted in his being committed to take his trial for manslaughter at the next criminal sessions.
>
> A public meeting was held on 26th February, at which over 80 Europeans were present, with Mr. C. H. Harrison in the chair, and remonstrances were addressed to the Governor, who however declined to restore the dismissed persons to the positions they had previously held in the Police force.
>
>   *   *   *
>
> The Inspector was brought to trial at the Criminal Session held in April, and after a trial lasting eight days was acquitted of the charge against him.

This fracas in Telok Ayer in 1857 and its unfortunate sequel, may be taken as the first recorded trial of strength between "Tabut" and the Police in Malaya. It is clear that there was in this case determined and organised resistance to Police authority, which had gained a much needed tonic from the India Act of 1856, introducing the principles of the Peel's new Police Act of 1829 into the Straits Settlements.

Resistance may have been stiffened among Indians which found its expression in India in the mutiny of that year, but of this there is no mention.

It is reasonable to assume that either the white or the red flag society,—there is nothing to enable us to guess which—was responsible for the riot.[4] In the course of the next few years both societies were to declare their presence in Singapore.

THE GREAT CONSPIRACY CASE (1865) AGAINST LEADERS OF THE WHITE AND RED FLAG SOCIETIES IN SINGAPORE

The earliest mention of the White and Red Flag societies by name occurs again in Buckley, under the years 1864 and 1865.

This reference (Buckley page 723) is as follows :—

> For some years there had been trouble arising at times from secret societies among the Klings, both Hindus and Mohamedans, called the Red and White Flag societies, which led to street fights and bloodshed, for the two societies were always at variance, although the Mohamedan members of both had the same religious tenets. In 1864, serious disturbances had taken place during the Moharrum festival, and in May this year (1865) Governor Cavenagh and Mr. Dunman forbade the procession. In October, what was called the Great Conspiracy Case,

---

Footnote.—(1) For the meaning of this name, *see* Footnote 2 page 185 *supra*.

Footnote.—(2) This refers to India Act No. 13 of 1856 "An act for regulating the Police of the towns of Calcutta, Madras and Bombay, and of the several stations of the settlement of Prince of Wales Island (*i.e.* Penang), Singapore and Malacca".

Footnote.—(3) Sir Herbert Dowbiggin has supplied this note :—"In Ceylon plantain trees are often cut down and stuck into the ground at the celebration of festivals". With the passing of the Moharram the practice seems to have died out in Malaya.

Footnote.—(4) In later Singapore records we learn that Telok Ayer has always been a Red Flag stronghold.

against six of the members was heard, two of whom, were men of standing, Mr. Duncan and Mr. Weir, giving them remarkably good characters in matters of business. They were all convicted, and sentenced to two years imprisonment. This practically broke up the societies, which had been established after the Chinese Ghi Hin and Ghi Hok societies, with which it was supposed they were connected.

We have not been able to find a record of this case, or the names of the six Indian accused, or any other reference thereto. If such were available it might shed much light on the subject of our enquiry.

Penang.—Although there is no mention of the Flag societies, as such in the records of Penang until 1867, there is ample evidence left on record by Vaughan as to their existence in Penang and Province Wellesley in fully developed form, as early as 1850 or perhaps earlier. The following extracts are taken from Vaughan's *Notes on the Chinese of Penang J.I.A.* VIII published in 1854, and refer to events several years before that date. These notes of Vaughan have been freely quoted in Chapter VI above, in reference to the Chinese hoeys in Penang at that date. The following extracts refer to the Malay and "Jawi-pekan" aspect of the subject:—

A very intelligent Malay Haji[1] who was educated at the Protestant Free School, and was well known at one time as a prominent member of several hoeys,[2] gave me the following particulars regarding his initiation and the object and construction of the society he belonged to. On his telling me his story, I asked if he was not afraid to divulge the secrets after taking an oath of fidelity? He replied, no—that being a Mohamedan, he did not consider the Chinese oath binding—that he was not sworn on the Koran and, therefore, did not care;[3] that for three or four years past he had deserted the fraternity, because his chief priest considered it to be contrary to their faith to belong to it, and he was then expiating his former wickedness by frequently attending the Musjid and implicitly obeying the injunctions of the Koran. I cannot vouch for the truth of his statement but give it verbatim. The Penghulu's[4] statement, which follows, corroborates the story in some points, and alludes to the Haji, as being the principal initiator on the night of his (the Penghulu's) admittance.

THE STATEMENT OF HAJI "X" 1854

What follows is all very vague and at this distance of time, not very helpful, except to show that such contacts between Triad and "Tabut" were being made in Penang ninety years ago. We are not told the name of the society to which the statement of Haji "X" refers. From internal evidence it is probable that it is intended to be a description of an initiation into the Toh Peh Kong ("Tokong") society under such truncated ceremonial as was customary at the period, to cover Malay initiation.

Comparison will show that the description of Haji "X" agrees, in many respects with Cooper's description of a Three Dot initiation (Chapter IX), which we have identified with "Tokong" and thence with what later became the Red Flag society under a separate Malay constitution. The statement of Haji "X" is as follows:—

Any person wishing to enter a hoey signifies his intentions to one of the members, who tells the chief or Toa Ko, who enters his name in a book. When a sufficient number are desirous of entering, a night for the initiation is fixed. When the night arrives the members of the hoe assemble in the principal room of the house, and the candidates are put into an adjoining apartment; each man pays 25 cents, and his name is entered in the books of the hoe. At the door leading into the hall stand two men, armed with swords and dressed in rich silk clothes, ornamented with divers figures of dragons, birds, etc.[5]

Half a dozen lighted Joss sticks are given to each candidate. They now advance in couples to the door, their right arm bared, and if Chinese, their queues opened out; they are not allowed to stand upright, but must advance in a stooping posture.[6]

On arriving at the door the following questions are put by the guards to each person:—

Q. What do you desire by entering the hoe?
A. I wish to become a brother of yours.
Q. Who told you to come?
A. I came of my own accord. No one told me to come.
Q. What do you hold those joss sticks for?
A. I wish to pray and swear before the hoe, that I will obey all its orders.

The candidates are then allowed to enter the hall in which is found a table before the "Tokong"[7] spread with eatables. A priest stands to the left (or one personating a priest). The Thoo Ah Koo[8] stands on the right.

Footnote.—(1) To avoid later confusion we will refer to this Malay Haji whose name is nowhere given, as Haji "X".

Footnote.—(2) As will be seen, there had not yet been evolved at this epoch a separate Malay ritual of initiation such as is used at the present-day. A truncated Chinese rigmarole was evidently used which would probably suit the admission of Malays to either Triad or "Tokong".

Footnote.—(3) Modern Malay initiations into the Red and White Flag societies are sworn on the Koran.

Footnote.—(4) To avoid later confusion we will refer to this Penghulu whose name is nowhere given, as Penghulu "Y".

Footnote.—(5) This description does not fit the Triad dress, which is white (mourning) for all. See page 118 *supra* and Ward and Stirling *op. cit.* Vol. I page 27 note 2 and page 56 note 2. Cooper Chapter IX *supra* does not describe the Three Dot dress, but *see* Hutson's reference to the dragon in the Ko Lao Hui (Chapter II *supra*).

Footnote.—(6) The stooping posture suggests Cooper's description of the Three Dot requirement (Chapter IX).

Footnote.—(7) i.e. The portrait of Kwan Ti *see* page 144 *supra*. This seems strong evidence that this was a Han league (Red Flag) initiation.

Footnote.—(8) Thoo Ah Koo (大 哥) = The President.

The second grade, called Jee-ko, sit in chairs on the right. The third grade or Sam-ko on the left. The fourth grade or ordinary members, called brothers, stand on either side, and in front.[1]

The candidates are then brought to the head of the table and are made to worship; this is done by stooping down three or four times and raising boths hands with the joss sticks over the head. Each candidate says that he will strictly obey all orders of the hoe and will not reveal to any one what he may see or hear. The priest then takes up a large book and says, "you come here unsolicited and wish to become a brother, and you have sworn before the God that you will strictly obey all orders and reveal nothing that you may see or hear this night?" All the candidates reply in the affirmative. The priest then says, "I will now read the rules of this hoe".

Rules.—

You will not reveal the proceedings of our meetings to any but a brother.

You must not cheat a brother or steal from him, you must not seduce the wife, daughter or any female relative of a brother......

If you break any of these rules, you must come before the hoe to be punished and on no account must you go to the police or to the Supreme Court. The hoe have the power of flogging you or imposing any other punishment they please.

* * *

If a brother commits the most serious crime, you must not inform against him but at the same time, you must not interfere with or obstruct the officers of justice in arresting him.

If a guilty brother is caught by the police, you must not assist in getting him off. But should the brother be innocent, you must make every exertion to get him off.

If you see a brother make a signal, it is your duty to answer it; if in need of assistance you must grant it.[2]

(Many other rules exist but the Haji had forgotten them).[2]

Signs.—

The following signs that will be shown you, must not be revealed.

If about to be assaulted in the street, roll up the right sleeve or the right leg of the trousers, or hold the right arm over the head with the fingers spread out.

* * *

On entering a house, if you wish to be known, put your *right*[3] foot in first over the thresh-hold and look up.

A handkerchief placed round the neck, and tied in the front with two knots, with the ends left hanging down, denotes a member of the Gee Hin. Junks on meeting at sea have a peculiar way of placing their sails and flags, so as to show what hoe they belong to.

After enumerating all the signs and signals, which are too numerous for any person to remember every member pricks the middle finger of the *right*[3] hand and drops a little blood into a bowl of arrack and each candidate is obliged to do the same. After this every member present drinks out of the bowl and the candidates are saluted as brethren.

Each newly initiated brother now pays a dollar and ten cents, gets a seal or chop on silk or paper, and he is then entitled to all privileges of the fraternity.

The Gee Hin and Ho Seng are nearly alike in their signs. To show yourself a member of the To-pe-kong draw the right hand across the mouth, and if in want of aid in a street row, hold the right arm up with the hand closed and point the thumb upwards. On refusing anything push it away with the open hand.[4]

Several months after hearing the Haji's story, I was on a visit to one of the country Police *Thannahs*,[5] and recollecting a report[6] that all the Mohammedan male inhabitants of the village had entered the Ho Seng hoe, I took the opportunity of questioning the Penghulu,[7] a highly respectable man, the son of a Haji named Haji Bruni,[8] he having been a native of Borneo. This man left some property and a large family, who are very influential. The Penghulu without any hesitation admitted it was quite true that about two or three years ago all the Mohammedan male inhabitants did join the Ho Seng, he being one of the number.[9]

As soon as Abdul Gunny, the priest,[10] heard of it, he repaired to the spot and assembled them all. He declared that they had all become kaffirs by joining heathens, and if they did not recant, he would close the Musjid, take the presiding priest away from the village, and excommunicate them all. On this they immediately renounced[11] the hoe and by the usual ceremonies were re-admitted into Islamism.

Footnote.—(1) This passage seems to confuse grades of initiation with the titles of lodge officials. The grading of initiates suggests the Ko Lao Hui of Hutson (Chapter II) and the Three Dot of Cooper (Chapter IX).

Footnote.—(2) These rules might belong to either Triad or "Tokong". They are of the normal pattern (secrecy, respect for women of members, mutual help) but are in any case "watered-down", and of little interest.

Footnote.—(3) The first-footing with the right; also the pricking of the right hand, belong to "Tokong". Both are the reverse of Triad, *cf.* Hutson and Cooper.

Footnote.—(4) The mention of these three societies by the deponent, two of them Triad and one of them "Tokong", does not disclose to which he belonged, but the passage seems to suggest that he belonged to all three, which is unlikely.

Footnote.—(5) The use of the Indian name for a Police Station reflects the Indian influence in the government of the time. It is a pity Vaughan does not give the name of the village or the Police Station. The mere fact of discussing secret societies seems to have affected him with an unusual air of mystery!

Footnote.—(6) This "report" appears to be something unconnected with the statement of Haji "X" above.

Footnote.—(7) *i.e.* Penghulu "Y", son of Haji Bruni.

Footnote.—(8) Vaughan in *J.I.A. II New Series* (1858) under "Notes on Malays of Penang", gives further information about this man's origin. His name was Haji Mohamed Salleh but he was known as Haji Brunei, a notable figure in Penang in the second quarter of the nineteenth century and one whom we guess from various references, to have belonged to the White Flag camp.

Footnote.—(9) The description by Penghulu "Y", purports, therefore, to be that of a Ho Seng initiation.

Footnote.—(10) There is reason to think from the scattered references to this man by Vaughan and others, that "Abdul Gunny the priest" belonged to the White Flag camp and may have succeeded Haji Brunei in its headship.

Footnote.—(11) This act of repudiation or repentance is called in Arabic *Taubat,* and is known in colloquial Malay as *Tobat,* a term with which we shall become more familiar in Chapter XXVI *infra.*

THE STATEMENT OF PENGHULU "Y" 1854

Penghulu "Y" says he entered the Ho Seng (和 勝 = Peaceful Victory) society, a note on which is given on page 103 *supra*. He also says (below) that it was a Chinese ceremony and that Haji "X" was present and acted as his sponsor and interpreter.

We have seen above that Haji "X" described a "Tokong" ceremony in his statement.

On page 103, we have given our *reasons* for thinking that the Ho Seng originally belonged to the Triad foundation and later changed flags and joined "Tokong" under whose red banner we definitely find it in Larut in 1870.

We do not know at what period the Ho Seng changed flags, but the change might have coincided with the renunciation of it by Penghulu "Y" described by Vaughan above.

The fact that "Abdul Gunny the priest" tends to identify himself (below) with the White Flag would be a further ground for the renunciation of Penghulu "Y", whose father Haji Brunei may have been an early White Flag leader.

Other evidence offered in Chapter XVI *infra*, suggests that the change of flags by the Ho Seng took place at a later date than 1850.

If the Ho Seng belonged to Triad in 1850, it would seem that Haji "X" was a member both of the Toh Peh Kong ("Tokong") and the Ho Seng (Triad) at that date which, although improbable, would explain Vaughan's description of him (above) as:—

> A very intelligent Malay ...... who was well-known at one time as a prominent member of several hoeys.

Whatever the correct explanation, it must be borne in mind that these were the formative years of the two flag associations, and the two Chinese camps were doubtless both angling for the support of such influential Mohamedans as they could attach to themselves with the bait of a truncated Chinese ceremony which meant no more either to Triad or "Tokong" than an acknowledgment of a loose affiliation.

Vaughan continues:—

> The following is the Penghulu's account of his initiation, but he said that it was so long ago, and not having been to a hoey since, he could not furnish a detailed account of the transaction, or the oath, signs, etc:—
>
> With 200 Malays or more I was persuaded to join the Ho Seng hoe. On the night of our initiation we assembled in the plantation of the chief of that hoey in the village. An attap shed was lighted up and a table spread with food was placed before a picture.[1] Two men with naked swords stood at the entrance of the shed, and held them overhead in the shape of a triangle,[2] which each candidate had to pass under; we had then to swear that we would not reveal any of the secrets or signs that would be communicated to us. All I can now recollect is that we were to call each other brother.
>
> We were not to injure the wife, daughter or any female relation or friend of a brother. If a false charge was brought against a brother we were to make every exertion to get him free. But if a brother was arrested on a true charge, the law was to take its course. If in a row or in want of assistance, raise the right arm, or roll up the right sleeve or one leg of the trousers.
>
> On setting tea before a man place three cups in a row, if he takes the middle cup he is a member of the Ho Seng.
>
> The ceremony of initiation was conducted in the Chinese language,[3] which the Penghulu did not understand, but Haji[4] conducted the business and interpreted the orders and signs.
>
> The Haji mentioned by the Penghulu was my informant stated above. During the day I paid the chief of the Ho Seng a visit and alluded to his having admitted the Malays into his hoey and their subsequent recantation. He denied their having been admitted into the hoey, but said that they had only formed a club to assist each other against the adjacent villages.[5] This of course was to put the Penghulu, (who was present) off the scent. If it had been merely a local club it is not likely that the Haji would have gone eleven miles from town to assist in the ceremony.

The foregoing is vague and not very profitable, but it gives a cross-section upon the process of evolution of the Red and White Flag societies among Malays under the tutelage of Triad and "Tokong", nearly a hundred years ago.

UNDERGROUND ISLAMIC INFLUENCES AT WORK IN PENANG 1830–1860

The two imported stems of Chinese "religious" or secret society organisation were clearly distinguishable in Penang by 1850 and were by then busily engaged in widening the circumference of their respective *imperia in imperio* by seducing the indigenous Sunni Mohamedan population to their allegiance. A somewhat similar process is discernable in the community of Islam at about the same epoch.

We have briefly reviewed in Chapter X, the secret sects of Islam and the place of sufism or mysticism in their organisation.

Sufism belongs to the Shiah "church" and was, like Triad and "Tokong", an importation into Sunni Malaya, where its practitioners have throughout been Arabs or those of Arab descent.

Footnote.—(1) This is again the picture of Kwan Ti and suggests the Three Dot ("Tokong") rite.

Footnote.—(2) The triangle suggests the Triad ceremony. The remainder might belong to either. The same principles of secrecy, protection of their own womenkind and mutual help are present in the rules.

Footnote.—(3) Initiations of Malays to the Flag associations are nowadays conducted in Malay and sworn on the Koran (*see* Chapter XXIX *infra*).
No doubt, if any genuine initiation of persons other than Chinese to either Triad or "Tokong" take place, the are conducted in Chinese.

Footnote.—(4) *i.e.* Haji "X".

Footnote.—(5) This is what we might have expected him to say. The same type of man is saying the same type of thing to-day.

This circumstance may have been the germinal cause of those rifts in the Sunni "church" of Malaya, which made their presence felt in Penang and Province Wellesley between 1830 and 1860.

Thus, Vaughan *Notes on the Malays of Penang J.I.A.* Vol. II (new series) published in 1858 has:—

> The following remarks refer only to customs peculiar to Malays in connection with their religious persuasion.
>
> A species of Hierarchy did at one time exist among them but at present each Musjid (or Mosque) has its own government and is independant of all others.
>
> The Hierarchy was thus constituted. A Kali (Kathi) or head priest governed the whole country, appointed his own prelates, granting them written orders to officiate in his stead, and stationed them in every village. Those only that had warrants from the Kali were recognised by the people as their spiritual chiefs.
>
> In Province Wellesley, the Kali of Telok-ayer-tawar still arrogates to himself this supremacy or popeship, but there are many Hajis bold enough to establish themselves as independant ministers, and they are resorted to by a great number who are wise enough to treat the Kali's threats with indifference. Many Hajis may be met with to this day bearing the official warrant or commission of the Kali of Telok-ayer-tawar.
>
> In Pinang, the same power was once exerted by the late Haji Macawi of Batu Uban, and now an Arab or a man of Arab descent, named Abdul Gunny is endeavouring to gain the ascendency but the spirit of liberty is abroad and it is probable he will never succeed.
>
> The Hierarchy above alluded to has been subverted in two ways; first by the Malays discovering that their priests had no power to execute their punishments under our rule, and secondly the local authorities have for some time refused to acknowledge any chief among the priests leaving the people to choose their own religious teachers. Such a course if persevered in will do much to ruin the Mahomedan religion.

From this we learn that "Abdul Gunny the priest", whom we have met already was an Arab or of Arab descent, and from another source we learn that "the late Haji Macawi", a prominent figure in Penang about 1825–1850 and a contemporary of Haji Brunei, was also an Arab.

Thus, Thomson *Some glimpses into Life in the Far East* 1864, referring to this man in Penang about the year 1839 on pages 41–42 (Vol. I) says:—

> Among the earliest of the native gentlemen I met was Meccawee, an Arab priest, a native of Mecca ...... and a man of influence among the Malay population, and patronised by the leading European residents, official and unofficial ...... Intimately acquainted with the various social and political movements of the natives, his conversation was interesting and entertaining. At this time the war of Tuanku Mahomed Saad was going on, on the opposite shores, against the Siamese, and this was a fertile subject of discussion between him and his friends. He would fulminate anathemas against the pigs of idolaters, who were now, with the assistance of a British frigate (Osborn's) crushing the spirit of independence that had long survived in Kedah, and he was thoroughly sympathised with by the European merchants and planters.

This passage proves that Haji Macawi was a supporter of Tengku Mohamed Said in the third Kedah rebellion 1838–39 from which we are entitled to infer from the evidence of Chapter XIII, that he was a supporter of that political faction which we identify with the Red Flag and "Tokong".

As we also know from Vaughan and Thomson above that he was a religious leader (Islam makes no distinction between religion and politics), we may assume that he was a leader of the religious faction which afterwards identified itself with the Red Flag.

There is no evidence to show what the personal relations of Haji Macawi with Triad and "Tokong" were, but we may be allowed to assume that as "Tokong" was assisting the Kedah Malay rebels, and Triad was aiding the Siamese, his friendship, if any, was with "Tokong".

Abdul Gunny[1] the Priest

We have seen this man in about 1853 call upon a whole kampong in Penang to renounce (*tobatkan*) its alleged membership of the infidel Ho Seng society. We shall now see that his righteous wrath was either less sincere than would at first appear, or else that after reflection, he took a leaf out of the Triad book and within a few years had organised a league on similar lines among his own followers, from motives which were not entirely those of pure Islam.

Vaughan at the same reference (1858) continues:—

> To regain the thousands that have in a manner forsaken their church, Abdul Gunny has formed a league and many have joined him. They bind themselves by an oath to obey implicitly the teaching of the Koran, and on no account to neglect the ancient usages of Mahomedans, they also promise to keep aloof from those that do not join them, or those that do and subsequently forsake them, they are not to attend feasts held by those that are not in the league, and above all they are not to attend the funerals of those that do not join them. The last provision induces more to join than any other rule, as there is nothing a Mahomedan dreads more than being treated with disrespect after death.

This passage shows that about 1855, in emulation of the former power exercised by Haji Macawi, Abdul Gunny the priest had organised a league bound by an oath under the cloak of Islam and in direct opposition to the teachings of the Prophet.

Two Religious Factions among Malays in Penang 1858

Vaughan concludes:—

> Abdul Gunny has an immense number of followers who hold him in the greatest reverence and to them his word is law; fortunately he appears an inoffensive man but such influence exerted by a bad man might lead to the most serious results. To counteract Abdul Gunny's league, a very

---

Footnote.—(1) Nowadays romanised as Abdul Ghani, or Abdulrani.

powerful party exists of men who may be called, Free-thinkers; educated enough to see the folly of blindly yielding to the will of others, and courageous enough to treat Abdul Gunny's threats with contempt. The leaders of the radical party are the wealthiest men in the place, and are much respected by their countrymen though regarded in the light of indifferent Mahomedans.

This passage is evidence of two distinct religious factions among the Malays of Penang and Province Wellesley about 1858, the leader of one of which was "Abdul Gunny the priest", and the other of which is described as the "radical party" or the "Free-thinkers". We are tempted to identify the latter with the followers of the late Haji Macawi who had mixed freely with Europeans and was obviously a free thinker and a powerful supporter of the Kedah Malay rebels.

Whether these two factions had already at this time adopted the flag distinctions, we are unable to say, but the following centrifugal influences were at work at the time to hasten the separation:—

    (1) The Indian criminal and Thug influence (the latter perhaps descending from the red and white colours of the Assassins of Alamut)—then being absorbed into the population (Chapter X) and tending to hasten the process of differentiation.

    (2) The transition of the Shiah religious festival of the Moharram into the rival secular Hasan and Husein "parties" under the colours white and red respectively (Chapter XII).

    (3) The Kedah-Siam war, tending to glorify "Tokong" in the eyes of the pure-bred Malays as supporting the red flag of the Kedah rebels against the Siamese infidels, their Chinese Triad allies and the pro-Siamese Court faction among the Kedah and Patani Malays themselves (Chapter XIII).

    (4) The intrigues of sufism for power within the congregation of Islam, as illustrated by the "leagues" organised by the two Arabs Haji Macawi and "Abdul Gunny the Priest" (Chapter XIV).

THE CHRYSALIS OF "TABUT" 1858

The inter-operation of these four processes seems to represent the chrysalis stage of "Tabut". How far devout Moslems may have engaged in any, or all of these evolutionary courses, we are unable to say.

It seems to have been the fact that all four of them drew their initial inspiration from imported sources, Indian, Chinese, Siamese and Arab, and that the indigenous Malays only later became involved in them, or exploited by them.

Even the Kedah-Siamese war about which, from the extract from Thomson (above) we know there was strong feeling among leading Mohamedans of Penang, seems to have been at the core more a struggle between Triad and "Tokong", who possessed the means of waging it and hoped for its spoils, than a secret crusade of Islam under the red banner of Kedah,[1] inspired by local hatred of the infidel Siamese.

It would probably be a true generalisation to say, that Tabut reached its chrysalis stage in Malaya through foreign agencies and imported influences.

STILL NO MENTION OF THE FLAG ASSOCIATIONS UP TO 1858

It is clear from the extracts from Vaughan given in Chapter XII that between 1850 and 1860 the Moharram festival in Penang was in process of degeneration, and that there were already two distinct rival parties associated in it, namely, the "devout worshippers" and "the desperate fellows" who baited the devout and carried their horse-play to the length of blood-shed.

According to Vaughan the celebration was even then confined to Indians and "Jawi-pekans", and the indigenous Malays still remained entirely aloof from it.

If we accept Vaughan, who makes no mention of the division into white and red, we are left to conclude either that the devout represented those who were later known as White Flag, and the "desperate fellows" represented the later Red Flag; or else that during the degeneration of the Moharram into the Boria, the devout became squeezed out of participation altogether, and at some stage during the transition period (about 1862) left the field entirely to the "desperate fellows" who were, and always had been divided amongst themselves into White and Red Flag parties. Once in full and undisputed possession of the field "the desperate fellows" fell to quarrelling among themselves in the annual "rag", which completed the metamorphosis of the Moharram festival into the Boria performance.

It is also clear from the extracts from Vaughan given in this chapter that between 1850 and 1855 Malays were freely in association with the Chinese secret societies in Penang, and although the names White Flag and Red Flag are not mentioned, it seems almost certain that they were in common use at this time, possibly (as suggested in Chapter XIII) as a "carry-over" from the Kedah-Siamese war. It is none the less curious that Vaughan does not mention the 'Flag' names, when his notes show that he knew so much else about them.

Footnote.—(1) Mentioned by Osborn (Chapter XIII).

It may have been the common knowledge of their existence that encouraged the leading Arabs of the period to organise them upon religious secret society lines, known to Shiah Islam but abhorrent to the teaching of the Prophet and to the Sunni doctrine, rather than allow their powerful infidel tutors to seduce them from Islam and exploit them to their own ends.

The four separate stems upon which the flag societies developed namely, the Thug deportees and the Moharram festival which provided the Indian element; and the Kedah-Siam war and the Arab-led leagues or religious *Jema'ah*[1] which supplied the Malay element, are thus clearly distinguishable at this point, before they became bridged over and intertwined with Triad and "Tokong", losing their separate identities in criminal and political alliances with the Chinese, which date from about 1860.

Before these four germinal processes become obliterated and Tabut finally emerges from its chrysalis, we may attempt to tabulate them, suggesting how the earlier religious *jema'ah* may have been the fore-runners of those two "religious factions" which played such a notable part in later Penang history. Thus, Hamilton in his article on the Boria (Appendix V) writing in 1920 has :—

> Formerly frequent collisions took place between the two factions of Red and White Flag, the followers of two noted Sayids of Acheen St. and Jelutong respectively, who had formed secret societies in imitation of, and in conjunction with, the Chinese.

May not Haji Macawi have been a founder of one of those societies and perhaps "Abdul Gunny the priest" a founder of the other?

The ingredients of the formative period of the Red and White Flag associations up to the end of the chrysalis stage, might have been something as follows :—

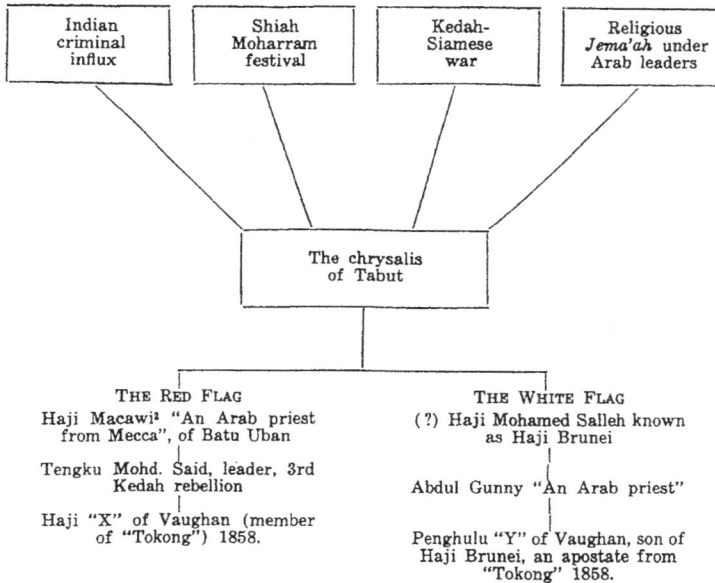

| Indian criminal influx | Shiah Moharram festival | Kedah-Siamese war | Religious *Jema'ah* under Arab leaders |

The chrysalis of Tabut

THE RED FLAG
Haji Macawi[2] "An Arab priest from Mecca", of Batu Uban

Tengku Mohd. Said, leader, 3rd Kedah rebellion

Haji "X" of Vaughan (member of "Tokong") 1858.

THE WHITE FLAG
(?) Haji Mohamed Salleh known as Haji Brunei

Abdul Gunny "An Arab priest"

Penghulu "Y" of Vaughan, son of Haji Brunei, an apostate from "Tokong" 1858.

In Chapter XXX *infra* we discuss the probable identity of the present heads of the Red and White Flag in Penang. After the year 1858, the separate identity of the two flag associations tends more and more to emerge and their respective alliances with Triad and "Tokong" to become evident.

For convenience, we call the two flag associations and their secret activities when referred to collectively, by the generic name of "Tabut", the literal and particular meaning of which word has been given in Chapter XI.

The emergence of "Tabut" in Penang slightly preceded its mention in Singapore by Buckley *op. cit.* in 1864–1865.

Footnote.—(1) Also spelled *Jumaat, Juma'ah,* etc., meaning "a general assembly of the faithful at the Friday mosque service". Thence loosely—and especially of Arab-led leagues such as that of "Abdul Gunny the priest" it can mean, a "congregation" or "body of followers of some particular religious teacher". For a fuller discussion of the term *see* Chapter XXIX *infra*.

Footnote.—(2) There may be a connection between this man and the foundation in 1835 of what is known to-day as the Mata Hari society, *see* Chapter XXVIII *infra*.

THE EMERGENCE OF THE WHITE FLAG

The Penang Riot Commissioners in 1868 printed a draft Report and a final Report. Only the latter is reproduced in Chapter XVI of this work. Para. 22 of the draft Report (*Minutes of Leg. Council 1867–69 Report page 8*) reads:—

The White Flag was established as a society about ten or twelve years ago (circa, 1855). It had existed in some other form, such as the party of performers during the Mohammedan festival of the Muharram for many years previous.

The second sentence is omitted from the final Report, which shows that the Commissioners were in some doubt about the connection between the flag societies and the Chinese secret societies on one side, and the Indian religious festival on the other.

The final Report continues:—

Para. 23.—The object of this (White Flag) society at the time of its establishment was a religious one, *viz*:—to attend and assist at the religious ceremonies of its members, such as marriages, funerals, circumcisions, etc. and its rules contained nothing bad, or injurious to the public. Of late years, the religious matters have been neglected and as described by a witness (No. 37):—

All manner of evil is done, mischief plotted and combination made, to help members out of trouble, instead of having recourse to the authorities.

From among the witnesses we find No. 68 Saiboo (page 73 of the *Penang Riot Commission Report*, Evidence section) who says:—

I am 34 years of age. The White Flag society was established before I was born. (This would give the date of foundation of White Flag as 1830 circa) I cannot say why the White Flag society was formed into a Kongsee. (*i.e.* a secret society).

And again witness No. 37 Mohd. Kader Houssain *alias* Pah Etam, an Indian Mohamedan (and second headman of the White Flag in 1867, although he refused to admit it) states:—

Q. How did people join the Kongsee to which you formerly belonged?
A. Mohammedans do not take an oath. They sign their names to an agreement. That is enough. Formerly the agreement related to religious matters and there was nothing bad in it, but now the agreement is not properly abided by and the consequence is that all manner of evil acts are done, mischief plotted, and combinations among the members made to get compensation for any of the members that may get into trouble, instead of having recourse to the proper authorities.

Again witness No. 44 Yeoh Whey Sew (page 57 of the record) when being questioned about the disappearance of some cloth which was the excuse for the riot, says:—

Q. Did you not get (the cloth) back again?
A. Yes, I got it back.
Q. When?
A. Two or three days afterwards. A Malay man brought it back.
Q. Was he a Red or a White Flag Malay?
A. He is a Mussulman priest[1] and lives half-way between the Red Flag and White Flag districts.

Lastly, we get the following evidence of actual White Flag alliance with Triad.

Para. 25 of the final Report reads:—

This (White Flag) society is composed of Malays and Klings, and during the late riots took part with the Ghee Hins ......

These extracts carry us right through the formative years from the early period before the White Flag had adopted its colour distinction, until we find it in open alliance with Triad in 1867.

THE EMERGENCE OF THE RED FLAG

Para. 26 of the *Penang Riot Commission Report* reads:—

The Red Flag is another society of Malays and Klings, and was established about eight years ago (*i.e.* 1860 circa) for religious purposes, but like the White Flag, it has lost its religious character, and adopted the same bad practices.

This finding like those above relating to the appearance of the White Flag, is no doubt correct, but rather suggests that the flag associations were peculiar to Penang.

We know from Buckley (above) that they were flourishing in Singapore in 1864 and probably for many years earlier. There was, too, the "Great Conspiracy Case" in Singapore of 1865 which brought the Red and White Flag societies to public notice, but this case is unnoticed in the *Penang Riot Commission Report* of 1868.

The process of disintegration and demoralisation of the Red Flag from a Shiah *jema'ah* for purposes of observance of the Moharram, into a criminal gang of Shiah Indian ticket-of-leave men, Sunni Malays and Hindu immigrants allied to "Tokong", took its final plunge in Penang about 1861.

Witness No. 36, before the Penang Riot Commission, named Vappoo Marican Noordin who was second headman of the Red Flag gives the following description as far as it may be believed, on page 52 of the evidence.

Footnote.— (1) This Mussalman priest is mentioned several times in the *Penang Riot Commission Report* but nowhere by name. The Commissioners were evidently unacquainted with Vaughan's writings, or at all events unaware of the secret society activities of the Arab-led religious *jema'ah*, one of which this Mussalman priest may have represented. We suggest that he may have been either "Haji X" or "Abdul Gunny the priest", both of whom we have met above in 1858, or perhaps he was a successor in office.

He states:—

> In 1861, I was one of the headmen of Che Long's *Jumahah* (Society). Some seven or eight months after that there was a fight between the societies of Che Long (Red) and Pah Etam (White). I said to some of the members, "This is a society for religious purposes, you have turned it into a fighting society, therefore, I must take my name off the books. I had not been a member of the society for more than two years. On leaving the society, I forwarded a notice to Mr. Plunket, the Police Magistrate, and to Mr. Waller, the Deputy Commissioner of Police, that I had no longer any connection with any society; this was in December, 1862. In Che Long's society, at the time I was a member, a roll-book was kept of the members in Penang, in which every one was obliged to sign his name; the headmen in the Province kept a similar roll of the members there. When I belonged to the society, there was not a single Kling or Chinese member; all were Malays, excepting a very few "Jawee-pukans": the entrance money was one dollar. I have been told that the old roll-book of the society was destroyed by a member called Arshad, on the occasion of a quarrel that he had with Che Long.

The foregoing extracts mark the definite emergence of Tabut in Penang under the colours White and Red, about 1860. The *Penang Riot Commission Report* is defective in that it makes no reference to the presence of "Tabut" in Singapore, nor to Vaughan's notes published in the *J.I.A.* 1854–1858, which record the association of Triad, "Tokong" and "Tabut" in Penang, ten to fifteen years earlier.

THE IDENTITY OF "TABUT" WITH THE BORIA

The following extracts identify "Tabut" with the Moharram festival in its degenerate form, the Boria:—

(1) In para. 35 of the final *P.R.C. Report* there is the following:—

> The first cause ...... (of the riots) ...... was a quarrel ...... between the Red Flag and White Flag Malays during the last Moharram festival.

(2) In para. 45:—

> *Conclusion* ...... The riots had their origin in a trifling quarrel between two rival Mohammedan societies during the late Moharram festival.

(3) In the printed evidence to the *P.R.C. Report* witness No. 37 Mohamed Kader Houssain *alias* Pah Etam, a Tamil Mohammedan, a hardened prevaricator who was known to be No. 2 in the White Flag at the time although he denied it, says:—

> I was formerly a member of the White Flag society. I joined the society in 1857 and left it in March, 1865.
> I go once a year to the Mosque in the Rope Walk in which they hold Taboot and ceremonies during ten days. After I left the society of which I was Headman,[1] some of the members joined the Red Flag, others the White Flag societies, others joined none, so that now in case of a disturbance, outside people say "Those are Pah Etam's men", referring to those that joined no society ...... Two months ago, a society was formed in Chulia Street. I did not know of it until after it had been arranged by (1) Shaik Madar (2) Mohamed Houssain (3) Che Mat and called "Kongsee Chulia Road".

Again witness 67 Vappoo Marican Noordin (page 73 of the *P.R.C. Report*) says:—

> The White and Red Flags are used by the Mussulmans during the month of Moharram.

This statement is untrue, no doubt, intentionally so, since all the witnesses at this enquiry were governed more by the oath of their particular society to disclose, than by their formal and to them meaningless oath to the Commission, to speak the truth.

We know from Herklots that the Moharram flags were green and red and they so remain to the present-day. To suggest that they were white and red misled the Commissioners into the erroneous belief that the White and Red Flag societies were innocent religious *jema'ah*, based on the observance of the Moharram.

To this impudent adoption of a borrowed religious sanction, which was accepted and became perpetuated by the *P.R.C. Report*, is due much of the subsequent immunity of the White and Red Flag societies from official investigation. We shall notice in later chapters how this immunity has persisted.

Lastly, witness No. 68 Saiboo (page 73 of the *P.R.C. Report*) says:—

> The Red Flag was formed into a Kongsee since the last 8 years. The object of it is that in case of death the members are to go and assist each other. These religious purposes are not carried out any longer: it was discontinued at the time of the riots, about three months after Moharrum time and two or three months before the riots. During Moharrum time the White Flag party goes on one side, but when they meet with the Red Flag party then a fight takes place like Hassan and Hussain parties.

This passage confirms the identity of "Tabut" with the Boria. It also, no doubt, helped to confirm the impudent imposture accepted by the Commissioners, that the flags of the Moharram were white and red. This is all the more surprising when we remember that the European officialdom of that day had an entirely Indian background.

This passage is interesting for another reason.

It is the first reference we have found to "the Hasan and Husein parties" as such, and also the first statement that the White and Red Flag societies of Penang claimed to be the local representation of those two pseudo-parties of the Indian Moharram.

There is, of course, no religious sanction in Shiah Islam for thus dividing the Alids (*see* Chapter X) into two hostile groups.

Footnote.—(1) He implies that it was a religious *jema'ah* of pre-flag-association vintage.

It was part of the process of distortion undergone by the Moharram in Penang that this local division developed and gained acceptance, until to-day in Malaya, the names of the Alids are synonymous with the flag associations, and are made to appear as separate and rival figures in the annual Boria, of which in the religious sense they are the central object of adoration.

The fights that resulted between the so-called Hassan and Husein parties, from this grotesque perversion, were from the very first the expression of the rivalries of the two secret societies of the White and the Red Flag and owed nothing to the Moharram but the borrowed prestige of the Alids. The riots that in later years disgraced the annual Boria season, completed the metamorphosis of a religious observance into a criminal orgy.

WHITE TRIAD, RED "TOKONG"

In Chapter XIII, we have seen the lining up of Triad with what became the White Flag, and of "Tokong" with what became the Red.

The *P.R.C. Report* makes the alliances of the two camps by 1867 quite clear. Para. 24 reads:—

> The White Flag society is in alliance with the Ghee Hins.

And para. 28:—

> In the year 1863, a fight took place between the Che Longs (Red Flag) and the Toh Peh Kong societies, after which these two societies became friendly and entered into an alliance for offensive and defensive purposes.

The *P.R.C. Report* is silent upon the origin of the colours, which is discussed in the next chapter, nor does it sufficiently emphasize the preponderating influence of the "Jawi-pekan" community in the flag societies at that date, an omission which the following paragraph may help to correct.

"JAWI-PEKANS" IN PROVINCE WELLESLEY 1867

In an article by J. R. Logan written in 1867 entitled *A Volunteer Police for Province Wellesley* and published in the *J.R.A.S.S.B.* for December, 1885, there occurs the following description of "Jawi-pekans" and their connection at that time with secret societies.

Page 185:—

> This Settlement is exposed to disturbances from three sources:—
> (1) The quarrels, originating here, or propagated from abroad, of the Chinese societies.
> (2) The quarrels of the Mohamedan *Jumahas*.
> (3) The existence of professional banditti in the adjacent Malay States ......
> The character and habits of our own population, especially of the immigrant and shifting classes make it very susceptible to such disturbances and a strong and active element of mischief is supplied in the case of allied Mohamedan and Chinese societies, by the ambition, craft and rapacity of a colonial class in which the subtlety of the Chinese, the effrontery of the Kling and the dissimulation and vanity of both are mingled with the boldness and suavity of the Malay. This class is known as the "Jawi-pekan".

Page 197:—

> A "Jawi-pekan"......inherits the boldness of the Malay and the subtlety, acuteness and dissimulation of the Hindoo (Indian). The same applies to all descendants of Indians, born and brought up in the Settlement.

> *   *   *

> The class of these men in the public offices are mostly related by blood or marriage. The progenitors were Jawi-pekans of Kedah, but while some of the present first and second cousins are not distinguishable from Malays, others are hardly distinguishable in person from Klings. The paid Police Penghulus, the collectors of Government rents and Municipal rates, the land measurers, the shroffs, Malay writers and Interpreters *have always largely belonged to this family alliance,* which also includes several of the leading men of the *jumahas*, many of the principal Malay and Kling (Pinang-born) merchants, and maintains a hereditary connection with the Kedah Court. Members of it are often employed by the Raja of Kedah as "kranis" and land measurers. Captain Light, in a despatch to the Supreme Government of India, dated 12th September, 1786, gives, in the course of a report on the state of affairs in Kedah, a strong instance of the extent to which the cunning of natives of India and their descendants sometimes enables them to rule Malays.

> "Datu Sri Raja (formerly named Ismal, and a common coolie) is now the King's merchant; he is a deep, cunning, villainous Chuliah. By working on the King's pusillanimity and raising jealousies, he reduced the power of the great men and engrossed the whole of the administration, by preferring only such as he thought attached to himself. To save the King from pretended assassinations, he built a small brick fort and built him up as in a cage; no one dares presume to go to audience without his knowledge. If he found any of the great men likely to get into favour, he bribed them to his interest. By monopolising every species of commerce, and oppressing the Malays, he found means to supply the King's necessities without his having the trouble to enquire how it (the money) came.

> He (the king) receives likewise a deal in presents and fines. Every person who has any demand to make, or suit to prefer first presents a sum of money which he thinks adequate to the demand; if the King approves of the sum he signs the paper, and his suit is obtained unless another person comes with greater sums".

> This would serve as an account of the administration of justice in the Malay States at the present-day (*i.e.* 1867).

> The Colonial Chinese (Babas) by intermarrying among themselves, and the women with pure Chinese, have largely eliminated the original Malay half-blood. They are distinguished by their conceit and forwardness; but have more softness and amenity of manner than the Jawi-pekans; retaining, in this respect, the impress of their Malay descent and association. They are intelligent, bold and pushing, and some of the secret societies, notably the head of the Twa-peh-kong, are drawn from this class. It is through their intimacy with the town Jawi-pekans and the Malay heads of the *jumahas* that the latter societies have been so easily brought into alliance with the former, notwithstanding the ban placed by Mohamedanism on all friendly

association with "infidels". It should be added that there is a considerable class composed of Jawi-pekans, Babas and Malays who are noted for their "fast" lives, and many of whom are led on from gambling and licentiousness to theft and other crimes. The recklessness and love of mischief and excitement render them a dangerous element in the societies to which large numbers of them belong.

The Chinese are gradually pushing their way among the Malays of north Province Wellesley, and as they increase in numbers and wealth, the Malays borrow money from them whenever they can, become more dependent on them and more liable to be seduced into joining their societies.

The foregoing might very well stand as a description of under surface conditions to-day in the secret society life of Malaya, as we shall have occasion to point out as we proceed with our story.

HINDU ELEMENT IN THE RED FLAG

The degeneration of the Moharram festival in Malaya by absorption of Hindu elements is illustrated by the secondary meaning given the word "Tabut" by Wilkinson (*see* definitions at beginning of Chapter XI) *viz:*—"A Hindu image or processional emblem".

There is constant reference to "Kling" membership of the flag societies in the *P.R.C. Report*. The name "Kling" at that time being applied in Malaya to all Indians, Hindu and Moslem, (Yule *Hobson-Jobson* page 372) and doubtless included "Chulias" (Indian Mohamedan traders) and "Jawi-pekans", the progeny of Indian settlers, many of whom were at this time ex-convicts and liberated Thugs.

This is illustrated by witness No. 36 Shamoo (page 47 of the *P.R.C. Report*) who although his religion is not recorded, may be accepted from his name as being a Hindu, "who came from Negapatam about nine years ago" and who states that he joined the Ghee Hin society in 1866, "because he lived in the midst of Ghee Hins". He does not say that he joined the White Flag society, but it is probable that this is what he either meant, or at any rate what he really did join.

Again witness No. 38 Saiboo (pages 51 and 73 of the *P.R.C. Report*) whose origin and religion are again not given, but who is recorded as being "a schoolmaster of Chulia Street", is quite definite that he was a member of the White Flag society only, and was not (page 73) a member of the Ghee Hin. We may surmise that he was also a Hindu.

Again witness No. 37 Mohamed Kader Houssain, *alias* Pah Etam (No. 2 of the White Flag) (page 50) states:—

> About the time of the riots more than 300 men, Klings and Malays joined the Red Flag society.

It is probable that a large percentage of those Klings were Hindus.

Again witness No. 67 Vappoo Marican Noordin (page 73) :—

> Two different societies were formed before they joined the Chinese societies. Many Klings belong to the Red Flag society.

We may presume that this witness was not referring in his last sentence to fellow-Indian Mohammedans like himself, but to Hindus.

Lastly, the *P.R.C. Report* para. 45 "Conclusion", has the following final sentence:—

> A notable circumstance, and one that has rendered these societies more harmful of late, is the combination of Mussulmans and Hindus with the Chinese, with whose customs their religious prejudices are so much at variance.

From the foregoing we may infer that by 1867 there was a large Hindu element among the membership of both White and Red Flag, but particularly the latter, and that a large proportion of these were Thugs, or the "Jawi-pekan" offspring of Thugs.

The period of the criminal influx from India 1830–1873, coincides with the rise of the criminal flag associations in Malaya, the date of whose emergence on organised lines we may place at 1860 or a little earlier. We may hazard the guess that a good many "foundation members" of these associations in their criminal form were Indian deportees, who shortly gained their freedom and became ordinary settlers. We have already noted in Chapter XII some elements of Thuggism in the Moharram festival, which have been reproduced in the Boria. These Thug elements obtrude themselves more markedly in the Red Flag initiation ceremony than in the White, a subject further discussed in Chapter XXIX.

It is clear that the Red Flag and its foster-parent "Tokong", and, we submit, "Tokong's" counterpart the Sa Tiam Hui (Chapters VIII and IX) whose sole purpose was criminality, would naturally attract to its standard the criminal, as distinct from the harmless coolie-type of Indian settler, and thus become, as it has remained, the more dangerous of the two flag associations.

Hutson (in Chapter II) referring to the Han Liu, from which we submit (Chapter VIII) "Tokong" and the Sa Tiam Hui have sprung, has:—

> Investigating the origin of this school, we find it begins in hoary antiquity, and probably represents the most ancient demon worship. The class tenaciously holds to natural depravity, resists external reforms, and through the ages has made licentious liberty the chief ideal of life.

And again:—

> The chief Han Liu ideal is liberty, which means to them anarchy, selfishness and depravity, and it may be said that the society is always "agin the Government".

This creed would find most followers among the liberated Indian criminals and Thugs in Penang of that day, in preference to the comparatively more respectable tenets and ancestry of Triad. Malays too, faced with the growing power of law and order, would freely join an association whose promise of organised plunder stirred again their pirate blood.

THE FINAL EMERGENCE OF "TABUT" IN MALAYA

The final emergence of "Tabut" between 1830 and 1867 and its conclusive identification with the Boria of the Malays, thence with those secret associations of "infidel" Hindus and Chinese, of whose existence the Boria is an established outward manifestation, has been sealed by the following *pantun:*—

> *Angkat tabut malam sa-puloh,*
> *Serunai gendang bunyi rioh,*
> *Bulan terang api di-suloh,*
> *Keling, China tempoh-menempoh.*

CHAPTER XV

THE HISTORICAL ORIGINS OF THE RED AND
WHITE FLAG SOCIETIES

Direct evidence upon the origin of the Flag societies and their colours, as they exist in Malaya to-day is nowhere to be found, but three theories are here presented to the reader's notice, namely:—

 (A) The Hare and Stirling *dictum.*—That they were from first to last nothing but appanages of the Chinese dangerous societies, (Triad and "Tokong"), deriving their names from the Chinese word "White" which means "loyalty" and the Chinese word "Red" which means "righteousness", and were merely local "mutual benefit associations" with criminal tendencies in imitation of their Chinese parent societies.

 (B) The Cowan and Luering *dictum.*—That they were of foreign origin, being local branches of secret societies common to the Pan-Islamic world, with headquarters in Mecca and representing the rival Mohamedan sects of Sunni and Shiah.

 (C) A new theory, now offered.—That whatever the source of the colours may be, and whatever the societies may have later become, they had their local origin in the struggle between Kedah and Siam which lasted from 1821 to 1848.

The evidence in support of the three different theories is as follows:—

(A) THE THEORY OF HARE

The only material in support of this theory is to be found in the writings of Hare and later Stirling, which are more in the nature of *ex-cathedra* statements than reasoned opinions supported by evidence, and appear to ignore the findings of the *Penang Riot Commission Report* (Chapter XVI).

Mr. G. T. Hare, Secretary for Chinese Affairs, Federated Malay States, wrote two memoranda on this subject dated 4th March, 1903 and 30th May, 1903 (reprinted *in extenso* in Appendix X).

The following are extracts from that of 4th March, 1903:—

"The White and Red societies spring from the old Gi Heng and Gi Hok Chinese societies in Singapore and from the old Gi Heng and Ho Sang societies in Penang. In their origin they were in both cases off-shoots of the Chinese dangerous societies. They were practically created by the Chinese headmen of the old societies as assistant branches to deal with the Colonial Police, many of whom were affiliated members of these flag associations. The word "red" means what is called in Chinese "righteousness" and the word "white" means "loyalty". "Righteousness" and "loyalty" are the two chief watchwords of the old Gi Heng and Gi Hok-Ho Seng dangerous societies, and the Malay words are really translations of the Chinese terms".

This view rests on the fact that the Chinese character 白 pe, pai, or paak, meaning "white", has a secondary meaning, "bright", "clear", or "pure". Upon this fact four assumptions are based:—

 (1) That the secondary meaning connotes the Chinese character 義 ghee, or yi = "righteousness", "loyalty", which is one of the characters of the Ghee Hin (義興) society.

 (2) That when the White Flag of the Malays allied itself with the Ghee Hin of the Chinese, it adopted by metalepsis the colour white to designate its affinity.

Similarly:—

 (3) That because the Chinese character 紅 hung, meaning, "red", is emblematic of "good-luck", joy and merrymaking, it connotes the Chinese character 福 hok, or fuk, = happiness, which is one of the characters of the Ghee Hok (義福) society.

 (4) That when the Red Flag allied itself with the Ghee Hok, it adopted, similarly, the colour red to bind the alliance.

Apart from the loose reasoning in Hare's proposition, which confuses the colour "red" with "righteousness", with which it has no affinity in Chinese, and also confuses the names of the Ghee Hin and Ghee Hok with their "watchwords" (discussed on page 84 *supra*), the general grounds for this view appear slender and far-fetched.

Further publicity has been given to what we consider this erroneous view of Hare, by Ward and Stirling who, in Vol. I *op. cit.* page 139, have the following :—

> The word "red" means "righteousness" in Chinese and the word "white", "loyalty". These two words play an important part in the Triad rituals and the Malay words are only translations of the Chinese terms.

Hare in his memo of 4th March, 1903 continues :—

> The Red and White Flag societies in Singapore and Penang included chiefly Jawa-Peranakans, Javanese, Boyanese, Klings and local Malays of the bully type. The Malays were always tools in the hands of the Presidents and Vice-Presidents of the old Chinese societies and they were engaged to do any dirty work that the Chinese society men did not want brought home to their own Chinese societies. The Red Flags and White Flags were recruited as opposition forces in Penang by the Gi Heng and Ho Seng, and in Singapore by the Gi Hok and Gi Heng, the four great antagonistic divisions into which the societies were then split up.
>
> During the 30 years that these Chinese dangerous societies flourished in the Straits, the Red Flag and White Flag Malay-Kling societies were treated as branches of the Chinese ones, though they were never registered by Government or recognised by the Police.
>
> It is quite a mistake to think that the Red and White Flag societies are independent Malay bodies or that they have any political aims. From first to last these Red and White Flag societies have never been anything than an appanage of the old registered Chinese dangerous societies, who supported them with funds on condition of being served by them.

We disagree with this view. In Chapters V and XIII, we have seen the beginnings of political intrigue in which those divisions, which later became the flag societies, took part.

Subsequent chapters will disclose the flag societies in political action in Perak and elsewhere from 1870 onwards under their colour distinctions.

Further currency has been given to this view by Ward and Stirling *op. cit.* Vol. I page 139 in the following passage :—

> Neither the Red nor the White society was ever officially recognised by the British Government in Singapore, wherein they differed from the old Ghee Hin.
>
> It seems probable that the White Flag society was founded by members of the Ghee Hin society in order to obtain control of members of the Malay Police and that the Red Flag society was founded by the Ghee Hok.

It is true that the Red and White Flag societies have never been officially recognised in the Malay States but they were suppressed in 1882 in the Straits Settlements where, in Section 3 of Ordinance IV of 1882,[1] we read :—

> The societies known as the Red Flag and White Flag and all similar associations by whatever name the same may be known, are hereby declared to be unlawful societies.

Further publicity was given to the same view by Stirling in an article published in the *J.M.B.R.A.S.* in April, 1925, in which the following passage occurs :—

> There can be no doubt that the Red and White Flag societies were created at the instance of the Headmen of the Ghee Hin and Ghee Hok Triad societies[2] and were used to deal with the local police (the majority of whom are still Malays) and such other Malays as headmen, schoolmasters, bailiffs and other Government employees. The word "Red" signified "righteousness" and the word "White" "loyalty". For righteousness and loyalty were the two watchwords of the Triad society. The colours of the flags, which were triangular in shape were red and white, such flags are in common use among Muslims. Votive flags of these colours are often found at sacred spots, where spirits are supposed to reside.
>
> The existence of these societies was purely local. Their members were mostly bullies and were engaged by the Chinese Triad society to do work, which the Chinese Triad society did not want brought home to it. The two societies were never recognised or registered by the Government in the same way as the Ghee Hin, Ghee Hok, and other Triad societies were recognised before 1890, when all of them were declared unlawful and dangerous, and compelled to hand over their seals and insignia to the Government. These Malay bodies had not political aims like the ordinary aims of the Triad society. From first to last they were appendages and conveniences of the latter. Some time after the suppression of the latter, they became insignificant, though at odd times they caused trouble by levying blackmail and causing disturbances. But their activities never caused serious concern, and I suppose they no longer exist to-day. The formation of these secret societies is rather alien to the Malay character, and must depend generally on a religious motive. The Red and White Flag societies were only kept alive by the knowledge that they had in the Triad society a powerful organisation behind them.

These views, evidently deriving in the first place from Hare, appear to have crystallised into the hitherto generally accepted version of the origin of the flag associations and have been thus expressed again by Ward and Stirling Vol. I page 137 :—

> The White Flag society was established about 1890,[3] its object being semi-religious, more especially to assist at religious funerals and circumcisions...... It also set out to help a brother in need and to assist him to redress his wrongs, real or supposed. It had some sort of treaty alliance with the Ghee Hin society, the mother lodge of the Hung society in Singapore, which in that very year (1890) was declared illegal by the Government.[4]
>
> The White Flag society consisted of Malays and of Tamils who had originally come from the Madras Presidency to work in the Straits Settlements. Later it seems to have lost its religious character and tended more and more to be diverted to unworthy objects.
>
> The Red Flag society was very similar and was established a little later[5] with almost precisely the same original objects. Both societies were mutual benefit clubs and among their avowed duties were those of assisting a brother against injustice and Police exactions and of aiding a poor brother in time of trouble.

Footnote.—(1) This Ordinance and that of 1885 are further discussed in Chapter XXI *infra.*
Footnote.—(2) Here we have the two rival camps both referred to by the name of one of them.
Footnote.—(3) The correct date is probably about 1830. The writers have forgotten the Penang riots of 1867.
Footnote.—(4) *See* Chapter XXI *infra.*
Footnote.—(5) It was going strong in 1863.

It is probably from this dictum of Hare and Stirling which has received much more publicity than any other view, that the general belief in the unimportance and moribund condition of the flag societies has arisen. In view of what is contained in Chapters X, XI and XII, we find ourselves unable to accept this dictum, for two primary reasons:—

Firstly, because although Malays are Sunnis, the Moharram festival and its later development into the Penang Boria is of definite Shiah origin and it must be satisfactorily explained how this Shiah celebration with which the flag societies are so closely bound up, came to take root in Penang, before we can feel that we are upon the right road to a correct solution of their origin.

Secondly, because the comfortable doctrine that the flag societies are harmless, being no more than local kampong mutual-benefit associations, or at worst "kongsi churi ayam", does not fit the facts.

Seeing the connection admitted also by Hare and Stirling, between the White Flag and Triad, and the Red Flag and "Tokong", it seems much more probable that all manifestations of mutual benefit clubs among Malays in the Peninsula are evidence of the activities of the flag societies, until the contrary is proved.   All the evidence presented in subsequent chapters supports this view.

In this connection Vaughan *Manners and Customs of the Chinese of the Straits Settlements* (1879) page 109 has:—

> It is said that the Red and White Flag societies amongst the Klings are affiliated to the Triad societies, the one to the Ghee Hin and the other to the Ghee Hok; but the Klings affirm that this is untrue. They say that their societies were brought from the Coromandel Coast and have no connection with the Chinese secret societies. It is a notorious fact that throughout the Colony, Malays and Klings and other races are members of the (Chinese) secret societies.

We do not know what societies amongst "Klings" of the Coromandel Coast may have existed in 1879, all of which are such vague terms, but as the reference is to Indian Mohamedans, it takes us back to the Moharram festival, and to the Sufi-Thug-Assassin link therewith.

(B) THE THEORY OF COWAN

Mr. William Cowan, Protector of Chinese, Perak, wrote a reply dated 9th April, 1903 (printed in full in Appendix X) to Hare's memorandum of 4th March, 1903.
The following are extracts from Cowan's memorandum:—

* * *

> *Para. 9.* I am of opinion the White and Red Flag societies are of exotic origin. They are not merely off-shoots of the Chinese dangerous societies as stated by Mr. Hare, but an inter-mixture of such societies, *viz.*, the Gi-Hin and Toa-peh-Kong with that of the two Muhammedan rival sects, *viz.*, the Sunnis and Shiah.
>
> *Para. 10.* I am informed by the Rev. Dr. Luering, an accomplished Malay and Arabic scholar, that all Muhammedan secret societies have taken their origin from the early political dispute which arose regarding the rightful succession in the early Caliphate, and which gave rise to the division of Islam into two rival sects, the Sunni and Shiah.[1] The enmity between them has existed unabated ever since, though it usually breaks out during the Muharram festival. On the 10th of this month (A.H. 61, A.D. 680) Hussain, the younger and then only surviving son of Ali, the son-in-law of the Prophet Muhammad, was killed in the massacre of Karbala, and the Shiah sect in their lamentations over the ill-fated brothers, Hassan and Husain, has annually revenged their undeserved and cruel murders.
>
> *Para. 11.* Please also refer to the evidence of Vapoo Marican Noordin and Saiboo, Nos. 67 and 68, page 73 of the book *re* the "Penang Riots of 1867",[2] where it says that the White and Red Flags are used by the Mussulmans during the month of Muharram, also that during the Muharram time the White Flag party goes on one side, but when they meet with the Red Flag party, then a fight takes place, like Hassan and Husain parties......

The Rev. Dr. Luering of Ipoh, in a letter to Cowan (printed in full in Appendix X) dated March 31st 1903, says:—

> 1. I have had the opportunity of a conversation with His Highness the Raja Muda, and have made private enquiries among a few influential Malays, which has convinced me that even here, the societies referred to by you, have not only been composed of the lower classes of Malays, but have had among their headmen the most influential inhabitants of the various districts. I have heard of penghulus, imams, Government pensioners, such as Police sergeants, school-teachers and others having taken a leading part in the management of these societies. His Highness the Raja Muda, as you know, felt great anxiety for his personal safety, but not from bullies or gang-robbers, belonging to this society. In his opinion the danger was much greater, and he felt compelled to take special precautions against the measures of the society. This tends to prove that in his opinion this society, in addition to whatever else may have been the particular purpose of the organisation, has also a political object in view.
>
> 2. I do not deny that in the Penang Riots (1867) and on other occasions, Malay and Chinese secret societies have gone hand in hand in their opposition against the Government and public safety. I also know that it has repeatedly been proved that Chinese societies have admitted Malays as members, but I do not think that this proves the identity of Chinese and Malay societies.

Footnote.—(1) *See* Chapter X *supra.*
Footnote.—(2) *i.e.* The *Penang Riot Commission Report* 1868.

3. Even the colours of the flags offer no conclusive proof thereof. "White" and "Red" flags have always been distinct emblems of true Muhammadan societies or *tarikahs*.[1] Literature on the subject of secret societies of the Muhammadans is rare, though these facts cannot be unknown to the student of the Muhammadan faith, but there is one English authority,[2] which I can quote on the subject of flags; C. W. Heckethorn, *Secret Societies*, Vol. I page 132, speaks of the Kadiriyeh society which I mentioned to you in a former letter, and gives as their outward marks, "white flags and turbans". The Said Badani, another organisation of this sort, is divided into different sections whose flags are red and white.

The Kadiriyeh and Said Badani sects of the dervishes are mentioned in Chapter X *supra*, where we have expressed the view that although there may be a superficial resemblance, it seems improbable that there is any direct connection between the dervish sects and the Malayan flag societies.

Dr. Luering continues:—

These *tarikahs* have made a considerable headway among Malay pilgrims. The centre of the organisation is in Mecca, and it is especially the Kadiriyeh (White Flag society) which is in favour among them. Several of the greatest Malay sheikhs in Mecca belong to this secret society, *see* Snouck Hurgronje, pages 351, 354, 372, 378 and *passim*.[3] I need not speak here of the real danger to Government which these societies present.

Dr. Snouck Hurgronje gives the text of a placard published in Mecca and posted up in 1885 at the very walls of the Kaaba, which incites the faithful to the murder of the Turkish Resident Othman Pasha, who by some strict but necessary measure had displeased a portion of the Meccan population. This paper is signed "Sharikat Islam"* *i.e.* on behalf of the Islamic Association. There are several organisations in Malaysia bearing the same name.

* This name is left blank in the original "Taiping Print" (Appendix X), presumably because it was illegible to the printer. Upon the clue provided by the phrase "on behalf of the Islamic Association", we have taken the liberty to suggest that the name intended is "the Sharikat Islam". Assuming this guess to be correct, we may mention here that evidence will be offered in Chapters XXVIII and XXXV *infra* showing recent connection between the Sharikat Islam in Mecca and in the Netherlands Indies with the White Flag in Malaya. This in turn suggests that the Sharikat Islam is an association of purely Sunni Islam, probably mainly religious and more or less secret and in any case unconnected with the dervish sects of Shiah Islam, such as the Kadirijeh or Said Badani mentioned by Dr. Luering.[4] This would help to explain the common use among Malays of the term *jema'ah* to describe their religious "schools" or assemblies in preference to the term *tarikah* which suggests a Shiah school of sufism. Dr. Luering concludes:—

I do not think that it would be politic for Government to make any hard and fast rules against Malay associations,[5] but I do think that for the peace and welfare of the country the Government should keep themselves fully informed with regard to the possible developments of such associations. This is the opinion of the eminent Dutch authority quoted above. His second volume closes with a wise and statesman-like warning which I take the liberty of translating (adding a few explanatory notes in brackets):—

The other consequences of the Haj (pilgrimage) are almost insignificant in comparison to the flourishing Malay colony in Mecca. The heart of the religious life of the Eastern Archipelago is there and an ever-growing number of arteries circulate the fresh blood in increasingly rapid pulsation through the whole body of the Muhammadan population. There the various ramifications of the mystic associations of the Jawah (Arabic for "Malays") come together, from there they get their literature which is taught in their (Koran) schools, there the people, through their friends and relatives resident in Mecca, take a part in the Pan-Islamic life and endeavour. As it is impossible, at this time, to dam up the continual stream of pilgrims, it is equally impossible to prevent that every coming and returning current (ships and other means of communications) which carries with it germs to Arabia, which develop there, and returns to us fully developed organisms which multiply here. It is, therefore, of importance that the Government should know what is developing in Mecca; which elements gather there from year to year, and how these elements, by wise treatment, may be won for the purposes of Government, or at least can be made harmless.

Hare, in a final reply to the views of Cowan and Luering, expresses disagreement with them in a memo dated 30th May, 1903 (reprinted in full in Appendix X) from which the following are extracts:—

1. It appears to me that Mr. Cowan and Dr. Luering both confound issues that are naturally distinct. As regards my previous remarks about the Malay Red and White Flag societies and

---

Footnote.—(1) The use of the word *tarikah* by Dr. Luering should be noted. It is the Malay form (also spelled *tarekat*) of the Arabic word *tarikat* = path, and means "the way of the mystic", the path to Truth through mysticism. The word is, therefore, wholly associated with sufism and thence with Shiah Islam. Cf. Wilkinson's Dictionary (1932). *Ilmu tarekat* = mystic doctrine: other synonyms are *ilmu sufi; ilmu tasawuf* and *ilmu suluk*. As used by Dr. Luering it has the same meaning as "religious *jema'ah*" *see* Chapter XIV footnote 1 page 221 *supra* and also Chapter XXIX *infra*.

Footnote.—(2) Heckethorn: *The Secret Societies of all ages and countries*, 2 Vols. first edition 1874; second edition (which is that quoted throughout this work and by Dr. Luering above) published in 1897, by George Redway, London. The best work of its kind in English up to that date and contains a useful bibliography in each volume.

Footnote.—(3) We have been unable to consult the original of this reference.

Footnote.—(4) Yeats-Brown *European Jungle* (published in May, 1939), page 236 has:—
"Strange how little we know of these mysteries of Islam...... If there is now to be a war in Europe, the world will hear more of the Dervish orders, for they are connected with a powerful pan-Islamic movement".

Footnote.—(5) Dr. Luering was evidently unaware of Colony Ordinance No. IV of 1885, suppressing the Red and White Flags in the Straits Settlements.

their connection with the Chinese Triad societies,[1] it is submitted there can be little question, as it is now a matter of history. Whether these Malay flag societies were off-shoots of the Triad societies[1] or independent Sunnite and Shiah organisations that joined the Chinese societies to get the benefit of the power and strength of the Chinese to forward their mutual animosity against one another, it is perhaps difficult to decide as there is little evidence extant about this. One fact, however, is clear, and that is that the Malays are practically all Sunnites (as far as they are educated in Muhammadan theology at all), and that very few Malays even know of the existence of the Shiah sect. It does not, therefore, seem likely that the Malay Red and White Flag societies are the rival parties of the Shiahs and Sunnites in disguise.

We agree that the local Red and White Flags are definitely not the rival schisms of Islam in disguise. We have attempted in Chapter XII to estimate the degree of religious influence to be found in them which has seeped through the Shiah channel of the Moharram festival.

Still less are they "the rival parties of Hasan and Husein", which do not exist in Shiah Islam. Nevertheless, some interested witnesses before the Penang Riot Commission in 1868, attempted, as we have seen, to foist this explanation upon unsuspecting European enquirers.

There is, indeed, independent support for the opposite view in Dr. Brewer's *Dictionary of Phrase and Fable* (20th edition) where the following definitions occur:—

Sunnites (page 864):—
Orthodox Mohometans who consider the Sunna or Oral law as binding as the Koran. They wear White turbans. The heterodox Moslems are called Schiites.

Schiites (page 794):—
Those Mohometans who do not consider the Sunna or Oral law of any authority, but look upon it as apocryphal. They wear Red turbans and are called "red heads".

The modern standard authorities, *Encyclopaedia of Islam*, etc., do not, however, support this colour distinction, which would be the explanation superficially most suited to fit the White and Red Flag societies of Penang. We merely draw attention here to the existence of this simple colour division, reminiscent of the distinguishing colours of Triad and "Tokong", but as it lacks confirmation and in other ways does not suit the circumstances of the birth of White and Red Flag societies in Penang, we must reject it.

Apart from this, there seems to be no evidence to support the belief that the origin of the White and Red Flags is to be found in the rivalries of the Sunni and Shiah schism, whose line of religious cleavage is no longer noticeable in Malaya, where the vast majority of Mohamedans are Sunnis and where the followers of the two rival flags are, therefore, of necessity professing members of the same religious faction. Added to this it can hardly be imagined, that if such a religious cleavage existed, it would seek to hide itself in alliance with infidel Chinese societies, and employ their rituals.

No doubt, the early system of government through the leaders of the different communities under the "Kapitan" system referred to in Chapter XIII, may have emphasised the cleavage between Sunni and Shiah in early Penang, where in 1804 the population contained 6,000 Sunni Malays and 4,000 Indians "chiefly Shiah traders known as Chulias". These would naturally remain apart and distinct in separate communities and with separate mosques.

The generally Indian background and atmosphere of Penang in those days would also tend to emphasise the racial and language differences of the two Mohamedan factions.

Evidence, however, is absent to help us to decide how far these circumstances may have incubated the germ of the White and Red Flag secret societies.

The fact that the Malays are Sunnis and that the flag associations have, in their restricted religious sphere, a Shiah origin, demands acknowledgment, nevertheless, of a certain degree and certain quality of Sunni-Shiah rivalry in the early stages of their development.

Hare concludes:—

* * *

I am also told that there are kinds of village clubs in some Malay kampongs formed by some leading headmen who have sufficient influence to force the rest of the Malays to combine to boycott enemies, engage counsel for litigation for those who get into trouble, prevent competition in securing contracts, etc. Such societies are very loosely organised and there is, too, an inherent weakness in such a society, as it entirely depends upon the personal influence of one man and rarely extends beyond the kampong. A headman of a secret society proper, however, is nearly always utterly insignificant outside his official position as "Headman of a Society", in fact it is impossible to treat such petty Malay clubs as "secret societies" at all, though their *modus operandi* may be clandestine, for there is little to shew where personal influence ends or society organisation begins.

In Chapter XIV, with the aid of Vaughan, we have attempted to show the growth of Tabut out of the complex elements which combined to form its chrysalis, into a separate stem of the undersurface cosmos allied to, but independent of, Triad and "Tokong".

We admit the importance of personal influence in this development, but subsequent evidence will show this influence to be the same to-day as we have seen it in its beginnings in Chapter XIV, namely, Arab. Not only is Tabut in modern Malaya Arab-inspired and Arab-controlled, but evidence will be offered (Chapter XXV) to show that each flag association is governed by an hereditary Arab hierarchy.

Footnote.—(1) Here we have the term Triad societies used in the plural officially for the first time. This error has since become a habit.

HIGH WATERMARK OF PAST ENQUIRY

The foregoing views represent the high watermark of past recorded official investigation into this subject.

The views remained divergent at the close of the 1903 correspondence, and no further comparison, discussion, or exploration of the different opinions appears to have been made since that date.

Neither Hare nor Cowan have presented much evidence in support of their views, and, while these each contain much that is doubtless correct, neither view, presents a satisfying explanation of the origin of the Flag societies, and we must, therefore, seek for the source elsewhere.

(C) A NEW THEORY

That whatever they may have later become, the White and Red Flag societies had their local beginning in the political struggle between Kedah and Siam, which opened in 1821 and closed in 1848.

Although it is our purpose in this work to confine ourselves as much as possible to fact and to the recorded opinions of others, we ask in this instance some latitude, in order to present such evidence as we have been able to find to support this theory.

The true origin of the Flag societies is a particularly obscure point, and also one of the greatest importance, in view of the political complexion which these societies assumed at the time of British intervention in Perak, and subsequently.

From points made in preceeding chapters we know as follows:—

Chapter V.—

In 1825–1830, when Siam was at war with Burma (Ava) and Kedah, the Siamese in the person of the Raja of Ligor, himself said to be half Chinese, were receiving aid from Ghee Hins and Hai Sans in Penang, Junk Ceylon, and even as far as Pegu (Rangoon), both societies being then chiefly Cantonese.

Chapter VI.—

Between the years 1830 and 1850, the Hai San changed its composition from Cantonese to Hakka, and became hostile to the Ghee Hins, probably due to events in China (Chapter IV). Meanwhile in 1844, a new society, the Toh Peh Kong, was formed by Hokkiens, and at the date of its foundation was also hostile to the Hai Sans, but later amalgamated with the Hai Sans as "Tokong", in hostility to the Ghee Hins (Triad). The President of the Ghee Hins in Penang in 1850 was Man Ah Fu, who had held this position for some thirty years had great influence and had originally come to Penang from Calcutta.

Chapter X.—

Between 1830 and 1870, large numbers of Indian convicts including Thugs who belong to an hereditary criminal sect, were absorbed into the population of Penang and Singapore and reared families known as "Jawi-pekans" or "Peranakans".

Chapter XII.—

Between 1800 and 1850, the Shiah festival of the Moharram became established in Penang. By 1850, it was being burlesqued by the "Jawi-pekans" and other "desperate fellows", and had entered its transitional period from religious festival to hooligan masquerade, now know as the Boria.

In 1850, it was still known as the Moharram, and was still disavowed and ignored by the genuine Malay population, while beginning to evince characteristics of Indian criminality.

Chapter XIII.—

About the year 1838, there is definite evidence of secret "associations" among the Malays of Penang, in connection with the rebellion against Siam of that year. There is also evidence that the banner of the Malays in this struggle was a red flag. The supplies, arms and ammunition for this rebellion came from Penang, and we are entitled to suppose that they were furnished at least in part, by that Chinese secret society faction ("Tokong") which was opposed to the Ghee Hin faction (Triad); which latter we have seen in Chapter V was in league with the Siamese during this period.

From the foregoing established facts, we suggest that the flag societies did not suddenly develop either as offshoots of Triad and "Tokong" in the second half of the nineteenth century as suggested by Hare, nor yet as Malayan branches of the Sunni and Shiah schisms as suggested by Cowan, although they are certainly secretly allied with Triad and "Tokong", and are certainly disguised under the spurious "rival banners", of Hasan and Husein in the annual Boria.

We suggest that the flag societies have undergone a number of processes in their development, which we might sketch as follows:—

1750–1800.—Process of inoculation taking place in Junk Ceylon; Malay and Siamese pirates being infused with the Ghee Hin virus.

1800–1825.—Same process in Penang and Province Wellesley.

1821–1830.—Hardening of Malay resistance to Siamese occupation of Kedah. Sympathy shown in Penang for Kedah rebels, and assistance rendered by Chinese of Penang to Kedah Malays.

1825–1830.—Siamese seeking aid of Penang Ghee Hin to further their schemes in Kedah and Perak. Many Malays and Chinese from Junk Ceylon, Ligor and Patani in Siamese service. Siamese receive British aid from Penang.

1830–1850.—While on the one hand the Ghee Hins (Triad) in Junk Ceylon and Penang were rendering help to the Siamese against the Kedah Malays, on the other, the Toh Peh Kongs ("Tokong") were aiding the Kedah Malays against the Siamese.

Triad and "Tokong" were both in the field, animated by the same motive, whilst backing different sides. That motive was what it always is with the Chinese, self-interest, prospects of trade, land settlement, concessions, "farms" and other spoils for the successful backer. It was during this period, naturally enough, that the split between Triad and "Tokong" in Penang became clearly distinguishable. They had taken opposite sides in a political quarrel which was not their quarrel, but which served as a wedge to keep them apart and to sharpen their differences, and divide them into two permanent camps of Triad (Ghee Hin) and "Tokong" (Toh Peh Kong and Hai San) which latter during these years, ceased to be a Cantonese foundation, and was absorbed by immigrant Hakka elements, sworn enemies of the "Punteis" who joined the Penang "Tokong" camp against the Triad Cantonese.

The suggestion that the Ghee Hin (Triad) supported Siamese interests in the north of the Peninsula against the Kedah Malays does not rest on mere surmise, nor upon the few extracts from the official correspondence of this period given in Chapter V. Song Ong Siang in *One hundred years of the Chinese of Singapore*, (1923) pages 66, 92 and 93, gives a sketch of the careers of Tan Tock Seng, Malacca-born Hokkien (1798–1850) and his eldest son Tan Kim Ching (1829–1892) who appear to have been leaders of the Ghee Hin (Hokkien branch) in Singapore, and the latter of whom was:—

"Consul General and Special Commissioner for Siam in the Straits Settlements, with great influence on the Chinese outside the Colony, especially in the northern states bordering on Siam, *viz.*, Kelantan and Patani".

The part played by Tan Kim Ching and the Ghee Hin society in the story of the Perak succession 1871–1873 is given in Chapter XVII.

1848.—This year saw the end of the Malay-Siamese struggle in Kedah and the restoration of the Malay dynasty. No one with a knowledge of the conditions of the period, can deny that the Chinese of Junk Ceylon (or Tongka, as it began to be called) and Penang, and later those of Singapore, played an important part in the struggle, by furnishing arms, ammunition, supplies, and even fighting-men, to the two belligerents. It is probable too, that this process was repeated further north in the simultaneous struggle which took place between the Siamese and Ava (Burma).

It is difficult to resist the conclusion that the two flag societies took birth during this period,—the Ghee Hins (Triad) with their Siamese and Malay *protégés* under the White Flag, from Penang to Ligor, and into Patani and up the coast to Junk Ceylon, and possibly as far as Rangoon (Pegu), of which we also have mention; and the Toh Peh Kongs and Hai Sans ("Tokong") with their Malay *protégés* under the Red Flag in Penang and across to the mainland into Province Wellesley and Larut, where the strongest Malay sympathies would naturally lie.

1848–1860.—If the foregoing represents in rough the true position, it is not difficult to imagine that during the period following this struggle, Triad and "Tokong" took steps to organise their whilom *protégés* into secret associations after their own pattern, which they would continue to use for their own ends. Both Triad and "Tokong" would have found a suitable and willing medium for the consolidation of their purpose in the number of "Jawi-bukans" or "Jawi-pekans" of Indian criminal antecedents, who from causes explained in Chapter X were at this period a numerous community in Penang.

Simultaneously with its growth, this Jawi-pekan community was already making its presence felt in another direction in the life of Penang. We have seen in Chapter XII how the Moharram festival first came to Malaya and how it took root in Penang. We have also seen later in the same chapter, how, about the year 1850, this festival was going through a transitional period of distortion from its original religious character into that of a hooligan orgy, and we have seen that the Jawi-pekan community were responsible for this transformation.

The picture presented is of two simultaneous processes at work during this formative period 1848–1860; the one collecting and organising on secret lines into two opposing camps, each under its Chinese parent, the scattered remnants of the two rival parties in the war of the Kedah succession; the other, identifying these two parties under rival banners in the annual Moharram festival.

In both these processes, the most likely medium at work for their consolidation would have been the "Jawi-pekan" community.

1860.—By the year 1860, the two processes seem to have been completed, although it was not until 1862, that we read, after a trial of strength, that the Red Flag society and "Tokong" finally made an alliance.

From 1860 onwards the line of cleavage for "offensive and defensive purposes" seems to be quite clear,—Triad and the White Flag on the one side, and "Tokong" and the Red Flag on the other—White Triad, and Red "Tokong", which remains the position to the present-day.

AND WHAT OF THE COLOURS?

There is no more evidence on this point than upon the origin of the societies themselves and here again we are forced back upon conjecture, guided by what we already know as fact. It seems probable that during the period 1800–1840, the Moharram festival remained a purely religious celebration in Penang, and that customary banners of green (Hasan) and red (Husein) were in use.

It also seems probable that during the war of the Kedah succession (1821–1848) the *protégés* of the Ghee Hin (Siamese and Patani Malays) and the *protégés* of the Toh Peh Kong (Kedah Malays) were distinguished under rival banners. We can find no reference to the colour of the banner of the Raja of Ligor, but it may well have been a variation of the White Elephant of Siam.[1] The banner of the Kedah Malays is mentioned by one writer of the period (Capt. Osborn R.N.) as red.[2] Following on this, when the two parties came to be identified with the celebration of the annual Moharram festival, then in its decadence, the parties may have decided to retain their former fighting flags—white for the Ghee Hins and red for the Toh Peh Kongs, rather than adopt the customary flags of the festival (green for Hasan and Ghee Hins, and red for Husein and Toh Peh Kongs), which would have had no meaning for them. Again the flags in the festival (green and red) are in no sense rival flags, as are the white and red of the Boria. The latter seem to us to disguise their fighting origin under the innocent religious banners of the Moharram, substituting white for green to provide the camouflage.

There are two facts admitted by all the authorities namely:—

(1) That the two flag societies have been mixed up with the two rival Chinese camps since at least 1860, and are the Mohamedan counterparts of the two Chinese organisations. (Chapters V and XIII).

(2) That the two flag societies have been mixed up with the celebration of the Moharram festival in the Straits Settlements since at least 1860. (Chapter XIV).

Added to these there is the further fact, sufficiently proved, we think, in Chapter XII, namely:—

(3) That the Penang Boria is the modern counterpart of the Shiah Mohamedan festival of the Moharram, distorted from its religious form to serve as cover for the perpetuation of the secret rivalries and criminal activities of the two Flag societies.

These three facts demonstrate the complex nature of the origin of the flag societies and appear to disprove the simpler theories of Hare and Cowan set out above namely:—

(a) That they are merely offshoots of their two hostile Chinese parents—a theory which ignores their early connection with the Moharram festival, and their later identification with the Boria.

(b) That they are the Malayan counterparts of the Sunni and Shiah schisms in the Mohamedan world—a theory which ignores their use of Triad and "Tokong" ceremonies of initiation, as well as their general association for criminal purposes, with their infidel Chinese parents.

We do not claim that the new theory (C) now propounded is entirely satisfactory, but at least it takes into account the complex nature of the probable origin of these societies.

Footnote.—(1) *See* page 204 *supra.*
Footnote.—(2) *See* page 210 *supra.*

Other possible origins of the colours Red and White

We have offered above the suggestion that the origin of the white and red flags may be found in the colours of Siam and Kedah in the War of succession, but it is as well to tabulate and examine the other sources from which the colours may come.

These are:—

  (1) An origin in the banners of Triad and "Tokong".
  (2) An origin in the banners of the Moharram festival.
  (3) An origin in the colours of the Knights Templar.
  (4) An origin in the Hindu concept of *Kama*.
  (5) An origin in the Malay (white) and Indian (red) colours representing "independent sovereignty".
  (6) An origin in the "archaic civilisation" of the Nile Valley.

(1) The banners of Triad and "Tokong"

In Chapter I, we have seen the colours of Triad lodges[1] to be:—Fukien—black; Canton—red; Yunnan—yellow; Hunan—white and Cheh Kiang—green.

According to the above, one should associate Triad in Malaya, which derives from the Canton lodge, with the red flag; whereas we know from all the foregoing evidence that it is definitely allied with the white.

In Chapter II page 31, we have seen that the colours of Ko Lao Hui "sections" (which, we have elsewhere identified with "Tokong") are, according to Heckethorn, white, black, red and yellow. Hutson also mentions red and black "flag leaders" at each "anchorage" of the Ko Lao Hui.

We think, therefore, that the original banners of Triad and "Tokong" provide no clue to the origin of the flag societies in Malaya.

(2) The banners of the Moharram festival

There is a considerable amount of evidence in support of the belief that we need look no further than this festival in its original form, for the idea of the white and red flags, although this does not help towards an explanation how these "rival parties in the Moharram" have come to be linked with Triad and "Tokong".

The evidence is as follows:—

Herklots, *op. cit.* page 159–160 gives a description of the standards (*alam*) and dignities (*maratib*) used in the Moharram festival in India, and their origin. Among these are the flags of Hasan and Husein.

Hasan's flag is triangular in shape and coloured plain *green* (for poison); Husein's flag is triangular and coloured *red* (for blood), with the device of the double sword presented by the Prophet to Ali (*Zu'l-faquar*) emblazoned thereon.[2]

From Herklots' general description of the festival in India, it is clear that three colours predominate therein, red, green and white.

Enquiry made from India (Aligarh University) as to present-day (1934) usage has elicited the following:—

> In India, the flags used in the Muharram are red and green; red for martyrdom (Hussain), green for poison (Hassan).

While red and green have their own explanations, there does not appear to be any special significance attaching to the use of the colour white, although mention of white and red in combination occurs frequently in Herklots, cf. in Chapter XI above, his description of the *Majnun Fakirs*, who wear a plaited queue of white and red paper hanging from their caps, or wear a white and red scarf as a necklet; or the *Bagla* who wear white paper caps on their heads: or the *Khogir Shah* who wear red and white strings round their heads; or again the *Ghagriwala* whose dress is either white or red and who have two standard bearers in their party who carry white, green or red "colours".

It may conceivably be with these latter, i.e., *the two standard-bearers of the Ghagriwala* who are mentioned by name by Haughton's informant (*see* Chapter XII), that the idea of the White and Red Flag parties in Penang and their respective colours originated.

Cowan above quotes the *Penang Riot Commission Report* 1868 and the reference therein, in the evidence of Vapoo Marican Noordin and Saiboo, to the use of the white and red flags during the Moharram festival, *viz*:—

> During the Muharram time, the White Flag Party goes on one side, but when they meet with the Red Flag Party, then a fight takes place, like Hassan and Husain parties.

It is just here that that further explanation was necessary, which has never been forthcoming, and has in consequence led to misunderstanding and confusion, and which may be summarized as follows:—

Footnote.—(1) *See* Schlegel pages 36–38 and Ward and Stirling Vol. I pages 156–158.
Footnote.—(2) These flags are illustrated in the Plate to face page 160 of Herklots *op. cit.*

By the year 1867, the celebration of the Moharram in Penang, had become a distortion of the original festival as introduced from India in the earlier part of the century. The original festival was, and still is, in Shiah countries one of mourning for the Alids (Ali, Hassan and Husain) whom the Shiahs revere even more than the Prophet himself: there is no element of rivalry between these three in the festival: despite its religious character, the festival in India contains comic elements, enjoyed by the riff-raff in which both Sunni Mohamedans and even Hindus join: this comic element takes the form of parties of celebrationists dressing themselves up to represent different types of Mohamedan Fakirs of whom Herklots mentions no less than fifty kinds: these parties indulge in horse-play and buffoonery and accompanied by the Ta'ziah or Tabut and by the various sacred emblems and standards of the Alids, form processions during the ten days of the festival, which have been likened to a "Lord Mayor's Show": the comic element has been seized upon by the Jawi-pekan or original Thug elements in Penang, to bastardise the festival to their own purposes and use it as a disguise for perpetuating their activities in the underworld of Penang.

Whether the white and red flags used, have their origin in the insignia of the original festival or whether they have an origin outside the festival as suggested in theory C (above) and have only been later imported into the Boria, must remain a moot point until further evidence becomes available.

(3) AN ORIGIN IN THE COLOURS OF THE KNIGHTS TEMPLAR

We have given in Chapter X, a brief historical sketch of the connection that existed between about A.D. 1100 and 1250 between the Knights Templar of the Crusades and the Assassins of Alamut: and of the descent of the Thugs of India from these same Assassins: and of the advent of the Thugs to Malaya between A.D. 1830 and 1870.

Having regard to the connection not only between the Templars and the Assassins, but also between the Templars and modern Freemasonry and to the interesting and still unexplained similarity between the ritual of the two latter and that of the Triad society[1] discussed by Schlegel and Ward and Stirling, we should not exclude the seemingly far-fetched notion that the colours may trace back to the white and red emblems of the Crusaders, of which the origin is given in Chapter X.

If this derivation is true, the origin may be ultimately found, not in the White of the Knights Hospitallers and the Red of the Knights Templar, but may be restricted to an origin exclusively in the colours of the Knights Templar, namely, the white surcoat with red cross thereon, and red skull-cap.[2]

That there was an identity between the white coat and red sash of the Assassins (Chapter X) and the white surcoat and red cross of the Templars has been emphasised by at least two authorities.

Von Hammer *History of the Assassins* page 80, mentions the resemblance between the Assassins and the Templars and Clavel *Histoire pittoresque de la franc-maçonnerie* (1843) page 356 has:—

> Oriental historians show us at different periods the Order of the Templars maintaining intimate relations with that of the Assassins and they insist upon the affinity that existed between the two associations. They remark that *they had adopted the same colours, white and red:* that they had the same organisation: the same hierarchy of degrees, etc., etc.

Whether this colour-analogy is merely accidental, or whether it has a common origin in something anterior to the Crusade period, we cannot of course say, but that there is an historical connection between the colours of the Templars and those of the Assassins, which may be repeated in the flag societies of Malaya through the Thugs of India, has to be remembered. Hence the possibility of an historical connection between the colours of the crusade period and those of the modern flag societies in Malaya is neither so remote nor so far-fetched as might at first appear. This aspect of our subject is further discussed in Chapter XXXIII.

(4) AN ORIGIN IN THE HINDU CONCEPT OF *Kama*

In a work by B. Z. Goldberg *The Sacred Fire*, a study of sex in religion (1931),[3] the following passage occurs on page 110:—

> "In India, there is a great spirit hovering over two drops of water. One of the drops is white and represents the masculine world. The other is red and symbolises the feminine element in creation. The two are separated and yet not unrelated, for both are touched by the great spirit *Kama*.[4] *Kama* is the great force that holds the universe together, for as the drops of water are drawn together by the attraction of *Kama*, they often unite and their union calls forth a spirit even greater than *Kama*. The union of the sexes brings down *Kama Kala* the highest deity of them all that has the sun for its face, fire and the moon for breasts and the *Hardha Kala* for organs of generation.

Footnote.—(1) *See* Introduction and Chapter XXXIII.
Footnote.—(2) *See* Lamb *The Crusaders: Iron Men and Saints* (1930) pages 259, 269 and 296–297.
Footnote.—(3) Published by Jarrolds, London.
Footnote.—(4) *Kama* (Sanscrit) = The god of love in the *puranas;* sensual desire. To be distinguished from *Karma*.

Here we seem to have the Yin Yang of the Chinese in a new setting; the dualism of man's origin associated in Hinduism with the colours red and white and in the same universal relationship *viz*:—

Red.—Left, female, earth, nature, dark.

White.—Right, male, heaven, god, light.

The colours, too, are represented by two drops of water, which again suggest the *water-motif* (page 131) of the nature school of the Han league.

We may, indeed, suggest that, if two drops of water represent the Yin Yang of the Han league, their union will produce a third drop representing man, the three drops together being the "Three drops of water", associated with the name of the Three Dot Brotherhood or the Han league (page 132) which are together symbolic of generation, or the process of Nature, namely Father, Mother, Child—the Nature School of Hutson.

This would be an attractive explanation both of the red and white flag as deriving from the dualism of Hinduism through Indian contacts,—just as their counterparts, the Han and Hung, derive from the Yin Yang of China—and of the *water motif* which is present in all Nature worship.

It would also provide a line of descent for the colours from the Vedic dualist concept of the Indo-Iranians through the Sumerians to the left Abrahamic succession (Aaronic): thence to Islam and the left Sufism of Abdullah bin Maimun: thence through Hasan Saba to the Assassins and perhaps to the Knights Templars and thence to the Thugs of India (*see* Introduction and Chapter X pages 152–53 and 160 *supra*).

Unfortunately, Goldberg's work although interesting and accurate is without individual documentation. We have been unable, therefore, to find authoritative confirmation of the foregoing concept. Goldberg's book has, however, a copious bibliography of standard works, on which it purports to be based.

We are reminded at this point of Dr. J. H. Cousins' discoveries (1935–37) in the old Palace at Padmanabhapuram, former capital of Travancore, where the well-preserved mural paintings depicting Hari-Hara (Vishnu-Shiva) and Ardhanareswara[1] (Parvati-Shiva) dating from c. A.D. 1750 present us, in the words of Dr. Cousins,[2] with:—

> What appears to be a single figure, but is found on examination to be composed of two figures in one, the left half female, the right half male, symbolic of the inner unity of the feminine and masculine principle of universal life.

These figures are, in fact, anthropomorphic representations of the Yin Yang of China or lingam-yoni of Hinduism. Their chief interest in this context lies in the fact that they are coloured and that the left, or female side, is that of a woman whose skin is black and clothing dark red and who holds in her hand the conch shell of Vishnu (*Hari*); the right, or male side, is that of a man whose skin is white and who holds in his hand the axe of Shiva (*Hara*).

It may perhaps be that if they exist at all, the "Red and White societies among the Klings" which, according to Vaughan above, writing in 1879, "they say were brought from the Coromandel Coast and have no connection with the Chinese", may yet be found to derive from the concept of Hari-Hara of Travancore which, at its core, is identical with the Uuniversism of China's Yin Yang (*see* Chapter III *supra*) and has an identical colour distinction.

(5) AN ORIGIN IN THE COLOURS OF MALAY (WHITE) AND INDIAN (RED) "INDEPENDENT SOVEREIGNTY"

Without wishing to seek for far-fetched derivations of the colours, there may be those who would lend support to the view that the colours may represent the idea of Malay (white) and Indian (red) independent sovereignty. The evidence in support of this view is as follows:—

White the colour of Malay sovereignty

    (1) Newbold in his *Account of the British Settlements in the Straits of Malacca* (1839) Vol. II page 288 (Footnote) has:—

> Royal blood is supposed by many Malays to be white. The title *Bedarah, Putih* is of the earliest origin.

    (2) In Wilkinson's dictionary, edition 1932, the following appears under the word:—

> '*Alam.*—Arabic. A standard. A flag regarded as an emblem. 'Alam, covers "banners". *Cf. Bendera puteh alam baginda*, the white banner that betokens independent sovereignty, and also the various solid tokens ('alam) of Hasan, Husein and Fatimah in the Moharram procession.

Footnote.—(1) *Ardha* = half: *nari* = goddess: *eswara* = god.

Footnote.—(2) Monograph "Past glories of Travancore" in *Illustrated Weekly of India* 8th January, 1939.

The suggestion may, we think, be safely dismissed that the colour white has any connection with "mourning" for the Alids.[1] It is true that white is used for mourning both by Chinese and Malays, but only in hangings or clothing and then in the case of the Chinese chiefly by women. (Cf. Skeat, *Malay Magic* page 34, "Puwadi" ceremony).

The colour *white* when used in a flag in Malaya is essentially that of *independent sovereignty*, as given by Wilkinson. Cf. Skeat *Malay Magic*, page 18 footnote, and page 37 :—

White......is considered by Malays to be the royal colour.[2]

Again the same authority *op. cit.* pages 33–34 :—

The white umbrella......was confined to the raja's person.

The use of the colour white is also appropriated by Malays to the conciliation of spirits (Skeat *op. cit.* page 51) and, curiously enough, is associated in Malay magic with their *white genii*, one of whom is declared, according to one account (quoted by Skeat *op. cit.* page 95) to be Maharaja Dewa or Mahadewa, the Malay name for the Hindu God Siva, whose connection with the Hindu "Durga-Puja" or Dussera festival and thence with the Moharram festival in India has already been noted in Chapter XI.

Red the colour of Indian sovereignty

All the authorities appear to be silent upon the use of the colour *red* among the Malays or its significance when used as a flag by them.

On the other hand, there is frequent reference to the use of the colour red among the Mohamedans of India, apart from the red flag of Husein and other appearances of the colour red in the Moharram festival as already noted.

Herklots *op. cit.* page 302–303 has :—

The screens surrounding the encampment of the Mughal Emperors were of scarlet: and a scarlet umbrella was carried over the Mussalman Kings of the Deccan.

This suggests that whereas among Mohamedans in Malaya white is the colour of independent sovereignty, in India it is red.

Again Herklots *op. cit.* on pages 72 and 228, refers to the ceremonial use of red among Indian Mohamedans in marriage and in magic for the purpose of "scaring away evil spirits", compared with the colour white, used by Malays for this latter purpose.

The Red Flag society from its foundation seems to have attracted a large number of "Jawi-pekans" and others with Indian criminal connections, which lends colour to the suggestion that the flag may have an Indian instead of a Malay origin. Until further evidence becomes available, no more can be said on the point.

(6) AN ORIGIN IN THE "ARCHAIC CIVILISATION", OR THE NILOTIC SYSTEM OF DUAL ORGANISATION

Lastly, we are reminded of the two territorial divisions of the predynastic Kingdom of Egypt, each with its distinctive flag and crown, white for upper and red for lower Egypt. These territorial divisions with their remarkable colour distinctions became merged under a single ruler of Egypt during the first four dynasties down to B.C. 2750. Thereafter, they gave rise in the sixth dynasty to the dual system of organisation of society known as the Children of the Sun, interpreted by Perry in his book of the same name.[3]

Of this system Sir Grafton Elliot Smith *In the Beginning* (1932) pages 76–77 says :—

The dual organisation was originally found in the earliest civilisation that was adopted in most parts of the world...... One manifestation of this system is revealed by the existence of what are called dual villages...... Each side of the village had a chief. The son of the chief of one side married the daughter of the chief of the other side...... One side had a sacred chief concerned with peace: the other had a secular chief associated with war. The Son of the Sun was originally the sacred chief. The two sides were constantly hostile. Each had a distinctive colour-label corresponding to the red and white of the two kingdoms of Ancient Egypt. This extremely complicated and bizarre form of civilisation was introduced throughout the world by the Children of the Sun wherever they went.

And on page 75 :—

Thus the territorial division became merged with the duality of rulers, bringing about the completion of the dual organisation of society...... This is found at the present-day in Macassar in the East Indies, in Samoa (in Polynesia) and elsewhere.

* * *

Footnote.—(1) As regards mourning colours customary among the Shiahs in India, Herklots, *op. cit.* page 106 has this:—

Dark blue is the mourning colour, black that of the Abbas-ide khalifas. Mourning dress however is not favoured and when it is worn, it is by women, not by men.

Footnote.—(2) *Cf.* also Hocart *Kingship* page 109, where reference is made to the coronation of King Charles I of England in white robes.

Footnote.—(3) W. J. Perry *Children of the Sun* (1923).

The effects of the historical event which took place in Egypt at the time of the sixth dynasty (B.C. 2500) must have been diffused in Asia, Oceania and America. It can be shown that the earliest form of social organisation adopted in these places was precisely this dual system.

This Egyptian association of the colours red and white in the sphere of politics is the earliest reference we can find to the subject. Whether it may have any connection through diffusion with the flag divisions in modern underground politics in Malaya, we are, of course, unable to say. Nevertheless, the system of mutation of succession rights, obtaining in Perak and elsewhere in Polynesia, would perhaps be explained by acceptance of the hypothesis of Nilotic diffusion. We refer again to this subject in Chapter XXII *infra*.

FINAL COMMENT ON THE COLOURS

(1) The fact that among the Chinese white is the colour of mourning and red the colour of happiness, does not appear to be relevant to the subject of our enquiry. The common custom among both Malays and Chinese in Malaya of festooning sacred places or *Keramat* with white and red pennants should perhaps be noted in this connection; although it is improbable that the custom has any direct connection with the flag societies or their colours.

(2) If an interpretation of the colours be sought in the Yin Yang or dualist principle (Chapter III) we get the following result:—

LEFT SIDE (YIN)		RIGHT SIDE (YANG)	
(The worship of Man)		*(The worship of God)*	
Black .. .. ⎫	Representing	White .. .. ⎫	Representing
Dark-red .. ⎬	Night, Earth	Yellow .. ⎬	Day, Heaven
Green .. .. ⎭	or Nature.		and the Sun.

This same colour distinction seems to run fairly constantly through the whole gamut of secret society praxis throughout the world, both ancient and modern and is also applicable to the flag societies of Malaya.

(3) The custom among Malays, which formerly prevailed until forbidden by proclamation after British intervention, of hoisting white or red flags on mosques in Perak is referred to on pages 342–343 *infra*.

HISTORICAL SPRINGS OF THE WHITE AND RED FLAG SOCIETIES

The main historical features of the nineteenth century which seem to have influenced the origin and development of the flag societies and led to their disguise in the present-day Boria parties, can, perhaps, be more clearly set out in tabular form. All dates refer to Penang unless obviously otherwise.

Chinese influences	*Local Penang influences*	*Neighbouring Political influences*
1795 TRIAD established.	1786–1810 System of Government through "KAPITANS" established.	1821 Conquest of Kedah by Siam.
1840 Alliance of Triad and White Flag.	1800–1820 MOHARRAM FESTIVAL introduced and confined to Shiah Indians.	1821–1840 Malay struggle to reconquer Kedah. Triad aids Siam. "Tokong" aids Kedah. Formative years of the White Flag (Triad) and Red Flag ("Tokong") societies. (Political stem).
1844 "TOKONG" established.	1825–1850 Advent of Thugs and Indian criminal deportees to Penang.	
	1850 Moharram Festival begins to decay. "Jawi-pekan" influence therein strong.	1840–1850 Formative years of the White Flag into a criminal society.
1850–1860 The Tai Ping Rebellion and The Dagger Rebellion in China.	1850–1860 Moharram Festival loses its religious character and becomes a cloak for White and Red rivalries and hooliganism.	1844–1860 Formative years of the Red Flag into a criminal society.
1862 Alliance of "Tokong" and Red Flag.	1857 The Indian Mutiny. Influx of Indian deportees thereafter.	1862–1873 The Larut Wars. Triad and White Flag *versus* "Tokong" and Red Flag.
	1867 Disclosure of alliances between Triad and White and "Tokong" and Red.[1] Distortion of Moharram Festival complete.	

Footnote.—(1) Officially established by *The Penang Riot Commission Report*. 1868.

Chinese influences	*Local Penang influences*	*Neighbouring Political influences*
1855–1868 The Hakka-Puntei War in South China.	1870–1890 Establishment of the "Boria". Continuance of White and Red Flag societies camouflaged under false colours in the "Boria".	1874 British intervention in Perak. Triad and "Tokong" intrigues in connection with the Perak succession.
	1890 to Present-day After suppression of dangerous societies 1890, change of disguise to social and sporting clubs and "mutual benefit" societies. Boria continued in association with these clubs.	

At the beginning of the Kedah-Siamese struggle it appears from the extracts given in Chapter V, that it was the Hai San under Low Ah Chong who were aiding the Siamese, the Hai San being at this period composed of Cantonese and friendly to Triad. They may even have been indistinguishable from Triad. It may have been the Wah Sang, composed of Hakkas, who first espoused the cause of the Malays in the struggle and supplied them with arms and assistance, but here there is nothing to guide us.

It becomes clear from Vaughan (extracts in Chapter VI) that by the end of the struggle (1850) the Hai San had become almost entirely Hakka and the Wah Sang had disappeared. We may be allowed to presume that as the Hai San underwent this change, so the Ghee Hin, with their preponderant interests along the coast, between Junk Ceylon and Penang, supported the Siamese to an increasing degree, while as their enemies the Hakkas absorbed the Hai San, the latter became more and more identified with the Kedah cause.

Conditions in China and the progress of the Hakka-Puntei war in Canton province doubtless hastened this re-orientation.

One might be tempted to think that there would be a more natural affinity between Triad and the Malays who were seeking to "drive out the Siamese and restore the Malay dynasty" in Kedah, but such considerations would be unlikely to exist in the conditions of that day and as they do not seem to conform with the meagre ascertained facts, it is idle to speculate upon them.

After the final triumph of the Malay cause in Kedah in 1848, it is probable that the loose associations between Triad and white flag, and "Tokong" and red flag to which the war had given rise (if we admit that they existed at all), remained dormant until they were organised, during the formative years 1850–1860, on secret society lines with the help no doubt of Chinese and Indian criminal elements, who had learnt something of each others language and underworld methods during earlier association in Penang gaol.

The formation of the two flags on secret society lines and their alliance with their Chinese parent societies of Triad and "Tokong", led naturally enough to all the subsequent hatred, warfare and intrigue in the secret society underworld of Malaya down to the present-day.

It is not possible to say, whether either or both or neither of the flag societies had an earlier independent connection with or even a genuine origin in the Indian Moharram festival in Penang. We know from witness No. 67 Vappoo Marican Noordin (page 73 of the evidence of the *Penang Riot Commission Report* 1868) that:—

> Two different societies were formed before they joined the Chinese societies. Many Klings belong to the Red Flag.

For the precise meaning of "Klings" at that epoch, *see* Glossary. These "Klings" doubtless included a number of Thugs and other criminals from India then at liberty. It is fairly safe to assume that the Red Flag at its foundation was more Indian than Malay and as years passed it attracted more of the Jawi-pekan or mixed Indian and Malay population than did the White, until the second period of its activity, (1870–1874) when it took sides in the Larut wars and supported the Mentri of Larut against Raja Abdullah and the White, up to the Treaty of Pangkor, since when there is probably as much Malay influence in the one as in the other, although the officials of the Red Flag are probably still of Indian or Arab descent. This aspect of the subject is further discussed in subsequent chapters.

ALTERNATIVE PRESUMPTIONS OF ORIGIN

Two main sets of presumptions not mutually destructive of one another, seem to offer themselves as the alternative origins of the two flag associations. The truth may lie somewhere between them. These alternatives both deriving from the chrysalis of Tabut, presented in the preceding chapter, are more easily set out in tabular form thus:—

THE CHRYSALIS OF TABUT

	THE RED FLAG		THE WHITE FLAG	
	A.—*Course of possible political origin in the Kedah-Siam war.*	B.—*Course of possible religious origin in the Indian Moharram festival.*	A.—*Course of possible political origin in the Kedah-Siam war.*	B.—*Course of possible religious origin in the Indian Moharram festival.*
(1)	May have had a political origin in the Kedah Malay struggle in which the Kedah Malays received help from "Tokong" in Penang.	May have had a religious origin in the Moharram festival, but evidently later than that (if any) of the White and of similar constitution to it, but centred at a different mosque or under the teaching of a different priest from the White.	May have had a political origin in the Kedah Malay struggle against Siam 1821-1848 in which Siam and Patani Malays received secret help from the Penang Triad.	May have had a religious origin in the Moharram festival between 1800 and 1830, centred perhaps at a particular mosque or under a particular religious teacher, the white flag being merely one of the emblems carried in that festival, and the society itself being confined entirely to Indians.
(2)	May have shown their gratitude to "Tokong" by accepting truncated membership of the "Tokong" foundation under the red flag of Kedah.	May have begun to change from a religious to a criminal association as soon as Indian ex-convict and Thug elements began to filter into the mosque from the gaols and introduced the tenets of "Tokong" and Thuggism.	May have shown their gratitude to Triad by accepting truncated membership of Triad under a Siamese flag.	May have begun to change from a religious to a criminal association as soon as Indian ex-convict elements began, about 1830-1850, to filter into the mosque from the gaols where they had made the acquaintanceship of Chinese criminals who were members of Triad.
(3)	May have changed from a political to a criminal association as soon as Indian ex-convict elements began to assume the leadership about 1860.	May have completed the change from a religious to a criminal society, when Indian criminal elements and Jawi-pekans began to assume the leadership about 1850-1860.	May have changed from a political to a criminal association as soon as Indian ex-convict elements began to assume the leadership about 1860.	May have completed the change from a religious to a criminal society when the Indian criminal elements and Jawi-pekans began to assume the leadership between about 1850 and 1860.
(4)	Had a dispute with "Tokong" in 1861, but finally allied themselves with "Tokong" in 1862 "for offensive and defensive purposes".	Quarrelled with "Tokong," in 1861, and then allied themselves with them in 1862, probably as a sett-off to a similar earlier alliance between White Flag and Triad and for a similar purpose, the exploitation of vice.	May have remained a purely criminal association under Indian and Jawi-pekan ascendency between about 1860 and 1870, still allied to Triad, and appearing openly under its original Siamese or Patani flag and its Indian leaders, at the annual Moharram festival during this period.	May during the same period, due to the former association in gaol of Indian White Flag leaders and Triad members, have cemented a mutual alliance between White Flag and Triad, largely for the exploitation of vice.

THE CHRYSALIS OF TABUT—*continued*

THE RED FLAG—*continued.*		THE WHITE FLAG—*continued.*	
A.—Course of possible political origin in the Kedah-Siam war.	*B.—Course of possible religious origin in the Indian Moharram festival.*	*A.—Course of possible political origin in the Kedah-Siam war.*	*B.—Course of possible religious origin in the Indian Moharram festival.*
(5) May have remained a purely criminal association under Indian and Jawi-pekan ascendency between about 1860 and 1870, still allied to "Tokong" and appearing openly during this period under its old red Kedah banner at the annual Moharram festival.	(5) Remained a purely criminal association under Indian and Jawi-pekan ascendency between about 1862 and 1870, still allied to "Tokong" and appearing openly under its original religious emblem at the annual Moharram festival.	(5) May have regained some of its original political character between 1870 and 1874, when it successfully espoused Raja Abdullah's candidature for the throne of Perak, supported by Triad, who in this campaign, were led by Tan Kim Cheng, leading merchant and "Siamese Consul" in Singapore.	(5) May have remained a purely criminal association under Indian and Jawi-pekan ascendency between about 1860 and 1870, still allied to Triad and appearing openly under its original religious emblem at the annual Moharram festival, at which its Indian leaders behaved like hooligans under the cloak of a religious pageant.
(6) May have regained some of its original Malay political character between 1870 and 1874 when it unsuccessfully espoused the cause of the Mentri of Larut supported by "Tokong" against Raja Abdullah's candidature for the throne of Perak.	(6) As the sources of Indian criminal inspiration began to dry up, at the closing of the Indian penal establishments in 1873 and the transfer of their members to the Andaman Islands, so the character of the Red Flag like that of the White, began to become more genuinely Malay, until we find it in 1875 and later, playing a leading part behind the scenes in Perak at the time of the British intervention, with its ally "Tokong" still further in the background, jealously guarding "Tokong's" interests against those of Triad, while the British reshuffle of 1874-1875 in Perak was taking place (*see* Chapters XVII to XX).	(6) May have shed most of its Indian criminal character as the flow of released Indian criminals from Penang and Singapore began to decrease about 1875, and as their leadership in the society began to pass to Arabs and Malays, during the Sultanship of Abdullah in Perak 1874-1876.	(6) May have become more identified with the indigenous Malays and have shed some of its Indian criminal characteristics and leadership, as the flow of released Indian criminals from the gaols began about 1875 to dry up, and resistance to British intervention in the Malay States in 1875-1876 hardened.
(7) May have deepened and widened its political character as resistance to British intervention in Perak hardened after 1875.			

It is only by reason of the fact that the White and Red Flags, evidently for the purpose of hiding their true character and thereby hoodwinking the authorities by proclaiming themselves "mutual benefit associations", have identified themselves with the annual Boria or distorted Moharram festival in Penang, that we have acceptance to-day of such an absurdity, as "rival Hasan and Husein parties", each under a separate and rival flag, Hasan having been made to exchange his classic green standard for the white, perhaps of Siam (or possibly for the white of the first Ghagriwala standard) while Husein by an accident has probably exchanged his classic red, emblazoned with the double sword of Ali, for the old red flag of Kedah or perhaps the plain red of the second Ghagriwala standard.

This superficial disguise:—

(a) As "mutual benefit" associations,

(b) As harmless participants in the annual Boria performances,

has kept alive and fostered the separate underground organisations of the White and Red Flag societies. Uncomfortable suspicions have arisen from time to time since the Treaty of Pangkor regarding the genuineness and harmlessness of this "mutual benefit" and annual Boria jamboree, but these suspicions have quickly been lulled to rest and the fabric of the imposture has remained almost intact up to the present-day.

We make no apology for attempting to make a full enquiry into the probable origins of the colours of the flag associations. It will be seen in later chapters that whatever their origins, by 1874, these two associations had thoroughly co-mingled with the indigenous Malay population and had taken sides with their respective Chinese allies in the Triad *versus* "Tokong" struggle for the possession of the Larut tin fields, and from thence had actually taken opposite sides in the purely political dispute over the Perak succession, which led to British intervention and the Treaty of Pangkor.

The next chapter will make it clear that in 1867, the two flag societies were already criminal secret associations, masquerading as *tarikah* or religious *juma'ah*, or "general assemblies of the faithful for Friday worship", or again as *madrasah* or "places of religious instruction connected with a mosque" or simply as "mutual benefit associations" and, under the cloak of "religious worship" and "mutual benefit", were claiming each year the right to break one another's heads under their secret society flags at the annual Moharram festival, a practice they have continued down to the present-day.

ABSENCE OF EARLY RECORDS TO GUIDE RESEARCH

It need not cause surprise that the records of early Penang supply so little material to assist our researches. The following extracts from Mills show the method of appointment of officers to Government service in those days.

Mills. *British Malaya* pages 92 and 93 has:—

> From about 1806 to 1830, the East India Company sent its own civil servants direct from Haileybury to Penang without previous training in India.
> After 1830, officials from the Bengal Civil Service were sent to fill the civil service posts in the Straits Settlements.

Mills page 95 has:—

> The Madras Army also supplied the Straits with some of its ablest officials. From an early date the garrison was drawn from Madras and a number of the officers studied Malay as a hobby. Those who became proficient were often detached from their regiments for administrative work.

Amongst these were:—

(1) Captain Burney, of the 25th Bengal Native Infantry who was stationed with his regiment in Penang 1811–1814 (Mills page 140).

(2) Colonel James Low of the Madras Native Infantry (unit not stated) who joined the Penang establishment in 1818 (Mills page 95).

(3) Colonel Butterworth, Deputy Quarter-Master-General of the Madras Army who was Governor of the Straits 1843–1855.

(4) Colonel Cavenagh who was Governor from 1858–1867.

Of the last two, Mills (page 95) remarks:—

> Neither had any previous experience of Malaya, since their whole careers had been spent in India. The appointments were for this reason unusual, but Butterworth and Cavenagh proved to be two of the most capable Governors sent to Malaya......
> In 1860, six out of the nineteen members of the administration, including the Resident Councillor of Malacca, were officers of the Madras Army.

It was only after 1867 that a separate Malayan Civil Service began to be built up, because, as Lord Canning expressed it in 1859 (Mills page 97):—

> Indian officers have no opportunity of acquiring experience of the habits or language of either Malays or Chinese and accordingly when officers are sent to the Straits, they have everything to learn...... It may be doubted whether Indian civil officers sent to the Straits ever become thoroughly well qualified for or heartily interested in, the duties they have to discharge. The character of the Chinese, the most important and at times a very unmanageable part of the population of the Straits Settlements, is quite different from that of any people with which Indian officers have to deal...... (They are) the very opposite of our Indian fellow subjects.

True as this appreciation of the position is, it is noteworthy from the *Penang Riot Commission Report* (Chapter XVI), that the Indian-trained civil servants of that day seemed to be equally in the dark about Indian customs (*e.g.* the Shiah festival of the Moharram and its origin) as they were about Chinese secret societies.

It is also noteworthy that although these India-trained servants of the Government of the Straits Settlements must have been aware of the existence and tenets of Thuggism and the fact that over 1,500 Thugs had been transported from India to Malaya between 1830 and 1850, where they and their descendants subsequently settled down, there does not appear in published contemporary records any reference to this fact or to its possible consequences, or to its possible connection with the Riots of 1867.

It must further be remembered that up to about 1870, the Chinese community, largely owing to the language difficulty, continued to rule itself almost entirely through the system of "Kapitans" (Chapter XIII) and that these Kapitans were usually if not exclusively the real heads of the Chinese secret societies.

It was not until the publication of Schlegel's work in 1866, that the Government obtained any insight into the working of the Triad society and it was not until the appointment of Pickering as the first "Protector of Chinese" in 1870, after the registration of dangerous societies in 1869, that the Government began to obtain reliable information sufficient to enable it to control them. Even after registration, the activities of Triad and "Tokong" remained largely underground until, the attempt at control failing, they were suppressed by law in 1890. Again throughout the whole period of their history in Malaya the flag societies of the Malays have remained almost entirely underground and very little reliable information has even been obtained about them, nor have they ever been officially registered. They were officially suppressed in the Colony by Ordinance IV of 1885, but this suppression was ineffective as it was applied to organisations of which little was known except the name, and the suppression was never brought into force in any of the native States.

Enquiries and search made among the primary sources for purposes of this work, have been by no means exhaustive, and evidence may yet be found in the archives of the East India Company filed in Calcutta or elsewhere, which will throw more light upon what must for the time being remain only a partial disclosure of the probable origins of the White and Red Flag societies, as presented in this and the foregoing chapter.

CHAPTER XVI

THE PENANG RIOTS OF 1867

We resume in this chapter the historical narrative on the Chinese side, at the point where it broke off at the end of Chapter VI, page 113 *supra*.

In the building up of our background the prominent features of this chapter have already to some extent been anticipated, for the reason that the Penang riots of 1867 and the report of the Commission of Enquiry[1] which followed them, is the first local official "fixed point" in the unravelment of our subject. In discussing events anterior to the publication of this report, we have, therefore, had frequent recourse to its findings.

From now onwards, it should be possible to unfold the story of Triad and Tabut with the aid of contemporary records.

In the month of July, 1867, Triad (Ghee Hin) and "Tokong" (Toh Peh Kong) in Penang came to loggerheads, and after a few preliminary skirmishes, they entered upon a regular war which lasted ten days, from August 3rd to 14th, and completely held up the town. In this war reinforcements were obtained in advance by both sides from Province Wellesley and "Junk Ceylon".

Perhaps no better introduction to a study of these riots can be offered than extracts[2] from the account of them given by Major-General Sir A. E. H. Anson, in his book *About Others and Myself*, published in 1920, who, as Colonel Anson first arrived in Penang as Lieutenant-Governor on 8th June, 1867, less than two months before the riots broke out.

Anson *op. cit.* pages 278–283 has :—

> There had been a bad feeling fermenting between two rival Chinese secret societies for some time before I arrived (8th June, 1867) in the Settlement, and this feeling had increased during the last Mohurrum festival, and led to constant assaults by individuals of the one party on those of the other. This had culminated in the murder of a Malay diamond merchant, a member of one of these societies. There were two societies among the Malays of the Settlement, named the Red Flag society and the White Flag society. These societies were originally of a religious character; but that character very soon ended, and they took to quarrelling and fighting with one another. The Red Flag Malays joined the Chinese Toh Peh Kong society, and the White Flag Malays the Ghee Hin secret society.

> About the beginning of July, (1867) a Toh Peh Kong Chinaman was looking through the palings bounding the premises of a White Flag Malay, when the Malay threw a rambutan (a Malay fruit) skin at the Chinaman, and called him a thief. The Chinaman went away, but returned with ten or twelve Toh Peh Kong friends. The Malay's friends then turned out and a fight with stones and clubs then took place. The Malays drove back the Chinese as far as their kongsee house, the meeting-place or club of their hoey. A kongsee is a company; a hoey, a secret society.[3] The stones thrown by the Malays then struck the Toh Peh Kong signboard, upon which the Toh Peh Kongs turned out in great number, and firearms were resorted to. The police interfered, and, for the moment, stopped the disturbance. After this, frequent assaults and murders were committed by both societies, and on the 1st, August a false charge was made by the head man of the Toh Peh Kongs, that some White Flag Malays and Ghee Hins had stolen some cloth, that, after being dyed, had been put out into the street to dry, by some Toh-Peh-Kong dyers. There is no doubt that this charge was made to bring about a *casus belli*, for which the headman had made every preparation. On the 3rd August, the Toh Peh Kongs attacked the Ghee Hins, and thus commenced the great Riot of 1867.

>   *   *   *

> When the riots broke out the Toh Peh Kong society made regulations for the pensioning of any of its members who might be injured, or the families of members who might be killed, transported, or imprisoned by the Government of the Colony.[4] The society had among its members most of the wealthy shopkeepers in the principal street in George Town, and included also the manufacturers and sellers of firearms and ammunition; and these were bound in times of disturbance, to supply the members with firearms; and it was in this manner that so many of the Toh Peh Kongs were armed during the riots.

> Having no house below on the plain, when the riots broke out, I was still living at the Government bungalow on the mountain; and looking down, I saw small parties of Toh Peh Kongs, armed with muskets, going about on the plain, and setting fire to the huts of the Ghee Hins. There was a party of some fifty Indian convicts on the mountain, employed in keeping the road up it in order, looking after the garden of the Government bungalow, fetching water for the bungalow, working the semaphore at the signal station, etc. I started off, down to the plain, escorted by a large party of these convicts, armed with sticks; and at the foot of the mountain got into my gharry, which I had telephoned for by semaphore, with one convict on the back of it, one on each side step, and the rest running by the sides of it.

Footnote.—(1) *The Penang Riot Commission Report* of 1868, hereafter referred to in this chapter as the *P.R.C. Report.*

Footnote.—(2) Some of these extracts were reprinted in the *Penang Gazette* of 22nd September, 1923, under the caption "Penang's Reign of Terror 1867".

Footnote.—(3) *See* pages 104–105 *supra.*

Footnote.—(4) *See* Appendix III.

Just before leaving England I had read the whole account of Governor Eyre's riots in Jamaica,[1] and having no one on whose advice I could rely, and having had no time to make myself acquainted with the customs and habits of the natives, I felt doubtful and somewhat nervous in regard to the measures I should take.[2] Added to my difficulties was the fact that the battery of artillery had just left for Rangoon, and its relief had not arrived; and the greater part of the Madras sepoy regiment had been sent, with two men-of-war to the Nicobar Islands.

* * *

At 8 o'clock (on 3rd August, 1867) I erected a barricade in one of the streets of the town and placed an armed police guard over it, to check one of the contending parties from making sallies upon the other in that neighbourhood. This barricade I formed of carts, timber, and anything available I found at hand.

The following day I erected barricades of *chevaux-de-frise*, and large blocks of firewood in the main street, over which guards of sepoys and special constables were placed. Every available European and some Eurasians, were sworn as special constables. I spent most of my time in a gharry going about the town, where firing was going on; and shot from muskets and small petards was flying about in all directions. Junks, flying their party flags,[3] were constantly arriving from Junk Ceylon and other native States to the north of the Malay Peninsula. . . . Rumours were brought to me that the Chinese threatened to blow up the civil powder magazine; then, that they proposed to attack some public building, and so on, and this necessitated parties of armed volunteers being sent off to guard these places. My head, too, became addled with the names of people and places that were continually being brought before me. These were Chinese names, Malay names, Mohammedan names, Hindoo names, etc.

* * *

These riots lasted ten days, then I at last got the headmen to agree to put a stop to them, and each society to pay a voluntary penalty of five thousand dollars (equal to about £1060), the dollar at that time being equal to four shillings and three pence.

A great many houses had been burnt down in both the town and country. I had then to make arrangements for sending 1,000 Ghee Hins across to the mainland from the south of the island, as they were afraid to pass up to the town through the Toh Peh Kong villages situated on the road.

On the tenth day of the riots the Governor of the Straits Settlements[4] arrived in one of the Government steamers from Singapore, with some of the Sepoy regiment stationed there on board.

* * *

I was successful in obtaining the voluntary penalty of 10,000 dollars which I had imposed on the two Chinese societies. With this money I built four police stations, capable of being defended, in those parts of the town which were most likely to be centres of disturbance.

These riots covered Penang island and a wide area of Province Wellesley and involved some 30,000 Chinese and 4,000 Malays, and were an outcrop of the struggle between Triad and "Tokong" for possession of the Larut tin fields which had already showed itself in the First Larut war of 1862 (*see* Chapter XVII *infra*).

The Penang riots came to an end when both sides had wearied of a conflict destined to flare up again a few years later 1872-74, in the second and third Larut wars.

The report of the Commission of Enquiry into these riots (of which Colonel Anson was Chairman), is a document which proves that the roots of the earliest secret society activity among peninsular Malays, are to be found in Penang.

This link with Penang continues; and the tap root of Malay secret society activity in the Peninsula to-day will be shown to be still in Penang.

The *P.R.C. Report* is supported by 70 printed pages of evidence taken by the Commission and is further embellished by an Appendix of 60 pages containing reprints of documents referred to in the evidence; and some pages of original translation of Triad ritual.

Some extracted portions of this "evidence" and other documents accompanying the report are reprinted as Appendices II, III, VII and VIII to this work. (*See* below page 250 footnote 2).

The Appendices to the Report itself are too voluminous for reproduction in full, but offer a wealth of information on the subject. They do not appear to have been consulted by Ward and Stirling in their work *The Hung Society* (1925).

The Penang Riot Commission of 1868 enjoyed the benefit of Schlegel's work published in 1866, which they had before them as a guide to the nature, aims and organisation of one of the warring factions but not of the other.

One defect in the Report and accompanying documents is the absence of Chinese characters and the variations in the romanised spelling of Chinese sounds, which make identifications difficult.

The Report is as follows:—

THE PENANG RIOT COMMISSION REPORT 1868

(*Published in Straits Settlements Legislative Council Proceedings Vol. 1868-69*)

The Commissioners appointed under Act XXI of 1867, to enquire into the origin and causes of the recent riots at Penang, have considered the matters referred to them, and have agreed to the following Report.

Footnote.—(1) Mr. E. J. Eyre was Governor of Jamaica 1862-1867. In 1865, there occurred a serious Negro rebellion in the island, which was firmly suppressed. A court of enquiry followed, as a result of which Mr. Eyre was recalled, prosecuted and acquitted. In 1872, the Government refunded to him the cost of his defence. He retired in 1874 and died in 1901.

Footnote.—(2) This was not surprising in view of what was just then happening to Mr. Eyre, whose case, no doubt, coloured the policy adopted towards the Penang riots and explains the leniency with which the leaders were subsequently treated.

Footnote.—(3) These were the flags of Triad and "Tokong" and were a common feature of the period up to the Treaty of Pangkor (1874). *See* below.

Footnote.—(4) Sir Harry Ord 1867-73.

Subjects of Enquiry

1. The subjects of enquiry as stated in Article I of the Act are—

    1st.—The origin and causes of the recent riots;

    2ndly.—How far the secret societies existing in Penang, have been concerned in instigating, or fostering such riots.

2. As the second subject treats of matters explanatory of the first, the Commissioners consider it better to report upon that subject in the first instance.

Societies concerned in the Riots

3. It is evident to the Commissioners, that there were four of the secret societies of Penang which were solely concerned in the late riots. Two of these societies are composed of Chinese, and two of Malay and Kling (natives of India) members.

4. The names of these four societies are the Ghee Hin, the Toh Peh Kong, (otherwise called Kien Teck) the White Flag and Red Flag.

Ghee Hin society

5. The Ghee Hin society or hoey, was formed in China, some centuries ago, for the purpose of overthrowing the Tartar rule, and replacing the Ming dynasty upon the throne of the country. This original object has been, practically, lost sight of by the branch at Penang, whose only real object has been, to carry on amongst its members a government of its own, as far as possible, independent of the Government of the Settlement.

6. The rules of this *imperium in imperio*, are given by two of the evidences before the Commission. One (No. 36) describing his initiation into the society says:—

    "A fowl's head was cut off and I was told, that whenever I was called by the society, I was to come immediately; when called on to subscribe, I was to do so; when there was a funeral, I was to attend, if called; if called to a marriage, I was to go; if called on at any time assistance was required, or to go and fight, I must go at once, and that if I did not obey these Rules, I would meet with the fate of the decapitated fowl then before me."

The other evidence (No. 53) gives these additional regulations:—

    "One member assaulted by another member, must bring his complaint before the headmen, and not before the Police; if he complained to the Police he would be punished. Should a member commit robbery, arson, or murder, the chiefs are bound to assist him in escaping from justice, and a chief would be punished, if he refused assistance. A criminal, assisted by the society to escape, has his passage paid, and a sum of money given him to make a new start in life."

7. The members of this society are bound by an oath, which is rendered more binding, in their estimation, by the ceremony of drinking one another's blood. The blood is extracted from their forefingers,[1] and mixed with spirits and water, in a bowl, from which all the new members drink.

8. There are three principal headmen, and a Sing Seng or secretary,[2] the latter of whom manages all matters of business.

9. There are also Councillors, whose number is not restricted, twenty of whom reside in George Town.

10. The number of members is stated, in evidence (No. 55) to be from 25,000 to 26,000, 14,000 to 15,000 of whom live in Province Wellesley: the total population of this Settlement being about 125,000. The members belonging to this society, consisting entirely of adult males, it must be evident, may, at any time, become highly dangerous to the peace of the Settlement.

11. The punishments awarded by the chiefs of the society against its offending members, are excommunication, flogging, cutting off the ears, and beheading; but the witness who gave the evidence (No. 8) regarding this adds: "But this is never done in this country". Another witness (No. 13) was present, not many months ago, when a member who was sentenced to 108 blows, the greatest number allowed, received 36 blows on the buttocks, with a stick 3 feet long and one inch in diameter. The punishment was for paying his addresses to another member's wife. This witness also states: "We don't inflict these extreme punishments (cutting off the ears and death) here". Another instance of flogging is given by witness (No. 36), for refusal to call members together when ordered to do so. Although there is no direct evidence, that the severer punishments have been carried out in this country, the Commissioners cannot but believe, that they have sometimes been enforced. Considering that the witnesses before the Commission have all struggled to conceal the worst features of their societies, it is not surprising, that there has been no direct evidence given on this point. It is enough, however, in support of the Commissioners' opinion, to state, that they have succeeded in obtaining sufficient evidence to prove how unscrupulously evil these societies are, and that the rules framed for the government of these societies in this very place, permit the infliction of these extreme and barbarous punishments.

12. The Ghee Hins of Penang consist chiefly of the labouring and artisan class, and are principally men from Canton.

Footnote.—(1) The middle finger of the *left* hand, *see* page 124 *supra*.
Footnote.—(2) The Sin Shang 先生 or master, *see* page 117 *supra*.

13. The Sing Seng or secretary of the Ghee Hins, appears to have been the leading and most influential person amongst them,—the chief being a very quiet man, and not disposed to be the cause of any disturbance. The secretary[1] has been deported from the Colony by order of the Government, in consequence of the prominent part he took in the bringing about of the late riots.

Toh Peh Kong society

14. The Toh Peh Kong society or hoey, was instituted in Penang about twenty-four years ago,[2] under one Khoo Ten Pang.

15. The society was founded by men from the Ho Kien province of China, who have always been antagonistic to the Cantonese, who form the greater part of the Ghee Hin society.

16. Khoo Ten Pang was succeeded, about fifteen years ago, by Khoo Thean Tek, who at the time of the riots was the headman of the society, and who is now a convict undergoing a sentence of seven years transportation, being a commutation of his original sentence of death, passed upon him for aiding and abetting in certain cases of murder during the riots.[3]

17. The Rules for admitting members, and the objects and regulations (see appendix)[4] of this society, are similar to those of the Ghee Hins.

18. The Rules for pensions and gratuities (see appendix),[4] to those who may be the sufferers, during their fights with other societies, would lead to the supposition, that the headmen, and better-to-do class of members, never intended to risk their own lives and persons on such occasions—the amounts of compensation being so small.

19. The Toh Peh Kongs number amongst their members most of the wealthy merchants and shop keepers of Beach Street, and include, also, the manufacturers and sellers of fire arms and ammunition. These proprietors of fire arms are bound, in times of disturbance, to supply the members of their society with muskets, and it was in this manner, that so many of the Toh Peh Kongs were armed during the late riots.

20. The number of Toh Peh Kongs in the Settlement, is about 5,000 to 6,000, the greater part of whom are in Prince of Wales' Island, very few residing in Province Wellesley.

21. The most influential person, next to Khoo Thian Tek, during the riots was Khoo Poh, a man described by one of the witnesses (No. 35) as clever and bold, and who gave advice to the headmen on all subjects. This man has been deported from the Colony by order of the Government.[5]

White Flag society

22. The White Flag was established as a society about ten or twelve years ago.[6]

23. The object of the society at the time of its establishment, was a religious one, *viz.*, to attend and assist at the religious ceremonies of its members, such as marriages, funerals, circumcisions, etc., and its rules contained nothing bad or injurious to the Public. Of late years the religious matters have been neglected, and as described by a witness (No. 37): "all manner of evil is done, mischief plotted, and combinations made, to help members out of trouble, instead of having recourse to the authorities".

24. The White Flag Society is in alliance with the Ghee Hins, and the head of it, Tuan Chee, and about thirty others, entered the Ghee Hin society about two years ago.

25. This society is composed of Malays and Klings, and during the late riots took part with the Ghee Hins. The town members of these two societies inhabit the same quarter of the town.

Red Flag society

26. The Red Flag is another society of Malays and Klings, and was established about eight years ago[7] for religious purposes, but like the White Flag, it has lost its religious character, and adopted the same bad practices.

27. The head of the society at the time of the riots, was Che Long, a Malay, who is described by one of the witnesses before the Commission, as a desperate character. Che Long is now a convict under sentence of 21 years transportation for the crime of arson, committed during the late riots. He appears to have taken an active part in the riots, and to have issued muskets, which were supplied to him on the order of Thean Tek, the head of the Toh Peh Kongs, to the members of his society.

Footnote.—(1) Named Boey Yoo Kong, *see* below.

Footnote.—(2) *See* page 106 ff. *supra.*

Footnote.—(3) This egregious rascal Khoo Thean Tek did not remain a convict long. The lawyers soon intervened on his behalf. He re-appears in the best Tammany manner in Chapter XX as a Government revenue monopolist in Perak in A.D. 1880. He died an immensely wealthy man c. 1887, as head of the Khoo Kongsi, one of the "big five" foundations of "Tokong" in Penang, which are also clan associations (*see* Chapters XVII, XXI and XXVII.)

Footnote.—(4) References to "appendix" in this report, are to those of the *P.R.C. Report* itself and not to those of this work. A few of the appendices of the report itself are, however, reproduced in this work (*see* below).

Footnote.—(5) Khoo Poh was very soon back again. *See* Chapters XVII and XX. This para. taken with para. 16 above shows the power of the Khoo Kongsi and the working of the hereditary principle (page 109 *supra*) in "Tokong" *viz*:—

    (i) Khoo Ten Pang 1844–1852.

    (ii) Khoo Thian Tek 1852–1867 and beyond (? 1887).

    (iii) Khoo Poh—Chief of Staff to No. 2 during 1867.

Footnote.—(6) *See* page 215 ff. *supra.*

Footnote.—(7) *See* page 222 ff. *supra.*

28. In the year 1863, a fight took place between Che Long's (the Red Flag), and the Toh Peh Kong societies, after which, these two societies became friendly, and entered into an alliance for offensive and defensive purposes.

29. The members of both societies occupy the same quarter of the town.

Erroneous opinion regarding hoeys

30. There is an opinion generally entertained, that the Chinese hoeys are necessary and beneficial to the Chinese community, as benefit societies. The Commissioners are, therefore, anxious before leaving the subject of the societies, to record that this opinion is erroneous.

31. Every Chinese tribe has its own benefit society, which is entirely free and independent of any hoey. It is only a member of a tribe, who can be the head of it, and he is appointed the head, in virtue of his social position in the tribe. The head of a hoey, on the contrary, may be a member of any tribe, and members of the same tribe are frequently to be found in different hoeys.[1]

Explanation of terms

32. The word *hoey* means "Brotherhood", "Society" or "Association", and the word *congsee* or *kongsee*, so frequently used in the evidence, means "company". A hoey is a secret society. A congsee is any company, but the word is frequently made use of to denote a hoey. The congsee house is the meeting house or club of the hoey.[2]

Origin and causes of the Riots

33. In order to ascertain the origin and causes of the recent riots, it is necessary to go back some years into the history of the societies concerned in them. It has already been mentioned, that the Toh Peh Kong, was, from the day of its foundation, antagonistic to the Ghee Hin society. It has latterly desired to gain the ascendancy over its rival, and its late chief, Thean Tek, appears to have been determined to carry out this object.[3]

34. It has also been mentioned that the Red Flag, and the White Flag societies, very soon dropped their religious character, and took to quarrelling and fighting, and that, lately, they had joined in alliance, the one with the Toh Peh Kongs, and the other with the Ghee Hins, for offensive and defensive purposes.

35. The first cause which appears to have brought about the particular riots, which are the subject of the present enquiry, was a quarrel about some trifle, between the Red Flag and White Flag Malays, during the last Mohurrum festival. This quarrel continued, and led to constant assaults, by individuals of the one party on those of the other, which resulted in the murder of a diamond merchant, a Malay, in the Toh Peh Kong quarter, by one of the Red Flag party.

36. This led to the Malay quarrel being taken up by the Chinese.

37. Thus things went on until about the 1st or 2nd July (1st of the 6th moon), when the peace was disturbed in the following manner—(*vide* evidence No. 4).

38. A Toh Peh Kong Chinaman was looking through the palings, bounding the premises of a White Flag Malay in Pitt Street. The Malay threw a rambutan skin at the Chinaman, and called him a thief. The Chinaman went away, but returned with ten or twelve Toh Peh Kong friends. The Malay's friends then turned out, and a fight with stones and clubs ensued. The Malay drove back the Toh Peh Kongs, as far as their congsee house, and then the stones thrown by the former, struck the Toh Peh Kong signboard, upon which the Toh Peh Kongs turned out in great numbers, and fire-arms are said to have been used. The Police interfered, and succeeded in putting a stop to the disturbance for the time.

39. About the 8th of the month (July), a meeting took place of the chiefs of the Toh Peh Kong, Ghee Hin, White Flag and Red Flag societies, who, assisted by arbitrators, patched up a settlement of grievances.

40. This settlement was, however, of no effect, for the following day the Toh Peh Kongs and Red Flag Malays, attacked and entered some of the houses of the White Flag Malays, and injured and destroyed their property.

41. After this, frequent assaults and murders were committed by both parties, and so matters continued until the 1st August, when a false charge was made by Thean Tek, the head of the Toh Peh Kong party, that some White Flag Malays and Ghee Hins, had stolen from the Toh Peh Kong cloth dyers, some cloth that had been put out in the street to dry, after having been dyed.

42. A meeting took place on the following day (at the house of Cheow Sew, one of the arbitrators, and a non-congsee man) of the headmen of the two Chinese societies and their arbitrators to try and settle the case of the stolen cloth; but in consequence of a quarrel between Thean Tek and the Sing Seng or secretary of the Ghee Hins, no settlement of differences was come to, and both these men left the meeting determined to fight.

43. There is no doubt, from the evidence, that Thean Tek was prepared and determined to do this beforehand, and that the false charge about the stolen cloth, was only made to bring about a *casus-belli*.

Footnote.—(1) This is an important conclusion and bears out the view that blood-brotherhood is thicker than clan association.

Footnote.—(2) This is rather confused. *See* page 104–105 *supra* where we have attempted a clearer exposition.

Footnote.—(3) The real dispute was in the Larut tin fields, *see* next chapter.

44. Accordingly, on the morning of the 3rd of August, the Toh Peh Kongs attacked the Ghee Hins, and thus commenced the riots, into the origin of which the Commissioners under Act XXI of 1867 were appointed to enquire.

45. The conclusion, arrived at by the Commissioners, is, that the late riots had their origin in a trifling quarrel between two rival Muhammadan societies during the late Mohurrum festival, and that they were fostered by two other rival societies of Chinese, with one of which, each of the former had joined in alliance. That all these societies joined in the riots by the direction, and under the instigation of their respective headmen or office-bearers, who directed their principal movements, and who, from the funds of their societies, supplied them with provisions and arms, with rewards for the heads of their enemies, and with gratuities and pensions for the wounded and for the relations of those who were killed when fighting. That the organisation and discipline of the societies appear to be as complete as that of any disciplined force of the Government. That it is therefore evident, that these secret societies are extremely dangerous to the peace and welfare of the community. A notable circumstance, and one which has rendered these societies more harmful of late, is, the combination of the Mussulmans and Hindoos with the Chinese, with whose customs their religious prejudices are so much at variance.

Suggestions

46. Although not required to do so by the Act, the Commissioners consider, that it is not altogether beyond their province, to make a few suggestions, concerning the means of preventing future injury to the Public, arising from secret societies in this Settlement. They would, therefore, recommend the entire suppression of these societies, which, it has been before stated, have no claim to be considered benefit societies, in the same manner as it has been done by legislation in Hongkong.[1] Should it, however, be found impossible to suppress the societies by legal enactment, the Committee would suggest:—

1st.—That all societies, of whatever nature, should be registered (under penalty) at the Office of the Commissioner of Police. The registration should furnish the names of the head, and other chiefs of the society, its object, number of members, etc. The registration should be annual, and a fee should be charged for registering, except in the case of benefit societies, and there should be a penalty for making a false registration.

2nd.—All oaths, of every description, should be prohibited, and any person guilty of administering an unlawful oath, should be liable to a penalty.

3rd.—The head of the Society or any of the chiefs, if the head is not forthcoming, should be liable, in case of any riot, in which his society should be concerned, to be prosecuted by any Police Officer, and to be fined in a penalty not less than $, and not exceeding $, without prejudice to the amount of any damage or injury committed, and in default of payment of the fine, the congsee or meeting house of the society, with all the premises attached thereto, and all other property, belonging to, or standing in the name of the society, should be forfeited to the Crown.

4th.—The head of the society, as well as every other member of it, should also be held liable in an action for any damage, or injury to property, committed by the congsee to which he belongs.

5th.—That a heavy penalty should be imposed upon any person found guilty of preventing by force or intimidation, any individual from making his complaint to the Police, or to any Magistrate, or other judicial authority, or from prosecuting any individual before any of the Courts of Law.

6th.—That a member of a society, forcing on any individual, a rule of his society, which is contrary to law, should be liable to a heavy penalty.

7th.—That all opportunities of collision between rival societies or religious sects, should, as far as possible, be prevented, by not authorizing processions of the members of such societies or sects, in the public streets, or high roads of the Settlement, and by confining such ceremonies to the grounds or compounds of such societies or religious communities.[2]

A. E. H. Anson,—
Lt.-Governor and President.

Lawrence Nairne.
Walter Scott.
James Lamb.
Bernard Rodyk.
Foo Tye Sin.
Nina Merican Noordin.
Ong Attye.
Lee Phee Chuan,
(Signed in Chinese characters.)

Prince of Wales' Island,
(Penang)
14th July, 1868.

Footnote.—(1) Referring to the Hongkong Ordinance of 1845 "For the Suppression of the Triad and other secret societies".

Footnote.—(2) Some of the documents annexed to the above Report are reprinted as Appendices to this work as follows :—

    (i) Kian Tek's new Instructions (Rules of the Toh Peh Kong society 1844) Appendix II.
    (ii) List of "War" pensions and gratuities payable by the Toh Peh Kong society. Appendix III.
    (iii) Extracts from the evidence. Appendix VII.
    (iv) Letter from Ghee Hin of Tongka to Ghee Hin of Penang, dated 11th of 6th Moon 1867. Appendix VIII.

OFFICIAL "DISCOVERY" OF THE TWO CAMPS OF TRIAD AND "TOKONG"

The *Penang Riot Commission Report* proves the existence in Penang in 1867 of the two hostile Chinese camps of Ghee Hin and Toh Peh Kong. For purposes of this work, we have called these two camps Triad and "Tokong", whose advent to and career in Malaya up to 1867, we have sketched in earlier chapters.

We propose from this point onwards to assume acceptance of this proof on the part of the reader and consequently to drop the use of inverted commas with the omnibus term Tokong, to express what is opposed to Triad.

The *P.R.C. Report* also establishes the co-existence of the two hostile Mohamedan camps of White and Red Flag independent of, but allied to the two Chinese camps, thereby reinforcing the proof of the two separate entities in the Chinese secret society world.

Two observations should perhaps be made here:—
(1) That this discovery was no sooner made than it appears to have been forgotten.
(2) That this discovery has never been applied to secret society conditions in Malaya outside Penang, in seeking an explanation for the cause of Chinese riots or Malay animosities elsewhere.

We submit that the discovery has only to be applied to secret society events in other Settlements both before and after 1867, to arrive at the conviction that what was true of Penang holds good for the whole Peninsula; and that the proposition put forward in earlier chapters[1] namely, that the Han and the Hung leagues are both represented throughout Malaya, the one by Tokong the other by Triad, has been proved.

We must now examine the "Evidence" section of the *P.R.C. Report* more closely and estimate its quality and see what other material of permanent value may be obtained from it. The following facts and figures are put together from the scattered body of the evidence. In all cases the original spelling is retained.

ANALYSIS OF THE "EVIDENCE" SECTION OF THE PENANG RIOT COMMISSION REPORT OF 1868

(1) The radical cause, and the precipitating cause of the riots:—

The only point on which we find ourselves in disagreement with the findings of the *P.R.C. Report* is under the head of "Origin and cause of the Riots" (paras. 33–41) which are generally too superficial. The nearest the report seems to get to the radical cause is in para 33 where it says:—

"The Toh Peh Kong was from the day of its foundation antagonistic to the Ghee Hin society".

This finding hardly sounds as if the two were merely different branches of one great secret brotherhood? The passage continues:—

"The Toh Peh Kong has latterly desired to gain the ascendency over its rival and its late chief Thean Tek appears to have been determined to carry out this project".

What the Commissioners did not know, or did not take into account, was that the first Larut war (*see* next chapter) had already been fought in 1862 between the same antagonists and had proved a complete victory on the field for Tokong, the aggressors, but was followed by their diplomatic defeat, inasmuch as Colonel Cavenagh, the Governor, put pressure on Tokong to re-admit Triad to their holdings in Larut and to pay Triad $17,000 compensation in addition.

This circumstance must have rankled in the minds of Tokong and explains why they were again the aggressors in the Penang riots, five years later.

The Penang outbreak might be called more accurately in history the second Larut war, but it was fought out in Penang instead of on the home ground, and was between the Toh Peh Kong or Hokkien section of Tokong instead of the Hai San or Hakka section, against the common enemy the Cantonese of Triad. It was fought with all the ferocity of the rival stems of the Han and Hung and with the contemporary background of the Hakka-Puntei war and the Taiping rebellion in China, both of which had their setting in the Canton province.

Land hunger and a claim by both Han and Hung to the exclusive right to exploit the wealth of the tin fields, these were the radical causes of the Penang riots just as they were of the Larut wars of which they formed one episode (*see* Chapter XVII).

The Penang riots of 1867 were, therefore, primarily a trial of strength between the two fundamental rivals of Triad and Tokong, represented by the Ghee Hin (Cantonese) and the Toh Peh Kong (Hokkien) respectively.

Tokong appears to have had its "country" headquarters at Jelutong[14] where, according to Appendix II of the *P.R.C. Report*, the Toh Peh Kong society was founded in December, 1844, and named Kian Tek. This foundation appears to have been identical with the Ghee Hok society of Singapore (*see* Chapters V and VI).

Footnote.—(1) *See* Chapter I page 14 (*c*)(1), Chapter II page 36 (foot) and Chapter VI page 11.

Footnote.—(2) At some time subsequent to the riots, Jelutong seems to have been abandoned by Tokong as its country Headquarters. Jelutong later becomes associated exclusively with Triad and White Flag.

The houses of Tokong at Jelutong were burnt by Triad in 1865.[1]

Tokong was numerically much weaker than Triad and decided to accumulate arms and ammunition in order to take revenge upon Triad for this attack.

The precipitating cause of the outbreak was a groundless quarrel picked by the Red Flag against the White Flag and instigated by Tokong who by August 1867, had provided themselves with a supply of arms, ammunition and fighting men from China and obtained further assistance from their sister lodge in Tongka (Junk Ceylon).

(2) The order of battle in 1867 was:—

Triad (Ghee Hin) supported by:—		Tokong (Toh Peh Kong) supported by:—
Ho Seng; and White Flag.	versus	Kian Tek; and Red Flag.

(3) The total strength was approximately:—

Triad:	Penang		10,000	Tokong:	Penang			6,000
	Province Wellesley	..	15,000		Province Wellesley	..		500
White Flag		..	3,000	Red Flag	..		..	1,000
	Total	..	28,000		Total	..		7,500

As Tokong was prepared and heavily armed with better weapons, this initial advantage made up for the disparity in numbers.

(4) The chief Chinese headmen at the outbreak of hostilities were:—

TRIAD	TOKONG
Lee Coyn (probably Lee Kwun), *President*;	Khoo Thean Teck, *President*;
Oh Wee Kee, *Vice-President*;	Khoo Poh, *Vice-President*;
Oh Ho Chong, *Vice-President*;	Neoh Oo Teoh, *Vice-President*;
Boey Yoo Kong, *Master*;	Lim Beng Kwa, *Master*;
Lim Kay Fat, *Clerk*; and	Khoo Mah Pean, *Clerk*; and
Twenty Counsellors.	Thirty Counsellors.

(5) The chief Malay and "Jawi-pekan" or Indian headmen were:—

WHITE FLAG	RED FLAG
(1) Tuan Chee (Chik) *alias* Sheik Omar *alias* Omar Abdul Rasul;	(1) 'Che Long *alias* Hadjee Mohamed Noor;
(2) Mohamed Kader Houssain *alias* Pak Etam;	(2) Tuan Mohamed (*Ref. evidence 29 page 42*).
(3) Shamoo;	
(4) Saiboo (a schoolmaster);	(3) Vapoo Merican Noordin;
(5) 'Che Abdul Karim;	(4) Abdul Kader Merican;
(6) Tungku Mat (Collector of Assessment, Ayer Hitam);	(5) 'Che Awang Pet.
(7) Mohamed Amin (Ayer Hitam);	(6) Said Mohamed Atas;[2]
(8) Hadjee Daoud;	(7) Said Houssain Ideed;[3]
(9) 'Che Omar;	(8) 'Che Awang Turkee;
(10) Joosoo;	(9) 'Che Aboo;
(11) Mohd. Ibrahim;	(10) Talip;
Prominent White Flag members:—	(11) 'Che Amboo;
(12) Hassan Besar;	(12) Wan Man;
(13) Karrim;	(13) Madarsah Merican ("Superintendent" and head fighting man);
(14) Mohd. Daoud;	
(15) Awang Moosah;	
(16) Nga Chee;	(14) 'Che Deen;
(17) Kling;	(15) Pawan Nerepoo;
(18) Mangay;	(16) Nadar (Police Peon).
(19) Houssain;	
(20) Mat;	
(21) Sahid;	
(22) Lah Rahaman.	

Footnote.—(1) This attack is evidently that referred to in the *Penang Administration Report* of 1865 (*see* pages 105–106 *supra*) and was not unconnected with contemporary events in Larut.

Footnote.—(2) He was no doubt a Sayyid and a member of the Arab family of Al-attas, whose connection with the Red Flag, down to the present-day is referred to in Chapters XXV and XXX *infra*.

Footnote.—(3) He was no doubt a Sayyid and a member of the Arab family of Ideed, whose connection with the Red Flag down to the present-day is referred to in Chapter XXX *infra*. This emphasises the hereditary principle peculiar to Tokong and Red Flag.

WHITE FLAG

And the following Police Peons, (*i.e.* Constables) :—

(23) Shenoo (Hindoo) ;
(24) Tahir (Malay) ;
(25) Pakareedin, a "duffadar".

White Flag district leaders:—

(26) Kader Bux, a cart-owner—Chulia Road.

(27) Shaik Madar; ⎫
(28) Mohamed Houssain; ⎬ Headmen between Chulia Road and Simpang Ampat.
(29) 'Che Mat; ⎭

(30) Tuanku Baidah; ⎫
(31) Abdul Karrim; ⎪
(32) Kadir; ⎬ Headmen of Hutton's Lane.
(33) Hadjee Houssain; ⎪
(34) Said Mohamed Sallie; ⎭

(35) Cassim; ⎫
(36) Mohamed Ghouse ⎬ Headmen of Macalister Road, and Jalan Bahru.
(37) Sultan; ⎭

(38) Maniah; } Pulau Tikus village.

(39) Hadjee Daoud; } Klawie.
(40) Hadjee;

(41) Tahir; } Tanjong Tokong.
(42) Ismail.

RED FLAG

The above all lived in Penang town, in or near Jalan Sampah.

In addition there were Red Flag headmen at the following fifteen "country" centres, whose names, except in one instance, are not recorded:—

(1) Titih Papan;
(2) Datu Kramat;
(3) Campong Lama;
(4) Ayer Etam;
(5) Sungai Penang;
(6) Batu Ooban (Headman, 'Che Oodin) ;
(7) Batu Man;
(8) Bayan Lepas;
(9) Penang Road;
(10) Dhobie Ghaut;
(11) Campong Bharu;
(12) Telok Jelutong;
(13) Sungai Glugor;
(14) Sungei Nibong;
(15) Telok Coomba.

The foregoing recital, although containing what are to-day but empty names, gives some idea of the grip the flag societies had upon the territory of Penang and Province Wellesley as long ago as 1867.

Portions of the evidence from which the foregoing information is taken are reprinted as Appendix VII, but there are numerous other references in the evidence, not included here or in Appendix VII, which provide further side-lights upon this aspect of our subject.

(6) The identity of the leaders of the belligerents:—

In the evidence, there appear the following particulars of *membership*:—

The names of mere members, except in a few cases, are not reproduced here:—

TRIAD		TOKONG	
Ghee Hin	—95 headmen and 95 members.	Toh Peh Kong	—119 headmen and members.
Ho Sang	— 7 headmen.	Hye San	—The society is mentioned but none of the headmen or members as such.
White Flag	—42 headmen and members.	Chin Chin	—Mentioned but no headmen or members.
		Red Flag	—16 headmen and members.

The Ho Hop Seah (和 合 社) is also mentioned, but there is nothing to show to which side it belonged, if either.

The names of the *leaders* only of Ghee Hin and Toh Peh Kong and *all* names of White and Red Flag mentioned in the evidence are given above, but some further identification is necessary.

We have not seen the record of the trials which followed the riots, but the following references thereto are given:—

P.R.C. Report para 16:—

Khoo Ten Pang was succeeded about 15 years ago (1848) by Khoo Thean Tek who, at the time of the riots was the Headman of the (Toh Peh Kong) society and who is now a convict undergoing a sentence of seven years' transportation being a commutation of his original sentence of death passed upon him for aiding and abetting in certain cases of murder during the riots.

Para 21:—

The most influential person next to Thean Tek during the riots was Khoo Poh,[1] a man described by one of the witnesses (No. 35) as clever and bold and who gave advice to the headmen on all subjects.—This man has been deported from the Colony by order of the Government.

Footnote.—(1) It appears from the "evidence" that this man came specially from Tongka for the riots as Generalissimo of Tokong.

Para. 27:—

> The head of the (Red Flag) society at the time of the riots was Che Long, a Malay who is described by one of the witnesses before the Commission as "a desperate character", Che Long is now a convict under sentence of 21 years transportation for the crime of arson committed during the late riots.

This man Che Long does not appear to have been examined by the Commissioners, which seems a pity.

Whatever these sentences of transportation may have amounted to, we find Khoo Thean Tek taking an active part in the Larut wars with his steamer the *Fair Malacca* in February, 1873, and later obtaining the monopoly of the opium farm in Perak at the hands of the British Resident.

Besides the above, one at least of the Ghee Hin headmen Boey Yu Kong appears to have been transported and we find that both he and Khoo Poh of the Toh Peh Kong had returned to the Colony in 1869, as the following extracts from Song Ong Siang *op. cit.* page 155 shows:—

> In September, 1869, a bill for amending the Preservation of the Peace Ordinance was introduced in the Legislative Council. Its real *raison d'être* was to provide indemnity to magistrates and Police officers who had imprisoned Boey Yu Kong and Ku Poh, the two headmen who had been deported in connection with the "Toa Pek Kong" riots at Penang and who had returned to the Colony.

Notwithstanding strong opposition from the Chief Justice the bill passed into law. This amending ordinance may have been inspired by events then taking place in London connected with the trial of Mr. E. J. Eyre, Governor of Jamaica, resulting from his suppression of the Jamaica rebellion of 1865.

(7) Tainted evidence:—

In studying the evidence recorded by the P.R. Commissioners, we must remember what has, perhaps, been insufficiently stressed by them namely, that practically the whole of it was tainted and unwillingly extracted from hostile witnesses, by a procedure foreign to them, under a formal "oath" meaningless to them and in the face of the vital, irrevocably binding and awe-inspiring oath of their own society, which forbade them, on pain of death, to disclose anything to the profane.   However much we may discount the infliction of the severer forms of secret society punishment, of the nature of which we have caught a glimpse in Chapters II, VII and IX, the fact remains that the societies retained the power of life and death over their members, against which fear of the special powers of investigation granted to the Commissioners under a temporary local law, was unlikely to prevail.

Added to this, most of the evidence was that of accomplices in the riots and was, therefore, inevitably tainted on that account.

For two cogent reasons, therefore, it was in the highest degree unlikely that the Commissioners could obtain anything but the minimum of information and that probably misleading, upon the finer points of Triad and Tabut organisation.

A third obstacle was the fact that the interrogators were themselves almost totally ignorant of the abstruse subject-matter of their investigation.

An admission of these difficulties is contained in the Report para. 11:—

> The witnesses before the Commission have all struggled to conceal the worst features of their societies.

We may be permitted to add that to a very large extent they probably succeeded.

(8) The link-up of Triad and Tabut:—

We should here note, for what it may be worth, the following testimony regarding the forging of that link between the Mohamedan societies (be their origin what it may) and the lodges of the Han and the Hung leagues, which we know to have taken place.

Witness No. 15, Oh Wee Kee on page 25 of the *P.R.C. Report* states:—

> Q. Now tell us (the Commission) truly about the White Flag society and their connection with the Ghee Hins.
> A. About two years ago (1866) the White Flag men joined our (Ghee Hin) society. It occurred in this way. There were some of our men of bad character who had combined to keep houses of bad repute (brothels), gambling houses, etc., etc., who got the White Flag Malays to assist them and secretly introduced them into our society as members.
> Q. Did these new members (Malay) take the oaths, pay the subscription, and have their names enlisted in the Ghee Hin books as members.
> A. Yes. One of our headmen told me that Tuan Chee (No. 1 White above) and about sixty or seventy of his men have entered our society (Ghee Hin).

This represents the probable channel by which the baser elements among the Chinese and the "Jawi-pekans", arrived at a common level of criminality.

In some such way Triad and Tokong induced the two Mohamedan societies to affiliate with them for purely criminal purposes to their mutual advantage, namely the exploitation of the weak and the propitation of the Police.   Thus, they established among themselves a complete *imperium in imperio* and reached under the cloak of "benevolence", the lowest depths of professional criminality from which they have never attempted to escape; and whose greed and rivalries have earned for them the apt caption of Mills "The Pirates' and Robbers' Co-operative association".

(9) Evidence of the ritual of initiation in use in 1867:—

We have caught a glimpse in Chapters XIV *supra* of the process already in operation about 1850 of initiation of Mohamedans to membership of Triad and Tokong. We have also had mention in the same chapter of one exclusively Mohamedan league, admission to which was by oath although contrary to Mohamedan law.

We are entitled to assume, therefore, that during the period 1850–1867 if not earlier, there arose two well recognised and entirely distinct processes of initiation of persons other than Chinese to the secret societies of the period, one a truncated form of the Triad or Tokong ceremony, conducted in Chinese with the aid of interpreters, and one a purely Mohamedan ceremony conducted in Malay.

These two ceremonies become more clearly distinguished at a later date and become known by the names of *The Wayang China* and *The Wayang Melayu (i.e.* the Chinese ceremony and the Malay ceremony). We discuss these two ceremonies in comparative detail in Chapter XXIX.

For the present, it will be sufficient to assume that both ceremonies were in use at the time of the *P.R.C. Report*, the Wayang Melayu being a direct admission of Mohamedans and others to the flag societies; and the Wayang China being a partial admission of Mohamedans and others to Triad or Tokong as the case might be, and representing, as it were, an advanced "degree" of flag association membership. The Wayang Melayu was and still is the true flag association admission ceremony, with an oath sworn in the Koran and is in use to-day side by side with the Wayang China of the pseudo-Chinese rite.

To return now to the *P.R.C. Report*, para. 6 of which refers to the rules of the societies and the ritual used, only four witnesses were questioned on this subject *viz:*—

(1) No. 15 Oh Wee Kee—Vice-President, Ghee Hin.
(2) No. 36, Shamoo, a native of Negapatam and presumably a Hindu, although it nowhere says so, and a member of the Ghee Hin.
(3) No. 49, Yeoh Yeng, a Tokong Counsellor.
(4) No. 53, Wong Sang Pah, Treasurer of the Ghee Hin.

Of these, the evidence of Shamoo is interesting. He explains how he came to join Triad and how Triad placed itself, according to its fixed habit, between him and the law.

In Schlegel *op. cit.* page 57, there is a reference to the accepted methods of recruitment employed by Triad and at top of page 113 *op. cit.* a record of what happened to those who refused to join. No wonder, therefore, that Shamoo soon found himself the unwilling recruit of "Tuangku Mat, a Collector of Assessment".

What Shamoo goes on to describe, (pages 47–48 of the "Evidence") is a Triad initiation ceremony held at Balik Pulau about September, 1866, for about 80 new members (30 Malays and 50 Chinese).

He says:—

> The Chinese paid 3.60 each (entrance fee) and the Malays and Klings 1.60, the reason of this difference I do not know.

The reason probably was that at one and the same initiation the 50 Chinese were admitted to the Ghee Hin proper, while the Malays and Klings took part only in the Wayang China.

By means of the Wayang China, members of the White and Red Flags became affiliated to Triad and Tokong in order to fetch and carry for them: and to get over the local language difficulty and to suborn the local police and so to safeguard in a foreign country the *imperium in imperio* of the Hung and the Han leagues.

The witness Shamoo also mentions:—

> Two months afterwards, I received a receipt for my entrance fee and a Poonchee (ticket of membership produced).

This document is not included among the "exhibits" appended to the Report. We know, however, that this Poonchee 本紙 pun chi, is the certificate or "Yellow Quilt" referred to on page 125 *supra*, which the Master hands to the initiate at the conclusion of the Triad initiation ceremony. Witness No. 49, Yeoh Yeng, a hard-boiled Tokong counsellor of 28 years standing, made under pressure unwilling and evasive admissions regarding the ceremony of Tokong initiation, from which we can gain little or no information.

(10) Officials of Tokong:—

Khoo Thean Tek, (Evidence 2) headman of the Toh Peh Kong (on page 6 of the record) makes the following admissions and references to Tokong officials:—

He gives:—
One President (himself);
One Vice-President;
One Second Vice-President;
One Master:

One Red Staff;
    Followed by—
Two Councils;
One Senior Council of four members; and
One Junior Council of twelve members;
    Followed by—
District headmen (number unlimited).

He denied the existence of a 先鋒 Sien Fung or Vanguard, an official whom we have seen is not included in the Tokong hierarchy (*see* page 150 (*c*) *supra*).

(11) Anti-law and anti-police characteristics of Tokong:—
    Admissions were wrung from Khoo Thean Tek (page 6) covering:—
        The infliction of punishment;
        The discipline demanded;
        The penalty for resort to the courts;
        The penalty for reporting to the Police;
        The penalty for giving evidence;
        The penalty for informing of a murder.

These characteristics are just as strong to-day as they were in 1867 and help to explain some of the police problems of Malaya.

(12) The tribe of Lim:—
    An interesting reference appears (on page 7) to the Hokkien or Teo Chew tribe of Lim (林), which furnishes a clue to its Ko Lao Hui and Tokong connections and criminal origins in China *viz*:—

    Q. You know of the arrival of some two or three hundred men from China of bad character.
    A. Yes. Two hundred more or less. For about two years they have been coming in, but the largest number arrived this year—at least a hundred.
    Q. Tell us what you know of them.
    A. They were fishermen by trade, but they and their women were really all pirates. They belonged to Kwa-Toh and Kwa Jin[1] in China, but were driven out of the country by their Government and came here. They all belonged to the tribe or surname of Lim.
    Q. To what societies do they now belong?
    A. Some to the Toh Peh Kongs, others to none.

Other interesting passages in the evidence, not specially noted in the Commission Report, are these:—

(13) Evidence of the flags of Triad and Tokong:—
    Evidence 4 (page 8) Oh Wee Kee says, "The flag of the Ghee Hin (Triad) is a red ground with white border", thus identifying it correctly with the flag of the Triad Mother lodge of Canton. (*See* Chapter I page 12 *supra*).

    Evidence 1 (para. 4) Khoo Thean Teck says, "The fighting flag of the Toh Peh Kongs (Tokong) is a triangle with a red ground and a black border". This was clearly not a Triad flag.

    Red and black are given by Hutson (Chapter II) as the colours of the flags of the Ko Lao Hui. This flag, (red with black border) will appear again in the Larut wars Chapter XVII.

(14) Evidence 4 (page 9) states that the agreement drawn up after the preliminary riots of July, 1867, between the Ghee Hins and the Toh Peh Kongs was in *English*, and that between the Red and White Flags was in *Tamil*.

(15) Officials of Triad:—
    Evidence 8 (page 13) sheds some light on the officials of Triad. Boey Yoo Kong, Master of the Ghee Hin lodge, gives the following:—

        One President (Lee Coyn).
        One Vice-President.
        One Second Vice-President.
        One Master (the witness, who says he is the first officer of the society and senior to all the rest).
        One Red Staff.
        One Treasurer and three Assistants.
        Twenty-five to thirty Counsellors.

Then follows this passage (page 14):—

    Q. Are there any other office-bearers?
    A. There are messengers called Chokie[2] in Town and in the country districts. Their duties are to call members to the society and to serve orders.
    Q. Have you no officers called Tai Ha[3] who search for new members and bring them to the society?
    A. There is such an office, but it is not filled up......whoever likes brings in new members and he gets a commission for it.

Footnote.—(1) Reference not identified.
    Footnote.—(2) This must represent the 草 鞋 (T'so Hai) or grass sandals (detectives) of a Triad lodge (page 117 *supra*).
    Footnote.—(3) This is a misprint and refers to the Tai Ma 渧 馬 (Horse leaders) or recruiters or bullies of a Triad lodge (page 117 *supra*).

(16) Anti-law characteristics of Triad:—

On page 4 Boey Yoo Kong says:—

Q. What is the punishment for disobedience?
A. The member is excommunicated.
Q. What is done to him on excommunication?
A. If the order is of importance he is flogged: if of more importance, his ears are cut off, and if of great importance, he is beheaded. But this is never done in this country.

Murder as a punishment is, as we know, of commonplace occurrence amongst secret society members in Malaya.

Again in Evidence 13, witness Khoo[1] Ah Soon (page 23) says:—

Q. Do you know of any instances of flogging taking place?
A. Yes, about three or four months ago in the country. It was because a member was paying attention to a fellow-member's wife.
Q. How many blows did he receive?
A. The punishment ordered was 108 blows upon his buttocks but only 36 blows were given with a stick about one inch in diameter and over three feet long. By the rules, not more than 108 or less than 36 blows, can be administered.
Q. What are the more severe punishments?
A. Cutting off the ears and death. The rules of our society are to this effect, but we don't inflict these extreme punishments here.
Q. Do not men seek to enter your society for the sake of protection?
A. Yes.
Q. Then when a member is dismissed he is no longer protected by the society?
A. No. He has no protection from us.

These admissions help the European reader of to-day to realise just why it is that secret societies, when their growth is unchecked, obtain the grip they do over a peasant population. An analysis of the Triad disciplinary code is given on pages 121-124, *supra*.

(17) Police membership of Tokong:—

On the top of page 91 *loc. cit.* there is a reference to Police membership of the Toh Peh Kong, and although this particular instance is not very convincing, it should be noted, as the subject will recur.

(18) Other features:—

In Evidence 22, Lim Beng Kwa (page 31) we learn of two other Hung Kwans (Red Staves) or inflictors of punishment of Tokong. We also find mention of "Kay" (*i.e.* Kheh or Hakka) members of the Toh Peh Kong for the first time.

We also gain some idea of the distribution of Tokong and Red Flag on Penang Island (confined to the town and northern coast areas) and in the Province, at Qualla Muda: Penaga: Telok Ayer Tawar: Lahar Ikan Mati: Permatang Sintu: all of which are in the North of Province Wellesley, suggesting an affinity with Kedah.

The Toh Peh Kong was also strong at Tongka (Junk Ceylon) at this time (page 32).

In Evidence 26, Lim Pick Teck (*loc. cit.* page 38) we read of a meeting, or rather council of war, held on 4th August, 1867, (during the riots) at which Tokong (Toh Peh Kong) and Red Flag Malays were present together. The identity of the Kian Hock society of Jelutong with the Toh Peh Kong is also referred to at the end of this evidence (page 39). We have already suggested (Chapter VI) the probable identity of the Kian Hock with the Ghee Hok society of Singapore, which also belonged to the Tokong foundation.

In Evidence 35, Lim Beng Kwa (page 46), we get an insight into the scale of compensation paid by the Toh Peh Kong to its followers, who lose their lives or get into trouble with the authorities. (*See* Appendix III *infra*).

As we shall see in Part II of this work, much the same system holds good to-day among Malay lodges.

We also learn that "seven-tenths of the Macao men are Ghee Hins", which we may take to mean that either:—

(a) seven-tenths of all Cantonese residents in Penang at that time were members of the Ghee Hin lodge, or more literally but less grammatically that;
(b) seven-tenths of the membership of the Ghee Hin lodge were Cantonese, the remaining three-tenths being "Chin Chews", *i.e.*, Hokkiens.

Again in Evidence No. 47, Teoh Chin Yen (page 59) says:—

Oh those men are Hokien men that have done this. Go to Wee Kee, the Hokien headman (in the Ghee Hin lodge); the fault was always laid on the Hokien men of whom a few belong to the Ghee Hin society. A great part of the members of the Ghee Hins are Macao men.

This shows that, quite as it should be, there was a Hokkien Branch of the Triad society functioning in Penang at that time, which would normally be hostile to the Hokkiens in Tokong.

(19) The link with Tongka (Junk Ceylon):—

An interesting feature of the *P.R.C. Report* is the casual evidence it furnishes of strong Triad and Tokong ties during the period 1860-1867, between Penang and "Junk Ceylon" (or Tongka as it is called in the evidence).

Footnote.—(1) This is a Triad witness and his surname was probably not Khoo (邱), but Kho (許) or Khaw (辜) or Gho (吳) or Ko (高), the romanisation being at fault.

K

These ties can be none other than a prolongation of those to which we have referred in Chapters IV, V, XIII and XV and which point to "Junk Ceylon" as the cradle of Triad and Tokong in Malaya.

Specific references to Tongka in the evidence are as follows:—

Page 2:—

Khoo Thean Teck Headman of Tokong.
"I then told him (a Ghee Hin Headman) that we must not allow the Tongka quarrel to extend to this place" (Penang).

Page 32:—

Lim Beng Kwa—Acting Secretary Tokong.
Q. What other books are kept there (i.e., in Khoo Thean Tek's house).
A. The payment of subscriptions book: the ledger: and the list of new members at Tongka, Junk Ceylon.

Page 35:—

Teoh Ching Yen—Councillor of Tokong.
Q. Do you know who wrote the new page in this book (a forged page of members' names)?
A. ......I heard that Khoo Poh's krani (clerk) did it.
Q. ......What are the names of his (Khoo Poh's) kranis?
A. One is called Toh Gan, the other Ching Thean Toon—The latter has just come from Tongka.

Page 44:—

Lim Hwa Cheam—Councillor of Tokong.
Thean Tek said Ching Thean Toon had done it (the forgery) ......he came lately from Tongka.

Page 56:—

Yeoh Whey Sew—Councillor of Tokong.
Q. Are the twenty muskets entered in your book as having been sold to Lim Beng Kwa and Khoo Mah Pean, the only ones you sold them in July and August last (1867)?
A. Yes.
Q. And the two tubs of gunpowder sold to those same parties—are they all?
A. Yes, I also sold eight barrels for Tongka.

Page 57:—

(The same witness).
Q. For what purpose had the Toh Peh Kongs prepared themselves with arms and ammunition?
A. We were afraid of the Ghee Hins—we had heard of the fighting in Tongka between the two societies, so we were determined to be prepared.

Page 59:—

Teoh Ching Yen—Councillor of Tokong (recalled).
Q. Had the fight between the Toh Peh Kongs and Ghee Hins at Tongka, nothing to do with the outbreak here?
A. Yes, I think so. The Ghee Hins at Tongka had so many men killed and wounded, that it had an influence.

Page 61:—

Yeoh Yeong—Councillor Tokong.
Q. How many men does your society muster in Tongka?
A. From four to five thousand.
Q. Has the society here sent arms and ammunition to the society in Tongka?
A. Yes. I have heard that two cases of muskets and ten kegs of gunpowder were sent.
Q. Are the societies here and in Tongka one and the same?
A. Yes. But they keep a separate account, a member going from here to Tongka is admitted a member without an entrance fee, but a member from Tongka wishing to join the society in Penang has to pay an entrance fee of $1.

Page 72:—

Lee Coyn (Kwun)—Headman of Ghee Hin.
Q. Do you recollect receiving an application from the Ghee Hins at Tongka for assistance in July last?

*   *   *

Q. What assistance did the Ghee Hins at Penang render to the Ghee Hins at Tongka?
A. ......We did not answer it (the letter) then. Some time after, three of the headmen from Tongka came to ask for assistance......I think the Tongka quarrel had nothing to do with the Penang affair.

Oh Wee Kee, Secretary of Ghee Hin.
Q. Had the fight in Tongka any influence upon the Ghee Hins here?
A. No.

All we know about the "fight in Tongka" is what is contained in a letter from Triad in Tongka to Triad in Penang, dated 11th of 6th (Chinese) Moon 1867, asking Penang at the instance of the Raja of Ujang Salang for arms and reinforcements against Tokong in Tongka, who had attacked Triad there.

This letter is that referred to in the last two extracts above and is printed as Appendix VII to the *P.R.C. Report* and is reproduced as Appendix VIII to this work.

These recurring references to Tongka would not have any special significance for the P.R. Commissioners, but they throw once again into relief that period of Siamese and Kedah history (1821–1848) (Chapter XIII) during which we know (Chapter V) that Triad and Tokong influence was active in Penang, Junk Ceylon, and Ligor. The nature of this activity has been the subject of our speculation in Chapters XIV and XV.

We see in the Tongka letter of 1867 (Appendix VIII) the same political alignment recurring, as we have suggested for the period of the Siam-Kedah war, namely support by the Siamese authorities for Triad and White Flag against Tokong and Red. This may be only a coincidence in the present case, but it is not an isolated one.

(20) General comment on the *P.R.C. Report:*—

This completes a brief survey of some relevant abstracts from the Notes of Evidence (which occupy 74 printed pages in the original Report). A few passages of the Evidence are reproduced *in extenso* in Appendix VII, in so far as such relate to the Red and White Flag societies.

The enquiry was conducted from the angle of the antagonism of Triad and Tokong (the principals) and not from that of the Malay societies (the auxiliaries or subsidiaries), which the Commission clearly regarded as being of very minor importance. This attitude of ignoring the importance of the Malay aspect of the Triad organisation has curiously persisted. We shall notice it again (Chapter XXI) when, at the time of the suppression of Chinese secret societies in 1890, the Malay auxiliaries are nowhere mentioned. We shall notice again in Chapters XXIV–XXVI that the whole history of the Malay Perak River society for the past thirty years has been one of official non-interference.

The *P.R.C. Report* established beyond question the connection between Triad and White Flag, and Tokong and Red Flag as far back as 1860–1870, a fact which has been lost sight of, thus leading to much doubt and empty argument in more recent years.

It was in the same year as the Penang riots (1867), that the "Transfer" took place, by which the rule of the Straits Settlements was transferred from the Government of India to the Colonial office and a separate administrative service (the Malayan Civil Service) was established for Malaya.

A further point to be remembered is that Triad and Tokong and their respective subsidiaries were at that period not only still tolerated by the Government of the day, but continued to be the main instruments by which the British Government exercised its functions through the "kapitans" of the communities concerned.

Uneasiness was felt after these riots and a measure of control was obtained by registration of societies in 1869, but suppression of secret societies did not become law until twenty-two years later (1890).

CHAPTER XVII

THE LARUT WARS 1862–1873

We have now to examine in this and the following chapter how Triad, Tokong and Tabut, operating from Penang, influenced the course of Malayan history and led to the reversal of the British policy of non-intervention on the mainland of the peninsula and ultimately to the Treaty of Pangkor.

The historical facts in this chapter are taken from the published references to the period.[1]

Before 1850, the district of Larut was almost uninhabited. About 1840, a Perak-born Malay, Che Long Jaafar, son of a minor chief whose brother had married a daughter of the Panglima, Bukit Gantang (or keeper of the pass between Larut and Kuala Kangsar) settled near the present township of Taiping. There were said then to be only three Chinese in the whole of Larut. Che Long Jaafar discovered a patch of rich mining-land at Kelian Pauh—the site of the present Taiping gaol—and soon Chinese miners from Penang were flocking into Larut.

Later new mining lands at Kelian Bahru, or present-day Kamunting, were discovered.

In 1850, Che Long Jaafar obtained from the then Sultan of Perak a title to the district of Larut as his own property.

In 1857, Long Jaafar died and was succeeded by his son Che Ngah Ibrahim who was recognised by the Sultan as the ruler of Larut in succession to his father. Swettenham *op. cit.* page 123 who knew him personally, says that Che Ngah Ibrahim was not a pure Malay, but was partly Indian and of a shrewdness and business capacity foreign to Malays. In 1864, he was granted the title of *Orang Kaya Mentri*, a title of the highest rank in Perak,[2] and a document recognising him as Ruler of Larut "from the Krian river in the north to the Bruas river in the south". From that date he was known as Raja of Larut, or Mentri of Larut, or Tengku Mentri.

Meanwhile the Chinese mining population at Klian Pauh and Klian Bahru were growing beyond the capacity of the Mentri who now lived at Bukit Gantang, to keep in order and disturbances began. History has labelled the two parties to these disturbances the "Four Districts" or See Kwan (四 郡) and the "Five Districts" or Go Kwan (五 郡). In doing so, history has been unkind to the student, for the reason that these names tend to confuse and to disguise the fact that the belligerents in the Larut Wars of 1862–1873 were identical with those of the Penang War of 1867.

That this was so, was perfectly well known to the authorities at the time and to subsequent historians, but until the appearance of Sir Richard Winstedt's *History of Perak* (1934 Chapter VII, "The Chinese miners of Larut") which revised and amplified "Wilkinson's *History of the Peninsular Malays* (2nd edition 1920 Chapter X), insufficient emphasis had been laid upon this important aspect of our subject.

EXPLANATION OF THE NAMES 四 郡 SEE KWAN AND 五 郡 GO KWAN

The first official mention of the belligerents under the convenient but misleading names of See Kwan and Go Kwan appears on page 8 of a memorandum by Skinner,

---

Footnote.—(1) These are:—
    (i) *Parliamentary Papers on the Malay States Vol. I* (Perak State Museum Library) which contains:—
        (*a*) Parliamentary Paper C 465 on the Selangor piracies—dated 1872.
        (*b*) Parliamentary Paper unnumbered, believed to be C 1111, chiefly on Perak affairs, in continuation of C 465 of 1872 dated 31st July, 1874.
        (*c*) Parliamentary Paper unnumbered in continuation of C 1111, chiefly on Negri Sembilan affairs dated 6th August, 1875.
    (ii) *Enquiry as to complicity of Chiefs in the Perak Outrages* (Singapore 1876).
    (iii) *Perak Papers 1874–79*. (Perak State Museum Library) which contains a good deal of correspondence prior to 1874.
    (iv) *British Malaya* Swettenham (1906) pages 104–126. The author took part in many of the events he describes.
    (v) *History of the Peninsular Malays*. Wilkinson (1923) pages 99–114.
    (vi) *History of Perak* Winstedt (1934) pages 78–90.
Footnote.—(2) From the sanscrit *Mantri* = official, romanised in Malay as *Mantĕri* or *mĕntĕri* and commonly spelled *mantri* or *mĕntri* and pronounced as the latter, meaning "Minister". The *Orang Kaya Mentri* is the fourth of the four principal ministers of State in Perak (*see* Chapter XVIII *infra*).

dated 10th January, 1874, entitled *Précis* of Perak affairs, published in *Perak Papers 1874–79*. The passage is as follows:—

> With August 1872 commences the second stage of the Larut disturbances. To understand what follows, the relation of the various Kwans (country divisions) with each other and with the great Hoeys (or Kongsees) whose headquarters are in Penang, should be made clear. The miners consist of Cantonese (here called Macaos) and Kehs, who are unfriendly and speak different dialects. These two great race divisions, though at the bottom of all the disturbances, have become much confused, many siding with the Kongsee to which they belong rather than with their own people. The present parties are best known by the names of See Kwan and Go Kwan as follows:—

SEE KWAN or Four Districts.		GO KWAN or Five Districts.	
Sin Neng		Cheng Sia	
Sin Whee	Mostly Ghee Hins	Poon Say	
Seow Keng	and Cantonese.	Soon Tek	Mostly Hye Sans and Khehs.
Whee Chew		Lam Hye	
		Tong Quan	

This important statement written ten days before the conclusion of the treaty of Pangkor, proves that at that time, the British Government was aware of the following facts:—

(1) that the Larut wars were fundamentally caused by the racial hatred of the Cantonese and Hakkas (Khehs).[1]

(2) that besides a racial or tribal animosity there was also a secret society or sectarian division between the belligerents of the Ghee Hin (Cantonese) and Hai San (Hakka) factions.

(3) that besides racial and sectarian division there was also a "China-side" territorial distinction between the two contestants in the Larut wars.

(4) that the tribal and territorial allegiance of individuals was less powerful than that of their membership of the two local secret society camps of Ghee Hin and Hai San.

These facts meant in a nutshell that although blood is thicker than water, sworn brotherhood in the circumstances prevailing in the secret society underworld of the day, was thicker than either.

This fact already established by para. 31 of the *P.R.C. Report* (page 249 *supra*) is of primary importance. It explains the phenomenon so frequently encountered in an examination of Chinese underworld cross-currents and hostilities in Malaya and, no doubt, elsewhere, and commented upon by Vaughan and other observers, namely, that men of the same tribe, clan and district of China,—even of the same family—may yet be found ranged against one another in mortal combat through the accident of their secret society allegiance.

This fact, no doubt, also explains the changes of allegiance or what appear to be total changes of allegiance from one camp to the other which come to notice not infrequently in this study, both among individuals and among the branches of the two main stems in the secret society underworld, when the preponderating influence for the time being demands such a change.

On page 113 *supra*, we have noted such a change or the appearance of such a change in the allegiance of the Hai San mentioned by Skinner, which in 1844 was (page 77) apparently chiefly composed of Cantonese and a member of the Ghee Hin camp in Penang, but which by 1872 was the spearhead of Tokong antagonism to Triad in Larut.

As we have shown (pages 60, 88 and 113) the name Hai San ("Sea and Land") seems to belong essentially to the Han stem and an explanation may be found in the speculation that the earliest members of the Hai San in Junk Ceylon and Penang (period 1780–1850) were Cantonese, whose allegiance to the Han stem was undermined by a factor still more potent even than that of blood brotherhood, namely the bitter internecine struggle (1855–1868) in the province of Canton between themselves and the irruptive Hakkas, a struggle known to history as the Hakka-Puntei war and referred to on pages 60–61 *supra*. It can easily be understood that such a prospect as the permanent loss of their land and ancestral homes to the marauding Hakkas would override Cantonese allegiance to the Han, to which their mortal enemies the Hakkas generally belonged and drove them overseas into the Hung camp to which the majority of their fellow Cantonese and fellow sufferers belonged.

Thus to the rising tide of Hakka immigration to Malaya during these fateful years and to the consequent clash of vested interests may be ascribed the exclusion of the Cantonese from the local Hai San and to this process the more or less wholesale absorption of that society by the Hakka immigrants would be but a natural corollary. We offer this speculation to cover a point of unique difficulty which is otherwise unexplained.[2]

Footnote.—(1) The cause of this hatred is given in Chapter IV *supra*.
Footnote.—(2) *See* also pages 77–78: 88–89 and 113 *supra*.

The complications of the Hakka-Puntei war in China may explain why, in recording the events of the Larut wars, history has chosen to emphasise the territorial division of the disputants which was in reality the least profound of the differences between them and only affected two out of many tribes engaged, whereas the fundamental division was the same as that of the Penang riots of 1867 namely between the two stems of Triad and Tokong. As history has made this choice, we find from 1874 onwards that the belligerents are continually referred to in official records as the Four Districts and the Five Districts respectively, resulting in further confusion regarding their true origin and characteristics. The names given by Skinner, therefore, require closer examination.

THE IDENTITY OF THE FOUR DISTRICTS (TRIAD) AND THE FIVE DISTRICTS (TOKONG)

China is divided into eighteen provinces (省 Shang), each province being subdivided into prefectures or departments (府 Fu) and each prefecture being subdivided again into districts of three classes according to importance, known as 縣 Yun (1st class), 州 Chau (2nd class) and 亭 Teng (3rd class).

The word *kwan* appearing in Skinner's memorandum with the meaning "district" is probably the Chinese character 郡 which, according to the lexicographers is an obsolete term for a prefecture or department (府 Fu) and not for a district. It is doubtless used colloquially meaning "the part of the country" a man hails from, and it is probably in this sense that it has come to be used in local history. As there are no characters to guide us in the original records and as we do not know the dialect from which the names recorded by Skinner were romanised, this may be a wrong assumption. There are, or were, fourteen prefectures 府 Fu in the province of Canton (excluding the island of Hainan) and some eighty districts. In a footnote below[1] we give the names of five of the more important prefectures of Kwangtung province from which immigrants to Malaya chiefly come, with the names of the districts in each, taken from a map to face page 6 of Meadows *The Chinese and their rebellions* (1856).

THE FOUR DISTRICTS (TRIAD)

Comparing Meadows' list with the names in Skinner's list of "Districts" we find that Skinner's "Four Districts" comprised :—

(1) Sin Neng (Sin Ning). A district in Kwang Chow prefecture.

(2) Sin Whee (San Wui or Sin Hwuy). Another district in Kwang Chow, contiguous to Sin Neng on the coast.

(3) Seow Keng. The whole of the Prefecture of Shaou King, or Shiu Heng contiguous to the districts of Sin Neng and Sin Whee, but itself containing thirteen districts.

(4) Whee Chew (Wai Chow or Hwuy Chow). The whole of the Prefecture of Wai Chow, containing ten districts and including the Treaty Port of that name opened in 1904.

If the above identifications are correct, the "Four Districts" faction in Larut included representatives of two complete prefectures and two districts of a third (the Kwang Chow prefecture), total 25 districts.

THE FIVE DISTRICTS (TOKONG)

Similarly examining Skinner's names of the "Five Districts" we find as follows :—

(1) Cheng Sia. A variant spelling of the district of Tsang Ching in the Kwang Chow prefecture in Meadow's list. This district appears to be variously spelled in the records as Chang Shiang or Chan Sung and of which the

---

Footnote.—(1) Names of certain prefectures and districts in the provinces of Kwangtung :—

Prefectures	Districts		Prefectures	Districts	
Kwang Chow	Tsing Yuen	Pwan Yu (Canton city district)	Kia Ying (Hakka country) ..	Ping Yuen	Hing Ning
				Chin Ping	Kia Ying
					Chang Lo
	Sam Shui	Hwa Yun		Tz Poo	Hae Yang
	Nan Hae	Tsung Hwa	Cha'ou Chow	Fung Shun	Ching Hae
	Shun Tih	Lung Mun	(Hakka and	Jaou Ping	Poo Ning
	Heang Shan	Tsang Ching	Teochew country)	Kee Yang	Chaou Yang
	Sing Hwuy	Tung Kwan			Hwuy Lae
	Sin Ning	Sin Gan (Kowloon)			
				Kwang Ning	Kaou Ming
				Kae Kin	Sin Hing
Hwuy Chow	Chang Ning	Yung Gan	Shaou King	Fung Chuen	Ho Shan
	Lin Peng	Po Lo	(read Shiu Hing)	Tak King	Kae Ping
	Ho Peng	Kwei Shan		Sze Hwuy	Gan Ping
	Lung Chuen	Hae Fung		Kaou Yaou	Yang Chun
	Ho Yuen	Luh Fung			Yang Keang

The above romanisation follows the orthography of Meadows *op. cit.* The common modern spelling of thirteen of the above districts is given in footnote (1) on page 100 *supra*.

modern spelling is Chang Seng (Cantonese) and Chen Shang (Hakka) and sometimes Chang Shang, a combination of both.

(2) Poon Say. Unidentified unless it be intended for the Pun Yu (Pwan Yu) district of the Kwang Chow prefecture.

(3) Soon Tek. Probably identifiable with the district of Shun Tih (Shun Tak) in Kwang Chow prefecture in Meadow's list.

(4) Lam Hye. Probably identifiable with Nan Hae (Nam Hoi) district of Kwang Chow in Meadow's list.

(5) Tong Quan. (Tung Kwun) a large district in the Kwang Chow prefecture lying between Hong Kong and Canton and containing many Hakkas (Khehs).

In another document in *Perak Papers 1874–79* Section "E" page 5 entitled:— "Agreement by the representatives of the Four Districts to place their affairs in Larut in the hands of the Governor of the Straits Settlements for solution" dated 16th January, 1874, the "Four Districts" are therein named as:—

Hway Chew;

Shew Hing;

Kong Chew;

Sin Neng.

These names probably stand for the three Prefectures of:—

Hwuy Chow (Wai Chow);

Shaou King (Shiu Heng);

Kwang Chow;

and the District of:—

Sin Neng (in the Prefecture of Kwang Chow)

and therefore except for substituting the whole prefecture of Kwang Chow for the district in it of San Wui, confirm Skinner's list.

This document was drawn up before Pickering (then just appointed from China) and was translated by him. The document is signed by twenty-four representatives of the "Four Districts" of Ghee Hins, each of whom has placed the name of his "district" after his signature. These district names include that of "Chao Chew" which suggest the presence of Teochew representatives from the Ch'aou Chow Prefecture; and "Kheh", which although a tribal and not a district name, suggests that there were still Hakkas to be found even among the Ghee Hins (Triad).

This assumption confirms Skinner's statement above, *viz:* "Many siding with the Kongsee to which they belonged, rather than with their own people". This is also the position revealed by the common experience of European officials. We should here note that the document drawn up before Pickering contains no mention of the Five Districts, whose representatives were evidently not present when it was made. This is not surprising seeing that they were already in possession of the mines and had nothing to gain and probably felt they had much to lose from the impending "settlement". *(See* Chapter XVIII *infra).*

Again, in another document in *Perak Papers* Section "C" page 17 para. 28 a year earlier than Skinner's list, Speedy in a letter dated 23rd October, 1872, reporting the arrival in Penang from Larut of Ghee Hin refugees of the Four Districts says:—

The refugees are of four classes, *viz.,* Sin Eng, San Ohee, Hoi Feng and You Feng and numbered 7,000 men.

These names seem to represent the Districts of San Ning and San Wui in the Kwang Chow prefecture and the Districts of Hoi Fung and Luk Fung in the Hwuy Chow (Wai Chow) prefecture. These four maritime Districts probably provide the origin of the term Four Districts or "See Kwan", which soon came to mean nothing more than the Ghee Hin army in Larut. Dyer Ball in *Things Chinese* page 207, remarks upon the peculiarities of the dialect spoken in two of these four districts. He says:—

Cantonese has numerous dialects and groups of dialects. One group consists of the San Wui (Sin Hwuy) San Ning (Sin Neng) Yan P'ing and Hoi P'ing a most peculiar class of dialects containing much that is very differet from the pure Cantonese.

We also find the Ghee Hin or the Four Districts (Triad) faction referred to in the correspondence of the period simply as "the Sinnengs", the name of one of the districts, probably because the majority of the Larut Ghee Hins came from it.

This faction is also sometimes referred to as the "See Yips", referring to a subdivision of the district of San Ning known as Sz Yap (四 邑) or the "Four Towns". In Malaya, and particularly Perak, the term Sz Yap is colloquially applied to those Cantonese who come from that dialectic area referred to by Dyer Ball above and comprising the districts of San Ning and San Wui and the sub-districts of Hoi P'ing and Yan P'ing.

We have not been able to find any official list of the Five Districts or Go Kwan (Tokong), other than that given by Skinner above, which if accepted would finally present the picture as follows:—

The Four "Districts".			The Five "Districts".		
1. Sin Neng	新寧	a district in Kwang Chow.	1. Cheng Sia	增城	a district in Kwang Chow.
			2. Poon Say— most likely Pun Yu	番禺	a district in Kwang Chow.
2. Sin Wee	新會	a district in Kwang Chow.	3. Soon Tek	順德	a district in Kwang Chow.
3. Seow Keng	肇慶	a prefecture.	4. Lam Hye	南海	a district in Kwang Chow.
4. Whee Chew	惠州	a prefecture.	5. Tong Quan	東莞	a district in Kwang Chow.

This "five" list is of adjoining districts in the Kwang Chow prefecture and can, therefore, be correctly referred to as the "Five Districts".

Nor are the Four and Five districts identified or even mentioned in the Pangkor engagement with the Chinese of 20th January, 1874 (Appendix IXB), where we might have expected to find their official identity established.

An interesting article on this subject entitled, "Hints on Investigation in the F.M.S." by C. R. Morrish appeared in the *Malayan Police Magazine* issue of June, 1929. This article includes a tabulated statement of Cantonese and Hakka districts in China with the general distribution of their representatives by occupation and area in Perak to-day.

The foregoing shows that the "Four" and "Five Districts" are misnomers and do not represent any clear-cut territorial or geographical boundaries in China as the names imply, but are probably innocent-sounding labels, used perhaps in the first instance by Triad and Tokong themselves, to suggest a harmless or excusable clan rivalry or dialectic difference and thus decently cloak the real underlying hatreds of the Hakka-Puntei War, which was then fighting itself out in south China (Chapter IV) and was mirrored in Larut.

We should dismiss from our minds, therefore, all idea of territorial, or clan rivalry as the cause of the Larut wars, and regard the names See Kwan and Goh Kwan merely as the hitherto accepted labels of the Triad and Tokong armies disputing possession of the Larut tin mines.

THE FIRST LARUT WAR 1862

Winstedt *A History of Perak* (1934) page 79[1] has:—

> It is a hard task to follow the trail of the truth through the maze of the Larut disturbances, but it is lightened if we keep closely to the main line of cleavage, that between the "Four Districts" who were members of the Ghi Hin Triad society; and the "Five Districts" who belonged to the Hai San and Toa-Peh-Kong organisation.[2]

Thus it was left to Wilkinson to re-discover in 1920 and to Winstedt to re-emphasise in 1934, what had already been officially recorded in Skinner's memorandum of 1874, namely that the true line of cleavage in almost all hostilities among the Chinese was that between Ghee Hin (Triad) and Toh Peh Kong (Tokong). We have already (Chapter VI) shown how the Hai San also belonged to the Tokong camp.

This cleavage had been officially proved in the *Penang Riot Commission Report* and had been re-stated by Skinner just before the Treaty of Pangkor and has since been forgotten, although it has coloured the whole history of the Chinese in Malaya throughout the period of the British connection.

Winstedt *op. cit.*[3] continues:—

> In 1862, the mines at Klian Pauh (now Taiping) were being worked by Hai San men under a leader named Chang Keng Kwi, while the Kamunting mines, a few miles away were the scene of the labours of Ghi Hin men under So Ah Chiang.

One day, a party of Ghee Hins visiting Klian Pauh became involved in a gambling dispute with some Hai Sans and immediately the cry of Tokong was raised "Kill these interlopers", an echo perhaps from the Hakka-Puntei war then raging in China. It should be borne in mind too, that in 1862 the Taiping rebellion (Chapter IV) which had sprung from the Hakkas of the Canton province was also at the zenith of its power. Here were two reasons, besides that of local jealousies, why the Ghee Hins might expect no mercy. They got none. Fourteen of the party were seized and barbarously murdered.

Winstedt *loc. cit.*[4] continues:—

> One man only of the fourteen lived to tell the tale. Kamunting was in a ferment at once. Any luckless Klian Pauh (Hai San) miner who happened to pass through the village was lynched, and tribal war broke out between the two villages. Both sides appealed to the

Footnote.—(1) Quoting Wilkinson *History of the Peninsular Malays* (1920) page 101.
Footnote.—(2) As a general rule the Hokkiens of Tokong belonged to the Toh Peh Kong and the Hakkas of Tokong to the Hai San.
Footnote.—(3) Quoting Wilkinson *op. cit.* page 101.
Footnote.—(4) *See* also Wilkinson *op. cit.* 102.

Malay head of the district. Ngah Ibrahim was an opportunist.[1] As soon as he saw that the Hai San men (who had begun the disturbances) were the stronger party he threw in his lot with them, put to death So Ah Chiang and drove the Ghi Hin men out of Larut. The dispossessed miners appealed to the British Government.

From this point, aggravated by the senseless murder of So Ah Chiang who was headman of the aggrieved party (Triad), the pendulum of Perak history began to oscillate and a bitter struggle opened between Triad and Tokong, for exclusive possession of the tin fields of Larut, with the British Government an unwilling and largely blindfold counterpoise between them. At this period Chinese in Perak, both Triad and Tokong members, claiming to come from Penang, were mostly regarded as British subjects, although in fact many of them were professional fighting men specially imported from China.

Winstedt *op. cit.* page 80 (quoting Wilkinson *op. cit.* page 102) concludes:—

Colonel Cavenagh, Governor of the Straits did not disregard the appeal. He sent a ship of war to the Perak coast to get settlement of a claim for damages by Go Kuan British subjects.[2] ...... When payment was not made, he ordered a blockade of the coast...... Ngah Ibrahim paid the money ($17,000) in May, 1862.

In consideration of payment Sultan Jaafar informed the Governor that he had restored the Government of Larut to Ngah Ibrahim, to whom the Sultan granted the title of *Orang Kaya Mentri* in October, 1863. Meanwhile the dispossessed Ghee Hins returned to occupation of the Kamunting mines and Triad appointed Ho Ghi Siu as their headman in Larut in succession to the murdered So Ah Chiang.

Thus ended the first Larut war.

PERIOD OF IRRUPTION OF TABUT INTO PERAK 1863–1871

With Triad and Tokong finally established in the Larut tin fields, there began in 1863, a period of seepage of their Malay counterparts, the White and Red Flag societies from Penang to Larut. During the next eight years, in the middle of which occurred the Penang riots of 1867 already discussed, the flag societies consolidated their position with their respective Chinese allies in the underground of Perak politics. We discuss below and in the following chapters the effect of this seepage upon the Perak succession and subsequent Perak history.

PERIOD OF THE GATHERING STORM 1863–1871

The Larut dispute remained quiescent in Perak between 1863 and 1871, but the main issues appear to have been transferred for solution to British territory during those years.

The diplomatic victory of Triad after British pressure had been exerted on Tokong following the first Larut war in 1863 probably rankled.

We have seen on pages 105–106 *supra*, how Triad burnt some Tokong houses at Jelutong, Penang, in 1865. Tokong was ripe for vengeance in 1867, when the riots discussed in Chapter XVI broke out, with Tokong the aggressors.

It seems probable that the leaders of Triad and Tokong in Penang during this period were interchangeable with their opposite numbers in Larut, some evidence of which is given below.

The Penang riots were, in effect, a prelude to the second Larut war and hastened that struggle to a decision.

THE SECOND LARUT WAR FEBRUARY–OCTOBER, 1872

Although he had made his peace with Triad and restored them to their holdings at Kamunting, under British pressure, the Mentri remained the ally of Tokong.

In the Penang Riots of 1867 the leaders in Penang were Lee Coyn (Triad) and Khoo Thean Tek (Tokong). Owing, perhaps, to the bad odour in which Lee Coyn found himself after the *P.R.C. Report*, or perhaps as a result of an order of transportation, such as we know was passed against the Tokong leader Khoo Thean Tek,[3] an exchange appears to have taken place between Ho Ghi Siu and Lee Coyn. At all events we find that at the beginning of the second Larut war in February, 1872, Ho Ghi Siu was the resident head of Triad in Penang and a certain Lee Ah Kun, whom we suggest was the "Lee Coyn" of the Penang riots, had replaced him as head of Triad in Larut.

At the same point of time we find that Chang Keng Kui head of Tokong in Perak during the first Larut war, had also been translated to Penang as head of Tokong there, *vice* Khoo Thean Tek, following, no doubt, upon the latter's court sentence of transportation.

We know that Khoo Thean Tek transferred himself to Perak as a result of his sentence but we have been unable to find any statement or evidence that he exchanged

Footnote.—(1) The real reason for his action may have been pressure from Hai San of which there is reason to think, he was himself a member (*see* below).
Footnote.—(2) An error seems to have crept in here. The claim was by the dispossessed See Kwan (Triad) faction in Penang, against the usurping Go Kwan (Tokong) faction, to whom Ngah Ibrahim had given possession of Klian Bahru (Kamunting).
Footnote.—(3) We have not been able to find an account of the court proceedings which followed the *P.R.C. Report*, so that uncertainty must remain on this point for the present.

places with Chang Keng Kui as head of Tokong in Larut, although it is reasonable to suppose that he did so. At all events he was very active in Perak during the second and third Larut wars on behalf of Tokong.

The latent cause of the second Larut war was a simmering dispute between Triad and Tokong over the boundary of certain tin bearing land lying between their respective holdings at Kamunting (Triad) and Klian Pauh (Tokong). The precipitating cause was an alleged intrigue between Lee Ah Kun and a woman of the Tokong camp at Klian Pauh who was said to be the wife of a close relative of Chang Keng Kui, then head of Tokong in Penang. It seems in the highest degree unlikely that the alleged intrigue was anything more than a framed-up *casus belli*, of the type we have seen in the Penang riots five years earlier. Lee Ah Kun and the woman were seized by Tokong and subjected to extreme indignities and finally drowned in a mining pool.

Meanwhile Ho Ghi Siu, Triad "boss" in Penang, was evidently aware that another trial of strength with Tokong in Larut could not be long postponed and although Triad was outnumbered in Perak in 1872, just as Tokong had been outnumbered in Penang in 1867, he had made preparations to meet the disparity of numbers by the importation of munitions and fighting men from China.

The murder of Lee Ah Kun was the signal for Ho Ghi Siu to order Triad to take the initiative in Perak, and, brushing aside attempts at arbitration, Triad in Kamunting attacked Tokong in Klian Pauh (modern Taiping) and by March 26th 1872, the Hai Sans although numerically superior were driven from Taiping back upon the Mentri's fort at Matang.

The Mentri was now in a dilemma. His allies Tokong were defeated and his mines were in the hands of his enemies Triad.

He thereupon temporised by evacuating to Penang the defeated Hai Sans at a cost to himsef in junk hire alone of $15,000, and made overtures to the victorious Ghee Hins. The Mentri also addressed the Governor Sir Harry Ord, explaining what had happened. The dispossessed Tokongs, who were largely British subjects of Penang, addressed the Government too, just as the dispossessed Triads had done in 1862.

The Governor replied to the Tokong petitioners declining to interfere and they thereupon began to arm in Penang in preparation for a counter-attack on Triad in Larut. Tokong opened their campaign in June, 1872, by blowing up the Penang residence of Triad's "boss" Ho Ghi Siu, but failed to kill him.

It was at this point that a further political complication arose in Larut.

Sultan Ali of Perak had died in May 1871 and the Perak chiefs had rejected the candidature of Raja Muda Abdullah, son of Raja Jaafar (predecessor of Sultan Ali) and had chosen instead Raja Ismail, the Bendahara, who had succeeded to the throne as Sultan Ismail in 1871.

The Mentri of Larut had supported the candidature of Raja Ismail against that of Raja Abdullah and when in March, 1872, the Mentri's allies had been driven out of Larut, Raja Abdullah supported the victorious Triads promising them the exclusive lease of the Larut mines and other concessions, when once he had gained the throne.

We examine this political twist introduced into the second Larut war in closer detail below.

Meanwhile Tokong preparations continued in Penang and in the second half of October a well-planned surprise attack upon Larut was launched by Tokong against Triad all unprepared.

The attack was completely successful, Winstedt *op. cit.* page 84 says:—

> Hundreds perished in the fighting: several hundred more died of exposure or privation in the jungle. In October, 1872, two thousand (Triad) refugees found their way to Penang of whom more than a hundred were wounded. All the Ghi Hin women fell into the hands of their enemies. A few preferred suicide to dishonour: the rest were divided up between the Hai San (Tokong) headmen and the Mentri's chiefs, for the Mentri had taken up once more his old policy of siding with the victors.[1]

So ended the second Larut war. The pendulum of fortune had swung away from Triad and left Tokong for the second time since 1862, in sole and undisputed possession of the Larut tin fields.

THE THIRD LARUT WAR DECEMBER 1872—JANUARY 1874

Then began the bitterest struggle of all, which only ended at the Treaty of Pangkor.

Inflamed at the victory of Tokong in October, 1872, and at the treatment of their womenfolk, Triad in Penang directed by Ho Ghi Siu made immediate preparations for a third campaign. In December, Triad blockaded the coast of Matang, preventing the export of tin and import of food. There ensued a pull-devil-pull-baker of moves and countermoves between the various interests involved, which are given in convenient form in the skeleton history of the campaign below, with the British Government in the position of anxious spectator, uncertain how to act because ignorant of the game in progress. It is worth noting as typical of the confusion of the day that in January 1873 a complaint was received in Penang that a small coasting vessel named the "Fair Malacca" registered in Penang and flying the British flag, had been fired on by the Ghee Hin "pirates"

Footnote.—(1) We suggest he did so because he was probably a member of the Hai San.

who were blockading the coast.   The Senior Naval Officer (Captain Denison R.N.) was thereupon called upon to protect British shipping against the "pirates" which he proceeded to do.   What was not made clear was that the "Fair Malacca" was the pride of the Tokong fleet and the personal property of Khoo Thean Tek, the most powerful Tokong leader of the day, whom we left in Chapter XVI condemned to death by a British Court for his share in the Penang war of 1867.   Nevertheless, at the beginning of 1873, we find him impudently invoking the aid of the British Navy as the ally of Tokong against the Triad "pirates" of Larut, two of whose leaders in Perak had been murdered by Tokong (So Ah Chiang and Lee Ah Kun) and whose leader in Penang Ho Ghi Siu living on British territory and under British protection had scarcely escaped with his life, when his residence in Penang had been blow up by Tokong in June, 1872.

The "Fair Malacca" appears to have been on a reconnaissance cruise in January, 1873, to see how she could break the Triad blockade and the fortunate chance of her being fired on while flying the flag of her port of register, enabled her to leave that rather ticklish job to the British Navy, with great profit to Tokong interests.

What is important to note in this is that Tokong thereby obtained the sympathy of the British Government in the third Larut war and was able to pose as the victim of Triad aggression.

It is true that Triad took the initiative in the third struggle by blockading Matang, but it was only after having suffered three reverses (1862; February, 1872, and October, 1872) at the hands of Tokong.   This comparatively mild precautionary measure was nevertheless whipped up by the wiles of the Tokong leaders in Penang, to appear to the British Government as piracy, thereby putting Triad in the wrong.

After eight months (December, 1872—August, 1873) of desultory fighting between Triad and Tokong, the Mentri of Larut and the Raja Muda Abdullah fishing in the troubled waters, finally openly emerged as they had secretly entered, Abdullah on the side of Triad and the Mentri of Tokong.

In these circumstances (August, 1873) the British Government countenanced a joint attempt by these two rather futile intermediaries to stop the war, by sending them from Penang to Larut in H.M.S. Midge to raise the blockade.

Triad blockaders took no notice of the order of Raja Abdullah to stop fighting. This put Triad still further in the wrong in the eyes of the British government, to whom Tokong now appeared as the most hopeful side to support.   In September, 1873, the Governor Sir Harry Ord took the decisive step and threw the whole weight of British support on the side of Tokong and the Mentri, and the British government thereupon found itself at war in support of the Mentri and Tokong against Raja Abdullah and Triad.   Up to the year 1867, when the Government of the Straits Settlements was transferred to the Crown, the East India Company had pursued a policy of strict non-intervention on the mainland of the peninsula.   This policy was continued by the Colonial office after the year 1867, but, no doubt, due in part to the circumstances of the third Larut war, a change was announced from London in August—September, 1873, to a policy of limited intervention.

In October, 1873, the Governor Sir Harry Ord left on retirement and in November, the new Governor Sir Andrew Clarke arrived charged with the task of intervention in the affairs of the Malay States and the establishment of the Residential system.

Meanwhile the third Larut war had reached stalemate until, by the decision of September, 1873, British Police under Captain Speedy were sent from Penang to Larut to aid the Mentri and at the same time British gunboats appeared off the Larut coast. The Triad blockaders now became themselves blockaded, to landward by Captain Speedy and his Police, to seaward by the Royal Navy.

From this point (September—October, 1873) the third Larut war became less a struggle between Triad and Tokong, than a political problem for solution involving:—
    (1) the cessation of hostilities among the Chinese.
    (2) disposal of the claim of Raja Abdullah to overlordship in Larut.
    (3) disposal of the spurious claim of Rajah Abdullah to the throne of Perak.

The second and third questions derived their importance largely from the support they received from Triad for selfish commercial ends.

Solution was to some extent found by the Treaty of Pangkor on 20th January, 1874, by which the See Kwans or Ghee Hins or Triad on the one hand, and the Goh Kwans, or Hai Sans or Tokong on the other agreed to lay down their arms and have their differences settled by a British Commission.

Thus ended the Larut wars, some features of which we must now examine in greater detail.

We would only repeat here that it is well nigh impossible to believe as presently accepted history would have us believe, that this struggle was carried on by two sections of one great secret brotherhood—the Hung league.   If we continue to accept that view, we must equally believe that the White and Red Flag societies are also one and the same fraternity.

Chinese leaders in Penang and Larut during the Larut wars

We should here make clear who were the Penang leaders, or "Towkays"[1] as they began to be called, during the Larut wars and their respective representatives at the mines, as far as the records show. It seems probable that for the purely business purpose of developing the mines, Triad or the Ghee Hins preferred to be known as the Four Districts, and Tokong or the Hai Sans as the Five Districts since this territorial distinction did not lay any unnecessary or unwelcome emphasis on the secret society aspect, which was the really binding factor in the struggle. The fact that the Four Districts were solid Triad and the Five Districts solid Tokong seems beyond dispute and explains why the headmen of each were interchangeable as between Penang and Larut, thus:—

	PENANG		LARUT	
	Triad	Tokong	Triad at Klian Bahru (later Kamunting)	Tokong at Klian Pauh (later Taiping)
First War March—May, 1862	Lee Coyn (李坤)	Khoo Tean Tek (丘天德)	(1) So Ah Chiang (蘇亞昌) murdered 1862 (2) Ho Ghi Siu (何義秀)	Chang Keng Kui (鄭景貴)
Second War Feb.—Aug., 1872	Ho Ghi Siu	Chang Keng Kui	(1) Li Ah Kun (? Lee Coyn) murdered 1872 (2) Koh Boo An (許武安)	Not mentioned, (probably Khoo Tean Tek)
Third War December, 1872— January, 1874	Ho Ghi Siu	Chang Keng Kui	(1) Koh Boo An (2) Chan Ah Yam (陳亞炎)	Not mentioned, (probably Khoo Tean Tek)

Chinese flags used in the Third Larut war December, 1872—January, 1874

The disputants in the third Larut war fought under separate flags and their flags can be identified as further evidence of the true nature of the struggle.

The flags of the Chinese belligerents in the Penang war of 1867 (page 256 section 13) were triangular and of the following colours:—

    Triad (Ghee Hin)   ..   ..   Red ground and White border ("Evidence" page 8).

    Tokong (Toh Peh Kong)   ..   Red ground and Black border ("Evidence" page 4).

Of these, the Ghee Hin is the flag of the Triad lodge of the Kwangtung Province (see Chapter I), while the Toh Peh Kong flag is not identifiable with that of any Triad lodge.

In the description of the Chinese flags in the third Larut war, Wilkinson op. cit. page 109 has:—

    "It was ceasing to be a question of "Ghi Hin" or "Hai San". A band of miscellaneous ruffians flying a red flag with a white border, would be recognised as "Koh Bu An's men": a black flag with a red border indicated that they were "Ho Ghi Siu's men" and so on".

These combinations of hostile colours repeat those of Triad and Tokong in the Penang war except that a slip appears to have been made in attributing a black flag with red border to Ho Ghi Siu who was the Ghee Hin leader in Penang and his flag in Larut would be the same as that of Koh Bu An viz:—Red with a white border.

Footnote.—(1) Anglicised from 頭家 Tau Ka = "head of the family", a polite form of address to a business man. In Malaya, it means a financier behind an enterprise. Thus, Wilkinson Dictionary (ed. 1932) has:—
    Tauke labur = Capitalist supplying funds to a group of workers.
    Tauke panglong = Resident agent of such a capitalist.
    These two Malay expressions exactly describe the relationship between the heads of the See Kwan and Go Kwan factions in Penang and their labour forces in Larut.

Other flags in use at this time in Larut are mentioned in C.S.O. Correspondence *Perak and Larut 1862–1873* (bound volume), where in a petition from some Teochews of Krian to the Lieut.-Governor of Penang dated 1st August, 1873, there is mention of the following flags being flown on junks participating in the third Larut war:—

The Toh Peh Kong Flag .. .. .. Red with black border.
The Ho Seng Flag .. .. .. Black with white border.

This description of the Toh Peh Kong Flag agrees with that of Khoo Tean Tek (*see* Chapter XVI page 256 *supra*).

The Ho Seng society which hitherto had been associated with the Ghee Hins and Triad camp, is referred to in a Penang Police Report dated 20th October, 1873, (in C.S.O. correspondence *Perak-Larut*) as having joined up with the Go Kwans (Tokong) in Larut about that date. Of this there is actual confirmation later on.

Lastly, in a statement taken by Pickering (in the same volume of C.S.O. correspondence) dated 25th August, 1873, a Chinese witness records that the flags flown on junks owned by Ho Ghi Siu were "Black with red edges". This is probably where Wilkinson obtained his reference above, but as Ho Ghi Siu was the Triad leader he could hardly have been sailing under Tokong colours and we must suspect an error here by Pickering's informant.

SKELETON HISTORY OF EVENTS IN PERAK 1850-1873

This was a pregnant period of Perak history, and it is necessary to get the sequence of the more important events quite clear, in order that we may distinguish those other cross-currents of secret society intrigue at work below. The following is a skeleton history of events in Perak from 1850—November, 1873, presented for easy reference:—

(1)	1850.	Appearance of Chinese miners in Larut from Penang where the secret societies of Triad and Tokong ruled the Chinese roost.
(2)	1862.	**First Larut war** in which Tokong were the aggressors. Tokong led by Chang Keng Kwee and working at Klian Pauh *versus* Triad led by So Ah Chiang and working at Klian Bahru.
(3)	1862.	The Mentri of Larut allied himself with Tokong. So Ah Chiang was murdered and Triad driven out of Larut to Penang.
(4)	1862.	The dispossessed Triads appealed for assistance and compensation to the Governor of the Straits (Cavenagh), who threatened a blockade of the coast, and the Mentri paid up $17,500 damages, and Triad returned to Larut.
(5)	1863.	Ho Ghi Siu succeeded the murdered So Ah Chiang as Triad leader in Larut.
(6)	1863–1870.	Spread of White and Red Flag influence in Larut among the Malays attracted to the mines in support of their respective Chinese allies Triad and Tokong. Swettenham *op. cit.* page 118 gives the population of Larut at this time as Chinese 20,000, Malays 2,000 or 3,000. Wilkinson *op. cit.* page 105 states that at this time Tokong who had remained in alliance with the Mentri since 1862, outnumbered Triad in the proportion of nearly two to one. Allow, therefore, the strengths to be Triad 7,000 Tokong 13,000.
(7)	1871. (25th May)	Sultan Ali of Perak died and the Raja Muda Abdullah son of Sultan Jaafar (predecessor of Ali) failed to attend the obsequies in accordance with custom.
(8)	1871. (July)	The Perak Chiefs rejected the absent Raja Muda Abdullah and installed the Bendahara, Raja Ismail, as Sultan Ismail.
(9)	1871. (August)	Sultan Ismail was recognised as Sultan of Perak by the British Government in Penang and by Raja Abdullah.
(10)	1872. (February)	**Second Larut war** in which Tokong are again the aggressors Murder of Li Ah Kun, Triad leader in Larut.
(11)	1872. (March)	Counterattack by Triad who although numerically inferior were well supplied with arms and specially imported fighting men. Tokong driven out of Larut and took refuge in Penang and appealed to the Governor of the Straits (Ord) for redress.
(12)	1872. (April)	Mentri made overtures for alliance with victorious Triad now in possession of his mines.
(13)	1872. (May)	Governor Ord unable to interfere or assist Tokong.
(14)	1872. (June)	Tokong blew up Ho Ghi Siu's house in Penang.
(15)	1872. (July)	Raja Muda Abdullah of Perak claiming to be the rightful Sultan of Perak arrived in Penang and began intriguing against the Mentri's authority in Larut. He sold "concessions", such as the Krian revenue farm, to adventurers and engaged lawyers to defend his actions.

(16)   1872.   Well-organised counterattack in Larut by Tokong from Penang
       (October)   against their defeat of the previous March. Mentri's warship
                     seized by Tokong lawyers under bogus action for debt. Total
                     defeat of Triad and seizure of their womenfolk by Tokong.
                     Triads flee to Penang.

(17)   1872.   Mentri allies himself again with victorious Tokong.
       (October)

(18)   1872.   Third Larut war in which Triad is for the first time the aggressor.
       (December)   Ho Ghi Siu having prepared a fleet of junks and enlisted fighting
                     men, blockaded the coast of Larut and seized Matang.
                     This struggle lasted for a year and led to British intervention
                     in Perak. Its character is similar to that of the Hakka-Puntei
                     war in China (1850–1868) between the same adversaries
                     Cantonese (Triad) and Hakkas (Tokong).

(19)   1873.   Mentri of Larut finding Larut unsafe, took up his residence in
       (January)   a boat at the mouth of the Krian River, where he met Raja
                     Muda Abdullah of Perak, his rival for the rulership and revenues
                     of Larut. They formed an alliance.

(20)   1873.   Mentri of Larut recognised Raja Abdullah as Sultan of Perak,
       (April)   and Raja Abdullah recognised Mentri as ruler of Larut with
                     title "Raja of Larut".

(21)   1873.   Raja Abdullah and the Mentri quarrelled and their alliance came
       (May)   to an end.

(22)   1873.   Larut gets too hot. Raja Abdullah retires to Penang, and makes
       (June)   an agreement with the Headmen of Triad in Penang, by
                     which he thinks he has gained Triad support and compliance.
                     The third Larut war between Triad and Tokong continues.

(23)   1873.   Abortive expedition by Raja Abdullah and the Mentri and others
       (August)   in a British gunboat "Midge" from Penang to Larut to command
                     Triad, the blockading force, to cease fighting. The Triads pay
                     no attention.

(24) 16- 8-1873.   Colonel Anson (Lieutenant-Governor of Penang) telegraphs to the
                     Governor, Sir Harry Ord, in Singapore reporting refusal of
                     Triad to comply with the orders of the titular Malay rulers
                     of Larut (Raja Abdullah and the Mentri of Larut) to cease
                     fighting against Tokong. Governor Ord leaves for Penang.

(25) 17- 8-1873.   Colonel Anson authorised the Mentri of Larut to recruit Indian
                     troops and to employ Captain Speedy of the Penang Police for
                     service in Larut.

(26) 21- 8-1873.   Raja Abdullah, furious at having been short-circuited by Colonel
                     Anson's action, wrote to Colonel Anson protesting against the
                     employment of British subjects in Perak and deposing the
                     Mentri from the rank and office of Raja of Larut.

(27) 24- 8-1873.   Governor Ord arrived in Penang and invited Raja Abdullah to a
                     conference. Raja Abdullah pleaded illness and sent a lawyer
                     who was rejected by the Governor. Raja Abdullah left Penang
                     for Larut with some of his Triad friends.

(28)   3- 9-1873.   Sir Harry Ord took the decisive step of recognising the Mentri
                     as the independent Ruler of Larut and of throwing the whole
                     weight of British support on the side of the Mentri and his
                     ally Tokong. This action demarcated the line of cleavage from
                     then on, for the next few months *viz*:—

                     British Government ⎫   ⎧ Abdullah
                     Mentri   ⎬ *versus* ⎨ Triad
                     Tokong   ⎩ White Flag
                     Red Flag   ⎭

(29) 15- 9-1873.   The British Government found itself at war in support of the
                     Mentri and Tokong against Raja Abdullah and Triad.

(30) 17- 9-1873.   After the British had sustained some naval casualties, Raja
                     Abdullah from Matang, made an appeal by letter, drafted by
                     his Triad lawyer, to Governor Ord to crush the Mentri and
                     Tokong, and to support him (Raja Abdullah) and Triad. The
                     appeal was refused.

(31) 24- 9-1873.   British gunboats shelled Triad stockades at Selinsing. The coast
                     got too hot for Raja Abdullah, who suddenly appeared in his
                     private steam launch near the British gunboats, was captured
                     and taken to Penang and released.

(32) 29- 9-1873.   Captain Speedy and his Sikhs sailed from Penang for Matang
                     as the first European Police Officer in the service of the Mentri
                     of Larut.

(33)   1873.   Change of policy of the Colonial Office, Whitehall, from one of
       (Aug.–Sept.)   non-intervention in the affairs of the native States, to a policy
                     of "limited intervention for the preservation of peace and

		security, the suppression of piracy and for the development of roads, schools and police, through the appointment of a Political Agent or Resident in each State".
(34)	3-10-1873.	Arrival in Singapore from Penang of Raja Abdullah as the guest of Triad (Tan Kim Cheng).
(35)	1873. (October)	**Execution of a bond by Raja Abdullah in favour of Tan Kim Cheng, making him his Collector of Revenue in Larut for ten years in return for Triad aid to gain the throne.**
(36)	1873. (October)	In pursuance of his bargain, Tan Kim Cheng introduced Raja Abdullah to W. H. Read, a member of the Legislative Council, and induced Read to support Abdullah's claim.
(37)	1873. (October)	Raja Abdullah sought an interview with the Governor (Ord) which was refused.
(38)	23-10-1873.	Departure of Raja Abdullah from Singapore for Perak.
(39)	1873. (October)	Departure on retirement of the Governor, Sir Harry Ord, an administrator "of knowledge, wisdom, tact and firmness", but who was very unpopular with the European community of Singapore.
(40)	4-11-1873.	Arrival in Singapore of the new Governor, Sir Andrew Clarke, charged by the Colonial Office with the task of intervention in the affairs of the Malay States and the duty of introducing the Residential system into the Native States.

Although the statement has been made, there is no evidence that W. H. Read and Tan Kim Cheng took Raja Abdullah to interview Sir Andrew Clarke in Government House sometime during November—December, 1873. Raja Abdullah left Singapore on 23rd October and there is no evidence that he returned there. It seems the fact that Sir Andrew Clarke met him for the first time at Pangkor at the signing of the Treaty in January, 1874.

EXAMINATION OF THE UNDERSURFACE HISTORY OF THE PERIOD 1850–1873

We will here leave the fortunes of Raja Abdullah in the hands of Read and Tan Kim Cheng in November, 1873 and trace the undersurface moves of Triad and Tokong during the foregoing period.

The three chief objects of rivalry between the two Chinese camps in Larut and between their leaders in Penang were:—

    (1) Possession of the mines themselves.
    (2) Possession of the monopoly of opium supply to the miners.
    (3) Possession of the monopoly of the revenue, liquor and other "farms" obtainable from the Ruler of Larut.

The first of these concerned both the leaders and the miners, representing the local struggle for satisfaction of that "land hunger" of the Hakkas (Tokong) which we have seen gave rise to the Hakka-Puntei war (Chapter IV) and of which the "Larut Wars" were a local prolongation, in which both sides joined with increased bitterness and persistence, because the land was rich and offered them far more than the pittance which would be their lot in China.

The second and third objects concerned only the leaders of the two camps, who saw in these monopolies the road to personal wealth and influence open out before them.

Even if the rank and file of the two camps had been willing to come to terms and find a *modus vivendi* seeing there was land enough for all, we can well suppose that nothing short of the total annihilation and exclusion of the other party would satisfy the greed of the leaders.

In these circumstances it became of great importance to the leaders to curry favour with and to support that local authority with whom they believed the grant of concessions and monopolies to lie.

During the period 1850—May, 1871, which included the first Larut war and the Penang war, Triad and Tokong endeavoured to hold the mines by force and to keep in with the *de facto* ruler of Larut, the only "local authority" from whom they had anything to hope. In this struggle Tokong, aided by the favourable result of their war in Penang in 1867, were mainly successful.

From the death of Sultan Ali (May, 1871) circumstances conspired to play into the hands of Triad and Tokong, because from that date "local authority" itself became divided owing to the dispute over the Perak succession.

In March, 1872, Triad for the first time since 1862, became paramount in Larut. Tokong on the other hand, with the Mentri, the *de facto* ruler, had been in alliance (as they were in possession) since 1862, became in March, 1872, outcasts in Penang.

In July, 1872, Raja Abdullah claiming to be the rightful ruler of Perak arrived in Penang, and, finding the Mentri's late allies now fugitives in Penang, began to undermine the Mentri's authority by offering "concessions" as Sultan in Larut.

It is probably at this point that Raja Abdullah identified himself with the Ghee Hins (Triad) against the Mentri and his Tokong allies. We are entitled to assume that the struggle which ensued for paramountcy in Larut was not confined to Triad and Tokong, but was shared by their allies of the last chapter, the White and the Red Flag Malays.

There is ample evidence that Raja Abdullah was supported by the White Flag Malays and the Mentri by the Red Flag. There is nothing on record to show that they were individually members of these organisations, but the presumption from their respective Chinese connections, is that they were.

The Mentri's membership of the Red Flag probably dated from his alliance with Tokong in 1862, and Raja Abdullah's membership of the White Flag probably from July, 1872.

At all events, from the date of the third Larut war (December 1872) onwards the Malays of Larut gradually became divided into two camps of the White and Red Flag according as they espoused the claims of Raja Abdullah or of the Mentri for the overlordship of Larut. Nor did the rival Malay camps dissolve at the Treaty of Pangkor (January 1874), which placed Raja Abdullah on the throne of Perak, nor yet at his deposition and banishment two years later, but have spread throughout Perak and persist to the present-day.

The undersurface moves of Triad and White Flag and Tokong and Red Flag during the period of the third Larut war December, 1872, to the Treaty of Pangkor January, 1874, can perhaps best be followed in a general way by a reference to the official record entitled *Enquiry into the complicity of Chiefs in the Perak Outrages* (1876),[1] from which the following is taken, page 2 of the *précis:*—

On the death of Sultan Ali, (25/5/1871), the officers of State, according to custom, were all summoned to attend the funeral. For some reason or other, neither Rajah Abdullah, then Rajah Muda, nor the Laxamana, nor the Shahbandar attended, and Rajah Ismail, then Bandahara,—but not of royal blood on the father's side—was elected Sultan, and the regalia given up to him, Rajah Usman (son of the late Sultan) being appointed Bandahara in his place. Rajah Abdullah did not acknowledge the election of Rajah Ismail as valid;[2] but having no money or following, was unable to assert his claims at the time. He however got a chop, or seal of office made for himself, with the full style of Sultan inscribed thereon, and was given a paper under the seal of the Laxamana and Shahbandar, acknowledging him as the rightful Sultan. There was another noble of royal blood Rajah Yusuf of Senggong, who was also dissatisfied with the election of Rajah Ismail as Sultan. He was the son of a former Sultan, Abdullah Mahomed Shah, and had twice already been passed over. He had considerable property, but on account of his violent and cruel disposition, none of the chiefs were with him, and like Abdullah, he was on that account obliged to keep quiet.

In October, 1872, a war broke out in Larut between two sections of the Chinese engaged in mining, one party being Macao Chinese of four districts, called See-kwans, or four-district men; and the other Keh Chinese of five districts, called the Goh-kwans, or five-district men. The See-kwans were members of the Ghee Hin society, and the Goh-kwans of the Hye-San society. The Hye-Sans after a few days fighting, drove the Ghee Hins from the mines, with great slaughter and put up a strong stockade at Kota, a village about two miles distant from the mines. The Ghee Hins retired on Permatang, the township of Larut, where the custom-house was, and also erected stockades. For some days there was severe fighting between the two parties, and the Mentri, fearing for his own safety, made a fort round his house on which he mounted *lelas* and cannon. After a short time as the fighting became more severe, he took refuge in Penang, where he entered into negotiations with the headmen of the Hye-San society, and actively assisted them in carrying on the war.

Just about this time Rajah Abdullah combined with the Shahbandar, Laxamana and Haji Musa—a wealthy trader—and attacked the Rajah Mahkota, an officer of the third class, who had been appointed by Rajah Ismail to collect the revenue at Sunghie Durian on the Perak river. The Rajah Mahkota, after a show of resistance, surrendered at discretion and gave up the official scales or badge of office as collector; and Abdullah, who having no house of his own, had up to this time been living miserably in his boat, went to reside at Battak Rabbit, the Shahbandar taking up his proper appointment as Collector at Tanjong Maidan, a little lower down the river. The fact, however that Abdullah was not in possession of the regalia, and that he was unsupported by any of the chiefs of the Ulu, prevented him from being generally recognised as Sultan, and he was usually termed, as before, the Rajah Muda. During the next two months after this event, the Mentri remained in Penang, but without being able to effect any decisive result in favour of his party. The Ghee Hins continued to hold possession of Permatang, where they made themselves comparatively safe from an attack from sea, by erecting a stockade and fort at a bend of the river where the channel was staked and secured by an iron chain and boom. In January, 1873, Rajah Abdullah went to Penang with the Laxamana, Shahbandar, and Rajah Driss (cousin of Abdullah), and in opposition to the Mentri, entered into a written engagement with the headmen of the Ghee Hins, dated 28th of February, by which he authorised them to vigorously prosecute the war, promising in return that, if they were victorious, he would farm out the mines at Larut to them, and pay half the expenses which might be incurred by them. On the 3rd of April, he removed with the Shahbandar, and Rajah Driss from Penang to the Krean where he lived, quietly watching the course of events, and was joined by Rajah Yusoof on whom he conferred in an informal way the title of Rajah Muda. After two months more of protracted warfare, the general state of things remained as bad or even worse than before. The mines were entirely neglected, trade with Penang was stopped, and the coast was infested with piratical boats, belonging to both factions.

At this juncture the Mentri and Abdullah both applied for assistance to Mr. Kim Ching a Chinese gentleman of considerable influence in the Native States, and the Siamese Consul at Singapore;[3] Abdullah desired to have himself properly installed, and recognised as the Sultan of Perak, and the Mentri wanted to be restored to his position as Governor of Larut.

Footnote.—(1) Hereinafter referred to as *E.P.O.*
Footnote.—(2) The evidence is that he did recognise Sultan Ismail at the outset.
Footnote.—(3) Tan Kim Ching, *see* note on him page 275 *infra.*

On being applied to, Mr. Kim Ching expressed himself willing to go to Penang and undertake the task of arbitrating between the Ghee Hins and the Hye-Sans (by which means he hoped peace might be restored, and the Mentri be able to return as Governor to Larut) if the Mentri on his part would acknowledge Abdullah as Sultan of Perak, and guarantee him the share of the Larut revenue to which he would be entitled as such.   The Mentri refused to listen to this proposal, his mind being bent on driving the Ghee Hins forcibly out of Larut, and becoming Governor of that district independent of Abdullah.   With that end in view, in July he secured the services of Captain Speedy, who resigned his appointment of Superintendent of Police at Penang, and went to India to raise Sepoys for the service of the Mentri.   Following up this energetic line of action, the Mentri on the visit of Sir Harry Ord to Penang in August, addressed a letter to him, representing that the Chinese in possession of the mines, i.e. the Hy-Sans, were those who had the real right to them, and were his supporters, while the other faction, the Ghee Hins, who were blockading the coast and keeping him out of the country, were his enemies.

The Governor-in-Council took this view of the case, rescinded an Order forbidding the exportation of arms to Larut, and despatched the "Midge" and the "Thalia" to cruise off the coast, and clear it of, as Sir Harry Ord termed it, "the marauding Chinese who infested it". The result was that on the 25th of September, Captain Woolcombe, Senior Naval Officer, was able to write in his despatch to the Secretary to the Admiralty—"I have now to report that on Sunday morning the 20th instant, the boats of this Ship, in conjunction with the "Midge" and her boats, engaged and captured, and totally destroyed, three large fighting junks, and two stockades in the Larut river, amounting in all to about between twenty-two and twenty-eight guns, and also armed with snider rifles.   The town of Larut, with nearly 4,000 men, surrendered to me unconditionally......   The Larut river is now clear, and the whole coast has been visited. A small steamer having the Rajah Muda of Perak on board, was captured by the "Midge" on the 22nd instant.   She is claimed by the Orang Kaya Mentri, and I have therefore sent her to Penang for the Lieutenant-Governor's investigation".   On his arrival in Penang, Abdullah was immediately released by order of Colonel Anson, but his position was pitiable.   The Ghee Hins, his supporters, were for the time defeated and driven from their strongholds on the sea-coast. Rajah Yusoof, whom he had left in charge at Bukit Gantang, had fled to Perak, and Captain Speedy with his Sepoys had occupied it.   Personally he had been subject to the indignity of being brought a prisoner to Penang on a charge of piracy, and upon being released, found himself stranded there without money or friends.   The Mentri on the contrary, was in high favour with the Government, had considerable property in Penang, and, in the present state of his fortune, could easily raise money to carry on the war; for, although driven from the sea-board and temporarily cowed, the Ghee Hins had not laid down their arms, and were still a formidable party.

In his distress, Abdullah turned to Mr. Kim Ching, the only friend of any influence he had left, and having, with difficulty raised a thousand dollars through the Shahbandar, took a passage for himself and fifteen of his followers to Singapore, where he arrived on the 3rd of October (1873).   Mr. Kim Ching received him well, provided him with a house, supplied him with funds, paid his lawyer's expenses, and energetically took up his cause.   Sir Harry Ord, however refused to receive him, and before he had been a month in Singapore, Mr. Kim Ching was obliged to urge him to return to Perak, as his demands for money were becoming excessive, and the dissolute life he was leading was creating a scandal.

On the 23rd of October, Abdullah returned to Perak, but before leaving Singapore he came to an understanding with Mr. Kim Ching, and, on the proviso that Mr. Kim Ching should succeed in getting him firmly established, and acknowledged as Sultan by our Government, executed a bond in his favour, by which Abdullah appointed him his Collector of Revenue at Larut for a period of ten years, with power superior, for that time, to any of the other officers of State.

On the 4th of November, Sir Andrew Clarke arrived in Singapore, and relieved Sir Harry Ord as Governor of the Straits Settlements.   The Native States question occupied his immediate attention, and Mr. Kim Ching lost no time in laying before him the claims of Rajah Abdullah, who, by his advice, addressed a letter to His Excellency requesting him to act as mediator between him and the Mentri, and to enter into a treaty with him, as the rightful Sultan of Perak, and to appoint a British Resident to assist him in governing the country. On the 12th of January, 1874, Sir Andrew Clarke arrived at Pangkor with the object of settling the disturbances in Larut, and of inviting the chiefs of Perak to a conference to decide between the rival pretensions of Rajah Abdullah and Rajah Ismail.   In carrying out this object the headmen of the two Chinese factions were brought to Pangkor in a man-of-war, and invitations were sent to the chiefs of Perak to attend at Pangkor on a given day.   Rajah Abdullah, the Bandahara, Laxamana, Shhbandar and the Rajah Mahkota, were towed down in their boats to the rendezvous: and the Mentri, together with the Tumongong,—his brother-in-law,—and the Datu Sagor,—his uncle,—arrived in his own steamer and kept apart from the other chiefs. The Mentri had Captain Speedy and his lawyer, Mr. R. C. Woods, also on board.   The principal chiefs absent were Rajah Ismail, Rajah Yusoof, and the Maharajah Lela.   After some days spent discussing the several points at issue, the heads of the rival Chinese factions bound themselves in a penal bond in the sum of $50,000, to give up fighting, and to refer their differences to Commissioners to be appointed for that purpose; and Abdullah and all the chiefs present entered into a Treaty by which Abdullah was recognised as Sultan of Perak, with a clause that a British Resident should be accredited to his Court, "whose advice must be asked and acted upon on all questions other than those touching the Malay religion and custom".   As soon as the proceedings were over, the Sultan's party were towed back to Battak Rabit, and Sir Andrew Clarke sent a letter to Rajah Ismail explanatory of what had taken place, and advised him to give up the Regalia to Sultan Abdullah.

From this official record the following additional facts command attention:—

(1) At the beginning of the third Larut war the Mentri was assisting Tokong in Penang.

(2) Raja Abdullah was joined in his candidature for the throne of Perak by—
      the Shahbandar;
      the Laxamana;
      and Haji Musa (a wealthy trader).

(3) In January, 1873, Raja Abdullah went from Batak Rabit, his home at the mouth of the Perak River (modern Telok Anson) to Penang accompanied by the Shahbandar, the Laxamana and his cousin Raja Dris (later Sultan Idris of Perak) and "in opposition to the Mentri, entered into a written engagement with the

headmen of the Ghee Hins, dated 28th February, 1873", thereby backing Triad for the victory in Larut, as Triad were backing him for the Sultanate. Whatever his previous relations may have been, from now on he and his adherents were definitely and openly identified with the fortunes of Triad and White Flag in Perak, as against the Mentri, Tokong and the Red Flag.

(4) In April, 1873, Abdullah moved to Krian and was there joined by Raja Yusop (his ultimate successor as Sultan of Perak) whom Abdullah recognised as Raja Muda.

(5) As the fortunes of war wavered (March—June, 1873), the Mentri (who was prepared to back either Triad or Tokong whichever was to prove ultimately triumphant and so restore him to his position in Larut) joined with Abdullah in seeking assistance of Tan Kim Cheng in Singapore.

(6) Tan Kim Cheng's terms for lending (as we may suppose) Triad aid to both Abdullah and the Mentri were, that the Mentri should acknowledge Abdullah as Sultan and that Abdullah should appoint the Mentri as Governor of Larut, with a guarantee of a share of the Larut revenues for himself.

(7) We should note here that these were the terms of the compromise ultimately decided upon by Sir Andrew Clarke, whose support of Raja Abdullah's cause was obtained through Tan Kim Cheng.

(8) These terms put the Mentri where Triad wanted him, namely, subordinate to Raja Abdullah who was Triad's nominee for the throne. Triad had, of course, in view the "farming" of the Perak revenues (including those of Larut) for themselves, so soon as Abdullah was successful in his candidature for the throne.

(9) The Mentri "refused to listen to this proposal", which explains why after the Abdullah-Mentri alliance of June, 1873, in the words of Wilkinson *op. cit.* page 109 "they fell out again a few weeks later".
It is also explains why, when the same terms were imposed by Sir Andrew Clarke at Pangkor, they were so bitterly opposed by the Mentri. The terms meant that Triad and White Flag were finally to triumph over Tokong and Red Flag in the struggle for the spoils of war.

(10) After the futile expedition to Larut of Raja Abdullah in the "Midge" 10th—14th August, 1873, by which he had hoped through his Triad friends to "command the cessation of hostilities" and so re-establish his political credit, the British authorities realising the impotence of Raja Abdullah, raised the ban on the import of arms to Larut, recognised the Mentri as ruler and authorised Captain Speedy to act as Police Officer for the Mentri in Larut. Raja Yusop who had been left at Bukit Gantang to represent Raja Abdullah, fled over the pass to the Perak river and the discomfiture of Raja Abdullah and his pretensions was completed by his own arrest at sea on 22nd September, when he was taken to Penang and there released.

(11) With his fortunes at their lowest ebb Abdullah went to Singapore on 3rd October with fifteen followers, whom we are entitled to suppose were White Flag Malays to make a personal appeal to Tan Kim Cheng for further Triad aid.

(12) With an eye to the main chance, Tan Kim Cheng promised him support in exchange for "a bond executed in Tan Kim Cheng's favour appointing him Raja Abdullah's Collector of Revenue in Larut for a period of ten years with power superior, for that time, to any other officers of State".
We have seen something of Tan Kim Cheng's earlier efforts at king-making in Kedah (Chapter XIII), but the pledge he extracted from Raja Abdullah as the price of his help, would have been among his better bargains, if it had come off.

(13) At the time of its execution there was not much prospect of turning the bond to account. Raja Abdullah's rival the Mentri had been recognised on 3rd September, 1873, by the Governor (Sir Harry Ord) as Ruler of Larut. Tan Kim Cheng sent his expensive and important visitor back to Perak on 23rd October, 1873.
On 4th November, 1873, the new Governor Sir Andrew Clarke arrived in Singapore with his instructions and seeking for an opening for intervention in Perak. "Tan Kim Cheng lost no time in laying before him the claims of Raja Abdullah".
This he did through W. H. Read, a member of the Legislative Council who, accompanied by Tan Kim Cheng, interviewed the new Governor on Raja Abdullah's behalf. It was, doubtless, at this interview that the conditions of British support for Raja Abdullah were determined.

(14) By Tan Kim Cheng's advice, which no doubt included these conditions, Raja Abdullah wrote a letter on 30th December, 1873, to the new Governor, who took up his cause and the star of Triad was once more in the ascendant.

Thus, by the astuteness of Tan Kim Cheng, the victory of Tokong four months before had been turned into a defeat, and within three weeks the Triad candidate was Sultan of Perak.

So much for the additional facts of Triad and Tokong intrigue brought out in the above extract. There remain one or two other incidents in this period which go to show that the real prize the leaders were angling for, was the monopoly of the revenue "farms" of Perak.

A letter in C.S.O. Singapore bound volume, *Perak and Larut Correspondence* from the Acting Lieut.-Governor of Penang (Campbell) to the Colonial Secretary, dated 19th February, 1873, is of interest. It should be borne in mind that the third Larut war which began in October, 1873, consisted of a blockade of the coast by Triad against Tokong who were bottled up in the interior without supplies. The "piracies" of that year were the efforts of Triad to prevent supplies reaching Tokong in the hinterland *via* the Larut coast.

An extract from the letter is as follows:—

"......Both these witnesses sympathise with the party of Tean Tek which at present is the beaten party in Larut. Again, Captain Webb of the "Fair Malacca" complains that on 14th inst., his steamer escaped with difficulty from......four piratical junks. But in this case also it must be borne in mind that the "Fair Malacca"......belongs to the side of Tean Tek's faction".

These references are to Khoo Thean Tek, the Tokong leader in the Penang riots of 1867 (Chapter XVI), who although officially "transported", was back again in the Colony in 1869 (*see* Chapter XX *infra*) and, as we shall see, was later a successful tenderer for revenue "farms" in Perak.

We shall see also how the conclusion of the Treaty of Pangkor was followed by a scramble by Triad and Tokong for revenue collecting rights and, according as one or the other was successful, so the influence of White or Red Flag became paramount in the locality of the parent "farm".

NOTE ON TAN KIM CHENG 陳金鐘

This man, a Straits-born Hokkien, and Consul-General for Siam in the Straits Settlements whom we have mentioned on pages 205 and 213 *supra* appears by inference to have been the Head of Triad in Malaya (*i.e.* elected from the Hokkien branch of the Ghee Hins in Singapore) although he nowhere appears in the records as such.

Song Ong Siang *op. cit.* page 93 records as follows:—

"As head of the Hokkien Huay Kuan in Telok Ayer Street, he was styled Captain China".

The following letter in C.S.O. Correspondence *Perak and Larut 1862–1873* from the Lieut.-Governor Penang to the Colonial Secretary, dated 4th July, 1873, indicates some of the activity of Tan Kim Cheng at this date:—

"In reply to your letter No. 2981 of 26/6/73 I have......to inform you that Mr. Kim Ching is neither in Penang nor Laroot, so far as I can learn.

I would recommend with a view to arranging matters in Perak that a government officer to sent to visit the Raja Bendahara (Raja Osman) at Great Perak (Kuala Kangsar) and also to see the principal chiefs there, and then to see the Laxamana at the mouth of the Perak river and after ascertaining their views, to confer with the Raja Muda (Abdullah) at Kreean and with the Tunku Mentri of Laroot, who is at present resident here.

I have little confidence in anything being satisfactorily arranged by Mr. Kim Ching.

I am informed that the Raja Muda (Abdullah) has declared in favour of the Ghee Hin party and has given over to them the use of his chop"......

We shall see in the next chapter how closely Tan Kim Cheng was associated with W. H. Read in obtaining the recognition of Sir Andrew Clarke to the claims of Raja Abdullah as Sultan of Perak (1874) and how throughout 1874 and 1875 he was active with his brother-in-law Lee Cheng Tee in procuring for Triad, first from Abdullah and later from Mr. Birch, the right of "farming" the revenues in the Perak River Valley.[1]

From what is on record of his activities in Siam at an earlier date and from the great influence he had in Singapore, and the influence he used in support of Raja Abdullah's candidature for the throne of Perak, it is not too great a stretch of the imagination to suppose that he was throughout his life 1829–1892, a leader if not the Head of Triad in Singapore. As the son of Tan Tock Seng, (founder of the Hospital which bears his name) he inherited a large fortune and although charged in Court and acquited of slavery towards the end of his career, he posed throughout his life as a philanthropist and the embodiment of all the Chinese virtues and died in 1892 full of riches and honour.

THE MURDER OF LI AH KUN (? 李亞坤). HIS PROBABLE IDENTITY WITH LEE COYN

Wilkinson *H.P.M.* pages 104–105 records this incident, the cause of the second Larut war (February—May, 1872) as follows:—

"At the time of the troubles of 1862, (first Larut war), the leading Hai San (Tokong) Chinese at Klian Pauh was Chang Keng Kwi, and the Ghee Hin (Triad) leader who succeeded So Ah Chiang (murdered 1862) at Kamunting was Ho Ghi Siu. Ten years later, both these (former) leaders (in Larut) were wealthy residents of Penang and their mines were managed by their attorneys.

Footnote.—(1) *See* Chapters XIX and XX *infra*.

Li Ah Kun, Ghi Siu's attorney was accused of an intrigue with the wife of a near relative of Ah Kwi. This scandal was the more dangerous because it came to light at a time when the passions of both sides were being inflamed by a boundary dispute. Ah Kwi's men seized Li Ah Kun and the accused lady, placed each of them in one of the curious crate-like baskets, used by Chinese for the transport of pigs and, after marching them about for some time in this ignominous guise, ended up by submerging the pair in the waters of a disused alluvial mine and holding them there till life was extinct. This outrage caused Ho Ghi Siu's men to take up arms at once...... There was now a small civil war in Larut".

We should examine this account more closely in the light of foregoing chapters. The leader of Triad in the Penang Riots of 1867 was a man whose name is recorded as "Lee Coyn".

We have not seen the record of the trial which took place as a result of the Penang riots, and we do not know whether "Lee Coyn" was charged at all and if so whether he was acquitted or convicted. The leaders of Tokong at that time were Khoo Tean Tek and Khoo Pah and we do know that the first of these was condemned to death, a sentence subsequently commuted to seven years transportation, which sentence together with a sentence of transportation on Khoo Pah and on Boey Yu Kong (梅 裕 廣 of Triad at the same time) was later annulled (1869) with the help of their lawyers. It seems probable that if "Lee Coyn" was charged he was not convicted, or if convicted he was not sentenced so heavily as the Tokong leaders, or his name would appear with theirs in the subsequent references to the annulment of their sentences.

Assuming that Lee Coyn was identical with Li Ah Kun, it would be in keeping with all we know of Tokong vengeance that they should wish to encompass his death to "save their face" for the death-sentence on Khoo Tean Tek.

If we now look at the facts of his death as recorded by Wilkinson we find these would be in keeping with a Triad-Tokong vendetta, and bear the complexion of an organised murder with the merest veneer of circumstantial excuse to cover it. The story of his "intrigue with the wife of a near relative of Chang Keng Kwi" is difficult to accept as genuine, when we consider the conditions at the mines in those days. The trade in women was part and parcel of the Triad-Tokong system and the Chinese women at the mines probably went to the highest bidder. Chinese coming overseas did not bring their wives with them and it is highly improbable that "the near relative of Ah Kwi" whose name is not given but who will have been a Hakka and a Tokong, would have had any woman in his household but a Cantonese (Triad) prostitute, whose death meant nothing to the Tokongs and was merely an added sacrifice incidental to the death of Li Ah Kun upon the altar of Tokong vengeance. If she was genuinely the wife of a close relative of Chang Keng Kwi—the stated excuse for the outrage— she would have been a Tokong-protected woman, and it is inconceivable that Tokong would have subjected a relative by marriage of their own leader to the ignominy described. The outrage was more in keeping with the pitiless hatred between the Cantonese and Hakkas engendered by the "Hakka-Puntei" wars in Kwangtung province (Chapter IV).

By the murder of Li Ah Kun in 1872, Tokong may have felt that the insult of the death sentence upon Khoo Thean Tek in 1868, had been avenged.

The Triad reply to the murder of Li Ah Kun was the third Larut war, and British intervention.

The difference in romanised spelling of Lee Coyn (1868) and Li Ah Kun (1872), who we suggest were one and the same man, may be found in the fact that the former spelling was made by officers unacquainted with the romanisation of Chinese sounds. In 1870, Pickering was appointed the first Chinese-speaking officer in the Straits Settlements Government and was closely associated with Chinese affairs in Perak at the time of British intervention. The change to the more orthodox romanisation Li Ah Kun may, therefore, be attributable to him.

NOTE ON:—

(1) CHANG KENG KWI 鄭景貴 (TOKONG).

(2) CHAN AH YIM 陳亞炎 (TRIAD).

We should here take note of two men who were destined to play an important part in the early days of British intervention in Perak.

The first, Chang Keng Kwi alias Ah Quee, a Hakka appears to have come first to official notice as the chief signatory to a petition, dated 26th September, 1872, addressed to Governor Ord from a party of "Chan Sung"[1] Chinese, "merchants of Penang and Larut" against a riotous faction of Sinneng Chinese who had caused them loss in Larut. This petition identifies him with Tokong, (Hai San) and in August, 1873, he appears as representative of Tokong (Hai San) on board the "Midge" in the abortive peace expedition of that month. From then on he is the spokesman of the Hakkas in Larut and after the Treaty of Pangkor at which he was present, he became "Kapitan China" in Larut and one of the leading Chinese under the British régime.

The second, Chan Ah Yim alias Ah Yam, a Cantonese from Sz Yap (Sinneng district) appears to come first to official notice as a signatory of a petition from the "See Yip tin-mining Kongsee lately of Laroote", dated 3rd May, 1873, addressed to Governor Ord

Footnote.—(1) i.e. the Hakka district of Chen Shang in the Kwang Chow prefecture of the Canton province.

complaining of the Mentri and his Chinese supporters who had seized the mines and caused loss and damage to the petitioners. This identifies him as a representative of Triad (Ghee Hin).

From this point onwards Chan Ah Yam appears to have taken the place of Ho Ghi Siu as Triad representative, and the latter disappears from the records, possibly because he became discredited with the British authorities after absenting himself from the "Midge" expedition, mentioned above.

Both these men were signatories to the "Engagement" (see Appendix IXB) made between the British and the Chinese Headmen of Larut at the time of the Treaty of Pangkor and under that engagement they were appointed to be the two Commissioners to see the engagement carried out. In this capacity we shall meet them again.

INFLUENCE OF TRIAD AND TOKONG UPON THE PERAK SUCCESSION 1871–1873

The following facts are taken from the authorities given at the beginning of this chapter except where otherwise noted. Anson in *About others and myself* on pages 287–288 has the following note upon the beginning of this period, in which he took an important part:—

> The relations between the Government and that of the native state of Perak, in the Malay Peninsula, had for many years been very unsatisfactory; and on my arrival at Penang (as Lieut.-Governor on 8/6/1867) complaints were continually being made to me by native British subjects (mostly Chinese) who resorted to that state on business or for trade, of the ill-treatment they received from the chiefs and head men; and there were many outstanding complaints of this nature still unsettled. The island of Pangkor, near the mouth of the Perak river, and about 90 miles south of Penang, which had been ceded to the Indian Government in 1826, had recently been occupied by three Malays, to whom permits to occupy and clear land to the extent of 400 acres had been given, and a small population, many of whom were escaped slaves from Perak, had sprung up there. There was also some question regarding a portion of the mainland of Perak opposite Pangkor, having also been ceded to the Government of India.[1]
>
>   *   *   *
>
> Shortly after my arrival at Penang, Sultan Ali, the then ruler of Perak, sent his Luxamana, or High Admiral, to me, with full powers to settle all questions in dispute between the two Governments: such as the boundaries between Perak and Patani, and Selangor, etc. These questions were in a fair way of being amicably settled between us, when Sir Harry Ord, the Governor of the Straits Settlements, made a sudden and unexpected visit up the Perak river, and endeavoured hurriedly to make a settlement of them with the Sultan on the spot. Now, questions could not be settled with Malays in an offhand manner. They were suspicious, and required time to consider them. The consequence was that they declined to come to any agreement. Almost immediately after that, stringent directions came from the Home Government to stop all further negotiations, and this put an end for the time being to all interference on our part in the affairs of the Malay native states.

Sultan Jaafar Muadzam Shah died about A.D. 1866, and was succeeded by his son-in-law (and second cousin), Sultan Ali-al-Kamal Riayat Shah, who died at Sayong on 25th May, 1871.

The heir to the throne of Perak was the Raja Muda, Raja Abdullah, son of Sultan Jaafar and brother-in-law of Sultan Ali, the same Raja Abdullah whose cause we left on the steps of Government House (in November 1873).

Upon the death of Sultan Ali, and in accordance with custom, the Bendahara (Raja Ismail) took possession of the regalia and, after seven days, sent a deputation to the Raja Muda (Raja Abdullah) inviting him as heir-presumptive to attend the obsequies of the late Sultan at Sayong, and be installed Sultan.

Raja Abdullah was of a weak, vacillating and timorous nature and feared to go to Sayong lest he be killed on his way upstream by a family rival, Raja Yusuf, who lived at Senggang and who bore him a grudge, connected with the succession to the throne. This circumstance is sufficient to illustrate the irresolute character of Raja Abdullah.

Whilst he was trying to make up his mind to go to Sayong and be crowned Sultan, his wife Raja Tipah, who was a sister of the late Sultan Ali and furious at her husband's delays and pusillanimity, was abducted down river by a Selangor Prince, Raja Daud. The fugitives escaped and the incident further discredited Raja Abdullah in the eyes of his people in a way peculiar to the Malay race. The incident made Raja Abdullah still more terrified to go to Sayong and still less acceptable to the chiefs as their new ruler. After forty days of waiting with the body of their Sultan still unburied, the Perak chiefs lost patience with the discredited Raja Abdullah and installed the Bendahara, Raja Ismail as Sultan.

Raja Abdullah's fear of Raja Yusuf arose from the fact that Raja Abdullah owed his position of Raja Muda to election more than to descent, Raja Yusuf being a more legitimate candidate, but unacceptable as Raja Muda to the Perak chiefs. This complication arose in this way. There were three branches of the Royal House that took it in turn to provide the Sultan and the Raja Muda. When the twenty-third Sultan died he should have been succeeded by a son of the twenty-first Sultan, and a son of the twenty-second Sultan should have been made Raja Muda. But the son of the twenty-second Sultan was Raja Yusuf who was unacceptable to the chiefs as Raja Muda, and whose branch of the family thus came to be passed over for the time in favour of Raja Abdullah, a son of the twenty-third Sultan, who

---

Footnote.—(1) For text of this treaty *see* Maxwell and Gibson *Treaties and Engagements affecting the Malay States and Borneo* (1924) page 23.

was appointed Raja Muda in 1868 instead of Raja Yusuf. Raja Yusuf then became a sort of legitimist claimant. Meanwhile, the Bendahara, Raja Ismail was installed as Sultan. Raja Yusuf recognised Sultan Ismail's title for the time being, but wished to be made the next heir to the throne.

We may anticipate events here by recording that, after the conclusion of the Perak war (December, 1876) which involved the removal from Perak politics of two Perak Sultans, namely, ex-Sultan Ismail, the former Bendahara, and Sultan Abdullah, the former Raja Abdullah, this Raja Yusuf supported by British assessors, sat as one of the Judges of the murderers of Mr. J. W. Birch, and was recognised by the British Government as Regent and later as Sultan of Perak. Swettenham remarks (*British Malaya* page 213) in reference to Raja Yusuf:—

> "Though his hereditary claim was......better than that of (Raja) Abdullah, he would probably never have become Sultan without the support of the British Government".

The decision to reject Raja Abdullah, the heir-presumptive, and the selection of Raja Ismail as Sultan in his stead, was a decision of the Perak chiefs themselves, made during an epoch (1871) prior to British intervention in Perak (1874) and uninfluenced by any considerations other than those of their own free choice and of the welfare of the State and without advice or pressure from the British Government.

The Mentri steadfastly supported the candidature of Ismail and except for the brief period in 1873 of his "alliance" with Abdullah, remained until the ultimate extinction of both of them, the ally and supporter of Ismail, from whom he had greater hope of confirmation as Ruler of Larut than from Abdullah. The following extract from a letter of Colonel Anson to the Colonial Secretary, dated 25th July, 1873, (in C.S.O. Perak and Larut) is interesting:—

> Tengku Oodin (Viceroy of Selangor) says that the Tungku Mantri is at the bottom of the present difficulties (disputed succession in Perak) and that under the existing state of things the Raja Muda (Abdullah) is principally supported by the Chinese at Laroot who are supplied with means from this Settlement, whilst the Raja Bendahara (Sultan Ismail) is supported by the Malays.

MEMBERSHIP BY MALAYS OF TRIAD AND TOKONG

The official records of the time nowhere mention the White and Red Flag societies during this period. The authorities appear not to have realised that there was any connection between the Triad and Tokong war in Penang of 1867 and the "See Kwan" and "Go Kwan" struggle in Larut, whereas we have seen that "See Kwan" and "Go Kwan" were in fact only other names for Triad and Tokong. We are entitled, therefore, to suppose from what we have seen above and from the after-history of the Flag societies in Perak, that the same alliance which existed between Triad and White Flag and Tokong and Red Flag in Penang in 1867, persisted in Larut during the same period and subsequently between the See Kwan and White Flag and Go Kwan and Red Flag in the second and third Larut wars.

There is no proof that the Mentri and his Malay adherents were members of the Red Flag, or that Raja Abdullah and his Malay supporters were members of the White, but subsequent chapters will show that this line of cleavage in the matter of the Perak succession which began in 1871, has persisted to the present-day. C. J. Irving writing on 24th July, 1872, (*Perak Papers* Section *B* page 2) on the subject of the second Larut war (February–May, 1872) has:—

> "At any rate it is clear that when the disturbances broke out in February last (1872) between the rival factions, the Chan Shiang (Tokong) and the Sin Heng (Triad), the Mentri's government was quite powerless to put a stop to them. In effect they did not stop until after the loss estimated at nearly 1,000 lives. One of the parties, the Chan Shiang, was entirely defeated and driven out of the country, the bulk of the survivors, to the number of nine or ten thousand, taking refuge at Penang, while the remainder took refuge in Quedah, Perak and other places. On the victory thus declaring itself, I have been told that the Mentri, who had previously been a member of the "Hai San" Kongsee or secret society of which the members chiefly belonged to the defeated party, withdrew from it and joined the "Habsia"[1] Kongsee the members of which were principally Sin Heng men. I will not vouch for the truth of this story, but I am inclined to believe it myself. I saw no reason to suspect my informant of a desire to mislead me, and besides it is not the first time I have heard of Malay Rajas becoming members of Chinese Kongsees.[2]
>
> If it really obtains, the practice is well worthy of notice, suggestive as it is of the political arrangements that are likely to arise when—as no doubt will be the case—the immense resources of the Peninsula attract a vast population of Chinese to the present almost uninhabited territories".

These were prophetic words.

The new ruler of Perak in June, 1871, took the title of Sultan Ismail Mu'abidin Shah and was recognised as Sultan by the Perak chiefs, by the British Government in Penang and by Raja Abdullah himself (August, 1871).

Footnote.—(1) *i.e.* the Ho Hop Seah (和合社).

Footnote.—(2) Irving's informant was not misleading him. He was referring to that period in April, 1872, when the Mentri "made overtures for alliance with victorious Triad, now in possession of his mines" (page 269 *supra*). Evidently to prove his *bona fides* and put him within the power of their vengeance if he should break faith, Triad required the Mentri to enter the Hung league before they would treat with him.

In Wilkinson *History of the Peninsular Malays* page 116, we read:—

> "It was only at a later date when Raja Abdullah's financial difficulties led him (in 1872, while still Raja Muda) to sell concessions as "Sultan", that concessionaires, their counsel and other interested parties began to cast doubts upon the validity of Ismail's Sultanate".

It was at this time too (1872) that we find Raja Abdullah in Penang interfering in the war in Larut, and from this time we first notice the tentacles of Triad and Tokong gaining a hold on matters of Perak State policy and, in particular, upon the affair of the Perak succession.

There is no direct evidence of this process, nor is this aspect of local history treated in any available work on the period, but it is a fair assumption to make, having regard to all the factors now known to have existed at that time, some of which were less clear then, than they are to-day.

In A.D. 1862, the Mentri of Larut (Che Ngah Ibrahim) was definitely allied with the Tokong (Hai San) faction and in A.D. 1872 (May) he transferred his allegiance to the Triad faction, which was then momentarily the stronger party in Larut.

Tokong, expelled from Larut to Penang in March, 1872, by the Mentri and Triad, returned to the attack in August, 1872. The success of this Tokong attack caused the transfer once again of the Mentri's support to Tokong.

There followed the counterattack of the Ghee Hins in October, 1872, still with the rather nebulous "support" of Raja Abdullah and the blockade of the Matang coast.

Stalemate ensued, and we find the Mentri in January, 1873, living in a boat at the mouth of the Krian River, while his Tokong allies hold the mines at Larut and the sea-board at Matang. Triad continued the blockade with their fleet in the hope of starving out Tokong, what time Raja Abdullah, titular ally of Triad, awaits the turn of events.

BRIEF ALLIANCE BETWEEN MENTRI AND RAJA ABDULLAH JUNE, 1873

We see in June, 1873, a brief "alliance" between the Mentri and Raja Abdullah, which came to an end when the Mentri refused to accept Tan Kim Cheng's terms for what we are entitled to believe was the promise of Triad help from Singapore.

Vetch *Life of Sir Andrew Clarke* gives another cause of quarrel page 148:—

> The Mentri of Larut, Ngah Ibrahim claimed his independence on the ground that he had been granted by the late Sultan Jaafar in 1862, full powers to govern the district of Larut with the advice of the Laksamana. Raja Muda Abdullah, on the other hand, claimed that the special powers granted to the Mentri were merely delegated powers, which lapsed on the late Sultan's death.[1]

> This grant of special powers to the Mentri was made in consideration of the Mentri having paid a fine for the Sultan, (Jaafar) which had been demanded by the British Governor (Cavenagh) as compensation to one of the Chinese factions (Triad) for losses inflicted by another faction (Tokong) with which the Mentri had sided.[2]

The Mentri and Raja Abdullah returned to Penang in June, 1873, having found the "war" too hot, leaving the struggle to Triad and Tokong for mastery of the mines.

ABORTIVE PEACE EXPEDITION OF H.M.S. "MIDGE" 10TH–14TH AUGUST, 1873

In August, 1873, we see these two again as members of an abortive peace "expedition" on H.M.S. "Midge" which included, or was intended to include, the Headmen of both Triad and Tokong in Penang, and we see their ineffectiveness.

The origin of the "Midge" expedition and its composition are interesting. Wilkinson *History of Peninsular Malays* page 110 has:—

> "In August, 1873, the fear of Chinese civil war in Penang forced Lieutenant-Governor Anson to take action.[3] On the 10th August, he called a meeting of rival leaders at his office. There were present:—
> (1) The Mentri of Larut.
> (2) Raja Abdullah.
> (3) Ho Ghee Siu (Headman in Penang of Triad).
> (4) Chang Ah Kwee (Headman in Penang of Tokong).
> (5) Commander Grant, H.M.S. "Midge".
> (6) Tengku Zia-ud-din, Regent of Selangor.

We have in the above list the same Chinese representation over again as we saw in Chapter XVI during the Penang Riots of 1867, namely:—

(1) Ho Ghee Siu   (Triad) ;
(2) Chang Keng Kwee   (Tokong) ;

the Heads of the rival camps, and the two men whose word was law among the Chinese in Penang and in Larut. These two men were almost entirely responsible in their capacity of President of the two societies, for the condition of civil war and anarchy to which Larut had been reduced and for the state of anger, anxiety and

---

Footnote.—(1) Sultan Jaafar died on 20/3/1865 and was succeeded by Sultan Ali (died 25/5/1871). Sultan Jaafar was the father of Raja Muda Abdullah, which, no doubt, influenced the latter in putting his own interpretation on his father's instrument, which he could not believe was intended to deprive him of his birthright.
Footnote.—(2) *See* First Larut war 1862 *supra.*
Footnote.—(3) He had already had a civil war in Penang in 1867, and did not want another.

impotence in which the British authorities found themselves. At a word or a nod, these two men, had they so willed it, could have called a truce and cut short the war and the wastage.

Their respective local titular allies:—
    (3) Raja Abdullah;
    (4) The Mentri;
appear to have stood in much the same relation to them in Perak in A.D. 1873 as:—
    (1) Lee Coyn (Triad);
    (2) Khoo Thean Teck (Tokong);
stood to:—
    (3) Tuan Chee (White Flag);
    (4) Che Long (Red Flag);
in Penang in A.D. 1867.

Wilkinson *op. cit.* continues:—

> The Lieutenant-Governor induced both parties to consent to an armistice pending arbitration by himself. But it was one thing to agree in Penang to an armistice and quite another matter to get the Larut belligerents to lay down their arms. The only member of the conference who was prepared to attempt the impossible was Raja Abdullah, who had nothing to lose and whose assurances were taken too seriously. He started at once for Larut on board H.M.S. Midge......
> He had counted on the help of Ho Ghi Siu whose word was law in Ghee Hin circles. Ho Ghi Siu was in no mood to support his chief. He gave everyone the slip and stayed behind in Penang. Raja Abdullah made excuses but was afraid to admit his weakness. He went unwillingly to Larut, refused to land lest his "followers" (the Ghee Hins blockading the coast) should fire on him and declined to authorise any attempt to force a passage up the river.
> Although the "Midge" was accompanied by two steamers full of rice for the starving miners (Tokong) in possession of the mines, the whole flotilla had to return to Penang with its mission unfulfilled. The Ghee Hin men refused to lay down their arms.
> On 14th August, Captain Grant returned to Penang and reported what had happened. Raja Abdullah wrote as follows to Colonel Anson:—
>   "We inform our friend that we went to Larut in the "Midge" accompanied by the Mentri. We wished to put a stop to the Chinese disturbances at Larut, but the Towkays and headmen did not go with us: moreover, at the time we met out friend, we stated that if those headmen did not go with us we should be unable to settle the disturbances. At the present time we are not well enough to meet our friend".
> The failure of this attempt to settle matters by arbitration put Ho Ghi Siu and his Ghee Hin associates in the wrong.
> Colonel Anson turned to the other side, telegraphed to Governor Ord (who left at once for Penang) and authorised the Mentri to recruit Indian troops and to employ Captain Speedy of the Penang Police for service in Larut".

BRITISH SUPPORT FOR TOKONG AND RED FLAG SEPTEMBER, 1873

On 3rd September, 1873, Governor Ord abandoned the position of counterpoise and lent British support to the Mentri and Tokong, while Raja Abdullah entered into closer relations with Triad in Penang and with Tan Kim Cheng in Singapore, and began to raise money from the latter by the sale of concessions as "Sultan".

Just at this juncture (October, 1873) Governor Ord left the Straits on retirement. His departure and the reversal of his policy by his successor who arrived in November, 1873, changed the course of history. At the date of Sir Harry Ord's departure the following was the position:—
    (a) The British Government had recognised Sultan Ismail as Sultan of Perak since his coronation at Sayong in July, 1871.
    (b) The British Government had recognised the Mentri of Larut (Che Ngah Ibrahim) as lawful ruler of Larut and independent of the Sultan of Perak, with effect from 5th September, 1873.
    (c) The British Government was aiding the Mentri with both men and military stores, to become master in his own house.

The only weakness in (c) was that it gave virtual possession of the wealth and prospects of Larut to the Tokong faction and it was not to be expected that Triad would accept such total exclusion, particularly since they had as their titular puppet leader, a claimant to the throne of Perak.

A CHANGE OF GOVERNORS AND A CHANGE OF POLICY

With British support the Mentri was soon in possession of Larut; the mines were set working and wealth and revenues began again to be produced. Raja Abdullah, bitterly disappointed as claimant both to the throne of Perak and the wealth of Larut, saw them both slip from his grasp through the turn in British policy decided on by Sir Harry Ord in September, 1873.

A change of Governors happened to coincide with these events and with a change of policy by the Colonial Office, which sent out Sir Andrew Clarke, in November, 1873, charged with the task of intervention and with the duty of introducing into the Malay States the residential system of British advisory officers.

Broken, discredited and disappointed, Raja Abdullah turned for help to Tan Kim Cheng and the new Governor.

We find his lost cause where we left it earlier in this chapter, being presented to Sir Andrew Clarke in November, 1873, by Read and Tan Kim Cheng with the support of Triad and White Flag behind it.

CHAPTER XVIII

THE TREATY OF PANGKOR AND THE UNSEEN
AGENCIES IN ITS MAKING

Wilkinson wrote in 1908[1]:—

> The line Sir Andrew Clarke elected to take led to the Perak war and to bitter controversies that make it even now inexpedient to discuss the history of Perak for the years 1874, 1875 and 1876.

The position remains much the same to-day.

It must be our task nevertheless to examine very closely the history of these three years, so that the reader may follow the thread of Triad, Tokong and Tabut intrigues which had so woven themselves into Perak politics, that at the end of 1873, Tokong and their shrewd and shifty Malay ally the Mentri of Larut, were, after twelve years of warfare, still in possession of the wealth of the Taiping mines; while Triad with their discredited Malay ally Raja Abdullah, were defeated and driven out of Larut back to their base in Penang. So great was the defeat that Triad's titular Malay leader went to Singapore in October, 1873, to seek further aid from Tan Kim Cheng and through the latter's intervention, became an object of interest to the new Governor, Sir Andrew Clarke.

The authorities for this chapter are:—

(1) *Perak Papers* 1874 (Perak State Museum Library).

(2) *Parliamentary Paper* unnumbered entitled, "Correspondence relating to the affairs of certain Native States in the Malay Peninsula", dated 31st July, 1874, (being a continuation of Command Paper 465 of 1872). It is probably C 1111, but is not so shown.

This latter Paper covers 270 printed pages and contains much of the material in (1) above. For brevity it will hereinafter be referred to as *Parliamentary Paper 465/74* and is to be found in *Parliamentary Papers on the Malay States* Vol. I 1872–75 in the Perak Museum Library.

RECOGNITION OF TRIAD, TOKONG AND TABUT INFLUENCE IN THE LARUT WARS

If any reader still doubts that Triad and Tabut influence ever existed in Perak politics, the following extracts from the above official sources seem to justify a different view:—

(a) Braddell, Attorney-General, Straits Settlements, in a statement of the past history of the Larut disturbances, written for the information of Sir Andrew Clarke in January, 1874, *Perak Papers* Section "G", page 5[2] says:—

> Matters were in this state when fresh disturbances broke out among the miners (of Larut) in February, 1872. The Mentri had found that his former allies (since 1862) the Hye-Sans or Go Kwans[3] were not comparatively so powerful as before, and he turned in favour of the See Kwans.[4] The result was that the Hye-Sans were driven out of the country.

> *   *   *

> The expelled Hye-Sans, after petitioning the Governor (in Penang), were active in making preparations to return to Larut and, in their turn, to expel the Ghee Hins. Great quantities of men and arms were collected in Penang and sent to Larut and at the same time the question of the disputed succession to the throne of Perak having risen, the Ghee Hins made common cause with the rejected Raja Muda (Abdullah) against the Hye-Sans, who adopted the side of the newly installed Sultan Ismail, who was supported by the Mentri.

(b) Again, in describing an interview with some of the Ghee Hin headmen on board the *Pluto* at Pangkor on 15th January, 1874, Braddell writes (*op. cit.* page 8)[5]:—

> They expressed their want of confidence in the Malays and asked that a British officer should be put in the mines to govern the people on principles of justice. They had fought enough and would have settled but they had got mixed up with Malay politics and found it now impossible to do anything without the assistance of the British Government.

(c) Again, in discussing preceding events, when on the visit to Penang of January, 1874, (*Perak Papers* Section "G" page 6). Braddell records:—

> It was thought that the Chinese factions had already suffered so much that they would be prepared to come to terms with each other and return to work at the mines, if they could be relieved from the complications arising out of their alliance with the contending Malay parties.

These official opinions, expressed on the eve of the Treaty of Pangkor, show that even then there was a fairly general feeling that the two parties to the Perak succession dispute were in league with the two camps of Chinese secret societies and Irving quoted on page 278 *supra* records his belief that the Mentri was actually a member of Tokong. It is equally clear that the exact nature of the influence wielded by these unseen agencies was not understood by the British Government. It seems safe to assume that the White and Red Flag societies were at this time in Larut as actively in alliance with Triad and Tokong as they had been a few years earlier in Penang (Chapter XVI *supra*), and that their continued existence, and influence in Perak politics, was not realised by the British authorities at the signing of the Treaty of Pangkor.

LEADERS OF TABUT IN THE PERAK SUCCESSION DISPUTE

We should here for convenience, tabulate the leading members of the two rival parties in this dispute, as we have seen them in the foregoing chapter and under the flags by which they must have been known, or later became known to one another, *viz* :—

RED FLAG	WHITE FLAG
Sultan Ismail.	Raja Abdullah.
The Mentri.	The Laxamana.
All the other territorial chiefs of Perak (except the Laxamana and the Shahbandar).	The Shahbandar.
	Haji Musa (a wealthy trader).
	Haji Hoosein (agent of Raja
Haji Ali.	Abdullah).
Haji Mat Yassin.	Tan Kim Cheng (Triad, Singapore).
Chang Keng Kwee (Tokong, Penang).	Chan Ah Yam (Triad, Penang).

From this line of cleavage we get a Nationalist party (Red Flag) supported by Tokong and an Interventionist Party (White Flag) supported by Triad.

There were some chiefs who apparently did not belong to either party, notably Raja Yusop, the legitimist claimant to the throne, who, like Abdullah, had also been passed over, and who, like him, ultimately became Sultan.

The line of cleavage between the adherents of the Interventionist and of the Nationalist parties became much more sharply defined after the signing of the Treaty of Pangkor.

THE FOUR "PROBLEMS"

The foregoing was probably the undersurface line-up in December, 1873, at the change of Governors. Braddell *Parliamentary Paper 465/74* page 165 para. 41, records the problems awaiting solution following upon the decision of the British Government to intervene, to be :—

First—The disputed succession to the throne of Perak.

Second—The position of the Mentri in Larut.

Third—The disputes at Larut between the Chinese.

Fourth—The action of the combatants at sea which had degenerated into piracy.

The first two "problems" appeared on the surface to concern the Malays alone; the second two, the Chinese. Through the intrigues of Triad and Tabut and unknown to Braddell, the four problems had, in fact, grown together into four facets of a single problem. As we shall see below, the first two "problems" were not genuine problems at all, and the two latter were but a single issue.

In his approach to a study of these questions Sir Andrew Clarke was guided largely by the presentation of the facts to him by Braddell and not by Anson. This presentation omitted mention of the two most important facts of all, namely, the recognition by Anson of Sultan Ismail as Sultan in July, 1871, and the recognition by Sir Harry Ord of the Mentri as independent ruler of Larut in September, 1873, which had been granted upon Anson's advice.

This recognition had meant to the unseen intriguers, British support for Tokong; but within three months it was reversed and by the Treaty of Pangkor, British support went unconsciously to Triad.

It is of the highest importance to a comprehension of the undersurface moves of this period, that the surface events and their chronological sequence should be clearly stated. This has been done by Winstedt *History of Perak* (1934) page 98 in the following passage :—

At the time of the Pangkor treaty Sir Andrew Clarke was probably ignorant that his predecessor had recognised the Mantri as the independent ruler of Larut. The papers on the subject were in Penang and were forwarded to him on 23 January, 1874, after the treaty had been signed.[1] Sir Harry Ord's statement in the Singapore Council had not been explicit. Sir Harry had regarded the Larut troubles as a Penang matter and had been guided largely by the advice of Lieutenant-Governor Anson; Sir Andrew Clarke, as a newcomer, was influenced by Singapore counsellors, especially by Mr. Braddell who had never been to Larut and could have only an imperfect acquaintance with the facts. The new Governor had been instructed and advised to introduce the residential system, but had not been told how to do it. He seized the first chance that presented itself. Raja 'Abdu'llah, after his capture by the men of the *Midge*, had been released by Colonel Anson, the Lieutenant-Governor, and after borrowing $1,000 through

Footnote.—(1) *See Parliamentary Paper 465/74*, pages 159–160.

the Shahbandar sailed to Singapore. He was a discredited man; and his rival, the Mantri was the recognized ruler of Larut. Raja 'Abdu'llah was ready to agree to the residential system or indeed to any other system that would secure his advancement. He lived at the expense of Kim Ching, the Chinese Consul for Siam in whose favour he executed a bond making his host collector of the Larut revenues for ten years, provided Kim Ching could get the British to recognize his Sultanate. Mr. W. H. Read, a member of Council, took 'Abdu'llah to the Governor[1] and induced him to write a letter dated 30 December, 1873 asking for a Resident at his court. This was the opening that Sir Andrew had desired. He took up Raja 'Abdu'llah's cause, thinking—on the facts before him—that it would be a fair compromise if Raja 'Abdu'llah recognized the Mantri as Mantri, and the Mantri recognized the Raja as Sultan.[2] It was not a fair compromise. The British Government had already recognized the Mantri as the independent ruler of Larut; and the Mantri demurred to being regarded as his rival's subordinate.[3] Sir Andrew Clarke and Mr. Braddell, unaware of this recognition and in all good faith, regarded the Mantri as an obstinate and recalcitrant individual who was making unnecessary difficulties and putting forward indefensible pretensions. Mr. Braddell's journal of the Pangkor negotiations has to be read in the light of what was known to the Governor and to himself, and not in the light of the true facts.

SKELETON HISTORY OF THE CIRCUMSTANCES SURROUNDING THE BRITISH APPROACH TO INTERVENTION

We must here notice in skeleton form and in correct chronological sequence the circumstances surrounding Sir Andrew Clarke's approach to the negotiations which ended at Pangkor and the share of Triad, Tokong and Tabut in creating those circumstances:—

(1) Aug., 1871.   The British Government recognised Sultan Ismail as Sultan of Perak.

(2) 3- 9-1873.   Sir Harry Ord, by Colonel Anson's advice, recognised the Mentri as independent ruler of Larut. Tokong thereby became paramount.

(3) 1-10-1873.   Departure of Raja Abdullah from Penang to Singapore as the guest of Triad (Tan Kim Cheng).

(4) 3/23-10-1873.   Execution of a bond by Raja Abdullah in Singapore in favour of Triad, making Tan Kim Cheng, his Collector of Revenue in Larut for ten years in return for the promise of Triad aid.

(5) Oct., 1873.   Refusal of Sir Harry Ord to interview Raja Abdullah at Government House.

(6) 20-10-1873.   Departure of Sir Harry Ord from Singapore on retirement.

(7) 23-10-1873.   Departure of Abdullah to Perak from Singapore where he had proved too expensive a guest for Triad to continue to entertain.

(8) 4-11-1873.   Arrival of Sir Andrew Clarke with a mandate for intervention.

(9) Nov., 1873.   Presentation of the facts of the Perak dispute to Sir Andrew Clarke by Braddell.

(10) Nov.-Dec., 1873.   Presentation of the claims of Raja Abdullah to the throne of Perak to Sir Andrew Clarke by W. H. Read and Tan Kim Cheng.

(11) Dec., 1873.   Acceptance of Raja Abdullah's claim by Sir Andrew Clarke.

(12) 30-12-1873.   Receipt by Sir Andrew Clarke of a letter from Raja Abdullah in Perak agreeing to sign a Treaty with the British Government and to accept a British Resident.

(13) 2- 1-1874.   Dispatch of Pickering from Singapore to Penang with a letter from Tan Kim Cheng to open unofficial negotiations with the contending Chinese.

(14) 4- 1-1874.   Receipt of a telegram by Sir Andrew Clarke from Pickering reporting agreement of the Ghee Hin Chinese in Penang to submit their claims to British arbitration.

(15) 5- 1-1874.   Receipt by Pickering of a telegram from the Colonial Secretary conveying the Governor's readiness to ratify Pickering's agreement with the Ghee Hins.

(16) 6- 1-1874.   Dispatch of Major McNair and Captain Dunlop from Singapore by Sir Andrew Clarke as emissaries to the two contending Chinese factions and the Perak chiefs inviting them all to a conference at Pangkor on 14th January, 1874.

Footnote.—(1) This seems unlikely. Raja Abdullah was in Singapore from 3rd to 23rd October, 1873. Sir Andrew Clarke arrived on 4th November and there is no evidence that Raja Abdullah returned to Singapore after that date, or that Sir Andrew Clarke met him until 16th January, 1874, at Pangkor. What seems more probable is that in November–December, 1873, Mr. W. H. Read took Tan Kim Cheng to the Governor as Raja Abdullah's representative in Singapore.

Footnote.—(2) As we have seen in the preceding chapter, these were Triad's original terms to the disputants, which would give Triad's puppet overlordship in Larut.

Footnote.—(3) It also ignored the fact that the British Government had already recognised Sultan Ismail as Sultan of Perak in August, 1871.

(17) 12- 1-1874. Sir Andrew Clarke arrived in the *Pluto* off Pangkor Island.

(18) 15- 1-1874. Arrival of Ghee Hin headmen and Raja Abdullah at Pangkor.
      (morning).

(19) 15- 1-1874. Interview of Chinese headmen with the Governor on board
      (afternoon). *Pluto* and terms of agreement drawn up.

(20) 16- 1-1874. First meeting of the Governor with the Raja Abdullah accom-
      (morning). panied by the Bendahara, Raja Osman.

(21) 16- 1-1874. Conference between the Governor and the Mentri.
      (afternoon).

(22) 17- 1-1874. Conference with all the chiefs present and confirmation of
      (Saturday). Raja Abdullah as Sultan.

(23) 19- 1-1874. Discussion of the terms of the Treaty.

(24) 20- 1-1874. Engagement with the Chinese (discussed separately below)
      11:0 a.m. signed. (Appendix IXB).

(25) 20- 1-1874. Treaty of Pangkor (discussed separately below) signed.
      3:0 p.m. (Appendix IXA).

(26) 20- 1-1874. Appointment of Captain Speedy as Assistant British Resident
      to see to the carrying out of the engagement with the
      Chinese to disarm. (The post of Resident was not filled
      until nearly a year later by the appointment of Mr. J. W. W.
      Birch in October, 1874).

(27) 20- 1-1874. Appointment of three Commissioners (Pickering, Swettenham
      and Dunlop) to assist Speedy in the disarmament of the
      Chinese. To this commission were added Cheng Keng Kui
      (Tokong) and Chan Ah Yam (Triad) the two headmen
      in Larut.

(28) 23- 2-1874. Report by the pacification commission that peace had been
      restored in Larut, disarmament completed and agreement
      reached upon the partition of the mines.

(29) Jan.-Feb., By the Treaty, Sultan Ismail was deposed, but as he was not
      1874. a signatory, he ignored it and continued to possess the
      regalia and to rule in the Upper Perak River *(Hulu)*
      supported by the non-signatory chiefs.

(30) Jan.-Feb., By the Treaty, Sultan Abdullah was recognised by the British
      1874. and by some of the signatory chiefs and took up his
      residence at Batak Rabit and began to rule in the lower
      reaches of the Perak River *(Hilir)*.

(31) Feb., 1874. Meeting of protest against the Treaty held by the Laxamana
      and other signatory chiefs.

(32) March, 1874. Sultan Abdullah began raising money for himself by selling
      concessions in land in Krian.

(33) April, 1874. Birch and Swettenham visited Sultan Ismail at Blanja and
      tried unsuccessfully to induce him to give up the regalia.

(34) April, 1874. The Mentri, a signatory chief, paid a lawyer (Woods) in
      Penang a retainer of $12,000 to put his case against the
      Treaty before the British Parliament.

(35) July, 1874. Braddell visited Sultan Abdullah at Batak Rabit and warned
      him against granting revenue concessions without the
      Governor's consent.

(36) July, 1874. A few days after Braddell's visit Abdullah obtained an advance
      of $13,000 from a Singapore Chinese, Lee Cheng Ti, a
      nominee of Tan Kim Cheng and Triad, for the right to
      collect taxes at the mouth of the Perak river. By this act
      Abdullah began to redeem his pledge to Triad (Item 4
      above) for their help in his candidature for the throne.

So much for a skeleton of the circumstances surrounding the Treaty, which we must now examine in closer detail.

THE NECESSITY FOR INTERVENTION

The year 1867 was the year of transfer of the Straits Settlements from the control of the Government of India to that of the Colonial office with the status of a Crown Colony.

The last Governor under the Government of India was Colonel Cavenagh (1859–1867) the first under the Colonial Office was Sir Harry Ord 1867–1878, throughout whose term of office the Colonial Office adhered to the non-intervention policy of the East India Company.

The second and third Larut wars had brought the tin trade between Penang and Larut to a standstill and had proved, with similar disturbances occurring concurrently in Selangor, the necessity for intervention of some kind.

The coming settlement was intended, therefore, to be primarily a treaty of agreement between the British Government and "the two Chinese factions", whom we now know to have been Triad and Tokong.

At the end of 1873, the third Larut war had reached stalemate. The revenues of Larut had fallen from $15,000 to $1,500 a month. The most pressing necessity was to conclude peace and re-establish the Larut-Penang tin trade.

By September, 1873, the Colonial office had recognised the necessity for intervention.

Sir Harry Ord did in fact restrictedly intervene in September, 1873, by supporting Tokong in Perak and by recognising the Mentri as the independent ruler of Larut.

Sir Andrew Clarke arrived in November, 1873, with a mandate from the Colonial office for general intervention and required only an opportunity to give effect to it.

THE OPPORTUNITY FOR INTERVENTION

Triad was quick to furnish that opportunity.

Tan Kim Cheng had shown a lively political sense and sharp business acumen in undertaking in October, 1873, to represent Raja Abdullah's cause to the new Governor in exchange for the right to become Abdullah's collector of taxes should anything come of the bargain.

The bond given to Tan Kim Cheng made him, in effect, Raja Abdullah's *wakil* or political agent in Singapore, whose claim to the sultanate he was pledged to further, because by doing so he was advancing his own commercial interests and the chance of a Triad victory in the third Larut war.

In furtherance of the scheme, Tan Kim Cheng invoked the aid of W. H. Read[1] a member of the Legislative Council, and, after introducing Raja Abdullah to Read in October, 1873, sent Abdullah back to Perak and induced Read to support Abdullah's pretensions.

Raja Abdullah's rejected claim was to be revived and was to receive a fresh hearing only through the support and intrigues of Triad for underground ends. Triad, through Kim Cheng and Read[2] had obtained the ear of Government in Singapore.

Winstedt *History of Perak* (1934) page 98 already quoted says:—

> Sir Harry Ord regarded the Larut troubles as a Penang matter and had been guided largely by the advice of the Lieutenant-Governor Anson. Sir Andrew Clarke as a newcomer was influenced by Singapore counsellors, especially by Mr. Braddell, who had never been to Larut and could have only an imperfect acquaintance with the facts.

Of the four Larut problems presented to Sir Andrew Clarke on arrival the first two *viz*:—the disputed Perak succession and the disputed position of the Mentri in Larut had already been solved.

Nevertheless, through the intrigues of Triad and White Flag, ousted from Larut by Sir Harry Ord's action in September, 1873, these two problems were resurrected as fresh issues on the arrival of Sir Andrew Clarke, and were tacked on to the only genuine problem awaiting solution, namely the conclusion of peace between the two Chinese factions in the third Larut war.

History has divided this latter problem into two separate questions namely, the Chinese war in Larut and the Chinese "piracy" on the coast. But as we have seen, the position was one of double blockade; the blockade of Tokong in Larut by Triad on the coast, and the counter-blockade of Triad on the coast by Speedy to landward and the Royal Navy to seaward. The settlement of the one would automatically settle the other. The question of piracy did not, therefore, arise.

It was with imperfect knowledge of the facts and without consultation with Colonel Anson that Sir Andrew Clarke proceeded to apply remedies to the "four problems", which he was led to believe awaited his solution.

Armed with the bond he had received from Raja Abdullah in Singapore in October, 1873, making him "collector of Larut revenue for ten years", Tan Kim Cheng awaited his opportunity to "get the British to recognise Raja Abdullah's sultanate".

In December, 1873, Read took Tan Kim Cheng to interview Sir Andrew.

Vetch *Life of Sir Andrew Clarke* page 149 has:—

> Through Mr. Read's instrumentality Sir Andrew, in due course, received a letter from Abdullah, (dated 30th December, 1873)[3] properly signed and "chopped", in which he made the following report:—
>
> > We and our great men request the Governor, who is now arbitrator and mediator, to aid us by inquiring into these disturbances with authority, so that they shall cease, and be settled properly and with justice. And if all these dissensions are brought

Footnote.—(1) For a sketch of his life 1818–1908, *see One Hundred Years of Singapore* (1921) Vol. II page 416 ff. He was a prominent freemason.

Footnote.—(2) This was no fortuitous combination. These two men had been in partnership in big business in Selangor since 1866 and by 1873 knew all the ropes. *See* page 418 *infra*.

Footnote.—(3) The letter is given, in translation, as Appendix I in the *E.P.O.* It is dated at the head 30th December, 1873 and at the foot 2nd January, 1874. If the latter date is correct, the letter could hardly have reached the Governor before 4th January, 1874, whereas Pickering's mission had already begun before that date. It seems probable that this letter was written under the guidance of Tan Kim Cheng and W. H. Read and the Governor may have received an earlier draft copy thereof, upon which he decided to dispatch the Pickering mission.

to an end and set right, and the country is restored to peace, we and our great men desire to settle under the sheltering protection of the English flag.

Further, we and our great men wish to make a new treaty of lasting friendship with the English Government, which will benefit both sides. And we, together with our great men, to show our good faith, ask of our friend, Sir Andrew Clarke, for a man of sufficient abilities to live with us in Perak, or at any fit place not far from us, and show us a good system of government for our dominions, so that our country may be opened up and bring profit, and increase the revenues as well as peace and justice.........

This was the opening Sir Andrew desired. He took up Raja Abdullah's cause and with it unconsciously the cause of the Ghee Hin and White Flag in Perak.

Sir Andrew was led by Read and Tan Kim Cheng to believe that a fair compromise would be for Raja Abdullah to recognise the Mentri as ruler of Larut and the Mentri to recognise Raja Abdullah as Sultan. These were the terms already offered to these two malcontents by Triad in April-May, 1873, in return for Triad aid to effect their confirmation and had been rejected by both parties (see page 273 (6) and (7) supra).

Raja Abdullah's cause was already lost, when it suddenly received through Triad intrigue and intervention the fortuitous and unexpected support of the Government of Singapore. Triad's terms were confirmed by the Treaty of Pangkor.

It was not possible for the Government of that day to realise the degree to which Triad and Tokong and their Malay auxiliaries had permeated local politics, and although there was the *Penang Riot Commission Report* of 1868 to give some indication of the possible presence of this unseen influence, the framers of the Treaty of Pangkor were doubtless unaware of it. The Treaty, we may make bold to suggest, sharpened the hostility of the two camps in their struggle for exclusive rights of exploitation in Perak, by introducing a directly political element into what had previously been primarily a commercial rivalry and the projection of an internecine strife between the two factions with roots in China. In this struggle the spoils had rested with Tokong (Red Flag) and their Malay ally, the Mentri who, by the very success of Tokong in the "war for possession" had gained his own independence of the Sultan of Perak and recognition of that independence by the British Government in Penang. The Treaty of Pangkor changed all this.

MISSION OF PICKERING[1] 3RD–20TH JANUARY, 1874.

Sir Andrew Clarke was aware that the most pressing need was to raise the blockade on the Larut coast and to bring the Chinese disputants to a conference.

Vetch *Life of Sir Andrew Clarke*, records the initial step he took to effect this, in the following passage, page 148:—

> Sir Andrew Clarke had good reason to believe that the Chinese were getting sick of the constant faction fighting, which was not only ruining the country of Perak, but also impoverishing themselves. He, therefore, took the first step in his Native States policy by sending the Official Chinese Interpreter to Government, Mr. Pickering, to open negotiations with the headmen of the Chinese factions in Perak, but with instructions to do so as if acting on his own authority, and not as delegated by the Governor.
>
> Mr. Pickering left Singapore for Perak in the steamer *Johore*, and at once set to work to find out whether the chiefs of the two parties could not be brought to settle their differences. His mission proved most successful. He gained the confidence of the headmen, and on the 4th January, 1874, was able to telegraph* to Sir Andrew that the chief headmen of both factions had agreed to submit their claims to the arbitration of the Governor, and to enter into an undertaking to surrender their rowboats, to dismantle their stockades, and to give up their arms.

* This telegram is given in *Parliamentary Paper 465/74*, page 74 and reads:—

> 4th January, 1874, Sinhengs gladly sign agreement: give boats, everything to your disposal in seven days, meanwhile beg orders.

It should be here noted that it was the Sinhengs *i.e.* "Four Districts" or Triad, to whom Pickering, armed with a letter from Tan Kim Cheng had first addressed himself and in the first place it was they only who signified their assent to his proposals in the above telegram.

MISSION OF MCNAIR AND DUNLOP 10TH–20TH JANUARY, 1874

Following upon the favourable telegram from Pickering of 4th January, 1874, Major McNair, Colonial Engineer and Captain Dunlop, Acting Inspector-General of Police, were entrusted with a mission by the Colonial Secretary (Birch) to proceed to Penang and Perak and arrange for the assembly at Pangkor on 14th January of:—

(a) The Chinese headmen of both factions;

(b) The major chiefs of Perak

in preparation for a conference with the Governor.

The letter of instructions given them dated 7th January, 1874, is in *Parliamentary Paper 465/74* pages 75–77.

Footnote.—(1) Pickering's report of his mission is given in *Parliamentary Paper 465/74*, pages 153–154.

Colonel Anson, Lieutenant-Governor of Penang, had received a telegram on 8th January, 1874, instructing him to summon the Chinese headmen in Larut and all the major chiefs of Perak to meet the Governor at Pangkor on 14th January and letters had thereupon been sent to them by the hand of Swettenham,[1] but Colonel Anson expressed a doubt as to the time being sufficient to enable them to be present. In addition, McNair and Dunlop who arrived in Penang on 10th January, 1874 brought a personal letter of summons to the conference from the Governor addressed to the following:—

(1) The Raja Bendahara;
(2) The Raja Abdullah Muda;
(3) The Mentri;
(4) The Laxamana.

This letter is given in *Parliamentary Paper 465/74*, page 155.

In the official correspondence of the period, by all except Colonel Anson, Sultan Ismail is referred to prior to the Treaty as the Raja Bendahara and sometimes as the *de facto* Sultan; and after the Treaty as the ex-Sultan Ismail. It is clear, therefore, that the above letter was intended for Sultan Ismail who did not comply with it.[2]

The report of McNair and Dunlop upon their mission is given in *Parliamentary Paper 465/74*, pages 77–80, and fully confirms the condition of alliance which then prevailed in Larut between the Mentri, his followers and Ah Quee's party, the Go Kwans (Tokong), on the one side; and Raja Abdullah, his followers and Ah Yam's party, the See Kwans (Triad) on the other.

From this time onwards, Ching Keng Kui *alias*-Ah Quee (Tokong) and Chan Ah Yim *alias* Ah Yam (Triad) a note upon whom is on page 275 *supra*, are the most prominent representatives of the two contending Chinese parties in Larut.

TWO ENGAGEMENTS CONCLUDED AT PANGKOR

It must here be emphasised that there were two distinct engagements drawn up at Pangkor:—

(1) *one in Malay* between the British and those Perak Chiefs present (who did not include the ruling Sultan), and known as the "Treaty of Pangkor" the terms of which are given in Appendix IXA.

(2) *one in Chinese* between the British and the Headmen in Penang and Larut of Triad and Tokong (who were also present at Pangkor) and referred to as a "Bond of $50,000 to keep the peace", the terms of which are reprinted as Appendix IXB.

THE ENGAGEMENT WITH THE CHINESE

The records show that this, the most pressing of the "problems", received prior attention at Pangkor.

The references in brackets in this section refer to the pages in *Parliamentary Paper 465/74*.

Pickering arrived in Penang on 3rd January, 1874 (page 165 para. 45) and the same day interviewed Chin Ah Yam and Koh Bu Ann, the two headmen of the Sinneng (Si-Kwan or Triad) faction in Penang and gave them the letter he had brought for them from Tan Kim Cheng (page 153). It will be noticed that Tan Kim Cheng still kept a directing hand upon the course of events. Later the same day Pickering interviewed Ho Ghi Siu, the former Triad leader, who had been discredited with the British Government since the abortive *Midge* expedition of August, 1873, (*see* Chapter XVI *supra*). A meeting of Triad leaders was held on the night of 3rd January, 1874, in Penang and on 4th January, 1874, Pickering met eight of them including their then plenipotentiary Chin Ah Yam. Pickering (*loc. cit.*) reports: "They had spent the night in their Kongsi house, considering Kim Cheng's letter and my advice". As a result of this meeting they conveyed to Pickering verbally the unconditional submission of their case to the British Government. This decision is what we would expect from the Triad side, who were the dispossessed party in Larut and whose acceptance of British intervention would help to force the political issue. Pickering reported to the Governor (*loc. cit.* page 154) that "the other party (Go Kwan or Tokong) will be just as glad, for during the last three or four years, the slain on both sides can be counted by thousands".

Pickering then sent his telegram of 4th January, 1874, and his written report to the Governor on 5th January, 1874, (pages 153–154).

On 10th January, 1874, Pickering met McNair and Dunlop who had arrived in Penang on their separate mission on that day (page 155). Subsequently all three of

Footnote.—(1) *Parliamentary Paper 465/74*, page 166 para. 49.
Footnote.—(2) The fact that it was addressed to the Bandahara may explain the attendance of the Bendahara, Raja Osman, at Pangkor. It is also noteworthy that, if the letter was intended for the four major chiefs, it should have been addressed to (i) The Bendahara; (ii) The Orang Kaya Besar; (iii) The Temenggong; (iv) The Mentri, in that order.

them interviewed Chang Keng Kui, the leader of the Cheng Sia faction of Tokong, who on 13th January, 1874, gave a written undertaking to McNair and Dunlop similar to that of Triad, and witnessed by Pickering, to abide by the Governor's arbitration (page 156). Meanwhile on 5th January, 1874, Pickering had received a telegram from the Colonial Secretary, Singapore (Birch) advising him in reply to his telegram of 4th January, 1874, that the Governor would ratify the verbal undertaking of the Triad faction conveyed in that telegram (page 74).

No doubt, Tokong was aware of the receipt of this communication which probably hastened their decision likewise to submit. Tan Kim Cheng had forced Tokong into a position from which they could not retreat.

On 6th January, 1874, the day following the receipt of the Colonial Secretary's telegram, the leaders of Triad in Penang had confirmed their verbal undertaking to Pickering by giving him a written undertaking[1] similar to that subsequently given by Tokong to McNair and Dunlop. This was signed by twenty-four members of the "Four Districts" including Chin Ah Yam and Koh Bu Ann (pages 74–75).

On 15th January, 1874, the Headmen of both sides came aboard the *Pluto* at Pangkor (page 167 para. 60) and interviewed the Governor, and the terms of an agreement between them were drawn up for signature later.

At 11.30 A.M. on 20th January, 1874, the agreement with the Chinese was executed (page 174 para. 109) and was signed by twenty-seven representatives of the two "contending parties". Unfortunately, the identity of the signatories as between Triad and Tokong was not shown on the final instrument (page 83 and Appendix IXB). Comparing the names on the Triad undertaking given to Pickering on 6th January, 1840, (page 75) with those on the final combined instrument (page 83), we may guess at some of the identities as follows :—

Go Kwan (Tokong)		Serial number on final instrument	Si Kwan (Triad)			Serial number on final instrument
Chang Keng Kui	..	14	Chin Ah Yam	..	..	2
Khoo Ah Chay	..	12	Wong Ah Chong		..	1
Khoo Ah Kway	..	20	Lee Chin Foey	..		6
Tan Ah Quay	..	3	Boo Ah Yen ⎫			10
Oh Kim Sin	..	4	? Koh Bu Ann ⎭			
Chiang Keng Bo	..	5	Ho Ah Chew	..		18
Ang Kang Sin	..	7	Lee Ah Fook	..	..	16
Ang Ah Kway	..	8	Li Ah Pow	..	..	17

The foregoing is only a guess, based on the similarity of surnames which, we have seen in the *Penang Riot Commission Report* (Evidence Section) Chapter XVI *supra*, to have belonged in the main to the one or the other faction. The remaining twelve signatures are not easily placed, but would seem mostly to belong to the Triad side.

Apart from this separate Chinese agreement, Triad and Tokong were, in fact, represented in the Treaty of Pangkor proper, through their respective Malay associates of the White and Red Flag, who were the signatories thereto.

THE MAJOR CHIEFS OF PERAK, JANUARY, 1874

It is necessary here to record the lists of the twelve Major Chiefs of Perak 1874–1876. A fuller note upon some of them is given in Chapter XXIII.

This is the list as given on page 1 of the *Précis* in the *Enquiry as to complicity of Chiefs in the Perak outrages* (E.P.O.) :—

The four superior Officers were styled in order of their precedence:—
  1. The Raja Bendahara, or Chief Executive Officer and lawgiver.
  2. The Orang Kaya Besar, or Keeper of the Privy Purse.
  3. The Tumengong, or Chief Magistrate.
  4. The Orang Kaya Mentri, or personal adviser to the Sultan.

The eight officers of second rank were styled:—
  5. The Maharajah Lela, or Commander-in-Chief.
  6. The Laxamana, or Admiral of the Fleet.
  7. The Shahbandar, Collector of Customs and Harbour Master.
  8. The Dato Sedika Raja, or Head of Public Works.
  9. The Panglima Kinta, or War Chief of the left bank of the river.
  10. The Panglima Bukit Gantang, or War Chief of the right bank.
  11. The Dato Sagor, Master of the Household.
  12. The Imam Paduka Tuan, or Head Priest.

These twelve officials are common to the constitution of several Malay States, although there is variation in the style of the title and in influence in individual cases. They are commonly referred to among Malays as the *Orang Duabelas* ("The Twelve") and with the Sultan constitute the Malay Government.

Footnote.—(1) The date of this document is given in *Parliamentary Paper* 465/74, page 75 as 16th January, 1874. This must be a misprint for 6th January, 1874, due to confusion with the Chinese date.

THE ROYAL PRINCES OF PERAK JANUARY, 1874

We have seen how, on the eve of the Treaty, there were two Sultans in Perak; Ismail, who had been reigning for over two years and Abdullah, who was about to be recognised by the British.

This complication tended to divide the *Orang Duabelas* into two factions according as they supported Ismail, or Abdullah. Again, to Ismail, Abdullah was still the Raja Muda; to Abdullah, Ismail was a usurper; he himself was Sultan and his cousin Raja Yusop was Raja Muda. The Bendahara appointed under Ismail was Raja Osman, son of the late Sultan Ali.

As the hereditary Shahbandar was a supporter of Abdullah, Sultan Ismail had appointed one of the sixteen minor chiefs Raja Mahkota the Shahbandar's son, to be his (Ismail's) Shahbandar or Collector of Customs at the mouth of the Perak river. Raja Mahkota had been driven out by Abdullah, but he nevertheless appears as one of the signatories to the Pangkor Engagement in support of Abdullah, in which he was, no doubt, influenced by his father.

Besides Sultan Ismail, whose title to the throne appears on closer examination to have been much clearer than history has hitherto admitted, there were the following Royal princes then in Perak:—

Raja Abdullah (Claimant) son of late Sultan Jaffar.

Raja Yusop (Claimant) son of the late Sultan Abdullah Mohamed Shah who preceded Sultan Jaffar.

Raja Osman (Bendahara) eldest son of late Sultan Ali. (Osman died 30th October, 1876).

Raja Ngah, son of Raja Osman Bendahara, known as Tengku Panglima Besar.

Raja Idris   } Elder and younger sons of late Bendahara Raja Iskandar—and
Raja Ahmad } cousins of Raja Abdullah.

Raja Abbas, son of Raja Abdullah's elder sister—(his nephew).

THE SIGNING OF THE TREATY OF PANGKOR

Vetch *op. cit.* page 149 has:—

> Having received Mr. Pickering's telegram and Abdullah's letter, Sir Andrew decided that he would himself go to Perak, and endeavour personally to settle, there and then, with the Perak chiefs all the questions at issue. He fixed the 14th January for the conference, and he selected Pulo Pangkor, at the Dindings, as the rendezvous.

Braddell's diary of the events at Pangkor 13th–20th January, 1874, leading up to the signing of the Treaty, is in *Perak Papers* Section G. pages 6–16[1] from which the following facts are taken:—

On 13th January, 1874, the Chinese Headmen arrived: the Hai San (Tokong) on H.M.S. *Avon* accompanied by Swettenham and the Ghee Hin (Triad) shepherded by Pickering, McNair and Dunlop on the s.s. *Johore*.

On 14th January, 1874, the Mentri arrived in his own steam yacht, accompanied by his Chief of Police, Captain Speedy and his lawyer, R. C. Woods.

On 15th January, 1874, Raja Abdullah arrived accompanied by the Bendahara (Raja Osman), Raja Ngah and Raja Abbas, the Laxamana, the Shahbandar, Raja Mahkota, "and other Chiefs and followers". This seems to have been the first meeting of Sir Andrew Clarke with Raja Abdullah.

On 17th January, 1874, there was a full conference of all the Chiefs present held in the Governor's ship *Pluto*, attended by the above-named and by the Temenggong and the Dato Sagor, who had meanwhile joined the Mentri in his yacht. The latter, though present, remained sulky and aloof.

Among others mentioned in Braddell's diary as having been present at this plenary meeting, were "Datoh Gapar, Datoh Rouah, Hajee Hussain, and Hajee Mohamed Syed", who all voted for the appointment of Raja Abdullah as Sultan. They appear to have been persons of no importance, who were not entitled to be present at all.

The names of the signatories to the Treaty are:—

Sir Andrew Clarke;
Sultan of Perak (Raja Abdullah);
Bendahara;
Temenggong;
Mentri of Perak;
Shahbandar;
Raja Mahkota;
Laxamana;
Dato' Sa'gor.

Footnote.—(1) Also *Parliamentary Paper* 465/74, pages 116–176.

L

The diary of events at Pangkor, recorded by Braddell, is in *Parliamentary Paper* *465/74*, pages 166–176 and the *verbatim* report of the confirmation of Raja Abdullah as Sultan is at *loc. cit.* page 172.

Sir Andrew's own account of the proceedings is contained in a letter to Mr. Childers of the Colonial Office, quoted by Vetch *op. cit.* page 154, in the following passage:—

On his return to Singapore after making the Pangkor Engagement he wrote to Mr. H. C. E. Childers:—

*   *   *

I feel I have done a good stroke; in short, all the people here say that nothing has been done so complete and equal to it since Raffles's time........

The Colonial Office may say that I might have submitted my scheme to them for their approval before putting it into force, but the only chance of success I had was to do what I did rapidly, so that not a soul knew my plans until I had almost pulled them through. The Chinese were moving and had no idea who was moving them. I had got hold of the heads of both parties, and neither knew that I knew the other.

I sent a steamer for the Malay chiefs telling them to come to see me at the Dindings, giving them no time to hesitate, nor telling them what I wanted them for, nor affording them time to send for their lawyers—nearly all Malay chiefs have Penang or Singapore lawyers retained by them. I was assured I could not get them together under six weeks or two months. I collected them in a week, and they were without their lawyers. One alone, the Mantri of Larut, had one;[1] but as none of the others had, I would not assent to his putting in an appearance.

CONSIDERATIONS INFLUENCING ATTENDANCE AT PANGKOR

It is as well to pause here and consider how it was that Raja Abdullah, already discredited with his own people, was able to muster such a comparatively imposing number of supporters for his conference with the Governor.

We suggest that the following considerations exercised an influence upon the attendance at Pangkor:—

(1) The Laxamana and the Shahbandar representing the Interventionists had, since 1871, supported Raja Abdullah's candidature. This was because his mother was the Laxamana's sister and the territorial as well as family influence of both the Laxamana and the Shahbandar was at the mouth of the Perak river, where Raja Abdullah had taken up his residence: and the actual venue of the Conference was in their territory.

(2) The mission of McNair and Dunlop may not have been conspicuously successful, but it must at least have aroused among the major chiefs curiosity, if not enthusiasm, for an event which was unique in the lives of all of them and in the history of the country.

(3) Sultan Ismail and those major chiefs representing the nationalists had no particular reason to expect that their non-appearance at this hastily summoned conference would have any decisive results. The Larut dispute was remote from the politics of the Perak river valley and was primarily the concern of the Mentri, whose title to Larut was not opposed by Sultan Ismail; and who, with his Indian blood, was more a businessman than themselves. Their sympathies were with the Mentri for the added reason that the dispute was no longer a purely Chinese one, but had been espoused by Raja Abdullah and his concession-hunting Chinese friends in opposition to the Mentri.

(4) The nationalists, no doubt, realised that if Abdullah's pretensions should be successful in raising him to power in Larut, their own position would be rendered less secure; but they had no reason to think that after so many years of dispute, settlement of the Larut issue would be reached in a few days. They nevertheless may have thought it wise to have an observer at the conference, which may explain the presence there of the Bendahara, Raja Osman, to whom they may have assumed the Governor's personal letter of summons was addressed. It was a proper choice by office and custom, but it was a bad individual choice for them, as Raja Osman was feeble-minded.

(5) The conference was the great opportunity for Triad to retrieve by settlement their lost position in Larut, and so win by diplomacy the third Larut war. We may, therefore, fairly assume that Triad agents directed by Tan Kim Cheng, whose hand was on the pulse of events, were busy canvassing the attendance of the opportunist chiefs, by pointing out the danger of their future position if the conference should result in appointing Raja Abdullah to be Sultan; or, by promising some pickings from the Revenue farms, once Triad got control of them, under Abdullah's bond to Tan Kim Cheng.

Some chiefs may, therefore, have thought it wise to make a show of supporting the candidate who looked like getting the job. This view may have accounted for the

_____

Footnote.—(1) Mr. R. C. Woods of Penang.

presence of the Mentri himself, the Temenggong, Raja Mahkota and the Dato' Sagor representing the opportunist party; and those other lesser fry who attended, but were not signatories to the Treaty.

Of these considerations influencing the attendance at Pangkor, the last would seem to have been the most powerful and we must here make a digression to show why.

LEE CHENG TEE (李清池) TRIAD'S AGENT FOR THE PERAK REVENUE FARM

We have seen above how Tan Kim Cheng as the price of his help, had obtained from Abdullah a document giving him (Tan Kim Cheng) a paramount position as Revenue Farmer for ten years in Perak. Winstedt *History of Perak* (1934) page 108 has the following in reference to this document:—

> Raja Idris then (May, 1875) tried to get Kim Ching to come and collect the Revenues of Larut under the document Abdullah had formerly given him......but Kim Ching also failed them: he had surrendered the document to the Governor and depended on the British to collect the money Abdullah owed him.

It seems, however, doubtful whether Tan Kim Cheng depended on the British to collect for him. The Chinese are, of course, adepts at erecting, in case of need, a screen of dummies and continuing their operations undisturbed behind this screen. We have seen, for example, in Chapter XVI how Khoo Thean Tek, leader of Tokong in Penang had been sentenced to death for his share in the Penang war of 1867, and yet, within a year or so, he was back again in the Colony, and we shall shortly make his acquaintance again as a Government Revenue Farmer in Perak!

Similarly, Tan Kim Cheng, when he gave up his document to the Governor, must have done so with his tongue in his cheek, because the following extract shows that he had already placed a dummy in the person of Lee Cheng Tee, in Perak as Revenue Farmer, contrary to the wishes of the Governor. *Enquiry into complicity of Perak chiefs* page 4 (foot) and page 5 has the following:—

> In the meantime[1] Sultan Abdullah had been endeavouring for some months to farm out the collection of taxes at the mouth of the Perak river and without having consulted Sir Andrew Clarke, was with this object, in treaty both with Che Ah Him, a merchant of Penang[2] and with Cheng Tee, a merchant in Singapore.
>
> In July, 1874, Mr. Braddell visited him at Batak Rabit and warned him to do nothing of the kind without the consent of the Governor. Notwithstanding this, Sultan Abdullah, two days after Mr. Braddell had gone away, gave the farm to Cheng Tee for $26,000, receiving $13,000, in advance but had the agreement made out in the name of the Shahbandar, in order that he might have an excuse ready in case he were brought to account for the transaction by our Government.
>
> Mr. Birch arrived in Perak on 4th November, 1874, and stopping at Kota Blanda for the night, sent for the Farmer Cheng Tee, and asked him by what right he was collecting taxes there. For some time Cheng Tee, knowing that he had taken the farm contrary to the wishes of the Government, tried to evade giving a direct answer, but at last confessed that he was collecting under an agreement with the Shahbandar.[3] Mr. Birch replied that such an arrangement would not be sanctioned, but that he would be very glad if Mr. Cheng Tee would compete for the farm when it was properly regulated and put up for tender and that he would see that he did not suffer by the change.

Triad had got their wedge in with the new Sultan, which is all that mattered.

Lee Cheng Tee (1833–1901) was the son-in-law of Tan Kim Cheng and was born in Malacca in 1833.

Song Ong Siang *op. cit.* gives a sketch of his career on pages 131, 155, 165 and 166. He was in partnership with Tan Seng Poh and others, who formed the Singapore Opium syndicate and were owners of the Tanah Merah gun-powder magazine in Singapore.

THE INTERVENTIONIST, THE NATIONALIST AND THE OPPORTUNIST CLIQUES AT PANGKOR, JANUARY, 1874

Wilkinson in *H.P.M.* page 121, gives a rather different version of this very important series of events, which he dismisses with only this brief reference. He says:—

> In the end every Perak chief present at Pangkor was led *nolens volens* to sign the treaty to accept Abdullah as Sultan and to agree to the presence of a British Resident, whose advice must be asked and acted upon, on all questions other than those touching Malay religion and custom.

Whether we accept the view or not, that Triad and White Flag influence was responsible for mustering so many chiefs to the support of Abdullah at Pangkor, it remains a fact otherwise nowhere properly explained, that the discredited outcast of November, 1873, was acknowledged Sultan in January, 1874, by some of those same chiefs who had so shortly before rejected him.[4]

All the chiefs of Perak with the exception of the Laxamana and Shahbandar had acknowledged Sultan Ismail in 1871.

Footnote.—(1) i.e. between 20th January, 1874, (date of the Treaty) and 4th November, 1874, (date of appointment of Mr. Birch, as first Resident of Perak).
Footnote.—(2) Unidentified, unless, perhaps, Chan Ah Yim is meant, but doubtless a Triad dummy.
Footnote.—(3) Sultan Abdullah had put up the Shahbandar as his dummy to treat with Triad's dummy Lee Cheng Tee.
Footnote.—(4) Sir Richard Winstedt comments (1936); "Sultan Abdullah was the son of a Telok Anson lady, daughter of the Laxamana and that helped him at Pangkor".

We must now notice who acknowledged and who refrained from acknowledging Abdullah in 1874. In doing so, we must remember that in the Perak political arena there was an Interventionist Party: a Nationalist Party: and an Opportunist Party. The Interventionists were, of course, led by Abdullah, the Nationalists by Ismail, and the Opportunists by the Mentri.

Under these heads, the Chiefs who were members of the *Orang Duabelas* and who signed the Treaty were:—

Interventionists.—
> The Laxamana;
> The Shahbandar.

Nationalist.—
> The Bendahara.

Opportunists.—
> The Mentri;
> The Temenggong (his brother-in-law);
> The Dato Sagor (his uncle).

The two other signatories to the Treaty, were:—

> Abdullah, as Sultan;
> Raja Mahkota, a minor chief, of little importance but belonging to the Nationalist group.

Those members of the *Orang Duabelas* who refused to have anything to do with the Treaty, and all of whom can be regarded as "Nationalists", were:—

The Maharaja Lela	First of the Eight.
The Sadika Raja	Fourth of the Eight.
The Panglima Kinta	Fifth of the Eight.
The Panglima Bukit Gantang	Sixth of the Eight.

There were two vacancies among the major chiefs at this time, *viz*:—

The Orang Kaya Besar	Second of the Four.
The Imam Paduka Tuan	Last of the Eight.

These two vacancies were filled shortly afterwards by Sultan Ismail.

CONSIDERATIONS INFLUENCING THE SIGNATORIES TO THE TREATY

The reasons for signing the Treaty can be guessed at as follows:—

Interventionists.—

The Laxamana, the Shahbandar: both Lower Perak Chiefs who were allied to Abdullah through his mother and whose influence was at the Kuala Perak where the Treaty was signed. They had never acknowledged Sultan Ismail and had always supported Abdullah's claims and were, therefore, probably the only sincere and undesigning Malay signatories to the Treaty.

Nationalists.—

The Bendahara: he may have been anxious by this means to secure his right of succession. He was probably at heart an adherent of the Sultan Ismail and the Nationalist Party. He was, perhaps, only present in reply to the Governor's letter of summons addressed to the Raja Bendahara, which was, in fact, intended for Sultan Ismail. In any case he had little personal influence and was wrong in the head. He died on 30th October, 1876.

The Raja Mahkota: belonged to the party of Sultan Ismail, who had appointed him his own Shahbandar or Collector of Customs at the mouth of the Perak River, because the hereditary Shahbandar was disaffected. He was not a major chief and was probably overawed by his surroundings. As he was on the spot in his official capacity, he seems to have been put in as a makeweight.

Opportunists.—

The Mentri, the Temenggong, his brother-in-law; the Dato Sagor, his uncle: the Temenggong was the senior of this trio, but it was the Mentri who probably carried the Temenggong with him.

The Mentri was in no sense an "officer of state". He was a wealthy semi-independent ruler and his only anxiety was to ensure that, if a Treaty was to be signed, his position and his wealth should be secured under it. His attitude to the Treaty can best be judged by the fact that he was unwilling to sign, but finally did so, and immediately afterwards began intriguing with lawyers against it. His two relatives were doubtless as anxious as he was to "keep the money in the family" by hook or crook and perhaps decided on the spur of the moment and with an eye on the main chance, that it might be safer to sign first and argue afterwards.

Two powerful absentees from the Treaty Conference which was so greatly to affect them were:—

Sultan Ismail—whose village was Blanja;
and
Raja Yusop of Senggang—the legitimist claimant who had been passed over.

Of these, Sultan Ismail must be identified with the Nationalist and Red Flag party, while it is doubtful if Raja Yusop belonged to, or cared about, either. He was appointed Raja Muda of Perak in 1877, Regent in 1878, and Sultan in 1884.

THE UNSEEN HAND OF TRIAD IN THE TREATY

In his letter to Mr. Childers Sir Andrew Clarke wrote:—

> The Chinese were moving and had no idea who was moving them. I had got hold of the heads of both parties and neither knew that I knew the other.

This claim seems untenable. As we have seen, the ground had been prepared by Triad before Sir Andrew Clarke's arrival in the country and in the subsequent developments covering a mere ten weeks, the hand of Triad can still be seen guiding events towards an ultimate Triad victory in the third Larut war. Even at the Conference itself there could be heard by those with ears to hear, the cooing of the Triad dove, whose nominee the Treaty placed on the throne and in the way of the big money.

The *Penang Riot Commission Report* (Chapter XVI) had proved the alliances in 1867 between Triad (Ghee Hin) and White Flag, against Tokong (Toh Peh Kong) and Red Flag.

Nothing had happened during the next six years to sever these alliances: much had happened to strengthen them.

The original Chinese hatreds of the Hakka-Puntei and Larut wars, had been intensified by a Malay political issue of the first importance to them—the overlordship of Larut—and, owing to the intervention of Triad "king-making", ultimately the Sultanate.

In this issue Tokong's patrons, Sultan Ismail and the Mentri were the *de facto* holders of office, while Triad's patron Sultan Abdullah, was challenging both. A decision was about to be given fatal to the prospects of the side that lost.

In steering events towards that decision, Triad's hand was at the wheel and the White Flag leader on the bridge.

We are entitled, therefore, to assume that the Interventionist chiefs were members of, or sympathisers with, White Flag, and that the Opportunist and Nationalist chiefs (both those who signed the Treaty and those who did not) were or became supporters of the Red Flag.

The line of flag cleavage was not conspicuous at the time of the Treaty in which the division between Triad and Tokong was the more strongly marked. Very soon afterwards the flag division made its presence felt.

THE WHITE FLAG AT THE TREATY

Perhaps it was only a co-incidence that at 3.0 P.M. on 20th January, 1874, at the conclusion of the signing of the Treaty, a salute was fired by H.M.S. *Avon* in honour of Raja Abdullah and the White Flag in the following circumstances recorded by Commander Petterson, R.N. (*Parliamentary Paper 465/74*, page 158 (foot)):—

> On the afternoon of the 20th instant His Excellency Sir A. Clarke requested me to be present on board H.M. Colonial Steamer *Pluto* at the signing of the new treaty on the occasion of the Raja Muda's installation as Ruler of Perak; also to fire a salute of eleven guns at the same moment, all of which I complied with, making a temporary flag of entirely white bunting.

We do not know what the state flag of Perak was at that date, but it may well have been pure white—the emblem of Malay royalty (*see* Chapter XV *supra*), as in the case of at least one other Malay State at the present date. In the latter case, the victory of white Triad over red Tokong symbolised by the Treaty, would only have received a vicarious acknowledgment from H.M.S. *Avon's* guns.

UNDERSURFACE EFFECTS OF THE TREATY

The change in undersurface political fortunes introduced by the Treaty operated in four main directions, *viz*:—

Firstly.—

It gave a quite unexpected victory to Triad and White Flag, by elevating their Malay patron to the throne of Perak, raising therewith their own secret influence and power in a new area of exploitation, namely the Perak River Valley, as distinct from Larut.

Secondly.—

It inflicted an equally unexpected political defeat upon Tokong and Red Flag by depriving them of their exclusive possession of the mines in Larut and by undermining influence with their Malay patron, Mentri Che Ngah Ibrahim.

Thirdly.—

It gave a political twist to the activities of the White Flag and Red Flag societies in Perak, which they had not hitherto possessed. The intrigues of king-making had previously been carried on by the Chinese through the heads of Triad and Tokong in their struggle for paramountcy in the Larut tin-fields. From the date of the Treaty it spread to the Malays themselves.

Fourthly.—

By deposing Sultan Ismail who had been freely and constitutionally elected Sultan of Perak two years before the era of British intervention and who refused to sign the Treaty, it occasioned deep-seated discontent among some of the Perak chiefs.

THE POSITION OF SULTAN ISMAIL

Fate seems to have decreed that this unhappy man should indemnify Triad through personal misfortune for all their losses in the Larut wars. History too seems to have added its share of misunderstandings to his load of sorrow.

The references below are to pages and paragraphs in *Parliamentary Paper 465/74*.

History has represented him as follows:—
  (1) That he was not of royal blood. (*Irving* page 130 para. 19).
  (2) That his title to the throne was bad.—
      (*Sir A. Clarke* page 71 para. 16; page 72 para. 27; page 79; page 113 para. 40. *Skinner* pages 117, 118 and 119. *Irving* pages 130, 131 and 136. *Braddell* pages 172 and 173).
  (3) That he was old and decrepit.—
      (*Sir A. Clarke and Braddell loc. cit.*). The Mentri also gave currency to this allegation (page 169 para. 67) evidently with the idea of delaying the proceedings at Pangkor.
  (4) That he was only acting temporarily as a stop-gap Sultan.—
      (*Sir A. Clarke* pages 71, 72, 79 and 113. *Skinner* pages 117, 118 and 119. *Irving* pages 130, 131 and 136. *Braddell* pages 169, 171, 172 and 173).
  (5) That he was not entitled to any higher title than that of Raja Bendahara.—
      (*Sir A. Clarke* page 157 and Article II of the Treaty).

All five allegations appear upon closer examination to be without any substance of fact. A detailed analysis of each is outside our present purpose, but we may briefly disprove two. Firstly, allegation (2); the overwhelming proof of his title to the throne was his possession of the regalia, to which he clung for months after he became a fugitive. Secondly, allegation (5); if he were only the Bendahara, how came it about that the Treaty of Pangkor was signed by the Bendahara (Raja Osman), who was not Bendahara Raja Ismail?

One explanation of this misrepresentation is to be found in the mouth of Triad giving currency to a tale of lies against a man who was a definite obstacle to the ripening of their schemes and whose disappearance would open the way to the throne for Triad's candidate, whose accession would signalise their final victory in the Larut wars.

The following facts should also be remembered:—
  (1) Triad, through Tan Kim Cheng, had the ear of Government in Singapore, and misrepresentation was, therefore, easy.
  (2) A study of the records seems to show that none of those officials who gave innocent credence to the foregoing allegations concerning Sultan Ismail, had ever so much as seen him.
  (3) Colonel Anson, alone, has recorded his mistrust of Tan Kim Cheng and of Raja Abdullah, and his respect for Sultan Ismail. But his voice was silent at Pangkor.

As a result of the changes which the Treaty brought in its train, the alliance of Triad and Tokong with the criminal elements of the White and Red Flag which we have seen in operation in Penang and Province Wellesley, quickly spread into Perak and other States.

Due to this development, there appears to have been added to each flag camp in Perak a political section, which enabled the succession feud to be perpetuated underground, the White in support of Sultan Abdullah, the Red in support of Sultan Ismail.

This speculation is of importance in attempting to follow the lines of subsequent political cleavage and the chain of misfortune of these two men, which so swiftly followed the signing of the Treaty.

SIGNS OF DISCONTENT WITH THE TREATY

It was clear from the first that the Treaty did not give satisfaction to any of its signatories.

Anson in *About Others and Myself* page 320 says:—

On 13th January, 1874, Sir Andrew Clarke arrived at the island of Pankor. He came in the Government steamer, *Pluto* accompanied by H.M. *Avon*. He had made arrangements that the chiefs of Perak should meet him there, but the Sultan did not come. The Rajah Muda, or Deputy Sultan,[1] who in the ordinary course would have been created Sultan, on the death of Sultan Ali, in 1871, was there. He had been passed over because of his exceedingly bad character. Wherever he had gone he had brought trouble and misery to the inhabitants. He was an opium smoker, and was unable to come to Penang on account of the debts he had incurred during a course of extravagance, dissipation, and folly, while on a visit there. In August 1873, I had endeavoured, with the aid of this Rajah Muda and other persons (Chinese and Malays) concerned, to put an end to the disturbances in Perak, and it was owing to the failure of the Rajah Muda to carry out the agreement he had signed with the rest that my efforts failed.[2] In consequence of this, and his notorious bad conduct, I told him he should never, so far as I had any influence, become Sultan of the country.[3] However, when Sir Andrew Clarke met him at Pankor, he seemed to be very favourably impressed by him, and on my meeting Sir Andrew a short time afterwards, he told me that directly he saw him, he saw he was "the right man".

In his despatch to the Earl of Kimberley, Sir Andrew stated[4]:—

> It was gratifying to me to find myself disappointed in the opinion I had formed of the Rajah Muda, who, to my surprise, I found a man of considerable intelligence and possessing perfect confidence that he should be able to maintain his position, if he were once placed in Perak as its legitimate ruler.

So at the meeting at Pankor with the Malay chiefs on board the Government steamer, and the man-of-war anchored close by, Sir Andrew induced them to agree to appointing the Rajah Muda to be Sultan, and to relegating the Sultan Ismail, who was not present, to the office of Rajah Muda. There can be little doubt that these chiefs did not fully realize what they were asked to agree to; or if they did, had no intention of acting up to it. One of them, with whom I was well acquainted, and whom I had always found very willing to comply with any request I made to him, came to me a few days after this affair at Pankor, and said he was so confused and upset at that meeting, that he did not rightly know what the Governor wanted him to do; and that, if he could know, he would be quite prepared to help to carry out his views. I suggested he should write to that effect, to the Governor. He said he did not know how to write such a letter, and asked me to draft one for him. This I did, and he got it translated into Malay by my interpreter, and sent it to the Governor at Singapore. It merely stated, in respectful language, what he had said to me. Some time after, Sir Andrew was at Penang, and he told me that he had received a most impertinent letter from this chief, and called him the d-est this, that and the other. I said "I wrote that letter". He looked at me but said nothing. Now Sultan Ismail was a very good and harmless man, and had he been treated, and dealt with, in a proper manner, would have been amenable, and willing to meet the views of the Colonial Government. However, the result of the arrangements that were made, including the sending to Perak, as Resident, Mr. Birch, a very able officer but one most unsuited for the appointment, was, that Mr. Birch was murdered; and this was the cause of the Perak War. It was only a month before his murder that Mr. Birch came to see me at Penang, and from what he then said to me, as to what he was doing in Perak it did not surprise me when I heard that the chiefs had conspired against him.

Sir Andrew Clarke's own account of the proceedings at Pangkor contained in his letter to Mr. Childers (above), would seem to endorse Anson's views in this passage.

The Dindings Clause (Article XI), referred to separately in the next Chapter, was particularly obnoxious and pleased no one.

CROSS-CURRENTS OF INTRIGUE FOLLOWING THE TREATY

The Treaty of Pangkor tended to induce the following undersurface cross-currents of Triad and Tabut intrigue:—

(1) By the recognition of Sultan Abdullah, White Flag influence was brought for the first time into the valley of the Perak river, and owing to the position of his home at Batak Rabit, that influence was first established in Lower Perak, around what is now Telok Anson, and the coast districts south thereof.

(2) By recognition of Sultan Abdullah as overlord of the Mentri of Larut, Triad and White Flag was made ascendant over Tokong and Red Flag, which latter had been paramount in Taiping, Krian and Selama from 1862–1872.

(3) This fact dismayed the Mentri and Tokong interests in Larut and drove them into the arms of the European lawyers in Penang, who had long been fishing in these troubled waters and who now set about finding means to smash the Treaty.

(4) That the signatories to the Treaty were not representative of the territorial Chiefs of Perak, tended to increase their reliance upon the hidden Triad influence behind them, which in other circumstances might have evaporated. This encouraged Sultan Abdullah to attempt to maintain his rather precarious position *vis-à-vis* his subjects, by an extension of White Flag influence through the medium of the revenue Farms, which, as we have seen above, were immediately let to Lee Cheng Tee.

TERRITORIAL INFLUENCE OF THE SIGNATORIES TO THE TREATY

Examining the territorial influence of the signatories more closely, we see that it would be, on paper, something as follows:—

Sultan Abdullah—Kuala Perak (modern Telok Anson).

The Bendahara (Raja Osman) was non-territorial.

Footnote.—(1) *i.e.* Raja Abdullah.
Footnote.—(2) This refers to the abortive *Midge* expedition to Larut.
Footnote.—(3) Anson was not present at Pangkor. This may be the reason for his absence.
Footnote.—(4) *Parliamentary Paper 465/74*, page 71 para. 22 (Dispatch of 26th January, 1874).
See also *loc. cit.* page 169 para. 72,

The Laxamana, the "Admiral".—At that time a powerful chief in Lower Perak, Mohamed Amin by name, the shrewdest and most active supporter of Abdullah and the White Flag, whose influence reached from up-river about Kuala Kinta down to the mouth of the river and all along the coast, including Bagan Datok, Rungkup and Kuala Bernam to the south; and to the north, Lumut, Sitiawan and the Dindings. Beyond the Dindings to the north, the coast-line of Matang—scene of so much fighting during the Larut wars—would come under the influence of the Mentri and the Red Flag.

The Shahbandar.—A non-territorial chief with few personal followers, but much influence. As Harbourmaster he controlled imports and exports at the mouth of the Perak river and as a supporter of Abdullah, his influence would naturally be on the side of the White Flag.

The Raja Mahkota.—The Laxamana's bespoke successor, and his second cousin, Tuan Haji Suleiman by name, who was known as the Dato Raja Mahkota or alternatively, the Dato Muda Laxamana and a chief of little importance.

It is noteworthy that the Secretary of State approved a seat on the Perak State Council to the "Dato Raja Mahkota" with effect from 5th July, 1880, and his name appears for the first time as a member of Council, in Council Minutes of 20th September, 1880, (*q.v.* Chapter XX).

The Mentri.—We already know about. He was head of the Red Flag in Perak and only signed the Treaty as an opportunist to save what he could of his wealth and position from the wreck of the Larut wars. Neither Sultan Abdullah, his hated personal rival, nor the White Flag, the rivals of his society, was likely to get a footing in Larut while he was there to prevent it.

Dato Sagor.—No. 7 of the "Eight" and one of the most powerful territorial chiefs in the Perak valley to sign the Treaty of Pangkor. His territory included both banks of the Perak river between Kampong Gajah and Pulau Tiga. He was executed for his complicity in Birch's murder in December, 1876. We do not know his motive in signing the Treaty and can only conjecture that he followed his nephew the Mentri. It is improbable that his signing the Treaty would have strengthened the influence of Triad and White Flag in his territory. His subsequent execution would, in any case, have thrown local sympathies back on the side of the Nationalist group of Red Flag and Tokong, or, as we shall henceforth call it in its political aspect, the non-treaty chiefs' party, or *Orang Duabelas*.

The Temenggong.—Wan Hasan, by name, No. 3 of the "Four". His descent is given in Winstedt *History of Perak* (1934) page 143.

Wilkinson *Papers on Malay Subjects* page 75 says:—

"The Temenggong was also a territorial chief. He was lord of the Mukim of Kota Lama, where he was all powerful".

It seems probable that Wan Hasan signed the Treaty from the same motives as the Dato Sagor—to share the fate and fortunes of the Mentri, his brother-in-law. Within a few weeks of the signing they were conspiring with other "Chiefs' Party" or *Orang Duabelas* members, and with an English lawyer to find means to break it. Wan Hasan had a brother Wan Hussain of Pasir Panjang, who, as will be seen in the next chapter, took an active part in opposing the British connection.

The Temenggong Wan Hasan was fortunate in that he was the only major chief who signed the Treaty, to survive it. All the others were banished, and the Dato Sagor executed. The Bendahara died in 1876, and the Raja Mahkota, the only other signatory who survived, was not a major chief. It would be safe to say that the Temenggong's adherence to the Treaty, and his survival of it, brought little or no support to the White Flag in Perak, because he was at heart a Red Flag man, and only signed the Treaty, because like the Mentri, he was a trimmer and wanted to be right either way. Whether his trimming affected politics in his territory of Kota Lama, it is not possible to say. A note on this turbulent Mukim is given in Chapter XXII.

Such were the signatories of the Treaty among the *Orang Duabelas*. The following with their territorial connections were absent:—

The Orang Kaya Besar (Penghulu Bendahari) the Treasurer and the second senior of the "Four". This post was vacant at the time of the Treaty, but in September–October, 1875, Sultan Ismail appointed Toh Syed Mahmood to the vacancy.[1]

The Maharaja Lela. (First of the "Eight") Commander-in-Chief. Territorial Chief of Pasir Salak and Sungei Dedap.

The Sadika Raja. (Fourth of the "Eight") Paramount chief in "the upper waters of the Perak river, where he held the same position that the Laxamana occupied near the sea. His authority extended from Kuala Temong above Kuala Kangsar to the white cotton tree, that marked the watershed between the Perak river and the Patani river" (Wilkinson).

The Panglima Kinta. (Fifth of the "Eight") Paramount chief of the Kinta Valley and Warden of the Eastern Marches.

The Panglima Bukit Gantang (Sixth of the "Eight").—Warden of the Western Marches. This post was vacant at the time of the Treaty, but in September–October, 1875, Sultan Ismail appointed Toh Muda Rappa to the vacancy.[1]

The Imam Paduka Tuan (Eighth of the "Eight").—Non-territorial. Add to these:—

> Sultan Ismail;
> Raja Yusop;
> Raja Idris;

and other Royal princes who were not present at the discussions, and it is easy to realise that the Pangkor Treaty was not representative of Perak opinion.

TERRITORIAL SUB-DIVISIONS OF THE RED AND WHITE FLAG CAMPS

Following upon the above survey, the territorial spheres of influence in Perak in 1874, as between the White and Red Flag societies and the chiefs' party, or, party of the *Orang duabelas* may be very roughly set down as follows after the Treaty:—

Red Flag		White Flag
Red	*Orang duabelas* (Non-treaty chiefs)	1. Lower Perak from Batak Rabit (Telok Anson) to Bagan Datok at the mouth.
1. Selama	1. The Perak River Valley solid, from the *Ulu* to Durian Sa' Batang.	2. Rungkup, Bernam and Slim.
2. Larut	2. The Kinta Valley.	3. Lekir, Lumut, and the Dindings coast.
3. Headquarters probably at Bukit Gantang (where the Mentri lived).	3. Bruas.	4. Headquarters probably at Batak Rabit (4th mile Telok Anson—Bagan Datok Road), where Sultan Abdullah lived.
	4. Headquarters either at Kota Lama (Temenggong) or Blanja, where Sultan Ismail lived.	

Doubtless to begin with, the non-Treaty Chiefs and their followers were held together by nothing more than the bond of mutual antipathy to, and exclusion from, the Treaty and loyalty to Sultan Ismail; and were not affected by the distinction of flags, which may have been strange to them. It cannot have been long, however, before the Mentri and his Tokong friends began to recruit for the Red Flag among the followers of the *Orang Duabelas*. Those who joined the Red Flag were doubtless initiated with the secret ritual and joined in the criminal practices of the society, while perhaps a residue of the original non-treaty party remained free of flag society contacts and if so, this residue may have formed the nucleus of the *Orang Duabelas* organisation of to-day. We are not able to say from present knowledge to what extent Tabut influence governs the present-day *Orang Duabelas* organisation in Perak. This aspect of the subject is discussed in Part II.

After the Treaty of Pangkor, Perak was left roughly divided as shown above and in a state of suspended animation and expectancy, with the elected-Sultan Ismail, still reigning in Kuala Kangsar where he had reigned since 1871, in possession of his seal of office and of the Perak regalia, and respecting ancient custom by continuing to live on the left bank of the river, while the treaty-Sultan Abdullah—the vanquished and discredited claimant of Larut—sat with his empty title and Ghee Hin influence at Batak Rabit, waiting upon events.

Events were soon to take place which will require us to re-adjust the spheres of influence both of the flag associations and of the chiefs' party as shown above.

THE COMMISSION OF SETTLEMENT OF THE LARUT DISTURBANCES

Under Clause XIII of the Treaty of Pangkor, a Commission was appointed to bring order into the chaos which had for so long obtained in Larut.

This pacification Commission was composed of Captain Dunlop, Mr. (afterwards Sir Frank) Swettenham, and Mr. Pickering. To the Commission were added Chang

Footnote.— (1) *E.P.O. Précis*, page 26.

Keng Kui, representing the Go-Kwans, (Tokong) and Chan Ah Yam, representing the See-Kwans (Triad). The Commission was assisted by Captain Speedy, Assistant Resident of Larut (*pro. tem.*), who had lately been in the service of the Mentri. The Commission was supposed to be aided also by the Mentri himself.

The Commission began its work on 23rd January, 1874, three days after the signing of the Treaty, and completed the work on 21st February. The Report of the Commissioners is contained in *Perak Papers, 1874–79* and includes a full and interesting journal kept by Sir Frank Swettenham, which contains plenty of evidence of the Mentri's and Chang Keng Kui's unwillingness to co-operate in the work, and intrigue between themselves. They, representing Tokong and Red Flag, and being the parties in possession, would, of course, have preferred to maintain the *status quo* and to keep the new Sultan and Triad and White Flag out of Larut.

Chang Keng Kui, with everything to lose by helping it, seems to have deserted the Commission about 10th February, but Chan Ah Yam, representing Triad and, therefore, with everything to gain, stuck on to the bitter end.

The obstacles put in the Commissioners' way, as described by Swettenham, were, as we can now see, the deliberate work of Tokong and Red Flag, who, no doubt, hoped by obstruction to mitigate for themselves the effects of the Treaty.

Tokong non-co-operation did not cease with the completion of the work of the pacification commission, but continued until the end of the next scene of the Perak drama, where it led to the murder of the first British Resident.

CHAPTER XIX

THE ASCENDANCY OF UNSEEN FORCES IN PERAK JANUARY, 1874
TO NOVEMBER, 1875

After the rush of events culminating in the Pangkor Engagement, the year 1874 was to a large extent one of suspended activity on the British side. Capt. Speedy, Chief of Police in the service of the Mentri for the three months immediately preceding the Treaty (under Governor Ord's recognition of the Mentri in September, 1873), was appointed by Sir Andrew Clarke "Assistant Resident" under the Treaty, but his functions were restricted to maintaining peace in Larut upon the terms of the Pacification Commission whose labours concluded in February, 1874. For the rest, the British were faced with the fact that there were now two Sultans in Perak, and a schism developed in the Perak River valley between the non-treaty party or the *Hulu* chiefs led by Sultan Ismail, and the treaty party or *Hilir* chiefs led by Sultan Abdullah. The schism was widened by the fact that the reigning-Sultan Ismail's title was unimpeachable, while the Treaty-Sultan Abdullah was freely referred to in the Malay records of the period as an illegitimate son, which was probably the real reason for the chiefs' original decision to reject him.

Two developments immediately followed the Treaty: Firstly, a prolonged attempt by the British Government to persuade Ismail to deliver up the Perak regalia, so that Sultan Abdullah might be installed. Secondly, a short-lived intrigue by Triad and White Flag hand-in-glove with Tokong and Red Flag to nullify the effects of the treaty by admitting Chinese capital to the country on Malay terms and not on those of the British Government.

There was also a move by Tokong and Red Flag, which did not pass the stage of a proposal and the retention of lawyers, to quash the Treaty by an appeal to the British Parliament.

In pursuance of the first objective Mr. J. W. W. Birch Colonial Secretary, Singapore,[1] accompanied by Swettenham, Assistant Secretary, Native States, was entrusted with a mission in April, 1874, to visit Sultan Ismail at his home at Blanja.

Birch came from the Ceylon Civil Service in 1870 and was unfamiliar with the Malay language and customs. It is not perhaps surprising that he was unsuccessful in his mission.

In pursuance of the second objective, after a preliminary exchange of views, Triad and the Hilir or White Flag chiefs attempted to exclude Tokong and the Hulu or Red Flag chiefs from any benefit from the inevitable penetration of Chinese capital throughout the State (which had previously been confined to Larut) by granting the exclusive monopoly of the revenue "farms" to Triad, under the terms of the bond given by Sultan Abdullah to Tan Kim Cheng in October, 1873. This move, if successful, would have had the effect of restricting Tokong's pickings to their old stamping ground in Larut, while leaving the rest of the State open to the undisputed exploitation of Triad.

THE PERIOD OF INTERREGNUM JAN.–NOV., 1874

No British Resident was appointed until November, 1874 and the period of suspended activity from the date of the Treaty 20-1-74 to the appointment of a Resident 1-11-74, gave a tactical advantage to Triad and Tokong which they were not slow to seize.

With no residential cat on the watch, tne Triad and Tokong mice had time to mobilise underground not only against one another, but also against the coming of the cat.

The interregnum, therefore, made Birch's difficulties, although he may not have realised it, all the greater. Pangkor was a triumph on paper for Triad and White Flag over Tokong and Red, but even the signatories made no attempt to keep the Treaty, and while Triad and White Flag sought to consolidate their position underground against the other camp, both camps were prepared to combine openly to oppose British intervention.

In February, 1874, meetings of protest against the Treaty were held by the Laxamana and other signatory chiefs, which suggests that they were not fully aware at the time, of the terms they had signed.

In March, 1874, the Mentri paid his lawyer R.C. Woods of Penang a retainer of $12,000 to prepare a case against the Treaty for presentation to Parliament. This move was vetoed by Sultan Abdullah, who feared for his newly won throne.

In June, 1874, Swettenham again visited Sultan Ismail at Blanja for the purpose of inducing him to meet the Governor at Penang, where it was hoped he would become a consenting party to the Treaty. The mission was again unsuccessful.

Footnote.—(1) For a sketch of his character and career in Malaya *see* Swettenham *Malay Sketches* (1895) Chapter XIX.

The appointment of Birch and the policy of Sir Andrew Clarke

Nevertheless, in discussing Sir Andrew Clarke's selection of Birch for the appointment of first Resident, Vetch *Life of Sir Andrew Clarke* page 176–177 has:—

> Mr. Birch's mission had been successful, and Sir Andrew felt himself justified in appointing him to be the first British Resident at Perak, Captain Speedy retaining the post of Assistant Resident at Larut. A letter from Sir Andrew to Mr. Birch shows with what care and personal attention the Governor watched the working of the new system:—
>
>   Singapore, 16th November, 1874.
>
> My dear Birch,
> "........ I must now content myself with saying that so far you seem to have done right well. I hope before you have got to Ismail you will have seen Yaha. Keep him with you, and make much of him, but be sure of him.
>
> Do not bother about the regalia, or any ceremony of making Abdullah sultan, and above all things I hope you will not forget to show every gentleness and deference to Ismail. Do not hurry him to any settlement of his own affairs, or to giving up anything. Interest him in inducing him to live where Abdullah will live, with a separate house, grounds, etc., and with all the honours of a sultan. Interest him in planting sugar, tobacco, etc. Swettenham has in this direction managed his old Sultan very well. The sooner you can get people to look at the land in Perak the better ....
>
> You will have to watch the Mentri with all your eyes, and urge Speedy to do the same. Speedy will still believe in him........ What is still more difficult for the Mentri to accept is that he could not have been in the position he is had we not interfered; and so in the same language you must gently but firmly tell Abdulla that I could never have given him any permission about the Krian or its revenues. I might have told him, and you can repeat it, that if he accepts in its entirety our advice, and by it rules his country justly, and keeps the peace to all and with all, what may be lost to him in the Krian will be more than made up elsewhere. I should make him, I mean induce him, to go with you everywhere. Tell him the Sultan of Selangor is doing it with Swettenham; that his doing so will make him stronger in his country, etc. In short, organise a regular "progress" with him, you, of course, taking care to be A. I. and the prominent figure.
>
> "P.S.—Why not make Abdullah his own Commissioner to settle boundaries with you?".

In further references to the views of the Colonial Office upon the method of intervention and to Sir Andrew Clarke's policy, Vetch *Life of Sir Andrew Clarke*, pages 162–164 has:—

> On the 6th March, 1874, the new Secretary of State for the Colonies, Lord Carnarvon, wrote his first brief official despatch to the Governor of the Straits Settlements, in which he gave a qualified approval of Sir Andrew Clarke's proceedings.
>
>   *   *   *
>
> At the same time Lord Carnarvon wrote semi-officially to assure him of the interest with which he watched Sir Andrew's action in the peninsula. He told him he was not disposed to quarrel with an extension of English influence rightly and easily developed, but he added the caution that we were entering upon new ground and relations of a somewhat delicate nature in our dealings with the Native States, and that though British Residents are an undoubted benefit to a State, yet through them we become much more closely connected than heretofore with things and persons and political combinations, that may easily lead us further than we intend to go. He impressed on Sir Andrew that this new phase of colonial policy needed careful watching by those on the spot, and would be easily jeopardised by precipitancy or immature ambition, and therefore much depended upon the personal character and ability of the Resident in each place. His anxiety he said, was that a policy so well begun should be continued on the same lines.
>
> Sir Andrew was in complete accord with the views expressed by Lord Carnarvon. The extension of British influence, he thought, should be very gradual, free from sensational development, inexpensive, and peaceful. No doubt some of his subordinates favoured stronger and more energetic measures, and were impatient at the slow development which was the Governor's policy, but Sir Andrew kept a tight control, and watched everything that went on in the Native States with a vigilant eye.

The main undercurrents of intrigue against the Treaty Jan.–Nov., 1874

It is not our purpose to attempt to label every individual of whom mention is made in these pages as being definitely either Triad and White or Tokong and Red Flag but enough has been disclosed to show, we believe beyond doubt, the two hostile underground camps into which Perak of those days was divided; so that if we are to follow the threads of this great underground intrigue it is only proper that we should indicate the camp, or colour of those whose probable attachments (if any) can be determined by inference.

It must be remembered that throughout the whole of official and unofficial records of the period 1870–1877, there is no mention of the White and Red Flag organisations which we have seen flourishing in Penang in 1867. It is only after Sir Hugh Low took charge in Perak that we find them again mentioned. Nevertheless during the period with which we are now dealing there will come to notice as actors in the Perak drama, some of the very same leaders of White and Red, whose acquaintance we made in Penang in 1867. The authorities in those days were clearly not aware of the extensive and unseen rival organisations of White and Red and Triad and Tokong into which the Malays and Chinese of Perak were divided. Their absence from the records need not, therefore, surprise us. During the interregnum period (Jan.–Nov., 1874) the main undercurrents of intrigue were:—

     (1) Triad and White Flag trying to establish Abdullah so as to make good their agreement with him about the farms and so establish their stake in the country.

(2) Tokong and Red Flag trying to maintain their *status quo;* while Ismail remained in possession of the regalia, and therefore *de facto* Sultan, thereby resisting the encroachment of Triad and White Flag, particularly upon their Larut interests.

(3) Both camps anxious to find ways and means of breaking the Treaty so as to keep the British out and themselves in.

Birch arrived at Batak Rabit as Resident on 4th of November, 1874 and thereafter whilst the above currents of intrigue continued, he was met, from different motives, by the combined current of opposition, open and secret, of both camps arrayed against him in pursuit of the third objective above.

His was an impossible task from the first and it required his own sacrifice and that "whiff of powder", referred to later by Raja Yusuf, to drive these forces underground, where they have since remained.

Reviewed from the angle of Triad and Tokong intrigue, the précis of evidence in the *E.P.O.* is a mine of revealing information.

In order to show that intrigue at work, it is necessary to present here in numbered sequence an outline of the historical events covering the period from the signing of the Treaty to the death of the First Resident appointed under it.

Comment has been added upon some of these events in the body of the summary, and other special features are discussed separately below it.

SKELETON SEQUENCE OF EVENTS FEB., 1874–NOV., 1875

(1)	21- 1-1874.	Sultan Abdullah returned to Batak Rabit well pleased with the Treaty except Article XI (the Dindings Clause) about which he had misgivings. This clause is discussed below.
(2)	Jan.-Feb., 1874. *(Ref. E.P.O. Precis page 4).*	The Laxamana at once became the spearhead of opposition to the Treaty among Sultan Abdullah's supporters and several meetings were held by him with other signatory chiefs to express their dissatisfaction particularly with the Dindings clause.
(3)	5- 2-1874. *(Ref. E.P.O. "Evidence", Section A, page 1).*	Tan Kim Cheng sent one of his Revenue Farm partners—a Bugis trader named Nakodah Traang—from Singapore to Perak to see Sultan Abdullah, with three letters *viz:*— (1) To Sultan Abdullah congratulating him upon his accession. (2) To Raja Yusuf reminding him that the writer's agreement with Abdullah had been fulfilled and expressing a hope that Raja Yusuf would be confirmed as Raja Muda. (3) To Bendahara Raja Osman, asking him to use his influence with Sultan Ismail to get him to surrender the regalia.

Comment.—This move shows clearly the hand of Tan Kim Cheng, the Triad kingmaker, still guiding events and anxious to consolidate Abdullah's precarious position as Sultan; and his own with Abdullah's likely successor, Raja Muda Yusuf.

It shows moreover that Tan Kim Cheng was perfectly well aware that Raja Osman was *de facto* Bendahara and Ismail *de facto* and *de jure* Sultan. Kim Cheng had won a slam at Pangkor and was anxious to have his score above the line chalked up to Triad. He had yet to win the rubber against Tokong.

(4)	February, 1874. *(Ref. E.P.O. Evidence page 1).*	Abdullah sent a message to Tan Kim Cheng that he would not recognise Raja Yusuf as Raja Muda and that, if he were firmly established as Sultan, he would hand over the country to the British.
(5)	18- 2-1874. *(Ref. E.P.O. Precis page 4).*	Sultan Abdullah sent an agent Haji Hoosein ("a native broker of Penang") to consult with Mr. Duke, the lawyer employed by Triad and White Flag in Penang, whether the Dindings clause could be rescinded.
(6)	25- 2-1874.	Sultan Abdullah sent a letter to Sir Andrew Clarke asking that a British Resident might be appointed at once, as well as a boundary Commissioner to fix the Dindings boundary.
(7)	March, 1874.	Sultan Abdullah began raising money for himself by selling concessions in land in Krian.
(8)	March, 1874.	The Shahbandar wrote to Nakodah Traang the White Flag associate of Tan Kim Cheng in Singapore, that Sultan Abdullah and the Laxamana were going to let the Perak Farms to Che Ah Him[1] of Penang.
(9)	April, 1874.	Lee Cheng Tee, Koh (? Goh) Soh Swee, Nakodah Traang and Dyang Ismail (Triad and White Flag tenderers for the Farms) went from Singapore to Perak to interview Sultan Abdullah.
(10)	April, 1874. *(Ref. E.P.O. Precis page 4).*	Birch and Swettenham undertook a joint mission to Sultan Ismail at Blanja to persuade him to give up the regalia. After a fortnight's stay they returned unsuccessful.

Footnote.—(1) Not identified under this spelling, but perhaps it stands for Chan Ah Yam (陳 亞 炎) titular leader of the Cantonese Triad lodge in Penang since August, 1873 (*see* Chapter XVIII). This person is described in the *E.P.O.* Glossary as, "Che Him, a Penang merchant".

Comment.—Their failure was attributed to the prompting of Ismail by the Mentri and the Laxamana, who saw in Ismail's refusal a means to break the Treaty.

(11)	April, 1874. (*Ref. E.P.O.* *Precis page 4*).	Birch and Swettenham had a cordial meeting with Sultan Abdullah at Batak Rabit and the latter expressed a strong wish on this occasion that Birch should be sent to Perak as Resident.
(12)	April, 1874. (*Ref. E.P.O.* *Precis page 4*).	The Mentri consulted Mr. R. C. Woods, the lawyer employed by Tokong and Red Flag in Penang, and paid him $12,000 to dispute the legality of the Treaty before Parliament. The Mentri also arranged for Woods to go to Blanja to interview Sultan Ismail and Raja Yusuf on the subject.
(13)	5- 6-1874.	Sultan Ismail addressed a letter for the first time to the Governor, regretting his inability to attend at Pangkor, not having received the summons in time; and putting forward his own claims to the Sultanate as the reason for his not having given up the regalia.
(14)	6- 6-1874.	Swettenham visited Blanja again for the purpose of inducing Sultan Ismail and Raja Yusuf to meet the Governor in Penang, where it was hoped they would become consenting parties to the Treaty. Ismail declined, but sent Raja Yusuf and Dato Nara with Swettenham to Penang as his representatives.
(15)	July, 1874.	Raja Yusuf and Dato Nara interviewed the Governor in Penang, but declined to accept on behalf of Sultan Ismail, the terms of settlement offered.
(16)	10- 7-1874.	The Governor in Penang wrote to Sultan Ismail in reply to his letter of 5-6-1874, offering him more favourable terms.
(17)	July, 1874.	Braddell visited Sultan Abdullah at Batak Rabit and warned him against granting revenue concessions without the Governor's consent.
(18)	July, 1874.	Two days after Braddell's departure, Abdullah granted the Perak Farms to Lee Cheng Tee (Tan Kim Cheng's nominee) for $26,000 for one year, receiving $13,000 in advance. The transaction was in the name of the Shahbandar in view of Braddell's warning.
(19)	18- 8-1874.	The Governor in Singapore wrote again to Sultan Ismail offering him still more definite terms of settlement and sent the letter by hand of Pickering and Raja Yahya,[1] adopted son of Ismail and one of his agents.
(20)	8- 9-1874.	Sultan Ismail replied to the Governor's letter of 18-8-1874 that he resigned all his affairs into the hands of the British Government.
(21)	5-10-1874.	The Governor received a report that Sultan Ismail had consulted Mr. Woods with a view to opposing the Treaty (*see* Item 12 above).
(22)	12-10-1874.	The Governor wrote to Sultan Ismail warning him of the folly of such action and sent the letter by hand of Raja Yahya. On his way to Blanja *via* Penang and Larut, Raja Yahya received confirmation that Woods was then on a visit to Ismail.

Comment.—Ismail was probably lukewarm and was being used by the Mentri who was thoroughly determined to set aside the Treaty.

(23)	16-10-1874. (*E.P.O. Precis* *page 5*).	Meeting at Blanja, at which the following non-Treaty (Red Flag) chiefs were present:— Sultan Ismail; R. C. Woods (Tokong lawyer in Penang); The Mentri; Raja Yusuf; The Temenggong; Panglima Kinta; Dato' Nara; Sadika Raja (Syed Mohamed); Sri Maharaja Lela; Tuan Chee (of Province Wellesley); Haji Aboobakar (of Province Wellesley). At which the following resolutions were passed:— (1) That the regalia was not to be surrendered to Sultan Abdullah. (2) That Raja Yusuf, Woods and Haji Aboobakar were to go to England to represent matters. (3) That if any attempt should be made by the Treaty party to obtain the regalia by force, Sultan Ismail should supply fighting men to oppose it, who should be under the command of Tuan Chee. (4) That arms, ammunition and a war chest for the purpose should be supplied by the Mentri. (5) That $25,000 should be paid to Woods by the Mentri as soon as possible.

Comment.—This shows that Red Flag was prepared on paper for a civil war against White Flag if need be, to break the Treaty, even before the arrival of the first Resident.

(24)	25-10-1874. (*E.P.O. Precis* *page 4 and* *Evidence Sec-* *tion A, page 1*).	Meeting at Lee Cheng Tee's "farm" (Item 18 above) at Kota Blanda at the mouth of the Perak River, at which were present Sultan Abdullah, the Mentri, the Laxamana, the Shahbandar, Raja Mahkota and the Dato' Mata Mata. At this meeting the Laxamana proposed that Sultan Abdullah should give full powers to the Mentri

Footnote.—(1) In much of the correspondence this man is referred to in error as Haji Yahya. His correct style appears to have been Raja Haji Yahya.

to govern the whole of Perak and to take up the matter of the Treaty and have it set aside, in England if necessary, because a British Resident was about to be appointed who would demand such powers from Sultan Abdullah, if he had not already given them to the Mentri. Abdullah at first agreed but on taking advice from Lee Cheng Tee who pointed out to him that he would no longer be Sultan if he did so, Abdullah though annoyed with Cheng Tee for the advice, finally refused.

Comment.—Here we see Tokong and Red Flag (represented by the Mentri) ten days after the Blanja meeting, scheming to oust Triad and White Flag from the big money, using the plausible argument of their mutual dislike of the Treaty as a means to persuade the fickle Abdullah and so avoid the danger of civil war. Only for the presence of Triad's agent Lee Cheng Tee who saw through the manœuvre, this scheme might have succeeded in further complicating the tangled skein of Perak politics, even before the arrival of the Resident.

(25)   4-11-1874.   Arrival of Mr. J. W. W. Birch, Colonial Secretary, Singapore as first British Resident, Perak (Item 11 above).

(26)   4-11-1874.   Birch spent the night at Kota Blanda and interviewed Lee Cheng Tee there, demanding by what right he was collecting taxes contrary to Braddell's recent instructions (Item 17 above). Cheng Tee was evasive, but under pressure confessed that he was collecting under an agreement with the Shahbandar. To this Birch replied that the arrangement would not be approved, but when the farm was put up for regular tender, he would be glad if Lee Cheng Tee would compete for it and Birch would see that Cheng Tee did not suffer by the change.

Comment.—And so from the first moment of his arrival, Birch was caught up in the swirls and eddies of Triad and Tabut intrigue.

How was he to know that Lee Cheng Tee was Triad's dummy and the place-man of Tan Kim Cheng? How was he to know that the "arrangement with the Shahbandar" had been made by Sultan Abdullah at Tan Kim Cheng's behest? This "arrangement" was one of the first-fruits of the Treaty of Pangkor and was made in fulfilment of Abdullah's bargain with Triad of October, 1873, (see page 271 Item 35 and page 283 Item 4 supra)—a fulfilment Abdullah had tried to evade, until Triad had installed Lee Cheng Tee on his doorstep. Birch could not know that long before his arrival as Resident the pitch had been queered against him, both in the political sphere which he had a right to think would be regulated by the terms of the Treaty; and much more so in the administrative sphere which he had come to develop. Everyman's hand was, for different reasons, politely but covertly against him from the start. He had no means of knowing that the men he came amongst were mostly the puppets of powerful unseen forces; Or that Tan Kim Cheng was other than what he had always taken him to be namely, a disinterested if influential Chinese resident of Singapore, who had helped the British to contrive the Treaty of Pangkor and who thereafter continued to enjoy confidence and to act as unofficial adviser on Chinese affairs to the Government in Singapore. The only European officer who seems to have suspected Tan Kim Cheng's bona fides was Colonel Anson, who on 4-7-1873 had written to the Colonial Secretary (Birch), vide Chapter XVII page 275 supra. "I have little confidence in anything being satisfactorily arranged by Mr. Kim Cheng".

(27)   5-11-1874.   Birch had his first meeting as Resident with Sultan Abdullah, the Shahbandar, Raja Mahkota and others; and laid before them the outline of his scheme for the better government of the country, which included:—
    (1) The establishment of a single opium "farm" for the whole of Perak.
    (2) The collection of taxes on all the rivers by Government officers.

(28)   8-11-1874.   Birch reached Bandar which he made his temporary headquarters. Three days association with Sultan Abdullah had caused him to alter his opinion of his character which he recorded as unstable, foolish and debauched.

(29)   16-11-1874.   Indignation meeting of signatory chiefs held at Durian Sa'batarg at which dissatisfaction was expressed at the proposals, Item 27 above.

(30)	21-11-1874.	Birch interviewed Sultan Ismail and the non-Treaty chiefs at Blanja with a view to arranging a meeting between Sultan Ismail and Sultan Abdullah, and received an outwardly favourable reception.
(31)	23-11-1874.	Before leaving Blanja, Sultan Ismail and Raja Yusuf stated verbally to Birch that they were willing to acknowledge Sultan Abdullah and sign the Treaty of Pangkor.

Comment.—The two immediately preceding items were, no doubt, the result of the Mentri's prompting, so as not to antagonise the Resident, until matters arranged on 16-10-74 (Item 23 above) had developed further.

(32)	24-11-1874.	Birch returned to Bandar and found a letter from Penang (presumably from Anson) reporting to him the meeting at Blanja of 16-10-1874 (Item 23 above).

Comment.—After this disclosure within three weeks of his arrival, Birch could have been no longer in any doubt of the extent of intrigue against him and the magnitude of the task before him.

(33)	25-11-1874.	Birch's second visit as Resident to Sultan Abdullah at Batak Rabit for the dual purpose of:— (a) Issuing a proclamation by Sir Andrew Clarke dated 2-11-1874, notifying the signatory chiefs that H.M. Government would hold them responsible for observing the provisions of the Treaty. (b) Reporting the success of his visit to the non-signatory chiefs upstream.

Comment.—A reaction against Birch had set in at Batak Rabit between 5-11 and 25-11-74 (E.P.O. Precis page 5, foot) as a result of his proposals for the better government of the country and his method of presenting them. The signatory chiefs had taken fright (Item 29 above).

(34)	26-11-1874. (E.P.O. Precis page 6 top).	While outwardly expressing pleasure at the reported success of Birch's visit to Sultan Ismail, the signatory chiefs sent urgent word to Ismail, on no account to sign the Treaty or surrender the regalia, lest Birch's authority would thereby be strengthened and he would be able to do what he liked in Perak.

Comment.—Within a month of Birch's arrival, Red and White Flag are thus shown to have been about to make common cause against him personally, as well as against the Treaty which was responsible for his presence.

(35)	13-12-1874.	Birch visiting Bidor burnt down the house of Tengku Panglima Besar (Raja Ngah) for levying "blackmail" on tin-miners.

Comment.—This was a hasty act to which Birch appears to have been moved by the false representations of the Laxamana, who sought thereby a means of antagonising the non-signatory chiefs against Birch and so undoing the effect of Item 31 above. In this the Laxamana was successful.

(36)	14—20-12-1874.	Birch sought to move Sultan Abdullah to accompany him upstream to Blanja to meet Sultan Ismail and receive the regalia.
(37)	18-12-1874.	Tuan Chee and Haji Aboobakar of the Red Flag went from Province Wellesley to Blanja to join with Raja Yusuf there in frustrating the meeting of the two Sultans, leaving a party of armed men at Bruas ready for any emergency.
(38)	19-12-1874.	Birch sent Speedy and a body of the Larut Sikh Police to Bruas to arrest these armed men.
(39)	24-12-1874.	Sultan Abdullah with Birch left Batak Rabit unwillingly for Blanja, with the expressed intention of not accepting the regalia from Ismail.
(40)	29-12-1874.	Birch and Abdullah reached Bota and Birch went ahead to Blanja and interviewed Sultan Ismail, Raja Yusuf, Tuan Chee and Haji Aboobakar and put the latter under open arrest.
(41)	30-12-1874.	The Mentri made contact with Sultan Abdullah at Bota during Birch's absence, to further ensure the frustration of the imminent meeting (E.P.O. Precis page 7). As a result, Abdullah sent a letter overland to Ismail saying he was coming upstream unwillingly at Birch's desire and that Ismail was on no account to give up the regalia; even if Abdullah were to ask him for it in the presence of Birch, he must refuse, otherwise "the country of Perak will be given over to the English".
(42)	31-12-1874.	Birch returned to Bota and was informed of the Mentri's visit and of the conversation he had with the Sultan. Birch enquired of Abdullah who admitted it, but concealed the fact that he had sent the above letter to Sultan Ismail.
(43)	2- 1-1875.	Birch and Abdullah arrived at Blanja, where the next eighteen days were spent in frozen negotiations for the surrender of the regalia.

(44)	18- 1-1875.	Birch wrote a formal letter to Ismail, informing him that he proposed to leave Blanja on the following day unless he received a satisfactory answer from him.
(45)	19- 1-1875.	To this ultimatum Ismail replied firmly but respectfully that in the peculiar circumstances of the making of the Pangkor Treaty, he was at a loss what to answer and asked for an interview with the Governor at Bruas.
(46)	20- 1-1875.	Birch and Sultan Abdullah left Blanja.

Comment.—All the objects of the meeting between the two Sultans were thus frustrated according to plan, by the unseen forces of the Red and White Flag. This is one of the rare occasions upon which they worked together for a brief time, for a given object.

(47)	21- 1-1875.	Sultan Abdullah stopped at Pasir Telor and Birch went on downstream without him. Abdullah entered into some negotiations with Ismail through the Laxamana whereby Ismail was to surrender the regalia to Abdullah without the intervention of the British. Raja Yusuf appears to have got wind of these negotiations and quashed them.
(48)	25- 1-1875.	Sultan Abdullah who feared Raja Yusuf above any one in Perak rejoined Birch at Pasir Panjang.
(49)	31- 1-1875.	A site for the Residency was chosen at Ayer Mati above Bandar, and was henceforth known as Bandar Bahru.
(50)	3- 2-1875.	Birch presented two proclamations to Sultan Abdullah on the subject of the collection of revenue, on the lines proposed in Item 27 above. Abdullah declined to sign them until after consultation with his chiefs.

Comment.—These proclamations became an acute bone of contention between Birch and Abdullah and his supporters for the next eight months. They or similar proclamations were finally "chopped" by the Sultan on 2nd October, 1875 (see items 145 and 157 below) and a month later Birch was dead.

(51)	10- 2-1875.	Birch went to Larut to arrange for the collection of taxes by authorised persons. Before leaving he pressed Abdullah to sign the two proclamations, the latter temporised.
(52)	11- 2-1875.	Birch took with him to Larut Haji Hoosein and two clerks of Sultan Abdullah, named Abdullah and Yusuf, to assist in keeping the revenue accounts there.
(53)	12—18- 2-1875.	Birch in Larut insisted against the advice of Speedy, upon the grant of mining land to an European (Mr. Knaggs) whose application had been approved by Sultan Abdullah. The Mentri disputed Sultan Abdullah's right to grant such approval in Larut.
(54)	18- 2-1875.	Birch left Larut for Penang and the clerk Yusuf asked leave to return to Bandar as he was afraid of the Mentri; who had warned him to leave Larut.
(55)	7- 3-1875.	Sultan Abdullah, having been informed by the Mentri that the clerk Yusuf was acting as a spy for Birch, had Yusuf murdered by Raja Musa at Bandar on the grounds that he could not be trusted.
(56)	10- 3-1875.	Abdullah visited Maharaja Lela at Pasir Salak; took over the Bendahara's revenue farm at Kuala Kinta for $300 a month; sent a trusted messenger Kundah Mat Yassin to Dato Nara with a letter saying that if Sultan Ismail was willing to give up the regalia and acknowledge him as Sultan, Abdullah was ready to go up the Kinta; sent another letter to Panglima Kinta asking him to come down and escort him up the Kinta.

Comment.—This move indicated an intention on the part of Abdullah and his supporters at that time to combine with Sultan Ismail in opposing Birch by force if necessary upon his return. The move did not, however, at that time lead to any definite developments.

| (57) | 15- 3-1875. | Sultan Abdullah convened his chiefs at Kuala Kinta to discuss the two proclamations (Item 50 above). It was then arranged that Abdullah should delegate Laxamana, Shahbandar, Orang Kaya Mat Arshad and Dato' Sago to represent him before Birch in all matters of State. A formal instrument (Kuasa) to this effect was prepared and signed by Abdullah. |
| (58) | 19- 3-1875. | Birch returned from Penang to Bandar and sent Nakodah Traang to Sultan Ismail with a letter from the Governor conferring upon him the title of Sultan Baginda. |

Comment.—This unhappy man had hitherto been known to the British authorities as the Bendahara, the temporary Sultan, the Deputy Sultan, the Sultan Muda, the Raja Muda, the Sultan Tua, the Ex-Sultan, and now this. It is true that had he been offered this particular title at the right time it might have mollified him into acceptance of the Treaty. The award came a year too late. He had already made his choice. His honorifics did not help him; within a year he was a fugitive, but he still clung to the regalia.

(59)	20- 3-1875.	Birch met Abdullah at Kuala Kinta and chided him upon his actions during Birch's absence. Abdullah expressed his desire to be free of the control of a British Resident and refused for several days to see Birch who returned to Bandar Bahru.
(60)	21- 3-1875.	The *Kuasa* (Item 57 above) was presented to Birch by the Laxamana and other delegates. Birch refused to recognise it.
(61)	25- 3-1875.	Upon Nakodah Traang's intervention Abdullah agreed to see Birch who again pressed Abdullah to sign the two proclamations. Abdullah again temporised.
(62)	25- 3-1875.	The Mentri arrived in his own steamer at Durian Sa'batang for the purpose of removing his family to a place of safety in anticipation of disturbances.
(63)	25- 3-1875.	The Mentri and Laxamana called on Birch who accompanied them to see Abdullah at Kuala Kinta, hoping that now the Mentri was present, Abdullah would decide to sign the two proclamations.
(64)	26- 8-1875.	Formal meeting of chiefs with Birch at Kuala Kinta. Present: Abdullah, Laxamana, Shahbandar, Mentri, Dato Sagor, Orang Kaya Mat Arshad. Birch again explained his proposals for revenue collection and general government. After a discussion of five hours, the chiefs rejected the proposals. After Birch had left, the Mentri renewed his proposal of 25-10-1874 (Item 24 above) that Abdullah should give him his authority to dispute the validity of the Treaty at law. Abdullah again refused to grant it.
(65)	27- 3-1875.	Birch went to Penang in connection with the letting of the opium farm.
(66)	30- 3-1875.	The Mentri returned to Larut taking with him all his family and dependents from Durian Sa'batang.
(67)	31- 3-1875.	Sultan Abdullah went to Pasir Salak to visit the Maharaja Lela, who was building a strong stockade round his house.

Comment.—The foregoing events marked a crisis in Birch's brief career in Perak. The points we have given make it clear that little blame could be laid upon him for finding himself baffled at every turn by the intangible hostility and opposition of both Red and White Tabut, of whose very existence he was ignorant. The trend of events also points to a hardening of the determination of both White and Red supporters to combine in resisting the British connection by force if need be. From this point the arena began to be prepared for combat.

After five months' effort, Birch felt that he had made no progress towards the fulfilment of the mission with which he had been charged. Quite wrongly he seems to have thought that some kind of written authority from the Sultan or delegation of powers to himself to act in the Sultan's name was necessary before he could hope to make progress. Insistence upon this *Kuasa* was the real reason of the breach that followed. In fact no such instrument was required nor has ever been given by a Sultan to his Resident. The Resident rules through the Sultan not the Sultan through the Resident. To seek to do so was Birch's only mistake.

It should also be remembered that his instruction contained the following:—

> "You will use your best exertions to put down, by force if necessary, all unlawful exactions of whatever nature so as to secure that whatever revenue is collected, shall be for the State alone and that freebooters, leviers of blackmail and chiefs pretending authority to levy duty, may be hindered in their extortions and all revenue collected may be paid into the general treasury of the country".

Birch, no doubt, took these instructions too literally. He was over-enthusiastic and forgot the virtue of *festina lente*. Anyone who knows the country to-day would hesitate to claim that after the labour of sixty-five years those instructions have even yet been entirely fulfilled. Birch failed to adjust himself to the Malays and expected them to adjust themselves to him. He was too sternly objective. He was greatly handicapped by having no first-hand knowledge of Malays and did not speak their language. With a little more understanding, sympathy and subjectivity he might have had the Perak world at his feet. Instead, he died with everyman's hand against him. It was at this time that he was insolently spoken of as, "Only a Dutch sailor, with nothing to fill his belly with, so he came to Perak to collect the livelihood of others".

(68)   11- 4-1875.   Birch returned from Penang (Item 65) and tried to induce Abdullah to return with him to Penang to see Sir Andrew Clarke, who was relinquishing his appointment in May, 1875, and returning to India. Abdullah refused and Birch went back to Penang taking the Laxamana with him.

(69)   21- 4-1875.   Sir Andrew left Penang for Singapore by the *Pluto* and stopped at Pangkor, where he wrote Abdullah a stiff letter of reproof for his conduct and reminding him of the terms of the Treaty.

(70)   24- 4-1875.   After receipt of the Governor's letter, Sultan Abdullah called upon Birch who was then back at Bandar Bahru and expressed penitence for his conduct and readiness to do anything he was called upon to do.

(71)   26- 4-1875.   Birch met Sultan Ismail in Kinta and was well received and gave him an invitation from the Governor to visit him in Singapore. Ismail declined for the genuine reason that his child was ill.

(72)   27- 4-1875.   Raja Yahya conveyed a message to Ismail from Birch, asking him to sign the Treaty or else to give Birch a *Kuasa* or authority of some kind. Ismail replied that he would never sign the Treaty, but would give Birch a *Kuasa* if he were recognised as Sultan.

(73)   26- 4-1875.   As soon as Birch's back was turned in Kinta, Sultan Abdullah by the advice of the Laxamana organised a deputation of three to go to Singapore and represent Sultan Abdullah's grievances against Birch to the Governor in person and also to get into touch again with Tan Kim Cheng.

Comment.—This move referred to again separately below was typical of Sultan Abdullah's double-dealing, two days after giving Birch a voluntary promise to co-operate. The deputation was composed of The Laxamana, Orang Kaya Mat Arshad and Raja Idris with Haji Hoosein co-opted and carried two letters (1) to the Governor Sir Andrew Clarke (2) to Tan Kim Cheng.

The letter to the Governor stated that Sultan Äbdullah was in great trouble and that the members of the deputation would explain his difficulties and grievances verbally to His Excellency. As Sir Andrew Clarke was relinquishing the Governorship, he asked for a written instrument confirming him in his title as Sultan, so that the new Governor could not repudiate him.

The points to be verbally submitted to the Governor were:—

    (1) That Birch should refrain from interference in matters of religion and custom.

    (2) That Birch should do nothing without consent of the Sultan and chiefs.

    (3) That Birch should not abolish hereditary taxes of the chiefs, which represented their customary dues.

    (4) That Birch should surrender certain run-away slaves and others who had taken sanctuary with him at Bandar Bahru.

    (5) That Birch should surrender all slaves who had escaped to Pangkor Island (British Territory) before his arrival in Perak.

The letter to Tan Kim Cheng requested him to come to Perak and undertake the collection of the revenue of Larut under the bond which Abdullah had given him in October, 1873 (*see* page 271 (35) and page 283 (4) *supra*), and so support Sultan Abdullah's authority against Birch.

We may also assume that this was a cunning attempt to get Triad into the Larut Revenue Farm and so effectually oust the Mentri and Tokong from their claims on the Larut revenues.

(74)   1- 5-1875. (*circa*).   The deputation left secretly for Singapore without Birch's knowledge. Raja Idris, Orang Kaya Mat Arshad and Haji Hoosein arrived some days earlier than the Laxamana and fearing the Laxamana was not coming they went first to Tan Kim Cheng, gave him the Sultan's letter and asked him, in the absence of the Laxamana, to take them before Sir Andrew Clarke.

Comment.—Thus when White Flag, left to their own devices in Perak for fifteen months under the Triad eye of Lee Cheng Tee at Kota Stia, found political complications becoming too acute after six months contact with the Resident, they turned again for guidance to Tan Kim Cheng. That astute gentleman as a proof of good faith had already after Pangkor handed over to the British the bond Abdullah had given him in October, 1873. This gesture, no doubt, strengthened Tan Kim Cheng's reputation with the British in Singapore as a straight-forward and reliable business man and cost him nothing. Triad interests were already secured in Perak by Lee Cheng Tee, while Abdullah's bond of October, 1873 was a useful document with which to impress the British authorities with the erroneous idea that Tan Kim Cheng had a just claim against Sultan Abdullah, and so make sure of juicy pickings when conditions stabilised. Tan Kim Cheng, therefore, declined to aid the deputation. He had nothing to gain by doing so and much prestige with the British to earn by being able to say afterwards that he had been approached to assist the now discredited Sultan Abdullah, but had declined to do so.

In the midst of these manoevres the hand on the helm was again changed.

(75)	7- 5-1875. (circa).	The Laxamana arrived in Singapore and headed the deputation to Sir Andrew Clarke, but had to wait for an interview as the new Governor's arrival was imminent.
(76)	10- 5-1875. (circa).	Arrival of the new Governor, Sir William Jervoise, who remained some days with Sir Andrew Clarke before taking office.
(77)	16- 5-1875.	Sir William Jervoise took office.
(78)	17- 5-1875. (circa).	The Laxamana and deputation had a long interview with Sir Andrew Clarke to whom they fully explained their grievances against Birch. They got no satisfaction. Sir Andrew rated them saying that Sultan Abdullah should have replied to his letter written from Pangkor (Item 69 above), before sending such a deputation and that all Sultan Abdullah's troubles were the result of his own fault in not following Birch's advice.
(79)	17 -5-1875.	Sir Andrew as the ex-Governor who had "lifted him out of his misery and sorrow, giving him position and honour", wrote a private letter to Sultan Abdullah, exhorting him as to his conduct towards the new Governor.
(80)	18- 5-1875.	The deputation had an interview with Sir William Jervoise, but made no complaint to him against Birch.
(81)	19- 5-1875. (Ref. E.P.O. Evidence C page 12).	The members of the deputation, angry at the result of their interview, called upon Nakodah Traang in Singapore (a member of White Flag and partner with Tan Kim Cheng in the Kota Stia farm) and asked him on behalf of Sultan Abdullah to offer Tan Kim Cheng a ten year Kuasa, if he would go to Perak and keep Birch in check. Nakodah Traang declined to give the message.
(82)	25- 5-1875. (circa).	The deputation returned from Singapore to Perak.
(83)	10- 5-1875.	Birch returned to Bandar Bahru from Kinta (Item 71 above) and learned from Haji Ali, a Red Flag adherent and supporter of Ismail, of the departure of the White Flag deputation secretly to Singapore.
(84)	10—17- 5-1875.	There was much rumour-mongering in Perak and an attack by Red Flag chiefs upon Bandar Bahru was anticipated. Lee Cheng Tee fortified the Customs House at Kota Stia. Nothing eventuated.
(85)	17- 5-1875.	Birch left Bandar Bahru for Penang to say good-bye to the departing Sir Andrew Clarke at Penang.
(86)	25- 5-1875.	Sir Andrew left Singapore for Penang on his way to India. On the same steamer were Raja Idris and the Laxamana, two members of the returning deputation. They gave Birch in Penang a garbled version of their interview at Government House.
(87)	4- 6-1875.	Birch returned to Perak, where the one-year lease of the Kota Stia farm by Abdullah through the Shahbandar to Lee Cheng Tee (Items 18 and 26 above) was shortly due to expire and there was a balance of $4,000 due to the Shahbandar which Birch had ordered Lee Cheng Tee not to pay. An altercation took place between Birch and the Shahbandar, Birch threatening him with expulsion from the country if he obstructed. This incident sharpened feelings against Birch.
(88)	8- 6-1875.	Birch interviewed Sultan Abdullah, Shahbandar and Raja Idris on the subject of taxation and threatened to have Sultan Abdullah and the Shahbandar turned out of the country if they continued to obstruct the measures he proposed. Birch gave them to 20th July to make up their minds.
(89)	11- 6-1875.	Birch went to Penang to get the Laxamana who was still there, to go to Krian and fix the boundaries under Article XII, of the Treaty. The Laxamana evaded Birch and returned to Durian Sa'batang.

Comment.—He had been in Penang since 28th May after leading his unfruitful deputation to Singapore and had seemingly been in touch with Red Flag leaders there during this time, as will appear later.

(90)	20- 6-1875. (circa).	Sultan Abdullah, seemingly at the instigation of the Laxamana, sent circulars to all the major chiefs both signatory and non-signatory, summoning them to an emergency meeting at Durian Sa'batang to consult about the affairs of Perak with reference to Birch.

(91)   10- 7-1875.   Birch met Tan Kim Cheng in Larut who had come to Perak to look after Triad interests and to see Sultan Abdullah as a result of Abdullah's letter to him of 1-5-1875 (Items 73 and 74).

(92)   14- 7-1875.   Birch reached Kuala Kangsar on his way back to Bandar Bahru overland from Larut, having arranged to meet Tan Kim Cheng again at Kota Stia on 22-7-1874.

At Kuala Kangsar, Birch received overtures from Raja Ngah, Tengku Panglima Besar, a cousin of Sultan Ismail (*see* Item 35), and separately from the Mentri, Temenggong and Bendahara and also independently from Raja Yusuf advising Birch of Sultan Abdullah's urgent summons to them to a council (Item 90 above) and hinting that they were in favour of the British taking over the country rather than allow "that puppet Abdullah", to remain on the throne.

Comment.—This was a move by the Red Flag chiefs to ingratiate themselves with Birch, whose patience with Abdullah was fast running out in which they saw the chance of substituting their patron Sultan Ismail for Abdullah under the Treaty, without forcing the issue to a decision by bloodshed. The reference to Abdullah as a "puppet" could only mean that they knew him to be the puppet of Triad, whose representative Tan Kim Cheng had again made his appearance in Perak just at that juncture. The reference could not have meant that they regarded Abdullah as the puppet of the British Government, seeing that the cause of the deadlock was Abdullah's refusal to be the latter's puppet.

(93)   18- 7-1875.   Birch reached Bandar Bahru and on 20th July, Raja Yahya following upon the above overtures, called upon him and said that Sultan Ismail was willing to allow the British to govern the country if only he were recognised as Sultan. Raja Yahya offered Birch four blank papers with Sultan Ismail's "chop" on them for Birch to fill up and address to himself (Ismail) or the new Governor, as Birch might think best, in order to strengthen Ismail's position. Birch declined to act as suggested and on the evening of 21-7-1875 left Bandar Bahru for Kota Stia to keep his appointment with Tan Kim Cheng (Item 92 above).

(94)   21- 7-1875.   The emergency meeting (Item 90 above) was held by Sultan Abdullah in the house of Haji Mat Yassin at Durian Sa'batang. There were present (1) Kundah Mohamed, with a written proxy from the Bendahara; (2) Wan Hussein with a proxy from the Temenggong; (3) Penghulu Mat Ali of Kurau with a proxy from the Mentri; and the following in person:—

(4) Laxamana;	(10) Raja Idris;
(5) Maharaja Lela;	(11) Raja Ahmat;
(6) Dato Sagor;	(12) Raja Musa;
(7) Shahbandar;	(13) Dato Muda Rappa;
(8) Orang Kaya Mat Arshad;	(14) Haji Mat Yassin
(9) Raja Mahkota;	and several others.

Comment.—This was a meeting of great importance and was held with formality, all present being seated according to rank. Sultan Abdullah opened the proceedings by reading a letter purporting to be from Sultan Ismail saying he would agree to whatever "his grandson" (*i.e.* Sultan Abdullah) and the Laxamana (*see* Items 89 and 90 above) might decide upon, in order to kill Birch. The Laxamana suggested poison, and after some discussion the Maharaja Lela volunteered to stab him. This decision was approved and confirmed by a secret oath. This meeting is further discussed separately below.

(95)   22- 7-1875.   Haji Hoosein arrived at Durian Sa'batang with a message for Sultan Abdullah from Tan Kim Cheng at Kota Stia saying that if Abdullah did not come at once for an interview he would wait no longer. Abdullah left for Kota Stia the same day with the Shahbandar, Raja Mahkota, Raja Idris and Dato Muda Rappa.

(96)   23- 7-1875.   Abdullah, Shahbandar and Raja Idris had a private interview with Tan Kim Cheng at Kota Stia, at which Birch was not present, and at which they related their grievances against Birch and asked Tan Kim Cheng's advice regarding Birch's revenue proposals. According to what Kim Cheng subsequently told Birch, which Birch recorded in his diary, Tan Kim Cheng rated the Sultan for his conduct and his breach of the Treaty. Abdullah in a huff returned to his boat.

(97)   24- 7-1875.   Sultan Abdullah still at Kota Stia renewed negotiations with Tan Kim Cheng and tried to induce him to enter into first one and then another agreement, drawn up by the Laxamana, antagonistic to Birch's policy and position as Resident. Tan Kim Cheng declined to consider these proposals and finally Sultan Abdullah agreed to sign certain of Birch's proposals but not others.

(98)   25- 7-1875.   Birch and Tan Kim Cheng decided to leave Kota Stia and seeing their preparations, Sultan Abdullah came ashore and signed certain notifications prepared by Birch, *viz*:—

    (1) Appointing the Laxamana a Commissioner for the Krian bounary question.

    (2) Appointing the British Resident and Raja Idris to be judges.

    (3) Granting the British Resident and the Shahbandar powers to abolish and impose taxes and appoint and dismiss headmen.

To avoid being bound by these decrees, Sultan Abdullah excused himself by a trick from putting his "chop" on them, saying it was broken.

(99)   25- 7-1875.   Abdullah gave Tan Kim Cheng an I.O.U. for $16,000 for advances previously received and made chargeable to the Perak Revenue. This document was endorsed by Birch as Resident; who made further proposals for a Civil List, which Tan Kim Cheng said should be approved by the Governor. Birch accompanied by Tan Kim Cheng returned to Bandar Bahru and made preparations for going to Singapore.

Comment.—In the foregoing sequence of events we see those who had just decided to kill Birch negotiating with him as if in good faith, while the guiding hand of Tan Kim Cheng eased events towards the solution most favourable to Triad interests. This visit of Kim Cheng to Perak showed him, of course, that Birch was out of his depth and that events were hastening towards a crisis and enabled Kim Cheng to take a leading part at the Kota Stia meeting. What Kim Cheng did not know was that Birch's life was already forfeit to White and Red Flag in secret combination against him. If he had known that, he could have saved Birch's life by warning the Governor.

(100)   26- 7-1875.   Raja Ngah called on Birch at Bandar Bahru with a message from Sultan Ismail much to the same effect as that delivered by Raja Yahya (Items 92 and 93 above). Birch received Raja Ngah's advances in a friendly spirit, but made no promises.

Comment.—At this visit Raja Ngah, no doubt, learnt what had transpired at Kota Stia 23–25th July. He may have feared that the documents which Sultan Abdullah had there signed would strengthen Abdullah on the throne; confirm White Flag in possession; give Birch the power he wanted, and so rivet the British connection and reverse the decision to kill him; besides finally excluding Sultan Ismail from the chance of recognition and Red Flag from final victory. These considerations, although ill-founded because the decrees signed by Abdullah at Kota Stia (Item 98) were in fact still-born, may have accounted for the apparent insincerity of Raja Ngah's immediately subsequent actions.

(101)   27- 7-1875.   Birch and Tan Kim Cheng left Bandar Bahru for Singapore to see the Governor about the Civil List (Item 99) and arrange for the Governor's (Sir William Jervoise) forthcoming visit to Perak. Birch left Bacon, his confidential interpreter, and Keyt his chief clerk, in charge of the Residency at Bandar Bahru.

(102)   27- 7-1875.   Raja Yahya went upstream carrying a draft letter entrusted to him by Birch for Sultan Ismail's signature. Raja Yahya also took a report written by himself for Sultan Ismail's information of the events of the Kota Stia interview of 25-7-1875 (Item 99) and reporting the decision of the chiefs at the Durian Sa'batang meeting of 21-7-1875 (Item 94).

(103)   1- 8-1875.   Raja Ngah (Tengku Panglima Besar) entered into a secret
(*Ref: E.P.O.* partnership with Haji Ali and Haji Mat Yassin and wrote letters to
Precis page 14 the headmen of the Hye San (Hai San) society of Penang and to
foot). Tuan Chee of Province Wellesley to borrow $20,000 on behalf of Sultan Ismail for the purpose of buying arms and provisions and to raise an army "in case of disturbances in Perak".

Comment.—These letters were addressed to (1) Chang Keng Kui and (2) Khoo Thean Tek whom we have met in Chapters XVI and XVII as the then leaders of Tokong and (3) to Tuan Chee of Province Wellesley referred to in the *E.P.O.* Glossary page 4 as "a Quedah chief engaged to Sultan Ismail's daughter". We here see history repeating itself, with Red Flag seeking aid from Tokong against the disasters anticipated in Perak from the intrigues of Triad and White Flag.

The letters were taken to Penang by Haji Mat Salleh another Red Flag stalwart, referred to in *E.P.O.* Glossary as "a follower of Ismail". Haji Mat Salleh was at the same time entrusted by Raja Yahya (Sultan Ismail's adopted son) with another mission, namely the purchase of a blank paper said to be in Penang allegedly bearing a genuine impress of Sultan Abdullah's "chop" which it was proposed to convert into a forged document with which to discredit Sultan Abdullah. This second mission again suggests that the Red Flag felt that the papers signed by Sultan Abdullah at Kota Stia on 25-7-1875 (Item 98) would strengthen his position with the British and weaken Ismail's and that therefore some drastic act of villainy was necessary in order finally to discredit him and re-open to Ismail the way to favour. In fact the position had not been altered by Abdullah's signature of the decrees of 25-7-1875, because of the trick used to avoid "chopping" them. Nor did it affect the decision to kill Birch. The contents of Raja Ngah's letters are given in *E.P.O.* Appendix Nos. XXXIII, XXXIV and XXXV. This important move is discussed separately below.

(104)	1- 8-1875. (*circa*). (*E.P.O. Precis page 15 top*).	Sultan Abdullah and the Laxamana entered into separate negotiations with the Mentri and Penghulu Mat Ali of Kurau to prepare men, boats, arms and ammunition for an attack upon Kota Stia immediately upon Birch's death.
(105)	28th July—20th August, 1875.	This was the period of Birch's absence in Singapore during which occurred a series of minor incidents connected with slave girls taking sanctuary at the Residency (a constant source of friction) : the marriage of Birch's "boy" to a local woman and other similar squabbles, heightened the hostility of the chiefs.
(106)	5- 8-1875. (*circa*).	Sultan Abdullah sent Haji Hoosein (a native broker of Penang, employed by Abdullah as an agent) to Penang to enquire of Mr. Duke, the lawyer employed by Triad and White Flag, whether he could get Birch removed by making a complaint to the Governor of his interference with slave-custom etc., upon the Governor's forthcoming visit to Perak.
(107)	7- 8-1875. (*circa*).	Sultan Abdullah sent Nakodah Ketek, a Perak trader of Batak Rabit, to Penang with $2,000 to buy arms and ammunition.
(108)	10- 8-1875.	Birch returned from Singapore, and immediately received two separate reports of the intention to kill him.
(109)	11- 8-1875.	Maharaja Lela and Pandak Indut, his brother-in-law, spent three days in close conference with Sultan Abdullah at Batak Rabit, during which Abdullah gave the Maharaja Lela an "authority" to kill Birch.
(110)	15- 8-1875.	Haji Ali and later Raja Ngah called on Birch and said that Sultan Ismail would do whatever Raja Ngah might arrange with Birch and was anxious for British protection and ready if necessary for annexation, but that he would never acknowledge Abdullah as Sultan. Birch made no promises.

Comment.—This was Red Flag's last overture. They, no doubt, felt that if they could gain Birch's support in time, Ismail might come into favour at the Governor's forthcoming visit to Perak. Meanwhile they continued to intrigue with White Flag to encompass Birch's murder, while preparing, with Tokong aid, for the war that would result.

(111)	18- 8-1875.	Birch left Bandar Bahru for Blanja to meet Sultan Ismail and arrange with him for the reception of the Governor who was expected to arrive overland from Larut about 11-9-1875.
(112)	21- 8-1875.	Birch arrived at Blanja and found Ismail away in Kinta. Birch sent Ismail a draft letter to the Governor for his signature expressing what Birch believed was in Ismail's mind (Item 110) and asking for the country to be taken over by the British. Raja Yahya took this draft to Ismail and subsequently reported that Ismail and the chiefs were ready to sign it, but were deterred therefrom by Tuan Chee of Province Wellesley, Ismail's prospective son-in-law, (Items 23 and 103) who was just then pressing Ismail to grant him authority to place the whole question of the Pangkor Treaty in the hands of lawyers. Ismail sent for the Mentri to advise him (Items 24 and 64).
(113)	25- 8-1875.	The Mentri arrived in Kinta from Larut and several meetings were held regarding the reply to be sent to Birch's draft. There were present at these meetings (1) Sultan Ismail (2) The Mentri (3) Dato Nara (4) Dato' Panglima Kinta (5) Tuan Chee and other Red Flag chiefs. The decisions arrived at were:— (1) that Ismail was to ignore Birch's letter, lest the signing of the draft should mean that Birch would take the whole country and give it over to the Governor on his visit to Blanja in September. (2) that the decision to kill Birch taken at Durian Sa'batang on 27-7-1875 (Item 94) was to be followed. (3) that Sultan Ismail was to send for the Maharaja Lela and give him an "authority" to kill Birch similar to that given him by Sultan Abdullah (Item 109). (4) that Sultan Ismail was to give Tuan Chee the authority he wanted to put the case in lawyers' hands (Item 112).
(114)	29- 8-1875.	Birch having waited a week at Blanja for a reply from Ismail in Kinta and receiving none, returned to Bandar Bahru.

Comment.—Meanwhile down-stream in the White Flag camp, other similar developments had been taking place.

(115)	20- 8-1875.	Nakodah Ketek (Item 107 above) returned from Penang to Batak Rabit with ten cases of muskets and eighty kegs of powder, which were taken by the Shahbandar and Laxamana to Durian S'batang.
(116)	24–26- 8-1875.	Sultan Abdullah held a *berhantu* ceremony, or sorcerer's seance, on these three nights at Batak Rabit conducted by the State shaman, Raja Ketchil Muda and his son Raja Ahmat, to decide by an appeal to the supernatural, when Birch's life should be taken.

There were present at these meetings (1) Sultan Abdullah (2) The Shahbandar (3) The Laxamana (4) Dato' Sagor (5) Raja Idris (6) Raja Ketchil Muda (7) Raja Ahmat (8) Syed Mashhor, a boon companion of Sultan Abdullah, (9) Orang Kaya Mat Arshad (son of the Laxamana) and others.

This important ceremony is discussed separately below.

Comment.—From the above sequence of events we see the Red Flag chiefs of the *Ulu* and the White Flag chiefs of the *Hilir* confirming concurrently the decision already taken by them in joint council on 2st July at Durian Sa'batang (Item 94). By these events Birch's fate was sealed by the unseen forces ranged against him.

(117)	31- 8-1875.	Birch left Bandar Bahru to meet the Governor by appointment in the Dindings and conduct him on a tour through Larut to Kuala Kangsar and thence down-stream to Blanja where he was to meet Sultan Ismail and to Kampong Gajah where he was to meet Sultan Abdullah.

Birch called at Batak Rabit and explained the programme to Abdullah who was suspicious of the new Governor's intentions and asked that the Laxamana should accompany the Governor's party, which was agreed to.

(118)	2- 9-1875.	Sir William Jervoise arrived in the *Pluto* off the Dindings and after picking up Birch and the Laxamana proceeded to Larut.
(119)	3- 9-1875.	Sultan Abdullah was suspicious that the Governor, by visiting the Ulu chiefs first, intended to recognise Sultan Ismail instead of himself. Abdullah, therefore, armed the boats of all his supporters and went upstream to await the Governor at Kampong Gajah as arranged, prepared to fight if what he feared should occur.

Comment.—Another suggested reason for these warlike preparations was that having decided to kill Birch and drive the British out of Perak, for which attempt Birch's death was to be the signal, the *ketika*, or auspicious moment, for the deed might present itself during the Governor's visit, when Sultan Abdullah was far from his base. He, therefore, wished to be ready for any eventuality.

(120)	7- 9-1875. (*circa*).	Sultan Abdullah reached Kampong Gajah and was there joined by Haji Hoosein and Mr. Duke, the Triad and White Flag lawyer from Penang (Item 106) to whom he showed all the papers he had received from Birch and asked Duke to present his case to the Governor on his arrival and have Birch removed. Duke replied that he could do nothing in Perak but that he would take a copy of the papers and present Abdullah's case to the Governor from Penang. Duke then left Kampong Gajah with Haji Hoosein for Batak Rabit where he remained until after the Governor's departure from Perak. During this time the Maharaja Lela and Pandak Indut were in constant attendance on Sultan Abdullah, and the Dato' Sagor in whose house Duke had stayed at Kampong Gajah, was building a stockade round it.
(121)	10- 9-1875.	Sir William Jervoise on his way down river interviewed Raja Yusuf at Senggang, who freely said that he wished the British to take over the Government of Perak as the only cure for present ills. The Governor was favourably impressed.
(122)	11- 9-1875.	Sir William Jervoise reached Blanja, interviewed Sultan Ismail and asked him if he was prepared to sign the draft letter Birch had sent him (Items 112, 113(1)). Ismail temporised.
(123)	12- 9-1875.	The Governor again interviewed Ismail and his advisers and asked them to sign a document he had prepared in Malay, by which the signatories agreed to hand over the government of Perak to the Governor, in the name of the Queen. Ismail again temporised.
(124)	12—13- 9-1875. (*Ref. E.P.O. Precis pages 19—20*).	That night a series of meetings were held between Ismail and the Ulu chiefs, the Laxamana by his presence representing Sultan Abdullah and the Hilir chiefs. The upshot was a decision to refuse to sign the Governor's draft and adherence to the plot to kill Birch. The Maharaja Lela said he would fulfil his promise upon getting a direct order from Sultan Ismail and Sultan Abdullah. The Laxamana undertook to obtain the latter from Abdullah (Item 109). Sultan Ismail said "If everyone is agreed, I will give my consent to it". The Laxamana said "Everything is settled here, I will rejoin Abdullah and the thing must take place". Final arrangements were made for a general rising upon Birch's death.
(125)	13- 9-1875.	Sultan Ismail sent a counter-proposal to the Governor that the Mentri should be given full powers to govern the country with the assistance of a Resident, saying that if the Governor approved, all the chiefs were ready to sign it. The Governor rejected the proposal. A full meeting of Ulu chiefs was then held and addressed by the Governor who proposed that the Government should be administered by British officers (Queen's Commissioners) and that suitable allowances should be paid to both Sultans and to those chiefs entitled thereto. The chiefs gave no decided reply and the Governor left Blanja, Bacon remaining behind to bring a reply by letter to his proposals.

(126)   15- 9-1875.   The Governor interviewed Sultan Abdullah and the Hilir chiefs at Kampong Gajah. There were present the Laxamana, Shahbandar, Dato' Sagor, Raja Mahkota, Raja Ahmat, Raja Abbas. The Governor invited them to accompany him to Bandar Bahru to discuss there the affairs of the country, but they made excuses and the Governor resumed his journey down river.

(127)   16- 9-1875.   Birch returned up-stream to fetch Abdullah to go to Bandar Bahru to interview the Governor. Abdullah unwillingly complied, saying to his armed followers, "if people want to do anything to me, you must help to set me free, and fight for me".

(128)   16- 9-1875.   Sir William Jervoise gave Sultan Abdullah a formal reception at the Residency and addressed him in similar terms to Sultan Ismail, suggesting that the Government of Perak should be taken over by British officers (Queen's Commissioners) and the Sultan and chiefs so entitled should receive fixed allowances. The Governor gave Abdullah a fortnight to which to consider the proposal with his advisers. Sultan Abdullah then returned to Kampong Gajah.

(129)   16- 9-1875.   The Governor left the Residency and embarked on the *Pluto* at Batak Rabit and returned to Singapore.

(130)   17- 9-1875.   Birch returned upstream to Kampong Gajah to arrange for Abdullah to go to Blanja and discuss the Governor's proposal with Sultan Ismail. Abdullah refused to receive Birch, who heard reports on all sides of the intention to kill him. He gave little credence to these reports and returned to Bandar Bahru.

(131)   18- 9-1875.   Raja Yusuf, who was anxious to be appointed Raja Muda, but whom Sultan Abdullah refused to recognise, called on Birch at the Residency, so as to follow up the favourable impression he had made on Sir William Jervoise (Item 121).

(132)   18- 9-1875.   Raja Idris, who had also shown friendliness to the Governor and had been threatened by Sultan Abdullah with removal from his office of judge in consequence, also arrived at the Residency to make terms with Birch.

(133)   18- 9-1875.   Letters for the Governor arrived at the Residency from Sultan Abdullah and Sultan Ismail, both temporising over the Governor's proposal for the appointment of Queen's Commissioners, but making it clear that they did not intend to accept it. Ismail's letter said he would never accept what had been done at Pangkor.

(134)   19- 9-1875.   Raja Yusuf and Raja Idris at the Residency signed a letter, addressed to the Governor drafted by Birch, assenting to the Governor's proposal and accepting fixed allowances. Birch thereupon paid Raja Yusuf $500 and Raja Idris $300 as a pledge of good faith.

Comment.—It was perhaps out of this incident that faith began to be reposed by the British in these two chiefs which resulted later in their both becoming Sultan (Yusuf, 27th Sultan 1876–1887; Idris, 28th Sultan 1887–1916). Thus they became the leaders of a new opportunist party, which began to take shape at this time in the distracted politics of Perak and which ultimately carried off the prizes.

(135)   19- 9-1875.   Raja Ngah (Tengku Panglima Besar) arrived at the Residency with a gift and a letter for the Governor expressing friendship and a desire for British protection and readiness to render assistance to the British (Items 100 and 103).

(136)   19- 9-1875.   Birch realising that agreement between Sultan Abdullah and Sultan Ismail to accept the Governor's proposal was impossible, telegraphed the Governor to that effect and suggested the dispatch of a small body of troops to Bandar Bahru and Kuala Kangsar supported by a gun-boat to prevent any attempt at disturbances, and added "There is a strong hope amongst the majority in Perak that you will carry out your promise".

Comment.—The dispatch of this telegram suggests that the Governor had made up his mind that should Ismail and Abdullah refuse his proposal, he would nevertheless impose it after precautions had been taken to prevent disturbances resulting.

(137)   20- 9-1875.   The standing problem of the chiefs' debt-slave women taking sanctuary under the advancing British power was accentuated at this time by an incident which further incensed Sultan Abdullah against Birch (Item 105).

(138)   24- 9-1875.   Sultan Abdullah, Raja Idris, The Shahbandar and Syed Mashhor who had now joined his advisers, visited Birch, no doubt as a result of the fruitful visit of Raja Yusuf and Raja Idris of 19th September (Item 134). Abdullah said he now felt he had no alternative but to write a letter to the Governor similar to that sent by Raja Yusuf and Raja Idris, and asking Birch's forgiveness for his past conduct. Sterile negotiations followed for the next few days upon the form Abdullah's letter to the Governor should take. Abdullah declined to sign a draft letter prepared for him by Birch. Swettenham who had now come from Selangor to assist Birch took part in these negotiations. Finally no letter was sent this time.

(139)   29- 9-1875.   The *Pluto* arrived from Singapore bringing a letter from the Governor reproving Sultan Abdullah for his evasive and obstructionist tactics and offering him a final proposal for his acceptance namely, that British officers should govern the country in his name and if he agreed he would continue to be recognised as Sultan and receive a large allowance.

(140)   29- 9-1875.   At the same time Birch received from Singapore:—
(1) a draft letter to be signed by Sultan Abdullah if he should accept the Governor's ultimatum.
(2) a letter to Raja Yusuf offering him the Sultanate. This second letter was only to be sent if Abdullah refused to accept the Governor's ultimatum.

(141)   30- 9-1875.   Birch decided to say nothing to Abdullah in the first place about the fresh letters from Singapore (Item 140) but made a final demand upon Abdullah to sign the draft already with him (Item 138).

(142)   1-10-1875.   Raja Idris brought Birch the original draft (Item 138) chopped by Abdullah, who had responded to the pressure.

(143)   1-10-1875.   Birch sent Abdullah two letters:—
(1) Confirming that Sultan Abdullah's allowance would be $2,000 p.m.
(2) Repeating what Sir William Jervoise had told Abdullah regarding debt-slaves, namely, that the whole subject would be investigated by British officers and the Waris Negeri: meanwhile Sultan Abdullah was not to interfere in cases of absconding debt slaves but, according to many witnesses, Birch gave a clear undertaking in this letter that in the event of any of Sultan Abdullah's own slaves absconding to British protection they would be returned to him.

(144)   1-10-1875.   Birch and Swettenham paid a congratulatory visit to Sultan
(evening).   Abdullah and informed him regarding the Singapore letters (Item 140) that the Governor had granted his request and that he was to remain Sultan and the country to be governed in his name.

(145)   2-10-1875.   As a sequel to Abdullah's acceptance of what were, in fact, the Governor's terms, Birch, not content, drafted a completely different letter for him to sign to that forwarded by Sir William Jervoise (Item 140(1) above) and, in addition, drew up in more stringent form the two proclamations (Item 50). Birch and Swettenham took these three documents to Pasir Panjang for Abdullah's signature. After much dispute and delay and only after Birch had threatened Abdullah that in the event of his refusal, the Governor's letter to Raja Yusuf (Item 140(2)) would be sent, did Abdullah finally "chop" the three documents.

Comment.—The three documents were:—
(1) Proclamation by the Sultan of Perak dated 2-10-1875 recognising Queen's Commissioners as Judges and Magistrates.
(2) Proclamation of the Sultan of Perak dated 2-10-1875 empowering the Resident and the Queen's Commissioners to govern in the Sultan's name.
(3) The Governor's Proclamation dated 15-10-1875 appointing Queen's Commissioners in Perak.
They are given in *E.P.O.* Appendix pages 31 and 32 as appendices LIV, LV and LVI.

(146)   3-10-1875.   Swettenham took Proclamations 1 and 2 by the *Pluto* to Singapore for printing, before posting up in Perak.

(147)   3-10-1875.   Birch went with him as far as Kota Stia and from there wrote to Abdullah that his orders for making a road from Kota Stia to Bandar Bahru were not being carried out. Abdullah ignored the letter.

(148)   5-10-1875.   Two slave girls of Sultan Abdullah and one of the Shahbandar
(circa).   bolted and 'took sanctuary at Bandar Bahru. Abdullah and the Shahbandar were greatly incensed (Items 105, 137 and 143(2)).

(149)   6-10-1875.   The Maharaja Lela and Dato' Sagor visited Sultan Abdullah in
(circa).   his boat at Pasir Panjang. The Maharaja Lela said others might follow Birch, but for himself he would adhere to the agreement to kill him, and that he had received a letter from Sultan Ismail and the Mentri telling him not to obey Birch. That night Sultan Abdullah gave the Maharaja Lela a written authority to kill Birch and they confirmed it by swearing an oath "by drinking water from a kris".

Comment.—This ceremony referred to separately below confirmed the sentence of death pronounced upon Birch both by the Red Flag and the White Flag chiefs. The oath mentioned, which is alien to Islam, seems to have been that of the *Wayang Melayu* (see Chapter XVI page 255 *supra*).

(150)   9-10-1875.   The Laxamana joined Abdullah at Pasir Panjang. Abdullah explained to him about the two proclamations he had signed and the Laxamana rated him roundly for having done so, saying he was no longer Sultan having signed away his powers to the British.

(151)   9-10-1875.   Sultan Abdullah, the Laxamana and Shahbandar went downstream to Bandar Bahru to look for the slave girls (Item 148) on the strength of Birch's promise to return such (Item 143(2)). They failed to find them, but Birch claimed that the new powers the Sultan had given him on 2-10-1875 enabled him to over-ride the promise he had given him of 1-10-1875. Birch also suggested to the Shahbandar and Laxamana the advantage if they were to sign a similar letter to that sent to the Governor by Raja Yusuf and Raja Idris (Item 134). In their exasperated state of mind they both refused.

(152) 10-10-1875. Sultan Abdullah and party moved to Bandar and met there Haji Mat Yassin on his way to Blanja on a summons from Sultan Ismail to attend a meeting of the Ulu chiefs.

(153) 11-10-1875. By agreement with Sultan Abdullah, the Laxamana sent a letter to Sultan Ismail by the hand of Haji Mat Yassin informing him that Abdullah had finally authorised Maharaja Lela to kill Birch.

(154) 12-10-1875. Birch left Bandar Bahru in the *Quedah* for the Bernam, taking with him as far as Pangkor the three run-away slave girls (Item 148) disguised as boat-men.

(155) 14-10-1875. Sultan Abdullah returned to Batak Rabit and began preparations for the armed conflict which was to follow Birch's murder.

(156) 18-10-1875. Birch returned from the Bernam and called at Batak Rabit. Sultan Abdullah obtained from him an order for a considerable quantity of supplies which were in fact to be used against him.

Comment.—This series of events mark a rising crescendo of mistrust and misunderstanding between Birch and both camps of the Malays. In the case of the White Flag this hatred rose to a positive frenzy on account of Birch's unwise protection of the royal slave-women, referred to separately below, which coincided with his assumption of increased powers under the proclamations of 2-10-75. These powers unwillingly granted, enabled him in turn to disregard the promise given to obtain them namely, to return Abdullah's own run-aways. However much Birch may have been exasperated, it is difficult at this point to absolve him of the appearance of bad faith, which was reciprocated by Abdullah in "laying Birch under contribution for supplies to be used by his enemies against himself" (*E.P.O. Précis* page 24).

(157) 19-10-1875. Meanwhile Birch no longer as Resident but as Queen's Commissioner under his newly acquired powers, had prepared seven notices all dated 2-10-1875 "in the name of the Sultan" and "by command of His Excellency the Governor" copies of which Swettenham had taken to Singapore, imposing import and export duties; a poll-tax (*hasil kelamin*) and other licences and fees. (*E.P.O.* Appendix pages 34–49). These he sent on 19-10-1875 to Raja Yusuf at Pasir Panjang to know if he approved of them. Raja Yusuf replied that he and Raja Idris approved of them, but warned Birch against the other chiefs (particularly the Laxamana, Shahbandar and Maharaja Lela) telling him his life was in danger and advising him to have more troops and Police in the country before the notices were promulgated. Birch paid little attention to these warnings.

(158) 26-10-1875. Swettenham returned from Singapore with printed copies of the three Proclamations (Item 145) and the seven notices (Item 157). At Kota Stia he was warned by the Police that disturbances were expected. On arrival at Bandar Bahru he informed Birch who did not share the view. The Laxamana and Shahbandar called to express their willingness to support the new *régime*, but probably more with the idea of diverting suspicion from themselves for complicity in coming events.

(159) 27-10-1875. Birch posted the Governor's proclamation at the Residency with a salute of 21 guns and went to Kuala Kinta and had the Bendahara's toll-house there pulled down and sent Penghulu Mat Akib to post the notices in Batang Padang and Bidor.

(160) 28-10-1875. Swettenham went upstream to Kuala Kangsar to post the proclamations and notices, Birch undertaking the work in the lower river.

(161) 28-10-1875. Sultan Abdullah held a meeting of chiefs at Durian Sa'batang. Present: The Laxamana, Shahbandar, Dato' Sagor, Maharaja Lela, Orang Kaya Mat Arshad, Raja Mahkota, Raja Idris[1] Raja Moosa. It was there agreed in confirmation of the decision taken at the same place on 21-7-1875 (Item 94) that the Maharaja Lela should kill Birch at Pasir Salak when he arrived to post notices there. The agreement was again confirmed by oath (*see* below).

Comment.—The decision to kill Birch was taken in July, but the impending visit of the Governor (August–September) seems to have slowed the action. The incidence of the Fasting month (Ramathan) in October referred to separately below, seems to have further delayed the maturing of plans.

(162) 29-10-1875. The Laxamana distributed arms and Sultan Abdullah cash and the supplies he had obtained from Birch (Item 156) in readiness for the rising. Abdullah returned to Batak Rabit to await events.

(163) 29-10-1875. Birch went to Kota Stia in the *Pluto* to post the proclamations and notices and to work upstream. He was there again warned by Nakodah Traang and others that there was going to be a disturbance after the Hari Raya Puasa (November 1st) and that it had been decided to kill him on his way upstream. Birch made light of these warnings.

Footnote.—(1) The presence or absence of Raja Idris at this last meeting became subsequently a subject of debate. It was finally decided that he was not present.

(164)   30-10-1875.   Birch called at Batak Rabit and sent Abdullah an instalment of his allowance of $1,500. The Shahbandar accompanied Birch as far as Durian Sa'batang, whence he sent up further supplies to the Maharaja Lela at Pasir Salak and then returned to Batak Rabit and reported to Sultan Abdullah and the Laxamana that all arrangements were made to kill Birch on his arrival at Pasir Salak.

(165)   31-10-1875   Sultan Abdullah and a few immediate followers went secretly by night to Pasir Panjang midway between Pasir Salak and Bandar Bahru.

Comment.—This move may have been to put himself in a better tactical position for getting news of Birch's death and attacking Bandar Bahru; or it may have been in fulfilment of an offer to keep in touch with Sultan Ismail and the Red Flag chiefs: (Items 94, 153 and 167) or perhaps even to ensure that they did not snatch from his grasp whatever advantage Birch's death might bring, or perhaps for all three reasons. Meanwhile the contact between the *Hilir* (White Flag) and *Ulu* (Red Flag) chiefs (last noticed at Item 153 above) was maintained.

(166)   15-10-1875. *(circa)*. (E.P.O. "Evidence", Section "H" page 52).   A meeting of the Ulu (Red Flag) chiefs was called at Blanja by Sultan Ismail (Item 152). Present:—

(1) Sultan Ismail;
(2) Dato Nara;
(3) Syed Mahmood;
(4) Panglima Perang Samaon;
(5) Dato Muda Rappa;
(6) Dato Panglima Kinta;
(7) Maharaja Dewa of Lambor;
(8) Dato Paduka of Sadong;
(9) Haji Ali;
(10) Haji Mat Yassin;
(11) Haji Mat Daud;
(12) Penghulu Telor of Telok Bakong.

At this meeting the following installations of chiefs were made:—

(a) No. 3 above, Syed Mahmood as Orang Kaya Besar (No. 2 of the "Four").

(b) No. 5 above, Dato Muda Rappa as Panglima Bukit Gantang (No. 6 of the "Eight"). (*See* Chapter XVIII).

Thereafter Sultan Ismail showed the assembly three letters from Sultan Abdullah (Item 153) in which it was stated that Birch was to be murdered and asked their opinion. They all agreed and said they would not submit to the rule of the British and would support a rising after the Fasting Month. By arrangement the Ulu chiefs were to take command of the Upper river, while the Hilir chiefs looked after the lower reaches. There were to be concerted attacks on Kuala Kangsar, Bandar Bahru and Kota Stia, with the object of driving the White people out of Perak.

(167)   22-10-1875. (E.P.O. "Evidence", Section "I" page 59).   Sultan Abdullah and the Laxamana sent a letter to Haji Mat Yassin at Blanja (Items 153 and 166) to inform Sultan Ismail that they were ready to go up river to Pulau Tiga or Lambor to meet him, and implied that the Hilir chiefs were ready to join forces with the Ulu chiefs, immediately upon Birch's death.

(168)   25-10-1875. *(circa)*.   Sultan Ismail sent cash and supplies to the Maharaja Lela together with a letter authorising him to kill Birch and sent messages to the Mentri, Temenggong and all the Hulu chiefs to come and celebrate Hari Raya Puasa (November 1st) at Blanja, so as to be in readiness for eventualities.

(169)   30-10-1875.   Swettenham arrived at Blanja on his way up-stream to Kuala Kangsar (Item 160) and handed out the proclamations and notices to be posted up. His reception was hostile. He proceeded up river.

(170)   1-11-1875.   Birch reached Pasir Salak in the evening on his way up river (Item 164) and tied up at a floating bath-house.

(171)   2-11-1875.   About 6.30 a.m., the Dato Sagor, from the Kampong Gajah side of the river, came to see Birch and had half-an-hour's interview after which he went to the Maharaja Lela's house at Pasir Salak. Birch ordered his clerk to begin posting the proclamations and notices on a neighbouring shop-house, after which the Dato Sagor returned with a party of armed Malays who began pulling down the notices. Birch meanwhile had entered the bath-house and his clerk called to him what was happening and Birch ordered him to repost fresh notices, which he did. As the clerk was returning to his boat a cry of *amok* arose and he was stabbed by the party of armed Malays, who then killed Birch in the bath-house.

Confusion ensued and his sepoy guard taken unprepared made a poor show of resistance. Besides Birch, and his clerk, one sepoy and one boatman were killed and several followers severely wounded.

The murder of Birch was no chance affray but the culmination of the Red and White Flag conspiracy traced above. The story of its retribution belongs to history.

EVENTS FOLLOWING BIRCH'S MURDER

The brief alliance of Red and White Flag broke down immediately after its main object was achieved and the concerted attacks upon Kuala Kangsar, Bandar Bahru and Kota Stia did not take place, due to the latent mistrust and jealousy between the two camps which immediately re-asserted itself. The Perak war which followed is sketched in the next chapter in its relation to the two flag camps.

No MENTION OF THE FLAG ASSOCIATIONS 1874–1876

The reader may be struck by the fact that, with the exception of a single reference to the Hai San (Tokong and Red Flag) society in the E.P.O. (Item 103 above), the official records of the period from the Treaty (January 1874) to the end of the Perak war (September 1876) are silent upon the existence of the flag associations, whose presence and activities in Penang and Perak had been so much in the official eye during the immediately preceding years 1867–1873 (see Chapters XVI and XVII supra).

The only reference to a flag of any colour in the records of this period occurs in Parliamentary Paper C 1709 ("Affairs of certain Native States in the Malay Peninsula, 1877) page 22, in the statement dated 21st May, 1876 of one Indut (not to be confused with Pandak Indut). This Indut is described in E.P.O. as "formerly a follower of Sultan Abdullah and now (1876) employed in the Perak Police Force".

He says:—

> One day (in August, 1875) I saw two boats with a white flag come to the landing place at Batak Rabit, and the Bandahara's son and five or six followers come ashore and go into Sultan Abdullah's fort.

This was no doubt the same white flag that was saluted by H.M.S. Avon upon the recognition of Sultan Abdullah at Pangkor on 20th January, 1874 (see page 293 supra) and was more likely to have been the flag of "independent Malay sovereignty" than that of the White Flag society. The Bendahara's son, mentioned in the extract, was Raja Ngah, the Tengku Panglima Besar, a rabid supporter of the Red Flag: and his visit to Sultan Abdullah at Batak Rabit in August, 1875, was, no doubt, connected with arrangements for the Berhantu ceremony (Item 116 above), at which both flags were represented and for which purpose Raja Ngah may have arrived in one of Sultan Abdullah's boats.

It was not until October, 1878, that the flag associations again broke surface in Perak and that their existence was again officially recognised and steps taken to control them. Those developments are recorded in the succeeding chapter.

We must here examine separately some of the ingredients in the foregoing historical recital, which prove that however little official attention was given them during the intervening years, the flag associations and their rivalries were nonetheless among the most active of the unseen forces at the time ranged against British intervention in Perak.

FURTHER EXAMINATION OF CERTAIN FEATURES IN THE ABOVE RECITAL

We must examine more closely the following matters mentioned in the foregoing historical sketch:—

(1) The Dindings Clause (Article XI) of The Treaty of Pangkor (Items 1, 2, 5 and 6).
(2) The broad grounds for Malay misgiving, following the Treaty.
(3) White Flag's appeal to Triad in Singapore, May, 1875 (Items 73 to 82 inclusive and 96 to 99).
(4) The Meeting of White and Red Flag chiefs at Durian Sa'batang on 21st July, 1875. (Items 89, 90 and 94).
(5) Red Flag's appeal to Tokong in Penang 1st August, 1875 (Items 89 and 103).
(6) White and Red Flag chiefs' appeal to the supernatural at Batak Rabit 24–26th August, 1875 (Item 116).
(7) The meaning of daulat, or the royal prerogative.
(8) The significance of the oath taken by the chiefs at Durian Sa'batang 21st July, 1875 (Item 94) and repeated at Pasir Panjang 6th October, 1875 (Item 149) and at Durian Sa'batang again 28th October, 1875 (Item 161).
(9) The effect of the fasting month (Ramathan) on the crisis of events.

(1) THE DINDINGS CLAUSE (ARTICLE XI) OF THE TREATY OF PANGKOR (ITEMS 1, 2, 5 AND 6)

This Article of the Treaty purported to clarify the boundaries of that area of Perak territory ceded to Britain under the First (1826) Treaty, signed by Captain Low, between the East India Company and the 20th Sultan Abdullah Muassam Shah of Perak on 18th October, 1826.[1] This Treaty refers only to "the Pulau Dinding and the islands of Pangkor".

It was obnoxious to the chiefs as yielding a strip of the mainland and thus invading the sovereignty of the State and was opposed at the signing of the Treaty, (Parliamentary Paper 465/74, page 174, paras. 107 and 108). It was particularly repugnant to Abdullah because the northern coast of Krian, Kurau and Matang was already denied him by the Mentri and, other things apart, it deprived him and his Triad friends of the farming rights of this large strip of coast, which would otherwise have been within the all-too-small sphere of Triad and White Flag influence and available for exploitation by Abdullah's revenue farmer.

Winstedt History of Perak (1934) page 99 has:—

> All chiefs objected to ceding more than the island of Pangkor to Great Britain, but to please his creditor Kim Cheng, Abdullah consented to cede a strip of the mainland too.

Footnote.—(1) See Maxwell and Gibson Treaties and Engagements affecting the Malay States (1924) page 23. The mainland is unmentioned in this Treaty.

The grounds for this view are not given and its correctness is open to some doubt. Tan Kim Cheng, as far as the records show, was not present at Pangkor and the terms of the Treaty then signed were not previously disclosed to the Malay chiefs. Tan Kim Cheng in Singapore may of course, have got to know the proposed terms and may have written to Abdullah ordering him to accept them unconditionally, including the Dindings clause, but this seems doubtful. The Dindings clause was not favourable to Triad because it not only deprived Tan Kim Cheng as prospective revenue farmer under Abdullah of this exploitation area, but delivered it over to his rivals Tokong, due to the following circumstances. When Sir Harry Ord recognised the Mentri as ruler—the weight of British influence, being at that moment, on the side of Tokong and Red Flag—this advantage was followed up by the Tokong revenue farmers of Penang (doubtless the appointees of Khoo Thean Tek whom we met in Chapter XVI), who in the person of Koh Seang Tat[1] appear from Enclosures 1 and 2 in *Parliamentary Paper* C 1505 ("Affairs of certain native States in the Malay Peninsula"), to have obtained at this time from Sir Harry Ord, the opium and spirit farms of Province Wellesley. From this it would only be a step for the Tokong farmer established in Province Wellesley and Krian in 1873 to take over the farming of the additional British territory acquired on the mainland in 1874 immediately to the south, namely the Dindings.

This process would bring the influence of the Red Flag to within a few miles of the mouth of the Perak river, and White Flag Headquarters at Batak Rabit.

The invasion of the Dindings at this epoch by the underground influences of Tokong and Red Flag exercised through the revenue farms, should be particularly noted, as it may explain subsequent happenings in that area, which included the murder of Captain Lloyd, first Superintendent of the Dindings on 26th October, 1878; and the wounding of two other European officials, Messrs. Burns and McKeown at Lumut in 1882.

(2) THE BROAD GROUNDS FOR MALAY MISGIVING FOLLOWING THE TREATY

The Treaty was made possible by the determination of Abdullah to avenge himself upon Ismail and the Mentri for his supersession; and by the shrewdness of Tan Kim Cheng in taking advantage of Abdullah's persistence. No sooner was the Treaty signed, however, than both Abdullah's party and Ismail's party were appalled by the prospect of what the Treaty meant to both. For a short time Abdullah tried to bluff himself into believing that the Treaty would involve little or no change to the *ancien régime* and he clearly relied upon Tan Kim Cheng to outwit the British if demands for change became too insistent, or beyond his power to resist. The long interregnum between the signing of the Treaty and the arrival of the first British Resident, no doubt encouraged him in these illusions. The presentation of Birch's proposals for the better government of the country on 5th November, 1874 (Item 27 above) finally dispelled them. Meanwhile the activities of the Mentri and Woods (Items 12 and 21–24) which had come to the ears of the Governor had left no doubt but that determined resistance to the Treaty from both the signatory and the non-signatory chiefs was to be expected. This knowledge, no doubt, coloured the instructions which Birch received upon his accepting office (Item 67 above). The prospect which slowly presented itself to the minds of all, was:—

    (1) Surrender of feudal privilege at the dictation of an "infidel" foreigner.
    (2) Deprivation of customary dues which in many cases represented the sole livelihood of the ancestral holders of these rights; and their substitution by "allowances" of uncertain value and unstated amount.
    (3) Introduction of a policy of *buka negeri* which is anathema to the unregenerate Malay mind, involving the admission of the "infidel" foreigner to the country on a basis of equality of opportunity and equality under the law.
    (4) The prospect of the exploitation of the natural wealth of the country at high pressure by foreign agency to the exclusion of the *anak watan* or "sons of the soil".
    (5) The transference of land-ownership to foreigners *in perpetuo*.
    (6) The transference of position, privilege and opportunity from the native aristocracy to a foreign plutocracy.
    (7) The submergence of Mohamedan law and the Malay language.

To a great extent these fears have been realised in the four States which later became "federated", and explains the hostility which so soon manifested itself unanimously against the Treaty and further explains the unresponsiveness of the independent States which in later years accepted protection, to invitations to any closer union. Probably the most bitter realisation of all was that the mineral wealth of the country, represented by gold and tin exports, was no longer fair game for personal Malay aggrandizment, but in future its exploitation and opportunities for fortune-hunting would be transferred to others better equipped.

As the *E.P.O. Précis* page 10 (top) says:—

"Twice within three months after taking up his appointment as Resident, had Mr. Birch asked the Sultan for such written authority under his seal as would have justified him, without

---

Footnote.—(1) We have not been able to identify this Koh Seang Tat, appointed revenue farmer for Penang 1873–1874 by Governor Ord, but he was doubtless either a partner, or a dummy of Khoo Thean Tek, who later comes into the picture again. He may have been identical with Khoo Syn Thuak (S.O.S. *op. cit.* page 101). He is referred to in the *E.P.O.* Glossary as "a Penang merchant".
    A reference to the Penang revenue farm records of that date, which are not available to us, would identify Koh Seang Tat and his associates.

straining his legitimate powers, in introducing a new system, by which the revenue was to be collected by salaried officers; a Police Force organised; roads opened up; paid Penghulus appointed, and all "squeezing" by the Datos stopped; and twice had the Sultan, after consultation with his principal chiefs, declined to grant these powers.

These were the earliest objectives of British intervention in Perak and it was therefore from the very first a matter of honour to ensure that once they had been achieved, no other forms of "squeezing", abuse of power, or corruption in public life, should take the place of the customary dues which the new system was to abolish. Comprehension of these considerations is necessary for an understanding of the events which immediately followed the Treaty and of much of the subsequent history of British relations with the Malay States.

Despite the safeguards of Article VI of the Treaty, which excluded Malay religion and custom from its orbit, it was inevitable that customs which rested on Islamic sanction, but which might offend the ethic of a Christian Resident, whose advice must be asked and acted upon, would undergo an unfavourable change, thereby weakening the sanction of Islam in the eyes of the people. However the Treaty was to be applied, it would involve a clash of religious ethics, before the Crescent would accept protection from the Cross. It is a tribute to both sides that the clash was not more severe, nor more longstanding.

It was nevertheless equally inevitable that those elements irreconcilable to the new order should seek colour-protection in that measure of exclusiveness afforded by Article VI, and it is there—under cover of "religious jema'ah", or disguised in the annual Boria and later camouflaged in social clubs and associations—that we find the political elements hostile to the British connection making common cause with the old-established underground organisations of Red and White Tabut.

(3) WHITE FLAG'S APPEAL TO TRIAD, MAY, 1875 (ITEMS 73–82 AND 96–99 INCLUSIVE)

It was natural, therefore, that when White Flag felt Birch to be getting out of hand, they should turn to Triad for aid in controlling him. The Laxamana, the shrewdest of Sultan Abdullah's advisers, was also the most implacable opponent of Birch among the White Flag chiefs. When at the end of March, 1875, after five months' experience, it was clear that what the British meant and what the Malays intended under the new *régime* were poles apart and that, in order to make progress towards his objective, Birch appeared ready to drop Abdullah and negotiate with Ismail, which would have meant a Tokong and Red Flag victory, the Laxamana saw that something must be done. He therefore suggested to Sultan Abdullah an appeal to the Triad contriver of the Treaty, in order to keep Birch in check. Under cover of a secret appeal to the Governor and unknown to Birch, the three White Flagateers betook themselves to Singapore to interview Tan Kim Cheng. Their journey started under bad auspices and their visit was abortive, largely perhaps because it coincided with the change in the Governorship, but also because their appeal to Tan Kim Cheng for practical aid was rejected, although it caused him to appear in Perak shortly afterwards to take stock of the position. The mission to Singapore having failed, the party returned to Perak disappointed and desperate and the Laxamana, determined to find another means, remained in Penang for the purpose. He saw that if Birch's overtures to Ismail were accepted, British influence might once again as in September, 1873, be transferred to the side of Tokong and Red Flag and the hope of Triad and White Flag gains would be gone. This fear seems to have quickened the *tempo* of intrigue and we find shortly afterwards the formation of an united Red and White front to kill Birch, sealed with an oath at Durian Sa'batang on 21st July, 1875. Although elated with the success of this manoeuvre—initiated it would seem by the Laxamana and the Mentri,—White Flag still placed their faith in the ultimate triumph of Triad. Thus, a little earlier we find Sultan Abdullah so firm in his belief in the power of Triad, that he seriously proposed to hand over the country to Tan Kim Cheng, so as to rid himself of Birch (early July, 1875). In this he was supported by the Shahbandar who said "Yes, Mr. Kim Cheng is more powerful than Mr. Birch, let us go and carry out the proposal" (*see E.P.O.* Evidence Section C page 18, top: also Items 81 and 97 above).

The events of 23rd–25th July, 1875, at Kota Stia (Items 96–99 above) were a great disappointment to the White Flag chiefs, who saw in Kim Cheng's attitude opposition to themselves and support of Birch. At this meeting Sultan Abdullah said he wanted Kim Cheng to help him against Birch but found that Kim Cheng was really on Birch's side (*E.P.O.* Evidence Section E, page 25, top). This was quite understandable. Once Abdullah was on the throne, Tan Kim Cheng had perforce to support the British, even against Abdullah—his own nominee for the Perak Stakes,—if he was to get any return on his investment in the revenue farms. For if Birch were to turn away from Abdullah and bring in Ismail in his place, Tokong might get the farms instead of Triad and Kim Cheng's outstanding claim of $16,700 would be irrecoverable.

(4) THE MEETING OF WHITE AND RED FLAG CHIEFS AT DURIAN SA'BATANG 21ST JULY, 1875 (ITEM 94)

The united front of Red and White Tabut, organised by the Laxamana and the Mentri against Birch was clinched by the meeting at the Laxamana's house at Durian Sa'batang on 21st July, 1875, at which both flags were fully represented and the common decision to kill Birch was sealed with an oath. It is doubtful whether either Sultan

Abdullah or Sultan Ismail was anxious at this point of time to have Birch removed by so drastic a means, but there can be no doubt of the determination of the Laxamana and probably the Mentri in the matter. The disappointing interview with Tan Kim Cheng at Kota Stia three days later probably hardened Abdullah's heart and made him feel there was no other alternative. At all events the oath then taken was twice confirmed by both parties to it in the following October. We see in these actions one of the few instances of Red and White Tabut combining to achieve a definite political object.

(5) RED FLAG'S APPEAL TO TOKONG 1ST AUGUST, 1875 (ITEM 103)

Although the die was cast at Durian Sa'batang on 21st July, 1875, jealousy and suspicion remained between the Hulu and the Hilir camps. Thus we see a week later, the Red Flag of the Hulu addressing Tokong in Penang so as to provide themselves with the means of preventing a runaway victory by White Flag following Birch's removal. These overtures throw into relief the underground alliance between Tokong and Red Flag in the political sphere, which we have seen in Chapter XVIII to obtain between Triad and White Flag and which was complementary to the similar alliance in the criminal sphere between the two partners in each camp, disclosed in preceding chapters.

The evidence of these overtures is referred to under Item 103 above, and is reinforced by three letters given in *E.P.O.* Appendix page xxii (Items XXXIII, XXXIV and XXXV) and in the statement of Haji Ali at the Enquiry. This witness is described in the *E.P.O.* as :—

> A Perak chief attached to Sultan Ismail, whose evidence is important on many points, but is not to be relied on when he had anything to conceal or any friend to screen.

This reservation does not apply to the interesting passage in his evidence in which he describes the Red Flag appeal to Tokong for aid (*E.P.O.* Evidence Section C page 18 top). He states that about 1st August, 1875, letters were sent to Penang on behalf of Sultan Ismail as follows :—

(a) To the Governor (Sir William Jervoise) asking for a loan of $10,000.

(b) To Vappoo Noordin asking him to interview the Governor in the matter of the loan to Sultan Ismail, (a) above.

(c) To Che Ah Quee (Chang Keng Kui) and Koh Teang Teck (Khoo Tean Tek) asking for $20,000 "to buy arms and collect men in case of there being disturbances in Perak on account of Sultan Abdullah.

(d) To Tuan Chee asking for $1,000 for a like purpose.

The four letters were then given to Haji Mat Salleh and Kandah Jabor (two Red Flag stalwarts) to take to Penang. Examining these letters further we find that:—

(a) The application to the Governor was evidently for a sort of "sweetener", which if he received it, Ismail would decide how far he would go to meet the British demands, to the exclusion of Sultan Abdullah.

(b) The addressee of the second letter may be identical with Vappoo Merican Noordin, the Indian or Jawi-pekan leader of the Red Flag in Penang, whose acquaintance we made in Chapter XVI (*see* page 252, subsection 5 (3) RED, *supra*).

(c) The third letter was addressed to Chang Keng Kui and Khoo Tean Tek, the two Tokong leaders of Penang whom we have already met in Chapters XVI, and XVII.

(d) The fourth was to Tuan Chee, the Kedah chief, resident in Province Wellesley and prospective son-in-law of Sultan Ismail, who appears from the scattered references to him to have been a leader of Red Flag spearmen of some importance. He should not be confused with Tuan Chee *alias* Sheikh Omar *alias* Omar Abdul Rasul leader of White Flag in Penang in 1867 (page 252 subsection 5 (1) *supra*) who would be a much older man and probably a Jawi-pekan.

This attempt to raise the wind does not appear to have been very successful. The Tokong leaders replied that they would not advance so much as $20,000 without knowing the purpose for which it was intended. Some funds were nevertheless collected. **The incident provides nevertheless conclusive proof that the same underground Sino-Malay contacts as we have seen in Penang in 1867 (Chapter XVI) were still in operation in the political sphere in Perak in 1875.**

(6) THE *Berhantu* CEREMONY AT BATAK RABIT 24TH, 25TH AND 26TH AUGUST, 1875 (ITEM 116)

Following upon the none too successful appeals for material aid made to their physical allies, Triad and Tokong, the White and Red Flag chiefs decided to make a joint appeal to the supernatural powers or spirits of the State (*jin keraja'an*) presided over by the State shaman, or Sultan Muda, who in Perak was the Raja Kechil Muda.[1] This ceremony was held at the house of Sultan Abdullah at Batak Rabit on the three successive nights 24th-26th August, 1875. The sources of information for what took place at this ceremony are:—

(1) *Perak Enquiry Papers* Vols. I and II (1876) (unprinted). *Straits Settlements Records;* Colonial Secretariat, Singapore.

Footnote.—(1) Winstedt, *Shaman, Saiva and Sufi* (1925) page 42.

(2) *E.P.O.* Evidence Section F, pages 32 and 33.
(3) Winstedt *History of Perak* (1934) page 111 and Appendix "I" page 172.
(4) Wilkinson *H.P.M.* (1923) pages 134 and 135.

A *main berhantu* is a ceremony of invocation of evil spirits for aid in sickness, an enterprise, etc., also known as *main puteri* (fairy performance) and its practice is of everyday occurrence among Malays of both high and low degree.

Some explanation is necessary to show how a race of orthodox Sunni Moslems are nevertheless so dependent in their daily life upon the power of the supernatural.

The authorities for our guidance in this further excursion into the realm of those unseen forces ranged against Birch are:—
(5) Skeat *Malay Magic* (1900).
(6) Gimlette *Malay poisons and charms* (1923).
(7) Winstedt *Shaman, Saiva and Sufi* (1925).

The first true Malays of the Peninsula (proto-Malays) came from Java and Sumatra, chiefly the latter, and were of mixed blood of whom Winstedt *Shaman* Introduction page 2 has:—

> The typical civilised Indonesian peoples, Malays and Javanese, are variants of a proto-type race with Indian, Arab and other foreign admixtures. In that proto-Malay race, whatever else may be its components, there is a Mongoloid strain.

Indonesian-Indian-Arab-Mongol, it is important to realise this mixture of blood and belief in order to understand Malay cosmogony. (*See* Introduction to this work).

The aboriginal inhabitants of the peninsula—the pagan tribes of *Orang laut* and *Orang bukit*—have a cosmogony of their own, which, although showing parallels with an earlier diffusion of belief (*see* Introduction *supra*), owes little or nothing to the Malay.

When the Malays began to filter into the Peninsula from Sumatra and elsewhere (*circa* B.C. 1000) they, no doubt, brought with them the primitive animism of that time. By about the opening of the Christian era Hinduism, kingship and the caste system had already been introduced from India into Java and Sumatra. (*See* Introduction *supra* under Mahameru). Later the Malay kingdom of Palembang in Sumatra introduced Maha-yana Buddhism into Java and the Malay peninsula, where it flourished from about A.D. 500 to A.D. 1250, when it began to give way to Islam. It is worth noting that Buddhism in China and Buddhism in Malaya were both the Maha-yana or Universitic form.[1]

The dualist principle of Father-Sun and Mother-Earth and much that emanates from it (Chapter III *supra*), is therefore very firmly established in the sub-conscious Malay mind, both through Indian and Chinese contacts. Shamanism, Hinduism, Buddhism, all had a place in the building up the Malay cosmogony, before the final ascendancy of Islam, from about A.D. 1450.

The earlier beliefs having the deeper roots, have maintained themselves against the anathemas of Islam and indeed, Sufism (*see* page 153 *supra*) or the mysticism of Shian Islam, which properly has no place among the orthodox Sunnis,—has become intertwined in Malaya with the spirits of the earlier animistic world and the gods and goddesses of the Hindu pantheon.[2]

To the One God of Islam the Malay medicine-man of every village adds to his incantations the names of the angels of the Old Testament and Koran and of the evil demons and spirits of the unseen world, all of, which are more powerful than man.

Of these we need only notice here the *jin*, or good or evil earth spirits, the children of Jan the serpent in the Koran.[3]

In Perak there are four chief Jin (*jin aruah* = exalted spirits) who are the unseen guardians of the Sultan and the State.

The chief of these is the State spirit (*jin Keraja'an*) also known as the Supporter of the Firmament (*junjong dunia udara*).[4]

So important a place does the spirit world occupy in Malaya, that on the fifth night of the Installation celebrations of a new Sultan, there frequently takes place the cognate ceremony of the installation of the State spirits (*tabal jin*).

This takes the form of the ceremonial lustration of the newly crowned Sultan and his consort on the topmost tier of the *pancha persada*, which, we have suggested in the Introduction page xl, derives from the tradition of Mount Meru (*see* also Introduction page xxvi–xxvii). In this connection it is of interest to note that according to one source, the *jin* of the Malay spirit world "were created from the soil of the mountain Mahameru, the Malay Olympus with the Hindu name".[5]

This strangely eclectic Malay cosmos can best be presented by the following diagram, which also suggests the place of association therein of the Red and White Flag societies.

Footnote.—(1) *See* de Groot *Religion in China* (1912) page 8 and this work page 37 *supra;* also Winstedt *Shaman, Saiva, Sufi* (1925) Introduction page 3.
Footnote.—(2) This is discussed fully by Winstedt *Shaman*, etc., Chapter XI "Magician and Mystic".
Footnote.—(3) *See* Winstedt *Shaman*, etc. page 32.
Footnote.—(4) For further particulars *see* Winstedt *History of Perak* (1934) where in Appendix "H" (page 166) he gives the names of 36 guardian genies of the State of Perak. *See* also Swettenham *Malay Sketches* (1895) pages 156–157.
Footnote.—(5) Winstedt *Shaman, Saiva and Sufi* page 32.

M

The Malay Cosmos

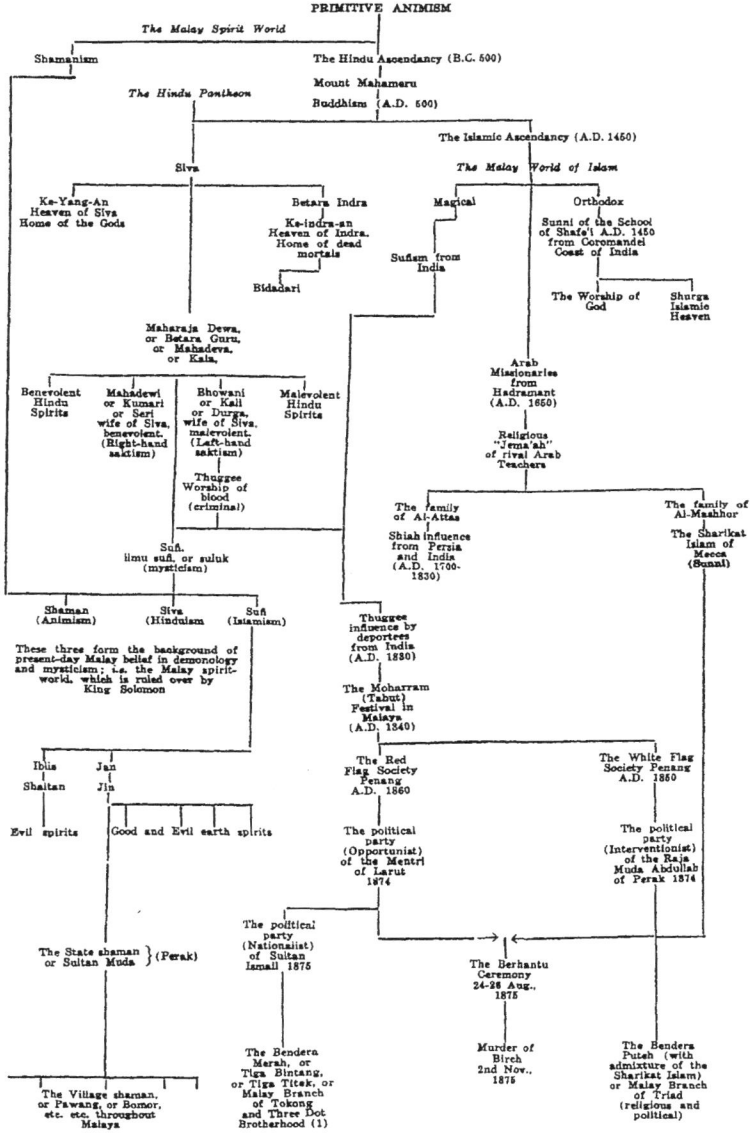

PRIMITIVE ANIMISM

The Malay Spirit World

Shamanism

The Hindu Ascendancy (B.C. 500)

Mount Mahameru

Buddhism (A.D. 500)

The Hindu Pantheon

The Islamic Ascendancy (A.D. 1450)

The Malay World of Islam

Siva

Magical   Orthodox

Ka-Yang-An
Heaven of Siva
Home of the Gods

Betara Indra
Ka-indra-an
Heaven of Indra.
Home of dead
mortals

Sunni of the School
of Shafe'i A.D. 1450
from Coromandel
Coast of India

Sufism from
India

Bidadari

The Worship of
God

Shurga
Islamic
Heaven

Maharaja Dewa,
or Betara Guru,
or Mahadeva,
or Kala,

Arab
Missionaries
from
Hadramaut
(A.D. 1850)

Benevolent
Hindu
Spirits

Mahadewi
or Kumari
or Seri
wife of Siva,
benevolent.
(Right-hand
saktism)

Bhowani
or Kali
or Durga,
wife of Siva,
malevolent.
(Left-hand
saktism)

Malevolent
Hindu
Spirits

Religious
"Jema'ah"
of rival Arab
Teachers

Thuggee
Worship of
blood
(criminal)

The family
of Al-Attas

The family of
Al-Mashhor

Shiah influence
from Persia
and India
(A.D. 1700-
1830)

The Sharikat
Islam of
Mecca
(Sunni)

Sufi.
ilmu sufi. or suluk
(mysticism)

Shaman
(Animism)

Siva
(Hinduism)

Sufi
(Islamism)

These three form the background of
present-day Malay belief in demonology
and mysticism; i.e. the Malay spirit-
world, which is ruled over by
King Solomon

Thuggee
influence by
deportees
from India
(A.D. 1830)

The Moharram
(Tabut)
Festival in
Malaya
(A.D. 1840)

The Red
Flag Society
Penang
A.D. 1860

The White Flag
Society Penang
A.D. 1850

Iblis

Shaitan

Jan

Jin

Evil spirits

Good and Evil earth spirits

The political
party
(Opportunist)
of the Mentri
of Larut
1874

The political
party
(Interventionist)
of the Raja
Muda Abdullah
of Perak 1874

The political
party
(Nationalist)
of Sultan
Ismail 1875

The State shaman
or Sultan Muda } (Perak)

The Berhantu
Ceremony
24-26 Aug.,
1875

The Village shaman,
or Pawang, or Bomor,
etc. etc. throughout
Malaya

The Bendera
Merah, or
Tiga Bintang,
or Tiga Titek, or
Malay Branch
of Tokong
and Three Dot
Brotherhood (1)

Murder of
Birch
2nd Nov.,
1875

The Bendera
Puteh (with
admixture of the
Sharikat Islam)
or Malay Branch
of Triad
(religious and
political)

Footnote.—(1) After losing the political struggle to White Flag, it became criminal upon absorption by Tokong.

This then was the motley crew whom Sultan Abdullah finally summoned to his aid to rid him of his too zealous adviser. History records the outcome of the seance to have been a promise from the spirits that Birch would be dead in three months.[1]

What is important to our subject in all this is the fact that not only were the unseen forces of Triad and Tabut mobilised against Birch, but also the supernatural powers of the spirit world of Perak, representing that "explosive material" handled by medicine men and referred to in the Introduction (page xx *supra*) as one of the human factors in Colonial administration, and the stuff from which wars and rebellions so often derive.

(7) THE MEANING OF DAULAT, OR THE ROYAL PREROGATIVE

Belief in the divinity of Kings (*see* Introduction page xxxi *supra*) is firmly held by the Malays, descending to them both through Hindu and Arab tradition from the common source of Mount Meru or the Nile. This attribute of royalty is known to Malays by its Arabic name of *daulat* = "the divine element in kingship"; a term only used in respect of princes of the Islamic faith. Of non-Moslem princes it is known to Malays as *andeka* = "the supernatural influence that protects kingship and punishes those who insult or injure the Lord's anointed".

In seeking to assess the power of unseen forces opposed to Birch in the Perak of that day, we cannot disguise the fact that in the eyes of his beholders his proposals for administrative reform amounted to a sacriligious infringement of *daulat*, or the divinity of kings, of which in its Malay setting, Birch was probably unaware. Not only were the proclamations (Items 27, 50 and 154 above) by which Birch sought to rule "in the Sultan's name" instead of "by advice through the Sultan", a challenge to the primary concept of *daulat* and the royal prerogative, but their very proposal was an act of lese-majesty as much in the eyes of Sultan Ismail and his supporters as in those of Sultan Abdullah and the White Flag chiefs.

To this was added the fact that although "Malay religion and custom" were specifically excluded by Article VI of the Treaty, from the sphere of advice of the British Resident, it was just in the sphere of custom that the sharpest conflicts arose. This was chiefly due to the existence of the Malay custom of debt-slavery (*hamba tanggongan hutang kepala*). Although Islam does not recognise slavery, it permits a man or woman to repay a debt by labour instead of in cash or goods and this had led to a pernicious and debased system under Malay feudal custom, whereby needy men and women and even children sold themselves and their future progeny to a wealthy neighbour or powerful chief, so as to repay a service or for no better reason than to get a good home. Much abuse resulted, especially in respect of marriageable young women.

The Residency building at Bandar Bahru, erected in Feb.–March, 1875, provided a physical sanctuary for any debt slave who, tiring of his or her debtor-status, chose to try the experiment of claiming protection there. Its completion coincided with the first crisis in Birch's career (Item 67 above), which arose from Birch's insistence upon his revenue reforms and his failure to obtain Sultan Ismail's adherence to the Treaty. Immediately afterwards, a new source of friction arose from Birch's refusal to surrender certain runaway slaves, who had taken sanctuary at the Residency. Whether these incidents were "arranged" in order to create further ill-feeling against Birch there is nothing to show, but they formed items (4) and (5) of the complaint to the Governor by the secret mission which left Perak on 1st May, 1875 (*see* Items 73 and 74 above) and returned unsatisfied. Other similar incidents followed in August and September, 1875 (Items 137, 143 above) and the climax of dispute was reached on 5th October, 1875 when two slave girls of Sultan Abdullah himself sought sanctuary at the Residency (Item 148). Birch's failure to return these women, from whatever cause it arose (*see* Items 143, 151 and 154 above), constituted in the eyes of both Malay factions not only a breach of that article of the Treaty which excluded Malay custom from the sphere of the Resident, but also an encroachment upon the royal prerogative and inflamed against him the popular feeling of outraged *daulat* and raised in its most acute form a challenge among the White flag chiefs to the divinity of kings (Item 156 above). That any royal slave-woman whose person was the property of the sovereign, should seek sanctuary with an unbeliever and should not be immediately given up for punishment, was a mortal wound to the dignity of royalty, and cut at once across the sanctity of custom and the position of womanhood under Islamic law and stirred to its depths, perhaps the most cherished of privileges that is to be found in any country.

In the Perak of that day the custom had been absolute for centuries and, in respect of the slave-women of the Sultan, was the birthright of *daulat*. This aspect of the debt-slave dispute in which Birch found himself unwittingly involved is not clearly presented in the evidence afterwards recorded by those who were probably equally with him unaware of its existence, but allowance must nonetheless be made for the presence of this "explosive material", in assessing the causes, which led to Birch's death and the Perak War.[2]

Footnote.—(1) We are not concerned here with the details of a *berhantu* performance. Those interested will find a general description of what takes place in Swettenham *Malay Sketches* (1895) Chapter XIV "Berhantu" page 147. Winstedt *Malayan Memories* (1916) page 70 "A Malay Seance" and a technical description in Gimlette *Malay Poisons and Charm Cures* (1923 ed.) page 86 *ff.*

Footnote.—(2) *See* also "Note" page 328 *infra* and Chapter XXII.

(8) THE SIGNIFICANCE OF THE OATH TAKEN BY THE CHIEFS AT DURIAN SA'BATANG ON 21ST JULY, 1875 (ITEM 94) AND REPEATED AT PASIR PANJANG ON 6TH OCTOBER, 1875 (ITEM 149) AND AGAIN AT DURIAN SA'BATANG ON 28TH OCTOBER, 1875 (ITEM 161)

We have seen in Chapter XIV (page 219 *supra*) that the taking of an oath on the Koran although forbidden by Islam, was already a commonplace during the decade 1850-60 among the organisers of the two religious factions of Malays in Penang and Province Wellesley, which emerged about that time as the White and Red flag societies. There is nothing to show that the oaths taken by the Perak chiefs in relation to the fate of Birch, were similar to oaths common to the flag associations, nor were the investigators of that day equipped to trace such a connection. Nevertheless the importance with which these oaths were regarded by the conspirators, the known connection of the conspirators with the flag associations and the fact that the oaths were taken "upon the Koran" and "by drinking water from a kris", both of which forms are forbidden by Islam and are common to the flag associations up to the present-day (*see* Chapter XXIX), compel our attention. It would seem from the narrative given in the *E.P.O.* that Birch's death was to be encompassed either (1) by the administration of poison (2) by the intervention of the *jin keraja'an*, or failing both these, (3) by stabbing, in that order; and that, after each had been decided upon an oath was taken to seal the compact. Hence we have the three occasions of oath-taking and three attempts on his life, the last of which only proved effective.

THE FIRST OATH (AT DURIAN SA'BATANG 21ST JULY, 1875)

In the *E.P.O.* (Evidence Section D, page 21) we have some description of the above compact, and the following oath which was taken:—

> The following is a draft from recollection of the secret oath of friendship given by Sultan Abdullah to eight chiefs, or their representatives...... We Sultan Abdullah give this paper to our chief, the Laxamana, who undertakes the work of poisoning Mr. Birch. If he cannot be poisoned, he must be killed, whenever there is a favourable opportunity and we approve of that being done. With this written oath, the Laxamana makes this binding document. Mr. Birch has not conformed with the Pangkor Treaty, nor with Malay customs or religion. Now, Sultan Abdullah and Sultan Ismail have approved of Mr. Birch being poisoned or killed. This is the oath of all their subjects who have placed their chops and signatures on this document. (Oath)......
> The parties then shook hands and swore never to reveal what had taken placed.

There is no mentioned in the record of the use of the Koran or a kris at this oath-taking.

THE SECOND OATH (AT PASIR PANJANG 6TH OCTOBER, 1875)

No oath of secrecy seems to have been taken at Batak Rabit after the *berhantu* ceremony held there in August, 1875. The second oath was taken at Pasir Panjang about 6th October, 1875, after what seems to have been a second *berhantu* ceremony of which no details appear in the records. Thus, in *E.P.O. Précis* page 23, referring to the actions of Sultan Abdullah in his boat at Pasir Panjang in early October, 1875 (Item 149 above) we read:—

> The Sultan told Mat Rouse to write out a paper from dictation......something similar to this. "We Sultan Abdullah......authorise the Maharaja Lela to kill Mr. Birch"...... Then he said to the Maharaja Lela "Let us now swear by drinking water from a kris".

Again in *E.P.O.* Evidence Section G page 37 in the evidence of Mat Rouse on the same incident we read:—

> Sultan Abdullah went down to Pasir Panjang, where they had a feast and a *main berhantu* at which the Shahbandar, Dato' Sagor and Syed Mashor were present...... Two days after this...... Sultan Abdullah dictated the above paper and Abdullah, Maharaja Lela and the Dato' Sagor took an "oath of secrecy by drinking water from a kris".

THE THIRD OATH (AT DURIAN SA'BATANG 28TH OCTOBER, 1875)

The third oath was taken at the second meeting of chiefs at Durian Sa'batang on 28th October, 1875 (Item 161 above). The *E.P.O. Précis*, page 25 (top) has:—

> The proceedings as at the former meeting at Durian Sa'batang were brought to a close by the chiefs taking a solemn oath of secrecy.

Again in *E.P.O.* Evidence Section G, page 38, in the evidence of Mat Rouse on the same incident, we read:—

> After that the four Datos, the Laxamana, Shahbandar, Dato Sagor and Raja Mahkota, took one another by the hand and swore never to reveal that the thing had been done by the order of Sultan Abdullah: never to reveal that they had held the present meeting: never to draw back from their present agreement...... Sultan Abdullah said "I am very glad to see that all you Datos are agreed". At the instance of the Laxamana they all bound themselves by another oath not to reveal their secret.

All this oath-taking and the manner of it—so alien to Sunni Islam and to the simplicity of Malay rural life suggests a background in the praxis of the *Wayang Melayu* of Triad and Tabut (*see* Chapter XVI page 255 *supra*).

(9) THE EFFECT OF THE FASTING MONTH (PUASA) ON THE COURSE OF THE CONSPIRACY

The fasting month of Ramathan (*bulan puasa*) under the Mohamedan lunar calendar coincided in 1875 with the month of October. During *bulan puasa* the kampong Malays of the peninsula are accustomed for the most part to sleep by day, except for the hours of prayer, and live by night. The first meal is taken at sundown and the last at about 4 a.m. Repetition of verses from the Koran chanted over and over at night (*berdikir* or *meratib*) induce a religious fervour during this month, which is absent at other seasons.

The liveliness of the hours of darkness provide a convenient background for intrigue; and enterprises of all kinds are commonly discussed during this month and put into execution after the *Hari Raya puasa*, or festival which marks the end of the fast. Many examples of this commonplace of Malay life could be quoted.

It was perhaps, therefore, unfortunate, if accidental, that Birch and Swettenham should have begun their campaign of proclamation-posting just at the end of the fasting month, when religious feeling against the measures proposed had been whipped up to fever pitch among the rayat.

Thus we see that Sultan Abdullah (Items 161, 162 and 165 above) was completing his arrangements in the last week of October for the rising that was to follow Birch's death; and that, similarly, Sultan Ismail (Items 166 and 168 above) took steps to have his followers around him for the Hari Raya festival (1st November, 1875). It may have been more than a coincidence, therefore, that Birch met his death on the following day. The incidence of the fasting month in October, 1875 may have delayed the maturing of plans, but may, at the same time, have added a psychological factor, which ensured their fulfilment.

THE LINE-UP OF RED AND WHITE FLAG INTRIGUE AGAINST BIRCH, NOVEMBER, 1874—NOVEMBER, 1875

Whereas the line of cleavage between Red and White Flag chiefs in Perak may not have been very distinct at the moment of Birch's arrival in Perak, when the predominant factor of cleavage was between the Treaty and the non-Treaty chiefs, or the interventionists *versus* the nationalist party, the events of the year of his administration and the intrigue which accompanied them, particularly the separate appeals of the Treaty chiefs to Triad in Singapore and of the non-Treaty chiefs to Tokong in Penang (noted separately above), tended to identify the chiefs at the moment of his death, with one or the other camp.

We may, therefore, suggest the following to have been the line-up of the Perak chiefs and their followers in November, 1875:—

Red Flag

1. Sultan Ismail.
2. The Mentri.
3. The Maharaja Lela.
4. Dato Sagor.
5. The Bendahara (Raja Osman).
6. The Temenggong.
7. Dato Nara (secretary of No. 1).
8. The Sadika Raja.
9. Orang Kaya Besar (Syed Mahmood).
10. Panglima Perang Samaon.
11. Dato Panglima Kinta.
12. Dato Panglima Bukit Gantang (Dato Muda Rappa).
13. Tengku Panglima Besar (Raja Ngah).
14. Raja Haji Yahaya (adopted son of No. 1).
15. Tuan Chee (of Province Wellesley, prospective son-in-law of No. 1).
16. Raja Yusuf.
17. Raja Idris } brothers—(cousins
18. Raja Ahmat} of Sultan Abdullah).
19. Raja Musa (brother of Sultan Abdullah).
20. Raja Ketchil Muda.
21. Haji Ali.
22. Maharaja Dewa of Lambor.
23. Dato Paduka of Sadong.
24. Penghulu Telor of Telok Bakong.
25. Haji Aboobakar.
26. Haji Mat Yassin.
27. Penghulu Mat Ali of Kurau (proxy of No. 2).
28. Kundah Mohamed of Bota (proxy of No. 5).
29. Wan Hussin (proxy of No. 6).
30. Haji Mat Salleh.
31. Dyang Moorwah.

White Flag

1. Sultan Abdullah.
2. The Laxamana.
3. The Shahbandar.
4. Raja Mahkota.
5. Raja Abbas (nephew of No. 1).
6. Orang Kaya Mat Arshad (son of No. 2).
7. Haji Hoosein.
8. Syed Mashhor.
9. Nakodah Traang.
10. Dyang Ismail.
11. Mat Rouse.
12. Alang Nor.
13. Indoot.
14. Nakodah Ketek.
15. Penghulu Haji Mat Akib.
16. Haji Mat Daud.

Of the above, No. 16 Raja Yusof and No. 17 Raja Idris of the Red Flag camp had already made tentative independent overtures to the British in Sept. 1875, (Item 134 above) and may perhaps be identified only superficially with the Red Flag with which their sympathies as adherents of the Nationalist party would more naturally lie.

To the above we might add the names of the Chinese capitalists or Revenue-Farmers belonging to the two camps who throughout the same period were striving for the "farms".

<table>
<tr><td>Tokong or Red Flag</td><td>Triad or White Flag</td></tr>
<tr><td>1. Khoo Thean Tek (page 252 supra).</td><td>1. Tan Kim Cheng.</td></tr>
<tr><td></td><td>2. Lee Cheng Tee.</td></tr>
<tr><td>2. Kho (?Khoo) Seang Tat, "a Penang merchant", who may have been Khoo Syn Thuak (see S.O.S. op. cit. page 101). One of the original Tokong rice firms in Singapore was that of Khoo Cheng Tiong of Chop Heng Chun, Boat Quay. In 1875 the proprietor was Khoo Cheng Teow of Chop Aik Seng, who employed Khoo Syn Thuak as manager in Penang.</td><td>3. Goh Siew Swee (also spelt in the records Koh Soh Swee).

The above three Chinese with the two Bugis Dyang Ismail and Nakodah Traang evidently formed the Singapore Revenue-farm Kongsi at this time.

4. Che Yim "a Penang merchant" who may possibly have been Chan Ah Yim (see pages 276 and 288 supra).</td></tr>
</table>

SIR ANDREW CLARKE'S MISGIVINGS

Before he left the Colony in May, 1875, Sir Andrew Clarke was beginning to have misgivings about the support he had given to Abdullah and his selection of Birch to be the instrument of his policy.

Anson *About Others and Myself* page 323 has:—

> Sir Andrew Clarke, before leaving the Colony, changed his opinion of Birch, for, in a letter he wrote to me, just before he left for India, he said:—
> "I am very much annoyed with Birch, and the head-over-heels way in which he does things; he and I will come to sorrow yet, if he does not mind. He has made a regular mull of the farms, and does not seem to have impressed either the Sultan or the ex-Sultan very favourably".

We have no clue to the nature of the "mull" over the farms referred to, but Birch could not have known that he had to contend in this matter not only with the scheming Abdullah, but with the unseen rival forces of Triad and Tokong.

Anson continues :—

> In my Report on the Settlement of Penang for the year 1874, I wrote an account of the affairs connected with the native state of Perak, so far as I was concerned with them; but as it indicated some of the failures in the policy which Sir Andrew Clarke had adopted, he requested me to withdraw two pages, which I did. My report without the part referred to, was in the usual course sent home to the Colonial Office.

COMPARISON BETWEEN THE POLICIES OF SIR ANDREW CLARKE AND SIR WILLIAM JERVOISE

Anson *op. cit.* page 324 has:—

> Sir Andrew Clarke went to India in May, 1875, and was relieved by Sir William Jervoise, R.E., as Governor of the Straits. It was arranged that Sir Andrew should remain at Singapore for a short time after Sir William's arrival, to give him any information he might require. This was a great mistake, for Sir Andrew wanted to dictate to Sir William the policy he should adopt, and Sir William declined to be dictated to. There was jealousy between the two, and I received the confidences of both of them.
> On leaving Singapore, Sir Andrew wrote to me at Penang as follows:—
> My dear Anson,
> Only one line to say that we leave this on or about the 26th,[1] and soon afterwards I hope to shake you by the hand, and thank you with all my heart for the loyal support, often when I fear you did not agree with my views, you have ever given me. Jervoise has plunged into native states head-over-heels. He seems determined to get along. I hope he may not go too far.
> In course of conversation with Clarke on one occasion he had told me that he should have had the command of the Ashanti Expedition, had he not stipulated that the country should be handed back to the native Government after the war was over.

In this context Vetch *op. cit.* page 181 has:—

> The murder of Mr. Birch and the war that followed caused a sharp controversy as to the respective policies of Sir Andrew Clarke and his successor, Sir William Jervoise. Both Governors were very able men, and did their duty to the best of their judgment. But their policies were essentially different and may be briefly stated as follows:—
> Sir Andrew's policy was very gradually to prepare the Malay States for coming into the British Empire by giving them British advisers, under the name of Residents, who should guide the chiefs, but not dictate to them, and while pointing out their duty and endeavouring to get them to perform it, should interfere as little as possible with their authority.

Footnote.—(1) *i.e.* 26th May, 1875.

In Sir Andrew's instructions to Mr. Birch he said:—

"Limit all your efforts to the sea-coast and navigable, waters, never mind the regalia, now and then have Ismail quietly told that he was losing money by holding back, but do not bother about the upper rivers where there are only Malays. Have patience with them. Debt-slavery is a bad thing, but until we are prepared to compensate in full and to show a better system to secure credit, let it for the present alone".

Again in writing to Mr. Childers in October, 1875, Sir Andrew said:—

To the Rt. Hon. H. C. E. Childers.

"I hear the new policy is to annex. This is foolish. The Resident system is far better; till each State pays we must be patient, and not hasten too much the ideas of how things should be done. Let us know the country well, and having established our police posts, our advance, when we make it, will be easy. If you annex you must be prepared to spend money and lose many lives".

On the other hand, Sir William Jervoise on visiting Perak in September, 1875, formed a very low opinion of the Malay chiefs. He considered them an illiterate, opium-smoking, indolent, self-indulgent lot. He found debt-slavery and other evils rampant, and he came to the conclusion that while the British Government had in every respect fulfilled their part of the compact under the Pangkor Engagement of 1874, and had incurred considerable pecuniary liabilities in so doing, the Perak chiefs had not met their treaty obligations. His policy was to hasten the development of the Native States by making them protected States, or, as he himself put it:—

"My proposal, therefore, is to govern the country in the name of the Sultan by means of officers to be styled Queen's Commissioners and Assistant Queen's Commissioners. I consider it very desirable that the change of policy from one of mere advice to one of control should be marked by a change in the titles of the British officers".

We have here a policy absolutely distinct from, and opposed to, that of Sir Andrew Clarke, and the controversy centred on the question whether the evils that existed in the Malay Native States could be patiently endured long enough to allow Sir Andrew Clarke's policy to succeed, and these Native States to be gradually absorbed into the Empire under their own governments; or whether it was necessary to start the drastic and coercive policy of Sir William Jervoise. As the sequel showed and as Sir Andrew maintained, to attempt to hasten annexation meant not only the expenditure of much money, but the loss of many valuable lives.

In consequence of Sir William Jervoise's new policy, the Malay chiefs were required to enter into agreements to accept his proposals; this they did, and on the 15th October, 1875, a proclamation was issued by the Governor's command establishing the new order of things in the Malay States. To Mr. Birch was entrusted the duty of distributing copies of it in Perak, and while engaged on this service he was murdered.

Vetch op. cit. page 178 records the following final judgment upon Sir Andrew Clarke's policy:—

During the eighteen months Sir Andrew held the government of the Straits Settlements, his attention had been engrossed with the pacification of the Native States and the initiation and development of the Resident system. It is for this policy that his short government is remembered in the East, and that he is honoured with a place next to Sir Stamford Raffles in public estimation, as the author of progress in the Malay Peninsula.

PROOF OF THE EXISTENCE OF THE TWO UNDERSURFACE CAMPS DURING BIRCH'S ADMINISTRATION

There is ample evidence in E.P.O. Sections G, H and I to show that the Hulu Chiefs and the Hilir Chiefs, each party acknowledging a different Sultan and each acting independently, reached the same decision—to murder Birch—that both Abdullah and Ismail ordered his murder; and that the Maharaja Lela was their common instrument. There is evidence, too, that the purpose of the alliance being accomplished, White and Red went their separate ways, although faced immediately with the common danger of revenge from without.

The following selections from the Appendices to the E.P.O. illustrate the foregoing and show still more clearly the workings of the Red and White Flag just prior to Birch's murder, albeit these names are nowhere applied to the two camps in the records of the period. E.P.O. Appendices page 28, No. 49 letter from the Governor (Jervoise) to Abdullah dated 27th September, 1875.

"When we met our friend at Kampong Gajah we informed our friend that we had seen ex-Sultan Ismail, Raja Muda, Raja Bendahara and the other chiefs of Perak. We have now to tell our friend that we see that our friend is only recognised in his position of Sultan by the people of the Ilir, and these bear but a small proportion to the people of the Ulu, and that ex-Sultan Ismail is still regarded as the Sultan by a large body of the people. Many of our friend's subjects are also leaving our friend because they are not well treated by our friend, and our friend only keeps his position as Sultan by the help and assistance of the British Government".

The two camps are here clearly seen.

Again E.P.O. Appendices page 22, No. 34 draft letter found in the possession of Haji Ali:—

"We Raja Ngah, Tengku Panglima Besar hand this letter to the bearer Haji Mat Salleh in order to introduce him to our friends in Penang such as Che Ah Quee (Chang Keng Kui), Koh Teang Tek (Khoo Thean Tek) and others. We have ordered Haji Mat Salleh to go to Penang to inform our friends......that the Yang-di-per-Tuan (i.e. Sultan Ismail) has surrendered the management of the affairs of the country of Perak into our hands. We beg, therefore, our friends to help us with ten, fifteen or twenty thousand dollars, for which Haji Mat Salleh, will give a receipt. Haji Mat Salleh is the same as ourselves, and we will bear the debt ...... It is in the service of Yang-di-per-Tuan.

Our friends must help and strengthen the country of Perak in its relations with the British Government. Our friends should consult with Haji Mat Salleh, who is a true man, and our friends must come and see us as soon as possible".

This shows Red Flag and Tokong in correspondence. Again (*op. cit.*) page 23, No. 37 draft letter to Raja Yahaya found in possession of Haji Ali:—

> "I beg to inform Your Highness regarding the arrangement of what we are going to do ...... Your Highness must come down quickly and......bring the money without delay for Raja Abdullah has given his power to Mr. Birch and Captain Kim Cheng...... If Your Highness is late it is almost impossible to carry out all the arrangements of what we are going to do".

This shows Red Flag intrigue against White Flag. The record does not give specimens of any of the letters passing between Abdullah and Tan Kim Cheng, which would show the correspondence between White Flag and Triad and thus complete the circuit.

The following final extract shows that the Government of the Straits Settlements was generally aware of the position:—*E.P.O.* Appendices page 33, Proclamation by the Governor appointing "Queens Commissioners" in Perak instead of a Resident dated 15th October, 1875:—

> Whereas the rajas and chiefs of Perak are divided into factions, parties, and individual interests, fostering and encouraging jealousies and enmities which they confess themselves unable to reconcile; and whereas certain persons, British subjects and others not subjects of the State of Perak have engaged, and are engaging in illegal transactions with certain chiefs of Perak, which tend to create interests subversive of order in the State and hostile to the interest of the Straits Settlements......

Birch's murder altered the circumstances to which this proclamation was intended to apply.

The first paragraph refers to the White and Red camps of the chiefs, the second to the Triad and Tokong camps of the Chinese revenue farmers. A note upon these syndicates of Chinese revenue farmers is given at the end of Chapter XX.

NOTE

THE SANCTITY (*Daulat*) OF MALAY ROYALTY AND COURT REGALIA

W. J. Perry *The Children of the Sun* (1923) pages 390–91 has:—

> The Malay rulers owe much of their great sanctity to their regalia. They are divine beings.

Skeat *Malay Magic* page 23 has:—

> The theory of the king as the Divine Man is held perhaps as strongly in the Malay region as in any other part of the world, a fact which is strikingly emphasized by the alleged right of Malay monarchs "to slay at pleasure, without being guilty of a crime".[1] Not only is the king's person considered sacred, but the sanctity of his body is believed to communicate itself to his regalia, and to slay those who break the royal taboos. Thus, it is firmly believed that anyone who seriously offends the royal person, who touches (even for a moment) or who imitates (even with the king's permission) the chief objects of the regalia, or who wrongfully makes use of any of the insignia or privileges of royalty, will *kena daulat*, i.e. be struck dead, by a quasi-electric discharge of that Divine Power which the Malays suppose to reside in the king's person, and which is called *daulat* or "Royal Sanctity".

Perry *loc. cit.* continues:—

> Professor van den Berg has made it clear that the great sanctity attaching to regalia belongs to the early stratum of kingship in Indonesia, to the rulers who are nearest in culture to the archaic civilization.[2] For he says: "Although the institution of regalia exists in the Javanese and Malay States, it nowhere has such a significance as in South Celebes. The superstitious reverence for regalia, which elsewhere is sporadic, is there a regular practice".[3]

> He says further that this custom is non-Mohammedan, and that a ruler must have possession of the regalia before he can reign.[4]

Footnote.—(1) W. Marsden *A History of Sumatra* London (1811) page 165.
Footnote.—(2) See Chapter XXII *infra*.
Footnote.—(3) L. W. C. van den Berg *De Mohamedansche Vorsten op Nederlandsch-Indie* page 74, published in *Bijdragen tot de taallanden Volkenkund van Nederlandsch-Indie*, 6th Series IX, 'S Gravenhage 1901.
Footnote.—(4) van den Berg *op. cit.* page 72.

CHAPTER XX

THE PERAK WAR AND THE INFLUENCE OF TRIAD AND TABUT ON ITS AFTERMATH

This is the saddest chapter in Perak history. It is the story of the retribution that followed the short-lived triumph of those unseen forces, which encompassed the death of Birch. The result was a war and an aftermath in which the hidden hand of Triad, Tokong and Tabut was at work.

The official history of the Perak war (November, 1875–December, 1876) is to be found in *Parliamentary Papers* C 1505 (1876); C 1512 (1876) and C 1709 (1877). The general narrative is given by Wilkinson and by Winstedt *op. cit.*

Swettenham was in Kota Lama on the day of Birch's murder and he was lucky to escape with his life at Blanja[1] on his way downstream. He reached the Residency safely and, with Lt. Abbott, R.N., put Bandar Bahru in a state of defence.

On 7th November, an unsuccessful attack was made by a small British force on the Maharaja Lela's stockade at Pasir Salak. Captain Innes, R.E. and Nakhoda Orlong were killed, and two other officers and several men were severely wounded.

On 16th November, a renewed attack with reinforcements was successfully made without casualties, and the village of Pasir Salak was burnt.

By the end of November, 1875, the following forces were collected at the scene of the disturbance:—

Major-General Colbourne, C.B., from Hong-Kong, Commanding; and Brigadier-General John Ross from India—

    300 all ranks of the 80th., Regiment
    200 all ranks of the 1/10th Regiment
    600 all ranks of the 3rd Regiment (the Buffs)
    450 strong 1st Gurkhas
     80 strong—one Company, of Bengal Sappers
A Battery and a half of Royal Artillery.

A Naval Brigade drawn from H.M. Ships, *Modeste, Thistle, Philomel, Ringdove* and *Fly.*

General Colbourne and the British troops from China, made Headquarters at Bandar Bahru. General Ross and the Indian troops were stationed at Kuala Kangsar.

After the capture of Pasir Salak (16th November, 1875), the Maharaja Lela and Dato Sagor and their followers went up-stream, and joined Sultan Ismail at Blanja and thence they established themselves at the village of Pengkalan Pigu on the Kinta River, 15 miles inland from the left bank of the Perak River.

General Colbourne's forces occupied Pengkalan Pigu on 17th December, 1875, with little loss, and all organised resistance was then at an end although a period of guerilla warfare followed, in which Sultan Ismail, the Maharaja Lela, the Dato Sagor and the other non-Treaty Chiefs were so persistently hunted by parties of military and irregulars, that they finally gave themselves up, as follows:—

    (1) Sultan Ismail to the Sultan of Kedah who handed him over to the Lieutenant-Governor of Penang on 20th March, 1876, together with the Perak regalia (*see* Chapter XXII). The regalia was placed in the Singapore Treasury until handed back to Perak in the reign of Sultan Idris. Sultan Ismail was banished from Perak and allowed to live in Johore where he died in 1889.

    (2) The Maharaja Lela and his father-in-law,

    (3) Pandak Indut, the actual murderers of Birch, after months of wandering in Upper Perak, gave themselves up in July, 1876.

    (4) The Dato Sagor had been secured about June, 1876.

A Commission of enquiry proved the complicity of the following Treaty Chiefs in the murder.

    (5) Sultan Abdullah
    (6) The Mentri of Larut
    (7) The Dato Laxamana
    (8) The Dato Shahbandar.

In September, 1876, Abdullah went to Singapore to explain his conduct to the Governor. The Governor proposed that he should appoint Raja Yusop to act as Regent for him. Abdullah demurred and was allowed to nominate Raja Osman the Bendahara instead (*Parliamentary Papers* C. 1709 (1877) page 71).

Footnote.—(1) *See* his *Malay Sketches,*—"A Personal Incident".

A Court was then set up to try Nos. 2, 3, and 4 above and others of their followers. This court was composed of Raja Yusop and Raja Alang Husein as judges, with Davidson and Maxwell as assessors.

The establishment of the Court is reported by the Governor as follows in Despatch No. 86, dated 11th January, 1877. *Parliamentary Papers* C. 1709 (1877) page 116:—

"As the proceedings of the inquiry into the complicity of Abdullah and the other Perak chiefs occupied a much longer time than I had anticipated, I determined to request the Raja Bendahara (the Regent)......to appoint judges to try the case. It was a matter of some difficulty, however, to nominate judges qualified for this duty, for the inquiry had by this time proved that nearly every chief in Perak had been more or less implicated in the conspiracy...... Eventually the Raja Bendahara nominated—

> the Raja Muda Yusuf
> Raja Allang Hoosein
> Raja Driss

as judges, any or all of whom had power to sit as such. As it subsequently appeared that Raja Driss was himself implicated in the general conspiracy, it was determined to try the case with the two first named chiefs as judges".

Nos. 2, 3 and 4 were found guilty, sentenced to death and hanged at Matang. The other accused were sentenced to life imprisonment.[1]

Nos. 5, 6, 7 and 8 were held in Singapore for complicity in the murder and were eventually banished to the Seychelles with their families. Ex-Sultan Abdullah died in Singapore in 1922, whither he had been allowed to return to end his days.

The Mentri's return from banishment is described by Swettenham in *The Real Malay* page 200 "An Old Master".

THE IMMEDIATE EFFECTS OF THE PERAK WAR ON THE MAJOR CHIEFS

We should pause here to consider the effect of these events upon the fortunes of the chief actors in the drama and upon the influence which they formerly exercised within the White and Red Flag societies.

We saw in Chapter XVIII the line of cleavage between the Perak chiefs caused by the Treaty of Pangkor.

The following was the result of the Perak war upon the principal leaders of the two parties:—

Treaty Chiefs—

(1) Sultan Abdullah (deposed and banished to the Seychelles).

(2) The Mentri of Larut

(3) The Shahbandar — banished to the Seychelles.

(4) The Laxamana

(5) The Dato Sagor (executed by hanging at Matang, 28th December, 1876).

Non-Treaty Chiefs—

(1) Sultan Ismail (deposed and banished to Johore).

(2) The Maharaja Lela

(3) Pandak Indut (father-in-law of No. 2). — (executed by hanging at Matang, 28th December, 1876).

Both sides were, therefore, losers. The Treaty was not a success. The war which followed it, brought to the throne the third Perak claimant, Raja Yusuf, one of the most unpopular chiefs in Perak, who had even been rejected for appointment as Raja Muda.

This second attempt at king-making by the British was, therefore, not calculated to allay the opposition of the remaining chiefs either Treaty or non-Treaty, who adopted an attitude of passive resistance to British intervention.

The banishment of ex-Sultan Abdullah must have weakened the influence of Triad and White Flag in Kuala Perak but the influence of the Triad "revenue-farm" remained and was soon to make its presence felt. To what extent the White Flag gained adherents from sympathy with the misfortunes of ex-Sultan Abdullah, his house and his banished companions, it is impossible to guess, but it is certain from later developments that the White Flag influence around Kuala Perak persisted among the ryot as the core of a vaguely conscious "restoration" Party.

The military remained in various parts of Perak until the end of 1876 when they were gradually replaced by a nondescript local Police Force hastily embodied.

The Governor, Sir William Jervoise, left for Australia early in 1877 and, after a two years' interregnum, was succeeded by Sir Frederick Weld from Tasmania 1879–1887.

Davidson a local lawyer was appointed in 1876 to be Resident of Perak in succession to Birch and resigned after a few months and was succeeded by Sir Hugh Low from Labuan 1877–1889, to whose wise administration the subsequent prosperity of Perak is largely due.

The aftermath of the war left the Perak Malays cowed, sullen and hostile.

Footnote.—(1) The village of Pasir Salak was destroyed and not allowed to be re-occupied. A memorial stone and inscription to this effect stands to-day on the bank of the Perak river at the deserted village of Pasir Salak to mark the place where Birch was murdered.

The graves of Captain Innes and others are hard by. The wisdom of such a perpetual reminder of this unhappy chapter of Perak's history is open to question.

Swettenham (*British Malaya* page 225) describes the position thus:—

> "Sir Hugh Low assumed his duties at a critical moment, for though the forces of disorder were broken, and the obstructive chiefs had been dealt with and both Abdullah and Ismail had been removed, there were still powerful chiefs in covert opposition to the Resident, if they dared not resort to open resistance.
>
> Their influence, however exercised, was sufficient to determine the attitude of large villages like Kota Lama (already mentioned as the most truculent Kampong in Perak at that time) and other villages, the headmen of which had either been punished for the part they had taken in the murder of Mr. Birch, and the subsequent fighting, or who were related to those who had paid this penalty. Most of the crime of the country could be traced to these places and whenever an arrest had to be made, the task was one of great delicacy and danger.
>
> (*B.M.* page 221) The period of "passive resistance" was eventually overcome by infinite patience and consistent firmness so that in the end the ever-decreasing band of irreconcilables found themselves without either sympathy or support and with no valid ground of complaint".

It is probably just as true to-day that the principal centres of crime in Perak are to be found in these "irreconcilable" village areas, but it would be incorrect to say that the "irreconcilable" element has entirely disappeared.

It is probably nearer the truth to suggest that the irreconcilable spirit of these early politically hostile areas of Perak has been kept alive up to the present-day by the power and influence of Triad and Tabut.

RAJA MUDA YUSUF AND THE FIRST STATE COUNCIL, SEPTEMBER, 1877

Raja Yusuf was appointed Raja Muda of Perak 1877–1878, and Regent from 1st September, 1878, and for his own safety he left his ancestral village of Senggang and took up his residence at Sayong on the opposite bank of the Perak river to Kuala Kangsar, where the British Resident now lived (1877).

We may here quote again from Swettenham (*British Malaya* page 226):—

> "The Regent Raja Yusuf knew the country better than any man, and his loyalty to the British Government was never questioned: but his unpopularity continued to the day of his death, when the posthumous title given him was *Marhum Ghafiru'llah* or "The late Sultan, may God forgive him".
>
> Fortunately a great safety-valve was discovered in the constitution of the State Council on which the Regent, the principal chiefs, two or three of the leading Chinese and the Resident and Assistant Resident had seats.[1]
>
> The functions of this Council were mainly legislative. They discussed and passed all the legislative enactments required by the State. All death sentences were referred to them and they decided whether they should be carried out or modified.
>
> They dealt with the appointments and salaries of all Malay chiefs and headmen and with civil and pension lists. The annual estimates of expenditure and revenue were laid before them for their information and the Resident discussed with the Council all matters of importance in which the members were likely to be interested. The institution served its purpose admirably. The Malay members from the first took an intelligent interest in the proceedings, which were always conducted in Malay, and a seat on the Council is much coveted and highly prized.
>
> A tactful Resident could always carry the majority with him and nothing was so useful or effective in cases of difficulty as for those who would have been obstructive, to find that their opinions were not shared by others of their own class and nationality. It was perhaps not altogether surprising that the Regent (Raja Yusuf) not infrequently found himself in a minority of one!

Further down on the same page Swettenham has:—

> "Sir Hugh Low had some difficulty with Chinese secret societies".

The nature of this difficulty we refer to below.

The first recorded Council Meeting was held at Kuala Kangsar on 10th September, 1877 (see *P. M. S. History* III, page 1) and the members of the first Perak State Council are given as follows:—

    Present:—

        The Raja Muda (Raja Yusuf)
        The Resident (Mr. Hugh Low)
        The Assistant Resident (Capt. Speedy)
        Raja Dris (Idris)
        The Orang Kaya Temenggong
        Capitan Ah Kwee
        Capitan Ah Yam

    Absent:—

        Che Karim of Selama.

The Raja Muda Yusuf had all along kept himself more or less aloof—doubtless due to his general unpopularity with all classes—from the earlier cleavages amongst the Perak Chiefs. He was not a signatory to the Treaty and hated Sultan Abdullah, so that he and his followers were unlikely to be supporters of the White Flag or to be influenced by the Ghee Hins, even if he was aware of their existence. As we have seen in Chapter XIX he was perhaps less unconnected with the Red Flag, which although mainly nationalist, was still dominated by the Mantri's followers and largely confined to the tin-fields of Larut.

Nor was he likely to be a sympathiser with the irreconcilables amongst the chiefs (or the Party of the *Orang Duabelas*), for was he not a gainer by the turn of fortune's

Footnote.—(1) We examine below the membership of the first Perak State Council more closely, in order to trace the continuance therein of Triad and Tabut influence.

wheel, which had brought to trial before himself and execution by his own command the more turbulent leaders of the non-Treaty chiefs, events which had led to the discomfiture of his enemies and his own elevation to the steps of the throne?

Historically, therefore, there is no reason why Raja Yusuf, whose leading position in Perak, first as Raja Muda, then as Regent and later as Sultan, lasted from 1877–1887, should not have been free from the hidden influence of either Triad, Tokong, Tabut or *Orang Duabelas;* nor was there any obstacle to his loyalty to the British connection, during his long association with it. This is the character history has given him.

Swettenham (*Malay Sketches* page 161) draws a picture of his position in modern Perak history, which explains his isolation amongst his own people and in consequence his comparatively loyal attitude to the British connection, at a time when the whole of Perak was sullenly hostile :—

> "The King (Raja Yusuf) was one with whom things had gone hardly until the appearance of the white man in his country. His character had not endeared him to the people who should have been his subjects but were almost without exception his enemies: and the consequence was that when he ought to have been elected to a high office (*i.e.* to Raja Muda in 1866 instead of Abdullah) and when his birth entitled him to be nominated Sultan (*i.e.* in 1871, instead of Ismail), his claims were ignored in favour of junior men. Up to the age of fifty or more he had passed his life in poverty and even in want, and often in open resistance to such authority as existed. These strained relations with his own people made him loyal to the British and, as his claims were indisputable and the opportunity came when they might be satisfied, he at last attained to the position which was his by right".

The last sentence refers to the position created by the Perak war, which removed both Sultan Abdullah and Sultan Ismail from the scene. Raja Yusuf had previously mentioned to the Governor, Sir William Jervoise, that nothing would be settled "until there had been a fight". Raja Yusuf had also recommended to Sir William Jervoise that after the "whiff of powder", the British should take over the whole administration of Perak. These two pieces of sage counsel appear to have obtained for Raja Yusuf the support of Sir William Jervoise and despite his personal unpopularity, ultimately gained for him the throne of Perak as the *protégé* of the British Government.

To return to the members of the first Perak State Council—

The next was Raja Idris, who had been a supporter of ex-Sultan Abdullah and to some degree had been involved in the conspiracy against Birch. His sympathies might, therefore, be expected to be with the White Flag. He acted as magistrate in Kuala Kangsar from 1877, and his former associations must have been an embarrassment to him. He can have had no affinity with the Red Flag, nor with the irreconcilables, or party of the *Orang Duabelas.*

The next member of Council was *The Temenggong* (Wan Hasan)—he was a signatory to the Treaty and was territorial chief of the notorious mukim of Kota Lama, at Kuala Kangsar. He also had close family ties with the Mentri and territorial interests at Prai. These divided loyalties might about balance one another, but it seems from the *F.P.O.* that he was in fact a powerful supporter of Red Flag interests, hand-in-glove with the Mentri, like whom he appears to have been a "trimmer", and yet to have retained the confidence of the British authorities sufficiently to be given a seat on the State Council. Having survived, and finding himself in this position, with Raja Idris as magistrate in Kuala Kangsar, he may as a matter of policy have given countenance to White Flag activity in his mukim of Kota Lama, but here we can only speculate.[1]

Next we have *Capitan Ah Kwee.* This is none other than Chang Keng Kui. He was now the head of Tokong in Penang and Larut and crowned his triumphs with a seat on the first State Council at Kuala Kangsar. The head of Tokong and Red Flag had made an official entry into the Perak River valley!

Next there is *Capitan Ah Yam*, who as Chan Ah Yam had been leader of Triad and White Flag in Penang and Larut ever since the murder of Li Ah Kun in 1872, and the eclipse of Ho Ghi Siu. The latter seems to have lost the confidence of the Penang authorities (Col. Anson) and with it the leadership of Triad, ever since he dodged the *Midge* peace mission in August, 1873.

Chang Keng Kui and Chan Ah Yam had been the two Chinese appointed to the Larut "Pacification Commission" in Jan.–Feb., 1874; and now Triad and Tokong took their seats side by side in the first Perak State Council.

Chinese secret societies had been registered in the Colony by Ordinance passed in 1869 as a result of the Penang Riots of 1867, and secret societies were "prohibited" by proclamation in Perak about this time. The appointment of these two men can, however, occasion no surprise, as the Chinese were still being governed under the *Capitan* system and these two leaders of Triad and Tokong took their seats in Council officially as the *Capitans* of their respective communities and not by virtue of their secret society associations, which were believed by a perhaps too trustful Government, to have been foresworn.

The last member of the Council was Che Karim of Selama. This man appears to have been granted a seat in order to represent the commercial interests of the now banished Mentri. He does not appear from the records to have attended any meetings of Council

---

Footnote.—(1) We make a fuller reference to this man and his family in Chapter XXII.

and seems to have been dropped from Council about Sept., 1878, when it was seen that he wished to embarrass Government with claims and actions arising out of the Larut Wars. He was probably a supporter of the Red Flag.

Such, then, were the members of the first Perak State Council constituted under the British connection from 1877, and such was in outline the probable degree of secret society influence and its interspersion in the Council itself, viz:—

(1)	Raja Muda Yusuf	Free.
(2)	Raja Dris	Sympathy with White Flag and fear of Red Flag.
(3)	Temenggong	Probably a member of the Red Flag.
(4)	*Capitan* Ah Kwee	Representative of Tokong and Red Flag interests.
(5)	*Capitan* Ah Yam	Representative of Triad and White Flag interests.
(6)	Che Karim of Selama	Probably Red Flag.

As the last mentioned was continually absent he exercised no influence in the Council.

We should notice that the Chiefs' Party or "irreconcilables" or non-Treaty Party or *Orang Duabelas*, were without direct representation on the Council at this time.

As regards the two Chinese members, emphasis is here laid upon their appointment, so as to bring to the reader's notice the existence of Triad and Tokong influence in the State Council, with Tokong in the ascendant, which has been wielded right from the beginning of British rule in Perak. This fact is liable to be overlooked after the lapse of nearly sixty years.

THE GROWTH OF SECRET SOCIETY INFLUENCE IN PERAK (1877–1882)

It will now be our duty to trace from the published records of the Perak State Council Minutes, such evidence of the growth of secret society influence in Perak during the next few years as shall be therein apparent, and to make some attempt to estimate the drift and importance of this growth and its ultimate significance.[1]

THE RED FLAG MUKIMS OF SA'YONG AND ULU KURAU
(Meeting of 6-2-1878)

This meeting was entirely concerned with the appointment of Penghulus and the arrangement of Mukims.

Details are not given, but this process must have had a wide effect upon the subsequent growth of Triad and Tabut influence in Perak.

In a footnote *loc. cit.* Sir Ernest Birch, writing in February, 1907, adds:—

> "It is noteworthy that the wishes of the people of the villages were consulted and that hereditary claims were generally recognised. Some of the Penghulus then appointed are in their places to-day (February 1907). A very famous old lady, still alive, Haji Wan Teh Sapiah was made Penghulu of Ulu Kurau. The large mukim of Sayong, opposite to Kuala Kangsar, was confirmed to the family of the Dato Sri Maharaja Lela".

We learn from C.S.O. Native 6500/82 (Perak) that Wan Teh·Sapiah, whose husband's name was Kulop Mohamed, was "Penghulu-ess" of Ulu Kurau in 1882, and was not in Sir Hugh Low's opinion at all satisfactory in her duties and in the payment of her revenue collections. From the same correspondence we also learn that without any notice she packed up her boxes and went to Mecca on 1st August, 1882, with her friend To Puan Anjang, wife of Dato Panglima Kinta. Her departure led Dato Mahomed Ali of Kurau, faithful follower of the ex-Mentri of Larut and who lost everything in consequence, to apply to Sir Hugh Low for appointment to the vacant Penghuluship of Kurau. He was recommended by Mr. R. W. Maxwell, Inspector of Police (Chief Police Officer), Penang.

As we have seen, this whole area was and has remained rabidly Red Flag.

TRIAD CLAIM OF $190,000 AGAINST RAJA ABDULLAH MAY, 1878
(Meeting of 4-5-1878)

In *P.M.S.* Part III page 10, we notice a claim entered by "certain Chinese including *Capitan* Ah Yam" for payment by Government of a sum of $190,000, being half an amount expended by them at the request of Raja Muda Abdullah (then ex-Sultan banished to the Seychelles) in Larut during the troubles (four years earlier). The Minute reads:—

> "After a full discussion of the matter......the members Raja Dris and Chan Ah Yam (*Capitan* Ah Yam) having special knowledge of the circumstances, the opinion of each member, beginning with the youngest, is taken down in writing and signed".

This item is instructive. Here we have Triad who had backed Abdullah to win the "Perak Stakes" during 1873–1876, and had lost (but who had nevertheless got a representative on the Perak State Council in 1877),—entering a claim against the winner, for, as it were, the "training fees" of their candidate. Surely a very impertinent claim, but one backed by the weight of Triad commercial interests in Singapore, Penang and Larut, presented with all the formality of a Council resolution, and sponsored by one of the interested parties, namely, *Capitan* Chan Ah Yam.

Footnote.—(1) The following extracts are taken from the printed Council Minutes, Perak, for the years 1877–1882, which have been published as *P.M.S. History* Parts III and IV in 1907 and 1909. In each case the page in the *P.M.S.* is given as reference with the relevant date in black type.

The whole claim looks as if it were made as a bare-faced "try-on" to test, thus early, the strength of Triad and White Flag influence in the counsels of the Perak Government, as a challenge to the encroachment of Tokong. The solution is equally interesting. We quote again from the Minutes:—

> "Chan Ah Yam says that the Raja Abdullah, not being Sultan at the time this debt was contracted, could not bind the ruler of the country, and it (the claim) ought not to be paid from its (the country's) finances but that the petitioners may justly claim repayment from any private property of Sultan Abdullah. *Capitan* Ah Kwee is of the same opinion".

This was a cunning move whereby Chan Ah Yam hoped to gain credit for himself for having released the Government from the obligation to pay the claim, thus gaining the goodwill, support and popularity of his fellow counsellors. At the same time he indicated a way whereby the claimants (who included himself) could be fully reimbursed and most important of all, the power of the Triad society be consolidated and increased in the Perak Valley, by obtaining in satisfaction of this claim, possession of the private property of the ex-Sultan.

> "The Orang Kaya Temenggong says: I think that as the Towkay Chin Ah Yam is one of the petitioners and was present and knows all the circumstances, we cannot do better than accept his opinion in which I concur".

Here we find Red Flag supporting Triad, which is unusual, but they were following Tokong's lead and were both kicking a man who was down.

> "Raja Dris says: this claim is founded on an agreement made while the country was convulsed by civil war. Neither the Sultan nor the Raja Muda were fully acknowledged and the Chinese were fighting against each other, and both the Raja Abdullah and the Chinese who were parties to the agreement were in the wrong. The Sultan himself—were there a fully acknowledged one—could not have bound the country to such an agreement; except with the consent of his principal chiefs. There is no case for enquiry, though much can be said against the claim if necessary".

This sounds like the view of the Resident using Raja Idris as his mouthpiece. If it is the genuine opinion of Raja Dris it looks as if he feared an increase in Triad and White Flag power in the Perak Valley which, as a "reconciled" chief, would not now suit him; besides creating a bad precedent if Chinese claimants were allowed to reimburse themselves by seizing Malay chiefs' property.

> "The Raja Muda Yusuf says it would not be proper to hold any enquiry; both parties to the agreement were acting illegally and against all Malay notions of right".

Here we have the healthy independent opinion of Raja Yusuf who, as has been pointed out, was probably less affected by "party" influence at this time than any other chief in Perak. The Council rejected the claim. History does not relate whether Counsellor Ah Yam and his fellow Ghee Hin claimants were able to obtain satisfaction of their claim by other means, but knowing the absolute undersurface power of Triad at that time, we may presume that Council's decision of 4th May, 1878, was not the last word on the subject.

KELIAN PAUH RE-NAMED TAIPING OR "GREAT PEACE", BETWEEN TRIAD AND TOKONG

It was about this time (June 1878) that Captain Speedy resigned and was succeeded as Assistant Resident, Larut, by Mr. W. E. Maxwell, with Headquarters in Taiping, the new Chinese name for Kelian Pauh, re-christened by Speedy in honour of the "Great Peace" which ended the Larut wars.

TOKONG'S CLAIM OF $166,000 AGAINST THE MENTRI JUNE, 1878
(Meeting of 26-6-1878)

We find a discussion at this meeting about the appointment of a Commission to enquire into the debts of the ex-Mentri of Larut.

The Tokong and Red Flag backers of the Mentri of Larut for the "Perak stakes", 1873–1876 (who, like Abdullah, also proved an "also-ran", the stakes going to the "outsider" Raja Yusuf) were now trying the same game (to a slightly different tune) as Triad had played at the previous Council meeting. They wanted the Mentri's debts to be paid by the State and asked for a Commission to be set up to fix the amount of those debts, so that claims could subsequently be made for at least the amount of the Commissioners' award. Having thus obtained in advance a measure of official recognition for them, such claims would have to be met. Tokong had learnt something from Triad precipitancy, *e.g.* to get the Government to agree first that a certain sum is due and then claim for it.

The Raja Muda again gave a refreshingly independent opinion (*P.M.S. History* III page 12):—

> "The Raja Muda Yusuf said that the Mentri's conduct had been ruinous to the country and he professed himself unable to understand on what principal his creditors could claim to have their debts paid by the State".

As Raja Yusuf's opinion upon the claims, first of Triad and now of Tokong, was that both should be rejected, we may safely absolve him from having any personal interest in either. This point is of importance in helping us to judge the weight of hidden influence of the two Flags upon subsequent Perak history.

The Resident (Sir Hugh Low) considered the claim of the Mentri's debtors to be in a different category to that of ex-Sultan Abdullah's debtors, but whether he was aware of the secret influences of Triad and Tokong at work is doubtful, seeing that he had only just come from Labuan, and could have had only a cursory acquaintance with the origins of the Penang riots and the Larut wars.

The Resident gave the following reasons for the establishment of a Commission to settle the Mentri's debts (page 12).

(1) The Mentri in his capacity of virtually independent Governor of Larut was justified in incurring liabilities on account of his district. This virtual independence was based upon the genuine powers granted him by Sultan Ja'afar.

(2) The Pangkor Treaty supported the principle on which the Chinese claims were based.[1]

(3) Government has recognised the principle by the appointment of a previous Commission.[2]

After a long discussion in which (page 12) the Raja Muda, Raja Dris and the Temenggong were clearly opposed to the appointment of a Commission, a Commission was appointed consisting of:—

(1) The Assistant Resident (Mr. W. E. Maxwell).

(2) Raja Dris.

We may hazard the guess that the objectors' motives were as follows:— Raja Muda Yusuf, because he objected on principle to paying the outstanding debts of any faction: Raja Dris—perhaps because the White Flag claim for payment had been rejected at the previous meeting of Council and he felt uncomfortable lest where his own side had lost, their rivals should be allowed to succeed.

Award of the Mentri's Debts Commission
(Meeting of 27-2-1879)

The sequel appears in *P.M.S. History* III pages 26–29 which records a very important meeting of Council on 27th February, 1879. This meeting marks the first real step towards the modern material development of Perak under British rule.[3]

Item 3 (a) and (b) of this meeting are relevant to our subject:—

Item 3—

"The Resident, by desire of the Regent, laid upon the table the following papers:—

(a) Report of the Commissioners appointed to enquire into the liabilities of the State of Perak in connection with the troubles in Larut.

(b) Report by his Britannic Majesty's Assistant Resident of Perak of two criminal prosecutions undertaken in Penang at the instance of the Government in pursuance of the recommendations of the Commissioners".

The amount awarded by the Mentri's Debts' Commissioners (page 29, Item 6) was $166,753, (as against the $190,000 claim by Triad which had been rejected at the Council Meeting of 4th May, 1878).

One of the claims (No. XVI) approved under the award was for a sum of $14,000 to Chang Ah Kwee (Tokong). This must have made his fellow counsellor, Chan Ah Yam (Triad), wince! Tokong was beating Triad at its own game!

Triad's false claims against the Mentri
(Meeting of 28-2-1879)

The next meeting (page 30) throws light upon Item 3 (b) above. Putting two and two together, we are left to infer (not a difficult process) that Triad as always, not to be outdone, sought to square accounts with their rivals by putting in a number of false claims to the Mentri's Debts Commission.

Ho Ghi Siew (Triad) is prosecuted by Maxwell

The fraud was spotted and Maxwell instituted proceedings for fraud and forgery, in the Penang Police Court, against our old acquaintance Ho Ghi Siew who had made the false claims. We know that Ho Ghi Siew although in political eclipse with the British, remained one of the most powerful leaders of Triad in Penang.

For some reason unexplained, but which surprised both Sir Hugh Low and Maxwell, Ho Ghi Siew was not committed for trial by the Penang Magistrate. It is here interesting to note that no leading Penang lawyers could be got to prosecute Ho Ghi Siew on behalf of the Perak Government. The hidden power of Triad was making itself felt in opposition to the Government of Perak. It is probable that neither the Resident nor the Assistant Resident was aware of these under-currents.

The Minute reads:—

"Mr. Maxwell could not secure the services of any barrister of consideration. The onus of conducting the whole case......fell upon him. It was ably managed by the Assistant Resident and to the last moment it was believed, even by Counsel for the prisoner, that Ho Ghi Siew would be committed for trial. The Government of Perak is under great obligations to the Assistant Resident for the zealous, fearless and able manner in which he exposed this attempt at criminal fraud".

Footnote.—(1) This refers to Articles IV, XIII and XIV of the Treaty, (Appendix IXA).
Footnote.—(2) This, no doubt, refers to the "Larut Pacification Commission 1874", mentioned above.
Footnote.—(3) Those interested are recommended to read the minutes for themselves.

Clearly the authorities did not realise the hidden powers arrayed against them. Triad had won its first trick against the Government of Perak, as always with the help of the lawyers in Penang.

Flushed with this success, Triad showed the cloven hoof. Ho Ghi Siew having escaped committal, Triad (doubtless with the knowledge of *Capitan* Ah Yam and by the advice of their Penang lawyers) tried the old Malay game of *da'wa balas*—a "save-face" proceeding, common both to Chinese and Malay legal formulæ.

Ho GHI SIEW (TRIAD) HITS BACK

(Page 30 Item 3). Ho Ghi Siew took a civil action against Mr. W. E. Maxwell in the Supreme Court Penang, to recover $15,000 damages for malicious prosecution!

It is interesting to note the amount of the sum claimed by Triad (*in persona* Ho Ghi Siew) as compensation for their wounded feelings. It is just $1,000 more than the sum awarded by Mr. W. E. Maxwell as member of the "Mentri of Larut Debt Commission" to Tokong (*in persona* Chang Ah Kwee). History does not relate what happened to this impudent suit.

The first important point to note in this incident is that here we have definite evidence of continued intrigue and wire-pulling at work between Triad and Tokong in Penang, in the struggle for ascendancy in the field of opportunity now fast opening out before them in Perak.

The second point is that the Government of Perak of that day must have been entirely unaware of this underground intrigue carried on with the knowledge of two of their State Counsellors, whom they believed to be honest men.

Triad must have felt secure that their intrigues would not be disclosed to the British Resident, either by their European lawyers or by their rivals Tokong, which might have led to an uncomfortable *dénouement* for all concerned and loss of profits all round. Otherwise they would not have dared the risk that the British Officers in Perak might get to know that the civil suit of Ho Ghi Siew was in reality only a bluff sponsored by the Triad lawyers in Penang (Duke) and the Triad representative in the Perak State Council (Chan Ah Yam), as a trial of strength between Triad and Tokong.

It seems certain that neither Sir Hugh Low nor Maxwell ever suspected the *bona fides* of the civil action of Ho Ghi Siew, or that Triad influence entered into it at all, or that Ho Ghi Siew was merely a figurehead in the action which was really being sponsored by Triad in Penang and its lawyers, for commercial and political purposes in Perak.

Had they suspected what we venture to think was the real position, *Capitan* Ah Yam would not have remained on the Council and Triad would have suffered a severe commercial and political defeat. We are entitled to believe that the mutual rivalries of Triad and Tokong and of their satellites the White and Red Flag were given full rein, limited only by the proviso that they must not break surface lest they bring the real underground game to the notice of the British authorities.

CHAN AH YAM (TRIAD) MAKES A CLAIM AGAINST TOKONG
(Meeting of 4-3-1879)

(Page 41). At this meeting of Council Chan Ah Yam is conveniently absent when a personal claim by him against the Government for payment of a sum not stated, for repairs alleged to have been done by him on the order of Sir Andrew Clarke (who had left the country in 1875), to the house at Permatang (Matang) of To' Puan Halimah, wife of the exiled Mentri is tabled, discussed and dismissed.

This looks like the Triad member of Council trying to get square on cash claims with the Tokong member, using a personal claim this time, instead of the united Lodge claims which had flopped so badly (*viz.*, Claim in Council $190,000 dismissed: Claim in Penang Court (damages) $15,000—apparently dismissed).

The Red star is in the ascendant, the White star on the wane.

THE FIRST OFFICIAL REFERENCE TO SECRET SOCIETIES IN PERAK
(Meeting of 5-9-1878)

(Page 7, Item 2). In the Minutes of this Meeting there is reference to "the frequency of night robberies in the various kampongs", and to, "the recent desecration of a grave at Bandar Bahru". This doubtless refers to the grave of one of the British victims of the fighting at Bandar Bahru in 1875 and is indicative of a continued spirit of unrest still seeking an outlet among the irreconcilables.

The existence of secret societies in Perak is mentioned for the first time at this meeting *viz.* (para. 4) :—

> "The question of secret societies and the course which it will be proper to take in regard to them is also ordered to stand over; the letter of his Excellency the Governor having been sent to Krian for Mr. Denison's information and not returned".

We are not privileged to know what this letter contained. It was probably written by Colonel Anson, who was Acting Governor about this date.

THE MURDER OF CAPTAIN LLOYD, SUPERINTENDENT OF THE DINDINGS AT PULAU PANGKOR
OCTOBER, 1878

We must here leave for a moment our survey of the first Perak State Council Minutes (resumed below) in order to record in its proper chronological order the murder of Captain Lloyd, first Superintendent of the Dindings on 26th October, 1878.

Whereas the murder of the first British Resident of Perak has been accorded its full measure of importance by the official historians, the murder of the first British Resident of the Dindings four years later has been passed over in silence. Just as the murder of Birch had its political background in the intrigues of White and Red Flag, so the murder of Lloyd may probably be laid at the door of Triad or Tokong.

We have seen how unpopular was the "Dindings Clause" (XIII) of the Treaty of Pangkor, particularly with Triad and White Flag whose sphere of exploitation through the revenue farm, was thereby so much restricted. We have seen the anxiety of both White and Red Flag to have the Treaty annulled, aided by the European lawyers of Triad (Duke) and Tokong (Woods), respectively.

It cannot be matter for surprise, therefore, if disappointment at their failure was marked by the murder of the first Dindings Resident. There is no mention in the Perak State Council Minutes of this incident, because it occurred just outside Perak territory but within what had been Perak before the Pangkor engagement and well within the sphere of influence of Triad and White Flag at Kuala Perak.

We have seen only two references to this murder *viz*:—

(a) *Paper laid before the Legislative Council 5th November, 1878*, entitled Correspondence regarding the murder of Captain Lloyd, Supt. of the Dindings".

(b) *The Golden Chersonese* by Isabella Bird (Mrs. Bishop) (1879).

In both of these, the secret society origin of the murder is referred to.

Mrs. Bishop *loc. cit.* writing from Penang on 21st February, 1879, gives the following account:—

"All the white residents have been greatly excited about a tragedy which has just occurred at the "Dindings", off this coast,[1] in which Captain Lloyd, the British Superintendent, was horribly murdered by the Chinese; his wife and Mrs. Innes (wife of the Superintendent of Durian Sa'batang) who was on a visit to her, narrowly escaping the same fate.

A Chinese gang swooped down upon the house from behind, beating gongs and shouting. Captain Lloyd got up to see what was the matter, and was felled by a hatchet, calling out to his wife for a revolver. This had been abstracted, and the locks had been taken off his fowling pieces. The Ayah fled to the jungle in the confusion, taking with her the three children, the youngest only four weeks old. The wretches then fractured Mrs. Lloyd's skull with the hatchet, and, having stunned Mrs. Innes, who was visiting her, they pushed the senseless bodies under the bed, and were preparing to set fire to it when something made them depart.

No more is likely to be known. The police must either have been cowardly or treacherous. The *Pyah Pekket*[2] called the next day and brought the frightfully mangled corpse, Mrs. Lloyd, whose reason was overturned, and Mrs. Innes, on here (to Penang). It is supposed that the Chinese secret societies have frustrated justice.

The following are extracts from the official accounts ((a) above):—

(1) *Report from Col. Anson, (Lt. Governor, Penang) to the Colonial Secretary, Singapore, dated 28th October, 1878*

* * *

"It appears that about 1-30 a.m. on 26th October, lights were seen approaching the Superintendent's bungalow (in Pulau Pangkor) and shots were fired by Chinese robbers to warn, it is supposed, persons not to interfere with them. Mr. Lloyd got up, went to the door and called out to the Police sentry, but received no reply. He then returned towards his bedroom where he was struck down from behind by a man with a hatchet and then dispatched with further blows......

* * *

"Before leaving the robbers had endeavoured to set fire to the building, but the Penghulu Haji Mohamed Akib had arrived in time to extinguish the torches and the flames they had lighted".

* * *

"The Police at Pangkor of whom there were twelve, appear to have done nothing, and their conduct will have to be enquired into and accounted for".

* * *

Mrs. Innes had only arrived at Pangkor on a visit to Mrs. Lloyd two days before the murder and was about to return to Durian Sa'batang the following day".

(2) *Report from Mr. H. Low, (Resident, Perak) at Pulau Pangkor to the Colonial Secretary, Singapore, dated 1st November, 1878*

I have the honour to report that having received his Excellency, the Governor's telegram through the Lieut.-Governor of Penang instructing me to proceed to the Dindings, at about noon on 28th ult., at Taiping, I left Matang in the "Kinta" at about 3 p.m. and arrived here (Pangkor) at 11 p.m. after a stormy passage.

On arriving at this place I heard from Mr. Karl and Mr. Riccard who had been engaged in making enquiries during the day, that suspicion pointed strongly to a Chinese of the Ho Seng secret society, named Sin Jan, who had been a contractor at the Lumut Sugar Estate, with about sixty *sinkeh* coolies and (who) had not returned to Penang with the other eight *kongsies* which had been working there, when they were provided with passages by the Government.

* * *

Footnote.—(1) She means, on Pulau Pangkor.
Footnote.—(2) A Government steam launch, the s.s. *Phya Puket.*

N

A servant of Mr. Lloyd, who had quarrelled with, and seemed to have a bitter feeling against his master, and who had absconded on 18th October, also was thought to have been concerned in the tragedy. Grave suspicions also appeared to rest on the serang of the Pangkor Water Police, who is said to belong to the Ho Seng society, and none of its members (*i.e.* the Police party), except perhaps the sentry, seem to have rendered any assistance. The furniture in the house, I was informed, had been smashed to pieces, showing that a feeling of spite had entered into the motions of the murderers. The next morning I examined the premises,......but on the whole it did not appear to my satisfaction, that spite had much weight with the robbers...... On the night of the 29th October, Sin Jan was arrested by a party of Perak Police under Mr. Innes...... Mr. Innes told me that this Sin Jan is a man who was troublesome when he dismissed the coolies from the Sugar Estate, and had said to him on that occasion, that if the white men did such things, not one of them would be left alive in the country...... Mr. Lloyd seems always to have kept two short Snider rifles in his front room, and a revolver pistol in his bedroom...... The gentlemen from Penang (Karl and Riccard mentioned above), in concert with whom I am conducting this enquiry, agree with me in opinion that the arms had been treacherously removed, or rendered useless before the attack, but we have been quite unable as yet to ascertain how this was done...... The serang of the Water Police who had been twelve years with Mr. Lloyd, will also be sent under arrest to Penang. The revolver was found upon him with its ammunition...... It is very doubtful where he was at the time of the commencement of the attack, though he was active after it was over.

* * *

"The Police say that on the night of the attack, seven of them were in their quarters, one on sentry and four gone away to get wood, to the north end of Pangkor. They all say that when they awakened, their barracks, which are not more than twenty yards distant from Mr. Lloyd's house, were surrounded by Chinese, who stabbed into the leaf walls with tridents and pointed nibongs, and prevented them, unarmed as they were, from getting in.[1]

My colleagues examined these walls before my arrival and could find no such marks as ought to have been perceptible if this statement were strictly true; but I think that there can be no doubt that the Police quarters were surrounded before any of the men had awakened. The sentry says he fired five shots at the robbers as they swarmed up to the knoll on which the house was built, but does not know if he hit any of them. The Penghulu told me he had examined the ground early in the morning and could see no trace of any casualty amongst the robbers......".

We have not seen any further reference to this murder. According to Mrs. Bishop:—

"No more is likely to be known".

"The Police must either have been cowardly or treacherous"......

"It is supposed that the Chinese secret societies have frustrated justice".

"A wretch is to be hanged here (Penang) for the crime this morning, on his own confession, but it is believed that he was doomed to sacrifice himself by one of these societies, in order to screen the real murderers".

We may perhaps hazard the guess that the murder of Lloyd was as much a political murder as the murder of Birch.

NOTE ON THE ALLEGIANCE OF THE HO SENG SOCIETY IN 1879

We have learned from Vaughan, (page 100 *supra*), how Malays of Penang and the Province were joining the Ho Seng in large numbers as early as 1854. We have noticed as we proceeded (*see* pages 103, 106, 112, 218 and 252 *supra*) that the Ho Seng was, up to 1873, identified with the Triad and White Flag camp.

But in that year there is evidence in C.S.O. correspondence (*see* page 269 above), that the Ho Seng changed its allegiance and joined up with Tokong and Red Flag in August, 1873, just before the outbreak of the third Larut war.

There are indications that this change of allegiance, as in the case of the Hai San at an earlier epoch (*see* page 113 *supra*), was due to the admission of Hakkas to the Ho Seng.

Granted that the Lloyd murder of 1879, in which the attack on the two women was not the least surprising feature, was the work of the Ho Seng society operating from Penang with a political motive, we are still left in doubt as to whether the Penang Ho Seng had changed allegiance in 1873 together with the Larut branch; and, therefore, the motive for the Lloyd murder remains too in doubt.

The alternatives are—

(*a*) If the Penang Ho Seng was still Triad and White Flag in 1879, the murder may have been instigated by that camp out of spite for the loss of the Dindings revenue, under the unpopular Dindings clause of the Treaty of Pangkor.

(*b*) As we shall see below ("The Telok Anson Tabut Trial, Sept., 1882"), the island of Pangkor was rabidly Ghee Hin and White Flag in 1882, and may be expected to have been so in 1878, which suggests that the murder might have been a general expression of Malay discontent at the Treaty, which took its name from the Island five years earlier.

(*c*) If the Penang Ho Seng was Tokong and Red Flag at this date, the outrage may have been a *riposte* against Triad for its continued prosperity in support of British intervention and despite the set-back of Birch's murder, and the downfall of Sultan Abdullah.

(*d*) If it was solely inspired by the Chinese element in the society, it may have had the pettier motive of a stroke against Triad finances, whose representative continued to hold the Dindings "farm", after the cession of the territory to the British, whereas Tokong held the revenue farms in the other British territory in the area, Penang and the Province (*see* below).

Footnote.—(1) The Police explanation as to how they came to be "unarmed" on this night with twelve muskets between them, is unconvincing, but too long to quote.

The evidence shows that the murder was committed with the cognisance of the Malay Police, and the treachery and callousness of the outrage, particularly towards the two women, bears all the marks of a Tokong and Red Flag crime.

POLICE MEMBERSHIP OF THE HO SENG SOCIETY, 1879

The suspicions of treachery by the Police, so prominent in the Lloyd murder, have been met with again and again by Police Officers of experience in Malaya, and the conduct of the subordinate Police in the Lloyd case and their excuses for it, is the measure of their own condemnation.

The general question of the membership of secret societies by subordinate Malay Police, and their position as "creatures" of the White and Red Flag societies, is discussed in a later Chapter.

Mrs. Bishop refers to the execution of a suspected scapegoat culprit, in order to placate the authorities. In an underworld where, as we have seen, the *Tai Ko* of a secret society still had the power of life and death over his members, the provision of "a victim" ready to confess and satisfy the law, becomes, when the occasion arises, a matter of routine simplicity, in which the Police dare not interfere.

There can be no reasonable doubt that, whoever were the actual instigators, the murder was a further challenge to the Treaty of Pangkor and to the growing power of British intervention, which was at this time beginning effectively, though perhaps unconsciously, to curb the power and pretensions of Triad and Tokong in Perak.

We must now resume our survey of the State Council Minutes.

REGISTRATION OF CHINESE COASTAL WORKERS IN PERAK DATED 1ST MARCH, 1879
(Meeting of 1-3-1879)

From 1st March, 1879, regulations for the "more effective control of the Chinese on the coast south of Larut and for the repression of crime and violence in that district, several instances of which have lately been reported"—were passed in the Perak State Council.

These regulations thirteen in number, amounted to registration and licensing of all Chinese employed in any *kongsi* (woodcutters, sawyers and fishermen), along the coast. (*See P.M.S. History* III page 37–38).

This measure was in effect an attempt to register aliens, but the easy submergence of individual identity among the Chinese at once defeated it. It was only with the introduction of the finger-print system twenty-five years later, that the establishment of Chinese identity was attained. No means has yet been devised for fixing the identity of Chinese *organisations*, and for insisting that they preserve their legally approved character and status.

THE TAIPING RIOTS OCTOBER 3RD–10TH, 1879
(Meeting of 20-10-1879)

The next challenge by Triad was the attempt to seize Taiping town, stronghold of Tokong, in what was known as the Taiping Riots of October, 1879.

Ever since the work of the Pacification Commission (Jan.-Feb., 1874), Triad had been relegated to Kelian Bahru (modern Kamunting), while Tokong were given Kelian Pauh (modern Taiping), claimed by Triad as originally theirs.

Page 54, Item 4, makes reference to these riots as follows:—

"The Resident laid upon the table a report by Lieutenant R. F. S. Walker, Commandant, Perak Armed Police, upon......the events of the 3rd October, and following days. The Resident regretted......the necessity of firing into a crowd the greater part of which was composed of people who had been misinformed and misled by wicked and designing persons"......

This is an unsatisfying reference to what we are justified in thinking was but another episode in the under-surface war between Triad and Tokong. Walker's Police report is re-published in the *Malayan Police Magazine*, issue of February, 1928, but it gives no clue to the origin of the riot, either surface or underground.

We have not seen any other report, and so are forced back upon speculation. The Minutes continue:—

"The steady conduct of the Police......prevented the probable destruction of the town at Taiping and ruin of the peace of the district...... The Chinese members, *Capitans* Ah Kwee and Ah Yam eagerly supported this resolution and said that anything less than had been done would have certainly involved the firing and plundering of the town on the 3rd instant".

These well-rounded phrases give us no inkling of the real motive that lay behind this sudden and unprovoked attack, which differed in no way from the many that had preceded it in the twenty years' struggle between Triad and Tokong for the wealth of Taiping.

It is not unreasonable to suppose that the Taiping riots of 1879 was a final attempt of Triad, who felt their influence in Larut to be in the wane owing to a series of rebuffs under the new Government. to seize again from Tokong the wealthy Taiping mines, which the Pacification Settlement that followed Pangkor (page 298 *supra*) had lost to them, and by re-opening the Larut wars, attempt to restore to full vigour the former power and influence of Triad and White Flag in Larut.

Walker's artillery gave the final answer to this Triad dream. His final salvo on 10th October, 1879, may be said to mark the end of the Larut wars.

We must not assume, however, that this last throw brought no profit to the thrower. The failure of Triad to oust Tokong from Larut may well have led to the transfer of Triad energies to fresh fields in Kinta and Selangor, where they are paramount to-day. Thus, Triad's ultimate defeat in Larut may have been one of the causes of that vast development in the Kinta tin-fields destined in a few years to eclipse those of Larut in wealth and importance, and lead ultimately to the transfer of the commercial capital of Perak from Taiping to Ipoh.

From 1880 onwards, the Chinese tin interests in Larut appear to have remained substantially in the hands of Tokong, while those of Kinta have throughout been predominently Triad. Thus, we see in Fermor, *Report upon the Mining Industry of Malaya (1940)*, page 23 (foot), that 1880 was the first year for which Kinta tin production figures are extant. In that year, 14,738 pikuls were produced, which rose to 33,572 pikuls in 1884 "in which year Kinta was still in its infancy". The Larut figure for 1884 was 126,999 pikuls. Fermor concludes:—

"During 1892, the Larut production (exports) had fallen to 71,974 pikuls, whilst the Kinta production (exports) had risen continuously to 192,671 pikuls".

And on page 24, (footnote 1) he has:—

"Only once between 1893–1929 did the Larut sales reach 100,000 pikuls in 1924. On the other hand, the Kinta Valley sales have increased enormously, reaching the maximum of 796,481 pikuls in 1924".

These historical facts seem to support the view that Triad, finally driven from Larut in 1880, moved to Kinta and Selangor, where they soon became paramount in the Chinese tin industry, a circumstance which perhaps explains the preponderance of Cantonese and K.M.T. influence in Ipoh and Kuala Lumpur to-day.

EARLIEST MENTION IN PERAK OF WHITE AND RED FLAG SOCIETIES
(Meeting of 20-10-1879)

That the Resident, Sir Hugh Low, scented the secret society origin of the Taiping riots of October, 1879, is probable from the next item in the minutes of the same meeting, (20th October, 1879), which reads, (page 55):—

"The Resident then brought to the notice of the Regent, Red and White Flag societies, which Mr. Denison reports as threatening the peace in the Krian and Kurau districts, and says he is not prepared to suggest legislation at this moment, but he wishes the members of Council to think over the matter, with a view to effective legislation at no remote date, and states that he himself is in favour of repressive measures".

We do not know what gave rise to this reference, but there are indications scattered through the records that Denison, whom we have already met as Commander of a gun-boat in the third Larut war, and who later accepted civil employment under the Perak Government as Superintendent of Krian and Kurau, was more aware of the probable underground conditions of intrigue of that day, than any other contemporary administrator. The power of the Red Flag in Krian and Kurau to-day is probably little changed since Denison's time.

The minute concludes:—

"The Regent says he quite agrees with the Resident, and that these institutions are quite illegal by the laws of the country, which punish membership with banishment".

In view of recent underground Perak history (*see* Chapter XXV *infra*), this reference to repressive measures is interesting. In point of fact, as far as our investigations go no legislation has ever been passed in the Native States against the Red and White Flag societies although a reference to such legislation was made at the meeting of 20-2-1880 below. As we shall see in the following Chapter, the Ordinance of 1882 which suppressed them by name in the Colony, had no counterpart in the legislation of the Malay States, and in the suppression of Chinese dangerous societies in the Colony, and the Malay States, which took place in 1890, they are also omitted.

It is perhaps significant that only the Raja Muda Yusuf is recorded as having commented upon this motion by the Resident. Raja Idris, the Temenggong, the Dato Panglima Besar, and the two Chinese members, apparently preserved a discreet silence at this reference by the Resident to "effective legislation" and to punishment with "banishment" by the Regent. It is hardly possible that either the Resident or the Regent was aware of the close but secret association between Triad and White and Tokong and Red Flag.

It was not until 1889 that a Perak Order-in-Council appeared suppressing "Chinese Secret Societies".

EXTENSION OF THE SYSTEM OF REGISTRATION OF CHINESE TO KRIAN, KURAU AND SELAMA, 3TH NOVEMBER, 1879
(Meeting of 3-11-1879)

The reply to the Taiping riot, October, 1879, is perhaps to be found in the following item in the minutes of the meeting of 3rd November, 1879, extending the system of registration introduced from 1st March, 1879 (page 61):—

"Item 11. The Resident proposes that the coast regulations for the registration of the Chinese on the coast and in outlying districts of Larut which passed the Council on 1st March, 1879, be extended to the north side of the Larut River, and include all the rivers and districts up to the northern boundary of the State, the registration to come into force from 1st April, 1880, and notices to be issued at once...... Unanimously agreed to".

PERAK REVENUE FARMS

But if the Resident was becoming aware of the hidden power of Triad and Tokong in the sphere of crime and was taking such measures as he could to combat these criminal activities amongst the coolies, he could not be expected to be on his guard against the all-pervading influence of Triad and Tokong in matters apparently so remote from crime as the letting of the Revenue Farms. Perak was bankrupt as a result of the war costs of 1875. Sir Hugh's greatest anxiety was the revenue, and the successful letting of the revenue farms was vital to his policy. His predecessor, Birch, had been accused of making "a mull" of the farms, when struggling to float them early in 1875, with the help of Triad, thwarted at every turn by the greed and private bargains of Abdullah with the Triad farmers Tan Kim Cheng and Lee Cheng Tee. It is quite possible that the motive for the murder of Lloyd in 1879 was revenge by the disappointed camp at the award of the revenue farms in the Dindings to their rivals. It is certain that Sir Hugh Low was not aware of the extent and ramifications of secret intrigue which encumbered the letting of the farms.

TOKONG AND RED FLAG CAPTURE ALL THE "FARMS" JANUARY, 1880

At this Council Meeting, 3rd November, 1879, Sir Hugh made a statement of the arrangements he had made. This statement which is too long to quote is recorded in *P.M.S. History* III pages 57 and 58, from which we gather that he had called for separate tenders for :—

(*a*) Larut;
(*b*) The Perak river Valley,

from "capitalists such as the Penang Opium farmers", for a period of three years 1st January, 1880—31st December, 1882.

The two successful tenderers appear to have been :—

(*a*) For Larut Farms—*Capitan* Chang Ah Kwee;
(*b*) For Perak River Farms—Khoo Thian Tek.

REAPPEARANCE OF KHOO THIAN TEK JANUARY, 1880

Here, there comes into the picture again Khoo Thian Tek, condemned to death for his share in the Penang riots of 1867 and later with the aid of the Tokong lawyer in Penang (Woods) pardoned. He had suffered a temporary eclipse between 1867 and 1880, during which years we have noticed him in the background of the Larut disturbances; in support of Chang Keng Kui and Tokong interests.

We now meet him again as a semi-Government official and one of the most influential men in Perak, a Government Revenue farmer, whose influence extended everywhere backed by Government support. His "opposite number" in Larut, Chang Keng Kui, was but another of the headmen of Tokong and probably junior in the society to himself. The revenues of Perak were for the next three years in the hands of Tokong. This development is interesting because it fixes the date and the manner of the first thorough penetration of Tokong and Red Flag influence throughout Perak.

Whereas with the advent of Sultan Abdullah in 1874, Triad and White Flag had obtained a temporary and precarious footing in the Perak river valley and along the south coastal areas, now with the coming of Khoo Thian Tek and his band of Tokong revenue-collectors six years later, the victory of Tokong over Triad in the struggle for place, patronage and wealth in Perak seemed assured. But if Triad had suffered a serious reverse, their allies the White Flag had not yet tried conclusions with the Red. So long as the Regency lasted neither Flag had much prospect of finding favour in high places, but things might alter at the next succession.

The political importance of the early sytem of revenue farms must by now have become clear to the reader and a separate note on the subject appears at the end of this chapter.

From 1880 onwards, it is probable that both Flags began to consolidate their positions in Perak and recruit adherents among the ryot, using the truncated ceremonies of initiation of Triad and Tokong, against the day when there would be a trial of strength between them.

RED FLAG IN KUALA KURAU FEBRUARY, 1880

(Meeting of 20-2-1880)

This assumption is strengthened by the following entry in the State Council minutes of 20th February, 1880 (*P.M.S. History* IV page 2) :—

Item 11. The Resident then lays upon the table a ticket book of the Red Flag secret society which had been seized at Sungai Siakap (near Kuala Kurau in Krian) in the possession of one Inche Adam, who is reported to have recently established a lodge of the society at that place during the absence of the Penghulu. The two sons of Penghulu Haji Sulaiman appeared as registered members on the counterfoil of tickets issued.

Mr. Denison had made frequent complaints of the trouble caused by these societies and the Council had on former occasions declared them illegal.[1]

Footnote.—(1) We have not been able to trace any legislation on the subject. This may refer to an *Ishtahar* or Proclamation long since buried. In the Annual Report of the Resident of Perak for 1889, however, there is reference to the repeal of the death sentence for membership of secret societies. This may, of course, refer to a provision of Mohamedan law,

Mr. Denison hoped the Council would be able to assist him by punishing the man Adam.

Item 12. H.H. the Regent says that there is no doubt of the illegality of these "Juma'ahs"[1] in the State of Perak as they are contrary to religion and policy. He recommends that the man Adam be sent before the High Court for trial.

Item 13. Raja Dris, the Temenggong and the Kadzi express similar opinions.

Item 14. It is unanimously ordered that the man Adam be put upon his trial before the High Court of Justice at Kuala Kangsar.

The Council minutes make frequent reference to Denison's trouble with Penghulus, all of which appears to have arisen from Red Flag influence in Krian and Matang.

PAYMENT FOR THE PERAK WAR 1875–1876
(Meeting of 20-9-1880)

Item 14. "At this meeting the Council received a bill from the British Government of $250,000, being cost of the Perak war. It was unanimously agreed to pay the amount, but *Capitan* Ah Yam stated that "it was not the Chinese but the Mentri who caused the war".

The bill was for the Perak war 1875–1876 and not for the Larut (Chinese) war 1862–1873. Despite this obvious fact which robbed *Capitan* Ah Yam's objection of any point it might have had, he could not apparently, as a good Ghee Hin (White Flag), let the claim pass without a challenge to the exiled Mentri (Red Flag).

THE TEMENGGONG VOICES DISCONTENT
(Meeting of 30-12-1880)

At this meeting, Item 9, we notice a significant wavering on the part of the Temenggong in his support of the new British regime. The minute reads:—

> "The Dato Temenggong says that he does not know why it should be so, but all his relatives and his people generally, were better off before the present Government was established, and they cannot bear taxation".

We may hazard the guess that as the revenue farms in the Perak valley, had now for just a year, been in the hands of Tokong collectors, the pickings and the tax evasions of the Temenggong, who by membership of the State Council had identified himself in the eyes of Tokong, as a White Flag supporter, had doubtless been materially reduced, which might have been the reason for this *cri de coeur*.

There were serious outbreaks of fire in Taiping in 1880, (*C.M.P.* II 17). These may have been accidental, but may have represented further efforts of Triad to get even with the Tokong "usurpers" and smoke them out of the fat mines of Kelian Pauh.

EXTENSION OF REGISTRATION OF CHINESE TO THE PERAK RIVER VALLEY 1ST JANUARY, 1881

Be that as it may, the Resident took steps at the meeting of 30th December, 1880, to increase his hold upon the Chinese population by extending the system of registration of Chinese to include the Perak valley.

Item 14 reads:—

> "The Resident proposes that the registration of Chinese should be enforced in all the districts on the Perak river and its tributaries (this would bring in Kinta), partly to facilitate the apprehension of contract labourers who escape from Larut to Perak proper or *vice versa*. Agreed to".

CHE KARIM OF SELAMA AND HIS FLAG AFFINITY 1872–1882
(Meeting of 31-12-1880)

From the minutes of the meeting held the next day, 31st December, 1880, at which there was a discussion of Che Karim's claims in Selama, we learn that the Temenggong was a relative of the exiled Mentri and formerly lived with him at Bukit Gantang. The following passage is also interesting (page 21):—

> "Raja Dris says that he was the friend and constant associate of Sultan Abdullah. He remembers the issue of authority to Che Karim to open Selama. The Mentri had previously been consulted. Che Karim, thinking that the Mentri was getting the worst of it in his fight with the Chinese (about 1872), came to Sultan Abdullah (who was on bad terms with the Mentri) for authority".

From this we may infer that as Che Karim, virtual chief of Selama (1872–1882), had at different times acknowledged the Mentri (Red) and Sultan Abdullah (White), a nucleus of both Red and White influence was formed in Selama from about 1872, onwards. The "Red" influence would naturally remain predominant as neighbouring districts were then, as now, almost wholly Red Flag.

THE USE OF FLAGS ON MOSQUES
(Meeting of 5-1-1881)

At this meeting we have the first recorded mention of the use of flags on mosques. The record unfortunately does not state the colour of the flag referred to, but it is important to note the incident, namely, that Haji Abdul Wahid, Deputy Kathi, Matang, complained that a flag had been taken down from the mosque at Matang by

---

Footnote.—(1) See page 221 *supra* and Chapter XXIX *infra*.

To' Puan Halimah, (principal wife of the ex-Mentri, then in exile) who climed that the mosque was hers. It might not be too wide of the mark to guess that it was a White Flag and, therefore, a challenge to the Red Flag of the Mentri.

We then get the following interesting record (page 23) :—

> "H.H. the Regent states that it has never been the custom to use flags in the mosques in Perak and he recommends that no flags be allowed for the present. The Kathi (Shaikh Mohamed Taib) thinks that a White Flag with black letters may be allowed at the mosque but no colour should be permitted other than black and white.
>
> The Dato Raja Mahkota thinks that flags should only be allowed on the application of the Imam to the Head of the Government.
>
> Raja Dris and the Temenggong vote with H.H. the Regent who accepts the Dato Raja Mahkota's amendment".
>
> Notice to be issued that no flags will be permitted on the mosques or at festivals except by permission of the Government".[1]

This reference appears to be of considerable interest and importance to the subject of our enquiry. It would perhaps not be too much to suggest that we here have in January, 1881, the first evidence that Triad and Tokong through their auxiliaries, White and Red, were attempting to extend that hidden influence in the religious life of the Malays in Perak, which we have seen in Chapter XIV, already existed in Penang and Province Wellesley 1850–1860.

From the subsequent entry in the record, it is evident that the Deputy Kathi, Matang, Haji Abdul Wahid was a rogue and he would not, therefore, be above mixing himself up in Malay secret society activities. The question of flags on mosques in Perak, and their secret society significance, did not end with this incident.[2]

THE CLAIM OF MEGAT PENDIA

At the same meeting there came up for discussion the petition of Megat Pendia of Kota Lama for the grant of a "pension" by Government in consideration of his ancestor having held the Bendaharaship. This claim is very interesting and will be discussed in Chapter XXII in connection with intrigues of this family of Megats.

EXTENSION OF REGISTRATION OF CHINESE TO THE WHOLE STATE 1ST JANUARY, 1882
(Meeting of 17-12-1881)

We should note at this meeting (pages 28–29) the final extension of the system of registration of Chinese inhabitants so as to include the whole State:—

> "The Resident, therefore, proposes that the registration system now in force in the coast districts and in Batang Padang, Kinta and Bidor, be extended to Larut and that every Chinese male of more than 16 years of age be registered throughout the State".

DISTRIBUTION OF REVENUE FARMS AS BETWEEN TRIAD AND TOKONG FOR THE PERIOD 1880–1885
(Meeting of 11-10-1882)

At this meeting a return was made to the subject of revenue farms, due for re-letting for a further period of three years 1st January, 1883—31st December, 1885.

The distribution of the farms for the preceding triennial period 1st January, 1880—31st December, 1882, was roughly as below, so far as the available records enable us to follow :—

DISTRIBUTION OF REVENUE FARMS (ALL TYPES), 1880–1882

Place	Successful tenderer or farmer	Position or past history	Lodge and Flag
Larut	*Capitan* Ah Kwee	Member of State Council	Tokong and Red
Ferak Valley	Khoo Thian Tek	Head of Penang Tokong	Tokong and Red
Kinta Valley (by later extension)	Khoo Thian Tek	Head of Penang Tokong	Tokong and Red

Footnote.—(1) Cf. Colony Ordinance No. IV of 1882, section 3 referred to in the next chapter.

Footnote.—(2) Sir Herbert Dowbiggin has kindly supplied this note:—

This is of interest, as in Ceylon, flags at political meetings or processions have led to disorder. After the last State Council elections in 1936 the hoisting of a flag of one candidate opposite the house of a supporter of another candidate and the waving of flags in processions by rival candidates who in one case, trailed the flag of the defeated candidate in the dust, led to disorder. It was recommended by the Police that at future State Council and Municipal elections the use of flags should be prohibited.

The distribution of the revenue farms for the ensuing triennial period 1883–1885 was something as follows as far as we can trace in C.S.O. Native (Perak) 6500/82, 7282/82, 7669/82 and 9172/82 examined in this connection:—

DISTRIBUTION OF REVENUE FARMS 1883–1885

Place	Farm	Successful tenderer	Reference C.S.O.	Lodge and Flag
1. Larut	Gaming and Pawn-broking	*Capitan* Chan Ah Yam and associate in chop "Tye Lee" Penang ..	9172/82	Triad (White)
	Opium and Tobacco	*Capitan* Chang Keng Kui, in association with Chen Eok (Penang Farmer) ..	7669/82	Tokong (Red)
	Spirits	Cheah Bun Hean ..	7669/82	Unidentified
2. Larut coast	All	Chang Keng Kui and Chen Eok	7669/82	Tokong (Red)
3. Selama ..	All	Lim Ah Min ..	7669/82	Probably Tokong
4. Kuala Kangsar	All	Khoo Eng	9172/82	Probably Tokong (Red)
5. Kinta ..	All	Yee Kong and associates in chop Yee Sang of Penang, Telok Anson and Gopeng	9172/82	Probably Tokong. Their tenders were throughout opposed by *Capitan* Ah Yam. The Opium farmer of Penang. There is nothing to show whether this was business or Triad rivalry. Probably the latter.
6. Lower Perak ..	Opium and Tobacco.	Yee Kong as above ..	9172/82	Tokong (Red) as above
	Gaming and Spirits	Ee Che Hok and Lee Kung Lian (possibly identical with Lee Keng Yam S.O.S. page 241) ..	9172/82	Definitely Tokong, because supported by *Capitan* Ah Kwee.
7. Bernam ..	All	Low Kim[1]	9172/82	Probably Tokong (Red)

POLICY OF WIDER DIVISION OF THE FARMS 1883–1885

At the meeting of 11th October, 1882, (page 48) the Resident explained the reasons for this new division of the "farms" as follows:—

"Item 10. The Resident explains the reasons for dividing the farms so very greatly on this occasion, the chief reason being a desire to give people who invest their money in the country a chance of sharing in the profits made by the revenue farmers.

Item 11. He adds that although he has advised this course on the present occasion—provided, of course, that proper prices were secured—he was personally of opinion that on the next allotment of the farms they should be divided up into only two primary divisions—*viz.*, Larut and Perak Besar (*i.e.* Perak river) farms. In each of these divisions there should be one chandu and opium farm, which should include the rights now conferred on the north and south Larut coast farms as regards opium, the rights of the opium import duty farmer, the rights of the chandu farmer in lower Perak, and the collection of the opium import duty in Lower Perak, a spirit farm extending over the whole of each division, and a joint gambling and pawnbroking farm, extending over the same area. Such an arrangement would attract greater capitalists to the country, if indeed they were not by that time to be found locally".

During the period 1880–1882, Chen Eok (Tokong) seems to have become opium farmer in Penang, a position long held by Tokong (Khoo Thian Tek and associates).

Footnote.—(1) Probably identical with Low How Kim (Song Ong Siang *op. cit.* pages 190–191) who was connected with the Singapore (Tokong) revenue farm. He had been established at Kota Setia for several years, probably under Khoo Thean Tek, where under Birch's administration, Triad had been paramount.

By the allotment of the gambling and pawnbroking farms, 1883–1885, Triad and White Flag once more obtained a footing—or rather this time an official standing—in Larut from which area their influence had been rigorously excluded since 3rd September, 1873, on which date Sir Harry Ord had thrown the whole weight of British support in Larut upon the side of the Mentri and the Tokong faction.

Similarly in Lower Perak, which since the Treaty of Pangkor (1874) had been a Triad and White Flag preserve, the allotment of the 1880–1885 farms unconsciously gave Tokong and Red Flag for the first time an entry and a semi-official standing in that area.

THE EFFECT ON TRIAD AND TABUT OF THE WIDER DIVISION OF REVENUE FARMS, 1883–1885

The greedy gangsters directing the fortunes of Triad and Tabut at that time, were not slow to jump at the new opportunities presented to consolidate their territorial advantages. They began active underground recruitment, by methods of terrorism, blackmail and oppression, among both the incoming flood of Chinese *sinkehs* seeking work in the mines; and among the indigenous Malay population, largely an impoverished ryot, to whom as bait for membership the promise of a share in the profits of smuggled opium or, in the pickings of a gambling farm, must have made a quick appeal.

The rapacious Triad and Tokong chiefs must have played their cards well; all the profits were soon flowing to the Penang capitalist "farmers" and the local Tabut share was little more than immunity from persecution and the right to batten on their non-member neighbours in their own kampongs, secure from Police interference, through the power of the parent lodges.

Thus we obtain here a glimpse of the secret history of Perak as written by the hidden hand of Triad and Tabut, and we shall notice in a later chapter that much the same system in lesser degree, obtains to-day, as then took shape fifty years ago. Triad and Tokong retain for themselves their own profits from their own secret sources of revenue, while admitting Tabut to a semi-partnership in this hidden kingdom, through the *Wayang Melayu* (*see* page 255 *supra*), the ceremony of initiation to membership of the White and Red Flag. Thereafter, Triad and Tokong expect Tabut to exercise the following functions:—

Firstly, to protect Triad and Tokong from Police interference by means of the peculiar power which Tabut can exercise over the local Police and over members of the Public who are non-members or would-be complainants.

Secondly, to fend for itself by depredations upon its own kind, secure from retribution through the exercise of the same peculiar power, leaving all revenues unimpaired for the full enjoyment of Triad and Tokong.

When we come to examine the criminal history of Perak during the past thirty years, we shall have to admit that the picture here given of the interaction of Triad, Tokong and Tabut is a fairly truthful one. We must at the same time be prepared to admit that it casts a severe reflection upon the Police administration of Perak during the same period.

RIVALRY OF WHITE AND RED FLAG FOR TERRITORIAL SPHERES OF INFLUENCE, 1882

It was not to be expected that the invasion in 1880 of the White Flag area of Lower Perak by the minions of the Tokong revenue farmer, Khoo Thian Tek, would be accepted without resistance.

We have not long to wait before the official records supply us with evidence of the fierce undersurface rivalry between White and Red Flag in the struggle for supremacy and the right of exploitation in the different parts of Perak.

THE TELOK ANSON TABUT TRIAL, 25TH SEPTEMBER, 1882
(*Meeting of 19-10-1882*)

This Council meeting records the trial at Telok Anson on 25th and 26th September, 1882, of the headmen of White and Red Flag in Lower Perak, before the following Bench of Judges:—

Mr. Denison	Dato Panglima Kinta and
Raja Dris	Orang Kaya Mat Arshad.
Dato Raja Mahkota	

The accused headmen were:—	*Place*	*Flag*	*Sentence*
1. Che Sarib	Bagan Nakhoda Omar		Four years' R.I.
2. Saiyid Hassan *alias* Saiyid Hassan Yahya		White	Two and a half years' R.I.
3. Udin	Sungei Bulu	Red	Ten years' R.I.

The record states—"These societies have their head offices in the Colony, but have recently ramified into Lower Perak".[1]

Footnote.—(1) This official asseveration of 1882 contains two statements, the truth of which has been amply proven in the preceding chapters.

And further down—"Udin had resisted the Police with force of arms and had called upon the ryots to assist him".

This completes our survey of the Perak State Council minutes as published by Wilkinson up to 1882—we have not examined subsequent minutes, which doubtless contain much similar information. The foregoing must suffice for our purpose.

The following are extracts from the C.S.O. correspondence relating to the above case (C.S.O. Penang 6890/82) :—

(Extract from Journal of Mr. J. B. M. Leech, Magistrate and Collector,
Sabak Bernam, August, 1882)

"Raja Indut brought me a man who confessed to belonging to the White Flag secret society, and stated that he had joined by the advice of the Che Sarib of Bagan Nakhoda Omar, who is the head of the society on the coast. Che Sarib had threatened to "boycott" him and his family if they did not join the society, so he very wisely paid his money and took tickets.

Started at once for Bagan Nakhoda Omar with Raja Indut and some Police.

August 11. Arrived at Bagan Nakhoda Omar where I found four white flags flying at various houses. Arrested Che Sarib and on searching his house, found two letters from Pawang Wahab, one of the Pangkor White Flag "terah kolis",[1] instructing Che Sarib, Syed Hassan, and Che Lebai Mat, to flog, fine and disgrace, some people who had committed offences against their "Jema'ah".[2]

These were the only documents found after a very careful search of Che Sarib's and three other houses, but several people gave up their tickets, all saying they had got them from Sarib. There were no books found and I doubt much if any were kept.

In the evening returned. Che Sarib confessed, saying that he had joined the society through fear, some four years ago, (1878). His son had at that time given evidence against a man named Kassim, a member of the society, who was imprisoned for stabbing a woman. Kassim complained to the society at Pangkor and on Sarib's son going there a short time after, he was set upon by the Ghee Hins[3] and beaten within an inch of his life. Sarib's son then went to Penang and joined, and was told by Habib Jahier (i.e. Syed Yahaya), that if his father joined also as he was the *Katuah* of his village, he would be appointed an officer of the society. Habib Jahier went on to say that if he did not join it would not be safe for him to go to Pangkor, Larut, or Penang. Sarib's statement I believe to be true, and goes to prove how very difficult it will be to put down the secret society in the Native States unless something more is done in British territory than has hitherto been attempted towards enforcing the new Ordinance.[4]

We are very grateful to Leech for this entry in his journal, which establishes the circumstances surrounding the Telok Anson Tabut case, in respect of two of the accused. We learn that Pawang Wahab was headman of White Flag in that area, with headquarters on Pangkor Island, and with jurisdiction, reminiscent of the Triad disciplinary code (Chapter VII *supra*), as far south as Bagan Nakhoda Omar, the Bernam and the Selangor border. It is not clear whether Habib Jahier *alias* Syed Yahya was:—

(1) The headman of White Flag in Penang, or

(2) Identical with Syed Hassan *alias* Syed Hassan Yahaya of Bagan Nakhoda Omar, No. 2 accused in the Telok Anson Tabut Trial of 25th September, 1882. Nor do subsequent references help us to a conclusion.

The passage demonstrates the operation of the Malayan under-world blackmail system with which we are now familiar, showing how, when once a citizen has fallen foul of the secret society net, (in this case, a lad who had innocently given evidence in Court against a White Flag member), his very existence is made unbearable to him, whole areas of territory in his own country forbidden to him, and his life endangered, until he breaks down and joins the under-world. Subsequent chapters prove how true this picture is at the present-day.

Leech's information met with that incredulity and detraction at the hands of the next Government official to receive it, with which workers in this field are all too familiar (*see below*). This type of criticism usually proceeds from the shallowness of ignorance rather than from a depth of knowledge of the subject.

The following is a record of the action taken by the Penang Government upon the above report in the same correspondence—

(1) "Inspector of Police:—

This discloses a serious state of things, be so good as to enquire, and make report.
1st September, 1882.   LIEUT.-GOVERNOR,
                                                        Penang.

(2) From Inspector of Police, Penang:—

To Honourable Lieut.-Governor, Penang.

I have made a careful enquiry with regard to this; I was already aware of the existence of the White Flag society at Pangkor, but I believe it will be found that Mr. Leech's informer

Footnotes.—(1) The term *terah kolis* is not fully identified. It may be of Sanscrit-Tamil origin, meaning literally "father cock", or in Malay, *bapa ayam* the domestic cock (as opposed to *ibu ayam*, the domestic hen), and thence = leader, or *pendekar* or *gagah perkasa*, deriving from the language of cockfighting in the earlier days in Malaya. Thence it could be applied in secret society argot to the local headman of the Red or White Flag society, meaning perhaps, "cock of the walk". The term is no longer in use to-day. It may, of course, have a Thuggee or Ramaseena origin. *See* page 172 *supra*.

Footnote.—(2) This tends to confirm the submission made in Chapter XIV that religious Jema'ah were but cover-protection for the flag societies. *See* Chapter XXIX *infra*.

Footnote.—(3) This clinches the alliance between White Flag and Ghee Hin on Pangkor Island in 1882.

Footnote.—(4) Referring to the *Dangerous Societies Amendment Ordinance No. IV of 1882.* Repealed in 1885.

is really only trying to serve his own ends. I have spoken to Syed Yahya and he tells me that Che Sarib joined the society since May, when all the headmen appeared before me, and had the Ordinance suppressing Mohammedan societies[1] explained to them. Syed Yahya declares that he has never threatened either Che Sarib's son, or anyone else. All the books of the Red and White Flag societies were deposited in my office during the month of June; if the heads of either of these societies have continued their working since then, I shall be only too glad to see them punished. I have had no trouble with them here. When the White Flag existed here it was split up into numberless little societies, each with its own chief. I believe something of the same kind is going on at Pangkor. A man named Pawang Wahab is the headman there and he is, I am informed, on bad terms with Nakhoda Mat Talib's son Mohamed Noordin. The latter was a member of the Red Flag here, but joined the White Flag at the Dindings: he came to me some months ago and asked me to have him appointed Khali (Kathi) there; his intention is to build a mosque at Dindings so as to avoid going to the one at Pangkor, and his wish no doubt is to oust Pawang Wahab so as to be appointed head of the White Flag society in his place. I believe that this man also is not on good terms with Penghulu Maakib.

In conclusion, I doubt whether the head of the former White Flag society in Penang has had anything to do with Che Sarib's son since his joining the society some years ago. If the Magistrate and Collector at Bernam will give us anything to work upon, he may trust upon the hearty co-operation of the Police here, but the reason that no steps have been taken to enforce the new Ordinance here, is that none have been necessary.

I had all the headmen of both societies in Pinang and Province Wellesley before me, and carefully explained every word of the Ordinance to them. I then gave them a month to collect their books; this was done, and they are now in my office. I have had no disturbance, no meetings, and hardly a case of assault amongst Malays since. I think this proves that no action has been necessary on my part.

11th September, 1882.   *(Sgd.)* R. W. MAXWELL,
                                                                Inspector of Police,
                                                                Penang.

The foregoing specious comment is typical of much that has been subsequently written in Government minute papers on this subject. The eradication of secret societies, some of which are as old as the history of man on this earth, is not, however, such a simple process as well-rounded phrases in Government correspondence might imply. The convictions obtained in the Telok Anson Tabut case against Che Sarib and others a fortnight after the above was written, is some proof of the truth of Leech's information, and some refutation of Maxwell's claim that Tabut had ceased to exist in compliance with a legislative command to do so. The record continues—

(3) Colonial Secretary:—

In transmitting this correspondence to His Excellency the Governor, as requested by the Resident of Perak, I have only to say that he and all his officers will receive the most cordial assistance from me and from Mr. Maxwell.

Upon the introduction of the Ordinance to suppress these societies,[2] it was anticipated by some sections of the Community that it would not have been possible to do so, without risking disturbance.

Mr. Maxwell, by tact and discretion combined with firmness, has so dealt with the leaders of these societies, both Red and White, as will, I trust, by degrees ensure their entire extinction, and thus rid us of one of the great pests of social life amongst this section of the people.

13th September, 1882.   LIEUT.-GOVERNOR,
                                                                Penang.

(4) In C.S.O. Native 6500/82 (Penang), Sir Hugh Low writes in his diary under date 28th August, 1882:—

Mr. Leech praises Raja Indut for much active assistance in getting hold of the secret society people by which Raja Indut has incurred much odium amongst the other Rajas and the people: the chief offender being also a near relative of his wife.

(5) In C.S.O. Native 7735/82 (Perak), the following para. occurs in Sir Hugh Low's letter of 10th October, 1882:—

Steady pressure will be kept upon persons acting as chiefs of these societies and enlisting members and it is believed they will give no further trouble in that part of Perak.

We shall see as we proceed with this record, what degree of "further trouble" in that part of Perak and elsewhere, the White and Red Flag have been capable of giving during the past fifty years.

THE SYSTEM OF REVENUE "FARMS" AND SYNDICATES IN MALAYA DURING THE NINE-TEENTH CENTURY

A whole Volume could be written upon this subject.

The first step towards introducing the British system into each unit of the dozen or so administrations which make up modern Malaya, was the transfer of the work of revenue collection from a feudal system of private exactions to an orderly system of public finance.

This change was effected in the early stages, in each administration, by employing the services of the revenue farmer. The "Farmer" was invariably a Chinese, or, more usually a group or syndicate of Chinese, who by public tender, obtained from the *de facto* if embryo British Government, the monopoly of the right to collect duty or revenue under certain fixed heads, in exchange for a fixed sum per annum tendered or "bid" and paid to the Government.

The duration of each such "farm", was usually three years. The Government got their fixed sum as revenue from the syndicate and the syndicate were left to make

Footnote.—(1) *i.e.* Ordinance No. IV of 1882, discussed in the next chapter.
Footnote.—(2) *i.e.* the Ordinance of 1882.

what they could out of their bargain.   Two facts tended to make the system of farms inevitable:—

(a) The bulk of the revenue-producing population were the Chinese who preserved their own language and customs and could, therefore, only be handled through their own nationals.

(b) The Government of each unit had to start from "scratch", or behind it and had no funds and no trained staff for the work of collection and supervision of revenue.

The "revenue farm" in the hands of a Chinese syndicate solved both difficulties and assured the Government a fixed revenue provided the syndicate was financially sound. The syndicate put in their own men to collect for them and also employed Malay and Indian traders in association with them to help in the collection of revenue from those nationals.

In administrations undergoing quick economic expansion, such as Malaya in the nineteenth century, the revenue farms brought their holders great wealth and there was keen competition between rival syndicates to obtain the farms.

The system also extended to the Dutch possessions and to the more remote States of the peninsula.

The chief "heads of revenue" which were thus "farmed" were:—

The opium monopoly;
The public gaming monopoly;
The "arack" or spirituous liquor monopoly; and
The pawn-shop rights.

THE RISE OF THE REVENUE FARMS

The following extracts show to some extent the growth of the revenue farms.

Extracts from *One Hundred Years of the Chinese of Singapore*, Song Ong Siang pages 9–10:—

> Colonel Farquhar in a private letter dated 31st March, 1820, to Raffles expressed himself:—
> "Nothing can possibly exceed the rising trade and general prosperity of this infant colony,......of only twenty months standing. One of the principal Chinese merchants here told me, in the course of conversation, that he would be very glad to give $500,000 for the revenue of Singapore five years hence......".
> With Chinese forming such a large element of the inhabitants, a great many of whom were addicted to the opium and gambling habits, the idea occurred to the Resident to follow the lead given by Penang and Malacca and establish opium, spirit and gambling farms, thereby obtaining revenue for police[1] purposes. In spite of a strong protest from Raffles, then at Bencoolen, the farms were sold, realising monthly $395 for four opium shops, $100 for arrack shops and $95 for gaming tables. A little later the gaming tables were placed under special control of the "Captain China" and a tax levied on them. The proceeds of the gaming tax were applied to keeping the streets clean. The farm revenues were kept as a separate fund and applied to local purposes until May, 1826, when they were ordered to be paid into the Treasury.

* * *

Page 17:—

> Legalised gambling went on during the whole term of office of Mr. Crawfurd (1823–26) and the revenue from the farm which was $15,076 in 1823 was double that amount in 1826, being $30,390. There were, however, still residents who did not look at the subject merely from the point of view of revenue, and in 1827 the Grand Jury made a presentment against the gaming farm as an immoral nuisance and were met by this remark;—"I did not think there were thirteen such idiots in this Island". Ten years later the first Recorder, Sir John T. Claridge, between whom and the Governor, Mr. Fullerton there had been a most violent quarrel, made a declaration from the Bench that the gambling farm was illegal, and the Government reluctantly suspended the gaming-farm system. A few months after the recall of Sir John Claridge, Mr. Fullerton brushed aside his decision and affirmed the legality of this method of raising the revenue. But his success was short-lived, for towards the end of the same year the Court of Directors[2] finally abolished the farm.
> Two attempts were made later to reintroduce the gaming farm, the first being made by Mr. Bonham, the Resident Councillor, in 1834, and the second by the press in 1836, but both failed.

* * *

Page 131:—

> Mr. Gulland, who had become acquainted with Tan Seng Poh[3] in the seventies, has this interesting sketch of him:—
> "At the time I write of, he was head of the opium farm. He was a well-groomed Chinaman, with all his appointments of the best. The opium farm consists of a syndicate of Chinese, and it was over the periodical letting of this monoply that the Executive Council in the eyes of its critics was always coming to grief. Neither wonder if they did, for it is no easy matter to go into any business transaction on his own ground with John Chinaman and come out of the deal on the right side. Moreover it is not to the advantage of the Colony to wring the last penny out of the farmer. The poor coolie that he serves has to be thought of as well as the amount of revenue that can be squeezed out of the farm, and it is generally best in the interests of all parties that the farm should be in strong hands, doing well for themselves by the business. If the Government can get two or three syndicates in the field anxious to secure the farm, then the letting is a comparatively easy matter, but on the principal that half a loaf is better than no bread these different factions combine and work together against the Government.

Footnote.—(1) The word is used in its wider sense, of Public utilities.
Footnote.—(2) *i.e.* of the East India Company.
Footnotes.—(3) One of the original Tokong revenue farmers of Singapore, *see* chart below.

It is the duty of the head of the farm to judge of the means and position of any probable opposition and to decide whether the new concern should be fought, squared or to what extent taken into partnership. A very anxious time Seng Poh must often have had, but he was a very able man and appeared to manage matters highly to the advantage of himself and his friends, all of whom seemed to grow rich......".

     *   *   *

Page 159:—

The *Daily Times* reports the amalgamation (as from 1st January, 1871) of the Singapore, Malacca, Rhio and Johore opium farms in November, whereby the Syndicate was able to establish a uniform price for chandu at the four Settlements. The co-operation of Mr. Tan Seng Poh, the Rhio opium farmer at the time, afforded valuable assistance to the Syndicate in crushing out the organised system of smuggling which had for some time robbed the farmers of a large portion of the lawful fruits of their monopoly.

     *   *   *

The following extract from Swettenham *British Malaya* pages 253–256 written in 1906, shows the variation in the system of revenue farms, as introduced into the Malay States on the west coast of the Peninsula:—

Reference has been made to the practice of "farming" certain sources of revenue, the principal amongst them being the right to prepare and sell opium for smoking, to manufacture and sell a Chinese spirit called "arak" or "samshu" and collect the duty on all imported spirits; to keep pawnshops and receive articles in pledge, and to open and manage halls where public gambling on certain games was carried on during certain prescribed hours. The regulations governing the right to open pawnshops and deal with pledges, and to tax, manufacture, and sell spirits, are practically the same as those in force in the neighbouring British Colony. As regards opium the Malay States adopted a method different to and perhaps less objectionable than the one recognised in the Straits Settlements. In the Straits the farmer alone has the right to deal with raw opium and convert it into the preparation called Chandu, which is used for smoking. With the consent of the Government, he issues licences for the retail of chandu, and the interference of the Government is practically confined to seeing that the chandu is up to a certain standard of purity, and that it is not sold at a higher price than that fixed by the Government contract. A chest of fine Indian opium contains forty balls of the raw product. While the price is constantly fluctuating from under $750 to $1,200 a chest, the forty balls of raw opium when "cooked", and made into chandu, will sell for $2,500 to $3,000, according to the limit of the Government price. It will be understood that when opium is cheap the farmer is likely to make very large profits, and will be adversely affected by a rise in price. On the other hand the farmer has to provide the whole preventive service to protect himself against smuggling, and though his profits are usually very large, his risks are greater than most speculators are prepared to run. This system is objectionable principally because of the enormous power it places in the hands of the farmer for a period of three years, during which he holds the monopoly. While, therefore, in order to give him a profit and a fair equivalent for the risks, the consumer has to pay rather a high price for his chandu; from one point of view, the moralist may urge that the more expensive the drug the better for the community.

The Residents in the Malay States understood this system and did not altogether favour it. The miners, the backbone of the revenue, declared that, if introduced, it would put a stop to their enterprise and ruin the country. They objected to the power which might be wielded by a monopolist who was also a miner, and they declared that unless the coolies could buy cheap opium, they would riot first and then leave the country. The truth or otherwise of these arguments was not put to the test, for the Resident adopted the following system.

The country, for the purpose of these revenue farms, was divided into a coast farm (where there were no mines, and into which it was exceedingly easy to smuggle such a portable and valuable drug as opium), and a rest-of-the-country farm, which of course included the mines and all the up-country. The coast farm was let and worked on the same system as that pursued in the Straits Colony, only that the maximum price of chandu was a good deal lower than that charged in any of the Colony's Settlements. The coast districts were, and still are of much less importance and contained much fewer inhabitants (principally Chinese wood-cutters and fishermen) than the mines. Except for use in the coast districts, anyone could import raw opium on paying the Government duty, which was at first about $7 a ball, and is now $14 a ball. The Government licenced all retail shops, while mine-owners and other large employers of Chinese labour imported their own opium, converted it into chandu, and dispensed it to their own employees. After a good many years the Government, in some States, farmed the collection of the opium *duty*, and while that policy made not the slightest difference to consumers it enabled the Government to calculate with certainty on the receipts from this source for each successive period of three years. The risks of opium smuggling are small as compared with those of chandu smuggling, because every chest of opium exported from India to the Straits, and thence to the Malay States, can be traced through every step of its passage. A great deal of inferior opium is, however, grown in China, and attempts are sometimes made to smuggle this stuff into the Colony and the Malay States.[1]

As regards public gambling, which is permitted to Chinese, and always has been permitted in the Malay States, anyone can supply reasons against it......

It is not necessary to do more than state briefly some of the causes why the British Advisers have supported the retention of the custom......

     *   *   *

Page 256:—

The Malay rulers and Chiefs strongly objected to the introduction of measures to make public gambling illegal; they said it was an old established custom, they knew the evils which would certainly follow its nominal suppression, and they declined to sacrifice the revenue which was derived from sanctioning the practice under strict control.

Therefore, the gambling farm has been continued. It is only permitted in places and buildings approved by the police, and during very limited hours. It is to the farmer's interest to see that no other form of gambling is carried on, and his servants, not the police, are engaged in preventive work. There is no particular inducement for the class of Chinese who indulge in this habit, to play in places other than those set apart for the purpose.[2]

Footnote.—(1) This refers to the famous Red Lion Brand opium which to the present-day is smuggled in large quantities into Malaya from China, and supplies the "illicit" opium market with its stock-in-trade at cheaper rates and lower quality than the "official" commodity manufactured from Indian opium, and supplied through the Government Opium Monopoly Department.

Footnote.—(2) Public Gaming was officially abolished in 1912.

THE RIVAL REVENUE FARM SYNDICATES OF TRIAD AND TOKONG

We have shown that the Chinese community in Malaya in the nineteenth centur was roughly divided, both openly and underground, into Triad and Tokong. It is n surprising, therefore, to find that the rival syndicates who tendered at different tim for the revenue farms in the different administrations, also represented the riv commercial interests of Triad and Tokong and constituted themselves an *imperium* i *imperio* within the Government machine, as the main source of its revenues. Th following chart devised from information contained in Song Ong Siang *op. cit.* rough] shows the two rival parent syndicates of "Revenue Farmers" between 1865 and 1890 :–

SINGAPORE REVENUE FARM SYNDICATES AND THEIR PENANG AND JOHORE ASSOCIATE 1865–1890

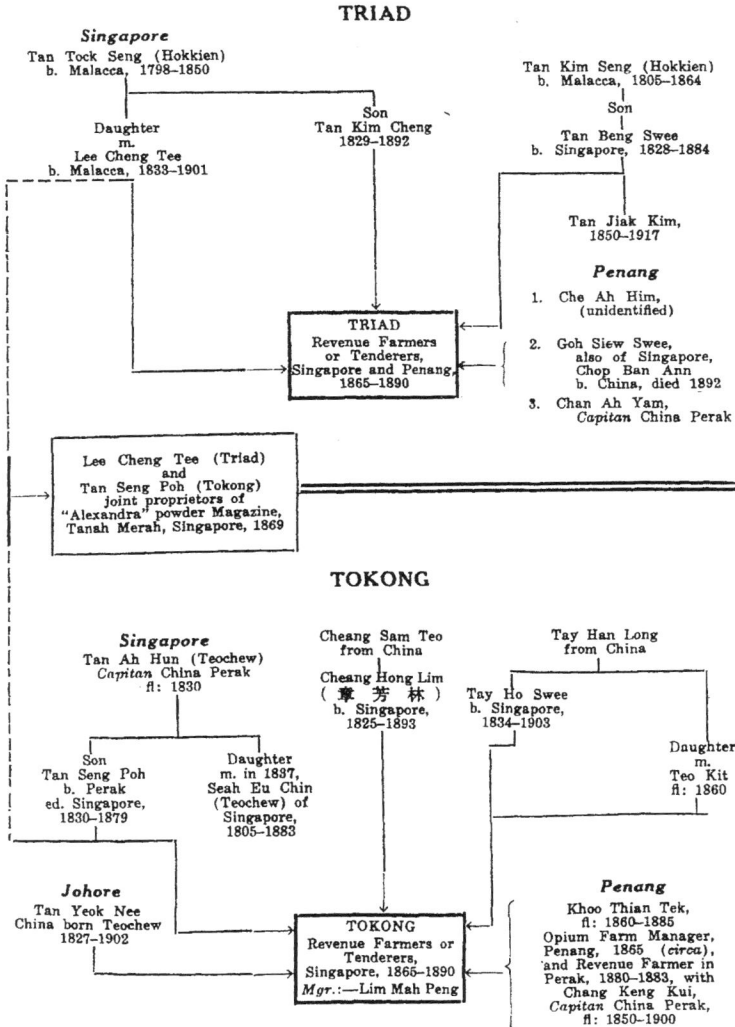

TRIAD

Singapore

Tan Tock Seng (Hokkien)
b. Malacca, 1798–1850

Tan Kim Seng (Hokkien)
b. Malacca, 1805–1864

Daughter
m.
Lee Cheng Tee
b. Malacca, 1833–1901

Son
Tan Kim Cheng
1829–1892

Son
Tan Beng Swee
b. Singapore, 1828–1884

Tan Jiak Kim,
1850–1917

Penang

1. Che Ah Him,
(unidentified)

2. Goh Siew Swee,
also of Singapore,
Chop Ban Ann
b. China, died 1892

3. Chan Ah Yam,
Capitan China Perak

TRIAD
Revenue Farmers
or Tenderers,
Singapore and Penang,
1865–1890

Lee Cheng Tee (Triad)
and
Tan Seng Poh (Tokong)
joint proprietors of
"Alexandra" powder Magazine,
Tanah Merah, Singapore, 1869

TOKONG

Singapore

Tan Ah Hun (Teochew)
Capitan China Perak
fl: 1830

Cheang Sam Teo
from China

Cheang Hong Lim
(章 芳 林)
b. Singapore,
1825–1893

Tay Han Long
from China

Tay Ho Swee
b. Singapore,
1834–1903

Daughter
m.
Teo Kit
fl: 1860

Son
Tan Seng Poh
b. Perak
ed. Singapore,
1830–1879

Daughter
m. in 1837,
Seah Eu Chin
(Teochew) of
Singapore,
1805–1883

Johore

Tan Yeok Nee
China born Teochew
1827–1902

TOKONG
Revenue Farmers or
Tenderers,
Singapore, 1865–1890
Mgr.:—Lim Mah Peng

Penang

Khoo Thian Tek,
fl: 1860–1885
Opium Farm Manager,
Penang, 1865 (*circa*),
and Revenue Farmer in
Perak, 1880–1883, with
Chang Keng Kui,
Capitan China Perak,
fl: 1850–1900

This association of well-known and respected Chinese with the two rival camps of Triad and Tokong does not impute anything improper to them, or cast any reflection upon their memories. At that period, every leading Chinese as we have seen, necessarily belonged to one camp or the other and the leaders of the community in both camps owed their positions as much to their society as to their business connections. This was the position openly up to 1870—less openly during the period of registration of Triad and Tokong 1870–1890, and has necessarily been altogether concealed since the official suppression of secret societies in 1890.

To take one or two examples from the "open" period:—

(a) Evidence *Penang Riots Commission Report* 1868 (Chapter XVI), Witness 44, Yeoh Whey Sew, Councillor of Toh Peh Kong (Tokong).

Page 57:—

> Q.—Why do you think Thean Tek could have prevented the fighting?
> A.—Because he has so much sway over the society that whatever he says, all the people will listen to.
> Q.—In your opinion why, if Thean Tek has so much influence did he not prevent the fighting?
> A.—I can't say.
> Q.—Was not Thean Tek very angry at losing the management of the Opium Farm?
> A.—Yes, he was.
> Q.—Do you think the late riots had any connection with Thean Tek's loss of the management of the Opium Farm?
> A.—Yes, I think so, because I have heard people say that Thean Tek and Lee Toh were partners in smuggling opium, and getting people to dispose of it.

Again page 60, Witness No. 49, Yeoh Yeong, a member, formerly Councillor of Toh Peh Kong:—

> "I am in the employ of the opium farmer and have charge of the prepared opium called chandu".

The foregoing suggests that Tokong interests quite openly held the Penang Opium Farm in 1867.

(b) We have seen in Chapters XVII, XVIII and XIX the manoevres of Tan Kim Cheng and Lee Cheng Tee to obtain the Perak river valley farms for Triad interests, when Birch was Resident of Perak.

(c) In this chapter we have seen the struggle between Triad and Tokong for the Perak farms under Sir Hugh Low 1877–1882.

These circumstances have repeated themselves with variations in all the administrations in Malaya and show how closely the early revenue farms were knit with the political development of British administration on the one hand, and with Triad and Tokong on the other.

Two other aspects of this subject demand our attention for a moment:—

Firstly.—The infiltration of Triad and Tokong into the Malay States by way of the revenue farms brought them, through their Chinese agents into close and semi-official contact with the *ryot* and thereby presented them with a ready means of extending their influence by recruitment to their Mohamedan auxiliary associations of White and Red Flag.

Secondly.—The fact that any one syndicate holding any particular farm, provided the opposition camp with a fair field for smuggling, promotion of illegal gaming and distillation of illicit liquor within the area of that farm to the detriment of their rivals. Hand in hand with this system went the exploitation of the only remaining vice, the trade in women and the "protection" of prostitutes.

To these causes may be ascribed much of the friction, gang-war and riots which are so common among the overseas Chinese.

This brief survey shows how the revenue farm system has helped to spread the secret net of Triad, Tokong, and Tabut throughout the length and breadth of Malaya.

CHAPTER XXI

TRIAD, TOKONG AND TABUT IN MALAYA 1868-1900
THEIR REGISTRATION AND SUPPRESSION

Several important results followed from the Penang riots of 1867 and the report of the Commission of Enquiry thereon (Chapter XVI).

First, there was the passing of the *Preservation of the Peace Ordinance* in 1867 as a temporary measure. Next, there was the criminal trial which followed the Riot Commission report, a record of which we have unfortunately been unable to consult for purposes of this work, but mention has been made above of the death sentence passed at this trial on Khoo Thean Tek and the sentences of transportation passed on others. From the records it appears that some of these sentences were remitted as a result of the activity of the lawyers Rodyk and Woods, and that two of those sentenced to transportation *viz;* Khoo Poh (Tokong) and Boey Yu Kong (Triad) returned to the Colony from banishment in 1869.

This gave rise on the Government side to a proposed amendment to the recently passed *Preservation of the Peace Ordinance* which led to hot debate in the Legislative Council (*see Council Proceedings 1869* pages 39–52), at the conclusion of which the amendment was apparently defeated as the result of representations by lawyers Rodyk and Woods.

THE REGISTRATION OF CHINESE SOCIETIES 1869

The next result of the *Penang Riots Commission Report* was the setting up of a Commission consisting of the Attorney-General (Braddell), W. H. Read, T. Scott, and F. S. Brown "to enquire into the secret societies".

The Commission, extracts from whose report follow, recommended that measures of control of secret societies be adopted. This led in turn to the introduction by Government of a bill for the suppression of secret societies. This bill aroused acrimonious debate, (*see Council Proceedings 1869*, pages 55-56, 63, 73-77, 91-100, 126-128) and finally *Ordinance No. XIX of 1869* was passed for the registration of secret societies, entitled "Ordinance for the registration of certain societies and the prevention of unlawful assemblies".

The report of the Commission which led to the registration of secret societies is as follows :—

REPORT OF THE COMMITTEE APPOINTED TO ENQUIRE INTO THE NATURE OF SECRET SOCIETIES
1869

Paper laid before the Legislative Council, 22nd July, 1869

(*Legislative Council Proceedings 1869.* Appendix "Y")

1. The Committee was appointed for the purpose of enquiring into the nature and objects of the secret societies which have so long existed in these Settlements, and of suggesting the measures to be adopted whether of total suppression or of restrictive regulations, in regard to the acknowledged evils which exist under their operation.

2. The labours of the Committee have been materially lightened by a valuable work by Mr. Schlegel on the *Thian Ti Hwei* published in Batavia in 1866. The descriptions contained in this work appear to be applicable to the Chinese societies existing in these Settlements, and the Committee have submitted portions of the work in Chinese characters to members of societies here, who recognise the signs, and inform us that the working of the societies detailed in the book, is similar to the state of things here.

3. The Committee have had the further advantage of perusing the reports and minutes of evidence taken by the Commission appointed in August, 1867, to enquire into the Penang riots and have derived much information from these important papers.

4. Considering that great weight ought to be attached to the opinions of the better classes of the Chinese community on the question of the total suppression or the regulation of secret societies, and that these opinions could best be arrived at through the form of answers to a circular letter, a Circular Letter was addressed to native gentlemen, and in reply a number of letters have been received. These have been written in many cases, on the express understanding that they were not published; they are, therefore, not added to the minutes of the proceedings, but the prominent feeling expressed is unfavourable to the societies; and while some desire their total suppression, in so far as any of them go beyond mere benevolent objects, all agree that they ought to be strictly watched, and prevented as far as possible from active subversion to the peace and good order of the Settlements.

5. The Committee have examined Mr. Dunman, the Commissioner of Police Straits Settlements, a gentleman of extensive experience extending over 25 years; during which time he has been at the head of the Singapore Police and has acquired great knowledge of the subject under investigation. Two Chinese headmen of societies at Singapore have also been examined.

6. The Committee have also had the further advantage of perusing the correspondence of this Government, in the year 1860 on the subject of the Chinese secret societies, and refers specially to the letters of the Hon. the Recorders of Singapore and Penang of 30th April, 1860, and the letter of His Honour the Governor to the Supreme Government of 5th of March, 1860.[1]

Footnote.—(1) This correspondence has not been seen for purposes of the present work.

7. All members of the Committee, moreover, have had a lengthened experience of the Chinese, and of the dangers arising from their secret societies (all in fact having been Magistrates in the Settlements for considerable periods), and in consequence have been enabled to bring to bear on the subject the knowledge and experience so acquired.

8. The Committee having thus detailed the means of knowledge at their disposal, proceed to intimate the results at which they have arrived.

9. The Committee consider it fully established that there are numerous secret societies in each of the Settlements, composed chiefly of Chinese, but that within the last few years numbers of Malays and natives of the Madras Coast, have been admitted as members; and these societies have a powerful organisation, and although some of them may have had their origin in benevolent motives, others have been founded on different principles, while from various causes many have degenerated into unlawful confederacies for objects altogether inconsistent with the public peace, and the due administration of Government by the constituted authorities; that although in most cases the hostility of the societies has been directed against rival societies, and that during their outbreaks they have not openly attacked the Government, the Committee consider that their persistent disregard of the authorities to be a serious evil, and one which is calculated to inspire the most serious alarm; and when to this is added the possibility of their hostility to each other abating, and of their acting in combination, the question assumes so grave an aspect as to require the most determined measures to be adopted for their control......

10. The societies at Singapore and Malacca have not lately appeared in so dangerous a light as in former years; but the organisation still exists, and is capable of being made use of against the public peace as well as against rival societies, and, therefore, the Committee recommend that the strictest control be exercised over all secret societies, whatever their original objects may have been.

11. The Committee consider it to have been fully established that the headmen, or chiefs of the societies, have such perfect control over the members, as to enable them to put an immediate stop to any outbreak of violence, and, indeed, to prevent such outbreaks on their part.

12. On these grounds, the Committee are of opinion that all secret societies of whatever nature, except Freemasons,[1] should be registered, and called upon to furnish returns once a year (or half year or quarter) stating the names and places of abode of the headmen and officers, the number of the members, and the days and places of meeting. Moreover the headmen should find ample security, not only for their own good conduct, but for that of the society to which they belong. The places of meeting should be open to the Commissioner of Police, and any Magistrate or Inspectors authorised by them. The headmen should be responsible for the production of accused persons, or of witnesses out on bail or recognizances, belonging to their several societies, in cases of trial before the Criminal, Civil or Magisterial Courts; and finally, the punishments should consist of forfeitures of securities, prosecution before the Criminal Courts, and the suppression of the delinquent society; the revival of a suppressed society being punished with transportation for a term of years.

13. The Committee feel confident that a law framed to carry out the above recommendations, would effectually put a stop to the obnoxious action of the secret societies, which form at present a just cause of complaint and apprehension; and while affording encouragement to those founded for benevolent or peaceful objects, would effectually restrain the turbulent, check the unruly, and at no distant period extirpate those whose influence has been hitherto fraught with danger to the peace and prosperity of the Settlements.

T. BRADDELL,
Attorney-General.

W. H. READ.

T. SCOTT.

Mr. Brown states that he agrees with this report so far as it goes, but as he thinks that it does not sufficiently meet the requirements of the case, he reports separately.

The foregoing document is a masterpiece of its kind. It demonstrates an axiom instead of proving a theorem. The first eight paragraphs add nothing to our knowledge, the ninth arrives at the conclusion already arrived at by Vaughan, Schlegel and the *P.R.C. Report* and which brought the Committee itself into being. The remaining paragraphs are padding for the single recommendation that "all secret societies of whatever nature except Freemasons, should be registered". As Read and Scott were both prominent freemasons, we can sympathise with their solicitude. The Committee was appointed "to enquire into the nature and objects of secret societies". It did neither.

The fourth member of the Committee, F. S. Brown of Penang, realised the deficiencies of the report and did what he could to remedy them. In a separate report of 10 printed pages too long and diffuse to reproduce in full, he got much nearer to the subject. He recognised that Penang's problem, with a large resident Malay population mixed up with the Chinese societies both in Penang island and in Province Wellesley, was a different problem from that of Singapore, where secret society activity was almost entirely confined to Chinese and Indians, the latter being mostly "Jawi-pekans" of Indian criminal ancestry, masquerading as "Malays".

What Brown pointed out in 1869 is substantially true to-day, and Penang has remained throughout the past sixty five years the cradle and nursery of secret society activity in Malaya. The following are extracts from Brown's report. The lists of Mohamedan societies in Penang he refers to, are unfortunately not attached to his report. The lists of Chinese societies (also not attached) are probably those given by Vaughan and referred to again below.

Brown says (*inter alia*) :—

1. "I agree generally with the opinions expressed in the joint report of the other members of the Committee, and, as they have long resided in Singapore, I would not presume to question the sufficiency of their proposals, if the intended legislation were to be confined to that

---

Footnote.—(1) W. H. Read and T. Scott, two members of the Commission were both prominent freemasons.

Settlement...... To these causes, as well as to the improvement which has been effected in the Police under the able management of Mr. Dunman, Singapore probably owes that immunity of late years, from dangerous feuds between Chinese societies to which reference is made in the 9th paragraph of the report.

2. I regret to say that our experience in Penang has been precisely the reverse. The societies have increased in numbers and boldness. Their leaders have become more domineering and reckless. It is seldom that two or three months pass over without breaches of the peace caused by their quarrels; and the permanent hostility thus kept up between some of the larger societies explodes every few years, in a general war between them, conducted, on each successive outbreak, with a more skilful organisation and better arms, with greater vindictiveness, ferocity,. and obstinacy, and with a more lamentable destruction of life and property, than on previous occasions. The regular force at the disposal of the local executive, Police and Military is wholly inadequate to deal with disturbances in which more than one half of the adult male population of the Settlement may be ranged on two sides, as was the case in those of August, 1867, and in the course of which, in addition to the hostile masses in town constantly attacking or trying to attack, each other in the streets, bands of hundreds, and sometimes of thousands, are marching about the country in different directions, in military array, and provided with muskets and field pieces......

3. ......A very considerable proportion of our Chinese, Malay, and Indo-Malay population, including many of the leaders and most influential members of the societies, are natives of Penang of the 1st, 2nd, 3rd, and even 4th generations. Numbers of them have been partially educated in our schools and speak English, and all are thoroughly aware of the freedom which English law secures to them. It is not surprising, therefore, that with the great increase in their numbers and wealth, the deference to their rulers which the earlier immigrants to the port felt, and which long continued to give a tone to the general character of the Asiatics in this respect, should have materially diminished in the town and in the island of Penang. The large Malay population of North Province Wellesley, drawn in great measure from Kedah, so late as 1821, and further recruited from that country in 1834, has long retained that strong sense of dependency and respect towards their superiors which they brought with them, and which was strengthened by their having found a refuge here from slavery in the Siamese Provinces. But with the great rise in the value of their lands and the consequent ability to gratify their ambition to make the pilgrimage to Mecca, or enable their children to do so, a very perceptible change in the same direction is steadily progressing among them also. The Malay, left in his own land and among his own people, is the least fanatical of Mohamedans, and he is very easily influenced, and many of the Hajis return from Arabia with new ideas and aspirations and with altered feelings towards Europeans. During late years the pernicious influence of the more ill-disposed or turbulent Indo-Malays and the Indo-Malay societies of the town has been greatly extended among the Malays of the Province, and all the villages on the coast facing Penang and for a considerable way inland, are now, more or less subject to them. It is to this change in the attitude of the Chinese and Mohamedan population to the Europeans that I would attribute the continually lessening sense of restraint which they show in the action of their societies......

*   *   *

Our Asiatic races have shaken off the sense of restraint and dependence that grew out of their native systems of law and government and the connection of these with the national religions, and found out that the system under which they live here, allows a great freedom in forming associations, and hence, great facilities to ambitious, turbulent and clever men to acquire power, and make it widely felt. They have learned that, on religious and benevolent pretexts, they may form leagues for almost any purpose without Government knowing, or caring, and engage in hostilities on a scale with which it is wholly powerless to cope, and which it can only put a stop to by appeals, direct or indirect, to the leaders. They have seen that out-break after out-break has occurred without any of the preventive and punitive measures called for by the well disposed inhabitants having been adopted by the Government, which on each new disturbance, is as little prepared to meet it as if it were without experience of any such crises, and had been taken by surprise......

*   *   *

12. The report also appears to me to be defective in not providing for compensation to be made for loss of, or injury to, life and property caused by the feuds of any of the societies. It has long been felt here that to make them pecuniarily responsible for all injury to property and impose heavy fines on murder, maiming or other injuries to the person caused by them—such fines to be applied in part for the benefit of the nearest relative of the person killed or injured,—would be, not only to apply a principle of natural justice recognised to a large extent by the law of England, but to hold over the members one of the most severe and effective restraints.

13. In the case of the Chinese in particular, there is no doubt that the leading and wealthier members of the societies would be much more influenced by the risk of heavy pecuniary penalties falling directly on themselves, than by that of a few scores or even hundreds among the mass of the members being imprisoned, or transported. They value the lives of the lower orders of their brethren—the fighting men—very lightly, and the latter appear to agree with them in this low valuation of themselves, if we may judge from the Twa-Pek-Kong scale of compensation for loss of life and wounds,[1] and the fact that needy Chinese may be found who are willing to take on themselves the guilt or punishment of others, for a price to be paid to them, or in the case of execution, to their families. Hitherto the chief restraint on the commission of crimes in the course of feuds of societies, has been the fear of retaliation at the hands of the opposite party, and it has had very little practical influence. But the Twa-Pek-Kong merchants would have hesitated to provoke the conflict of 1867 in the deliberate and determined way they did, and to begin it by issuing the order "to attack the Macaos wherever met", and as it proceeded, to supply muskets and cannon so as to make the destruction of the lives and properties of their opponents unprecedentedly great, and the Ghi Hin leaders would have been less ready to direct their society "to fight the Twa-Peh-Kongs wherever they met them; to kill, burn, and destroy; and do as much other damage to them as they could", if they had been made a law making their own property and that of other members of their respective societies answerable for every injury inflicted on their opponents......

14. The report would confine legislation to the Chinese secret societies but the disturbances which occurred here in 1867, were more protracted and dangerous and less under the control of Government than any previous ones, owing in a very considerable degree, to two of the Mohamedan societies having taken part in them. These, like all the other Malay societies are not secret. They were in their origin, merely *Jumahas*—religious associations, assemblies, or

---

Footnote.—(1) *See* Appendix III.

congregations; but equally in the town, the country districts of the island, and North Province Wellesley we have found, of late years, how easily they may be diverted to bad purposes. In their ordinary action they overawe and persecute those Mohamedans in the districts where they are strong, who refuse to join them, and they provoke quarrels and set up a power above the law. We have now seen with what facility their leaders, some of them intimates from boyhood of the Penang-born leaders of the Chinese societies, can induce them to join in the feuds of the latter. It was remarkable that the Indo-Malays and Malays were, as might have been expected, much more reckless and wanton in firing shots, even when only two or three were together,—more regardless of the interference of the police, and the Europeans who served as Special Constables,—and much less under the control of their office-bearers,—than the Chinese. There are many Chinese societies,—religious and quasi-religious, tribal and in the nature of trade guilds,—besides the secret ones, possessed of large property and having numerous members; and new ones are formed yearly. All, or many of the members of certain of these societies are members of secret societies, also, and may, at any time, be led to aid in the working of these. The Tie-Chu Chinese have lately formed themselves into a society, numbering upwards of ten thousand, and are now building a large hall in the town. Nearly all of them belong to the Ghi Hin. On one of the headmen being lately asked whether, in the event of quarrels between members, he and his fellow office-bearers had a kind of concurrent jurisdiction with the chiefs of the Ghi Hin, he replied, "The case would first come before us, and if we could not settle it, or either party were dissatisfied with our decision, it might be taken before the Ghi Hin Council". In the event of the Ghi Hin feeling itself hampered by an Act confined to the secret societies, it is easy to see how so closely allied societies might be made instrumental in carrying on its operations.

15. We must also look to the possibility of an Act confined to the secret societies being entirely evaded by the office-bearers, when required to find security, professing that their societies had abandoned the practices and rescinded the rules by which secrecy is maintained. Such societies as the Ghi Hin and Twa-Peh-Kong would thus continue free from any greater restraints than the law already imposes. They would remain the same in members, leaders and organisation, and the same also, there can be little doubt, in their constitution. For without being made subject to such an Act as is considered necessary in Penang, it would be difficult, or impossible for Government to prevent their retaining their present rules in secrecy, or to prove that they did retain them......

* * *

17. The learned labour of Mr. August Schlegel of Batavia and the evidence taken by the Commission of Enquiry have proved that there are now in existence in Chinese communities of Penang powerful societies, some of the objects of which are essentially criminal. We know that similar societies exist in Junk Ceylon and Larut, affiliated with the Penang societies, and of which indeed, they would appear to be branches. We know also that they exist in Singapore and Malacca. We have reason to believe that they exist in every Chinese community that has been established in the European and native countries of the Archipelago......

* * *

It is notorious that the Penang societies send aid in men, arms and vessels to the branches in Junk Ceylon and elsewhere, and that this aid rendered the feud that occurred in Junk Ceylon in 1867 nearly simultaneously with that of Penang, much more obstinate, sanguinary and savage than it would otherwise have been, the Siamese Local Government being driven into even a smaller corner than what was held by that of Penang, placed in a state of siege, and the warehouse of the Governor used by the Twa-Peh-Kongs as a prison for a number of Ghi Hin captives, in which they were deliberately burnt and suffocated to death. Piratical vessels were also fitted up here to plunder and burn the Junks owned by members of the hostile society and destroy the crews. The Penang societies in the same way drew on the branches in the Malay and Siamese territories for the aid of fighting men and the desperadoes or so-called "braves", who are placed in the front of the array.

18. These societies are thus criminal and dangerous in their objects or practices in the following respects. They are criminal conspiracies against a Government with which ours is in amity. They are criminal conspiracies to commit or aid and abet the commission of murder, mutilation, arson and robbery in the adjacent Siamese and Malay countries and on the high seas. They are criminal conspiracies against the liberty of individuals whom they threaten and persecute into becoming members. They are criminal conspiracies of the most formidable kind against the peace of the Colony. They are criminal conspiracies against the jurisdiction of the Magistrates and Courts for the maintenance of illegal tribunals of their own. They are criminal conspiracies to aid members, indirectly if not directly,—as accessories after, if not before, the fact, in the commission of crimes. They facilitate the joint action of members in the actual commission, and all the members are under the most solemn and binding obligation to harbour the criminals, to aid them in escaping arrest, and if arrested, in escaping conviction by subornation or perjury; they form, or facilitate and protect the formation of companies for smuggling, for the maintenance of gambling houses and brothels, and for the importation and hiring out of prostitutes from China, thereby adding to the seductions which they hold out to the worse, and corrupting the better classes of the Malay population, and powerfully promoting vice and crime. It does not appear to me that we should be justified in limiting our legislation to a measure that would leave the criminal objects of these societies untouched. It is our duty to suppress these societies, either directly and at once, by proscribing them by name under heavy penalties, as is done in China (I do not of course mean by Chinese penalties) or indirectly, by provisions that will only admit of their continued existence subdivided into bodies of moderate dimensions, with everything criminal or dangerous eliminated from their rules, and subjected to such surveillance by Government, at once searching and elastic as will speedily, or by degrees, according to the mode which Government may, and can, use the machinery furnished to it, put an end to their criminal action.

* * *

23. It appears to me that the contemplated legislation is of such paramount importance, and is calculated to have so great an influence in moulding the character of our mixed Asiatic population, that we cannot proceed with too much deliberation. It is less objectionable to leave things as they are a little longer than to act hastily and with insufficient light. The report of the Penang Committee is confined to two of the secret societies. It is very desirable that such information as can be readily obtained respecting the other secret societies, of which there are four at present in Penang (the Ho-Seng, Hai-San, Chin-Chin, and Hoh-Hap-Siah, the last a recent off-shoot from the Ghi-Hin) and the various other Chinese, Mohamedan and Hindoo associations, should be placed before the Council. Among the papers which append[1] will be found a list of the principal Chinese societies in Penang in 1857 with additions to the present time, and a list,

---

Footnote.—(1) These are not attached; probably he refers to Vaughan's paper.

compiled by the Magistrate of Police about the same time, of the Mohamedan societies. With the Chinese list are joined lists of other societies, some of which would come under the operation of the Act,—including the larger Mohamedan societies in which many of the smaller ones of 1857 have now merged,—or be desirous of availing themselves of the facilities given by it for the tenure and transmission of property, the protection of their rights, etc. The Commissioner of Police might readily compile similar, but more exhaustive lists, with short notes on the objects of the different societies.

25. ....Many years ago the Malays of Bayan Lepas who had been seduced into entering the Ghi Hin in large numbers, were withdrawn from it, and have since kept aloof from it and the other town societies. After the disturbances of August, 1867, the leading men of the Mohamedan community, at my request exerted themselves successfully to engage a large portion of the Malay population of the island not to enter the Chinese societies, and numbers who had done so were expurgated and took the same engagement. During the disturbances of February, 1865, between the Ghi Hin and the Twa-Peh-Kong it was found that the only practicable mode of preventing bands of armed Chinese assembling in different districts and crossing from one part of the island to another on their expeditions for murder, plunder and burning, was to station parties of neutrals at the proper points and patrol the roads so as to make sure of intercepting the gangs whatever direction they took, and opposing them by a force sufficient to overawe, disarm, capture, and disperse them. This plan was had recourse to as soon as the two societies, finding that the authorities had obtained the full command of the town, showed an intention to shift the field of conflict to the country. The Malays turned out zealously and in large numbers at Glugor, Batu Uban, Bayan Lepas, and most of the eastern villages, but in the middle of the island Ayer Itam, Paya Trubong, and Arlau they were found to be either friendly to the Ghi Hin, or too much intimidated by them to give effective assistance......

*   *   *

This was so obvious to the European gentlemen who were engaged in restoring the peace as Justices and Special Constables, that the Grand Jury at the next Criminal Session made a presentment, a portion of which I quote here:—

"That there have recently been riots of the most serious nature among the Chinese population leading to robbery, arson and murder in broad daylight by gangs of armed men. That this is only an aggravated repetition of outrages that have for years disgraced this station, and are evidently increasing in magnitude, and threaten the most serious conse-quences to all classes of the community. In practice it is found that the present state of the law and the defective organisation of the Police totally fail to prevent the recurrence of these outbreaks. They are solely the effects of Chinese secret societies whose pernicious influence has been often denounced by Grand Juries of the Straits Settlements......

The Grand Jury considering the inability of the Police force (expensive as it is), to deal with this evil, are of opinion that it should be empowered to secure at once in emergencies, the assistance of the ryots through their Penghulus under a suitable organization".[1]   (17th February, 1865).

......That there are no considerable obstacles in carrying it into effect is proved by the ready acceptance of a similar system by the Malays of a large portion of North Province Wellesley soon after the disturbances of August, 1867. It was most favourably received except in some villages near the coast having an Indo-Malay element in which there were branches of the town societies. The Telok Ayer Tawar society, the fourth in the appended list[2] agreed to dissolve itself, and the members living at Permatang Bogah, Permatang Sintu, and Permatang Rambi, voluntarily asked to be allowed to join in the movement, and signed the engagement not to enter any such society in future, and to aid in keeping the peace under head-men elected by themselves (subject to confirmation by Government) whenever called on to do so......

*   *   *

26. My recommendations substantially agree with those of the Penang Commissioners under Ordinance 21 of 1867. They recommended the entire suppression of the secret societies (and under this name they included the Mohamedan Red and White Flags which are not secret, so that they appear to have classed with the secret societies, all Religious, Benevolent, or Benefit societies that may be instrumental in disturbing the peace) and, failing that, their registra-tion......

*   *   *

PENANG, 21st August, 1869.

(Signed) F. S. BROWN.

Brown's style is diffuse which makes it difficult to prune brief and clear extracts from his undoubtedly able report. The report seems to show a clearer understanding of the true facts, especially as they relate to Malays, than any other document of the period.

EVEN AFTER REGISTRATION (1869) TOKONG REMAINED IDENTIFIED WITH TRIAD

The system of registration introduced in 1869, necessarily implied a measure of official recognition of secret societies, a fact quickly taken advantage of by the societies to increase their extortion and blackmail.

Pickering in an article published in *Fraser's Magazine, August, 1876*. entitled "The Chinese in the Straits Settlements" says:—

"The opinion of every respectable Chinese in the Straits Settlements is that the recognition of the Triad Society is a disgrace to our Government".

Pickering changed his view when writing in *J.R.A.S.S.B. No. 1* (1878) and *No. 3* (1879) on the same subject, and seems then to have favoured registration. The *Registration Ordinance No. 19 of 1869* was strengthened by *Ordinance 5 of 1877*, but it was soon found that any form of recognition was a direct encouragement to the spread of secret society influence. The "Rules" and even the "Thirty Six Oaths" were polished up for purposes of registration, objectionable items omitted, and polite references to the British Government and Chinese Protectorate officials inserted, so as to appear as innocuous and pleasing as possible to the official eye. Registration thus became a

Footnote.—(1) We have not been able to consult any report of the 1865 disturbances in Penang.
Footnote.—(2) No list appended.

farce. One good result which might have been expected from registration would have been the disclosure of the existence of the two camps of Triad and Tokong, with separate rules and different ritual.

Such a disclosure would have explained a great deal to the authorities, but it was not in the interest of either Triad or Tokong that the authorities should become fully enlightened. It suited both camps that the fiction should be maintained that the Ghee Hok was "a branch of the Ghee Hin". This fiction has been maintained to the present-day, by, we submit, a deliberate policy of hoodwinking the authorities.

Schlegel had exposed the Triad in 1866, but Tokong remained unexposed until Hutson published his article in 1920. (Chapter II *supra*).

Thus, for fifty-four years Tokong seems to have succeeded in concealing itself in Malaya within the folds of Triad, to the mutual advantage of the leaders of both.

From Hutson's article and from what we have seen of the rules of the Toh Peh Kong society in Penang (page 109 *supra* and Appendices II and III), we can imagine the terrifying quality of the real Rules and Oaths of Tokong, none of which, according to Hutson, have ever come to light.

The way Tokong got over the difficulty of registering even an expurgated copy of its rules during 1869–1890 is explained by the following extract from Vaughan *Manners and Customs of the Chinese of the Straits Settlements* (1879) where, on pages 112–119, he gives the rules of the Ghi Hok society as submitted for registration. These comprise a list of exhortations to virtue, dished up to look like the Thirty Six Oaths of the Triad Society, the whole being in every way unexceptionable, thus:—

> Rule 8. "If the concubine of a member of the Ghi Hok society run away with another man, he must not secretly call the brethren to come forward and break the laws by fighting. It is his own business, and he must manage it. The headman will not interfere. But if his lawful wife run away with another man he should acquaint the headman, and if he has no money to take proceedings in Court, they will provide him with a sufficient sum to take out a summons, and so let the Government punish the offender".

> Rule 12. "If any member of the Ghi Hok society introduce an offender against the Company's[1] law into the society, the headman, knowing of the fact will immediately dismiss such member from the society".

> Rule 30. "If any member of the Ghee Hok society, by quarrelling and fighting with the members of another Kongsee offend against the Company's laws, the headman will admonish and reprove him; if he refuses to listen they will dismiss him from the society and will not be responsible for any trouble he may get into afterwards".

It seems surprising that such stuff was accepted as genuine, but the registration of these dangerous societies left no other course open to either side. The registrar probably had to wink at a great deal.

Vaughan *op. cit.* introduces these rules with the following remarks page 112:—

> "The following rules and oaths are registered by the Ghi Hok society as *bona fide*, but are supposed to be manufactured for the purpose of deceiving the Police authorities. This may be so, but it is a remarkable fact that the writer has, during the numerous enquiries he has made on the subject, elicited from people of all classes professing to be members of the Ghi Hin society, rules and oaths to a similar effect".

In this passage Vaughan seems more than usually naïve. Granted that Tokong camouflaged itself in this rather obvious way by confusing itself in the eyes of authority, with Triad; it still seems amazing that throughout the long history of battle, murder and sudden death which ensued between Triad and Tokong in Larut and elsewhere during the twenty years of "registration", there was no sufferer from the inhumanity and extortion of these societies found to come forward and denounce the imposture, and declare Tokong to be what, we submit, it is.

The only explanation we can suggest for this amazing conspiracy to silence, is the certainty of death—and probably a very unpleasant death—to whomsoever in Malaya should denounce Tokong to the authorities. Even this seems a very inadequate explanation.

Registration had effect only in the three Settlements; but after 1878, in Perak and the other States, and after 1882 in the Straits Settlements, various measures were taken to control and suppress Chinese secret societies altogether.

TRIAD AND TOKONG IN THE COLONY AND ELSEWHERE IN THE PENINSULA 1868–1890

We must now take up again the story of secret society activity both in the Colony and in Perak and the other States from 1868 to 1890.

We will pursue this record in the following order:—

Singapore
Penang
Malacca
Perak
Selangor
Negri Sembilan

Singapore.—We here continue where we broke off in Chapter VI page 113 *supra* and Chapter XVI page 259 *supra*. The years 1868 to 1869 in Singapore were occupied with framing legislation for the control and registration of secret societies referred to at the beginning of this Chapter.

Footnote.—(1) The Company = The East India Company, *i.e.*, the British Government.

THE TANAH MERAH POWDER-MAGAZINE, 1869—A JOINT TRIAD-TOKONG TRADING CONCERN

The supply of gunpowder was an important factor in the preparations for the campaign which Triad and Tokong were organising against one another in Larut about this time (*i.e.* second and third Larut wars). They probably drew their supplies from Singapore, and victory would clearly lie with whichever side held a monopoly licence for a gunpowder magazine. It is curious and interesting to note, therefore, as recorded in Song Ong Siang *op. cit.* page 155 that on 31st July, 1869, the gunpowder magazine at Tanah Merah, Singapore, was opened with a public luncheon, the joint proprietors being Tan Seng Poh and Lee Cheng Tee. A glance at the chart of the revenue farm syndicates in Singapore (circa 1870) given at the end of Chapter XX shows how, evidently, there was a compromise between Triad and Tokong over the magazine licence, and one representative of each camp became the nominal holders of the licence. This is mere speculation and assumes that Government would approve only one magazine licence. It is none the less relevant and interesting for that.

REVISION OF THE LAW TO COVER CASES OF BOEY YU KONG AND KHOO POH

Song Ong Siang *op. cit.* page 155 refers to the amendment to the *Preservation of the Peace Ordinance 1867* mentioned at the beginning of this chapter in the following terms:—

> "In September, 1869, a bill for amending the *Preservation of the Peace Ordinance* was introduced into the Legislative Council. Its real *raison d'être* was to provide indemnity to Magistrates and Police Officers who had imprisoned Boey Yu Kong and Ku Poh, the two headmen who had been deported in connection with the Toa-Pek-Kong riots at Penang and who had returned to the Colony. There was strong opposition at the second reading of the bill by the Chief Justice (Sir Benson Maxwell) who was supported by the two unofficial members, owing to the penal and retrospective character of the measure".

As we have seen in Chapter XVI, Boey Yu Kong was No. 2 of Triad and Ku Poh No. 2 of Tokong in the Penang riots, 1867.

The following is an extract from the debate which took place in the Legislative Council upon the proposed amendment. On 28th August, 1869 the Chief Justice (Sir Benson Maxwell) speaking against the amendment to the *Preservation of the Peace Bill* in reference to the action of the Penang Justices after the riots of 1867, (*Legislative Council Proceedings 1867* page 43), said:—

> "If I am not misinformed those Justices at first sent up another man's name instead of Koh Poh's (Khoo Poh) and, I confess, having resided long in Penang, if I might state my private opinion, I think it is not unlikely that in that instance they were perhaps not far wrong, but then they were not acting judicially but on a mere *fama clamosa*. This man however was a natural-born subject and, therefore, your law was not able to reach the most dangerous of the place, but only persons of very inferior position and powers of mischief".

The "other man" here referred to must be Khoo Thean Tek. In this connection W. R. Scott speaking on the same subject in the Legislative Council on 28th September, 1869, (*Legislative Council Proceedings 1869* page 76), said:—

> "The Penang riots ought to have been put down with a stronger hand. After they were over, what occurred? One man was tried for murder and sentenced to death but his sentence was commuted to seven years penal servitude, and now he has received a free pardon! (This must be Khoo Thean Tek). Then a special act was passed for the Preservation of the Peace, and under that two men were deported and I hear now that they have both been pardoned! (This must be Khoo Poh and Boey Yu Kong). That is more dangerous to the peace of the community than strong-handed power".

SINGAPORE RIOTS 1870–1872

Song Ong Siang *op. cit.* page 158, mentions further Ghee Hok (Tokong) trouble in Singapore in 1870.

Again page 166 (*op. cit.*) Song Ong Siang refers to the Singapore riots of 21st–26th October, 1871, during which public flogging was resorted to and Tan Seng Poh (Tokong) and Tan Beng Swee (Triad) were appointed additional Police Magistrates to try the rioters.

TAN KIM CHENG A MAGISTRATE IN SINGAPORE 1872

Again at the same reference there is mentioned the serious Hokkien-Teochew riots of October, 1872, in which Tan Kim Cheng "sat as a Magistrate in the Police Court and tried many cases, invariably sentencing the guilty offenders to be flogged".

A commission was appointed to enquire into the Singapore riots of 1872 and their findings are recorded in Song Ong Siang *op. cit.* page 166 as follows:—

> "(1) That it was desirable to establish a system of Chinese immigration.
> (2) That the best way of governing the Chinese was through the Chinese, following the practice in vogue in the Dutch possessions, and in Saigon".

We have not seen the report of this Commission, but it is possible even at this distance to hazard the guess that the Singapore riots of 1872, were a sympathetic reflection of the fierce struggle then taking place in Perak between Triad and Tokong, and known as the third Larut war, which broke out in October, 1872, and led to British intervention. (Chapters XVII *supra*).

Within a few months of his appearance as a Magistrate in Singapore we find Tan Kim Cheng accepting the position of mediator between Raja Muda Abdullah and the

Mentri of Perak, with a strong bias towards the former, who was already in alliance with the Ghee Hins. The relevant passage taken from *E.P.O.* page 2 has already been quoted in full in Chapters XVII and XVIII. The following sentences will serve to refresh the recollection:—

"In October, 1872, a war broke out in Larut......between the Ghee Hins (Triad) and Hai Sans (Tokong)......

In January, 1873, Raja Abdullah went to Penang and in opposition to the Mentri entered into a written engagement with the headmen of the Ghee Hins dated 28th February, 1873, by which he authorised them to vigorously prosecute the war, promising in return that if they were victorious he would farm out the mines at Larut to them...... After two months more of protracted warfare the general state of things remained as bad, or even worse than before.......

At this juncture (June, 1873) the Mentri and Abdullah both applied for assistance to Mr. Kim Cheng, a Chinese gentleman of considerable influence in the Native States, and the Siamese Consul at Singapore...... On being applied to, Mr. Kim Cheng expressed himself willing to go to Penang and undertake the task of arbitrating between the Ghee Hins and the Hai Sans......if the Mentri......would acknowledge Abdullah as Sultan of Perak and guarantee him the share of the Larut revenue to which he would be entitled to as such. The Mentri refused to listen to this proposal, his mind being bent on driving the Ghee Hins forcibly out of Larut and on becoming Governor of that district independent of Abdullah".

Following this up, the Mentri obtained the support of the Governor (Sir Harry Ord.) and the services of Captain Speedy. In October, 1873, Abdullah went to Singapore as the guest of Tan Kim Cheng, and the result of this visit was the Treaty of Pangkor, after which Tan Kim Cheng continuously pulled Triad and White Flag strings in Perak, as shown in Chapters XVIII, XIX and XX.

REGISTRATION OF SOCIETIES A FAILURE 1875

Song Ong Siang (henceforward quoted in this Chapter as S.O.S.) *op. cit.* page 175, refers to a small riot which occurred on 24th May, 1874 at a funeral in Neil Road which arose:—

"Out of rivalry between the Hai San (Tokong) and Ghi Hin (Triad) kongsis as to which should have the honour of carrying the remains of the deceased who had two sons, one in each kongsi".

This reference is interesting as it corroborates the fact already established *vide* page 261 *supra*, that sworn brotherhood takes precedence over clan or family ties. Nevertheless as a general guide, particularly in Penang and in the native States, the following primary indications of the probable secret society allegiance of an individual Chinese might be accepted *viz*:—*Cantonese*, Triad and White; *Hakka*, Tokong and Red.

It is clear from the foregoing recital of secret society activity in Singapore alone, where control under the system of registration might be expected to be better than in less concentrated areas, that registration as a means of putting a stop to riots was a failure.

S.O.S. page 182 refers to Pickering's article "The Chinese in the Straits of Malacca" which appeared in *Fraser's Magazine for October, 1876*, in which he dealt with the subject of secret societies, making the following points:—

(1) The system of registration was a mere farce, books and lists being faked to mislead the Government. The real wire-pullers were unknown and the Government had no hold upon them.

(2) He advocated the introduction of responsible Government among the Chinese by the division of the community into Wards with headmen and a Captain over all.

In view of what, we submit, was the real position it seems unlikely that a single "Captain" system would have worked, when there were in fact two rival camps. The erroneous belief that the societies were all more or less branches of the same stem is clearly seen in this proposal, an idea which has persisted to the present-day, but which we submit is a fundamental misconception of the true position.

THE POST OFFICE RIOT SINGAPORE DECEMBER 1876

In December, 1876, occurred the Chinese Post Office riot recorded by S.O.S. pages 184–188.

This brought into prominence again a certain Teochew named Chua Moh Choon, a man whom Song Ong Siang credits with having been the head of the Ghee Hok (Tokong) in Singapore between about 1850 and 1880. It seems at least doubtful whether this man who was known to everyone to be a rascal, was the real head of Tokong. (*See* below).

Assuming for the moment that the Ghee Hok in Singapore was in fact a lodge of the Han Liu and not of the Triad society, we see from Hutson's article in Chapter II what a large number of office-bearers there are in such a lodge, and it seems more probable that Chua Moh Choon was a subordinate headman only, who bore the nominal title of head to forestall curiosity and supply cover to the real chiefs above him.

WHO WAS THE HEAD OF TOKONG IN SINGAPORE IN 1876?

The real head of Tokong in Singapore was more likely to have been a man of the calibre of Tan Kim Cheng, the head of Triad. The most likely man to have filled the bill in Singapore 1860–1880 was perhaps Tan Seng Poh, (*see* his relative position in the chart of revenue farm syndicates page 350 *supra*).

In suggesting the names of the real leaders of Triad and Tokong we do not seek to besmirch the memory of any individual. The whole of the Chinese community of Malaya (as of most other overseas Chinese communities) was entirely organised, for its own protection and its own governance, within a secret society framework and this was tacitly acknowledged up to 1870, in which year registration ultimately gave it official recognition.

The Chinese in Malaya, who by 1870 had become wealthy and influential, all owed their position, like the Highbinders and their Tammany counterparts in America of the same day, to the power of their secret societies. They could not otherwise have become influential. Triad and Tokong made them or broke them. No aspersion is, therefore, cast upon anyone in naming him a headman in this or that secret society. The leaders of the Chinese community in each centre of population were of necessity the headmen of the "Hoeys", otherwise they would not have been the leaders. We see this clearly in Penang in 1867 and at the Treaty of Pangkor in 1874, and the position remained more or less thus, until 1890 when the secret societies were officially suppressed, and declared unlawful under the British flag,—thereby reversing the position which had previously obtained throughout Malaya.

Are we then to suppose that the societies thereupon ceased to exist? that the men who were the leaders of the Chinese community in Malaya and the heads of Triad and Tokong in 1889, ceased to be the leaders and "resigned their membership" of Triad and Tokong as from 1890?

We have seen something of the ritual of initiation of Triad in Chapter VII and of Tokong in Chapters II, VIII and IX and it is not reasonable to suppose that any of these leaders could, even if they wished to, resign from those societies to which they owed their positions of wealth and influence *vis-à-vis* the British Government, merely upon the passing of a measure making illegal to-day what had been legal from time immemorial up till yesterday. It would be on all fours with asking the District Grand Master of a Freemason's lodge to resign overnight his position and to repudiate entirely his masonic associations on grounds which to him would seem unjust and impossible.

CHUA MOH CHOON (TEOCHEW) (蔡茂春)

This man is referred to by W. H. Read and Buckley *op. cit.* and by S.O.S. pages 88, 175, 187 and 203. He is stated by S.O.S. to have been the acknowledged headman of the Ghee Hok in Singapore between 1850 and 1880. He first came into prominence in the riot of 1854. S.O.S. *op. cit.* page 203 continues:—

> After that date his name appears again more than once in unsavoury prominence, but he was always careful to keep within the four corners of the law. He was mentioned in the 1871 "directory" as carrying on business under the style of Moh Choon & Co., Chop Hong Lee at Boat Quay, and he was one of the principal traders having dealings with Europeans.
> The fact that he was already a prominent figure in the Ghee Hok Hoey in 1854 and was the headman of that society for many years until his death on 26th January, 1880, would show that he must have been a man of ability and force of character.

When we have seen the power of Tokong in Penang and Perak, where it fought wars, made kings, owned a fleet, ran tin mines and held the revenue farms of the country, we cannot agree that such a comparatively small man as Chua Moh Choon was the real head of Tokong in Singapore.

Curiously enough, S.O.S. records page 202 the death of Chua Moh Choon on the same date (26th January, 1880) as Tan Seng Poh, who, as we have suggested above was a much more likely chief of Tokong in Singapore throughout the contemporary period. Their funerals took place on the same day.

THE CHINESE SECRET SOCIETY PICTURE IN SINGAPORE 1850–1878

The following general observations by Vaughan upon Chinese secret societies in Singapore 1850–1878 are taken from his *Manners and Customs of the Chinese* (1879).

His view that clan allegiance was stronger than secret society allegiance when it came to fighting, is not born out by the facts submitted in the foregoing chapters.

Vaughan *op. cit.* pages 7, 8 and 94, has:—

> Sir John Davis says in his work on China, "There is a peculiar turbulance about the character of the people on the sea coast of this province Quantung, as well as the adjoining one of Fuhkeen, which distinguishes them from other Chinese, and has been frequently noticed in the Government proclamations, especially in regard to the spirit of clanship which is a frequent source of so much disorder. This difference may be perhaps attributed to the seafaring habits which distinguish them from the rest of the Empire. The most notorious place for these excesses is the district of Chaou-Chaou on the frontiers of Canton and Fuhkeen but still in the former province. One of the inhabitants some years since carried his appeal even to Pekin against the magistrates, who either would not, or could not, restrain the outrages.
> The immense fleets of pirates who have often continued for years to infest the southern coasts, may partly account for the existence of a maritime population in these two provinces distinguished by a ferocity of character so different from the peaceful mildness of the other Chinese". One need scarcely be surprised with such a population at the outbreaks that have occurred so frequently in the Straits between the natives of these two provinces; the only wonder is that the Colony is so peaceful as it is. The outrages so graphically described by Davis were enacted to the very letter in the riots of 1854 in Singapore which occurred between the Cantonese and Hokkiens and were not suppressed until the island was placed under martial law. The speedy appearance of the military in 1871, when a riot broke out between the same people, has tended much to restrain the turbulent disposition of the unruly inhabitants.

Mr. Pickering writes in an article on The Chinese in the Straits Settlements, published in *Fraser's Magazine* issue of August, 1876:—

"The Chinese emigrants to the Straits consist for the most part, of the lowest classes of the population of the two most turbulent provinces of China, Kwantung and Fuhkien. The miners and artisans are from the former province, and belong to two distinct tribes speaking different dialects, *viz.*, the Puntis or Macaos, and the Hakkas or Khehs; these two tribes have been at enmity in China for years. The agriculturists, boatmen and small shop-keepers come from the districts around Chu-Chao-Foo, or Tay-Chew in Quangtung, or from the province of Fuh-Keen. Tay-Chews and Hokiens are often engaged in their own country in petty feuds. Every emigrant on leaving China carries with him, if nothing else, the prejudice of race, or the remembrance of his clan or district feud; these are elements of discord in any mixed Chinese community, but small compared with the baneful influence of the Heaven and Earth societies for the interests of which, the Chinese is obliged and willing to forget his family, clan and district".

Again, Vaughan *op. cit.* pages 95, 96 and 97 has:—

It is a popular error that most of the riots that have from time to time disturbed the peace of this colony originated with the secret societies; such is not the case, the greatest riot we ever had in Singapore *viz.*—that of 1854 occurred between the natives of Fuhkien and Kwangtung. The former under the generic term Hokiens were ranged against four races on the other side, *viz.*, the Macaos, Kehs, Tay Chews, and Hylams. The solemn obligations of the secret societies were cast to the winds, and members of the same Hoey fought to the death against their brethren.[1] In 1870–71 and again in 1872, the riots were between the Hokiens and Tay Chews; and so in 1876.

In 1854, the riots were not suppressed until martial law was proclaimed after the lives of thousands of men, women and children were sacrificed, and a vast deal of property destroyed.

In 1871, troops were called out immediately the riot broke out and had a most salutary effect on the Chinese population. The whole affair was virtually over in a day, but the fact of the soldiers having been called out so quickly had done much to preserve the peace of the town since.

In 1876, the riots were also between the Hokiens and Tay Chews but were quickly suppressed through the intervention of the headmen of those tribes.

Riots have occurred frequently between the great clans of Tans and Lims; the Lees and Choas; the Gohs and Hohs; the Lees and Tans; the Pohs and Choas; and between other clans. In all these disturbances the vows of the secret societies were sacrificed to the claims of family and district feuds.

The secret societies are additional elements of discord it is true, but so are any elements introduced amongst such an inflammable population.

The Chinese converts to Christianity, Roman Catholics, regard themselves as a distinct brotherhood,[2] they are called Hong Kahs[3] and any quarrel occurring amongst their members and outsiders *is at once* adopted by the whole body, and riots ensue. We have had disturbances between the Hong Kahs and Ghi Hins; and Hong Kahs and Ghi Hoks. The latter was a formidable affair which lasted several days and was put down with much difficulty.

Between secret societies we have had riots between Ghi Hins and Ghi Hoks; Ghi Hoks and Ghi Soons; Ghi Hoks and Hok Mengs; Ghi Hocks and Hok Heens; Ghi Hins and Hok Heens. The great riot in Penang in 1867 was between the Toh-peh-kongs and Ghi Hins.

In Malacca in 1875, they were between the Ghi Hins and Ghi Boos. In both these settlements there have also been disturbances between tribes and races.

To suppress certain elements of discord it would certainly be advisable to crush secret societies, but on the other hand, for the same reason it would be necessary to crush the Hong Kahs, and put a stop to all proselytism; and insist that all distinctions of clans should be abolished on Chinese landing in the colony.

Mr. Pickering observes in his paper that the opinion of every respectable Chinese in the Straits Settlements is that the recognition of the Hoey or Heaven and Earth societies is a disgrace to our Government. The writer has heard many respectable Chinese say the reverse.[4] They hold that the Hoeys do a great deal of good, and that it would be absolutely impossible to uproot them. They say the chiefs and members of the secret societies are loyal to the British Government and do their utmost to preserve the peace. It is only a few unscrupulous rascals who take advantage of their influence, as chiefs of the Hoeys, to squeeze certain sections of the community, and exercise a degree of terrorism over women and weak people whom they terrify. These do so in spite of the rules of the society, and might be dealt with personally by the Government and deported to China to put a stop to their nefarious practices.

The deportation of one of the heads of a secret society in 1876, for his supposed connection with the post office riots, though as far as the writer has been able to ascertain, an innocent man, has done a vast deal of good; it has shown the heads of the secret societies, that any breach of the peace might lead to any of them being sent away from the colony to the ruin of their business and families.

The registration of the members of the secret societies also has done much good. It is a remarkable fact that in all the riots we have had, the greatest respect has been shown to us. The presence of one native policeman in a street has been sufficient to maintain the peace there, and in no case have the police been attacked wantonly or with intention by the Chinese. The writer only knows of one instance, in 1875 or 1876 when an *emeute* took place by the Chinese against the native police for certain arbitrary proceedings on the part of the latter.

* * *

Footnote.—(1) We cannot accept this statement. We have dealt with the 1854 riots in Chapter VI *supra.* They were caused by the same division of Triad and Tokong or Hung league *versus* Han league, with which we are now familiar.

Footnote.—(2) *i.e.* the *tertium quid*, the refuge of escapists from both Triad and Tokong.

Footnote.—(3) The characters for this name are probably 紅教 Hung Kau = foreign religion men, *i.e.* converts to Christianity; the character 紅 hung = red, being used in its vulgar meaning. *Cf.* 紅毛人 hung mo yan = red haired man = foreigner. The term should in any case be clearly distinguished in sound and meaning from 洪家 hung ka = flood family, a name for the Triad society (page 1 *supra*).

The correct term for Roman Catholic is 天主教 Tin Chu Kau or Heaven's Lord religion.

Footnote.—(4) Pickering was throughout antagonistic to Triad (Tin Tei Hui) although he later became an honorary member of a Triad lodge in Singapore.

Page 107:—

The greatest danger to the peace of the colony lies in the hatred that exists between the lower orders of the great tribes of Hokiens and Cantonese, who have at present no recognised leaders, but fortunately in Singapore are kept in check by the influence and good advice of such men as the Hon. Mr. Whampoa, Tan Kim Ching, Seah Eu Ching and his sons, Tan Beng Swee, Tan Seng Poh, and other influential men of both sections;[1] whose advice is constantly sought by their countrymen, and who are ever ready at great sacrifice to themselves, to attend to their complaints and advise them, always in favour of peace and quietness. Doubtless, in Penang and Malacca the rabble are kept in check by the same influence. One of the greatest objections the writer can urge against the secret societies is that, it gives the head men of unscrupulous character the opportunity of establishing a reign of terror amongst the people. They have always at their command a number of *samsings* or rowdies who are ready to obey their behests to the letter. These generally take possession of the brothels; act as protectors as they say to the women; and take the opportunity of fleecing these poor creatures for the benefit of themselves and their masters. All the brothels in Singapore are under the protection of certain chiefs of various secret societies, and the inmates are forced to contribute money not only for matters relating to themselves, but as a kind of blackmail for the protection afforded them. This tax is levied not only on the women, who are however the largest contributors, but on petty shopkeepers. Many of the chiefs and officers of the secret societies subsist solely on this blackmail and the monies they can squeeze out of the peaceful inhabitants of the colony. The influence of these scoundrels can only be shaken by a counter influence exercised by the police and other authorities. The writer does not agree with Mr. Pickering that secret societies can be suppressed by legislation. This has been tried with reference to gaming and proved an utter failure; and were it to be tried with secret societies, a principal of antagonism would be initiated between the Chinese and the Government which at present does not exist, and which it would be unwise to invoke.

The following secret societies at Singapore are registered as dangerous:—

Ghi Hin,	Tay Chew	⎫
"	Hokien	⎪
"	Macao—called "Kong-foo-sin"[2]	⎬ The Ghi Hin emanated from the Triad society of China.
"	Hylam	⎪
"	Keh, "Song Pek Kwan"	⎭

Ghi Kok		⎫
Ghi Kee	"Kong Hok"	⎬ These four are branches of the Ghi Hin and connected with that institution; but between some and the Mother society, no good feeling exists.[3]
Hok Hin		⎪
Ghi Sin		⎭

Hye San
* Hin Beng Hong†
* Yeat Tong Koon
* Tong Ngu Hong.

The three marked * are not considered dangerous. In the writer's opinion these tribal societies are quite as dangerous to the peace of the colony as the Ghi Hin. The Tan society, Hin Beng Hong has fought with the Lims and Lees, and is powerful enough in numbers to face any of the tribal or secret societies.

† This society admits men of the seh, or clan Tan only.

* * *

Page 108:—

It is said that in Singapore more than forty thousand Chinese belong to the Triad societies. The Ghi Hin claim about fourteen thousand at least; the Ghi Kee, Hok Hin, Ghi Sin and Hye San about three or four thousand each. The Ghi Hoks number about ten thousand at least.

* * *

The Ghi Hin society at Singapore has a fine lodge at Rochore. It is a large upper roomed building about sixty feet wide, and one hundred and twenty feet long, with extensive kitchens on each side thirty to forty feet wide extending the whole length of the building, capable of cooking dinner for several hundred men. The following nine societies are branches of the Ghi Hin and are intimately connected with it *viz*:—the Ghi Hin Macao, the Ghi Hin Hokien, the Ghi Hin Tay Chew, the Ghi Hin Keh or Song Pek Kwan, the Ghi Hin Hylams, the Ghi Hok, the Ghi Kee, the Ghi Sin and Hok Hin.

No event of any importance can be carried into effect by any of these without communicating with the parent society. Such as the election of an elder brother or a sinsay, or other officer; and on the 22nd of the 7th moon, and 22nd of the 12th moon in each year, the members of all these societies feast together at this lodge.[4]

So much for Vaughan's careful analysis of the problem in 1879. He was handicapped in his observations by an incomplete picture of the Chinese under-world of his day.

PICKERING'S ANNUAL REPORT OF 1878

The following excerpt from Pickering's 1878 annual report shows the position and power of the societies at that time, the opinion which Pickering then held of them, and the attitude of Government towards them:—

During the year 1878, the headmen of the various Hoeys have almost without exception afforded prompt and efficient assistance when called upon by the Inspector-General of Police or myself, and they have shown a marked and growing disposition to refer their disputes and quarrels to the Government instead of, as heretofore, fighting on every possible occasion. The Lodge meetings of the different societies have been visited several times during the year and

Footnote.—(1) Vaughan was unaware that "the influential men of both sections", were themselves the real heads of the two stems of the secret society world.

Footnote.—(2) This is a misprint for Kong Foo Siu, or Shiu (廣府肇) the name by which the Cantonese Branch of Ghee Hin was known.

Footnote.—(3) Vaughan is conscious of a difference, but does not know what it is. We submit that it is the difference between Triad and Tokong.

Footnote.—(4) This statement seems open to doubt, but we cannot dispute it.

an initiation ceremony in its integrity lasting from 10 p.m. to 3 a.m. has been witnessed by the Colonial Secretary, the Inspector-General of Police, the Assistant Protector of Chinese and myself. In cases where the headmen of a lodge offend against the general laws of the Gi Hin (or mother) society they are tried at the Rochore Kongsi house before a General Council of the nine branches, and Major Dunlop and myself have several times been requested to attend these trials to see fair play. The services of the headmen are continually called for in the hundreds of cases of petty disputes and debts which are referred to this office, as the lower class of Chinese in the Colony almost invariably belong to some Hoey. The improvement in the conduct of the chiefs of societies has not been effected without a certain diminution of their power and authority and has resulted in reducing largely the revenues of the different Kongsis. The inferior office-bearers and members, knowing that there is always an appeal from any injustice perpetrated by their chiefs, are apt to obey them only when their orders coincide with their own wishes; and, feeling that no severe punishment can follow, they are exceedingly lax in the payment of the half-yearly subscriptions. Thus, for instance, the best disciplined society in Singapore—the Gi Hok—now contains 3,294 registered members; yet the whole amount of subscriptions (nominally at $1 per head) received during 1878 only amounted to $2,363. The original Gi Hin society again has on our register 3,425 members but is at present in a disorganized state and the subscriptions only amount to about $1,000. In fact, the sums now received scarcely suffice to pay the working expenses of the lodges, and continual complaints are made that the district headmen hold back the subscriptions collected from their respective members. It may be said indeed that the secret societies of Singapore are far from flourishing and their power for evil is comparatively small. The Police, however, will I think bear me out when I say that the Hoeys are often very useful in assisting the Government to deal with the lower classes of the Chinese. That such societies when left to themselves and allowed to acquire power and wealth are undoubtedly dangerous is shewn by the riot at Nibong Tebal in Province Wellesley and the late Dindings tragedy.[1] The Gi Hin, Toa Peh Kong, and Ho Seng societies of Penang control most of the Chinese population of that Island and the adjoining province. The Gi Hin has large funds invested in house or land property and the Ho Seng virtually rules the coast population of Larut, the Dindings and Perak. The riot at Nibong Tebal was caused by an attack on a Gi Hok village by the Gi Hins, and Mr. Low, H. B. M. Resident at Perak, attributes the murder of Captain Lloyd to the intrigues of the Ho Seng society. If milder measures do not succeed in breaking the mischievous and unruly spirit of these societies, it is surely time that the Government suppressed them with a strong hand. It is unjust to the European community and to the well-disposed and really respectable portion of the Chinese that the public peace should be disturbed, life endangered, and the law set at defiance by semi-savages whom hunger, poverty, or the punishment due to crimes committed in their own country have forced to seek the protection and immunity afforded by our too lenient rule. It is all very well to call the Chinese "the backbone of the Colony"; but it must be recollected that the flag made the Settlements and that Chinese flock to them only for their own advantage. Take away our Government and the result would be a state of anarchy of which Larut has afforded an expensive example. Singapore and Penang having but few natural resources and being for the most part entreports for European trade would relapse into a state of jungle, inhabited only by piratical fishermen; and the mines of the Malay States under similar conditions would be worked only by a population of Chinese adventurers, subject to periodical diminution by massacre.

In his 1879 report, Pickering first hints at the necessity for amendment to *Ordinance XIX of 1869* (see below):—

> Through the decrease of power in the headmen, one or two societies in Singapore are becoming very troublesome, and require constant supervision to prevent them from being a nuisance. Under the present Ordinance (1869) there is no provision for suppression of any of these societies after they have once been registered; a slight alteration of section 4 of *Ordinance XIX of 1869*, giving the Governor power to suspend or cancel the registration of any society, would enable the Executive to have a better check on Hoeys dangerous to the public peace, or (if found advisable) to suppress the whole of the societies in this Colony.

Pickering's 1879 report also gives for the first time the figures for the Penang societies. There were six societies registered with 46,795 members: the Penang Ghee Hin was the leading society with 27,498 members. The Singapore Ghee Hin total had meanwhile increased to 33,103.

DIVERGENT VIEWS OF VAUGHAN AND PICKERING

We might perhaps notice here the conflict of views expressed by Vaughan and Pickering who were both prolific writers on this subject in their day.

Pickering had the advantage of a knowledge of colloquial and written Chinese, but Vaughan was a close observer of both Chinese and Malay life and had experience as a local magistrate. Both men were equally indebted to Schlegel, whose work appeared in 1866.

Vaughan held at different times:—

(1) That family, clan and tribal ties over-rode the blood-brotherhood of the "Hoeys".

(2) That clan associations can be as mischievous as recognised dangerous secret societies, and in the 1854 riots over-rode the blood-brotherhood of the secret societies.

(3) That so-called "Friendly" or "Mutual benefit" societies are seldom what they avow, but as in China proper, are common disguises adopted by the dangerous secret societies to flout the law.

(4) That the Chinese secret society under-world although based on the Triad society was clearly divided into two rival and hostile factions, to each of which belonged a number of the individual secret societies. In Penang and Singapore those two factions were represented by the Ghee Hins and the Ghee Hoks and their respective affiliations.

Footnote.—(1) The murder of Captain Lloyd page 337 *supra*.

Pickering held at different times:—

    (1) That blood-brotherhood over-rides family, clan and tribal ties; and territorial and race distinctions.

    (2) That clan associations were useful instruments of governance and should be encouraged.

    (3) That "Friendly" or "Mutual benefit" societies were both friendly and of mutual benefit to their members, but were liable to become unfriendly and a nuisance to others.

    (4) That the Chinese under-world was based on the Triad society, the character of which was such that its recognition in the Straits Settlements was a disgrace to the British Government. He must have revised this view later because he is said to have become a member of Triad in Singapore about 1880—doubtless a very "honorary" member, during the farcical registration period 1869-1882 when Triad was considered to be not only respectable but an essential instrument of Government.

We now come to a period 1880-1890, for which the regular annual reports of Pickering are available to give us a clearer official picture of our subject in Singapore and Penang during those years.

REGISTERED CHINESE SECRET SOCIETIES AND THEIR MEMBERSHIP IN SINGAPORE, 1880-1890

    One Hundred Years of Singapore (1921) Vol. I page 280 says that in the 1881 census there were 153,532 Chinese in the three settlements, and out of this total Pickering gives the membership figures of Chinese secret societies for that year (*see* G.N. 144/82) as:—

Singapore	..	..	..	..	33,103
Penang	..	..	..	..	46,705

In 1888, the membership of registered Chinese secret societies was officially given as:—

		Societies	*Office bearers*	*Members*
Singapore	..	11	1,122	62,376
Penang	..	5	361	92,581
Total	..	16	1,483	154,957
			Grand Total ..	156,440

Allowing for the growth of the Chinese population between 1881 and 1888, the figures remain startling.

We must now examine this period of secret society history in Singapore in closer detail. In doing so we shall see running throughout as the one constant and undeviating factor, the rivalry and hatred of Triad and Tokong. This, if we accept it as a guiding principle, will give form and meaning to what must otherwise remain a senseless jumble of warring clans and clashing factions, continually at one another's throats, seemingly without purpose, aim, or plan and all regarded by the authorities as being but segments of a single blood-brotherhood. If we refuse to accept the evidence so far deduced, showing the existence of the two great rival fraternities, a closer analysis of the secret society history of this period will be unprofitable. If we do accept it, the picture presented becomes coherent and the problem of subsequent control becomes clarified and rationalised in a manner otherwise impossible.

THE SINGAPORE PICTURE IN 1881

    Thus, in his Annual Report upon secret societies in Singapore for the year 1881 (*Gazette* Notification 144/1882) Pickering has:—

                   *   *   *

    There are several secret societies which are very troublesome through their disorganisation, and a quarrel between the Ghee Hocks and Malays at Buddoh, during which a Chinese was fatally injured, together with some small fights between rival kongsis, shew that the state of things is not yet all that could be wished, and the Chief of the Police and Registrars of dangerous societies are looking anxiously for the passing of an amendment on *Ordinance XIX of 1869*. This legislation, we believe, will give the Government a thorough and beneficial control over the Thian-te-Hui, and all other societies which are, or may become, dangerous to the public peace; then it is to be hoped that the hoeys will only be conspicuous as a means whereby the lower orders of the Chinese can be kept in hand, in default of legislation which would seem to be incompatible with our notions of just rule.

Pickering's 1881 report is supported by a statement of particulars of those Chinese societies registered in that year in Singapore as dangerous under Section 3 of the Ordinance of 1869. Chinese characters are unfortunately still absent.

We have to go back to 1825 to find such a similar statement covering Penang, prepared by Caunter and reproduced on page 75 *supra*. After 1881, these statements, both for Singapore and Penang, a few of which we reproduce below, became a regular feature of the Annual Reports of the Chinese Protectorate of the Colony and help us to realise the magnitude which the problem of control had assumed before final suppression in 1889.

The 1881 statement for Singapore is as follows:—

CHINESE SECRET SOCIETIES REGISTERED UNDER SECTION 3 OF ORDINANCE NO. XIX OF 1869 IN SINGAPORE FOR THE YEAR 1881

Name of society	Kongsi House	Name of President of society	Occupation	Residence	No. of Office Bearers	No. of members in register book	No. of actual subscribers during the year 1881
Ghee Hin (Hokkien)	No. 4, China Street	Tok Chong Poh	Tailor	No. 591, North Bridge Road	214	5,438	3,157
Ghee Hin (Tiechiu)	No. 13, Carpenter Street	Lee Ah Ah	Trader	No. 189, Beach Road	57	2,012	1,177
Ghee Hin (Hailam)	No. 487-1, North Bridge Road	Ong Chee Tek	Trader	No. 59-14, North Bridge Road	70	2,324	979
Ghee Hok	No. 25-4, Carpenter Street	Lee Ah Hoey	Rice Shop-keeper and Manager of Theatre	No. 23, Hongkong Street	336	6,750	3,921
Ghee Sin	No. 33, Jalan Sultan	Tan Leng Su	Guardian of Temple	No. 33, Jalan Sultan	63	1,413	Nil
Ghee Khee Kwang Hok	No. 140, Beach Road	Teoh Mah Tek	Gambier Trader	No. 116, Beach Road	62	3,065	1,531
Hok Hin	No. 41, North Canal Road	Tan Chu Se	Trader	— Kallang	105	4,809	1,932
Kong Fooy Sew	No. 475, North Bridge Road	Wong Ah Siah	Carpenter	No. 191, South Bridge Road	64	2,108	1,367
Song Peh Kwan	No. 32, Upper Nankin Street	Leong Ah Phan	Sawyer	No. 85, Upper Nankin Street	52	3,231	1,275
Hai Sant	No. 26, Upper Cross Street	Siah Kiat Seng	Geomancer	No. 81, Havelock Road	37	1,953	856
				Total 1881	1,060	33,103	16,195
				Total 1880	979	28,317	16,151
				Increase	81	4,786	44

Footnote.—(1) Suppressed on 31st October, 1882. (G.N. 1/83).

We recognise a number of old friends in this list of societies and may roughly divide them as follows:—

Tokong	Triad
Ghee Hok	Ghee Hin (Hokkien)
	Ghee Hin (Teochew)
Hok Hin	Ghee Hin (Hailam)
	Ghee Sin
Song Peh Kwan	Ghee Khee Kwang Hok
	Kong Fooy Sew
Hai San	

In 1882, there was passed an amendment to the *Ordinance of 1869* enabling the Government to order the suppression of any registered society which was considered dangerous. (*See* below under the "Suppression Section" pages 389–390). The first to fall under this ban was the Singapore Hai San.

SUPPRESSION OF THE HYE SAN SOCIETY SINGAPORE, DECEMBER, 1882 (G.N. 1/83)

By Order in Council dated 31st October, 1882, the Hye San society was declared to be an unlawful society under the *Dangerous Societies Ordinance, 1882*, and was called upon to show cause why it should not be suppressed and having done so, it was still considered dangerous and was suppressed on 28th December, 1882.

The G.N. is dated Colonial Secretary's Office, Singapore, 2nd January, 1883, and must have been intended to apply to Singapore only, although it does not say so. In this connection, Colonel Dunlop, I.G.P., S.S., in his Annual Report for 1882 (G.N. 308/83) has under secret societies:—

> "The secret societies have been comparatively quiet during the past year, but the utmost vigilance is required to prevent petty quarrels among members assuming serious proportions through the machinations of unscrupulous headmen. The amendment of the *Dangerous Societies Ordinance 1869*, by *Ordinance IV of 1882* has borne good fruit in all the Settlements as regards the Red and White Flag societies and I have every confidence that in a few years, these dangerous confederations will have died out.
>
> Under the provisions of the same Ordinance in Singapore an unruly Chinese hoey—the Hye San[1]—has been suppressed and its only property, its meeting house, taken possession of by the Government.
>
> Its members still give considerable trouble, but there is little doubt they will ere long be absorbed into other and better managed societies.

This passage shows that it was only the Singapore Branch of the Hai San that was suppressed... This is confirmed by the fact that the Hai San appears in the Table of registered societies in Penang for the year 1883 with 22 office bearers and 542 members (G.N. 18/4/1884 page 461) *see* below under "Penang" Section.

Perhaps the Police and Protectorate at that time did not realise that the Hye San of Singapore and the Hai San of Penang were lodges of the same society. They could not have known that that society was the Ko Lao Hui or Han league of China. Nor could they have been aware of the part played by the Hai San in the Penang Riots of 1867 and in the Larut wars of 1872–1874.

In the Singapore Protectorate Report for 1883, Powell who was acting for Pickering writes:—

> The year 1883 has passed without any serious disturbances in Singapore between societies as such although a number of petty quarrels have occurred.
>
> Two Headmen of the Hai-San society (suppressed last year), Tan Si-Koe and Tan Kok-Chi, who were banished under the *Peace Preservation Ordinance*, on 28th May, 1881, returned to Singapore some time before the departure of Colonel Dunlop and Mr. Pickering for Europe. The former was arrested in a house in Kampong Glam: he was subsequently sentenced to penal servitude for life. The other Headman, Tan Kok-Chi, who was living on a gambier plantation on the other side of the island, managed to escape to Johore, and has probably, by this time, found his way back to China.
>
> Almost simultaneously with the return of these men, some disturbances took place in the neighbourhood of Smith Street and Sago Street between *samsengs* formerly belonging to the Hai-San and members of the Kong Fui Siu. These men went about for a day or two with a short iron bar concealed up the sleeve, with which they attacked obnoxious persons. A number of these rascals being sentenced to two months' imprisonment without the option of a fine, and, in addition being bound over for a term, the rest were at once restored to good order.
>
> In accordance with the Dangerous Societies Ordinance, 1882, the Straits-born Chinese have, at least ostensibly, given up all connection with the Hoeys.
>
> The total number registered as members of dangerous societies to the end of the year 1883, is, in Singapore, 43,881; and in Penang, 57,996; the number of new members during the year being 8,364 and 6,995.

Footnote.—(1) Dunlop had a hand in the preliminaries of the Treaty of Pangkor (*see* page 286 *supra*) but evidently did not connect the Hye San and Go Kwan of Larut in 1874 with the Hye San of Singapore nine years later.

The number belonging to each of the different societies is given in the accompanying tables.[1]

In the report of R. W. Maxwell, Acting Inspector General of Police for the Colony in 1883, we read:—

> Watching and, to some extent, controlling the working of these societies, is one of the most difficult duties the Chief Police Officers have to perform, and it is only by the most constant and troublesome work that disturbances are prevented. An ordinary assault, which in other countries is thought nothing of, will in the Straits often lead to serious riots, unless carefully enquired into, and some arrangement come to between rival societies.

> There is no doubt that these societies are most dangerous, and I should be glad to see them suppressed.

> I would strongly urge the necessity of dealing more severely with headmen of societies. It is seldom indeed that they ever give any sort of assistance to the Police in tracing out serious crimes, such as murders and gang robberies, even though the names of members of their societies are given. I am certain that if heavy fines were inflicted upon societies for every gang robbery committed where any of the offenders were proved to be members of such societies, this particular crime would cease. It is one of the rules of every society that members are bound to assist each other, and they certainly carry it out to the letter, where offenders are concerned.

THE DEVELOPMENT OF "ILLICIT" HOEYS

The system of registration (1869) and partial suppression (1882) had one curious result, which complicated the whole question of control, particularly in the larger towns.

When first introduced in 1869, both sides came to regard registration as a farce, and Triad and Tokong continued as before, while sending faked rules and other documents for official registration.

In 1882, the registration Ordinance of 1869 was amended to give power to the Registrar to refuse to register any section of Triad or Tokong which had made itself particularly obnoxious to him. This refusal to register was supposed automatically to dissolve the branch and render its further existence illegal or "illicit". Of course, the particular sections refused registration under this rule, merely submerged and carried on just as before. They then began attacking the registered branches of their parent stems to whom they ceased to bear allegiance, and the greatest confusion resulted between registered branches of secret societies and unregistered or "illicit" branches. The latter free-lanced as gangs of roughs, causing as much trouble to the registered branches of their own Mother lodge as they did to the Registrar, yet always preserving the radical distinction between the Han and Hung camps.

This is well illustrated in the following extracts from Pickering's report for the year 1884 upon the state of the Chinese secret societies in Singapore (*Straits Settlements Gazette* 1885 page 151) :—

> The year 1884 has, with minor exceptions, been characterised by the continuance of good order amongst the Chinese of Singapore, and has contributed another annual argument proving that, in spite of the existence of continual petty quarrels and rivalries which some years ago would have resulted in serious and prolonged disturbances, the Chinese can be kept in good order by the enforcement of exceptional legislation suited to their condition and habits, and the very elements of former disorder forced to contribute to the preservation of peace.

> 2. That the present comparatively peaceful state of things is owing to the repressive legislation now enforced and not to the absence of disturbing causes, is shewn by the fact that several societies have lately been established which, by registering as "Friendly" have taken advantage of their immunity from Government supervision to increase their strength in order to squeeze brothel-keepers, gain money from gambling and to oppose and rival the Thian-Te Hoeys.[2]

> 3. During the past year, these associations have given much trouble; by their provocations and attacks, the headmen of the registered dangerous societies[3] (who, with few exceptions, do all in their power to assist the Police and Protectorate and to control their refractory members) have been much tried, and have had some difficulty to prevent serious quarrels.

> 4. Authority has lately been given by His Excellency the Acting Governor, to register five of these *soi-disant* Friendly societies,[4] under Section 3 of *Ordinance No. XIX of 1869*. This will doubtless have the effect of checking their increase in members and will render them amenable to law and order.

> 5. With a population annually recruited by an immigration of some 120,000 full-grown Chinese of the lower classes, ignorant of our laws, and containing every element of disorder as well as of prosperity to the Colony, we can only hope to preserve order by laws fitted to their condition.

Footnote.—(1) Except for the disappearance of the Hai San society, the schedule shows no change from that for 1881.

Footnote.—(2) Pickering did not, of course, distinguish between Triad and Tokong, but lumped all Chinese dangerous societies into Triad, where they have remained. It was, of course, the essential rivalry of Hung and Han, or Triad and Tokong, that was the real cause of the brawling and dissention of which he complained.

Footnote.—(3) *i.e.* Licit, or lawful Hoeys.

Footnote.—(4) *i.e.* "Illicit Hoeys".

This development hastened the disintegration of the officially registered branches of Triad and Tokong and discipline was impaired so greatly that the headmen of the registered branches complained to the Registrar. This condition of affairs was described in Pickering's Annual Report for 1886 quoted by S.O.S. pages 225–226. Such turmoil could not last, and already a commission was sitting whose recommendation was that all the Chinese dangerous societies should be suppressed.[1]

THE DANGEROUS SOCIETIES AMENDMENT ORDINANCE IV OF 1885

In 1885, the *Dangerous Societies Ordinance of 1882* was repealed and re-enacted with wider powers, still under the original *Dangerous Societies Suppression Ordinance of 1869*. Under Section 10, of the 1885 law powers were taken to restrict membership of any named society to Chinese subjects born in China of Chinese parents. This was an attempt to lever out Straits-born Chinese and non-Chinese who were unbanishable, but whose increasing membership of the dangerous societies was fast becoming a serious minor problem of its own.

Needless to say this well meant measure failed because it did not comprehend the problem to be met.

THE SINGAPORE PICTURE IN 1885

The following is from Pickering's Report for Singapore in 1885 (G.N. 61/1886) :—

On the morning of the Chinese New Year (15th February, 1885) a fight occurred between two gangs of coolies employed on the Trafalgar Estate, Seranggong, during which fire-arms were used, one man was killed and several wounded. Though the parties belonged respectively to the Ghee Hok and the Teo-Kun Ghee Hin societies, the quarrel was the result of rivalry in work and not from any society dispute. As an incentive to labour, one gang had been pitted against the other in piece-work, and the defeated party having been derided by the victors, an altercation ensued which led to blows and finally to the fatal affray. Lim-Ka-Koe, the Chief of the Teo-Kun Ghee Hin, not only neglected to obey our orders himself, or to take any steps in the matter, but he also failed to send any of his influential headmen to settle the quarrel. For this behaviour and on account of a long course of refractory conduct, and inability to manage his society, Lim-Ka-Koe was called before the Governor in Council to shew cause why he should not be deported, and was only spared from banishment, by relinquishing all connection with secret societies, and promising to behave well for the future.

The Teo-Kun Ghee Hin and Ghee Sin societies having yearly become more dangerous to the public peace, through disorganisation, and the incompetency of their managers and office-bearers, were suppressed, together with two societies—the Kwang-Kit-Tong and Ng-Fuk-Tong recently established for the purposes of intriguing against the Thian-Te-Hoe, and creating disturbances amongst brothels in order to extort money from the keepers.

Three Friendly societies—the Li Seng Hong, Hong Ghee Tong and Ut Tong Kun—by their conduct rendered it necessary to register them as dangerous societies.

Six thousand six hundred and four (6,604) new members have joined the Singapore societies during 1885, making a total of 49,891 members on our register.

While the dangerous societies are giving comparatively little trouble, I regret to have to state that, several times during the year, petty fights have taken place between Friendly societies composed of Straits-born Chinese, the members of which are, in many cases, cashiers, store-keepers or clerks in the employ of the principal European firms. These societies have given much trouble, by their young members (in emulation of the former behaviour of the Thian-Te-Hoe) fighting with sticks, etc. in various parts of the town, or by roistering at night in the vicinity of the licensed brothels.

If this state of things should continue, the Registrars will be obliged to apply for power to register these Hoeys under section 3 of *Ordinance XIX of 1869*, and then all Straits-born Chinese will be obliged to leave them under penalty of fine or imprisonment.

The alternative to this measure would be, that the office-bearers should be called out as special constables in time of disturbance, and made to patrol the streets for the preservation of order.

This course, besides being objectionable for other reasons, would cause much inconvenience to European business in the Square, were, on some mail day, the heads of firms to find their Chinese clerks, etc. taken away from office and engaged on Police duty.

This report is interesting for several reasons.

Pickering's faith in registration—so wishfully expressed in earlier reports—is beginning to waver in this one. The game of faked rules and faked rites and initiations by which he had been bluffed for many years, was beginning to rub thread-bare. But he still believed it possible that by the formality of an empty promise to the Governor, a hard-boiled Triad gangster, such as Lim Ka Kui obviously was, could be made "to relinquish all connection with secret societies and to behave well in future". Pickering evidently believed that such a promise was both possible of fulfilment and worth cancellation of banishment to obtain. Such views disclose a total misconception of the nature and potency of the secret society virus.

Footnote.—(1) For further comment upon this period *see* Ward and Stirling *op. cit.* Vol. I pages 9–12.

Again in the 1885 report, we see that no sooner were the Teo-Kun Ghee Hin and the Ghee Sin (both Triad-camp factions) suppressed, than their places were taken by three so-called "Friendly societies"—the Li Seng Hong: Hong Ghee Tong: Ut Tung Kun, seemingly also Triad foundations with perhaps a little extra veneer of "Benefit society" in their make-up, to get them past the Registrar.

They, too, soon showed their true colours and quickly came under the official ban. They were in fact, no doubt, the two societies just suppressed, divided into three, with new nominal office-bearers to provide some decent degree of camouflage. These so-called friendly societies soon became more dangerous than the dangerous societies, as this report shows.

Again we see the Kwang Kit Tong and the Ng Fuk Tong, doubtless anchorages of the Han league, (certainly the latter *vide* Chapter II *supra*) "recently established for the purpose of intriguing against the T'in Tei Hui", just as we would have expected. Altogether, a good many facets of the major problem are presented in this report.

PICKERING'S VIEWS ON THE CONNECTION BETWEEN SECRET SOCIETIES, PUBLIC GAMING, AND POLICE CORRUPTION, 1885

In the following extract from his Annual Report for 1885 (G.N. 61/1886) Pickering suggested the connection then existing between secret society activities and the spread of Public gaming and the effect of both upon Police morale. He pressed for the inclusion of promoters of Public gaming among those subject to the Banishment Ordinance, a provision of law in force to-day.

He says:—

In our Reports for the years 1882 and 1883, Mr. Powell and I brought to notice the prevalence of gambling, and I would again bring forward for the consideration of the Government, the existence of some hundred and more common gaming houses throughout Singapore, where gambling is carried on openly (in some cases, day and night) without, it would seem, any fear of detection.

I have seen in a quarter-of-an-hour's walk, some 70 of these houses; at the doors of many were touts calling on the passers-by to "come up and make their fortunes", at the various games played inside. The Chinese newspaper Lat Pau has spoken very plainly of this state of things, which is causing great danger to the welfare and good order of the Chinese, and is certainly demoralising the native portion of the Police force.

Apart from the natural desire to see removed the reproach which now exists in the eyes of the Chinese against the vigilance of the Police and the efficacy of our laws, as Registrar of dangerous societies, and to a certain extent responsible for their good order, I feel that gambling, as it now exists in Singapore, is a danger to the peace, and may, if allowed to go on, undo all the good work which the Inspector-General of Police and I have been trying to do during the last twelve years. Nothing is more likely to create quarrels and jealousy between the secret societies than the emulation which is aroused to share in the great profits accruing from the establishment of gaming houses in the various districts of the Settlement.

Gambling has existed, and will, no doubt, to a certain extent always exist, amongst an Asiatic population, but I can bring all the Chinese of Singapore to bear me witness when I say that, whereas formerly people did their gambling in secret, now, in both Singapore and Penang, the vice is openly practised without any apparent fear on the part of the people who organize and carry on the business.

In default of any amendment of the present law, there is no doubt that the banishment of some dozen bad characters (who, as headmen of secret societies, are carrying on the organization of gaming-houses) would have a beneficial effect in reducing the evil.

I am sure the Inspector-General of Police will agree that these men are as dangerous to the public peace, and to the prosperity of the Colony, as if they were political offenders.

They, however, have very lately (after taking advice) got the idea that unless they make themselves objectionable by fomenting society quarrels, there is no danger of penalty of deportation.

As there seems to exist a sensitiveness towards, and a shrinking from, this kind of punishment, I feel it my duty to endeavour to place the question in what I consider its true light.

In these Settlements, we have an Asiatic population of which at least 50 per cent. are alien Chinese, and who, till within the last twelve years, were accustomed periodically to put a stop to business by riots, either on account of quarrels amongst themselves or for the purpose of protesting against some new measure of the Government.

This population is annually recruited by an emigration from China of some hundred thousand adults; a large proportion of these adults have been accustomed to obey the laws only just so far as their Mandarins have been strong enough to enforce them; and besides this, many have been in the habit of engaging in cruel clan fights.

Amongst the immigrants, there are also not a few men who, by a long course of crime, have made their native land too hot to hold them, yet all the new-comers, on landing here, are admitted to nearly every privilege, and to all the protection enjoyed by British subjects. These Chinese who have never known liberty in its true sense, are suddenly endowed with the same privileges and immunities as Englishmen who, through ancestors, have received during several centuries chastisement and training, before obtaining, or being able to appreciate the present conditions of social and political freedom.

Surely it is not too much to expect from the Chinese, that in return for the protection and assistance they receive so freely here, they should be obliged to obey our laws, and live peaceably and quietly under our Flag.

o

After fifteen years' experience of the Chinese in this Colony and the Native States, I should be guilty were I not to advocate with all my might, the judicious and impartial use of this great safeguard to the peace of the Settlements, and a very grave responsibility will certainly rest on the Registrars, if we do not urge the exercise of the powers now vested in the Governor in Council, or were we to fail to recommend the deportation of any Chinese alien, who by his conduct may constitute a standing danger to the peace, good order or even to the moral interests of the large Chinese population, even if the offender should not belong to a dangerous society, or possess sufficient intellectual powers to entertain in his mind a political idea.

The same elements of disorder which caused trouble and continual disturbances amongst the Chinese in former years, exist now, but they are kept down, chiefly by the fear of deportation. Another element of discord has raised its head, which also is paralyzing the hands of the guardians of our peace, thus adding to the difficulties with which we have to contend.

On these accounts I trust that I am not overstepping my duty when I express the hope that the habitual criminal and the organiser of gambling establishments, may be added to the list of those who (if absolutely necessary) are liable to banishment from the Colony.

COMMISSION OF ENQUIRY INTO PUBLIC GAMING IN THE COLONY 1886

As a result, no doubt, of Pickering's efforts, a Commission of Enquiry was appointed in 1886 to report upon Public Gaming and Public Lotteries in the Colony.

G.N. 50/1887 contains the Governor's decision upon the Report of this Commission dated 8-1-1887, which disclosed the extent of corruption in the Police of Singapore and Penang due to the organisation of illicit gaming by the headmen of registered secret societies.

THE SINGAPORE PICTURE IN 1886

The following is the picture given by Pickering in his Annual Report on Singapore Chinese secret societies in 1886 (G.N. 80/1887) :—

The so-called Friendly societies Tong Meng, Kim Hok, Hok Tek Choon, Ghee Lan Tong, and Eng Chuan Tong, mentioned in my last Report, were called upon to furnish further particulars according to section 3 of *Ordinance XIX of 1869*, as being dangerous to the public peace; on receiving the due notices from the Registrars, they took legal advice, and contrived to evade supervision by dissolving themselves, and handing their books and paraphernalia over to the Government.

The headmen, however, secretly keep up their organizations, and cause much trouble by enlisting members from the registered societies, quarrelling with each other, and fomenting such trouble that, if some steps are not taken to break them up and to punish the Straits-born Chinese who manage them, these unlawful associations will, in a short time, become a very serious element of disorder in the Settlement.

To complicate matters, the Teo-Kun Ghee-Hin society, suppressed two years ago, has revived, and some of its most turbulent headmen have kept the members together, and, in connection with the above-mentioned societies, carry out their designs against the registered branches of the Thian-Te Hoey.

The Chiefs of the registered dangerous societies are often put to great straits to keep their men from retaliating against the attacks made by illicit Hoeys; they also complain that, whilst they themselves are kept under strict supervision, and have not only to obey the law, but also to be responsible for their members, the managers of the unrecognised societies (free from restraint and responsibility) are allowed to evade the law, and to carry on their intrigues with impunity.

The number of new members of dangerous societies during the year 1886 was 6,350, making a total in our books of 56,241.

The "so-called friendly societies" mentioned in this report were, of course, what they have always been since the Sacred Edict in China of A.D. 1670 (page 7 above),—polite fictions, intended to deceive no one but the authorities. From the transitional period of the Hung league A.D. 1644–1700 (*vide* page 9 *supra*) throughout the political period A.D. 1700–1865 (page 9 *supra*) and on into the degenerate period, from 1865 to the present-day (page 13 *supra*), the same use of camouflage titles for protective purposes has become part and parcel of the secret society praxis of China, with which to beguile established authority and maintain intact the *imperium in imperio* of the Chinese under-world. (*See* also page 31 *supra*).

In short, in this business, names and avowed objects mean nothing. They are but the cloak demanded by officialdom in which is disguised the operations of an underground autarchy as old as the world itself.

We reproduce Pickering's schedule of Singapore registered societies in 1886, for comparison with that of 1881. It will be seen that the Teochew Ghee Hin and the Ghee Sin have disappeared and the last four "friendly societies" have been added. They too were soon to disappear.

CHINESE SECRET SOCIETIES REGISTERED UNDER SECTION 3 OF ORDINANCE NO. XIX OF 1869

IN SINGAPORE FOR THE YEAR 1886

Name of society	Kongsi House	Name of President of society	Occupation	Residence	No. of Office Bearers	No. of members in register book	No. of subscribers during the year 1886
Ghee Hin (Hokkien)	No. 4, China Street	Gam Kam Lian	Druggist	No. 157, South Bridge Road	330	12,675	4,240
Ghee Hin (Hailam)	No. 31, Malabar Street	Liom Hong Ji	Trader	No. 56, North Bridge Road	62	4,236	1,860
Ghee Hok	No. 3, River Valley Road	Lee Ah Hoey	Rice Shop-keeper and Manager of Theatre	No. 23, Hongkong Street	320	12,410	5,161
Ghee Khee Kwang Hok	No. 140, Beach Road	Tiun Mah Tek	Gambier Shop-keeper	No. 10, North Bridge Road	78	4,737	2,120
Hok Hin	No. 41, North Canal Road	Poh Kin Thak	Opium and Spirit Shop-keeper	No. 3, Carnie Street	121	10,631	2,925
Kwang Fui Siu	No. 475, North Bridge Road	Wong Ah Siah	Eating Shop-keeper	No. 229, South Bridge Road	53	3,589	1,672
Song Peh Kwan	No. 32, Upper Nankin Street	Khew Choe	Sawyer	No. 60, Upper Nankin Street	54	6,180	1,623
Hong Ghee Tong	No. 3, Upper Chin Chew Street	Cheong Ah Hong	Spirit Shop-keeper	No. 13, Sago Street	15	402	250
Lee Seng Hong	No. 163, South Bridge Road	Yong Ah Lam	Carpenter	No. 181, South Bridge Road	5	407	360
Yet Tong Kun	No. 35, North Canal Road	Kong Pak Weng	Opium Shop-keeper	No. 16, Banda Street	8	415	238
Heng Sun	No. 119, Amoy Street	Lim Ee Ek	Doctor	No. 119, Amoy Street	42	559	280
				Total 1886	1,086	56,241	20,729
				Total 1885	1,303	49,891	20,037
				Increase	..	6,350	692
				Decrease	217	..	..

Note.—(i) The Teochew Ghee Hin and (ii) The Ghee Sin disappear from the registered list and the last four are added.

THE RISE OF ASIATIC SOCIAL "CLUBS", 1886

In 1886, it was also realised that the results hoped for from the amending Ordinance of 1885 were not to be achieved. In the Annual Report of 1886 by Col. Dunlop, the Inspector-General of Police we read:—

> During the year, considerable anxiety was caused by certain societies kept up and managed in Singapore by Straits-born Chinese. It seems impossible to suppress these and cognate societies. Our difficulties, I fear, can only be overcome by increasing the powers of the Registrars, and by assuming that all such societies from the very first are dangerous to the public peace.
>
> In Penang, similar associations under the name of clubs exist in considerable numbers, and there seems little doubt they are gambling clubs, and have been brought into existence solely to evade the Gaming House Ordinance.

The attempts to restrict Chinese societies to China-born members by the 1885 Ordinance and the attempt to restrict gaming by the Gaming House Ordinance of the same year, had the effect, common to such legislation, of forcing the evil into fresh channels.

It is from about this period that we see the rise of the social "clubs" among Asiatics in imitation of European clubs, but designed to provide in another form the facilities for underground intrigue and relaxation which the growing volume of legislation was denying to certain sections of the Asiatic community. These "clubs" avowing a vast variety of purpose, multiplied exceedingly after the final suppression of secret societies in 1890 and led to a state of chaos in subsequent attempts to control them, which is the condition under which they exist to-day.

A modern home parallel is seen between restriction of liquor selling hours and the rise of the "bottle-party".

ATTEMPTED MURDER OF PICKERING BY TOKONG JULY, 1887

Meanwhile there occurred in 1887, an attempt to murder Pickering which helped to seal the fate of the Hoeys.

S.O.S. *op. cit.* page 231 gives the following account:—

> "In July 1887, a very grave attempt was made to murder Mr. Pickering, C.M.G., while he was seated at work in his office in the Chinese Protectorate, by Chua Ah Siok, a Teochew carpenter, who appeared to have been instigated to commit the crime by certain members of the Ghee Hok society. He walked up to the front of Pickering's desk and threw at his face the iron head of a carpenter's axe, which struck Pickering with its butt-end full on the forehead causing a severe wound. The assailant who was arrested on the spot stated that although hired to cause death he had determined not to kill a public officer, but to do such an injury only as he could by throwing an axe without its handle. He was tried at the November Assizes on the charge of voluntarily causing grievous hurt instead of the graver charge of attempted murder. He pleaded guilty and was sentenced to seven years' rigorous imprisonment.
>
> In connection with this affair three members of the Ghi Hok society were committed for trial for abetting this murderous attack, but the charge was withdrawn. They were afterwards banished for being concerned in the murder of the "Lieutenant" China of the Karimons[1] in April, 1887".

These events pointed to a concerted attempt by Tokong in 1887 to damage the prestige of Triad. We know Pickering to have been admitted freely to meetings of the "reformed" or registered Triad in Singapore and we may presume that the "Lieutenant" (*i.e.* Captain) China of the Kerimons was also a member of Triad as he was murdered by Tokong. Pickering must have been mystified by these attacks as the Ghee Hok was, of course, then regarded as a "branch" of Triad.

Pickering never fully recovered from this dastardly attempt on his life by enemies whom he believed to be friends. He retired the next year 1889 and died in 1898.

We have not seen any of the official papers dealing with this attempt on his life, nor the report of the Commission of Enquiry which followed it, but the name of his assailant as given by S.O.S. suggests a possible connection between him and Chua Moh Choon (page ... *supra*) alleged head of Singapore Ghi Hok 1850–1880, having regard to the hereditary principle in Tokong.

THE SINGAPORE PICTURE IN 1887

Pickering's report for 1887 has the following:—

> During the past year, owing to visits to the other Settlements and to absence from the Colony on sick leave, I have only been able to attend the Singapore office for about five months, but I will endeavour to give a report of the general state of the Chinese population for the year 1887 as far as regards their secret societies.
>
> With one exception, the registered dangerous societies have given very little trouble, but in other respects the state of things complained of in paragraphs 3 to 6 of my last Report still exists.
>
> The principal headmen of the Ghee Hok society interested in gambling, continued their lawless career, and although they did not, as I predicted, revenge themselves on the headmen who appeared as witnesses before the Commission,[2] there is no doubt, from evidence in the possession of Government, that, presuming on their continued immunity from banishment, they determined to get rid of my opposition to their schemes, by inciting Choah Ah Sioh to attack me in my office on the 18th July, in such a manner that I only escaped providentially with my life.

Footnote.—(1) The Group of Dutch Islands to the west of Singapore.

Footnote.—(2) *i.e.* The Commission on Gaming and Lotteries 1886 referred to above.

Owing to the liberality of the Government, I was, however, enabled to enjoy a complete rest in Ceylon, which, I am thankful to say, has entirely restored my health.

There is reason to believe that the Ghee Hok Kongsi was used as a meeting house for the conspirators, not only against me, but against the Chinese officer who was murdered in Karimons.

The sentence of banishment passed on the Ghee Hok headmen was, there is no doubt, richly deserved, and had good results amongst others, in the diminution of gambling, it was also a significant fact that after their arrest and detention, the daily receipts of the Opium Farm sensibly increased.

Owing to the trouble caused by the chiefs of the Ghee Hok society during the past two years, I have felt it my duty to officially recommend its suppression as a warning to the others, the reasons for doing this being far graver than have existed in the cases of those societies which have been abolished during the past seven years.

I have at the same time stated my opinion that the time has arrived when the Government should take serious measures for the gradual abolition of all the existing dangerous societies, and to forbid, under severest penalties, their revival, or the establishment of any new societies of a similar nature.

I have always been of opinion that the existence of the Thien-Te-Hoe in our dominions is an anomaly and a reproach, yet, considering that they had been allowed to flourish here unchecked since the establishment of the Colony, and that, by cordial co-operation between the Heads of the Police and the Chinese Protectorate Departments, we have not only been able for some years to keep them in order, but also in many ways to make them useful to the Government, I have not, since 1878, urged their suppression.

Late experience has shown me that, in the absence of the above-mentioned co-operation, these societies would soon become as dangerous as ever, and for this reason I am obliged to recommend their suppression.

Knowing, however, as I do, how strongly the passion for forming clandestine societies exists in the Chinese breast, and having in view Netherlands India and China, where in spite of the severest penalties (in China that of decapitation) the Thien-Te-Hoe still exists and occasionally gives very much trouble, I cannot take the responsibility of recommending that the Government should by one sudden and bold stroke suppress all the existing societies at once.

Such a measure, unless the Police have sufficient knowledge of the subject, and unless the Chief of that Department is prepared to undertake the greatest share of the responsibility, would be merely to throw on a very few individuals of the Chinese Protectorate the burden of keeping down and watching a number of societies only nominally abolished, and which consequently being un-recognised, we should be deprived of the powers of control and supervision we now possess under *Ordinance XIX of 1869*, as amended by *Ordinance IV of 1885*.

Of course, if the Government should decide on putting down all dangerous societies at one stroke, we must do our duty to the utmost, but I feel bound to point out the difficulties in the way, and also to say that, in order to carry out suppression effectually, the great desideratum will be an Ordinance authorising the penalties of long terms of imprisonment, fine and banishment against persons engaged in any way in keeping up a suppressed society, or in opening a new one, and that the onus of proof of innocence must rest on the defendants. As far as mere nominal suppression, the present Ordinance gives the necessary powers.

The number of new members of dangerous societies during the year 1887 was 6,135, making a total in our books of 62,376.

In this revealing report Pickering recommends the suppression of the Ghee Hok, the faction responsible for the attack upon him, whose character he suggests, as it was later described by Hutson, as:—

"Natural depravity and resistance to reform which, through the ages, have made licentious liberty the chief ideal of life".

This is the Tokong or Han league ethic, *see* Chapter II page 32 *supra*. Pickering falls into error when he ascribes the attack upon him to the T'in Tei Hui, of which he himself was an "honorary" member in Singapore.

Such an attack by Triad would have been inexplicable and contrary to all the canons of secret society law. He attempts no explanation of this point, for the reason that without a knowledge of the presence of Tokong no explanation was possible. He goes on to recommend the complete suppression of all secret societies, of which he clearly felt the most dangerous to be Triad.

THE SINGAPORE PICTURE IN 1889

Powell in his Report on the Chinese Protectorate for the year 1889 has:—

During the year 1889, 5,000 new members of dangerous societies were registered in Singapore, making a total since 1877 of 68,316.

* * *

4. In Singapore, for some months, there were considerably strained relations between the Hokkien Gi Hin and Gi Hok societies, and numerous assaults took place. Both sides were Te Chiu and the trouble arose from the fact that on the abolition, some years ago, of the Tio Kun Gi Hin, a Te Chiu society, a good many of its members joined the Hokkien Gi Hin. The matter was finally settled by arbitration in the central lodge at Rochor, and the squabbles ceased. Had they not done so, I should have been obliged to recommend certain headmen on each side by whom the ill-feeling was fostered for deportation.

5. Later in the year, the Hokkien Gi Hin and the Chong Pak Koan kongsis fell out, but the dispute was soon settled.

6. A society formerly abolished—the Thong Meng—made a bold attempt to re-establish a mixed organization headed by Straits-born Chinese, and succeeded in enlisting some thousands of members, for which purpose they had a number of lodges in the town. Assaults on people who would not join them were frequent, and there was a good deal of disturbance in the streets.

Colonel Dunlop and myself, after considerable trouble, were, in April, able to get sufficient evidence to convict before a Court of two Magistrates, and four headmen were fined $250 each. These four were the farmer of one of the Municipal markets, a clerk to a well-known lawyer, an interpreter of the Police Court, and another influential Straits-born Chinese. Five Counsel were engaged for the defence, and an appeal was the natural consequence, but on the case being inquired into in the Supreme Court the Judge declined to alter the decision of the Magistrates.

Comment.—Winstedt (quoted on page 264 *supra*) has said—"It is a hard task to follow the trail of truth through the maze of the Larut disturbances, but it is lightened if we keep closely to the main line of cleavage".

The same applies in even greater degree to the task which presents itself to the student of local secret society history from the year 1890 onwards.

The Protectorate report for 1889 covers the last year of toleration in any form and in it we catch the last official glimpse of that main line of cleavage, which has been our guide hitherto, that between Triad and Tokong, before they plunge into the unseen under-world where we have to continue to wrestle with them in the darkness, amidst a continual kaleidoscope of broken ends and bits and pieces; an encyclopaedia of new names, mushroom-growths, joinings, partings, friendships, enmities, alliances, bickerings, squabblings, warfares and peace-makings; a chiaroscuro of plots, counter-plots, revelations, obscurities, disclosures, theories and counter-theories, informations, arrestings, releasings, prosecutions and deportations; a seething cauldron of under-world intrigue in which cause and effect, the why and the wherefore have become inextricably mixed-up in a seemingly endless chain of meaningless hatreds and rivalries, wherein a blind application of the Banishment Ordinance and a constant sentry-go maintained by the Police are the only safeguards against the outbreak of that age-old open warfare which we have tried to outline in the foregoing chapters.

The outlook from 1890 onwards might well daunt the student, but if we keep closely to the main line of cleavage, our task will be lightened and the probability of our arriving at right conclusions upon the present-day position will be enhanced.

Thus we see in para. 4 of the above report a reference to a squabble between the Teochew members of the Hokkien Ghee Hin and the Teochew members of the Ghee Hok which presents an initial difficulty until we follow the main line of cleavage.

The Teochew Branch of the Ghee Hin (the Tio Kun Gi Hin), Triad, had been suppressed in 1885 and as the Teochews have a close geographical affinity with the Hokkiens, the Teochew Ghee Hin upon its suppression had joined the Hokkien Ghee Hin (Triad) and had, of course, remained hostile to those of their own clansmen, who had all along belonged to the Ghee Hok (Tokong).

Again in para. 5, the Hokkien Ghee Hin (Triad) had a dispute with the Chong Peh Koan (Song Peh Kwan) or Tokong, which was settled by arbitration.

These squabbles were, no doubt, part of that process of disintegration which began with the presence of the "licit" and "illicit" Hoeys already noted above, which, in turn, arose as a consequence of the partial suppression policy begun in 1885.

THE TUNG MENG (同盟) SOCIETY SINGAPORE 1889

Para. 6 of the above report refers to the Tong Meng society of Singapore as having been "previously abolished". We cannot find any reference to its earlier demise, but a society of the name Tong Beng, which may be identical, appears in G.N. 224/1886 as one whose membership was restricted to China-born Chinese under Section 10 of *Ordinance VI of 1885*. A "so-called Friendly Society" of the same name, is referred to in Pickering's 1886 report (above) as having dissolved itself.

In the present context the society is shown as a Straits-born revival of a formerly "mixed" organisation which probably means "composed of both China-born and Straits-born Chinese".

The reference shows us that the ramification of secret societies among Straits-born Chinese is no new thing, but dates at least from the decade before suppression (1890). But mention of a society of this name in Singapore at this period (1885–1890) is interesting for another reason. It introduces us to the name if not to an actual branch of that secret political organism which, more than any other agency perhaps, was responsible for the political revolution in China of October, 1911 and whose head and inspiration was Dr. Sun Yat Sen. We draw attention, therefore, to its early mention here, because we shall meet the Tung Meng Hui (同盟會) again in Chapter XXVI *infra*, where we introduce it as the directing agency of the great Chinese Revolution which changed the face of Asia.

In that chapter we shall find it to have been not only "mixed" in the sense ascribed to it by Powell, but to have been mixed in the vastly wider and unique sense, that it included in its revolutionary ranks the leaders of both Triad and Tokong.

THE SIGNIFICANCE OF THE NAME TUNG MENG HUI

We might here dive into esoterism for a moment, to glance at the significance of its name.

Tung 同 means—"all: all together: agreement: covenant".

Meng 盟 means—"bright: a solemn declaration before the bright spirits: to swear a covenant with the use of blood: faithful".

The character 盟 is composed of the 72nd radical 日 =Sun and the 74th radical 月 =Moon above the 108th radical 皿 (Ming) =dish.

The latter is similar to the form of the 143rd radical 血 Hüt = blood and becomes the more so in this combination due to the toe of the moon above it, suggesting perhaps both the dish and the blood within it, used at the initiation ceremony or making of the covenant. But the character 明 Meng, also meaning "bright", is itself the character for the Ming Dynasty (明朝 Ming Ch'iu or 大明 Tai Ming A.D. 1368–1628) which it was the declared intention of the revolutionary leaders of 1911 and the theme of the political slogan of the Triad society during its revolutionary period (A.D. 1700–1865) to restore.

Hence the significance of the Hung league slogan, Faan Ts'ing Fu Ming (反清復明) = "Overturn the Ts'ing and restore the Ming dynasty", becomes again evident. (See pages 9 and 12 supra also pages 42–43 supra).

Again, as we shall see in Chapter XXVI, the Tung Meng Hui combined under its revolutionary banner of 1911, both Triad and Tokong elements who themselves in their esoteric sphere, represented respectively the Sun and the Moon: or Day and Night: or Light and Darkness: or Father Sun (god) and Mother Earth (goddess).

No more appropriate name both in form, sound and meaning could possibly have been devised, therefore, than that of the Tung Meng Hui, to convey both openly and esoterically the idea for which it stood.

Its ultimate achievements justified its choice of name.

THE ABOLITION OF DANGEROUS SOCIETIES 1889

Powell's Report for 1889 concludes:—

7. The year has been a memorable one in the history of Straits societies by the passing of a new Societies Ordinance, which came into force on the 1st day of January, 1890.

8. The object of the Ordinance is to effect the abolition chiefly of the Triad, but also of other dangerous societies, some of which have existed in Singapore since 1821, and in Penang for a much longer period.

9. Towards the end of 1889 proclamations were widely issued in the three Settlements to prepare all classes for the change, and special notices were given to the societies registered as dangerous under the old Ordinance—viz; ten in Singapore, five in Penang, and three in Malacca—that they would not be registered under the new Ordinance, but must wind-up their affairs by the 30th of June.

10. One society house was in consequence sold even before the end of the year in Singapore, one or two in January, and others are in a fair way of following on the same track.

11. The Singapore societies do not own any other property than the kongsi houses, in which respect they are widely different from the Penang societies, which, in one or two cases, are very wealthy.

12. All the Singapore and Penang societies have in 1890 delivered up their chops and books, and Mr. Hare and myself were present at the central lodge the other day when the headmen of the six Triad branches made formal renunciation by the burning of the original diplomas which constituted them part of the mother-organization—the Gi Hin.

The following references in Powell's Report for 1890 complete the rather smug official description of suppression. As history and experience have shown, the real picture was far different and the societies then officially suppressed are as active and alive to-day as they were a thousand years ago and will be a thousand years hence.

Powell's 1890 Report has:—

Perhaps the most important work of the Department during the year 1890 has been in the suppression of the dangerous societies. I have already sent in two interim reports regarding this subject.

The members of these large and dangerous associations, numbered by thousands, through persuasion and argument, seeing the Government firm in a matter which received the full approval of the general population, European and Chinese, have peacefully dissolved.

The insignia, registers and seals of all were, about the middle of the year, handed over to the Protectorate, and a formal renunciation of the membership of the parent Gi Hin—to which all Singapore dangerous societies belonged—was made at the central lodge at Rochore by the burning of the original diplomas by the headmen.

All the meeting houses, except one, which is in the hands of the Official Assignee, have been sold. In Singapore and Malacca, few of the societies had any surplus, in some cases indeed a subscription having to be made to pay their debts; but in Penang a sum of over $100,000 from the sale of the property was paid into the Supreme Court, which is now deciding in what way it is to be spent.

While I am not prepared to say that societies which have lasted as long as these, with their extended organizations, are no longer a danger to the peace, and may not at some future date shew themselves again and again, yet I have no hesitation in asserting that the majority of the members have accepted and have obeyed the order of the Government in ceasing to belong to the Hoeys. By the general population the suppression has been looked upon with relief.

* * *

We conclude this section with the schedule of Chinese registered societies in Singapore in 1889 on the eve of suppression. This is the last such schedule ever to be gazetted for Singapore.

CHINESE SECRET SOCIETIES REGISTERED UNDER SECTION 3 OF ORDINANCE NO. XIX OF 1869

IN SINGAPORE FOR THE YEAR 1889

Name of society	Kongsi House	Name of President of society	Occupation	Residence	No. of Office Bearers	No. of members in register book	No. of subscribers during the year 1889
Ghee Hin (Hokkien)	No. 4, China Street	Gan Kam Lian	Druggist	No. 175, South Bridge Road	478	18,973	Nil
Ghee Hok	No. 3, River Valley Road	Ang Ah Hiang	Coffin-maker	No. 32, Macao Street	396	14,487	3,650
Ghee Khee Kwang Hok	No. 140, Beach Road	Tiun Mah Tek	Gambier Shop-keeper	No. 10, North Bridge Road	97	6,466	Nil
Hok Hin	No. 45, North Canal Road	Poh Kim Thak	Opium	No. 3, Carnie Street	162	14,317	3,100
Kwong Fui Siu	Victoria Street	Wong Ah Si	Carpenter	No. 229, South Bridge Road	61	4,877	Nil
Song Peh Kwang	No. 32, Upper Nankin Street	Khew Choe	Sawyer	No. 60, Upper Nankin Street	60	7,413	1,279
Hong Ghee Tong	No. 3, Upper Chin Chew Street	Cheang Ah Hong	Spirit Shop-keeper	No. 13, Sago Street	15	402	..
Lee Seng Hong	No. 163, South Bridge Road	Yong Ah Lam	Carpenter	No. 181, South Bridge Road	5	407	..
Yet Tong Kun	No. 22, Banda Street	Ng Yaw Seng	Shoe-maker	No. 22, Banda Street	5	415	..
Heng Sim	No. 41, Havelock Road	Sau Kim	Cargo-boat-man	No. 3, Club Street	42	559	..
				Total 1889	1,321	68,316	8,029
				Total 1888	1,223	63,316	9,872
				Increase	98	5,000	..
				Decrease	..	..	1,848

Powell's report for 1890 concludes:—

One result of the suppression of the dangerous societies has been to give rise to a number of small brothel societies (also mixed up with gambling) who are perpetually dispersing and re-forming under different names.

The origin of these is in the mulct undoubtedly formerly paid by the brothels to the dangerous societies. These being now dispersed, different sections have attempted to levy a similar tax, using threats of creating a disturbance and assault.

In Kreta Ayer, from time to time different societies of this sort have appeared, causing very numerous breaches of the peace, and the Police have not been very successful in implicating the headmen or suppressing the kongsis.

The brothel-keepers from this district came in a body some little time ago and asked me to put up a notice in all the brothels that it was unnecessary for them to pay to any one, whoever he might be, the tax formerly levied by the dangerous societies.

In Upper Hokkien Street, a similar association of Chiun Pho (a district of Hokkien) men attempted to be formed by a man Ko Kim Liong, a headman of the Hok Hin dangerous society, and a disturbance took place. I was able to get sufficient evidence against him to procure his banishment in May.

The new Ordinance is working smoothly as regards the registration of friendly societies. Of these, 37 have been allowed to register in Singapore, 89 in Penang, and 34 in Malacca. A number of other societies of a harmless character were exempted from registration.

The Report of the Inspector-General of Police, S.S. for the year 1890 has the following reference to official suppression:—

Secret societies have all been suppressed during the year without any trouble. In Penang, an attempt was made to resuscitate the old Red and White Flag Muhammadan societies, and there was a great deal of ill-feeling between the rival parties and a good deal of rowdyism took place, ending in one unfortunate boy being killed. Several cases were brought up and published, and the end of the year found matters much quieter. A Chinese society called the Sui-Lok-Peng-On gave a great deal of trouble in Penang, and had such influence that those who suffered at its hands, were afraid to come forward and complain. After some months of work, however, sufficient evidence was placed before the Executive Council to enable them to banish the two principal headmen, and since then the society has almost come to an end, but it has required constant vigilance to prevent it again becoming a serious nuisance.

No doubt, the attack upon Pickering hastened the decision to suppress all secret societies, but before examining that feature of our subject, we must trace their history in Penang and Malacca during the period 1868 to 1890.

Penang

PENANG, 1868–1890

The extracts from F. S. Brown's report of 21st August, 1869 given at the beginning of this chapter, furnish a second opinion to Vaughan quoted in Chapter VI above, upon secret society affairs in Penang at this time.

The records of secret society activity in Penang for the ten years 1870–1880 appear to be no longer in existence, but this must have been a prolific period coinciding as it did with the intrigues leading up to the Treaty of Pangkor (1874) and with Birch's administration in Perak (1875): the Perak war (1876) and the consolidation of British rule in Perak, 1877–1880.

Penang, the cradle of Sino-Malay secret society conspiracies and the base and sally-port of the Larut wars, must have been buzzing with excitement in these active years, during which the parent societies of Triad and Tokong and their White and Red auxiliaries were watching lynx-eyed political developments around them. Later, after suppression in 1890, they took up permanent positions underground in the northern settlement and carried on their *imperium in imperio:* their warfare and their hatreds: their trade rivalries and their struggle for place and power, out of sight and hearing of the authorities who had suppressed them.

In *Manners and Customs of the Chinese* published in 1879 Vaughan has the following reference to Penang in 1878 on page 108:—

"In Penang are registered as dangerous the following societies:—

Ghi Hin	Hye San
Toh-peh-kong	Hoh Hak Seah (Ho Hop Seah)
Ghi Hok	Choon Ghe Seah
Ho Seng	

In the decade 1880–1890, we get a clearer picture of the Penang under-world from the reports of Pickering.

THE PENANG PICTURE IN 1881

Pickering's Report on Penang for 1881 (G. N. 144/82) contains the following:—

Apart from an insignificant attempt by the Ghee Hocks at Balik Pulau to renew, at the beginning of last year, the old feud between them and the Ghee Hengs, the public conduct of Penang secret societies has been most orderly. 2,417 new members were registered. The total number of the six Chinese secret societies in Penang is 46,705.

A schedule of the six registered societies referred to is appended. We may roughly divide them as follows:—

Tokong	Triad
Toh Peh Kong	Ghee Hin
Ho Seng	
Ghee Hock	
Tsun Sim	
Hai San	

On this division Tokong would number about 19,000 members and Triad about 27,000.

We may assume that the names recorded as those of the Headmen, are those of dummies. This was a common practice during the "fake" period of registration 1870–1882. In preceding chapters we have made the acquaintance of some of the redoubtable leaders of Triad and Tokong in Penang during this decade, but their names do not appear in the official Schedule for 1881 which is as follows:—

CHINESE SECRET SOCIETIES REGISTERED UNDER SECTION 3 OF *ORDINANCE NO. XIX OF 1869*

IN PENANG FOR THE YEAR 1881

Name of Society	Lodge	Principal	Occupation	Residence	No. of Office Bearers	Total No. in 1880	Registered during 1881	Total No. at the end of 1881
Ghee Hing	31, Church Street	Vong Tsun Tsong	Baker	Market Street	177	25,973	1,525	27,498
Toa Peh Kong	57, Armenian Lane	Tsng Thien Tun	Writer	Armenian Lane	85	8,834	294	9,128
Ho Seng	53, King Street	Go Bun Eng	Opium Farm Officer	Market Lane	46	5,442	414	5,856
Ghee Hock	Rope Walk	Gim Sam	Lime-dealer	Beach Street	49	1,785	115	1,900
Tsun Sim	40, King Street	Cheah Yin Tsai	Shop-keeper	Beach Street	25	1,950	69	2,019
Hai San	393, Beach Street	Lo Vun Tsen	Blacksmith	Beach Street	22	394	Nil	394
Total					404	44,378	2,417	46,795

The Red and White Flag societies in Penang 1881–1882

Ordinance XIX of 1869 "to provide for the suppression of dangerous societies" discussed more fully below, did not name any particular society for suppression, such as did the Hongkong Ordinance of 1845 suppressing the Triad society. It is clear that the 1869 measure was aimed primarily at the Chinese societies as the principal culprits in the Penang riots of 1867. As a result, the Malay flag societies appear to have escaped notice for a decade or so, until their activities in Penang became so obnoxious as to bring them to official notice. We have already seen something of those activities, chiefly in the political sphere, on the Perak-Penang shuttle between 1870–1882 in Chapters XVIII, XIX and XX *supra*, and the Teluk Anson Tabut Case of 1882, cited in the latter chapter, is some indication of their activities in the purely criminal sphere.

At all events, by 1880, they had made themselves so objectionable that a measure of suppression was decided upon. The following are extracts from the Annual Reports 1881–1882 of the Inspector General of Police, relating to Malay Red and White Flag activity in Penang in those years:—

1881. The Malay secret societies have not given much trouble during the year. Their influence for evil amongst the most ignorant classes of the community is still great and it is to be hoped that the proposed amendment of the Dangerous Societies Ordinance will soon become law. The time has come when all British-born or naturalised subjects should be obliged to be on the side of Government and order, and not members of societies whose objects are, for the most part, opposed to our ideas of right Government.

1882. The Malay secret societies have been comparatively quiet during the past year, but the utmost vigilance is required to prevent petty quarrels amongst members assuming serious proportions through the machinations of unscrupulous Headmen. The amendment of "The Dangerous Societies Ordinance 1869", by Ordinance No. IV of 1882, has borne good fruit in all the Settlements as regards the Red and White Flag societies, and I have every confidence that, in a few years, these dangerous confederations will have died out.

By Section 1 of *Ordinance IV of 1882* discussed more fully under the "Suppression" section of this chapter below, the Red and White Flag societies were indicted and suppressed by name in the Colony. Seeing that they were already ramified all over the Peninsula in both the political and criminal sphere and were not simultaneously suppressed outside the Colony, the ineffectiveness of the Colony measure against them was pre-determined.

We now return to the Chinese societies in Penang.

The Picture in Penang in 1883

In the Protectorate report by Powell in 1883 we read:—

During the year under review, the secret societies have been unusually troublesome to the Registrars in Penang, especially the Ghee-Hing society, by its incessant attacks on members of other societies.

The Report of the Committee appointed to enquire into the charges made against certain Headmen of the Ghee-Hing Kongsi, mentioned above, is already in the hands of Government.

Similarly, Khoo Mah Pian former clerk of the Toh Peh Kong in 1867 (*see* page 252 *supra*) re-appears from his former hiding place to prove the hereditary principle of Tokong.

In the sixteen years that had elapsed, the authorities—to whom one "Chinaman" was much the same as another, had probably forgotten all about the Penang riots and their leaders all of which was by then ancient history, just as most Europeans in Malaya to-day have forgotten, if they ever knew, what happened in this country in 1917.

The Chinese, however, are great respecters of custom and continuity, and can afford to wait.

In the interval the old gang had retired underground and dummies had been put up for registration and to bear the "loss of face" that such a procedure involved; while the old gang remained in charge just the same.

When their position was liable to be compromised or jeopardised by the Ordinance of 1882, they again declared themselves, and re-appeared above-ground after sixteen years.

This incident illustrates a common feature of secret society praxis in Malaya, which is often denied by the uninformed, and should be the more carefully noted on that account.

We should also notice that the Hai San, suppressed in Singapore by *Gazette* Notification No. 1 of 1883 (page 366 above), remained on the official Penang list for that year.

The Year 1884 in Penang

Pickering has the following in his report for 1884:—

In Penang there were several affrays between members of secret societies, viz:—between Ghi Hings and Ghi Hoks at Nibong Tebal on the 19th February; between the Ghi Hings and members of the Fo-Hap-Sha[1] Friendly society at Bukit Mertajam on the 14th June; between the Ghi Hings and the Ho Sengs at Damar Etam, Balik Pulau, on the 17th, 18th and 20th June; between the Ghi Hings and Ghi Hoks at Nibong Tebal on the 29th September; but the most serious affray occurred at Simpang Ampat in the Trans-Krian on the 2nd December, when several houses belonging to the Ghi Hoks were looted, and one was burned by the Ghi Hings.

There were 4,766 new members of secret societies registered during 1884, thus raising the total number of members of secret societies registered in Penang to 62,764, the Ghi Hings alone numbering 35,764.

Footnote.—(1) i.c. Ho Hop Seah.

The Schedule of Penang societies accompanying the 1883 report although comprising the same six societies as in the 1881 Schedule, has other interesting features.

The Schedule is as follows:—

CHINESE SECRET SOCIETIES REGISTERED UNDER SECTION 3 OF *ORDINANCE NO. XIX OF 1869*

IN PENANG FOR THE YEAR 1883

Name of Society	Lodge	Principal Headmen	Occupation	Residence	No. of Office Bearers	No. of Members on Registered Books 1883
Ghee Hing	Church Street	Vong Tsin Tsung, Boey Yau Kong[1], Lim Khai Fat[2]	Baker, Writer, Clerk	Market Street, Church Street, Penang Street	177	33,773
Twa Peh Kong	Armenian Lane	Tsug Thien Tun, Khoo Mah Phan[3], Ong Loon Tek	Writer, Shop-keeper, Trader	Armenian Lane, Acheen Street, Beach Street	85	11,485
Ho Seng	King Street	Goh Boon Eng, Tsew Ho Kiet, Lim Boon Tsin	Trader, Shop-keeper, Pastry Cook	King Street, China Street, China Street	46	7,671
Tsun Sim	King Street	Yap Hap Kiet, Po Tsun Guan, Tan Siu An	Trader, Opium retailer, Chop Sin Tek Ho	Beach Street, Beach Street, Beach Street	25	2,088
Ghee Hok	Rope Lane	Sim Yau Chiang, Ngun Tek Bun, Kwa Ah Ha	Mandore, Shop-keeper, Trader	Prye, Beach Street, Beach Street	49	2,437
Hai San	Beach Street	Lo Vun Tsen, Chah Luk, Ng Sien	Blacksmith, Planter, Trader	Beach Street, Pulau Betong, Pitt Street	22	542
				Total 1883	404	57,996
				Total 1882	404	51,001
				Increase	—	6,995

The interest in this Schedule lies in the fact that whereas that of 1881 under *Ordinance IV of 1882*, mindful perhaps of the threats and thunderings in that Ordinance, entered upon the list of Ghee Hin and Toh Peh Kong headmen names of those who were very far from being nobodies in the Penang under-world. And so we meet again unexpectedly with—

     Boey Yau Kong and

     Lim Khai Fat

of Triad who as Boey Yoo Kung and Lim Kay Fat were Master and Clerk respectively of the Ghee Hins in the Penang Riots of 1867 (*see page* 252 *supra*).

Footnote.—(1) He was "Master" of Triad in Penang, 1867 (*see* page 252 *supra*).
Footnote.—(2) He was clerk of Triad in Penang, 1867 (*see* page 252 *supra*).
Footnote.—(3) Previously mentioned in para 252 *supra*.

The following occurs in the Annual Report of the Acting Inspector-General of Police for 1884 :—

> The secret societies have given the usual amount of trouble. There have been several disturbances, but none of a very serious nature excepting in Province Wellesley. The good services of the Chinese Protectorate have been invaluable in keeping these associations under control. Several of the so-called Friendly societies, many of whose members are Straits-born Chinese, have been troublesome, and in one or two instances have been the cause of quarrels with the Dangerous societies. I have no hesitation in saying that banishment has acted as a most wholesome deterrent, as it is now to the advantage of the headmen to keep their societies in good order.

The I.G.P. quotes *inter alia* the following 1884 secret society case which illustrates the smouldering hatred of the two factions of Triad and Tokong only waiting an excuse to burst into flame :—

> On the 8th of December, a serious riot took place at Sempang Ampat. The riot was caused by a dispute about $1.60 which a Ghee Hock owed a Ghee Hin. The Ghee Hock refused to pay, abuse followed. and the friends on both sides joined in.
>
> The Ghee Hocks, seeing they were in the minority, retired, and next day they attacked some Ghee Hins who were working in a plantation, one of whom was wounded. The Ghee Hins then collected their men, and next morning attacked the Ghee Hock houses, killing and mutilating their pigs and smashing their furniture. Twelve men were arrested and sent up for trial.
>
> The leader was sentenced to eighteen months' rigorous imprisonment, two others to one year, and the remainder discharged. The heads of both societies were also bound over by the Magistrate to keep the peace for three months in $500 each.

THE YEAR 1885 IN PENANG

Following is from Pickering's report on Penang societies for 1885 (G.N. 61/86) :—

> In Penang, several quarrels and fights have taken place between the Ho-Sengs and Ghee Hins, and the Ho-Sengs and Toa Peh Kongs, but they have been generally nipped in the bud by the Police.
>
> A branch of the Singapore Ghee Hok society was established in Penang and Province Wellesley some ten years ago, and has been a continual source of trouble, having no *raison d'être*, and being considered as an interloper by the older established societies. Having become a nuisance by its numerous quarrels and by the incompetency of its chiefs, the Ghee Hok society in Penang was suppressed in September.
>
> There is no doubt that in Penang and Province Wellesley the secret societies need to be dealt with very firmly. The Ghee Hin society is very powerful and possesses ample funds and large property; it and the Toa Peh Kongs are backed by wealthy Chinese, and unless they are kept in order by a strong hand, they may give much trouble. In any future complications or disturbance, deportation judiciously applied, will have an excellent effect in keeping good order amongst the Chinese in Penang and the Province.

The first paragraph of this report indicates the uncertain loyalty of the Ho Seng society, a note upon whose allegiance in Perak about this time as between Triad and Tokong is given on page 338 *supra*.

The Ho Seng (和 勝) was one of the three earliest societies in Penang of which we have a record. It is mentioned in the *Burney Papers* (*see* page 72 *supra* (foot)) and by Caunter in 1825 (page 75 *supra*) and by Pattullo in 1829 (page 77 *supra*). The latter records it as "the secret society of the Wai Chow Cantonese allied at that time to Ghee Hin and Triad. It may, like the Hai San (*vide* page 113 *supra*), have changed its complexion in later years. It certainly seems to have joined the Tokong camp in Perak during the Larut wars (about 1873).

The second paragraph of Pickering's report refers to the foundation in Penang of the Ghee Hok from Singapore "some ten years ago" (*i.e.* about 1875). The Ghee Hok appears in the first "Pickering List" of Penang societies published in 1881 and given on page 378 above.

We have no record of its first appearance in Penang, but the year 1875 suggests itself as most likely because, following the Treaty of Pangkor, we can well imagine that Tokong would be anxious to strengthen itself in Penang for the exploitation of the newly-opening territory of Perak, where there was promise of "good hunting" in the under-world of the tin-mining industry. The Larut wars had recently ended and Triad influence, which had been so powerful a factor in concluding the Treaty of Pangkor (Chapter XIX), might be expected to make large strides in the absence of stronger numerical opposition from Tokong. The foundation of Ghee Hok in Penang, where Tokong had hitherto been represented by its Toh Peh Kong and Hai San battalions, was much like raising another battalion of local recruits for the Tokong under-world-army in Penang, under the Ghee Hok banner from Singapore. The suppression of the Ghee Hok in Penang under the Ordinance of 1885 is noted below.

The third paragraph of Pickering's 1885 report is once again an unconscious admission of the presence of the two camps of Triad and Tokong, which were constantly at one another's throats.

SUPPRESSION OF THE GHEE HOK SOCIETY IN PENANG SEPTEMBER 1885. (G.N. 508/85)

By Order dated 15th September, 1885, the Ghee Hok society of Penang was suppressed under the *Dangerous Societies Ordinance 1885*, after having been called on to shew cause why it should not be suppressed, and having thereafter still been regarded as dangerous.

The Schedule of registered societies in Penang for the year 1886 is as follows:—

CHINESE SECRET SOCIETIES REGISTERED UNDER SECTION 3 OF ORDINANCE NO. XIX OF 1869

IN PENANG FOR THE YEAR 1886

Name of Society	Lodge	Principal Headmen	Occupation	Residence	No. of Office Bearers	No. of Members 1886
Ghi Hing	Church Street	Vong Tsin Tsung Tan Ah Pau Lim Kui Choon	Baker Trader Cigar-seller	Church Street Beach Street Church Street	183	48,247
Twa Peh Kong	Armenian Lane	Inn Kam Lor Khu Mah Pien Cheng Thien Tun	Rice Shop-keeper Shop-keeper Writer	Beach Street Acheen Street Armenian Lane	85	15,545
Ho Seng	King Street	Li Chung Fuk Chew Ho Kiet Lim Sam Ki	Trader Shop-keeper Writer	Chulia Street China Street Market Street	46	11,220
Tsun Sim	King Street	Chia Yew Chai Tok Sok Bu Teh Hai Tong	Trader Sit-planter Writer	Beach Street Pulau Tikus Beach Street	25	2,359
Hai San	Beach Street	Chan Ah Shin Yi Ah Fah Chin Ah Choi	Tin-miner Writer Tailor	Church Street Beach Street Pitt Street	22	674
				Total 1886	361	78,045
				Total 1885	355	68,691
				Increase	6	9,354

Note.—Ghee Hok has disappeared from this list having been suppressed by G.N. 508/85.
Footnote.—(1) One of the Khoo Kongsi, previously mentioned on page 252 supra.

THE PENANG PICTURE 1886–1889

From 1886, the name of the Ghee Hok society disappears from the Penang records, but as the membership of the six registered societies in 1883 was 58,000 and the five remaining societies in 1886 was 78,000 rising to 92,000 in 1887 and to 104,000 in 1888, (see Schedules) one may assume that the suppression of the Ghee Hok made no difference to the actual strength of Tokong in Penang in the years following its suppression.

THE YEAR 1886 IN PENANG

Pickering's report for 1886 has:—

> In Penang, there were 9,354 new members of secret societies registered during 1886, thus raising the total number of members of secret societies registered in that Settlement to 78,045.

THE YEAR 1887 IN PENANG

Pickering's report for this year (G.N. 261/88) has:—

> During the year 1887, 14,536 new members of secret societies were registered in Penang, giving a total number up to date since 1877 of 92,581.

> The year opened with a riot between Ghi Hins and Ho Sengs[1] in King Street, where one man was badly injured. Several hundreds took part, and the street, after the disturbance was finished, was an instructive sight, being covered with broken bottles, stones, sticks and brickbats. Had it not been for the prompt action of the Police at the time, more than one life would probably have been lost. A large number of rioters were arrested on the spot, and Assistant Superintendent Cuscaden and myself afterwards seized some others, so that more than ninety were brought on one day to the Police Court, most of them being convicted.

> This and a good many previous disturbances were, I have little doubt, chiefly due to the action of Chiu Ho Kiat, the Ji Ko of the Ho Seng society. Mr. Maxwell, the Superintendent of Police, and myself strongly recommended his deportation to the Government, but this was not allowed. He went so far in his sympathy with Ching Keng, one of the chief rioters, who was sentenced to three months' imprisonment and $100 fine, as to appeal against the decision of the Magistrate in the case. Again, during my absence in Singapore in October last, he was without doubt instrumental in causing a disturbance at a meeting held at the Chinese Town Hall to consider as to the management of the Chinese Temple in Pitt Street, where many leading Babas were put into a great state of trepidation by sudden cries of *Pah, Pah*, when the meeting broke up in disorder.

> The Ji Ko[2] of this society having so distinguished himself, the new Toa Ko[3] (elected in April)—Li Chong Fok—could not rest in obscurity and shortly after his installation was nearly cut to pieces in a serious riot between Ghi Hin and Ho Seng tin miners in Salak near Kwala Kangsa in the State of Perak. The result of the case there was that he was banished from the State and heavy security taken that he should not return. Since then he has been living peacefully in Penang.

> With the exception of the riot in January and the affair of the Temple, the societies have been restricted to very small collisions during the rest of the year. A slight friction at Penaga in Province Wellesley between Ghi Hins and Toa Peh Kongs, which might have come to be serious, was stopped by prompt intervention on the part of the Police and Protectorate.

> Two headmen—Ng Theng Sui and Wong Wa—of the Li Seng Hang society, (mentioned in my last report), a society which is registered as a dangerous society in Singapore,[4] but which attempted to open a Kongsi house here without first making a report, were fined $200 each, and no more has been heard of the society since.

THE PENANG PICTURE AT THE TIME OF SUPPRESSION 1889

Powell's Protectorate Report for 1889 has:—

> The Acting Assistant Protector in Penang approximately estimates the total registration there, for the year 1889, at 113,300.

> As regards Penang, Mr. Wray reports no serious friction during the year between the societies. One unregistered society—the Tian Thien Sia—that commenced to form was dispersed on the first attempt.

> The Assistant Protector at Penang has received the chops of the five dangerous societies, whom it is intended to abolish under the new Societies Ordinance, and is in hope that they "will cease to exist as working organizations" by the 30th June, 1890.

The Annual Report of the Resident Councillor, Penang for 1889 has:—

> 119. There has been no serious friction between the secret societies during the year and the few petty quarrels and disturbances which have occurred have been settled by the Police and Protectorate.

> 120. The passing of the Societies Ordinance caused little excitement amongst the ranks of the dangerous societies. The Assistant Protector of Chinese (Mr. Wray), by means of meetings and discussions with the various headmen, prepared their minds for the dissolution of the societies, and explained thoroughly the motives and intentions of the Government, at the same time indicating the best methods of disposing of their property. The majority of the headmen appear anxious to get rid of their responsibilities.

> 121. The five dangerous societies have surrendered their chops to the Assistant Protector and are now taking measures to dispose of their property.

Footnote.—(1) This suggests that the Ho Seng in Penang as in Perak (page 338 *supra*) had also joined Tokong at this date.

Footnote.—(2) The 二 哥 or Vice President see page 117 *supra*.

Footnote.—(3) The 大 哥 or President see page 117 *supra*.

Footnote.—(4) Shown as the Lee Seng Hong in the Singapore schedules 1886–1889 above.

The following Schedule accompanies Pickering's report for 1888 and presents the semi-final surface picture of secret societies in Penang, before their final disappearance underground following their official abolition from 1st January, 1890:—

CHINESE SECRET SOCIETIES REGISTERED UNDER SECTION 3 OF *ORDINANCE NO. XIX OF 1869*

IN PENANG FOR THE YEAR 1888

Name of Society	Lodge	Principal Headmen	Occupation	Residence	No. of Office Bearers	No. of Members Registered during the year 1888	No. of Members
Ghi Hing	Church Street	Wong Tsui Tsung, Lim Ah Thia, Ang Ah Khai	Baker, Trader, Depôt-keeper	Church Street, Beach Street, King Street	183	9,188	68,658
Toa Peh Kong	Armenian Lane	Ion Kam Lo, Khu Mah Pien[1], Tiun Eng Liau	Rice Shop-keeper, Nil, Nil	Beach Street, Acheen Street, Armenian Street	49	1,547	19,175
Ho Seng	King Street	Li Chung Fuk, Chew Ho Kiet, Khau Ah Chia	Rice Shop-keeper, Sundry Shop-keeper, Nil	Rope Walk, China Street, Carnarvon Street	88	864	13,266
Tsun Sim	King Street	Chia Ju Chai, To Sok Gu, Teh Whai Ki	Sundry Shop-keeper, Retail Opium Shop-keeper, Engraver	Beach Street, Pulau Tikus, Beach Street	9	44	2,403
Hai San	Beach Street	Yi Win Hin, Kok Fuk, Chia Luk	Nil, Tailor, Fruit Dealer	Penang Street, Acheen Street, Beach Street	9	79	801
				Total 1886	338	11,722	104,303
				Total 1887	361	14,536	92,581
				Increase	—	—	11,722
				Decrease	23	2,814	—

Footnote.—(1) A member of the Khoo Kongsi previously mentioned on page 252 *supra*.

There follows the last gazetted Schedule of registered Chinese societies in Penang which was published with Powell's report for 1889. Among the "principal Headmen", we can recognise some old friends who have been with us in this survey since 1867. It was unlikely that they would now go out of business in meek compliance with an official order which meant less to them than the drastic Sacred Edict of their own Emperor in 1772 which had so signally failed to smoke them out of their underground haunts:—

CHINESE SECRET SOCIETIES REGISTERED UNDER SECTION 3 OF *ORDINANCE NO. XIX OF 1869*
IN PENANG FOR THE YEAR 1889

Name of Society	Lodge	Principal Headmen	Occupation	Residence	No. of Office Bearers	No. of Members Approximate
Ghi Hing	Church Street	Vong Tsui Tsung / Lim Ah Thial / Ang Ah Thail	Baker / Trader / Depôt-keeper	Church Street / Beach Street / King Street	245	75,000
Twa Peh Kong	Armenian Lane	Khu Ma Tieul / Lan Kuang Li	Shop-keeper / Nil	Acheen Street / China Street	50	21,000
Ho Seng	King Street	Li Chung Fuk / Ang Kim Lew / Khaw Ah Chia	Trader / Sugar Planter / Nil	Rope Walk / Beach Street / Carnavon Street	92	14,000
T'sun Sim	King Street	Chia Yew Chai / Fok Sok Bu / Teh Hai Tong	Trader / Siri Planter / Writer	Beach Street / Pulau Tikus / China Street	9	2,450
Hai San	Beach Street	Teom Tek Lok / Lim Hiang Long	Tailor / Nil	Beach Street / Beach Street	13	850
				Total 1889	409	113,300
				Total 1888	338	104,300
				Increase	71	9,000

Footnote.—(1) Although we cannot guarantee the identity owing to variations in romanised spelling and the vagaries of the printer's devil, these three headmen seem to have stayed the course from 1867 to 1890 and, no doubt, so continued till their death.

Malacca

MALACCA IN 1870–1878

The following references, taken from *Parliamentary Papers C 1505* (1876) and *C 1709* (1877), give particulars of four days secret society riots in Malacca in December 1875, in which eight Chinese were killed. These Triad *versus* Tokong riots are particularly interesting as marking the first officially recorded case of Triad and Tokong fighting in Malaya under the banners of White and Red, which we have hitherto associated only with their Mohammedan auxiliaries. In these riots Triad was represented by two factions recorded as Ghee Hin and Ghee Boo, the latter not identified, and Tokong by a society recorded as Ho Beng, which may or may not be a dialectic variant of the Ho Seng society, discussed above.

TRIAD AND TOKONG RIOTS UNDER WHITE AND RED FLAGS DECEMBER 1875

It should be remembered that these riots occurred during the period of unrestricted registration 1870–1882, when all societies were recognised.

In *Parliamentary Paper C 1505* page 239, Plunket, then acting Lieut.-Governor of Malacca, in a report to the Governor dated 25th December, 1875, says:—

"On 7/12/75 ...... a member of the Ghee Boo society got into a row while attending a Malay *Jogay (joget)* at Bunga Raya in the town of Malacca and was beaten by a man named Kim Choo nephew to Boon Swee[1] the head of the Ho Beng society.

* * *

On 8/12/75 ...... Kim Choo got beaten in town by some Ghee Boo men.

* * *

On 10/12/75 two men belonging to the Ho Beng society were beaten ...... in turn by men of the Ghee Boo society. The two Ho Beng men reported the matter to their headman Boon Swee.

Boon Swee referred the matter to Boon Teong,[2] the manager of the opium farm, a very influential man in settling all such quarrels......"

Page 240:—

"On 13/12/75 ...... a report was brought in that (there were) in the Durian Tunggul road, mobs of Chinese armed with sticks and spears with pieces of red cloth tied to them. The red cloth is considered an emblem of the Ho Beng society and Supt. Hayward sent out the Sergt.-Major and six constables accompanied by Boon Swee (head of the Ho Beng society) to disperse the mob.

* * *

On 14/12/75 ...... I ordered Boon Swee who is the interpreter in my court to go and apologise according to the Chinese fashion to the Ghee Hin society ......

* * *

On 16/12/75 Mr. Martin Velge arrived ...... and reported that ...... a mob under a red flag had twice attacked some shops in Durian Tunggal ...... Numbers of men also came to complain of attacks having been made during the night ...... by men under the red flag.

* * *

At about 10 p.m. a report came in that the Ghee Hins under the white flag were coming down in great force from Tanjong Kling to attack the opposite party.

* * *

On 18/12/75 ...... In the course of the day a report was received from Inspector Cartwright that a party of men under the red flag had taken possession of the village of Sepatai ...... robbing, plundering, and burning all around, and in one of their fights they killed one of the white flag party and beheaded him".

In the court-case which resulted from this riot the following evidence, recorded in *Parliamentary Paper C 1709* page 32 was given:—

Ung Piow states:—

    I am a mandore in Chin Hoon's plantation at Kalamat ...... I belong to the Ghee Hin Kongsee. Some of the coolies belonged to the Ghee Hins and some not. There were disturbances between the Hok Bengs and the Ghee Hins. The Ghee Hin men fly white flags and the Hok Bengs red.

* * *

The Ghee Hins are composed of Hokkiens, Macaos and Hylams. I don't know if there are any Malays.

* * *

Dolemat states:—
    I saw one red flag up. I did not see any white ones.

Page 37:—

Cassim states:—
    ...... I saw the Chinese conversing, they had two red flags.

These references show that Triad and Tokong were at this period (the murder of Birch had just taken place) beginning to fight one another under the banners of their Malay subsidiaries and not under their own flags. We shall have further evidence of this development later. There do not appear to be any other Malacca secret society activities recorded up to 1900.

Footnote.—(1) For reasons given elsewhere we think this Boon Swee is identical with Chong Bun Sui, a Malacca-born Hakka, author of the "Powell Report" of 1884, (*see* below).

Footnote.—(2) Elsewhere and for reasons given, we identify this man as Seet Bun Tiong. He was probably the real head of Tokong in Malacca and Chong Boon Swee merely a junior headman.

THE MALACCA PICTURE IN 1879–1889

Vaughan in *Manners and Customs of the Chinese* page 108 has the following about Malacca in 1879:—

"In Malacca the dangerous societies are:—

Ghi Hin	Ghi Boo
Hok Beng	Hye San
Ho Seng	

It is said that the red and white flag societies amongst the Klings are affiliated to the Triad societies the one to the Ghi Hin and the other to the Ghi Hok; but the Klings affirm that this is untrue; they say that their societies were brought from the Coromandel Coast and have no connection with the Chinese secret societies. It is a notorious fact that throughout the colony, Malays and Klings, and other races are members of the secret societies".

We have discussed this suggested origin of the Red and White Flag societies in Chapter XV pages 229 and 237 *supra.*

From the foregoing the following would seem to have been the division of Triad and Tokong camps in Malacca in 1880:—

Triad *(Under a White Flag)*	Tokong *(Under a Red Flag)*
Ghee Hin	Ho Beng
Ghee Boo	Hok Beng
	Ho Seng
	Hai San
Headman[1] *(Probably)*	Headmen[1]
(1) Tan Tek Guan younger brother of Tan Kim Cheng of Singapore.	(1) Seet Bun Tiong
	(2) Chong Bun Swee
	(3) Chan Tek Cheang

Malacca does not bulk largely in the records of this period as far as we have seen them, and is almost unmentioned in the Chinese Protectorate reports of this decade. There can, however, be no doubt that the same underground warfare was constantly at work. The following extract is from Pickering's annual report for 1885 (G.N. 61/1886):—

In Malacca, during the first part of the year, some trouble arose between the dangerous societies. Mr. Wray, Acting Assistant Protector of Chinese, Singapore, was sent to enquire into the affair; the enquiry resulted in the suppression of the Hok Beng and Ghee Boo societies, and the re-registration of the others.

The suppression of these two societies in Malacca by G.N. 412/85 and 411/85 respectively is referred to again below. They represented, of course, the same old rivalry of Triad and White Flag *versus* Tokong and Red, with which readers are by now familiar.

The Colony Government had also by 1885, become aware of this rivalry, if not with the cause of it and, when no improvement resulted from the amended *Ordinance No. IV of 1885,* the necessity for total suppression began to gain acceptance as the only solution left. The attack upon Pickering of 1887, no doubt, clinched this decision.

Although a little awkward in chronology, we will, therefore, here interpolate the story leading up to the suppression of secret societies in the Colony in 1890, before proceeding to the record of Triad, Tokong and Tabut in the other parts of Malaya between 1870 and 1900.

THE APPROACH TO TOTAL SUPPRESSION

The decision for total suppression of secret societies in the Straits Settlements taken in 1889, was not a sudden one. The approach to it had moved in leisurely fashion through a period of seventy years in the following well-defined phases:—

(1)	Period of toleration	1786–1868
(2)	So-called suppression of dangerous societies	1869
(3)	Period of unrestricted registration	1870–1881
(4)	Suppression of the Red and White Flag societies	1882
(5)	Period of restricted registration, or partial suppression of Chinese secret societies	1882–1889
(6)	Total suppression of Chinese secret societies	1890
(7)	Period of selective registration, exemption and refusal of registration	1890 to present-day.

The decision for final suppression was sponsored by Sir Cecil Clementi Smith the first Governor of the Straits Settlements possessing an intimate personal knowledge of the Chinese. In China proper secret societies, and particularly the Triad society had been in suppression since the promulgation of the Sacred Edict by the Manchu Emperor, Kang Hsi in A. D. 1662 (*see* page 9 *supra*) and similar action had been taken by the British

Footnote.—(1) *See* below this Chapter, under "Selangor" where the evidence upon which these deductions rest is given.

Government in Hong Kong in 1845 within three years of the foundation of that Colony (*see* page 8 *supra*). It was perhaps due to the fact that the Straits Settlements were, until 1867, governed from India by officers appointed from India who did not understand the Chinese, that the power of Triad and Tokong grew to such immense proportions in Malaya before the curb began to be applied after the "transfer" of 1867 and the appointment of Pickering as the first "Protector" in 1870.

We have also seen in Chapter XX the introduction into Perak during the years 1879–1882 of a system of registration of individual Chinese in an effort to control the intangible power of Triad and Tokong; and the issue of a Perak Order in Council of 1st September, 1889, prohibiting all Chinese secret societies in Perak.

On the Mohamedan side there was, of course, the standing prohibition of Islam against all secret oaths and associations. This we have seen (page 218 *supra*), was evaded by the cover-protection afforded by religious Jema'ah, which were firmly established from about 1830. As a first measure of control of Mohamedan secret societies in the Colony, there was passed *Ordinance IV of 1882* noted more fully below suppressing the Red and White Flag societies.

This Ordinance attempted by a general measure to achieve two things:—

    (*a*) To confine the membership of recognised secret societies to immigrant Chinese and so prevent Straits-born Chinese who were non-banishable from becoming entangled in them.

    (*b*) To abolish the existence of secret societies from among all other communities and to prevent their re-growth.

It failed to achieve either purpose and was re-enacted by *Ordinance IV of 1885* noted more fully below which sought to obtain the same ends by more particular methods. The second measure also failed.

Then came total suppression in the Colony under the *Ordinance of 1889* (which had effect from 1st January, 1890).

The 1889 Ordinance was a compromise, providing for:—

    (1) The dissolution and prohibition of Chinese dangerous societies.

    (2) The exemption of harmless societies.

    (3) The registration of others.

Complementary legislation was for the first time, introduced into Perak, *vide* Perak Orders in Council of 1/9/1889 and No. 1 of 1892, in respect of Chinese secret societies only, and this was followed by the *Registration of Societies Enactment, Perak 1895*. Similar measures were adopted in the other Malay States which, with a multitude of amendments and re-enactments remain the body of the law to-day.

THE MACHINERY OF SUPPRESSION

We now come to an examination of the seven years immediately preceding total suppression. There had been passed a *Suppression of Dangerous Societies Ordinance* in 1869 as a result of the Penang Riot Commission Report 1868, and this had been prolonged in 1870, 1872 and was extensively amended in 1882. It should be noted that this measure as passed referred to dangerous societies, whether Chinese or otherwise and not to secret societies as such. We must examine it more closely.

"AN ORDINANCE TO PROVIDE FOR THE SUPPRESSION OF DANGEROUS SOCIETIES NO. XIX OF 1869"

This piece of legislation began as "a bill to provide for the suppression of secret societies", in seventeen sections, published on pages 589–593 of the *Straits Settlements Gazette* of 15th October, 1869.

It was drafted by Sir Thomas Braddell then Attorney-General and according to the "objects and reasons" was presented by the Committee appointed to prepare a Bill on the subject of secret societies, in accordance with the instructions of the Legislative Council. It was as we have seen the direct outcome of the Penang Riot Commission Report of 1868 (Chapter XVI *supra*).

The bill was completely re-cast in Committee and in its final form contained 32 sections intituled as above, and much good sense.

It was finally published on pages 767–772 of the *Straits Settlements Gazette* of 24th December, 1869 and was in force for one year, subsequently prolonged by the 1870 amendment.

This measure did not, as we might think from its title, order the suppression by name of any society either "dangerous" or secret.

The following features of this important Ordinance should be noted:—

    (1) It was essentially a measure for the registration of all societies and associations of ten or more persons, except commercial companies (Section 1) and lodges of British freemasonry (Section 27).

(2) If any society whether registered or not, should appear to the Governor to have an illegal object or to be likely to prove dangerous to the public peace, it could be called upon to furnish additional particulars (Section 3) *viz*:—

    (i) Name, residence and occupation of all office-bearers and all members, with proof of the correctness of such lists.

    (ii) Copy of rules, orders, instructions, by-laws and regulations of the society.

    (iii) Statement of all payments required by members and the sources of all income of the society from whatever source derived.

    (iv) Copy of all engagements, obligations or promises taken and given, proposed or tendered by members.

    (v) Explanation of all signs and pass-words used by members.

    (vi) Statement and explanation of all insignia, banners, paintings, drawings, writings or other articles intended to be used by the society.

    (vii) Description of ceremonies to be used for the purpose of the society.

    (viii) Particulars of every change, alteration or addition to the above, proposed.

(3) The Registrar was given power to refuse registration when the above particulars were of a warlike or aggressive character or showed an illegal purpose (Section 4).

(4) The Governor could require bonds with two sureties up to one thousand dollars from the manager or office-bearers of any society registered under the Ordinance (Section 5).

(5) The administration of oaths of any kind was prohibited (Section 6).

(6) Notice of meetings of any registered society was to be given to the Registrar (Section 7).

The practical result of this Ordinance was not suppression or dissolution; but formal registration. The name of the Ordinance is, therefore, misleading. No suppression that we have been able to trace took place under it and its title is therefore a misnomer. It inaugurated that period of unrestricted registration 1870–1882, which led to conditions of bogus returns and faked membership already noted, during a decade when the immigrant Chinese population of Malaya was increasing by hundreds of thousands, following British intervention in Perak and the rise of the tin-mining industry.

THE GROWTH OF TABUT IN THE COLONY 1867–1882

Side by side with the growth of Triad and Tokong during this period, there was the corresponding growth of White and Red Tabut both in the Colony and in the Native States, which we have already traced in Chapters XVII, XVIII, XIX and XX *supra*.

As the Flag societies had hitherto remained outside the efforts of Government to control secret societies, despite the exposure of Tabut in the *Penang Riot Commission Report* of 1868, it is not perhaps surprising that Tabut activities became more and more aggressive between 1870 and 1882, until in the latter year an amending Ordinance to that of 1869 was introduced.

The general purpose behind this measure was to restrict membership of secret societies in Malaya to the stream of immigrant Chinese, who were already on arrival immersed in secret society lore, and to prevent the spread of the secret society virus among Straits-born Chinese and among the other resident communities in Malaya who could not be banished.

SUPPRESSION OF RED AND WHITE FLAG IN THE COLONY MARCH 1882

The Dangerous Societies Suppression Ordinance No. IV of 1882

Ordinance IV of 1882, printed on page 251 of the *Straits Settlements Government Gazette* 1882, amended and re-enacted the 1869 Ordinance and is of importance as it contains the first reference in the body of Colony law, to the suppression of the Red and White Flag societies by name.

The preamble reads:—

Whereas secret associations of Chinese based on, or connected with, the association known as the Triad society in China, have long existed in these Settlements; and Whereas persons not connected by origin or language with China have been admitted as members of such secret associations; and Whereas separate secret associations of persons not connected by origin or language with China have of late been established at the several Settlements, under the name, at present, of the Red Flag society and the White Flag society; and Whereas such secret associations have for their object purposes incompatible with the maintenance of good order and constituted authority and afford, by means of secret agencies, facilities for the commission of crime and for the escape of criminals; and Whereas it is desirable to prevent British subjects and Chinese and others who may have been naturalised as British subjects and persons of other than Chinese descent or nationality from being members of societies which are recognised as dangerous; and Whereas it is expedient to make better provision by law for the suppression of all such secret associations.

It is hereby enacted ....

This measure aimed at:—

    (1) Abolition of the Red and White Flag societies root and branch.

    (2) Prevention of British born or British naturalised persons or any person not a Chinese from being a member of a dangerous society.

    (3) Restriction of membership of Chinese secret societies to China-born Chinese.

Section 1 reads:—

> The societies known as the Red Flag society and the White Flag society and all similar secret associations by whatever name the same may be known, having among their members persons not born in China of Chinese parentage, or having among their members any British born subjects or persons who are naturalised British subjects, are hereby declared to be unlawful societies and the said societies shall not be registered under *Ordinance XIX of 1869*.

This section denied registration and, therefore, legal existence to the Red and White Flag societies by whatever name and in whatever form they might be found.

It, therefore, attempted to suppress at one blow the prototype and antitype secret society among communities other than Chinese, conducted on the Chinese model.

Seeing that the authorities knew all about these "type" societies in 1868 after presentation of the *Penang Riots Commission Report* of that year, their suppression under this Ordinance fourteen years later seems a little delayed.

Section 5 says:—

> When any of the banners or insignia, or writings of any society declared to be unlawful under this Ordinance are found in the possession, custody or control of any person ...... it shall be presumed ...... that he is a member of such unlawful society.
>
> If any such banners, insignia or writings are found at any mosque it shall be presumed that they are in the possession, custody or control of the Penghulu Mukim, or Bilal of the Mosque.

This section suggests that at that time the authorities were aware of some connection between Mohamedan mosques (or religious *jema'ah*) and Mohamedan secret societies.

We do not know how this awareness arose, nor upon what evidence the suspicion rested, but that it was not misplaced, this work helps to prove. The Telok Anson Tabut Trial of September, 1882, (page 345 *supra*) was a case in point.

Section 11 reads:—

> Any person not born in China of Chinese parentage and any person being a British-born subject, and any person being a British naturalised subject, who is found to be a manager, or office-bearer, or member of any society, as to which additional particulars are required to be furnished under Section 3 of *Ordinance XIX of 1869*, shall be liable on conviction to a penalty not exceeding $500.

The purpose of this section was to attempt to restrict membership of all Chinese societies, secret or otherwise, which were registered under the 1869 Ordinance, to China-born Chinese.

That the section did not fulfil its purpose is shown by the amending section 10 of Ordinance 1885 referred to below.

ORDINANCE IV OF 1885[1]

Ordinance IV of 1882 was repealed and re-enacted by *Ordinance IV of 1885*, being "An Ordinance to amend the law relating to Dangerous Societies". It remained based upon the original *Dangerous Societies Suppression Ordinance No. XIX of 1869* some of which sections it amended.

The 1885 Ordinance was also directed against the Red and White Flag societies which are again named in the preamble, expanded from that of 1882.

Section 1 of the 1882 Ordinance was much strengthened by section 3 of 1885 which reads as follows:—

> The societies known as the Red Flag society and the White Flag society and all similar associations, by whatever name the same may be known, are hereby declared to be unlawful societies, and shall not be registered under the Principal Ordinance[2] and any person acting as manager or office bearer or assisting in any way in the conduct of the business of or in managing the affairs of any such unlawful society shall be liable to a fine not exceeding one thousand dollars or to imprisonment of either description for any period not exceeding twelve months or to both fine and imprisonment, and any person who is a member of or who attends any meeting of any such unlawful society or who subscribes or pays money or gives aid or procures from others subscription money or aid for or towards the maintenance of any such unlawful society shall be liable to a fine not exceeding five hundred dollars or to imprisonment of either description for any period not exceeding six months or to both fine and imprisonment.

We have Maxwell's assurance of 11th September, 1882, quoted in Chapter XX page 347 *supra* that the Ordinance of 1882 finally disposed of the Red and White Flag in Penang and yet we see the same Ordinance being strengthened in 1885.

Footnote.—(1) Under this Ordinance the following earlier experiments were repealed:—

    The *Dangerous Societies Suppression Ordinance No. XIX of 1869* (Sections 2, 4, 28 and 31 only).
    The *Dangerous Societies Suppression Continuation Ordinance No. XVI of 1870*. The whole.
    The *Dangerous Societies Suppression Ordinance No. V of 1872*. The whole.
    The *Dangerous Societies Ordinance No. IV of 1882*. The whole.

Footnote.—(2) *i.e.* The *Dangerous Societies Suppression Ordinance No. XIX of 1869*, which introduced the principle of registration and under which secret societies were registered and societies considered to be dangerous were refused registration.

RESTRICTION OF MEMBERSHIP OF CHINESE SOCIETIES TO CHINESE NATIONALS

In one particular the 1885 Ordinance introduced a novelty, in order to strengthen the third aim of the 1882 measure.

The preamble and Section 11 of the 1882 Ordinance (both quoted above) sought to restrict membership of Chinese societies to China-born Chinese. The 1885 measure expanded Section 11 of the 1882 Ordinance by taking powers to gazette the names of Chinese societies, membership of which was forbidden to all except China born Chinese.

Section 10 of the 1885 Ordinance reads:—

"The Governor in Council may from time to time by Order declare with respect to any Chinese society or Hoey in such Order mentioned that it is unlawful for any person other than a Chinese subject born in China of Chinese parents to be a member thereof. Any person not being a Chinese subject born in China of Chinese parents who after the expiration of fourteen days from the date of the publication of such Order in the *Government Gazette* shall be found to be a member of such society shall, in the absence of proof that he had no knowledge of such Order, be liable to a fine not exceeding five hundred dollars or to imprisonment of either description for a period not exceeding six months or to both fine and imprisonment."

This section aimed at keeping "proto-type" secret society members, deprived of their own Red and White societies, out of the ranks of named Chinese registered societies secret and otherwise. This is rather wishful legislation, and in any case belongs more to the approved rules of a registered society than to the Statute Book.

CHINESE SOCIETIES IN THE COLONY SO RESTRICTED

As a sequel to Section 10 of *Ordinance IV of 1885*, we find Orders published in the *Gazette* declaring that "no person other than a Chinese subject born in China of Chinese parents is permitted to be a member of any of the following Chinese societies or Hoeys", all of which were at that time registered under the 1869 Ordinance. These lists of Chinese societies were, of course, published without Chinese characters, which we have suggested in the Schedule on pages 426–428 below.

Many of them have already been met with in preceding chapters. The lists are:—

(1) **In Singapore**
   (G.N. 306/85)

   Hok-Kien Ghee Hin   Teo Kun Ghee Hin
   Ghee Hok   Kwang Kit Tong
   Hok Hin   Ng Fuk Tong
   Song Peh Kwan   Hong Ghee Tong
   Kong Fui Siew   Lee Seng Hong
   Ghee Khee or Kwang Hok   Yet Tong Kun
   Hylam Ghee Hin   Keng Soon
   Ghee Sin

   (G.N. 224/86)

               Eng Chuan Tong
               Gi Lan Tong
               Kim Hok Tong
               Tong Beng
               Hok Tek Choon

(2) **In Malacca**
   (G.N. 339/85)   (G.N. 105/87)
      Ghee Hin   Baba Eng Hoh Malacca
      Ghee Boo   Ghee Siew
      Macao Ghee Hin
      Hai San
      Hoh Beng

(3) **In Penang**
   (G.N. 413/85)
      Ghee Hin   Ghee Hok
      Twa Peh Kong   Tsun Ghee Seah
      Ho Seng   Ho Hap Seah
      Tsun Sim   Keng Hok Tong
      Hysan

ACTIVE SUPPRESSION OF CERTAIN CHINESE SOCIETIES, 1885–1889

Apparently within a few months it was realised that neither registration nor restriction of membership was achieving the desired measure of control over certain societies which had been registered since 1869 and whose membership had been restricted earlier in the current year. At all events, there shortly followed in 1885 under the amended powers given by Section 4 of the 1885 Ordinance, the active suppression for the first time of societies registered under the 1869 Ordinance.

Thus, we find the suppression of the following societies throughout the Straits Settlements, gazetted on 19th June, 1885, and subsequent dates (again no Chinese characters are given) :—

Teo Kun Ghee Hin	(G.N. 352/85)
Ghee Hin	(G.N. 353/85)
Kwang Kit Tong	(G.N. 354/85)
Ng Fuk Tong	(G.N. 355/85)
Ghee Boo society of Malacca	(G.N. 411/85)
Hok Beng society of Malacca	(G.N. 412/85)
Ghee Hok society of Penang	(G.N. 508/85)
Hainan Ghee Hin of Singapore	(G.N. 115/88)
Heng Beng society (no Settlement mentioned)	(G.N. 353/88)

To this list must be added the suppressions already noted, *viz*:—

The Hai San society of Singapore	(G.N. 1/82)
The Red and White Flag societies in all three Settlements	(Section 1 of *Ordinance IV of 1882*)

The foregoing represents the total of discriminatory suppression enforced prior to the introduction of general suppression in 1890, the approach to which we must now examine.

THE SUPPRESSION OF SECRET SOCIETIES, 1889

The Case for Suppression

The case for total suppression is best given in the dispatch of the Governor (Sir Cecil Clementi Smith) himself a Chinese scholar, who addressed the Secretary of State for the Colonies on 20th June, 1888, in the following terms:—

Paper No. 292 laid before the Legislative Council (12/12/1888)
(Council Proceedings 1888)

My Lord,—I have the honour to request your Lordship's consideration to the subject of the Chinese secret societies in this Colony, about which I intimated in a recent despatch, that I should specially report, and I must beg your Lordship to bear with me while I explain the extent and character of these societies, the objects they have in view, and the effect that they have on the welfare of the Colony.

2. According to the last returns, there are eleven secret societies in Singapore, having 1,122 office bearers and 62,376 members enrolled in the register book. In Penang there are five secret societies, having 361 office bearers and 92,581 enrolled members. There was an increase in the number of members in the two Settlements in 1887, as compared with 1886 of 20,771. The total number of registered members is 156,440. The estimated Chinese population of Singapore and Penang (including Province Wellesley) according to the last Census (1881) was 153,532, but it is known to be much in excess of those figures. It will be at once seen to what extent the secret societies affect the Chinese communities in Singapore and Penang.

3. Now what are these secret societies? They are branches of the great Chinese secret society "Thien-Ti-Hui", or Triad society, which was established in China in the 17th century. To belong to it in China renders a person liable to decapitation, and every endeavour is made by the Chinese authorities to stamp it out. The origin of the Triad society was political,—namely to dethrone the Manchu Dynasty—but its power and influence was felt to be baneful in regard to almost every branch of the administration of the Government.

4. There can be little doubt but that the Authorities at Hongkong must have been early warned of the danger arising from the operations of this and similar societies, for among the very first series of enactments in the Statute Book of that Colony is one "for the suppression of the Triad and other secret societies". The immunity which that Colony—though on the very borders of China—enjoys up to this time from the harmful effect of secret societies, is due to the fact that they were never allowed to get foothold in the Colony. The preamble of the Hongkong Ordinance accurately describes these societies as "associations having objects in view which are incompatible with the maintenance of good order and constituted authority and with the security of life and property, and afford by means of a secret agency increased facilities for the commission of crime and the escape of offenders". That description, which was written in 1845, holds good to this day, and it is, in my opinion, to be regretted that the policy indicated in that Ordinance has not been carried out in these Settlements. It was eminently a sound policy for any part of the British Empire where Chinese congregate, not only in the interests of the Government, but of the Chinese themselves, and any other policy can only be construed by the Chinese Government as unfriendly to their country, and may at any time form the subject of diplomatic remonstrance.

5. It was in 1869, that the Government of the Straits Settlements first legislated on the subject of the secret societies. Riots, had in 1867, taken place in Penang between members of certain secret societies which resulted in great destruction of property and loss of life. From the correspondence, I gather that the influential residents desired that strong measures should be adopted for their suppression, but I presume that the Government did not feel itself in a position at the time to take that course, for the result of the deliberations was the passing of *Ordinance No. XIX of 1869*. This elaborate enactment is styled "an Ordinance to provide for the suppression of dangerous societies", but in effect it provides mainly for the registration and control of such societies. It has been amended more than once, but the position remains almost the same, and the Government recognises that there exist in the Colony certain Chinese societies which are emphatically dangerous to the public peace.

6. I will now cull a few extracts from recent reports of the Inspector-General of Police and of the Protector of Chinese in regard to secret societies.[1]

* * *

7. I may here state that the Protector of Chinese recommends that the Ghee Hok society should be suppressed, and adds that it is time that Government should use all possible means towards the gradual abolition of dangerous societies throughout the Colony. Upon this recommendation the Inspector-General of Police wrote the following minute:—"I have given this matter my most serious consideration, and I submit that the time has come for Government to suppress entirely Chinese dangerous societies. It may be possible to do it piecemeal, as suggested in this letter, but in my opinion it would be better to make a bold stroke and suppress all the existing dangerous societies at once. By the suppression of the Ghee Hok branch of the great Ghee Hin society, as proposed by the Protector of Chinese, we would, I fear greatly strengthen the remaining branches of the same society (branches not so well managed even as the one supposed to be suppressed). There is nothing to choose between these societies. They are all equally dangerous, and all are engaged in the management and protection of gaming-houses and brothels. If Government is satisfied that the Ghee Hok society has perpetrated the crimes laid to its charge in this letter, I feel satisfied no better opportunity could be found for suppressing it and the other societies with which it is affiliated".

8. The Acting Attorney-General also informs me that it is well known to all who practice in the Courts that these secret societies constantly interfere with the course of justice, sometimes to prevent and hinder it by screening offenders, sometimes it may be to assist it by yielding them up. He instances a case tried at the last Assises at Singapore in which two Chinese were charged with murder. The evidence showed that the deceased, Chan Yu Haing, had been knocked on the head with an iron tool in a stonemason's shed situated in a crowded thoroughfare and near a Police Station. The neighbour of the injured man saw the blow struck, but instead of taking him to the Police Station, where they might both have made immediate and uninfluenced statements, the neighbour took the man past the Police Station to the meeting house of the Kongsi to which they both belonged. Here the neighbour handed the injured man over to one of the Headmen of the society, who after some delay, took the man to the Police Station and laid a charge against the accused. Council for the accused contended that the charge was a false one, got up by this Headman against one of the accused, in order to injure a trade rival, and one who was not a member of the society. However this may be, the case affords an illustration of the way in which important cases are submitted to secret societies previous to their being brought before the recognised Government Authorities.

9. Such an incident as is above detailed is not unusual. It is as much as anything the outcome of fear of doing what may not accord with the wishes of the secret society. No one who has witnessed the initiation of members, as I have been able to do, can fail to appreciate the species of terrorism exercised over the ignorant beings who are made members of a society on their arrival in this Colony. A lodge is held. They are admitted one by one under an arch of drawn swords. Pass-words are taught them as they go on from stage to stage round a lofty altar decorated with the insignia of the society. Subsequently the oath is read out to them from a paper, which is burnt, and the ashes are mixed in a cup with water, into which a drop of blood is made to fall from the pricked finger of each novice. A portion of this herrible mixture is then drunk by every one, and, after a cock has been strangled[2] and thrown out into the street,—one of the officers of the society shouting "May ye perish like that cock if you break the oath you have taken",—the ceremony is concluded.

10. But not only is the existence of these societies a danger to the peace of the Colony, they seriously affect the peace of the Protected Native States. Very many instances could be quoted to show that from the head-quarters of the secret societies in Penang emissaries go forth to the Native States and enrol members in large numbers, who at the slightest provocation—a dispute in a brothel, a fight between two men belonging to rival societies—create a riot. A very serious riot arising from some such small cause occurred in November last year in Perak. The report of the Commandant of the Perak Sikhs on the riot contains the following passages:—"originating in a quarrel at a brothel in Papan, through the agency and perfect organisation of the secret societies the quarrel developed into a serious and what would have been a desperate struggle between the Ghee Hin and Hai San secret societies ...... so perfect appeared the organization of these societies, that a message sent round on the evening of the 28th resulted in the Ghee Hins marching down upon Papan from Lahat and the adjoining mining centres in large numbers and attacking the Kongsis occupied by the Hai San men, to which society belonged one of the leading parties in the brothel dispute. At about 7 a.m. on the 29th November a large force of Ghee Hins, with tokens marched into Papan from Lahat direction, dashed through Papan, looted two Kongsis, but on the Hai Sans mustering, retired. One man was killed, and several desperately wounded. The rioters were armed with parangs, knives, sticks, etc. Two men were hanged for their share in the murders (for some of these wounded subsequently died) committed in the riot. Others were sentenced to death for being active agents of the Penang secret societies, but their sentences were commuted. And "the Secretary for Chinese affairs in Perak enters largely", as the Resident states in his Report for 1887, "into the important question of secret societies in Perak, the organisation of which, the number of their members, and their being bound upon all occasions to support each other in defiance of the laws of the State, enables worthless characters at any time to create serious disturbances, and imperil its peace". In accordance with the law of Perak, any one convicted of being the agent of a secret society is liable to the penalty of death.[3]

11. I could multiply the number of cases of a similar character, but I have doubtless quoted enough to show the actual danger of allowing these secret societies to continue in our midst. That they should be suppressed has been over and over urged by some of the most able of the Unofficial Members of the Legislative Council, and the same view strongly commends itself to the respectable portion of the Chinese community of the Colony, though they will abstain, for reasons

Footnote.—(1) These have mostly been given above under the respective Settlements for the various years and are therefore not repeated here.

Footnote.—(2) Strangulation as we have seen pages 138, 146 and 148 *supra*, belongs to the Tokong ceremony and not to the Triad.

Footnote.—(3) We have not traced this law. That it existed between about 1882 and 1889 is proved by Perak Order-in-Council No. 24 of 1889 abolishing it.

to be easily understood, from publicly advocating any such measure. These societies are, as I have stated, prohibited in China,—the Mother Country of those who form the societies in this Colony. They are prohibited in Hongkong. They are prohibited in the Malay States in our immediate neighbourhood, which are under British protection. They are prohibited in the Dutch Colonies in these seas. It is, in short, only in the Straits Settlements that they are allowed to exist, to flourish, and to increase in number and power—a standing menace to all good government, and a great scandal to British administration. The policy adopted up to this time as regards these societies is one that I have never ceased to regret since my first connection with this Colony ten years ago, for I believe it to be a weak policy, and most detrimental to the public interests. It has however been carried on by the support, and on the advice of, local officers of ability and experience, whose faith in it has, at last, been seriously shaken.

12. It will be urged that if these societies are suppressed, the Government will have no machinery to put in their place, and that in consequence the assistance which the officers of the Government now obtain—I should more correctly say, occasionally obtain—from headmen, in the detection of crime, in the arrest of accused persons, and in the controlling of large numbers of Chinese who may be under some temporary excitement, will be lost. Assuming this to be true, for the purposes of argument, I should still unhesitatingly advise that these societies should be suppressed. In a Colony properly administered, it is not prudent to have an *imperium in imperio*. The Government must be the paramount power, and it is not so in the eyes of many thousands of the Chinese in the Straits Settlements.

13. The Government is not now weak in regard to Chinese affairs, as it was when in 1869 the first Ordinance dealing with these secret societies was passed. I believe that I am right in saying that, at that time there was not a single Officer of the Government who had any knowledge of the Chinese language, or of their habits or customs. Since 1871, it had the very marked advantage of the services of Mr. Pickering who possesses extraordinary qualifications for the post of Protector of Chinese and of adviser to the Government on all matters connected with the Chinese community. His department has grown by degrees, until it is second to none in importance, and there are now other offices which are presided over by gentlemen who have passed in the Chinese language, and have been trained in the public service. This strengthening of the Government Departments in the direction referred to will continue, and the Government can and will give to the Chinese inhabitants a real and honest protection in lieu of that protection which they believe they obtain by joining a secret society. They will learn more and more that, as in Hongkong, without being "squeezed" they can obtain easy and ready access to a Government Official who knows their language, and their complaints will be attended to with promptitude, and their grievances redressed. The organization for replacing the societies is ready at hand and has only to be developed.

14. I cannot but believe that your Lordship will concur in the opinion that the time has come for suppressing these secret societies, and hence I have had a draft Ordinance prepared for that purpose, and I now submit it to your Lordship's consideration. Its principles are approved of by my Executive Council. It requires but little in the way of explanation, and I have only to draw special attention to one or two sections. By Section 5, it is provided that no society, with certain exceptions, shall be registered without the previous approval of the Governor in Council, while by Section 4 no society unless registered can lawfully exist. Under Section 10 the Governor in Council will be able to dissolve all the existing secret societies. Certain other sections provide for the punishment of those who manage, assist in managing, or are members of an unlawful society, and it is specially provided that the power of banishment may be exercised in the case of those convicted of managing, or assisting in the management of such societies, which power might properly be brought into force, in my opinion against any person of Chinese origin, even though he might be a British subject. Special provision has been made by Section 11 for dealing with the property of any society which may be dissolved, and it will be so dealt with that the Executive Government will have nothing to do with it. It seems to me of the highest importance that the Chinese should see that, in taking the action which I have recommended, the Government has taken care to ensure that it should receive no material benefit from the disposal of the property of any suppressed society.

15. Such is, in a few words the character of the Bill. I am quite alive to the fact that its introduction will create a considerable commotion among a large number of Chinese. There will probably be disturbances, because the headmen of the societies, who have for years been living and fattening on the gambling-houses and brothels, and on the money they have been able to squeeze out of their ignorant and superstitious countrymen, will find their occupation gone, and they will not give up their influential position without a struggle. Time will, of course, be given to enable the object and intention of the Government to be thoroughly well understood, and every means will be adopted to ensure publicity of the actual effect of the measure, before it is brought into operation. Happily, the Government will have on its side the great strength arising from the support of the respectable and law-abiding portion of the community, and I have no fear of a successful issue of the policy which I have advocated, should it be adopted. Of this I feel quite confident—that the complete suppression of the secret societies must be, at one time or another, carried out, and the longer it is delayed, the more difficult will be the task, and the more serious will be the conflict between the Government and the societies.

I have, &c.,

CECIL C. SMITH.

20th June, 1888.

This despatch contains many features of interest too numerous to comment upon, but the reference to Pickering's Annual Report for 1885 wherein he mentions "the Ng Fuk Tong (Five Happinesses lodge) "as having been recently established for the purpose of intriguing against the Triad society" should be noted.[1]

The Ng Fuk (五 福) is the name of one of the eight lodges of the Ko Lao Hui (Tokong) mentioned by Hutson in Chapter II and the passage clearly shows that the local gang which took this name were Tokong roughs engaged in that anti-Triad campaign of which Pickering himself was a victim two years later.

Footnote.—(1) This reference is given on page 368 under the year 1885 in Singapore and is omitted from the above reprint of the Governor's despatch in consequence.

S.O.S. *op. cit.* page 257 has the following in reference to the suppression of secret societies:—

> The great event of the year 1889 was undoubtedly the passing into law of the Societies Ordinance. The bill attracted the deepest interest on account of the great change it was to effect in the nature of the organisation of a large mass of the Chinese of the Colony. While it was generally felt that the abolition of the secret societies was absolutely necessary, there was uncertainty as to what the practical outcome of such an irrevocable step as their complete suppression might be. The unofficial members had solidly opposed this second reading, but in the progress of the bill through Committee, the Government made certain concessions...... After some delay caused by the consideration of the Secretary of State of a memorial against the Bill forwarded by the Ghee Hin society, the Royal assent was finally notified and the Ordinance came into force on 1st January, 1890, with six months grace for the secret societies to wind up their affairs and distribute or otherwise dispose of their property and funds.

The memorial from the Ghee Hins mentioned above has not been seen by us and might contain something of interest.

THE ORDER FOR GENERAL SUPPRESSION

The Societies Ordinance 1889

Ordinance No. 1 of 1889 entitled "An Ordinance to amend the law relating to societies", gave effect to the decision for general suppression. It was passed on 21st February, 1889, and came into force from 1st January, 1890, by G.N. 551/89 under the title *The Societies Ordinance 1889.*

Its main provisions were:—

(1) By Section 2 it repealed—

    (a) *The Dangerous Societies Suppression Ordinance, 1869.*

    (b) *The Dangerous Societies Ordinance, 1885.*

(2) Companies, businesses and Freemasons' lodges were excluded from the definition of society (Section 3).

(3) Any individual society or class of societies could be *exempted* from the provisions of the Ordinance by Governor's Order in Council (Section 3 (d)).

(4) With the exception of the above, every society existing at the coming into force of the Ordinance was required to apply for Governor in Council's approval to become registered (Section 5 (1)).

(5) Approval of registration did not make a society lawful, whose purposes and objects were unlawful (Section 5 (2)).

(6) Societies existing at the date of coming into force of the Ordinance, which were not exempted under Section 3 (d), were required to be *registered* within six months failing which they were deemed unlawful (Section 6 (2)).

(7) Societies formed after the date of coming into force were required to be either exempted under Section 3 (d) or registered under Section 5 (1), failing which they were unlawful (Section 6 (1)).

(8) The Governor in Council could order the *dissolution* of any registered society by *Gazette* Notification (Section 11).

The preamble reads:—

> "Whereas great danger has arisen from the existence of societies having among their objects purposes incompatible with the peace and good order of the Colony and it is expedient to provide against such danger ......".
> It is hereby enacted ......

The same might be said with equal truth of conditions to-day, after forty-five years test of this legislation.

The essential difficulty and fatal flaw in all such legislation, is to be found in the fact that one can legislate to dissolve a registered or exempted society, but one cannot legislate to dissolve an unregistered one. The one is tangible and has an established official identity, the other has not. The new Ordinance introduced the principle of the three alternatives:—exemption, registration or dissolution. What was neither exempted nor registered was in theory dissolved by *Gazette* Notification—so far as such a procedure has power to affect such an end.

The new Ordinance dropped the useful provision of surety-bonds for office-bearers, provided by the 1869 Ordinance, and omitted mention of any particular societies or class of societies by name, such as the Red and White Flag or the Triad society, specifically referred to in earlier legislation.

By G.N. 735/89 of 18th December, 1889, all managers and Committees of societies formed for:—

    Recreation
    Charity
    Religion
    Literature

were called upon to apply for exemption under Section 3 (d) of the new Ordinance. This move provided the dangerous societies with a most welcome loop-hole for survival and furnished them with that very cover-protection of which at the moment they were in such need.

We shall see as we proceed how societies and clubs among Asiatics for recreation, charity, religion and literature have since 1890 been continuously organised. Some of these have been exempted and some registered, but of very few can it be said that they have not at one time or another become hosts for secret society·intrigue.

This circumstance arises from the principle implicit in all secret society praxis namely, that the illegal can co-exist within the legal.

THE CAMPAIGN OF SUPPRESSION IN 1890 IN THE STRAITS SETTLEMENTS

The sources of information on this subject covering the Colony are:—

(1) The *Government Gazettes* of the period.

(2) A list given in Ward and Stirling *op. cit.* Vol. I page 180.

(3) A book. *Impressions of the seals and tickets of membership of those Chinese secret societies in the Straits Settlements suppressed in 1889-1892.*

The history of this book is given on pages 101-104 *supra* and it is briefly referred to as *The Clementi-Smith woodprints.*

The first two sources present the usual difficulty of identification, by reason of the absence of Chinese characters, which the third fortunately in part supplies.

THE EARLIEST EXEMPTIONS FROM REGISTRATION

Rather paradoxically, the campaign of suppression began by the publication in the *Gazette* of lists of societies to which *exemption* from registration was granted under Section 3 (*d*) of the new Ordinance.

Thus, G.N. 196/90, 258/90 and many others began the negative process of exemption and an examination of the lists of names shows the rise of numerous Football, Cricket and Social clubs among the Asiatic communities which, right from the beginning of the campaign, gained exemption and hence freedom from further official scrutiny.

A list of some eighty exempted clubs and associations, European, Chinese and Indian appears on page xxxii of the Index to the *Straits Settlements Gazette* for the year 1890.

Similar lists appear in Powell's report on the Chinese Protectorate for 1890 at the following references in the *Straits Settlements Gazette* for 1891:—

For Singapore—Schedule F page 1095.

For Penang   —Schedule G page 1104.

For Malacca   —Schedule A page 1107.

Examination of these lists shows that initial exemptions ranged in Singapore from the Singapore and Tanglin clubs to the Ban Choon Hwee, the Kwan Chui Hui and the Soo Lim Wee "clubs"; in Penang from the Penang Cricket club to the Kong Hock Tong, the Hoi Tsoo Soo, Tai Pak Kong, and the Hindoosin; and in Malacca from the Malacca club to the Sam To Thong and the Tiong Lan Hoe.

Granted that the majority of those Chinese associations exempted were, or appeared to be harmless, there is a familiar ring about the selected names above which suggests that in some cases "new presbyter was but old priest writ large". This is particularly noticeable among the new generation of clubs in Penang to which the Ordinance gave birth, a large number of which adopted the term 社 she = society, to describe themselves. This term literally means "An altar of the spirits of the ground" or "A place of sacrifice to the earth spirits", which immediately suggests the Yin, the Toh Peh Kong and the Han league discussed in Chapter VI pages 101 and 106 and in Chapter VIII *supra*.

There is a flavour about the Penang exemptions which, subject to correction, suggests that they may have concealed the inner ring of Tokong and Red Flag in Penang, the historical matrix of secret society intrigue in Malaya.

When we consider the antiquity of Triad and Tokong; their astonishing powers of self-preservation and recuperation; their virile history in China under the suppression ban of the Sacred Edict: their basis in religious belief and their social necessity as insurance agencies among overseas Chinese as described in preceding chapters, we must concede that the dangerous societies against which the new Ordinance was aimed, no doubt took advantage of the exemption clause to preserve their identity by changing their name and outward appearance during the transition period of 15 months from the passing of the Ordinance (21/2/89) to the latest date for registration under Section 6 thereof (30/6/90).

How far this chameleon-like process may have taken place and official exemption have thereby been obtained, cannot, of course, at this distance of time be discovered; but in view of the close connection between Triad and Tokong and their stem temples of Buddhism and Taoism already noted (Chapter III), retirement for a space within the folds of a local temple would have been simplicity itself.

Knowing the power behind the dangerous societies and the ease with which the authorities both in China and overseas have ever been persistently hoodwinked by them, it would be surprising indeed if their leaders did not take advantage of such an opportunity to obtain at one stroke official recognition and official freedom from further interference, under some innocent sounding name of a temple or a club, invented on the spur of the moment for the purpose.

It would perhaps be worth while to examine all the earlier exemptions between 1890–1893 in this light.

THE EARLIEST REGISTRATIONS UNDER ORDINANCE NO. 1 OF 1889

The same criteria might be applied to the earliest registrations under the new Ordinance. These are given in Powell's Report on the Chinese Protectorate for the year 1890 at the following references in the *Straits Settlements Gazette* of 1891:—

> For Singapore—Schedule H page 1097.
>
> For Penang   —Schedule I page 1105.
>
> For Malacca —Schedule C page 1108.

POSITIVE DISSOLUTIONS UNDER THE 1889 ORDINANCE

Action under this head was taken in two ways:—

> (a) By declaration of unlawfulness after effluxion of the six months' time limit under Section 6 (2) above.
>
> (b) By direct order of dissolution under Section 11 above.

A list of the societies dealt with under (a) and (b) above during the year 1890 appears on page xxxii of the Index to the *Straits Settlements Gazette* for that year. We will take the first category first.

A.—Societies declared unlawful in the Colony on and after 1st July, 1890, under Section 6 (2) of Ordinance No. 1 of 1889

Examination of the *Gazette* shows the following societies declared unlawful under this category with the relevant *Gazette* Notification. The Chinese characters are, of course, not given in the *Gazette*.

> (1) **Singapore**
>
> > (Under G.N. 381/90 of 1st July, 1890)—
> >
> > > Gi Hok
> > >
> > > Heng Sun
> > >
> > > Hok Hin
> > >
> > > Hokkien Ghee Hin
> > >
> > > Hong Ghee Thong
> > >
> > > Kong Fui Siew
> > >
> > > Kwang Hok Ghee Khee
> > >
> > > Li (Lee) Seng Hong
> > >
> > > Song Peh Kwan
> > >
> > > Yet Tong Kun

See also Powell's Report on the Chinese Protectorate for 1890, Singapore Section, Appendix *G*, on page 1096 of the *Straits Settlements Gazette* 1891.

> (2) **Penang**
>
> > (Under G.N. 473/90 of 21st August, 1890)—
> >
> > > Ho Hap Seah
> > >
> > > Tsuan Ghee Seah

> (3) **Malacca**
>
> > (Under G.N. 443/90 of 5th August, 1890)—
> >
> > > Hai San
> > >
> > > Macao Ghi Hin
> > >
> > > Sin Ghi Hin

See also Powell's Report for 1890, Malacca Section, Appendix *B*, on page 1107 of *Straits Settlements Gazette* for 1891.

B.—Societies dissolved in the Colony in 1890 by Governor's Order in Council under Section 11 of Ordinance No. 1 of 1889

(1) Singapore

(Under G.N. 373/90 of 20th June, 1890)—
Gi Hok society of Singapore

(Under G.N. 494/92)—
The Tin Bu society of Singapore (Not previously come to notice)

(2) Penang

(Under G.N. 472/90 of 21st August, 1890)—
Ghee Hin
Ho Seng
Kean Tek
Hai San
Chun Sim

See also Powell's Report on the Chinese Protectorate for 1890, Penang Section, Appendix *H*, on page 1104 of *Straits Settlements Gazette* 1891.

(3) Malacca

(Under G.N. 444/90 of 5th August, 1890)—
The Macao Ghi Hin society of Malacca (*i.e.* the Cantonese Branch of Triad)
(Under G.N. 1/91 of 5th January, 1891)—
The Sin Gi Heng society at Malacca.

These *Gazette* Notifications show that a rather wide-meshed net was thrown over the dangerous societies at the time of their suppression, enabling them to survive without much inconvenience in another form and under another name, and the piecemeal application of the law in the different Settlements resulted in what was officially suppressed in one Settlement, being ignored in another.

These measures struck a direct if ill-aimed blow at both Triad and Tokong in the Colony, particularly in Penang, but the nature of the forces aimed at, their power of survival underground, their agility in evading the legal steam-roller and the whole history of Triad and Tabut in Malaya since that date, go to prove that the blow was not a knock-out.

This was perhaps inevitable at a time when information upon the form and substance of Triad and Tokong was so meagre.

THE SIN GHEE HIN IN MALACCA 1890

We should perhaps notice that a society of this name was evidently flourishing in Malacca in 1890, because we find it both declared unlawful by G.N. 443/90 on 5th August, 1890, and also dissolved by G.N. 1/91 on 5th January, 1891. These notifications prove that a society of this name, with which we shall become more familiar in subsequent Chapters, existed at that date at least in Malacca if not elsewhere in Malaya.

Some authorities have held that the Sin Ghee Hin (or "New Ghee Hin") is a revival of the former Ghee Hin suppressed in 1890 and dating only from the early years of the present century. The fact that both the Ghee Hin and the Sin Ghee Hin were suppressed contemporaneously in 1890 disproves this theory. This, in turn, has some bearing upon the question which arises in a later chapter namely, whether the modern Sin Ghee Hin society belongs to the Triad or the Tokong camp.

VARIOUS SUPPRESSIONS OF THE GHEE HIN (TRIAD)

The method adopted in carrying out the campaign of suppression appears at this distance of time to have been haphazard.

For instance we have seen page 392 above, that between 1882 and 1888 some twelve dangerous societies had been suppressed by notification in the *Gazette* and those suppressions remained effective under the new Ordinance of 1889.

Nevertheless several of those already suppressed societies were again *Gazetted* as unlawful or dissolved under the new Ordinance.

Furthermore the scope of the notifications varied in respect of the societies named, some being confined to a named Settlement, others embracing the Colony and others again wherein no territorial limitation was mentioned.

Thus we find that the Ghee Hin was suppressed throughout the Straits Settlements by G.N. 353 of 1885. The Hainan Ghee Hin of Singapore was suppressed by G.N. 115 of 1888. Again the Hokkien Ghee Hin in Singapore was declared unlawful by G.N. 381 of 1890. Again the Cantonese Ghee Hin in Malacca was declared unlawful by G.N. 443 of 1890. Again the Ghee Hin in Penang was dissolved by G.N. 472 of 1890 while the Cantonese Ghee Hin in Malacca was dissolved by G.N. 444 of 1890.

No *Gazette* Notification has been traced which dissolved the Ghee Hin of Singapore under the Ordinance of 1889 other than G. N. 353 of 1885. This may be due to official oversight, or to our own failure to trace the relevant notification.

VARIOUS SUPPRESSIONS OF THE GHEE HOK (TOKONG)

The Ghee Hok and its subsidiaries similarly underwent a piece-meal attack by officialdom. Thus, the Hai San society of Singapore was suppressed by G.N. 1 of 1882. The Ghee Hok society of Penang was suppressed by G.N. 508 of 1885. Again the Gi Hok of Singapore was declared illegal by G.N. 381 of 1890. The Hai San of Malacca was declared illegal by G.N. 443 of 1890. Again the Gi Hok society of Singapore was dissolved by G.N. 373 of 1890, while the Hai San of Penang was dissolved by G.N. 472 of 1890.

The fact remains that in spite of all this "swatting" over nearly a decade, Ghee Hin (Triad) and Ghee Hok (Tokong) have continued to flourish, and, at the present-day the secret society mosquito that survived the swatting campaign of 1890, continues to sting the administration that has so vigorously sought to squash it.

THE WARD AND STIRLING LIST OF SOCIETIES DISSOLVED IN SINGAPORE IN 1890

Our next reference is to the list given by Ward and Stirling, again without Chinese characters. We have been unable to trace the authority for this list and it does not agree with the records in the *Gazette* Notifications quoted above.

In Vol. I page 180 Ward and Stirling *op. cit.* have:—

"At the suppression of the Triad society in Singapore there were nine lodges of the society which had been registered, and which in that year surrendered their seals, etc. They were all branches of the Ghee Hin society ...... which was the Mother lodge in Malaya and from her were descended all the other lodges......

The names of the lodges suppressed were as follows:—

		Suggested Chinese Characters
(1) Hokkien Ghee Hin	福 建 義 興	
(2) Hok Hin	福 興	
(3) Tie Kun Ghee Hin	潮 郡 義 興	
(4) Kwong Hok or Ghee Khee	廣 福 (or 義 記)	
(5) Siong Peh Kuan	松 柏 館	
(6) Kwong Hui Sian	廣 海 山	
(7) Ghee Sin	義 新 (or 義 先)	
(8) Ghee Hok	義 福	
(9) Hailam Ghee Hin.	海 南 義 興	

"The Ghee Hok became a very powerful lodge and was- inclined to be hostile to the Mother Temple of the Ghee Hin".

Apart from the official *Gazette* notifications referred to above, this is apparently the only published list of suppressed societies and it refers only to Singapore. We have suggested the Chinese characters for the names, but some of these may be incorrect.

We disagree with the comment quoted above accompanying the list, as it perpetuates what we believe to be a fallacy, namely that all these societies were branches of Triad. With very little to guide us we would divide them thus:—

Triad   Comment
    (1) Hokkien Ghee Hin ..
    (2) Tie Kun Ghee Hin ..   Presumably intended for the Teochew Ghee Hin.
    (3) Hailam Ghee Hin ..

Tokong
    (4) Kwong Hui Sian ..   Evidently meant to represent "Kwong Hai San"—
                      the Cantonese branch of the Hai San society.
    (5) Ghee Hok ..

Uncertain
    (6) Hok Hin ..
    (7) Kwong Hok ..   Unidentified. Probably Tokong according to
         or   Vaughan's list above.
        Ghee Khee ..

                        The Ts'ung Pak Kwun or "Cypress and Fir tree
                        society" discussed in Chapter V, and although
    (8) Siong Peh Kuan .. always referred to as the Hakka branch of
                        the Ghee Hin, seems more likely to have
                        belonged to Tokong.
    (9) Ghee Sin ..   Unidentified. Might be either.

THE CLEMENTI-SMITH WOODPRINTS

Our third source is the book of impressions of Chinese "chops" recorded by Sir Cecil Clementi-Smith himself in 1890, and kindly lent in 1938 for purposes of this work by Sir Cecil Clementi, former Governor of the Straits Settlements.

It does not purport to be a complete record and the impressions appear in no particular order. Only the names of the separate societies appearing in the book are given below, without particulars of all the seals etc., contained in the book, which is entitled:—

Impressions of the Seals and Tickets of Membership of the Chinese secret societies in the Straits Settlements which have been suppressed 1889–1892:—

Ho Sing	和	勝	
Kian Tek	建	德	
Chun Sim	存	心	
Hok Hin	訊	興	
Gi Hok	義	福	
Kwong Wai Siu (Ghee Hin)	廣	惠	肇
Kwong Hok Ghee Khee (Ghee Hin)	廣	福	義	記
Sun Peh Kwan	松	柏	館
Li Seng Hong	利	坡	行
Yut Tung Kuan	粵	東	館
Hung Yi Thong	洪	義	堂
Ying Fuk Thong	英	福	堂

Besides giving us the authentic Chinese characters for these societies, the book provides us with one of the only two copies we have seen of the seal and membership ticket of the Kian Tek society. These are reproduced in Chapter VI *supra*.

It will be noticed that this list again does not agree very closely with the *Gazette* Notifications nor with the Ward and Stirling list.

Further, this list covers the Straits Settlements and not any particular Settlement as do the *Gazette* Notifications.

Dividing out the two camps in this list we get:—

Triad   Comment

Kwong Wai Siu   .. ⎫   These both bear the endorsement "Ghee Hin" in
                            ⎬   the original in the handwriting of Sir Cecil
Kong Hok Ghee Khee .. ⎭   Clementi-Smith. The Kong Hok Ghee Khee
                                  is mentioned in Vaughan's list above as "Ghi
                                  Kee 'Kong Hok' ".

Tokong

Kian Tek   ..   ..   ——

Gi Hok   ..   ..   ——

Uncertain

Ho Sing   ..   .. ⎰   Discussed in Chapter V. Was apparently ori-
                       ⎱   ginally Triad and changed flags in 1870.

Chun Sim   ..   ..   Not identified.

Hok Hin   ..   .. ⎰   Unidentified. Probably Tokong according to
                       ⎱   Vaughan's list above.

Sung Peh Kwan .. ⎰   "The Cypress and Fir tree society", discussed in
                     ⎱   Chapter V. Probably Tokong.

Li Seng Hang   .. ⎫   A clan association registered as dangerous in
    or   ⎬   Singapore in 1886 and dealt with in court in
Lee Seng Hong .. ⎭   Penang the same year. It was probably Triad.

Yut Tung Kuan .. ⎫   Mentioned by Vaughan above (as Yeat Tong
    or   ⎬   Koon) but not then considered dangerous. A
Yet Tong Kun   .. ⎭   "Friendly" society registered as dangerous in
                        Singapore *vide* 1886 Schedule.

Hung Yi Thong .. ⎫   A Friendly society with a strong Triad flavour,
    or   ⎬   registered as dangerous in Singapore *vide*
Hong Ghee Tong .. ⎭   1886 Schedule.

Ying Fuk Thong .. ⎫   Evidently that "Friendly" society of Penang
    or   ⎬   restricted to Chinese membership by G.N.
Keng Hok Tong .. ⎭   413/85 (above).

TRIAD, TOKONG AND TABUT 1890–1900

From this point we resume the survey of Triad and Tabut in the following places and between the dates shown, adding notes on individual suppressions and exemptions of interest as they occur in the records:—

The Colony	..	..	..	1890–1900
Perak	..	..	..	1883–1900
Selangor	..	..	..	1850–1900
Negri Sembilan	..	..	..	1865–1900
Pahang	..	..	..	1884–1900
Siam	..	..	..	1895–1900
Sarawak	..	..	..	1885–1900

The Colony 1890–1900—If registration from 1869 onwards gave rise to "illicit hoeys" as we have seen above, total suppression in 1890 give full rein to the camouflaged social club.

These two bugbears of public administration in Malaya flourish to-day almost as never before, due to three things:—

(a) The fact that the illegal can co-exist with the legal;

(b) The increase in the Chinese immigrant population;

(c) The increase in the Straits-born Chinese population.

The combination of the illicit hoey and the camouflaged club provided respectively the underground and the surface "host" in which Triad and Tokong continued to maintain their grip upon the social and commercial life of the overseas Chinese community after their official abolition in 1890.

In Chapter I pages 3 and 13 *supra* we have referred to this period as falling within the "degenerate age" of the Hung league.

It would perhaps be more accurate to describe this particular period from 1890 onwards, as the era of seeming disintegration.

Soon after the introduction of registration in 1869, which gave official recognition to officially approved patterns of Triad and Tokong which as we have seen were mostly bogus, the "illicit hoeys" or unofficial and unrecognised although no doubt the more genuine pattern of Triad and Tokong, immediately made their presence felt as "rivals" of the registered or sealed patterns. In truth the "illicit hoey" was in each case more likely to have been the real Triad and Tokong, forcing the pace from below upon its officially recognised and, therefore, "respectable" shadow-self whose counterfeit character left the latter in an uncomfortable and anomalous position between official patronage and the smiles and frowns of the Registrar on the upper side and the pressure of communal blackmail on the under.

Thus, registration and suppression for different reasons hastened the process of seeming disintegration particularly in the towns, where the presence of gangs of roughs, like the Mohocks in London a century earlier, made themselves a pest to the inhabitants under the name of a secret society. These gang-names appear to have been made deliberately confusing in order to blanket any distinguishing characteristics as between Triad and Tokong, so that the authorities would continue in ignorance of their true nature and separate origin.

Thus, in the Annual Report for 1891 Wray wrote:—

The introduction of Ordinance I of 1889 has resulted in the disappearance of the old "Dangerous Societies" as working organisations, though it will take many years for the Triad element and traditions to become extinct in these Settlements, and if any special cause for the revival of inter-society hostilities were to arise, attempts would doubtless be made to rally round the flags of the respective societies.

Every year, however, the process of disintegration progresses, and with incessant watchfulness on the part of the Protectorate and Police, we may hope to see the day when the Straits branch of the "Hung Family" will be a thing of the past.

There have, however, sprung up (especially in Singapore) many small societies (off-shoots of the expiring parent kongsees), whose existence is a real menace to the welfare and liberties of our Chinese settlers. Mr. Powell, in the Annual Report for 1890, alludes to their formation.

Their methods are to send parties of *samsengs*[1] (or roughs) round to brothels, cooly-depôts, music-halls and shops, demanding the payment of various monthly sums of money as "subscriptions" under the threat of coming in force and interrupting the business of the establishment if payment is refused. The fighting men of these societies are kept in the lodges by the headmen on the proceeds of the monies collected.

Since my arrival on 29th December, I have had an opportunity of raiding one of these societies, and I have hopes of being able, with the assistance of Mr. Hare (who has collected most valuable information on the subject), to keep them all under.

Footnote.—(1) This is one of the first official uses of this term we have encountered, *see* page 135 *supra.* It seems properly applicable to the fighting men of Tokong only.

P

Proceedings were taken during the year against the Tong Beng Kongsee, a dangerous society of some 4,000 members which had been suppressed twice and was again revived in 1891. Several headmen were sent to gaol by the Supreme Court, and two deported, of whom one appealed in vain against the sentence of banishment.

Mr. Evans, Acting Assistant Protector in Penang, reports that there have been no serious affrays or breaches of the peace during the year, and that several thousand dollars of the assets of the Ghi Hin Kongsee have been handed over to various institutions in Penang, including $3,000 to the Free School, and $2,000 each to the Pauper Hospital and Leper Asylum at Pulau Jerejak.

The Societies Ordinance has worked well in the three Settlements. During the year, 6 societies have been registered in Singapore, 70 in Penang, and 7 in Malacca.[1] Altogether 155 have been registered since the introduction of the Ordinance, and 109 have been exempted from registration.

Thus, the Tong Beng (同 盟) society re-appears in the Protectorate report for 1891 and it is also mentioned by S.O.S. *op. cit.* pages 262–263 under this year.

Although a new-comer to the secret society stage of Singapore at a time when the curtain was being officially rung down upon its elder brethren, it would seem from its evident vitality to have been without much doubt, the foundation-branch of that Tung Meng Hui which was the spearhead of Chinese revolutionary political secret societies in the last decade of the nineteenth century and the first decade of the twentieth, and from which the National Government and most other pseudo-republican Governments of China—have since sprung. (*See* Chapter XXVI *infra*).

POLITICAL RENASCENCE OF CHINESE SECRET SOCIETIES BETWEEN 1891 AND 1900

In China Proper, the period between 1891 and 1900 witnessed the political renascence of secret societies after their decimation during the Taiping Rebellion (1850 to 1865), a process which led by different roads to the "Boxer" rising of 1900 (pages 34–35 and 66 *supra*) and to the revolutionary explosion of 1911 (Chapter XXVI *infra*). In the Straits Settlements during the same period the social fabric of the dangerous societies was undermined by the suppression edict of 1890, but their criminal activities remained unimpaired throughout.

THE COLONY PICTURE IN 1892

In the Protectorate report for 1892 Wray wrote:—

The year 1892 has shewn the large Triad societies[2] of these Settlements the hopelessness of attempting any revival, and, as long as the Government are prepared to encounter them promptly and with determination, there is little danger that these once powerful secret organisations will cause trouble.[3]

The inherent clannish propensities of the Chinese are, however, so strong, and the profits obtainable by agitators so enticing, that attempts will be made again and again whenever the authorities shew symptoms of laxity in crushing the hydra-headed "Hung" league.

A dangerous off-shoot of the Gi Hok society which had been blackmailing and terrorising over one district in the heart of Singapore for some time, was dealt with summarily during the year, and was completely routed by the sudden banishment of several of its headmen. Subsequent attempts to re-open have been reported by the inhabitants of the district in question, and have been promptly frustrated by the exercise of the provisions of "The Societies Ordinance 1889".[4]

Valuable information collected by Mr. Hare has enabled the Government to practically extirpate the much-dreaded "Coffin-breaking" (*i.e.* Box-breaking), or Sui Liok Peng On society, with its ramifications in Hongkong, Shanghai and Rangoon. This was a gang of a few hundred ship-thieves and sharpers—ruffians who did not hesitate to drug and murder passengers when deemed expedient. Some of the gang have been caught and banished, others warned and photographed and many have fled. The Registrar-General in Hongkong has assisted this Department in the work of exterminating the gang.

THE COFFIN-BREAKING SOCIETY

The Shiu Lok Peng On (上 落 平 安) lit. "Peace-on-the-Waters Society", popularly known as the "Coffin-breaking" *i.e.* "Luggage pilferers' Union", was clearly a Tokong criminal organisation for robbing Chinese overseas passengers travelling back and forth. Its brief description by Wray bears all the *stigmata* of the Ko Lao Hui as given by Hutson in Chapter II *supra*, with some of the features of Thuggee.

POINTERS IN THE PROTECTORATE SCHEDULES OF REGISTERED SOCIETIES IN 1892

In the schedules of registered societies under the 1889 Ordinance accompanying the 1892 Protectorate Report we should perhaps notice the following:—

Under Singapore—

(1) Page 19 Item No. 34:—
    Name—Tin Bu Bio society.
    Place of Meeting—The Chinese Temple, Havelock Road.
    Registered—27th November, 1890.
    Suppressed—9th September, 1892, under G.N. 494/92.

Footnote.—(1) We should notice how from the very first, Penang leapt into the lead in the registered society racket.

Footnote.—(2) Here we have the use of the plural for something that was not only singular, but unique, finding its way into official reports, where the usage has remained.

Footnote.—(3) This forecast has proved a little optimistic.

Footnote.—(4) This is all very vague and contradicts the first paragraph. He is probably referring to the Tung Meng (同 盟) society as the off-shoot of the Ghee Hok.

This suggests that the old dangerous societies which had run to hide themselves in the respectability of a Chinese Temple when registration came into force, soon showed their real character again.

On 30th December, 1892, Singapore had a total of 62 societies of all kinds among all nationalities registered.

Under Penang—

(2) Page 21 Item No. 17:—

Name—Chu Gi Seah (She).
President—Khoo Thian Lye.
Occupation—Revenue Farmer Kulim, Kedah.
No. of members in Register—34.

This man was, no doubt, a member of Tokong like others of his surname we have met. The combination of Tokong headman and revenue farmer which we have seen flourish in Perak under Khoo Thian Tek seems also to have been developed in Kedah, no doubt with much profit.

(3) Page 22 Item No. 37:—

Name—Seh Khoo Kongsi.
President—Khoo Sin Boe.
Meeting Place—Kongsi house, Beach Street.
No. of members in Register—Unknown.

Here we have the Toh Peh Kong society (Tokong) raising its ugly head and with an unlimited membership under the "Kongsi" name of the Khoo clan, who we have seen were its hereditary headmen.

We have more to say about the Khoo Kongsi of Penang later on.

(4) Page 23 Item No. 38:—

Name—Boon San Tung.
President—Khoo Thian Poe.[1]
Meeting Place—Kongsi house, Beach Street.
No. of members in Register—Unknown.

Here is another branch of the Khoo Kongsi coming out into the open with a revival of the Toh Peh Kong society with unlimited membership and under another name, which we shall soon meet with again.

(5) Page 25 Item No. 96:—

Name—Ng Fuk Hong.
President—Ho Thin Khin.
Occupation—Goldsmith.
Meeting Place—Kongsi house, Church Street.
No. of members in Register—Unknown.

Here is another familiar Tokong foundation re-appearing in its new disguise with an unlimited membership.

On 31st December, 1892, Penang had 99 societies of all kinds registered, of which some 75 were allegedly "clan" associations. We shall see how this registration of "clan" associations, as colour-protection for the revived dangerous societies, grew apace in Penang during the next few years.

The Protectorate Annual Reports for 1893 and 1894 are not procurable.

THE POSITION IN SINGAPORE IN 1895

In his Protectorate report for 1895 Capper has:—

6. The abolition of the registration of brothels having given rise to a belief amongst the lower criminal classes that the Government did not intend in future to give ordinary Police protection to the inmates of brothels, has resulted, as was anticipated, in a great increase of black-mailing and bullying, both in Singapore and Penang.

7. At the close of the year 1894 and through the first few months of 1895, a determined attempt was made in Singapore by the lawless Cantonese in Kreta Ayer, Hokkien Street, Kampong Malacca and Kampong Glam, to re-organise the brothel-squeezing societies that were suppressed in 1891 and 1892.

8. During these disturbances, the Keng Tak Hong or registered society of boiler-makers and others working at Tanjong Pagar Dock and other ironworks, joined one of these bands of brothel-squeezers, and one of the chief of the boiler-makers was arrested, but was subsequently released, as there was not sufficient evidence against him.

9. Two rival parties struggled for the monopoly of the extortion aimed at, and were dealt with by the Government, the ring-leaders being banished, while a number of their agents were bound over by the Police Magistrate to keep the peace.

This is the first official admission of the re-appearance of racketeering on a large scale, since the official suppression of 1890.

The lawless Cantonese in Kreta Ayer and Hokkien Street, Singapore were perhaps former members of the Ghi Hok (Tokong), those in Kampong Malacca and Kampong Glam perhaps former members of the Ghee Hin (Triad). We learn from the Report

---

Footnote.—(1) This may be Khoo Poh whom we met in 1867, *see* page 248 *supra* footnote (5).

for 1896 (below) that the Keng Tak Hong (敬德行) which, in its sound if not in its Chinese characters, is reminiscent of the Kian Tek (Tokong) society of Penang (pages 101–102 and 106–107 above) was allied at this period in Singapore with the Kreta Ayer *samsengs* (Tokong) which is just as we would have expected—*Plus ça change, plus c'est la même chose.*

We see again in the 1895 report, "Two rival parties struggling for the monopoly of extortion". We are now fairly familiar with the character and composition of these two rival parties, which we are unable to agree were two branches of the Triad society. Such an explanation does not make sense. We know them to have been and to remain, the rival forces of Hung and Han.

THE PENANG PICTURE IN 1895

In his report for 1895 Capper wrote:—

In Penang, the rikisha coolies of the surnames Tan and Chia, in Penang Road and the vicinity, gave some trouble on several occasions, and there was some fighting, but they were dealt with by the Police without any serious difficulty. There was also some rioting on Weld Quay on two occasions, the parties implicated being the coolies employed by rival indigo firms.

One Tan Thoan, against whom an order of banishment was issued in 1892 for being implicated in the formation of the Tai Te Ia[1] society at Jelutong, was arrested in Penang in August and deported to China.

In Penang, there is a large number of *samsengs* who infest Campbell Street, practising extortion not only on keepers and inmates of brothels, but even on shop-keepers and hawkers. Assaults are committed in broad daylight, knuckle-dusters being frequently used.

Such is the fear inspired by these men, that the victims are reluctant to make any complaint. In a considerable number of cases, however, brothel-keepers have given information, and the Department has assisted them by the arrest of men on the spot, watching cases in the Police Court, and otherwise.

Towards the end of the year, information was received of at least one Cantonese society in Penang organised for the purpose of squeezing brothel-keepers and others, assaulting obnoxious persons, arranging for bail in the Police Court, intimidating witnesses, and getting up false charges. The ring-leaders usually describe themselves as goldsmiths,[2] but have really no fixed residence or trade. They are being watched with a view to a case for deportation being established.

POINTERS IN THE PENANG SCHEDULE OF REGISTERED SOCIETIES IN 1895

In the Penang schedule of registered societies accompanying the 1895 report we should notice the following:—

(1) Page 23 Item No. 40:—
>   *Name*—Hang Kong Ki Beo or Techiu Kongsi.
>   *President*—Kho Bu An, Planter, Nibong Tebal.
>   *Place of Meeting*—Temple, Chulia Street.
>   *No. of Members.*—Unknown. A district association.

This may perhaps have been the Kho Bu An—leader of Triad in Larut and second Triad member of the Perak State Council in succession to Chan Ah Yam (*see* pages 268 and 331–333 *supra*). This is another example of a Temple being used as cover for the continuance of suppressed society activity.

THE KHOO KONGSI AGAIN 1895

(2) Page 23 Item No. 52:—
>   *Name*—Khu (Khoo) Kongsi: Ban San Tong.
>   *President*—Khu (Khoo) Cheah, Merchant.
>   *Place of Meeting*—Kongsi house, Beach Road.
>   *No. of Members*—Unknown.

(3) Page 23 Item No. 53—
>   *Name*—Khu (Khoo) Kongsi: Liong San Tong.
>   *President*— { Khu Thien Po / ? Khoo Thian Poh } merchant, Malay Street.
>   *Place of Meeting*—Kongsi house, Beach Road.
>   *No. of Members*—Unknown.

Here we seem to have the re-appearance of the Toh Peh Kong of 1867 in the guise of twin "clan" associations, officially described in the schedule as Ji Seh (字姓) or family or "surname", both of unlimited membership, and both under the direction of the Khoo Kongsi.

We shall meet these two associations, the Ban San Tong (文山堂) and the Liong San Tong (龍山堂) again in their modern setting in Chapter XXVII *infra*. The latter name takes us back to that document of the Ko Lao Hui recorded by Playfair and reproduced on page 29 (Chapter II) *supra*.

Footnote.—(1) 大帝爺 Tai Tai Ye = The Great Judge, "God".

Footnote.—(2) This is a characteristic that persists. The "profession" of bogus itinerant goldsmith affords cover-protection for crime preparation and secret society activity.

(4) Page 24 Item No. 95:—
> *Name*—Ng Fuk Thong.
> *President*—Phon Yan, Trader, Market Street.
> *Place of Meeting*—Kongsi house, Church Street.
> *No. of Members*—Unknown.

Although officially described as a district association this may have been a lodge or anchorage of the Ko Lao Hui of unlimited membership under a name with which we are now familiar, *see* Hutson Chapter II page 25 (8) *supra*.

Under the schedule of societies exempted from registration 1895 we find—

(5) Page 29 Item No. 136:—
> *Name*—Kong Hok Tong.
> *Settlement*—Penang.
> *Date of Exemption*—21st August, 1895.

The name suggests a revival in Penang of the Cantonese and Hokkien branches of Triad under a disarming "mutual benefit" title and enjoying the full freedom of action provided by exemption under the Societies Ordinance of 1889.

THE COLONY PICTURE IN 1896

And so to 1896, where in the Annual Report of W. Evans then Protector of Chinese, Straits Settlements we meet with official Chinese characters for the first time upon the long road we have travelled since 1800.

Evans writes in his 1896 report:—

Ordinance I of 1889, for the suppression or regulation of societies, continues to work smoothly and successfully; so that, after nearly eight years' experience, I can confidently assert that there exists at present no society which is in any way dangerous to the peace of the Colony.

There are, however, and always will be, where Chinese congregate, many societies existing for unlawful purposes and having among their objects purposes incompatible with the peace and good order of the Colony. Such societies require constant watchfulness on the part of the Protectorate by which alone they are kept within safe limits, or, on breaking out are seized and dealt with according to law.

During the year 1896, in Singapore two attempts were made to form secret and unlawful societies, one long-existing unlawful society was discovered, and various disturbances occurred amongst some of the registered societies.

The most formidable of the two new societies formed was the "Gi Leng" (義 鈴) composed of Hokkiens and Teochius and headed by a Straits-born Hokkien, a lawyer's clerk. A peculiar feature of this society was that it was largely joined by Teochius surnamed Tan (陳). This society occupied the Kampong Saigon and Havelock Road districts.

At the same time the old "Tong Beng" (同 明) was revived in the Gelang district, and joined hands with two registered societies—the "Ho Keng Sia" (和 慶 社) and "Bun Heng" (文 興). These two societies, when applying for permission to register, alleged that they were formed for friendly purposes, such as attending weddings and funerals of members. The former was confined to Straits-born, and the latter to Hailams. These three societies having united occupied the Kampong Bencoolen and Kampong Glam districts, recruiting large numbers of members.

About February however, the "Gi Leng" (義 鈴) and "Tong Beng" (同 明) quarrelled, and fighting between the rival parties was frequent. Then a society of Straits-born Chinese registered under the name of "Sun Tek Hoe" (順 德 會) also joined the "Tong Beng" (同 明) alliance, until finally sufficient evidence was obtained to enable the protectorate to take action, with the result that the China-born leaders on both sides were banished, the Straits-born leaders were convicted before the Supreme Court, and the three registered societies were, by order of the Governor in Council, dissolved.

In Malacca, an unlawful society called the "Chiau Eng Si" (招 應 祠) was started by certain Hailams of doubtful character. Several hundreds of members were recruited in the up-country plantations, and serious affrays took place between them and the registered Hailam society. Mr. Hare, Assistant Protector of Chinese, Singapore, visited the Settlement in June and July, and successfully broke up the organization, arresting five of the leaders, who were subsequently banished.

In December, the existence of the "Yun Shin Tong" (永 盛 堂), or Rattan Chair-makers' guild, came to the notice of the Protectorate, owing to its interference with the trade. As this guild has existed in ignorance or defiance of the law for nearly eight years, I considered it advisable to institute proceedings against certain of the leading members, who finally pleaded guilty and received light punishment.

The guild of boiler-makers at Tanjong Pagar, registered under the name of "Keng Tak Hong" (敬 德 行), became disorganized and turbulent. The headmen were mixed up with the Kreta Ayer *samsengs*, and the society was under no proper control, so it was also dissolved by order of the Governor in Council (*c.f.* paragraph 8, Report for 1895).

* * *

In Penang, disturbances amongst the rikisha-pullers in Penang Road and Bridge Street, between the coolies employed by rival indigo firms on Weld Quay, amongst the residents of Gertak Sanggui, that notorious village, and others, have given this Department some work.

A society formed for aggressive purposes by servants employed in lodging-houses was broken up on the Assistant Protector taking action for its suppression.

The total number of societies registered at the end of the year was 226—in Singapore 57, in Penang 135, and in Malacca 34; and exempted in Singapore 125, in Penang 44, and in Malacca 25.

The comparatively much larger number of registered societies in Penang should be noted, indicating the relatively much greater volume of suspicious society activity in Penang than elsewhere which is explained by the grip that sodalities, partisanship and clannishness have historically had upon the Chinese of the Northern Settlement.

POINTERS IN THE PENANG SCHEDULE OF REGISTERED SOCIETIES IN 1896

(1) Page 23 Item No. 15:—
    Name—Chu Gi Siah.
    President—Khu (Khoo) Thien Lai, Opium Farmer, Malay Street.
    No. of Members—30.
    Cf. Item (2) under year 1892 above.
    The combination of Khoo clan and opium farmer continues. This society is officially described as a "parental" one.

(2) Page 26 Item No. 104:—
    Name—Hui Liong Siah.
    Headmen—Lim Bu and Tan Ju of Jelutong.
    Place of Meeting—Temple of Tai Te Ia, Jelutong.
    No. of Members—43. Described as a "parental" society.
    This may have been a revival under Temple cover of the Tai Te Ia
    (大帝爺) secret society of Jelutong referred to under the year 1895 (above) as having been suppressed in 1892.

(3) Page 26 Item No. 128:—
    Name—Hok Tek Tong.
    Headman—Liang Eng, Jelutong.
    Place of Meeting—Toh Peh Kong Temple, Jelutong.
    Date of Registration—16th April, 1896.
    No. of Members—36.
    Purpose—Religious.
    This is an interesting registration.

Here we have what seems to be the old Toh Peh Kong society shyly peeping out from behind the temple pillars at Jelutong and taking us straight back to the earlier foundation in Penang (1842–1867), discussed on page 106 ff. *supra.*

The Chinese characters of the new foundation are not given, but we may guess Hok Tek Tong to stand for 福德堂 a variation, no doubt, from the names Kien Tek (建德) Kien Hok (建福) and Hok Kien (福建) by which it had been previously known (page 106 *supra*).

Its meeting place too, is another exemplar of temple cover for the revival of Tokong. Its number of members has the esoteric meaning referred to in earlier chapters and common both to Triad and Tokong and its "religious" purpose is on all fours with what preceding chapters have presented for our consideration.

It would probably be safe to date the open revival of Tokong in Penang, suppressed in 1890, from 16th April, 1896, the date of the registration of the Hok Tek Tong.

THE PROBLEM OF THE STRAITS-BORN SECRET SOCIETY GANGSTER

The 1896 Protectorate Report emphasises the growing problem of the Straits-born gangster.

We have seen the earlier attempt to restrict membership of Chinese secret societies to China-born Chinese (*Ordinance IV of 1882*, pages 389–390 *supra*) and so to prevent British-born, or naturalised persons from becoming members of dangerous societies; and we have seen that attempt even in its revised form as *Ordinance IV of 1885* (pages 390–391), again fail.

Total suppression in 1890 (page 395 *supra*) equally failed to touch the problem, which took cover in the exemption afforded by the Ordinance for associations formed for recreation, charity, religion and literature.

Already we have seen (page 367) the development of the "illicit" Hoey, the germ of the free-lance racketeer brigade during the earliest control period 1869–1882. This phase was followed by the rise of the European-type social club among Straits-born racketeers, commented upon by Colonel Dunlop in his report for 1886 (page 372). It was also about this year that we notice the rise of the Tung Meng Hui (pages 374–75) which was the political forerunner of the Chinese Revolution of 1912 (Chapter XXVI) and on that account alone embraced in its ranks both China-born and Straits-born Chinese in large numbers.

Although the flood-waters of the revolution have now abated, there remains among its many fresh unsolved problems that of Straits-born Chinese membership of dangerous societies, both criminal and revolutionary.

THE COLONY IN 1897

The following are extracts from Evan's report for 1897, included because of the Chinese character given:—

Singapore—

Frequent complaints were made of the existence of gangs of *samsengs* in the different brothels streets, notably Fraser Street, Upper Hokkien Street and Hongkong Street.

In August, I recommended the dissolution of the "Tong On Wui Kun" (東 安 會 舘) or society for natives of Tong-Kun and San-On districts of the Canton province. The facts were briefly these:—A case of assault was determined before the Magistrate: one party was dissatisfied with the decision of the Court: on his application the society issued a notice to the other party to the case to appear before the society and have the matter enquired into again: a fine of $1 in default of appearance.

The society was accordingly dissolved by order of His Excellency the Governor in Council, and the balance, after paying all claims, etc. was handed to a Committee of three Trustees (including the Protector of Chinese) to be spent in assisting poor and infirm natives of the said districts to return home.

During the year, four new societies have been registered in Singapore, in Penang four, and in Malacca five.

In Singapore, three have ceased to exist, in Penang one, and in Malacca nil. The total number of societies registered is now 232—in Singapore 55, in Penang 138, and in Malacca 39. Exempted from registration in Singapore (and still in existence), 100, in Penang 44, and in Malacca 25.

Penang—

Mr. Capper reports from Penang:—

(1) In August, I became aware of the existence of a Hailam fighting society "Tiong Hin" (中 興) in Kuala Kangsar Road. I raided the house and had a warrant issued for the arrest of the principal offenders, but they all absconded.

(2) In March, I instituted proceedings against a man named (Iun Chui 楊 水) for being concerned in an unregistered society at Jelutong, the "Hong Khai Sia" (鳳 開 社) He was fined $100, in default, three months' rigorous imprisonment. This man was before the Executive Council in connection with the "Tai Te Ia" society (大 帝 爺) in 1892.

(3) In October, I raided two houses in Jelutong Road and subsequently applied for the fiat of the Attorney-General to prosecute two men in connection with the society called "Siun Kang Kong" (相 公 公).

(4) In November, I raided a house in Rope Walk, and a prosecution was subsequently instituted against one man. He has just (January, 1898) been convicted of being a member of a Hailam society called the "Theng Hong Ko" (廳 芳 閣).

The registered clubs in Penang in 1897 numbered 138 and are given on pages 27 to 30 of the Protectorate Report for that year. All except one (No. 98 on the list, the Penang Peranakan, a Jawi-pekan club of which Mohamed Sahat was "president") were Chinese and all of these except a few, such as the Chinese Cycling Club (No. 132) and the George Town Reading Room (No. 138), were either Temple, Clan or District foundations any of which, if not all of which, could act as secret society "host", Some 50 of the total are recorded as being of "unknown" membership, which gave them free rein to recruit in unlimited numbers.

It is from about this year that the Chinese secret societies in Penang, clothed in the respectability of registration, appear to have regained in full measure the power and prestige they lost at the suppression in 1890.

Those old friends whose seeming re-appearance in legal garb is particularly mentioned under the years 1892, 1895 and 1896 above, have remained established to the present-day.

THE COLONY 1898–1900

Unfortunately, Evans dropped Chinese characters from his reports after that of 1897. The following extracts are from his 1898 report:—

The registered societies have given no trouble during the year, though some of them are reaching larger proportions than was perhaps contemplated.

A Tiechiu society has been started in Penang and has caused some disturbance by fights and assaults in various parts of the town. Orders of Banishment have, however, been issued against 13 of the leading men, and there will quickly be an end of the society. It was known as the "Pang Long" society as it had its origin in the timber yards (in Chinese "Pang Long").[1]

The Seh Tan society in Penang is in trouble as the trustees and would-be trustees have fallen out. The serious part of it is that the Seh Tan is a very large clan, and the ill-feeling between the leaders may extend to their followers and the result will be a disturbance.

During the year 1898, there were registered in Singapore 6 societies, in Penang none, and in Malacca none.

There were exempted from registration, in Singapore 12, in Penang 2, and in Malacca none.

The total numbers now are:—

Singapore 58 registered societies, 109 exempted from registration and still in existence.
Penang 138 registered, 46 exempted.
Malacca 39 registered, 25 exempted.

Footnote.—(1) The Chinese characters for this term are 枋 廊 pang long *lit.* timber yard. The word however is now absorbed into the Malay language—(*see* Wilkinson's Malay Dictionary, 1932 edition) with the meaning: "A coolie-gang working a plantation under a landlord who provides the advances". The common meaning of the term in Singapore is: A coolie depôt: a secret society meeting place, den, or hide-out.

Evans' 1899 report has for Singapore:—

There have been two prosecutions for managing unlawful societies:—

(1) The "Sin Gi Hoe" or Rangoon Road society.

The existence of this society was brought to my notice towards the end of 1898 and at intervals during this year, I received complaints which satisfied me of its continued existence. I made two unsuccessful raids and finally in November, obtained Orders for the Banishment of 9 persons alleged to be concerned in the management of the society. Six of these were arrested, and 3 out of the 6 were duly banished.

(2) The "Hau Fuk Thong" or Cantonese tailors Guild.

The Cantonese tailors without the sanction of the law formed themselves into a Guild and after a dispute with the master tailors as to prices for piece work called a general strike. I then prosecuted 5 of the leading men for managing this unlawful society and they were all committed to the Assizes. A compromise was then arranged by which the Guild applied for permission to register under the Societies Ordinance.

In Kreta Ayer, I hear of the existence of one or two gangs which scarcely deserve the name of society. They will be taken in hand and dispersed as soon as they begin to cause trouble.

Under Penang in 1899 Evans has:—

In Penang the "Panglong" or timber-yard society[1] gave some trouble until the arrest of the ring-leaders in February. After enquiry 6 out of the 8 arrested were banished.

The affairs of the Penang Seh Tan Kongsi are still unsettled, no advance having been made in the litigation which was pending last year. The two parties[2] cannot agree on the question of trustees and the Kongsi will probably have to be dissolved.

Evans records nothing of importance in Singapore in his report for 1900, but has the following under Penang for that year:—

From Penang, Mr. Firmstone reports that "there has been a revival of society activity and aggression".

The "Buan An Thai" society which came into existence on the break up of the "Panglong" society has been dealt with unsuccessfully in the Courts, (owing to legal requirements not being exactly fulfilled) but successfully before the Executive Council, 4 men being banished for life.

THE GATHERING OF THE CLANS 1900

The position of registered and exempted societies in the Colony remained fairly constant at the turn of the century, *viz*:—

Registered

Singapore	..	..	..	.. 68
Penang	..	..	..	.. 140
Malacca	..	..	..	.. 40

Exempted

Singapore	..	..	..	.. 115
Penang	..	..	..	.. 50
Malacca	..	..	..	.. 25

The large preponderance of registered societies remained in Penang and the great majority of these were registered as "clan" associations.

But there is a catch in this registration of clan associations, for the reason that although the lexicographers give some 1,800, there are in every-day use among the Chinese only about 150 clan, or family names, or "surnames" as we understand the term; and of these only about 100 are really common, so much so that the ordinary Chinese term for "the people" is 百姓 paak seng, or "the hundred families". If there is unrestricted registration of clan associations up to the limit of every-day clan names, opportunity is given to the bullies and blackmailers of the under-world to force the whole population of Chinese into one or other of the "clan associations", which are in many cases but legal cover for illegal and unwilling association, made to appear legal by registration, but in fact controlled by the heads of Triad and Tokong.

The flood of registration which we see took place in Penang at the end of last century has re-established and maintained that Settlement in its historical position as the fountain-head of secret society intrigue throughout Malaya.

Realisation of this fact is necessary to understand the special position occupied by Penang in the modern secret society picture and it also explains the peculiar position of Penang in the crime world of Malaya: as well as the notorious clannishness and intransigence of its Chinese inhabitants.

This concludes the Colony survey of Triad and Tokong down to 1900. We have heard little of Tabut since its "suppression" in 1882, but there are a few references to indicate its presence during the same period.

Footnote.—(1) *See* footnote page 407 *supra*.
Footnote.—(2) No doubt, the Tans of Triad and the Tans of Tokong.

TABUT IN PENANG 1890–1900

The following extracts from the Annual Reports of the Inspector-General of Police, Straits Settlements between 1890 and 1900 show the drift of Tabut undercurrents in Penang during this decade:—

1890—
20. The Dangerous Societies. In Penang, an attempt was made to resuscitate the old Red and White Flag Muhammadan societies, and there was a great deal of ill-feeling between the rival parties and a good deal of rowdyism took place, ending in one unfortunate boy being killed. Several cases were brought up and punished, and the end of the year found matters much quieter.

1891—
62. In several cases of unprovoked assault among Malays it was shewn that the parties concerned were known to formerly belong to the Red and White Flag societies. It would be very remarkable indeed if all party feeling had already disappeared.

1892—
78. Although the Red and White Flag societies in Penang no longer exist, petty feuds are still kept up amongst the lower classes of Malays and Jawi-Pekans. These feuds often result in cowardly assaults upon unarmed persons, and during one of these, an old man was beaten to death. His two assailants were arrested, and hanged. It is to be hoped that this will be a lesson to the many cowardly roughs who infest the town of Penang. I mention this case under this heading, as although the cause of the assault was not traced to secret societies, the petty associations existing among the Malays and Jawi-Pekans are akin to them.

No further mention of Tabut in Penang appears in these reports until after 1900.

Triad and Tokong in Perak 1883–1900

The period of British consolidation following the Perak war may be said to have ended in 1882, down to which point we have traced the influence of Triad and Tabut in Perak in Chapter XX.

The records of the succeeding period are meagre, but there may be much undisclosed material in Secretariats and other Government offices in Malaya which has not been included in the present work.

CONDITIONS IN PERAK IN 1882

We have seen by his measures of registration of the Chinese population referred to in the preceding Chapter, that Sir Hugh Low was apprehensive of the power of the immigrant Chinese population to combine against the Government. He had the murder of Capt. Lloyd (1879) and the Taiping riots (1879) as grounds for his misgiving.

There is also reference by Boyle (given below) to Sir Hugh having been himself threatened by the societies, but we have not been able to find any confirmation of this.

In his annual report for Perak for 1882 (para. 72), Sir Hugh mentions that "30,000 Chinese might be assembled in a few hours in Taiping, the chief seat of commerce and government in Larut" and again in paras. 102–103 he has:—

The number of Chinese miners have increased from about 9,000 in 1877 to probably 50,000 at the time I am writing, and they are still arriving in crowds...... Having been imported direct from the inland districts of China they were of all men the most rude, conceited and ignorant, with no confidence in Europeans, easily oppressed and misled by their own country-men who employed them and who were themselves greatly influenced by the secret societies in Penang, especially the coast districts of Perak.

As a result of these misgivings, Sir Hugh appears to have obtained approval for the appointment of Secretary for Chinese Affairs, Perak in 1883 and the first holder of the office was C. A. Schultz who took up his duties about he beginning of 1884. Meanwhile a proclamation forbidding the existence of secret societies in Perak appears to have been published in 1882 or 1883 on the lines of the Colony Ordinance No. IV of 1882 discussed above.

In his annual report for 1883 Powell, who was then acting for Pickering, mentioned the probable existence of Chinese secret societies in Perak. This innocent reference, which one might have thought hardly needed emphasis, drew a disclaimer from the newly-appointed Schultz, who in reply wrote a report dated 3rd May, 1884, for the information of the Acting Resident of Perak (Swettenham) which appears in C.S.O. Perak Correspondence (3574/84, entitled *Report on Chinese Friendly societies and secret societies in Larut* and is as follows:—

Friendly societies.—The Friendly societies existing in Taiping, Kota and Kamunting were established at different times, as will be seen from the enclosed list.[1] I do not think that they have ever, as such, given any trouble to Government; on the contrary I believe, that they have done and are doing good both by assisting their poorer countrymen, and by adjusting minor disputes between members.

They have no political object whatever and are principally established for the following purposes:—

1st. To give shelter to newcomers, who are friendless and without any engagement.
2nd. To have a place for the performance of sacrificial rites.
3rd. To assist their countrymen (*i.e.* men from the same districts in China) who die without means, to obtain a respectable funeral.
4th. To settle amicably matters of dispute between the members.

The societies are supported by entrance fees and donations of members.

Footnote.—(1) List not found in the correspondence.

As I thought it inadvisable that any Chinese societies should exist, after the establishment of this office, without their existence being officially known by Government, I proposed (in my letter No. 18/84 of 20th January) to Her Majesty's Resident that these Friendly societies should be registered at this office and this was sanctioned by Her Majesty's Resident in his letter China No. 305/84 and in a Government notification it was made known to the societies.

As it is a considerable work to enter all the names of the members in the registration books, 6 societies with 3,272 members have only been registered hitherto, but all the others have been summoned to appear with their books and they will all be registered in due time.

Secret societies are not allowed to exist in the state; it is however, more than probable that there are a good many members of such societies here, who have been initiated in Penang or elsewhere, and it is also possible that these members hold secret meetings in the jungle, although none have ever been discovered by the Police; as far as I have been able to ascertain no serious disturbance or riot has taken place here,[1] that could be put down directly to the influence of these societies.

TAIPING, 3rd May, 1884.

C. A. SHULTZ,
Secretary for Chinese Affairs,
Perak.

This trite and artless document if they ever saw it, must have gladdened the hearts of Chang Keng Hui and Chan Ah Yam then both members of the Perak State Council.

The report was sent to the Colonial Secretary by Swettenham with the following covering letter:—

C.S.O. PERAK 3574/84.

RESIDENCY,
KUALA KANGSAR.
6th May, 1884.

Sir,

In reply to your letter India 2413/84 of the 22nd ultimo, I have the honour to enclose a report by the Secretary for Chinese Affairs from which it appears there are no Chinese secret societies in Perak, and as far as I am aware, the existence of such societies is prohibited.

2. In Selangor, where also there are no secret societies, I believe certain clans have in Kuala Lumpur what they call a Kongsi house, which corresponds to our Rest House, and they assist each other in making temples and in burying the dead.

3. I should be much obliged if His Excellency the Acting Governor would allow me to be informed of the authority on which the Acting Protector of Chinese (Powell) has made the statement to which my attention has been called, and also for the substance of the information he has received with reference to Chinese secret societies in Perak.

I have etc.,
(Signed) FRANK SWETTENHAM,
H.B.M.'s Acting Resident,
Perak.

Powell was called on to justify his casual remark and did so in the following minute dated 26th May, 1884:—

Honourable Colonial Secretary,

1. When writing the paragraph which has called for animadversion (vide paragraph 3 of Resident of Perak's letter of 6th May, 1884 above) what was chiefly in my mind was a Chinese document sent down by the Resident of Sungei Ujong in August last (vide 7765–83).

Mr. Paul wrote to say that he suspected a secret society was being formed there at the time and asked for a translation of the document to see whether it could throw any light on the subject. The document was the appointment by the "Sungei Ujong Gi Hin society" of a headman in 1877.

2. With regard to Perak and Selangor, I am not I regret to say, able to speak from personal experience. I have always understood from Chinese that societies were existent there as in other places and the statement seemed to me to be worthy of belief.

3. On receipt of the above minute accompanied by Mr. Roger's strong disclaimers as regards Selangor—Mr. Swettenham and Captain Schultz are, I observe, more guarded,—I sent for Chong Bun-sui, the second interpreter in the Supreme Court; whom I knew had an intimate knowledge of all the States, and asked him whether he could give me any information as regards societies there. He immediately confirmed my opinion and offered to give me a list of societies, as well as the names of such headmen as he knew. This document I enclose with a translation.[2]

4. Bun-sui, I may state is a Malacca-born Chinese of Kheh descent with considerable natural ability, and has had special opportunities of obtaining a knowledge on the subject; having been employed in the Government Service in all three States.

In Perak he was much used and appreciated by Sir Hugh Low in connection with the Chinese, and had to do so much travelling and jungle work in consequence, that he got disgusted and preferred to take an appointment in Singapore on less salary. His statement is, I believe worthy of all credence.

Footnote.—(1) He had forgotten, if he ever knew of them, the Larut wars 1862–1874 and the Taiping riots of 1879.
Footnote.—(2) See below "The Powell Report".

5. The result of my enquiries would show that the following societies at least are represented:—

    In Perak.   Hai San,
                     Gi Hin.

These are not distinct societies but part and parcel of the Penang societies of the same name under recognised headmen in Perak.

    In Selangor.   Ghi Hin,
                     Hai San,
                     Song-pak-kun (a branch of the Ghi Hin).

The two first are Malacca societies, and the third a Singapore one. The Hok-beng, another Malacca society appears also to have extended to Selangor, but my informant is unable to give me the names of the headmen.

    In Sungei Ujong. Gi Hin,
                     Hai San.

(both these are probably connected with Malacca but the first is sufficiently independent to have a recognised kongsi house of its own at a place called Tanjong. It was probably from this that the document above referred to issued.

6. The headmen in Larut and Selangor are appointed by the societies in Penang, Malacca or Singapore, and act something after the fashion of District Headmen in the Straits, only that they have greater powers in respect of having a more independent command and being the recipients of initiation fees and subscriptions. This money, a percentage to the collector, and working expences being deducted, is forwarded to headquarters.

7. In face of the Government prohibition there are of course no recognised kongsi-houses either in Perak or Selangor, but if a meeting is required the house of one or other headman, or member is made use of. Sinkhehs coming into the country have often their entrance fees paid for them by the towkay, the amount being debited to the Sinkheh in his account.

8. Mr. Paul will no doubt be able to give some further information as regards societies in Perak. It is worthy of remark that the Hai San kongsi is not in Penang a strong one, having registered up to last year only 542 members. It would appear to be as strong, if not stronger in Perak than it is in Penang.

                                           F. POWELL,
                               Acting Protector of Chinese,
                                            Singapore.

26th May, 1884.

CHONG BUN SUI (莊文瑞) THE COMPILER OF THE POWELL REPORT, MAY 1884

This man's identity and some of his history is given in the above extract. The explanation why a man evidently otherwise so well informed, was unable to give Powell the names of the headmen of the Hok Beng society of Malacca, is perhaps to be found in the fact that we identify Chong Bun Sui with that Boon Swee mentioned by Plunket as being his interpreter in the Malacca riots of December, 1875 (*see* above page 386 footnote (1) and *Parliamentary Paper*, C 1505, page 239).

At that time Chong Boon Swee was himself the headman of the "Hoh Beng" society in Malacca and no doubt he so remained, under the hereditary principle of Tokong, until he died. Besides being "bad form" in Chinese eyes to make such an admission and thus cause himself some loss of "face", it might also have affected his official appointment as interpreter in the Supreme Court, Singapore!

THE POWELL REPORT 1884

Despite its origin, there is no reason to disbelieve Chong Bun Sui's report to Powell of May, 1884, which we have for convenience labelled the Powell Report.

The original in Chinese is still in C.S.O. Correspondence 3574/84.

The report is as follows:—

Perak—

The Hai-sans first came to Perak and Larut and afterwards the Gi-hins. Chi Long (貴郎) who was then the Ruler,[1] entered the Hai-san kongsi at Penang. At the present time there are a great many Gi-hins and Hai-sans in Larut. There are no kongsi houses but there are without doubt private meeting places.

The following are the headmen of the Gi-hin kongsi in Larut:—

    Chan A Yam   (陳亞豔) (Captain—Macao)

    Lo A Phang   (羅亞朋) (Kheh)

    Lok Yau   (陸 友) (Macao)

The headmen of the Hai-san kongsi at Larut are:—

    Cheng Kui   (鄭 貴) (Captain)

    Cheng Kiu-shin (鄭景勝)

    Fong Kun-po   (馮觀保)

The headman of the Hai-san kongsi at Gopeng in Kinta is Chan Ah Tong (陳亞同) (Kheh). There is no kongsi house. Chu Ng (朱吾) (Kheh) is the headman of the Gi-hin kongsi at Papan in Kinta. There is no kongsi house.

Footnote.—(1) *i.e.* Che Long Jaafar first Ruler of Larut. *See* page 260 and 278 *supra.*

Selangor—

The Gi-hin kongsi has existed in the town of Klang from the year Jun Ngo (壬戌) corresponding to the English year 1862, when Hiu Siu (邱秀) was the captain. The Gi-hin kongsi house was at Umpang. The men who established the Gi-hin were:—

Koan Kui	(關 貴)
Lim Hiong-kak	(林宏學) and
Lim Jit-seng	(林日生)

together with a Malay named Unku Kit (吾孤吉). This Malay was A.D.C. to the Yam Tuan (炎端) and was called the Penglima Prang (邦里麻吧零). Afterwards in the year Kah Chu (甲子) (1864) Lau Yim-kong (劉壬光) was Captain and he was a Hai-san. He went and petitioned the Yam Tuan and Unku Samat (吾孤沙末) that they should not allow the establishment of two kongsis, Hai-san and Gi-hin, in Klang as it would lead to fighting and disturbances. Therefore from that time to the present there has been no regular kongsi-house but there are without doubt private places of meeting.

The following are the headmen of the Gi-hin kongsi in Klang:—

Chhiu Hin	(趙 興)	(Macao)
Chhiu Yok	(趙 育)	(Macao)
Ye Hong piu	(余紅表)	,,
Lim Jit-seng	(林日生)	(Baba)

The headmen of the Hai-san kongsi in Klang are:—

Yap Shak	(葉 石)	(Kheh)
Yap Tek-loi	(葉德來)	(Captain—Kheh)
Chia Fat	(謝 發)	(Macao)
Chiong Si	(張 四)	(Kheh)

In Kanching (干津) in Selangor the Gi-hin kongsi is chiefly composed of Ka-Eng-Chiu (嘉應州) men. These belong to the Singapore Song-pak-kun (松柏舘) Society (a branch of the Gi-hin) and are in considerable number. The headman of the Gi-hin (here) is Ch'in Chon-shen (陳泉生) (Kheh). There is no kongsi-house.

There are also many Hai-sans at Kanching. The headman of the Hai-san kongsi (here) is Yap Ng (葉五) (Kheh). There is no kongsi-house.

At Samuntan in Selangor there are a great many Hai-sans. The headman is Chu Sam-hin (朱三興) (Kheh). There is no kongsi-house. There are also Gi-hin members at this place taken from the mining class.

Sungei Ujong—

The Gi-hin kongsi (義興公司) in the town of Sungei Ujong (*i.e.* Seremban) was in existence as long ago as the year Pian Chu (丙子) (1876). The kongsi house was at Tanjong and had a gilt-chop above the door.

Afterwards in the year Bo In (戊寅) (1878), because the Hai-san (海山) had no kongsi-house, their members became angry and went to the Gi-hin kongsi-house and pulled down the gilt-chop. From that time to the present they have not put up the gilt-chop again, but they have a red paper above the door on which is inscribed "This is the Gi-hin Kongsi". This is still at Tanjong. The following are the headmen of the Gi-hin kongsi:—

Chiong Ng-chai	(鍾五仔)	(Kheh)
Chiong Fong-Chhiong	(鍾鳳昌)	,,
Ng Chhium-Lip	(黃倉立)	(Hokkien)
Liu Lam-ko	(劉林哥)	(Kheh)

The Hai-san kongsi has been in Sungei Ujong town for 20 or 30 years (*i.e.* say since about 1860 or so). They have members but no kongsi-house. The following are the headmen of the Hai-san kongsi in Sungei Ujong:—

Wong Ying	(黃英)	(Captain—Macao)	
Hiu Sam	(邱三)	(,,	Kheh)
Lam Sam	(林三)	(Kheh)	
Lim Be	(林馬)	(Hai-lok-hong) (海陸豐)	

Comment on the Powell Report 1884

This interesting document confirms from an independent source a good deal of what we already know. The following comments are necessary:—

(1) The mention of Che Long, the first ruler of Larut, father of Che Ngah Ibrahim confirms that he joined Tokong in Penang. We may the more readily conclude that his son the Mentri was also an initiated member of Tokong, and so corroborate Irving's informant, pages 278-279 *supra*.

(2) Powell confirms that in 1884 Chan Ah Yam and Chang Keng Kui were the two heads in Perak of Triad and Tokong respectively, and as we know, were also on the State Council.

(3) Comment upon the references to Selangor and Negri Sembilan is reserved for those sections below.

(4) The report as a whole is the earliest clear, and apparently unbiassed statement upon record, touching the identity of the leaders of Triad and Tokong in the Malay States.

(5) It gives for the first time the tribe of each man mentioned and shows what we might expect to find, namely that Triad is predominantly Cantonese or Hokkien, and Tokong is predominantly Hakka. There is no hard and fast rule about this, and all tribes are probably to be found in both camps, but the main lines of cleavage in Perak, for reasons recorded, (the Hakka-Puntei War, etc.) have made the division there as stated.

THE S.C.A. PERAK'S REJOINDER TO THE POWELL REPORT 16TH JULY 1884

Schultz S.C.A. Perak, was moved to write another memo (C.S.O. Perak 6795/84) in which he comments further upon the Powell Report in the following terms:—

Whether the societies referred to by the Assistant Protector of Chinese *viz*; the Hai San and Gi Hin societies have recognised headmen for Perak on their books in Penang, I am unable to say, but of those mentioned in the document translated by Mr. Powell, the three *viz*:—

Chan Ah Yam,
Cheng Kui (*Capitan*),
Cheng Kui Shin,

deny ever having been headmen.[1]

Chan Ah Yam stated to me that he had been a member of the Gi Hin for over twenty years and that he had never denied having been so; that the said society had no necessity of having headmen here, as there was no branch or Kongsi established in the State and that he had on several occasions when applied to by the society in Penang, replied that no branch could be opened here as it was contrary to the laws of the country. The two other men Cheng Kui, and Cheng Kui Shin stated the same thing and the former added that he had resigned his membership of the Hai San in the beginning of the year, a fact which is known to me.

*   *   *

(*Signed*) C. A. SCHULTZ.

16*th July*, 1884.

Triad and Tokong having hoodwinked the British authorities as to their real character up to that date, were determined to keep up the "good boy" pretences with the new S.C.A. in Perak, in which, with their tongues in their cheeks, they appear to have been most successful.

Regarding the foregoing, Pickering has the following minute in the same paper:—

My remarks in minute of 7th August, 1884, in Selangor 5722/84 equally apply to this paper and I have no doubt that Ah Yam and Ah Kui still are members and can enter their respective Kongsi houses in Penang and take part in business.

*   *   *

It is a pity that Mr. Powell's carefully considered and trustworthy statements should have called forth something like feelings of resentment from Messrs. Schultz and Rodgers. It cannot reflect anything on them to suppose that with their short experience they cannot know everything about a question so secret and complicated as Chinese secret societies. Mr. Powell did what he did for the public good, but his statements are not likely to be corroborated by Ah Yam, Ah Kui or the others whose names are mentioned.

(*Signed*) W. A. PICKERING.

13*th August*, 1884.

This correspondence has been quoted at some length as it is typical of much else written on the subject.

Schultz's view was that because there had been passed a law forbidding secret societies in Perak and because former known leading members had assured him that they had "resigned" and that the societies had been disbanded,—therefore it was so.

Things of course do not happen like that, however comforting it may be to imagine from an official chair that they do.

In the two extracts given above, the contrast is complete between the bureaucratic and the practical mind.

Footnote.—(1) Who signed the Chinese engagement at the Treaty of Pangkor 20th January, 1874?

The one resents and regards as a personal affront information which it conceives may reflect unfavourably upon itself or its omniscience—the sharper the truth the deeper the resentment.

The other seeks truth for its own sake for the good of the job, careless of what shadows may be cast in the pursuit of fact and reality. As a result, the big guns of ruffled vanity were soon spitting defence, defiance and denial, regardless of the truth.

On a subject so abstruse, in respect of which every European must necessarily remain abysmally ignorant, one would have thought that in very shame the bureaucrats might have paused to consider their own imperfect knowledge. Schultz is probably not the only officer who has been similarly hoodwinked by Triad and Tokong. All that happened in Perak, when the official wrath blew upon them, was what has happened to them everywhere else,—they submerged, where they have since remained flourishing in their natural habitat, the under-world.

EVIDENCE OF TRIAD AND TOKONG ACTIVITY IN PERAK 1884–1887

Powell and Pickering had not long to wait for justification of their view.

There were riots in Tanjong Piandang in 1884, but we have not been able to see a report upon them. This is in the Kuala Kurau area already mentioned, pages 340–341 *supra*.

Again, the Acting British Resident, Perak (Swettenham) in his Annual Report for 1884 wrote:—

> A gang of desperate Chinese attacked and looted the house of the Penghulu at Pangkor, and almost immediately afterwards (12th January, 1885) attacked the Police Station and looted the Revenue Farmers' house at Sabak Bernam. Acting on information received from an informer in Penang, the greater portion of this gang was very energetically and successfully traced and arrested by Major Walker and the Perak Police, assisted by the Acting Superintendent of the Dindings (Mr. Dew). At the recent Assizes in Penang, ten men accused of participation in the Pangkor robbery were all convicted and sentenced to various terms of imprisonment, a result which cannot fail to have an excellent moral effect on a class of Chinese who for years have infested the south of Province Wellesley and Kedah and the coast of Perak. The leaders of these gang-robbers are supposed to have their Head-Quarters in Penang, and it is there the plunder is disposed of, while Kedah is selected as a haven of refuge, after the commission of an unusually daring crime.

Although these outrages were not officially attributed to secret societies, the above description of them speaks for itself to the discerning.

We will complete our survey of Perak up to 1900 with extracts from the Perak Annual Reports, so far as we have been able to consult them.

In the Resident's report for 1887 we read:—

> There were two riots, one at Padang Balak in the Kuala Kangsar district[1] on the 19th April between members of the Hoh Seng and Ghee Hin secret societies for which the respective representatives were heavily fined and deported, and others sentenced to terms of imprisonment.

The reference shows that Triad and Tokong were fighting it out for supremacy in the Kuala Kangsar area in 1887. As we shall see, Tokong and Red Flag won.

THE PAPAN RIOT 29TH NOVEMBER, 1887

The report continues:—

> A riot took place at Papan in the Kinta District on the 29th November, arising from a quarrel between members of the Ghee Hin and Hoh Seng secret societies, who, during the preceding night, called in many hundreds of their members; and, had it not been for the prompt and vigorous action of the Magistrate and his officers, supported by the Police and the Malays of the neighbourhood, the disturbance would have spread over the whole district.
>
> The rioters were armed with pointed sticks, spears and knives, wearing white or red badges, and carrying banners. About 500 of the Ghee Hins arrived from Lahat in the early morning, and immediately attacked and looted two kongsis of the opposite faction, desperately wounding six persons, one of whom afterwards died in hospital.
>
> The Magistrate and Collector arrived in time to prevent more serious fighting, although one other man was knocked down and severely wounded in a fight which took place in the street. Many of the rioters taken with arms in their hands were flogged at once and dismissed, while the headman and leaders were reserved for trial, which took place before His Highness the Sultan, the Resident, and the Chief of Kinta a few days afterwards. Two men were sentenced to death for "culpable homicide amounting to murder" and executed in Thaipeng, nine men received sentences of rigorous imprisonment, varying from six months to two years, and twelve stripes with a rattan. Twelve kongsis were fined in sums varying from $36 to $5,000, amounting in all to $11,916, and the Bail Bond of one towkay, who had become security for his kongsi to $1,500 was estreated.

In Pickering's report for Penang in 1887 (above) he refers to this riot as being between the Ghee Hin and the Hai San.

Whether it was Ghee Hin *versus* Ho Seng or Hai San is of little consequence because both the latter were Tokong. We have referred at pages 269 and 338 above to the change of allegiance of the Ho Seng in Perak in 1873 from the Triad to the Tokong branch.

It seems probable that the change-over was general and applied as much to Penang and elsewhere as to Perak, and was probably due to absorption of the Ho Seng by the inflowing Hakka hordes. The appearance of white and red badges in this riot, to distinguish the two camps will be noticed.

Footnote.—(1) Not identified. Perhaps Salak is meant—modern Salak North. In the days before typewriters, printers took liberties with proper names in manuscript.

THE DEATH-PENALTY FOR MEMBERSHIP OF SECRET SOCIETIES IN PERAK 1887

The Resident's report for 1887 contains the following under the heading "Chinese Secretariat" :—

> The Secretary for Chinese Affairs enters largely into the important question of secret societies in Perak, the organisation of which, the numbers of their members, and their being bound upon all occasions to support each other in defiance of the laws of the State, enable worthless characters at any time to create disturbances and imperil its peace. These societies all have their headquarters in Penang and send travelling agents, who have power to hold lodges in the State, distribute tickets, initiate members and collect subscriptions, which is done to a large amount. Such proceedings are contrary to the laws of Perak, by which they are punishable with death, and three persons were actually sentenced during 1887, but in the Council of State, in consideration of the full sentence not having recently been carried out, the punishment was commuted to imprisonment for 24 years, a proclamation having been published that in future the death penalty would be enforced.

The name of the writer of this report is not recorded, but it could hardly have been Schultz. Once again, it points to the uncomfortable truth, which, having been revealed, seems to have been promptly forgotten.

The mention of the death-penalty is interesting and probably unique and its inception may have been due to the influence of Mohamedan law.

It would seem that the death-penalty had been imposed by proclamation at an earlier time (probably in 1883 following the Colony Suppression Ordinance of 1882) and had, like all drastic legislation, become a dead-letter and was "warmed-up" after the disclosures of the Papan riot of 1887. Chan Ah Yam and Chang Keng Kui must have felt uncomfortable as they helped this legislation through the State Council. The council minutes of this year must be interesting, read in this light.

The Resident's report for 1887 represents a big change from three years earlier, when it was officially reported that there were no secret societies in Perak.

In the Resident's Report for 1888 we read:—

> In September, the Commandant (of the Perak Sikhs) in consequence of disquieting reports received from the Acting Magistrate and Collector, visited the Kinta District, accompanied by a show of force. He made a most careful inspection and sent in to Government a very interesting report. He called at 246 kongsis containing 8,447 Ghee Hins and 5,394 Hai San coolies, from which the rioters of November 1887 were principally drawn. He found that there was no reason whatever to suspect that further trouble was likely to take place.

The surface policy of the big stick was beginning to be adopted in place of the more intimate underground method of prevention by observation, and disruption by means of methodical application of banishment.

It is also interesting to note that whereas the death-penalty for membership of a secret society was to be enforced, the old names Ghee Hin (Triad) and Hai San (Tokong) were still being officially used, the reason being the belief that these societies, by virtue of their registration, had undergone a metamorphosis, or purification which rendered them innocuous and no longer secret societies. Whatever they may have been on paper, they continued to demonstrate their typical characteristics in the Chinese under-world.

REGISTRATION IN PERAK 1895

The death-penalty in Perak was evidently repealed by Perak Order-in-Council No. 24 of 1889. Another Order-in-Council No. 1 of 1892 followed (*see* below).

Both these Orders-in-Council (24 of 1889 and 1 of 1892) were repealed by Order-in-Council No. 8 of 1895, which introduced into Perak registration on the same lines as the Colony Ordinance of 1889.

We should here glance at the process and policy of suppression as it affected Perak.

SUPPRESSION INTRODUCED INTO PERAK 1889–1895

The first move towards suppression in Perak actually preceded the Colony measure. This was an Order-in-Council dated 5th August, 1889, gazetted as No. 24/1889 (Perak Government Gazette 1889 page 734) issued by Sir Frank Swettenham then British Resident and containing six clauses which said in effect:—

(1) On and after 1st September, 1889, all Chinese secret societies are absolutely prohibited in the State of Perak and any one attempting to organise them is liable to fine ($1,000) : imprisonment (5 years) : flogging (30 strokes) : deportation and confiscation of all property.

(2) Any one joining them is liable to similar but lesser punishment.

(3) The use of flags of any secret society whether ashore or afloat and the possession of insignia, tickets, or rules of any secret society is prohibited.

For reasons repeatedly given in this work, this measure was ineffective because, firstly, insurance in some form for one's own preservation is a law of human nature; and secondly the illegal can always co-exist and operate within the legal.

Aware, perhaps, of its ineffectiveness, and following upon the suppression Ordinances in the Colony, the Perak Government issued a second Order-in-Council No. 1 of 1892, a copy of which we have not been able to obtain.

Next followed the Registration of Societies Enactment (Order-in-Council No. 8 of 1895, published in the Perak Government Gazette of 1895 page 329)— a comprehensive measure on the lines of the Colony Ordinance of 1889, and providing for exemption, registration and dissolution.

POINTERS TO THE POLICY OF EXEMPTION IN PERAK

Examining the Perak Gazette of the period, we find that G.N. 563/95 exempted from the provisions of the Registration Enactment, 21 Chinese temples in Kinta and one club in Ipoh. Again, the Annual Report of the Assistant Protector of Chinese, Taiping for 1896, mentions that in that year there were exempted in the Larut district, 37 Chinese clubs and temples.

In the light of present knowledge by which the sources of Chinese belief and the sources of Chinese secret societies have been drawn much closer together,—the Toh Peh Kong temple towards Tokong and the Buddhist temple towards Triad,—it would seem that a too generous exemption of temple foundations at the outset of total suppression, unconsciously handed back with one hand the cloak of concealment, which abolition had removed with the other.[1]

We see that official suppression in Perak had no more practical result than in the Colony. Thus in the annual report of the Protector of Chinese, Perak, for the year 1895 we read:—

> The new Order in Council, No. 8 of 1895, drafted on the lines of the Straits Ordinance, came into force during the year and I hope soon to have a complete register of all the societies in the State.
>
> The old secret societies are not so much to the fore, but more trouble is to be apprehended from the clubs, like those of the boatmen at Teluk Anson, or the Gambling Farm employees at Ipoh; some care will have to be exercised in admitting societies of this nature on the register.
>
> So far registration has been attempted only at Ipoh and Taiping; 18 clubs have been registered, with a membership of 20,000. Thirty temples and social clubs have been exempted from registration.
>
> I would point out that while the law empowers the Registrar to call upon the headmen of any society about to be registered to give particulars and all the information which may be required, there is no penalty for disobedience of that Order. There is, at times, some difficulty in getting the responsible men to come forward when required. It would be possible, of course, to prosecute them for being members of an unregistered society, but something simpler than that is needed.

We see here in Perak what we have already noted in the Colony—the rise of the Asiatic "club" as registered cover and the use of the temple foundations as exempted cover for the continuance of secret society organisation. Further, the difficulty mentioned "in getting the responsible men to come forward" was common to Colony experience under the 1889 Ordinance which caused puppets to be registered as headmen of "substitute" and harmless-sounding "clubs", which, in effect, were the standard secret societies decked out to fit the law with the real heads of the real organisations deep in the background and beyond the clutches of the Registrar.

A returning sense of reality is noticeable in the Report of the Assistant Protector of Chinese, Kinta, (unnamed) for the year 1896. He says:—

> I am of opinion that about 70 per cent of the Chinese population of Kinta are members of secret societies, principally the "Gi Hins". In consequence of arrests of members for being in possession of tickets the Chinese are now very crafty. They have other secret places than their pillow-boxes for their tickets. As regards the agents, they are full of cunning. They require constant watching.
>
> The "Hai San" secret society during the year attempted to organise a branch at Tronoh, but its plans were frustrated by the prompt action of this department and the police.
>
> The suspected headmen were summoned before me, and duly cautioned. This seems to have had an excellent effect upon them. During the year the Gambling Farms in some parts of Kinta were harassed a great deal by bad characters, who attempted to boycott and levy blackmail. From information received these men are instigated by petty towkays, who are reputably headmen or members of the "Hai San" secret society. A list of names has been given to the police by the Revenue Farmers, who are certainly deserving of every protection.

This is the position discussed in Chapter XX supra. When the revenue "farm" was held by the Ghee Hin (Triad), it was attacked and boycotted by the Hai San (Tokong), and vice-versa, as much, no doubt, for the purpose of discrediting their hereditary under-world enemies, as for preparing the way for their own syndicate's success at the next tender for the "farms".

The report continues:—

> I shall be very pleased to see the Perak Government, at an early date, adopt the same procedure as in the Colony in regard to the disposal of notorious and undesirable characters. I believe this class of men in the Colony is, on the joint report of the Chief Police Officer of the district and the Protector or Assistant Protector of Chinese, arraigned before the Executive Council instead of a law Court. This is certainly, with an alien population, an excellent procedure. As headmen of secret societies and blackmailers of brothels are so very cunning in their actions, and as it is the duty of the society, on the arrest of any of their headmen to do its utmost at all costs to get them off, either by retaining Counsel or obtaining false witnesses; and further, as we cannot get informers and respectable men to give their evidence in open Court, I think

---

Footnote.—(1) It would be tedious to the reader to quote particulars of these temple exemptions. They may be found by those interested under the following Perak *Government Gazette* notifications among others:—192/95, 411/95, 366/96, 411/96, 436/96, 477/96, 34/97, 60/97, 192/97 and 724/97.

the Government cannot do better than follow the Colonial procedure, *viz.*, trial before His Highness the Sultan in Council, who has the power, under Order in Council No. 5 of 1894, of banishing such persons for the public safety and welfare.

I submit that this is the only and best way of supervising secret societies, blackmailing of brothels, and boycotting of the Revenue Farms, in a mining district like Kinta, where they have excellent places, like some of the limestone caves and the distant mining kongsis, offering every facility for the holding of secret societies.

. This department is expected to suppress secret societies. There is an elaborate Order in Council. In the old days, the Discharge Ticket system materially assisted the police in tracing up crime, particularly the possession of secret society tickets and documents. Things are now changed, but just as much good work is expected of this department. The "golden key", *viz.*, the offer of a reward for valuable information given, is no longer in my possession.

A Chinaman is not so foolish as to give information gratis, or on credit, regarding secret societies, and run the risk of losing his life, or having his business damaged, simply for the sake of being thanked by a Government Officer. I had lately to get a donation from the "Fai Wong Lui" Fund to send an informer to China, as it was not safe for him to stay in Kinta.

I shall also be glad if arrangements could be made with the police in the different divisions to send this department a fortnightly or monthly return of the habitual bailers, so that their movements can be watched.

As secret society meetings are invariably held at night, I am of opinion that it will be an excellent thing to re-introduce the system of night-passes, as in Hongkong. In former days persons travelling about on foot at night had to carry lights.

The photographing of bad characters will also tend to put down a lot of crime.

This report refers to several features of secret society praxis with which we were familiar prior to 1890 and which had indeed led to the necessity for official suppression, and which it would seem official suppression had, after all, done little to abate.

Again, in the report of the Assistant Protector of Chinese, Taiping, for 1896 we read:—

No secret society case of any importance came before the Taiping Protectorate. Though there is little doubt that these societies still exist, their power for evil has been much weakened. Thirty-seven Chinese clubs and temples were exempted from registration.

For the remaining years of the century in Perak, the Annual Report of the Resident has the following references:—

1896—
There were few cases in connection with secret societies brought before the Courts, but there is, doubtless a strong organisation of such societies in the State, the Ghee Hins probably in the majority. No disturbances were directly traced to secret societies during the year.

1897—
Very little trouble was given by secret societies and the only attempt made to organise a new society in the Kinta district was successfully frustrated.

1898—
Secret societies gave but little trouble. Mr. Hare writes "With the abolition of secret societies in Penang and the sale of their property, the whole organisation broke up, and is as defunct in Perak as it is in Penang".

1899—
Attempts to form two secret societies, one in Kinta, the other in Larut were discovered and frustrated by the joint exertions of the Protector and the Deputy Commissioner of Police, to both of whom much credit is due. In one case five and in the other six of the ring-leaders of the society in question were arrested, and after full investigation, banished for life from the State.

1900—
Secret societies gave no trouble during the year, though the Protector of Chinese says periodical attempts are still made, and will always continue to be made, to start small, unlawful organisations. Evidence to ensure prosecution or banishment is difficult to obtain. Incessant vigilance on the part of the Protector and the Police are now sufficient guarantee against any such unlawful organisation.

This concludes our survey of Perak condition up to the close of the century.

We must now turn to Selangor and make a brief examination of Chinese secret society conditions in that State from 1850 to 1900.

Triad and Tokong in Selangor 1850–1900

Winstedt *History of Selangor, J.R.A.S.S.B.*, October, 1934, page 16 has:—

As in Perak so in Selangor, it was Chinese immigration on a large scale that finally broke down Malay administration.

In 1837, we get an echo of the old Perak troubles in a letter from Sultan Muhammed (of Selangor) to Mr. Salmond, Resident Councillor of Penang, reporting that a Chinese named Koh Chai an agent of the Chau Phya of Ligor (Raja of Ligor) had entered Perak in a ship with 200 men to collect Siamese debts.

This Koh Chai or Kok Chai as he is also referred to is mentioned by Thomson *op. cit.* *see* Chapter XII and was an influential resident of Penang. We are entitled to assume from the evidence in Chapters V and XIII above, that Kok Chai was a member of the Triad society. (*See* page 205 *supra* under (*a*)).

The death of Sultan Muhammed occurred in 1857 and left an indeterminate succession, which led to civil war and internal disturbance much as we have seen in Perak between 1871–1874. Sultan Abdul Samad succeeded to the throne of Selangor in 1860 on a disputed title.

Winstedt *op. cit.* page 19 continues:—

On 6th March, 1866, Sultan Abdul Samad wrote that he had arranged with W. H. Read and Kim Cheng to collect the taxes at Klang, each of the two collectors to retain one-tenth of the revenue; and on 20th March, 1866, the Sultan's brother-in-law Raja Abdullah, *alias* Dollah originally of Riau, wrote Cavenagh (the Governor) to the same effect. Raja Abdullah had been given charge of Klang, by Sultan Muhammed, had introduced Chinese, opened tin mines up-river and, though he himself lived at Pangkalen Batu, had founded Kuala Lumpur and was collecting a large revenue. His success excited the jealousy of Raja Mahdi whose father, Sulaiman, had ruled Klang before Raja Abdullah superseded him and had made no profit out of the Malay fossikers and tin-washers, who then represented the tin mining industry. Even a monthly allowance from Raja Abdullah failed to appease Raja Mahdi and now a feud between Bugis and Mandilings......at Kuala Lumpur provided him with forces.

THE REVENUE COLLECTING FIRM OF W. H. READ AND TAN KIM CHENG IN OPERATION IN SELANGOR 1866

This is an illuminating passage disclosing that the hand played by Read and Tan Kim Cheng in the destinies of Perak in 1873–1874 (pages 271–280; 283–285: and Chapters XIX and XX *supra*), was not an accidental one, nor was it their first partnership in the political arena of the Malay States. Here we find them eight years earlier, engaged in a very profitable mutual undertaking which, no doubt, provided them with valuable experience for similar enterprise in Perak at a later date.

Winstedt *loc. cit.* continues:—

Raja Mahdi lacked money and provisions......but a Straits-born Malacca Chinese Baba Tek Cheng supplied his needs accepting only interest.on his outlay, till victory should put his client in a position to grant limitless concessions of land.

There were losses on both sides but towards the end of the year 1866 Raja Mahdi starved his enemies into admitting defeat.[1]

In December, 1866, Sultan Abdul Samad......informed the British Government that he was ready to consider the claims of Mr. W. H. Read and Towkay Kim Cheng and other British subjects for damages due to the disturbances at Klang.

TRIAD AND WHITE FLAG *versus* TOKONG AND RED FLAG IN SELANGOR 1866

These extracts are very informative. They show the same process taking place in Selangor as we have seen developed with such unhappy results in Perak *viz*:—the grasping hand of Triad angling for concessions through the channel of the revenue farm monopoly; the development of civil war in which Triad and Tokong gave their support to the opposing factions, keeping the war going with supplies and provisions and awaiting the chance to dig themselves in on the side of the victor.

We meet again Tan Kim Cheng (Triad) in partnership with W. H. Read as holders of the Klang revenue farms on a 10% basis each, after Chinese had been introduced into Selangor by Raja Abdullah. We may hazard the guess that Raja Abdullah like his namesake in Perak was supported by Triad (seeing that Tan Kim Cheng had been behind him) and was, therefore, White Flag; while his opponent Raja Mahdi was supported by a Malacca Chinese "Baba Tek Cheng", whom we identify as Chan Tek Cheang, J.P. of Malacca. This man we identify below by implication as Tokong, while we may surmise that Raja Mahdi was therefore Red Flag. In *Parliamentary Paper* C 1505 pages 239 and 240, in connection with the Malacca riots of 1875 already mentioned above, Plunket in one of his dispatches (page 239) has:—

I wish particularly to bear witness to the untiring zeal with which Mr. Boon Teong, manager of the opium farm, Mr. Tek Cheang a Justice of the Peace and Mr. Tek Guan brother to the Siamese Consul at Singapore, have assisted me in dealing with these riots.

The Tek Guan mentioned was Tan Tek Guan (陳德源)[2] younger brother of Tan Kim Cheng of Singapore, the kingmaker, and therefore Triad. Both were sons of Tan Tock Seng who was born in Malacca in 1798 and whose career in Singapore is given by S.O.S. *op. cit.* page 66.

The Boon Teong mentioned was Seet Boon Tiong (薛文仲) also referred to as See Boon Tiong, who was foundation member No. 21 of the Keng Tek Whay, an association of Malacca-born Hokkiens founded in Singapore in 1831, which we discuss fully in Chapter XXVII *infra*, where we identify it with Tokong.

The fact that Tan Tock Seng, although a Hokkien born in Malacca and a man of 33, at the height of his business career in Singapore in 1831, is not among the foundation members of the Keng Tek Whay, suggests that he was ineligible on some other ground. This we may assume was because he belonged to Triad, the most likely camp in which to find the father of Tan Kim Cheng and Tan Tek Guan.

The same applies to Tan Kim Seng another leading Hokkien merchant of Singapore 1805–1864, who was born in Malacca but whom we have placed in the Triad camp (*see* page 350 *supra*).

Again Tan Seng Poh, whom we have suggested (pages 359–360 *supra*) was probably the real Head of Tokong in Singapore during the middle years of the nineteenth century, was not a foundation member of the Keng Tek Whay. The explanation in his case is, no doubt, because he was ineligible being a Teochew born'in Perak, son of Tan Ah Hun the first *Kapitan* China of Perak (1837) *see* page 350 *supra*.

Footnote.—(1) Raja Abdullah had meanwhile fled to Malacca and taken up permanent residence there.

Footnote.—(2) S.O.S. refers to the career of Tan Tek Guan in *op. cit.* pages 178–179, and 293–294 and 367.

THE CAMP IDENTITY OF CHAN TEK CHIANG (曾德昌), J.P.

There remains to be decided the camp identity of "Baba Tek Cheng" or Chan Tek Cheang, J.P. of Malacca, whom circumstantial evidence suggests was Tokong during the period 1866–1875.

In *Parliamentary Paper* C 1505, page 240 Plunket has:—

> Upon this, the headmen of the three societies, Ghee Hin (Triad) Ghee Boo (Triad) and Hoh Beng (Tokong), went to the opium farm the same evening (13/12/1875) and declared before Superintendent Hayward, Mr. Boon Teong (opium farmer) and Mr. Chan Tek Cheang, J.P. that their quarrels were at an end.

This incident is referred to by S.O.S. *op. cit.* page 178 in the following passage under date 14th April, 1876:—

> Mr. Tan Teck Guan, a brother of Tan Kim Cheng, had become a prominent citizen of Malacca, and he along with Mr. Chan Teck Chiang received a graceful tribute in the form of a letter, signed by all the leading Malacca Chinese merchants and published in the *Daily Times* on 14th April, 1876, for having succeeded in settling a dispute between two rival secret societies in Malacca and in getting the headmen to sign a bond to keep the peace, or forfeit $500.

We have not been able to find any other evidence to help to identify Chan Teck Chiang's secret society affinities. He is not among the foundation members of the Keng Tek Whay, where we would expect to find him if he were a member of Tokong, but he may have succeeded one of the foundation members *viz:*—either No. 3 Chan Beng Tin ((曾明徵) or No. 4 Chan Buay Seng (曾梅生), one of whom may have been his father. (*See* Chapter XXVII *infra*).

The two facts that:—

(1) He supported Raja Mahdi in the Selangor Civil War 1869–1874;
(2) He was responsible for settling the secret society war in Malacca in 1875 in collaboration with Tan Tek Guan whom we know to have been Triad and White Flag;

must remain for the present sufficient reason for identifying him by implication with Tokong and Red Flag, until further evidence which appears below, pointing to the same conclusion, is taken into consideration.

THE SELANGOR CIVIL WAR 1869–1874

Winstedt *History of Selangor* page 20 continues:—

> The second protagonist, a new and potent figure, now entered the stage of Selangor politics...... In 1867, the Sultan of Selangor's daughter (Raja Arfah) married Tengku Zia-ud-din (or Kudin for short) younger brother of Ahmad Tajuddin Mukaram Shah, Sultan of Kedah.[1]
>
> This Tengku Kudin was energetic and educated and had acquired European ideas of administration and development. Accordingly on 12th June, 1868, his father-in-law gave him a document......the purport of which was that Tengku Kudin was appointed viceroy of the whole state of Selangor and was given Langat for his own. Langat had always been the personal property of the donor Sultan Abdul Samad. The Sultan's sons Yaakob and Kahar soon became jealous of their brother-in-law and Raja Mahdi was already a believer in the rule that those should "take who have the power, and those should keep who can".

The course of the domestic war which developed in Selangor between 1869–1874 from these circumstances is described by Winstedt *op. cit.* pages 21–32 and led finally to British intervention by much the same path as in Perak. The two Malay factions were throughout each supported by a faction of Chinese whom we can only suppose were Triad and Tokong, although the facts recorded by history are insufficient to enable us to identify them definitely. Further research would be necessary before this could be indisputably established.

The flag allegiance seems to have remained constant, somewhat as follows:—

White	Red
1. Raja Abdullah.	1. Raja Mahdi.
2. Tengku Zia-ud-din *alias* Tengku Kudin of Kedah known as the Viceroy.	2. Syed Mashhor (an Arab fighting-man from Pontianak).
3. Raja Ismail (son of No. 1) (supported by "A Chinese merchant of Malacca" (Winstedt *op. cit.* page 21) name not stated, but as we know Tan Kim Cheng was in support of this faction, the "Malacca merchant was probably his brother Tan Tek Guan (Triad)).	3. Raja Mahmud (supported by Chan Tek Cheng, Tokong, of Malacca).

With the advent of Sir Andrew Clarke as Governor (4th November, 1873), a new policy was approved by the Secretary of State for the Colonies and British intervention in the affairs of Selangor only awaited a suitable opportunity. In September, 1874, as a

---

Footnote.—(1) *See* Chapters V and XIII above.

result of representations of both Sultan Abdul Samad and the Viceroy Tengku Kudin, who by now had triumphed over Raja Mahdi, the Governor sent Sir Frank Swettenham then a young civil servant, to Langat to give informal advice to the Sultan. So successful was this arrangement that a Resident J. G. Davidson was appointed in December, 1874, while Swettenham remained as Assistant Resident.

Winstedt *op. cit.* page 32 continues:—

> Raja Mahmud now surrendered and loyally served Mr. Swettenham through the Perak troubles (of a year later) and later Mr. Hugh Clifford in Pahang. Syed Mashhor also served the British in Perak. Rajah Mahdi refused to accept a pension to live in Johore and still demanded Klang, fomenting disturbances that at the end of 1875 led to his detention in the civil prison in Singapore; his death from tuberculosis removed the last of the old-world disturbers of Selangor's peace. One item of Selangor's earliest budget was $300,000 owing by the Viceroy to a Malacca Chinese merchant for munitions of war.

We have not been able to trace the name of this "Malacca Chinese merchant" but we may be fairly sure that, whoever he was, he was acting on behalf of Tan Kim Cheng of Singapore and represented Triad and White Flag interests as against the Raja Mahdi and Chan Tek Cheang clique. The merchant was quite likely Tan Kim Cheng's own brother Tan Tek Guan, who died a wealthy man in 1891 (*see* S.O.S. *op. cit.* page 178).

TRIAD AND TOKONG IN SELANGOR 1884

So much for published historical references to Triad and Tokong in Selangor. There remains consideration of the references to Selangor in the Powell Report (page 412 above) in which Chong Bun Sui (himself a member of Tokong) records as follows:—

(1) The establishment of the Ghee Hin in Klang in 1862 by Lim Jit Seng (a baba, probably Cantonese) and two others, together with "Ungku Kit" the Panglima Perang and A.D.C. to Sultan Abdul Samad of Selangor. This strengthens the earlier submission made above that the Sultan's and Tengku Kudin's party in the civil war of 1869–1874 was probably White Flag. It is also a further pointer to the practice believed to have been common, of Malay Rajas entering Chinese secret societies. (*See* pages 211–213, 278 and 281–282 *supra*).

(2) The next point of interest is the mention of the mining village of Kanching (near Kuala Lumpur) where Ghee Hins (Triad) were composed of Kia Eng Chiu Hakkas from the Hakka branch of the Triad society in Singapore, (which he says was called the Song Pak Kun); while the Hai Sans (Tokong) were also Hakkas, presumably from other districts—an example of the same tribe in the same place but under divided secret society allegiance.

It seems at least doubtful whether the Song Pak Kun or Tsung Pak Kwun (The Cypress and Fig tree society, *see* Chapter VI) was in fact a "branch" of the Triad. Its name and associations suggest Tokong.

(3) The reference to Semantan is interesting (over the border of Selangor and in Pahang). It was from Semantan that the Malay rebels in the Pahang war of 1893 originated, who gave Sir Hugh Clifford so much trouble and whom we shall have occasion to mention later. They may well have been Red Flag Malays who had caught the infection from the Chinese miners there, mentioned in the Powell report, the majority of whom were Hai Sans (Tokong).

(4) Lastly, the Powell report mentions Yap Tek Loi (葉德來) as being one of the headmen of Hai San in Klang between about 1864 and 1884 and also the *Kapitan* of the Hakkas in Selangor during the same period.

The Annual Report of the Acting British Resident, Selangor for the year 1884 has:—

> An attempt was also made to establish an illegal secret society among the Chinese, but the ring-leaders were arrested before they had succeeded in inducing many persons to join them.
>
> The Superintendent reports that he received great assistance, in the suppression of this illegal society, from Captain Yap Tek Loy, the recognised head of the Chinese community in Selangor, who, on this as on all other occasions, cordially co-operated with the Police in maintaining order in the State.

The Resident reposed more trust in the good faith of Yap Tek Loy than the history of the *Kapitan* system justifies. The position was that at that period Tokong was paramount in Selangor and its headman Yap Tek Loy much to his own advantage, actively supported the authorities in keeping out Triad influence, which, since its collapse in Larut in 1880, had been seeking fresh fields of development further south (*see* page 340 *supra*).

Negri Sembilan (Sungei Ujong)—The area of Lukut which lies in modern Negri Sembilan between Port Dickson and the Selangor border, had long been famous as a mining centre capitalised by Malacca Chinese. The area formerly belonged to Selangor and the riots which occurred there in about 1834 have already been referred to in Chapter V. These events had from an early date attracted Triad and Tokong into an area which is now part of Negri Sembilan. The next mention we have is in Winstedt *History of Negri Sembilan, J.A.S.B.*, October, 1934, page 68:—

> "In 1865, the Penghulu of Johol wrote offering Gemencheh to the British if they would attack that mining centre and oust one Penghulu Jaafar who had become offended with the writer because the writer had leased the mines to Baba Bom Tiong and Towkay Cham and had attacked the writer on a dark night and killed and wounded his men".

We identify these two Chinese as See (or Seet) Boon Tiong, Malacca opium farmer, 1875, mentioned above under Malacca, and Chan Tek Cheang, J.P. of the same place, both of whom appear to have been Tokong headmen. The above extract suggests that Triad interests may have prompted Penghulu Jaafar's action. It also helps to identify Chan Tek Cheang with Tokong.

There is no other published historical reference to the early entry of Chinese into Negri Sembilan, but reference to Powell's Report above shows that Tokong was established in Seremban about 1860 and that Triad was not recognised there until much later (1878).

This looks as if Lukut had been a Tokong and Red Flag preserve until after British intervention in 1877, at which date Chinese immigration into Negri Sembilan became general, and Triad rivalry to Tokong soon became established.

This was aided, too, by the Triad drift to the south which followed their final economic defeat in the Larut wars, which we date from about 1880, discussed above (pages 339–340).

The Powell Report under Sungei Ujong gives the position of Triad and Tokong in Seremban in 1884 and shows Tokong paramount and furnishing both a Cantonese and Hakka *Kapitan.*

Pahang—Swettenham *British Malaya* page 270, says that in 1888 Pahang had a population of fifty thousand Malays and a few hundred Chinese. It is probable that the majority of the latter were engaged in tin mining at Bentong. In October, 1888, the first British Resident J. P. Rodger was appointed to Pahang and was faced with the same difficulties as had confronted Birch in Perak in 1875. Winstedt *History of Malaya, J.A.S.B.*, March, 1935, page 247 has:—

> As in Perak so in Pahang the substitution of political allowances for ancient rights caused great heart-burning...... (In 1893) Bahman, chief of Semantan[1]......flouted the Government by continuing to collect taxes, had his title taken away by the Sultan, and collected a few followers...... Rumour whispered that the Sultan, who had taken the field with a thousand men, would follow his chief's entreaty to change sides and expel the British...... Rebellion spread...... The cool courage of Hugh Clifford saved Kuala Lipis...... The rebels scattered...... A general amnesty was proclaimed and even Bahman was promised his life ......but he put more trust in a Trengganu Sayid[2] who promised him success and invulnerability in a holy war.
>
> In June, 1894, Bahman invaded Pahang (from Trengganu) but......the Malay chiefs were tired of fighting and prepared to resist their rebel brother...... Forty rebels fell. In vain Hugh Clifford pursued the rest into Trengganu. Siamese Commissioners co-operated with Clifford......and at the end of 1895 Bahman and his few surviving followers were captured and removed to Bangkok.

Swettenham *British Malaya* page 271 referring to this incident, known as the Pahang war, says:—

> Some chiefs took up arms against all that the new regime stood for, and the consequence was a long and harrassing and an expensive "war", which was only brought to a conclusion by hunting the rebels out of Pahang and even following them into the independent neighbouring states Kelantan and Trengganu, where they were eventually secured, mainly by the efforts of Mr. Hugh Clifford. Some of the rebels lost their lives in these prolonged operations, some were done to death by the Siamese, who took part in their arrest, and the remainder were deported to Siam where a number of the survivors remain to the present time (1900).

These two extracts are interesting as they link the Pahang rebellion of 1893 with a certain Trengganu Sayid who fostered it, and with the Siamese who helped half-heartedly to suppress it. The State of Trengganu was then and until the Treaty of 1909, under the protection of Siam.

We shall show in a subsequent Chapter XXVIII the influence which this Trengganu Sayid (Ungku Sayid of Chabang Tiga) and his followers wielded in connection with a minor rising in Trengganu in 1928.

We suggest that Red Flag infection may well have been brought to the East Coast for the first time by Bahman and his fellow rebels from Semantan in 1894.

Again we see the Siamese, whom throughout we have identified with the White Flag, taking a willing part in the arrest of the Pahang rebels of 1895 whom we may suppose belonged to the other camp.

Siam—The T'oung Pao (通報) Series I Vol. VII for the year 1898, has, on page 472, a reference to serious Chinese secret society riots at Chantabun in August, 1896, "due to the visit of an important secret society leader to that place".

Footnote.—(1) *See* reference to Semantan in the Powell Report of 1884 page 412 above.
Footnote.—(2) Ungku Sayyid of Chabang Tiga who died in 1924, *see* Chapter XXVIII *infra.*

We have already referred in Chapter XIII *supra* to the preponderance of Triad among the Chinese in Siam and the probable historical explanation for this predominance. We have also noted in the same chapter how this ascendency over Tokong has persisted in Siam to the present-day.

Sarawak—The following reference to Triad and Tokong in Sarawak, is found in Heckethorn *Secret Societies of all Ages* Vol. II page 133. It is included here as being the earliest published reference which we have been able to find to the name Sa Tiam Hui or Three Dot Brotherhood:—

> *The Straits Times* of the 17th September, 1889, contained full particulars of the trial of a number of prisoners who were proved to be members of the Ghee Hin or Sam Tian secret society of Sarawak. The six leaders were shot; eleven being active members, carrying out orders of the leaders, beating, frightening, or murdering non-members, were sentenced to receive six dozen strokes of the rattan, to have their heads shaved, to be imprisoned during the Rajah's pleasure; seven others against whom no specific charges were made out, were dismissed on swearing to have no further dealings with the society.

Here again the name is used by Heckethorn as a synonym for the Ghee Hin or Triad society, the official view held of the Sa Tiam Hui down to the present-day. This view which we hold to be erroneous, would explain why it was possible for the "seven others to swear to have no further dealings with the society",—an absurd enough demand when we know the meaning of the secret oath and the power it holds. The explanation may be that they were not members of the Triad society, but of its rival Tokong, and so it was easy for them to swear dissociation from their enemies.

In Chapters VIII and IX *supra* we have offered for acceptance what we believe to be the true origin of the name Sa Tiam Hui, but its use seems to have become common in Malaya only after the suppression of secret societies in 1890.

THE NETHERLANDS INDIES 1850–1900

Clarified since 1866 by the labour of Schlegel (Chapter I), the experience of our Dutch friends *vis-à-vis* Chinese secret societies in the Netherlands Indies, particularly in the social and criminal spheres, has been much the same as our own in Hong Kong and Malaya, but the policy applied by the Dutch Colonial authorities to the control of the *imperium in imperio* created by these overseas sodalities among the Chinese, has been different from our own. The reason for this difference of treatment is probably to be found in the vast disparity in population-ratio as between Malaya and the Netherlands Indies.

Thus, the present population of Malaya is about 4,500,000 of whom 1,800,000 or 40% are Chinese; while the present population of the Netherlands Indies is about 61,000,000 of whom 1,250,000 or about 2% are Chinese.[1] With such an insignificant population-ratio, the problems of the Chinese in the Netherlands Indies are of comparatively less importance, although the total Chinese population is only some half million less than that of Malaya.

To what extent Triad and Tokong have made themselves separately distinguishable in the Netherlands Indies in the social and criminal sphere during the past century we are unable without separate study of the subject to say; but the economic influence of Chinese *kongsis* in Java during the last two centuries receives casual reference by Dr. W. G. Cator *The Economic position of the Chinese in the Netherlands Indies* (1936).[2]

This concludes our survey of Triad and Tokong up to 1900.

BOYLE'S VIEWS UPON THE POLICY OF SUPPRESSION

The following are comments by Boyle upon the policy of suppression. In common with all other commentators he writes from the view-point that there is only one clandestine confederacy among the Chinese, namely Triad, and that all manifestations of secret organisation are but branches of the Triad society, whereas we believe it to be amply demonstrated in this work that there were and still are, two separate distinct and rival secret sodalities in the Chinese secret society under-world both in China proper and among Chinese overseas. The following are Boyle's comments in his article *Chinese Secret Societies* published in *Harper's Magazine* September, 1891, pages 599–600:—

> Having traced the history of the T'ien Ti, glanced at its organisation, and observed too briefly the objects it professes, we have to consider what in effect is its influence. Certain articles of the oath assist us here. The first after enjoining obedience, commands every member to mind his own affairs; the second forbids him under direct penalties, to confide in any

---

Footnote.—(1) Emerson: *Malaysia*, a study in direct and indirect rule (1937) page 43.

Footnote.—(2) Other references, unobtainable for purposes of this work, are:—
  (i) W. A. van Rees: *Montrado* (Gebr. Muller, s'Hertogenbosch 1858).
  (ii) S. H. Schaank: *De Kongsi's van Montrado*, published in the *Tijdschrift voor Indische Taal-Land-en Volkenkunde* Vol. XXXV (Mart. Nijhof, 'S Gravenhage 1893).
  (iii) Dr. J. J. M. de Groot: *Het Kongsiwezen van Borneo* (Mart. Nijhof, 'S Gravenhage 1909).
  (iv) H. Borel: *Chineesche Vereenigingen* (Published in the periodical *Moederland en Kolonien* of 1913 Vol. VI.
  (v) J. C. Mollema: *The development of the island of Billiton and of the Billiton Coy.* (Published Martinius Nijhof, 1918).

The above works are to be found in the Library of the Koninklijke Bataviaasch Genootschap van Kunsten en Wetenschappen at the Batavia Museum.

uninitiated person whatsoever; the thirty-fourth sentences him to a cruel death if he calls upon police, magistrates, or jurisdiction of any kind, under any circumstances; the thirty-fifth pronounces an awful doom if he gives evidence in a court of law unless be it understood, by direction of his superior—that is, generally false witness. In the Master's address to candidates after initiation, he tells them to lay before him any wrong or grievance they may have, and justice shall be done. These principles, the repudiation of all jurisdictions, and the assumption of their power by an irresponsible tribunal, constitute an *imperium in imperio*, the foulest, the bloodiest, the most oppressive of which there is record, on such a scale.[1]

Schlegel says, the Hung league has carried civil war and murder wherever it has gone. Milne says, "They engage to defend each other against the police, to hide each other's crimes, to assist detected members in making their escape from justice". Pickering says the T'ien-Ti is a "combination to carry out private quarrels, and to uphold the interests of the members in spite of law; and lastly, to raise money by subscription, or by levying fees on brothels or gaming houses". The Inspector-General of Police for Singapore says, "They are a standing danger to the peace of the Settlement". And so on. Their government is a reign of terror, which the law itself maintains in its own despite, for if it be not thought advisable to take active steps against one who has incurred the ill will of the society, such as murder, torture, or a pitiless beating, a false charge is brought, and supported, if needful, by a thousand witnesses.

The Colonial branches of the T'ien-Ti are murderously hostile among themselves. They have, in fact, no *raison d'être*—beyond that enmity to the Manchu, very vague in practice—save internecine war.

This statement illustrates once again the contradiction that members of one great brotherhood could be "murderously hostile among themselves", or that "internecine war" could be their sole *raison d'être* which would make the existence of a single brotherhood meaningless. These conditions can only be explained by acceptance of the hypothesis of the two great rival brotherhoods of Triad and Tokong

Boyle continues :—

Their chiefs accumulate enormous wealth. Chang Ah Kwi, a leading member of the Gin-Seng branch at Penang,[2] was proved to possess two millions sterling when tried for murder. His fellow prisoner, Chin Ah Yam, was said to be as rich.[3] The District Grand Master, Khu-Tan-Tek, who was actually sentenced by the Supreme Court, declared that the government dared not hang him, and he proved right, so far, at least, that the government did not. These cases arose out of the tremendous riot which I must refer to presently, when the town was occupied for more than a week by warring Hweys, forty thousand strong. Perak was a native state at the time, rich in antimony mines, which had attracted fifty thousand Chinamen, every single one belonging to a society established at Penang. Freed from all restraint, they followed their own instincts. The Malay Rajah did not interfere so long as they paid their dues. Pitched battles were incessant. On one occasion thirty thousand men engaged, of whom two thousand were left dead upon the field. The mother lodges at Penang took up these quarrels and attacked one another. At length the Governor of the Straits Settlements proposed to occupy Perak, and the Rajah accepted. But the societies remained. At a conference in his own drawing-room, they once threatened to hang Sir Hugh Low.[4]

One of the very earliest enactments in the Statute-book of Hongkong decrees "the suppression of the Triad and other secret societies"; it was passed in 1845. The preamble describes them as "associations having objects in view incompatible with the maintenance of good order and constituted authority, and with the security of life and property". But nothing was done in the Straits. Month by month the streets of Singapore, even more especially of Penang, were held by mobs, fighting to the death. Scores of times the garrison was called out. Murders were discovered weekly, suspected daily. One man boasted to Mr. Pickering that he had released seventy-two of his confederates from jail. Petitions were sent to the Governor and to the Colonial Office, until respectable inhabitants, Chinese as well as European, were sick of petitioning. At length came the crisis. Penang was the headquarters of several associations, the chiefs residing there in safety, whilst they directed wholesale murder and civil war in the native States. In 1867, they had a grand quarrel. Not less than forty thousand men took up arms, a thousand at least were killed, whole streets looted, women outraged, and houses burnt. Two years afterwards the Colonial Office assented at last to decree, not the suppression of secret societies as was demanded, but their registration.

It worked some good, no doubt. Mr. Pickering, the Registrar, declared himself satisfied, because, as he ingenuously confessed, no better could be had. Even an attempt on his own life by the chiefs of the Ghee Hok society did not shake his faith. But the public, which saw crime still rampant in all directions, could not wait longer than nine years for the beneficent effects of registration. Backed by the police, and in fact, everybody else, it demanded stronger measures, and in 1888 the societies were suppressed. The despatch of Sir Cecil Clementi-Smith urging this measure points out that eleven secret societies were registered in Singapore by last returns, having 1122 office-bearers and 62,376 members enrolled; in Penang, five secret societies with 361 office-bearers and 92,581 members—an increase of 20,771 in the twelve months. This will be thought startling, but when, as has been said, the whole Chinese population by the census of 1881 was but 153,532, it shows in the first place that the census is inexact, and in the second that very nearly all the males must be enrolled in one or other branch of this tremendous conspiracy.

It is satisfactory so far as it goes, to learn that no bad results have followed. I have seen a letter from Sir Cecil Clementi-Smith dated December 29, 1890, which says: "you will be glad to know that the policy has been quite successful. I have made careful inquiry since I

Footnote.—(1) We think the record of the Thugs of India discussed in Chapter X *supra* which was perhaps unknown to Boyle, was even fouler and bloodier than either Triad or Tokong.
Footnote.—(2) He seems to be getting mixed up here between the Ghee Hin and a gin-sling! Chang Ah Kwi (Chang Keng Kui) was, of course, the head of the Hai San (Tokong) in Penang and Larut and not of the Ghee Hin (Triad).
Footnote.—(3) Boyle is confusing Chang Keng Kui (Tokong) and Chan Ah Yam (Triad) with Khoo Poh (Tokong) and Boey Yu Kong (Triad) who, with Khoo Thean Tek (Tokong) appear to have been the only persons committed to trial for the Penang Riots of 1867, with the results we have seen.
Footnote.—(4) We have found no official confirmation of this statement although Boyle appears to have been generally well-informed.

came back and am quite satisfied that there has been no attempt at resuscitation, and that the dangerous societies are entirely blotted out. Of course, a careful watch must be maintained". May this cheering view prove exact.

HECKETHORN'S VIEW

The following are Heckethorn's comments published in 1897 in *Secret Societies of all Ages* Vol. II page 138:—

A law passed in 1889 in the Straits Settlements for the suppression of Chinese secret societies, according to a report issued in 1892 by the Protector of Chinese in those settlements, has led to the disappearance of those dangerous organisations. But it is admitted that it will take many years for the Triad element to become extinct; the action of the Hung league is merely suspended, and out of it have sprung many minor societies, as off-shoots from the parent society, who send gangs of roughs to brothels, coolie-depôts, music halls and shops, demanding monthly contributions, under threat of coming in force, and interrupting the business of the establishment. The fighting men of these societies are kept in the lodges by the headmen on the proceeds of the exactions thus levied. The expulsion of the headmen, as the speediest remedy of these evils, has been tried, with as yet only partial success.

Comment on the Policy of Suppression

(1) The two vast clandestine confederacies, the Hung league and the Han league into which we believe the overseas Chinese to be mainly divided, are of too ancient origin and have beliefs, prejudicies, and interests too widespread and deeply rooted in China proper, for it to be possible ever to suppress, or uproot them by local legislation overseas.

(2) We have tried to show that up to the year of official suppression, all the leading Chinese in Malaya were members of one or the other; their individual success in commerce depending no less upon their Triad or Tokong associations, than upon their business acumen.

(3) The power of these cabals, or sodalities (to use Hutson's word), was vastly greater than the power of any particular Chinese merchant, or combination of merchants in a British Colony or elsewhere overseas, to break them, however much individual merchants may have wished to set themselves free from the tentacles of this under-surface octopus. The effect of suppression, we may with reason suppose, was to leave everything exactly as it was before, except that Triad and Tokong went quietly underground, a position they had been accustomed to occupy for centuries in China; and where they have remained in Malaya for the past forty-five years. The leaders of Triad and Tokong who were in positions of power and influence in 1890, which they owed to their societies, just could not, we must suppose, repudiate their allegiances, but, in order to appear to comply with the law, had openly to simulate their dissociation from all things connected with Triad and Tokong, while maintaining in secret their former relationships, to attempt to sever which, however much they individually may have wished to do so, would probably have brought a swift retribution.

(4) To imagine fondly that this influential direction of Triad and Tokong in Malaya ceased from the date of the official "suppression" of Chinese secret societies in 1890, is to deny the evidence of history, and the evidence of the present-day. The rules of Tokong as far as we know them, appear to include an hereditary principle (see Rules 11, 12, and 20 of the Toh Peh Kong society of Penang 1844, Appendix II). We have seen from Hutson's researches the antiquity and the ruthlessness of Tokong and we may be permitted to assume that it is under this hereditary principle that leaders are chosen to-day, to direct the destinies of Tokong and Red Flag in Malaya.

(5) Up to the date of official suppression in Malaya there was no legal reason for the leading Chinese to deny their membership of these societies, but the wealthiest and the most influential Chinese, even during the period of registration 1870-1890, appear to have increasingly preferred to pose outwardly as being unassociated therewith and to allow smaller fry of the society, such as Chua Moh Choon of the Singapore Ghee Hok, (pages 359-360 *supra*) to be officially recorded as the headmen; thus giving cover to the real heads in case of disturbances for which they might be held pecuniarily responsible, or perhaps in preparation for the day of official suppression.

(6) This device may have been adopted as a direct result of the Penang riots of 1867 and the Larut wars of 1872-1874 and the fear which grew with increasing business prosperity, that if such disturbances were to occur again, and the real heads of the two camps in Malaya were officially known, it would mean financial ruin and expulsion from the country; whereas, no harm would be done if the blame fell on a few dummy headmen.

(7) The only channels which appear to have been open to the individual Chinese of that period anxious to cut free from the humiliation of his secret society associations, seem have been either, conversion to the Christian religion,

or naturalisation as a British subject: and it is interesting to note how many of the leading Chinese in Malaya in the last century adopted this way of cutting themselves free from under-surface entanglements. In viewing this aspect of our subject, we have to remember that both Triad and Tokong, according to the authorities quoted, were definitely religious, and their rejection in favour of the Christian faith involved, therefore, a spiritual change, as well as conferring a material benefit.

(8) Official suppression in 1890 of the societies mentioned in the earlier part of this Chapter, drove Triad and Tokong underground and doubtless loosened society discipline and gave the small fry more opportunity for free-lancing as the heads of semi-independent gangs of blackmailers and bullies, than was possible either under the period of tolerance (1800–1870), when society discipline was very strict and when the societies were themselves an integral part of the governance of the Chinese through the *Kapitan* system; or again under the period of unrestricted registration (1870–1882), when Triad and Tokong were officially recognised; or again under the period of limited registration (1882–1889) during which some of the most dangerous gangs which had sprung up during the earlier period of unrestricted registration, were actually "suppressed".

(9) So soon as both Triad and Tokong and all their works were officially driven underground, their discipline was undermined, their individual cohesion was loosened and their disintegration in Singapore into groups of freelance gangsters was hastened. But their separate identities remained.

(10) It would be a mistake, we think, to imagine that the disintegration so noticeable at the present-day in Singapore, has been general over the whole of Malaya. Penang has been shown to be the cradle of Triad and Tokong and of their Malay auxiliaries, the White and the Red Flag societies, and the strong line of cleavage between these in modern Malaya—outside perhaps of Singapore— is to-day evidence both of the permanence and solidarity of the two rival camps. The reason for this is probably to be found in the following two facts :—

    (a) Penang has remained the *primum mobile* of Triad and Tokong activity in Malaya and more particularly of White and Red Flag intrigue.

    (b) The White and Red Flag societies although suppressed in the Straits Settlements by Ordinance IV of 1882, were not included in the official suppression of 1890 and have retained their virility underground unimpaired.

(11) A noticeable feature of the history of Triad and Tokong in Malaya (and doubtless elsewhere also), is the fact that Tokong almost always appear as the aggressors; and it is only after Triad have had great provocation that they have joined battle with them. This fact is in keeping with the character for brutality, pugnaciousness, and callousness, which Hutson, in his illuminating article (Chapter II), has given to members of the Ko Lao Hui, to which, we submit, Tokong belongs.

(12) By comparison, Triad throughout appear almost inoffensive until roused, which is again in keeping with their more respectable ancestry and with the morality of their ritual and aspirations, compared with what Hutson calls the depravity of the Ko Lao Hui.

NAMES APPLIED TO THE HAN AND HUNG LEAGUES IN MALAYA BETWEEN 1868–1900

For convenience of reference and identity we should perhaps here attempt to divide the multitude of fresh names met with since 1868 into the two camps of Han and Hung.

The following schedule is very much subject to correction, but is offered as a guide in continuation of that appearing on page 112 *supra*. The only society mentioned in this chapter which is not included herein is the Tung Meng Hui (同盟會) which, as we suggest in Chapter XXVI *infra*, was probably composed of elements of both Triad and Tokong. This fact, we suggest, enabled it to effect enough underground combination— if only temporarily—to set the Revolution of 1911 in motion.

NAMES APPLIED TO THE HAN LEAGUE (TOKONG) AND THE HUNG LEAGUE (TRIAD) IN MALAYA BETWEEN 1868 AND 1900

The Han League (Tokong)

Serial No.	Common Name	Characters	Place in use	Authority
1	Ghee Hok	義福	Singapore, 1830–1891	All commentators
2	Ghee Soon	義順	Singapore, 1878	Vaughan
3	Hok Meng (Hoh Beng)	福明	Singapore and Malacca, 1878	Vaughan
4	Hai San (Hye San)	海山	Singapore, Penang, Perak and Selangor, 1850–1890	Vaughan, Pickering and Official records
5	Ghee Kok	義閣	Singapore, 1878	Vaughan
6	Song Peh Kwan	松柏館	Singapore and Selangor, 1850–1890	All commentators
7	Hok Hin	福興	Singapore, 1850–1890	All commentators
8	Ho Seng	和勝	Penang, Malacca and Perak, 1870–1890	All commentators
9	Tsun Sim / Chun Sim	存心	Penang, 1881–1890	Pickering, Clementi-Smith, and Official records
10	Toh Peh Kong	大伯公	Penang, 1842–1890	All commentators
11	Ho Beng	和明	Malacca, 1870–1890	Vaughan, Plunket, Powell
12	Hok Beng	福明		

The Hung League (Triad)

Serial No.	Common Name	Characters	Place in use	Authority
1	Ghee Hin (All tribal branches)	義興	Universally	All commentators
2	Ghee Khee Kwang Hok	義記廣福		
3	Ghee Sin	義新	Singapore, 1875–1890	Vaughan, Pickering and Clementi-Smith
4	Kong Fui Shiu	廣惠肇		
5	Hong Ghee Tong	洪義堂		
6	Lee Seng Hong	利城行	Singapore, 1886–1890	Pickering, Clementi-Smith and Official records
7	Yet Tong Kun	粵東館		
8	Heng Sun (Sim)	—	Singapore, 1886–1890	Pickering and Official records
9	Ghee Boo	義務		
10	Ghee Siew	義肇	Malacca, 1870–	Vaughan, Plunket, Official records and Gazettes
11	Baba Eng Ho	峇峇永和		

NAMES APPLIED TO THE HAN LEAGUE (TOKONG) AND THE HUNG LEAGUE (TRIAD) IN MALAYA BETWEEN 1868 AND 1900—continued

THE HAN LEAGUE (TOKONG)

Serial No.	Common Name	Characters	Place in use	Authority
13	Ng Fuk Tong	五福堂	Singapore, 1870–1890	Official records and Govt. Gazettes
14	Kim Hok Tong	—		
15	Hok Tek Choon	—		
16	Tsun Ghee Seah	存義社	Penang, 1870–1890	Official records and Govt. Gazettes
17	Ho Hap Seah	和合社		
18	Shui Lok Peng On or "Coffin-breaking" society	上落平安	Shanghai, Hong Kong, Singapore and Rangoon, 1890–1915	Wray Protectorate Report 1892
19	Tin Bu Beo	—	Singapore, 1890–1892	Wray
20	Chu Gi Seah	—	Penang, 1892–1896	Wray and Capper
21	Seh Khoo Kongsi	姓邱公司	Penang, 1892–1935	Wray
22	Bun San Tong	文山堂	Penang, 1892–1935	
23	Ng Fuk Hong	五福行	Penang, 1892–1900	
24	Keng Tak Hong	敬德行	Singapore, 1895–1900	Capper Protectorate Report, 1895
25	Tai Te Ia	大帝爺	Penang, 1892–1895	Capper, 1895
26	Liong San Tong	榴山堂	Penang, 1895–1935	Capper, 1895
27	Ng Fuk Thong	五福堂	Penang, 1895	Capper, 1895

THE HUNG LEAGUE (TRIAD)

Serial No.	Common Name	Characters	Place in use	Authority
12	Kwang Kit Tong	—	Singapore, 1870–1890	Official records and Govt. Gazettes
13	Keng Soon	—		
14	Eng Chuan Tong	—		
15	Ying Fuk Thong / Keng Hok Tong	英福堂	Penang, 1870–1890	Official records and Govt. Gazettes
16	Gi Lan Tong	義蘭堂	Singapore, 1870–1890	Official records and Govt. Gazettes
17	Kong Hok Tong	廣福堂	Penang, 1895	Capper
18	Hang Kong Ki Beo	—	Penang, 1895	Capper
19	Gi Leng	義鈴	Singapore, 1896	Capper
20	Ho Keng Sia	和慶社	Singapore, 1896	Capper
21	Bun Heng	文興	Singapore, 1896	Capper
22	Tung On Wui Kun	東安會館	Singapore, 1897	Evans
23	Hau Fuh Thong	—	Singapore, 1898	Evans

NAMES APPLIED TO THE HAN LEAGUE (TOKONG) AND THE HUNG LEAGUE (TRIAD)
IN MALAYA BETWEEN 1868 AND 1900—*continued*

THE HAN LEAGUE (TOKONG)

Serial No.	Common Name	Characters	Place in use	Authority
28	Sun Tak Hoe	順德會	Singapore, 1896	Capper
29	Chiau Eng Si	招應祠	Malacca, 1896	Capper
30	Yun Shin Tong	永盛堂	Singapore, 1896	Capper
31	Hui Liong Siah	一	Penang, 1896	Capper
32	Hok Tek Tong	福德堂	Penang, 1896	Capper
33	Tiong Hin	中興	Penang, 1897	Evans
34	Hong Khai Sia	鳳開社	Penang, 1897	Evans
35	Siun Kang Kong	相公閣	Penang, 1897	Evans
36	Theng Hong Ko	騰芳閣	Penang, 1897	Evans
37	Sin Gi Hoe	新義會	Singapore, 1898	Evans

THE HUNG LEAGUE (TRIAD)

Serial No.	Common Name	Characters	Place in use	Authority
24	Panglong (Timber yard)	枋廠	Penang, 1899	Evans
25	Buan An, Thai (? Maan On Tui)	萬安隊	Penang, 1899	Evans

Comment upon the Legislative Control of Societies

The policy of alternative exemption, registration, or refusal of registration of societies, introduced by the Ordinance of 1889, has remained as it began—a compromise, and a very unsatisfactory compromise, which has never worked smoothly for three outstanding reasons:—

(1) It has ignored the basic principle of secret societies discussed fully in Chapter XXXIII *infra*, which is as old as the world namely, that the illegal can co-exist with the legal.

(2) It has ignored the co-existence of illegal Mohamedan with illegal Chinese secret societies, both in alliance and both subsisting within a legal envelope.

(3) There has never been established a Department of Government fully informed upon this difficult subject and exclusively charged with the administration of legal societies and of the anti-secret-society law and with the control and suppression of illegal developments and tendencies within its legal frame-work.

The result during the past fifty years in the sphere of society registration has been a perpetual game of "bob-apple", or "same-man-different-hat", in which illegal and dangerous associations are regularly suppressed and as regularly re-appear under a different name, and in which the powers of subversion have been continually in command of the situation and the efforts of Government continually at a disadvantage and lagging behind the realties of control.

The inherent weakness of toleration is encouragement; of registration recognition; and of suppression, evasion. Halifax, Secretary for Chinese Affairs, Hongkong, early in the present century is believed to have summed up the position as follows:—

"Toleration is impossible, registration is impossible, and suppression is impossible. The more you tolerate, register and suppress the more they flourish",

or words to that effect. We forget for the moment whether he was referring to Chinese secret societies or to Chinese prostitutes, but the analogy is a close one!

Of recent years a fourth estate under the Societies Ordinance has been unofficially added to the presently officially-existing three (of exempted, registered and refused), namely "recorded". A modern "recorded" society does not in fact differ in status in any marked degree from any of the other three. They all four proceed above and below ground, pretty much as they please, with little or no official interference unless they draw attention to themselves by some clumsiness—otherwise they are largely immune.

The present chaotic state of society registration in Malaya, much of which is being used illegally as cover for subversive propaganda and for the flotation of unlawful combinations under the appearance of legality, demands a revision of the problem in the light of modern requirements, in which the following points merit attention:—

(1) The purpose of all legislation in Malaya for the control of societies, which began with Ordinance XIX of 1869, is to gain and maintain control of all their activities open and hidden.

(2) Amending legislation in 1882, 1885 and 1889, was all to the same end. The registration of societies, which began in 1869, has continued in various forms for the past seventy years up to the present-day without giving any satisfaction. For this there must be a reason.

(3) The reasons, we submit, are mainly two:—
The fact that the illegal can co-exist within the legal.
The fact that control only begins with registration and does not end there.

(4) If legislation does not give Government complete hold over societies we are better without any legislation, because partial supervision is exercised only over the legal or open activities of any given registered society. This partial supervision gives the society a legal status, which, in turn, provides that very cover for its hidden and illegal activities, which it is the whole purpose of all legislation on the subject to deny.

(5) To provide complete control would require a separate department of Government staffed by a corps of inspecting officers, familiar with every ruse employed to evade the purpose of registration, and with powers to recommend the instant dissolution of any society suspected of harbouring illegal activities within its legal status.

(6) There is not, in fact, and never has been, any whole-time supervision of the activities of registered societies. The most perfunctory returns are made to the Registrar when demanded and there the matter usually ends. It is only when a registered society draws attention to itself by allowing the illegal *corpus* within to break surface and take charge, and evidence of its illegal activities thereby becomes patent, that action for dissolution ensues.

(7) Indeed, in most cases, the illegal hardly troubles to hide itself so long as official attention is not attracted to it.   It may often be found lying upon the surface of the legal.

(8) Asiatic clubs, societies and associations as we know them to-day, came into existence in 1890, following the Ordinance of 1889. A few— very few—registered clubs are genuine, long-established, mutual-benefit associations.   The remainder—the vast majority—not even excluding some registered and exempted so-called Sports Clubs, exist solely either for the less harmful purpose of gaming and racketeering, or for the more harmful purpose of subversive political activities; in both cases contrary to the terms of their registration.

(9) The dictum of certain Registrars of societies:—"when in doubt, register", does nothing to combat the real dangers, because registration of itself effects nothing.

(10) In Chapter XXXIII *infra* we have recommended the try-out of a system of suspended registration, by the introduction of a period of probation, as it were, before application for registration of any society, whose *bona fides* are suspect, is finally disposed of.   Opportunity might be taken too, to return to the useful provision of Section 5 of Ordinance XIX of 1869 by imposing a bond, or cash deposit for good behaviour upon the promoters, or office-bearers of any suspect society as a condition of registration.   Such restrictions combined with :—

    (i) limitation of membership in numbers and area;

    (ii) prohibition of affiliation;

    (iii) personal responsibility of office-bearers for all activities, both legal and illegal of their members

should do much to reduce the present dangerous abuse of the Societies Ordinance, as a curtain for illegality both social, economic and political.

These restrictions should also help towards reducing and controlling the power of Triad and Tokong to organise and extend their two camps at will, while paying lip-service only to the requirements of the Societies Ordinance.

THE CONSPIRACY TO SILENCE OF TRIAD AND TOKONG

One of the most surprising features of the Chinese under-world in Malaya is the fact that the two opposing camps of Triad and Tokong have continued so long not only in existence but also in power, without exposure.

It could only be by collusion that a conspiracy so vast could continue to remain undisclosed.

Throughout the history of modern Malaya, every member of Triad must have been perfectly well aware of the existence of Tokong as a separate, hostile and rival sodality, and *vice versa;* and yet, there has never been a breach between the other to the authorities.   It has been throughout officially accepted that they were all branches of the Triad society; and no information has been proffered to the Government to explode what we believe to be this fallacy.   We can only suppose that both Triad and Tokong realised long ago that whatever their own differences might be, it would mean the ruin of both for one to expose the other.

As a result, we submit, a vast conspiracy to silence has been imposed upon the members of both clandestine confederacies as well as upon the members of the White and Red Flag, who must be equally well aware of the imposture,—whereby the Government has been kept in ignorance of the true position all these years.

The success of such a conspiracy, if in fact it has existed, could only be insured, if there were very powerful interests behind it.

A consideration of these implications is reserved for Part II.

Made in the USA
Las Vegas, NV
07 February 2025

598cda93-835d-4716-880e-e9d29b67167aR01